Adolescence
and
Emerging Adulthood

Adolescence
and
Emerging Adulthood

A Cultural Approach

Jeffrey Jensen Arnett
University of Maryland

Prentice Hall

Upper Saddle River, New Jersey 07458

Library of Congress Cataloging-in-Publication Data

Arnett, Jeffrey Jensen,
    Adolescence and emerging adulthood : a cultural approach/Jeffrey Arnett.—1st ed.
      p. cm.
    Includes bibliographical references and index.
    ISBN 0-13-089444-3 (alk. paper)
    1. Adolescence—Cross-cultural studies. 2. Teenagers—Cross-cultural studies.
    3. Young adults—Cross-cultural studies. I. Title.
HQ796 .A7255 2000
305.235–dc21   00-058874

VP/Editorial Director: Laura Pearson
Senior Acquisitions Editor: Jennifer Gilliland
Editorial Assistant: Nicole Girrbach
AVP and Director of Production and Manufacturing:
    Barbara Kittle
Managing Editor: Mary Rottino
Editorial Production Supervisor: Lisa M. Guidone
Production Assistant: Meredith Gnerre
Prepress and Manufacturing Manager: Nick Sklitsis
Prepress and Manufacturing Buyer: Tricia Kenny
Creative Design Director: Leslie Osher
Art Director: Carole Anson
Interior Designer: Paul Gourhan

Cover Design: Paul Gourhan
Art Manager: Guy Ruggiero
Line Art Coordinator: Mirella Signoretto
Photo Research: Linda Sykes
Image Specialist: Beth Boyd
Manager, Rights and Permission: Kay Dellosa
Director, Image Resource Center: Melinda Reo
Director of Marketing: Beth Gillett Mejia
Senior Marketing Manager: Sharon Cosgrove
Copyeditor: Kathy Pruno
Proofreader: Rainbow Graphics
Indexer: Linda Buskus, Northwind Editorial Services

Acknowledgments for copyrighted material may be found beginning on
p. 493, which constitutes an extension of this copyright page.

This book was set in 10/12 New Baskerville Roman by TSI Graphics and was printed by Von Hoffman Press.
The cover was printed by Von Hoffman Press.

© 2001 by Prentice-Hall, Inc.
A Division of Pearson Education
Upper Saddle River, New Jersey 07458

Printed in the United States of America
10 9 8 7 6 5 4 3 2 1

ISBN 0-13-089444-3

Prentice-Hall International (UK) Limited, *London*
Prentice-Hall of Australia Pty. Limited, *Sydney*
Prentice-Hall Canada, Inc., *Toronto*
Prentice-Hall Hispanoamericana, S.A., *Mexico*
Prentice-Hall of India Private Limited, *New Delhi*
Prentice-Hall of Japan, Inc., *Tokyo*
Pearson Education Asia Pte. Ltd., *Singapore*
Editora Prentice-Hall do Brasil, Ltda., *Rio de Janeiro*

To Robin, Kelly,
Nathan, Raina,
Paris, and Miles—
so much to look
forward to!

Brief Contents

Contents

Special Focus Boxes

CULTURAL FOCUS

HISTORICAL FOCUS

RESEARCH FOCUS

Preface

Adolescence is a fascinating time of life, and for most instructors it is an enjoyable topic to teach. For many students taking the course, it is the time of life they have just completed or are now passing through. Learning about development during this period is a journey of self-discovery for them, in part. Students who are many years beyond this period often enjoy reflecting back on who they were then, and they come away with a new understanding of their past and present selves. What students learn from a course on adolescence often confirms their own intuitions and experiences, and sometimes contradicts or expands what they thought they knew. When it works well, a course on adolescence can change not only how students understand themselves, but also how they understand others and how they think about the world around them. For instructors, the possibility the course offers for students' growth of understanding is often stimulating. My goal in writing this textbook has been to assist instructors and students in making illuminating connections of understanding on this dynamic and complex age period.

This is a first edition textbook so it may be useful to outline the features that distinguish it from existing textbooks. I wrote this book with the intention of presenting a fresh conception of the field of adolescence—a conception reflecting what I believe to be the most promising and exciting new currents. There are four essential features of the conception that guided this book: (1) a focus on the cultural basis of development; (2) an extension of the age period covered to include "emerging adulthood" (roughly ages 18 to 25), as well as adolescence; (3) an emphasis on historical context; and (4) an interdisciplinary approach to theories and research.

The Cultural Approach

In teaching courses on adolescence, from large lecture classes to small seminars, I have always brought a considerable amount of research from other cultures into the classroom. My education as a postdoctoral student at the Committee on Human Development at the University of Chicago included a substantial focus on anthropology. Learning to take a cultural approach to development greatly expanded and deepened my own understanding of adolescence, and I have seen the cultural approach work this way for my students as well. Through an awareness of the diversity of cultural practices, customs, and beliefs about adolescence, we expand our knowledge of the range of developmental possibilities. We also gain a greater understanding of adolescent development in our own culture by learning to see it as only one of many possible paths.

Taking a cultural approach to development means infusing discussion of every aspect of development with a cultural perspective. I present the essentials of the cultural approach in the first chapter, and it serves as a theme throughout the book. Each chapter also includes a *Cultural Focus* box in which an aspect of development in a specific culture is explored in-depth—for example, adolescents' family relationships in India, Germany's apprenticeship program, and media use among young people in Nepal.

My hope is that students will learn not only that adolescent development can be different depending on the culture, but also how to *think culturally*—that is, how to analyze all aspects of adolescent development for their cultural basis. This includes learning how to critique research for the extent to which it does or does not take the cultural basis of development into account. I provide this kind of critique at numerous points throughout the book.

Emerging Adulthood

Not only is adolescence an inherently fascinating period of life, but we are also currently in an especially interesting historical moment with respect to this period. One distinguishing feature of adolescence in our time is that it begins far earlier than it did a century ago, because puberty begins for most people in industrialized countries at a much younger age. Yet, if we measure the end of adolescence in terms of taking on adult roles such as marriage, parenthood, and stable full-time work, then adolescence also ends much later than it has in the past because many people postpone these transitions until at least the mid-twenties. My own research over the past few years has focused on development among young Americans from their late teens through their mid-twenties, including Asian Americans, African Americans, Latinos, and Whites. I have concluded on the basis of this research that this period is neither adolescence nor adulthood, nor even "young adulthood." In my view, the transition to adulthood has become so prolonged that it constitutes a separate period of the life course in industrialized societies lasting about as long as adolescence.

Thus, a second distinguishing feature of the conception guiding this textbook is that the age period covered includes not only adolescence but also "emerging adulthood"—the period extending from the late teens through the mid-twenties. In a recent paper in *American Psychologist* (Arnett, 2000a), I presented a theory of emerging adulthood, conceptualizing it as a period characterized by instability and by exploration of possible life directions in love, work, and worldviews. I describe this theory in some detail in the first chapter of this book, and use it as the framework for discussing emerging adulthood in the chapters that follow. Since there is not nearly as much research on emerging adulthood as there is on adolescence, the balance of material in each chapter tilts quite strongly toward adolescence. However, each chapter contains material that pertains to emerging adulthood.

The Historical Context

Given the differences between adolescence now and adolescence in the past, knowledge of the historical context of development is crucial to a complete understanding of adolescent development. Students will have a richer understanding of adolescent development if they are able to contrast the lives of young people in the present with the lives of young people in other times. Toward this end, I provide historical material in each chapter. Each chapter also contains a *Historical Focus* box that focuses on young people's development during a specific historical period—for example, adolescents' family lives during the Great Depression, the "Roaring Twenties" and the rise of youth culture, and work among British adolescents in the 19th century.

The emphasis on the historical context of development is especially important now with the accelerating pace of cultural change that has taken place around the world in recent decades due to the influence of globalization. In economically developing countries, the pace of change in recent decades has been especially dramatic, and young people often find themselves growing up in a culture that is much different than the one their parents experienced in their own adolescence. Globalization is a pervasive influence on the lives of young people today, in ways both promising and troubling, and for this reason I have made it one of the unifying themes of the book.

An Interdisciplinary Approach

The cultural approach and the emphasis on historical context are related to a fourth distinguishing feature of the conception offered in this book—the interdisciplinary approach to theories and research. Psychology and education are naturally represented abundantly because these are the disciplines where the most research on adolescent development takes place. However, I also integrate materials from a wide range of other fields. Much of the theory and research that is the basis for a cultural understanding of adolescence comes from anthropology, so anthropological studies are strongly represented. Students often find this material fascinating because it effectively challenges their assumptions about what they expect adolescence to be like. Interesting and important cultural material on adolescence also comes from sociology, especially with respect to European and Asian societies, and these studies find a place here. History is notably represented for providing the historical perspective discussed above. Other disciplines drawn from include psychiatry, medicine, and family studies.

The integration of materials across disciplines means drawing on a variety of research methods. The reader will find many different research methods represented here from questionnaires and interviews to ethnographic research and biological measurements. Each chapter contains a *Research Focus* box, in which the methods used in a specific study are described in detail.

Chapter Topics

My goal of presenting a fresh conception of young people's development has resulted in chapters on topics not represented as strongly in most other textbooks. Most textbooks include a discussion of moral development, but this textbook has a chapter on cultural beliefs (Chapter 4), including moral development, religious beliefs, political beliefs, and a discussion of individualistic and collectivistic beliefs in various cultures. This chapter provides a strong basis for a cultural understanding of adolescent development, because it emphasizes how the judgments we make about how adolescents should think and act are almost always rooted in cultural beliefs.

While most textbooks also include a discussion of gender issues at various points, and some include a separate chapter on gender, this textbook includes a chapter on gender (Chapter 5) that focuses on cultural variations and historical changes in gender roles, in addition to discussions of gender issues throughout the book. Gender is a key defining guideline for life in every culture, and the vivid examples of gender roles and expectations in non-Western cultures should help students become more aware of how gender acts as a defining guideline for young people's development in their own culture as well.

This textbook also has an entire chapter on work (Chapter 11), which is central to the lives of adolescents in developing countries because a high proportion of them are not in school. In industrialized societies, the transition from school to work is an important part of emerging adulthood, and this transition receives special attention in this chapter. An entire chapter on media is included (Chapter 12) with sections on computer games and the Internet. In most societies today, media are a prominent part of young people's lives, but this is a topic that receives surprisingly little attention in most textbooks. Finally, this textbook closes with a chapter on adolescence and emerging adulthood in the 21st century, in which the futures awaiting young people around the world are considered. In this chapter, we take a sweeping tour of the future prospects facing young people in every part of the world, and we see once more how dramatically different the lives of young people in different cultures can be.

One chapter found in most other textbooks but not in this one is a chapter on theories. In my view, having a separate chapter on theories gives students a misleading impression of the purpose and function of theories in the scientific enterprise. Theories and research are intrinsically related, with good theories inspiring research and good research leading to changes and innovations in theories. Presenting theories separately turns theory chapters into a kind of "Theory Museum," separate and sealed off from research. Instead, I present theoretical material throughout the book, always in relation to the research the theory has been based on and has inspired.

Each chapter contains a number of critical thinking questions under the heading *Thinking Critically*.

Critical thinking has become a popular term in academic circles and it has been subject to a variety of definitions, so I should explain how I used the term here. The purpose of the critical thinking questions was to inspire students to a higher level of analysis and reflection about the ideas and information in the chapters—higher, that is, than they would be likely to achieve simply by reading the chapter. With the critical thinking questions I sought to encourage students to connect ideas across chapters, to consider hypothetical questions, and to apply the chapter materials to their own lives. Often, the questions have no "right answer." Although they are mainly intended to assist students in attaining a high level of thinking as they read, they may also serve as lively material for class discussion.

Supplements to the Textbook

The supplements for this textbook have been prepared by Dr. Kimberly Schonert-Reichl and her graduate students in the Department of Education at the University of British Columbia. Kim is a respected scholar on adolescence who had years of experience as a high school teacher before becoming a professor, and she has made fruitful use of her skills as both a scholar and a teacher in preparing the Instructor's Resource Manual. I have worked with her in choosing the topics for the Manual so that it would complement the textbook.

The Instructor's Resource Manual with Tests and Web site (www.prenhall.com/arnett) was prepared carefully and thoroughly by Kimberly Schonert-Reichl, Helen Novak, and Sandra Jarvis Selinger under Kim's direction, and special care has been taken to ensure that the items are clear and accurate.

I have also prepared a book of readings to accompany this textbook entitled *Readings in Adolescence and Emerging Adulthood*. The sections in the book of readings parallel the chapters in the textbook so that the two books complement each other. My selections for the book of readings followed a concept similar to the textbook. Consequently, the readings incorporate studies from a variety of cultures, on emerging adulthood as well as adolescence, and draw from a variety of disciplines. Instructors may wish to use the book of readings to supplement the textbook, especially for upper-level undergraduate courses.

Acknowledgments

Preparing a first-edition textbook is an enormous enterprise that involves a wide network of people, and I have many people to thank for their contributions. Becky Pascal, my original editor at Addison-Wesley, recruited me to write the book, and it was her excitement over my new ideas for a textbook that, in part, persuaded me to take on the project. Jennifer Gilliland, who took over as editor when the book was transferred to Prentice Hall, has supported the book wholeheartedly and has repeatedly gone the extra mile to provide me with the resources I've requested in my efforts to make the book as good as I could possibly make it.

The review process for the book was long and exacting, and the reviewers were indispensable for the many comments and suggestions for improvement they provided. I'm very grateful for the time and care expended by these reviewers to give me detailed, well-informed reviews. In the first two rounds of reviews, the reviewers were:

Denise M. Arehart, University of Colorado–Denver; Belinda Blevins-Knabe, University of Arkansas–Little Rock; Curtis W. Branch, Columbia University; Gary Creasey, Illinois State University; Bonnie B. Dowdy, Dickinson College; Julia A. Graber, Columbia University; Virginia Gregg, North Adams State College; Daniel Houlihan, Minnesota State University; Sharon Page Howard, University of Arkansas–Little Rock; Karen G. Howe, The College of New York; Joline N. Jones, Worcester State College; Steven Kirsh, SUNY–Geneseo; Joseph G. Marrone, Siena College; Terry Maul, San Bernardino Valley College; Merryl Patterson, Austin Community College; Daniel Perkins, University of Florida; Daniel Repinski, SUNY–Geneseo; Merry Sleigh-Ritzer, George Mason University; Lisa Turner, University of South Alabama; Randy Vinzant, Hinds Community College; Niobe Way, New York University; Belinda Wholeben, Rockford College; Missi Wilkenfeld, Texas A & M University; and Joan Zook, SUNY–Geneseo.

Following the first two rounds of reviews, each chapter was reviewed by an outstanding scholar in the area covered by the chapter in order to provide the highest level of evaluation of the accuracy and currency of the material. These expert reviewers were:

Chapter 1: Shirley Feldman, Stanford University; Chapter 2: Christy Buchanan, Wake Forest University; Chapter 3: Janis Jacobs, Pennsylvania State University; Chapter 4: Jim Youniss, Catholic University of America; Chapter 5: Nancy Galambos, University of Victoria; Chapter 6: Susan Harter, University of Denver; Chapter 7: Reed Larson, University of Illinois; Chapter 8: David Kinney, Central Michigan University; Chapter 9: Paul Florsheim, University of Utah; Chapter 10: Andrew Fuligni, New York University; Chapter 11: Jeylan Mortimer, University of Minnesota; Chapter 12: Jane Brown, University of North Carolina–Chapel Hill; and Chapter 13: Jennifer Maggs, University of Arizona.

Following the expert reviews, the book was reviewed by a copyeditor, Kathy Pruno, who provided additional helpful suggestions. The production editor for the book was Lisa Guidone, who was exemplary in her competence and professionalism. The photo researcher was Linda Sykes, who came up with many a marvelous photo, as you will see.

I also wish to thank my parents, Marjorie and Calvin Arnett, who were remarkably patient (I see that now) during my own adolescence and emerging adulthood. Thanks to my wife, Lene Jensen, a developmental psychologist at Catholic University of America, who was a sounding board for many of my ideas for the book and who provided numerous good ideas as well. Finally, thanks to our twin babies Miles and Paris, who provided inspiring squeals at key moments and who showed their enthusiasm for the project by trying to eat the page proofs. Many thanks, all of you.

Jeffrey Jensen Arnett
Department of Human Development
University of Maryland
June 2000

About the Author

The author and his proofreading assistants, Paris (left) and Miles.

Jeffrey Jensen Arnett is a Visiting Associate Professor at the University of Maryland. He has also taught at the University of Virginia, Oglethorpe University, and the University of Missouri, and he has been a Visiting Scholar at the Center on Adolescence at Stanford University. He was educated at Michigan State University (undergraduate), the University of Virginia (graduate school), and the University of Chicago (postdoctoral studies). His research interests are in risk behavior in adolescence, media use in adolescence, and a wide range of topics in emerging adulthood. Currently, he serves on the Editorial Board of *Journal of Youth and Adolescence* and *Youth & Society*. He lives in University Park, Maryland, with his wife, Lene Jensen, and their infant twins, Paris and Miles.

Adolescence
and
Emerging Adulthood

CHAPTER 1

Introduction

In the dim dawn light of a simple reed house in Tehuantepec, Mexico, 16-year-old Conchita leans over an open, barrel-shaped oven. Although it is just dawn, she has already been working for 2 hours making tortillas. It is difficult work, standing over the hot oven, and hazardous, too; she has several burns on her arm from the times she has inadvertently touched the hot steel. She thinks with some resentment of her younger brother, who is still sleeping and who will soon be rising and going off to school. Like most girls in her village, Conchita can neither read nor write, because it is only the boys who go to school.

But she finds consolation in looking ahead to the afternoon, when she will be allowed to go to the center of town to sell the tortillas she has made beyond those that her family will need that day. There she will see her girlfriends, who will be selling tortillas and other things for their families. And there she hopes to see the boy who spoke to her, just a few words, in the town square two Sunday evenings ago. The following Sunday evening she had seen him waiting in the street across from her home, a sure sign that he is courting

3

her. But her parents would not allow her out, so she hopes to get a glimpse of him in town (Chinas, 1991).

In a suburban home in Highland Park, Illinois, 14-year-old Jodie is standing before the mirror in her bedroom with a dismayed look, trying to decide whether to change her clothes again before she goes to school. She has already changed once, from the blue sweater and white skirt to the yellow and white blouse and blue jeans, but now she is having second thoughts. "I look awful," she thinks to herself, "I'm getting so fat!" For the past 3 years her body has been changing rapidly, and now she is alarmed to find it becoming rounder and larger seemingly with each day. Vaguely she hears her mother calling her from downstairs, probably urging her to hurry up and leave for school, but the stereo in her room is playing a Sheryl Crow CD so loud it drowns out what her mother is saying. "All I wanna do is have some fun," Sheryl sings, "I've got a feeling, I'm not the only one."

In Amakiri, Nigeria, 18-year-old Omiebi is walking to school. He is walking quickly, because the time for school to begin is near, and he does not want to be one of the students who arrive after morning assembly has started and are grouped together and made to kneel throughout the assembly.

In rural Mexico, a girl and her mother cook tortillas.

Up ahead he sees several of his fellow students, easily identifiable by the gray uniforms they are all required to wear, and he breaks into a trot to join them. They greet him, and together they continue walking. They joke nervously about the exam coming up for the West African School Certificate. Performance on that exam will determine to a great extent who is allowed to go on to university.

Omiebi is feeling a great deal of pressure to do well on the exam. He is the oldest child of his family, and his parents have high expectations that he will go to university and become a lawyer, then help his three younger brothers go to university or find good jobs in Lagos, the nearest big city. Omiebi is not really sure he wants to be a lawyer, and he would find it difficult to leave the girl he has recently begun seeing. However, he likes the idea of moving away from tiny Amakiri to the university in Lagos, where he has heard that all the homes have electricity and all the latest American movies are showing in the theaters. He and his friends break into a run over the last stretch, barely making it to school and joining their classes before the assembly starts (Hollos & Leis, 1989).

Three adolescents, in three different cultures, with three very different lives. Yet all are adolescents: all have left childhood but not yet reached adulthood, all are developing into physical and sexual maturity and learning the skills that will enable them to take part in the adult world.

Although all of them are adolescents, what makes these three adolescents so different is that they are growing up in three very different cultures. Throughout this book we will take a cultural approach to understanding development in adolescence by examining the ways that cultures differ in what they allow adolescents to do and what they require them to do, the different things that cultures teach adolescents to believe, and the different patterns that cultures set out for adolescents' daily lives. Adolescence is a cultural construction, not simply a biological phenomenon. Puberty—the set of biological changes involved in reaching physical and sexual maturity—is biological and universal, and the same biological changes take place in puberty for young people everywhere, although with differences in timing and in cultural meanings. But adolescence is more than the events and processes of puberty. **Adolescence** *is a period of the life course between the time puberty begins and the time adult status is approached, when young people are preparing to take on the roles and responsibilities of adulthood in their culture. To say that adolescence is culturally constructed means that cultures vary in how they define adult status and in the content of adult roles and responsibilities. Almost all cultures have some kind of adolescence (Schlegel & Barry, 1991), but the length and content and daily experience of adolescence varies greatly among cultures.*

In this chapter, we will lay a foundation for understanding the cultural basis of adolescence by beginning with a look at how adolescence has changed through the history of Western culture. Historical change is also cultural change; for example, the United States of 2000 is different culturally from the United States of 1900 or 1800. Seeing how adolescence changes as a culture changes will illustrate the cultural basis of adolescence.

Another way this chapter will lay the foundation for the rest of the book is by introducing the concept of emerging adulthood. This textbook covers not only adolescence—roughly ages 10 to 18—but also emerging adulthood—roughly ages 18 to 25. Emerging adulthood is a new idea, a new way of thinking about this age period. In this chapter I describe what it means. Each chapter that follows will contain information about emerging adulthood as well as adolescence.

This chapter also sets the stage for what follows by discussing the scientific study of adolescence and emerging adulthood. I will present some of the basic features of the scientific method as it is applied in research on these age periods. It is important to understand adolescence and emerging adulthood not just as periods of the life course but as areas of scientific inquiry, with certain standard methods and certain conventions for determining what is valid and what is not. In every chapter of the book you will find a Research Focus box that explores a specific study in depth and discusses specific aspects of the methods used in research.

Finally, this chapter will provide the foundation for the chapters to come by previewing the major themes of the book and the framework of the book. These sections will introduce you to themes that will be repeated often in subsequent chapters, and will let you know where we are headed through the course of the book.

But before we get started, there are a few terms used throughout the book that you should be sure you know.

Culture. Culture is the total pattern of a group's customs, beliefs, art, and technology. Thus, a culture is a group's common way of life, passed on from one generation to the next.

The West. The United States, Canada, Western Europe, Australia, and New Zealand make up the West. They are all industrialized countries, they are all representative democracies with similar kinds of governments, and they share to some extent a common cultural history. In the present, they are all characterized by secularism, consumerism, and capitalism, to one degree or another. The West usually refers to the majority culture in each of the countries, but each country also has cultural groups that do not share the characteristics of the majority culture and may even be in opposition to it.

Industrialized countries. The term industrialized countries includes the countries of the West along with Eastern countries such as Japan and South Korea. All of them have highly developed economies that have passed through a period of industrialization and are now based mainly on services (such as law, banking, sales, and accounting) and information (such as computer-related companies).

Majority culture. The majority culture in any given society is the culture that sets most of the norms and standards and holds most of the positions of political, economic, intellectual, and media power. The term *American majority culture* will be used often in this book to refer to the mostly White middle-class majority in American society.

Society. A society is a group of people who interact in the course of sharing a common geographical area. A single society may include a variety of different customs, religions, family traditions, and economic practices. Thus, a society is different from a culture: Members of a culture share a common way of life, whereas members of a society may not. For example, American society includes a variety of different cultures, such as the American majority culture, African American culture, Latino culture, and Asian American culture. They share certain characteristics in common by virtue of being Americans—for example, they are all subject to the same laws, and they go to similar schools—but there are differences among them that make them culturally distinct.

Traditional cultures. The term traditional culture refers to a culture that has maintained a way of life based on stable traditions passed from one generation to the next. These cultures do not generally value change but rather place a higher value on remaining true to cultural traditions. Often traditional cultures are "preindustrial," which means the technology and economic practices typical in the industrialized countries are not widely used. However, this is not always true; Japan, for example, is still in many ways traditional, even though it is also one of the most highly industrialized countries in the world. When we use the term *traditional cultures*, naturally this does not imply that all such cultures are alike. They differ in a variety of ways, but they have in common that they are firmly grounded in a relatively stable cultural tradition, and for that reason they provide a distinct contrast to cultures of the West.

Developing countries. Most previously traditional, preindustrial cultures are becoming industrialized today as a consequence of globalization. The term developing countries is used to refer to countries where this process is taking place. Examples include most of the countries of Africa and South America, as well as Asian countries such as Thailand and Vietnam.

Socioeconomic status. The term socioeconomic status (SES) is often used to refer to social class, which includes educational level, income level, and occupational status. For adolescents and emerging adults, because they have not yet reached the social class level they will have as adults, SES is usually used in reference to their parents' levels of education, income, and occupation.

Young people. In this book the term young people is used as shorthand to refer to adolescents and emerging adults together.

Adolescence in Western Cultures: A Brief History

Seeing how people in other times have viewed adolescence provides a useful perspective for understanding how adolescence is viewed in our own time. In this brief historical survey, we begin with ancient times 2,500 years ago and proceed through the early 20th century.

Adolescence in Ancient Times

Ideas about adolescence as a stage of the life course go back a long way in the history of Western cultures. In ancient Greece (4th and 5th centuries B.C.), the source of so many ideas that influenced Western history, both Plato and Aristotle viewed adolescence as the third distinct stage of life, after infancy (birth to age 7) and childhood (ages 7 to 14). In their views, adolescence extended from age 14 to age 21. Both of them viewed adolescence as the stage of life in which the capacity for reason first developed. Writing (in 4 B.C.) in *The Republic*, Plato argued that serious education should begin only at adolescence. Prior to age 7, according to Plato, there is no point in beginning education because the infant's mind is too undeveloped to learn much, and during childhood (ages 7 to 14) education should focus on sports and music, which children can grasp. Education in science and math should be delayed until adolescence, when the mind is finally ready to apply reason in learning these subjects.

> "THE YOUNG ARE IN CHARACTER PRONE TO DESIRE AND READY TO CARRY ANY DESIRE THEY MAY HAVE FORMED INTO ACTION. OF BODILY DESIRES IT IS THE SEXUAL TO WHICH THEY ARE MOST DISPOSED TO GIVE WAY, AND IN REGARD TO SEXUAL DESIRE THEY EXERCISE NO SELF-RESTRAINT."
> —ARISTOTLE, *RHETORIC*, CA. 330 B.C.

Aristotle, who was a student of Plato's during his own adolescence, had a view of adolescence that was in some ways similar to Plato's. Aristotle viewed children as similar to animals, in that both are ruled by the impulsive pursuit of pleasure. It is only in adolescence that we become capable of exercising reason and making rational choices. However, Aristotle argued that it takes the entire course of adolescence for reason to become fully established. At the beginning of adolescence, in his view, the impulses remain in charge and even become more problematic now that sexual desires have developed. It is only toward the end of adolescence—about age 21, according to Aristotle—that reason establishes firm control over the impulses.

THINKING CRITICALLY

Plato and Aristotle argued that young people are not capable of reason until about age 14. Give an example of how the question of when young people are capable of reason is still an issue in our time.

Adolescence From Early Christian Times Through the Middle Ages

A similar focus on the struggle between reason and passion in adolescence can be found in early Christianity. One of the most famous and influential books of early Christianity was Saint Augustine's autobiographical *Confessions*, which he wrote in about 400 A.D. In his *Confessions*, Augustine described his life from his early development until his conversion to Christianity when he was 33. A considerable portion of the autobiography focused on his teens and early twenties, when he was a reckless young man living an impulsive, pleasure-seeking life. He drank large quantities of alcohol, spent money

> "FOR THIS SPACE THEN (FROM MY NINETEENTH YEAR, TO MY EIGHT AND TWENTIETH), WE LIVED SEDUCED AND SEDUCING, DECEIVED AND DECEIVING, IN DIVERSE LUSTS."
> AUGUSTINE, *CONFESSIONS*, 400 A.D.

extravagantly, had sex with many young women, and fathered a child outside of marriage. In the autobiography, he repents his reckless youth and argues that conversion to Christianity is the key, not only to eternal salvation but to the establishment of the rule of reason over passion here on earth, within the individual.

Over the following millennium, from Augustine's time through the Middle Ages, the historical record on adolescence is sparse, as it is on most topics. However, one well-documented event that sheds some light on the history of adolescence is the Children's Crusade, which took place in 1212. Although termed the "Children's Crusade," it was actually composed mostly of young people in their teens, including many university students (Sommerville, 1982). In those days, university students were younger than today, usually entering between ages 13 and 15.

The young crusaders set out from Germany for the Mediterranean coast, believing that when they arrived there the waters would part the way the Red Sea had for Moses. They would then walk over to the Holy Land (Jerusalem and the areas where Jesus had lived), where they would appeal to the Muslims to allow Christian pilgrims to visit the holy sites. Several Crusades had already been conducted by adults, attempting to take the Holy Land by military force. The Children's Crusade was an attempt to appeal to the Muslims in peace, inspired by the belief that Jesus had decreed that the Holy Land could be gained only through the innocence of youth.

> "THE VERY CHILDREN PUT US TO SHAME. WHILE WE SLEEP THEY GO FORTH JOYFULLY TO CONQUER THE HOLY LAND."
> —POPE INNOCENT III, 1212, REFERRING TO THE CHILDREN'S CRUSADE

Unfortunately, the "innocence" of the young people—their lack of knowledge and experience—made them a ripe target for the unscrupulous. Many of them were robbed, raped, or kidnapped along the way. When the remainder arrived at the Mediterranean Sea, the sea did not open after all, and the shipowners who promised to take them across turned around and sold them to the Muslims as slaves. The Children's Crusade was a total disaster, but the fact that it was undertaken at all suggests that many people of that era viewed youth as a time of innocence and saw that innocence as possessing a special value and power.

Adolescence From 1500 to 1890

Beginning in about 1500, young people in some European societies typically took part in what historians term **life-cycle service**, a period in their late teens and twenties in which young people would engage in domestic service, farm service, or apprenticeship in various trades and crafts (Ben-Amos, 1994). Life-cycle service involved moving out of the family household and into the household of a "master" to whom the young person was in service for a period lasting (typically) 7 years. Young women were somewhat less likely than young men to engage in life-cycle service, but even among women a majority left home during adolescence, most often to take part in life-cycle service

Life-cycle service was common in Western countries from about 1500 to about 1800. This woodcut shows a printer's apprentice.

as a servant in a family. Life-cycle service was also common in the United States in the early colonial period in New England (beginning in the 17th century), but in colonial New England such service was less common and usually took place in the home of a relative or family friend (Rotundo, 1993).

In the young United States, the nature of adolescence soon began to change. Life-cycle service faded during the 18th and 19th centuries. As the American population grew and the national economy became less based in farming and more industrialized, young people increasingly left their small towns in their late teens for the growing cities. In the cities, without ties to a family or community, young people soon became regarded as a social problem in many respects. Rates of crime, premarital sex, and alcohol use among young people all increased in the late 18th and early 19th centuries (Wilson & Herrnstein, 1985). In response, new institutions of social control developed—religious associations, literary societies, YMCAs, and YWCAs—where young people were monitored by adults (Kett, 1977). This approach worked—in the second half of the 19th century, rates of crime, premarital pregnancies, alcohol use, and other problems among young people all dropped sharply (Wilson & Herrnstein, 1985).

The Age of Adolescence, 1890–1920

Although I have been using the term *adolescence* in this brief history for the sake of clarity and consistency, actually *adolescence* became a term widely applied to young people in their teens and early twenties only toward the end of the 19th century and the beginning of the 20th century (Kett, 1977). Before this time, young people in their teens and early twenties were more often referred to as **youth** or simply as young men and young women (Modell & Goodman, 1990). However, toward the end of the 19th century important changes took place in this age period in Western countries that made a change of terms appropriate.

In the United States and other Western countries, the years 1890–1920 were crucial in establishing the characteristics of modern adolescence. Key changes during these years included the enactment of laws restricting child labor, new requirements for children to attend secondary school, and the development of the field of adolescence as an area of scholarly study. For these reasons, historians call the years 1890–1920 the "Age of Adolescence" (Tyack, 1990).

Toward the end of the 19th century, the industrial revolution was proceeding at full throttle in the United States and other Western countries. There was a tremendous demand for labor to staff the mines, shops, and factories. Adolescents and even preadolescent children were especially in demand, because they could be hired to work cheap and because they were physically resilient and could withstand working conditions that were often terrible. The 1900 U.S. census reported that three-quarters of a million children aged 10 to 13 were employed in factories, mines, and other industrial work settings. Few states had laws restricting the ages of children in the workplace, even for work such as coal mining (Tyack, 1990). Few states restricted the number of hours children or adults could work, so children often worked 12 hours a day for as little as 35 cents a day.

As more and more young people entered the workplace, however, concern for them also increased among urban reformers, youth workers, and educators. In the view of these adults the young people were being exploited and harmed (physically and morally) by their involvement in adult work. These activists successfully fought for legislation that prohibited companies from hiring children as labor and severely limited the number of hours that could be worked by young people in their early teens (Kett, 1977).

Along with laws restricting child labor came laws requiring a longer period of schooling. Up until the late

RESEARCH FOCUS
Don't Call Them "Kids"

This chapter describes how the use of the term *adolescence* is fairly new historically, becoming common only in the early 20th century. A Gallup (1990) study indicates that, nearly a century later, today's adolescents have mixed feelings about the term. Only 19% of 13- to 17-year-olds—fewer than one in five—polled by the Gallup organization said they considered it "very acceptable" to be referred to as adolescents (see Table 1.1).

Although they are not especially fond of being called adolescents, they are even less fond of being referred to as *boys and girls*, *kids*, or *children*. This is not hard to interpret. All these terms make them sound young and place their status in the childhood they are leaving behind. Understandably, they view these terms as no longer accurate in describing them.

The terms they find most acceptable are also interesting: *young adults*, followed by *teenagers* and *young men and women*. Perhaps they like these terms because, at least for *young adults* and *young men and women*, these terms make them sound more grown-up and mature.

This kind of study is called a **national survey**. A **survey** is a questionnaire study that involves asking people questions about their opinions, beliefs, or behavior (Thio, 1997). Usually, closed questions are used, meaning that participants are asked to select from a predetermined set of responses, so that their responses can be easily added and compared.

If it is a national survey, that does not mean, of course, that every person in the country is asked the survey questions! Instead, as this chapter describes, researchers seek a sample—that is, a relatively small number of people whose responses are taken to represent the larger population from which they are drawn. Usually, national surveys such as the one described here use a procedure called **stratified sampling**, in which they select participants so that various categories of people are represented in proportions equal to their presence in the population (Goodwin, 1995). For example, if we know that 52% of the 13- to 17-year-olds in the United States are female, we would want the sample to be 52% female; if we know that 13% of 13- to 17-year-olds are African American, the sample should be 13%

TABLE 1.1: WHAT TEENS PREFER TO BE CALLED

	Very Acceptable	Somewhat Acceptable	Not Acceptable
Young adults	64%	30%	6%
Teenagers	60	35	4
Young men and women	59	34	4
Teens	53	40	6
Youth	29	55	16
Adolescents	19	60	19
Boys and girls	10	40	49
Kids	10	40	49
Children	7	21	71

Responses to the question, "What terms do you consider acceptable for describing people your own age?," asked in a national survey of young people aged 13–17.

Gallup (1990).

African American; and so on. The categories used to select a stratified sample often include age, gender, ethnic group, education, and income. For adolescents, their parents' levels of education and income are typically used, because education and income are intended to represent socioeconomic status (SES), and adolescents are not old enough to have reached a level of education or income that accurately reflects their SES.

The other characteristic of a national survey is usually that the stratified sample is also a **random sample**, meaning that the people selected for participation in the study are chosen randomly—no one in the population has a better or worse chance of being selected than anyone else (Shaughnessy & Zechmeister, 1985). You could do this by putting all possible participants' names in a hat and pulling out as many participants as you need or by paging through a phone book and putting your finger down in random places, but these days the selection of a random sample for national surveys is usually done by a computer program. Selecting a random sample enhances the likelihood that the sample will be genuinely representative of the larger population.

19th century, many states did not have any laws requiring children to attend school, and those that did required attendance only through elementary school (Tyack, 1990). However, between 1890 and 1920 states began to pass laws requiring attendance not only in elementary school but in secondary school as well. As a consequence, the proportion of adolescents in school increased dramatically—in 1890, only 5% of young people aged 14 to 17 were in school, but by 1920 this figure had risen to 30% (Arnett & Taber, 1994).

This change contributed to making this time the "Age of Adolescence," because it marked a more distinct separation between adolescence as a period of continued schooling and adulthood as a period that begins after schooling is finished.

Some scholars have claimed that laws restricting child and adolescent labor and requiring them to attend school amounted to a kind of plot against them. According to this **inventionist view**, adolescence was invented during the early 20th century as a way of keeping young people excluded from useful and income-producing work, instead keeping them in educational institutions where they would be dependent on adults and learn to be passive and compliant to adult authority (Lapsley, Enright, & Serlin, 1985). However, other scholars have argued that working in a coal mine for 35 cents a day was no bargain for young people, and education was a way for them to prepare themselves for the better jobs available in a more developed economy (Stedman & Smith, 1983). Nevertheless, the inventionists are right that the new laws concerning work and school did change adolescence, making it more isolated from adults and from the world of work.

During the 19th century, adolescents often worked under difficult and unhealthy conditions.

Laws requiring children to attend school were passed in the early 20th century.

volume set entitled *Adolescence*, Hall's textbook covered a wide range of topics, including physical health and development, adolescent development cross-culturally and historically, and adolescent love. Much of what he wrote is dated and obsolete now. To a large extent he based his ideas on a now-discredited theory of **recapitulation**, which held that the development of each individual recapitulates or reenacts the evolutionary development of the human species as a whole. He believed the stage of adolescence reflected a stage in the human evolutionary past when there was a great deal of upheaval and disorder, with the result that adolescents experience a great deal of **storm and stress** as a standard part of their development. (For more on the "storm and stress" debate, see the Historical Focus box.) No reputable scholar believes the theory of recapitulation anymore. However, Hall did a great deal to focus attention and concern on

The third major contributor to making the years 1890–1920 the Age of Adolescence was the work of G. Stanley Hall and the beginning of the study of adolescence as a distinct field of scholarship (Modell & Goodman, 1990). Hall was an impressive person whose achievements included obtaining the first Ph.D. in psychology in the United States, becoming the founder of the American Psychological Association, and serving as the first president of Clark University. In addition, Hall was the initiator of the child study movement in the United States, which advocated research on child and adolescent development and the improvement of conditions for children and adolescents in the family, school, and workplace.

Among his accomplishments, Hall also wrote the first textbook on adolescence. Published in 1904 as a two-

> "AT NO TIME OF LIFE IS THE LOVE OF EXCITEMENT SO STRONG AS DURING THE SEASON OF ACCELERATED DEVELOPMENT OF ADOLESCENCE, WHICH CRAVES STRONG FEELINGS AND NEW SENSATIONS."
> — G. STANLEY HALL, *ADOLESCENCE*, 1904, VOL. I, P. 368

G. Stanley Hall, the founder of the scholarly study of adolescence.

adolescents, not only among scholars but among the public at large. Thus, he was perhaps the most important figure in making the years 1890–1920 the Age of Adolescence.

This brief history of adolescence provides only a taste of what adolescence has been like in various eras of history. However, as the history of adolescence is one of the themes of this book, historical information will appear in every chapter.

HISTORICAL FOCUS
The "Storm and Stress" Debate

One of G. Stanley Hall's ideas that is still debated today among scholars is his claim that adolescence is inherently a time of storm and stress. According to Hall, it is normal for adolescence to be a time of considerable upheaval and disruption. As Hall described it (Arnett, 1999a), adolescent storm and stress is reflected in especially high rates of three types of difficulties during the adolescent period: *conflict with parents*, *mood disruptions*, and *risk behavior* (antisocial or reckless behavior such as substance use and crime).

Hall (1904) favored the **Lamarckian** evolutionary ideas that were considered by many prominent thinkers in the early 20th century to be a better explanation of evolution than Darwin's theory of natural selection. In Lamarck's now-discredited theory, evolution takes place as a result of accumulated experience. Organisms pass on their characteristics from one generation to the next not in the form of genes (which were unknown at the time Lamarck and Darwin devised their theories) but in the form of *memories and acquired characteristics*. Thus, Hall, considering development during adolescence, judged it to be "suggestive of some ancient period of storm and stress" (1904, vol. 1, p. xiii). In his view, there must have been a period of human evolution that was extremely difficult and tumultuous; the memory of that period had been passed ever since from one generation to the next and was recapitulated in the development of each

individual as the storm and stress of adolescent development.

In the century since Hall's work established adolescence as an area of scientific study, the debate over adolescent storm and stress has simmered steadily and boiled to the surface periodically. Anthropologists, led by Margaret Mead (1928), countered the claim that a tendency toward storm and stress in adolescence is universal and biological by describing non-Western cultures in which adolescence was neither stormy nor stressful. In contrast, psychoanalytic theorists, particularly Anna Freud (1946, 1958, 1968, 1969), have been the most outspoken proponents of the storm and stress view.

Anna Freud (1958, 1968, 1969) viewed adolescents who did *not* experience storm and stress with great suspicion, claiming that their outward calm concealed the inward reality that they must have "built up excessive defenses against their drive activities and are now crippled by the results" (1968, p. 15). She viewed storm and stress as universal and inevitable, to the extent that its absence signified a serious psychological problem: "To be normal during the adolescent period is by itself abnormal" (1958, p. 267).

What does more recent scholarship indicate about the validity of the storm and stress view? A clear consensus exists among current scholars that the storm and stress view proposed by Hall and made more extreme by Anna Freud and other psychoanalysts is not valid for most adolescents

(Arnett, 1999a; Offer & Schonert-Reichl, 1992; Steinberg & Levine, 1997). The claim that adolescent storm and stress is characteristic of all adolescents, and that the source of it is purely biological, is clearly false. Scholars today tend to emphasize that most adolescents like and respect their parents, that for most of them their mood disruptions are not so extreme that they need psychological treatment, and that most of them do not engage in highly reckless behavior on a regular basis.

On the other hand, studies in recent decades have also indicated some support for what might be called a "modified" storm and stress view (Arnett, 1999a). Research evidence supports the existence of some degree of storm and stress—at least for adolescents in the middle-class American majority culture—with respect to conflict with parents, mood disruptions, and risk behavior. Not all adolescents experience storm and stress in these areas, but adolescence is the period when storm and stress is *more likely* to occur than at other ages. Conflict with parents tends to be higher in adolescence than it is before or after adolescence (Paikoff & Brooks-Gunn, 1991). Adolescents report greater extremes of mood and more frequent changes of mood, compared with preadolescents or adults (Larson & Richards, 1994), and depressed mood is more common in adolescence than it is in childhood or adulthood (Petersen et al., 1993). Rates of most types of risk behavior rise sharply during adolescence and peak during late adolescence or emerging adulthood. The different aspects of storm and stress have different peak ages: conflict with parents in early adolescence to midadolescence, mood disruptions in midadolescence, and risk behavior in late adolescence and emerging adulthood (Arnett, 1999a).

We will explore each of the aspects of storm and stress in more detail in later chapters. For now, however, it should be emphasized that even though there is evidence to support a modified storm and stress view, this does not mean that storm and stress is typical of all adolescents in all places and times. Cultures vary in the degree of storm and stress experienced by their adolescents, with storm and stress relatively low in traditional cultures and relatively high in Western cultures (Arnett, 1999a). Also, within every culture there is variability among individuals in the amount of adolescent storm and stress they experience.

Adolescence and Emerging Adulthood

"When our mothers were our age, they were engaged. . . . They at least had some idea what they were going to do with their lives. . . . I, on the other hand, will have a dual degree in majors that are ambiguous at best and impractical at worst (English and political science), no ring on my finger and no idea who I am, much less what I want to do. . . . Under duress, I will admit that this is a pretty exciting time. Sometimes, when I look out across the wide expanse that is my future, I can see beyond the void. I realize that having nothing ahead to count on means I now have to count on myself; that having no direction means forging one of my own."

—*Kristen, age 22 (Page, 1999, pp. 18, 20)*

In the various eras of history described in the previous section, when people referred to adolescents (or youth or whatever term a particular era or society used), they usually indicated that they meant not just the early teen years but the late teens and into the twenties as well. This was as true during the age of adolescence, when the term adolescence first became widely used, as it had been in earlier times. When G. Stanley Hall (1904) initiated the scientific study of adolescence early in the 20th century, he defined the age range of adolescence as beginning at *14* and ending at *24* (Hall, 1904, vol. 1, p. xix). In contrast, today's scholars generally consider adolescence to begin at about age 10 and end by about age 18. Studies published in the major journals on adolescence rarely include samples with ages higher than 18 (Arnett, 2000a). What happened between Hall's time and our own to move scholars' conceptions of adolescence forward chronologically in the life course?

Two changes stand out as possible explanations. One is the decline that has taken place during the 20th century in the typical age of the initiation of puberty. At the beginning of the 20th century, the median age of **menarche** (the term for a girl's first menstruation) in Western countries was about 15 (Eveleth & Tanner,

1976). Because menarche takes place relatively late in the typical sequence of pubertal changes, this means that the initial changes of puberty would have begun somewhere in the range of ages 13 to 15 for most boys and girls (usually somewhat earlier for girls than for boys), which is just where Hall designated the beginning of adolescence. However, the median age of menarche (and, by implication, other pubertal changes) declined steadily between 1900 and 1970 before leveling out, so that by now the typical age of menarche in the United States is 12.5 (Brooks-Gunn & Paikoff, 1997). The initial changes of puberty begin about 2 years earlier, thus the designation of adolescence is beginning at about age 10.

As for when adolescence ends, the change in this age may have been inspired not by a biological change but by a social change: the growth of high school attendance to a normative experience for adolescents in the United States. As noted earlier, in 1890 only 5% of persons aged 14 to 17 were enrolled in high school. However, this proportion rose steeply and steadily throughout the 20th century to 95% by 1985 (Arnett & Taber, 1994). Because attending high school is now nearly universal among American adolescents and because high school graduation usually takes place at age 18, it makes sense for scholars studying American adolescents to designate the end of adolescence as age 18. In contrast, Hall did not choose 18 as the end of adolescence because for most adolescents of his time no significant transition took place at that age. Education ended earlier, work began earlier, leaving home took place later. Marriage and parenthood did not take place for most people until their midtwenties (Arnett & Taber, 1994), which may have been why Hall designated the end of adolescence as age 24.

Hall viewed the late teens and early twenties as an especially interesting time of life. I agree, and I think it would be a mistake to cut off our study of adolescence in this book at age 18. A great deal happens in the late teens and early twenties that is related to development earlier in adolescence, and that has important implications for the path that development takes in adulthood. I have called this period **emerging adulthood**, and I consider it to include roughly the ages 18 to 25 (Arnett, 1998a, 2000a; Arnett & Taber, 1994). This is a transitional period, in American society as well as in many other societies, of moving out of adolescence and into adulthood.

Although a great deal of variability exists among emerging adults, perhaps the most distinctive characteristic of emerging adulthood is that it is a period of experimentation and exploration. Emerging adults are more independent of their parents than adolescents are, and most of them have not yet entered into the long-term commitments in love and work that most adults have. During emerging adulthood, in between the reliance on parents of adolescence and the commitments and responsibilities of adulthood, young people often try out a variety of life possibilities in love, work, education, and worldviews (Arnett, 2000a, 2000b; Erikson, 1968).

The exploratory nature of emerging adulthood is reflected in emerging adults' living arrangements. Most young Americans move out of their parents' household by age 18 or 19 (Goldscheider & Goldscheider, 1999). During emerging adulthood, from ages 18 to 25, they have the highest rate of residential change of any age group (Figure 1.1). This reflects the experimentation and exploration going on in their lives. They may attend college for a while, then stop for a while to work full-time, then perhaps resume college. Some move to another part of the country or the world to study or work. Some try graduate school after college. They experiment and explore in love as well: The majority have sexual intercourse for the first time in their late teens and have a series of love relationships from their late teens until they marry in their late twenties. About two-thirds of American emerging adults also cohabit with a romantic partner before marriage (Michael et al., 1995). For about 40% of emerging adults, their residential changes include moving back in with their parents at least once (Goldscheider & Goldscheider, 1999).

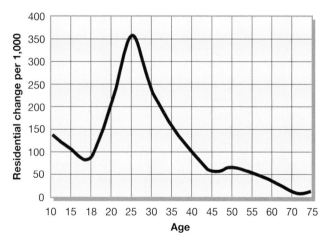

FIGURE 1.1 *Rate of residential change by age.*
Source: U.S. Bureau of the Census (2000).

Although experimentation and exploration are characteristic of the lives of many emerging adults, such opportunities are not available to all of them. The young woman who has a child outside of marriage at age 16 and spends her late teens and early twenties alternating between welfare and low-paying jobs has little chance for experimentation and exploration; nor does the young man who drops out of school and spends most of his late teens and early twenties unemployed and looking unsuccessfully for a job. Also, some young people choose not to experiment and explore during their late teens and early twenties, but prefer to enter adult role commitments relatively early. We will use the term *emerging adulthood* in this book to refer to persons aged 18 to 25, and will sometimes focus on the experimentation and exploration that characterizes this age period for most young people, while also recognizing that emerging adults are diverse in their life situations and life choices.

Another distinctive feature of emerging adulthood is that most emerging adults themselves experience it as an in-between period, not adolescence but not quite adulthood, either. When asked "Do you feel that you have reached adulthood?" the majority of emerging adults respond neither yes nor no, but the ambiguous "in some respects yes, in some respects no" (Arnett, 1994a, 1997, 1998a, 2000a). As Figure 1.2 shows, it is only when people reach their late twenties and early thirties that a clear majority feel they have reached adulthood. Most emerging adults have the subjective sense of being still in a stage of exploration, of not yet taking on the roles and responsibilities that come with adulthood (Arnett, 1998a).

Emerging adulthood does not exist in all cultures. Cultures vary widely in the ages that young people are expected to enter full adulthood and take on adult responsibilities (Schlegel & Barry, 1991). Emerging adulthood exists only in cultures in which young people are allowed to postpone entering adult roles such as marriage and parenthood until at least their mid-twenties (Arnett, 2000a). Thus, emerging adulthood exists mainly in industrialized societies such as the United States, Canada, most of Europe, Australia, New Zealand, and Japan (Arnett, 2000a; Chisholm & Hurrelmann, 1995). However, in many other areas of the world, emerging adulthood is growing in prevalence as cultures become more industrialized and more integrated into a global economy. This topic will be addressed often in the chapters to come.

Emerging adulthood is a recent phenomenon historically. In the United States, the median ages of marriage is at a record high—about 25 for women and 27 for men (Arnett, 2000a)—and has risen steeply over the past 40 years (see Table 1.2). Also, a higher proportion of young Americans than ever before attends at least some college—currently, over 60% (Bianchi & Spain, 1996). Similar changes have taken place in recent decades in other industrialized countries (Arnett, 2000d; Chisholm & Hurrelmann, 1995; see Table 1.3). This postponement of adult responsibilities into the mid- to late twenties makes possible the experimentation and exploration of emerging adulthood. With growing industrialization and economic integration worldwide, emerging adulthood is likely to become increasingly common

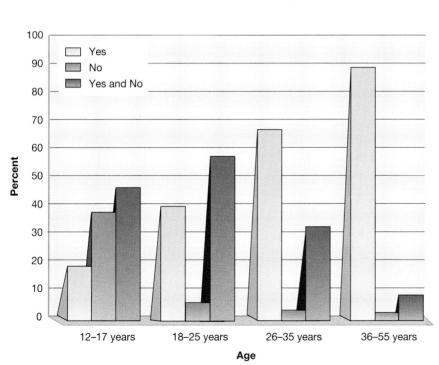

FIGURE 1.2 *Age differences in response to the question, "Do you feel that you have reached adulthood?"*

Source: Arnett (2000a).

TABLE 1.2: MEDIAN AGE OF FIRST MARRIAGE AND FIRST BIRTH IN THE UNITED STATES, 1890–1997

Year	Marriage		First Birth
	Men	*Women*	*Women*
1997	26.8	25.0	25.0
1988	25.9	23.6	23.7
1980	24.7	22.0	23.0
1970	23.2	20.8	22.1
1960	22.8	20.3	21.8
1950	22.8	20.3	22.5
1940	24.3	21.5	23.2
1930	24.3	21.3	—*
1920	24.6	21.2	—
1910	25.1	21.6	—
1900	25.9	21.9	—
1890	26.1	22.0	—

*Median age at first birth is not available before 1940.

Sources: U.S. Bureau of the Census (1991) (marriage) and U.S. Department of Health and Human Services (1990) (first birth).

around the world in the 21st century (Arnett, 2000a, 2000d).

In this book, then, we will cover three periods: **early adolescence**, from age 10 to about age 14; **late adolescence**, from age 15 to about age 18, and emerging adulthood, from about age 18 to about age 25. Including all three of these periods will allow us to examine across a broad age range the various aspects of young people's development—the biological, psychological, and social changes they experience over time. Studies on early and late adolescence are more abundant than studies of emerging adulthood, so most of the information in the book will refer to adolescence, but each chapter will contain some information on emerging adulthood.

THINKING CRITICALLY

Is 25 a good rough upper age boundary for the end of emerging adulthood? Where would you put the upper age boundary, and why?

The Transition to Adulthood

Adolescence is generally viewed as beginning with the first noticeable changes of puberty (Feldman & Elliott, 1990). The end of adolescence, as we have defined it here, is also quite clear: age 18, when most Americans reach the end of their high school education. Age 18 also marks the beginning of emerging adulthood, as most young people leave home shortly after high school and begin the exploratory activities that characterize emerging adulthood. But what marks the end of emerging adulthood? If emerging adulthood is in many ways a period of transition from adolescence to full adulthood, how does a person know when the transition to adulthood is complete? The answer to this question is complex and varies notably among cultures. First, we examine the transition to adulthood in American society, then in non-Western cultures.

> "BUT WHEN, BY WHAT TEST, BY WHAT INDICATION DOES MANHOOD COMMENCE? PHYSICALLY, BY ONE CRITERION, LEGALLY BY ANOTHER. MORALLY BY A THIRD, INTELLECTUALLY BY A FOURTH—AND ALL INDEFINITE.
> —THOMAS DE QUINCEY, *AUTOBIOGRAPHY*, 1821

TABLE 1.3: MEDIAN MARRIAGE AGE (FEMALES) IN SELECTED COUNTRIES, 1995

Industrialized Countries	Age	Developing Countries	Age
Canada	26.0	Egypt	21.9
Germany	26.2	Ghana	21.1
France	26.1	Nigeria	18.7
Italy	25.8	India	20.0
Japan	26.9	Indonesia	21.1
Australia	26.0	Brazil	22.6

Source: Noble, Cover, & Yanagishita (1996).

A young person in three periods: early adolescence (age 10–14), late adolescence (age 15–18), and emerging adulthood (age 18–25).

THINKING CRITICALLY

In your view, what marks the attainment of adulthood for yourself? For others, generally?

The Transition to Adulthood, American Style

“*Sometimes I feel like I've reached adulthood, and then I'll sit down and eat ice cream directly from the box, and I keep thinking, 'I'll know I'm an adult when I don't eat cream right out of the box anymore.' . . . But I guess in some ways I feel like I'm an adult. I'm a pretty responsible person. I mean, if I say I'm going to do something, I do it. Financially, I'm fairly responsible with my money. But there are still times where I think, 'I can't believe I'm 25.' A lot of times I don't really feel like an adult.*”

—Lisa, age 25 (Arnett, unpublished data)

In industrialized societies, there are a variety of possible ways one could define the transition to adulthood. Legally, the transition to adulthood takes place in most respects at age 18. This is the age at which a person becomes an adult for various legal purposes, such as signing legally binding documents and being eligible to vote. One could also define the transition to adulthood as entering the roles that are typically considered to be part of adulthood: full-time work, marriage, and parenthood (Hogan & Astone, 1986).

But what about young people themselves? How do young people in industrialized societies conceptualize the transition to adulthood? Four recent studies tell us what most young people in the American majority culture view as the key markers of the transition to adulthood (Arnett, 1994a, Arnett, 1998a; Greene, Wheatley, & Aldava, 1992; Scheer, Unger, & Brown, 1994). The results of the four studies were very similar. Young people from their midteens to their late twenties agreed that the most important markers of the transition from adolescence to adulthood are *accepting responsibility for one's self, becoming capable of making independent decisions,* and *becoming financially independent,* in that order. Note the similarity among these three criteria: All three are characterized by **individualism**, all three emphasize the importance of learning to stand alone as a self-sufficient individual without relying on anyone else. Thus, they reflect the individualistic values of the American majority culture (Bellah et al., 1985; Triandis, 1995).

The Transition to Adulthood, Other Perspectives

What about traditional cultures? Do they have different ideas about what marks the beginning of adulthood, compared to industrialized societies? The answer appears to be yes. Anthropologists have found that in virtually all traditional, non-Western cultures, the transition to adulthood is clearly and explicitly marked by *marriage* (Schlegel & Barry, 1991). It is only after marriage that a person is considered to have attained adult status and is given adult privileges and responsibilities. In contrast, few of the young Americans in the four studies mentioned above indicated that they considered marriage to be an important marker of the transition to adulthood.

What should we make of that contrast? One possible interpretation would be that traditional cultures elevate marriage as the key transition to adulthood because they value **interdependence** more than independence, and marriage signifies that a person is taking on new interdependent relationships outside the family of origin (Arnett, 1995a, 1998a; Markus & Kitiyama, 1991; Turnbull, 1983). Marriage is a social event rather than an individual, psychological process, and it represents the establishment of a new network of relationships with all the kin of one's marriage partner. This is especially true in traditional cultures, where family members are more likely than in the West to be close-knit and to have daily contact with one another. Thus, cultures that value interdependence view marriage as the most important marker of leaving adolescence and entering adulthood be-

cause of the ways marriage confirms and strengthens interdependence.

Still, these conclusions about traditional cultures are based mainly on the observations of the anthropologists who have studied them. If you asked young people in these cultures directly about their own conceptions of what marks the end of adolescence and the beginning of adulthood, perhaps you would get a variety of answers other than marriage. For example, Susan Davis and Douglas Davis (1989) asked young Moroccans (aged 9 to 20) "How do you know you're grown up?" They found that the two most common types of responses were (1) those that emphasized chronological age or physical development, such as the beginning of facial hair among boys; and (2) those that emphasized character qualities, such as developing self-control (see the Cultural Focus box). Few of the young people mentioned marriage, even though Davis and Davis (1989) stated that in Moroccan culture generally, "after marriage, one is considered an adult" (p. 59). This suggests that further investigation of young people's conceptions of the transition to adulthood in traditional cultures may prove enlightening, and that their views may not match the conceptions of adulthood held by adults.

THINKING CRITICALLY

How is the Moroccan conception of adolescence similar to and different from the view stated by Plato and Aristotle?

Marriage is of great significance as a marker of adulthood in traditional cultures. Here, a Burmese bride and groom (center) and their attendants.

The Scientific Study of Adolescence and Emerging Adulthood

One can gain insights into development during adolescence and emerging adulthood in many ways. There are some excellent autobiographies of these periods such as *This Boy's Life* by Tobias Wolff (1987) and the autobiography of Anne Frank (1942/1997). Journalists have written accounts of various aspects of these periods, often focusing on a particular young person or a small group (for a recent example, see Hersch [1998]). Some terrific novels have been written that focus on adolescence and emerging adulthood, such

CULTURAL FOCUS
Moroccan Conceptions of Adolescence

Anthropologists Susan Davis and Douglas Davis (1989) have been studying adolescents in Morocco for nearly three decades, originally as part of the Harvard Adolescence Project described in this chapter. One of the questions that has interested them in their research concerns the qualities Moroccans see as characteristic of adolescence.

The most important concept in Moroccan views of adolescence is the concept of 'aql. This is an Arabic word that has connotations of reasonableness, understanding, and rationality. Self-control and self-restraint are also part of 'aql—to possess 'aql means to have control over your needs and passions and to be able and willing to restrain them out of respect for those around you. Moroccans see 'aql as a quality expected of adults and often lacking in adolescents.

'Aql is expected to develop in both males and females during adolescence, but males are believed to take a decade longer to develop it fully! However, do not assume that this is for biological reasons. Unlike males, females are given a variety of responsibilities from an early age, such as household work and taking care of younger siblings, so it is more important for them to develop 'aql earlier to meet the demands of these responsibilities. It is quite common, not just in Morocco but worldwide in traditional cultures, that much more work is required out of females in adolescence than out of males (Schlegel & Barry, 1991; Whiting & Edwards, 1988).

Another term Moroccans use in reference to adolescence is *taysh*, which means reckless, rash, and frivolous. This quality is especially associated with awakening sexuality and the possible violations of social norms this awakening may incite (female virginity before marriage is very important to Moroccans). Taysh is a quality associated with adolescence in the views of many Moroccans, as illustrated in this exchange between Susan Davis and Naima, a mother of two adolescents:

Susan: What does this word taysh *mean?*

Naima: It starts at the age of fifteen, sixteen, seven-

Moroccan adolescents.

teen, eighteen, nineteen until twenty. [It lasts] until she develops her 'aql. *She is frivolous [taysha] for about 4 years.*

Susan: How do you know they have reached that age? How would you know when Najet [her daughter, age 13] gets there?

Naima: You can recognize it. The girl becomes frivolous. She starts caring about her appearance, dressing well, wearing fancy clothes and showy things, you understand. . . . She also messes up her school schedule. She either leaves too early or comes too late [i.e., she may be changing her schedule to meet boys]. You have to be watchful with her at that juncture. If you see she is on the right path, you leave her alone. If you notice that she is too late or far off the timing, then you have to set the record straight with her until the age of adolescence is over. When she is twenty years of age, she recovers her ability to reason and be rational.

Susan: When your son Saleh [age 14] reaches the age of adolescence, how would you know it?

Naima: I will notice that he doesn't come home on time, he will start playing hookey. . . . He will start

> *following girls. . . . Girls will start complaining,*
> *'Your son is following me.' This is the first conse-*
> *quence.*
>
> *Susan: So it's similar to the girl—the girl will dress*
> *in a fancy way, while the boy will start getting inter-*
> *ested in her.*
>
> *Naima: That's it.*
>
> Moroccans explicitly state that marriage marks
> the end of adolescence and the entry into adult-
> hood. However, from their use of the terms *'aql* and
> *taysh*, we can see that the transition to adulthood
> also involves intangible qualities similar to the ones
> important to American adolescents and emerging
> adults. Can you see the similarities between *'aql* and
> *taysh* and the qualities important in Americans' con-
> ceptions of the transition to adulthood discussed in
> this chapter?

as J. D. Salinger's *Catcher in the Rye* (1951/1964), and Russell Banks's *The Rule of the Bone* (1995).

I will draw on sources in all these areas for illustrations and examples. However, the main focus in this book will be on the scientific study of adolescence and emerging adulthood. You will be learning about development during adolescence and emerging adulthood as an area of the social sciences. You will read about the most important and influential studies that have contributed to this field.

What does it mean for scholars to engage in the scientific study of adolescence and emerging adulthood? It means to apply the standards of the **scientific method** to the questions we investigate (Cozby, Worden, & Kee, 1989; Goodwin, 1995; Shaughnessy & Zechmeister, 1985). The scientific method includes standards of **sampling**, **procedure**, and **measures**.

With respect to sampling, scholars who study adolescents and emerging adults seek to obtain a **sample** that represents the **population** they are interested in. Suppose, for example, a scholar wants to study adolescents' attitudes toward contraception. A Planned Parenthood clinic offering contraceptive services would probably not be a good place to look for a sample, because the adolescents coming to such a clinic are quite likely to have more favorable attitudes toward contraception than adolescents in general—otherwise, why would they be coming to a place offering contraceptive services? Instead, if a scholar wanted to know about the attitudes of adolescents *in general* toward contraception, it would be better to sample adolescents through schools or through a telephone survey that selected households randomly from the community.

On the other hand, if a scholar was particularly interested in attitudes toward contraception among the population of adolescents who are already using or planning to use contraception, then a Planned Parenthood clinic would be a good place to find a sample. It depends on the population the scholar wishes to study and on the questions the scholar wishes to address. The goal is to seek out a sample that will be **representative** of the population of interest (Goodwin, 1995; Shaughnessy & Zechmeister, 1985). If the sample is representative of the population, then the findings from the sample will be **generalizable** to the population. In other words, the findings from the sample will make it possible to draw conclusions about not just the sample itself, but the larger population of adolescents that the sample is intended to represent.

The procedure of the study is the second consideration of the scientific method. The procedure refers to the way the study is conducted and the data is collected. One standard aspect of the procedure in scientific studies of human beings is **informed consent** (Goodwin, 1995). Human subjects participating in any scientific study are supposed to be presented with a **consent form** before they participate (Shaughnessy & Zechmeister, 1985). Consent forms typically include information about who is conducting the study, what the purposes of the study are, what participation in the study involves (e.g., filling out a questionnaire on contraceptive use), what risks (if any) are involved in participating, and what the person can expect to receive in return for participation. Consent forms also usually include a statement indicating that participation in the study is voluntary, and that persons may withdraw from participation in the study at any time.

The use of consent forms is not always possible (for example, in telephone surveys), but whenever possible they are included in the procedure for scholars studying adolescents and emerging adults. For adolescents under age 18, the consent of one of their parents is also usually required as part of a study's procedures.

Another aspect of the procedure is the circumstances of the data collection. Scholars try to collect data in a way that will not be biased. For example, scholars must be careful not to phrase questions in an interview or questionnaire in a way that seems to lead people toward a desired response. They must also assure participants that their responses will be confidential, especially if the study concerns a sensitive topic such as sexual behavior or drug use.

The measures used in the study are the other key aspect of the scientific method. In the next section, we will consider a variety of measures used in research on development in adolescence and emerging adulthood. This will also be a way of introducing some of the major studies on adolescence and emerging adulthood, studies that I will be referring to often in the course of the book.

THINKING CRITICALLY

You have probably read about topics concerning adolescence and emerging adulthood in newspapers and magazines. In general, do these journalistic pieces meet the criteria for scientific research?

Measures Used in Research

Scholars conduct research on adolescence and emerging adulthood in a variety of academic disciplines, including psychology, sociology, anthropology, education, and medicine. They use a variety of different measures in their investigations.

Two key issues with all measures are **reliability** and **validity**. There are a variety of types of reliability, but in general, a measure has high reliability if it obtains similar results on different occasions (Shaughnessy & Zechmeister, 1985). For example, if a questionnaire asked girls in their senior year of high school to recall when their first menstrual period occurred, the questionnaire would be considered reliable if most of the girls answered the same on one occasion as they did when asked the question again 6 months later. Or, if adolescents were interviewed about the quality of their relationships with their parents, the measure would be

reliable if the adolescents' answers were the same for two different interviewers (Goodwin, 1995).

Validity refers to the truthfulness of a measure (Shaughnessy & Zechmeister, 1985). A measure is valid if it measures what it claims to measure. For example, IQ tests claim to measure intellectual abilities, but as we shall see in Chapter 3, this claim is controversial. Critics claim that IQ tests are not valid (i.e., that they do not measure what they claim to measure). Notice that a measure is not necessarily valid even if it is reliable. It is widely agreed that IQ tests are reliable—people generally score about the same on one occasion as they do on another—but the validity of the tests is disputed. In general, validity is more difficult to establish than reliability.

We will examine questions of reliability and validity throughout the book. For now, we turn to the measures.

Questionnaires The most commonly used measurement approach in social science research is the questionnaire (Sudman & Bradburn, 1989). Usually, questionnaires have a **closed question** format, which means that participants are provided with specific responses from which to choose (Sudman & Bradburn, 1989). Sometimes the questions have an **open-ended question** format, which means that participants are allowed to write in their response following the question. One advantage of closed questions is that they make it possible to collect and analyze responses from a large number of people in a relatively short time (Shaughnessy & Zechmeister, 1985). Everyone responds to the same questions with the same response options.

For this reason, closed questions have often been used in large-scale surveys conducted on adolescents and emerging adults. One of the most valuable of these surveys is the Monitoring the Future survey conducted by the Institute for Social Research at the University of Michigan (Bachman et al., 1997; Johnston, O'Malley, & Bachman, 1995; O'Malley, Bachman, & Johnston, 1988). Since 1974, the Monitoring the Future (MTF) survey has collected data on over 10,000 high school seniors every year. The survey focuses on drug use, but it also contains a variety of questions on topics from educational aspirations to socializing with friends (e.g., Osgood et al., 1996; Schulenberg et al., 1995). Since 1990, the MTF survey has included a sample of 8th grade and 10th grade adolescents as well as high school seniors. Also, MTF follow-up studies of adolescents who were high school seniors in the 1980s now extend to nearly age 30 (e.g., Bachman et al.,

1997). This makes the MTF survey an extremely valuable resource on emerging adulthood as well as adolescence.

Interviews   Although questionnaires are the dominant method used in the study of adolescence and emerging adulthood, the use of questionnaires has certain limitations (Sudman & Bradburn, 1989). When a closed question format questionnaire is used, the range of possible responses is already specified, and the participant must choose from the responses provided. The researcher tries to cover the responses that seem most plausible and most likely, but it is impossible in a few brief response options to do justice to the depth and diversity of human experience. For example, if a questionnaire contains an item such as "How close are you to your mother? A. very close; B. somewhat close; C. not very close; D. not at all close," it is probably true that an adolescent who chooses "very close" really is closer to his/her mother than the adolescent who chooses "not at all close." But this alone does not begin to capture the complexity of the relationship between an adolescent and a parent.

Interviews are intended to provide the kind of individuality and complexity that questionnaires usually lack (Briggs, 1989). An interview allows a scholar to hear adolescents and emerging adults describe their lives in their own words, with all the uniqueness and richness that such descriptions make possible. An interview also allows a scholar to know the whole person and see how the various parts of the person's life are intertwined. For example, an interview on an adolescent's family relationships might reveal how the adolescent's relationship with her mother is affected by her relationship with her father, and how the whole family was affected by certain events—perhaps a family member's loss of a job, psychological problems, medical problems, or substance abuse.

Interviews provide **qualitative** data, as contrasted with the **quantitative** data of questionnaires, and qualitative data can be interesting and informative. However, like questionnaires, interviews have limitations (Sudman & Bradburn, 1989; Shaughnessy & Zechmeister, 1985). Because interviews do not typically provide preclassified responses the way questionnaires do, interview responses have to be coded according to some plan of classification. For example, if you asked the interview question, "What occupation do you plan to have by age 30?" you might get a fascinating range of responses from a sample of adolescents or emerging adults. Those responses would help to inform you

about the entire range of occupations young people imagine themselves having as adults. However, to make sense of the data and present it in a scientific format, at some point you would have to code the responses into categories—business, arts, professional/technical, trades, and so on. Only in this way would you be able to say something about the pattern of responses among your sample.

Coding interview data takes time, effort, and money. This is one of the reasons far more studies are conducted using questionnaires than using interviews. However, some excellent studies have been conducted using interview data. For example, William Julius Wilson, a sociologist, has conducted studies of hundreds of African American emerging adults in poor neighborhoods in Chicago (Wilson, 1987, 1996). The focus of his research is on the difficulties many young urban African Americans face in pursuing educational and occupational opportunities. He analyzes the connections between high unemployment among young urban African Americans and the schools they attend, the neighborhoods they live in, their beliefs about work and about education, their family circumstances, and employers' views of them as potential employees. In his books, he combines quantitative and qualitative data to portray the lives of young African Americans in a way that is extremely lively, insightful, and enlightening. Wilson's quantitative data provide the reader with a clear understanding of the overall pattern of young people's lives in urban ghettos, but at the same time his qualitative examples bring to life the individual perspectives and circumstances of the people he studies. We will talk more about Wilson's studies, especially in Chapter 11 on work.

Ethnographic Research   Another way scholars have learned about adolescence and emerging adulthood is through **ethnographic research** (Jessor, Colby, & Shweder, 1996). In ethnographic research, scholars spend a considerable amount of time among the people they wish to study, usually by living among them. Information gained in ethnographic research typically comes from scholars' observations, experiences, and informal conversations with the people they are studying. Ethnographic research is commonly used by anthropologists, usually in studying non-Western cultures. Anthropologists usually report the results of their research in an **ethnography**, which is a book that presents an anthropologist's observations of what life is like in a particular culture.

Margaret Mead and a Samoan adolescent.

The first ethnography on adolescence was written by Margaret Mead (1928). Mead studied the people of Samoa, which is a group of islands in the South Pacific. One of the inspirations of her study was to see whether the "storm and stress" said by G. Stanley Hall to be typical of American adolescents would also be present in a non-Western culture where life was much different than in American society. She reported that, contrary to Hall's claim that adolescent storm and stress was biologically based and therefore universal, most adolescents in Samoa passed through adolescence smoothly, with little sign of turmoil or upheaval.

After Mead's ethnography of Samoan adolescence, several decades passed before anthropologists gave much attention to adolescence. However, in the 1980s two eminent anthropologists at Harvard University, Beatrice and John Whiting, set out to remedy this neglect. They initiated the **Harvard Adolescence Project**, in which they sent young scholars to do ethnographic research in seven different cultures in various parts of the world. The cultures included the Inuit (Eskimos)

of the Canadian Arctic; aborigines in Northern Australia; Muslims in Thailand; the Kikuyu of Kenya; the Ijo of Nigeria; rural Romania; and Morocco.

The project produced a series of extremely interesting and enlightening ethnographies (Burbank, 1988; Condon, 1987; Davis & Davis, 1989; Hollos & Leis, 1989). These ethnographies show not only the enormous variation that exists in the nature of adolescence in cultures around the world, but also the ways that cultures even in remote areas are being influenced by the West and by globalization. I will be drawing from these ethnographies often in the course of the book.

Biological Measurement   The biological changes of puberty are a central part of adolescent development, so research on adolescence includes measurement of biological factors. One area of this research has focused on the timing and pace of different aspects of physical development during puberty, such as genital changes and the growth of pubic hair. Several decades ago a British physician, J. M. Tanner, conducted a series of studies that carefully monitored adolescents' physical changes and established valid information about the timing and sequence of these changes (Eveleth & Tanner, 1976; Tanner, 1962). More recently, scholars have conducted research measuring hormonal levels at various points during adolescence and looking at the ways hormonal levels are related to adolescents' moods and behavior (Brooks-Gunn & Reiter, 1990; Susman, 1997). We will examine biological research on adolescence in various chapters of the book, especially Chapter 2 (Biological Foundations).

Daily Records   All the methods described so far have been around for many decades in the social sciences. One new method that shows great promise for providing insights into adolescence and emerging adulthood is the **Experience Sampling Method (ESM)** developed by Csikszentmihalyi and Larson (1984; Larson & Richards, 1994). This method involves having young people wear beepers, usually for one week. When they are beeped at random times during the day, they record a variety of characteristics of their experience at that moment, including where they are, who they are with, what they are thinking, and what they are feeling. The results provide a unique perspective on adolescents' daily experiences. The ESM studies have been especially important in providing insights into adolescents' emotional lives and their experiences in their families. I will refer to these studies often, especially in Chapter 6 (The Self) and Chapter 7 (Family Relationships).

Other measures are also used in research on adolescence and emerging adulthood, such as laboratory experiments and observations. Throughout the book, I will present studies using a wide variety of methods. For now, the measures described above provide you with an introduction to some of the measures used most often.

THINKING CRITICALLY

Choose a topic on adolescence and emerging adulthood that you would be interested in studying. What methodological approach would you use, and why?

Theories and Research

A crucial part of the scientific process in any field is the development of theories. A good theory presents a set of interconnected ideas in an original and insightful way and points the way to further research. Theories and research are intrinsically connected: A theory generates research, and research leads to modifications of the theory, which generates further research. A good example of this is G. Stanley Hall's storm and stress theory. His theory has generated a great deal of research in this century; in turn, this research resulted in modifications of his theory because research has showed that storm and stress was not as extreme and was not universal in adolescence as he had proposed. Research still continues on the questions his theory provoked, such as the extent to which conflict with parents is common in adolescence (Arnett, 1999a; Laursen, Coy, & Collins, 1998).

There is no separate chapter on theories in this book, not because I do not think theories are important but because I think theories and research are intrinsically connected and should be presented together. Theories are presented in every chapter in relation to the research they have generated and the questions they have raised for future research.

Themes of the Book

In the course of the book we will be addressing a variety of different topics on adolescence and emerging adulthood, from puberty to education to problems of various kinds. However, a number of themes will be part of every chapter: cultural contrasts, historical contrasts, interdisciplinary approach, gender issues, and globalization.

Cultural Contrasts

The cultural approach is a central part of this book. It is essential to be aware of cultural issues and cultural differences in order to gain a complete understanding of development in adolescence and emerging adulthood. What it is like to be an adolescent or an emerging adult in the American middle class is different in many ways from being a young person in Egypt, or Thailand, or Brazil—and also different from being a young person in certain American minority cultures, such as urban African American culture or the culture of recent Mexican American immigrants. Although the physical changes of puberty are similar everywhere, cultures differ greatly in how they respond to these changes and in what they allow and expect from their adolescents. Cultures also differ in how much freedom for experimentation and exploration they allow emerging adults.

Until recently, scholars focused almost exclusively on adolescents and emerging adults in the White American middle class. However, in the past two decades this has changed dramatically. By now, scholars have presented descriptions of development in adolescence and emerging adulthood in places all over the world, and scholars focusing on American society have increased their attention to cultures in the United States that are outside of the White middle class.

Throughout the book, I present examples from many different cultures for each of the topics we address. Also, each chapter has a box called Cultural Focus, which looks in more detail at one particular culture with respect to the topic of the chapter.

Historical Contrasts

In the same way that we can learn a lot about adolescence and emerging adulthood from comparing different cultures, we can also learn a lot by comparing the lives of adolescents and emerging adults today to adolescence and emerging adulthood as it was experienced in other times. Throughout the book, I provide historical information on each of the topics we discuss. Also, each chapter has a box entitled Historical Focus that provides more detailed information on a specific issue in a specific historical period.

Interdisciplinary Approach

Most scholars studying adolescence and emerging adulthood are psychologists. They have been trained in psychology, and they work as professors in the psychology departments of colleges and universities. However, many scholars in other disciplines are also studying adolescence and emerging adulthood. Anthropology's recent studies we have already discussed. Sociology has a long tradition of scholarship on adolescence and emerging adulthood, and some of the most important studies in such areas as peer relations, delinquency, and the transition to adulthood come from sociology. Physicians, especially in psychiatry and pediatrics, have also made important contributions, especially concerning the biology of adolescence and emerging adulthood and the treatment of medical disorders that may occur during these age periods, such as anorexia nervosa. Scholars in education have contributed insightful work on adolescents' and emerging adults' development in relation to school, as well as other topics. In recent years historians have published a number of excellent studies on adolescence and emerging adulthood.

The boundaries we set up between different disciplines are useful in some ways, but they are essentially artificial. If you want to understand development in adolescence and emerging adulthood, you should seek insights wherever you can find them. I want you to have as full an understanding of adolescence and emerging adulthood as possible by the time you finish this book, and toward that goal I will use material from psychology, anthropology, sociology, psychiatry, education, history, and other disciplines.

Gender Issues

In every culture known to us, gender is a key issue in development throughout the life span (Carroll & Wolpe, 1996; Chinas, 1992). The expectations cultures have for males and females are different from the time they are born (Maccoby, 1990). Children become aware of their own gender by the time they are about 2 years old, and with this awareness they grow sensitive to the differences in what is considered appropriate behavior for each gender. Differences in cultural expectations related to gender typically become more pronounced at puberty (Brooks-Gunn & Reiter, 1990). Adolescence and emerging adulthood are, among other things, periods of preparation for taking on adult roles in the family and in work. In most cultures these roles differ considerably depending on whether you are male or female, so the expectations for male and female adolescents and emerging adults differ accordingly. Roles in the courtship and sexual behavior that are typically part of adolescence and emerging adulthood also differ considerably between males and females in most cultures.

Although all cultures have different expectations for males and females, the *degree* of the differences varies greatly among cultures. In the majority cultures of the West these days, the differences are relatively blurred: Men and women hold many of the same jobs, wear many of the same clothes (e.g., blue jeans, t-shirts), and enjoy many of the same entertainments. If you have grown up in the West, you may be surprised to learn how deep gender differences go in many other cultures. For example, in Morocco, boys are more or less expected to become sexually experienced before marriage (Davis & Davis, 1989). Girls, on the other hand, are expected to be virgins on their wedding night. Thus, the boys' first sexual experience is typically with a prostitute. The morning after the wedding, bride and groom are obliged to hang the sheet from their bed out the window, complete with a bloody stain on it to prove that the girl's hymen was broken on the wedding night, thus confirming she had been a virgin until that moment.

Nothing comparable to this exists in the West. However, gender-specific expectations exist in the West, too. Even now, there are few male nurses or male secretaries or full-time fathers, and there are few female truck drivers or female engineers or female U.S. Senators. The differences in expectations for males and females may be more subtle in the West than in some other cultures, but they remain powerful, and they are a key part of adolescence and emerging adulthood. Throughout the book, I bring up gender differences for each of the topics we address, and Chapter 5 is devoted specifically to gender issues. By the end of the book, I want you to have a broader sense of how males and females are treated differently in cultures around the world, and of how your own culture has shaped your development in gender-distinctive ways you may not have realized before now.

Globalization

Researchers on adolescence have recently begun giving more attention to cultural influences on development in adolescence and emerging adulthood. It is ironic, however, that this attention to culture comes at a time in world history when the boundaries that give cultures their distinctiveness are becoming steadily fainter (Clausen, 1996; Fukuyama, 1993), and the world is becoming increasingly integrated into a global culture—a "global village," as the social philosopher Marshall McLuhan put it some years ago. No traditional culture has remained exempt from these changes. You can go to the remotest rain forest culture in Venezuela, the northernmost Arctic village in Canada, the smallest mountain village of New Guinea, and you will find that every one of them is being drawn inexorably into a common world culture. Our exploration of development in adolescence and emerging adulthood would not be complete without including an account of these changes, which reflect the **globalization** of adolescence and emerging adulthood (Schlegel, 2000).

> "HUNGARIANS, CZECHOSLOVAKS AND BULGARIANS TRY TO IMITATE EVERYTHING THAT IS AMERICAN—AND I MEAN *EVERYTHING.* . . . IF WE KEEP GOING LIKE THIS, OUR SMALL COUNTRIES WILL GRADUALLY LOSE THEIR NATIONAL CULTURES."
> —MIKLOS VAMOS, HUNGARIAN JOURNALIST, 1994

Globalization of adolescence: A Venezuelan adolescent's t-shirt depicts characters from the American TV show "The Simpsons."

THINKING CRITICALLY

Have you traveled to another country in recent years? If so, can you think of examples you have witnessed that reflect the globalization of adolescence? If not, can you think of examples you have read about or heard about? What positive and negative consequences do you anticipate from the globalization of adolescence?

Globalization means that increasing worldwide technological and economic integration is making the world "smaller," more homogeneous. As a consequence of the globalization of adolescence and emerging adulthood, young people around the world experience increasingly similar environments. Adolescents and emerging adults all over the world are growing up listening to much of the same music, watching many of the same movies, going to school for an increasing number of years, learning how to use personal computers, drinking the same soft drinks, and wearing the same brands of blue jeans (Barber, 1995; Schlegel, 1998). The appeal of being connected to a global culture appears to be especially high among adolescents and emerging adults (Barber, 1995). Perhaps this is because they are more capable than children of seeking out information beyond the borders of their own culture—through travel and the Internet, for example—

> "KIDS ON THE STREETS OF TOKYO HAVE MORE IN COMMON WITH KIDS ON THE STREETS OF LONDON THAN THEY DO WITH THEIR PARENTS."
> —SUMNER REDSTONE, OWNER OF MTV, 1994

and less committed to established roles and a set way of life than adults are.

Throughout the book, I present examples of how the lives of adolescents and emerging adults are being affected by globalization. We will consider how their future lives are likely to be affected by this trend, in both positive and negative ways.

Framework of the Book

Following this introductory chapter, the book is divided into three sections. The first section, Foundations, includes chapters on five different areas of development: Biological Foundations, Cognitive Foundations, Cultural Beliefs, Gender, and the Self. These chapters describe the areas that form the foundation for young people's development across a variety of aspects of their lives. Together, these chapters form the basis for understanding development as it takes place in the various contexts in which young people live.

Thus, the first section sets the stage for the second section, called Contexts. **Context** is the term that scholars use to refer to the environmental settings in which development takes place. This section has chapters on six different contexts for adolescents' and emerging adults' development: Family Relationships; Friends and Peers; Dating, Love, and Sexuality; School; Work; and Media.

The third section is entitled Problems and Prospects. The first chapter in this section, Problems, addresses problems ranging from risky automobile driving to drug use to depression. The second chapter in this section, and the final chapter in the book, is on Adolescence and Emerging Adulthood in the 21st Century. In this chapter we look ahead to the future of development in adolescence and emerging adulthood, and consider the opportunities as well as the perils that may be experienced by the young people of the century to come.

Summing Up

This chapter has introduced you to the central ideas and concepts that we will be considering throughout the rest of the book. The following summarizes the key points we have discussed:

- The cultural approach taken in this book means that adolescence and emerging adulthood will be portrayed as being culturally constructed, in the sense that cultures determine what the experience of these age periods is like. Consequently, what it is like to be an adolescent or an emerging adult varies widely among cultures.

- Adolescence has a long history in Western societies as a specific period of life between childhood and adulthood. However, it was only during the years 1890–1920 that adolescence developed into its modern form, as a period of life when young people are largely excluded from adult work and spend their time mostly among their peers.

- Emerging adulthood is the term for the period from ages 18 to 25. It is a period during which many young people are more independent from their parents than they were as adolescents, but they have not yet taken on adult role responsibilities; consequently, they often have the opportunity to engage in experimentation and exploration in a variety of areas of life.

- A variety of different methods are used in the study of adolescence and emerging adulthood, ranging from questionnaires and interviews to ethnographic research to biological measurements.

- The book is divided into three major sections: Foundations, Contexts, and Problems and Prospects.

In each chapter, this Summing Up section restates the main points of the chapter, then offers some reflections on what we know at this point and what we have yet to learn.

The study of adolescence and emerging adulthood is relatively new. Adolescence has been established as a distinct field only since G. Stanley Hall's work was published a century ago; emerging adulthood is only just now becoming a distinct area of study. As you will see in the chapters to come, a remarkable amount has already been learned about these age periods. However, so far most research has focused on young people in the American majority culture. That focus is now broadening to include other groups in American society as well as young people in other cultures around the world. One of the goals of this books is to make you familiar with research on adolescence and emerging adulthood from many different cultures, so that you will be able to take a cultural approach in your own understanding of how young people develop during these years.

Key Terms

adolescence	survey	interdependence	closed question
culture	stratified sampling	scientific method	open-ended question
the West	random sample	sampling	interview
industrialized countries	inventionist view	procedure	qualitative
majority culture	child study movement	measures	quantitative
society	recapitulation	sample	ethnographic research
traditional culture	storm and stress	population	ethnography
developing countries	Lamarckian	representative	Harvard Adolescence
socioeconomic status	menarche	generalizable	Project
(SES)	emerging adulthood	informed consent	Experience Sampling
young people	early adolescence	consent form	Method (ESM)
life-cycle service	late adolescence	reliability	globalization
youth	individualism	validity	context
national survey			

For Further Reading

Hall, G. S. (1904). *Adolescence: Its psychology and its relation to physiology, anthropology, sociology, sex, crime, religion, and education* (Vols. I & II). Englewood Cliffs, NJ: Prentice-Hall. These are two thick volumes, each over 500 pages, but you may find it enjoyable to browse through them to get a sense of Hall's ideas. This will also give you a sense of how the scientific approach to the study of adolescence has changed since Hall's time.

Kett, J. F. (1977). *Rites of passage: Adolescence in America, 1790 to the present.* New York: Basic Books. A highly readable analysis of the history of adolescence in the United States by historian Joseph Kett.

Modell, J. (1989). *Into one's own: From youth to adulthood in the United States, 1920–1975.* Berkeley: University of California Press. Historian John Modell shows how the timing of marriage and parenthood has changed in the course of the 20th century. This lively book contains excerpts from magazines, letters, and other sources to illustrate the statistics.

Schlegel, A. (2000). The global spread of adolescent culture. In L. Crockett & R. K. Silbereisen (Eds.), *Negotiating adolescence in a time of social change.* Cambridge: Cambridge University Press. An excellent, up-to-date analysis of how globalization is influencing adolescence.

Applying Research

Elkind, D. (1984). *All grown up and no place to go: Teenagers in crisis.* New York: Addison-Wesley.

In this book, developmental psychologist David Elkind addresses the problems that result from adolescence beginning earlier than in the past. According to Elkind, many young people are facing issues such as sexuality and substance use before they are developmentally ready to deal with them.

Biological Foundations

"I had my first period at twelve, knew about it before and wasn't scared. I thought I was feeling pretty good, because then I would know I was growing up to be a lady, you know. And I really had a nice feeling."

> —African American adolescent girl (quoted in Konopka, 1976, p. 48)

"I didn't know about [menstruation]. [My mother] never told me anything like that. I was scared, I just started washing all my underclothing hoping that my mother won't find out but she came in and caught me washing it, and she started laughing at me. But she never did tell me what it was. . . . I mean she told me it wasn't anything to worry about, it's something that happens, you know, but she didn't tell me what it meant and stuff like that."

> —Latina adolescent girl (quoted in Konopka, 1976, pp. 47–48)

"Since I've gotten more physically mature I get a lot of stares when I go out. Sometimes it feels nice or funny when I'm with my friends, especially when it's someone nice. But when it's some weirdo or when some older man says something like "Ooooooooh,"

31

then it's scary and I want to say, 'I'm only twelve, leave me alone.'"

—Denise, age 12 (quoted in Bell, 1998, p. 24)

"I can't stand what I look like right now! Sometimes I just want to put a bag over my head to hide my face. It's all broken out with zits and oily places. I can wash it ten times a day and it's still the same."

—Pablo, age 15 (quoted in Bell, 1998, p. 10)

"Pubic hair scared the shit out of me. I saw all these little bumps and I didn't know what they were. I thought maybe I had VD but I hadn't even had sex."

—Juan (quoted in Bell, 1998, p. 20)

"[The first time I ejaculated] I'm almost positive that it was a wet dream. The problem was that I didn't know what it was. I was surprised that I had wet my bed—what did I do? I only found out a year later what it was."

—White American adolescent boy (quoted in Stein & Reiser, 1993, p. 377)

These examples illustrate the wide range of reactions that young people have to some of the events that indicate the development of physical and sexual maturity. They also suggest the ways that cultures influence young people's interpretation of the biological events of puberty, in part by informing them or neglecting to inform them about the changes that will be taking place in their bodies.

Although adolescence is a culturally constructed period of life, the physical and biological changes of puberty are a central part of development during adolescence in all cultures. Many changes take place, and they are often dramatic. There you are, growing at a more or less steady rate through childhood, and then suddenly the metamorphosis begins—growth spurt, pubic hair, underarm hair, acne, changes in body shape, breast development and menarche in girls, first ejaculation in boys, and much more. The changes are often

exciting and joyful, but adolescents often experience them with other emotions as well—fear, surprise, annoyance, and anxiety. Reaching the key changes earlier or later than most peers is especially a source of anxiety.

The biological changes of puberty are similar across cultures, but we will see in this chapter that even biological events interact with cultural influences. Culture influences the timing of biological events, and cultures respond in a variety of ways to the biological changes that signify adolescents' attainment of sexual maturity. Adolescents, in turn, rely on information provided by their cultures for interpreting the changes taking place within their bodies and in their physical appearance.

In this chapter we will begin with a description of the hormonal changes that initiate puberty and lead to the physical and biological changes of puberty. This will be followed by a description of the physical changes that happen to the body during puberty, including changes in height, weight, muscle-to-fat ratio, and strength. Next will be a description of primary sex characteristics (sperm and egg production) and secondary sex characteristics (such as growth of pubic hair and the development of breasts). Finally, we will examine cultural, social, and psychological responses to puberty, including the different experiences of adolescents who mature relatively early or relatively late.

The Biological Revolution of Puberty

The word **puberty** is derived from the Latin word *pubescere*, which means "to grow hairy." But adolescents do a lot more in puberty than grow hairy. After developing gradually and steadily during childhood, with puberty the body undergoes a biological revolution that dramatically changes the adolescent's anatomy, physiology, and physical appearance. By the time adolescents enter emerging adulthood, they look much different than before puberty, their bodies function much differently, and they are biologically prepared for sexual reproduction. These physical and biological changes result from changes that occur in the endocrine system during puberty.

The Endocrine System

The **endocrine system** consists of glands in various parts of the body. These glands release chemicals called **hormones** into the bloodstream, and the hormones affect the development and functioning of the body. Let us take a look at each of the glands that are part of the endocrine system, and the hormones they secrete during puberty (see Figure 2.1).

The Initiation of Puberty in the Hypothalamus

The hormonal changes of puberty begin in the **hypothalamus**, which is located in the lower part of the brain, beneath the cortex. The hypothalamus has profound and diverse effects on physiological and psychological motivation and functioning in areas such as eating, drinking, and the experience of pleasure, including sexual pleasure. In addition to these functions, the hypothalamus also stimulates and regulates the production of hormones by other glands (Petersen, 1988). To initiate puberty, the hypothalamus begins gradually to increase its production of the **gonadotropin-releasing hormone (GnRH)**, releasing GnRH in pulses at intervals of about 2 hours. The increase in GnRH begins early, in middle childhood, at least a year or two before even the earliest bodily changes of puberty (Petersen & Taylor, 1980). Researchers do not yet know what causes the hypothalamus to begin increasing GnRH production (Brooks-Gunn & Reiter, 1990). However, poor nutrition and low weight both early in

life and at the age of puberty can delay the onset of puberty (Brooks-Gunn & Reiter, 1990).

The Pituitary Gland and the Gonadotropins The increase in GnRH affects the **pituitary gland**, which is a gland about half an inch long located at the base of the brain. GnRH is appropriately named gonadotropin-releasing hormone, because that is what it does when it reaches the pituitary gland—it causes hormones called **gonadotropins** to be released from the pituitary. The two gonadotropins are **follicle-stimulating hormone (FSH)** and **luteinizing hormone (LH)**. FSH and LH stimulate the development of **gametes**—egg cells in the ovaries of the female and sperm in the testes of the male (Villee, 1975). FSH and LH also influence the production of sex hormones by the ovaries and testes, which will be described in more detail below.

The Gonads and the Sex Hormones The ovaries and testes are also known as the **gonads**, or sex glands. In response to stimulation from the FSH and LH released by the pituitary gland, the gonads increase their production of the **sex hormones**. There are two classes of sex hormones, the **estrogens** and the **androgens**. With respect to pubertal development, the most important estrogen is **estradiol** and the most important androgen is **testosterone** (Villee, 1975). Increases in the production of these hormones are responsible for most of the observable bodily changes of puberty, such as breast growth in females and facial hair in males (Petersen & Taylor, 1980).

Estradiol and testosterone are produced by both males and females, and throughout childhood the levels of these hormones are about the same in boys and girls (Money, 1980). However, once puberty begins the balance changes dramatically, with females producing more estradiol than males and males producing more testosterone than females (see Figure 2.2). By the midteens, estradiol production is about 8 times higher in females than it was prior to puberty, but only about twice as high for males (Nottelmann et al., 1987; Susman, 1997). Similarly, in males testosterone production is about 20 times higher by the midteens than it was prior to puberty, but in females it is only about 4 times higher (Nottelmann et al., 1987; Susman, 1997).

Androgens are produced not only by the sex glands but also by the adrenal glands. At puberty, the pituitary gland increases production of a hormone known as **adrenocorticotropic hormone (ACTH)**, and ACTH causes the adrenal glands to increase androgen production (Brooks-Gunn & Reiter, 1990). The androgens

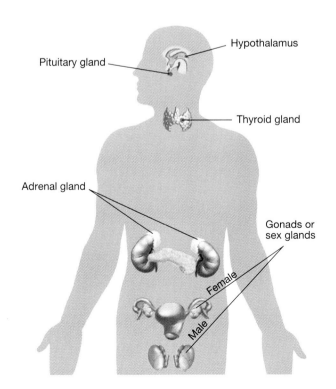

FIGURE 2.1 *The major glands involved in pubertal change.*

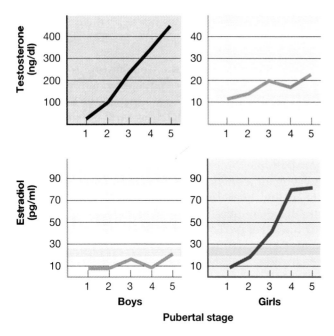

FIGURE 2.2 *Sex differences in hormonal changes during puberty.*

Source: Nottelmann et al. (1987).

70 degrees, when the temperature falls below that level the furnace comes on. As the furnace heats the rooms, the temperature rises, and when it reaches 70 degrees again the furnace turns off. In your body, when the levels of the sex hormones fall below their set points, their production by the gonads increases. Once the levels rise again to the set points, their production decreases.

What happens when puberty begins is that the set points for androgens and estrogens *increase* in the hypothalamus, with the set point for androgens rising higher in males than in females and the set point for estrogens rising higher in females than in males. In other words, during childhood the gonads produce only a relatively small amount of sex hormones before the set point of the hypothalamus is reached and the

released by the adrenal gland have the same effects as the androgens released by the testicles, contributing to bodily changes such as the development of increased body hair.

The Feedback Loop in the Endocrine System Although it is not known what triggers the hypothalamus to set puberty in motion by increasing its production of GnRH, quite a bit is known about other aspects of the interactions between the glands of the endocrine system during puberty (Brooks-Gunn & Reiter, 1990). From infancy onward, a **feedback loop** runs between the hypothalamus, the pituitary gland, the gonads, and the adrenal glands which monitors and adjusts the levels of the sex hormones (see Figure 2.3). The hypothalamus monitors the levels of androgens and estrogens in the bloodstream, and when the sex hormones reach an optimal level, called the **set point**, the hypothalamus reduces its production of GnRH. The pituitary responds to the reduction in GnRH by reducing its production of FSH, LH, and ACTH and the gonads and adrenal glands, in turn, respond to lower levels of FSH and LH by reducing the amount of sex hormones they produce.

A commonly used metaphor for the set point is a thermostat. If you set the thermostat where you live at

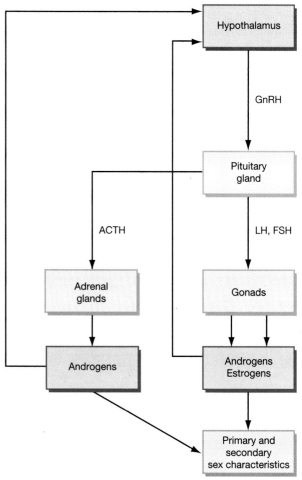

FIGURE 2.3 *The feedback loop.*

Source: Adapted from Grumbach et al. (1974).

hypothalamus signals the gonads to decrease production of the sex hormones. As puberty begins, however, and the set points for the sex hormones rises in the hypothalamus, the gonads can produce an increasing amount of the sex hormones before the hypothalamus instructs them to decrease production. To return to the thermostat metaphor, it is as if the thermostat were set at 40 degrees during childhood, and the "heat" of sex hormone production is triggered only occasionally. In the course of puberty, it is as if the thermostat rises to 80, and the "heat" of sex hormone production rises accordingly. But keep in mind that the set points for estrogens and androgens differ for males and females.

Physical Growth During Puberty

The increases in the levels of the sex hormones discussed in the previous section result in a variety of dramatic changes in the bodies of adolescents. One aspect of these changes is the rate of physical growth. After proceeding at an even pace since infancy, growth suddenly surges when puberty arrives. In fact, one of the earliest signs of puberty for both girls and boys is the

adolescent growth spurt, the rapid increase in height that takes place at the beginning of adolescence. Figure 2.4 shows the typical rate of growth in height from birth through age 19, including the adolescent growth spurt. At **peak height velocity**, when the adolescent growth spurt is at its maximum, girls grow at about 3.5 in. (9.0 cm) per year, and boys grow at about 4.1 in. (10.5 cm) per year (Tanner, 1971). For both girls and boys, the rate of their growth at peak height velocity is the highest it has been since they were 2 years old.

As Figure 2.4 shows, girls typically reach the beginning of their growth spurt as well as their peak height velocity about *2 years earlier* than boys. This is true of other aspects of physical development in puberty as well—girls mature about 2 years ahead of boys. Until the growth spurt begins, throughout childhood girls and boys are almost identical in their average height (Marshall, 1978). Girls become taller on average for about 2 years in early adolescence, from age 11 to age 13, the 2 years when they have hit their growth spurt while boys have not. However, the earlier maturation of girls contributes to their smaller adult height, because the adolescent growth spurt also marks the beginning of the end of growth in height. Because

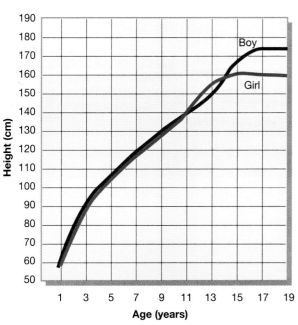
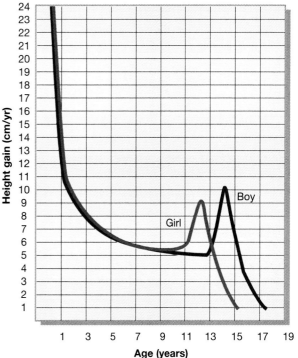

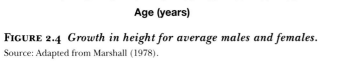

FIGURE 2.4 *Growth in height for average males and females.*
Source: Adapted from Marshall (1978).

girls begin their growth spurt earlier, they also reach their final height earlier—about age 16, as you can see in Figure 2.4, compared with about age 18 for boys (Tanner, 1962). Higher levels of testosterone also contribute to a higher average final height in boys (Underwood & Van Wyk, 1981).

THINKING CRITICALLY

What are some of the social and psychological implications of the fact that girls mature about 2 years earlier than boys during puberty?

During the adolescent growth spurt, not all parts of the body grow at the same pace. A certain amount of **asynchronicity** in growth during this time explains why some adolescents have a "gangly" look in early adolescence, as some parts of the body grow faster than oth-

Girls typically reach their growth spurt 2 years earlier than boys.

ers. The **extremities**—feet, hands, and head—are the first to hit the growth spurt, followed by the arms and legs (Tanner, 1971). Some parts of the head grow more than others. The forehead becomes higher and wider, the mouth widens, the lips become more full, and the chin, ears, and nose become more prominent (Mussen et al., 1990). The torso, chest, and shoulders are the last parts of the body to reach the growth spurt, and therefore the last to reach the end of their growth.

In addition to the growth spurt, a spurt in muscle growth occurs during puberty (Tanner, 1971), due primarily to the increase in testosterone. Because boys experience greater increases than girls in testosterone, they also experience greater increases in the growth of their muscles (Grumbach et al., 1974). As Figure 2.5 shows, prior to puberty girls and boys are very similar in their amounts of muscle mass.

Levels of body fat also surge during puberty, but body fat increases more for girls than for boys, as Figure 2.5 shows. As a consequence of these sex differences in muscle and fat growth, by the end of puberty boys have a muscle-to-fat ratio of about 3:1, whereas the muscle-to-fat ratio for girls is 5:4 (Grumbach et al., 1974). Other sex differences in body shape also develop during puberty. Hips and shoulders widen among both girls and boys, but hips widen more than shoulders in girls and shoulders widen more than hips in boys (Petersen & Taylor, 1980).

THINKING CRITICALLY

Given that girls naturally develop a lower muscle-to-fat ratio than boys during puberty, why would any culture create physical ideals that demand thinness in females once they reach puberty?

Similarly, in both boys and girls the heart becomes larger during puberty—on average, its weight almost doubles (Litt & Vaughan, 1987)—and the heart rate falls, but boys' hearts grow more than girls' hearts do and their heart rates fall to a lower level (Tanner, 1971). By age 17, the average girl's heart rate is about five beats per minute faster than the average boy's (Eichorn, 1970; Neinstein, 1984). A similar change takes place in the growth of the lungs. A measure of lung size called **vital capacity**, which means the amount of air that can be exhaled after a deep breath, increases rapidly for

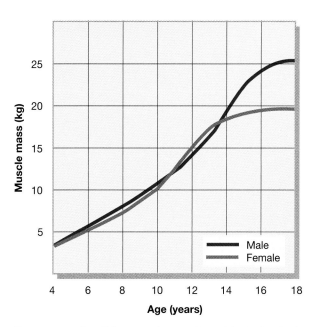

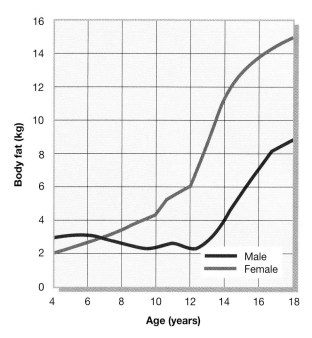

FIGURE 2.5 *Sex differences in muscle and body fat during puberty.*

Source: Adapted from Grumbach et al. (1974).

both boys and girls during puberty, but increases more for boys than for girls (Litt & Vaughan, 1987).

These sex differences in physical growth and functioning result in sex differences in strength and athletic ability during adolescence and beyond. Prior to puberty boys and girls are about equal in strength and athletic performance (Tanner, 1971), but during puberty boys overtake girls, and the difference remains throughout adulthood.

Gender differences also exist in cultural expectations for physical activity in many cultures, with adolescent girls sometimes being discouraged from participating in sports in order to conform to cultural ideas of what it means to be "feminine" (Petersen & Taylor, 1980). Boys are more likely to exercise in adolescence, and this gender difference contributes to the difference between adolescent boys and girls in their athletic performance (Smoll & Schutz, 1990). This has remained true even in recent years, despite an increase in organized athletic activities for girls from childhood onward. A 1999 survey by the World Health Organization of 15-year-olds in 26 Western countries found that in every country boys were more likely than girls to say they exercised vigorously at least twice a week outside of school (Smith, 2000). Across countries, about three-fourths of boys exercised at least twice a week, compared with about one-half of girls. In

studies that take amount of exercise into account, the muscle-to-fat ratio is still higher for boys than for girls, but the difference is not as large as in studies that do not take exercise into account (Woods et al., 1977).

Physical Functioning in Emerging Adulthood Although most people reach their maximum height by the end of adolescence, in other ways emerging adulthood rather than adolescence is the period of peak human physical functioning. Even after maximum height is attained, the bones continue to grow in density (Tanner, 1971), and maximum calcium levels are reached in the twenties. A measure of physical stamina called **maximum oxygen uptake**, or **VO$_2$ max**, which reflects the ability of the body to take in oxygen and transport it to various organs, also peaks in the early twenties (Plowman, Drinkwater, & Horvath, 1979). Similarly, **cardiac output**, the quantity of blood flow from the heart, peaks at age 25 as measured during exercise (Lakatta, 1990). Reaction time is also faster in the early twenties than at any other time of life. Studies of grip strength among men show the same pattern, with a peak in the twenties followed by a steady decline (Kallman, Plato, & Tobin, 1990).

Of course, like the sex differences in adolescence discussed above, most aspects of optimal physical functioning in emerging adulthood could be due in part to greater physical activity and exercise among emerging adults compared with adolescents or older adults (Goldberg, Dengel, & Hagberg, 1996). However, taking physical activity and exercise into account explains only a small portion of the peak of functioning in emerging adulthood. Altogether, for most people emerging adulthood is the time of life when they are at the peak of their health, strength, and vigor (Bee, 1998).

One way to demonstrate this is at the extreme, in terms of peak performances in athletic activity. Several studies have been conducted of the ages of athletes' best performances (Ericsson, 1990; Schultz & Curnow, 1988; Stones & Kozma, 1996). The peak ages have been found to vary depending on the sport, with swimmers youngest (the late teens) and golfers oldest (about age 31). However, for most sports the peak age of performance comes during the twenties.

Emerging adulthood is also the period of the life span with the least susceptibility to physical illnesses (Gans, 1990). This is especially true in modern times, when vaccines and medical treatments have dramatically lowered the risk of diseases such as polio that used to strike mainly during these years (Hein, 1988). Emerging adults are no longer vulnerable to the illnesses and diseases of childhood, and with rare excep-

tions they are not yet vulnerable to diseases such as cancer and heart disease for which rates rise later in adulthood. The immune system is at its most effective during this time. Consequently, the late teens and early twenties are the years of fewest hospital stays and fewest days spent sick in bed at home (Gans, 1990). In many ways, then, emerging adulthood is an exceptionally healthy time of life (Millstein, Petersen, & Nightingale, 1993).

However, this is not the whole story. Although emerging adulthood is the period of least susceptibility to health problems resulting from illness and disease, it is the period of *greatest* susceptibility to a variety of health problems resulting from *behavior* (Sells & Blum, 1996). Especially in the United States, the late teens and early twenties are the years of highest incidence of many types of disease and death due to behavior. Automobile accidents are the leading cause of death among emerging adults in the United States (National Highway Traffic Safety Administration, 1999), and injuries and deaths from automobile accidents are higher in the late teens and early twenties than at any other period of the life course (U.S. Department of Transportation, 1995). Homicide is another common cause of death in the United States during emerging adulthood, especially among young Black men (National Center for Health Statistics, 1999). Rates of contracting sexually transmitted diseases, including HIV, are highest in the early twenties (Stein et al., 1994).

We will discuss the causes of these problems in Chapter 13. For now, it is worth noting that a consensus has developed in recent decades among health experts that the source of most physical health problems in the teens and early twenties is in young people's behavior (e.g., Gans, 1990; Millstein, 1989; Irwin, 1993). As a result, programs emphasizing **health promotion** during these years have become more common (Millstein, Petersen, & Nightingale, 1993; Susman et al., 1993). Programs in health promotion tend to emphasize *prevention* of problems through encouraging changes in the behaviors that put young people at risk (e.g., driving at high speeds, having unprotected sex). Many of these programs focus on the early adolescent years, in the belief that these are years when patterns of behavior are being established that may endure into late adolescence, emerging adulthood, and beyond. The success of such programs has been limited so far (Millstein et al., 1993), as we will see in more detail in Chapter 13.

For most people, the peak of their physical functioning comes during emerging adulthood.

Primary Sex Characteristics

In addition to the changes in physical growth and functioning described so far, two other kinds of changes take place in the adolescent's body in response to increased sex hormones during puberty. **Primary sex characteristics** involve the production of eggs and sperm and the development of the sex organs. **Secondary sex characteristics** are other bodily changes resulting from the hormonal changes of puberty, not including the ones related directly to reproduction.

Egg and Sperm Production As noted, increases in FSH and LH at puberty cause eggs to develop in the ovaries of females and sperm to be produced in the testes of males. Although the same hormones are involved for both males and females, the development of the gametes is otherwise quite different for the two sexes. Females are born with about 400,000 immature eggs, called **follicles**, in each ovary. By puberty, this number has declined to about 80,000 in each ovary. Once a girl reaches menarche (her first menstrual period) and begins having menstrual cycles, one follicle develops into a mature egg, or **ovum**, every 28 days or so. Females release about 400 eggs over the course of their reproductive lives.

In contrast, males have no sperm in their testes when they are born, and they do not produce any until they reach puberty. The first production of sperm in boys is called **spermarche** (Laron et al., 1980). Once spermarche arrives in boys, they produce sperm in astonishing quantities—there are between 30 and 500 *million* sperm in the typical male ejaculation, which means that the average male produces millions of sperm every day. If you are a man, you will probably produce over a million sperm during the time you read this chapter—even if you are a fast reader!

Why so many? One reason is that the environment of the female body is not very hospitable to sperm. The female's immune system registers sperm as foreign bodies and begins attacking them immediately (Carroll & Wolpe, 1996). A second reason is that sperm have, in relation to their size, a long way to go to reach the ovum. They have to make their way along and through the various structures of the female reproductive anatomy. So it helps to have a lot of sperm wiggling their way along toward the ovum, because that increases the likelihood that some of them may make it to the ovum at the appropriate time.

The Male and Female Reproductive Anatomy
The changes of puberty prepare the body for sexual re-

production, and during puberty the sexual organs undergo a number of important changes as part of that preparation. In males, both the penis and the testes grow substantially in puberty. The penis doubles in length and diameter, on average (Carroll & Wolpe, 1996). In its mature form, the flaccid (limp) penis averages 3 to 4 inches and about 1 inch in diameter. The tumescent (erect) penis averages $5\frac{1}{2}$ to 6 inches in length and $1\frac{1}{2}$ inches in diameter. The growth of the testes is even more pronounced—they increase $2\frac{1}{2}$ times in length and $8\frac{1}{2}$ times in weight, on average (Carroll & Wolpe, 1996). The dramatic growth of the testes is necessary for them to be able to produce and contain the many millions of sperm described above.

In females, the external female sex organs are known as the **vulva**, which includes the **labia majora** (Latin for "large lips"), **labia minora** (Latin for "small lips"), and the **clitoris**. The labia majora, labia minora, and clitoris all grow substantially in puberty (Carroll & Wolpe, 1996). The ovaries also increase greatly in size and weight. Just as the testes grow to accommodate sperm production, the growth of the ovaries reflects the growth of maturing follicles. Furthermore, the uterus doubles in length during puberty, growing to a mature length of about 3 inches, about the size of a closed fist. The vagina also increases in length, and its color deepens.

As noted earlier, once ovulation begins a mature follicle is released from the ovaries in each monthly cycle. The two ovaries typically alternate months, with one releasing an ovum and then the other. The ovum moves along the fallopian tube and travels to the uterus. During this time, a lining of blood is building up in the uterus in preparation for the possibility of receiving and providing nutrients for the fertilized egg. If the egg becomes fertilized by a sperm during its course along the fallopian tube, the fertilized egg begins dividing immediately. When it reaches the uterus it implants itself in the wall of the uterus and continues developing. If the follicle is not fertilized, it is evacuated during menstruation along with the blood lining in the uterus.

Although menarche is a girl's first menstruation, it is not the same as the first ovulation. On the contrary, girls often menstruate before they begin ovulating, and many girls ovulate inconsistently for up to 2 years after menarche, even if they menstruate consistently (Petersen & Taylor, 1980). For example, one study of early adolescent girls in Finland found that over half of their cycles during their first 2 years after menarche did not involve ovulation (Apter & Vihko, 1977). This inconsistency can unfortunately persuade some sexually active adolescents that the early adolescent girl is "infertile" or somehow "can't get pregnant," but this is far from the truth. Fertility may be inconsistent and unpredictable during the first 2 years after menarche, but it is certainly possible for most girls (Petersen & Taylor, 1980). Whether boys experience a similar lag between spermarche and the production of sperm capable of fertilizing an egg is not known.

Secondary Sex Characteristics

> "I WAS ABOUT SIX MONTHS YOUNGER THAN EVERYONE ELSE IN MY CLASS, AND SO FOR ABOUT SIX MONTHS AFTER MY FRIENDS HAD BEGUN TO DEVELOP (THAT WAS THE WORD WE USED, DEVELOP), I WAS NOT PARTICULARLY WORRIED. I WOULD SIT IN THE BATHTUB AND LOOK DOWN AT MY BREASTS AND KNOW THAT ANY DAY NOW, ANY SECOND NOW, THEY WOULD START GROWING LIKE EVERYONE ELSE'S. THEY DIDN'T. . . .
> 'DON'T WORRY ABOUT IT,' SAID MY FRIEND LIBBY SOME MONTHS LATER, WHEN THINGS HAD NOT IMPROVED. 'YOU'LL GET THEM AFTER YOU'RE MARRIED.'
> 'WHAT ARE YOU TALKING ABOUT?' I SAID.
> 'WHEN YOU GET MARRIED,' LIBBY EXPLAINED, 'YOUR HUSBAND WILL TOUCH YOUR BREASTS AND RUB THEM AND KISS THEM AND THEY'LL GROW.'"
> —NORA EPHRON 2000, *CRAZY SALAD*, PP. 2–4

All the primary sex characteristics are directly related to reproduction. In addition to these changes, numerous other bodily changes take place as part of puberty but are not directly related to reproduction. These changes are known as secondary sex characteristics.

Some secondary sex characteristics develop for only males or only females, but for the most part the changes that happen to one sex also happen to the other, to some degree. Both males and females grow hair in their pubic areas and underneath their arms. Both also grow facial hair—you knew that males do, but you may not have realized that females also grow hair, just a slight amount, on

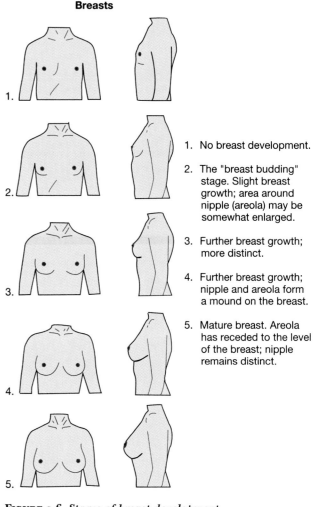

Breasts

1. No breast development.

2. The "breast budding" stage. Slight breast growth; area around nipple (areola) may be somewhat enlarged.

3. Further breast growth; more distinct.

4. Further breast growth; nipple and areola form a mound on the breast.

5. Mature breast. Areola has receded to the level of the breast; nipple remains distinct.

FIGURE 2.6 *Stages of breast development.*
Source: Marshall and Tanner (1969).

their faces during puberty. Similarly, increased hairiness on the arms and legs is more pronounced in males, but females also grow more hair on their limbs at puberty (Petersen & Taylor, 1980). However, boys also begin to grow hair on their chests, and sometimes on their shoulders and backs as well, whereas girls do not.

Both males and females experience various changes in their skin and bones (Eveleth & Tanner, 1990; Tanner, 1971). The skin becomes rougher, especially around the thighs and upper arms. The sweat glands in the skin increase production, making the skin oilier and more prone to acne, and resulting in a stronger body odor. Also, bones become harder and more dense throughout the body. Males and females also experience a deepening of the voice as the vocal cords lengthen, with males experiencing the steeper drop in pitch.

Even breast development, although obviously a secondary sex characteristic that occurs in females, also occurs in a substantial proportion of males. About one-fourth of boys experience enlargement of the breasts about midway through puberty (Bell, 1998; Tanner, 1970). This can be a source of alarm and anxiety to adolescent boys, but for the majority of them the enlargement recedes within a year.

For girls, the breasts go through a series of predictable stages of development (see Figure 2.6). The earliest indication of breast development, a slight enlargement of the breasts known as **breast buds**, is also one of the first outward signs of puberty in girls (Tanner, 1971). During this early stage there is also an enlargement of the area surrounding the nipple, called the **areola**. In the later stages of breast development the breasts continue to enlarge, and the areola first rises with the nipple to form a mound above the breast, then recedes to the level of the breast while the nipple remains projected (Marshall & Tanner, 1969).

Table 2.1 provides a summary of our discussion on the physical changes in males and females during puberty.

THINKING CRITICALLY

Puberty involves the development of sexual maturation. Among the secondary sex characteristics described here, which are viewed in your culture as enhancing sexual interest and attractiveness between males and females? Which are not?

The Order of Pubertal Events

Puberty is comprised of many events and processes, typically stretching out over several years (see Table 2.2). A great deal of variability exists among individuals in the timing of pubertal events. Among young people in industrialized countries such as the United States, the first pubertal events may occur as early as age 8 in girls and age 9 or 10 in boys, or as late as age 13 (Brooks-Gunn & Reiter, 1990; Hermans-Gidden et al., 1997). The duration between the initiation of the first pubertal event and full pubertal maturation can be as short as a year and a half or as long as 6 years (Tanner, 1962). Consequently, among a population of adolescents, some are likely to have finished their pubertal development before others have even begun. Because adolescents experience their first events in

TABLE 2.1: PHYSICAL CHANGES DURING ADOLESCENCE

Both sexes	Males only	Females only
Pubic hair	Sperm production	Ovulation/menstruation
Underarm hair	Wider shoulders and chest	Breast development
Facial hair	Increased proportion of muscle to fat	Broader hips/pelvis
Arm and leg hair		Increased proportion of fat to muscle
Rougher skin (especially thighs, upper arms)	Chest hair	
Oilier skin, stronger body odor	Shoulder and back hair	
Harder bones		
Lower voice		
Growth spurt		
Larger forehead		
Wider mouth		
Fuller lips		
More prominent chin, ears, nose		

puberty at different ages and proceed through puberty at different rates, age alone is a very poor predictor of an adolescent's pubertal development (Tanner, 1962).

More consistency can be seen in the order of pubertal events than in the ages they begin or the amount of time it takes to complete them (Eichorn, 1975). For girls, downy pubic hair is often the first sign of the beginning of puberty (Harlan, Harlan, & Grillo, 1980), followed closely by the appearance of breast buds. (For about 20% of girls, breast buds precede the first sign of pubic hair; Brooks-Gunn & Reiter, 1990). The next event for girls is usually the growth spurt (Petersen & Taylor, 1980), along with the growth of the sexual and reproductive organs (clitoris, labia, uterus, and vagina; Tanner, 1971). Menarche, the development of underarm hair, and the secretion of increased skin oil and sweat occur relatively late in puberty for most girls (Brooks-Gunn & Reiter, 1990; Goldstein, 1976).

For boys, the first outward sign of puberty is usually the growth of the testes, along with or closely followed by the beginning of pubic hair (Neinstein, 1984; Tanner, 1971). These events are followed (usually about a year later) by the initiation of the growth spurt and the increased growth of the penis (Tanner, 1970), along

with the beginning of the deepening of the voice (Goldstein, 1976). Spermarche takes place sometime between ages 12 and 14 for most boys (Laron et al., 1980). In boys as in girls, the growth of underarm hair and the secretion of increased skin oil and sweat take place relatively late in puberty. For boys, facial hair is also one of the later developments of puberty, usually beginning about 2 years after the first outward events of puberty (Goldstein, 1976; Neinstein, 1984; Tanner, 1991).

Virtually all the studies we have been considering in this section on changes in physical growth and functioning during puberty have been conducted with White adolescents in the West. In fact, the main source of our information about physical growth and functioning remains the studies of J. Tanner and his colleagues (see the Research Focus box), which were mostly conducted 30 to 40 years ago on British adolescents who were in foster homes. Tanner's findings have been verified in numerous studies of White adolescents in the United States (Brooks-Gunn & Reiter, 1990), but we do not have similarly detailed information on other ethnic and cultural groups around the world.

Two studies indicate the variations that may exist in other groups. In a study of Chinese girls, Lee, Chang,

TABLE 2.2: THE SEQUENCE OF PHYSICAL CHANGES AT PUBERTY

Boys		Girls	
Characteristic	*Age of first appearance (years)*	*Characteristic*	*Age of first appearance (years)*
1. Growth of testes, scrotal sac	9½–13½	1. Growth of pubic hair	8–14
2. Growth of pubic hair	10–15	2. Growth of breasts	8–13
3. Growth spurt	10½–16	3. Growth spurt	9½–14½
4. Growth of penis	10½–14½	4. Menarche	10–16½
5. Change in voice	11–15	5. Underarm hair	10–16
6. Spermarche	12–14	6. Oil- and sweat-producing glands, acne	10–16
7. Facial and underarm hair	12–17		
8. Oil- and sweat-producing glands, acne	12–17		

Source: Adapted from Goldstein (1976).

and Chan (1963) found that pubic hair began to develop in most girls about 2 years after the development of breast buds, and only a few months before menarche. This is a sharp contrast to the pattern for the girls in Tanner's studies, who typically began to develop pubic hair at about the same time they developed breast buds, usually 2 years before menarche (Tanner, 1971). Also, in a recent American study (Herman-Giddens et al., 1997), many Black girls were found to begin developing breast buds and/or pubic hair considerably earlier than White girls. At age 8, nearly *50%* of the Black girls had begun to develop breasts or pubic hair or both, compared with just 15% of the White girls. This was true even though Black and White girls were similar in their ages of menarche. Studies such as these indicate that it is important to investigate ethnic differences in the rates, timing, and order of pubertal events.

RESEARCH FOCUS
Tanner's Longitudinal Research on Pubertal Development

J. M. Tanner was a British biologist who studied the pattern and sequence of various aspects of physical development during puberty (Marshall & Tanner, 1969; Marshall & Tanner, 1970; Tanner, 1962, 1971, 1991). His research took place mainly during the 1960s and 1970s, and involved White boys and girls who were living in state-run foster homes in Britain. Through the use of direct physical evaluations and photographs, he made careful assessments of growth and development during puberty. By following adolescents over a period of many years, he was able to establish the typical ages at which various processes of pubertal development begin and end (as shown in Figure 2.7), as well as the range of variation for each process. His work on adolescents' physical development is widely accepted by scholars on adolescence; in fact, the stages of various aspects of pubertal development are known as "Tanner stages," as shown in the examples for breast development in females (see Figure 2.6) and genital development in males (see accompanying photo).

Tanner and his colleagues focused on specific aspects of physical development during puberty: the growth spurt, the development of pubic hair, genital maturity in boys, the development of breasts in girls, and menarche in girls. For breast development (girls), genital maturity (boys), and pubic hair, Tanner described a sequence of five stages. Stage 1 for each of these areas of development is the prepubertal stage, when no physical changes have

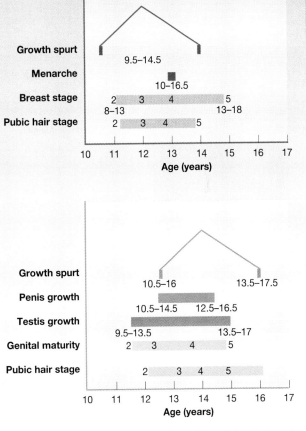

FIGURE 2.7 *Typical age ranges for pubertal development.*
Source: Adapted from Marshall & Tanner (1970), p. 22.

appeared. Stage 5 is the stage when maturity has been reached and growth is completed. Stages 2, 3, and 4 describe the levels of development in between. In addition to the stages, Tanner described other bodily changes such as muscle growth and the composition of the blood (Tanner, 1971).

The adolescents Tanner studied were mainly from low socioeconomic status (SES) families, and many of them probably did not receive optimal physical care during childhood (Marshall & Tanner, 1970). They were living in foster homes, which indi-

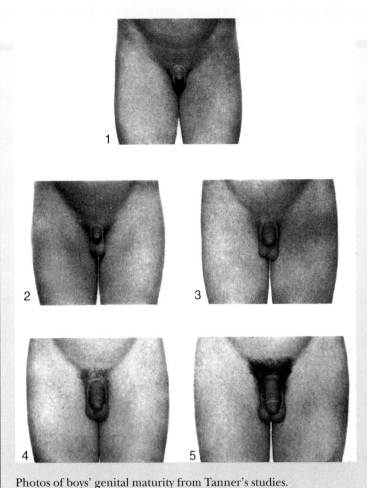

Photos of boys' genital maturity from Tanner's studies.

cates that there had been problems of some kind in their families. Thus, the adolescents in Tanner's studies were not selected randomly, and were in many ways not truly representative of the larger population of adolescents, even the larger population of White adolescents. Nevertheless, Tanner's description of development in puberty has held up very well. Studies of normal White American adolescents have found patterns very similar to the ones Tanner described (Lee, 1980; Brooks-Gunn & Reiter, 1990). Since his original studies, Tanner and his colleagues (Eveleth & Tanner, 1990) have also researched development during puberty in other countries in various parts of the world and found that the timing and pace of development during puberty vary widely depending on the levels of nutrition and medical care available to adolescents.

Tanner's research was longitudinal. A **longitudinal study** is a study in which *the same individuals are followed across time,* and data on them is collected on more than one occasion. The range of time involved can vary from a few weeks to an entire lifetime. This kind of study is different from a **cross-sectional study**, which *examines individuals at one point in time.* Both kinds of studies are valuable, but there are certain kinds of information that can only be gained with a longitudinal study. For example, in Tanner's research, the only way to find out how long it typically takes for females to develop from Stage 1 to Stage 5 of breast development is through a longitudinal study. If breast development were assessed with a cross-sectional study, it would be difficult to tell for each girl how long it had taken for her to develop to that stage and how long it would take for her to develop to the next stage. With a longitudinal study, this can be assessed quite precisely.

Given a similar environment, variation in the order and timing of pubertal events among adolescents appears to be due to genetics (Petersen & Taylor, 1980). The more similar two people are genetically, the more similar they tend to be in the timing of their pubertal events, with identical twins the most similar of all (Mar-

shall, 1978). However, the key phrase here is "given a similar environment." In reality, the environments adolescents experience differ greatly, both within countries and between countries. These differences have profound effects on the timing of puberty, as we will see in detail in the following section.

Cultural, Social, and Psychological Responses to Puberty

Whatever their culture, all humans go through the physical and biological changes of puberty. However, even here culture's effects are profound. Cultural diets and levels of health and nutrition influence the timing of the initiation of puberty. Perhaps more importantly, cultures define the meaning and significance of pubertal change in different ways. These cultural definitions in turn influence the ways that adolescents interpret and experience their passage through puberty. We will look at culture and pubertal timing first, then at culture and the meaning of puberty. Then we will examine social and psychological responses to puberty, with a focus on differences between adolescents who mature relatively early and adolescents who mature relatively late.

Culture and the Timing of Puberty

How do cultures influence the timing of the initiation of puberty? The definition of culture includes a group's technologies. Technologies include food production and medical care, and by now we know that the age at which puberty begins is strongly influenced by the extent to which food production provides for adequate nutrition and medical care provides for good health throughout childhood (Brooks-Gunn & Reiter, 1990). In general, puberty begins earlier in cultures where good nutrition and medical care are widely available (Eveleth & Tanner, 1990).

Persuasive evidence for the influence of technologies on pubertal timing comes from historical records showing a steady decrease in the average age of menarche in Western countries over the past 150 years. This kind of a change in the characteristics of a population over time is called a **secular trend** (Bullough, 1981). As you can see from Figure 2.8, a secular trend downward in the age of menarche has occurred in every Western country for which records exist. Menarche is not a perfect indicator of the initiation of puberty—as we have discussed, the first outward signs of puberty appear much earlier for most girls, and of course menarche does not apply to boys. However, menarche is a reasonably good indicator of when other events have begun, and it is a reasonable assumption that if the downward secular trend in the age of puberty has occurred for females, it has occurred for males as well. Menarche is also the only aspect of pubertal development for which we have records going back so many decades. Scholars

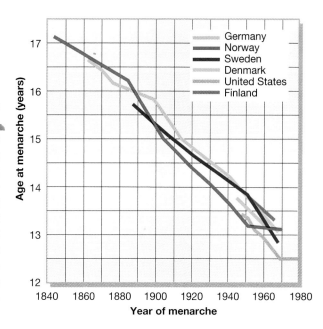

FIGURE 2.8 *The decline in the age of menarche in Western countries.*

Source: Adapted from Eveleth & Tanner (1990).

believe that the secular trend in the age of menarche is due to improvements in nutrition and medical care that have taken place during the past 150 years (Bullough, 1981; Brooks-Gunn & Reiter, 1990).

Further evidence of the role of nutrition and medical care in pubertal timing comes from cultural comparisons in the present. When we look around the world, we find that the average age of menarche is lowest in industrialized countries, where adequacy of nutrition and medical care is highest (Eveleth & Tanner, 1990). For girls in the United States, the average age of menarche is 12.5 (Brooks-Gunn & Reiter, 1990; Brooks-Gunn & Paikoff, 1997). In contrast, the average is higher in economically less-developed countries, where nutrition may be limited and medical care is often rare or nonexistent (Eveleth & Tanner, 1990).

One illuminating contrast is between African girls in Africa and African American girls in the United States. In African countries the average age of menarche varies widely, but in none of them is it as low as for girls in the United States, and in some African countries the average age of menarche is as high as 15, 16, or even 17 years old (Eveleth & Tanner, 1990). In contrast, the average age of menarche for African American girls is just 12.2 (Hermans-Gidden et al., 1997). It is very likely that the lower age of menarche for African American girls compared with African girls is due to African American girls receiving considerably better nutrition and medical care.

Studies also show that *within* countries, adolescent girls from affluent families tend to menstruate earlier than girls from poorer families, in places as diverse as Hong Kong, Tunis, Iraq, South Africa, and the United States (Eveleth & Tanner, 1990; see Figure 2.9). Again, we can infer that economic differences result in differences in the adequacy of the nutrition and medical care these girls receive, which in turn influences the timing of menarche.

With respect to nutrition in particular, substantial evidence shows that girls who are involved in activities in which there is a great deal of pressure to keep down their weight, such as ballet and gymnastics, experience later menarche and have inconsistent periods once they do begin to menstruate (Picard, 1999). The body responds to their low weight as a nutritional deficiency and delays menarche.

In addition to the influence of cultural technologies on pubertal timing, studies suggest that the immediate social environment may also influence pubertal timing. Several studies indicate that puberty occurs earlier in girls who grow up in an environment where there is a high level of family conflict (Ellis, 1991; Graber et al.,

1995; Moffitt et al., 1992; Steinberg, 1988). Some evidence also suggests that girls who grow up in a home where the father is not present (due to divorce or death) reach puberty earlier (Surbey, 1990). At this point it is not known why family conflict or father absence may induce earlier onset of puberty.

THINKING CRITICALLY

In your view, what potential social and psychological problems may develop as a consequence of girls showing signs of reaching puberty (such as initial breast development) as early as 8 or 9 years old?

Given that the secular trend in the age of menarche was steadily downward for over a century in industrialized countries, will girls someday begin menstruating in middle childhood or even earlier? Apparently not. In most industrialized countries the median age of menarche has been more or less stable since about 1970 (Brooks-Gunn & Reiter, 1990; Bullough, 1981; Herman-Giddens et al., 1997). Human females appear to have a genetically established **reaction range** for the age of menarche. This means that genes establish a range of possible times when menarche may begin and environment determines the actual timing of menarche within that range.

In general, the healthier the environment, the lower the timing of menarche. However, the reaction range has boundaries: Even under relatively unhealthy conditions, most girls will reach menarche eventually, and even among conditions of optimal health there is a lower threshold age that menarche is unlikely to fall below. Because the timing of menarche in industrialized countries has changed little in recent decades, it appears that populations of girls in these countries have reached the lower threshold age of their reaction range for menarche.

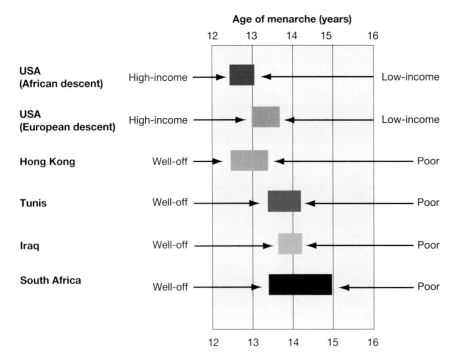

FIGURE 2.9 *Age of menarche in relation to socioeconomic status (SES) in various countries.*

Source: Adapted from Eveleth & Tanner (1990).

Cultural Responses to Puberty: Puberty Rituals

Puberty has been marked with rituals in many cultures through history as the departure from childhood and the entrance into adolescence, particularly in traditional cultures. Not all traditional cultures have such rituals, but they are quite common, especially for girls. Schlegel and Barry (1991) analyzed information on adolescent development across 186 traditional cultures and reported that the majority of them had some kind of ritual initiation into adolescence at the beginning of puberty—68% had a puberty ritual for boys, 79% for girls (Schlegel & Barry, 1991).

For girls, menarche is the pubertal event that is most often marked by ritual (Schlegel & Barry, 1991). In many cultures, menarche initiates a monthly ritual related to menstruation that lasts throughout a woman's reproductive life. It is remarkably common for cultures to have strong beliefs concerning the power of menstrual blood. Such beliefs are not universal, but they have been common in all parts of the world, in a wide variety of cultures. Menstrual blood is often believed to present a danger to the growth and life of crops, to the health of livestock, to the likelihood of success among hunters, and to the health and well-being of other people, particularly the menstruating woman's husband (Buckley & Gottlieb, 1988; Kitahara, 1982). Consequently, the behavior and movement of menstruating women is often restricted in various ways, for example

Menarche is often marked by a ritual in traditional cultures. Here, girls of the N'Jembe tribe of West Africa prepare for their initiation.

by requiring them to remain secluded in a menstrual hut during their periods.

However, the views that cultures have toward menstrual blood are not uniformly negative (Buckley & Gottlieb, 1988). Often, menstrual blood is viewed as having positive powers as well. For example, it is sometimes viewed as promoting fertility and is used in fertility rituals. Some cultures use menstrual blood in the treatment of medical conditions, and some use it to make love potions (Ladurie, 1979). Sometimes both positive and negative beliefs about menstruation exist within the same culture.

An example of cultural ambivalence toward menstruation can be found among the Asante, a culture in the African nation of Ghana (Buckley & Gottlieb, 1988). Among the Asante, menstruating women are subject to numerous stringent regulations concerning where they may go and what they may do, and the penalty for violating these taboos can be death. However, the Asante also celebrate girls' menarche with an elaborate ritual celebration. The menarcheal girl sits in public view under a canopy (a symbol of honor usually reserved for royalty), while others come before her to congratulate her, present her with gifts, and perform songs and dances in her honor. Thus, on this occasion menstruation is celebrated, even though the rest of the time it is viewed with a great deal of dread and fear.

Practices among Orthodox Jews show a similar ambivalence, with a shift toward a more positive balance in recent decades. Traditionally, when girls told their mothers they had reached menarche, mothers responded with a sudden ritualistic slap on the face (Brumberg, 1997). This gesture was intended to inform the daughter of the future difficulties awaiting her in her life as a woman. Following menarche, each time they menstruated Orthodox women were obliged to have a ritual bath called **mikveh** 7 days after their period was finished, as a way of ridding themselves of the uncleanness believed to be associated with menstruation. Today, the slap has been retired. The mikveh still exists, but today the bath has more positive connotations. Orthodox Jewish women report that it makes them feel connected to other Jewish women—their current Jewish friends as well as Jewish women of history (Kaufman, 1991). Also, because sexual intercourse is prohibited among Orthodox Jewish couples from the time a woman begins her period until the time she completes mikveh, mikveh also marks the woman's readiness for resuming lovemaking with her husband, and consequently it has connotations of sexual anticipation (Kaufman, 1991).

Puberty rituals for males do not focus on a particular biological event comparable to menarche for females, but the rites for males nevertheless share some common characteristics. In particular, they typically require the young man to display courage, strength, and endurance (Gilmore, 1990). Daily life in traditional cultures often requires these capacities from young men in warfare, hunting, fishing, or other tasks, so the rituals could be interpreted as letting them know what will be required of them as adults and testing whether they will be up to adulthood's challenges.

The rituals for boys are often violent, requiring boys to submit to and sometimes engage in bloodletting of various kinds. Among the Sambia of New Guinea, for example, boys climb on the back of a "sponsor" who runs through a gauntlet of older men who beat the boy on his back until it is bloody (Herdt, 1987). The Samburu of West Africa have a public circumcision ritual for boys on the threshold of adolescence (Spencer, 1965). Among the Amhara of Ethiopia, boys were forced to take part in whipping contests in which they faced off and lacerated each other's faces and bodies (LeVine, 1966). Some boys went further in proving their fortitude by scarring their arms with red-hot embers. Among the Tewa people of New Mexico (also known as the Pueblo Indians), at some point between the ages of 12 and 15 boys were taken away from their homes, purified in ritual ceremonies, and then stripped naked and lashed on the back with a whip that drew blood and left permanent scars.

Puberty rituals for boys often require them to endure physical pain. Here, the traditional stick fight between adolescents in the Xhosa tribe of Southern Africa.

Although these rituals may sound cruel if you have grown up in the West, adults of these cultures have believed that the rituals are necessary for boys to make the passage out of childhood toward manhood and be ready to face life's challenges. In all these cultures, however, the rituals have declined in frequency or disappeared altogether in recent decades as a consequence of globalization (e.g., Herdt, 1987; see Cultural Focus box). Because traditional cultures are changing rapidly in response to globalization, the traditional puberty rituals no longer seem relevant to the futures that young people anticipate (Burbank, 1988).

■ _____ **THINKING CRITICALLY**

Are there any rituals in Western cultures that are comparable to the puberty rituals in traditional cultures? Are there ways that Western cultures should recognize puberty that they do not do now?

Social and Psychological Responses to Puberty

The West does not have puberty rituals like those of traditional cultures. Nevertheless, in the West as in traditional cultures, the people in adolescents' social environment respond to the changes in adolescents' bodies that signify puberty and the development of sexual maturity. Adolescents in turn form their personal responses to puberty in part on the basis of the information provided to them by the people in their social environment. First, let's examine the adjustments that take place in parent–adolescent relations when puberty begins, then the adolescents' personal responses to puberty.

Parent–Adolescent Relations and Puberty When young people reach puberty, the metamorphosis that takes place affects not only them personally but their relations with those closest to them, in particular their parents. Just as

CULTURAL FOCUS
Coming of Age in Samoa

One interesting example of a puberty ritual that both males and females participate in comes from the islands known as Samoa, in the Pacific Ocean near New Zealand. Samoa became known to many Americans earlier in this century when the anthropologist Margaret Mead wrote a book about Samoan adolescence, *Coming of Age in Samoa* (1928), that was widely read in the United States (and, in fact, all over the world). Many people were fascinated by the stark contrast between adolescence in Samoa and adolescence in the West.

One of the ways Samoa differed from the West was in having a ritual to mark the beginning of adolescence. The traditional rite of passage into adolescence involved an elaborate process of tattooing sometime between ages 14 and 16 (Cote, 1994). The tattoos were made in elaborate geometric patterns and extended from the waist to the knees (see accompanying photo). Having the tattoos put on was painful, especially for males, whose tattoos were more elaborate than the ones for females and usually took 2 to 3 *months* to complete, whereas the tattoos for females took 5 to 6 days. But the young men experienced it together and took satisfaction in sharing the ordeal of it and supporting one another. In spite of the pain, few young men or young women declined to take part in it, because being tattooed was considered essential to sexual attractiveness and to being accepted as a legitimate candidate for eventual full adult status.

This tattooing ritual has been profoundly affected by the globalization of adolescence. In the past 100 years, Samoan culture has changed a great deal (Cote, 1994). Missionaries arrived and sought to stamp out a variety of native practices they considered immoral, including the ritual of tattooing. The rise of secondary education and the widening of economic opportunities for Samoans who immigrated to nearby New Zealand undermined the traditional economy and caused the tattooing ritual to be viewed as irrelevant or even shamefully "primitive" by some Samoans. By now, most Samoans have abandoned their cooperative, traditional ways for participation in the wage labor of the global economy.

Recently, however, tattooing for young men has undergone a revival. Currently, the majority of young men get tattoos in their teens to demonstrate their pride in the traditional ways of their culture, as part of an explicit attempt to resist the total absorption of their indigenous culture into the global culture (Cote, 1994).

Tattooing is a traditional rite of passage for Samoan adolescents.

adolescents have to adjust to the changes taking place in their bodies, parents have to adjust to the new person their child is becoming.

How do parent–adolescent relations change at puberty? For the most part, studies of adolescents and their parents in the American majority culture find that their relationships tend to become cooler when pubertal changes become evident (Buchanan, Eccles, & Becker, 1992; Holmbeck & Hill, 1991; Larson & Richards, 1994; Paikoff & Brooks-Gunn, 1991). Conflict increases and closeness decreases. Parents and adolescents seem to be less comfortable in each other's presence when puberty is reached, especially in their physical closeness. In one especially interesting study demonstrating this, researchers went to a shopping mall and an amusement park and observed 122 pairs of mothers and children aged 6 to 18 (Montemayor & Flannery, 1989). For each pair, the researchers observed them for 30 seconds and recorded whether they were talking, smiling, looking at, or touching each other. The most notable result of the study is shown in Figure 2.10. Among early adolescents (ages 11–14) and their mothers, there was a steep decline in how much they touched each other compared with younger children and their mothers, and the decline continued through late adolescence (ages 15–18). Mothers and early adolescents

talked more than mothers and younger children, suggesting that parent–child communication styles shift toward talking and away from touching as puberty is reached.

Other studies have found that it is the physical changes of puberty that lead to the change in parent–adolescent relations, not age alone (Paikoff & Brooks-Gunn, 1991). If a child reaches puberty relatively early, relations with parents change relatively early; if a child reaches puberty relatively late, relations with parents change relatively late. For example, one study of 10- to 15-year-olds found that regardless of age, those who had reached puberty felt less close to their mothers and less accepted by their fathers (Steinberg, 1987a, 1988). Studies have also found that conflict with parents tends to be especially high for young people who mature early (Laursen & Collins, 1994; Sagestrano et al., 1999).

What is it about reaching puberty that causes parent–child relations to change? At this point, scholars are uncertain. Some scholars have suggested that increased distance between parents and children at puberty may have an evolutionary basis (Steinberg, 1987b, 1989). According to this **distancing hypothesis** (Steinberg, 1989), it may be adaptive for young people to move away from closeness to their parents once they reach sexual maturity, so that they mate and reproduce with persons outside the family, thus avoiding the genetic problems that often result from incest. This hypothesis seems supported by evidence that in most species of monkeys and apes, the young of the species spend less time with their parents and have less physical contact with them upon reaching puberty (Steinberg, 1987b). However, if the distancing hypothesis were true, one would also expect that emotional distance at puberty would especially increase between adolescents and their opposite-sex parent, and this is not the case. Both boys and girls tend to have both greater closeness and greater conflict with their mothers during adolescence than with their fathers (Claes, 1998; Larson & Richards, 1994).

If the distancing hypothesis were true, one would also expect to find distancing between adolescents and their parents in nearly all cultures, but again this is not the case. In fact, the studies that have found distancing to take place at puberty have been mainly studies of two-parent White American families and one recent study of African American families (Sagestrano et al., 1999). Distancing is not as common in Latino families or divorced mother-headed families (Anderson, Hetherington, & Clingempeel, 1989; Molina & Chassin,

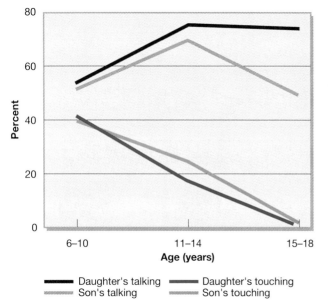

FIGURE 2.10 *Frequency of adolescent–mother touching and talking.*

Source: Montemayor & Flannery (1989).

1996). Distancing is also not typical in traditional cultures. Schlegel and Barry's (1991) survey of traditional cultures found that girls in traditional cultures often grow closer to their mothers during adolescence, because they often spend much of their days side by side in shared labor. Furthermore, in traditional cultures as in the American majority culture, adolescents of both sexes tend to be closer to their mothers than to their fathers. Thus, the unanswered question appears to be, what is it about the American majority culture that leads to greater distancing between parents and children when children reach puberty?

Personal Responses to Menarche and Semenarche Although menarche occurs relatively late in pubertal development for most girls, girls' responses to it have received a great deal of attention from researchers. This may be because menarche is more momentous as an *event* than other female pubertal changes are. The growth of pubic hair, the development of breasts, and most other pubertal changes occur gradually, almost imperceptibly from one day to the next, whereas menarche is suddenly *there* one day, when there was nothing to herald it the day before. Similarly, menarche is easier for scientists to measure—it is easier to identify when menarche begins than the beginning of other more gradual changes. Menarche also holds a special significance in that it signifies that ovulation is beginning and therefore reproductive maturity is arriving. Of course, boys' first ejaculation holds a similar significance, but it has received far less research, perhaps because of its relation to masturbation, a taboo topic in the West as it is in most cultures (Michael et al., 1994).

How do girls respond to menarche? Almost all the research on this topic has been conducted on girls in the American majority culture, and for them the short answer would be: positively for the most part but with shades of ambivalence. In a study of over 600 girls, Brooks-Gunn and Ruble (1982) found that girls often reported that menarche makes them feel more "grown up." Many girls also indicated that reaching menarche is welcomed because it catches them up to peers who have already begun menstruating and signifies their capacity to bear children. Studies that follow girls over time find that menarche is followed by increases in social maturity, prestige with peers, and self-esteem (Brooks-Gunn & Reiter, 1990).

> "EACH TIME I HAVE A PERIOD . . . I HAVE THE FEELING THAT IN SPITE OF ALL THE PAIN, UNPLEASANTNESS, AND NASTINESS, I HAVE A SWEET SECRET AND THAT IS WHY, ALTHOUGH IT IS NOTHING BUT A NUISANCE TO ME IN A WAY, I ALWAYS LONG FOR THE TIME THAT I SHALL FEEL THAT SECRET WITHIN ME AGAIN."
> —ANNE FRANK (1942/1997), *DIARY OF A YOUNG GIRL*, P. 117

However, not all reactions to menarche are positive. Both culture and biology may shade girls' reactions. Cultures may provide girls with no information to help them anticipate it, or with a negative view that leads them to anticipate it in a negative way. During the 19th century in American society, many girls received no information about menarche before it occurred, and they often responded with shock and fear when they were one day surprised by it (Brumberg, 1997; see the Historical Focus box). Across cultures, evidence from anthropological studies in cultures as diverse as rural Turkey, Malaysia, and Wales suggests that even in the

HISTORICAL FOCUS
Menarche as a Taboo Topic

Some traditional cultures have had false beliefs about menstruation, such as the belief that menstrual blood has magical power that can cause crops to fail. However, people in traditional cultures aren't the only ones that have had false beliefs about menstruation. In the United States, erroneous and bizarre beliefs about menstruation have been widespread until relatively recent times. Furthermore, menarche has been shrouded in shame and secrecy, leaving many girls entirely ignorant of it until they suddenly found themselves bleeding incomprehensibly. The history of American beliefs about menstruation and menarche is described in *The Body Project: An Intimate History of American Girls* by Joan Jacobs Brumberg (1997).

Throughout the 19th century, menstruation and menarche were regarded as taboo topics in most middle-class American families. An 1895 study of Boston high school girls indicated that 60% had no knowledge of menarche before it occurred. A popular 1882 advice book for mothers railed against the "criminal reserve" and "pseudo-delicacy" that led mothers to fail to prepare their girls for menarche. Another 19th-century advice writer reported that "numbers of women" had written to tell her that they were totally unprepared for menarche, including one who wrote that "It has taken me nearly a lifetime to forgive my mother for sending me away to boarding school without telling me about it." A Cornell professor and author of books for young people reported that many college girls believed they were internally wounded when menarche arrived. At the time, menarche was later than it is now (typically age 15 or 16) and college entrance was earlier (16 or 17), so many girls would have experienced menarche at college.

Why such secrecy? Because middle-class Americans of that era believed they had a duty to protect girls' "innocence" for as long as they could. Children who grew up on farms learned a lot about the facts of life by observing and caring for farm animals, but parents in the middle-class sought to protect their children from such raw realities. They associated menarche with budding sexuality, and they were zealous about protecting girls' virginity until marriage. As part of this effort, they often attempted to delay menarche by having girls avoid sexually "stimulating" foods such as pickles! Menarche came anyway, of course, but they believed it was best to keep girls in ignorance of menarche—and sexuality—for as long as possible.

In the course of the 20th century, as the sexual restrictiveness of the 19th century faded, menarche and menstruation gradually became more openly discussed. The Girl Scouts was among the first organizations to discuss menstruation openly. Beginning in the 1920s, attaining the Health Winner merit badge required young Girl Scouts to read about menarche and talk to their troop leader about it. A substantial amount of information was communicated through the media. In the 1920s, as mass-produced sanitary napkins became popular (previously, cotton rags or cheesecloth had been typically used), ads for sanitary napkins helped to open up discussion of menstruation. Companies making sanitary napkins distributed pamphlets on menstruation to girls through mothers, teachers, and the Girl Scouts during the 1930s and 1940s. In the 1940s a cartoon produced by Disney, "The Story of Menstruation," was seen by 93 million American school girls. Magazines for girls, such as *Seventeen*, provided advice on how to handle menstruation while remaining active.

Today, it has become rare for an American girl to experience menarche in total ignorance of what is happening to her body. Cultural beliefs in American society no longer associate menarche with sexuality, but rather with health and hygiene. It may be, in fact, that dissociating menarche from sex has been important in allowing it to be discussed more openly. As we will see in future chapters, open discussions of adolescent sexuality remain rare in American society.

Nineteenth-century mothers rarely discussed menarche with their daughters.

present girls often are provided with no information at all to prepare them for menarche, with the result that it often comes as quite a surprise and is experienced with fear and dismay (Appell, 1988; Delaney, 1988; Skultans, 1988). This is an example from an Egyptian woman's memoir:

> It would be difficult for anyone to imagine the panic that seized hold of me one morning when I woke to find blood trickling down beneath my thighs. . . . I was obliged to overcome the fear and shame which possessed me and speak to my mother. I asked her to take me to a doctor for treatment. To my utter surprise she was calm and cool and did not seem to be affected by her daughter's serious condition. She explained that this was something that happened to all girls and that it recurs every month for a few days. On the last day when the flow ceased, I was to cleanse myself of this 'impure blood' by having a hot bath. . . . I was therefore to understand that in me there was something degrading which appeared regularly in the form of this impure blood, and that it was something to be ashamed of, to hide from others. (Saadawi, 1980, p. 45)

Within the American majority culture, research indicates that most girls have talked about menstruation with their mothers before menarche arrives, or received information from friends or from school, but girls who are unprepared for menarche experience it more negatively (Brooks-Gunn & Reiter, 1990). Girls who mature earlier than others are more likely to be unprepared for it. Because it takes place earlier for them than for other girls, they are less likely to have learned about it from peers and their mothers may not yet have told them about it. Research also indicates that girls who have been led by their mothers, peers, or other sources to expect (before menarche) that menstruation will be unpleasant report greater discomfort once menarche occurs (Brooks-Gunn & Ruble, 1982).

The results of studies of girls' responses to menarche indicate vividly that the degree to which cultures provide knowledge and shape expectations for menarche can have important effects on how girls experience it. However, studies also indicate that most girls and women experience some degree of biologically based discomfort associated with menstruation. Among adolescent girls, most report some degree of **premenstrual syndrome (PMS)**, which is the term for the combination of behavioral, emotional, and physical symptoms that occur in the week before menstruation. Various studies have found that from one-half to three-fourths of adolescent girls experience discomfort related to their menstrual cycles, with symptoms including backaches, headaches, fatigue, and depression, as well as general discomfort (Brooks-Gunn & Ruble, 1982; Fisher, Trieller, & Napolitano, 1989; Klein & Litt, 1983; Wilson & Keye, 1989). Even among girls whose experience of menarche is mostly positive, many dislike the messiness of dealing with menstrual blood and the obligation of carrying around supplies to deal with it every month (Brooks-Gunn & Ruble, 1982). Also, some girls report disliking the fact that menstruation places limits on what they can do.

Seen in this light, it is easier to understand the ambivalence girls often experience when they begin menstruating. They like the confirmation that they are developing normally toward reproductive maturity, but they may not like the discomfort and practical requirements that accompany menstruation each month. However, adolescent girls and adult women experience a great range of physical responses to menstruation. At the extreme, a very small proportion of girls and women experience premenstrual symptoms that are severe enough to interfere with their daily functioning; on the other hand, some experience no symptoms at all, and there is a great deal of variability in between these two extremes. Poor diet, high stress, alcohol use, insufficient sleep, and lack of exercise all make PMS symptoms more severe, but orgasms relieve

> "A GIRL COULD CLAIM TO HAVE HER PERIOD FOR MONTHS AND NOBODY WOULD EVER KNOW THE DIFFERENCE. WHICH IS EXACTLY WHAT I DID. ALL YOU HAD TO DO WAS MAKE A BIG FUSS OVER HAVING ENOUGH NICKELS FOR THE KOTEX MACHINE AND WALK AROUND CLUTCHING YOUR STOMACH AND MOANING FOR THREE TO FIVE DAYS A MONTH ABOUT THE CURSE AND YOU COULD CONVINCE ANYBODY. . . . 'I CAN'T GO. I HAVE CRAMPS.' 'I CAN'T DO THAT. I HAVE CRAMPS.' AND MOST OF ALL, GIGGLINGLY, BLUSHINGLY: 'I CAN'T SWIM. I HAVE CRAMPS.' NOBODY EVER USED THE HARD-CORE WORD. MENSTRUATION. GOD, WHAT AN AWFUL WORD. NEVER THAT. 'I HAVE CRAMPS.'"
> —NORA EPHRON 2000, *CRAZY SALAD*, PP. 2–3

menstrual cramps for many women (Carroll & Wolpe, 1996).

For boys, perhaps the closest analogue to menarche is first ejaculation, sometimes known as **semenarche** (not to be confused with spermarche, which was described earlier in this chapter). Very little research has taken place on this topic. Two small studies (Gaddis & Brooks-Gunn, 1985; Stein & Reiser, 1993) found that boys' reactions to semenarche were mostly positive. They enjoyed the pleasurable sensations of it and, like girls' experience of menarche, it made them feel more grown up. However, ambivalence existed for boys as well. Many reported that surprise or fear was part of the experience.

Culture certainly influences boys' interpretation of semenarche. Semenarche may occur through "wet dreams" or masturbation, and there is a long history of shame and censure associated with masturbation in the West (Michael et al., 1994). Perhaps for this reason, American boys tend to tell no one after they experience semenarche (Gaddis & Brooks-Gunn, 1985). A study of boys in Nigeria found that there, in contrast, boys tended to tell their friends about semenarche soon after it took place (Adegoke, 1993), perhaps reflecting less of a stigma associated with masturbation in Nigerian culture.

THINKING CRITICALLY

What kind of preparation for menarche/semenarche would you recommend be provided for today's adolescents? At what age? If schools provide information on menarche/semenarche, should that information include a discussion of the relation between these events and sexuality?

Early and Late Pubertal Timing

"Everybody thought there was something wrong with me because I still looked like a ten-year-old until I was fifteen or sixteen. That has been really a bad experience for me, because everybody was changing around me and I was standing still. I was changing in my head but not my body. My parents were even going to take me to the doctor to see if I was deformed or something like that, but they didn't, and finally last year I

started to grow. My voice started changing and everything, so I guess I'm normal after all, but I think it's going to be awhile before I stop feeling like I'm different from everybody else."

— *Steven, age 17 (quoted in Bell, 1998, p. 14)*

In some respects, social and personal responses to puberty are intertwined. That is, one factor that determines how young people respond to reaching puberty is how others respond to them. In industrialized societies, one aspect of others' responses that adolescents seem to be acutely aware of concerns perceptions of whether they have reached puberty relatively early or relatively late compared with their peers.

One interesting feature of puberty rites in traditional cultures is that eligibility for them is not typically based on age, but on pubertal maturation. This is obvious with regard to rites related to menarche; a girl participates the first time she menstruates. However, boys' participation in puberty rites is also based on maturation rather than age. Typically, the adults of the community decide when a boy is ready, based on his level of physical maturation and usually on their perceptions of his psychological and social readiness as well (Turnbull, 1983).

In contrast, chronological age has much more significance in industrialized countries. One important reflection of this is that the school systems in industrialized countries are **age-graded**—children are grouped on the basis of age rather than on the basis of developmental maturity. As a result, the seventh grade (for example) includes children who are all 12 or 13 years old, but their pubertal development is likely to vary widely, from those who have not experienced any

Adolescents of the same age may have much different levels of physical maturity.

pubertal changes to those who are well on the way to full maturity. Grouping them together in the same classrooms for many hours each day adds to the intensity of comparisons between them and makes them highly aware of whether they are early, late, or "on time," compared with others.

A great deal of research has been conducted on early versus late maturation among adolescents in the West, especially in the United States, extending back over a half century. The results are complex. They differ depending on gender, and the short-term effects of maturing early or late appear to differ from the long-term effects. The effects also differ depending on the area of development considered: self-image, popularity, school performance, and behavior problems. To help clarify, we will look at the results of these studies separately for girls and boys.

Early and Late Maturation Among Girls

The effects of early maturation are mostly negative for girls, although there are some positive effects initially. The good part is that early-maturing girls tend to be more popular than other girls during the time they have the maturational advantage (Simmons, Blyth, & McKinney, 1983). However, in the long run early maturation tends to be more negative than positive for girls. With regard to popularity and body image, as puberty progresses other girls "catch up," and because early maturation typically results in a shorter and heavier appearance it is ultimately a disadvantage in cultures like those of the West, which place such a high value on thinness (Petersen, 1988). Findings from studies in several Western countries indicate that by high school, early-maturing girls generally have a poorer self-image and higher rates of depression, anxiety, and eating disorders compared with other girls (Caspi et al., 1993; Ge, Conger, & Elder, 1996; Graber et al., 1994; Graber, Brooks-Gunn, & Warren, 1997; Simmons & Blyth, 1987). Early maturation is especially difficult for girls when it is combined with other transitions, such as the entry to junior high school or parents' divorce or remarriage (Simmons & Blyth, 1987).

Late maturers, in contrast, tend to experience anxiety about their lateness when they are in their early teens, but by their late teens they tend to have a more favorable body image than other girls (Simmons & Blyth, 1987), probably because they are more likely to end up with the lean body build that tends to be favored for females in Western majority cultures. They are also more likely to be seen by others as attractive and sociable in their late teens (Livson & Peskin, 1980).

Pubertal timing effects not only self-image and popularity, but also behavior. Girls who mature early are more likely to be involved at an early age in sexual activity, drug and alcohol use, and delinquency (Caspi & Moffitt, 1991; Magnusson, Stattin, & Allen, 1986). Because they look older than other girls, they tend to attract attention from older boys, who then introduce them to these activities (Petersen, 1993). Researchers have speculated that the sexual pressure early-maturing girls experience from older boys may be partly responsible for the higher levels of depression and anxiety they report (Blyth, Simmons, & Zakin, 1985).

However, it is not only others' perceptions that are important but also self-perceptions. Girls who *perceive* themselves as early maturers are more likely than other girls to see themselves as ready to engage in smoking, drinking, and alcohol use, and this perception is more important than their *actual* pubertal timing in predicting their participation in these behaviors (Dubas, Graber, & Petersen, 1991).

"I THINK IT'S DISGUSTING THAT YOU ALL PICK ON ME BECAUSE I'M BIG!" LAURA SAID, SNIFFLING. . . . "DON'T YOU THINK I KNOW ALL ABOUT YOU AND YOUR FRIENDS? DO YOU THINK IT'S ANY FUN TO BE THE BIGGEST KID IN THE CLASS?"

"I DON'T KNOW," I SAID. "I NEVER THOUGHT ABOUT IT."

"WELL, TRY THINKING ABOUT IT. THINK ABOUT HOW YOU'D FEEL IF YOU HAD TO WEAR A BRA IN FOURTH GRADE AND HOW EVERYBODY LAUGHED AND HOW YOU ALWAYS HAD TO CROSS YOUR ARMS IN FRONT OF YOU. AND ABOUT HOW THE BOYS CALLED YOU DIRTY NAMES JUST BECAUSE OF HOW YOU LOOKED."

I THOUGHT ABOUT IT. "I'M SORRY, LAURA," I SAID.

"I'LL BET!"

"I REALLY AM. IF YOU WANT TO KNOW THE TRUTH . . . WELL, I WISH I LOOKED MORE LIKE YOU THAN LIKE ME."

"I'D GLADLY TRADE PLACES WITH YOU."

—FROM *ARE YOU THERE, GOD? IT'S ME, MARGARET* BY JUDY BLUME (1970)

■

THINKING CRITICALLY

In the light of the difficulties often experienced by early-maturing girls, can you think of anything families, communities, or schools could do to assist them in early adolescence?

Early and Late Maturation Among Boys Like the findings for girls, the findings for boys indicate that early maturation is often a mixed blessing. However, overall, early maturation tends to be more positive for boys than for girls. Early-maturing boys tend to have more favorable self-images, fewer psychological problems, and higher popularity than other boys (Graber, Lewinsohn, Seeley, & Brooks-Gunn, 1997; Petersen, 1985). This may be because early-maturing boys get their burst of growth and muscular development before other boys do, which gives them a distinct advantage in the sports activities that are important to male popularity in middle school and high school (Brown, 1990; Kinney, 1993). Also, the earlier development of facial hair, lowered voice, and other secondary sex characteristics may make early-maturing boys more attractive to girls. Unlike early-maturing girls, for whom the early bloom of popularity has usually wilted by midadolescence, early-maturing boys' advantages persist through the teens (Graber et al., 1997; Petersen, 1987).

However, not everything about being an early-maturing boy is favorable. Like their female counterparts, early-maturing boys tend to become involved earlier in sex and substance use (Andersson & Magnusson, 1990; Silbereisen et al., 1989), and they are more likely to have problems in school (Duncan et al., 1985). Like the findings for girls, these findings for boys are consistent in studies from several Western countries. Early maturers also tend to have more temper outbursts (Livson & Peskin, 1980). Late maturers, in contrast, rate higher on measures of intellectual curiosity and social initiative (Livson & Peskin, 1980).

Late-maturing boys may also have an advantage over early maturers in the long run, at least in some respects. One study of pubertal timing followed boys from their early teens all the way to the threshold of middle age (Peskin, 1967; Livson & Peskin, 1980). This study found that by their late thirties, males who had been early maturers in adolescence had become more cooperative, self-controlled, and sociable than other males, but they were also more likely to be conventional and humorless. Late maturers, on the other hand, had turned out to be more insightful, inventive, and playful than other males.

Why pubertal timing would have these kinds of long-term effects is not entirely clear, but one interpretation is that early maturation caused some boys to be pushed into adult roles and responsibilities earlier than others—perhaps because, due to their physical maturity, others assumed they were ready. Early assumption of adult roles may have, in turn, shortened the period where they might have experimented with various roles and identities, with the result that their capacities for creativity and psychological flexibility were squelched early. Late maturers, with their younger appearance, may have been allowed more

TABLE 2.3: SUMMARY OF STUDIES ON EARLY AND LATE MATURATION

	Early	Late
Females, short-term	More popular, more attention from boys; more likely to be involved in early sexual activity, substance use	Anxiety about lateness
Females, long-term	Poorer self-image; higher rates of depression, anxiety, eating disorders	More favorable body image; considered more attractive and sociable
Males, short-term	More favorable self-image, more popular; earlier involvement in sex and substance use, more temper outbursts	Higher in intellectual curiosity, social initiative
Males, long term	More cooperative, self-controlled, sociable; more conventional, humorless	More impulsive; more insightful, inventive, playful

time to experiment and explore possible life directions, which may have promoted their creativity and adaptability as adults.

Keep in mind, as you read about these studies of the consequences of early and late maturation, that a great deal of variance exists in each of these groups. Although early and late maturation are related to certain kinds of general outcomes on a group level (see Table 2.3), the effects for individuals will naturally depend on their particular abilities, experiences, and relationships.

Also keep in mind that so far, all the studies conducted on pubertal timing have involved adolescents in the majority cultures of Western countries. I suggested above that the effects of maturing relatively early or relatively late may be due to the age-grading that exists in these countries, but right now we do not really know. How do adolescents and adults respond to pubertal timing in cultures where no age-graded schooling exists? In Western countries, do the cultural characteristics of minorities lead adolescents in these cultures to respond differently to early or late maturation than adolescents in the majority culture, even though they also experience age-graded schools? These are questions to challenge researchers in the years to come.

Biological Development and the Environment: The Theory of Genotype–Environment Interactions

For many years in the social sciences, scholars have debated the relative importance of biology and the environment in human development. In this **nature–nurture debate**, some scholars have claimed that human behavior can be explained by biological factors (nature) and that environment matters little, whereas others have claimed that biology is irrelevant to most aspects of human behavior and that human behavior can be explained by environmental factors (nurture). In recent years, most scholars have reached a consensus that both biology and environment play key roles in human development, although scholars continue to debate the relative strength of nature and nurture (cf. Baumrind, 1993; Scarr, 1993).

Given the profound biological changes that take place in adolescence and emerging adulthood, nature–nurture issues are perhaps especially relevant to these periods of life. One influential theory on this topic that I will be relying on occasionally in this book is the **theory of genotype-environment interactions** (Scarr, 1993; Scarr & McCartney, 1983). According to this theory, both genetics and environment make essential contributions to human development. However, the strength of the influences of genetics and the environment are difficult to unravel because our genes actually influence the kind of environment we experience. Based on our genotypes, we *create our own environments*, to a considerable extent. These genotype–environment interactions take three forms: passive, evocative, and active.

Passive Genotype–Environment Interactions

Passive genotype–environment interactions occur in biological families when *parents provide both genes and environment for their children.* This may seem obvious, but it has profound implications for how we think about development. Take this father–daughter example. Dad has always been good at drawing things, ever since he was a boy, and now he makes a living as a commercial illustrator. One of the first birthday presents he gives to his little girl is a set of crayons and colored pencils for drawing. She seems to like it, and he provides her with increasingly sophisticated materials as she grows up. He also teaches her a number of drawing skills as she seems ready to learn them. By the time she reaches adolescence, she's quite a proficient artist herself, and draws a lot of the art for school clubs and social events. She goes to college and majors in architecture, and goes on to become an architect. It is easy to see how she became so good at drawing, given an environment that stimulated her drawing abilities so much—right?

Not so fast. It is true that Dad provided her with a stimulating environment, but he also provided her with half of her genes. If there are any genes that contribute to drawing ability—such as genes that contribute to spatial reasoning and fine motor coordination—she may well have received those from Dad, too. The point is that in a biological family, it is very difficult to separate genetic influences from environmental influences because *parents provide both*, and they are likely to provide an environment that reinforces the tendencies they have provided to their children through their genes.

Evocative Genotype–Environment Interactions

Evocative genotype–environment interactions occur when a person's inherited characteristics *evoke* responses from others in their environment. If you had a son who started reading at age 3 and seemed to love it, you might buy him more books; if you had a daughter who could sink 20-foot jump shots at age 12, you might arrange to send her to basketball camp. Did you ever baby-sit or work in a setting where there were many children? If so, you may have found that children differ in how sociable, cooperative, and obedient they are. In turn, you may have found that you reacted differently to them, depending on their characteristics. That is what is meant by evocative genotype–environment interactions—with the crucial addition of the assumption that characteristics such as reading ability, athletic ability, and sociability are at least partly based on genetics.

Active Genotype–Environment Interactions

Active genotype–environment interactions occur when people seek out environments that correspond to their genotypic characteristics. The child who reads easily may ask for books as birthday gifts, the adolescent with an ear for music may ask for piano lessons, the emerging adult for whom reading has always been slow and difficult may choose to begin working full-time after high school rather than going to college. The idea here is that people are drawn to environments that match their inherited abilities.

Genotype–Environment Interactions Over Time

The three types of genotype–environment interactions operate throughout childhood, adolescence, and emerging adulthood, but their relative balance changes over time (Scarr, 1993). In childhood, passive genotype–environment interactions are especially pro-nounced, and active genotype–environment interactions are relatively weak. This is because the younger a child is, the more parents control the daily environment the child experiences and the less autonomy the child has to seek out environmental influences outside the family. However, with age, especially as children move through adolescence and emerging adulthood, the balance changes. Parental control diminishes, so passive genotype–environment interactions also diminish. Autonomy increases, so active genotype–environment interactions also increase. Evocative genotype–environment interactions remain relatively stable from childhood through emerging adulthood.

The theory of genotype–environment interactions is by no means universally accepted by scholars on human development. In fact, it is currently the source of vigorous debate in the field. In 1993, there was a powerful exchange on this topic between two of the most prominent developmental psychologists, Sandra Scarr (1993) and Diana Baumrind (1993). Many scholars (such as Baumrind) question the theory's claim that characteristics such as sociability, reading ability, and athletic ability are substantially inherited. However, it is currently one of the most important new theories of human development, and you should be familiar with it as part of your understanding of development during adolescence and emerging adulthood. I find the theory provocative and useful, and I will be referring to it in the chapters to come.

THINKING CRITICALLY

Think of one of your abilities in relation to the genes and environment provided to you by your parents, and describe how the various types of genotype–environment interactions may have been involved in your development of that ability.

Summing Up

This chapter has presented the biological changes that take place during puberty and some of the cultural, social, and personal responses that result from these changes. Here are the main points we have covered in this chapter:

- During puberty, a set of remarkable transformations takes place in young people's bodies. Hormonal changes lead to changes in physical functioning and to the development of primary and secondary sex characteristics. In many respects, these changes reach full fruition in emerging adulthood, which is a time of peak physical functioning for most people.

- Cultures influence young people's experience of puberty through cultural technologies in health and nutrition, which influence the timing of the initiation of puberty; through rituals that give meaning to pubertal changes; and through providing or failing to provide young people with information about what is happening to their bodies. In industrialized countries, the cultural practice of age-graded schooling means that the timing of puberty has important consequences for adolescents who begin puberty relatively early or relatively late.

- According to the theory of genotype–environment interactions, the influences of genetics and the environment are difficult to separate because in some ways genes shape the kind of environment we experience. During adolescence and emerging adulthood, greater autonomy allows young people to seek out the environmental influences that will enhance their inherited abilities—active genotype–environment interactions increase, in the terminology of the theory.

Perhaps the most notable single fact in this chapter is that the typical age of reaching puberty has declined steeply in industrialized countries over the past 150 years, so that now the first evident changes of puberty take place between ages 10 and 12 for most people, and even earlier for some. Reaching puberty means reaching sexual maturity, and in many ways the cultural beliefs and practices of industrialized countries still have not adjusted to the fact that young people now reach the threshold of sexual maturity at such an early age. Parents are often unsure of when or how to talk to children about their changing bodies and their sexual feelings. School officials are often equally unsure about what to communicate to children. Adolescent peers exchange information among themselves, but what they tell each other is not always accurate or healthy. Consequently, adolescents often experience their biological changes with limited information about what is happening to them.

Still, in this area even more than in most of the areas we will discuss in this book, we know little about the experiences of young people outside of the middle-class majority cultures of Western countries. How do young people in traditional cultures respond to the biological changes of puberty? And what about adolescents in minority cultures in Western societies? In the decades to come, research on these questions may provide us with better information about the different ways that cultures may enhance young people's passage through the dramatic transformations of puberty.

Key Terms

puberty	estradiol	secondary sex	premenstrual syndrome
endocrine system	testosterone	characteristics	(PMS)
hormones	adrenocorticotropic	follicles	semenarche
hypothalamus	hormone (ACTH)	ovum	age-graded
gonadotropin-releasing	feedback loop	spermarche	nature–nurture debate
hormone (GnRH)	set point	vulva	theory of genotype–
pituitary gland	adolescent growth spurt	labia majora	environment
gonadotropins	peak height velocity	labia minora	interactions
follicle-stimulating	asynchronicity	clitoris	passive genotype–
hormone (FSH)	extremities	breast buds	environment
luteinizing hormone	vital capacity	areola	interactions
(LH)	maximum oxygen uptake	longitudinal study	evocative genotype–
gametes	(VO$_2$ max)	cross-sectional study	environment
gonads	cardiac output	secular trend	interactions
sex hormones	health promotion	reaction range	active genotype–
estrogens	primary sex	mikveh	environment
androgens	characteristics	distancing hypothesis	interactions

For Further Reading

Brooks-Gunn, J., & Reiter, E. O. (1990). The role of pubertal processes. In S. S. Feldman & G. R. Elliott (Eds.), *At the threshold: The developing adolescent*. Cambridge, MA: Harvard University Press. A useful summary of development during puberty.

Brumberg, J. J. (1997). *The body project: An intimate history of American girls*. New York: Random House. A highly readable history of changes in American beliefs and attitudes regarding the physical development of adolescent girls. Includes fascinating information about menarche and menstruation (see Historical Focus box), skin care, standards of body shape and size, and sexuality. For each topic, changes from the early 19th century to the present are discussed.

Eveleth, P., & Tanner, J. (1990). *Worldwide variation in human growth*. Cambridge, MA: Cambridge University Press. A fascinating survey of development during puberty in countries around the world. Shows how the timing of puberty varies depending on the quality of adolescents' nutrition and medical care.

Applying Research

Bell, R. (1998). *Changing bodies, changing lives: A book for teens on sex and relationships* (3rd ed.). New York: Random House. A lively account of the changes of puberty, including bodily changes as well as sexuality and relationships. Written to help adolescents understand their changing bodies, it includes many illuminating quotes.

Blume, J. (1970). *Are you there, God? It's me, Margaret.* New York: Yearling. This book does not exactly apply research, but it is worth knowing about because it has been highly popular with early adolescent girls for 30 years. It is considered a classic book on girls' development during puberty, with over 6 million copies sold, and it is still highly popular. The main character is 11-going-on-12-year-old Margaret, who lobbies God for two biological favors: periods and bigger breasts. At her school, Margaret makes friends with other late-maturing girls. In secret club meetings, they try dubious breast-augmenting techniques and discuss (not always honestly) who has and has not reached menarche.

Cognitive Foundations

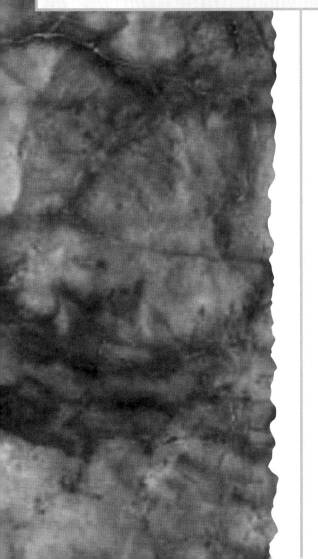

Namo has a problem. It is early morning and he is standing with some friends on the shore of Truk Island in the South Pacific. The friends (all in their late teens) have planned a spearfishing trip for today, but as Namo looks out over the ocean he notices signs that disturb him. The movement and color of the clouds, the height and activity of the waves, all suggest a storm on the way. He looks over their equipment—spears, a small outboard motorboat with a single motor (no oars or sails), some liquid refreshments.

If they were planning with safety in mind they would at least take oars, but he knows that a large part of the appeal of the trip is the risk involved, with the opportunity it presents to demonstrate their courage. The small boat, the dubious weather, and the large sharks common in the area where they will be swimming as they spearfish—they will have ample opportunity today to test their bravery, but as he matches the anticipated challenges with their capacities, he is confident they will measure up to it. Quelling his doubts, he jumps in the boat and they set off (Marshall, 1979).

63

Eva has a problem. She is sitting in the staff room of a hospital in Bremen, Germany, and analyzing the medical charts of a patient being treated for ovarian cysts. Something is not quite right—the diagnosis is ovarian cysts, but the levels of certain of the patient's hormones are much higher than normal and suggest that something else besides the cysts is problematic. At age 22, Eva has been studying medicine for 3 years and she has learned a great deal, but she is well aware that she has not yet accumulated the knowledge and experience the doctors have. She wonders, should she tell them what she thinks?

Mike has a problem. He is sitting in his ninth-grade classroom in San Francisco, California, and puzzling over the problems on the math quiz in front of him. "Amy received 70% of the votes in the election for class president," reads the first one. "If her opponent received the remaining 21 votes, how many people voted in the election?" Mike stares at this and tries to remember how to solve such problems. There was one he was working on last night that was just like this, how did it go? He has difficulty recalling it, and his attention begins to drift off to other topics—the basketball game coming up this Friday, the Smashing Pumpkins CD he was listening to on the way to school, the legs of the girl in the white skirt two rows in front of him—wow! "Ten minutes," intones the teacher from the front of the room. "You have ten more minutes." Seized with panic, he focuses intently again on the problem in front of him.

Adolescents and emerging adults all over the world confront intellectual challenges as part of their daily lives. Often, as in the cases of Namo and Eva above, their challenges are similar in type and magnitude to the challenges faced by adults, although usually with less authority and responsibility than adults have. In industrialized countries, many of adolescents' intellectual challenges take place in the setting of the school, as in Mike's case. As we shall see, however, the changes that take place in cognitive development during adolescence and emerging adulthood affect all aspects of their lives, not just their school performance.

In this chapter we will look at changes during adolescence and emerging adulthood in how young people think, how they solve problems, and how their capacities for memory and attention change. These changes entail what scholars call **cognitive development**. We will begin by talking about Jean Piaget's theory of cognitive development and some of the research that is based on it. Piaget's theory describes general changes in mental structures and problem-solving abilities that take place during childhood, including adolescence. Next we will discuss some of the cognitive changes that take place during emerging adulthood, changes referred to by scholars as postformal thinking. Then we will consider theory and research on information processing. In contrast to the Piagetian approach, which describes general changes in cognitive development, the information-processing approach focuses on a detailed examination of specific cognitive abilities such as attention and memory.

Later in the chapter we will look at the practical use of cognitive abilities in critical thinking and decision making, and the ways that ideas about cognitive developments can be applied to social topics. Following this we will examine what intelligence tests measure. This will include a detailed discussion of the strengths and limitations of standard IQ tests, as well as a discussion of alternative approaches to conceptualizing and measuring intelligence. Finally, we will discuss the role of culture in cognitive development.

Piaget's Theory of Cognitive Development

Unquestionably, the most influential theory of cognitive development from infancy through adolescence is the one developed by the Swiss psychologist **Jean Piaget** (pronounced pee-ah-*jay*), who lived from 1896 to 1980. Piaget was quite the adolescent prodigy. He developed an early fascination with the workings of the natural world, and he published articles on mollusks while still in his early teens.

However, after receiving his Ph.D. at age 21 from his studies of mollusks, his interests shifted to human development. He took a job that involved intelligence testing with children, and he was intrigued by the kinds of wrong answers children would give. In particular, it seemed to him that children of the same age not only answered the questions in similar ways when they gave the correct answer, but also gave similar kinds of wrong

Jean Piaget.

answers. He concluded that age differences in patterns of wrong answers reflected differences in how children of various ages thought about the questions. Older children not only *know more* than younger children, he decided; they also *think differently* than younger children.

This insight became the basis of much of Piaget's work over the next 60 years. Piaget's observations convinced him that children of different ages think differently, and that changes in cognitive development proceed in distinct **stages** (Piaget, 1972). Each stage involves a different kind of thinking about the world. The idea of stages means that each person's cognitive abilities are organized into one coherent **mental structure**; a person who thinks within a particular stage in one aspect of life should think within that stage in all other aspects of life as well, because all thinking is part of the same mental structure (Keating, 1991). Because Piaget focused on how cognition changes with age, his approach (and the approach of those who have followed in his tradition) is known as the **cognitive-developmental approach**.

According to Piaget, the driving force behind development from one stage to the next is **maturation** (Inhelder & Piaget, 1958). Each of us has within our genotype a prescription for cognitive development that prepares us for certain changes at certain ages. A reasonably normal environment is necessary for cognitive development to occur, but the effect of the environment on cognitive development is limited. You cannot teach a 9-year-old something that only a 13-year-old can learn, no matter how sophisticated your teaching techniques. In the same way, by the time the 9-year-old reaches age 13, the biological processes of maturation will make it easy for him or her to understand the world as a typical child of 13 understands it, and no special teaching will be required.

Piaget's view stressing the importance of maturation contrasted with other theorists who believed that there were no inherent limits to development, or that environmental stimulation could override any inherent limitations on what children are capable of learning at any given age (Flavell, Miller, & Miller, 1993). The emphasis on maturation also separated Piaget from other theorists in that Piaget portrayed maturation as an active process, in which children seek out information and stimulation in the environment that matches the maturity of their thinking. This contrasted with the view of other theorists such as the behaviorists, who viewed the environment as acting on the child through rewards and punishments rather than seeing the child as an active agent in the environment.

Stages of Cognitive Development in Childhood and Adolescence

Based on his own research and his collaborations with his colleague Barbel Inhelder, Piaget devised a theory of cognitive development to describe the stages that children's thinking passes through as they grow up (Inhelder & Piaget, 1958; Piaget, 1972; see Table 3.1). The first 2 years of life Piaget termed the **sensorimotor stage**. Cognitive development in this stage involves learning how to coordinate the activities of the senses (such as watching an object as it moves across your field of vision) with motor activities (such as reaching out to grab the object). Next, from about age 2 to about age 7, is the **preoperational stage**. Here the child becomes capable of representing the world symbolically, such as through the use of language. However, children in this stage are still very limited in their ability to use **mental operations**, that is, in their ability to manipulate objects mentally and reason about them in a way that accurately represents how the world works. For example, children of this age are easily enchanted by stories about how a pumpkin changed into a stagecoach or a frog into a prince, because with their limited understanding of the world these are not just fanciful tales but real possibilities.

TABLE 3.1: PIAGET'S STAGES OF COGNITIVE DEVELOPMENT

Age	Stage	Characteristics
0–1	Sensorimotor	Learn to coordinate the activities of the senses with motor activities.
2–7	Preoperational	Capable of symbolic representation, such as in language, but limited ability to use mental operations.
7–11	Concrete operations	Capable of using mental operations, but only in concrete, immediate experience; difficulty thinking hypothetically.
11–15 (20)	Formal operations	Capable of thinking logically and abstractly, capable of formulating hypotheses and testing them systematically; thinking is more complex, and can think about thinking (metacognition).

Concrete operations is the next stage, lasting from about age 7 to about age 11. Children become more adept at using mental operations during this stage, and this leads to a more advanced understanding of the world. For example, they understand (in the classic demonstration) that if you take water from one glass and pour it into a taller, thinner glass, the amount of water remains the same. However, children in this stage focus on what they can experience and manipulate in the physical environment around them (Flavell et al., 1993; Gray, 1990). They have difficulty transferring their reasoning to situations and problems that require them to think systematically about possibilities and hypotheses. That is where the next stage, formal operations, comes in.

Formal Operations in Adolescence

The stage of **formal operations** begins at about age 11 and reaches completion somewhere between age 15 and age 20, according to Piaget (1972), so this is the stage most relevant to cognitive development in adolescence. Children in concrete operations can perform simple tasks that require logical and systematic thinking, but formal operations involves taking concrete operations one step further. Three major types of abilities are present in formal operations that are not present in concrete operations (Keating, 1991): (1) the **isolation of variables**, systematically changing one variable while the others are held constant; (2) **combinatorial reasoning**, generating all possible combinations of a set of elements; and (3) **proportional reasoning**, understanding how different variables in a given situation are related to each other. In this way, formal operations involves the development of the ability to think *scientifically* and apply the rigor of the scientific method to cognitive tasks.

To demonstrate how this works, let us look at one of the tasks Piaget used to test whether a child has progressed from concrete to formal operations. This task is known as the **pendulum problem** (Inhelder & Piaget, 1958; see Keating, 1975). Children and adolescents are shown a pendulum (consisting of a weight hanging from a string and then set in motion) and asked to try to figure out what determines the speed at which the pendulum sways from side to side. Is it the heaviness of the weight? The length of the string? The height from which the weight is dropped? The force with which it is dropped? They are given various weights and various lengths of string to use in their deliberations.

Children in concrete operations tend to approach the problem with random attempts, changing more than one variable on each attempt. So, they might try the heaviest weight on the longest string dropped from medium height with medium force, then a medium weight on the smallest string dropped from medium height with lesser force. When the speed of the pendulum changes, it remains difficult for them to say what caused the change, because they altered more than one variable. If they happen to arrive at the right answer—it's length of string—they find it difficult to explain why. This is key, for Piaget; cognitive advances at each stage are reflected not just in the answers children devise for problems, but in their explanations for *how* they arrived at the solution.

It is only with formal operations that we become able to find the right answer to a problem like this, as well as to understand why it is the right answer and explain it. The formal operational thinker approaches the pendulum problem by utilizing the kind of hypothetical thinking involved in a scientific experiment. "Let's see, it could be weight; let me try

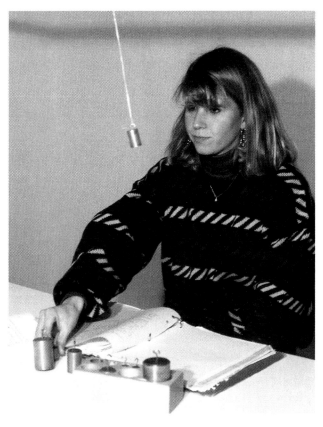

The pendulum problem.

and similar tasks (Keating, 1990). The transitional period from concrete operations to formal operations on these tasks usually takes place from age 11 to 14 (Keating, 1990).

The problems Piaget used to assess the attainment of formal operations were essentially scientific problems, involving the capacity to formulate hypotheses, test them systematically, and then make deductions (that is, draw conclusions) on the basis of the results (Inhelder & Piaget, 1958; Piaget & Inhelder, 1969). However, a number of other aspects to formal operations focus less on scientific thinking and more on logical or applied reasoning (Keating, 1990; Ginsberg & Opper, 1988). These include the development of capacities for **abstract thinking**, **complex thinking**, and thinking about thinking (called **metacognition**). All of these capacities were discussed by Piaget, but in recent years there has been considerable research on them by other scholars as well.

changing the weight while keeping everything else the same. No, that's not it; same speed. Maybe it's length; if I change the length while keeping everything else the same, *that* seems to make the difference; it goes faster with a shorter string. But let me try height, too; no change; then force; no change there, either. So it's length, and only length, that makes the difference." Thus, the formal operational thinker changes one variable while holding the others constant (isolation of variables), considers all possible combinations of variables (combinatorial reasoning), and considers how the variables might be related to one another (proportional reasoning). Through this process the formal operational thinker systematically tests the possible solutions and arrives at an answer that can be defended and explained. The capacity for this kind of thinking, which Piaget (1972) termed **hypothetical-deductive reasoning**, is at the heart of Piaget's concept of formal operations.

In Piaget's research, as well as in the research of many others, adolescents perform significantly better than preadolescent children at the pendulum problem

Abstract Thinking

Something that is *abstract* is something that is strictly a mental concept or process; it cannot be experienced directly, through the senses. Abstract concepts include, for example, time, friendship, and faith. You were introduced to several abstract concepts in Chapters 1 and 2, including culture, the West, and adolescence itself. You cannot actually see, hear, taste, or touch these things; they exist only as *ideas. Abstract* is often contrasted with *concrete*, which refers to things you *can* experience through the senses, and the contrast is especially appropriate here, because the stage preceding formal operations is termed *concrete* operations. Children in concrete operations can apply logic only to things they can experience directly, concretely, whereas the capacity for formal operations includes the ability to think abstractly and apply logic to mental operations as well (Piaget, 1972; Keating, 1990).

Suppose I tell you that A = B and B = C, then ask you, does A = C? It is easy for you, as a college student, to see that the answer is yes, even though you have no idea what A, B, and C represent. However, children thinking in terms of concrete operations would be likely to be mystified by this problem. They would need to know what A, B, and C represent; they would probably need to *see* A, B, and C in front of them. In contrast, you realize that it does not matter what they are. The same logic applies to A, B, and C no matter what they represent.

But abstract thinking involves more than just the capacity to solve this kind of logical puzzle. It also involves the capacity to think about abstract concepts such as justice, freedom, goodness, evil, and time. Adolescents become capable of engaging in discussions about politics, morality, and religion in ways they could not when they were younger, because with adolescence they gain the capacity to understand and use the abstract ideas involved in such discussions (Adelson, 1961; Kohlberg, 1976).

Complex Thinking

Formal operational thinking is more complex than the kind of thinking that occurs in concrete operations. Concrete operational thinkers tend to focus on one aspect of things, usually the most obvious and concrete, but formal operational thinkers are more likely to see things in greater complexity and perceive multiple aspects of a situation or idea. This greater complexity can be seen in the use of metaphor, sarcasm, and satire.

Metaphor With formal operations, adolescents become capable of understanding metaphors that are more subtle than metaphors they may have understood earlier (Sternberg & Nigro, 1980). Metaphors are complex, because they have more than one meaning. They have the literal, concrete meaning, and then they have one or more less obvious, more subtle meanings. Poems and novels are full of them. Consider, for example, this passage in a poem by T. S. Eliot entitled "A Dedication to My Wife":

> No peevish winter wind shall chill
> No sullen tropic sun shall wither
> The roses in the rose-garden which is ours and
> ours only.

On one level, the meaning of the passage is about the hardiness of the roses in a garden. But there is a second meaning as well—the roses are a metaphor of the author's optimism for the enduring vitality of the love between him and his wife. Adolescents can grasp multiple meanings such as this to a degree that children usually cannot (Sternberg & Nigro, 1980).

Sarcasm Sarcasm is another example of complex communication. As with metaphors, there is more than one interpretation possible. "Nice pants," someone says to you as they greet you. That has a literal meaning, as a compliment for your fine taste in fashion. But depending on who says it, and how they say it, it could have another, quite different meaning: "What an ugly pair of pants! You sure look like a fool." Adolescents become capable of understanding (and using) sarcasm in a way children cannot, and as a result sarcasm is more often part of adolescents' conversations Eder (1995).

One study examined how understanding of sarcasm changes from middle childhood through adolescence (Demorest et al., 1984). Participants of various ages were presented with stories in which they were asked to judge whether a particular remark was sincere, deceptive, or sarcastic. Children aged 9 or younger had difficulty identifying sarcastic remarks, but 13-year-olds were better than the younger children, and college students were better than the 13-year-olds.

> "[Ackley] was even more stupid than Stradlater. Stradlater was a goddam genius next to Ackley. . . . I reached up from where I was sitting on the floor and patted him on the goddam shoulder. 'You're a prince, Ackley kid,' I said. . . . 'You're a real prince. You're a gentleman and a scholar, kid. . . . Tell me the story of your fascinating life, Ackley kid,' I said."
> —Sarcasm in "The Catcher in the Rye" (Salinger, 1951), pp. 47-49.

Satire Satire is a kind of complex communication that contains elements of both metaphor and sarcasm. For example, the story *Alice in Wonderland* is highly entertaining as a children's story, but Lewis Carroll also intended it as a metaphor for the political situation in 19th-century Britain, and it contains many remarks that can be read as sarcasm directed toward various political figures of the day. Political cartoons also have this kind of double-edged bite, employing both metaphor and sarcasm. Adolescents who have reached formal operations have the capacity to understand the multiple meanings in political cartoons (Linn, De Benedictus, & Delucchi, 1982; Lave, 1988), whereas children in concrete operations would per-

Reprinted with special permission of King Features Syndicate.

ceive only the literal meaning of it and would probably not see the humor in it.

Metacognition: Thinking About Thinking

One of the abstractions adolescents develop the capacity to think about with formal operations is their own thoughts. They become aware of their thinking processes in a way that children are not, and this enables them to monitor and reason about those processes. This capacity for "thinking about thinking," known as metacognition, enables adolescents to learn and solve problems more efficiently (Chalmers & Lawrence, 1993; Keating, 1991; Kuhn, 1999).

You probably use metacognition to some degree as you read; almost certainly you use it when studying for an exam. As you move along from sentence to sentence, you may monitor your comprehension and ask yourself, "What did that sentence mean? How is it connected to the sentence that preceded it? How can I make sure I remember what that means?" As you study for an exam you look over the material you are required to know, asking yourself if you know what the concepts mean and determining which are most important for you to know.

Metacognition applies not only to learning and problem solving, but also to social topics—thinking about what you think of others and what they think of you. We will explore these topics in the section on social cognition later in the chapter.

Limitations of Piaget's Theory

Piaget's theory of cognitive development has endured remarkably well. Decades after he first presented it, Piaget's theory remains the dominant theory of cognitive development from birth through

Adolescents can understand the satire in political cartoons in a way younger children cannot.

Toles © 1993 The Buffalo News. Reprinted with permission of UNIVERSAL PRESS SYNDICATE. All rights reserved.

adolescence. However, that does not mean that the theory has been verified in every respect. On the contrary, Piaget's theory of formal operations is the part of his theory that has been critiqued the most and that has been found to require the most modifications, more than his ideas about development at younger ages (Flavell, 1992; Keating, 1990, 1991). The limitations of Piaget's theory of formal operations fall into two related categories: individual differences in the attainment of formal operations, and the cultural basis of adolescent cognitive development.

Individual Differences in Formal Operations
Recall from earlier in the chapter that Piaget's theory of cognitive development puts a strong emphasis on maturation. Although he acknowledged some degree of individual differences, especially in the timing of transitions from one stage to the next, Piaget asserted that most people proceed through the same stages at about the same ages, because they experience the same maturational processes (Inhelder & Piaget, 1958). Every 8-year-old is in the stage of concrete operations; every 15-year-old should be a formal operational thinker. Furthermore, Piaget's idea of stages means that 15-year-olds should reason in formal operations in all aspects of their lives, because the same mental structure should be applied no matter what the nature of the problem (Keating, 1991).

Abundant research indicates decisively that these claims were inaccurate, especially for formal operations (Overton & Byrnes, 1991). In adolescence and even in adulthood, a great range of individual differences exist in the extent to which people use formal operations (Blasi & Hoeffel, 1974; Keating, 1991). Some adolescents and adults use formal operations over a wide range of situations, others use it selectively, still others appear to use it rarely or not at all. One review indicated that by eighth grade, only about one-third of adolescents can be said to have reached formal operations (Strahan, 1983). Other reviews find that, on any particular Piagetian task of formal operations, the success rate among late adolescents and adults is only 40% to 60%, depending on the task and on individual factors such as educational background (Keating, 1991). Some evidence suggests that this proportion increases during the teens but even in the late teens and into adulthood a large proportion of people use formal operations either inconsistently or not at all.

Even people who demonstrate the capacity for formal operations tend to use it selectively, for problems and situations in which they have the most experience

and knowledge (Flavell, Miller, & Miller, 1993). For example, adolescents who are experienced chess players may apply formal operational thinking to chess strategies, even though they may not have performed well on standard Piagetian tasks such as the pendulum problem (Chi, Glaser, & Rees, 1982). An adolescent with experience working on cars may find it easy to apply principles of formal operations in that area but have difficulty performing classroom tasks that require formal operations.

A specific kind of experience, in the form of science and math education, is also important to the development of formal operations. Adolescents who have had courses in math and science are more likely than other adolescents to exhibit formal operational thought (Keating, 1991), especially when the courses involve hands-on experience. This makes sense, if you think about the kinds of reasoning required for formal operations. The hypothetical-deductive reasoning that is so important to formal operations is taught as part of science classes; it is the kind of thinking that is the basis of the scientific method. It is easier for adolescents to develop this kind of thinking if they have systematic instruction in it, and the more they have applied hypothetical-deductive thinking to problems in science classes, the more likely they are to perform well on tasks (such as the pendulum problem) used to assess formal operations (Keating, 1991).

Gray (1990) suggests that Piaget underestimated how much effort, energy, and knowledge it takes to use formal operations. According to Gray (1990), concrete operations are sufficient for most daily tasks and problems, and because formal operations are so much more difficult and taxing, people often will not use formal operations even if they have the capacity to do so. Formal operations might be useful for scientific thinking, but most people will not go to the time and trouble to apply it to every aspect of their daily lives. Thus, the concept of formal operations is inadequate for describing how most people—adolescents as well as adults—solve practical problems and draw causal inferences in their everyday lives (Keating, 1991; Kuhn, 1992; Lave, 1988).

Culture and Formal Operations   In the same way that questions have been raised about whether adolescents and adults apply formal operations to all aspects of their lives, questions have also been raised about the extent to which cultures differ in whether their members reach formal operations at all. By the early 1970s numerous studies indicated that cultures varied widely in the prevalence with which their members displayed an understanding of formal operations on the kinds of tasks that Piaget and others had used to measure it. A consensus had formed among scholars that in many cultures formal operational thought (as measured with Piagetian tasks) does not develop, and that this was particularly true in cultures that did not have formal schooling (Cole, 1996).

Piaget responded to these criticisms by suggesting that it may be that, although all persons reach the *potential* for formal operational thinking, they apply it first (and perhaps only) to areas in which their culture has provided them with the most experience and expertise (Piaget, 1972). In other words, it may not make sense to give such tasks as the pendulum problem to people in all cultures, because the materials and the task may be unfamiliar to them. However, if you use materials and tasks familiar to them and relevant to their daily lives, you may find that they display formal operational thinking under those conditions.

Studies like the ones described in the Cultural Focus box indicate that Piaget's ideas about cognitive development in adolescence can be applied to non-Western cultures, as long as they are adapted to the ways of life of each culture. There is widespread support among scholars for the proposition that formal operations constitute a universal human potential but the forms it takes in each culture are derived from the kinds of cognitive requirements people in that culture

In traditional cultures, practical activities sometimes require formal operations. Here, adolescents in the South Pacific help build the roof of a shelter.

CULTURAL FOCUS
Formal Operations Among the Inuit

Until recent decades, Inuit (formerly known as Eskimo) children and adolescents of the Canadian Arctic had never attended school (Balikci, 1970; Condon, 1987). If Inuit adolescents had tried to perform the tasks of formal operations or taken a standard IQ test, they probably would have done poorly (Cole, 1996).

But did they, nevertheless, possess and use formal operational thinking? Consider the kind of work adolescent boys and girls performed by the age of 12 or 13 (Balikci, 1970; Condon, 1987):

Boys	Girls
Harnessing dog team for sledge	Cutting fresh ice
Pushing and pulling sledge when stuck in snow	Fetching water
Preparing bows and arrows, harpoons, and spears for hunting	Gathering moss for fire
Helping to build snowhouses	Caring for infants and small children
Helping to erect skin tents	Sewing
Hunting polar bears, seals, etc.	Tanning animal skins
Fishing	Cooking

Many of the daily tasks of Inuit life require formal operations.

Not all these tasks would require formal operations. Assigning them to adolescents (rather than children) may have been appropriate simply because adolescents' larger physical size meant they could perform many tasks better than children, such as fetching water and helping to move a sledge that was stuck in the snow. Other tasks, however, would be likely to demand the kind of thinking involved in formal operations.

Take the hunting trips that adolescent boys would participate in with their fathers, or sometimes undertake by themselves. To become suc-cessful, a boy would have to think through the components involved in a hunt and test his knowl-edge of hunting through experience. If he were unsuccessful on a particular outing, he would have to ask himself why. Was it because of the location he chose? The equipment he took along? The tracking method he used? Or were there other causes? On the next hunt he might alter one or more of these factors to see if his success improved. This would be hypothetical-deductive reasoning, altering and testing different variables to arrive at the solution to a problem.

Or take the example of an adolescent girl learn-ing to tan animal hides. This is an elaborate process, involving several complicated steps. Girls were given responsibility for doing it on their own beginning about age 14. If a girl failed to do it properly, as would sometimes happen, the hide would be ruined, and her family would be disappointed and angry with her. She would have to ask herself, where did the process go wrong? Mentally, she would work her way back through the various steps in the process, trying to identify her error. This, too, is formal operational thinking, mentally considering various hypotheses in order to identify a promising one to test.

In recent decades, globalization has come to the Inuit, and adolescents spend most of their day in school rather than working alongside their parents (Condon, 1987). This has provided them with a greater range of opportunities than they had before. Some of them go to larger nearby cities after high school to receive professional training of vari-ous kinds. By now, they face many of the same cog-nitive demands as adolescents in the Canadian majority culture.

However, as has so often happened in the course of globalization, there have been negative repercus-sions as well. Many adolescents find school boring and irrelevant to their lives, and some of them look to alcohol, glue sniffing, and shoplifting to add excitement. Inuit young people are "not only in transition between childhood and adulthood but also in transition between two distinct ways of life" (Condon, 1987, p. 188), and the transition has not been easy to make.

face (Cole, 1996). However, in every culture there is likely to be considerable variation in the extent to which adolescents and adults display formal operational thought, from persons who display it in a wide variety of circumstances to persons who display it little or not at all.

THINKING CRITICALLY

If abstract thinking is required for the formation of ideas about politics, morality, and religion, how could you explain why such ideas exist even in cultures in which the development of formal operations is rare?

Cognitive Development in Emerging Adulthood: Postformal Thinking

In Piaget's theory, formal operations is the end point of cognitive development. Once formal operations is fully attained, by age 20 at the latest, cognitive maturation is complete. However, like many aspects of Piaget's theory regarding formal operations, this view has been altered by research. In fact, research indicates that cognitive development often continues in important ways during emerging adulthood. This research has inspired theories of cognitive development beyond formal operations, known as **postformal thinking** (Sinnott, 1998). Two of the most notable aspects of postformal thinking in emerging adulthood concern advances in pragmatism and reflective judgment.

Pragmatism

Pragmatism involves adapting logical thinking to the practical constraints of real-life situations. Theories of postformal thought emphasizing pragmatism have been developed by several scholars (Arlin, 1989, 1990; Basseches, 1984, 1989; Labouvie-Vief, 1982, 1990, 1998). The theories have in common an emphasis that the problems faced in normal adult life often contain complexities and inconsistencies that cannot be addressed with the logic of formal operations. The theories also have in common that, to date, only a limited amount of research has been conducted on them.

According to Labouvie-Vief (1982, 1990, 1998), cognitive development in the early twenties is distinguished from adolescent thinking by a greater recognition and incorporation of practical limitations to logical thinking. In this view, adolescents exaggerate the extent to which logical thinking will be effective in real life. In contrast, the early twenties bring a growing awareness of how social factors and factors specific to a given situation must be taken into account in approaching most of life's problems.

A similar theory of cognitive development in emerging adulthood has been presented by Michael Basseches (1984, 1989). Like Labouvie-Vief (1982, 1990), Basseches (1984) views cognitive development in emerging adulthood as involving a recognition that formal logic can rarely be applied to the problems most people face in their daily lives. **Dialectical thought** is Basseches' term for the kind of thinking that develops in emerging adulthood, involving a growing awareness that most problems do not have a single solution and that problems must often be addressed with crucial pieces of information missing (Basseches, 1984). For example, a person may have to decide whether to return to college for more education without knowing whether jobs will be available in their intended field by the time they complete their education.

Another approach to postformal thinking has been proposed by Patricia Arlin (1989, 1990). Arlin argues that formal operations is a stage of problem solving, and it is followed at least for some people by a stage of **problem finding**. Problem finding involves generating a variety of possible solutions to complex problems and seeing old problems in new ways. Thus, it is more effective than formal operations for addressing the problems of real life, which often have either no clear solution or multiple solutions. However, Arlin (1990) acknowledges that a stage of problem finding is reached by only a small proportion of adults.

THINKING CRITICALLY

Think of a problem you have had in your life lately. Can you apply the insights of Labouvie-Vief, Basseches, and Arlin to the problem?

Reflective Judgment

Reflective judgment, another cognitive quality that has been found to develop in emerging adulthood, is the capacity to evaluate the accuracy and logical coherence of evidence and arguments.

Reflective judgment tends to improve during college.

An influential theory of the development of reflective judgment in emerging adulthood has been proposed by William Perry (1970/1999), who based his theory on his studies of college students in their late teens and early twenties. According to Perry (1970/1999), adolescents tend to engage in **dualistic thinking**, which means that they often see situations and issues in polarized terms—an act is either right or wrong, with no in-between; a statement is either true or false, regardless of the nuances or the situation to which it is being applied. In this sense, they lack reflective judgment. However, reflective judgment begins to develop for most people in their late teens. First a stage of **multiple thinking** takes place, in which young people tend to be more aware than dualists that there are two or more sides to every story, two or more legitimate views of every issue, and that it can be difficult to justify one position as the true or accurate one. In this stage people tend to value all points of view equally, even to the extent of asserting that it is impossible to make any judgments at all about whether one point of view is more valid than another.

By the early twenties, according to Perry, multiple thinking develops into **relativism**. Like people in the stage of multiple thinking, relativists are able to recognize the legitimacy of competing points of view. However, rather than denying that one view could be more persuasive than another, relativists attempt to compare the relative merits of competing views. Finally, by the end of their college years, many young people reach a stage of **commitment**, in which they commit themselves to certain points of view they believe to be the most valid, while being open to reevaluating their views if new evidence is presented to them.

Research on reflective judgment indicates that significant gains may take place in the late teens and twenties (Kitchener et al., 1993; Pascarella & Terenzini, 1991). This research also indicates that formal operations is a necessary but not sufficient condition for reflective thinking (Kitchener & King, 1990). However, the gains that take place in emerging adulthood appear to be due more to education than to maturation (Kitchener & King, 1990)—people who pursue a college education during emerging adulthood show greater advances in reflective judgment than people who do not. Also, Perry and his colleagues acknowledged that the development of reflective judgment is likely to be more common in a culture that values pluralism and whose educational system promotes consideration of diverse points of view (Perry, 1970/1999). However, thus far no cross-cultural research has taken place on reflective judgment.

THINKING CRITICALLY

The Constitution of the United States specifies a minimum age of 36 before a person can be elected president. Why do you suppose this is so? What sort of cognitive qualities might be insufficiently developed prior to that age for a person to be capable of exercising the duties of the office?

The Information-Processing Approach

The approach of Piaget and the scholars who have continued his line of theory and research describes how adolescents and emerging adults develop capacities such as hypothetical-deductive reasoning, abstract thinking, and reflective judgment. The focus of the theory is on how the development of these general cognitive capacities is reflected in young people's performance on specific tasks such as the pendulum problem described in the previous section. Piaget also emphasized the way cognitive abilities change with age, from preadolescence to adolescence, from concrete operations to formal operations.

The **information-processing approach** to understanding cognitive development in adolescence is quite

HISTORICAL FOCUS
Gender and Cognitive Development in Emerging Adulthood

In most cultures throughout history, opportunities for enhancing cognitive development through education have been much more limited for females than for males. In the United States and other Western countries, this issue pertains particularly to emerging adulthood. Historically, these countries have conceded that girls should at least receive education at younger ages, so that they can learn to read and write. However, there has been much more debate over and resistance to the idea that females should receive higher education. Many people in the 18th and 19th centuries were vehemently opposed to the idea that females should be allowed to attend colleges and universities.

Historian Linda Kerber (1997) distinguishes three periods in the history of higher education for women. The first extended from 1700 to 1775. During this time, female literacy grew (as it did for males), but no colleges or universities accepted female students. Of course, it was also rare for males to receive higher education at that time, but at least the more privileged males had this opportunity. Females were barred entirely.

The second period extended from 1776 to 1833, and Kerber calls it the "Era of the Great Debate over the Capacities of Women's Minds." The question of whether women were cognitively capable of benefiting

In the 19th century, there were strong prejudices against women with regard to their intellectual abilities.

from higher education was hotly debated during this time. The final year of this period, 1833, is the year that the first women entered higher education, at Oberlin College, which was founded as a women's college. The third period, from 1833 to 1875, was marked by a steady expansion in opportunities for women to pursue higher education. By 1875, dozens of institutions accepted female students, and the debate over whether women should be allowed to pursue higher education had turned in favor of the proponents.

Arguments against allowing young women the opportunity for higher education had two main features. One was the claim that "too much" education for young women would be hazardous to them, because it would spoil their feminine qualities and because it might exhaust them and even make them ill. A second was the claim that women were inherently inferior to men intellectually, and therefore higher education would be wasted on them.

The first claim, that intellectual stimulation was hazardous to young women, was especially prevalent in the 18th century. A popular verse during that century read:

Why should girls be learn'd and wise?
Books only serve to spoil their eyes.
The studious eye but faintly twinkles
And reading paves the way to wrinkles.

About the same time, an influential Boston minister declared, "Women of masculine minds have generally masculine manners, and a robustness of person ill calculated to inspire tender passion."

During the 19th century, this argument continued to be stated, but as women began to break through the barriers to higher education some men claimed that women were "scientifically" shown to be cognitively inferior. A lot of scientific activity took place in the 19th century, and a lot of pseudoscience, too. Some of the worst pseudoscience attempted to establish biologically based group differences in intelligence (Gould, 1981). Even scientists who were otherwise respectable were infected by pseudoscientific reasoning when it came to issues of intelligence. Paul Broca, perhaps the most important figure in neurology in the 19th century, claimed that the smaller brains of women demonstrated their intellectual inferiority. He knew very well that brain size is related to body size, and that women's smaller brain size simply reflected their smaller body size rather than inferior intelligence, but his prejudice against the cognitive capacities of women allowed him to talk himself out of it:

> We might ask if the small size of the female brain depends exclusively on the small size of her body. . . . But we must not forget that women are, on average, a little less intelligent than men. . . . We are therefore permitted to suppose that the relatively small size of the female brain depends in part upon her physical inferiority and in part upon her intellectual inferiority. (1861, quoted in Gould, 1981, p. 104)

The pseudoscientific claims got even worse than that. Gustave Le Bon, the French scholar who was one of the founders of social psychology, commented:

> In the most intelligent races, as among the Parisians, there are a large number of women whose brains are closer in size to those of gorillas than to the most developed male brains. This inferiority is so obvious that no one can contest it even for a moment; only its degree is worth discussion. All psychologists who have studied the intelligence of women . . . recognize today that they represent the most inferior forms of human evolution and that they are closer to children and savages than to an adult, civilized man. They excel in fickleness, inconstancy, absence of thought and logic, and incapacity to reason. Without doubt there exist some distinguished women, very superior to the average man, but they are as exceptional as the birth of any monstrosity, as, for example, of a gorilla with two heads; consequently we may neglect them entirely. (1879, quoted in Gould, 1981)

Keep in mind that Broca and Le Bon were not regarded as cranks or fools, but were two of the most important scholars of their time. They both reflected and affected attitudes toward the cognitive capacities of females that many people held in those days.

Things have changed now in the West. In all Western countries, females excel over males on nearly every measure of educational achievement (Arnett, 2000d; Chisholm & Hurrelmann, 1995). However, it remains true in most of the world that females receive less education than males (Mensch, Bruce, & Greene, 1998). It is also true that certain prejudices against females' cognitive abilities continue to exist in the West, as we will discuss in the chapters on gender and school.

different. Rather than looking at general cognitive capacities, the information-processing approach seeks to delineate the steps involved in the thinking process, and describe how each step is connected to the next (Sternberg, 1988). The information-processing approach does not have a developmental focus (Rebok, 1987); the focus is not on how mental structures and ways of thinking change with age but on the thinking processes that exist at all ages. However, some studies of information processing do compare adolescents or emerging adults to people of other ages. In any case, an understanding of information processing is necessary for a complete understanding of the way cognition works in any particular age period, including adolescence and emerging adulthood.

The model for the information-processing approach is the computer (Hunt, 1989). Information-processing researchers and theorists try to break down human thinking into separate parts in the same way that the functions of a computer are separated into capacities for *attention, processing, storing,* and *retrieving* information (see Figure 3.1). In the pendulum problem, someone taking the information-processing approach would examine how adolescents draw their attention to the most relevant aspects of the problem, process the results of each trial, remember the results,

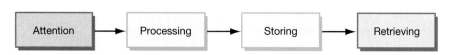

FIGURE 3.1   *The sequence of steps in information processing.*

and retrieve the results from previous trials to compare to the most recent trial. In this way the information-processing approach is a **componential approach** (Sternberg, 1983), meaning that it involves breaking down the thinking process into its various components. Let us look at each of the components of information processing and how they change during adolescence. For all of them, adolescents are better than children and there are few substantial changes from midadolescence through emerging adulthood and into adulthood.

Attention

Have you ever read a textbook while someone else in the same room was watching television? Have you ever had a conversation at a party where music and other conversations were blaring loudly all around you? These are tasks that require **selective attention**, which is the capacity to focus on relevant information while screening out information that is irrelevant (Casteel, 1993). Adolescents tend to be better than preadolescent children at tasks that require selective attention, and emerging adults are generally better than adolescents (Manis, Keating, & Morrison, 1980; Sexton & Geffen, 1979). Adolescents are also more adept than preadolescents at tasks that require **divided attention**—reading a book and listening to music at the same time, for example—but even for adolescents divided attention may result in less efficient learning than if attention was focused entirely on one thing (Schiff & Knopf, 1985).

One aspect of selective attention is the capacity to analyze a set of information and select the important parts of it for further attention. When you listen to a lecture in class, for example, your attention may fluctuate. You may monitor the information being presented and increase or decrease your level of attention according to your judgment of the information's importance. This aspect of selective attention is also a key part of problem solving; one of the initial steps of solving any problem is to decide where to direct your attention. For example, if your computer fails to boot up, the first thing you try to do is to decide where the source of the problem is—the monitor, the plug, or the computer itself. Adolescents are better than children at focusing on the most relevant aspects of a problem (Casteel, 1993; Miller & Weiss, 1981).

THINKING CRITICALLY

Design a simple study to assess adolescents' or emerging adults' abilities for selective attention, and a separate study on their learning abilities under conditions of divided attention.

Processing Information: Speed, Capacity, and Automaticity

Once attention is drawn to the relevant aspects of a situation, the information is processed. Adolescents generally process information with greater speed, capacity, and automaticity than children (Case, 1985, 1997). With regard to *speed*, think of the example of a video game. Adolescents are generally better at such games than children, because the games typically require the player to respond to the changing circumstances of the game, and adolescents are faster at processing

Capacities for selective attention and divided attention improve during adolescence.

Video games require speed of information processing.

information as those changes occur. In experimental situations involving tasks such as matching letters, there is an increase in speed of processing from age 10 through the late teens (Fry & Hale, 1996; Hale, 1990; Kail, 1991a, 1991b), with the largest gains coming in the early part of this age period.

Processing **capacity** refers to how many aspects of a situation you can keep in your mind at once. For example, if you are cooking two or three dishes at the same time, you have a lot to process simultaneously—how each dish is coming along, what the next step is for each one, and whether they look like they will all be ready at the same time. Adolescents are generally believed to have a larger processing capacity than children, although there has been less research in this area than on other aspects of information processing (Case, 1997).

Another aspect of processing is **automaticity**, that is, how much cognitive effort the person needs to devote to processing the information (Case, 1997). For example, if I give you a few computational problems—100 divided by 20, 60 minus 18, 7 times 9—you can probably do them without writing them down and without straining yourself too much. This is partly because you have done problems like this so much in the course of your life that they are almost automatic—much more than they would be for a preadolescent child.

Adolescents show greater automaticity of processing in a variety of respects, compared with preadolescent children. However, automaticity depends more on experience than on age alone. This has been shown in studies of chess players. Expert chess players have been found to process the configurations on chess boards with a high degree of automaticity, which enables them to remember the configurations better and analyze them much faster and more effectively than novices do (Bruer, 1993; Chase & Simon, 1973; Chi, Glaser, & Rees, 1982). Furthermore, expert chess players who are children or adolescents demonstrate greater automaticity in processing chess configurations than novice adults do (Chi et al., 1982).

Automaticity is closely related to speed and capacity (Barsalou, 1992). The more automatic a cognitive task is, the faster you are likely to be able to do it. Also, the more automatic a task is, the less processing capacity it takes, leaving more room for other tasks. For example, you may be able to read a magazine while you watch TV, but you would probably find it harder to fill out your tax forms while watching TV. This is because reading the language on tax forms, filled as it is with terms you are likely to see only on tax forms, is much less automatic to you than reading the language of a magazine.

■   **THINKING CRITICALLY**

Think of an example of a task you performed today in which you used automaticity.

Storing and Retrieving Information: Short-Term and Long-Term Memory

Memory is a key part of information processing, perhaps even the most important part. Drawing your attention to something and processing information about it would not do you much good if you could not store the results in your memory and call them back into your mind when you needed them. Because memory is so important to learning, a great deal of research has taken place on it. One important distinction scholars have made is between short-term and long-term memory. **Short-term memory** is memory for information that is currently the focus of your attention. It has a limited capacity and retains information for only a short time, usually about 30 seconds or less. **Long-term memory** is memory for information that is committed to longer-term storage, so that you can draw on it again after a period when your attention has not been focused on it. The capacity of long-term memory is unlimited, and information is retained indefinitely. You can probably think of things you experienced 10 or more years ago that you can still call up from your long-term memory.

Both short-term and long-term memory improve substantially between childhood and adolescence (Dempster, 1984; Fry & Hale, 1996). The most common test of short-term memory capacity is to recite lists of numbers or words, gradually increasing the length, and see how many the person can remember without making a mistake. So, if I give you the list "1, 6, 2, 9," you can probably remember that pretty easily. Now try this: "8, 7, 1, 5, 3, 9, 2, 4, 1." Not so easy, is it? But you are certainly better at this kind of test now than when you were 8 or 10. Short-term memory capacity increases throughout childhood and early adolescence until the midteens and remains stable after about age 16 at an average of 7 units of information (Dempster, 1984).

In a series of elegant experiments, Robert Sternberg and his colleagues demonstrated how increases in short-term memory between childhood and adolescence have implications for problem-solving abilities (Sternberg, 1977; Sternberg & Nigro, 1980; Sternberg & Rifkin, 1979). They presented analogies to third-grade, sixth-grade, ninth-grade, and college students. For example, "Sun is to moon as asleep is to . . . ?"

1. Star
2. Bed
3. Awake
4. Night

There was improvement with age, especially between the younger (third and sixth grade) and older (ninth grade and college) students. Sternberg attributed the differences to short-term memory capacities. Analogies take a considerable amount of short-term memory space. You have to keep the first set of words ("sun is to moon") and the nature of their relationship in your short-term memory continuously as you consider the other possible pairings ("asleep is to star . . . asleep is to bed. . .") and analyze their relationships as well. Prior to adolescence, people do not have enough short-term memory capacity to perform tasks like this very effectively. (The correct answer is "awake," in case you are wondering.)

Long-term memory also improves in adolescence. Adolescents are more likely than preadolescent children to use **mnemonic devices** (memory strategies), such as organizing information into coherent patterns (Siegler, 1988). Think of what you do, for example, when you sit down to read a textbook chapter. You probably have various organizational strategies you have developed over the years (if you do not, you would be wise to develop some), such as writing a chapter outline, making notes in the margins, organizing information into categories, underlining key passages, and so on. By planning your reading in these ways, you remember (and learn) more effectively.

Another way long-term memory improves in adolescence is that adolescents have *more experience* and *more knowledge* than children do, and these advantages enhance the effectiveness of long-term memory (Keating, 1990). Having more experience means that more tasks are processed automatically, which means that you can focus on remembering less familiar information. For example, if you read Spanish fluently, you are more likely than a novice to remember the details of a story in Spanish, partly because you can focus on the plot and the characters, whereas the novice would have to devote more short-term memory capacity to translating the words. The more short-term memory capacity you can free up through automaticity, the more effectively you can move new information from short-term to long-term memory (Case, 1997).

Having more knowledge also helps you learn new information and store it in long-term memory. This is a key difference between short-term and long-term memory. The capacity of short-term memory is limited, so the more information you have in there already, the less effectively you can add new information to it. With long-term memory, however, the capacity is essentially unlimited, and the more you know the easier it is to learn new information (Keating, 1990). What makes it easier is that you already have information in your memory that you can use to form associations with the new information, which makes it more likely that the new information will be remembered (Pressley & Schneider, 1997). For example, if you have already had a course in child development or human development, some of the concepts (such as concrete operations) and big names (such as Piaget) presented here may be familiar to you. If so, the new information you come across here will be easier for you to remember than for someone who has never had a related course before, because you can make associations between the new information and the knowledge you already have.

THINKING CRITICALLY

Among the courses you have taken in your college education, for which have you found information easiest to remember, and for which hardest? In what ways do the memory concepts presented here help explain why some courses are easier than others for you to retain the information?

Limitations of the Information-Processing Approach

Like Piaget's theory of cognitive development, the information-processing approach has not been without its critics. According to the critics (e.g., Kuhn, 1992), information-processing theorists and researchers are guilty of **reductionism**, which means breaking up a phenomenon into separate parts to such an extent that the meaning and coherence of the phenomenon as a whole becomes lost. From this perspective, what information-processing scholars see as a strength—the focus on the various separate components of cognitive processes—is actually a weakness. It leads to the reductionist claim that human cognition is *nothing but* the activity of these separate components. In the words of one critic, this approach leads scholars to the false conclusion that "the performance is *nothing but* the serial execution of a specified set of individual processes" (Kuhn, 1992, p. 236).

According to the critics, by taking a reductionist approach, information-processing scholars have lost the **holistic perspective** that characterized Piaget's work. That is, they fail to consider how human cognition works as a whole rather than as a set of isolated parts. The analogy of a computer, favored by information-processing scholars, is misguided because human beings are *not* computers. Computers have no capacity for self-reflection, no awareness of how their cognitive processes are integrated, organized, and monitored. Because this capacity is a central part of human cognition, critics argue, overlooking it leaves the information-processing approach insufficient and inadequate.

Computers also lack emotions, and according to some scholars, emotions must be taken into account when considering cognitive functioning. Evidence suggests that adolescents' emotions tend to be more intense and more variable than either children's or adults' emotions (Larson & Richards, 1994), so this would seem to be an especially important consideration with regard to adolescent cognition. In one study, researchers presented three dilemmas to high school students, college students, and adults (Blanchard-Fields, 1986). The dilemmas were intended to vary in the degree of emotional involvement they elicited from the participants—the low-involvement dilemma concerned conflicting accounts of a war between two fictitious nations, whereas the high-involvement dilemmas concerned a conflict between parents and their adolescent son over whether he should join them on a visit to his grandparents, and a man and a woman disagreeing over whether their unintended pregnancy should end in abortion. The researchers found that the high school and college students showed less advanced reasoning about the high-involvement dilemmas than about the low-involvement dilemmas, whereas the adults showed similar reasoning levels for all three dilemmas. This study indicates both that emotions can affect cognition and that the affect may be greater for adolescents and emerging adults than for adults.

Practical Cognition: Critical Thinking and Decision Making

Both the cognitive-developmental approach and the information-processing approach have been highly influential in the study of cognitive development, and both have generated an enormous amount of research.

However, other research on cognitive development in adolescence and emerging adulthood has been more concerned with how cognition operates in real life, as applied in practical situations. Two areas of research on practical cognition in adolescence and emerging adulthood are critical thinking and decision making.

The Development of Critical Thinking

In combination, the changes in cognitive development during adolescence that we have described thus far have the potential to provide adolescents with a greater capacity for **critical thinking**, thinking that involves not merely memorizing information but analyzing it, making judgments about what it means, relating it to other information, and considering ways in which it might be valid or invalid.

According to cognitive psychologist Daniel Keating (1990; Keating & Sasse, 1996), cognitive development in adolescence provides the potential for critical thinking in several ways. First, a wider range of knowledge is available in long-term memory, across a variety of domains; thus, the ability to analyze and make judgments about new information is enhanced because more previous knowledge is available for comparison. Second, the ability to consider different kinds of knowledge simultaneously is increased, which makes it possible to think of new combinations of knowledge. Third, more cognitive strategies are available for applying or gaining knowledge, such as planning and monitoring one's own comprehension; these strategies make it possible to think more critically about what one is learning.

However, Keating and others stress that critical-thinking skills do not develop automatically or inevitably in adolescence. On the contrary, critical thinking in adolescence requires a basis of skills and knowledge obtained in childhood, along with an educational environment in adolescence that promotes and values critical thinking. According to Keating (1990), gaining specific knowledge and learning critical-thinking skills are complementary goals. Critical thinking promotes gaining knowledge of a topic because it leads to a desire for underlying explanations, and gaining knowledge of a topic makes critical thinking possible because it makes relevant knowledge available for analysis and critique.

Given the potential usefulness of critical thinking in the learning process, one might expect that critical-thinking skills would be a primary goal of teaching in schools. However, observers of the American educational system generally agree that American schools do a poor job of promoting critical thinking (Keating, 1990; Linn & Songer, 1991; Steinberg, 1996). Assessments of adolescents' critical-thinking skills generally find that few adolescents develop such skills and use them capably, in part because such skills are so rarely promoted in the classroom (Linn & Songer, 1991). Instead of promoting the complementary development of knowledge and critical thinking as described by Keating (1990), nearly all secondary school teaching is limited to promoting the rote memorization of concrete facts, with the limited goal that students will be able to remember those facts until a test is taken (Linn & Songer, 1991).

The promotion of critical thinking would require small classes and a classroom environment in which focused discourse between teachers and students is the norm (Keating, 1990; Keating & Sasse, 1996). These characteristics are not typical of American secondary schools (Linn & Songer, 1991, 1993). European secondary schools have been argued by some scholars to be better at providing a classroom environment that promotes critical thinking (Hamilton, 1990). American colleges also tend to have more success than American secondary schools in promoting critical thinking, especially in relatively small classes (Magolda, 1997). In this textbook, the Thinking Critically questions in each chapter are intended to promote critical thinking on adolescence and emerging adulthood. They also provide you with examples of what critical thinking means.

THINKING CRITICALLY

Did your high school successfully promote critical thinking? If not, why do you think it did not? What practical barriers existed to the promotion of critical thinking?

Can Adolescents Make Competent Decisions?

We saw in Chapter 1 that making independent decisions is one of the things that most adolescents and emerging adults in American society consider to be a crucial part of becoming an adult (Arnett, 1998a). What do studies tell us about whether adolescents possess the cognitive abilities to make decisions competently? The answer to this question has important implications, given that adolescents in modern societies are confronted with decisions about whether to use drugs (including alcohol and cigarettes), when to become sexually active, and which educational path to pursue.

This area also has political and legal implications, in debates over whether adolescents should have the right to make independent decisions about using contraception, obtaining an abortion, or pursuing various medical treatments. Currently, adolescents (under age 18) are prohibited in many states from making independent decisions about medical treatments (Steinberg & Cauffman, 1996). Also, legal contracts entered into by adolescents under age 18 do not have the same power as contracts signed by persons aged 18 or over; adolescents may disavow a contract any time they wish, whereas adults may not (Nurcombe & Parlett, 1994). Furthermore, crimes committed by adolescents are treated under a different legal system than crimes committed by adults, and usually more leniently, a tacit recognition that adolescents should not be held responsible for bad decisions in the same way adults are (Steinberg & Cauffman, 1996). Increasingly, states are narrowing this distinction and trying juveniles under the same rules as adults for many crimes, but most states have maintained at least some distinction in the legal system that recognizes differences in decision-making capabilities between adolescents and adults.

Are adolescents competent to make major decisions, such as about legal or medical issues?

One of the most prominent current perspectives on adolescent decision making is **behavioral decision theory** (Beyth-Marom et al., 1993; Beyth-Marom & Fischoff, 1997; Byrnes, Miller, & Reynolds, 1999; Fischoff, 1992; Furby & Beyth-Marom, 1992). According to this perspective, the decision-making process includes (1) identifying the range of possible choices; (2) identifying the consequences that would result from each choice; (3) evaluating the desirability of each consequence; (4) assessing the likelihood of each consequence; and (5) integrating this information.

Studies indicate that competence in this process varies substantially with age. Compared with preadolescent children, early adolescents generally identify a wider range of possible choices, are better at anticipating the consequences of the possible choices, and are better at evaluating and integrating information (Keating, 1990). In each of these respects, however, early adolescents are less skilled than late adolescents or emerging adults (Byrnes et al., 1999). Transitions in decision-making competence tend to occur at about ages 11 to 12 and again at ages 15 to 16 (Keating, 1990).

For example, Lewis (1981) presented adolescents in grades 8, 10, and 12 with hypothetical situations regarding decisions about medical procedures. The 12th graders were more likely than the 10th or 8th graders to mention risks to be considered (83%, 50%, and 40%, from oldest to youngest), to recommend consultation with an outside specialist (62%, 46%, and 21%), and to anticipate possible consequences (42%, 25%, and 11%).

Most studies comparing late adolescents and adults have found few differences between them in the decision-making processes they use (Beyth-Marom et al., 1993; Beyth-Marom & Fischoff, 1997; Furby & Beyth-Marom, 1992). Why is it, then, that adolescents are so much more likely than adults to take risks such as driving while intoxicated or trying illegal drugs? One possible explanation is that adolescents and adults make different evaluations about the desirability of the different consequences (Maggs, 1999). For example, in deciding whether to try an illegal drug that is being handed around at a party, both adolescents and adults may identify the same range of choices and the same possible consequences from these choices (Quadrel, Fischoff, & Davis, 1993), such as the possible pleasurable feelings from the drug and the possibility of being considered daring or timid by others (for trying it or not trying it). However, adolescents and adults may evaluate these consequences differently. Adolescents may be more attracted to the possible sensation-seeking pleasure of the

drug (Arnett, 1994b), more eager to be considered daring by others, and more worried about being considered timid by others. As a consequence, adolescents would be more likely than adults to try illegal drugs even though both adolescents and adults would be going through the same decision-making process (Quadrel et al., 1993).

Another explanation has been proposed by Steinberg and Cauffman (1996). They argue that differences in decision-making abilities between adolescents and adults should be divided into two broad categories: those attributed to cognitive factors and those attributed to psychosocial factors (i.e., social and emotional maturity). According to Steinberg and Cauffman (1996), most studies of decision-making abilities among adolescents and adults have explored only cognitive factors. However, they view this approach as too narrow and as likely to underestimate the differences between adolescents and adults. Instead, they propose that mature decision making should be viewed as the product of the interaction between cognitive and psychosocial factors, with competent decision making potentially undermined by a deficiency in either area.

The implication of their theory is that even though adolescents may be able to show the same level of cognitive ability as adults in making a decision, adolescents may make different decisions because they are more likely than adults to be affected by psychosocial factors, such as the emotions of the moment and the desire to be accepted by peers. To continue with the drug use example, adolescents may be able to state the same pros and cons about drug use as adults would. However, when offered a drug by a friend, an adolescent might be more likely than an adult to be affected by the excitement of being out with friends and the desire to fit in with them; consequently, the adolescent may make the decision to try the drug when the adult would not. Steinberg and Cauffman's (1996) initial research using this model supports the theory, by showing that various aspects of psychosocial development predict decision-making competence among adolescents.

■ **THINKING CRITICALLY**

By what age, if at all, should adolescents be allowed to decide whether to get a tattoo, whether to use birth control, and whether to live on their own? Justify your answer in terms of the decision-making concepts presented here.

Social Cognition

The reason cognitive development is discussed in an early chapter of this book is that it is one of the areas of development that provides a foundation for a wide range of other aspects of development, from family relations and friendships to school performance and risky behavior. As one pair of scholars put it, cognitive development in adolescence functions as an **organizational core** that affects all areas of thinking, no matter what the topic (Tomlinson-Keasey & Eisert, 1981).

This means that the cognitive development concepts we have discussed in relation to the physical world can be applied to social topics as well. **Social cognition** is the term for the way we think about other people, social relationships, and social institutions (Flavell, 1985; Lapsley, 1989). Because social cognition (like cognitive development generally) is reflected in so many other aspects of adolescent development, we will be discussing aspects of social cognition throughout the book. Here, as an introduction, we examine three aspects of social cognition: perspective taking, implicit personality theories, and adolescent egocentrism.

Perspective Taking

Have you had a conversation lately with a young child? If you have, you may have found that such conversations tend to go most smoothly when the focus of the conversation is on them rather than you. Young children tend to assume that topics that focus on themselves are of great interest not only to themselves but to all others, and it rarely occurs to them to ask themselves how your interests might differ from theirs. As children grow into adolescents, they become better at **perspective taking**, the ability to understand the thoughts and feelings of others (Selman, 1980). Of course, understanding the thoughts and feelings of others remains a challenge even for most adults. But most people improve at this as they grow up, and adolescence is an especially important period in the development of perspective taking.

Robert Selman (1976, 1980; Selman & Byrne, 1974) has done considerable research on the development of perspective taking. On the basis of this research, he has proposed a theory describing how perspective taking develops through a series of stages, from early childhood through adolescence. In these stages, according to Selman, the egocentrism of childhood gradually develops into the mature perspective-taking ability of adolescence.

Selman has used mainly interviews as the method of his research. In the interviews, children and adolescents are provided with hypothetical situations and asked to comment on them. For example: "Dr. Miller has just finished his training to be a doctor. He was setting up an office in a new town and wanted to get a lot of patients. He didn't have much money to start out with. He found an office and was trying to decide if he should spend a lot of money to make it fancy, by putting down a fancy rug, buying fancy furniture, and expensive lighting, or if he should keep it plain, with no rug, plain furniture, and a plain lamp" (Selman, 1980, p. 42).

Responses indicating perspective-taking abilities are then elicited by asking questions about the doctor's thinking about attracting new patients, and asking about the point of view of patients and of society in general on the doctor's behavior ("What do you think society thinks about doctors spending money to make their offices fancy to attract people?").

Selman's research indicates that until adolescence, children's capacity for perspective taking is limited in various ways. Young children have difficulty separating their own perspective from the perspective of others. When they reach ages 6 to 8, children begin to develop perspective-taking skills, but have difficulty comparing perspectives. By preadolescence (ages 8 to 10), most children can understand that others may have a point of view that is different from their own. They also realize that taking another's perspective can assist them in understanding other's intentions and actions.

According to Selman, in early adolescence, about ages 10 to 12, children become capable for the first time of **mutual perspective taking**. That is, early adolescents understand that their perspective-taking interactions with others are *mutual*—just as you understand that another person has a perspective that is different from your own, you also realize that other persons understand that you have a perspective that is different from theirs. Also, unlike preadolescents, early adolescents have begun to be able to imagine how their view and the view of another person might appear to a third person. In the Dr. Miller example, this stage would be reflected in the ability to explain the doctor's perceptions of how his patients might view him and also how others might view both him and his patients.

According to Selman's theory, social cognition develops further in late adolescence. After mutual perspective taking comes **social and conventional system perspective taking**, meaning that adolescents come to realize that their social perspectives and those of others are influenced not just by their interaction with each other but also by their roles in the larger society. In the Dr. Miller example, this stage would be reflected in an understanding about how the role of doctor is perceived by society and how that would influence the perspective of the doctor and his patients.

In general, Selman's research has demonstrated that perspective-taking abilities improve from childhood through adolescence. However, his research also shows that there is only a loose connection between age and perspective-taking abilities. Adolescents may reach the stage of mutual perspective taking as early as age 11 or as late as age 20 (Selman, 1980). In fact, people of any given age vary a great deal in their perspective-taking abilities.

Other studies of perspective taking have found it plays an important role in adolescents' peer relationships. For example, studies have found that adolescents' perspective-taking abilities are related to their popularity among peers (Kurdek & Krile, 1982) and to their success at making new friends (Vernberg et al., 1994). Being able to take the perspective of others helps adolescents to be aware of how the things they say and do might please or displease others.

Implicit Personality Theories

Part of social cognition involves making judgments about what other persons are like and why they behave the way they do. Scholars call these kinds of judgments **implicit personality theories** (Barenboim, 1981). People of all ages form implicit personality theories, but these theories change in a variety of ways from childhood to adolescence.

A classic study on this topic was conducted in England in the early 1970s by Livesley and Bromley (1973). They interviewed 320 children and adolescents aged 7 to 15, asking them various questions about their perceptions of other persons. In the book they wrote describing the results of the study (Livesley & Bromley, 1973), they presented many examples of how young people describe others and used those examples as illustrations of the ways implicit personality theories change with age.

They found that the youngest children, aged 6 to 7, tended to describe others in terms of concrete, external characteristics. They also described others egocentrically, by referring to themselves. Here is an example of one 7-year-old child's description of a neighbor:

> She is very nice because she gives my friends and me toffee. She lives by the main road. She has

fair hair and she wears glasses. She is 47 years old. (Livesley & Bromley, 1973, p. 214)

By middle childhood (ages 8 to 10), children began to describe others in terms of internal traits and abilities rather than solely in terms of their external characteristics. However, their descriptions of others were usually not well-integrated and could be inconsistent. For example, here is a 10-year-old's description of a classmate:

> She is quite a kind girl. . . . Her behavior is quite good most of the time but sometimes she is quite naughty and silly most of the time. (Livesley & Bromley, 1973, p. 218)

In contrast to the younger children, adolescents' descriptions of others were more *abstract*. Even more than children in middle childhood, adolescents tended to describe others in terms of their abstract personality traits rather than in terms of their behavior or their outward appearance. Adolescents' descriptions of others were also more *complex*. Their comments reflected an awareness that the aspects of personality that people exhibit to others may depend on the situation, and people may exhibit different and even contradictory traits in different situations. Finally, adolescents' descriptions of others were more *organized* than the descriptions of younger children. That is, the different parts of their description were more likely to be integrated and to be explicitly connected by the adolescent. Here is an example of a 15-year-old adolescent's description of a classmate:

> Andy is very modest. He is even shyer than I am when near strangers and yet is very talkative with people he knows and likes. . . . He tends to degrade other people's achievements, and yet never praises his own. . . . He easily gets nervous. (Livesley & Bromley, 1973, p. 221)

Livesley and Bromley (1973) included emerging adults in a smaller study they conducted as part of their research. They found that in the late teens and twenties, young people's implicit personality theories continued to grow in complexity. For example, one emerging adult described a friend by stating

> She is curious about people but naive, and this leads her to ask too many questions so that people become irritated with her and withhold information, although she is not sensitive enough to notice it (Livesley & Bromley, 1973, p. 225)

However, the most significant changes in implicit personality theories took place between childhood and adolescence.

Since Livesley and Bromley's classic study, other studies have confirmed their descriptions of the differences in implicit personality theories between children and adolescents (Barenboim, 1981; Hill & Palmquist, 1978; Shantz, 1983). Notice that the characteristics that distinguish adolescents from younger children in their social cognition—more abstract, more complex, more organized—are also characteristics that distinguish adolescents from younger children in the other aspects of cognitive development we have discussed.

Adolescent Egocentrism

"I remember a time in high school when everybody who was anybody wore Guess jeans. I was pretty poor back then and couldn't afford to pay $50 or $75 for a pair of jeans, so I went without. Every time I was walking down the hall with my non-Guess jeans on and heard anyone whispering or giggling behind me, I was convinced they were laughing at me because I wasn't wearing Guess jeans. It's pretty sad—now I own two pairs of Guess jeans and nobody (including myself) cares."

—*Dawn, age 20 (Arnett, unpublished data)*

"During early adolescence I believed/pretended that a movie crew was following me around and taping everything I did. They personally picked me because I was the most popular girl in school and had the most interesting life. Or so I thought!"

—*Denise, age 21 (Arnett, unpublished data)*

"I had never really had an acne problem, but one morning in my junior year of high school I woke up with a zit so horrifying! It was a huge one on my chin. I refused to go to school, because I knew everyone would look at me and say, "That is the biggest, ugliest zit I have ever seen!" So for 30 minutes I cried and pleaded with my mom not to make me go. I explained to her how it would ruin my social life. Finally, she grew tired of me and let me stay home. I was so relieved that no one would be able to see me."

—*Hannah, age 20 (Arnett, unpublished data)*

"When I was in high school a group of us would go to the cliffs at the lake and 'blind jump' at night. Usually everyone had been drinking. To add an element

of danger, about 60 feet or so down the cliff there was a shelf that stuck out about six feet that you had to avoid. There was one guy we knew, 18 years old, who tripped when he was jumping, landed on the shelf, broke his neck and died. We all thought he must have done something stupid and that it couldn't happen to us."

—*Ryan, age 22 (Arnett, unpublished data)*

We have seen that adolescents become less egocentric than younger children as they learn to take the perspective of others, and we have also seen that implicit personality theories become less egocentric in middle childhood and adolescence. However, cognitive development in adolescence also leads to new kinds of egocentrism that are distinctly adolescent.

We have noted that cognitive development in adolescence includes the development of metacognition—the capacity to think about thinking. This development includes the ability to think about not only your own thoughts but also the thoughts of others. When these abilities first develop, adolescents may have difficulty distinguishing their thinking about their own thoughts from their thinking about the thoughts of others, resulting in a distinctive kind of **adolescent egocentrism**. Ideas about adolescent egocentrism were first put forward by Piaget (1967) and were developed further by David Elkind (1967, 1985). According to Elkind, adolescent egocentrism has two aspects: the imaginary audience and the personal fable.

The Imaginary Audience The **imaginary audience** results from adolescents' limited capacity to distinguish between their thinking about themselves and their thinking about the thoughts of others. They have a hard time determining where the boundary is between their thoughts about themselves and their thoughts about other's thoughts. Consequently, they may confuse the two. Because they think about themselves so much and are so acutely aware of how they might appear to others, they conclude that others must also be thinking about them a great deal. Because they exaggerate the extent to which others think about them, they imagine a rapt audience for their appearance and behavior.

This exaggeration makes them much more self-conscious than they were prior to formal operations. Do you remember waking up in seventh or eighth grade with a pimple on your forehead, or discovering a mustard stain on your pants and wondering how long it had been there, or saying something in class that

Adolescents sometimes believe an "imaginary audience" is acutely conscious of their behavior and appearance.

everybody laughed at (even though you didn't intend it to be funny)? Of course, experiences like that are not much fun as an adult, either. But they tend to be worse in adolescence, because the imaginary audience makes it seem like *everybody* knows about your humiliation and will remember it for a long, long time.

The imaginary audience is not something that simply disappears when adolescence ends. Adults are egocentric, too, to some extent. Adults, too, imagine (and sometimes exaggerate) an audience for their behavior. It is just that this tendency is stronger in adolescence, when formal operations are first developing and the capacity for distinguishing between our own perspective and the perspective of others is at a particularly undeveloped stage.

The Personal Fable The **personal fable** is built on the imaginary audience, according to Elkind (1967, 1985). The belief in an imaginary audience that is highly conscious of how you look and act leads to the belief that there must be something special, something unique, about you—otherwise why would others be so

preoccupied with you? Adolescents' belief in the uniqueness of their personal experience and their personal destiny is the personal fable.

The personal fable can be the source of adolescent anguish, when it makes them feel that "no one understands me" because no one can share their unique experience (Elkind, 1978). It can be the source of high hopes, too, as adolescents imagine their unique personal destiny leading to the fulfillment of their dreams to be a rock musician, or a professional athlete, or a Hollywood star, or simply successful in the field of their choice. It can also contribute to risky behavior by adolescents whose sense of uniqueness leads them to believe that adverse consequences from behavior such as unprotected sex and drunk driving "won't happen to me" (Arnett, 1992a). We will discuss the relationship between the personal fable and risky behavior in more detail in Chapter 13.

Like the imaginary audience, the personal fable diminishes with age, but it never disappears entirely for most of us. Even most adults like to think there is something special, if not unique, about their personal experience and their personal destiny. People of all ages exhibit what is known as the **optimistic bias**, which is a tendency to assume that accidents, diseases, and other misfortunes are more likely to happen to other people than to ourselves (Weinstein, 1998). But the personal fable and the optimistic bias tend to be stronger in adolescence than at later ages, because with age our experiences and conversations with others lead us to an awareness that our thoughts and feelings are not as exceptional as we had thought (Elkind, 1978).

THINKING CRITICALLY

Do you think most emerging adults have outgrown adolescent egocentrism? Give examples of the imaginary audience and the personal fable that you have witnessed among your peers or experienced yourself.

Quite a few studies of adolescent egocentrism have taken place in the last decade or so, based on Elkind's ideas. In general, these studies have not supported Elkind's prediction that the imaginary audience and the personal fable should peak in early adolescence, when formal operations first appear, and then decline in the mid- to late teens. Instead, studies find that egocentrism remains more or less stable throughout the teens and early twenties (Goossens, Seiffge-Krenke, & Marcoen, 1992; Quadrel et al., 1993).

Few studies have been conducted thus far comparing adolescents and emerging adults to adults on scales measuring the imaginary audience and the personal fable. However, a number of studies have compared adolescents and emerging adults to adults on the optimistic bias. These studies indicate that the optimistic bias is stronger among adolescents and emerging adults than among adults; adolescents and emerging adults tend to be less likely than adults to believe that they would suffer negative consequences from behavior such as driving while intoxicated or smoking cigarettes (Arnett, 1992a, 2000e). Also, *within* groups of adolescents and emerging adults, people are more likely to engage in risky behavior if they believe that negative consequences from taking risks are more likely to happen to others than to themselves (Arnett, 1992a, 2000e; Weinstein, 1998).

The Psychometric Approach: Intelligence Testing

Thus far, we have looked mostly at group patterns in cognitive functioning, describing the cognitive functioning of adolescents and emerging adults in general. Another way to look at cognitive development is to look at **individual differences**, that is, how various individuals within a group (all 16-year-olds, for example) might differ in their cognitive abilities. This is the goal of intelligence tests. Attempting to understand human cognition by evaluating cognitive abilities using intelligence tests is known as the **psychometric approach**.

Let us begin by looking at the characteristics of the most widely used intelligence tests, then look at some of the research on intelligence tests that pertains most directly to adolescence. Following that we will consider two alternative ways of conceptualizing and measuring intelligence.

The Stanford-Binet and Wechsler Intelligence Tests

The first intelligence test was developed in 1905 by a French psychologist named **Alfred Binet** (pronounced bee-*nay*). Binet's test was brief, just 30 items, and assessed performance in areas such as memory and abstract thinking (Gould, 1981). In the years since its original development it has been revised and expanded several times. Some of the most important revisions were conducted by Louis Terman of Stanford University in the 1920s, and the test is now known as the **Stanford-Binet**. The most recent revision of the test includes four content areas: verbal reasoning, quantitative reasoning, abstract/visual reasoning, and short-term memory. It can be given to people from age 2 through adulthood. The test results in an overall score called the IQ (for **intelligence quotient**).

The other widely used IQ tests are the Wechsler scales, including the **Wechsler Intelligence Scale for Children (WISC-III)** for children aged 6 to 16 and the **Wechsler Adult Intelligence Scale (WAIS-III)** for persons aged 16 and up. The Wechsler tests contain two kinds of subtests, **Verbal subtests** and **Performance subtests**. The results of the Wechsler tests provide a Verbal IQ and a Performance IQ as well as an overall IQ. More detail on the WISC-III and the WAIS-III are provided in the Research Focus box.

As the Research Focus box indicates, the **relative performance** on IQ tests is very stable—people who score

RESEARCH FOCUS
The Wechsler IQ Tests

Among the most widely used IQ tests are the Wechsler scales. Children and early adolescents (ages 6 to 16) are typically tested using the Wechsler Intelligence Scale for Children (WISC-III), and older adolescents and adults (ages 16 and up) with the Wechsler Adult Intelligence Scale (WAIS-III). The "III" in the names indicates that this is the third version of the tests that has been developed. Because the two previous versions of the tests were criticized for being culturally biased against American minority cultures (Miller-Jones, 1989), special efforts were made in the third version of the tests to eliminate any items that might require a particular cultural background (Psychological Corporation, 2000).

The Wechsler scales consist of 11 subtests, 6 of which are Verbal subtests and 5 of which are Performance subtests. The results of the test include an overall IQ score, a Verbal IQ score, a Performance IQ score, and scores for each of the 11 subtests. More detail on each of the subscales of the WAIS-III is provided in Table 3.2, so you can get an idea of what IQ tests really measure.

A great deal of research has gone into the development of the Wechsler scales. One of goals of this research was to establish **age norms**. Age norming means that a typical score for each age is established by testing a large random sample of people from a variety of geographical areas and social class backgrounds. An individual's IQ score is determined by comparing the individual's performance on the test to the "norm," or typical score, for people of his or her age. The **median**—the point at which half of the population scores above and half below—is designated as having the score of 100, and other scores are determined according to how high or low they are in relation to the median.

Two other important considerations in the research to develop the Wechsler tests were reliability and validity. As discussed in Chapter 1, reliability is a measurement of the extent to which responses on a measure are consistent. There are a number of kinds of reliability, but one of the most important is **test-retest reliability**, which examines whether a person's scores on one occasion are similar to their scores on another occasion. The Wechsler IQ tests have high test-retest reliability, and it improves as people get older (Psychological Corporation, 2000). For most people, little change in IQ scores takes place after about age 10 (Gold et al., 1995; Hertzog & Schaie, 1986).

Of course, that does not mean that your mental abilities never advance after age 10! Keep in mind that IQ is a *relative* score. It indicates how you compare with other people *your age*. So, people who score better than their peers at age 10 are also likely to score above average at age 20, 30, 40, and so on; people whose IQs are below average at age 10 are also likely to score below average as they become older, relative to other people of the same age. There are exceptions to this general pattern. Some people change dramatically in IQ during childhood or adolescence, for better or worse (Moffitt et al.,

---

TABLE 3.2: THE WAIS-III: SAMPLE ITEMS

Verbal Subtests

Information: General knowledge questions, for example, "Who wrote 'Huckleberry Finn'?"

Vocabulary: Give definitions, for example, "What does 'formulate' mean?"

Similarities: Describe relationship between two things, for example, "In what ways are an apple and an orange alike?" and "In what ways are a book and a movie alike?"

Arithmetic: Verbal arithmetic problems, for example, "How many hours does it take to drive 140 miles at a rate of 30 miles an hour?"

Comprehension: Practical knowledge, for example, "Why is it important to use zip codes when you mail letters?"

Digit Span: Short-term memory test. Sequences of numbers of increasing length are recited, and person is required to repeat them.

(Continued)

TABLE 3.2: THE WAIS-III: SAMPLE ITEMS   (CONTINUED)

Performance Subtests

For all the Performance tests, scores are based on *speed* as well as accuracy of response.

Picture Arrangement: Cards depicting various activities are provided, and the person is required to place them in an order that tells a coherent story.

Picture Completion: Cards are provided depicting an object or scene with something missing, and the person is required to point out what is missing (for example, a dog is shown with only three legs).

Matrix Reasoning: Patterns are shown with one piece missing. The person chooses from five options the one that will fill in the missing piece accurately.

Block Design: Blocks are provided having two sides all white, two sides all red, and two sides half red and half white. Card is shown with a geometrical pattern, and person must arrange the blocks so that they match the pattern on the card.

Digit Symbol: At top of sheet, numbers are shown with matching symbols. Below, sequences of symbols are given with empty box below each number. The person must place matching number in box below each symbol.

Source: Tavris & Wade (1997).

1993), but the more typical pattern is one of great stability in IQ scores.

The validity of an instrument is the extent to which it measures what it claims to measure. For IQ tests, the validity question would be, do IQ tests really measure intelligence? Some evidence regarding this question is presented in this chapter. However, questions about validity are much harder to answer than questions about reliability, and the validity of IQ tests remains hotly debated among scholars and in the general public.

higher than average in childhood tend to score higher than average as adolescents and adults, and people who score lower than average in childhood tend to score lower than average as adolescents and adults. However, some interesting patterns of change occur in **absolute performance** from midadolescence through young adulthood (Moffitt et al., 1993). Figure 3.2 shows how scores on the WAIS changed from age 16 to age 38 in one longitudinal study (Bayley, 1968). Notice how absolute scores on the Verbal subtests generally improved from ages 16 to 38, whereas absolute scores on the Performance subtests tended to peak in the midtwenties and then decline.

These patterns reflect a distinction that some scholars have made between fluid and crystallized intelligence (Horn, 1982). **Fluid intelligence** refers to mental abilities that involve speed of analyzing, processing, and reacting to information, which is the

THINKING CRITICALLY

What aspects of "intelligence" does the WAIS-III *not* include, in your view?

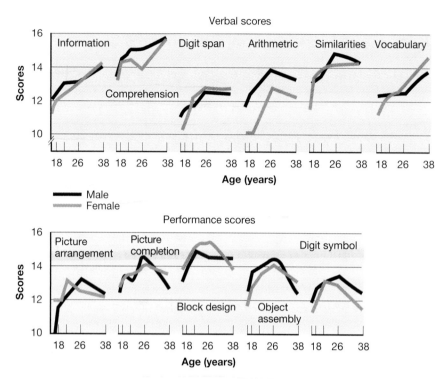

FIGURE 3.2 *Changes in scores on IQ subtests, ages 16 to 38.*
Source: Bayley (1968).

kind of ability tapped by the Performance subtests (Performance tests reward speed of response, whereas Verbal tests do not). IQ tests indicate that this kind of intelligence peaks in emerging adulthood. **Crystallized intelligence**, in contrast, refers to accumulated knowledge and enhanced judgment based on experience. Subtests like Information, Comprehension, and Vocabulary assess this kind of intelligence, and absolute scores on these subtests tend to improve through the twenties and thirties.

Intelligence Tests and Adolescent Development

An enormous amount of research using IQ tests has been conducted since they were first developed. With respect to adolescence, the most notable results concern adoption studies.

Adoption studies take advantage of an extraordinary **natural experiment**. A natural experiment is a situation that exists naturally—in other words, the researcher does not control the situation—but that provides interesting scientific information to the perceptive observer. Adoption is a natural experiment in the sense that, unlike in most families, children in adoptive families are raised by

adults with whom they have no biological relationship. As a result, similarities between adopted children and their adoptive parents are likely to be due to the environment provided by the adoptive parents (Weinberg, 1989). In contrast, similarities between adopted children and their biological parents are likely to be due to genetics, because the environment the children grew up in was not provided by the biological parents.

An interesting pattern occurs in adoption studies that follow children from birth through adolescence (Rowe, 1995). In early and middle childhood, a substantial correlation in IQ exists between adopted children and their adoptive parents. However, by the time adopted children reach adolescence, the correlation between their IQs and the IQs of their adoptive parents has declined, even though the number of years they have all been in the same family has increased. How could this be?

What may explain it is a gradual decline with age in the influence of the immediate family environment on intellectual development, and a gradual increase in active genotype–environment interactions—that is, in the degree to which children choose their own environmental influences (Scarr & McCartney, 1983). In early and middle childhood, parents have a great deal of control over the kind of environment their children experience. Parents control decisions about how much time their children spend on homework, how much television they watch, what they do for fun on the weekends, whom they play with, and so on. However, by adolescence, many of these decisions are made by the adolescents themselves (Rowe, 1995). Parents still have important influences on adolescents, but adolescents have much more autonomy than younger children. Adolescents have a greater say in how much time they spend on homework, in how much of their free time they spend reading or watching television, and in choosing friends who match the level of their own intellectual interests. All these decisions contribute to intellectual development, and as a consequence adolescents resemble their adoptive parents in IQ to a lesser extent than younger adopted children do.

A particularly interesting line of adoption research concerns Black children who have been adopted by White parents. One of the most bitter controversies surrounding intelligence tests concerns racial differences in IQ (Gould, 1981). African Americans and Latinos generally score lower than Whites on the most widely used IQ tests (Anastasi, 1988), from childhood through adulthood. However, scholars disagree vehemently over the source of this group difference. Some assert that the difference is due to inherited ethnic/racial differences in intelligence (e.g., Herrnstein, & Murray, 1995). Others assert that the differences simply reflect the fact that IQ tests concern knowledge obtained in the majority culture, which Whites are more likely than minorities to have grown up in (e.g., Brody, 1992; Gould, 1981; Miller-Jones, 1989). Interracial adoption represents an extraordinary natural experiment, in that it involves raising African American children in the White-dominated majority culture.

And what do these studies find? In general, they indicate that when Black children are raised in adoptive White families, their IQs are as high or *higher* than the average IQ for Whites (Weinberg, Scarr, & Waldman, 1992). Their IQ scores decline somewhat in adolescence, but their IQs nevertheless remain relatively high. This indicates that overall differences in IQ between Whites and African Americans are due to cultural and social class differences rather than to genetics.

Other Conceptions of Intelligence

For many centuries of Western history, intelligence has been viewed as the degree of a person's knowledge and reasoning abilities (Kail & Pellegrino, 1985). This conception of intelligence underlies the construction of intelligence tests, and it is the one that most people hold, scholars and nonscholars alike. In one study (Sternberg et al., 1981), scholars and nonscholars indicated the abilities they believed to be characteristic of an intelligent person. The scholars (psychologists studying intelligence) and nonscholars (from a variety of backgrounds) provided similar responses. Both groups viewed intelligence as comprised of verbal abilities (e.g., "good vocabulary," "high reading comprehension") and problem-solving skills (e.g., "reasons logically," "can apply knowledge to the situation at hand").

However, in recent years alternative theories of intelligence have been proposed. These theories have sought to present a conception of intelligence that is

Black children raised by White parents tend to have higher-than-average IQs.

much broader than the traditional conception. Two of the most important alternative theories of intelligence have been presented by **Robert Sternberg** and **Howard Gardner**. Sternberg's (1986, 1988, 1990, 1997) **triarchic theory of intelligence** includes three distinct but related forms of intelligence. **Componential intelligence** is Sternberg's term for the kind of intelligence that IQ tests measure, which involves acquiring, storing, analyzing, and retrieving information. **Experiential intelligence** involves the ability to combine information in creative ways to produce new insights, ideas, and problem-solving strategies. **Contextual intelligence** is practical intelligence, the ability to apply information to the kinds of problems faced in everyday life, including the capacity to evaluate social situations.

Sternberg has conducted extensive research to develop tests of intelligence that measure the three types of intelligence he proposes. These tests involve solving problems, applying knowledge, and developing creative strategies. Sternberg's research has demonstrated that each person has a different profile of the three intelligences that can be assessed (Sternberg, 1990, 1997). However, so far these tests are not widely used among psychologists (Gardner, 1999), in part because they take longer to administer and score than standard IQ tests do.

Gardner's (1983, 1989, 1999) **theory of multiple intelligences** includes eight types of intelligence. In Gardner's view only two of them, linguistic and logical-mathematical intelligences, are evaluated by intelligence tests. The other intelligences are spatial (the ability to think three-dimensionally); musical; bodily-kinesthetic (the kind that athletes and dancers excel in); naturalist (ability for understanding natural phenomena); interpersonal (ability for understanding and interacting with others); and intrapersonal (self-understanding). As evidence for the existence of these different types of intelligence, Gardner (1983, 1989) argues that each involves different cognitive skills, that each can be destroyed by damage to a particular part of the brain, and that each appears in extremes in geniuses as well as in *idiots savants* (the French term for people who are mentally retarded but who possess an extraordinary ability in one specialized area).

Gardner argues that schools should give more attention to the development of all eight kinds of intelligence, and develop programs that would be tailored to each child's individual profile of intelligences (Gardner, 1999). He has proposed methods for assessing different intelligences, such as assessing musical intelligence by having people attempt to sing a song, play an instrument, or orchestrate a melody (Gardner, 1999). How-

ever, thus far neither Gardner nor others has developed reliable and valid methods for analyzing the intelligences he proposes. Gardner has also been criticized for extending the boundaries of intelligence too widely. When an adolescent displays exceptional musical ability, is this an indication of musical "intelligence" or simply of musical talent? Gardner himself has been critical of the concept of "emotional intelligence" proposed by Daniel Goleman and others (Goleman, 1997), arguing that the capacity to empathize and cooperate with others is better viewed as "emotional sensitivity" rather than intelligence (Gardner, 1999). However, Gardner is vulnerable to a similar criticism for proposing "interpersonal" and "intrapersonal" intelligences.

THINKING CRITICALLY

Do you agree that all the mental abilities described by Gardner are different types of intelligence? If not, which types would you remove? Are there other types you would add?

The underlying theme in both Sternberg's and Gardner's theories of intelligence is the question of how intelligence should be defined. If intelligence is defined simply as the mental abilities required to succeed in school, the traditional approach to conceptualizing and measuring intelligence is generally successful. However, if one wishes to define intelligence more broadly, as the entire range of human mental abilities, the traditional approach may be seen as too narrow, and Sternberg's or Gardner's approach may be preferred.

Culture and Cognitive Development

Although they differ in many ways, the three major perspectives on cognitive development discussed in this chapter—cognitive-developmental, information processing, and psychometric—have in common that they underemphasize the role of culture in cognitive development during adolescence. The goal of both the theories and the research from these perspectives has been to discover principles of cognitive development that apply to all people in all times and all cultures—in other words, to strip away the effect of

According to Howard Gardner, there are eight different kinds of intelligence. These dancers would be demonstrating bodily-kinesthetic intelligence.

culture on cognition in an effort to identify universal human cognitive characteristics (Cole, 1996).

However, in recent years some scholars have called this approach into question. According to the perspective that has come to be known as **cultural psychology**, cognition and culture are inextricably related (Cole, 1996; Shweder et al., 1998; Stigler, Shweder, & Herdt, 1990). Rather than trying to strip away the effect of culture on cognition, cultural psychologists seek to examine the ways that culture and cognition are interrelated, and the profound effects that culture has on cognitive development. Rather than seeking to develop tests of cognitive abilities to examine underlying structures that apply to all aspects of thinking, cultural psychologists seek to analyze how people use cognitive skills in the actual activities of their daily lives (Cole, 1996; Hutchins, 1983; Retschitzki, 1989). Cultural psychology is being applied to an increasing range of topics, but thus far the main focus in cultural psychology has been on culture and cognition (Cole, 1996).

The presence and content of formal schooling is one way that cultures influences cognitive development. As we have seen earlier in this chapter, successful performance on Piagetian tasks assessing formal operations is related to the amount of schooling a person has experienced, especially education in math and science (Cole, 1996). In most traditional cultures in developing countries, few young people are still in school by the time they reach adolescence (Schlegel & Barry, 1991). Consequently, they often do poorly on standard Piagetian tasks of formal operational reasoning (Hollos & Richards, 1993; Rogoff, 1993, 1997). One would also expect schooling to influence information-processing abilities for processing and storing information, by teaching memory strategies and by increasing the amount of knowledge that adolescents have available to assist them in learning new information. However, thus far few studies of information processing have been conducted outside the American majority culture.

Another cultural influence with important implications for adolescents' cognitive development is electronic media. Radio, television, and computers were unknown until the 20th century, and have only recently been introduced in many traditional cultures (Barber, 1995). As we will see in detail in Chapter 12, adolescents are especially avid users of electronic media, from MTV to the Internet.

How does daily exposure to these media influence the way adolescents think? Some scholars have suggested that the intense daily exposure to electronic media that most Western adolescents experience has the effect of diminishing their information-processing abilities for attention and memory, because these media often present vast quantities of information in a barrage of constantly changing stimulation (e.g., Postman, 1985). Music videos and television commercials are especially well-known for presenting rapidly changing images and sounds. Scholars have also suggested that media discourage the development of critical thinking in adolescence, because the emphasis of much media content is on emotion and high-sensation stimulation rather than on presenting information that would promote reflective thought (Keating, 1990). An example would be "action" shows in television and movies that portray frequent car chases and explosions.

However, few studies have been conducted to test scholars' claims of the effects of media on young people's cognitive development. One promising opportunity currently exists in developing countries. As a result of globalization, adolescents in many parts of the world have been exposed to electronic media only recently. Studies of their cognitive abilities before and after the introduction of electronic media may provide interesting insights into the influences of media on adolescent cognition.

Summing Up

In this chapter we have examined a variety of aspects of cognitive changes in adolescence and emerging adulthood. The following summarizes the key points we have discussed:

- Piaget's theory of formal operations explains many of the changes that take place cognitively between preadolescence and adolescence, in areas including

abstract thinking, complex thinking, and metacognition. However, research has shown that not all persons in all cultures reach formal operations, and most people do not use formal operations in all aspects of their lives.

- Cognitive development in emerging adulthood is distinguished by the development of certain aspects of postformal thinking, especially pragmatism and reflective judgment.

- The information-processing approach focuses on separating cognitive processes into different components, including attention, various aspects of processing information, and various aspects of memory. However, the information-processing approach has been criticized for losing a sense of the overall thinking process by breaking it down into components.

- Two aspects of practical cognition are critical thinking and decision making. Adolescents reach the potential for critical thinking, but teaching techniques in secondary schools rarely bring this potential out; colleges have more success with emerging adults. Adolescents appear to be capable of making some decisions using the same processes as adults, although with adolescents psychosocial factors such as the emotions of the moment may be more likely to influence their decisions.

- Social cognition also changes during adolescence, in areas including perspective taking, implicit personality theories, and adolescent egocentrism.

- Absolute scores on intelligence tests improve throughout the teens and twenties for Verbal tests, but scores on Performance tests peak in the midtwenties. Sternberg and Gardner have proposed alternatives to traditional conceptions of intelligence.

- Most research on cognitive development in adolescence and emerging adulthood has ignored culture in seeking universal principles of cognition. However, the new field of cultural psychology emphasizes the cultural context of cognition.

The three major approaches discussed in this chapter—cognitive-developmental, information processing, and psychometric—should be thought of as complementary rather than oppositional. The cognitive-developmental approach provides an overall view of cognitive changes in adolescence and emerging adulthood. From this approach we gain insights into how mental structures change with age and how changes in mental structures result in a wide range of other cognitive changes, from hypothetical-deductive reasoning to the use of sarcasm to reflective judgment. The information-processing approach focuses on the components of cognitive functioning, in areas including attention, processing, and memory. From this approach we learn how these aspects of cognition work at their most basic level; we also learn how capacities for performing these functions change with age from childhood through adolescence and emerging adulthood. The psychometric approach focuses on measuring individuals' cognitive abilities. From this approach we learn about the range of individual differences in various cognitive abilities at any given age and also how the typical level of these cognitive abilities changes with age.

Together, these three approaches provide a broad understanding of cognitive changes in adolescence and emerging adulthood, especially when combined with other areas of study that are derived from these approaches, such as practical cognition and social cognition. However, the glaring omission in our understanding is the cultural approach. Because all three approaches have neglected cultural factors in seeking universal principles of cognitive development, at this point we know relatively little about the role of culture in cognitive development during adolescence and emerging adulthood. This neglect is now being rectified in the new field in cultural psychology, which has already begun to change our understanding of cognitive development in childhood (e.g., Rogoff, 1990) and which is likely to do the same for adolescence and emerging adulthood in the years to come.

Key Terms

cognitive development	concrete operations	metacognition	information-processing
Jean Piaget	formal operations	postformal thinking	approach
stage	isolation of variables	pragmatism	componential approach
mental structure	combinatorial reasoning	dialectical thought	selective attention
cognitive-developmental	proportional reasoning	problem finding	divided attention
approach	pendulum problem	reflective judgment	capacity
maturation	hypothetical-deductive	dualistic thinking	automaticity
sensorimotor stage	reasoning	multiple thinking	short-term memory
preoperational stage	abstract thinking	relativism	long-term memory
mental operations	complex thinking	commitment	mnemonic devices

reductionism
holistic perspective
critical thinking
behavioral decision
    theory
organizational core
social cognition
perspective taking
mutual perspective taking
social and conventional
    system perspective
    taking
implicit personality
    theories

adolescent egocentrism
imaginary audience
personal fable
optimistic bias
individual differences
psychometric approach
Alfred Binet
Stanford-Binet
intelligence quotient
Weschler Intelligence
    Scale for Children
    (WISC-III)

Weschler Adult
    Intelligence Scale
    (WAIS-III)
Verbal subtests
Performance subtests
relative performance
age norms
median
test-retest reliability
absolute performance
fluid intelligence
crystallized intelligence

natural experiment
Robert Sternberg
Howard Gardner
triarchic theory of
    intelligence
componential intelligence
experiential intelligence
contextual intelligence
theory of multiple
    intelligences
cultural psychology

For Further Reading

Case, R. (1985). *Intellectual development: Birth to adulthood.* New York: Academic Press. Case is one of the few scholars on information processing who takes a developmental approach, examining how information-processing abilities change with age.

Gardner, H. (1983). *Frames of mind: The theory of multiple intelligences.* New York: Basic Books. This is the original statement of Gardner's influential theory. At this time he included seven intelligences in his theory. Only recently has an eighth type, naturalist, been added (Gardner, 1999).

Gould, S. J. (1981). *The mismeasure of man.* New York: Norton. In this book, Gould describes the history of intelligence testing and how the tests have often been used to discriminate against women and minority groups in American society. Gould is a superb writer, highly readable and highly insightful.

Keating, D. (1990). Adolescent thinking. In S. S. Feldman & G. R. Elliott (Eds.), *At the threshold: The developing adolescent* (pp. 54–89). Cambridge, MA: Harvard University Press. An excellent, well-written, insightful summary of the research and theory in adolescent cognitive development up to 1990.

Piaget, J. (1972). Intellectual evolution from adolescence to adulthood. *Human Development, 15,* 1–12. I recommend that you read something Piaget has written, instead of simply reading how others describe his ideas. He has an insightful and original style of expressing his ideas. This article would be a good choice, because it focuses on issues related to adolescence and emerging adulthood.

Applying Research

Beyth-Marom, R., Fischoff, B., Jacobs, M., & Furby, L. (1990). *Teaching decision-making skills to adolescents.* Washington, DC: Carnegie Council on Adolescent Development. Describes and evaluates various programs designed to teach decision-making skills to adolescents. Provides recommendations for improving such programs.

King, P.M., & Kitchener, K.S. (1994). *Developing reflective judgment: Understanding and promoting intellectual growth and critical thinking in adolescents and adults.* San Francisco: Jossey-Bass. The authors have done research for many years on reflective judgment, which they view as an aspect of critical thinking. Here they present a summary of the research using their Reflective Judgment Model, describing how reflective judgment develops from adolescence through emerging adulthood and the role education plays in promoting reflective judgment. They emphasize the practical applications of their model, encouraging educators to recognize young people's capacities for critical thinking and providing ideas for promoting young people's skills in making reflective judgments.

Cultural Beliefs

CHAPTER 4

- *Should young people accept their parents' authority without question? Or do parents have an obligation to treat their children as equals or near-equals by the time the children reach adolescence and emerging adulthood?*

- *When making decisions about the future, which should come first, young people's individual desires and ambitions or the well-being of their families?*

- *Should young people spend their leisure time—Friday and Saturday evenings, for example—with their parents at home or with their friends in unsupervised activities?*

- *Is it best for young people to date a variety of persons before marriage in order to become experienced at intimate relationships? Or is it better if young people do not date before marriage and instead allow their parents to investigate potential partners for them when it comes time for them to marry?*

- *Is it acceptable for young people to become sexually active prior to marriage? Is the acceptability of premarital sexual activity any different for girls than for boys?*

Most likely, you have opinions about each of these issues. And your particular view on these issues is probably typical of the people in your culture. However, whatever the view held by your culture on these issues, it is certain that there are other cultures whose beliefs are considerably different. Cultures vary greatly in their views about the proper standards of behavior for adolescents and emerging adults. Each culture is characterized by **cultural beliefs** that provide the basis for opinions about issues such as the ones presented above (Arnett, 1995a).

Throughout this book we emphasize the cultural approach to understanding development in adolescence and emerging adulthood. Adolescence and emerging adulthood are culturally constructed periods of life. As we have seen in Chapters 2 and 3, even biological and cognitive development in adolescence and emerging adulthood are shaped profoundly by cultural influences. Every chapter of this book emphasizes the cultural basis of development and presents a variety of examples of differences and similarities among adolescents and emerging adults in various cultures.

In this chapter we will focus on cultural beliefs. Why is it important to examine cultural beliefs as part of gaining a full understanding of development in adolescence and emerging adulthood? One reason is that cultural beliefs form the foundation for every aspect of socialization that takes place in a culture (Arnett, 1995a). The kinds of rules and responsibilities parents set for adolescents, the materials schools teach and the way schools are run, the kinds of laws cultures have to restrict young people's behavior—all these practices and more are founded on cultural beliefs about what is morally right and what is morally wrong, which behaviors should be rewarded and which punished, and what it means to be a good person.

A second reason for focusing on cultural beliefs is that in many cultures adolescence and emerging adulthood are times when knowledge of these beliefs is communicated with particular intensity. Adolescence brings changes in cognitive development that allow people to grasp abstract ideas and concepts in a way they could not when they were younger. Cultural beliefs are abstract—they typically include ideas about good and evil, right and wrong, justice and virtue, and so on. The fact that cultures often choose adolescence as a time for teaching these beliefs seems to reflect a widespread intuitive awareness that this is when children are ripe for learning and embracing cultural beliefs.

What Are Cultural Beliefs?

Before proceeding further we need to specify what we mean when we refer to cultural beliefs. Cultural beliefs are *the commonly held norms and moral standards of a culture, the standards of right and wrong that set expectations for behavior.* These beliefs are usually rooted in the culture's **symbolic inheritance**, which is a set of "ideas and understandings, both implicit and explicit, about persons, society, nature and divinity" (Shweder et al., 1998, p. 868). So, cultural beliefs include both the beliefs that constitute a culture's symbolic inheritance and the norms and moral standards that arise from these beliefs.

Cultural belief systems include the **roles** that are appropriate for particular persons. All cultures have gender roles, that is, beliefs about certain kinds of work, dress, and other aspects of behavior that are appropriate for women, and the different standards that are believed to be appropriate for men. Cultures may also have age-related roles—a man may be expected to be a warrior in his youth, for example, but to give up that role by middle adulthood and become part of a council of elders. Cultures may also have roles related to social status or social class—for example, members of the British upper class have historically considered it contemptible to work for a living, whereas the lower and middle classes have found it contemptible *not* to work. Young people become more aware of their culture's beliefs about such roles in the course of adolescence. This is partly because of increasing cognitive capacities for abstract thinking and self-reflection and partly because reaching adolescence means that the threshold of adulthood is approaching and young people will soon be expected to adapt themselves to the role requirements for adults in their culture.

A culture's symbolic inheritance is the basis for its norms and standards (Shweder et al., 1998). The symbolic inheritance usually includes beliefs about the ultimate meaning of things, about the place of an individual's life in the vast scheme of things. Sometimes these beliefs are religious and include ideas about where the soul of the individual came from and where it goes after death. (The idea of the soul—an intangible, individual human identity that is distinct from our bodily natures—is nearly universal in cultures' religious beliefs.) Sometimes these beliefs are political, with ideas about how the individual is part of a great historical movement heading toward an inevitable conclusion. The Communist beliefs that were so influential in the 20th century are an example of this. Sometimes

CULTURAL FOCUS
The Bar and Bat Mitzvah

In Jewish tradition, an important event at age 13 signifies the adolescents' new responsibilities with respect to Jewish beliefs. The event is a ceremony called the **Bar Mitzvah**, and it has existed in some form for over 2,000 years. Of course, the details have changed over the centuries, and today the ceremony differs in some respects from one synagogue to another. Until recently, for example, only boys participated in the Bar Mitzvah. However, in recent decades, in many Jewish congregations girls have participated as well (although it is still more common for boys). For them, the ceremony is called the **Bat Mitzvah.**

Although they vary among synagogues, Bar and Bat Mitzvahs share some common elements:

• Prayers are recited stating belief in the one and only God and promising allegiance to God's com-

The Bar Mitzvah.

mandments. Further prayers praise God and reaffirm the sacredness of the Sabbath.

• The Torah is passed from one generation to the next, literally and figuratively. (The Torah consists of the first five books of the Hebrew Bible. These are also the first five books of what Christians call the Old Testament.) The initiate and his/her parents and grandparents come to the front of the synagogue. The Torah is taken from the ark (where it is normally kept) and passed from the grandparents to the parents to the initiate.

• The initiate carries the Torah around the room so that people may touch it with their hands or with a prayer book or prayer shawl, which they then kiss. The congregation remains standing as it is taken around the room.

• The Torah is returned to the front and unwrapped. Often younger children perform the unwrapping.

• The initiate recites a portion of the Torah, then reads from the Haftorah, which consists of the teachings of Jewish prophets.

• The initiate receives the blessings of his/her parents and rabbi.

• The initiate gives a brief talk on some aspect of Jewish teachings. Often, the talk focuses on some of the implications that might be drawn from the portions of the Torah and the Haftorah the initiate has just recited.

• The young person's initiation is celebrated with a festive meal.

In Jewish tradition, completing the Bar/Bat Mitzvah means that the young person can now participate fully in the religious activities of the community. After their Bar/Bat Mitzvah young people can be counted toward the minimum of 10 required for holding religious services. Also, they are now obliged to carry out the same religious rituals as adults, and their word is now valid in sessions determining violations of Jewish law.

Furthermore, they are now "subject to the commandments." That is, they are now responsible for their own actions, as children are not. (Recall from Chapter 1 the importance of responsibility for one's actions in contemporary views of the transition to adulthood.) In fact, the Bar Mitzvah sometimes includes a part where the parents declare, "Blessed is He who has freed me from responsibility for this child's conduct." Perhaps this reflects an intuitive awareness in Jewish tradition of the cognitive advances of adolescence, which make young people capable of a new level of self-reflection and decision making.

Notice how the ceremony works to inculcate cultural beliefs. The beliefs are passed, quite literally, from one generation to the next during the ceremony, as the parents and grandparents pass the Torah to the initiate. The initiate's new responsibility for carrying on those beliefs is signified by the fact that he/she takes the Torah around the room to be blessed. The initiate also reads from the holy books, and this act—declaring aloud before the community a portion of their shared beliefs—is crucial to attaining full status as a member of the community.

these beliefs are familial and communal, with the significance of an individual life being derived from its place in a larger organization that existed before the individual was born and will continue to exist after the individual has passed on. Adolescence is a time of particular importance for cultures to communicate these beliefs about the ultimate meaning of things and to encourage their young people embrace them wholeheartedly.

In this chapter, we will first discuss the role that cultural beliefs play in the socialization of adolescents. Following this we will consider specific aspects of cultural beliefs, including religious beliefs, moral beliefs, and political beliefs.

Cultural Beliefs and Socialization

One important aspect of cultural beliefs is the set of beliefs that specifically concerns standards of right and wrong for raising children, adolescents, and emerging adults. Should young people be taught that individuals should be independent and self-sufficient, following their own individual desires rather than complying with the norms of the group; or should they be taught that the group comes first, that the needs and requirements of the family and community should have higher priority than the needs and desires of the individual? Should individuals be allowed and encouraged to express themselves, even when what they say or do may offend other people; or should individuals strive to conform to the accepted standards of their culture?

All cultures have answers to these questions as part of their cultural beliefs, and the kinds of answers cultures devise vary widely. At the heart of these answers are cultural beliefs about **socialization**, the process by which people acquire the behaviors and beliefs of the culture they live in (Arnett, 1995a; Clausen, 1966). Three outcomes are central to this process (Arnett, 1995a). **Self-regulation** is the capacity for exercising self-control in order to restrain one's impulses and comply with social norms. This includes the development of a conscience, the internal monitor of whether you are complying adequately with social norms; when your conscience determines that you are not, you experience guilt. **Role preparation** is a second outcome of socialization. This includes preparation for occupational roles, gender roles, and roles in institutions such as marriage and parenthood. The third outcome of socialization is the cultivation of **sources of meaning**, which indicate what is important, what is to be valued, what is to be lived for. Human beings are uniquely existential creatures—unlike other animals, we are capable of reflecting on our mortality and on what our lives mean in light of the hard fact that we all die some day (Becker, 1973). Sources of meaning provide consolation, guidance, and hope to people in confronting existential questions.

These outcomes of socialization are shared by all cultures. To survive and thrive and perpetuate themselves from one generation to the next, cultures must teach these things to their members. However, this does not mean that cultures express these goals explicitly, or that cultural members are even consciously aware of these as outcomes of socialization. Much of what cultures teach about what people should believe and value is taught implicitly, through the practices and behaviors young people are taught (Shweder et al., 1998).

The Three Goals of Socialization

A. Self-regulation.

B. Role preparation.

C. Sources of meaning.

Adolescence and emerging adulthood are important periods of development with respect to each of these socialization outcomes. Self-regulation is something that begins to be learned in infancy, but it adds a new dimension in adolescence as regulation of sexual impulses rises in importance with puberty and sexual maturity. Also, as puberty progresses and young people reach their full size and strength, it becomes more important for cultures to ensure that they have learned self-regulation so that they will not disrupt or endanger the lives of others. Role preparation also becomes more urgent in adolescence and emerging adulthood. These years are crucial for young people to prepare themselves for the occupational and social roles they will be expected to take on as adults. Adolescence and emerging adulthood are also key times for the development of sources of meaning, because adolescents are capable of grasping and understanding the abstract ideas about values and beliefs that are part of the meanings for life that cultures teach.

THINKING CRITICALLY

Do you think that the beliefs of all cultures are equally good and true, or do you think that the beliefs of some cultures are better and truer than the beliefs of others? If you believe that some are better/truer than others, on what standard would you base your evaluation, and why?

Cultural Values: Individualism and Collectivism

Although all cultures share similar socialization *outcomes*, cultures differ widely their socialization *beliefs*. A central issue with respect to cultural beliefs about socialization concerns whether cultures value individualism and self-expression most highly in the

> "THE NAIL THAT STANDS OUT GETS POUNDED DOWN."
> —JAPANESE PROVERB

characteristics they wish to promote in their children, or whether they value obedience and conformity most highly. This is sometimes portrayed as a contrast between individualism and **collectivism**, with individualistic cultures giving priority to independence and self-expression and collectivist cultures placing a higher value on obedience and conformity (Triandis, 1995).

A great deal of research has taken place on individualism and collectivism in the past 25 years (Trommsdorff, 1994), especially focusing on cultural contrasts between the majority cultures of the West and Eastern cultures such as the Chinese, Japanese, and Korean cultures (Hofstede, 1980; Triandis, 1995). Scholars have examined differences in values and beliefs among people in a wide range of cultures and have consistently found people in the West to be more individualistic and people in Eastern cultures to be more collectivistic (Triandis, 1995). Scholars have also discussed the development of the self in individualistic and collectivistic cultures (Markus & Kitiyama, 1991; Shweder et al., 1998). Collectivistic cultures promote the development of an **interdependent self**, such that people place a strong value on cooperation, mutual support, maintaining harmonious social relations, and contributing to the group. In contrast, individualistic cultures promote the development of an **independent self**, such that people place a strong value on independence, individual freedoms, and individual achievements.

However, several points should be kept in mind regarding individualism and collectivism. First, most cultures' belief systems are not "pure types" of one or the other, but a combination of the two in various proportions. Although the contrast between the individualistic West and the collectivistic East holds up quite well in research, some scholars have pointed out that most Western cultures, too, have elements of collectivism (e.g., Killen & Wainryb, 1998), and most Eastern cultures have elements of individualism (Mines, 1988; Spiro, 1993). In Eastern cultures, this blend is increasingly complex as they are influenced by the West through globalization (Barber, 1995).

A second point is that individualism and collectivism describe overall tendencies for the beliefs of cultures as a whole, but individual differences exist in every culture (Killen & Wainryb, 1998; Spiro, 1993). A culture that is individualistic overall is likely to have some individuals who are more collectivistic than individualistic; and a culture that is collectivistic overall is likely to have some individuals who are more individualistic than collectivistic.

A third and related point is that diversity also exists within individuals. Most people are probably not purely individualistic or purely collectivistic in their be-

Collectivism is especially strong in Asian cultures. Here, a Korean family takes a walk together.

liefs and behavior, but have some combination of the two tendencies, which they may use in different settings (Killen & Wainryb, 1998; Smetana, 1993). For example, a person may be relatively individualistic at work or in school, striving for individual achievement and recognition, but relatively collectivistic at home, seeking to cooperate and maintain harmony with family members. Individualism and collectivism are not necessarily mutually exclusive, but may coexist within individuals (Killen & Wainryb, 1998).

Keep these qualifiers in mind as we discuss individualism and collectivism in this chapter and throughout the book. As long as you remember these limitations, the concepts of individualism and collectivism remain highly useful and valid as a "shorthand" way of describing the general patterns and contrasts in beliefs among various cultures.

Broad and Narrow Socialization

In this book, we will discuss the contrast in socialization patterns between individualistic and collectivistic cultures in terms of broad and narrow socialization (Arnett, 1995a). Cultures characterized by **broad socialization** favor individualism. They encourage individual uniqueness, independence, and self-expression. Cultures characterized by **narrow socialization** favor collectivism. They hold obedience and conformity as the highest values and discourage deviation from cultural expectations. Individualism and collectivism describe the general differences in values and beliefs among cultures; broad and narrow socialization describe the *process* by which cultural members come to adopt the values and beliefs of an individualistic (broad) or collectivistic (narrow) culture.

The terms *broad* and *narrow* refer to the range of individual differences cultures allow or encourage—relatively broad in broad socialization, relatively narrow in narrow socialization. All socialization involves some degree of restrictiveness on individual preferences and inclinations. As Scarr (1993) notes, "cultures set a range of opportunities for development; they define the limits of what is desirable, 'normal' individual variation. . . . Cultures define the *range* and *focus* of personal variation that is acceptable and rewarded" (pp. 1335, 1337; emphasis in the original). Socialization inevitably means the establishment of limits, but cultures differ in the *degree* of restrictiveness they impose, and the degree of cultures' restrictiveness is central to the contrast between broad and narrow socialization.

Because Western cultural beliefs emphasize individualism, Western cultures tend toward broad socialization. The West has a long history of emphasizing individualism in a variety of aspects of life (Bellah et al., 1985), and this includes cultural beliefs about socialization. In contrast, socialization in non-Western cultures tends to be narrower, with a greater emphasis on promoting the well-being of the family and community rather than the individual, and often including hierarchies of authority based on gender, age, and other characteristics (Markus & Kitiyama, 1991; Whiting & Edwards, 1988). The term *non-Western cultures* includes preindustrial cultures as well as cultures in Asia, Africa, the Middle East, and South America.

Most cultures with narrow socialization are less economically developed than the West. Narrow socialization is emphasized in these cultures partly because young people's work is necessary for families' survival; conformity and obedience are demanded to ensure that young people will make their necessary contributions. However, narrow socialization is also characteristic of some highly industrialized Asian cultures, such as Japan, although socialization in these societies may be becoming broader in response to globalization (Feldman, Mont-Reynaud, & Rosenthal, 1992).

The same qualifiers that apply to individualism and collectivism also apply to broad and narrow socialization. All cultures have a considerable amount of variability, based on individuals' personalities and preferences. If we say socialization in a particular culture is broad, that does not mean that everyone in the culture has the same beliefs about the desirability of individualism. It simply means that the culture *as a whole* can be described as tending toward broad socialization, although individuals within the culture may vary in their beliefs. Think of the concepts of broad and narrow socialization as a simple, shorthand way for referring to an essential contrast in socialization, *not* as absolute categories that every culture in the world fits into cleanly.

It is important, too, to state explicitly that individualism–collectivism and broad–narrow socialization are not meant to be terms that imply moral evaluations. With each general type of socialization there are tradeoffs. Under broad socialization, because individualism is encouraged there is likely to be more creativity and more innovation, but also a higher degree of loneliness, social problems, and disorder (Arnett, 1995a; Bellah et al., 1985). Under narrow socialization, there may be a stronger sense of collective identity and greater social order, but at the cost of greater repressiveness and suppression of individual uniqueness (Arnett, 1995a; Ho & Chiu, 1994). Each form of socialization has its merits as well as its negatives.

THINKING CRITICALLY

Do you agree or disagree with the viewpoint that there are pros and cons to both broad and narrow socialization? Explain your view.

Sources of Socialization

Socialization involves many aspects of a culture. You may think of parents most readily when you think of socialization, and parents usually are central to the socialization process. However, socialization involves other sources as well. The sources of socialization include *family* (not just parents but siblings and extended family, too), *peers and friends, school, community, workplace, media, legal system,* and *cultural belief system* (Arnett, 1995a). In general, the influence of the family on socialization diminishes in adolescence (Scarr & McCartney, 1983), while the influences of peers, school, community, media, and the legal system increase. Family influence in Western majority cultures diminishes further in emerging adulthood, when most emerging adults move out of their family household. Nevertheless, the family remains a powerful influence on socialization in adolescence and emerging adulthood (O'Connor et al., 1996), even if its influence is not as powerful as earlier in development.

Individualism and collectivism are promoted in distinctive ways by each source of socialization. In this book, a specific chapter will be devoted to several socialization sources, including family, peers and friends, school, workplace, and media. Information on socialization in the community and the legal system will be presented in a variety of chapters. Table 4.1 provides a summary description of broad and narrow socialization.

TABLE 4.1: BROAD AND NARROW SOCIALIZATION

Source	**Broad Socialization**
Description	
Family	Few restrictions on adolescents' behavior; adolescents spend considerable time away from family in unsupervised leisure; parents encourage independence and self-sufficiency in adolescents.
Peers/Friends	Adolescents are allowed to choose their own friends. Adolescents make friends of different ethnic groups and social classes, based on their similar interests and attractions as individuals.
School	Teachers promote students' individuality and attempt to adapt curriculum to each student's individual needs and preferences; low emphasis is placed on order and obedience to teachers and school authorities; no uniforms or dress code are required.
Community	Community members do not know each other well, and adult community members exercise little or no social control over adolescents; independence and self-expression of the individual is valued more highly than conformity to the expectations and standards of the community.
Workplace	Young people are allowed to choose for themselves among a wide range of possible occupations. Workplaces generally promote creativity and individual achievement.
Media	Media are diverse and media content is mostly unregulated by governmental authorities; media promote gratification of individual desires and impulses.
Legal System	Legal restrictions on behavior are minimal; rights of the individual to a wide range of self-expression are highly valued; punishments for most offenses are light.
Cultural Beliefs	Individualism, independence, self-expression.

Source	**Narrow Socialization**
Description	
Family	Duty and obligation to family are valued highly; adult family members command respect and deference; responsibility to family is considered more important than individual's autonomy or achievements.
Peers/Friends	Adults exercise control over adolescents' friendship choices, in part by disapproving of friendships between adolescents of different ethnic groups and social classes.
School	Emphasis is on learning standard curriculum rather than on independent or critical thinking; firm discipline is used in the classroom; uniforms or conformity to strict dress code may be required.
Community	Community members know each other well and share common cultural beliefs. Adherence to the standards and expectations of the community is highly valued; nonconformity is viewed with suspicion and treated with ostracism.
Workplace	Young people's job choices are constrained by the decisions of adults (e.g., parents, governmental authorities). Workplaces promote conformity and discourage innovative thinking that might challenge the status quo.
Media	Media are tightly controlled by governmental authorities; media content is generally restricted to socially acceptable themes that do not threaten common moral standards.
Legal System	Legal restrictions are placed on a wide range of behavior, including sexuality and political views, and are backed by swift and severe punishment.
Cultural Beliefs	Collectivism, obedience, conformity.

Cultures can vary in their socialization from these different sources—a culture may be relatively broad in family socialization, for example, and relatively narrow in socialization through the school. However, usually a culture's sources are consistent in their socialization, because the cultural belief system is the foundation for the socialization that takes place through the other sources. Parents, teachers, community leaders, and other socialization agents in a culture carry out common socialization practices because of their shared beliefs about what is best for children and adolescents (Arnett, 1995a; Harkness & Super, 1995).

An Example of Socialization for Cultural Beliefs

So far, our discussion of cultural beliefs and the different forms of socialization has been abstract, describing the nature of cultural beliefs and distinguishing two general cultural approaches to socialization. Now let us look at a specific example of socialization for cultural beliefs, as an illustration of the ideas we have introduced.

An ethnography on adolescence among the indigenous people of Australia, known as the Aborigines (a-bor-*ih*-gen-ees), was written by Victoria Burbank (1988) as part of the Harvard Adolescence Project. Until about 50 years ago, the Aborigines were nomadic hunters and gatherers. They had no settled residence, but moved their small communities from one place to another according to the seasons and the availability of food such as fish and sea turtles. They had few possessions; shelters and tools were manufactured easily from materials widely available.

A key part of adolescent socialization among the Aborigines involves the ritual teaching of a set of cultural beliefs known as the Law. The Law includes an explanation of how the world began and instructions for how various ritual ceremonies should be performed, such as the male circumcision ritual that is one of the rites of passage that initiates adolescent boys into manhood. The Law also includes moral precepts for how interpersonal relations should be conducted. For example, there are complex rules about who may have sex with whom and who may marry whom, and at what age people should marry; also, it is viewed as best if marriages are arranged by the parents rather than chosen by the young people themselves.

The Law is presented in a series of three public ceremonies. Each of the ceremonies represents a stage in the initiation of adolescent boys into manhood. (Although both boys and girls learn the Law, only boys participate in the rituals of initiation.) In the ceremonies, various aspects of the Law are taught. Songs, dances, and the painted bodies of the performers present stories that illustrate the Law. The whole community attends. Following the ceremonies, the adolescent boys experience an extended period of seclusion in which they are given little to eat and have almost no contact with others. Following their learning of the Law and this period of seclusion, they have a new, higher status in the community.

In the traditional teaching of the Law we can see illustrations of the principles of socialization and cultural beliefs we have discussed. The Law is at the center of the symbolic inheritance of the Aborigines; it contains ideas about relations between the individual, society, and divine forces. The Law stresses self-regulation, especially with regard to sexual desire, by specifying rules for sexual contact. Information about roles is taught as part of the Law; adolescent boys learn the expectations for behavior that they must follow in their role as adult men. The Law also provides a source of meaning, by explaining the origin of the world and by providing adolescents with a clear and secure place in their communities.

In this dance ceremony, young Australian Aborigines act out tenets of the Law.

The cultural beliefs expressed in the Law are collectivistic. Adolescents are taught that they have obligations to others as part of the Law, and that they must allow others to make important decisions that affect them, such as whom they shall marry. Because their beliefs are collectivistic, socialization among the Aborigines is narrow; conformity and obedience to the Law and to elders is emphasized. Adolescent boys do not decide for themselves whether to take part in the ceremonies of the Law; they *must* take part, or be ostracized.

However, like so many of the practices of traditional cultures, the relationship between adolescents and the Law has been dramatically affected by globalization. The ceremonies still exist, and adolescents still take part. But the period of boys' seclusion that follows, which used to last about 2 months, now lasts only a week. Furthermore, there is increasing resistance among adolescents to learning and practicing the beliefs and rules of the Law at all. To many of them, the Law seems irrelevant to the world they live in, which is no longer a world of nomadic hunting and gathering but of schools, a complex economy, and modern media. Adolescents now develop beliefs based not just on the Law but on their other experiences as well, and these experiences have made their beliefs more individualistic. Learning about the rest of the world through school and media has led many of them to question their native cultural practices, such as arranged marriages. As Burbank (1988) observes, "Today . . . the Law must compete with the lessons of school, church, movies, and Western music. Initiation may no longer be viewed by the initiate himself as a means to a desired end—the achievement of adult male status. Rather, it may be seen as a nonsensical ordeal of pain and privation. Under these circumstances, its ability to affect subsequent behavior may be minimized" (pp. 37–38).

In recent years, young Aborigines have also begun to display many of the modern problems of adolescence and emerging adulthood, such as unmarried pregnancy in their teens, substance use, and crime. The power of the Law has diminished as a source of self-regulation, roles, and meaning, and for young Aborigines their new problems signify that nothing yet has arisen to take its place.

Socialization for Cultural Beliefs in the West

Can you think of anything comparable to the Aborigines' teaching of cultural beliefs for adolescents in your own community? If you grew up in the West, it may be difficult. There is no formal, ritual teaching of individualism. In a way, that would be contrary to the whole spirit of individualism, because ritual implies a standard way of doing things and individualism stresses independence from standard ways. You could find evidence of implicit teaching of individualism in adults' practices with regard to adolescence—the kinds of freedoms parents allow adolescents, or the range of choices adolescents are allowed for the courses they take at school. We will discuss these and other practices reflecting individualism in future chapters. But what about *beliefs*? What evidence do we have of cultural beliefs that reflect individualism?

One interesting piece of evidence comes from a famous study conducted by Helen and Robert Lynd in the 1920s (Lynd & Lynd, 1929), describing life in a typical American community they called "Middletown" (actually Muncie, Indiana). The Lynds studied many aspects of life in Middletown, including women's beliefs about the kinds of qualities they considered most important to promote in their children. Fifty years later, another group of researchers (Caplow et al., 1982) returned to Middletown and asked the residents many of the same questions, including the ones about child-rearing beliefs.

As you can see from Table 4.2, the results indicate that the child-rearing beliefs of the American majority culture had changed dramatically (Alwin, 1988). Narrow socialization values such as obedience and loyalty to the church had declined in importance, whereas broad socialization values such as independence and tolerance had become central to their child-rearing beliefs. This change was reflected in behavioral differences in Middletown adolescents, particularly girls. By 1978, adolescent girls had become substantially more independent from their parents, spending more of

TABLE 4.2: CHILD-REARING VALUES OF WOMEN IN MIDDLETOWN, 1928–1978

	1928	1978
Loyalty to church	50	22
Strict obedience	45	17
Good manners	31	23
Independence	25	76
Tolerance	6	47

The table indicates the percentage of women in 1928 and 1978 who listed each of the indicated values as one of the three most important to them, out a list of 15 values.

Source: Alwin (1988).

their time away from home and depending less on their parents for money and for information about sex. Other studies have confirmed this trend in the cultural beliefs of the American majority culture over the 20th century, away from obedience and conformity and toward individualism (Alwin, Xu, & Carson, 1994; Cohn, 1999). Even though the United States has a long tradition of valuing individualism (Bellah et al., 1985), the strength of individualistic beliefs has evidently grown during the past century, and adolescents in the American majority culture today are growing up at a time when individualism is stronger than in the past.

HISTORICAL FOCUS
The Origin of the Boy Scouts and Girl Scouts

One of the points discussed in this chapter is that, for the most part, Western cultures have little in the way of formal teaching of cultural beliefs. Many adolescents in the United States receive some formal instruction in religious beliefs, but in other Western cultures religion is much less a part of the lives of adolescents. Even in the United States, fewer than half of adolescents take part regularly in religious activities (Wallace & Williams, 1997).

The absence of formal moral training was discussed with particular intensity in public forums in the early 20th century in the United States as well as in Europe. Adults worried greatly that, with the decline of religion, young people would grow up without a moral orientation strong enough to guide them through an increasingly complex and dangerous world (Kett, 1977).

In Great Britain, a man named Robert Baden-Powell had an idea for how to address this perceived danger of moral decline among young people. In 1908, he started an organization, called the Boy Scouts, that would be dedicated to teaching moral precepts to adolescent boys aged 11 to 17. Boy Scouts would learn how to do wood crafts, how to swim, how to set up a camp, how to cook outdoors, and various other outdoor survival skills. However, Baden-Powell made it clear that these activities were all intended to have a moral purpose: to socialize boys so that they would become good citizens with a high moral character (Rosenthal, 1986).

This purpose is reflected explicitly in two key parts of the Boy Scout program: the Scout Oath and the Scout Law, which all boys are required to learn (by memory) to become Scouts. The Scout Oath is as follows:

On my honor I will do my best
To do my duty to God and my country
And to obey the Scout Law;
To help other people at all times;
To keep myself physically strong,
Mentally awake, and morally straight.

The Scout Law is as follows:

A Scout is:
Trustworthy
Loyal
Helpful
Friendly
Courteous
Kind
Obedient
Cheerful
Thrifty
Brave
Clean
and Reverent.

Scouting was begun with the explicit purpose of teaching values to young people.

and a total of over 25 million boys in virtually every country in the world (www.bsa.scouting.org). The country with the largest number of Boy Scouts is Indonesia, which has nearly 10 million. Membership in the Girl Scouts is about half the size of the Boy Scouts. Boy Scouts and Girls Scouts are the largest voluntary organizations of adolescent boys and girls in the world.

Of course, Scouting has changed considerably from its early days when, as one scholar described it, the organization stressed "glorification of discipline" and had an "obsession . . . with inculcating obedience" (Rosenthal, 1986, pp. 8, 112). The Scouting movement has adapted to the broadening of socialization in the 20th century in Western cultures by becoming less strict and focusing more on each Scout's individual development (Rosenthal, 1986). Goals of the Girl Scout program now include helping each girl "Develop to her full potential" as well as more collectivistic values. Nevertheless, the focus of Scouting remains on relatively narrow socialization in contemporary societies.

Notice that these are mostly collectivistic rather than individualistic values. Nothing here about self-esteem or individual achievement. Instead, values such as being trustworthy, loyal, helpful, courteous, kind, and obedient are all values that are oriented toward consideration for and service to others. In a sense, the creation of the Boy Scouts can be seen as an attempt to create an organization that would maintain some elements of collectivism in Western cultures that were becoming increasingly individualistic.

Baden-Powell's idea was instantly and phenomenally successful. Within a few years after the origin of the Boy Scouts in 1908, the organization had spread all over the world and involved millions of early adolescent boys. In 1912, the Girl Scouts was created on similar principles, and quickly spread around the world to include millions of early adolescent girls. Parallel organizations were created for preadolescent boys (Cub Scouts) and preadolescent girls (Brownies/Junior Girl Scouts) as well as for older adolescents (Venturing for boys and girls, Senior Girl Scouts for girls only).

The Scouting movement continues to thrive today. Membership in the Boy Scouts has remained more or less steady for the past two decades at about one million adolescents in the United States

Note that Scouts was created for young people reaching adolescence, the same period that cultures such as the Australian Aborigines choose for their own socialization rituals communicating cultural beliefs. This may be because people in many cultures have intuitively realized that this is the period of life when the time is ripe for such socialization, because the young person's cognitive capacities have matured to a point capable of grasping abstract ideas such as duty and obligation. The initiation practices of many cultures seem to reflect a view that when young people reach adolescence, it is imperative to ensure that they have understood and embraced the beliefs of their culture before they take on the responsibilities of adult life.

Cultural Beliefs and the Custom Complex

The examples of the Aborigines and Middletown portray the cultural beliefs that adults hold explicitly and teach intentionally to their young people. However, cultural beliefs are also contained in people's everyday practices, even when they are not conscious of it. Every aspect of development is influenced by the cultural context in which it takes place, and every pattern of behavior reflects something about cultural beliefs.

This means that every aspect of development and behavior in adolescence and emerging adulthood can be analyzed as a **custom complex** (Shweder et al., 1998). This term was coined a half century ago by Whiting and Child (1953), who stated that a custom complex "consists of a customary practice and of the beliefs, values, sanctions, rules, motives and satisfactions associated with it" (1953, p. 27). More recently, scholars have placed the custom complex as the central focus of the growing field of cultural psychology (Shweder et al., 1998), which examines human development from a perspective that combines psychology and anthropology.

To put it simply, a custom complex consists of normative practice in a culture and the cultural beliefs that provide the basis for that practice. I will use this term at various points in the book, but for illustration here let us briefly consider dating as an example of a custom complex.

Dating is something you may be used to thinking about as something that is **ontogenetic**—when adolescents reach the ages of 13, 14, or 15, it is "natural" for them to begin dating. However, analyzing dating as a custom complex shows that it is not simply a natural part of development, but a custom complex that reflects certain cultural beliefs. We can begin by noting that dating is by no means a universal practice. It is more common in the United States than in Europe (Alsaker & Flammer, 1999b), and it is discouraged in most non-Western cultures—although the practice is growing in non-Western cultures in response to globalization (Schlegel, 2000). Furthermore, even in the United States it is a recent practice. Prior to the 20th century, young people in the United States typically engaged not in dating but in courtship, which was structured and monitored by adults (Bailey, 1989).

A custom complex involves both a set of practices and the cultural beliefs that underlie those practices. What cultural beliefs underlie the Western practice of dating? First, dating reflects a cultural belief that adolescents and emerging adults should be allowed to have a substantial degree of independent leisure time. This is in contrast to cultures which believe that young people should spend their leisure time with their families. Second, dating reflects a cultural belief that young people should have a right to decide for themselves the persons with whom they wish to have intimate relationships. This is in contrast to cultures whose beliefs specify that young people should allow their parents to make those decisions for them. Third, dating reflects a cultural belief that some degree of sexual experience before marriage is acceptable and healthy for young people. This is in contrast to

Dating is not universal, but is part of the custom complex that reflects certain cultural beliefs.

cultures that believe young people's sexual experiences should begin only after they are married.

All aspects of development in adolescence and emerging adulthood can be analyzed in this way. Family relationships, peer relations, school experiences, and more—all of them consist of a variety of custom complexes that reflect the beliefs of the cultures in which young people live. Thus, in the chapters to come we will use the idea of the custom complex as a way of revealing and exploring the cultural beliefs that underlie socialization.

Cultural Beliefs in Multicultural Societies

In describing cultural beliefs, *cultures* should not be confused with *countries*. Many countries contain a variety of cultures with a variety of different cultural beliefs. For this reason, we speak in this book not of an "American" cultural belief system, but of the cultural beliefs of the American *majority culture*, as well as the cultural beliefs of minority cultures within American society.

A variety of studies have shown that the cultural beliefs of American minority cultures tend to be less individualistic and more collectivistic than the cultural beliefs of the American majority culture. Among Latinos, obedience to parents and obligations to family are strongly emphasized. Adolescents in Latino families generally accept the authority of the parents and express a strong sense of obligation and attachment to their families (Suarez-Orozco & Suarez-Orozco, 1996). Asian American adolescents are also considerably more collectivistic and less individualistic than adolescents in the American majority culture. Compared with adolescents in the majority culture, they spend considerably more time carrying out family chores, and they express a strong sense of duty and obligation to their families (Fuligni, Tseng, & Lam, 1999). In their conceptions of what it means to

be an adult, Asian American emerging adults are more likely than their counterparts in the majority culture to believe that becoming capable of supporting their parents financially is a key criterion for becoming an adult (Arnett, 1998a); this belief is one aspect of their collectivism. With respect to African Americans, little research has been conducted on the individualism–collectivism dimension. However, there is some evidence that African American young people are more individualistic than young people in other American minority groups, but less individualistic than young people in the majority culture (Phinney, Ong, & Madden, 2000).

Most other Western countries also have substantial minority populations whose cultural beliefs tend to be considerably more collectivistic and less individualistic than the Western majority culture. Canada has a substantial Inuit (or "Native Canadian") population; Australia has a Chinese Australian population; and New Zealand has a substantial number of Maoris. There is a Turkish minority culture in Germany, an Algerian minority culture in France, a Pakistani minority culture in England—many other examples could be given. In every case, the cultural beliefs of the minority culture tend to be more collectivistic and less individualistic than in the Western majority culture.

Because cultural beliefs typically provide the foundation for socialization from all other sources, usually

Latino families tend to be more collectivistic than families in the American majority culture. Here, a Latino extended family in San Antonio, Texas.

a great deal of consistency of socialization exists across sources. In a culture characterized by broad socialization, because the cultural beliefs center on individualism, individualism is likely to be promoted in the family, the school, the media, and other sources of socialization. In a culture characterized by narrow socialization, because obedience and conformity are highly prized, these values are likely to be promoted not only in the family but from other sources of socialization as well.

But what happens when the socialization young people experience is not consistent across sources? What happens when young people are part of a minority culture whose beliefs differ from the majority culture? When this is the case, they may find themselves being exposed to a kind of socialization within the family that is different from the socialization they experience from sources such as school, the media, and the legal system, because sources of socialization outside the family tend to be controlled by the majority culture (Arnett, 1995a).

Because the United States has been a multicultural society from its beginnings, many adolescents throughout American history have experienced this kind of contrasting socialization environment. In recent decades, a new surge of immigration has steeply increased the proportion of people from minority cultures living in the United States, especially Latinos and Asian Americans. Projections indicate that White Americans of European background will cease to be a majority in American society by the second half of the 21st century, for the first time ever (O'Hare, 1992). In other Western countries as well, immigration from non-Western countries has increased in recent decades and is expected to increase further in the decades to come. All over the West, the status and well-being of people in minority cultures is likely to be an important issue of the 21st century.

To explore the ways that the beliefs of young people in minority cultures may be influenced by their own culture as well as the majority culture, in the next section we examine in detail a study on Chinese adolescents in Hong Kong, the United States, and Australia.

When East Meets West: Chinese Adolescents in Australia and the United States

"I've really had a bad experience with having friends that are not Chinese or not Asian, just in terms of them not understanding how I think of my family and how important they are to me and my family obligations. . . . 'Cause my family comes first with me always, and I'll drop everything to help them out. So sometimes I've canceled on my White friends and said, 'I can't come to this because I have to do something with my family.' And they would never understand that. Or if I wanted to go somewhere and my parents said no, and I would not go, they would say, 'Well, just go. Why do you have to listen to them?' You know, 'What do you mean, they said no?' And I'm trying to explain this to them and they don't understand. But if I said that to one of my friends who was Chinese, she'd be like, 'Oh, okay. You can't go.'"

—*Elisa, age 22 (Arnett, unpublished data)*

One of the contrasts in cultural beliefs discussed most by scholars is the contrast between East and West. Eastern cultures such as Chinese and Japanese cultures have long been viewed as placing a high emphasis on collectivistic values such as obedience to authority, respect for elders, and conformity to group expectations (Hsu, 1983; Trommsdorff, 1994). Eastern cultures tend to value service to the group more highly than individual achievement. Individual achievements are valued only to the extent that they bring honor to the group of which the individual is a part (Lau, 1988). In contrast, as we have discussed, the cultural beliefs of the West tend to center on the broad socialization values of individualism and self-expression (Bellah et al., 1985; Hofstede, 1980; Trommsdorff, 1994). Although young people in Eastern cultures are becoming more individualistic in response to globalization (Lau, 1988; Lin & Fu, 1990), differences continue to be found consistently between young people in Eastern and Western cultures.

The contrast between Eastern and Western cultural beliefs makes for an especially interesting and complex socialization environment when adolescents are exposed to both beliefs. Shirley Feldman and her colleagues studied this situation among Chinese adolescents whose families had immigrated to Australia or the United States (Feldman et al., 1992). The sample included adolescents from both **first-generation families** (the adolescents and their parents were born in China before immigrating) and **second-generation families** (the adolescents were born in the West but their parents and grandparents were born in China). For comparison, Feldman and her colleagues also included White adolescents in Australia and the United States and Chinese adolescents in Hong Kong. The adolescents were aged 15 to 18, in 10th and 11th grades. They completed questionnaires on various aspects of their values and beliefs, including a questionnaire on individualism–collectivism.

The results indicated that even for first-generation Chinese adolescents in the United States and Australia, their values and beliefs were more similar to White Western adolescents than to Chinese adolescents in Hong Kong. In a number of respects, Chinese adolescents in the West were more individualistic and less collectivistic than Chinese adolescents in Hong Kong. First-generation Chinese adolescents living in the West differed from Hong Kong Chinese adolescents in that they placed less value on tradition (e.g., taking part in traditional rituals) and more value on outward success (e.g., attaining wealth and social recognition). There were few differences between first-generation and second-generation Chinese adolescents, and few differences between either of these groups and the White Western adolescents.

The one collectivistic value that endured for Chinese adolescents living in Western countries concerned the variable Feldman and her colleagues (1992) called "family as residential unit," which included the belief that aging parents should live with their adult children and the belief that unmarried children should live with their parents until they marry. Chinese adolescents were more likely than White adolescents to hold these beliefs, not only Chinese adolescents in Hong Kong but also first- and second-generation Chinese adolescents in Australia and the United States. However, there was a steady decline in the strength of this value with acculturation into the majority culture in both the United States and Australia. Hong Kong Chinese adolescents were more likely to hold these beliefs than first- or second-generation Chinese adolescents. Furthermore, first-generation Chinese adolescents were more likely to hold these beliefs than second-generation Chinese adolescents. Nevertheless, even second-generation Chinese adolescents were more likely to hold these beliefs than White Western adolescents. Figure 4.1 illustrates the pattern.

THINKING CRITICALLY

Describe how the Asian practice of parents living with their adult children constitutes a custom complex.

Overall, the results of this study show that many first- and second-generation Chinese adolescents em-

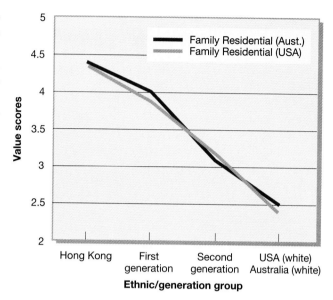

FIGURE 4.1 *Cultural differences in valuing family as a residential unit.*

Source: Feldman, Mont-Reynaud, & Rosenthal (1992).

brace the individualistic beliefs of the Western culture they live in rather than the culture they and their families have come from. Other studies also demonstrate this, and show that the differences in beliefs between immigrant parents and their adolescent children can be a source of parent–adolescent conflict (Cashmore & Goodnow, 1987; Rosenthal, 1984, 1987), as adolescents resist their parents' beliefs and parents feel frustrated and threatened as their adolescents embrace beliefs that are different than their own. More generally, these studies provide good examples of the importance of conceptualizing socialization as a cultural process that has a variety of sources—not only the family, but also peers, school, community, and media, with all of these sources ultimately rooted in cultural beliefs. Even though Chinese adolescents continue to live with their families in their new country, their beliefs and values change because they are also exposed daily to contrary socialization influences outside the family.

Religious Beliefs

"*My parents were atheists. They didn't believe in God. I started going to church when I was a sophomore in high school because I dated a boy that I had a really big crush on, and when he broke up with me I was devastated and I was like, 'I'll just go to his church, and that way, we'll have something in common.' So I started going, and I thought, 'My gosh, I like this.' And so by a year later, I was saved."*

—Stacy, age 23 (from Arnett & Jensen, 1999)

"*I was brought up as a Christian. I was baptized when I was seven years old, went to church every Wednesday, every Sunday, and Sunday night. I had to go for years and years in a row. . . . I'm surprised I'm not a complete saint right now, as much church as I went to and I was subjected to. . . . [But now] I'm not religious at all. Zero. I question the credibility of religion now. I can't say for sure if I believe there is a supreme being out there or not. I just don't know."*

—Tom, age 24 (from Arnett & Jensen, 2000)

In most cultures throughout human history, cultural beliefs have mainly taken the form of religious beliefs. Although the content of cultures' religious beliefs is extremely diverse, virtually all cultures have religious beliefs of some kind. These beliefs typically include explanations for how the world began and what happens to us when we die.

Religious belief systems also typically contain prescriptions for socialization, related to the three main outcomes: self-regulation, role preparation, and sources of meaning. Religions typically specify a code for behavior, and these codes usually contain various rules for self-regulation. For example, the Ten Commandments that are part of the Jewish and Christian religions state explicit rules for self-regulation—thou shalt not kill, steal, covet thy neighbor's wife, and so on. For role preparation, gender roles especially are emphasized in religious belief systems. Most religious belief systems contain ideas about distinct roles for males and females. Finally, with respect to sources of meaning, most religious belief systems contain ideas about the significance of each individual's life in relation to an eternal supernatural world—for example, gods, supernatural forces, or the souls of one's ancestors.

In general, adolescents and emerging adults in industrialized societies are less religious than their counterparts in traditional cultures. Industrialized societies such as Japan and Western countries tend to be highly **secular**, which means based on nonreligious beliefs and values. In every industrialized country, religion has gradually faded in its influence over the past two centuries (Bellah et al., 1985). Religious beliefs and practices are especially low among adolescents in Eu-

rope. For example, in Belgium only 30% of adolescents aged 17 to 18 believe in God and only 10% attend religious services weekly (Goossens, 1994).

Americans are more religious than people in virtually any other industrialized country, and this is reflected to some extent in the lives of American adolescents and emerging adults. For a substantial proportion of Americans, including young people, religion plays an important part in their lives (Youniss, McLellan, & Yates, 1999). According to a national survey, 95% of American adolescents aged 13 to 17 believe in God (or a universal spirit), 93% believe that God loves them, 91% believe in heaven, 75% believe in hell, and 86% believe that Jesus Christ is God or the son of God (Gallup & Bezilla, 1992).

THINKING CRITICALLY

Why do you think Americans generally are more religious than people in other industrialized countries?

The proportion of American adolescents who take part in religious practices is lower than the proportion who report religious beliefs, but a substantial proportion do report regular religious practices. Thirty-two percent of American high school seniors report weekly attendance at religious services (Wallace & Williams, 1997) and 50% report attending services within the past 7 days (Gallup & Lindsay, 1999). Forty-one percent of adolescents aged 13 to 17 say they are currently involved in Sunday school, and 36% report being involved with a church youth group (Wallace & Williams, 1997). Even if their actual participation may not be quite as high as the participation they report (see the Research Focus box), these figures indicate a strikingly strong positive view of religion among American adolescents. In a 1997 national poll, 80% of adolescents aged 16 to 18 indicated that they believe it is important for children to attend religious services (Wildavsky, 1997).

However, religiosity declines from adolescence through emerging adulthood. Both religious participation and religious beliefs decline throughout the teens (Wallace & Williams, 1997) and are lower in the late teens and early twenties than at any other period of the life span (Roof, 1993; Hoge, Johnson, & Luidens, 1993). This may be a reflection of the importance of individualistic criteria to young people making the transition to adulthood, as we saw in Chapter 1. Adolescents and

RESEARCH FOCUS
Religious Practices and Social Desirability

According to the surveys presented in this chapter, a substantial proportion of American adolescents are actively involved in religious practices. One half report attending religious services in the past 7 days, 41% report being involved currently in Sunday school, and 36% report weekly Bible reading (Gallup & Lindsay, 1999; Wallace & Williams, 1997).

These are strikingly high numbers, if valid. But are they valid? Recently, a controversy has developed among scholars on religion over the accuracy of people's self-reported religious behavior. Polls conducted by the Gallup organization over the past half century have indicated that the proportion of American adults reporting weekly attendance at religious services has remained remarkably stable during that time, at about 40% (Gallup & Castelli, 1989; Gallup & Lindsay, 1999). However, other scholars have questioned the accuracy of those self-reports. In a 1993 study, a team of sociologists measured religious participation by counting people at services and concluded that the actual rate of attendance was 20% rather than 40% (Hardaway, Marler, & Chaves, 1993).

In 1998, a study was published that investigated people's religious behavior through examining their time-use diaries (Presser & Stinson, 1998). The diaries were not kept for the purposes of recording religious practices, but the daily record of activities over several months revealed, among other things, the extent of people's attendance at religious services. Thousands of diaries were available from 1965 to 1994. Analysis of the diaries showed that the rate of weekly attendance had dropped from 42% in 1965 to 26% in 1994. Although similar analyses have yet to be conducted for adolescents, the results of these studies suggest that current self-reports of religious participation among adolescents may also be inflated.

Why would people report their behavior inaccurately? Because they respond to their perceptions of what scholars call **social desirability** (Sudman & Bradburn, 1989). Socially desirable behavior is behavior that you believe would be approved by others. Adolescents and adults may exaggerate the extent to which they attend religious services because they believe that other people would approve of them if they did attend religious services. As sociologist Mark Chaves observes, "Most people believe going to church is a good thing to do and, when surveyed, often say they did go to church even when they didn't" (Woodward, 1993).

Social desirability is an issue for research not just on religious practices but for many of the other types of behavior we will examine in the course of this book. Drug use is generally stigmatized; for this reason, young people may not always report the full extent of their drug use. Having numerous sexual partners tends to be more socially desirable for boys than for girls; perhaps for this reason, boys often report more sexual partners than girls in surveys of young peoples' sexual behavior. Each time you read about a study, ask yourself: Is there any reason why the young people in this study may have reported their behavior inaccurately to make it appear more socially desirable?

---

emerging adults may feel that they need to make a break with their parents' religious beliefs and practices to establish that they have reached a point where they are making their own decisions about their beliefs and values (Arnett & Jensen, 2000). By emerging adulthood there is little long-term relationship between the beliefs of emerging adults and the beliefs of their parents. One longitudinal study found that parents' frequency of church attendance when their children were in early adolescence was unrelated to their children's religiosity 11 years later, as emerging adults (Willits & Crider, 1989). Another reason for the decline in religiosity in emerging adulthood may be that by the time they reach their late teens young people are no longer pressured by their parents to attend church, and they resume again (if at all) only when they have young children of their own (Arnett & Jensen, 2000; Hoge et al., 1993).

Religious faith and religious practices tend to be especially strong among African Americans.

Family factors are important, too. Adolescents are less likely to be religious when their parents disagree with each other about religious beliefs (Clark & Worthington, 1987) and when their parents are divorced (Gallup & Castelli, 1989). Ethnicity is another factor. In American society religious faith and religious practices tend to be stronger among African Americans than among Whites (Wallace & Williams, 1997).

The relatively high rates of religiosity among African American adolescents helps explain why they have such strikingly low rates of alcohol and drug use (Wallace & Williams, 1997). However, it is not only among minority groups that religiosity is associated with favorable adolescent outcomes. In the American majority culture, adolescents who are more religious report less depression and less likelihood of premarital sex, drug use, and delinquent behavior (Benson, Donahue, & Erickson, 1989; Donahue, 1994; Wright, Frost, & Wisecarver, 1993). Also, adolescents who value religion are more likely than other adolescents to perform volunteer service to their community (Youniss et al., 1999).

Religious Beliefs and Cognitive Development

Cognitive development between childhood and adolescence leads to changes in how young people think about religion. Specifically, adolescents' ideas about religious faith tend to be more abstract and less con-

crete, compared with younger children. In one study, Elkind (1978) interviewed several hundred Jewish, Catholic, and Protestant children from ages 5 to 14. They were asked various questions about religion, such as "What is a Catholic?," "Are all boys and girls in the world Christians?," and various questions about the religious beliefs of themselves and their families. By the time they reached their early teens and the beginning of formal operations, children's responses were more abstract and complex than at younger ages. Younger children tended to emphasize external behavior in explaining what it means to be a member of a particular faith—persons are Catholic if they go to mass regularly, for example. In contrast, the adolescents emphasized internal and abstract criteria, such as what people believe and their relationship with God.

Another scholar, James Fowler, has proposed a theory of stages of religious development from birth through adulthood that is linked to cognitive development (Fowler, 1981; 1991). According to Fowler, early adolescence is a stage of **poetic-conventional faith**, in which people become more aware of the symbolism used in their faith. In this stage, according to Fowler, religious understanding becomes more complex in the sense that early adolescents increasingly believe that there is more than one way of knowing the truth. Late adolescence and emerging adulthood are a stage of **individuating-reflective faith**, in which people rely less on what their parents believed and develop a more individualized faith based on questioning their beliefs and incorporating their personal experience into their beliefs. Of course, movement into this stage could also reflect an integration of religious faith with the individualistic values of the American majority culture. Fowler's theory is based on studies of people in the American majority culture, and it is difficult to say whether people in less individualistic cultures would also go through the "individuating" process Fowler describes.

One contrast to the individuating process of religious development in the American majority culture can be found in cultures where Islam is the dominant religion. In Islam, the most important change that occurs at adolescence involves the holy month that Muslims call **Ramadan** (Davis & Davis, 1989). Ramadan commemorates the revelation of the Muslim holy book, the **Koran**, from God to the prophet Muhammad. During this month each year, Muslims are forbidden from taking part in any indulgences, and they are required to fast (that is, refrain from eating, drinking, and sexual activity) from sunrise to sunset every

When they reach adolescence, Muslims are expected to participate in the month-long fast of Ramadan.

considered shameful for a person who has clearly reached sexual maturity not to fast. Thus, in adolescence, religious practices among Muslims become less open to individual choice, more guided by social pressures. Socialization for their religious behavior becomes narrower—less individual variability is tolerated in whether they observe the fast.

In some urban areas, there have been recent reports that some adolescents are rebelling by refusing to observe the fast; but in the smaller rural communities, the narrow socialization pressures of family and community can be intense, and few adolescents resist (Davis & Davis, 1989). Or, more accurately, because they have been raised in a culture where fasting at Ramadan is valued, by the time young people reach adolescence nearly all of them eagerly take part in the fast. They have made the beliefs of their culture their own beliefs, and they usually do not have to be coerced or pressured into participating.

■ _____ **THINKING CRITICALLY**

How could you apply Fowler's theory of changes in religious beliefs in adolescence to the beliefs and practices of Muslim adolescents with respect to Ramadan?

day. The final day of Ramadan is celebrated with a great feast. There are nearly a billion Muslims in the world's population, and Muslims all over the world observe Ramadan. (Most of the world's Islamic population is not in the Middle East but in Asia—Indonesia has the largest Muslim population of any country in the world, and India and Pakistan are second and third.)

Prior to puberty, young Muslims have no obligation to participate in fasting. Girls are supposed to fast for the first time after they reach menarche. The judgment of whether a boy is old enough to be expected to fast is based on signs such as beard growth and changes in body shape (Davis & Davis, 1989).

Preadolescent children sometimes fast for a day or a few days, especially around the time they are nearing puberty. They are commended for doing so by older children and adults, but they are not obligated to do it. However, once they have reached puberty young people are expected to fast during Ramadan. In fact, it is

Cultural Beliefs and Moral Development

Religious beliefs are usually learned from one's culture, although the development of adolescents' religious thinking is based in part on passage through stages of cognitive development. What about moral development? To what extent are adolescents' moral beliefs dependent on their cultures' beliefs, and to what extent are adolescents' moral beliefs a result of cognitive processes common to adolescents everywhere?

For the most part, scholars who have studied and theorized about adolescents' moral development have viewed it as rooted in universal cognitive processes. This is true of the ideas of the two most influential scholars on adolescent moral development, Jean Piaget and Lawrence Kohlberg. However, their views have recently begun to be challenged by scholars who emphasize the role of cultural beliefs in moral development. We will consider Piaget's and Kohlberg's ideas first, then other points of view, including the cultural approach.

Piaget's Theory

Piaget (1932) developed his ideas about moral development using several different methods. He watched children play games (such as marbles) to see how they practiced and discussed the rules. He played games with them himself and asked them questions during the games (e.g., Can rules be changed? How did the rules begin?) to investigate how they would explain the origin of rules and how they would react to violations of the rules. Also, he presented children with hypothetical situations involving lying, stealing, and punishment to see what kinds of judgments they would make about how to determine whether an action was right or wrong.

On the basis of his research, Piaget concluded that children have two distinct approaches to reasoning about moral issues, based on the level of their cognitive development. **Heteronomous morality** corresponds to the preoperational stage, from about age 4 to about age 7. Moral rules are viewed as having a sacred, fixed quality. They are believed to be handed down from figures of authority (especially parents) and can be altered only by them. **Autonomous morality** is reached at the beginning of adolescence with the onset of formal operations at about age 10 to age 12 and involves a growing realization that moral rules are social conventions that can be changed if people decide they should be changed. (From age 7 to age 10 there is a transitional stage between heteronomous and autonomous moral thinking, with some properties of each.)

The stage of autonomous morality also involves growing complexity in moral thinking in the sense that autonomous moral thinkers take into account people's motivations for behavior rather than focusing only on the consequences. For example, a child who breaks a dish by accident is seen as less guilty than a child who breaks a dish while doing something wrong such as stealing.

Piaget's interest in the rules of children's games reflected his belief that moral development is promoted by interactions with peers. In Piaget's view, peers' equal status requires them to discuss their disagreements, negotiate with one another, and come to a consensus. This process gradually leads to an awareness of the rules of games, and from there to an awareness of moral rules more generally. According to Piaget, parents are much less effective than peers in promoting children's moral development, because parents' greater power and authority make it difficult for children to argue and negotiate with them as equals.

Kohlberg's Theory

Lawrence Kohlberg (1958) was inspired by Piaget's work, and he sought to extend it by examining moral development through adolescence and into adulthood. Like Piaget, he viewed moral development as based on cognitive development, such that moral thinking would change in predictable ways as cognitive abilities developed, regardless of culture. Also like Piaget, he presented people with hypothetical moral situations and had them indicate what behavior they believed was right or wrong in that situation, and why.

Kohlberg began his research by studying the moral judgments of 72 boys aged 10, 13, and 16, from middle-class and working-class families in the Chicago area (Kohlberg, 1958). He presented the boys with a series of fictional dilemmas, each of which was constructed to elicit their moral reasoning. Here is one of the dilemmas:

> During [World War II], a city was often being bombed by the enemy. So each man was given a post he was to go to right after the bombing, to help put out the fires the bombs started and to rescue people in the burning buildings. A man named Diesing was made the chief in charge of one fire engine post. The post was near where he worked so he could get there quickly during the day but it was a long way from his home. One day there was a very heavy bombing and Diesing left the shelter in the place he worked and went toward his fire station. But when he saw how much of the city was burning, he got worried about his family. So he decided he had to go home first to see if his family was safe, even though his home was a long way off and the station was nearby, and there was somebody assigned to protect the area where his family was.
>
> Was it right or wrong for him to leave his station to protect his family? Why? (Kohlberg, 1958, pp. 372–373)

In each interview, the participant would be asked to respond to three stories such as this one. To Kohlberg, what was crucial for understanding the level of people's moral development was not whether they concluded that the actions of the persons in the dilemma were right or wrong, but *how they explained* their conclusions.

Kohlberg (1976) developed a system for classifying their explanations into three *levels* of moral development, with each level containing two *stages*, as follows:

*Level 1: **Preconventional reasoning**.* At this level, moral reasoning is based on perceptions of the likelihood of external rewards and punishments. What is right is what avoids punishment or results in rewards.

- *Stage 1: Punishment and obedience orientation.* Rules should be obeyed to avoid punishment from those in authority.

- *Stage 2: Individualism and purpose orientation.* What is right is what satisfies one's own needs and occasionally the needs of others, and what leads to rewards for oneself.

*Level 2: **Conventional reasoning**.* At this level, moral reasoning is less egocentric, and the person advocates the value of conforming to the moral expectations of others. What is right is whatever agrees with the rules established by tradition and by authorities.

- *Stage 3: Interpersonal concordance orientation.* Care of and loyalty to others is emphasized in this stage, and it is seen as good to conform to what others expect in a certain role, such as being a "good husband" or a "good boy/girl."

- *Stage 4: Social systems orientation.* Moral judgments are explained by reference to concepts such as social order, law, and justice. It is argued that social rules and laws must be respected for social order to be maintained.

*Level 3: **Postconventional reasoning**.* Moral reasoning is based on the individual's own independent judgments rather than on what others view as wrong or right. What is right is derived from the individual's perception of objective, universal principles rather than the subjective perception of either the individual (as in Level 1) or the group (as in Level 2).

- *Stage 5: Community rights and individual rights orientation.* The person reasoning at this stage views society's laws and rules as important, but also sees it as important to question them and change them if they become obstacles to the fulfillment of ideals such as freedom and justice.

- *Stage 6: Universal ethical principles orientation.* The person has developed an independent moral code based on universal principles. When laws or social conventions conflict with these principles, it is seen as better to violate the laws or conventions than the universal principles.

Kohlberg followed his initial group of adolescent boys over the next 20 years (Colby et al., 1983), interviewing them every 3 or 4 years, and he and his colleagues also conducted numerous other studies on moral reasoning in adolescence and adulthood. The results verified Kohlberg's theory of moral development in a number of important ways:

- Stage of moral reasoning tended to *increase with age.* At age 10, most of the participants were in Stage 2 or in transition between Stage 1 and Stage 2; at age 13, the majority were in transition from Stage 2 to Stage 3; by ages 16 to 18, the majority were in Stage 3 or in transition to Stage 4; and by ages 20 to 22, 90% of the participants were in Stage 3, in transition to Stage 4, or in Stage 4. However, even after 20 years, when all of the original participants were in their thirties, few of them had proceeded to Stage 5, and none had reached Stage 6 (Colby et al., 1983). Kohlberg eventually dropped Stage 6 from his coding system (Kohlberg, 1986).

- Moral development proceeded in the predicted way, in the sense that the participants did not skip stages but proceeded from one stage to the next highest.

- Moral development was found to be cumulative, in the sense that the participants were rarely found to slip to a lower stage over time. With few exceptions, they either remained in the same stage or proceeded to the next highest stage.

The research of Kohlberg and his colleagues also indicated that moral development was correlated with SES, intelligence, and educational level. Middle-class boys tended to be in higher stages than working-class boys of the same age, boys with higher IQs tended to be in higher stages than boys with lower IQs (Weinreich, 1974), and boys who received a college education tended reach higher stages than boys who did not (Mason & Gibbs, 1993).

The research of Kohlberg and his colleagues has also included cross-cultural studies in countries all over the world such as Turkey, Japan, Taiwan, Kenya, Israel, and India (Snarey, 1985). Many of these studies have focused on moral development in adolescence and emerging adulthood. In general, the studies confirm Kohlberg's hypothesis that moral development as classified by his coding system progresses with age. Also, as in the American studies, participants in longitudinal studies in other cultures have rarely been found to regress to an earlier stage or to skip a stage of moral reasoning.

However, Stage 5 postconventional thinking has been found to be even more rare in non-Western cultures than in the United States (De Mey et al., 1999; Kohlberg, 1981; Snarey, 1985). Does this mean that people in non-Western cultures tend to reason at lower levels of moral reasoning than people in the West, perhaps because of lower educational levels (Kohlberg, 1986)? Or is the absence of Stage 5 reasoning in non-Western cultures a reflection of a cultural bias built into Kohlberg's classification system, a bias in favor of Western secularism and individualism (Shweder, Mahapatra, & Miller, 1990)? These questions have been the source of some controversy, as we will see in more detail when the cultural approach is described below.

Critiques of Kohlberg

It would be difficult to overstate the magnitude of Kohlberg's influence on the study of moral development in adolescence. Not only was he highly productive himself and in his collaborations with colleagues, but he also inspired many other scholars to investigate moral development according to the stage theory he proposed (e.g., Rest, 1986; Walker, 1984, 1989). However, his theory has also been subject to diverse criticisms. The critiques can be divided into three general types: the structure versus content critique, the gender critique, and the cultural critique.

The Structure Versus Content Critique   As noted, Kohlberg was interested in how people reason about moral issues, not in whether they consider certain types of behavior right or wrong. That is, Kohlberg was interested in exploring the *structure* of people's moral reasoning, rather than the *content* of their moral judgments. He presented people with hypothetical moral dilemmas so that the content would be the same for everyone, and differences between them in their responses would reflect differences in the structure of their moral reasoning.

However, some scholars have questioned this assumption that structure rather than content is the key to moral development. Kohlberg's dilemmas concern issues such as stealing in order to save a life, the mercy killing of a terminally ill person, and a soldier's sacrifice of his life for his fellow soldiers, but how often do people actually confront these kinds of dilemmas in their own lives? Several studies indicate that when adolescents and adults are asked to describe their responses to moral dilemmas they have actually experienced, most often they generate dilemmas concerning friendships, family relationships, sexual relations, and

work-related issues, rather than the kinds of life-and-death dilemmas Kohlberg used (Jensen, 1995; Walker, 1989; Walker, de Vries, & Trevethan, 1987; Yussen, 1977). Scholars who have conducted these studies question the relevance of Kohlberg's system to people's actual moral judgments and behavior.

However, several studies indicate that stage of moral development as assessed by Kohlberg's system is related to real-life moral judgments. The stage of moral reasoning people apply to Kohlberg's hypothetical dilemmas tends to be similar to the moral reasoning they apply to moral dilemmas they describe from their own lives (Walker et al., 1987). Also, stage of moral reasoning on Kohlbergian dilemmas is related to moral behavior. Adolescents and emerging adults who rate relatively high in Kohlberg's coding system are also less likely to engage in antisocial behavior, less likely to engage in cheating, and more likely to assist others who are in need of help (Rest, 1983).

The Gender Critique   Did you notice that Kohlberg's original research sample included only males? Later, when he began to study females as well, he initially found that in adolescence females tended to reason at a lower level (most typically Stage 3) than males of the same age (most typically Stage 4). This finding inspired a former student of his, Carol Gilligan, to develop a critique that claimed his theory was biased toward males, undervaluing the perspective of females, whom she viewed as having a different moral "voice" than males.

According to Gilligan (1982), Kohlberg's theory of moral development is biased in favor of a **justice orientation**. This orientation places a premium on abstract principles of justice, equality, and fairness when judgments are made about moral issues. The primary consideration is whether these principles have been followed—for example, in the sample dilemma described above, a person reasoning with the justice orientation would focus on whether the fire chief was being fair in checking on his family first, and on whether justice would be better served if he went to his post instead. Gilligan argued that males are more likely than females to approach moral issues with a justice orientation, with the result that males tend to be rated as more "advanced" in Kohlberg's system.

However, according to Gilligan, the justice orientation is not the only legitimate basis for moral reasoning. She contrasts the justice orientation with what she terms the **care orientation**, which involves focusing on relationships with others as the basis for moral

Carol Gilligan has proposed that adolescent girls' moral reasoning is based on a care orientation.

reasoning. For example, in the sample dilemma someone reasoning from the care orientation would focus on the relationships between the fire chief and his family and community, viewing the dilemma in terms of the relationships involved and the needs of each person rather than in terms of abstract principles. Gilligan claimed that the care orientation is more likely to be favored by females, and that Kohlberg's system would rate moral reasoning from this perspective as lower than moral reasoning from the justice orientation.

Gilligan particularly focused on early adolescence as a period when girls come to realize that their concerns with intimacy and relationships are not valued by a male-dominated society, with the result that girls often "lose their voice," that is, become increasingly insecure about the legitimacy of their ideas and opinions (Gilligan, Lyons, & Hanmer, 1990). Gilligan criticized Kohlberg's theory of moral development, as well as other prominent theories of human development by Freud, Piaget, and Erikson, as being too male-oriented in presenting the independent, isolated individual as the paragon of mental health, thus undervaluing females' tendencies toward interdependence and relational thinking.

Gilligan's gender critique has inspired a great deal of attention and research since she first articulated it in 1982. What does the research say about her claims? For the most part, studies support Gilligan's contention that males and females tend to emphasize somewhat different moral concerns (Galotti, 1989; Galotti, Kozberg, & Farmer, 1991; Skoe & Gooden, 1993). For example, when adolescents are asked to consider their personal moral dilemmas, girls are more likely than boys to report dilemmas that involve interpersonal relationships (Galotti, 1989; Skoe & Gooden, 1993).

However, evidence generally does not support her claim that Kohlberg's system is biased in favor of males. In the most comprehensive test of this claim, Lawrence Walker (1984, 1989) analyzed the results from 108 studies that had used Kohlberg's system to rate stages of moral development. Walker combined the results from the various studies statistically to see whether any overall differences existed in how males and females were rated. The results indicated that no significant differences existed between males and females as rated by Kohlberg's system.

In Kohlberg's (1986) own response to Gilligan's critique, he disputed her claim that considerations of justice exclude or undervalue the care orientation. On the contrary, he argued, concerns with justice also imply concern for the needs and well-being of others. Nevertheless, he revised his scoring system in the early 1980s, partly in response to her critique, to address the possibility of a male bias (Colby & Kohlberg, 1987; Walker, 1984). Scholars on moral development are increasingly emphasizing that even if gender differences in moral reasoning exist, the differences are not absolute or mutually exclusive, and both males and females use both justice and care principles in their moral reasoning.

THINKING CRITICALLY

From your experience, do you think that there are overall differences between males and females in the basis of their moral reasoning (justice vs. care)? Give an example.

The Cultural Critique   Although Kohlberg did not deny that culture has some influence on moral development, in his view the influence of culture was limited to how well cultures provide opportunities for individuals to reach the highest level of moral development (Jensen, 2000). To Kohlberg, cognitive development is the basis for moral development. Just as cognitive development proceeds on only one path (given adequate environmental conditions), so moral development also has only one natural path of maturation (Kohlberg, 1976, 1986). As development proceeds and individuals' thinking becomes progressively more developed, they rise inevitably along that one and only path. Thus, the highest level of moral reasoning is also the most rational. With an adequate education that allows for the development of formal operations, the individual will realize the inadequacies and irrationality of the lower levels of moral reasoning, and embrace the highest, most rational way of thinking about moral issues.

Recently, these assumptions have been called into question by scholars taking a cultural approach to moral development. The most cogent and penetrating critique has been presented by cultural psychologist Richard Shweder (Shweder et al., 1990; Shweder et al., 1998). According to Shweder, the postconventional level of moral reasoning described by Kohlberg is not the only rationally based moral code and is not higher or more developed than other kinds of moral thinking. In Shweder's view, Kohlberg's system is biased in favor of the individualistic thinking of "Western elites" of the highest social classes and highest levels of Western education. Like Gilligan, Shweder objects to Kohlberg's classification of detached, abstract individualism as the highest form of moral reasoning.

Shweder notes that in research using Kohlberg's system, very few people are classified as postconventional thinkers. As we saw above, in studies examining moral thinking across cultures very few people outside the West are classified as reaching the postconventional level, and even in the West postconventional thinking is rare. However, in Shweder's view this is not because most people in the world have not fully developed their capacities for rational thinking. On the contrary, the fault is in Kohlberg's system, and in what the system classifies as the highest level of rational moral thought.

Although Kohlberg claims that postconventional thinking is supposed to rely on objective, universal principles that form the basis of moral right and wrong regardless of the perspectives of either individuals or groups, in fact only a *particular kind* of objective principles get classified as postconventional under Kohlberg's system—those that reflect a secular, individualistic, Western way of thinking about moral issues. Shweder argues that people in many cultures in fact routinely make reference to objective, universal principles in their moral reasoning. However, because they view these principles as being established by tradition or religion, Kohlberg's system classifies their reasoning as conventional. Shweder sees this as a secular bias in the system.

This bias makes it difficult for people in most cultures to be classified as reaching the highest level of rationality, Level 3, because people in most cultures

outside the West invoke principles of tradition and/or a religious authority. However, Shweder argues, it is no less rational to believe in objective principles established by a religiously based divine authority and handed down through tradition than to believe in objective principles that have a secular, humanist basis. To argue otherwise would be to assume that all rational thinkers must be atheists or that it is irrational to accept an account of truth from beings believed to have superior powers of moral understanding, and to Shweder neither of these assertions is defensible.

Shweder supports his argument with data from a study comparing American children, adolescents, and adults with persons of similar ages in India (Shweder et al., 1990). Here, I will focus on the results specific to adolescents (aged 11 to 13), but the results were similar across all age groups. Shweder and his colleagues took a different approach to the study of moral reasoning than the one taken by Kohlberg. Rather than ask people about hypothetical situations, they asked people about specific real-life practices known to be typical in one or both countries (a sample of these is shown in Table 4.3). Because they believed that it was a mistake to assume that "content" does not matter in moral reasoning, they recorded whether the participants viewed each practice as right or wrong. Because they believed that Kohlberg's system erred by classifying any reference to tradition or divine authority as conventional, they classified responses as postconventional if the participant made reference to universal moral principles, even if those principles were based on tradition or religious beliefs.

As you can see from Table 4.3, Indian and American adolescents often disagreed about the kinds of behavior that are right or wrong. Similar patterns were found for younger children and adults. To Shweder, these sharp divergences call into question Kohlberg's notion that moral development proceeds through similar age-related stages in all cultures. On the contrary, children learn the moral beliefs specific to their culture by an early age, and these beliefs are well-ingrained by adolescence and remain stable through adulthood. Within each culture, beliefs about right and wrong were highly correlated regardless of age, but across cultures there was little agreement between Indians and Americans in any age group.

Although the Indians and Americans often disagreed about whether various practices were right or wrong, there were strong similarities between them in the kind of moral reasoning they used. However, contrary to findings using Kohlberg's system that postconventional reasoning is rare in any culture, Shweder

TABLE 4.3: VIEW OF MORAL ISSUES BY AMERICAN AND INDIAN ADOLESCENTS

Disagreement: Indians view it as right, Americans as wrong

   A father's inheritance goes more to his son than to his daughter.

   A husband beats his wife for disobeying his commands.

   A father beats his son for skipping school.

Disagreement: Indians view it as wrong, Americans as right

   A woman sleeps in the same bed as her husband during her menstrual period.

   A 25-year-old son addresses his father using his father's first name.

   A person eats beef regularly.

Agreement: Indians and Americans think it is wrong

   Incest between brother and sister.

   A man kicks a dog sleeping on the side of the road.

   A father asks his son to steal flowers from a neighbor's garden, and the boy does it.

Source: Schweder et al. (1990).

and his colleagues found postconventional reasoning to be characteristic of the *majority* of moral reasoning statements of children, adolescents, and adults in *both* countries. This is because Shweder classified moral reasoning as postconventional when people based their reasoning on any type of universal moral obligation. Kohlberg's system would have classified most of those statements as conventional, because they often referred to tradition or religious beliefs.

Recently, Shweder and his colleagues (Shweder et al., 1997; Jensen, 1997a, 1997b, 2000) have presented an alternative to Kohlberg's coding system. In Shweder's system, three types of ethics form the basis for people's moral judgments.

The *Ethic of Autonomy* defines the individual as the primary moral authority. Individuals are viewed as having a right to do as they wish so long as their behavior does no direct harm to others.

The *Ethic of Community* defines individuals as members of social groups to which they have commitments and obligations. In this ethic, the responsibilities of roles in the family, community, and other groups are the basis of one's moral judgments.

The *Ethic of Divinity* defines the individual as a spiritual entity, subject to the prescriptions of a divine authority. This ethic includes moral views based on traditional religious authorities and religious texts (e.g., the Bible, the Koran).

Research conducted thus far has shown that emerging adults in the United States rely especially on the ethic of autonomy. Jensen (1995) found that emerging adults relied more than midlife or older adults on the ethic of autonomy when explaining their views about issues such as divorce and suicide. Also, Haidt, Koller, and Dias (1993) found that college students in both the United States and Brazil used autonomy more than community on a variety of moral issues. However, one recent study found that emerging adults used autonomy and community in roughly equal proportions (and divinity rarely) in response to questions about the values that guide their lives and the beliefs and values they would like to pass on to the next generation (Arnett, Ramos, & Jensen, in press). Research using the three ethics has only begun in recent years, and it remains to be seen how use of the three ethics changes in different cultures from childhood through emerging adulthood.

THINKING CRITICALLY

Having read about Kohlberg's theory and Shweder's cultural critique of it, which do you find more persuasive, and why?

Political Beliefs

Cultural beliefs include political beliefs about desirable and undesirable features of political institutions, about what kind of political arrangements are fair or unfair, and about the extent to which human rights such as free speech and freedom of the press should be allowed. In cultures such as the American majority culture, political beliefs tend to be one part of a larger individualistic worldview. This worldview includes cultural beliefs about the rights of individuals and the obligations of individuals to their community or nation.

Because political thinking often involves a consideration of abstract ideas such as justice, law, and the distribution of wealth, it seems reasonable to expect that political thinking in Western majority cultures develops in adolescence toward greater abstraction and complexity, in a manner similar to religious thinking and moral thinking. Research on the development of political thinking seems to support this expectation. However, research in this area is not abundant, and it provides few insights into the cultural basis of political thinking.

One scholar who has done extensive work on political development in adolescence is Joseph Adelson (1971, 1991). Adelson's research was in the tradition of Piaget and Kohlberg. He used hypothetical situations to elicit adolescents' thinking about political arrangements and ideas, and he explained political development in terms of the cognitive changes of adolescence.

Adelson's main hypothetical situation was this: "Imagine that a thousand men and women, dissatisfied with the way things are going in this country, decide to purchase and move to an island in the Pacific where they must devise laws and modes of government." Based on this hypothetical situation, the researchers asked adolescents numerous questions to gather information about their political views. Each adolescent was asked about the merits of different possible forms of government for the island (democracy, dictatorship, etc.), and about the purpose and enforcement of laws. Adolescents were asked to consider what should be done if the government wanted to build a road across the island and a person who owned part of the land where the road was to be built refused to sell; if a law was passed to forbid smoking and people continued to smoke; and what to do about the rights of minority citizens on the island.

Adelson and his colleagues looked at political development in relation to age, gender, social class, and IQ, but the only one of these variables that was found to be related to political thinking was age. Studying adolescents aged 11 to 18, he found a profound shift in political thinking beginning at ages 12 to 13 and completed by ages 15 to 16. The shift involved three key changes: a change in what Adelson called "cognitive mode," a

sharp decline in support for authoritarian political systems, and the development of the capacity for ideology.

The change in cognitive mode, as Adelson described it, included several changes related to the development of formal operations, such as increased use of abstract ideas and increased tendency to see laws as human constructions rather than as absolute and unchangeable. Older adolescents were more likely than younger adolescents to use abstract ideas instead of concrete examples. For example, when asked about the purpose of laws, a typical older adolescent responded "to ensure safety and enforce the government," whereas a typical younger adolescent said laws are necessary "so people don't steal or kill." Similarly, when asked questions about the nature of government, older adolescents were more likely to refer to abstract ideas such as community or society, whereas younger adolescents' statements were more concrete and specific, referring, for example, to the president or the mayor.

Adolescents' views of laws also changed with age. The youngest adolescents viewed laws as eternal and unchangeable. If people did not obey the laws, the authorities should enforce them with greater and greater punishments. However, by about age 15 adolescents were more likely to see laws as social constructions that could be changed if the people governed by them wished to change them. In Adelson's view, this reflected the development of formal operations and a growing tendency to see laws less as concrete objects and more as social arrangements subject to change. This is similar to what Kohlberg described in moral development as the development from Level 1 thinking, emphasizing a fixed moral code, to Level 2 thinking, emphasizing the changeable, socially created quality of moral and legal rules. Both Kohlberg and Adelson found a similar change at a similar time, from ages 10 to 15.

The second key change observed by Adelson and his colleagues between early and late adolescence was a sharp decline in authoritarian political views. Younger adolescents tended to be remarkably authoritarian. For example, to enforce a law prohibiting cigarette smoking, they approved of procedures such as hiring police informers and hiding spies in the closets of people's homes! "To a large and various set of questions on crime and punishment," noted Adelson, "they consistently propose one form of solution: punish, and if that does not suffice, punish harder" (Adelson, 1971, p. 1023). Older adolescents' thinking was, again, more complex—they tried to balance the goal of the law with considerations such as individual rights and long-term versus short-term costs and benefits. On an index of authoritarianism used in the study, 85% of the youngest participants were rated in the highest category, compared with only 17% of those in their senior year of high school.

The third key change involved the capacity to develop an ideology. This means that the older adolescents had developed a set of beliefs that served as the basis for their political attitudes. In addressing Adelson's questions, they spoke of principles reflecting a belief in some combination of individual and community rights, rather than being limited to a focus on immediate and concrete solutions as the younger adolescents were.

More recent studies of the development of political thinking in adolescence have confirmed many of Adelson's findings (Flanagan & Botcheva, 1999). For example, Judith Torney-Purta (1990, 1992) has described how political thinking becomes increasingly abstract and complex during adolescence, progressing from the concrete, simple views of preadolescence to the more coherent, abstract ideology of late adolescence. Several scholars have confirmed Adelson's finding that authoritarianism declines in adolescence (Flanagan & Botcheva, 1999). For example, tolerance of opposing or offensive political views increases from childhood to adolescence and peaks in late adolescence (Sigelman & Toebben, 1992). Recent studies on political development have also touted the promise of the Internet as a source of international knowledge which, under a teacher's guidance, could promote tolerance and perspective taking in adolescents' political views (Flanagan & Botcheva, 1999; Torney-Purta, 1990, 1992).

Political Ideas as Cultural Beliefs

Like Piaget and Kohlberg, Adelson was seeking to establish a path of development through stages that would apply to young people everywhere. However, neither Adelson nor others have attempted to apply his ideas to cultures other than the American majority culture, so it is difficult to say how similar the developmental path of political thinking he described would be to the path followed by adolescents in a much different culture. However, if we borrow a little from the research and critiques on moral development, we can state two likely hypotheses. One hypothesis is that there would be some common changes in political thinking with age from early adolescence to late adolescence across cultures, because the abstract ideas invoked by the older adolescents in Adelson's studies reflects their more advanced cognitive abilities. The second hypothesis is that it is also likely that the pat-

tern observed by Adelson reflects adolescents' socialization into the political ideas that are part of the cultural beliefs of the American majority culture (Bellah et al., 1985).

Adelson and his colleagues studied adolescents in three different countries, but they were similar countries—the United States, Great Britain, and West Germany, countries with similar laws and political institutions. What would they find if they asked similar questions of adolescents in China, in Saudi Arabia, or among the Australian Aborigines? It seems likely that the political ideas of adolescents in those cultures would reflect the dominant political ideas of their societies and would differ accordingly from American adolescents. Aristotle, the ancient Greek philosopher, was one of the most brilliant persons who ever lived, yet he believed that dictatorship was superior to democracy, that some men were born to be slaves, and that women were inferior to men in virtually every respect. Was he less developed or less logical than other people of his time, or than the typical 16-year-old of our time? Not likely. What is more likely is that he, like us, reflected the cultural beliefs of his time and place.

Political Socialization in Communist Countries

For adolescents and emerging adults in Western countries, political socialization is only one part of the exposure they receive to cultural beliefs. Although they learn democratic political ideals at school, they receive little direct political socialization outside of the school setting. Also, political cultural beliefs must compete with religious beliefs and family moral instruction in their influence on the cultural beliefs of adolescents and emerging adults. However, in some parts of the world, such as in Communist countries, political beliefs are central to cultural beliefs. In countries such as China and the former Soviet Union, governments have attempted to make political beliefs the basis of ideological thinking in all other spheres of life. Religious ideas, moral reasoning, even ideas about family and personal life were supposed to be replaced by an all-encompassing Communist ideology.

The practices of the former Soviet Union and the Eastern European countries controlled by it until 1989 provide a vivid example of intensive political socialization in Communist countries. Under Soviet rule, two large youth associations controlled political socialization. The "Pioneers" organization was for children and early adolescents from ages 7 to 14, and the "Young Communist League" was for young people from age 14 through their early twenties (Mirchev,

Political beliefs are central to cultural beliefs in Communist countries. Here, members of a Soviet youth organization.

1994; Podolskij, 1994). These youth organizations provided a setting not only for political indoctrination, but also for social activities, sports, arts and music, and outdoor activities. However, the primary purpose of the youth organizations was explicitly political—to teach children, adolescents, and emerging adults to be obedient citizens who would believe the Communist ideology and follow the instructions of the Communist government.

The youth organizations were run by the government and included instruction in Communist ideology along with their other activities. No privately run, potentially competing youth organizations were allowed to exist (Mirchev, 1994). Potentially competing beliefs were also suppressed—for example, religious practices were generally forbidden, and atheism was taught both within the schools and within the youth organizations (Macek & Rabusic, 1994). The goal of the youth organizations was to make socialization in Communist countries extremely narrow, so that there would be little variability in political views and little deviation from the Communist political belief system.

However, this intensively narrow political socialization was never entirely successful. Even before the fall of Communism in the Soviet Union and Eastern Europe in the late 1980s and early 1990s, youth cultures existed in these countries whose resistance to Commu-

nist ideology was subtle but unmistakable. For example, many young people would wear Western styles and listen to and play Western rock music (Mirchev, 1994), as a custom complex symbolizing their rejection of Communism and their ideological affinity with the West.

And when the collapse of Soviet Communism began in 1989, it was initiated by emerging adults. The "Velvet Revolution" in Czechoslovakia began with a massive student-led strike and demonstration (Macek & Rabusic, 1994). When some of these students were beaten, shot, and killed, the rest of Czechoslovakian society rose up in outrage. The Communist government soon resigned in the face of the massive protests, and from there the dominoes fell all across Eastern Europe and throughout the Soviet Union as Communist governments resigned or were thrown out. Young people played a prominent role in the revolutions that led to the fall of Communism in many of these countries (Flanagan & Botcheva, 1999; Macek & Rabusic, 1994). In Hungary, young people organized demonstrations agitating for independence, and the first new political party after the fall of Communism was an explicitly youth-centered party with membership restricted to persons under age 35. In Bulgaria, young people were active in the strikes and demonstrations that led to the fall of the Communist government, and representatives of student movements took a prominent role in the new parliament. The events of this period demonstrate that the intensive political socialization of young people in these Communist countries was limited in its effectiveness, and that many young people rejected it in spite of begin subjected to it from childhood onward.

THINKING CRITICALLY

How would you explain why emerging adults were more likely than adolescents to be involved in the revolutions that overthrew Communist governments in Eastern Europe?

In the years since the transition to democracy, young people in Eastern Europe have become disillusioned and frustrated by the pace of change and by the substantial social costs that have accompanied democracy and the transition to a market economy. By now, they have largely turned away from conventional politics, like their counterparts in western Europe and North America (Flanagan & Botcheva, 1999).

Summing Up

In this chapter we have examined various aspects of the cultural beliefs underlying the socialization of adolescents and emerging adults, and you have been introduced to many of the ideas that are part of the cultural approach that will be taken in the chapters to come. The key points of the chapter are as follows:

- Socialization is the process by which people acquire the behaviors and beliefs of the culture they live in. Three outcomes central to this process are self-regulation, role preparation, and the cultivation of sources of meaning.

- Cultural beliefs usually tend toward either individualism or collectivism, with individualistic cultures giving priority to individualism and self-expression and collectivist cultures placing a higher value on obedience and conformity. Broad and narrow socialization are the terms for the process by which cultural members come to adopt the values and beliefs of an individualistic or collectivistic culture. Sources of socialization include family, peers and friends, school, community, media, workplace, legal system, and cultural beliefs.

- A custom complex consists of a distinctive cultural practice and the cultural beliefs that are the basis for that practice. Many aspects of development and behavior in adolescence and emerging adulthood can be understood as custom complexes.

- Cultural beliefs are often based on religious beliefs. Most industrialized countries today tend to be secular rather than religious, but religiosity is stronger in the United States than in European countries. Ideas about religious faith tend to become more abstract and less concrete in adolescence, compared with preadolescence.

- Kohlberg's theory of moral development proposed that moral development occurs in a universal sequence regardless of culture. However, Shweder has disputed this assumption and has proposed his theory of three ethics as a culturally based alternative to Kohlberg's theory.

- Like religious and moral beliefs, in the course of adolescence political beliefs become more abstract and complex. Communist countries have attempted to place Communist political beliefs at the center of cultural beliefs, but these attempts have often been resisted by adolescents and emerging adults.

The ideas about cultural beliefs presented in this chapter form a foundation for understanding development in adolescence and emerging adulthood using a cultural approach. Individualism and collectivism provide a useful way of distinguishing between two general types of cultural beliefs, although these are rough categories and cultures do not necessarily fit neatly into one or the other. Broad and narrow socialization describe the process through which beliefs of individualism or collectivism become beliefs that are held by adolescents and emerging adults. The idea of the custom complex is useful for directing our attention to the cultural beliefs that lie behind everything that people in a culture do as a customary practice. Religious, moral, and political beliefs are different kinds of cultural beliefs that people use for guiding their behavior and making sense of the world around them.

The development of ideas about cultural beliefs has mostly proceeded separately from research on adolescence and emerging adulthood. Only in recent years have cultural beliefs begun to be recognized by scholars on adolescence and emerging adulthood as an essential part of understanding these age periods. This new melding of the cultural approach with research on adolescence and emerging adulthood is producing a great deal of provocative and exciting research, which we will be examining in the chapters to come.

Key Terms

cultural beliefs	interdependent self	social desirability	conventional reasoning
symbolic inheritance	independent self	poetic-conventional faith	postconventional
roles	broad socialization	individuating-reflexive	reasoning
Bar Mitzvah	narrow socialization	faith	justice orientation
Bat Mitzvah	custom complex	Ramadan	care orientation
socialization	ontogenetic	Koran	
self-regulation	first-generation families	heteronomous morality	
role preparation	second-generation	autonomous morality	
sources of meaning	families	preconventional	
collectivism	secular	reasoning	

For Further Reading

Gilligan, C. (1982). *In a different voice: Psychological theory and women's development.* Cambridge, MA: Harvard University Press. Even though Gilligan's predictions of male–female differences in moral reasoning have not been borne out in research, this book is worth reading for its thought-provoking critique of the male model that has often been used in theories of human development, including development in adolescence and emerging adulthood.

Kohlberg, L., & Gilligan, C. (1971, Fall). The adolescent as a philosopher: The discovery of the self in a postconventional world. *Daedalus, 100,* 1051–1086. An engaging statement of Kohlberg's conception of moral development in adolescence. Written with his student, Carol Gilligan, before she developed her critique of his theory.

Shweder, R. A., Goodnow, J., Hatano, G., Levine, R. A., Markus, H., & Miller, P. (1998). The cultural psychology of development: One mind, many mentalities. In W. Damon (Ed.), *Handbook of Child Development* (Vol. 1, 5th ed., pp. 865–937). An excellent overview of cultural psychology. Defines cultural psychology, describes the custom complex, and applies cultural psychology to moral development, language development, cognitive development, and the development of the self.

Trommsdorff, G. (1994). Parent–adolescent relations in changing societies: A cross-cultural study. In P. Noack, M. Hofer, & J. Youniss (Eds.), *Psychological responses to social change* (pp. 189–218). New York: Walter de Gruyter. The introduction to this chapter presents a useful overview of the literature on individualism and collectivism in relation to adolescence. Then Trommsdorff presents a study comparing adolescents in Germany, Scotland, Japan, and Indonesia with respect to the relation between the individualism or collectivism of their culture and their relationships with their parents.

Applying Research

Scholars studying other cultures have written books providing insights on how to conduct such research. Below are two useful books on this topic, the first a classic book by an anthropologist and the second a recent book edited by two psychologists.

Geertz, C. (1973). *The interpretation of cultures.* New York: Basic Books.

McLoyd, V. C., & Steinberg, L. (1998). *Studying minority adolescents: Conceptual, methodological, and theoretical issues.* Mahwah, NJ: Erlbaum.

Gender

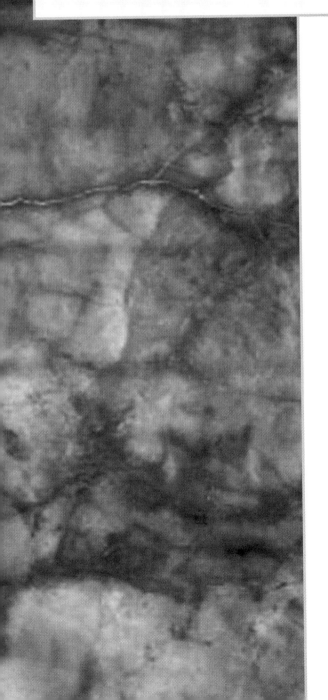

Tracy undresses, feeling nervous and apprehensive, and then feels silly. After all, the photographer is a professional and has probably seen a thousand naked bodies, so what is one more. All that work in the weight room, the aerobics—why not show off, after all the work it took to get such a tight body? "I should be proud," Tracy thinks, slipping into the robe thoughtfully provided by the photographer. Once exposed to the lights of the studio, Tracy gets another pang of doubt but dismisses it and drops the robe. The photographer suggests a seated pose, and Tracy strikes it, but he drops his hands to cover his genitals. "Move your hands to your knees, please," the photographer says gently. After all, she is a professional and knows how to put her models at ease (adapted from Carroll & Wolpe, 1996, p. 162).

The purpose of this story, as you have probably guessed, was to show how readily our minds slip into assumptions about male and female roles and how surprised we are when our gender stereotypes turn out to be wrong. Thinking about the world in terms of gender comes so easily to most of us that we do not even realize how deeply our assumptions about gender shape our perceptions. The first thing most people ask when they hear someone they know has had a baby is, "Is it a boy or a girl?" From birth onward—and these days, with prenatal testing, even before birth—gender organizes the way we think about

129

people's traits and abilities and how people behave. And at adolescence, when sexual maturity arrives, consciousness of gender and socialization pressures related to gender become especially acute.

In every chapter of this book, gender is an important topic. From family relationships to school performance to sexuality, gender similarities and differences merit our attention. Because gender is so important for so many aspects of development, we also must focus directly on gender as one of the foundations of development during adolescence and emerging adulthood. Many issues need to be addressed: What sort of gender-specific requirements do different cultures have for young people when they reach adolescence? In what ways does gender become especially important to socialization in adolescence, and how is gender socialization expressed in the family and other settings? What are the consequences for adolescents of conforming or refusing to conform to cultural expectations for gender role behavior? These are the sorts of questions we address in this chapter.

Because information on gender is relevant to all the chapters of this book, in this chapter I present especially extensive sections on cultural and historical patterns of gender socialization in adolescence, as a foundation for the chapters to come. These sections will be followed by an examination of gender socialization in modern Western societies. Then we will consider gender stereotypes in emerging adulthood and reasons for the persistence of gender stereotypes even when the evidence supporting them is weak. Finally, we will consider the ways globalization is changing gender expectations for adolescents and emerging adults in traditional cultures.

Before we proceed, however, let's clarify the difference between gender and sex. In general, social scientists use the term **sex** to refer to the *biological status of being male or female*. **Gender**, in contrast, refers to the *social categories of male and female* (Gentile, 1993; Unger & Crawford, 1996). Use of the term *sex* implies that the characteristics of males and females under consideration have a biological basis. Use of the term *gender* implies that characteristics of males and females may be due to cultural and social beliefs, influences, and perceptions. For example, the fact that males grow facial hair at puberty and females develop breasts is a sex difference. However, the fact that girls tend to have a more negative body image than males in adolescence is a gender difference. In this chapter, our focus will be on gender.

Adolescents and Gender in Traditional Cultures

For adolescents in traditional cultures, gender roles and expectations infuse virtually every aspect of life, even more so than in the West. Adolescent boys and girls in traditional cultures often have very different lives and spend little time in each other's presence. The expectations for their behavior as adolescents and for the kind of work they will be expected to do as adults are sharply divided, and as a result their daily lives do not often overlap (Schlegel & Barry, 1991). Furthermore, for both males and females the gender requirements tend to intensify at adolescence and tend to allow for very little deviation from the norm. In cultures where socialization is narrow, it tends to be narrowest of all with regard to gender expectations.

Let's look first at the gender expectations for girls in traditional cultures, then at the gender expectations for boys.

From Girl to Woman

Girls in preindustrial traditional cultures typically work alongside their mothers from an early age. Usually by age 6 or 7 they are helping to take care of younger siblings and cousins (Whiting & Edwards, 1988). By 6 or 7 or even earlier they are also helping their mothers obtain food, cook, make clothes, gather firewood, and all of the other activities that are part of running a household. By adolescence, girls typically work alongside their mothers as near-equal partners (Schlegel & Barry, 1991). The authority of mothers over their daughters is clear, but by adolescence daughters have learned the skills involved in child care and running a household so well that they can contribute an amount of work that is more or less equal to their mothers' work.

One important gender difference that occurs at adolescence in traditional cultures is that boys typically have less contact with their families and considerably more contact with their peers than they did prior to adolescence, whereas girls typically maintain a close relationship with their mothers and spend a great deal of time with them on a daily basis (Schlegel & Barry, 1991). This difference exists partly because girls are more likely to work alongside their mothers than boys are to work alongside their fathers, but even when adolescent boys work with their fathers they have less contact and intimacy with them than adolescent girls typically have with their mothers. This interde-

By adolescence, girls in traditional cultures often work alongside their mothers as near-equals. Here, they are picking lichee nuts in southern China.

pendence between mothers and daughters does not imply that girls remain suppressed in a dependent, childlike way. For example, Schlegel (1973) describes how among the Hopi, a Native American tribe, mother–daughter relationships are extremely close throughout life, yet adolescent girls are exceptionally confident and assertive.

Nevertheless, in traditional cultures socialization becomes broader for boys in adolescence and stays narrow or becomes even narrower for girls. In the company of their mothers and often with other adult women as well, adolescent girls' daily lives remain within a hierarchy of authority. All adult women have authority over the girls because of their status as adults and because of their older age (e.g., Chinas, 1991; Davis & Davis, 1989).

Another reason for the narrower socialization of girls at adolescence is that the budding sexuality of girls is more likely to be tightly restricted than is the budding sexuality of boys (Whiting, Burbank, & Ratner, 1986). Typically, adolescent boys in traditional cultures are allowed and even expected to gain some sexual experience before marriage. Sometimes this is true of girls as well (e.g., Burbank, 1988; Coté, 1994), but for girls more variability exists across cultures, from cultures that condone or encourage them to become sexually active before marriage to cultures that punish girls' loss of virginity before marriage with death, and every variation in between (Whiting et al., 1986). When adolescent girls are expected to be virgins and adolescent boys are expected not to be, boys sometimes gain their first sexual experience with prostitutes or with older women who are known to be friendly to the sexual interests of adolescent boys (e.g., Davis & Davis, 1989). However, this double standard

also sets up a great deal of sexual and personal tension between adolescent girls and boys, with boys pressing for the girls to relax their sexual resistance and girls fearful of the shame and disgrace that will fall on them (and not on the boy) if they should give in.

An excellent example of gender-specific expectations for adolescent girls in traditional cultures comes from the work of Chinas (1991), who has studied adolescent girls and women in a village in Mexico. In Chinas' description, socialization becomes narrower for girls once they reach puberty. Prior to puberty, girls are often sent to the town plaza to shop for food at the outdoor market. In the course of performing this task they become shrewd shoppers, adept at making change and at calculating mental additions and subtractions of money. However, in Mexican culture virginity is demanded for girls prior to marriage. Consequently, once they reach puberty girls are no longer allowed to go to the town plaza alone and are generally kept under close surveillance to reduce the likelihood of premarital sexual adventures.

During adolescence, the activities of the girls in the village mainly involve learning how to run a household. Middle childhood is a time of learning how to care for children (usually the girls' younger siblings), but by adolescence other girls in middle childhood take over some of the child care, and adolescent girls spend their time learning household skills such as making and cooking tortillas, sewing, and embroidery. School is not a part of the adolescent girl's experience. If she has had the opportunity to go to school at all, it would have been only for a year or so at age 6 or 7, just long enough to become literate. Boys, in contrast, are much more likely to be allowed to attend school until age 12 or older.

Girls are allowed few opportunities to interact with boys from about age 10 to about age 16. Talking to boys at these ages is strongly discouraged, and in small villages a girl's behavior can be monitored almost constantly, if not by her parents or her brothers than by other adults who know her. However, around age 16 girls are considered to be reaching marriageable age, and they begin to be allowed to attend public fiestas under the watchful eye of an older female relative—mother, aunt, or grandmother. The girl of this age will also be allowed to attend the Sunday evening *paseo*, in which the people of the village gather in the public square and stroll around the plaza, those on the outer edge in one direction and those on the inner edge in the other direction. This provides a rare chance for young people to look each other over and maybe even exchange a few words.

CULTURAL FOCUS
Male and Female Circumcision in Adolescence

Circumcision, which involves cutting some portion of the genitals so that they are permanently altered, is an ancient practice. We know that male circumcision goes back at least 2,500 years among the ancient Jews and other cultures in what is now known as the Middle East. For many Jews then and now, circumcision has had great religious and communal significance, as a visible sign of the covenant between God and the Jewish people and as a permanent marker of a male's membership in the Jewish community. Among the Jews, circumcision takes place on the eighth day of the infant's life.

If you are a male who has grown up in the United States, it is likely that you were circumcised as an infant, whether you are Jewish or not. Today, circumcision is routinely performed shortly after birth for hygienic reasons, as a way of preventing certain diseases that are slightly more likely to develop in uncircumcised males.

However, in several parts of the world, circumcision takes place not in infancy but in adolescence, and not just among boys but among girls as well. Cultures with adolescent circumcision exist in the Middle East and in Asia, but are most prevalent in Africa (Hatfield & Rapson, 1996). In most cultures that have circumcision in adolescence, it takes place for both boys and girls. However, the nature of it and the consequences of it are quite different for males and females.

Male circumcision in adolescence typically involves cutting away the foreskin of the penis. This is intensely painful, and no anesthetic of any kind is used. Boys are supposed to demonstrate their courage and fortitude by enduring the circumcision without resisting, without crying, and without flinching (Gilmore, 1990). There is a great deal of social pressure to be stoic. Circumcision usually occurs as a public ritual, observed by the community, and if a boy displays resistance or emotion he will be disgraced permanently before his community, and his family will be disgraced as well.

Although male circumcision is painful and traumatic, and emotional and social effects of failure

can be great, the physical effects of male circumcision are not harmful in the long run. Once the cut heals, the boy will be capable of experiencing the same pleasurable sensations in his penis as he did before the circumcision. Also, if a boy endures the circumcision without visible emotion, afterward he will receive the benefit of an increase in his status, as he is considered to have left childhood and entered adolescence.

For adolescent girls, the procedure and the consequences of circumcision are considerably more traumatic physically and emotionally. Female circumcision takes a variety of forms, but nearly always the clitoris is affected. In some cultures the hood of the clitoris is cut off, in some the entire clitoris is cut off, and in some the clitoris is cut off along with parts of the labia minora and the labia majora (Hatfield & Rapson, 1996). Figure 5.1 shows the rates of female circumcision in various African countries.

Although the circumcision of adolescent girls is not done publicly as it usually is for boys, and although girls are not expected to remain silent and stoic during the procedure, the physical consequences of circumcision are much more severe for girls. Typically, a great deal of bleeding occurs, and the possibility of infection is high. Afterward many girls have chronic pain whenever they menstruate or urinate, and their risks of urinary infections and childbirth complications are heightened. Furthermore, the operation virtually ensures that the girl will never have an orgasm. In fact, every act of intercourse is likely to be painful to her for years afterward, perhaps all her life.

Why would cultures inflict this on women? In part because of the inertia of cultural practices—in general, people grow up believing the practices and beliefs of their culture are good and right, and do not often question the ultimate ethical foundation for them (Arnett, 1995a). However, another motivation for males may be that, without the possibility of orgasm, wives may be less likely to have sex with other men (Hatfield & Rapson, 1996). Female

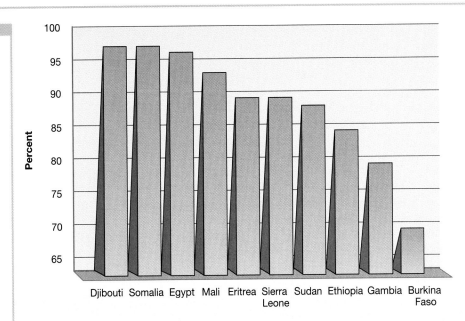

FIGURE 5.1 *Rate of female circumcision in various countries.*
Source: The Economist (1999).

submit "voluntarily" because they have no other real choice.

In recent years, female circumcision has become an extremely controversial issue of global concern. Critics have termed it **genital mutilation** and have waged an international campaign against it. International organizations such as the United Nations have issued reports condemning it (Bernard, 1987). The writer Alice Walker has written a novel depicting the practice, *Possessing the Secret of Joy* (Walker, 1992), and has become a leader in the fight to end it. Some defenders have argued that the West should not impose its values and practices on developing countries (El-Bakri & Kameir, 1983). However, the critics respond that respect for cultural differences can go only so far, and that practices that cause suffering to large numbers of people should be condemned and abolished in whatever culture they take place (Hatfield & Rapson, 1996; Nussbaum, 1992). Nevertheless, as of this writing female circumcision continues tobe inflicted on the adolescent girls of many African cultures.

circumcision is a particularly brutal way for men to exercise control over women's sexuality.

Why would women submit to it? In part because they have no choice. If they do not submit willingly, they may be held or tied down (Hatfield & Rapson, 1996). However, another reason is that girls in these cultures grow up knowing that a man will not marry a girl who is uncircumcised (French, 1992), and they know furthermore that they must marry to have an accepted social place in their culture. So, they may

If a boy is interested in a girl, he will begin to wait outside her home on Sunday evenings in the hopes of being allowed to escort her to the *paseo*. This is a critical point, and although the boy is always the initiator of the courtship, here the girl has the power to make or break it. If she discourages him, he is obliged to give up the courtship. If she allows him to escort her, they are considered more or less engaged. Thereafter, he will spend most of his free evenings waiting concealed outside her home in hopes that she will emerge on some errand. After some months of this, representatives of the boy ask the girl's parents for permission for

him to marry her. Although the girl is not asked about her own feelings, she has already indicated her consent indirectly by allowing the boy to court her.

Chinas' description of the girls in this Mexican village illustrates several themes often found in the socialization of adolescent girls in traditional cultures: early work responsibilities, close relationships with monitoring female adults, and a focus in adolescence on preparing for marriage and gender-specific adult work. The gender socialization of boys in traditional cultures is similar in some ways and different in others, as we will see in the next section.

From Boy to Man

One striking difference between gender expectations for girls and gender expectations for boys in traditional cultures is that for boys manhood is something that has to be *achieved*, to a much greater extent than girls have to achieve womanhood. It is true that girls are required to demonstrate various skills and character qualities before they can be said to have reached womanhood. However, in most traditional cultures womanhood is seen as something that girls attain naturally during adolescence, and their readiness for womanhood is viewed as indisputably marked when they reach menarche. In contrast, adolescent boys have no comparable biological marker of readiness for manhood. For them, the attainment of manhood is often fraught with peril and carries a definite and formidable possibility of failure.

As an illustration of this, it is striking to observe how many cultures have a term for a male who is a failed man. In Spanish, for example, a failed man is *flojo* (a word that also means flabby, lazy, useless), a *gamberro*. Similar words exist in a wide variety of other languages (Gilmore, 1990). (You can probably think of more than one example in English.) In contrast, although there are certainly many derogatory terms applied to women, none of them have connotations of *failure at being a woman* the way *flojo* and other terms mean *failure at being a man*.

So, what must an adolescent boy in traditional cultures do to achieve manhood and escape the stigma of being viewed as a failed man? Anthropologist David Gilmore (1990) has written a splendid book, *Manhood in the Making: Cultural Concepts of Masculinity*, in which he analyzes this question across traditional cultures around the world. He concludes that in most cultures an adolescent boy must demonstrate three capacities before he can be considered a man: *provide, protect,* and *procreate*. He must **provide** in the sense that he must demonstrate that he has developed skills that are economically useful and that will enable him to provide economically for the wife and children he is likely to have as an adult man. For example, if what adult men mainly do is fish, the adolescent boy must demonstrate that he has learned the skills involved in fishing, and learned them adequately enough to provide for a family.

Secondly, he must **protect**, in the sense that he must show that he can contribute to the protection of his family, kinship group, tribe, and other groups to which he belongs, from attacks by human enemies or animal predators. He learns this by acquiring the skills of warfare and the capacity to use weapons. Conflict between human groups has been a fact of life for most cultures throughout human history, so this is a pervasive requirement. Finally, he must learn to **procreate**, in the sense that he must gain some degree of sexual experience before marriage. This is not so he can demonstrate his sexual attractiveness but simply so that he can demonstrate that in marriage he will be able to perform sexually well enough to produce children.

Manhood requirements in traditional cultures typically involve not just the acquisition of specific skills in these three areas, but also the development of certain *character qualities* that must accompany these skills to

In traditional cultures, adolescent boys must learn to provide, protect, and procreate. Here, Mbuti boys in central Africa learn to hunt.

> "WHEN WE SEE GUYS ACTING IN CERTAIN GUY WAYS, WE MUST NOT JUDGE THEM TOO HARSHLY. WE MUST VIEW THEM THE SAME WAY WE VIEW ANY OTHER CREATURES OF NATURE, SUCH AS SNAKES. THEY DO THINGS THAT SEEM INAPPROPRIATE IN A CIVILIZED WORLD, BUT THEY ARE ONLY FOLLOWING BEHAVIORAL PATTERNS THAT WERE EMBEDDED EONS AGO. IF WE ARE PATIENT AND UNDERSTANDING WITH THEM, IF WE SEEK TO UNDERSTAND WHAT 'MAKES THEM TICK,' WE CAN SUCCEED IN MODIFYING THEIR BEHAVIOR AND BRINGING THEM MORE 'IN TUNE' WITH MODERN SOCIETY. I'M TALKING ABOUT SNAKES HERE. GUYS ARE HOPELESS."
> —FROM BARRY(1995), P. 41

make them useful and effective (Arnett, 1998a). Learning to provide involves developing not just economic skills, but also the character qualities of diligence and stamina. Learning to protect involves not just learning the skills of warfare and weapons, but also cultivating the character qualities of courage and fortitude. Learning to procreate involves not just sexual performance, but also the character qualities of confidence and boldness that lead to sexual opportunities.

Gilmore (1990) gives many fine examples in his book. For example, the *Mehinaku* live in the remotest part of the world's largest rain forest in central Brazil. Where they live is so remote that they are one of the few remaining cultures that has been affected very little by globalization. Other than the occasional visit from a missionary or an anthropologist, they have been (so far) left alone.

For an adolescent male among the Mehinaku, learning to provide means learning to fish and hunt, which are the two main male economic activities (the females tend vegetable gardens, care for children, and run the household). Depending on the local food supply, fishing and hunting sometime involve going on long expeditions to promising territory, sometimes for days or weeks at a time. Thus, learning to provide means not only learning the skills involved in fishing and hunting but also developing the character qualities of diligence, stamina, and courage (because the expeditions are sometimes dangerous). Adolescent boys who fail to accompany their fathers

Do you think the manhood requirements common in traditional cultures—provide, protect, and procreate—also exist in a modified form for adolescent boys in Western societies? Are there other qualities that you think are part of the requirements for manhood—not just adulthood, but manhood specifically—in Western societies?

on these trips out of laziness or weakness or fear are ridiculed as a "little girl" and told that women will find them undesirable.

Learning to protect means learning to fight and wield weapons against men of neighboring tribes. The Mehinaku themselves prefer peace and are not aggressive toward their neighbors, but their neighbors attack them on a regular basis and the men are required to defend themselves and their women and children. The men must also learn to defend themselves on their food-finding trips, as this often means traveling through the territory of more aggressive tribes.

As part of their preparation for protecting, Mehinaku boys and men engage in almost daily wrestling matches. These matches are fiercely competitive, and each time a male wins he elevates his status in the community, whereas repeated losing is deeply humiliating and a threat to his manhood status. This puts considerable pressure on adolescent boys, because boys who cannot compete well at these matches find their progress toward legitimate manhood called into question, and they find themselves considerably less attractive to adolescent girls as potential husbands.

With regard to learning to procreate, sex is perhaps the most popular topic of conversation among adolescent boys and men. They joke and brag about it, but they are also deeply concerned about potential failures, because in their small community any failures to "perform" quickly become public knowledge. Because impotence is so formidable, they use numerous and elaborate magical rituals to prevent or cure it, such as rubbing the penis with various animal or plant products. As with providing and protecting, there is considerable pressure on adolescent boys to show they can perform sexually, and they are ridiculed and ostracized if they cannot.

One other thing about Mehinaku manhood bears mentioning, because it is quite common in other cultures as well. Men and adolescent boys are supposed to spend their leisure time with each other, not at home with their mothers or wives and children. Adolescent boys and men gather daily in the public plaza to talk, wrestle, and make collective decisions, whereas girls and women are generally supposed to keep out of this central public place. A male who prefers the company of women, even of his wife, is ridiculed as a "trash yard man," a man who is not truly a man. (This is a good example of a term for a failed man, as described earlier.) Again, the pressure on adolescent boys to conform to this norm is intense. Whatever his own inclinations may be, this narrow socialization for the male role demands his conformity.

The themes of providing, protecting, and procreating can be seen clearly in adolescent boys' gender socialization among the Mehinaku. This example also illustrates the intense gender socialization pressure that often exists for adolescent boys in traditional cultures and the dire social consequences for boys who fail to measure up to culturally prescribed norms for manhood. For both boys and girls in traditional cultures, adolescence is a time when gender roles are clarified and emphasized. As we will see in the next section, increased emphasis on gender roles in adolescence has long been characteristic of American society as well.

Adolescents and Gender in American History

In the same way that looking at adolescence in traditional cultures reveals sharp disparities in the socialization of males and females, looking at adolescence in American history reveals a similar pattern. As in traditional cultures, in the history of American society what it means to grow from girl to woman has been very different from what it means to grow from boy to man.

From Girl to Woman

"I'm so tired of being fat! I'm going back to school wearing 119 pounds—I swear it. Three months in which to lose thirty pounds—but I'll do it—or die in the attempt."

—Excerpt from the diary of a 15-year-old American girl in 1926 (in Brumberg, 1997, pp. 102–103)

Adolescent girls growing up in the American middle class in the 18th and 19th centuries faced expectations that both constricted and supported them more than for American adolescent girls today. They were narrowly constricted in terms of the occupational roles they were allowed to study or enter. Few professions other than teacher, nurse, or seamstress were considered appropriate for a woman. In fact, no profession at all was considered best, so that a young woman could focus on her "proper" future roles of wife and mother.

Adolescent girls were also constricted by cultural perceptions of females, especially young females, as fragile and innocent. One key reason they were discouraged from pursuing a profession was that intellectual work was considered "unhealthy" for women. This view was connected to beliefs about menstruation, specifically the belief that intellectual work would draw a woman's energy toward her brain and away from her ovaries, thus disrupting her menstrual cycle and endangering her health (Brumberg, 1997). This is a good example of something that was claimed to be a sex difference—biologically, women were viewed as less capable of intellectual work—but that turned out to be a gender difference instead (rooted in cultural beliefs).

This view of adolescent females as too fragile and innocent to do strenuous work is in sharp contrast to the expectations we have seen in traditional cultures, where adolescent girls work alongside their mothers with near-adult responsibilities. However, it is likely that this exclusion from work applied mainly to American adolescent girls in the growing middle class. Until the mid-19th century the majority of American families were small-scale farmers (Hernandez, 1994), and in those families the lives of adolescent girls were very much like their counterparts in traditional cultures, working alongside their mothers doing useful and necessary work every day.

A third area where the lives of adolescent girls were narrowly constricted historically in American society is sexuality. In American history until about the 1920s, virginity until marriage was considered essential for adolescent girls. The word *hymen* was rarely used, but adolescents girls were taught that they possessed a "jewel" or "treasure" that they should surrender only on the night of their wedding (Brumberg, 1997). Until marriage, young women were kept as innocent as possible in body and in mind.

The goal of keeping girls innocent was taken so far that many adolescent girls were not even told about menarche. Historians estimate that before the mid-20th century up to 65% of American adolescent girls were entirely unprepared for menarche (Brumberg, 1997)—and we have seen, in Chapter 2, how disturbing it can be to girls who do not know it is coming. Mothers believed that by saying nothing about it they were shielding their girls for as long as possible from the dark mysteries of sex. It was only in the 1920s, sometimes called "the first American sexual revolution," that virginity began to lose its near-sacred status. And it was only in the late 1940s that the majority of girls learned about menstruation from school, their mothers, or other sources before menarche actually arrived (Brumberg, 1997).

A fourth area of constriction for adolescent females historically was physical appearance. We have discussed how the current slim ideal of female appearance can be difficult for girls when their bodies reach puberty, but irrational ideals of female appearance are not new. Until the early 20th century most middle-class adolescent girls and women in the West wore some version of the corset, which was designed to support the breasts and to pinch the waist tightly to make it look as small as possible. By the 1920s corsets were rarely used,

replaced by bras, but the 1920s also witnessed new requirements for female appearance—shaving the legs and underarms became the convention for American women, and dieting also became a common practice in an effort to attain a slim, boyish figure.

By the 1950s boyishness was out and big breasts were in. Adolescent girls' diaries from the 1950s show a preoccupation with bras and breasts and a variety of dubious techniques for increasing breast size (Brumberg, 1997), from exercise programs to creams to exposing them to moonlight. In each era, adolescent girls have striven for the female ideal they have been socialized to desire, and often experienced the normal course of their biological development during puberty as a great source of frustration.

However, developing from girl to woman also had some advantages historically as compared to the present, according to Joan Jacobs Brumberg (1997), a historian and the author of a thoughtful book called *The Body Project: An Intimate History of American Girls.* Brumberg acknowledges, and describes in some detail, how girls in the 18th and 19th centuries in American society were constricted and sheltered and left largely ignorant of the workings of their own bodies. However, she argues that girls of those times also benefited from the existence of a wide range of voluntary organizations, such as YWCA, the Girl Scouts, and the Camp Fire Girls, in which adult women provided a "protective umbrella" for the nurturing of adolescent girls. In these organizations the focus was not on girls' physical appearance or their bodies but on service projects in the community, on building relationships between adolescent girls and adult women, and on the development of character, including self-control, service to others, and belief in God. Brumberg (1997) observes:

Whether Christian or Jew, black or white, volunteer or professional, most women in this era shared the ethic that older women had a

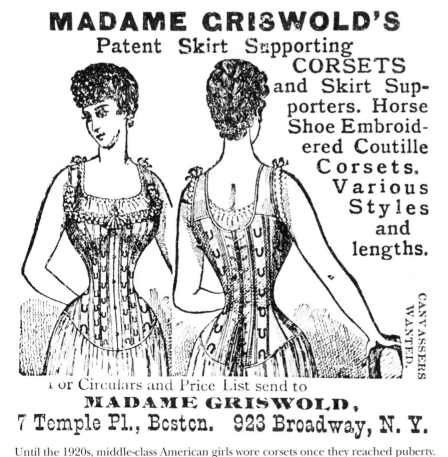

MADAME GRISWOLD'S Patent Skirt Supporting **CORSETS** and Skirt Supporters. Horse Shoe Embroidered Coutille Corsets. Various Styles and lengths.

CANVASSERS WANTED.

For Circulars and Price List send to **MADAME GRISWOLD,** 7 Temple Pl., Boston. 923 Broadway, N. Y.

Until the 1920s, middle-class American girls wore corsets once they reached puberty.

special responsibility to the young of their sex. This kind of mentoring was based on the need to protect all girls, not just one's own daughters, from premature sexuality and manipulation at the hands of men. Although the ethic generated all kinds of censorious directives about sexual behavior and its consequences . . . it also gave a cooperative and expansive tone to American community life. In towns and cities across the United States, middle-class matrons and young adult women, in the time before they married, performed countless mundane acts of guidance and supervision, such as showing girls how to sew, embroider, or arrange flowers, or helping them to organize collections of food and clothing for impoverished families. In all of these settings, there were chattering girls along with concerned adults, bound together by both gender and common projects. (pp. 19–20)

Today, in Brumberg's view, adolescent girls are less constricted, but also more vulnerable and less integrated into the lives of adult women outside their families.

THINKING CRITICALLY

Would it be possible today to reconstruct the "protective umbrella" provided for adolescent girls by adult women in previous times, or would today's adolescent girls find such protection patronizing and restrictive?

From Boy to Man

Like gender expectations for adolescent girls, gender expectations for adolescent boys have changed markedly in the past two centuries but have also retained some consistent features. In his book *American Manhood*, historian Anthony Rotundo (1993) describes the transformations that have taken place between the American Revolution and the present in how Americans view the passage from boyhood to manhood.

In Rotundo's account, the 17th and 18th centuries in colonial America were characterized by communities that were small, tightly knit, and strongly based in religion. In this phase of what Rotundo terms **communal manhood**, the focus of gender expectations for

adolescent boys was on preparing to assume adult role responsibilities in work and marriage. Rotundo calls this "communal manhood" because preparing to take on responsibilities toward community and family was considered more important than striving for economic success and individual achievement. Preparing to become "head of the household" was seen as especially important for adolescent boys, because as adult men they would be expected to act as provider and protector of wife and children. Note the striking resemblance to the requirements of manhood in traditional cultures, with the common emphasis on learning to provide and protect.

During the 19th century, as American society became more urbanized, young men became more likely to leave home in their late teens for the growing American cities to make it on their own without much in the way of family ties. Rotundo calls the 19th century the era of **self-made manhood**. This was a time in American history when individualism was growing in strength and males were increasingly expected to become independent from their families in adolescence and emerging adulthood as part of becoming a man, rather than remaining closely interdependent with other family members. Although becoming a provider and protector remained important, an explicit emphasis also developed on the importance of developing the individualistic character qualities necessary for becoming a man. *Decision of character* became a popular term to describe the passage of a young man from high-spirited but undisciplined youth to a manhood characterized by self-control and a strong will for carrying out independent decisions (Kett, 1977).

One interesting historical similarity between gender expectations for young males and females was the creation during the 19th century of a wide range of voluntary organizations that brought young people together. The organizations for girls were described above. For males, the organizations included literary societies (where young men would meet to discuss books they had read), debating societies, religious groups, informal military companies, fraternal lodges, and the YMCA.

Like the organizations for girls, the organizations for boys stressed the importance of developing self-control, service to others, and belief in God. However, the male organizations were less likely to be run by adults and more likely to be run by the adolescents and emerging adults themselves (Kett, 1977). Perhaps for this reason, the male organizations tended to involve not just sober camaraderie but also occasional boisterous play, rowdy competition, and (in some organizations) fighting and drinking alcohol, in spite of the professed commitment to self-control (Kett, 1977).

Another feature of the organizations for young males was an emphasis on strenuous physical activity. Populations in the big cities were growing rapidly, but many men voiced concerns that growing up in a city made boys soft and weak. They advocated activities such as military training, competitive sports, and nature trips for young males because they believed that becoming a man meant becoming tough and strong (Kett, 1977). As discussed in Chapter 4, the creation of the Boy Scouts also arose from this belief.

Rotundo calls the 20th century the era of **passionate manhood**, in which individualism has increased still further. Although individualism grew in American society in the 19th century, adolescent boys at that time were nevertheless expected to learn self-control and self-denial as part of becoming a man, so that they would maintain control over their impulses. In contrast, during the 20th century passionate emotions such as anger and sexual desire became regarded more favorably as part of the manhood ideal. Self-expression and self-enjoyment replaced self-control and self-denial as the paramount virtues young males should learn in the course of becoming a man.

Socialization and Gender in the West

So far we have looked at gender socialization in traditional cultures and in American history. What about the contemporary American majority culture and other similar cultures in the West? What sort of socialization for gender goes on in these cultures at adolescence? We address this question by looking first at a hypothesis about gender socialization in adolescence. Then we look at American cultural beliefs about gender and at gender socialization with respect to family, peers, school, and the media.

The Gender Intensification Hypothesis

Psychologists John Hill and Mary Ellen Lynch (1983; Lynch 1991) have proposed that adolescence is a particularly important time in gender socialization, especially for girls. According to their **gender intensification hypothesis**, psychological and behavioral differences between males and females become more pronounced at adolescence because of intensified socialization pressures to conform to culturally prescribed gender roles. Hill and Lynch (1983) believe that it is this intensified socialization pressure, rather than the biological changes of puberty, that results in increased differences in behavior between males and females as adolescence progresses. Furthermore, they argue that the increase in the intensity of gender socialization at adolescence is greater for females than for males, and that this is reflected in a variety of ways in adolescent girls' development.

In support of their hypothesis, Hill and Lynch (1983) offered several arguments and sources of evidence. During adolescence, girls become notably more self-conscious than boys about their physical appearance, because looking physically attractive becomes an especially important part of the female gender role. Girls also become more interested and adept than boys in forming intimate friendships; to Hill and Lynch this is because adolescents have been socialized to believe that having intimate friendships is part of

For both boys and girls, voluntary organizations were popular in the 19th century. Shown here are young men at a YMCA.

the female gender role but is inconsistent with the male gender role.

Since Hill and Lynch (1983) proposed this hypothesis, other studies have been presented that support it (Wichstrom, 1999). In one study, boys and girls filled out a questionnaire on gender identity each year in sixth, seventh, and then eighth grades (Galambos, Almeida, & Petersen, 1990). Over this 2-year period, girls self-descriptions became more "feminine" (e.g., gentle, affectionate) and boys' self-descriptions became more "masculine" (e.g., tough, aggressive). However, in contrast to Hill and Lynch's (1983) claim that gender intensification is strongest for girls, the pattern in this study was especially strong for boys and masculinity. Another study found that increased conformity to gender roles during early adolescence took place primarily for adolescents whose parents influenced them toward gender conformity (Crouter, Manke, & McHale, 1995). This study indicates that gender intensification does not occur equally for all adolescents, but especially for adolescents who are exposed to socialization pressures to conform to traditional gender roles.

Cultural Beliefs About Gender

What sort of cultural beliefs about gender exist for adolescents and emerging adults currently growing up in American society? Since 1972 the National Opinion Research Center (NORC) has conducted nationwide surveys of adult Americans' beliefs about gender roles and a variety of other topics. Table 5.1 shows the results of some of the items on gender for the years 1972–1982 combined and for 1994 (the most recent year available).

The results of these surveys show that the gender expectations in American society have changed considerably since the period 1972–1982. Today's American adolescents and emerging adults are entering an adult world in which traditional gender beliefs are weaker than in the past. However, the results also show that a considerable proportion of Americans—about one-fourth—continue to have beliefs about gender roles not unlike the ones we have seen in traditional cultures: Men should hold the power and be out in the world doing things, and women should focus on caring for children and running the household. The existence of traditional gender role beliefs in American

TABLE 5.1: AMERICAN'S BELIEFS ABOUT GENDER ROLES

	1972–1982 % Agree	1994 % Agree
Do you agree or disagree that:		
It is much better for everyone involved if the man is the achiever outside the home and the woman takes care of the home and family.	66	35
Women should take care of running their homes and leave running the country up to men.	34	14
It is more important for a wife to help her husband's career than to have one herself.	57	22
	1972–1982 % Disapprove	1994 % Disapprove
Do you approve or disapprove of a married woman earning money in business or industry if she has a husband capable of supporting her?	29	18
	1972–1982 % No	1994 % No
If your party nominated a woman for president, would you vote for her if she were qualified for the job?	20	8

Source: www.norc.uchicago.edu/gss

society is also indicated in studies of gender socialization and gender stereotypes, as we shall see in the following sections.

Gender Socialization: Family, Peers, and School

We talked in the previous chapter about cultural differences in socialization. However, differences in socialization also occur within cultures, especially in the socialization of boys and girls. **Differential gender socialization** is the term for socializing males and females according to different expectations about the attitudes and behavior appropriate to each gender (Burn, 1996). We have seen how intense differential socialization can be in traditional cultures and how intense it has been in American history. It also exists currently in the West in more subtle but nevertheless effective forms.

Differential gender socialization begins early, in virtually every culture. Parents dress their boys and girls differently, give them different toys, decorate their bedrooms differently. One study found that 90% of the infants observed at an American shopping mall were wearing clothing that was gender-specific in color and/or style (Shakin, Shakin, & Sternglanz, 1985). In another study (Sidorowicz & Lunney, 1980), adults were asked to play with a 10-month-old infant they did not know. All adults played with the same infant, but some were told it was a girl, some were told it was a boy, and some were given no information about its gender. There were three toys to play with: a rubber football, a doll, and a teething ring. When the adults thought the child was male, 50% of the men and 80% of the women played with the child using the football. When they thought the child was female, 89% of the men and 73% of the women used the doll in play.

Throughout childhood children get encouragement from parents, peers, and teachers to conform to gender roles. Numerous studies attest that parents encourage gender-specific activities in their children and discourage activities they see as inconsistent with their child's gender (Lytton & Romney, 1991). Children (especially boys) who deviate from gender norms in play suffer peer ridicule and are less popular than children who conform to gender roles (Berndt & Heller, 1986).

During middle childhood, gender rules often become temporarily more flexible (Basow & Rubin, 1999). However, with the gender intensification of adolescence, differential socialization becomes more pronounced. Parents tend to monitor and restrict adolescent

Pressures to conform to traditional gender roles intensify in adolescence.

girls more strictly than adolescent boys with respect to where they are allowed to go and with whom (Papini & Sebby, 1988). Peers punish with ridicule and unpopularity the adolescents who deviate from gender role expectations (Eder, 1995; Huston & Alvarez, 1990)—the boy who decides to take up the flute, the girl who wears unstylish clothes and no makeup.

In school, some studies have found that adolescent boys receive more attention from teachers than girls do (Sadker & Sadker, 1994), but the most recent studies indicate that girls generally feel greater acceptance and encouragement from teachers than boys do (Sommers, 2000). There may be differences, depending on the subject area. For example, Matyas (1987) found that in college classes, professors of math, science, and engineering paid more attention to male students and were more likely to encourage them to become involved in research and to pursue graduate studies.

The findings about differential socialization at home and at school do not mean that parents and teachers consciously and intentionally treat adolescent girls and boys differently. Sometimes they do, but often differential socialization simply results from the different expectations that parents and teachers have for males and females as a consequence of their own gender socialization. In their differential gender socialization of adolescent girls and boys, parents and teachers reflect their culture's beliefs about gender, and they may do so without even thinking consciously about what they are doing.

THINKING CRITICALLY

Based on your experience, give examples of differential socialization in childhood, adolescence, and emerging adulthood.

Media and Gender

"I read Seventeen *magazine and like that's mostly how I got to do all my make-up, just from looking at magazines, looking at models, and seeing how they're doing it. Like I'd sit for two hours doing my make-up for something to do. It was fun."*

—Margaret, age 17 (in Currie, 1999, p. 3)

The television shows, movies, and music most popular with adolescents promote many stereotypes about gender, as we will see in Chapter 12 on media. However, magazines are worth discussing here because they are the media form with the most obvious focus on gender socialization, especially the magazines read by adolescent girls. Magazines for adolescent girls have a combined annual circulation rate of over 3 million copies in the United States, and one study found that three-fourths of white girls aged 12 to 14 read at least one magazine regularly (Klein et al., 1993). Boys read magazines, too, but their favorite magazines—Sport, Gamepro, Hot Rod, Popular Science—are not as clearly gender focused. For girls, every issue of their favorite magazines is packed with gender-specific messages about what it means to be an adolescent girl (Currie, 1999).

What sort of gender messages do adolescent girls get when they read these magazines? Several analyses have been made of the content in girls' magazines, and they have reported highly similar findings (Currie, 1999; Duffy & Gotcher, 1996; Durham, 1998; Evans et al., 1991; Pierce, 1993). One study (Evans et al., 1991) analyzed the content in ten issues of three magazines for adolescent girls: *Seventeen* (the most popular), *Young Miss,* and *Sassy.* The analysis showed that the magazines relentlessly promote the gender socialization of adolescent girls toward the traditional female gender role. Physical appearance is stressed as being of ultimate importance, and there is an intense focus on how to be appealing to boys. Figure 5.2 shows the proportion of articles devoted to each of six topics. Fashion was the most common topic in all three magazines, with a proportion from 27% to 41%. Another 10% to 13% of the articles were devoted to beauty, and most of the articles on "health" (3% to 6%) were about weight reduction and control. Altogether for each of the magazines, from 44% to 60% of the content focused directly on physical appearance.

This percentage actually understates the focus on physical appearance, because it does not include the advertisements. In the three magazines taken together 46% of the space was devoted to advertisements (with a high of 57% in the most popular magazine, *Seventeen*). The ads were almost exclusively for clothes, cosmetics, and weight-loss programs.

In contrast to the plethora of articles and advertisements on physical appearance, there were few articles on political or social issues (although *Sassy* had more than the other two magazines). The main topic of "career" articles was modeling. There were virtually no articles on possible careers in business, the sciences, law, medicine, or any other high-status profession in which the mind would be valued more than the body. Of course, no doubt the magazine publishers would carry an abundance of articles on social issues and professional careers if they found they could sell more magazines that way. They pack the magazines with articles and ads on how to enhance physical attractiveness because that is the content to which adolescent girls respond most strongly.

Why? Perhaps because early adolescence—the time when these magazines are most popular—is a time of gender intensification (Basow & Rubin, 1999). Girls become acutely aware when they reach adolescence that others expect them to look like a girl is supposed to look and act like a girl is supposed to act—but how is a girl supposed to look and act? These magazines promise to provide the answers. Wear this kind of blouse, and this kind of skirt, and style your hair like this, and wear this kind of eye shadow and this kind of lipstick and this perfume, and be sure to stay or get *THIN*. The message to adolescent girls is that if you buy the right products and strive to conform your appearance to the ideal presented in the magazines, you will look and act like a girl is supposed to look and act

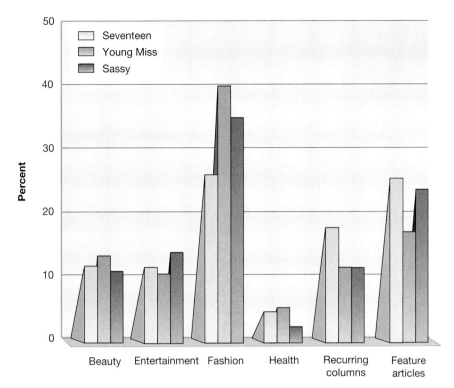

FIGURE 5.2 *Content distribution of three teen magazines.* The content of girls' magazines strongly emphasizes physical appearance.
Source: Evans et al. (1991).

and you will attract all the boys you want (Durham, 1998; Evans et al., 1991).

Of course, the appeal of girls' magazines involves not only gender intensification but also culture (Heilman, 1998). Girls respond to their portrayal in the magazines as appearance-obsessed slaves to love because they have been taught through the gender socialization of their culture to see themselves that way, and by adolescence they have learned their lesson well (Durham, 1998). Analyses of a popular magazine for British girls called *Jackie* show that the content has changed substantially in recent years, from a previous focus on appearance similar to American magazines to a much different portrayal of girls as strong, responsible, independent thinkers (McRobbie, 1994). But even recent analyses of the most popular magazines for American and Canadian girls show little change in content, with physical appearance and boy catching still predominant (Currie, 1999; Durham, 1998).

Gender Socialization as a Source of Problems

For both girls and boys, the intensified gender socialization they experience in adolescence can be a source of

problems. For girls, the focus on physical appearance that is the heart of the female gender role can produce a variety of kinds of distress (Wichstrom, 1999). Girls are more likely than boys to develop a negative body image in adolescence (Harter, 1989; Rosenblum & Lewis, 1999)—hardly surprising, given the magazine ideals to which they compare themselves. The emphasis on thinness that is part of the female ideal of physical appearance leads the majority of girls to diet in adolescence (French et al., 1995), and at the extremes, some girls develop serious eating disorders that threaten their health and even their lives (Striegel-Moore & Cachelin, 1999). Adolescent girls who are unfortunate enough to be overweight or regarded by their peers as physically unattractive suffer merciless ridicule (Burns & Farina, 1992; Cash, 1995). This ridicule can be vicious, and it comes not only from boys but from other girls (Eder, 1995). Even long after adolescence, close to half of women are dissatisfied with their physical appearance (Cash & Henry, 1995).

For boys, the problem at the core of their gender role in adolescence is aggressiveness (Pollack, 1998). Boys are more aggressive than girls from infancy onward, partly for biological reasons but also because of their gender socialization (Maccoby, 1990). During adolescence boys are expected by their peers to be verbally aggressive, directing half-joking insults at other boys on a regular basis (Eder, 1995). Often these insults involve manhood itself; adolescent boys commonly use insults such as "wimp," "weenie," "pussy," and "faggot," calling the manhood of other boys into question. From this we can see that it is not just in traditional cultures that adolescent boys face the intimidating prospect of being regarded as a failed man. They defend themselves by using verbal aggressiveness in return, and by being physically aggressive when necessary. Boys who demonstrate physical aggressiveness successfully in sports such as football frequently have the highest status among their peers (Brown, 1990; Brown & Lohr, 1987; Stone & Brown, 1999).

A variety of problems stem from this emphasis on aggressiveness in the male role. Aggressiveness is used as a

Aggressive behavior is a source of certain problems in adolescence and emerging adulthood for males.

way of establishing social hierarchies among adolescent boys, and low-status boys suffer frequent insults and humiliations from other boys (Eder, 1995). Furthermore, aggressiveness is a source of problem behaviors in adolescence and emerging adulthood such as vandalism, risky driving, fighting, and crime (Arnett, 1992a; Wilson & Herrnstein, 1985). Joseph Pleck (Pleck, 1983; Pleck, Sonnenstein, & Ku, 1998) has shown that adolescents who value aggressiveness as part of the male gender role are especially likely to engage in problem behavior. In Pleck's analysis of data from a national study of 15- to 19-year-old boys (Pleck et al., 1998), boys who agreed with statements such as "A young man should be tough, even if he is not big" were more likely than other boys to report school difficulties, alcohol and drug use, and risky sexual behavior.

Cognition and Gender

Socialization interacts with cognitive development to produce adolescents' ideas about gender. Lawrence Kohlberg, whose ideas about moral development were discussed in Chapter 4, also proposed an influential theory of gender development known as the **cognitive developmental theory of gender**. Kohlberg (1966) based this theory on Piaget's ideas about cognitive development, applied specifically to gender. According to Kohlberg's theory, gender is a fundamental way of organizing ideas about the world. By the time children are about 3 years old, they understand **gender identity**, that is, they understand themselves as being either male or female.

Once children possess gender identity, they use gender as a way of organizing information obtained from the world around them. Certain toys become "toys that girls play with," whereas others are "toys that boys play with." Certain clothes become "clothes that boys wear" and others become "clothes that girls wear." By age 4 or 5 children identify a wide range of things as appropriate for either males or females, including toys, clothing, activities, objects, and occupations (Serbin, Powlishta, & Gulko, 1993). Furthermore, according to cognitive developmental theory, children seek to maintain consistency between their categories and their behavior. Kohlberg (1966) called this process **self-socialization**. Boys become quite insistent about doing things they regard as boy things and avoiding things that girls do; girls become equally intent on avoiding boy things and doing things they regard as appropriate for girls (Bussey & Bandura, 1992).

How does cognitive developmental theory pertain to adolescence? The hallmark of cognitive development in adolescence is formal operations, which includes the development of self-reflection and idealization. As a consequence, reaching adolescence leads to asking oneself questions about what it means to be a woman and what it means to be a man, and to making judgments about how one measures up to expectations for one's gender. This is a continuation of self-socialization, but more self-reflectively than in childhood. Reaching adolescence also means having fantasies about the ideal woman and the ideal man. The posters of entertainment and sports stars that are typical decorations in the bedrooms of adolescents reflect these fantasies.

Since Kohlberg (1966) presented his theory, another cognitive theory of gender has been presented that builds on his ideas and also uses more of Piaget's ideas. This theory is known as **gender schema theory**. Like Kohlberg's theory, gender schema theory views gender as one of the fundamental ways that people organize information about the world. A **schema** is Piaget's term for a structure for organizing and processing information.

According to gender schema theory, gender is one of our most important schemas from early childhood onward. By the time we reach adolescence, on the basis of our socialization we have learned to categorize an enormous range of activities and objects and personality characteristics as "female" or "male." This includes not just the obvious—vaginas are female, penises are male—but many things that have no inherent "femaleness" or "maleness" and are nevertheless taught as possessing gender—the moon as "female" and the sun as "male" in traditional Chinese culture, or long hair as "female" and short hair as "male" in many cultures, for example.

Sandra Bem (1981a, 1993), one of the foremost proponents of gender schema theory, stresses that people apply gender schemas not just to the world around them but to themselves. Once they have learned gender schemas from their culture, they monitor their own behavior and attitudes and shape them so that they conform to cultural definitions of what it means to be male or female. In this way, according to Bem, "cultural myths become self-fulfilling prophesies" (1981a, p. 355). Thus, Bem, like Kohlberg, sees gender development as taking place in part through self-socialization, as people strive to conform to the gender expectations they perceive in the culture around them.

The gender intensification of adolescence means that adolescents increasingly think of themselves and others in terms of what is masculine and what is feminine. Boys experience pressure to become more masculine and avoid what is feminine; girls experience pressure to become more feminine and avoid what is masculine. What sort of characteristics and behavior do adolescent boys and girls see as being feminine or masculine? And how is their evaluation of their own femininity and masculinity related to their overall sense of self?

Traits regarded by most members of the American majority culture as masculine or feminine are shown in Table 5.2. These traits are taken from the Bem Sex Role Inventory (BSRI; Bem, 1974), the most widely used measure of gender role perceptions. The BSRI was originally developed on the basis of college students' ratings of the traits most desirable for an American man or woman (Lips, 1993), but since it was developed similar responses have been obtained in

---

■ **THINKING CRITICALLY**

> Give an example (one for males and one for females) of a custom complex for gender—a cultural practice that reflects cultural beliefs related to gender roles in your culture.

Masculinity, Femininity, and Androgyny

"*In our health class, the guys and the girls had to switch roles for a day. We were supposed to try to imagine what it's like to be the other one and act that way. The guy I switched with said he thought it would be so much easier to be a girl, because you wouldn't have to worry about knowing what to do or have to be smooth and cool and all that crap. . . . I just couldn't believe he was saying those things, because I always thought how much easier it would be to be a guy. You wouldn't have to worry about how you looked or how you acted. You could do whatever you felt like doing without worrying about your reputation. But he said, of course guys worry about their reputation, but it's the opposite kind of reputation. He said they have to put on this big act about how experienced they are. . . . He worries that he won't do the right thing or say the right thing.*"

— *Penny, 11th grade, New York*
(in Bell, 1998, p. 106)

TABLE 5.2: MASCULINE AND FEMININE TRAITS (FROM THE BEM SEX ROLE INVENTORY)

Masculine	Feminine
Self-reliant	Yielding
Defends own beliefs	Cheerful
Independent	Shy
Athletic	Affectionate
Assertive	Flatterable
Strong personality	Loyal
Forceful	Feminine
Analytical	Sympathetic
Has leadership abilities	Sensitive to the needs of others
Willing to take risks	Understanding
Makes decisions easily	Compassionate
Self-sufficient	Eager to soothe hurt feelings
Dominant	Soft-spoken
Masculine	Warm
Willing to take a stand	Tender
Aggressive	Gullible
Acts as a leader	Childlike
Individualistic	Does not use harsh language
Competitive	Loves children
Ambitious	Gentle

Source: Bem (1974).

studies of other age groups, including adolescents. A cross-national study of young people in 30 countries found similar gender role perceptions across the countries, with remarkable consistency (Williams & Best, 1990).

The items in the scale show a clear pattern. In general terms, femininity is associated with being nurturing (sympathetic, compassionate, gentle, etc.) and compliant (yielding, soft-spoken, childlike, etc.). In contrast, masculinity is associated with being independent (self-reliant, self-sufficient, individualistic, etc.) and aggressive (assertive, forceful, dominant, etc.). This difference in traits associated with each gender role has been described by scholars as a contrast between the **expressive traits** ascribed to females and the **instrumental traits** ascribed to males (Lips, 1993). An emphasis on emotions and relationships is reflected in the expressive traits at the center of the female gender role (DeLisi & Soundranayagam, 1990). In contrast, an emphasis on action and accomplishment is reflected in the instrumental traits at the center of the male gender role.

Another reflection of what adolescents view as masculine or feminine is in their gender ideals, that is, their views of what their ideal man or woman would be like. Psychologist Judith Gibbons has done a cross-cultural study of adolescents' gender ideals indicating that adolescents in many different parts of the world have similar views of these ideals. Gibbons and her colleagues (Gibbons & Stiles, 1997; Stiles, Gibbons, & Schnellman, 1990) have surveyed over 12,000 adolescents aged 11 to 19 in 19 countries around the world, including countries in Europe, Central America, Asia, and Africa. In their survey, adolescents rate the importance of 10 qualities as characteristics of the ideal man or woman.

In nearly all the countries, the most important and least important qualities for the ideal man and the ideal woman were not gender specific after all. The most important quality was being "kind and honest." In contrast, having a lot of money and being popular were rated low as ideal qualities, for both the ideal man and the ideal woman. However, some differences were seen in male and female gender ideals. In all countries it was considered more important for the ideal man to have a good job than for the ideal woman to have one. Also, in nearly all countries it was viewed as more important for the ideal woman to be good looking than for the ideal man to be.

Generally, adolescent boys and girls had similar views of the ideal man and the ideal woman, but there were some differences. In all countries, girls were more likely than boys to think it was important for the ideal man to like children. Girls were also more likely to think it was important for the ideal woman to have a good job. In contrast, boys were more likely than girls to think it was important for the ideal woman to be good looking. Both the similarities and differences between adolescent girls' and boys' views of gender ideals are paralleled in cross-cultural findings of adults' gender ideals (Buss, 1989, 1995).

But must we think of people as being either masculine *or* feminine? If an adolescent girl possesses "feminine" traits, does that mean that she must be low on "masculine" traits, and vice versa for boys? Some scholars have argued that the healthiest human personalities contain both masculine and feminine traits. **Androgyny** is the term for the combination of masculine and feminine traits in one person.

The idea of androgyny first became popular in the 1970s (e.g., Bem, 1977; Spence & Helmreich, 1978). The **women's movement** of the 1960s (see Historical Focus box) had led many people in the West to reconsider ideas about male and female roles, and one outcome of this thinking was that it might be best to transcend the traditional opposition of masculine and feminine traits and instead promote the development of the best of each. In this view, there is no reason why a man could not be both independent ("masculine") and nurturing ("feminine"), or why a woman could not be both compassionate ("feminine") and ambitious ("masculine"). Androgynous persons would rate themselves highly on traits from both the "feminine" column and the "masculine" column in Table 5.2.

Advocates of androgyny have argued that being androgynous is better than being either masculine or feminine because an androgynous person has a greater repertoire of traits to draw on in their daily lives (Bem, 1977). In a given situation, it might be better on some occasions to be gentle ("feminine") and on other occasions to be assertive ("masculine"). More generally, it might be better to be ambitious ("masculine") at work and affectionate ("feminine") at home. Advocates of androgyny point to research evidence that androgynous children are more flexible and creative than other children (Hemmer & Klieber, 1981), and that androgynous women are better at saying "no" to unreasonable requests (Kelly et al., 1981). In contrast, highly feminine women have been found to be higher in anxiety and lower in self-esteem (Bem, 1975).

But what about adolescents? Is androgyny best for them? Here the answer is more complex. In general, research evidence indicates that in adolescence, an-

PLATONIC FORMS IN THE LATE 20TH CENTURY

LESSON 6: *The Wonderful Man*, IDEAL VS REAL

IDEAL (WHAT YOU WANT)

REAL (WHAT YOU'RE LUCKY TO GET)

♥ INTELLECTUAL — READS "INTERESTING ARTICLES" IN PLAYBOY
♥ ARTISTIC — OFTEN WEARS MATCHING SOCKS
♥ CONSIDERATE — SPLATTERS JUST A BIT; ONLY LEAVES SEAT UP 50% OF THE TIME
♥ INTERESTED IN YOUR MIND — SOMETIMES LOOKS UP FROM YOUR CHEST
♥ FAITHFUL — ONLY LOOKS AT OTHER BABES IN YOUR ABSENCE
♥ HOPELESSLY ROMANTIC — ABLE TO DISTINGUISH BETWEEN CACTUS & ROSE
♥ CLASSY — KEEPS PLAYBOYS HIDDEN
♥ SENSITIVE — NOTICES WHEN YOU CRY
♥ COMMUNICATES WELL — ANSWERS PHONE SOMETIMES
♥ CROSS-CULTURAL — SWEARS IN SPANISH
♥ PROGRESSIVE — KNOWS DIFFERENCE BETWEEN "WOMAN" & "GIRL"
♥ GREAT LOVER — SEX LASTS LONGER THAN CIGARETTE
♥ CLEAN — ONLY HAS HERPES AND IT'S "UNDER CONTROL"
♥ ATHLETIC — GETS HIS OWN SECONDS
♥ LOVES KIDS & PETS — HAD SNAKE HE FED LIVE THINGS TO
♥ GOOD TASTE IN MUSIC — HAS ONE GOOD DYLAN TAPE THAT A FRIEND GAVE HIM

Jennifer Berne ©1989

cultural gender expectations. It is revealing that not only self-image but also peer acceptance is highest in adolescence among androgynous girls and masculine boys (Massad, 1981). In both respects, adolescents' perceptions reflect cultural beliefs.

These patterns also may indicate that for American boys, as for their counterparts in traditional cultures, manhood is a status that is more insecure and fraught with potential failure than womanhood is for girls, so that any mixing of masculine and feminine traits in their personalities is viewed as undesirable and threatening, by themselves and others. Some scholars have also argued that, despite the changes inspired by the women's movement, males continue to have higher status in American society than females. Consequently, for a girl to act more "like a boy" means that her self-image and status among peers improves because she associates herself with the higher-status group—males—whereas for a boy to act more "like a girl" means that his self-image and peer status declines because he is associating himself with the lower-status group—females (Unger & Crawford, 1996).

Since the 1970s, androgyny has fallen out of favor among scholars. The main criticism is that the concepts of masculinity, femininity, and androgyny are usually portrayed as characteristics of the person, rather than as a reflection of the gender socialization of the culture they live in. In the view of some scholars, this has drawn attention away from the ways that Western societies continue to be **sexist** and **patriarchal**, meaning that males dominate and that women are often discriminated against. Sandra Bem (1993), one of the scholars best known for promoting androgyny, has stated that "By focusing on the person rather than the patriarchy, androgyny provides no conceptual or political analysis of gender inequality; in fact, it diverts attention away from such analysis" (p. 124). Nevertheless, Bem and others continue to believe that androgyny is valuable as an ideal:

At a certain historical moment for feminist theorists, and even today for many people confused about how to behave as a man or a woman, androgyny provides both a vision of utopia and a model of mental health that does not require the individual to banish from the self whatever

drogyny is more likely to be related to a positive self-image for girls than for boys. Androgynous girls generally have a more favorable self-image than girls who are either highly feminine or highly masculine, but highly masculine boys have more favorable self-images than boys who are feminine or androgynous (Markstrom-Adams, 1989; Orr & Ben-Eliahu, 1993).

Why would this be the case? Probably because adolescents' views of themselves are a reflection of how they measure up to cultural expectations. Due in large part to the women's movement, people in the West have become more favorable toward females who are androgynous. It is regarded more favorably now than it was 40 years ago for females to be ambitious, independent, athletic, and other "masculine" traits. However, males are still expected to avoid being soft-spoken, tender, and other "feminine" traits. Adolescents view themselves, and others, in terms of how they fit these

HISTORICAL FOCUS
The Women's Movement of the 1960s

The women's movement, seeking equality of rights and opportunities for women, has a long history in the United States, dating back over a century to the time when women first organized in an effort to gain the right to vote. One especially important period in the history of the women's movement was the 1960s. The 1960s were a time of dramatic social changes in many ways—the civil rights movement, the War on Poverty, and the sexual revolution are examples—and the women's movement was one of these changes. The greatly expanded range of opportunities in education and employment that exist for adolescent girls and emerging adult women today in American society are rooted in the changes in gender role attitudes that were inspired by the women's movement in the 1960s.

Here are some of the key events of the women's movement during this period (Linden-Ward & Green, 1993; Weatherford, 1997):

- 1963: After more than 300 years in existence, Harvard University grants its first degrees to women.
- 1964: The passage of the 1964 Civil Rights Act includes a provision banning discrimination on the basis of sex. First inserted by the bill's opponents in the hopes it would kill the entire legislation, this provision becomes the basis of substantial gains in women's legal rights over the following decades.
- 1966: The National Organization for Women (NOW) is founded. NOW remains the leading organization in the women's movement to this day.
- 1968: Feminists picket the Miss America contest in Atlantic City, New Jersey, carrying signs such as "Cattle Parades are Degrading to Human Beings." Outside the auditorium, women dump symbols of their treatment as sexual objects into a "freedom trash can"—bras, high-heeled shoes, curlers, make-up, and magazines such as *Cosmopolitan* and *Playboy*. As the winner is crowned, feminists in the

balcony unfurl a large banner declaring "Women's Liberation." Because the contest was televised, the protests received enormous attention and greatly expanded public attention—positive and negative—to the women's movement.

- 1970: To commemorate the 50th anniversary of the ratification of the 19th Amendment, which allowed women to vote, NOW sponsors a nationwide strike for women's rights. Thousands of women in cities across the country march for equal rights for women.

Issues related to women in emerging adulthood were part of the women's movement in the 1960s, as the example of the protest at the Miss America contest indicates. Also, many of the movement's most energetic and prominent members were young women. One of the most important books of the period was *Sexual Politics*, by Kate Millett (1970/2000), who was a graduate student at the time she wrote it. A critique of the sexism of American society, the book became a widely discussed best-seller and an inspiration to an entire generation of feminists. However, the importance of the women's movement of the 1960s for adolescence and emerging adulthood is not only that young people played a part in it but that young women growing up today have far more opportunities and are far less restricted by gender roles than any generation of Americans before them, due substantially to the changes that began during the 1960s. Sexism is still strong in many ways in American society (Faludi, 1991), but young women growing up today have many opportunities in education, occupations, and leisure that their predecessors could only imagine.

attributes and behaviors the culture may have stereotypically defined as appropriate for his or her sex. To my mind, that revolution in the discourse of the culture was—and is—a worthy political accomplishment. (Bem, 1993, p. 124)

We can say in any case that for adolescents and emerging adults, androgyny remains useful as a way of describing those who do not fit neatly into conventional gender roles and who instead combine "masculine" and "feminine" qualities in their personalities and behavior.

Gender Roles in American Minority Groups

Most of the studies on masculinity, femininity, and androgyny have taken place on mostly White samples of young people, especially college undergraduates (Lips, 1993). However, numerous scholars have written more generally on gender roles in American minority cultures. What kinds of gender roles are presented to young people in these cultures?

For African Americans, some scholars have argued that the female role among African Americans contains a variety of characteristics that reflect the difficult challenges that Black women have faced historically, from the era of slavery to the present. These characteristics include self-reliance, assertiveness, and perseverance (Hooks, 1981; Terrelonge, 1989). Similar strengths are found in Black adolescent girls, who tend to have higher self-esteem and less concern with physical appearance than white girls do (Basow & Rubin, 1999; Vasquez & Fuentes, 1999).

The gender role of Black men also reflects African American history, but in a different way. In American history, Black men have been frequently subjected to insults to their manhood, from their status as property during slavery to being denigrated as "boys" (no matter what their age) in some parts of the United States,

until recently. Even today, economic conditions in many American cities make it difficult for Black men to fill the traditional "provider" aspect of the male role through stable employment (Wilson, 1987, 1996).

As a consequence of these humiliations, according to some scholars, many young Black men adopt extreme characteristics of the male role in order to declare their masculinity in spite of the discrimination they experience (Billson, 1996). These characteristics include physical toughness, risk taking, and aggressiveness (Franklin, 1984). Richard Majors (1989; Majors & Billson, 1992) describes the "Cool Pose" common to young Black men in urban areas of the United States. The "Cool Pose" is a set of language and behavior intended to display strength, toughness, and detachment. This style is demonstrated in creative, sometimes flamboyant performances in a variety of settings, from the street to the basketball court to the classroom. These performances are meant to convey pride and confidence. According to Majors (1989), although this aggressive assertion of masculinity helps young Black men guard their self-esteem and their dignity, it can be damaging to their relationships because it requires a refusal to express emotions or needs that they fear would make them vulnerable.

In recent years, adult Black men in some urban areas have attempted to provide an alternative ideal of manhood for young Black men, an ideal that emphasizes responsibility and diligence rather than aggressiveness (Ferrier, 1996). In Washington, DC, a group called the Alliance of Concerned Black Men focuses on establishing personal relationships with boys in poor neighborhoods. Boys in these neighborhoods typically have no father present—overall, nearly 70% of Black children are born to single mothers—and the Alliance seeks to provide boys with male guidance and positive male role models, as well as job training and placement.

Research has not yet been conducted on how well such groups work, but some individual examples are

Young Black males sometimes adopt the "Cool Pose" as a way of guarding against threats to their manhood.

impressive. One recent article in the *Washington Post* described the experiences of some of the boys in the program. One boy, named Michael, had been involved with gangs, violence, and drug dealing before he became involved with the Alliance. Now, through the assistance of men in the Alliance, he has obtained his high school equivalency degree and he has a job in an information services company—although he admits that he still feels the lure of the excitement of the streets every day.

Among Latinos, gender roles have been highly traditional until recently, much along the lines of the traditional cultures described earlier in this chapter (Almquist, 1989; Garcia, 1991; Vasquez & Fuentes, 1999). The role of women was concentrated on caring for children, taking care of the home, and providing emotional support for the husband. The Catholic Church has been very strong among Latinos historically, and women have been taught to emulate the Virgin Mary by being submissive and self-denying. The role of men, in contrast, has been guided by the ideology of **machismo**, which emphasizes males' dominance over females. Men have been expected to be the undisputed head of the household and to demand respect and obedience from their wives and children. The traditional aspects of manhood have been strong among Latinos—providing for a family, protecting the family from harm, and procreating a large family (Astrachan, 1989).

However, in recent years evidence has emerged that gender expectations among Latinos have begun to change, at least with respect to women's roles. Latina women are now employed at rates similar to Whites,

and a Latina feminist movement has emerged (Espin, 1997; Garcia, 1991). This movement does not reject the traditional emphasis on the importance of the role of wife and mother, but seeks to value these roles while also expanding the roles available to Latinas.

Adolescents and emerging adults who are members of American minority cultures are exposed not only to the gender roles of their own culture but also to the gender roles of the majority culture, through school, media, and friends and peers who may be part of the majority culture. This may make it possible for young people in American minority cultures to form a variety of possible gender concepts based on different blends of the gender roles in their minority culture and the gender roles of the larger society. However, moving toward the gender roles of the majority culture often results in conflict with parents who have more traditional views, especially for girls and especially concerning issues of independence, dating, and sexuality (Fuentes & Vasquez, 1999).

Gender Stereotypes in Emerging Adulthood

Given the differential gender socialization that people in American society experience in childhood and adolescence, it should not be surprising to find that by the time they reach emerging adulthood they have definite, and different, expectations for males and females. Most research on gender expectations in adulthood has been conducted by social psychologists, and because social psychologists often use college undergraduates as their research participants much of this research pertains to emerging adults' views of gender. Social psychologists have especially focused on gender stereotypes. A **stereotype** occurs when people believe others possess certain characteristics simply as a result of being a member of a group. Gender stereotypes, then, attribute certain characteristics to others simply on the basis of whether they are male or female. Gender stereotypes can be viewed as a particular type of gender schema, applied specifically to persons (rather than to clothes, toys, and so on).

One area of particular interest with regard to emerging adulthood is research on college students' gender stereotypes involving work. Generally, this research indicates that college students often evaluate women's work performance less favorably than men's. In one classic study, Goldberg (1968) asked college women to evaluate the quality of several articles supposedly written by professionals in a variety of fields. Some of the articles were in stereotypically female fields such as dietetics, some were in stereotypically male fields such as city planning, and some were in gender-neutral fields. There were two identical versions of each article, one supposedly written by, for example, "John McKay" and the other written by "Joan McKay." The results indicated that the women rated the articles more highly when they thought a man was the author. Even articles on the "female" fields were judged as better when written by a man. Other studies have found similar results with samples of both male and female college students (Cejka & Eagly, 1999; Paludi & Strayer, 1985). Although not all studies have found a tendency for men's work to be evaluated more favorably, when differences are found they tend to favor men (Lips, 1993; Top, 1991).

THINKING CRITICALLY

Do you think your professors evaluate your work without regard to your gender? Does it depend on the subject area?

However, some studies have also found that when a person's behavior violates stereotypical gender expectations this may create a "boomerang effect" that works in their favor (Weber & Crocker, 1983). In one study, college students were presented with photographs supposedly from finalists in two photography contests, one for football and one for tennis (Heilman, Martell, & Simon, 1988). Some students were told the photographs were taken by a female finalist, and some were told they were taken by a male finalist; actually, both groups of students were shown the same photographs. In the football photography contest, photos supposedly taken by females were evaluated more highly than photos supposedly taken by males, whereas in the tennis photography contest no gender-related difference in evaluations was found. Because football (unlike tennis) is strongly associated with the male gender role, the researchers concluded that the females in the football contest were **overevaluated** because they had violated gender role expectations.

Similarly, in a study in which students evaluated two female and two male speakers on a strongly female-specific topic, "sex bias in the counseling of women," the male speakers were evaluated more highly (Gilbert, Lee, & Chiddix, 1981). Again, this indicates that an overevaluation of performance resulted from

defying gender role expectations. These findings show that gender-related evaluations of performance can be complicated, and often depend on the specific characteristics of the person and on the specific area in which the person is being evaluated.

The Persistence of Beliefs About Gender Differences

Although some gender differences exist in adolescence and emerging adulthood with respect to various aspects of development, for the most part the differences are not large. Even when there is a statistically significant difference between males and females, for most characteristics there is nevertheless more similarity than difference between the genders. For example, even if it is true overall that adolescent girls are more affectionate than adolescent boys, there are nevertheless many adolescent boys who are more affectionate than the typical adolescent girl.

Most human characteristics fall into something resembling what is called a "normal distribution" or a bell curve—a small proportion of people rate much higher than most other people, a small proportion rate much lower than most people, but most people fall somewhere in the middle, somewhere around average. Think of height as a concrete example. You may have a friend who is 4 foot 10 inches and another friend who is 6 feet 10 inches, but most of the people you know are probably between five feet and six feet tall.

The point, with regard to gender, is that even when gender differences exist between males and females, the portion of the two bell curves that overlaps is a lot greater than the portion that is distinctive to either gender, for most characteristics. (The same is true among children and adults as well as adolescents.) For example, Figure 5.3 shows the distribution of male and

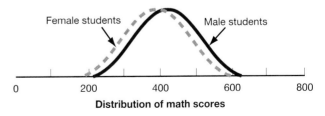

FIGURE 5.3 *Overlap of bell curves.* Although the difference in math performance between males and females in this study was statistically significant, there was a great deal of overlap in performance between the two groups.
Source: Benbow & Stanley (1980).

female adolescents from a famous study that found a significant gender difference in math performance (Benbow & Stanley, 1980). As you can see, the two distributions overlap far more than they differ. When people hear that "adolescent boys do better at math than adolescent girls," they tend to think of the two distributions as mostly or entirely separate, without realizing that the similarity between the genders is actually greater than the difference between them. Indeed, whenever you read about studies reporting gender differences (including in this textbook), keep in mind that the distributions of males and females usually overlap a great deal (Tavris, 1992).

Why, then, do so many enduring stereotypes exist about gender? Why do so many people persist in thinking of the genders as radically different in many ways, as "opposite" sexes?

Two reasons can be offered for the persistence of the perception of gender differences. One reason stems from the development of gender schemas. Gender schemas tend to shape the way we notice, interpret, and remember information according to our expectations about the genders. Once we have formed ideas about how males and females are different, we tend to notice events and information that confirm our expectations and disregard or dismiss anything

---

RESEARCH FOCUS
Meta-Analyses of Gender Differences

Usually, doing research on adolescence and emerging adulthood means collecting data through methods such as questionnaires or ethnographic observation. However, sometimes a scholar will approach a research question by taking data that other scholars have collected in a variety of studies and combining it into one analysis to obtain an overview of studies in an area. **Meta-analysis** is the term for the statistical technique that integrates the data from many studies into one comprehensive statistical analysis. Meta-analyses have been used frequently in research on gender differences (e.g., Friedman, 1989; Maccoby & Jacklin, 1974), including on gender differences in adolescence (e.g., Baker & Perkins-Jones, 1993). Meta-analysis is used more often in research on gender than in most other areas, partly because there are so many studies published on gender differences—over 20,000 in the past 20 years (Myers, 1990). However, it can be used on any topic for which numerous studies exist.

A meta-analysis indicates whether a difference exists between groups (e.g., males and females) and also indicates the size of the difference. The difference between the groups is called the **effect size**, and it is usually represented by the letter d. In a meta-analysis, the effect size is computed for each study by subtracting the mean of one group (e.g.,

females) from the mean of the other group (e.g., males) and then dividing the result by the within-group standard deviation for the two groups combined (Hyde, 1992). The within-group standard deviation is a measure of how much variability exists within each group. The convention in these analyses is that a d of .20 indicates a small effect size, .50 a medium effect size, and .80 a large effect size (Cohen, 1969). First a d is calculated for each study, and then the ds are averaged across all the studies included in the meta-analysis.

Table 5.3 shows the results of a meta-analysis of gender differences on mathematics achievement tests for eighth-grade adolescents in 19 countries. As you can see, for the most part the effect sizes are very small—only three of the studies found an effect size above .20 in favor of males, and only one found an effect size above .20 in favor of females. Overall, the average effect size for the seven countries where boys' performance was significantly better than girls was .18, and the average effect size for the four countries where girls' performance was significantly better than boys was .16. Thus, the meta-analysis provides a useful overview of cross-national gender differences on math performance and shows that, overall, the differences between boys' and girls' math performance in eighth grade is neither large nor consistent.

TABLE 5.3: NATIONAL SEX DIFFERENCES ON EIGHTH-GRADE MATHEMATICS TEST

Country	Mean for boys	Mean for girls	X_M-X_F difference	Effect size
Superior Performance of Boys				
France	17.02	14.18	2.84*	.37
Israel	18.79	17.74	1.05*	.11
Luxembourg	13.34	11.74	1.60*	.25
Netherlands	22.00	20.23	1.77*	.17
New Zealand	14.60	13.51	1.09*	.10
Ontario, Canada	17.72	16.94	.78*	.08
Swaziland	9.29	7.89	1.40*	.21
Equal Performance				
British Columbia	19.55	19.27	.28	.03
England-Wales	15.38	14.92	.46	.04
Hong Kong	16.59	16.09	.50	.05
Japan	23.84	23.80	.04	.004
Nigeria	9.50	9.05	.45	.07
Scotland	16.83	16.68	.15	.01
Sweden	10.70	11.18	−.48	−.06
United States	14.98	15.12	−.14	−.01
Superior Performance of Girls				
Belgium-French	19.44	20.54	−1.10*	−.12
Finland	13.24	14.87	−1.63*	−.17
Hungary	22.36	23.62	−1.26*	−.13
Thailand	12.09	14.16	−2.07*	−.22

*Indicates female and male scores were significantly different according to an F test, $p < .01$. Note effect sizes, which are all in the small range.
Source: Baker & Perkins-Jones (1993).

that does not. In several studies of children and adolescents, for example, boys and girls recalled gender-stereotyped people and activities better than those that were nonstereotyped, and this tendency was strongest for the boys and girls who already possessed the strongest gender stereotypes (Furnham & Singh, 1986; Stangor & Ruble, 1987, 1989). Also, studies of college students have shown that when they are shown males and females performing an equal number of gender-stereotyped and non-gender-stereotyped behaviors, they consistently overestimate the number of gender-

stereotyped behaviors performed (Martin, 1987). These studies illustrate the way our gender schemas draw our attention to examples that confirm our expectations, so that we perceive the behavior of others to be more gender consistent than it actually is.

A second reason for the persistence of our beliefs about gender differences in capabilities is that the social roles of men and women seem to confirm those beliefs. According to **social roles theory**, social roles for males and females enhance or suppress different capabilities (Eagly, 1987). Differential gender socialization leads males and females to develop different skills and attitudes, which leads to different behaviors. The differences in behavior seem to confirm the appropriateness of the different roles.

For example, caring for children is part of the female gender role in most cultures, including the American majority culture. In the American majority culture most girls are given dolls as children, and many are given some responsibility for caring for younger siblings. When they reach early adolescence, girls learn that baby-sitting is one of the options available to them as a way to earn money; boys, in contrast, learn that baby-sitting is something girls do but not boys. When they reach emerging adulthood, women are more likely than men to enter child care as a profession, perhaps including majoring in early childhood education in college. When they have children of their own, young women are also more likely than young men to devote themselves to full-time care of their own children.

Thus, as a consequence of differential gender socialization, and because girls grow up with caring for children as a possible future role but boys do not, girls are more likely to develop skills and attitudes that involve caring for children. As a consequence of developing these skills and attitudes, they are more capable of and more interested in devoting themselves to child care in their personal and professional lives as adolescents and emerging adults. The different behavior of women and men regarding child care confirms cultural beliefs that women are "naturally" more loving and nurturant than men. So, we see males and females doing different things, and we conclude that it must be because they are inherently different (Deaux & Lewis, 1984), overlooking the way their behavior has been shaped by differential gender socialization and by the social roles offered by their culture.

■ ### THINKING CRITICALLY

Consider the overlapping bell curves of math abilities in adolescence. Then use social roles theory to explain why so few women are in fields such as engineering and architecture.

Gender and Globalization

As today's adolescents grow into adulthood, what kind of world will they face in terms of gender roles? In the West, adolescent girls today have opportunities that were unknown to women in previous eras of Western history. Formal prohibitions no longer exist to women becoming doctors, lawyers, professors, engineers, accountants, athletes, or anything else they wish. As we have seen in this chapter, it is not quite that simple. Direct and indirect gender role socialization often steers adolescent girls away from math- and science-oriented careers. Nevertheless, statistics show definite signs of change. The proportion of females in fields such as medicine, business, and law are considerably higher than 20 years ago (Bianchi & Spain, 1996; Dey & Hurtado, 1999) and are remarkable compared with 50 or 100 years ago. Whether similar changes will occur in other male-dominated fields such as engineering and architecture is difficult to predict. However, women tend to earn less money than men even when they are doing similar work, which shows that gender equality has a ways to go.

In countries outside the West, for the most part adolescent girls have much less in the way of educational and occupational opportunities, not only compared with boys in their own countries but compared with girls in the West. In most developing countries adolescent girls are considerably less likely than adolescent boys to go to secondary school (Mensch, Bruce, & Greene, 1998), because adolescents' education requires families to sacrifice the labor of an otherwise potentially productive adolescent (and sometimes families must also pay for the schooling); families tend to be less willing to make this sacrifice for adolescent girls than for adolescent boys.

However, discrimination against girls may change as globalization proceeds and traditional cultures become increasingly industrialized and connected to the global economy. In one study illustrating this process, Williams and Best (1990) surveyed perceptions of gender roles in 14 countries, including industrialized countries as well as developing countries. They used the Sex-Role Ideology Scale (Kalin & Tilby, 1978), which contains 30 items such as "For the good of the family, a wife should have sexual relations with her husband whether she wants to or not," and "Women's work and men's work should not be fundamentally different in nature." The results of their study showed considerable variation among countries in gender role perceptions, with the Netherlands, Germany, and Finland the most egalitarian and India, Pakistan, and Nigeria the least egalitarian (the United States and Canada were right in the middle). Furthermore, the authors analyzed the results in relation to each coun-

In traditional cultures, boys are more likely than girls to be able to attend secondary school.

opportunities for girls. Traditional gender roles are often rooted partly in biological differences that determine the kind of work that men and women can perform in a preindustrial economy. Men's greater size and strength give them advantages in work such as hunting and fishing. Women's biological capacity for childbearing restricts their roles mainly to childbearing and childrearing; when they are unable to control their reproductive lives through contraception, they spend most of their late teens, twenties, and thirties either pregnant or nursing.

As economies become more developed and complex, brain matters more than brawn and men's physical advantage ceases to matter in work that involves analyzing and processing information. Economic development also usually includes increased access to contraception; in turn, access to contraception makes women's adult roles less focused on childbearing and childrearing alone. Because traditional cultures likely will continue to move further in the direction of economic development, their gender roles likely will become more egalitarian as well. And there is evidence that adolescents may lead the way, in studies that find adolescents in developing countries to have less conservative perceptions of gender roles than adults (e.g., Mensch et al., 1998; Yang, 1986).

try's level of economic development and found a strong relationship between economic development and egalitarian perceptions of gender roles.

This suggests that, as traditional cultures proceed toward economic development, they may offer more

Summing Up

In this chapter we have examined theories and research concerning the significance of gender in development during adolescence and emerging adulthood. The information in this chapter provides an introduction to many issues concerning gender that will be explored in more detail in the chapters to come. The main points of the chapter are as follows:

- In traditional cultures, gender roles tend to be sharply divided, and in adolescence, boys' and girls' daily lives are often separate. Girls spend their time with adult women learning skills important for child care and running a household, whereas boys learn the skills necessary for the requirements of the male role: provide, protect, and procreate.

- In earlier periods of American history, adolescent girls were constricted in many ways, but they also benefited from a "protective umbrella" of involvement and concern by adult women. Ideals of manhood have also changed in the course of American

history, from "communal manhood" to "self-made manhood" to the "passionate manhood" that is the current ideal.

- In American society today, boys and girls receive differential gender socialization from birth, and gender-related socialization pressures intensify at adolescence. Research shows that pressures to conform to gender expectations come from the family, peers, and teachers. For girls, the magazines they like best relentlessly emphasize physical appearance.

- The cognitive developmental theory of gender and gender schema theory state that we tend to organize our perceptions of the world according to schemas for male and female, and we categorize a wide range of behavior and objects on this basis.

- Research indicates that there is a widespread tendency across cultures to classify some traits as "feminine" and others as "masculine." Androgyny is the term for combining "feminine" and "masculine" traits within one person. Among adolescents, androgyny tends to be more acceptable for girls than for boys.

- Although research generally finds few substantial differences between males and females in most respects, perceptions of gender differences persist, partly because gender schemas are resistant to change once established and partly because males' and females' social roles seem to confirm stereotypes about gender differences in some respects.

- Views of gender have changed substantially in the West in the past century and are likely to change in developing countries in the future as a result of economic development and globalization.

Theory and research have established quite well how gender socialization takes place and have identified the specific influences in adolescence that promote conformity to gender expectations. The evidence portrays quite vividly the costs that gender expectations exact from adolescents and emerging adults. For girls, the emphasis on physical appearance in adolescence is a frequent source of anxiety and distress. Also, girls are sometimes dissuaded from pursuing certain high-status, high-paying educational and occupational paths because they learn to regard these paths as unfeminine and incompatible with being female; as emerging adults, their work may be regarded less favorably simply because they are female. In traditional cultures, girls are often excluded even from opportunities to attend secondary school.

Adolescent boys face different sorts of gender-based restrictions and obstacles, no less daunting. Boys in traditional cultures have to achieve manhood by developing the required skills for providing, protecting, and procreating. The price of failing to meet these requirements is humiliation and rejection. In the West, gender socialization pressures on boys are less formal but nevertheless formidable. Whatever their personal inclinations, adolescent boys must learn to use verbal and physical aggressiveness to defend themselves against insults to their manhood from other boys. Adolescent boys who cross the gender divide and display "feminine" traits such as sensitivity to the feelings of others risk ridicule and rejection, like their counterparts in traditional cultures.

You might wonder, given the negatives associated with gender socialization in adolescence and emerging adulthood, and given the limitations that gender roles place on the development of young people's potentials, why gender socialization is so highly emphasized and conformity to gender roles is so highly valued across virtually all cultures and across history as well. Perhaps the answer lies in the ways that gender roles provide us with schemas, with frameworks for understanding how the world works. For adolescents and emerging adults, because these periods of life are the time when sexual maturity is reached, they are eager for information about what their potential mates may find attractive. Gender schemas and gender roles provide them with that information.

At this point, however, we know relatively little about how young people themselves perceive the gender socialization process. Future studies may investigate this question. It may be especially interesting to investigate this question with emerging adults. We have discussed emerging adulthood as a period when experimentation and exploration are common and when critical-thinking skills are more developed than in adolescence. Does this mean that some emerging adults may begin to question the gender expectations of their culture? Do emerging adults feel less constricted by gender roles and more comfortable with androgyny? Or is this true of only some emerging adults, in some peer groups, in some cultures?

Key Terms

sex	passionate manhood	self-socialization	patriarchal
gender	gender intensification	gender schema theory	machismo
genital mutilation	hypothesis	schema	stereotype
provide	differential gender	expressive traits	overevaluated
protect	socialization	instrumental traits	meta-analysis
procreate	cognitive developmental	androgyny	effect size
communal manhood	theory of gender	women's movement	social roles theory
self-made manhood	gender identity	sexist	

For Further Reading

Brumberg, J. J. (1997). *The body project: An intimate history of American girls.* New York: Random House. A fascinating examination of gender role expectations for girls in the United States over the past 200 years.

Gilmore, D. (1990). *Manhood in the making: Cultural concepts of masculinity.* New Haven: Yale University Press. Gilmore's superb account of the gender expectations for adolescent boys in a variety of traditional, nonindustrialized cultures.

Tavris, C. (1992). *The mismeasure of woman: Why women are not the better sex, the inferior sex, or the opposite sex.* New York: Simon and Schuster. A highly readable, skeptical, and insightful summary of social science research on gender differences.

Books Applying Research Knowledge

Pipher, M. (1994). *Reviving Ophelia: Saving the selves of adolescent girls.* New York: Ballantine. A best-selling book on the perils facing adolescent girls in American society, based on Pipher' work as a clinical psychologist. Her portrayal is extreme at times; she states that "all girls feel pain and confusion. . . . Like Ophelia, all are in danger of drowning" (p. 73). Nevertheless, she is a perceptive and eloquent critic of the forces in American society that undermine the selves of adolescent girls.

Pollack, W. (1998). *Real boys: Rescuing our sons from the myths of boyhood.* New York: Henry Holt. Pollack's book was intended as the boys' counterpart to Pipher's *Reviving Ophelia,* and his book shares the same liabilities and virtues as Pipher's book. Like Pipher, his portrayal is extreme, with all adolescent boys depicted as troubled or potentially troubled, but like Pipher his book contains much in the way of insights and good advice for helping adolescents.

The Catcher in the Rye, *by J. D. Salinger (1951/1964), is probably the best-known novel of adolescence. It consists entirely of one long self-reflective monologue by the main character, Holden Caulfield, as he tries to figure out himself and his place in the world. Here are a few examples:*

"I act quite young for my age sometimes. . . . I'm seventeen now, and sometimes I act like I'm about thirteen. . . . Sometimes I act a lot older than I am—I really do—but people never notice." (p. 9)

"I'm the most terrific liar you ever saw in your life. It's awful. If I'm on my way to the store to buy a magazine, and somebody asks me where I'm going, I'm liable to say I'm going to the opera. It's terrible." (p. 16)

"I thought probably I'd get pneumonia and die. I started picturing millions of jerks coming to my funeral and all. . . . Then I thought about the whole bunch of them sticking me in a goddam cemetery and all, with my name on this tombstone and all. Surrounded by dead guys. Boy, when you're dead, they really fix you up. I hope to hell when I do die somebody has sense enough to just dump me in the river or something. Anything except sticking me in the goddam cemetery. People coming and

putting a bunch of flowers on your stomach on Sunday, and all that crap. Who wants flowers when you're dead? Nobody." (pp. 154–155)

"Anyway, I keep picturing all these little kids playing some game in this big field of rye and all. Thousands of little kids, and nobody's around—nobody big, I mean—except me. And I'm standing on the edge of some crazy cliff. What I have to do, I have to catch everybody if they start to go over the cliff—I mean if they're running and they don't look where they're going I have to come out from somewhere and catch them. That's all I'd do all day. I'd just be the catcher in the rye and all. I know it's crazy, but that's the only thing I'd really like to be. I know it's crazy." (p. 173)

Holden Caulfield is not a typical adolescent. It is his atypical sensitivity and wit that makes him such a compelling character in Catcher in the Rye. *However, he provides a good example of how issues of the self come to the forefront of development in adolescence. He engages in* **self-reflection** *about his maturity (or lack of it). He evaluates himself, sometimes negatively ("I'm a terrific liar . . ."). He has moments of elation, but more moments of loneliness and sadness, in which he broods about death and the cruelties of life. He tries to work out issues of identity, of who he is and what he wants out of life, concluding—at least for now—that the only future that appeals to him is the imaginary one of being the "catcher in the rye," the guardian of playing children.*

The issues Holden confronts in his monologue are the kinds of issues we will address in this chapter on the self. As we saw in Chapter 3, on cognitive development, moving into adolescence results in new capacities for self-reflection. Adolescents can think about themselves in a way that younger children cannot. The ability for abstract thinking that develops in adolescence includes asking abstract questions about one's self, such as "What kind of person am I? What are my essential characteristics? What am I good at? How do other people perceive me? What kind of life am I likely to have in the future?" Younger children can ask these

questions, too, but only in a rudimentary way. With adolescents' growing cognitive capacities, they can now ask these questions of themselves more clearly, and they can come up with answers that are more complex and more insightful.

This enhanced cognitive capacity for self-reflection has a variety of consequences. It means that adolescents change in their *self-conceptions*, that is, in their answers to the question "What kind of person am I?" It means that adolescents change in their *self-esteem*, that is, in their capacity for evaluating their fundamental worth as a person. It means that adolescents change in their *emotional understanding*, as they become more aware of their own emotions, and as their enhanced understanding of themselves and others affects their daily emotional lives. It also means that adolescents change in their *identities*, that is, in their perceptions of their capacities and characteristics and how these fit into the opportunities available to them in their society. All of these changes continue through emerging adulthood, but identity issues are especially central to emerging adulthood, even more than in adolescence in many respects.

We will discuss each of these aspects of the self in this chapter, and end with a look at young people's experiences and states of mind when they are by themselves. First, however, we consider the cultural approach to concepts of the self. Although self-reflection increases in adolescence as a part of normal cognitive development, the culture young people live in has profound effects on how they experience this change.

Culture and the Self

The general distinction introduced in Chapter 4, between individualistic and collectivistic cultures, between broad socialization values and narrow socialization values, comes into play in considerations of the self, and perhaps especially on this topic. In discussing cultural differences in conceptions of the self, scholars typically distinguish between the independent self promoted by individualistic cultures and the interdependent self promoted by collectivistic cultures (Markus & Kitayama, 1991; Shweder et al., 1998).

Cultures that promote an independent, individualistic self also promote and encourage reflection about the self. In such cultures it is seen as a good thing to think about yourself, to consider who you are as an independent person, and to think highly of yourself (within certain limits, of course—no culture values selfishness or egocentrism). Americans are especially known for their individualism and their focus on self-oriented issues. It was an American who first invented the term *self-esteem* (William James, in the late 19th century), and the United States continues to be known to the rest of the world as a place where the independent self is valued and promoted (Triandis, 1995).

However, not all cultures look at the self in this way and value the self to the same extent. In collectivistic cultures, characterized by narrow socialization, an interdependent conception of the self prevails. In these cultures, the interests of the group—the family, the kinship group, the ethnic group, the nation, the religious institution—are supposed to come first, before the needs of the individual. This means that it is not necessarily a good thing, in these cultures, to think highly of yourself. People who think highly of themselves, who possess a high level of self-esteem, threaten the harmony of the group because they may be inclined to pursue their personal interests regardless of the interests of the groups to which they belong.

Thus, children and adolescents in these cultures are socialized to mute their self-esteem and to learn to consider the interests and needs of others at least as important as the interests and needs of themselves (Whiting & Edwards, 1988). By adolescence, this means that the "self" is thought of not so much as a separate, independent being, essentially apart from others (Schlegel & Barry, 1991), but as *defined by* relationships with others, to a large extent. This is what it means for the self to be interdependent rather than independent (Markus & Kitayama, 1991). In the perspective of these cultures, the self cannot be understood apart from social roles and obligations.

We will learn in more detail about different ways of thinking about the self as we move along in this chapter. Keep in mind, however, that cultures vary in the way their members are socialized to think about the self.

THINKING CRITICALLY

Based on what you have learned so far in this book, what would you say are the economic reasons preindustrial cultures would promote an interdependent self?

Self-Conceptions

Adolescents think about themselves differently than younger children do, in a variety of respects. The changes in self-understanding that occur in adolescence have their foundation in the more general changes in cognitive functioning discussed in Chapter 3. Specifically, adolescent self-conceptions, like adolescent cognitive development overall, become more *abstract* and more *complex.*

More Abstract

> *"The hardest thing is coming to grips with who you are, accepting the fact that you're not perfect—but then doing things anyway. Even if you are really good at something or a really fine person, you also know that there's so much you aren't. You always know all the things you don't know and all the things you can't do. And however much you can fool the rest of the world, you always know how much bullshit a lot of it is."*
>
> —*Nan, age 17 (in Bell, 1998, p. 78)*

Harter (1999) describes the development of self-conceptions from childhood through adolescence. According to Harter (1999), with age children describe themselves less in concrete terms ("I have a dog named Buster and a sister named Carrie.") and more in terms of their traits ("I do well in school, but I'm not so good at sports."). In adolescence, self-conceptions become still more trait-focused, and the traits become more abstract, as they describe themselves in terms of intangible personality characteristics (Harter, 1990a, 1999). For example, one 15-year-old girl in a study on self-conceptions described herself as follows:

"What am I like as a person? Complicated! I'm sensitive, friendly, outgoing, popular, and tolerant, though I can also be shy, self-conscious, even obnoxious. . . . I'm a pretty cheerful person, especially with my friends. . . . At home I'm more likely to be anxious around my parents." (Harter, 1990b, p. 352)

Notice the use of all the abstractions. "Sensitive." "Outgoing." "Cheerful." "Anxious." Adolescents' capacity for abstraction makes these kinds of descriptions possible.

One aspect of this capacity for abstraction in adolescents' self-conceptions is that they can distinguish between an **actual self** and **possible selves** (Markus & Nurius, 1986; Martin, 1997; Oyserman & Markus,

1990). Scholars distinguish two kinds of possible selves, an ideal self and a feared self (Martin, 1997; Oyserman & Markus, 1990). The **ideal self** is the person the adolescent would like to be (for example, an adolescent may have an ideal of becoming highly popular with peers or highly successful in athletics or music). The **feared self** is the person the adolescent imagines it is possible to become but dreads becoming (for example, an adolescent might fear becoming an alcoholic, or fear becoming like a disgraced relative or friend). Both kinds of possible selves require adolescents to think abstractly. That is, possible selves exist only as abstractions, as *ideas* in the adolescent's mind.

The capacity for thinking about an actual, an ideal, and a feared self is a cognitive achievement, but this capacity may be troubling in some respects. If you can imagine an ideal self, you can also become aware of the degree of discrepancy between your actual self and your ideal self, between what you are and what you wish you were. If the discrepancy is large enough, it can result in feelings of failure, inadequacy, and depression. Thus, depression is very rare prior to adolescence, but rates of depressed mood rise in early adolescence and are higher in midadolescence than at any other point in the entire life span (Petersen et al., 1993). Similarly, one study found that the discrepancy between the actual and the ideal self is greater in midadolescence than in either early or late adolescence (Strachen & Jones, 1982).

However, awareness of actual and possible selves can have more favorable consequences as well. This awareness provides some adolescents with a motivation to strive toward their ideal self and avoid becoming the feared self (Cota-Robles, Neiss, & Hunt, 2000; Markus & Nurius, 1986; Oyserman & Markus, 1990). Most scholars who have studied this topic see it as healthiest for adolescents to possess both an ideal self and a feared self. One study that compared delinquent adolescents to other adolescents found that the nondelinquent adolescents tended to have this balance between an ideal self and a feared self. In contrast, the delinquent adolescents possessed a feared self but were less likely than other adolescents to have a clear conception of an ideal self to strive for (Oyserman & Markus, 1990).

More Complex

A second aspect of adolescent self-understanding is that it becomes more complex. Again, this is based on a more general cognitive attainment, the formal operational ability to perceive multiple aspects of a situation or idea. Scholars have found that adolescents' self-conceptions become more complex especially from early adolescence to middle adolescence. One scholar who has done extensive work on self-conceptions in childhood and adolescence, Susan Harter, conducted a study in which she asked adolescents in 7th, 9th, and 11th grades to describe themselves (Harter, 1986). The results showed that the extent to which adolescents describe themselves in contradictory ways (e.g., shy and fun-loving) increased sharply from 7th to 9th grade and then declined slightly in 11th grade.

Harter and her colleagues have found that recognizing these contradictions in their personalities and behavior can be confusing to adolescents, as they try to sort out "the real me" from these different aspects of themselves that appear in different situations (Harter, 1999; Harter, Bresnick, Bouchey, & Whitesell, 1997). However, adolescents' contradictory descriptions do not necessarily mean that they are confused about which of the two contradictory descriptions apply to their actual selves. To some extent, the contradictions indicate that adolescents, more than younger children, recognize that their feelings and their behavior can vary from day to day and from situation to situation (Harter, 1990a). Rather than simply saying "I'm shy" as a younger child might, an adolescent might say "I'm shy when I'm around people I don't really know, but when I'm around my friends I can be kind of wild and crazy."

A related aspect of the increasing complexity of self-conceptions in adolescence is that adolescents become aware of times when they are exhibiting a **false self**, a self that they present to others while realizing that it does not represent what they are actually thinking and feeling (Harter, 1990a; Harter, Marold, Whitesell, & Cobbs, 1996; Harter et al., 1997). With whom would you think adolescents would be most likely to exhibit their false selves—friends, parents, or dates? Harter's research indicates that adolescents are most likely to put on their false selves with dating partners, and least likely with their close friends, with parents in between. Most adolescents in Harter's research indicate that they sometimes dislike putting on a false self, but many also say that some degree of false self behavior is acceptable, and even desirable, to impress someone or to conceal some aspect of the self they do not want others to see.

Adolescents are most likely to show a false self to dating partners.

THINKING CRITICALLY

Why do you think a false self is most likely to be shown to dating partners? Would the false self be gradually discarded as the dating partner becomes a boyfriend or girlfriend, or not?

Self-Esteem

Self-esteem is a person's overall sense of worth and well-being. **Self-image, self-concept,** and **self-perception** are closely related terms, referring to the way a person views and evaluates himself or herself. A great deal has been written and discussed about self-esteem in the past 40 years in American society, especially concerning adolescents. In the 1960s, self-esteem enhancement programs for young people became popular, based on the idea that making children and adolescents "feel better" about themselves would have a variety of positive effects on other aspects of functioning, such as school achievement and relationships with peers (DuBois & Tevendale, 1999; Harter, 1990b). In the 1980s, particular concern developed about self-esteem among girls and about evidence

showing that girls often experience a drop in self-esteem as they enter adolescence (American Association of University Women, 1993; Gilligan, Lyons, & Hanmer, 1990).

All this concern about self-esteem is a distinctly American phenomenon. Even among Western countries, Americans value high self-esteem to a far greater extent than people in other Western countries (Triandis, 1995), and the gap between Americans and non-Western countries in this respect is even greater (Whiting & Edwards, 1988). The American concern with self-esteem is part of American individualism (Bellah et al., 1985).

The cultural focus on self-esteem in American society has led to a considerable amount of research on adolescent self-esteem by scholars in recent decades. This research has shed light on a number of issues concerning self-esteem in adolescence, including changes in self-esteem from preadolescence through adolescence, different aspects of self-esteem, self-esteem and physical appearance, and influences on self-esteem.

Self-Esteem From Preadolescence Through Adolescence

Several longitudinal studies of self-esteem have followed samples from preadolescence through adolescence, and these studies generally find that self-esteem declines in early adolescence, then rises through late adolescence and emerging adulthood (Block & Robins, 1993; O'Malley & Bachman, 1983; Savin-Williams & Demo, 1984; Zimmerman, Copeland, Shope, & Dielman, 1997). There are a number of developmental reasons why self-esteem might follow this pattern. The "imaginary audience" that we have discussed as part of adolescents' cognitive development can make them self-conscious in a way that decreases their self-esteem when they first experience it in early adolescence (Elkind, 1967; 1985). That is, as adolescents develop the capacity to imagine that others are especially conscious of how they look and what they say and how they act, they may suspect or fear that others are judging them harshly.

And they may be right. Adolescents in Western cultures tend to be strongly peer-oriented and to value the opinion of their peers highly, especially on day-to-day issues such as how they are dressed and what they say in social situations (Berndt, 1996). But their peers have developed new cognitive capacities for sarcasm and ridicule, which tend to be dispensed freely toward any peer who seems odd or awkward or uncool (Eder, 1995). So, the combination of greater peer-orientation, greater self-consciousness about evaluations by peers,

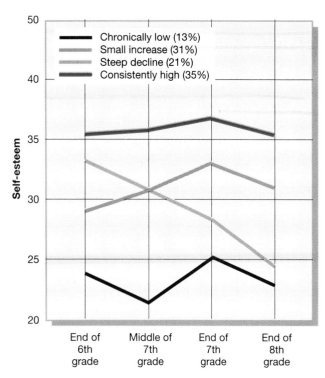

Self-esteem (y-axis)

- Chronically low (13%)
- Small increase (31%)
- Steep decline (21%)
- Consistently high (35%)

End of 6th grade — Middle of 7th grade — End of 7th grade — End of 8th grade

FIGURE 6.1 *Self-esteem in early adolescence.* Self-esteem can go in a variety of different directions in early adolescence.
Source: Hirsch & Dubois (1991).

and peers' potentially harsh remarks contributes to declines in self-esteem at adolescence.

On the other hand, the degree of decline in adolescents' self-esteem should not be exaggerated. Although a substantial proportion of adolescents experience a decline in self-esteem during adolescence, many others do not. One study followed a sample from 6th grade through 8th grade, and showed that different children have different patterns of change in self-esteem as they move into adolescence (Hirsch & DuBois, 1991). Figure 6.1 shows the patterns. Only a small proportion of adolescents (about one-fifth) followed a pattern of steep decline. The majority of adolescents were either consistently high or increased in self-esteem during the period of the study. Other studies have reported similar patterns (Deihl, Vicary, & Deike, 1997; Pahl, Greene, & Way, 2000; Zimmerman et al., 1997).

Different Aspects of Self-Esteem

As scholars have studied self-esteem, they have concluded that self-esteem has different aspects, in addition to overall self-esteem. Morris Rosenberg, the scholar who developed the widely used Rosenberg Self-

Esteem Scale, distinguished between baseline self-esteem and barometric self-esteem (Rosenberg, 1986). **Baseline self-esteem** is the stable, enduring sense of worth and well-being a person has. Persons with high baseline self-esteem might have an occasional bad day in which they feel incompetent or self-critical, but still have high baseline self-esteem because most days they evaluate themselves positively. In contrast, persons with low baseline self-esteem might continue to have a poor opinion of themselves even though they have days when things go right for them.

Barometric self-esteem is the fluctuating sense of worth and well-being people have as they respond to different thoughts, experiences, and interactions in the course of a day. According to Rosenberg, early adolescence is a time when variations in barometric self-esteem are especially intense (Rosenberg, 1986). An adolescent might have a disagreement with a parent over breakfast and feel miserable, then go to school and have some fun with friends before class and feel good, then get back a test in biology with a poor grade and feel miserable again, then get a smile from an attractive potential love interest and feel great—all in just a few hours. The Experience Sampling Method (ESM) studies, in which adolescents carry beepers and record their moods and activities when beeped, confirm Rosenberg's insights by showing just this kind of rapid fluctuation of moods among adolescents in a typical day (Larson & Richards, 1994). ESM studies find that adults and preadolescents experience changes in their moods as well, but not with the same frequency or intensity as adolescents. Other studies confirm that adolescents' self-esteem varies depending on whom they are with (Harter, Waters, & Whitesell, 1998).

Further aspects of adolescent self-esteem have been investigated by Susan Harter (1988, 1989, 1990a, 1990b, 1997, 1999). Her *Self-Perception Profile for Adolescents* distinguishes the following eight domains of adolescent self-image:

- Scholastic competence
- Social acceptance
- Athletic competence
- Physical appearance
- Job competence
- Romantic appeal
- Behavioral conduct
- Close friendship

RESEARCH FOCUS
Harter's Self-Perception Profile for Adolescents

The most widely used measure of self-image in adolescence is Susan Harter's (1988, 1999) *Self-Perception Profile for Adolescents*. The scale consists of nine subscales of five items each, for a total of 45 items. Eight of the subscales assess specific domains of self-image, and the ninth subscale assesses overall ("global") self-worth. The format of the items is to present two statements about "teenagers"; the adolescent then selects which of the statements most applies to him or her, and then whether the statement is "sort of true for me" or "really true for me." Examples of items from each subscale are shown in Table 6.1.

Notice that for some items, the response that signifies high self-esteem comes first (before the

TABLE 6.1: SAMPLE ITEMS FROM THE SELF-PERCEPTION PROFILE FOR ADOLESCENTS

Scholastic Competence

Some teenagers have trouble figuring out the answers in school BUT Other teenagers almost always can figure out the answers.

Social Acceptance

Some teenagers are popular with others their age BUT Other teenagers are not very popular.

Athletic Competence

Some teenagers do not feel that they are very athletic BUT Other teenagers feel that they are very athletic.

Physical Appearance

Some teenagers think that they are good looking BUT Other teenagers think that they are not very good looking.

Job Competence

Some teenagers feel that they are ready to do well at a part-time job BUT Other teenagers feel that they are not quite ready to handle a part-time job.

Romantic Appeal

Some teenagers feel that other people their age will be romantically attracted to them BUT Other teenagers worry about whether people their age will be attracted to them.

Behavioral Conduct

Some teenagers often get in trouble for the things they do BUT Other teenagers usually don't do things that get them in trouble.

Close Friendship

Some teenagers are able to make really close friends BUT Other teenagers find it hard to make really close friends.

Global Self-Worth

Some teenagers are happy with themselves most of the time BUT Other teenagers are often not happy with themselves.

Source: Harter (1988).

"BUT"), whereas for other items the high self-esteem response comes second (after the "BUT"). The reason for this variation is to avoid a **response bias**, which is the tendency to choose the same response for all items. If the high self-esteem response comes first for all items, after a few items an adolescent may start simply checking the first box without reading the item closely. Altering the arrangement of the items helps to avoid a response bias.

Reliability and validity are two qualities sought in any questionnaire. To establish the reliability of the subscales, Harter calculated the **internal consistency** of each one. Internal consistency is a number that indicates the extent to which the different items in a scale or subscale are answered in a similar way. Harter's subscales showed high internal consistency, which means that adolescents who reported a positive self-perception on one item of a subscale also tended to report a positive self-perception on the other items of the subscale, and adolescents who re-

ported a negative self-perception on one item of a subscale also tended to report a negative self-perception on the other items.

What about the validity of the scale? One way to establish validity is to see whether findings using the measure are consistent with findings using other methods. Research using the Harter scale has found that girls rate themselves lower than boys on physical appearance and global self-worth, but higher than boys on close friendships (Harter, 1988, 1999). Because these findings are consistent with findings from other studies, the findings appear to support the validity of the Harter scale. However, Harter's research has taken place mostly on adolescents in the American middle class. The measure may not be as valid for adolescents in other cultures, especially in Eastern cultures such as Japan and China, in which it is socially disapproved to evaluate yourself positively (Shweder et al., 1998).

Examples of items from each subscale are provided in the Research Focus box, along with more information about the scale. In addition to the eight subscales on specific domains of self-esteem, Harter's scale also contains a subscale for global (overall) self-esteem.

Harter's research indicates that adolescents do not need to have a positive self-image in all domains to have high global self-esteem. Each domain of self-image influences global self-esteem only to the extent that the adolescent views that domain as important. For example, some adolescents may view themselves as having low athletic competence, but that would only influence their global self-esteem if it was important to them to be good at athletics. Nevertheless, some domains of self-esteem are more important than others to most adolescents, as we will see in the next section.

Self-Esteem and Physical Appearance

Which of Harter's eight aspects of self-image would you expect to be most important in adolescence? Research by Harter and others has found that physical appearance is most strongly related to global self-esteem, followed by social acceptance from peers (DuBois et al., 1996; Harter, 1988, 1989, 1990b, 1999; Wright, 1989). Adolescent girls are more likely than boys to emphasize physical appearance as a basis for self-esteem. This gender difference largely explains the gender difference in self-esteem that occurs at adolescence. Girls have a more

negative body image than boys in adolescence, and are more critical of their physical appearance. They are less satisfied with the shape of their bodies than boys are, and the majority of them believe they weigh too much and have attempted to diet (Irwin, Igra, Eyre, & Millstein, 1997; Simmons & Blyth, 1987). Because girls tend to evaluate their physical appearance negatively, and because physical appearance is at the heart of their self-esteem, girls' self-esteem tends to be lower than boys during adolescence (DuBois et al., 1996).

The prominence of physical appearance as a source of self-esteem also helps explain why girls' self-esteem is especially likely to decline as they enter early adolescence. As we have seen in Chapter 2, girls in American society are often highly ambivalent about the changes that take place in their physical appearance when they reach puberty. Reaching puberty means becoming more womanly, which is good, but becoming more womanly means gaining weight in certain places, which—in the American majority culture, at least—is not good. Because the physical ideal for American females is so thin, reaching an age where nature promotes rounder body development makes it difficult for adolescent girls to feel good about themselves (Graber et al., 1994; Keel et al., 1997; Rosenblum & Lewis, 1999). The focus on physical attractiveness as a source of self-esteem is further promoted by the fact that reaching adolescence also means facing evaluations from others as a potential

> "GIRLS COMPARE THEIR OWN
> BODIES TO OUR CULTURAL
> IDEALS AND FIND THEM
> WANTING. DIETING AND
> DISSATISFACTION WITH BODIES
> HAVE BECOME NORMAL
> REACTIONS TO PUBERTY. . . .
> GIRLS ARE TERRIFIED OF BEING
> FAT, AS WELL THEY SHOULD BE.
> GIRLS HEAR THE REMARKS
> MADE ABOUT HEAVY GIRLS IN
> THE HALLS OF THEIR SCHOOLS.
> NO ONE FEELS THIN ENOUGH.
> BECAUSE OF GUILT AND SHAME
> ABOUT THEIR BODIES, YOUNG
> WOMEN ARE CONSTANTLY ON
> THE DEFENSIVE. . . . ALMOST
> ALL ADOLESCENT GIRLS FEEL
> FAT, WORRY ABOUT THEIR
> WEIGHT, DIET AND FEEL GUILTY
> WHEN THEY EAT."
>
> —MARY PIPHER (1994), *REVIVING
> OPHELIA: SAVING THE SELVES OF
> ADOLESCENT GIRLS*, PP. 184–185

romantic/sexual partner, and for girls especially, physical attractiveness is the primary criterion for this evaluation (Galambos, Almeida, & Petersen, 1990; Hill & Lynch, 1983).

However, the research that has found a decline in girls' self-esteem in adolescence and a gender difference in perceived physical appearance has been mainly on White adolescents. Some evidence indicates that African American girls evaluate their physical appearance quite differently than White girls do. In one study of junior high and high school students, 70% of the African American girls were satisfied with their bodies, compared with just 10% of the White girls (Parker et al., 1995). Furthermore, a majority of the African American girls (64%) and very few of the White girls agreed that "it is better to be somewhat overweight than somewhat underweight." However, some evidence suggests that Black and Asian young women evaluate themselves according to skin color, with those having relatively dark skin also having negative perceptions of their attractiveness (Bond & Cash, 1992; Sahay & Piran, 1997).

Influences on Self-Esteem

What causes some adolescents to have high self-esteem and other adolescents to have low self-esteem? Feeling accepted and approved by others—especially parents and peers—is the factor identified by theorists and researchers as the most important (Harter, 1990b, 1999; Hoge, Smit, & Hanson, 1990; Robinson, 1995). Although adolescents often spend less time with their parents and have more conflict with them than prior to adolescence, adolescents' relationships with parents remain highly important to them (Allen & Land, 1999; Larson & Richards, 1994). If parents provide love and encouragement, adolescent self-esteem is enhanced; and if parents are denigrating or indifferent, adolescents respond with lower self-esteem. As peers become especially important in adolescence, they gain considerable power over self-esteem in adolescence compared with earlier ages (Harter, 1990b). Approval from adults outside the family, especially teachers, contributes to self-esteem as well (Hill & Holmbeck, 1986).

School success has also been found to be related to self-esteem in adolescence (Bachman & O'Malley, 1986; DuBois & Tevendale, 1999), especially for Asian American adolescents (Szezulski, Martinez, & Reyes, 1994). But which comes first? Do adolescents gain in self-esteem when they do well in school, or does self-esteem directly influence adolescents' performance in school? In the 1960s and 1970s, the predominant belief in American education was that self-esteem is more of a cause of school success than a consequence. Numerous programs were instituted to try to enhance students' self-esteem, by praising them and trying to teach them to praise themselves, in the hopes that this would raise their school performance. However, scholars eventually concluded that these programs did not work (Harter, 1990b). More recent studies have shown that school success tends to be a cause rather than a consequence of self-esteem (DuBois & Tevendale, 1999; Liu, Kaplan, & Risser, 1992; Rosenberg, Schooler, & Schoenbach, 1989). In fact, adolescents who have inflated self-esteem—that is, they rate themselves more favorably than parents, teachers, and peers rate them—tend to have greater conduct problems in the classroom, compared with their peers (DuBois et al., 1998). The best way to improve adolescents' school-related self-esteem is to teach them knowledge and skills that can be the basis of real achievements in the classroom (Bednar, Wells, & Peterson, 1995).

THINKING CRITICALLY

Americans generally consider it healthy to have high self-esteem. Is it possible for self-esteem to be too high? If so, how would you be able to tell when that point is reached? Is it subjective, based simply on each person's opinion, or could you define that point objectively?

The Emotional Self

Among the issues of the self that adolescents confront is how to understand and manage their emotions. One of the most ancient and enduring observations of adolescence is that it is a time of heightened emotions. Over 2,000 years ago, the Greek philosopher Aristotle observed that youth "are heated by Nature as drunken men by wine." About 250 years ago, the French philosopher Jean-Jacques Rousseau made a similar observation: "As the roaring of the waves precedes the tempest, so the murmur of rising passions announces the tumultuous change" of puberty and adolescence. Around the same time that Rousseau was writing, a type of German literature was developing that became known as "sturm und drang" literature—German for "storm and stress." In these stories, young people in their teens and early twenties experienced extreme emotions of angst, anguish, and romantic love. Today, too, most American parents see adolescence as a time of heightened emotional fluctuations (Buchanan et al., 1990; Buchanan & Holmbeck, 1998).

What does contemporary research tell us about the validity of these historical and popular ideas about adolescent emotionality? Probably the best source of data on this question is the ESM studies (Csikszentmihalyi & Larson, 1984; Larson & Ham, 1993; Larson & Richards, 1994) in which people record their emotions and experiences when they are "beeped" at random times during the day. What makes the ESM method especially important for the question of adolescent emotionality is that it assesses emotions at numerous specific moments, rather than having adolescents make an overall judgment of their emotional fluctuations. Furthermore, ESM studies have also been conducted on preadolescents and adults. Thus, if we compare the patterns of emotions reported by the different groups, we can get a good sense of whether adolescents report more extremes of emotions than preadolescents or adults.

The results indicate that they do (Larson, Csikszentmihalyi, & Graef, 1980; Larson & Richards, 1994). Adolescents report feeling "self-conscious" and "embarrassed" two to three times more often than their parents and are also more likely to feel awkward, lonely, nervous, and ignored. Adolescents are also moodier when compared to preadolescents. Comparing preadolescent 5th graders to adolescent 9th graders, Larson and Richards (1994) describe the emotional "fall from grace" that occurs during that time, as the proportion of time experienced as "very happy" declines by 50%, and similar declines take place in reports of feeling "great," "proud," and "in control." The result is an overall "deflation of childhood happiness" (p. 85) as childhood ends and adolescence begins.

However, it would be a mistake to attribute this emotionality entirely to "raging hormones." Although hormonal changes appear to make some contribution to increased emotionality in early adolescence, most scholars see these emotional changes as due to cognitive and environmental factors more than to biological changes (Buchanan et al., 1992). According to Larson and Richards (1994), adolescents' newly developed capacities for abstract reasoning "allow them to see beneath the surface of situations and envision hidden and more long-lasting threats to their well-being" (p. 86). Larson and Richards (1994) also argue that experiencing multiple life changes and personal transitions during adolescence (such as the onset of puberty, changing schools, and beginning to date) contributes to adolescents' emotional volatility. However, Larson and Richards (1994) emphasize that it is not just that adolescents experience potentially stressful events but *how* they experience and interpret them that underlies their emotional volatility. Even in response to the same or similar events, adolescents report more extreme and negative moods than preadolescents or adults.

Negative moods become more common in adolescence.

Gender and the Emotional Self: Do Adolescent Girls Lose Their "Voice"?

One of the most influential theorists on the self-development of girls in adolescence in recent years has been Carol Gilligan. In Chapter 4, we discussed how Gilligan and her colleagues have proposed that adolescent girls and boys tend to think differently about moral issues, with girls emphasizing the importance of care and boys emphasizing the importance of justice. Gilligan and her colleagues have also argued that there are gender differences in the self in adolescence. They claim that early adolescence is a crucial turning point in self-development, in which boys learn to assert their opinions whereas girls lose their "voice" and become reticent and insecure (Brown & Gilligan, 1992; Gilligan, Lyons, & Hanmer, 1990).

In Gilligan's view, girls and boys differ from early childhood onward in their emotional responses to social relationships. She sees girls as more sensitive to the nuances of human relationships from an early age, more observant of the subtleties of social interactions, and more interested in cultivating emotional intimacy in their relationships with others. Girls have a "different voice" than boys, not just in their views of moral issues but in their views of human relationships more generally.

According to Carol Gilligan, girls risk losing confidence in themselves when they reach adolescence.

Early adolescence is crucial because it is at this point that girls become aware of an irreconcilable conflict in the gender expectations that the American majority culture has for females. On the one hand, girls perceive that independence and assertiveness are valued in their culture, and that people who are ambitious and competitive are most likely to be rewarded in their education and in their careers. On the other hand, they perceive that their culture values females mainly for their physical appearance and for feminine traits such as nurturance and care for others, and rejects as "selfish" females who show the traits the culture rewards most, such as independence and competitiveness. As a result, girls in early adolescence typically succumb to the gender socialization of their culture and become more insecure and tentative about their abilities, more likely to mute their voices in an effort to be socially accepted. At the extremes, according to Gilligan, the muting of girls' voices is reflected in an escalation in such problems as depression and eating disorders when girls reach adolescence.

In her views of adolescent girls' emotional development, Gilligan's influence has been profound. Her writings have received a wide audience, not just in the social sciences but also among the general public. A clinical psychologist, Mary Pipher (1994), wrote a book called *Reviving Ophelia* drawing heavily on Gilligan's ideas about the emotional selves of adolescent girls, and it became a best-seller. One of the schools in which Gilligan has conducted her research, a private girls' school in upstate New York, was so impressed by Gilligan's findings that school authorities revised the entire school curriculum in an effort to preserve girls' voices in adolescence by emphasizing cooperation over competition and making special efforts to encourage girls to express themselves.

However, here as in her research in moral development, Gilligan has attracted nearly as many critics as admirers. These critics have argued that Gilligan exaggerates the differences between boys and girls in adolescence (Greene & Maccoby, 1986; Sommers, 2000; Tavris, 1992). For example, it is true that girls' self-esteem declines at adolescence, but boys' self-esteem declines as well, although not usually to the same extent (e.g., DuBois et al., 1996). A related criticism is of Gilligan's research methods. As in her studies of moral development, her studies of gender differences in the self in adolescence have rarely included boys. She studies girls and then makes assumptions about how they differ from the patterns that might be found among boys (e.g., Brown & Gilligan, 1992; Gilligan et al.,

1990). Also, she typically presents the results of her research only in the form of excerpts from the interviews she and her colleagues have conducted, and commentaries on those excerpts. Critics find this approach weak methodologically and hard to judge for reliability and validity (Sommers, 2000).

Although Gilligan's research methods can be criticized for certain flaws, other researchers have begun to explore the issues she has raised using more rigorous methods. In one study, Susan Harter and her colleagues examined Gilligan's idea of losing one's voice in adolescence in a study that included both males and females (Harter et al., 1997; Harter, Waters, Whitesell, & Kastelic, 1998). Harter and colleagues gave the adolescents a questionnaire to measure the degree of their "voice" (expressing an opinion, disagreeing, etc.), and another questionnaire to measure the degree of their self-reported masculinity and femininity. The results indicated some support for Gilligan's theory, in that "feminine" girls reported lower levels of "voice" than boys did. In contrast, androgynous girls—who reported having both masculine and feminine traits—were equal to boys in "voice." However, Harter's research does not support Gilligan's claim that girls' "voice" declines as they enter adolescence (Harter, 1999).

THINKING CRITICALLY

Based on your experience and observation, do you agree or disagree with Gilligan's view that girls lose their "voice" in adolescence? Do boys?

Identity

One of the most distinctive features of adolescence is that it is a time of thinking about who you are, where your life is going, what you believe in, and how your life fits into the world around you. These are all issues of **identity**. It is the adolescents' nascent capacity for self-reflection that makes consideration of identity issues possible. Adolescents are able to consider themselves in the abstract, in the "third person," in a way that younger children cannot. During adolescence, and continuing through emerging adulthood, explorations are made into various aspects of identity, culminating in commitments that set the foundation for adult life.

Adolescence and emerging adulthood are crucial periods for identity development, and for this reason theorists and researchers have devoted a considerable amount of attention to this topic. In this section, we will look first at Erikson's theory of the adolescent identity crisis, then at the research that has been conducted to explore Eriksons's theory. After that, we will consider the roles of gender and culture in adolescent identity development, with a special focus on ethnic identity among minorities in American society.

Erikson's Theory (PSYCO ANALYSIS)

Erik Erikson (1902–1994) is one of the most influential scholars in the history of the study of adolescent development. Indeed, he has had a substantial influence on the study of human development from infancy to old age. Drawing on his diverse experience as a teacher, psychoanalyst, ethnographer among Native Americans, and therapist of World War II veterans, he developed a comprehensive theory of human development across the life span. However, the primary focus of Erikson's work was on adolescence, and adolescent development is where he has had his greatest influence.

In Erikson's theory of human development across the life span, each period of life is characterized by a distinctive developmental issue or "crisis," as he described in his classic book *Childhood and Society* (Erikson, 1950). Each of these issues presents a healthy path of development and an unhealthy path. For example, infancy is viewed by Erikson as a period of *trust versus mistrust*. The healthy path of infant development, in Erikson's theory, is establishing a secure sense of trust with at least one person who can be counted on to provide protection and loving care. The alternative, the unhealthy path, is mistrust, which results from a failure to establish that secure sense of trust.

Each stage of life has a central issue of this kind, according to Erikson (1950). In adolescence, the central issue is **identity versus identity confusion**. The healthy path in adolescence involves establishing a clear and definite sense of who you are and how you fit into the world around you. The unhealthy alternative is identity confusion, a failure to form a stable and secure identity. Identity formation involves sifting through the range of life choices available in your culture, trying out various possibilities, and ultimately making commitments. The key areas in which identity is formed are love (personal relationships), work (occupation), and ideology (beliefs and values) (Erikson, 1968). In Erikson's view, a failure to establish commitments in these areas by the end of adolescence reflects identity confusion.

HISTORICAL FOCUS
Young Man Luther

Among Erik Erikson's many innovative contributions to the field of human development were his studies in **psychohistory**, which is the psychological analysis of important historical figures. His most extensive works of psychohistory were his analyses of the development of Mohandas K. Gandhi, the leader of the independence movement in India in the mid-20th century, and Martin Luther, the theologian and leader of the Protestant Reformation in the 16th century. His study of Luther is of particular interest for our purposes, because he focused on Luther's development during adolescence and emerging adulthood. In fact, the title of his book on Luther is *Young Man Luther* (1958).

According to Erikson, two events were especially important in Luther's identity formation. The first event took place in 1505, when Luther was 21. He was about to begin studying law. Since his childhood his father had decreed that he would become a lawyer, and he was on the verge of fulfilling his father's dream. However, shortly before the beginning of his first semester of law school, as he was traveling to the college where he was to be enrolled, he was caught in a severe thunderstorm. A bolt of lightning struck the ground close to where he was taking shelter from the storm and may even have thrown him to the ground. In his terror, he cried out to St. Anne for protection and promised that he would become a monk if he survived the storm. The storm abated, and a few days later Luther entered a monastery in accordance with his promise to St. Anne—without informing his father, who was enraged when he learned what Luther had done.

The second event took place 2 years later, when Luther was 23. He was with his fellow monks in the choir of the monastery, listening to a reading from the Bible that described Jesus's cure of a man who was possessed by a demon (Mark 9:17). Suddenly, Luther threw himself to the ground, raving and roaring "It isn't me! It isn't me!" This event is interpreted by Erikson (and others) as indicating the depth of Luther's fear that he could never eradicate the sense of moral and spiritual inadequacy that he felt, no matter what he did, no matter how good a monk he

was. By shouting "It isn't me!," Luther "showed himself possessed even as he tried most loudly to deny it" (Erikson, 1958, p. 23). Erikson and others have seen this event as pivotal in Luther's identity development. His sense that nothing he could do would be good enough to make him holy in the eyes of God eventually led him to reject the Church's emphasis on doing good works to earn entry into heaven, and to create a new religious doctrine based on the idea that faith and faith alone was enough to make a person worthy and saved before God.

Erikson's study of Luther illustrates several aspects of his theory of identity formation. First, Erikson viewed identity formation as centering on an identity crisis. More recent theorists and researchers tend to use the term *exploration* rather than crisis to describe the process of identity formation, but Erikson used the term *crisis* deliberately. As he wrote in *Young Man Luther*:

> Only in ill health does one realize the intricacy of the body; and only in a crisis, individual or historical, does it become obvious what a sensitive combination of interrelated factors the human personality is—a combination of capacities created in the distant past and of opportunities divined in the present; a combination of totally unconscious preconditions developed in individual growth and of social conditions created and recreated in the precarious interplay of generations. In some young people, in some classes, at some periods in history, this crisis will be minimal; in other people, classes, and periods, the crisis will be clearly marked off as a critical period, a kind of "second birth," apt to be aggravated either by widespread neuroticisms or by pervasive ideological unrest. . . . Luther, so it seems, was a rather endangered young man, beset with a syndrome of conflicts. (pp. 14–15)

Thus, Erikson viewed Luther's youth, including the two crisis events described above, as an extreme example of the identity crisis that all adolescents go through in one form or another.

Secondly, Erikson's study of Luther shows his sensitivity to the cultural and historical context of identity development. Throughout the book, Erikson emphasizes the match between Luther's unusual personality and the historical and cultural circumstances in which he lived. Had Luther grown up in a different time and place, he would have developed a much different identity. In analyzing Luther, Erikson shows the importance in identity development of the person looking inward and assessing his or her individual abilities and inclinations, then looking outward to possibilities available in the social and cultural environment. Successful identity development lies in reconciling the individual's abilities and desires with the possibilities and opportunities offered in the environment.

Third, in describing Luther's development Erikson shows that identity formation reaches a critical point during the identity crisis, but it begins before that time and continues well after. In explaining Luther, Erikson describes not only his adolescence and emerging adulthood but also his childhood, particularly his relationship with his loving but domineering father. Also, Erikson describes how Luther's identity continued to develop through his adulthood. The two key crises took place in his early twenties, but it was not until his early thirties that he broke away from the Catholic Church and established a new religious denomination. In the decades that followed, his identity developed further as he married, had children, and continued to develop his religious ideas.

Erikson did not assert that adolescence is the only time when identity issues arise and that once adolescence is over identity issues have been resolved, never to return. Identity issues exist early in life, from the time children first realize they have an existence separate from others, and continue far beyond adolescence as adults continue to ask themselves questions about who they are and how they fit into the world around them. Erikson observed, "A sense of identity is never gained nor maintained once and for all. . . . It is constantly lost and regained" (1959, p. 118).

Nevertheless, Erikson saw adolescence as the time when identity issues are most prominent and most crucial to development. Furthermore, Erikson argued that it is important to establish a clear identity in adolescence as a basis for initial commitments in adult life and as a foundation for later stages of development. Erikson viewed this as true of all his stages—developing via the healthy path provides a stable foundation for the next stage of development, whereas developing via the unhealthy path is problematic not only in that stage but as a foundation for the stages to come.

How does an adolescent develop a healthy identity? In Erikson's view, identity formation is founded partly in the **identifications** the adolescent has accumulated in childhood (Erikson, 1968). Children *identify* with their parents and other loved ones as they grow up—that is, children love and admire them and want to be like them. When adolescence comes, adolescents reflect on their identifications, rejecting some and embracing others. The ones that remain are integrated into the adolescent self, combined of course with the adolescent's own individual characteristics. Thus, adolescents create an identity in part by modeling themselves after parents, friends, and others they have loved in childhood, not simply imitating them but integrating parts of their loved ones' behavior and attitudes into their personality.

The other key process that contributes to identity formation, according to Erikson, is experimenting with various possible life options. Erikson described adolescence as often including a **psychosocial moratorium**, a

Erik Erikson proposed that the central developmental issue of adolescence is identity versus identity confusion.

period when adult responsibilities are postponed as young people try on various possible selves. Thus, dating and falling in love are part of identity formation, because during this process you get a clearer sense of yourself through intimate interactions with other persons. Trying out various possible jobs—and, for college students, various possible majors—is part of identity formation, too, because this experimentation gives you a clearer sense of what you are good at and what you truly enjoy. Erikson saw ideological experimentation as part of identity formation as well. "Trying out" a set of religious or political beliefs by learning about them and participating in organizations centered around a particular set of beliefs serves to clarify for adolescents who they are and how they wish to live. In Erikson's view, the psychosocial moratorium is not characteristic of all societies but only those with individualistic values, in which individual choice is supported (Erikson, 1968).

Most young people in Western societies go through the experimentation of the psychosocial moratorium and then settle on more enduring choices in love, work, and ideology as they enter adulthood. However, some young people find it difficult to sort out the possibilities that life presents to them, and they remain in a state of identity confusion after their peers have gone on to establish a secure identity. For many of these adolescents, according to Erikson, this may be a result of unsuccessful adaptation in previous stages of development. Just as identity formation provides the foundation for further development in adulthood, development in childhood provides the basis for development in adolescence. If development in any of the earlier stages has been unusually problematic, then identity confusion may be the outcome of adolescent development. For other adolescents, identity confusion may be the result of an inability to handle all the choices available to them and an inability to decide among them.

At the extreme, according to Erikson, such adolescents may develop a **negative identity**, "an identity perversely based on all those identifications and roles which, at critical stages of development, had been presented to them as most undesirable or dangerous" (Erikson, 1968, p. 174). Such adolescents reject the range of acceptable possibilities for love, work, and ideology offered by their society, and instead deliberately embrace what their society considers unacceptable, strange, contemptible, and offensive. Youth subcultures such as skinheads and "metalheads" (fans of heavy metal music) are often formed by adolescents who share a negative identity (Arnett, 1996; Roe, 1992).

Research on Identity

"For me, I'm exploring who I am—trying to find out more who I am, because I'm not really sure any more. Because up till about seventh grade, I was just a kid. I was me and I never really thought about it. But now I've thought about it a lot more and I'm starting to have to make decisions about who I want to be."

—Conrad, age 13 (in Bell, 1998, p. 72)

Erikson was primarily a theoretical writer and a therapist rather than a researcher, but his ideas have inspired a wealth of research over the past 30 years. One of Erikson's most influential interpreters has been James Marcia (1966, 1980, 1989, 1993, 1994, 1999). Marcia constructed a measure called the Identity Status Interview that classified adolescents into one of four identity statuses: *diffusion, moratorium, foreclosure,* or *achievement*. This system of four categories has also been used by scholars who have constructed questionnaires to investigate identity development in

> "IS THE SENSE OF IDENTITY CONSCIOUS? AT TIMES, OF COURSE, IT SEEMS ONLY TOO CONSCIOUS. FOR BETWEEN THE DOUBLE PRONGS OF INNER NEED AND INEXORABLE OUTER DEMAND, THE AS YET EXPERIMENTING INDIVIDUAL MAY BECOME THE VICTIM OF A TRANSITORY EXTREME IDENTITY CONSCIOUSNESS, WHICH IS THE COMMON CORE OF THE MANY FORMS OF 'SELF-CONSCIOUSNESS' TYPICAL FOR YOUTH. WHERE THE PROCESSES OF IDENTITY FORMATION ARE PROLONGED (A FACTOR WHICH CAN BRING CREATIVE GAIN), SUCH PREOCCUPATION WITH THE 'SELF-IMAGE' ALSO PREVAILS. WE ARE THUS MOST AWARE OF OUR IDENTITY WHEN WE ARE JUST ABOUT TO GAIN IT AND WHEN WE (WITH THAT STARTLE WHICH MOTION PICTURES CALL A 'DOUBLE TAKE') ARE SOMEWHAT SURPRISED TO MAKE ITS ACQUAINTANCE; OR, AGAIN, WHEN WE ARE JUST ABOUT TO ENTER A CRISIS AND FEEL THE ENCROACHMENT OF IDENTITY CONFUSION."
>
> —ERIK ERIKSON (1968), P. 165

adolescence rather than using Marcia's interview (e.g., Adams, 1999; Benson, Harris, & Rogers, 1992; Grotevant & Adams, 1984). The interview provides rich qualitative data, but coding it is time consuming. The questionnaire approach is quicker and easier, although it does not provide the richness of the qualitative approach.

As shown in Table 6.2, each of these classifications involves a different combination of **exploration** and commitment. Erikson (1968) used the term **identity crisis** to describe the process through which young people construct their identity, but Marcia and other current scholars prefer the term *exploration* (Adams et al., 1992; Grotevant, 1987; Marcia, 1994; Waterman, 1992). Crisis, in the view of these scholars, implies that the process inherently involves anguish and struggle, whereas exploration implies a more positive investigation of possibilities.

Identity diffusion is a status that combines no exploration with no commitment. For adolescents in identity diffusion, no commitments have been made among the choices available to them. Furthermore, no exploration is taking place—the adolescent at this stage is not seriously attempting to sort through potential choices and make enduring commitments. Any choices made at this point are brief and transitory.

Identity moratorium involves exploration but no commitment. This is a stage of active experimentation, the active trying-out of different personal, occupational, and ideological possibilities. This classification is based on Erikson's (1968) idea of the psychosocial moratorium. Different possibilities are being tried on, sifted through, some discarded and some selected, in order for adolescents to be able to determine which of the available possibilities are best suited to them.

Adolescents who are in the **identity foreclosure** classification have not experimented with a range of possibilities but have nevertheless committed themselves to certain choices—commitment, but no exploration. This is often due to a strong influence on the part of parents. Marcia and most other scholars tend to see ex-

ploration as a necessary part of forming a healthy identity, and therefore see foreclosure as an unhealthy course of identity development. This is an issue we will discuss further below.

Finally, the classification that combines exploration and commitment is **identity achievement**. Identity achievement is the classification for young people who have made definite personal, occupational, and ideological choices. By definition, identity achievement is preceded by a period of identity moratorium in which exploration takes place. If commitment takes place without exploration, it is considered identity foreclosure rather than identity achievement.

Two findings stand out from the many studies that have been conducted using this four-category system of identity development in adolescence. One is that adolescents' identity status tends to be related to other aspects of their development (Berzonsky, 1992; Marcia, 1980; Papini, Micka, & Barnett, 1989; Swanson, Spencer, & Petersen, 1998). The identity achievement and moratorium statuses are notably related to a variety of favorable aspects of development. Adolescents in these categories of identity development are more likely than adolescents in the foreclosure or diffusion categories to be self-directed, cooperative, and good at problem solving. However, adolescents in the achievement category are rated more favorably in some respects than adolescents in the moratorium category. As you might expect, moratorium adolescents are more likely than achievement adolescents to be indecisive and unsure of their opinions (Marcia, 1980).

In contrast, adolescents in the diffusion and foreclosure categories of identity development tend to have less favorable development in other areas as well (Adams, 1999; Berzonsky, 1992; Josselson, 1989). Compared with adolescents in the achievement or moratorium statuses, adolescents in the diffusion status are lower in self-esteem and self-control. Diffusion status is also related to high anxiety, apathy, and disconnected relationships with parents. Diffusion is considered to be the least favorable of the identity statuses and is viewed as predictive of later psychological problems (Akhtar, 1984; Marcia, 1980; Meeus, Iedema, Helsen, & Vollebergh, 1999).

The foreclosure status is more complex in its relation to other aspects of development (Papini et al., 1989; Phinney, 2000). Adolescents in the foreclosure status tend to be higher on conformity, conventionality, and obedience to authority than adolescents in the other statuses. These are generally considered negative outcomes as measured by the values of Western majority cultures because broad socialization values of independence and individualism view negatively anything

TABLE 6.2: THE FOUR IDENTITY STATUSES

		Commitment	
		Yes	*No*
	Yes	Achievement	Moratorium
Exploration	*No*	Foreclosure	Diffusion

that reflects values of conformity and obedience. Also, adolescents with the foreclosure status tend to have especially strong attachments to their parents, which may lead them to accept their parents' values and guidance without going through a period of exploration as adolescents with the achievement status have done (Phinney, 2000). Again, this is sometimes portrayed as negative by those who believe it is necessary to go through a period of exploration in order to develop a mature identity, but this view rests partly on values that favor individualism and independent thinking.

The other prominent finding in research on identity formation is that it takes longer than scholars had expected to reach identity achievement, and in fact for most young people this status is reached—if at all—in emerging adulthood rather than in adolescence. Studies that have compared adolescents from ages 12 through 18 have found that although the proportion of adolescents in the foreclosure category decreases with age and the proportion of adolescents in the identity achievement category increases with age, even by the end of high school only about one-third of adolescents are classified as having reached identity achievement (Christopherson, Jones, & Sales, 1988; Meeus et al., 1999; Waterman, 1999). Studies of college students find that progress toward identity achievement also takes place during the college years, but mainly in the specific area of occupational identity rather than for identity more generally (Waterman, 1992). One study indicated that identity achievement may come faster for emerging adults who do not attend college (Munro & Adams, 1977), perhaps because the college environment tends to be a place where young people's ideas about themselves are challenged and they are encouraged to question previously held ideas (Arehart & Smith, 1990; Lytle, Bakken, & Romig, 1997). Some evidence also suggests that females progress toward identity achievement somewhat faster than males, especially in the personal domain (Dyk & Adams, 1990). However, even for noncollege emerging adults and even for females, the majority have not reached identity achievement by age 21, and few studies have extended beyond this age (Kroger, 1999).

Several decades ago, Erikson observed that identity formation was taking longer and longer for young people in industrialized societies. He commented on the "prolonged adolescence" that was becoming increasingly common in such societies and how this was leading to a prolonged period of identity formation, "during which the young adult through free role experimentation may find a niche in some section of his society" (1968, p. 156). Considering the changes that have taken place since he made this observation in the 1960s, including much higher ages of marriage and parenthood and longer education, Erikson's observation applies to far more young people today than it did then (Coté, 2000). Indeed, the conception of emerging adulthood as a distinct period of life is based to a considerable extent on the fact that, over recent decades, the late teens and early twenties have become a period of "free role experimentation" for an increasing proportion of young people (Arnett, 2000a). The entrance to full adulthood has become postponed, compared with earlier generations, as many emerging adults use the years of their late teens and early twenties for explorations in love, work, and ideology.

THINKING CRITICALLY

Think of one of the non-Western cultures that have been featured in earlier chapters of this book, and consider how the process of identity formation takes place in that culture.

Gender and Identity

Some scholars have argued that gender differences exist in identity formation (Gilligan, 1982; Waterman, 1992). The difference appears to exist especially in relation to occupational exploration. That is, some evidence suggests that females are more willing than males to constrain their occupational exploration to maintain their relationships (Archer, 1989; Cooper & Grotevant, 1987; Marcia, 1993; Patterson et al., 1992). For example, females might be less willing than males to take advantage of an educational or occupational opportunity that would require them to move a great distance, because that would mean leaving their parents, their friends, perhaps their romantic partner.

This gender difference was especially strong in earlier studies of identity formation. More recent studies have found that gender differences in identity formation have diminished (Archer & Waterman, 1994; Lacombe & Gay, 1998). Nevertheless, some gender differences remain in the extent of young people's occupational explorations (Archer, 1989; Josselson, 1988; Marcia, 1994; Patterson et al., 1992). Young women tend to have more difficulty than young men in successfully integrating their aspirations for love with their aspirations for work, in part because of gender double standards in American society decreeing that in a romantic partnership, his occupational aspirations usually take priority over hers.

In Erikson's theory, this means that intimacy is often a higher priority than identity for females, whereas for males identity tends to come before intimacy (Gilligan, 1982; Lytle et al., 1997; Miller, 1991; Scheidel & Marcia, 1985; Surrey, 1991). According to Erikson, **intimacy versus isolation** is the central issue of young adulthood. Establishing intimacy means uniting your newly formed identity with another person in an intimate relationship. The alternative is isolation, characterized by an inability to form an enduring intimate relationship. Research on the relation between identity and intimacy has often focused on gender differences, with most studies indicating that intimacy issues arise earlier for females than for males, so that females often accomplish intimacy before identity (Scheidel & Marcia, 1985) or that developmental processes of identity formation and establishing intimacy are integrated for females (Lytle et al., 1997; Miller, 1991; Surrey, 1991), whereas males tend to achieve identity before intimacy. However, the findings are not entirely consistent, and one recent study found that high school girls tended to be higher in identity and lower in intimacy than high school boys (Lacombe & Gay, 1998), so more research is needed.

Culture and Identity

Erik Erikson's background was diverse—he was the son of Danish parents, raised in Germany, and spent most of his adult life in the United States—and he was acutely aware of the relation between culture and identity formation. He spent time as an ethnographer among the Sioux and Yurok tribes of Native Americans, and he devoted a chapter in *Childhood and Society* (1950) to adolescent identity development in these tribes. Nevertheless, virtually all of the research inspired by Erikson's theory has taken place among White middle-class adolescents in the United States. What can we say about identity development among adolescents in other cultures?

One observation that can be made is that the psychosocial moratorium, the period of experimentation that Erikson viewed as a standard part of identity formation, is considerably more possible in some cultures than in others. In today's industrialized societies, there are few pressures on young people to become economic contributors in childhood or adolescence. Young people in these societies are generally allowed a long psychological moratorium in adolescence and emerging adulthood to try out various possible life choices in love, work, and ideology. However, the experience of adolescence is often much different in traditional cultures. Experimentation in love is clearly limited or even nonexistent in cultures where dating is not allowed and marriages are either arranged by parents or strongly influenced by them. Experimentation in work is limited in cultures where the economy is simple and offers only a limited range of choices.

Limitations on exploration in both love and work have been tighter for girls in traditional cultures than for boys. For love, some degree of sexual experimentation is encouraged for adolescent boys in most cultures, but for girls there is more variability, with some traditional cultures allowing girls sexual experimentation and some punishing it severely (Whiting et al., 1986). For work, in most traditional cultures and for most of human history in every culture, adolescent girls have been designated by their cultures for the roles of wives and mothers, and these were essentially the only choices open to them (Mensch, Bruce, & Greene, 1998).

In terms of ideology, too, a psychosocial moratorium has been the exception in human cultures rather than the standard. In most cultures, young people have been expected to grow up to believe what adults teach them to believe, without questioning it. It is only in recent history, and mainly in industrialized Western countries, that these expectations have changed, and that it has come to be seen as desirable for adolescents and emerging adults to think for themselves, decide on their own beliefs, and make their life choices independently (Bellah et al., 1985). For modern young people in the West, then, identity development is a longer and more complex process than in the past and compared with traditional cultures. But this is increasingly true for the rest of the world as well, as industrialization increases worldwide and as Western values of individualism influence traditional cultures through globalization (Barber, 1995; Schlegel, 2000).

Identity Development Among Ethnic Minorities

In discussing identity, we have noted that in Erikson's theory the three key areas of identity formation are love, work, and ideology. For a large and growing proportion of adolescents in American society, one aspect of ideology is beliefs about what it means to be a member of an ethnic minority within a society dominated by the White majority culture. Although scholarly attention to this topic is not abundant, it has increased in recent years as the number of people who are members of ethnic minorities in American society has grown and as scholars have begun to devote greater attention to cultural issues in development (Phinney, 1990, 2000; Spencer & Dornbusch, 1990).

Like other identity issues, issues of ethnic identity come to the forefront in adolescence because of the cognitive capacities that adolescents develop (Kurtz, Cantu, & Phinney, 1996; Wong, 1997). One aspect of the growing capacity for self-reflection, for adolescents who are members of ethnic minorities, is likely to be a sharpened awareness of what it means for them to be a member of their minority group. Group terms such as *African American*, *Chinese*, and *Latino* take on a new meaning, as adolescents can now think about what these terms mean and how the term for their ethnic group applies to themselves. Also, as a consequence of their growing capacity to think about what others think about them, adolescents become more acutely aware of the prejudices and stereotypes that others may hold about their ethnic group.

Because adolescents who are members of ethnic minorities have to confront such issues, their identity development is likely to be more complex than adolescents who are part of the majority culture (Phinney, 2000; Phinney & Alipuria, 1987). Consider, for example, identity development in the area of love. Love—along with dating and sex—is an area where cultural conflicts are especially likely to come up for adolescents who are members of ethnic minorities. Part of identity development in the American majority culture means trying out different possibilities in love by dating different people, developing intimate relationships with them, and gaining sexual experience with them. However, this model is in sharp conflict with the values of certain American ethnic minority groups. In most Asian American groups, for example, recreational dating is frowned on, and sexual experimentation before marriage is considered disgraceful—especially for females (Miller, 1995; Sung, 1985; Wong, 1997). Similarly, among Latinos, gaining sexual experience in adolescence is considered wrong for girls, and they are often highly restricted by their parents and by their brothers to prevent any violation of this norm (Inclan & Herron, 1990). Young people from these ethnic groups face a challenge in reconciling the values of their ethnic group on such issues with the values of the majority culture, to which they are inevitably exposed through school, the media, and peers (Markstrom-Adams, 1992; Miller, 1995; Phinney & Rosenthal, 1992).

How, then, does identity development proceed for young people who are members of minority groups within Western societies? To what extent do they develop an identity that reflects the values of the majority culture, and to what extent do they retain the values of their minority group? One scholar who has done extensive work on these questions is Jean Phinney (Kurtz, Cantu, & Phinney, 1996; Phinney, 1990, 2000; Phinney & Alipuria, 1987; Phinney & Devich-Navarro, 1997; Phinney & Rosenthal, 1992). On the basis of her research, Phinney has concluded that adolescents who are members of minority groups have four different ways of responding to their awareness of their ethnicity (see Table 6.3; Phinney, Devich-Navarro et al., 1994). **Assimilation** is the option that involves leaving behind the ways of one's ethnic group and adopting the values and way of life of the majority culture. This is the path that is reflected in the idea that American society is a "melting pot" that blends people of diverse origins into one national culture. **Marginality** involves rejecting one's culture of origin but also feeling rejected by the majority culture. Some adolescents may feel little identification with the culture of their parents and grandparents, nor do they feel accepted and integrated into American society. **Separation** is the approach that involves associating only with members of one's own ethnic group and rejecting the ways of the majority culture. **Biculturalism** involves developing a dual identity, one based in the ethnic group of origin and one based in the majority culture. Being bicultural usually means moving back and forth between the ethnic culture and the majority culture, and alternating identities as appropriate to the situation.

TABLE 6.3: FOUR POSSIBLE ETHNIC IDENTITY STATUSES

		Identification With Ethnic Group	
		High	*Low*
Identification With Majority Culture	*High*	Bicultural	Assimilated
	Low	Separated	Marginal

Examples:

Assimilation: "I don't really think of myself as Asian American, just as American."

Separation: "I am not part of two cultures. I am just Black."

Marginality: "When I'm with my Indian friends, I feel White, and when I'm with my White friends, I feel Indian. I don't really feel like I belong with either of them."

Biculturalism: "Being both Mexican and American means having the best of both worlds. You have different strengths you can draw from in different situations."

Source: Based on Phinney & Devich-Navarro (1997).

Adolescents with a bicultural ethnic identity are able to alternate their identities depending on the group they are with.

Which of these ethnic identity statuses is most common among American minority adolescents? One study of high school students looked at ethnic identity among White, African American, Latino, and Asian American adolescents (Rotheram-Borus, 1990). Overall, minority adolescents were most likely to view themselves as bicultural (40% to 50%). However, differences were seen among the ethnic groups. Mexican American and Asian American adolescents most often viewed themselves as bicultural, whereas African American and Puerto Rican adolescents were more likely than adolescents in the other groups to have a separation orientation. Similar results were obtained in a study by Phinney (Phinney, DuPont et al., 1994). Marginality is common among Native American adolescents (see the Cultural Focus box). Each of these ethnic groups are diverse and contain adolescents with a variety of different ethnic identity orientations (Hemmings, 1998).

Does one approach to ethnic identity formation tend to be healthier or more favorable than the others? In general, the answer appears to be no. Ethnic identity status has been found to be unrelated to characteristics such as self-esteem, grades in school, and social competence (Rotheram-Borus, 1990). However, the answer is more complicated than this. Some scholars have argued that, for Black adolescents in particular, cultivating pride in their ethnic identity is an important part of their identity formation, especially in a society where they are likely to experience discrimination for being Black (Spencer &

Markstrom-Adams, 1990; Ward, 1990). The study by Rotheram-Borus (1990) described above seems to confirm this, in that minority adolescents who preferred separation also had the strongest ethnic identification and ethnic pride. However, other scholars have argued that promoting ethnic identity may lead adolescents to cut themselves off from the majority culture in a way that inhibits their personal growth (Phinney & Rosenthal, 1992). These scholars express concern that some minority adolescents may come to define themselves in opposition to the majority culture—developing a negative identity, in Erikson's (1968) terms—in a way that may interfere with developing a positive identity of their own.

The separation response is, at least in part, a result of the discrimination and prejudice that minorities often face in American society, and that young people become more fully aware of as they reach adolescence. Their awareness of discrimination may also increase with the length of time their family has been in the United States. An interesting finding in this research is that foreign-born adolescents tend to believe in the American ideal of equal opportunity more than minority adolescents whose families have been in the United States for a generation or more (Phinney, DuPont et al., 1994; Suarez-Orosco & Suarez-Orozco, 1996). This suggests that recent immigrants may have high hopes for becoming assimilated into the great American melting pot, but after a generation or two many of them come up against the realities of ethnic prejudice in American society. Black adolescents tend to be more in favor of separation than adolescents from other ethnic groups (Phinney, Devich-Navarro et al., 1994), perhaps because most of them are from families who have been in the United States for many generations and who have experienced a long history of slavery, racism, and discrimination (Hemmings, 1998).

The Self, Alone

One of the reasons that adolescents are able to engage in the frequent self-reflection that allows them to consider their self-conceptions, self-esteem, emotional

CULTURAL FOCUS
The Native American Self

Native American young people exhibit greater difficulties in many respects than any other American minority group. They have the highest prevalence rates for use of alcohol, cigarettes, and illicit drugs (Bachman et al., 1991; May, 1996). They have the highest school dropout rate and the highest teenage pregnancy rate (John, 1998; Laframboise & Low, 1989). Especially alarming is the suicide rate among Native American young people aged 15 to 24, which is three times as high as the rate for Whites (John, 1998). Suicide is the leading cause of death among young Native Americans. Native Canadians are similar to Native Americans in their levels of substance use, dropping out of school, teenage pregnancy, and suicide (Galambos & Kolaric, 1994).

To a large extent, the difficulties of Native American young people are viewed by scholars as rooted in problems of the self (Katz, 1995; Lefley, 1976). The self-esteem of Native American adolescents tends to be substantially lower than in other ethnic groups (Dinges, Trimble, & Hollenbeck, 1979; Dodd, Nelson, & Hofland, 1994; Liu et al., 1994). Young Native Americans have also been found to have problems forming an identity in adolescence and emerging adulthood, as they attempt to reconcile the socialization of their Native American cultures with the influences and demands of the dominant White majority culture (Dodd et al., 1994; Lefley, 1976; Liu et al., 1994).

The explanation for problems of the self among young Native Americans is partly historical and partly contemporary. In historical terms, during the 19th century Native American cultures were decimated and finally overcome by the spread of European American settlement into the vast areas of the United States that Native Americans once dominated. The devastation of their cultures was deep and thorough, as they were betrayed repeatedly by the U.S. government, killed in large numbers, forced to leave their homelands, and ultimately herded onto reservations in the most desolate parts of the country. This alone would be enough to explain substantial disruption to their cultural life in the present, with

consequent effects on the socialization and development of their young people.

In the 20th century, additional practices of the federal government added to and prolonged the cultural destruction suffered by Native Americans. For most of the century, Native American children were forced to attend schools run not by the adults of their community but by the Bureau of Indian Affairs (BIA), a federal agency. The goal of these schools was complete assimilation of Native American children and adolescents into the ways of the majority culture—and, correspondingly, the annihilation of their attachment to their own culture's beliefs, values, knowledge, and customs (Unger, 1977). Often, these schools were boarding schools where the children lived during the school year, completely isolated from their families and communities.

Given these conditions, and given that constructing the self requires a cultural foundation (Shweder

The self-development of young Native Americans is often fraught with difficulties.

et al., 1998), many Native American young people found it difficult to construct a stable and coherent self. These educational practices finally changed in the 1970s, when federal legislation was passed giving Native Americans substantial control over their schools (John, 1998). Still, like the effects of losing their lands and being forced to enter reservations a century ago, the damage from the cultural annihilation practices of the schools have endured in Native American cultures.

In the present, threats to the selves of Native American young people remain from the historical legacy of cultural destruction and from the bleak conditions that face them as they look ahead to adulthood. The legacy of cultural destruction makes it difficult for them to form a bicultural identity; Native American cultures and the American majority culture are difficult to combine, because for many young Native Americans accepting White society even as part of a bicultural identity would amount to a betrayal of their own people in the light of the suffering they have endured at the hands of Whites (Deyhle, 1995). At the same time, government practices undermining Native American cultural socialization over the 20th century have been effective, so

that many young people no longer share their culture's traditional beliefs or know much about their culture's traditional way of life. As Deyhle (1998) observes, "On the one hand, due to the racism against [Native Americans] in the Anglo community and youth's insistence on cultural integrity, the Anglo world is not available to them. On the other hand, the traditional lives of their ancestors no longer exist" (p. 6).

Thus, many young Native Americans find themselves with a marginal ethnic identity status, alienated from the majority culture as well as from their own culture, living between two worlds and at home in neither. Conditions in their communities are grim—rates of poverty and unemployment among Native Americans are exceptionally high (John, 1998)—but the predominantly White majority culture does not accept them and is not accepted by them. Their high rates of substance use, dropping out of school, teenage pregnancy, and suicide reflect their difficulties in constructing a self under these conditions. Although some recent hopeful signs have been seen—for example, in rising rates of college enrollment—overall the prospects facing young Native Americans remain formidably bleak.

states, and identity is that they are often by themselves. Studies of time use among American adolescents indicate that they spend about one-fourth of their time alone, which is more time than they spend with either their families or their friends (Larson, Csikszentmihalyi, & Graef, 1982; Larson & Richards, 1994).

The ESM studies provide some interesting data on adolescents' experiences of being alone (Larson et al., 1982; Larson & Richards, 1994). These studies find that a substantial proportion of adolescents' time alone is spent in their bedrooms, with the door closed. Is this a lonely time for them? The answer to this question is not simple. During their time alone their moods tend to be low—they are more likely than at other times to report feeling weak, lonely, and sad. However, after a period alone their mood tends to rise. Larson and Richards (1994) conclude that adolescents use their time alone for self-reflection and mood management. They listen to music, they lie on their beds, they groom themselves in the mirror, they brood, they fantasize. When their time alone is done, they tend to feel restored, ready to face the slings and arrows of daily life again.

Larson and Richards (1994) provide a revealing example of one adolescent girl's experience of being alone. She was alone about one-fourth of the times she was beeped, the typical rate. Often, she reported feeling lonely during her times alone. She brooded over her looks, she brooded over how all the girls except herself seemed to have a boyfriend. Yet, she reported, "I like to be by myself. I don't have to be worried or aggravated by my parents. I have noticed that when I'm alone I feel better sometimes." Then she added, in large print, "*!NOT ALWAYS!*," reflecting her ambivalence (Larson & Richards, 1994, p. 102).

Being alone can be constructive, then, as long as an adolescent does not have too much of it. Studies have found that adolescents who spend an unusually high proportion of their time alone tend also to have higher rates of school problems, depression, and other psychological difficulties (Achenbach & Edelbrock, 1986; Larson & Richards, 1994). However, the same studies have found that adolescents who are rarely alone also have higher rates of school problems and depression. Time alone can be healthy for adolescents because, as

Adolescents spend more time by themselves than with family or friends.

Larson and Richards (1994) observe, "After a long day in which their emotions are played upon by peers, teachers, and family members, a measured period of time by themselves, to reflect, regroup, and explore, may be just what they need" (p. 103).

Just as being alone does not necessarily mean being lonely, a person can be lonely even when among others. Robert Weiss (1973) has made an important and influential distinction between two types of loneliness, social loneliness and emotional loneliness. **Social loneliness** occurs when people feel that they lack a sufficient number of social contacts and relationships. This may occur, for example, for a person who has few friends or companions and therefore spends a great deal of time alone. In contrast, **emotional loneliness** occurs when people feel that the relationships they have lack sufficient closeness and intimacy. Thus, social loneliness reflects a deficit in sheer *quantity* of social contacts and relationships, whereas emotional loneliness reflects a deficit in the emotional *quality* of a person's relationships (Adams et al., 1988; Asher et al., 1990; DiTommaso & Spinner, 1997; Larson, 1990; Russell et al., 1984). Young people may experience either or both of these types of loneliness in their teens and early twenties.

Emerging adulthood is a period when time spent alone is especially high. According to ESM studies across the life span, young people aged 19 to 29 spend more of their leisure time alone than any persons except the elderly, and more of their time in productive activities (school and work) alone than any other age group under 40 (Larson, 1990). Although studies are lacking that indicate the extent to which emerging adults are lonely during their time alone, there are good reasons why these years might be expected to be lonelier. Most emerging adults move out of the home by age 18 or 19 (Goldscheider & Goldscheider, 1994) to go to college or just to live independently. This move may have many advantages, such as giving emerging adults more independence and requiring them to take on more responsibility for their daily lives, but it also means that they are no longer wrapped in the relative security of the family environment. They may be glad to be on their own in many ways, but nevertheless they may find themselves to be lonely more often than when they had lived at home (DiTommaso & Spinner, 1997). Most young people in American society do not enter marriage—and the emotional support and companionship that usually go along with it—until their mid- to late twenties (Arnett, 1998a). For many young people, emerging adulthood is a period between the companionship of living with family and the companionship of marriage or some other long-term partnership (Arnett, 2000a).

The college environment is one in which emerging adults rarely experience social loneliness, but emotional

Emotional loneliness is common in the first year of college, even though college students are often around other people.

loneliness is common (Wiseman, 1995). The first year of college has been found to be an especially lonely period for many young people (Cutrona, 1982; Larose & Boivin, 1998), even though they are meeting many new people. For example, a college freshman living in a dormitory may have people around virtually every moment of the day—while sleeping, eating, studying, working, and going to class—but still feel lonely if those social contacts are not emotionally rewarding or significant.

THINKING CRITICALLY

Compared with young people in Western cultures, do you think young people in traditional cultures would be more or less likely to experience loneliness?

Summing Up

In this chapter we have addressed a variety of aspects of the self in adolescence and emerging adulthood, including self-conceptions, self-esteem, the emotional self, identity, and being alone. The main points of the chapter are as follows:

- Self-conceptions become more abstract in adolescence. This includes the development of the capacity to distinguish between an actual self, an ideal self, and a feared self. Self-conceptions in adolescence also become more complex, with an increased awareness that different aspects of the self might be shown to different people and in different situations. This includes an awareness that one may show a false self to others at times.

- Research indicates that self-esteem tends to decline in early adolescence and rise in late adolescence and emerging adulthood. Self-esteem does not decline among the majority of adolescents, but it is more likely to decline for girls than for boys. The aspects of self-esteem that are most influential in adolescents' overall self-esteem are physical appearance and social acceptance.

- The ESM studies show that adolescents tend to experience more extremes of emotions, especially negative ones such as feeling embarrassed or awkward, compared with preadolescents or adults. Carol Gilligan has argued that gender differences exist in emotional self-development during adolescence, as girls "lose their voice" in the course of conforming to cultural pressures for the female role, rather than asserting their authentic selves.

- According to Erik Erikson, the key issue in adolescent development is identity versus identity confusion, and the three principal areas of identity formation are love, work, and ideology. For adolescents in Western societies, identity formation usually involves a psychosocial moratorium, that is, a period of experimentation with various life possibilities.

- Adolescents who are members of ethnic minorities face the challenge of developing an ethnic identity in addition to an identity in the areas of love, work, and ideology. Four possible alternatives of ethnic identity formation are assimilation, marginality, separation, and biculturalism.

- The ESM studies find that adolescents are alone about one-fourth of the time. Although their moods tend to be low during these times, they often use these times for reflection and regeneration. Emotional loneliness tends to be high among college freshmen.

Studies of the self in adolescence and emerging adulthood are difficult to find outside of American society. Because of the American tradition of individualism, issues of the self have been of more interest and concern to Americans than to people in other societies, and this is reflected in the interests of American scholars. The distinction between the independent self that is emphasized in American society (and to a lesser extent in other Western cultures) and the interdependent self that is emphasized in non-Western societies is an important one, but so far this idea has not been applied much to research on adolescence and emerging adulthood.

Key Terms

self-reflection
actual self
possible selves
ideal self
feared self
false self
self-esteem
self-image
self-concept

self-perception
baseline self-esteem
barometric self-esteem
response bias
internal consistency
identity
identity versus identity
    confusion
psychohistory

identifications
psychosocial moratorium
negative identity
exploration
identity crisis
identity diffusion
identity moratorium
identity foreclosure
identity achievement

intimacy versus isolation
assimilation
marginality
separation
biculturalism
social loneliness
emotional loneliness

For Further Reading

Erikson, E. (1968). *Identity: Youth and crisis.* New York: Norton. Erikson's classic book on the development of identity during adolescence and emerging adulthood.

Gilligan, C. (1982). *In a different voice: Psychological theory and women's development.* Cambridge, MA: Harvard University Press. Gilligan's best-known book. Provides a good critique of male-oriented developmental research as well as a good example of how Gilligan presents her work.

Livesley, W. J., & Bromley, D. B. (1973). *Person perception in childhood and adolescence.* New York: Wiley. This book on conceptions of self and others is loaded with vivid qualitative examples.

Markus, H. R., & Kitayama, S. (1991). Culture and the self: Implications for cognition, emotion, and motivation. *Psychological Review, 98,* 224–253. Presents the authors' now widely used cultural distinction between independent and interdependent selves.

Applying Research

Seligman, M. E. P. (1993). *What you can change and what you can't: The complete guide to successful self-improvement.* New York: Fawcett. This book was written by Martin Seligman, who is a prominent researcher on depression, so it is not the usual self-help book. Well-informed and witty, Seligman's book can be helpful to people struggling with issues of the self at many periods of life, including adolescence and emerging adulthood.

"When my first boyfriend broke up with me last year, I was really depressed and he kept saying I should talk to my mom. So I did. And she made me feel a lot better. . . . My mom and I are really close now. I feel like she's a friend, not just my mother."

—Gretchen, age 17 (Bell, 1998, p. 70)

"[My mother] says, 'I just don't want to hear anymore; go back to your room.' And I think, as a human being, she shouldn't be able to say that to me without getting my response back; I just don't feel that's right."

—14-year-old girl (Konopka, 1985, p. 67)

"Everything was going along like usual and then all of a sudden my dad started doing crazy things—like staying out real late, not telling my mom where he was, showing up late for work or not showing up at all. My parents were arguing a lot and he would get real defensive, so it just kept building up and up. . . . And pretty soon my dad came to me and said, 'Well, you know me and your mom are having problems and I think I'm going to have to

185

leave.' And we both started crying. . . . I didn't want to cry, I was trying not to cry, but I couldn't help it."

—*Gordon, age 17 (Bell, 1998, p. 67)*

Family life! It can be the source of our deepest attachments, as well as our most bitter and painful conflicts. For young people and their parents, frequent adjustments are required in their relationships as adolescents and emerging adults gain more autonomy, inexorably moving away from their families toward the larger world and new attachments outside the family. These adjustments do not always proceed smoothly, and conflicts can result when young people and their parents have different perceptions of the most desirable pace and scope of this growing autonomy. For many adolescents and emerging adults in Western societies, family life is further complicated by their parents' divorce and perhaps remarriage, which require further adjustments that many young people find difficult, at least in the short run.

Despite these complications, for most young people the family remains a crucial source of love, support, protection, and comfort (Allen & Land, 1999; Steinberg, 1990). Family members, especially parents, are most often the people adolescents and emerging adults say they admire most (Offer & Schonert-Reichl, 1992; Steinberg, 1990) and are among the people to whom they have the closest attachments (Allen & Land, 1999; Claes, 1998). Adolescents and emerging adults also typically attribute their core moral values to the influence of their parents (Offer, 1969; Offer & Schonert-Reichl, 1992).

In this chapter, we will explore many aspects of the family lives of adolescents and emerging adults. We will begin with a look at various aspects of the family system in which adolescents develop, including parents' development at midlife, sibling relationships, and relationships with extended family members. Then we will focus on the central relationships in adolescents' family systems, their relationships with their parents. This will include a discussion of the effects of various parenting styles on adolescents' development and an examination of adolescents' attachments to parents. Emerging adults' relationships to parents will be examined as well.

In the second half of the chapter we will turn to challenges and difficulties in young people's relationships with parents. We will examine the basis for conflict with parents in adolescence. We will also look at the historical context of adolescents' family lives, including changes in family life over the past 200 years as well as more recent family changes—rising rates of divorce, remarriage, single-parent households, and dual-earner families—and how these changes have influenced adolescents' development. The chapter will close with a look at the causes and effects of physical and sexual abuse in the family and the problems faced by adolescents who run away from home.

The Adolescent in the Family System

One useful framework for making sense of the complex ways family members interact with each other is the **family systems approach**. According to this approach, to understand family functioning one must understand how each relationship within the family influences the family as a whole (Minuchin, 1974). The family system is composed of a variety of subsystems (Kramer & Lin, 1997; Piotrowski, 1997). For example, in a family consisting of two parents and an adolescent, the subsystems would be mother and adolescent, father and adolescent, and mother and father. In families with more than one child, or with extended family members who are closely involved in the family, the family system becomes a more complex network of subsystems, consisting of each **dyadic relationship** (a relationship of two persons) as well every possible combination of three or more persons (Kramer & Lin, 1997; Piotrowski, 1997).

The family systems approach is based on two key principles. One is that each subsystem influences every other subsystem in the family (Minuchin, 1974). For example, a high level of conflict between the parents effects not only the relationship between the two of them but also the relationship that each of them has with the adolescent (Emery & Tuer, 1993; Wilson & Gottman, 1995).

A second, related principle of the family systems approach is that a change in any family member or family subsystem results in a period of **disequilibrium** (or imbalance) until the family system adjusts to the change (Minuchin, 1974). When a child reaches adolescence, the changes that accompany adolescent development make a certain amount of disequilibrium normal and inevitable. A key change is the advent of puberty and sexual maturity, which typically results in a certain amount of disequilibrium in relationships with each parent (Paikoff & Brooks-Gunn, 1991), as we saw in

RESEARCH FOCUS
The Daily Rhythms of Adolescents' Family Lives

In several chapters so far I have referred to research using the Experience Sampling Method (ESM), which involves having people carry wrist-watch beepers and then beeping them randomly during the day so that they can record their thoughts, feelings, and behavior. This method is an exceptionally creative and unusual approach to studying adolescents' lives. Some of the most interesting and important findings so far using this method concern the interactions and relationships between adolescents and their families. Here, let's look at ESM research in greater detail.

Reed Larson and Maryse Richards are the two scholars who have done the most to apply the ESM to adolescents and their families. In their book, *Divergent Realities: The Emotional Lives of Mothers, Fathers, and Adolescents* (Larson & Richards, 1994), they described the results of a study that included a sample of 483 fifth through ninth graders and another sample of 55 fifth through eighth graders and their parents. They included fifth through ninth graders in the study to gain insights into the changes that take place in family experience from preadolescence through midadolescence. All were two-parent, White families. (Larson and Richards are currently collecting data on single-parent African American families.) All three family members (adolescent, mother, and father) were beeped at the same time, about 30 times per day between 7:30 in the morning and 9:30 at night, during the week of the study.

When beeped, they paused from whatever they were doing and recorded a variety of information in the notebooks that the researchers had given them for the study. The notebooks contained items about their *objective situation* when beeped: where they were, who they were with, and what they were doing. There were also items about their *subjective situation*: they rated the degree to which they felt happy to unhappy, cheerful to irritable, and friendly to angry, as well as how hurried, tired, and competitive they were feeling. The results provide "an emotional photo album . . . a set of snapshots of what [ado-lescents] and [their] parents go through in an average week" (Larson & Richards, 1994, p. 9).

What do the results tell us about the daily rhythms of adolescents' family lives? One striking finding of the study was how little time adolescents and their parents actually spent together on a typical day. Mothers and fathers each averaged about an hour a day spent in shared activities with their adolescents, and their most common shared activity was watching television. The amount of time adolescents spent with their families dropped by 50% between fifth and ninth grades. In turn, there was an increase from fifth to ninth grade in the amount of time adolescents spent alone in their bedrooms.

The study also revealed some interesting gender differences in parent–adolescent relationships. Mothers were more deeply involved with their adolescents, both for better and for worse. The majority of mother–adolescent interactions were rated positively by both of them, especially experiences such as talking together, going out together, and sharing a meal. Adolescents, especially girls, tended to be closer to their mothers than their fathers and had more conversations with them about relationships and other personal issues. However, adolescents' negative feelings toward their mothers increased sharply from fifth to ninth grade, and certain positive emotions decreased—for example, the proportion of interactions with mother in which adolescents reported feeling "very close" to her fell from 68% in fifth grade to just 28% by ninth grade. Also, adolescents reported more conflicts with their mothers than with their fathers—although fathers were often called in if mom's authority failed to achieve the results she desired—and the number of conflicts between mothers and adolescents increased from fifth to ninth grades.

As for fathers, they tended to be only tenuously involved in their adolescents' lives, a "shadowy presence," as Larson and Richards put it. For most of the time they spent with their adolescents, the mother was there as well, and the mother tended to be more directly involved with the adolescent when the three of them were together. Moms were usually on the "front lines" of parenting, whereas for fathers parenting was more of a voluntary, leisure-time activity. Fathers averaged only 12 minutes per day alone with their adolescents, and 40% of this time was spent watching TV together. Fathers and their adolescents did not talk much, and when they did sports was the most common topic.

THINKING CRITICALLY

Why do you think fathers tend to be less involved than mothers in the lives of their adolescents? Do you think this will remain true when the current generation of adolescents grows up and has adolescents of their own?

Fathers usually reported being in a good mood during the rare times they and their adolescents were doing something together. In contrast, adolescents' enjoyment of their time with their fathers decreased with age between fifth and ninth grades, especially for girls. Fathers tended to dominate when they were with their adolescents, and adolescents often resented it. Dad may have been enjoying their time together, but by ninth grade the adolescent usually was not. The "divergent realities" experienced in adolescents' families seem to be especially sharp between fathers and adolescents.

The authors used the term "the Six O'Clock Crunch" to describe what happens when mom and dad come home from work in the early evening and face a barrage of demands—greeting each other, fixing dinner, taking care of household chores, and dealing with the emotions each has piled up during the day. The burden of household tasks fell mostly on mothers rather than fathers, even when both parents worked an equal number of hours. Adolescents were even less help than fathers—they did only half as much household work as fathers, who already did a lot less than mothers. And even when they helped out, they often felt annoyed when asked to do so; they interpreted requests for help as harassment. As the authors put it, "Many of these adolescents, especially boys, felt little responsibility for their family's needs, and were therefore annoyed when asked to do their part" (Larson & Richards, 1994, p. 100).

At the same time, however, the study showed that parents are often important sources of comfort and security for adolescents. Adolescents brought into the family their emotions from the rest of the day. If their parents were responsive and caring, adolescents moods improved and their negative emotions were relieved. In contrast, if adolescents felt their parents were unavailable or unresponsive, their negative feelings became even worse.

Thus, the study demonstrates the enduring importance of parents in the lives of adolescents. Also, because the study included the perspectives of fathers and mothers as well as adolescents, interacting in pairs as well as all together, the results provide a vivid sense of the interconnected emotions and perspectives within the family system.

Chapter 2. Changes also take place as a result of adolescents' cognitive development, which may lead to disequilibrium because of the way cognitive changes affect adolescents' perceptions of their parents (Collins, 1990).

THINKING CRITICALLY

Think of an example of disequilibrium that occurred in your family during your adolescence or emerging adulthood. How did the various family members adapt?

When emerging adults leave home, the disequilibrium caused by leaving may change their relationships with their parents for better or worse (Graber & Dubas, 1996). Parents change, too—most parents are reaching midlife as their children reach adolescence, and the changes of midlife may result in disequilibrium in their relationships with their children (Steinberg & Steinberg, 1994). Other, less normative changes that may take place in adolescence or emerging adulthood can also be a source of disequilibrium—the parents' divorce, for example, or psychological problems in the adolescent or in one or both parents. For both normative and nonnormative changes, adjustments in the family system are required to restore a new equilibrium.

In the following sections, we will examine three aspects of the family system that have implications for adolescents' development: changes in parents at midlife, sibling relationships, and extended family relationships.

Parents' Development During Midlife

"I'm ready for a giant change, because a little change just won't do it for me. My kids are getting ready to leave home soon, and I want to sell the house and do something crazy, like go around the world for a year, or move back into the city and get a job or go back to school. I'm not willing to wait till I get cancer or until somebody dies, or until Peter and I divorce to make a change. At least now we can still enjoy ourselves."

—*Ellie, 39-year-old mother of three adolescents*
(Bell, 1998, p. 67)

For most parents, their children's development during adolescence and emerging adulthood overlaps with their own development during midlife. As noted in Chapter 1, the median age of marriage and first childbirth in industrialized societies today is quite high, usually in the mid- to late twenties. If adolescence begins about age 10, this means that most parents in industrialized societies are nearing age 40 when their first child enters adolescence, and age 40 is usually considered the beginning of midlife (Levinson, 1978; Shweder, 1998). Of course, a great deal of variability exists in most industrialized societies—a substantial proportion of people have children as young as their teens or as old as their forties. But even for people who have their children relatively early or relatively late, their children's development in adolescence and emerging adulthood is likely to overlap at least in part with their own development during midlife, if it can be said that midlife lasts roughly from age 40 to 60.

What kinds of developmental changes take place during midlife that may have an impact on the family system? For the past several years, a consortium of distinguished scholars has collaborated on a major investigation of development during midlife (Shweder, 1998). This consortium, known as MIDMAC (because their work is sponsored by the MacArthur Foundation) has confirmed and extended studies by earlier scholars in finding that, for most people in most respects, midlife is an especially satisfying and enjoyable time of life. Despite popular beliefs that midlife is typically a time of **"midlife crisis"** and decline, for most people midlife is in fact the prime of life.

At midlife, most parents of adolescents are reaching the prime of life in many respects.

This is true in a variety of aspects of life. Job satisfaction peaks in middle adulthood, as does the sense of having job status and power (Gallagher, 1993; Shweder, 1998; Tamir, 1982). Earning power tends to increase, so that many couples who struggled financially when their children were younger find themselves financially secure for the first time during midlife (Gallagher, 1993). Marital problems decline (Gallagher, 1993; Shweder, 1998; Swensen, Eskew, & Kohlhepp, 1981). Gender roles become less restrictive and more flexible for both men and women, not only in the West but in non-Western cultures as well (Gutmann, 1987; Nash & Feldman, 1981).

People's personalities also tend to become more flexible and adaptive when they reach midlife. For example, in one large study of German adults at midlife, during their forties and fifties most people reported a steady rise in what the researchers called "flexible goal adjustment," as defined by affirmative responses to items such as "I can adapt quite easily to changes in a situation" (Brandstadter & Baltes-Gotz, 1990; Brandstadter & Greve, 1994). It appears, then, that as their children reach adolescence, most parents are likely to be flexible enough to adapt their parenting to adolescents' changing development and growing autonomy. The results of studies on midlife adults also suggest that adolescents' growing autonomy may be welcomed by most parents, in that it may give parents more time for enjoying their own lives.

One change that has been much-discussed in popular culture is the *empty-nest syndrome*, referring to the adjustments that parents must make when their youngest child leaves home. Although popular stereotypes suggest that this is a difficult time for parents, in fact most parents handle it easily. For example, in one study of women's responses to the "empty nest," only one-third reported that a significant adjustment was required when their last child left home, and of this one-third, more of them reported it as a positive adjustment than as a negative adjustment (Harris, Ellicott, & Holmes, 1986). In general, parents' marital satisfaction and overall life satisfaction improves when their adolescent children move into emerging adulthood and leave the nest (White & Edwards, 1990). Disequilibrium is not necessarily negative, and for most parents the disequilibrium in the family system that results from children leaving home is experienced as positive.

THINKING CRITICALLY

Why do you think parents respond favorably when their children leave home?

About one-fourth of emerging adults "return to the nest" to live at least once after they leave (Goldscheider & Goldscheider, 1999). Thus far, no research has examined how young people and their parents respond when this occurs.

Although reaching midlife is positive for most adults, there is variability at midlife as there is at other ages. For men in blue-collar professions that require physical strength and stamina, such as construction or factory work, job performance becomes more difficult to sustain in middle adulthood and job satisfaction declines (Sparrow & Davies, 1988). Although marital problems decline at midlife for couples who stay married, some couples divorce at midlife. Only about one-fourth of divorces take place after age 40, but midlife divorces tend to be even more emotionally and financially difficult than divorces at younger ages, especially for women (Cherlin, 1992). Also, although a midlife

crisis does not take place for most adults, for the minority of adults who experience an unusually intense period of reevaluation and reappraisal at midlife, their relationships with their adolescents tend to be negatively affected by it (Hauser et al., 1991; Steinberg & Steinberg, 1994). In short, evaluating the influence of parents' midlife development on the family systems that adolescents and emerging adults experience requires taking into account the specific characteristics of the parents' lives.

Sibling Relationships

For about 80% of American adolescents, and similar proportions in other industrialized societies, the family system also includes relationships with at least one sibling (U.S. Bureau of the Census, 1998). The proportion of families with siblings is even higher in developing countries, where birth rates tend to be higher and families with only one child are rare (Noble, Cover, & Yanagishita, 1996).

Scholars have described five common patterns in adolescents' relationships with their siblings (Stewart, Beilfuss, & Verbrugge, 1995). In the **caregiver relationship**, one sibling serves parental functions for the other. This kind of relationship is most common between an older sister and younger siblings, in both Western and non-Western cultures (Whiting & Edwards, 1988). In the **buddy relationship**, siblings treat each other as friends. They try to be like one another, and they enjoy being together. A **critical relationship** between siblings is characterized by a high level of conflict and teasing. In a **rival relationship**, siblings compete against each other and measure their success

Adolescents tend to have more conflict with siblings than with anyone else.

against one another. Finally, in a **casual relationship** between siblings, the relationship between them is not emotionally intense, and they may have little to do with one another.

Adolescents' relationships with their siblings can take any one of these forms, or any combination of them. A conflict relationship between siblings is common. In fact, in one study that compared adolescents' relationships with siblings to their relationships with parents, grandparents, teachers, and friends, adolescents reported more frequent conflicts with their siblings than with anyone else (Furman & Buhrmester, 1985). Common sources of conflict include teasing, possessions (e.g., borrowing sibling's clothes without permission), responsibility for chores, name-calling, invasions of privacy, and perceived unequal treatment by parents (Goodwin & Roscoe, 1990).

However, even though adolescents tend to have more conflicts with siblings than in their other relationships, conflict with siblings is lower in adolescence than at younger ages (Buhrmester & Furman, 1990). Over the course of adolescence, relationships with siblings become more casual and less emotionally intense (Anderson & Starcher, 1992; Buhrmester & Furman, 1990), partly because adolescents spend less time with their siblings (Buhrmester & Furman, 1990). Adolescents' involvement in friendships and employment takes them outside the family environment for an increasing amount of time (Larson & Richards, 1994), resulting in less time and less conflict with siblings.

Adolescents in traditional cultures often take care of younger siblings.

THINKING CRITICALLY

Thus far, no research has taken place on sibling relationships in emerging adulthood. Based on your own observations and experience, what would you expect research to indicate about sibling relationships during this period?

Nevertheless, many adolescents have a buddy relationship with their siblings and feel close to them (Seginer, 1998). Most adolescents list their siblings when asked to list the most important people in their lives (Blyth, Hill, & Thiel, 1982), and siblings are often an important source of emotional support (Seginer, 1998). Adolescents who have more than one sibling may be closer to one sibling than to others. With respect to

their "favorite" brother or sister, adolescents rate the level of closeness as similar to their relationship with their best friend (Greenberger et al., 1980). However, for sibling relationships in general, adolescents rate the level of closeness as lower than their relationships with parents or friends (Buhrmester & Furman, 1987).

In traditional cultures, the caregiver relationship between siblings is the most common form. Adolescents in traditional cultures often have child-care responsibilities. In Schlegel and Barry's (1991) analysis of adolescence in traditional cultures, over 80% of adolescent boys and girls had frequent responsibility for caring for younger siblings. This responsibility promotes close attachments between siblings. Time together, and closeness, is especially high between siblings of the same gender (Schlegel & Barry, 1991), mainly because in traditional cultures daily activities are often separated by gender.

Conflict tends to be low between adolescent siblings in traditional cultures, because age serves as a powerful determinant of status (Whiting & Edwards, 1988). Older siblings are understood to have authority over younger ones, simply by virtue of being older. This lessens conflict because it is accepted that the older sibling has the right to exercise authority—although of course sometimes younger siblings resist their older siblings' authority (Schlegel & Barry, 1991). Also, siblings in traditional cultures often rely on one another economically throughout life, which means that they all have an interest in maintaining harmony in the relationship (Schlegel & Barry, 1991). For example, Hollos and Leis's (1989) ethnography of Nigerian adolescents described how they frequently rely on older siblings to provide them with connections that will lead to employment.

Extended Family Relationships

In traditional cultures, young men generally remain in their family home after marriage, and young women move into their new husband's home (Schlegel & Barry, 1991). This practice has been remarkably resistant to the influence of globalization, so far. It remains the typical pattern, for example, in the majority cultures of India and China, the two most populous countries in the world, as well as for most other traditional cultures in Asia and Africa. Consequently, in these cultures children typically grow up in a household that includes not only their parents and siblings but also grandparents, and often uncles, aunts, and cousins as well.

These living arrangements promote closeness between adolescents and their extended family. In Schlegel and Barry's (1991) cross-cultural analysis, adolescents in traditional cultures were often closer to their grandparents than to their parents. Also, for both boys and girls, daily contact was as high with grandparents as with parents, reflecting the grandparents' presence in the home. Overall, boys were slightly closer to their grandmothers than to their mothers, and considerably closer to their grandfathers than to their fathers; girls were generally as close to their grandmothers as to their mothers, and (like boys) considerably closer to their grandfathers than to their fathers. Perhaps this is because parents typically exercise authority over adolescents, which may add ambivalence to adolescents'

relationships with their parents, whereas grandparents are less likely to exercise authority and may focus more on nurturing and supporting adolescents.

Similar patterns of closeness to grandparents have been found among adolescents in American minority cultures. Asian American adolescents typically grow up with grandparents either in the home or living nearby, and they report high levels of nurturing and support from their grandparents (Fuligni, Tseng, & Lam, 1999; Sung, 1979). Many Mexican American adolescents have grandparents living in their household, and closeness in extended family relationships is highly valued in Mexican American families (Fuligni, Tseng, & Lam, 1999; Suarez-Orozco & Suarez-Orozco, 1996).

African American families also have a tradition of extended family households (Wilson, 1989). Several studies of African American families have described how their extended families provide mutual support, sharing financial resources and parenting responsibilities (McAdoo, 1996; Taylor, 1997). About 70% of African American adolescents are in single-parent families, and extended family support has been found to be especially important in reducing the emotional and economic stresses of single parenthood (Wilson, 1989). The effects of this support are evident in the lives of adolescents. For example, research by Ronald Taylor has found that extended family support in African American families is negatively related to ado-

Grandparents tend to be important figures in the lives of African American adolescents.

lescents' involvement in problem behavior and positively related to their grades in school (Taylor, 1994, 1996, 1997).

Extended family members are also important figures in the lives of adolescents in Western majority cultures. About 80% of American adolescents list at least one member of their extended family among the people most important to them (Blyth et al., 1982). However, in the American majority culture adolescents' contact with extended family members is relatively infrequent (Feiring & Lewis, 1991), in part because extended family members often live many miles away. American adolescents have significantly less contact with their extended family members compared with adolescents in European countries, because members of European extended families are more likely to live in close proximity (Alsaker & Flammer, 1999b; Arnett & Balle-Jensen, 1993). Also, for American adolescents closeness to extended family members declines substantially between childhood and adolescence (Buhrmester & Furman, 1987; Levitt, Guacci-Franco, & Levitt, 1993).

An exception to this pattern occurs among adolescents in divorced families, who tend to have increased rather than decreased contact with their grandparents during adolescence, especially with their maternal grandfather (Clingempeel et al., 1992). This suggests that the maternal grandfather fills in for the father's role in these families, to some extent, by spending more time with his grandchildren than he would if the father were present. Similarly, mothers and adolescents may have greater need for the grandfather's support and assistance, given the economic and emotional strains that often occur in divorced families (Hetherington et al., 1998).

Parenting Styles

"*My parents are never home. They're either off on a trip or away at work or something. Like, I get home from school and there's a note on the table about what I can make myself for supper and not to expect them. They don't show up at my games or band concerts. I mean, am I an orphan or what?*"

—*Julian, age 14 (Bell, 1998, p. 57)*

Because parents are so important to the development of children, social scientists have devoted a great deal

of research to the quality of parent–child relationships and to the effects that parents have on the development of children and adolescents. One branch of this research has involved the study of **parenting styles**, that is, the kinds of practices that parents exhibit in relation to their children and the effects of these practices. For over 50 years scholars have engaged in research on this topic, and the results have been quite consistent (Maccoby & Martin, 1983; Steinberg, 2000). Virtually all of the prominent scholars who have studied parenting have described it in terms of two dimensions: demandingness and responsiveness (also known by such other terms as control and warmth, restrictiveness and love). Parental **demandingness** is the degree to which parents set down rules and expectations for behavior and require their children to comply with them. Parental **responsiveness** is the degree to which parents are sensitive to their children's needs and the extent to which they express love, warmth, and concern for their children.

Many scholars have combined these two dimensions to describe different kinds of parenting styles. Currently, the best-known and most widely used conception of parenting styles is the one articulated by Diana Baumrind (1968, 1971, 1991a, 1991b). Her research on middle-class American families, along with the research of other scholars inspired by her ideas (see Maccoby & Martin, 1983; Steinberg, 2000), has identified four distinct parenting styles (see Table 7.1).

Authoritative parents are high in demandingness and high in responsiveness (Maccoby & Martin, 1983; Steinberg, 1996). They set clear rules and expectations for their children. Furthermore, they make clear what the consequences will be if their children do not comply, and they make those consequences stick if necessary. However, authoritative parents do not simply "lay down the law" and then enforce it rigidly. A distinctive feature of authoritative parents is that they *explain* the

TABLE 7.1: PARENTING STYLES AND THE TWO DIMENSIONS OF PARENTING

		Demandingness	
		High	*Low*
	High	Authoritative	Indulgent
Responsiveness	*Low*	Authoritarian	Indifferent

Source: Based on Maccoby & Martin (1983).

reasons for their rules and expectations to their children (Steinberg, 1996), and they willingly engage in discussion with their children over issues of discipline, sometimes leading to negotiation and compromise. Authoritative parents are also loving and warm toward their children, and they respond to what their children need and desire.

Authoritarian parents are high in demandingness but low in responsiveness (Dornbusch et al., 1987; Maccoby & Martin, 1983; Steinberg, 1996). They require obedience from their children, and they punish disobedience without compromise. None of the verbal give-and-take common with authoritative parents is allowed by authoritarian parents. They expect their commands to be followed without dispute or dissent. Also, they show little in the way of love or warmth toward their children. Their demandingness takes place without responsivenesss, in a way that shows little emotional attachment and may even be hostile.

Indulgent parents are low in demandingness and high in responsiveness (Lamborn et al., 1991; Maccoby & Martin, 1983; Steinberg, 1996). They have few clear expectations for their children's behavior, and they rarely discipline them. Instead, their emphasis is on responsiveness. They believe that children need love that is truly "unconditional." They may see discipline and control as having the potential to damage their children's healthy tendencies for developing creativity and expressing themselves however they wish. They provide their children with love and warmth and give them a great deal of freedom to do as they please.

Indifferent parents are low in both demandingness and responsiveness (Maccoby & Martin, 1983; Steinberg, 1996). They seem uninvolved and even uninterested in their children's development. Their goal may be to minimize the amount of time and emotion they have to devote to parenting. Thus, they require little out of their children and rarely bother to correct their behavior or place clear limits on what they are allowed to do. They also express little in the way of love or concern for their children. They may seem to have little emotional attachment to them.

An American Parenting Style?

*"**M**y mom's just starting her career now. She's going to become a legal assistant and she's going back to school and all, but she's saying, 'All these years you kids have been able to do what you wanted,*

and I've always been there putting you first. Well, now I'm coming first for a while. . . . Now I need you to take care of the house.' And I say, 'Gee, Mom, that's great for you, but where am I supposed to come from now?'"

—Wendy, age 17 (Bell, 1998, p. 67)

How common are each of these parenting styles among the parents of adolescents in American society? Is a particular parenting style typical among American parents? The best evidence on these questions comes from a study of over 4,000 American adolescents aged 14 to 18 (Lamborn et al., 1991). The adolescents were diverse, coming from working-class as well as middle-class backgrounds, from urban, suburban, and rural communities, and including African Americans (9%), Asian Americans (14%), and Latinos (12%). The adolescents completed a questionnaire asking about various aspects of their parents' demandingness and responsiveness, and on the basis of their reports their parents were classified as falling into one of the four parenting styles described above.

Figure 7.1 shows the results. As you can see, the most common parenting style among the parents of the adolescents in the study was the indifferent style (37%), followed closely by the authoritative style (32%). Authoritarian (15%) and indulgent (15%) styles were less common. Authoritative parenting was somewhat more

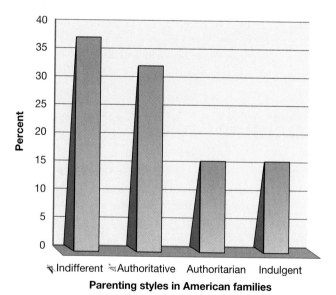

FIGURE 7.1 *Percentage of parents using each parenting style.*

common in middle-class families than in working-class families, and in White families than in minority families. Authoritarian parenting was more common in minority families than in White families.

Thus, we might conclude that the parents of American adolescents have diverse parenting styles, tending toward styles that either combine demandingness and responsiveness (authoritative) or lack both of these qualities (indifferent). We might also conclude that the family socialization of American adolescents tends toward broad rather than narrow socialization—only the authoritarian style emphasizes obedience and conformity, and that style is used by only a small proportion of parents. The other three styles all place a higher value on individualism, independence, and self-expression, although in different ways and to different degrees.

The high proportion of indifferent parents in the study (Lamborn et al., 1991)—37%—is striking. Perhaps this is related to the aspects of parents' midlife development discussed earlier in this chapter. At midlife, many parents feel they are reaching an enjoyable time of life, and they may wish to pursue their own interests now after many years of raising young children.

These parenting styles can also be looked at as custom complexes. As described in Chapter 4, a custom complex consists of a typical cultural practice and the beliefs underlying it. What beliefs are reflected in the parenting styles described above? Research on parents' child-rearing goals shows that American parents tend to value independence highly as a quality they wish to promote in their children (Alwin, 1988; Hoffman, 1988). Authoritarian parenting clearly discourages independence, but the other three parenting styles—authoritative, indulgent, and indifferent, which accounted for 85% of the parenting styles in the study described above (Lamborn et al., 1991)—reflect parents' beliefs that it is good for adolescents to learn **autonomy**, that is, to learn to be independent and self-sufficient, to learn to think for themselves and be responsible for their own behavior.

Authoritative parents promote autonomy in positive ways, through encouraging discussion and give-and-take that teaches adolescents to think independently and make mature deci-

sions. Indifferent and indulgent parents promote this outcome in a negative way, that is, through the absence of restraint that allows adolescents a great deal of autonomy without parental guidance. As we will see shortly, the differences in how these parenting styles promote autonomy result in different effects on adolescents' development. Nevertheless, in combination the prominence of these parenting styles in the families of American adolescents reflects the prominence of individualism in American cultural beliefs (Alwin, 1988).

The Effects of Parenting Styles on Adolescents

A great deal of research has been conducted on how parenting styles influence adolescents' development. A summary of the results is shown in Table 7.2. In general, authoritative parenting is associated with the most favorable outcomes, at least by American standards. Adolescents who have authoritative parents tend to be independent, self-assured, creative, and socially skilled (Baumrind, 1991a, 1991b; Fuligni & Eccles, 1993; Lamborn et al., 1991; Steinberg et al., 1994; Steinberg, 2000). They also tend to do well in school and to get along well with their peers and with adults (Steinberg, 1996, 2000).

All the other parenting styles are associated with some negative outcomes, although the type of negative outcome varies depending on the specific parenting style (Baumrind, 1991a, 1991b; Dornbusch et al., 1990; Durbin et al., 1993; Lamborn et al., 1991; Steinberg et al., 1994; Steinberg, 1996, 2000). Adolescents of authoritarian parents tend to be dependent, passive, and conforming. They are often less self-assured, less creative, and less socially adept than other adolescents. Adolescents of indulgent parents tend to be immature and irresponsible. They are more likely than other adolescents to conform to their peers.

TABLE 7.2: ADOLESCENT OUTCOMES ASSOCIATED WITH PARENTING STYLES

Authoritative	Authoritarian	Indulgent	Indifferent
Independent	Dependent	Irresponsible	Impulsive
Creative	Passive	Conforming	Delinquent
Self-assured	Conforming	Immature	Early sex, drugs
Socially skilled			

Adolescents of indifferent parents tend to be impulsive. Partly as a consequence of their impulsiveness, and partly because indifferent parents do little to monitor their adolescents' activities, adolescents of indifferent parents tend to have higher rates of problem behaviors such as delinquency, early sexual involvement, and use of drugs and alcohol.

Authoritative parenting tends to be better for adolescents for a number of reasons (Steinberg, 2000). Adolescents are at a point in their lives when they have become capable of exercising more autonomy and self-regulation than when they were younger (Steinberg, 1990, 1996). In order to be able to move into adult roles after adolescence, they need to be given a greater amount of autonomy and required to exercise a greater amount of responsibility (Steinberg & Levine, 1997). At the same time, they lack the experience with the world and with their own impulses and abilities that adults have, and consequently an excess of autonomy may leave them aimless or even lead them into harm (Dornbusch et al., 1990). Authoritative parenting achieves a balance between allowing enough autonomy for adolescents to develop their capacities while at the same time requiring them to exercise their increased autonomy in a responsible way. All the other parenting styles either fail to allow as much autonomy or allow it without requiring the kind of responsibility that is associated with healthy development.

Authoritative parenting combines demandingness with responsiveness, which includes affection, emotional attachment, love, and concern for the adolescent's needs and well-being. Parents' responsiveness helps adolescents to learn to believe in their own worthiness as people (Baumrind, 1991a, 1991b). It also leads adolescents to identify with their parents and seek to please them by embracing the values their parents hold and by behaving in ways that the parents will approve (Baumrind, 1991a, 1991b). The other parenting styles either lack responsiveness or provide it without requiring an adequate level of demandingness.

Inconsistency between parents also tends to be related to negative outcomes for adolescents. Most studies of parenting in adolescence simply combine ratings for the two parents into one rating, but studies that examine differences have produced interesting results. For example, Johnson, Shulman, and Collins (1991) had 5th, 8th, and 11th graders rate their parents on various items. Parents were categorized into two general types, authoritative or permissive. Fifth

graders generally viewed their parents as similar—only 9% rated them in different categories—but the proportion perceiving a discrepancy rose with age, to 23% of 8th graders and 31% of 11th graders. Adolescents who perceived inconsistency between their parents were lower on self-esteem and school performance compared not only with those who perceived both parents as authoritative but also with those who perceived both parents as permissive. A study by Wentzel and Feldman (1993) produced similar results: Adolescents who perceived inconsistency in the parenting styles of their parents were lower than other adolescents on self-control and academic motivation.

THINKING CRITICALLY

How would you categorize the parenting style of your parents when you were in adolescence? Was it the same for you as for your siblings (if you have any)? To what extent did their parenting influence you, and to what extent did you evoke certain parenting behaviors from them?

A More Complex Picture of Parenting Effects

Although parents undoubtedly affect their adolescents profoundly by their parenting, the process is not nearly as simple as the cause-and-effect model just described. Sometimes discussions of parenting makes it sound as though Parenting Style A automatically and inevitably produces Adolescent Type X (Collins, Maccoby, Steinberg, Hetherington, & Bornstein, 2000). However, enough research has taken place by now to indicate that the relationship between parenting styles and adolescent development is considerably more complex than that. Adolescents not only are affected by their parents, but also affect their parents in return. This principle is referred to by scholars as **reciprocal or bidirectional effects** between parents and children (Mussen et al., 1990).

Recall our discussion of evocative genotype–environment interactions in Chapter 2. Adolescents are not like billiard balls who head reliably in the direction they are propelled by their parents. They have personalities and desires of their own that they bring to the parent–adolescent relationship (Scarr, 1992). Thus, adolescents may evoke certain behaviors from their parents. An especially aggressive adolescent may evoke authoritarian parenting—perhaps the parents find that authoritative explanations of the rules are simply ignored, and their responsiveness diminishes as a result of the adolescent's repeated violations of their trust. An especially shy adolescent may evoke indulgent parenting—parents may see no point in laying down specific rules for an adolescent who has no inclination to do anything outrageous anyway.

Research involving siblings suggests that reciprocal effects occur in parent–adolescent relationships. Most research on the effects of parenting styles involves only one adolescent per family, and this research indeed finds a consistent correlation between what adolescents say their parents do and what adolescents report about their own characteristics and behavior. However, a few studies have included more than one adolescent per family, and those studies make the picture considerably more complex. The interesting finding of these studies is that adolescent siblings *within the same family* often report very different things about what their parents are like toward them (Daniels et al., 1985; Hoffman, 1991; Plomin & Daniels, 1987). One study investigated families with two adolescents aged 11 to 17 and found that siblings perceived significant differences in their parents'

love for them, their parents' closeness to them, their parents' use of discipline, and the degree to which their parents involved them in family decisions (Daniels et al., 1985).

Thus, one adolescent may see her parents as admirably demanding and responsive, the epitome of the authoritative parent, whereas her brother describes the same parents as dictatorial, unresponsive, authoritarian parents. These differences in how adolescents perceive their parents' behavior are in turn related to differences in the adolescents: The ones who perceive their parents as authoritative tend to be happier and to be functioning better in a variety of ways (Daniels et al., 1985). Overall, little similarity in personality exists between adolescent siblings (Plomin & Daniels, 1987), which suggests that whatever effect parents have, it may be different for different adolescents within the same family.

Does this research discredit the claim that "parenting styles" influence adolescents? No, but it modifies this claim (Collins et al., 2000). Parents do have beliefs about what is best for their adolescents, and they try to express those beliefs through their behavior toward their adolescents (Alwin, 1988). However, parents' actual behavior is affected not only by what they believe is best but also by how their adolescents behave toward them and how their adolescents seem to respond to their parenting. Being an authoritative parent is easier if your adolescent responds to the demandingness and responsiveness you provide, and not so easy if your love is rejected and your rules and the reasons you provide for them are ignored. Parents whose attempts to persuade their adolescents through reasoning and discussion fall on deaf ears may be tempted either to demand compliance (and become more authoritarian) or give up trying (and become indulgent or indifferent).

Adolescent siblings within the same family often report different experiences with their parents.

Parenting in Other Cultures

Almost all the research on parenting styles has taken place in American society, and most of it has taken place on families in the American majority culture.

What do parent–adolescent relationships look like if we step outside of the American experience and look around the world, especially toward non-Western cultures?

Probably the most striking difference in parenting styles is how rare the authoritative parenting style is in non-Western cultures. Authoritative parents do not rely on the authority of the parental role to ensure that adolescents comply with their commands and instructions. They do not simply lay down the law and expect to be obeyed. On the contrary, a key feature of authoritative parenting is that parents *explain the reasons* for what they want adolescents to do and *engage in discussion* with their adolescents over the guidelines for their adolescents' behavior (Baumrind, 1971, 1991a; Steinberg & Levine, 1997).

Outside of the West, however, this is an extremely rare approach to adolescent socialization. In traditional cultures, parents expect that their authority will be obeyed, without question and without requiring an explanation (Whiting & Edwards, 1988). This is true not only of nonindustrial traditional cultures but also of industrialized traditional cultures outside the West, most notably Asian cultures such as China, Japan, Vietnam, and South Korea (Fuligni et al., 1999; Zhou, 1997). In traditional cultures, the *role of parent* carries greater inherent authority than it does in the West. Parents are not supposed to provide reasons why they should be respected and obeyed. The simple fact that they are parents and their children are children is viewed as sufficient justification for their authority (see the Cultural Focus box for an example).

CULTURAL FOCUS
Young People and Their Families in India

India is currently the second-most populous country in the world, with a population of over one billion. By the middle of the 21st century, it is projected to pass China and reach a population of one and a half billion, more than five times the projected population of the United States. India is an astonishingly diverse country, with a wide variety of religions, languages, and regional cultures. Nevertheless, scholars generally believe that a common Indian culture can be identified (Segal, 1998), including with regard to young people and their families. The features of the Indian family provide a good illustration of young people's family lives in a traditional culture.

Indian families have many features in common with other traditional cultures discussed in this book. Collectivistic values are strong, and the well-being and success of the family is considered more important than the well-being and success of the individual (Saraswathi, 1999). There is a strong emphasis on sacrifice, and children are taught from an early age to relinquish their own desires for the sake of the interests of the family as a whole. Interdependence among family members is stressed throughout life, emotionally, socially, and financially (Gupta, 1987; Kakar, 1998; Shukla, 1994).

As in most traditional cultures, the Indian family has a clear hierarchy based on age (Kakar, 1998; Reddy & Gibbons, 1999; Segal, 1998). Respect for elders is strongly emphasized. Even in childhood, older children are understood to have definite authority over anyone younger than they are; even in adulthood, older adults are considered to merit respect and deference from younger adults simply on the basis of being older. Because it is common for young married couples to live with the husband's parents rather than establishing a separate residence, many households with children contain grandparents and often uncles, aunts, and cousins as well. This pattern is changing, because Indian society is becoming increasingly urbanized, and extended family households are less common in urban areas than in rural areas. Nevertheless, even now 80% of India's population is rural and tends to live according to traditional family arrangements (Carson et al., 1999).

One feature that is distinctive to the traditional Indian family is the idea that the parents, and especially the father, are to be regarded by their children as a god would be regarded by a devotee. The Hindu religion, which most Indians believe, has many gods of varying degrees of power, so this is not like stating that the father is like "God" in a Western sense. Nevertheless, the analogy of a father being like a god to his children effectively symbolizes and conveys the absolute nature of his authority within the family.

These features of the Indian family have important implications for the development of adolescents and emerging adults. The inherent authority of parents and the emphasis on respect for elders means that parents expect obedience even from adolescents and emerging adults. Traditional Indian families include little of the explanation of rules and discussion of decisions that characterize the relationships between adolescents and parents in authoritative Western families. For parents to explain the reasons for their rules, or for young people to demand to take part in family decisions, would be considered an offense to the parents' inherent authority. This does not mean the parents are "authoritarian," in the scheme of parenting styles described by Western social scientists. On the contrary, warmth, love, and affection are known to be especially strong in Indian families (Kakar, 1998; Larson et al., 2000). Indian parenting is better described by the term *traditional* discussed in this chapter.

The authority of parents in Indian families also means that there are not the same expectations of autonomy for adolescents and emerging adults as there are in Western families (Gupta, 1987; Larson et al., 2000; Reddy & Gibbons, 1999; Segal, 1998; Shukla, 1994). Indian adolescents spend most of their leisure time with their families, not with peer friends, cliques, and crowds. Dating and sexual relationships before marriage are almost nonexistent (Kakar, 1998). Most marriages are arranged by the parents, not chosen independently by the young people themselves. Emerging adults often remain in their parents' homes until marriage.

What are the consequences of these family practices for the development of Indian adolescents and emerging adults? A Western reader may be tempted to regard the practices of Indian families as "unhealthy" because of their hierarchical, patriarchal quality and because of the way that the autonomy of young people is suppressed. However, it is probably more accurate to view Indian family socialization as having both costs and benefits, like other cultural forms of socialization (Arnett, 1995a). For young people in India, there are clearly costs in terms of individual autonomy. To be expected to be obedient to your parents even in your teens and twenties (and beyond), to be discouraged from ever questioning your parents' authority and judgment, and to have your parents control crucial life decisions in love and work clearly means that young people's autonomy is restricted in Indian families.

However, Indian family practices have clear benefits as well. Young people who grow up in a close, interdependent Indian family have the benefit of family support and guidance as they enter adult roles. For example, even now in India, even among well-educated, urban Indians, most young people continue to prefer to have their parents arrange their marriage rather than choosing a marriage partner themselves (Kakar, 1998). Having a strong sense of family interdependence also provides Indian young people with a strong family identity, which may make them less lonely and vulnerable as they form an individual identity. Indian adolescents have low rates of delinquency, depression, and suicide compared with Western adolescents (Kakar, 1998).

The influence of globalization can be seen in Indian culture as in other traditional cultures. Western styles of dress, language, and music are popular among young Indians. In urban middle-class families, the traditional Indian pattern of parental authority is changing, and parents' relationships with their adolescents increasingly involve discussion and negotiation (Larson et al., 2000; Reddy & Gibbons, 1999). Nevertheless, young Indians remain proud of the Indian tradition of close families, and they express the desire to see that tradition endure (Mullatti, 1995).

Does this mean that the typical parenting style in traditional cultures is authoritarian? No, although sometimes scholars have made the mistake of coming to this conclusion. Keep in mind that authoritarian parenting combines high demandingness with *low responsiveness*. Parents in traditional cultures are indeed high in demandingness, and their demandingness is often of a more uncompromising quality than is typical in the West. However, it is not true that parents in traditional cultures are typically low in responsiveness. On the contrary, parents and adolescents in nonindustrialized traditional cultures often develop a closeness that is nearly impossible in Western families, because they spend virtually all of their days together, working side by side (boys with their fathers, girls with their mothers), in a way that the economic structure of industrialized societies prevents (Schlegel & Barry, 1991). Parents and adolescents in industrialized traditional cultures such as Asian cultures also maintain a strong degree of closeness, reflected in shared activities and mutual obligations (Fuligni et al., 1999).

However, parental responsiveness outside the West may be expressed quite differently in non-Western cultures. For example, parents in non-Western cultures rarely use praise with their children (Whiting & Edwards, 1988). But are typical parents of adolescents in non-Western cultures responsive—do they have deep emotional attachments with their adolescents, do they love them, are they deeply concerned with their well-being? Unquestionably the answer is yes.

If parents in non-Western cultures cannot be called authoritarian, what *are* they? The fact is, they do not fit very well into the parenting scheme presented above. They are generally closest to authoritative parents, because like them they tend to be high in demandingness and high in responsiveness. However, as noted, their demandingness is very different than the demandingness of the authoritative American or Western parent.

Diana Baumrind (1987), the scholar who originally invented the terminology for the parenting styles we have been discussing, has recognized the problem of fitting traditional cultures into her scheme. In fact, she has proposed the term **traditional parenting style** to describe the kind of parenting typical in traditional cultures—high in responsiveness and high in a kind of demandingness that does not encourage discussion and debate but rather expects compliance by virtue of cultural beliefs supporting the inherent authority of the parental role (Baumrind, 1987).

The difficulty of fitting other cultures into Baumrind's scheme applies not only to non-Western traditional cultures, but also to ethnic minority cultures that are part of American society. Studies indicate that African American, Latino, and Asian American parents are less likely than White parents to be classified as authoritative and more likely to be classified as authoritarian (e.g., Chao, 1994; Dornbusch et al., 1987; Feldman et al., 1991; Steinberg et al., 1991; Steinberg, Dornbusch, & Brown, 1992). However, because none of these studies used Baumrind's more recent "traditional" category as one of the classifications, it is somewhat difficult to say what this means. If parents in these

studies were high in responsiveness and also high in an uncompromising demandingness that rejects discussion and explanation, they would not have fit well into either the authoritative or the authoritarian categories used by the researchers.

Asian American psychologist Ruth Chao (1994) has argued that designations of authoritative and authoritarian cannot be easily applied to Asian American parents. She suggests that White researchers may misunderstand Asian American parenting and mislabel it as authoritarian, because it involves a degree and type of demandingness that is typical of Asian families but that may be perceived as wrong by a White researcher unfamiliar with Asian cultural beliefs. Asian American adolescents show none of the negative effects typically associated with authoritarian parenting. On the contrary, they have higher educational achievement, lower rates of behavioral problems, and lower rates of psychological problems, compared with White adolescents (Feldman et al., 1991; Steinberg, 1996). This suggests that the cultural context of parenting is crucial to predicting the effects parenting will have on adolescents.

Latino parents in American society have also typically been classified as authoritarian (Busch-Rossnagel & Zayas, 1991). The Latino cultural belief system places a premium on the idea of *respeto*, which emphasizes respect for and obedience to parents and elders, especially the father. The role of the parent is considered to be enough to command authority, without requiring that the parents explain their rules to their children. Again, however, this does not mean that their parenting is authoritarian. Another pillar of Latino cultural beliefs is **familism**, which emphasizes the love, closeness, and mutual obligations of Latino family life. This hardly sounds like the aloofness and hostility characteristic of the authoritarian parent, and in fact studies confirm the positive effects of familism on Latino adolescents (Fuligni et al., 1999; Suarez-Orozco & Suarez-Orozco, 1996).

Attachments to Parents

"[M]y parents are] always there and I feel I can always go to them and they always say something that will make me feel better."

—*17-year-old girl (Konopka, 1985, p. 71)*

We have noted that adolescents consistently state that their parents are among the most important figures in their lives, and that most young people maintain a sense of emotional closeness to their parents throughout adolescence and emerging adulthood. An influential theory describing the emotional relationships between parents and children is **attachment theory**. Attachment theory was originally developed by British psychiatrist John Bowlby (1969, 1973, 1980), who argued that among humans as among other primates, attachments between parents and children have an evolutionary basis in the need for vulnerable young members of the species to stay in close proximity to adults who will care for and protect them. Bowlby's colleague, American psychologist Mary Ainsworth (1967, 1982), observed interactions between mothers and infants and described two general types of attachment: **secure attachment**, in which infants use the mother as a "secure base from which to explore" when all is well, but seek physical comfort and consolation from her if frightened or threatened; and **insecure attachment**, in which infants are less confident in exploring the environment and resist or avoid the mother when she attempts to offer comfort or consolation.

Although most of the early research and theory on attachment focused on infancy, both Bowlby and Ainsworth believed that the attachment formed with the **primary caregiver** in infancy forms the foundation for attachments to others throughout a person's life. Bowlby quoted a phrase from Sigmund Freud to describe this, in which Freud stated that the relationship with the mother is "the prototype of all [future] love relations" (Freud, 1940/64, p. 188). According to Bowlby (1969), in the course of interactions with the primary caregiver in infancy, the infant develops an **internal working model** that shapes expectations and interactions in relationships to others throughout life. This implies that in adolescence and emerging adulthood, the quality of relationships with others—from friends to teachers to romantic partners to the parents themselves—will all be shaped, for better or worse, by the quality of the attachments to parents the young person experienced in infancy.

This is a provocative and intriguing claim. How well does it hold up in research? First, abundant research indicates that a secure attachment to parents *in adolescence* is related to a variety of favorable outcomes. Secure attachments to parents are related to a variety of aspects of adolescents' well-being, including self-esteem and psychological and physical health (Allen & Kuperminc, 1995; Allen & Land, 1999; Juang & Nguyen, 1997). Adolescents who have secure attachments to parents also tend to have closer relationships to friends

Secure attachments to parents are related to adolescents' well-being in a variety of respects.

and romantic partners (Allen & Bell, 1995; Allen et al., 1994; Laible, Carlo, & Rafaelli, 2000). Security of attachment to parents in adolescence has also been found to predict a variety of outcomes in emerging adulthood, including educational and occupational attainment, psychological problems, and drug use (Allen et al., 1998; O'Connor et al., 1996). Adolescents with secure attachments to their parents tend to perceive their parents as responsive, and as we have seen responsiveness is one aspect of the authoritative parenting style, which tends to be related to positive outcomes in adolescence.

Another prediction of attachment theory involves the compatibility between autonomy and relatedness in adolescence. According to attachment theory, autonomy (being capable of self-direction) and **relatedness** (feeling close to parents emotionally) should be compatible rather than opposing dynamics in relations with parents. That is, in infancy as well as in adolescence, if children feel close to their parents and confident of their parents' love and concern, they are likely to be able to develop a healthy sense of autonomy from parents as they grow up (Allen & Bell, 1995). Rather than promoting prolonged dependence on parents, a secure attachment gives children the confidence to go out into the world, using the comfort of that attachment as a "secure base from which to explore."

This prediction from attachment theory is supported by research. Adolescents who are the most autonomous and self-reliant also tend to report close, affectionate relationships with their parents (Allen et al., 1994; Ryan & Lynch, 1989). Adolescents who have trouble establishing autonomy in adolescence also tend to have more difficulty maintaining a healthy level of relatedness to parents. An imbalance between autonomy and relatedness (i.e., too little of one or both) tends to be related to a variety of negative outcomes, such as psychological problems and drug use (Allen et al., 1994).

However, these studies do not really test the heart of attachment theory, which is the claim that attachments *in infancy* form the basis for all later relationships, including those in adolescence and emerging adulthood. What do studies indicate on this crucial issue? Because the infants in the earliest attachment studies have only recently grown into adolescence, there is limited data available so far. A series of studies of college students, mostly by Roger Kobak and his colleagues, has attempted to reconstruct the students' early attachments by having them recall various aspects of their childhood relationships with their parents (Kobak & Cole, 1994; Kobak et al., 1993; Kobak & Sceery, 1988). These scholars have found that college students' who remember having secure attachments in childhood also report (in the present) lower rates of depression (Kobak & Cole, 1994), more stable romantic relationships (Davis & Kirkpatrick, 1998), and closer friendships (Kerns, 1994) compared with students who report having insecure attachments in childhood. This seems consistent with the prediction of attachment theory that a secure attachment in infancy provides a solid foundation for later development. However, this research approach relies on having people recall memories from childhood, which other research has found to be an unreliable enterprise, often distorted by failures of memory and by the quality of present relationships.

The only study thus far that has followed a sample from infancy to adolescence has found that attachment classification in infancy predicted the quality of interactions with others at ages 10 and 15 (Sroufe, Carlson, & Schulman, 1993). When the children in the original infancy study reached age 10, the researchers invited them to attend a summer camp where their relations with peers could be examined. At age 10, the children who had been securely attached in infancy were judged to be more skilled socially, more self-confident, and less dependent on other campers. Five years later, the researchers arranged a camp reunion where the children could again be evaluated. At age 15, adolescents who had been securely attached in infancy were more open in expressing their feelings and were more likely to form close relationships with peers. However, some studies have failed to find a relation between infant attachment and behavior even 2 years later. At this point, then, the answer to the question of whether infant attachment is a foundation for adolescent development awaits further studies following up samples from infancy into adolescence.

Emerging Adults' Relationships With Parents

In Western majority cultures, most young people move out of their parents' home sometime during emerging adulthood. In the United States, leaving home typically takes place around ages 18 to 19 (Goldscheider & Goldscheider, 1999). This is earlier than in most other Western countries. For example, in Germany the median age of leaving home is 23 for males and 21 for females (Silbereisen, Meschke, & Schwarz, 1996), and median ages in other Western countries are similar. In the United States as well as in other Western countries, few emerging adults remain in their parents' home until marriage. The most common reasons for leaving home stated by emerging adults are going to college, cohabiting with a partner, or simply the desire for independence (Goldscheider & Goldscheider, 1999; Silbereisen et al., 1996).

When a young person leaves home, a disruption in the family system takes place that requires family members to adjust. As we have seen, parents generally adjust very well, and in fact report improved marital satisfaction and life satisfaction once their children leave (White & Edwards, 1990). What about the relationship between parents and emerging adults? How is it influenced by the young person's departure?

Typically, relationships between parents and emerging adults *improve* once the young person leaves home. In this case, at least, absence makes the heart grow fonder. Numerous studies have confirmed that emerging adults report greater closeness and fewer negative feelings toward their parents after moving out (e.g., O'Connor et al., 1996; Shaver, Furman, & Buhrmester, 1985; Sullivan & Sullivan, 1980). Furthermore, among emerging adults of the same age, those who have moved out tend to get along better with their parents than those who remain at home. For example, Dubas and Petersen (1996) followed a sample of about 246 young people from age 13 through age 21. At age 21, the emerging adults who had moved at least an hour away (by car) from their parents reported the highest levels of closeness to their parents and valued their parents' opinions most highly. Emerging adults who remained home had the poorest relations with their parents in these respects, and those who had moved out but remained within an hour's drive were in between the other two groups.

Relationships with parents tend to improve when emerging adults leave home.

of Italians aged 15 to 24 live with their parents, the highest percentage in the European Union (EU). However, only 8% of them view their living arrangements as a problem—the lowest percentage among EU countries. Many European emerging adults remain at home contentedly through their early twenties, by choice rather than necessity.

Thus, studies in both the United States and Europe show that emerging adults can maintain or enhance the closeness they feel to their parents even as they become more autonomous. This is similar to the pattern we have already seen for adolescents. For both adolescents and emerging adults, autonomy and relatedness are complementary rather than opposing dimensions of their relationships with their parents (O'Connor et al., 1996).

What explains these patterns? Some scholars have suggested that leaving home leads young people to appreciate their parents more (Katchadourian & Boli, 1985). Another factor may be that it may be easier to be fond of someone you no longer live with. Once emerging adults move out, they no longer experience the day-to-day frictions with their parents that inevitably result from living with others. They can now control the frequency and timing of their interactions with their parents in a way they could not when they were living with them. They can visit their parents for the weekend, for a holiday, or for dinner, enjoy the time together, and still maintain full control over their daily lives.

In European countries, emerging adults tend to live with their parents longer than in the United States, especially in southern and eastern Europe (Chisholm & Hurrelmann, 1995). There are a number of practical reasons for this. European university students are more likely than American students to continue to live at home while they attend university. European emerging adults who do not attend university may have difficulty finding or affording an apartment of their own. However, also important are European cultural values that emphasize mutual support within the family while also allowing young people substantial autonomy. Young Europeans find that they can enjoy a higher standard of living by staying at home rather than living independently, and at the same time enjoy substantial autonomy. Italy provides a good case in point (Chisholm & Hurrelman, 1995). Ninety-four percent

Parent–Adolescent Conflict

"This is a dangerous world, what with all the drugs and drunk drivers and violent crime and kids disappearing and you name it. I know my kids are pretty responsible, but can I trust all their friends? Are they going to end up in some situation they can't get out of? Are they going to get in over their heads? You can never be sure, so I worry and set curfews and make rules about where they can go and who they can go with. Not because I want to be a tough dad, but because I want them to be safe."

—*John, father of a 16-year-old son and a 13-year-old daughter (Bell, 1998, p. 54)*

"My father is very strict and had a great deal of rules when I was in high school, which usually could not be bent for anything. My father was very worried about the fact that I was getting older and interested in boys so much. This worrying led him to lay down strict rules which led to many arguments between us. He wouldn't let me date until I was 16—by this he meant 'don't even speak to a boy until you're 16!' He would hardly let me go anywhere."

—*Danielle, age 19 (Arnett, unpublished data)*

The course of family life does not always run smooth, and this seems to be especially true for families with adolescents. For a variety of reasons, adolescence can be a difficult time for relationships with parents.

However, the degree of parent–adolescent conflict should not be exaggerated. Early theories of adolescence, such as by G. Stanley Hall (1904) and Anna Freud (1946), made it sound as though it was universal and inevitable that *all* adolescents rebel against their parents and that *all* parents and adolescents experience intense conflict for many years. Anna Freud (1946) even believed that adolescents would not develop normally without this kind of turmoil in their relationships with their parents.

Few scholars on adolescence believe this anymore. Over the past few decades, numerous studies have indicated that it is simply not true. In fact, adolescents and their parents agree on many of the most important aspects of their views of life and typically have a great deal of love and respect for one another (Offer & Schonert-Reichl, 1992). Two studies in the 1960s were among the first and most important in dispelling the stereotype about pervasive and fierce conflict in parent–adolescent relationships (Douvan & Adelson, 1966; Offer, 1969). Both studies found that the great majority of adolescents like their parents, trust them, and admire them. Both studies also found that adolescents and their parents frequently disagreed, but that their arguments were usually over seemingly minor issues such as curfews, clothes, grooming, and use of the family car. These arguments usually did not seriously threaten the attachments between parents and their adolescents.

More recent studies confirm this pattern (e.g., Collins, 1990; Hill, 1987; Offer, Ostrov, & Howard, 1981; Steinberg, 1990, 2000). These studies report that adolescents typically love and care about their parents and are confident that their parents feel the same about them. Like the earlier studies, recent studies find that arguments between parents and adolescents generally concern seemingly minor issues such as curfews, clothing, musical preferences, and the like (Hill & Holmbeck, 1987; Smetana, 1988; Steinberg & Levine, 1997). Parents and adolescents may disagree and argue about these issues, but they usually agree on key values such as the importance of education, the value of hard work, and the desirability of being honest and trustworthy (Gecas & Seff, 1990).

However, let's not get carried away with the rosy portrait of family harmony, either. Studies also indicate that conflict with parents increases sharply in early adolescence, compared with preadolescence, and remains high for several years before declining in late

THINKING CRITICALLY

Apply the idea of the custom complex to parent–child conflict in the American majority culture. How do the typical topics of conflict reflect certain cultural beliefs?

adolescence (Paikoff & Brooks-Gunn, 1991). One study found that high school sophomores had an argument with a parent about once every three days, lasting an average of 11 minutes (Montemayor, 1982). Frequency of conflict between *typical* adolescents and their parents is higher than between *distressed* marital couples (Buchanan, Maccoby, & Dornbusch, 1991). Conflict in adolescence is especially frequent and intense between mothers and daughters (Montemayor, 1982; Steinberg, 1990). Both parents and adolescents report more frequent conflict in early adolescence than prior to adolescence (Paikoff & Brooks-Gunn, 1991; Smetana, 1989); by midadolescence, conflict with parents tends to become somewhat less frequent but more intense (Laursen, Coy, & Collins, 1998). It is only in late adolescence that conflict with parents diminishes substantially (Laursen et al., 1998).

Conflict in adolescence is especially frequent and intense between mothers and daughters.

Perhaps as a consequence of these conflicts, parents tend to perceive adolescence as the most difficult stage of their children's development (Buchanan et al., 1990; Pasley & Gecas, 1984; Silverberg & Steinberg, 1990). Although midlife tends to be an especially fruitful and satisfying time for adults, for many of them their satisfaction with their relationships with their children diminishes when their children reach adolescence (Gecas & Seff, 1990).

Although most parent–adolescent conflict is over apparently minor issues, some issues that seem trivial on the surface may in fact be substitutes for more serious underlying issues (Arnett, 1999a). For example, most American parents and adolescents have limited communication about sexual issues. Especially in the era of AIDS and other sexually transmitted diseases, it would be surprising indeed if most parents did not have some concerns about their adolescents' sexual behavior (Eccles et al., 1993), yet they find it difficult to speak to their adolescents directly about sexual issues. As a result, they may say "You can't wear that to school" when they mean "That's too sexually provocative." They may say "I don't know if it's a good idea for you to date him" when they really mean "He has that lean and hungry look—I worry that he will want you to have sex, and I worry that you'll like the idea." And "You have to be home by 11:00" may mean "The movie ends at ten, and I don't want you to have time to have sex between the time the movie ends and the time you come home."

Sexual issues are not the only issues that may be argued about in this indirect way. "I don't like that crowd you're hanging around with lately" could mean "They look like the type who might use drugs, and I worry that they might persuade you to use them, too." Arguments about curfews may be parents' attempts to communicate that "The sooner you come in, the less likely it is that you and your friends will have drunk enough beer to put yourselves at risk for a terrible automobile accident."

Seen in this light, these arguments are not necessarily over trivial issues, but may be proxies for arguments over serious issues of life and death (Arnett, 1999a). Parents have legitimate concerns about the safety and well-being of their adolescents, given the high rates of adolescents' risky behavior (Arnett, 1995a), but they also know that in the American majority culture they are expected to loosen the reigns substantially when their children reach their teens. The result may be that they express their concerns indirectly, through what seem to be less serious issues.

Sources of Conflict With Parents

"One minute my mother treats me like I'm old enough to do this or this—like help her out at home by doing the marketing or making dinner or babysitting my little brother. And she's always telling me, 'You're thirteen years old now, you should know better than that!' But then the next minute, when there's something I really

Chores are a common source of conflict between parents and adolescents.

want to do, like there's a party that everyone's going to, she'll say, 'You're too young to do that.'"

> —*Elizabeth, age 13*
> *(Bell, 1998, p. 55)*

But why do parents and adolescents argue more than they did earlier? Why would early adolescence be a time when conflict with parents is especially high? Part of the explanation may lie in the biological and cognitive changes of adolescence. Biologically, adolescents become bigger and stronger physically with puberty, making it more difficult for parents to impose their authority by virtue of their greater physical presence. Also, puberty means sexual maturity, which means that sexual issues may be a source of conflict—at least indirectly—in a way they would not have been earlier (Arnett, 1999a; Steinberg, 1990).

Cognitively, increased capacities for thinking abstractly and with more complexity makes adolescents better arguers than preadolescents and makes it more difficult for parents to prevail quickly in arguments with their children. Conflict may also be a reflection of cognitive changes experienced by adolescents and their parents in their expectations for one another. Psychologists Andrew Collins and Judith Smetana have studied these mutual cognitions in relation to parent–adolescent conflict, from different perspectives. According to Collins (1997), conflict may occur when parents' expectations are violated as their child reaches adolescence and wants to behave differently—for example, stay out later, spend more time with friends, wear different clothes. Adolescents' expectations of their parents change at the same time, in terms of what they expect their parents to allow them to do. Thus, adolescents' development may result in a mismatch between parents' and adolescents' expectations, and conflict between parents and adolescents may occur in the course of revising their expectations for one another. Although parents and adolescents are likely to experience conflict as distressing, Collins' (1997) insights suggest that conflict can be constructive and useful, as it promotes the development of a new equilibrium in the family system that allows adolescents greater autonomy.

Smetana (1988) argues that parent–adolescent conflict results from the different ways that parents and adolescents understand and define the range of adolescents' autonomy. Issues of conflict are frequently viewed by parents as matters of desirable social convention but viewed by adolescents as matters of personal choice. Research indicates that, especially in early adolescence, parents and adolescents often disagree about who should have the authority over issues such as dress and hair styles,

whom the adolescent's friends should be, and what state of order or disorder should be maintained in the adolescent's bedroom (Smetana, 1989; Smetana & Asquith, 1994). Parents tend to see these as issues they should decide, or at least influence and set boundaries for; adolescents, however, tend to see the issues as matters of personal choice that should be theirs to decide by now. Perhaps the peak of conflict occurs in early adolescence because that is the time when adolescents are first pressing for a new degree of autonomy, and parents are adjusting to their adolescents' new capacities and struggling over how much autonomy they should allow.

Culture and Conflict With Parents

Although the biological and cognitive changes of adolescence may provide a basis for parent–adolescent conflict, this does mean that such conflict is therefore universal and "natural." Biological and cognitive changes take place among adolescents in all cultures, yet parent–adolescent conflict is not typical in all cultures (Arnett, 1999a). Culture can take the raw material of nature and shape it in highly diverse ways. This is no less true for parent–adolescent conflict than for the other topics we will address in this book.

In traditional cultures, it is rare for parents and adolescents to engage in the kind of frequent, petty conflicts typical of parent–adolescent relationships in the American majority culture (Schlegel & Barry, 1991; Whiting & Edwards, 1988). Part of the reason for this is economic. In nonindustrialized traditional cultures, family members tend to rely a great deal on each other economically. In many of these cultures family members spend a great deal of time together each day, working on family economic enterprises (Schlegel & Barry, 1991). Children and adolescents depend on their parents for the necessities of life, parents depend on children and adolescents for the contribution of their labor, and the larger network of relatives are all expected to assist one another routinely and help one another in times of need. Under such conditions, the pressure to maintain family harmony is intense, because the economic interdependence of the family is so strong (Schlegel & Barry, 1991).

However, more than economics and the structure of daily life are involved in the lower levels of parent–adolescent conflict in traditional cultures. Levels of conflict are low in parent–adolescent relationships not only in nonindustrialized traditional cultures but also in highly industrialized traditional cultures, such as Japan and Taiwan (Zhou, 1997), and in the Asian American and Latino cultures that are part of American society (Chao, 1994; Suarez-Orozco & Suarez-

THINKING CRITICALLY

How would you predict parent–adolescent conflict in traditional cultures will be affected by globalization?

Orozco, 1996). This indicates that even more important than economics are cultural beliefs about parental authority and the appropriate degree of adolescent independence. As discussed earlier, the role of parent carries greater authority in traditional cultures than in the West, and this makes it less likely that adolescents in such cultures will express disagreements and resentments toward their parents (Arnett, 1999a).

This does not mean that adolescents in traditional cultures do not sometimes feel an inclination to resist or defy the authority of their parents, to question their demands and argue with them. Like Western adolescents, they undergo biological and cognitive changes at puberty that may incline them toward such resistance. But socialization shapes not only the way people behave but their cultural beliefs, their whole way of looking at the world (Arnett, 1995a). Someone who has been raised in a culture where the status and authority of parents and other elders is taught to them and emphasized constantly in direct and indirect ways is unlikely at adolescence to question their parents' authority, regardless of their new biological and cognitive capacities. Such questioning is simply not part of their cultural beliefs about the way the world is and the way it should be.

A key point in understanding parent–adolescent relationships in traditional cultures is that the independence that is so important to Western adolescents is not nearly as much of an issue in non-Western cultures. In the West, as we have seen, regulating the pace of adolescents' autonomy is often a source of parent–adolescent conflict. However, although there may be conflicts about the pace of adolescents' autonomy, parents and adolescents in the West agree that independence is the ultimate goal for adolescents as they move into adulthood (Alwin, 1988). Individuals in the West are supposed to reach the point, during emerging adulthood, where they no longer live in their parents' household, no longer rely on their parents financially, and have learned to stand alone as self-sufficient individuals (Arnett, 1998a). The pace of the adolescent's growing autonomy is a source of contention between parents and adolescents not because parents do not want their adolescents eventually to become independent of them, but because the ultimate

goal of self-sufficiency that both of them value requires continual adaptations and adjustments in their relationship as they move toward that goal (Steinberg, 1990). Increasing autonomy prepares adolescents for life in a culture where they will be expected to be capable of independence and self-sufficiency. The discussion, negotiation, and argument typical of parent–adolescent relationships in the West may help prepare adolescents for participation in a politically diverse, democratic society.

Outside of the West, independence is not highly valued as an outcome of adolescent development (Schlegel & Barry, 1991). Financially, socially, even psychologically, interdependence is a higher value than independence, not only during adolescence but throughout adulthood (Markus & Kitayama, 1991). According to Schlegel and Barry (1991), in traditional cultures "independence as we know it would be regarded as not only egocentric but also foolhardy beyond reason" (p. 45), because of the ways that family members rely on each other economically. Just as a dramatic increase in autonomy during adolescence prepares Western adolescents for adult life in an individualistic culture, learning to suppress disagreements and submit to the authority of one's parents prepares adolescents in traditional cultures for adult life in cultures where interdependence is among the highest values and where throughout life each person has a clearly designated role and position in a family hierarchy.

Historical Change and the Family

To gain a complete understanding of adolescents' and emerging adults' family relationships today, it is necessary to understand the historical changes that are the basis for current patterns of family life. Many of the changes that have taken place in Western societies over the past two centuries have had important effects on families. Let's take a look briefly at these changes, considering how each has affected adolescents' and emerging adults' family lives. We will focus on the American example, but similar changes have taken place in other industrialized countries in the past two centuries and are taking place today in economically developing countries. First we will examine changes over the past two centuries, then focus on changes during the past 50 years.

Patterns Over Two Centuries

Three of the changes that have influenced family life over the past two centuries are a lower birth rate, longer life expectancy, and a movement from predominantly rural residence to predominantly urban residence. In contrast to young people today, young people of 200 years ago tended to grow up in large families; in 1800, women in the United States gave birth to an average of *eight* children (Harevan, 1984)! As a consequence, adolescents who were among the eldest children were much more likely to have responsibility for younger children than they are today, when the average number of births per mother is just two (Noble et al., 1996). In this respect, adolescents' family lives 200 years ago in the West were like the lives of adolescents in traditional cultures today (Schlegel & Barry, 1991).

Longer life expectancy is another change that has affected the way young people experience family life. Up until about 1900, the average human life expectancy was about 45 (Kett, 1977); now it is over 70 and still rising (U.S. Bureau of the Census, 1999). As a consequence of the lower life expectancy in earlier times, marriages frequently ended in the death of a spouse in young or middle adulthood, and remarriage

TABLE 7.3: THE CHANGING FUNCTIONS OF THE FAMILY

Function	Performing Institution, 1800	Performing Institution, 2000
Educational	Family	School
Religious	Family	Church/Synagogue
Medical	Family	Medical profession
Economic Support	Family	Employer
Recreational	Family	Entertainment industry
Affective	Family	Family

of a widowed spouse was common (Hetherington, Arnett, & Hollier, 1986). Thus, adolescents frequently experienced the death of a parent and the remarriage of their widowed parent.

Increased urbanization has also resulted in changes in family life. Up until about 200 years ago, most people lived and worked on a family farm. As recently as 1830, nearly 70% of children lived in farm families (Hernandez, 1997). By 1930, this figure had dropped to 30%, and today it is less than 2%. This means that the majority of adolescents growing up 200 years ago would have grown up in a rural area in a farm family, with their daily lives structured around farmwork and spent almost entirely with their families. As people moved off the farms, they moved increasingly to the cities. Emerging adults often led the way, leaving their farm families to head for the bright lights of the big city (Kett, 1977). This meant new opportunities for education and employment, as well as greater exposure to opportunities for premarital sex, alcohol use, and other temptations of urban life (Wilson & Herrnstein, 1985).

Each of these changes has had effects on young people's family lives. Overall, we can say that the range of functions the family serves has been greatly reduced, many of them taken over by other social institutions (Coleman, 1961). The family in our time has mainly emotional, or **affective functions**—the family is supposed

Between 1830 and the present, the proportion of farm families fell from about 70% to less than 2%.

to provide its members with love, nurturance, and affection above all else.

Table 7.3 shows some of the functions the family once served and the institutions that now serve those functions. As you can see, the only one of those functions that still remains mainly within the family is the affective function. Although the family also contributes in the other areas, the main context of those functions has moved out of the family. Most young people living in industrialized countries do not rely on their parents to educate them, treat their medical problems, make a place for them in the family business, or provide recreation. Rather, young people look to their parents mainly for love, emotional support, and some degree of moral guidance (Allen & Land, 1999; Hoffman, 1988; Offer & Schonert-Reichl, 1992).

The Past 50 Years

Contemporary family life not only is much different than it was 200 years ago, but also has changed dramatically in the past 50 years. During this time the most dramatic changes have taken place in the rise in the divorce rate, the rise in the proportion of children in single-parent households, and the rise in the prevalence of dual-earner families. Once again, let's look at each

HISTORICAL FOCUS
Adolescents' Family Lives in the Great Depression

The Great Depression was the most severe economic cataclysm of the 20th century. It began with a plunge in the American stock market in 1929 and soon spread around the world. In the United States by 1932, at the depth of the Depression, stocks had dropped to just 11% of their 1929 value, thousands of companies had collapsed, thousands of banks had failed, and hundreds of thousands of families had been evicted from their homes (Manchester, 1973). One-third of adult men were unemployed, and homelessness and malnutrition were rampant. The average family suffered a decline in family income of 40% (Elder, 1974/1999).

What sort of effects did these historical events have on adolescents' development? Sociologist Glen Elder and his colleagues have analyzed longitudinal data from a study that followed families for 7 years beginning in the early 1930s (Elder, 1974/1999; Elder, Caspi, & Van Nguyen, 1986; Elder, Van Nguyen, & Caspi, 1985). Known as the Oakland Growth Study, the project followed the families of 167 adolescents born in 1920–1921, from 1932 when the adolescents were 11 to 12 years old until 1939 when they were 18 to 19 years old. Later follow-ups took place in the 1950s and again in the 1960s. All the families were White, and slightly more than half were middle-class prior to the Depression.

The families varied greatly in how much they suffered economically during the Depression, and many of the scholars' comparisons concerned "deprived" versus "nondeprived" families. Most deprived families suffered income declines of half or more of their 1929 income. The nondeprived families suffered a loss averaging about 20% of their 1929 income—certainly substantial, but not as devastating as in the deprived families.

Economic difficulties affected adolescents' family lives in a variety of ways. The economic upheaval of the Depression put a considerable strain on family relationships, especially in deprived families. Many of the fathers in the deprived families were frustrated and ashamed because of their inability to find work and support their families, and their relationships with their wives and children often deteriorated as a result. Fathers often became more punitive toward their children and more prone to anger and irritability toward their wives as well as their children. The more angry and punitive the fathers became, the more their children were likely to suffer declines in social and psychological well-being.

For other family members, the effects of economic deprivation were more complex and varied and were surprisingly positive in many ways. As the father's status in deprived families declined, the mother's often rose. On average the mother in deprived families was viewed by her adolescent children as more powerful, supportive, and attractive than the father.

Economic deprivation tended to bring adult responsibilities into the lives of adolescents at an early age. By age 14 or 15, adolescents in deprived families were more likely than those in nondeprived families to be employed in part-time jobs—about two-thirds of boys in deprived families and nearly half of girls in deprived families were employed by that age. For example, one boy in Elder's study washed dishes in the school cafeteria after school, then supervised the work of six newspaper delivery boys. Adolescent girls often worked in baby-sitting or in local stores. Adolescents' earnings were usually contributed to the family's needs. Deprived families also required more household work from adolescents, especially girls, in part because mothers in these families were more likely to be employed. Adolescents from deprived families tended to marry earlier than adolescents from nondeprived families.

The effects of these early family responsibilities were generally positive. Adolescents who were employed displayed more responsible use of money and more energetic and industrious behavior compared with those who were not. In general, adolescents in deprived families felt that they played an important role in the lives of their families. Although they were required to take on responsibilities at an early age, those responsibilities were clearly important and meaningful to their families.

However, some negative effects were seen as well, especially for adolescent girls in deprived families. Girls in deprived families showed greater moodiness, lower social competence, and greater feelings of inadequacy compared with girls in nondeprived fam-

During the Great Depression, many adolescents took on adult responsibilities within their families.

ilies. These effects were especially strong for girls who felt rejected by their fathers. Girls in deprived families were also less likely than other girls to take part in social activities such as dating, in part because of their greater household responsibilities.

Taken together, the results of Elder's study show the complex interactions that take place between historical events and adolescents' family lives. The study also shows that even under conditions of extreme adversity, many adolescents are highly resilient and will thrive in spite of—or even because of—the adversity.

of these changes with an eye to their implications for development in adolescence and emerging adulthood.

Rise in the divorce rate.   Fifty years ago divorce was relatively rare in American society, compared with the present, and the rate of divorce actually declined between 1950 and 1960 (Figure 7.2). However, between 1960 and 1975 the divorce rate more than doubled, before leveling out and remaining about the same between 1975 and the present. Americans have the highest divorce rate of any country in the world (McKenry & Price, 1995). The current rate is so high that nearly half of the current generation of young people (born in the

1980s) are projected to experience their parents' divorce by the time they reach their late teens (Hernandez, 1997). Furthermore, over three-fourths of those who divorce eventually remarry (Furstenberg, 1990), with the result that over one-fourth of young people spend some time in a stepfamily by the time they reach age 18 (Glick, 1989; Hernandez, 1997). Within American society, the divorce rate is especially high among African Americans (Hernandez, 1997).

Rise in the rate of single-parent households.   The rise in the divorce rate has contributed to a simultaneous rise in the rate of single-parent households.

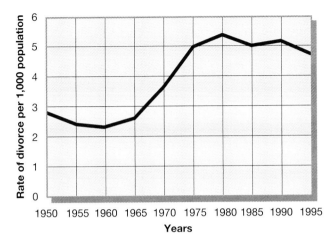

FIGURE 7.2 *Changes in divorce rate.*

Source: Hernandez (1997).

Although most divorced parents remarry (Furstenberg, 1990), they have a period between marriages as single parents. Usually, it is the mother who is the **custodial parent**, that is, the parent who lives in the same household as the children following the divorce; this is true in about 90% of divorces (Furstenberg, 1990).

In addition to the rise of single-parent households through divorce, there has been a rise in the proportion of children born outside of marriage. This is true for both White and Black families in American society, but as you can see from Figure 7.3 it is especially true

for Black families. Combining the rates of divorced single-parent households and the rates of single-parent, never-married households for young people born in the 1980s, only 20% of Blacks and 40% to 45% of Whites grow up through age 18 living with both of their original parents (Hernandez, 1997).

Rise in the rate of dual-earner families.   In the 19th and 20th centuries, the rise of industrialization took most employment outside of the home and farm into factories, larger businesses, and government organizations. However, it was almost exclusively men who obtained this employment. Women were rarely employed in the economic enterprises of industrialization. During the 19th century their designated sphere became the home, and their designated role was cultivation of a family life that their husband and children would experience as a refuge from the complex and sometimes bruising world of industrialized societies (Lasch, 1979).

This trend changed about 50 years ago with the rise of **dual-earner families**, as mothers followed fathers out of the home and into the workplace. Over the past 50 years, employment among women with school-aged children has increased steadily, from about one-fourth to over three-fourths (Hernandez, 1997). Mothers of adolescents are more likely than mothers of younger children to be employed outside of the home (Hernandez, 1997). Part of the increase is related to the increase in rates of divorce and single parenthood discussed above, which have often left the mother as the only source of the family's income—among single mothers, over 80% are employed (Hofferth, 1992). Mothers in nondivorced families may also work to help the family maintain an adequate income.

Of course, noneconomic reasons are often involved as well. Many educational and occupational opportunities have opened up to women in the past 50 years that had been denied to them before, and they have taken advantage of them by entering the workplace. Research indicates that most employed mothers would continue to work even if they had enough money (Scarr, Phillips, & McCartney, 1989). Professional women as well as

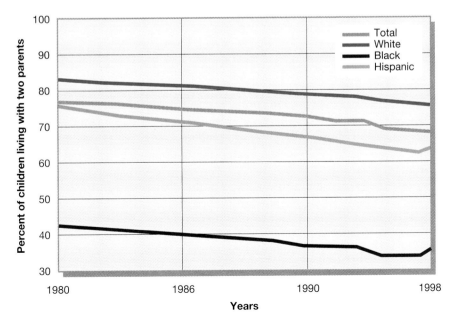

FIGURE 7.3 *Ethnic differences in living with a single parent.*

Source: Federal Interagency Forum on Child and Family Statistics (1999).

waitresses and factory workers generally report that they are committed to their jobs, enjoy having a work role as well as family roles, and desire to continue to work (Scarr et al., 1989).

Effects of Divorce, Remarriage, Single Parenthood, and Dual-Earner Families

Now that we have reviewed the historical background of the current American family, let's take a look at how divorce, remarriage, single parenthood, and dual-earner families are related to young people's behavior and to their perceptions of their family lives.

Divorce

"When I was 15 my parents separated. I continued to live with my mother but would visit my father on Sunday. During that time we would do something 'entertaining,' like go to a movie, which relieved the pressure from us to actually interact. . . . My parents are now divorced and my father calls me every Sunday night. We talk about school, my job, and things in the news. But when I need advice or just want to talk, I always call my mother. She is more aware of my everyday life and I feel very comfortable with her. With my father, on the other hand, our relationship is more forced because he is not up-to-date on my life and hasn't been for some time."

— *Marilyn, age 21 (Arnett, unpublished data)*

"My parents were divorced, so the money was pretty thin. My father was a psycho and didn't pay child support. When I was in junior high I wanted everything that the other kids had—Liz Claiborne purses, designer clothes, etc. I would pester my mother for money constantly, sometimes to the point where she would be in tears because she wanted to give me things but couldn't afford to do so."

— *Dawn, age 20 (Arnett, unpublished data)*

Because the rate of divorce is so high in American society and has risen so dramatically in recent decades, scholars have devoted a great deal of attention to inves-

tigating the effects of divorce. These studies consistently find that young people whose parents have divorced are at higher risk for a wide variety of negative outcomes compared with young people in nondivorced families, in areas including behavior problems, psychological distress, and academic achievement (Amato & Keith, 1991; Buchanan, 2000). With regard to behavior problems, adolescents whose parents have divorced have higher rates of using drugs and alcohol (Needle, Su, & Doherty, 1990) and tend to initiate sexual intercourse at an earlier age, compared with adolescents in nondivorced families (Dornbusch et al., 1985). With regard to psychological distress, adolescents with divorced parents are more likely to be depressed and withdrawn. Those who feel caught in a loyalty conflict between their parents are especially likely to be anxious and depressed following the divorce (Buchanan et al., 1991; Buchanan, Maccoby, & Dornbusch, 1996). Adolescents in divorced families also are more likely to report having psychological problems, and more likely to receive mental health treatment (Buchanan, 2000; Chase-Landsdale, Cherlin, & Kiernan, 1995; Cherlin, 1999). With regard to academic achievement, young people from divorced families tend not to do as well in school as their peers (Amato, 1993; Zimiles & Lee, 1991), and they are less likely to attend college than young people from nondivorced families (Furstenberg, 1990; Astone & McLanahan, 1995).

Although the findings on the effects of divorce are consistent, a great deal of variability exists in how adolescents and emerging adults respond to divorce. As one prominent research team observed, "the fact that a young person comes from a divorced family does not, in itself, tell us a great deal about how he or she is faring on embarking into adulthood" (Zill, Morrison, & Coiro, 1993, p. 100). To say that a young person's parents are divorced tells us only about **family structure**. Family structure is the term scholars use to refer to the outward characteristics of the family—whether the parents are married, how many adults and children live in the household, what the degree of biological relationship is between the family members (e.g., in stepfamilies), and so on. However, in recent years most of the attention of scholars studying divorce has been focused on **family process** (Emery, 1999)—that is, the quality of family members' relationships, how much warmth or hostility there is between them, and so on. So, instead of asking the simple question, why does divorce have negative effects on children and adolescents, let's ask the more complex and more enlightening question:

How does divorce influence family process in ways that, in turn, influence child and adolescent development?

Perhaps the most important aspect of family process with regard to the effects of divorce on children and adolescents is *exposure to conflict between parents* (Emery, 1999). Divorce involves the dissolution of a relationship that is, for most adults, at the heart of their emotional lives and their personal identities (Wallerstein & Blakeslee, 1989). Because the marriage relationship carries such a large freight of hopes and desires, it rarely sinks without numerous explosions occurring along the way. Living in the household where the divorce is taking place, children and adolescents will likely be exposed to their parents' hostility and recriminations before and during the divorce, and this exposure is often painful, stressful, and damaging to them (Amato & Keith, 1991; Long et al., 1988).

In nondivorced families, too, parents' conflict has damaging effects on children's development (Emery, 1999; Long et al., 1988). In fact, numerous studies have found that adolescents and emerging adults in high-conflict nondivorced households have poorer adjustment than adolescents and adults in low-conflict divorced households (Amato, Loomis, & Booth, 1995; Emery, 1999; Margolin, 1988; Mechanic & Hansell, 1989). Longitudinal studies that include data before and after divorce indicate that adolescents' problems

Exposure to conflict between parents leads to a variety of problems in children and adolescents.

after divorce often began long before the divorce, as a consequence of high conflict between their parents (Buchanan, 2000; Cherlin, Chase-Lansdale, & McCrae, 1998; Cherlin et al., 1991). Thus, it is exposure to parents' conflicts, rather than the specific event of divorce, that is especially damaging to children and adolescents (Amato, 1993).

A second important aspect of family process to consider with regard to the effects of divorce is that *divorce affects parenting practices*. Divorce is highly stressful and painful to most of the adults who experience it (Jacobs, 1983; Wallerstein & Blakeslee, 1996; Weinraub & Wolf, 1983), and not surprisingly it effects many aspects of their lives, including how they carry out their role as parents. The burdens fall especially on mothers. As the sole parent in the household, the mother has to take on all the parenting that was previously shared with the father, and often has increased employment responsibilities now that the father's income no longer comes directly into the family—not to mention handling by themselves the leaky roof, the sick pet, the disabled car, and all the other typical stresses of daily life.

So, it is understandable that mothers' parenting tends to change following divorce, usually for the worse. Especially in the year following divorce, mothers tend to be less affectionate, more permissive, and less consistent in their parenting than they were before the divorce took place or than they will be after a few years have passed (Buchanan, 2000; Hetherington, 1991; King, 1992; Smetana et al., 1991; Wallerstein & Corbin, 1991). Mothers may have difficulty being authoritative parents following divorce, with all of the stresses piling up on them, and as a result they may become indulgent or indifferent (Dornbusch et al., 1985; McLanahan & Bumpass, 1988). Adolescents in divorced families consequently have greater freedom than adolescents in nondivorced families, in matters such as how to spend their money and how late to stay out, but younger adolescents especially may find it to be more freedom than they can handle wisely (Turner, Irwin, & Millstein, 1991).

Another way parenting may change after divorce is that the mother may rely on the adolescent as a confidant. This is a mixed blessing for adolescents—they may enjoy becoming closer to their mothers while at the same time finding it difficult to hear about their parents' marital troubles and their mothers' difficulties in the aftermath of the divorce (Buchanan, Eccles, & Becker, 1992). Emerging adults may be able to handle this role better; some studies find that emerging adults who experience their parents' divorce become closer to their mothers after the divorce (White, Brinkerhoff, & Booth, 1985), and are closer to their mothers than young people in nondivorced families (Cooney, 1994).

As for young people's relations with their fathers after divorce, in most families children's contact with their father declines steadily in the years following the divorce (Amato & Keith, 1991). Consequently, adolescents and emerging adults whose parents divorced years earlier often see their fathers only rarely (Amato & Keith, 1991; Cooney, 1994). Divorced fathers complain that it often becomes difficult to arrange meetings as young people become increasingly involved in activities of their own (Dudley, 1991). Also, divorced fathers are frequently the target of young people's resentment and blame following divorce (Cooney, 1994; Cooney et al., 1986). Children often feel pressured to take sides when their parents divorce (Bonkowski, 1989), and because mothers are usually closer to their children prior to the divorce, children's sympathies and loyalties are more often with the mother than with the father following divorce (Furstenberg & Cherlin, 1991). Thus, young people in divorced households tend to have more negative feelings and fewer positive feelings toward their fathers compared with young people in nondivorced families (Cooney, 1994; Peterson & Zill, 1986; Zill et al., 1993).

A third factor in considering the effects of divorce on young people is the *increase in economic stress* that typically results in the aftermath of divorce (Furstenberg, 1990). With the father's income no longer coming directly into the household, money is often tight in mother-headed households following divorce. In the aftermath of divorce, the income in mother-headed families decreases by an average of 40% to 50% (Smock, 1993). The economic strains in divorced families may have negative effects on parent–child relationships. Some studies claim that the problems children and adolescents exhibit following divorce are due largely to these economic problems (Blum, Boyle, & Offord, 1988).

Several factors help to ameliorate the negative effects of divorce on adolescents (Buchanan et al., 1992,

1996; Donnelly & Finkelhor, 1992). Adolescents who maintain a good relationship with their mothers following divorce tend to function well in the aftermath of divorce (Buchanan, 2000; Buchanan et al., 1996; Tschann et al., 1990). Also, when divorced parents are able to maintain a civil relationship and communicate without hostility about issues involving their children, their children and adolescents are less likely to exhibit the negative effects of divorce (Buchanan et al., 1996; Maccoby, Depner, & Mnookin, 1988). A related factor of importance is the degree of consistency of parenting between the separate households of the mother and the father. If parents maintain consistency with each other in parenting—which they are more likely to do if they are communicating well—their adolescents benefit (Buchanan et al., 1992, 1996). In general, adolescents show fewer negative effects of parental divorce than younger children do (Buchanan, 2000; Hetherington, 1991, 1993), perhaps because adolescents are less dependent on their parents, spend more time with their peers outside of the family household, and have greater cognitive capacities to understand and adapt to what is happening.

Remarriage

In the light of those factors that seem to be most strongly related to adolescents' problems following divorce—parental conflict, disruptions in parenting, and economic stress—you might think that the mother's remarriage would greatly improve the well-being of adolescents in divorced families. (We focus on mothers' remarriage because it is usually the mother who has custody of the children.) The mother and her new husband have just chosen to get married, so presumably they are getting along well. The mother's parenting could be expected to become more consistent, now that she's happier in her personal life (Coleman & Ganong, 1990; Ganong & Coleman, 1999). And she is not on her own as a parent anymore, now that she has her new husband to help her with parenting and daily household tasks. As for economic stress, presumably it eases now that the stepfather's income is part of the family income.

Although some studies do find that adolescents respond favorably when their mothers remarry (Studer, 1993), for the most part studies find that adolescents typically take a turn for the worse. In general, adolescents in stepfamilies have a greater likelihood of a variety of problems compared with their peers, including depression, anxiety, and conduct disorders (Allison & Furstenberg, 1989; Freeman, 1993; Hetherington &

■ **THINKING CRITICALLY**

In addition to the factors mentioned here, can you think of other things that might influence adolescents' responses to divorce for better or worse?

Clingempeel, 1992; Kasen et al., 1996; Lee et al., 1994). The academic achievement of adolescents in stepfamilies tends to be lower than in nondivorced families, and in some studies lower than in divorced families (Jeynes, 1999). Adolescents in stepfamilies are also more likely to be involved in delinquent activities, not only compared with adolescents in nondivorced families but also compared with adolescents in divorced families (Dornbusch et al., 1985; Steinberg, 1987c).

Furthermore, although following divorce adolescents tend to have fewer problems than younger children, following remarriage the reverse is true—adolescents have *more* problems adjusting to remarriage compared with younger children (Hetherington, 1993; Zill & Nord, 1994). Adolescent girls tend to have an especially negative reaction to their mothers' remarriage (Hetherington, 1993). The reasons for this are not clear, but one possibility is that the girls develop a closer relationship with their mothers following divorce, and this closeness is disrupted by the mother's remarriage (Hetherington, 1991).

Why do adolescents often respond unfavorably to their mother's remarriage? Scholars who have studied remarriage emphasize that, although remarriage may seem as though it should be positive for children and adolescents in some of the ways discussed above, it also represents another disruption of the family system, another stressful change that requires adjustment (Capaldi & Patterson, 1991; Hetherington, 1993). The toughest time for families after divorce tends to be one year following the divorce (Hetherington, Stanley-Hagan, & Anderson, 1989; Hetherington et al., 1998). After that, family members usually begin to adjust, and their functioning typically improves substantially after 2 years have passed. Remarriage disrupts this new equilibrium. With remarriage, family members have to adapt to a new family structure and integrate a new person into a family system that has already been stressed and strained by divorce. The precarious quality of this integration is illustrated by the fact that many stepfathers and adolescents do not even mention each other when describing their family members, even 2 years following the remarriage (Ganong & Coleman, 1999; Hetherington, 1991)!

With remarriage as with divorce, adolescents' responses are diverse, and the influence of family process as well as family structure must be recognized. A key issue is the extent to which the stepfather attempts to exercise authority over the adolescent (Hetherington et al., 1989; Hetherington, 1993). A stepfather who attempts to remind an adolescent that the curfew hour is

11:00 P.M. or that it is the adolescent's turn to do the laundry may well receive the withering retort, "You're *not* my father!" Younger children are more likely to accept a stepfather's authority, but adolescents tend to resist or reject it (Hetherington, 1991; Hetherington et al., 1989; Vuchinich et al., 1991; Zill et al., 1993).

Relationships between stepparents and adolescents have a number of other hazards to overcome in addition to the issue of the stepfather's authority (Ganong & Coleman, 1999; Hetherington, 1991; Visher & Visher, 1988). Establishing an attachment to a stepparent can be difficult at an age when adolescents are spending less time at home and becoming more peer oriented. Adolescents (and younger children as well) may also have divided loyalties and may fear that establishing an attachment to the stepfather amounts to a betrayal of their father. Also, because adolescents are reaching sexual maturity, they might find it difficult to welcome their mother's new marriage partner into the household. They are more likely than younger children to be aware of the sexual relationship between mother and stepfather and are likely to be uncomfortable with this awareness.

All of these considerations mean that it is a formidable challenge for stepfathers and adolescents to establish a good relationship. However, many stepfathers and adolescents do meet these challenges successfully and establish a relationship of warmth and mutual respect (Ganong & Coleman, 1994, 1999).

Single Parenthood

In addition to the single-parent households created through divorce, there is an increasing number of single-parent households in which the mother has never married (Burns, 1992; U.S. Bureau of the Census, 1999). Just as in divorced families, adolescents in never-married, single-parent households are at greater risk for a variety of problems, including low school achievement, psychological problems such as depression and anxiety, and behavioral problems such as substance use and early initiation of sexual activity (McLanahan & Sandefur, 1994). However, just as in divorced families, family process is at least as important as family structure. Many never-married single parents have relationships with their adolescent children that are characterized by love, mutual respect, and mutual support, and adolescents in these families tend to be doing as well or better than adolescents in two-parent families.

Also, looking at family structure only in terms of the parents can be misleading. As noted earlier in the chapter, African American families have a long tradition of extended family households, in which one or more grandparents, uncles, aunts, or cousins also live in the household (McAdoo, 1998). An extended family structure has been found to provide important assistance to single-parent African American families, through the sharing of emotional support, economic responsibilities, and parenting responsibilities (Barbarin & Soler, 1993; McAdoo, 1993; Wilson, 1989). Extended family members not only provide direct support to adolescents, but also help adolescents indirectly by supporting the single parent, which enhances her parenting effectiveness (Taylor, Casten, & Flickinger, 1993).

Dual-Earner Families

With both parents gone from the household for at least part of a typical day in most Western families, and with parents so important in the socialization of their children and adolescents, scholars have turned their attention to the question: What happens when both parents are employed? What are the consequences for adolescents' development?

For the most part, few substantial effects have been seen on adolescents from living in a dual-earner family as compared with a family where only one parent is employed (Galambos & Ehrenberg, 1997). The ESM studies indicate that no differences exist between dual-earner families and families in which the mother is not employed, in terms of both the quantity and quality of time that mothers spend with their adolescents (Richards & Duckett, 1994). Other studies have also reported few differences in the functioning of adolescents based on whether or not both parents are employed (Galambos & Maggs, 1991).

However, studies have found that the effects of dual-earner families depend on the gender of the adolescent and on whether both parents are working full-time. The effects of being in a dual-earner family are often quite positive for adolescent girls. These girls tend to be more confident and have higher career aspirations than girls whose mothers are not employed (Hoffman, 1984), perhaps because of the model the mother provides through her participation in the workplace.

In contrast, several studies have found that adolescent boys in dual-earner families do not function as well as boys in families with only one employed parent. Adolescent boys (but not girls) in dual-earner families tend to have more arguments with their mothers and with their siblings compared with boys whose mothers are not employed (Montemayor, 1984). Apparently, these conflicts result from the greater household responsibilities required from adolescents when the mother is employed, and the fact that boys resist these responsibilities more than girls do. Having two full-time working parents is also associated with poorer school performance for boys in middle-class and upper-middle-class families (although not for boys in lower social classes; Bogenschneider & Steinberg, 1994).

However, boys' school performance is not affected if one parent works part-time. The amount of hours worked by the parents is an important variable in other studies as well. Adolescents, both boys and girls, are at higher risk for various problems if both parents work full-time than if one parent works just part-time. The risks are especially high for adolescents who are unsupervised by parents or other adults on a daily basis for several hours between the time school ends and the time a parent arrives home from work. These adolescents tend to have higher rates of social isolation, depression, and use of drugs and alcohol (Carnegie Council on Adolescent Development, 1992; Galambos & Maggs, 1991; Richardson et al., 1993; Steinberg, 1986). In one study of nearly 5,000 eighth graders, the ones who were on their own for at least 11 hours a week were twice as likely to be using alcohol and other drugs (Richardson et al., 1989).

Another key variable in considering the effects of dual-earner families is the quality of the relationships between the parents and the adolescent (Galambos & Ehrenberg, 1997). Adolescents in dual-earner families are more likely to function well if parents maintain

Most American adolescents today live in a dual-earner family.

monitoring from a distance for example, by having their children check in with them by phone (Galambos & Maggs, 1991; Pettit et al., 1999). If parents can manage to maintain adequate levels of demandingness and responsiveness even when both of them are working, their adolescents generally function well (Galambos & Maggs, 1991; Steinberg, 1986).

Physical and Sexual Abuse in the Family

Although most adolescents and emerging adults generally have good relationships with their parents, some young people suffer physical or sexual abuse from their parents. Rates of abuse in American society are difficult to establish, because this is an area for which social desirability is especially strong—physical and sexual abuse involve behaviors that most families would not readily disclose to others. However, numerous studies indicate that physical abuse is more likely to be inflicted on adolescents than on younger children (Garbarino, 1989; Kaplan, 1991; Williamson, Borduin, & Howe, 1991). Sexual abuse typically begins just prior to adolescence, and then continues into adolescence. Six to ten percent of American college students indicate they have been sexually abused by a parent (Haugaard, 1992; Haugaard & Reppucci, 1988). Similar figures were reported in a national survey of Canadian adolescents aged 13 to 16 (Holmes & Silverman, 1992).

Physical Abuse

What leads parents to inflict physical abuse on their adolescent children? One well-established finding is that abusive parents are more likely than other parents to have been abused themselves as children (Kashani et al., 1992; Simons, Whitback, et al., 1991). They are also more likely to have experienced parental conflict, harsh discipline, or the loss of a parent as they were growing up (Cicchetti & Carlson, 1989).

This does not mean that children who are abused are destined to grow up to abuse their own children—in fact, the majority of them will not (Zigler & Hall, 1989). It does mean that being abused is a strong risk factor for becoming an abusive parent, perhaps because some children who are abused learn the wrong lessons about how to parent their own children (Cappell & Heiner, 1990; Kashani et al., 1992). However, children who are physically abused only in adolescence are less likely than those who are abused throughout

childhood to grow up to abuse their own children (Garbarino, 1989).

Other factors that are related to parents' physical abuse of their children and adolescents tend to involve family stresses or problems in the parents' lives. Abuse is more likely to occur in poor than in middle-class families, in large than in small families, and in families where parents have problems such as depression, poor health, or alcohol abuse (Hansen, Conaway, & Christopher, 1990; Whipple & Webster-Stratton, 1991). Abusive parents also tend to be poorly skilled at parenting and at coping with life stresses (Hansen & Warner, 1992; Wolfe, 1985).

Physical abuse is related to a variety of difficulties in the lives of adolescents. Abused adolescents tend to be more aggressive in their interactions with peers and with adults (Ammerman & Hersen, 1992; Eckenrode, Laird, & Doris, 1993). This may occur as a result of modeling the aggressive behavior displayed by their parents, although it is also possible that passive genotype–environment interactions are involved (i.e., that abusing parents may pass down genes to their children that contribute to aggressiveness). Abused adolescents are more likely than other adolescents to engage in antisocial behavior (Bensley, Van Eeenwyk, Spieker, & Schoder, 1999; Garbarino et al., 1986; Lewis et al., 1989). They are also more likely than other adolescents to have low self-control, to perform poorly in school, and to have difficulty in their peer relationships (Alexander, Moore, & Alexander, 1991; Salzinger et al., 1993; Weiss et al., 1992). However, these consequences are not inevitable; many abused adolescents are surprisingly resilient and grow up to be normal adults and nonabusive parents (Corby, 1993; Zigler & Hall, 1989).

Sexual Abuse

The causes of sexual abuse by parents are quite different from the causes of physical abuse. Physical abuse is more commonly inflicted on boys than on girls, whereas sexual abuse takes place mainly between girls and their fathers or stepfathers (Briere, 1992; Haugaard, 1992; Holmes & Silverman, 1992; Watkins & Bentovim, 1992). Unlike physically abusive parents, sexually abusive fathers are usually not aggressive, but rather tend to be insecure and socially awkward around adults (Briere, 1992; Finkelhor, 1990). Because they feel inadequate in their relationships with adults—including, usually, their wives—they prefer to seek sexual satisfaction from children, who are easier for them to control (Haugaard, 1992). Sexual abuse usually results from motives such as these, rather than being an expression of affection that got out of control. On the contrary, fathers who abuse their adolescent daughters tend to have been detached and distant from them when they were younger (Parker & Parker, 1986). Sexual abuse is more likely to be committed by stepfathers than by fathers, perhaps because there is no biological incest taboo between stepfathers and their stepdaughters (Briere, 1992; Watkins & Bentovim, 1992).

The effects of sexual abuse tend to be even more profound and pervasive than the effects of physical abuse. Parental sexual abuse constitutes an ultimate breach of trust—rather than providing care and protection, the parent has exploited the child's need for nurturance and protection for the sake of his own needs. Consequently, many of the effects of parental sexual abuse are evident in the victim's social relationships. Adolescents who have been sexually abused tend to have difficulty trusting others and forming intimate relationships (Brown & Finkelhor, 1986; Lundberg-Love, 1990). During the period of sexual abuse and for many years afterward, many victims of sexual abuse experience depression, high anxiety, and social withdrawal (Graystone, de Luca, & Boyes, 1992; Kiser et al., 1991; McLeer et al., 1992). Adolescent victims may react with one extreme or the other in their sexual behavior, either highly avoidant of sexual contacts or highly promiscuous (Green, 1991; Tharinger, 1990). Other consequences of sexual abuse include substance abuse, higher risk for a variety of psychological disorders, and suicidal thoughts and behavior (Bensley et al., 1999; Briere & Runtz, 1989, 1991; Finkelhor, 1990; Yoder, Hoyt, & Whitbeck, 1998).

■ **THINKING CRITICALLY**

Explain the effects of sexual abuse in terms of attachment theory.

Although sexual abuse is among the most harmful things a parent can do to a child, one-third of sexually abused children demonstrate few or no symptoms as a result (Finkelhor, 1990; Kendall-Tackett, Williams, & Finkelhor, 1993). Support from the mother after a father's or stepfather's sexual abuse has been disclosed is especially important to girls' recovery from sexual abuse; daughters cope far better if their mothers believe their account of the abuse and comfort and reas-sure them, rather than rejecting them or blaming them (Briere, 1992; Haugaard & Reppucci, 1988). Psychotherapy can also contribute to the girl's recovery (Rust & Troupe, 1991).

Running Away From Home

“*I skipped out of school two days and my dad found out and he just gave it to me with his belt. I had bruises all over my hands and all over my legs. And my mother couldn't do anything about it and she was upset with me at the time, so that Friday I ran away.*”

— *15-year-old girl (Konopka, 1985, p. 78)*

For some adolescents, family life becomes unbearable to them for one reason or another, and they run away from home. It is estimated that about one million adolescents run away from home each year in the United States (Flanagan & Maguire, 1992; Tomb, 1991). About one-fourth of these adolescents are not so much runaways as "throwaways"—their parents have forced them to leave home (Kufeldt & Nimmo, 1987; Tomb, 1991). In any case, about 80% to 90% of adolescents who leave home stay within 50 miles of home, often staying with a friend or relative, and return within a week (Tomb, 1991). Adolescents who stay away from home for weeks or months, or who never return at all, are at high risk for a wide variety of problems (McCarthy & Hagan, 1992; Rotheram-Borus, Koopman, & Ehrhardt, 1991; Whitbeck & Hoyt, 1999).

Not surprisingly, adolescents who run away from home have often experienced high conflict with their parents, and many have experienced physical or sexual abuse from their parents (Rotheram-Borus et al., 1991). For example, in one study of runaway adolescents in Toronto, 73% had experienced physical abuse and 51% had experienced sexual abuse (McCarthy, 1994). Other family factors related to running away from home include low family income, parental alcoholism, high conflict between parents, and parental neglect of the adolescent (Rotheram-Borus et al., 1991; McCarthy, 1994; Windle, 1989; Whitbeck & Hoyt, 1999). Characteristics of the adolescent also matter. Adolescents who run away are more likely than other adolescents to have been involved in criminal activity, to use illegal drugs, and to have had problems at school (Fors & Rojek, 1991; Windle, 1989). They are also more likely to have had psychological difficulties such as depression and emotional isolation (Rotheram-Borus, 1993; Whitbeck & Hoyt, 1999).

Although leaving home often represents an escape from a difficult family life, running away is likely to lead to other problems. Adolescents who run away from home tend be highly vulnerable to exploitation. Many of them report being robbed, physically assaulted, and malnourished. In their desperation they may seek money through prostitution and pornography (Rotheram-Borus et al., 1991). A study of 390 runaway adolescent boys and girls demonstrated the many problems they may have (McCarthy & Hagan, 1992). Nearly half had stolen food and over 40% had stolen items worth over $50. Forty-six percent had been jailed at least once, and 30% had participated in prostitution. Fifty-five percent had used hallucinogenic drugs, and 43%

had used cocaine or crack. Other studies have found that suicidal behavior is common among runaway adolescents (Rotheram-Borus, 1993; Yoder et al., 1998).

Many urban areas have shelters for adolescent runaways. Typically, these shelters provide adolescents with food, protection, and counseling (McCarthy & Hagan, 1992). They may also assist adolescents in contacting their families, if the adolescents wish to do so and if it would be possible and safe for them to go home. However, many of these shelters lack adequate funding and have difficulty providing services for all the runaway adolescents who come to them (McCarthy & Hagan, 1992).

Summing Up

In this chapter we have explored a wide range of topics related to the family lives of adolescents and emerging adults. Following are the main points of the chapter:

- Adolescents generally have higher conflict with siblings than in their other relationships, but most adolescents have a casual relationship with siblings in which their contact is limited. In traditional cultures, a caregiver relationship between siblings is the most common form. Because grandparents in traditional cultures often live in the same household as their children and grandchildren, adolescents tend to be as close to their grandparents as to their parents.

- The two key dimensions of parenting styles focused on by scholars are demandingness and responsiveness. Authoritative parenting, which combines high responsiveness with high demandingness, has generally been found to be related to positive outcomes for adolescents in the American majority culture. Studies of non-Western cultures indicate that the "traditional" parenting style is most common in those cultures.

- According to attachment theory, attachments formed in infancy are the basis for relationships throughout life. Although this claim is in question, studies of attachment involving adolescents and emerging adults indicate that attachments to parents are related to young people's functioning in numerous ways and that autonomy and relatedness in relationships with parents are compatible rather than competing qualities.

- Emerging adults who move away from home tend to be closer emotionally to their parents and experience less conflict with them than those who remain at home.

- Research shows that conflict between parents and children tends to be highest during early adolescence, and most parents experience their children's adolescence as a difficult time. Parent–adolescent conflict tends to be lower in traditional cultures because of greater economic interdependence of family members and because the role of parent holds greater authority.

- Profound social changes in the past two centuries have influenced the nature of adolescents' family lives, including decreasing family size, lengthening life expectancy, and increasing urbanization. Changes over the past 50 years include increases in the prevalence of divorce, single-parent households, and dual-earner families.

- Parents' divorce tends to be related to negative outcomes for adolescents, including behavioral problems, psychological distress, problems in intimate relationships, and lower academic performance. However, there is considerable variation in the effects of divorce, and the outcomes for adolescents depend not just on family structure but on family process.

- Adolescents tend to respond negatively to their parents' remarriage, but again a great deal depends on family process, not just family structure.

- Dual-earner families have become much more common since World War II. For today's adolescents, having two parents who work tends to be unrelated to most aspects of their functioning. However, some studies have found some negative effects for boys and for adolescents in families where both parents work full-time.

- Adolescents who are physically abused are more aggressive than other adolescents, more likely to engage in criminal behavior, and more likely to do poorly in school, among other problems.

- Sexual abuse in families takes place most commonly between daughters and their fathers or stepfathers, who are often incompetent in their relationships with adults. Sexual abuse has a variety of negative consequences, especially in girls' abilities for forming intimate emotional and sexual relationships.

- Running away from home is most common among adolescents who have experienced family problems such as physical or sexual abuse, high conflict, or parents' alcoholism. Adolescents who stay away from home for more than a week or two are at high risk for problems such as physical assault, substance use, and suicide attempts.

Even though adolescents spend considerably less time with their families than they did when younger and even though emerging adults typically move out of the family household, family relationships play a key role in development during adolescence and emerging adulthood, both for better and for worse. Home is where the heart is, and where a part of it remains; adolescents and emerging adults continue to be attached to their parents and to rely on them for emotional support, even as they gain more autonomy and move away from their families literally and figuratively.

The power of the family on development is considerable, but family life is not always a source of happiness. Conflict with parents is higher in adolescence than at other ages. Adolescents and emerging adults often experience pain and difficulties when their parents divorce or remarry, although most young people adjust to these family transitions after a few years. The family is sometimes the setting for physical or sexual abuse, and some adolescents find their family lives so unbearable that they run away from home.

The many cultural changes of the past two centuries have resulted in profound changes in the kind of family lives young people experience. Rates of divorce, single-parent households, and dual-earner families all rose dramatically in the second half of the 20th century. In many ways, the family's functions in the lives of adolescents and emerging adults have been reduced in the past century, as new institutions have taken over functions that used to be part of family life. Still, the family endures as the emotional touchstone of young people's lives, not only in American society but all over the world.

Key Terms

family systems approach	casual relationship	autonomy	primary caregiver
dyadic relationship	parenting styles	reciprocal or	internal working model
disequilibrium	demandingness	bidirectional effects	relatedness
midlife crisis	responsiveness	traditional parenting style	affective functions
caregiver relationship	authoritative parents	familism	custodial parent
buddy relationship	authoritarian parents	attachment theory	dual-earner families
critical relationship	indulgent parents	secure attachment	family structure
rival relationship	indifferent parents	insecure attachment	family process

For Further Reading

Allen, J., & Land, P. (1999). Attachment in adolescence. In J. Cassidy & P. R. Shaver (Eds.), *Handbook of attachment*. New York: Guilford. An up-to-date summary of research on adolescent attachments.

Hetherington, E.M. (1999). *Coping with divorce, single parenting, and remarriage: A risk and resiliency perspective.* Mahwah, NJ: Erlbaum. A recent book summarizing the research on these topics.

Furstenberg, F. (1990). Coming of age in a changing family system. In S. S. Felman & G. R. Elliott (Eds.), *At the threshold: The developing adolescent.* Cambridge, MA: Harvard University Press. A good summary of changes in the family in recent decades and their effects on adolescent development.

Larson, R., & Richards, M. H. (1994). *Divergent realities: The emotional lives of mother, fathers, and adolescents.* New York: Basic Books. This book describes the results of Larson and Richards's research using the ESM. It provides an excellent, insightful, and vivid portrayal of adolescents' family lives in the American majority culture. It is also very well-written, a pleasure to read.

Applying Research

Comer, J. P., & Poussaint, A. E. (1992). *Raising black children*. New York: Plume. Two prominent professors of psychiatry provide advice to parents of Black children on how to help their children confront racism, handle anger and conflict, and maintain an African American identity in American society.

Kalter, N. (1990). *Growing up with divorce*. New York: Free Press. Kalter, a clinical psychologist who has worked with children, adolescents, and their families, offers strategies to parents for helping their children cope with the aftermath of divorce. Addresses differences in the risks likely for children and adolescents and for boys and girls.

Steinberg, L., & Levine, A. (1997). *You and your adolescent: A parent's guide for ages 10 to 20*. New York: Harper Perennial. Advice for parents of adolescents from Laurence Steinberg, one of the most eminent scholars on adolescence. Chapters include "Family Communication and Problem-Solving," "Sexual Awakening," "How Young Adolescents Think," and "Your Role in Your Adolescent's Education."

Friends and Peers

"A best friend to me is someone you can have fun with and you can also be serious with about personal things—about girls, or what you're going to do with your life or whatever. My best friend Jeff and I can talk about things. His parents are divorced too, and he understands when I feel bummed out about the fights between my mom and dad. A best friend is someone who's not going to make fun of you just because you do something stupid or put you down if you make a mistake. If you're afraid of something or someone, they'll give you confidence."
(Bell, 1998, p. 80)

This statement, made by a 13-year-old boy, is an eloquent expression of the value of friendship in adolescence—or any age, for that matter. At all ages, we value friends as people we can both have fun with and be serious with. We look for friends who understand us, in part based on common interests and experiences. We rely on friends to be gentle on us when we make mistakes and to support us and prop up our confidence when we are in doubt or afraid.

However, friendship is of special value and importance during adolescence and emerging adulthood. These are periods of life in which the emotional center of young people's lives is moving away from their immediate families and into

223

Friendships are especially important during adolescence and emerging adulthood.

relationships with persons outside the family (Youniss & Smollar, 1985). This does not mean that parents cease to be important—as described in the previous chapter, the influence of parents remains prominent in many ways throughout adolescence, and attachments to parents remain strong for most emerging adults as well. Nevertheless, gradually but inevitably the influence of parents diminishes as young people become more independent and spend less and less of their time at home. Eventually, most young people in Western societies move away from home and, at some point, form an enduring romantic partnership. However, during their teens and early twenties few adolescents or emerging adults have yet formed the kind of enduring romantic partnership that will extend into adulthood. Friends provide a bridge between the close attachments young people have to their family members and the close attachment they will eventually have in a romantic partnership. Friends can also be an emotional refuge for adolescents who have difficult relationships with their parents (Berndt, 1996).

Friends contribute to identity formation, too (Erikson, 1968). Because people tend to choose friends who are like themselves, young people clarify their own traits in the course of choosing friends. And in conversations with friends, young people often explore identity issues of who they are and what goals they have for their lives.

During adolescence, it is not only close friends who become important but also the larger world of peers. In Western societies, adolescents typically attend large middle schools and high schools with a complex peer culture. These schools are usually much larger than the elementary schools they attended as children (Entwisle, 1990; Hechinger, 1993). In these schools group hierarchies are established, with some adolescents clearly understood to be high in status and others clearly viewed as having low status. Being an adolescent in Western societies means, in part, learning to navigate through this school-based peer culture.

In this chapter we will consider both close relationships with friends and social relationships in the larger peer culture. We will begin by examining friendships. First adolescents' relationships with friends and family will be compared and contrasted. Then we will explore various developmental changes that take place in friendships from middle childhood through adolescence, with a special focus on intimacy as a key quality of adolescent friendships. We will also examine the factors involved in choosing friendships, particularly the similarities that draw adolescent friends to one another. This will be followed by a discussion of "peer pressure," or "friends' influence" as it will be discussed here. There will also be a section on friends and leisure activities in emerging adulthood.

In the second half of the chapter we will examine larger peer social groups, including cliques and crowds. This will include a discussion of popularity and unpopularity in adolescence, and interventions that have been devised to help unpopular adolescents. Finally, the idea of a common youth culture will be examined, in its latest forms and in how youth culture reflects historical changes in the influence of parents and peers.

Peers and Friends

Before we proceed, we need to distinguish *peers* from *friends*, because the two terms are sometimes erroneously believed to be the same. Peers are simply people who have certain aspects of their status in common. For example, Louis Armstrong and Dizzy Gillespie are peers, because they are generally considered to be two of the greatest trumpet players who ever lived. When social scientists use the term *peers*, they usually are referring to the more concrete aspects of status, especially *age*. So, for our purposes, **peers** are people who are about the same age. For adolescents, peers consist of the large network of their same-age classmates, community members, and coworkers.

Friends, of course, are something quite different. For adolescents, their friends tend to be peers—people who are about their age. However, not all their peers are friends. **Friends** are people with whom you develop a valued, mutual relationship. This is clearly different from simply being in the same age group.

Family and Friends

In the previous chapter we talked about how, in the American majority culture, the amount of time spent with family decreases in the course of adolescence, while the amount of conflict with parents increases (Larson & Richards, 1994; Youniss & Smollar, 1985). Parents remain important figures in the lives of adolescents, but the level of warmth and closeness between parents and their children typically declines during adolescence (Larson & Richards, 1994). As they move through their teens, American adolescents move steadily away from the social world of their families.

As they move away from their parents, adolescents become increasingly involved with their friends. We have noted that from the age of 6 or 7, all children in industrialized societies spend the better part of a typical day in school with their peers. However, during adolescence, young people increasingly spend time with other young people their age not only at school but in their leisure time after school, in the evenings, on weekends, and during the summer and other breaks from school.

The Experience Sampling Method (ESM) studies testify to the change in proportion of time spent with friends and parents that occurs during adolescence (Larson et al., 1996). As you can see from Figure 8.1, the amount of time spent with family decreases by about half from 5th to 9th grade, then declines even more steeply from 9th through 12th grade. In contrast, time spent with friends increases, as does time alone, especially for boys. Another study found similar results, using a slightly different method (Buhrmester & Carbery, 1992). Adolescents aged 13 to 16 were

interviewed daily over a 5-day period about how much time they spent in interactions with parents and friends. The average with parents was 28 minutes per day, whereas the average with friends was 103 minutes per day—almost four times greater.

Relationships with family and friends during adolescence change not only in quantity but also in quality. Adolescents indicate that they depend more on friends than on their parents for companionship and intimacy (Bibby & Posterski, 1992; Furman & Buhrmeister, 1992).

> "A FAITHFUL FRIEND IS THE MEDICINE OF LIFE."
> —ECCLESIASTES 6:16

Friends become increasingly important people during adolescence—the source of adolescents' happiest experiences, the people with whom they feel most comfortable, the ones they feel they can talk to most openly.

One of the best studies comparing the quality of adolescents' relationships with friends and parents was carried out by Youniss and Smollar (1985), who surveyed over a thousand adolescents aged 12 to 19. Over 90% of these adolescents indicated that they had at least one close friend "who means a lot to me." In addition, the majority (about 70%) agreed with each of these statements:

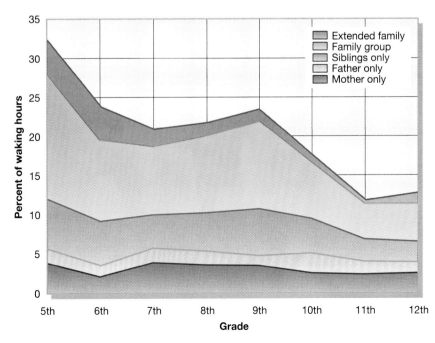

FIGURE 8.1 *Changes in time spent with others during adolescence.*
Source: Larson et al. (1996).

My close friend understands me better than my parents do.

I feel right now in my life that I learn more from my close friends than I do from my parents.

I'm more myself with my close friends than with my parents.

Youniss and Smollar (1985) also asked adolescents to indicate whether they would prefer parents or friends as the ones they would go to for discussion of various issues. The results are shown in Figure 8.2. Parents were preferred for issues related to education and future occupation, but for the more personal issues friends were preferred by large margins.

THINKING CRITICALLY

Why do you think adolescents find it more difficult to be close to their parents than to their friends?

In another study comparing orientations to parents and friends, young people in 4th grade, 7th grade,

10th grade, and college were asked to indicate which relationships provided them with the most emotional support (Furman & Buhrmester, 1992). For the 4th graders, parents were their main sources of support. However, for the 7th graders—moving into adolescence—same-gender friends were equal to parents as sources of support, and for the 10th graders same-gender friends had surpassed parents. For the college students—now in emerging adulthood—the pattern changed again. By that time, romantic partners were the main sources of support.

European studies comparing relationships with parents and friends show a pattern similar to American studies. For example, a study of Dutch adolescents (aged 15 to 19) asked them with whom they "communicate about themselves, about their personal feelings, and about sorrows and secrets" (Bois-Reymond & Ravesloot, 1996). Nearly half of the adolescents named their best friend or their relationship partner, whereas only 20% named one or both parents (only 3% their fathers). Studies in other European countries confirm that adolescents tend to be happiest when with their friends and that they tend to turn to their friends for advice and information on social relationships and leisure, although they tend to come to parents for advice about education and career plans (Hurrelmann, 1996).

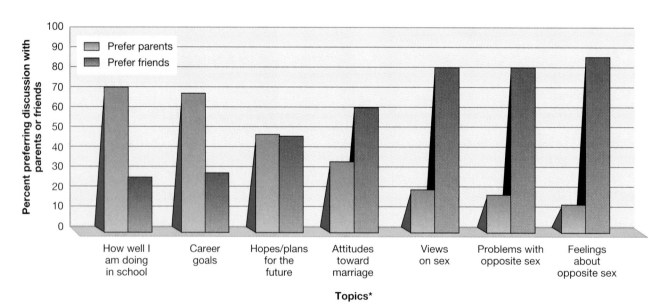

FIGURE 8.2 *Percentage of adolescents preferring to discuss topics with friends or family.*
Source: Youniss & Smollar (1985), p. 294.

The results of the studies comparing relationships with parents and friends suggest that not only are friends highly important in young people's lives, in many ways they are even more important than parents (Harris, 1999). However, this does not necessarily mean that close relationships with parents are incompatible with having close friendships (Youniss & Smollar, 1985). On the contrary, studies indicate that adolescents who have strong attachments to their parents are also more likely to develop strong attachments to friends. The more likely adolescents are to be able to trust and confide in their parents, the more likely they are to describe the same qualities in their relationships with their friends (Blain, Thompson, & Whiffen, 1993; Gold & Yanof, 1985; Raja, McGee, & Stanton, 1992).

Although the direct influence of parents diminishes during adolescence, parents shape their adolescents' peer relationships in a variety of indirect ways (Harris, 1999; Mounts, 1997; Smith & Crockett, 1997). Through parents' choices of where to live, where to send their adolescents to school (e.g., public versus private school), and where to attend religious services (or whether to attend at all), parents influence the peer networks their adolescents are likely to experience and the pool of peers from which adolescents are likely to select their friends (Cooper & Ayers-Lopez, 1985; Ladd & LeSieur, 1995). Also, parents influence adolescents' personalities and behavior through their parenting practices, which in turn affect adolescents' friendship choices. For example, in one study of 3,700 adolescents by Bradford Brown and his colleagues (Brown et al., 1993), adolescents with parents who encouraged academic achievement and who monitored their adolescents' activities were found to have higher grades and lower levels of illicit drug use; grades and illicit drug use were in turn related to adolescents' choices of friends.

Emotional States With Friends: Higher Highs, Lower Lows

In the ESM studies, adolescents report that their happiest moments take place with friends, and they are generally much happier with friends than with family. Larson and Richards (1994) describe two principal reasons for this. One is that in a close friend adolescents find someone who mirrors their own emotions. One seventh-grade girl described her friend by saying "She feels the same about the same things, and she understands what I mean. Mostly, she is feeling the same

things. . . . And if she doesn't, she'll say 'Yeah, I understand what you're talking about'" (Larson & Richards, 1994, p. 92). This girl and her friend both took part in the ESM study, and when they were "beeped" together their moods were usually the same, usually highly positive. This is in sharp contrast to adolescents' moods with parents, as we saw in the previous chapter. Adolescents often experience negative moods when with parents, and there is often a deep split in moods between the parent who is enjoying their time together and the adolescent who feels low and would like to be somewhere else.

A second reason why adolescents enjoy their time with friends so much more than their time with parents, according to Larson and Richards (1994), is that adolescents feel free and open with friends in a way they rarely do with parents. Perhaps this is the essence of friendship—friends accept and value you for who you really are. For adolescents, sometimes this means being able to talk about their deepest feelings, especially about their budding romantic relationships. Sometimes it means getting a little crazy, goofing around, letting loose with adolescent exuberance. Larson and Richards (1994) described an escalating dynamic of manic joy they sometimes captured in "beeped" moments, when adolescents would be feeding on each other's antics to their increasing delight. In one episode, a group of boys were hanging around in one of their backyards when they started spraying each other with a hose, taunting each other and laughing. In another episode, adolescent girls at a sleepover were found dancing on the ping-pong table, laughing and hugging each other. Shared enjoyment among adolescent friends is especially high on weekend nights, which Larson and Richards (1998) call "the emotional high point of the week" for adolescents (p. 37).

Of course, adolescent friendships are not only about emotional support and good times. In the ESM studies, friends were the source not only of adolescents' most positive emotions but also of their most negative emotions—anger, frustration, sadness, and anxiety. Adolescents' strong attachments to friends and their strong reliance on friends leave them vulnerable emotionally. They worry a great deal about whether their friends like them, whether they are popular enough (Larson & Richards, 1994). Larson and Richards (1994) observed that "Triangles, misunderstandings, and conflicting alliances were a regular part of the social lives of the [adolescents] we studied" (p. 94). For example, when one boy showed up an hour and a half late to meet his friend, the friend angrily rejected him and avoided him for days. During this time the boy spent much of his time alone, feeling guilty—"I'll just think about it and I'll get upset" (p. 95)—until they reconciled.

Family and Friends in Traditional Cultures

As in the West, adolescence in traditional cultures also entails less involvement with family and greater involvement with peers. Schlegel and Barry (1991), in their cross-cultural analysis, reported that this pattern is typical in cultures worldwide:

> At all stages of life beyond infancy, from the rough-and-tumble play group of childhood to the poignant, ever-diminishing cluster of aged cronies, persons of similar ages congregate. Such groups take on special meaning in adolescence, when young people are temporarily released from intense identification with a family. In childhood, people depend for their very life on the natal family; in adolescence, they are neither so dependent as they were nor so responsible as they will be. It is then that peer relations can take on an intensity of attachment that they lack at other stages of the life cycle. (p. 68)

Although this pattern applies widely around the world, an important difference between Western cultures and the traditional cultures described by Schlegel and Barry (1991) is that traditional cultures are more

likely to have substantial gender differences in adolescents' relationships to peers and family. Specifically, in traditional cultures, involvement with peers and friends tends to be much greater for boys than for girls. Adolescent girls spend more time with same-sex adults than boys do; they have more contact and more intimacy with their mothers than boys do with either parent, and they also have more contact with their grandmothers, aunts, and other adult females than boys do with adult males. Among the Zapotecs of Mexico, for example, adolescent girls spend their days in the household among adult women, learning cooking, sewing, and embroidery, whereas boys work alone or in groups in the fields during the day and congregate with each other in the village in the evening (Chinas, 1991). However, Schlegel and Barry stress that although these gender differences exist, for both male and female adolescents in traditional cultures more of their time is spent with their families than in the West, where schooling takes adolescents away from their families and into a peer society for the better part of each day.

Developmental Changes in Friendships

We have seen that friends become more important in adolescence than they had been prior to adolescence. But what is it about development from late childhood to adolescence that makes friends increasingly important? And how is friendship different in adolescence than in late childhood?

Intimacy in Adolescent Friendships

"When I was younger [my friends and I] just played. Now we talk over things and discuss problems. Then it was just a good time. Now you have to be open and able to talk."

— *15-year-old boy (Youniss & Smollar, 1985, p. 105)*

Probably the most important distinguishing feature of adolescent friendships, compared with friendships in late childhood, is intimacy. **Intimacy** is the degree to which two people share personal knowledge, thoughts, and feelings. Adolescent friends talk about their thoughts and feelings, confide hopes and fears, and help each other understand what is going on with their parents, their teachers, and other friends to a far greater degree than younger children do.

In traditional cultures, adolescent boys spend more time with friends than adolescent girls do. Here, boys of the Abouri tribe of Ghana, West Africa.

Harry Stack Sullivan (1953) was the first theorist to develop ideas on the importance of intimacy in adolescent friendships. In Sullivan's view, the need for intimacy with friends intensifies in preadolescence and early adolescence. Around age 10, according to Sullivan, most children develop a special friendship with "a *particular* member of the same sex who becomes a chum or close friend" (Sullivan, 1953, p. 245). Children at this age become cognitively capable of a degree of perspective taking and empathy they did not have earlier in childhood, and this new capacity enables them to form friendships where they truly care about their chums as individuals rather than simply as play partners.

Over the next few years, during the transition to adolescence, a relationship with a chum enhances development in a variety of ways. Chums promote further the development of perspective taking, as they share their thoughts. Their mutual attachment gives them the motivation to try to see things from one another's point of view. Also, chums provide honest evaluations of each others' merits and faults. This con-

> "TO MAKE A FRIEND, CLOSE
> ONE EYE. TO KEEP A FRIEND,
> CLOSE THE OTHER EYE."
> —JEWISH PROVERB

tributes to identity formation, as adolescents develop a more honest and accurate self-evaluation of their abilities and personalities.

Since Sullivan described his theory, numerous scholars have presented research supporting his assertion of the importance of intimacy in adolescent friendships. We have already noted how adolescents tend to rely more on their friends than on their parents as the ones to whom they confide important personal information, especially as it pertains to the opposite sex. Similarly, adolescents are more likely than younger children to disclose intimate and personal information to their friends (Berndt, 1996; Buhrmester & Furman, 1987). When adolescents are asked what they would want a friend to be like or how they can tell that someone is their friend, they tend to mention intimate features of the relationship. They state, for example, that a friend is someone who understands you, someone you can share your problems

Friendships in preadolescence tend to be based on shared activities, whereas adolescents are more likely to rely on friends for intimacy and support.

with, someone who will listen when you have something important to say (Berndt & Perry, 1990; Bukowski, Newcomb, & Hoza, 1987). Younger children are less likely to mention these kinds of features and more likely to stress shared activities—we both like to play basketball, we ride bikes together, and so on. Adolescents also describe their friends as the ones who help them work through personal problems (such as conflicts with parents or the end of a romance) by providing emotional support and advice (Savin-Williams & Berndt, 1990).

Adolescents rate trust and loyalty as more important to friendship than younger children do (Berndt & Perry, 1990; Hartup & Overhauser, 1991). Adolescents describe their friends as the ones who won't talk behind their backs or say nasty things to others about them. This is related to the emphasis on intimacy. If you are going to be opening up your heart to someone and telling them things you would not tell anyone else, you would want to be especially sure that they would not use your openness against you. In fact, when they explain why a close friendship has ended, adolescents most often mention some form of the breaking of that trust as the reason—failing to keep a secret, breaking promises, lying, or competition over a romantic partner (Youniss & Smollar, 1985).

Let's take a closer look at two studies that indicate the development of intimacy in adolescent friendships: one that looks at differences between late childhood and early adolescence, and another that looks at differences from late adolescence into emerging adulthood. In one study (Diaz & Berndt, 1982), pairs of best friends in fourth grade (late childhood) and eighth grade (early adolescence) were asked to provide information about each other's background characteristics (birth date, telephone number, etc.), preferences (favorite sport, favorite subject in school, etc.), and thoughts and feelings (what the friend worries about, gets mad about, etc.). Late childhood best friends knew as much as the early adolescent best friends about each other's background characteristics, but early adolescent friends knew more about each other's preferences, thoughts, and feelings.

In another study (Fischer, 1981), late adolescent high school students and emerging adult college students were compared in how they described their relationship with the person closest to them (not including family members). Their descriptions were coded into one of four categories: *friendly* (focus on shared activities), *intimate* (focus on affection, emotional attachment, communication), *integrated* (combination of friendly and intimate), or *uninvolved* (focus on neither shared activities nor intimacy). College students were more likely than high school students to be rated as having an intimate or integrated relationship.

Intimacy and Adolescent Development

One way of explaining the increased importance of intimacy in adolescents' friendships is in terms of cognitive changes. Recall from Chapter 3 that thinking during adolescence becomes more *abstract* and *complex*. As we discussed, these advances influence not only how adolescents solve problems but also how they understand their social relationships, that is, their social cognition. Greater ability for abstract thinking makes it possible for adolescents to think about and talk about more abstract qualities in their relationships—affection, loyalty, and trust, for example (Berndt, 1992; Hartup & Overhauser, 1991; Youniss & Smollar, 1985). Greater ability for complex thinking can be applied to adolescents' social relationships—your best friend is the one you can't wait to talk to about who just broke up with whom, who just asked whom to the school dance, who the new English teacher seems to like best (and least), and so on. Adolescents are newly aware of all the complex webs and alliances and rivalries that exist in human relationships, and friends are the ones they can talk to about it all (Adler & Adler, 1998; Eder, 1995). Talking about these social cognitive topics promotes the kind of exchange of personal knowledge and perspective that constitutes intimacy.

Also consider that many events are taking place as part of puberty and sexual maturity that lend themselves to the development of intimacy between friends. We have seen how much difficulty adolescents have talking to their parents about sexual issues. Friends are much preferred. Momentous things are happening—the changes in the body, first romances, first kisses, and so on. Sharing personal thoughts and feelings about these topics promotes intimacy between friends.

Gender is also important in the development of intimacy in adolescent friendships. Although both boys and girls go through the cognitive changes of adolescence to a similar degree, and both go through different but comparable bodily changes, there are consistent gender differences in the intimacy of adolescent friendships, with girls tending to have more intimate friendships than boys (Connolly & Konarski, 1994; DuBois & Hirsch, 1993; McNelles & Connolly, 1999; Shulman, Laursen, Kalman, & Karporsky, 1997). Girls spend more time than boys talking to their friends (Raffaelli & Duckett, 1989), and they place a higher value on talking together as a component of their friendships (Apter, 1990;

Youniss & Smollar, 1985). Girls also rate their friendships as higher in affection, helpfulness, and nurturance, compared with boys' ratings of their friendships (Lempers & Clark-Lempers, 1993). And girls are more likely than boys to say they trust and feel close to their friends (Raja, McGee, & Stanton, 1992; Shulman et al., 1997). In contrast, boys are more likely to emphasize shared activities as the basis of friendship, such as sports or hobbies (Connolly & Konarski, 1994; DuBois & Hirsch, 1993; Youniss & Smollar, 1985).

What explains these gender differences? Thus far, not many studies have looked for the reasons behind gender differences in the intimacy of adolescent friendships. However, there is ample research on gender differences in socialization that has implications here. From early in life, girls are more likely than boys to be encouraged to express their feelings openly (Maccoby, 1990). Boys who talk openly about how they feel risk being called a "wimp," a "wuss," or some other unflattering term. This is even more true in adolescence than earlier, because with puberty and sexual maturity both males and females become more conscious of what it means to be a male and what it means to be a female. Intimate conversation is something usually associated with being female, according to Western cultural beliefs about gender roles, so adolescent girls may cultivate their abilities for it whereas adolescent boys may be wary of moving too much in that direction. Nevertheless, intimacy does become more important to boys' friendships in adolescence, even if not to the same extent as for girls.

Other Developmental Changes in Adolescent Friendships

Degree of intimacy is the most notable developmental change in friendships from childhood to adolescence, but it is not the only one. Bradford Brown (1990), a prominent scholar on adolescent friendships, has specified four other developmental changes:

- Adolescents spend more time with their friends, compared with preadolescent children. We noted earlier that time spent with family decreases during adolescence; that time goes partly to increased time with friends (along with increased time alone). Time spent with friends peaks in the midteens, then declines gradually in late adolescence and emerging adulthood as people pair off into intimate couples. Compared with adolescents, adults have fewer friends and see them less often.

- Adolescent friends have less adult supervision and control than preadolescent friends. Parents in the American majority culture tend to allow more independence for adolescents than for preadolescents, but adolescents are also more likely to actively avoid adult monitoring and seek out places where they can be together without being watched or overheard by adults.

- Adolescents spend more time with friends of the opposite sex. Early adolescents spend most of their time in same-sex pairs or groups, but the amount of time spent in mixed-sex pairs or groups increases steadily during the teens.

- Adolescents are more aware than preadolescents of the social structure of peer groups, that is, they are more likely to view their peers as being members of distinct crowds such as "jocks," "populars," and "nerds." We will discuss crowds in detail later in this chapter.

Choosing Friends

Why do people become friends? For adolescents, as for children and adults, one of the key reasons identified in many studies is *similarity*. People of all ages tend to make friends with people who are similar to them in age, gender, and ethnicity, among other characteristics (Aboud & Mendelson, 1998; Hartup & Overhauser, 1991; Lempers & Clark-Lempers, 1993; Luo, Fang, & Aro, 1995). The role of ethnicity in friendships is somewhat different in adolescence than at other ages, as we will discuss below. First we will take a look at three similarities particular to adolescent friendships: educational orientation, media and leisure preferences, and participation in risk behavior.

> "TO LIKE AND DISLIKE THE SAME THINGS, THAT IS INDEED TRUE FRIENDSHIP."
> —SALLUST, CA. 50 B.C.

Educational Orientation

Adolescent friends tend to be similar in their educational orientations, including their attitudes toward school, their levels of educational achievement, and their educational plans (Berndt, 1996). Adolescents who like school, study a lot, and plan to go to college tend to have friends who feel the same. Adolescents who dislike school, rarely study, and look forward to being done with it all also tend to have friends who view it the way they do.

In adolescence and emerging adulthood, friends tend to be similar in educational goals.

This does not simply end with high school (Osgood et al., 1996; Osgood & Lee, 1993). In the college setting there are often groups of friends who study a lot together and seem very serious about getting a good education, and other groups of friends who party a lot together and seem very intent on having a good time. Not that studying and partying are always mutually exclusive, but the degree of a person's educational orientation tends to structure their time in high school and college. You may have friends who expect you to study with them the night before the big biology exam, or you may have friends who expect you to join them for Dollar Pitcher Night at the local nightspot and to heck with the biology exam. Adolescents and emerging adults tend to prefer as friends people who would make the same choice as they would in this kind of situation (Osgood et al., 1996; Osgood & Lee, 1993; Urberg, Degirmencioglu, & Tolson, 1998).

Media and Leisure Preferences

Another common similarity in adolescent friendships is in preferences for media and leisure activity. Adolescent friends tend to like the same kinds of music, wear the same styles of dress, and prefer to do the same things with their leisure time (e.g., Arnett, 1996; Wulff, 1995a). Again, this makes certain logical sense. If you like to listen to the rap station and your friend prefers classic rock, that could result in quite a few loud discussions when you are driving places together. If you prefer to play chess on Saturday evenings whereas your

friend prefers to go out on the town, you will probably not be spending many of your Saturday evenings together, and you will not likely stay friends for long (Urberg et al., 1998).

Risk Behavior

A third common similarity among adolescent friends is risky activities. Adolescent friends tend to resemble each other in the extent to which they drink alcohol, try drugs, drive dangerously, get in fights, shoplift, vandalize, and so on (Berndt, 1996; Cairns et al., 1988; Dishion et al., 1991; Osgood et al., 1996; Stone et al., 2000). Adolescents engage in these risk behaviors to varying degrees—some on a regular basis, some now and then, some not at all. Because adolescents usually take part in risk behavior with friends, adolescents tend to choose friends who resemble themselves in the extent to which they participate in risky activities (Urberg et al., 1998). We will talk in more detail about this aspect of adolescent friendships in the section on peer pressure later in this chapter.

Ethnicity

Although ethnic similarity between friends is typical at all ages, adolescence is a time when ethnic boundaries in friendships become sharper between the various cultural groups in American society. During childhood ethnicity is related to friendship, but not strongly. However, as children enter adolescence friendships become less interethnic, and by late adolescence they are generally ethnically segregated (Peshkin, 1991; Shrum, Cheek, & Hunter, 1988).

Why would this be so? The reasons are not clear. One possibility that has been suggested is that it may be difficult for adolescents of different ethnicities to be friends because they often differ not only in ethnic group but in family socioeconomic status (SES) background and neighborhood. Even when adolescents have interethnic friendships at school, they rarely see those friends outside of school (DuBois & Hirsch, 1990), perhaps because they live in different areas of town and because their families may be different in incomes, occupations, and levels of education. This makes sense, but it does not explain why the division would be greater in adolescence than earlier.

Another possible reason is the stereotypes and prejudices that young people may have about people of other ethnic backgrounds. Keep in mind that adolescents' parents do not commonly have interethnic friendships, either, and neighborhoods in American towns and cities are often ethnically segregated, so that

CULTURAL FOCUS
Interethnic Friendships Among British Girls

In Europe a considerable proportion of young people's interactions with peers takes place through youth clubs (Alsaker & Flammer, 1999a). Time in school is focused solely on education. Extracurricular activities such as sports teams, dances, and parties are sponsored not by schools but by youth clubs. In most Western European countries, a majority of young people belong to a youth club (Alsaker & Flammer, 1999a).

Helena Wulff (1995a) has studied interracial friendships among adolescent girls in a youth club in a working-class section of London, England. Wulff, a Swedish anthropologist, used interviews as the main method of her research, along with observations of the girls in the youth club. She focused especially on the friendships among 20 Black and White girls aged 13 to 16. The Black girls were the English-born daughters of immigrants from former British colonies such as Jamaica and Nigeria. Wulff was especially interested in exploring the interethnic friendships among the girls, which she noticed were very common at the club.

In many ways the friendships among the girls had little to do with ethnicity and were similar to the friendships described among adolescent girls in the United States and other countries. Their most common activity together was talking, mostly about boys and about male celebrities (e.g., singers, actors) they admired. They also talked a great deal about aspects of appearance—the latest hairstyles, clothes, cosmetics, and jewelry. Other favorite shared activities were listening to recorded music and dancing in their bedrooms and at parties and teen nightclubs.

They occasionally took part in risky activities together such as shoplifting or smoking marijuana.

Although they spent a great deal of time together enjoying shared activities, when they spoke to Wulff about their friendships the girls emphasized not shared activities but the importance of intangible qualities, especially trust. A friend, they told Wulff, is "someone you can share things with, like problems, and also someone you can trust," as well as "someone you can talk to, tell secrets and all that and you know they won't . . . tell anybody else" (Wulff, 1995a, p. 68). Again, this is highly similar to the perspective reported in studies of American adolescent friends (Berndt, 1996; Youniss & Smollar, 1985).

However, the girls were also conscious of ethnic issues and explicitly addressed those issues in some ways in their friendships. They were well aware that racism and ethnic inequality are pervasive in British society. In reaction to this, and in resistance to it, they deliberately emphasized Black elements in their youth styles, taking "an interesting revenge against the low-class position of most Blacks" (Wulff, 1995a, p. 71). Thus, they listened especially to predominantly Black forms of music such as reggae, ska, and "jazzfunk." Some—White as well as Black—wore their hair in a mass of thin plaits most often worn by Blacks. They mixed Black and White components in their clothing and their jewelry. In the various aspects of their common style, according to Wulff (1995a), "the concern with and the search for ethnic equality run through them all. . . . they cultivated their own aesthetic of ethnic equality through their youth styles" (pp. 72–73).

young people may reach adolescence without ever having had much contact with peers of other ethnic groups (Taylor, 1998). This lack of familiarity may make it difficult for adolescents of different ethnic backgrounds to find the kind of comfortable similarities that form the basis of most friendships. Again, however, this would seem to be no different in adolescence than earlier in childhood.

One factor specific to adolescence may be that as they grow into adolescence, young people in American society become increasingly aware of the long, troubled history of interethnic relations in the United States, and this awareness fosters mutual suspicion and mistrust. Similarly, as adolescents begin to form an ethnic identity, they may begin to see the divisions between ethnic groups as sharper than they had perceived them before (Phinney, 1990). These are possibilities, but more research is needed to investigate them.

Ethnic segregation in friendships does not end when adolescence ends. On most college campuses, too, students of different ethnic backgrounds tend to hang out in homogeneous groups without much mixing. And beyond college, too, throughout adulthood, interethnic friendships are fairly uncommon in American society (Taylor, 1998).

Friends' Influence and Peer Pressure

"Friends can push you into doing stuff you know you shouldn't be doing. You try and say no and they'll probably end up beating you up or something. My friends tell me to do something and I do it. They're a lot older than me. Like they'll tell me we're going to play basketball, so they come by and pick me up and we end up going to the liquor store. And I say, 'Hey, man, what's in the bag?' and they say, 'Gin. Now shut up and take a drink.'"

—*Lionel, age 14 (Bell, 1998, p. 74)*

"If the kids in my group are smoking marijuana they say, 'You want to try it?' If you say no, they say 'Fine.' That's all there is to it. No one forces you. And no one puts you down."

—*Aaron, age 14 (Bell, 1998, p. 76)*

One of the topics on adolescents' peer relationships that has received the most attention is peer pressure. Scholars on adolescence have devoted considerable theoretical and research attention to it, and the general public (at least in the United States) believes that peer pressure is a central part of adolescence, something all adolescents have to learn to deal with in the course of growing up (Berndt, 1996).

Friends' influence is a more accurate term than peer pressure for the social effects adolescents experience. Remember the difference between friends and peers: Peers are simply the more or less anonymous group of other people who happen to be the same age as you are; friends are emotionally and socially important in a way that peers are not. When people talk about peer pressure, what they really mean is friends' influence. When we think of an adolescent girl standing around

with a group of other adolescents as they pass around a joint, and we imagine them handing it to her expecting her to take a puff, we assume that the people she is hanging around with are her friends, not merely her peers. If we overhear an argument between an adolescent boy who wants to get his navel pierced and his parents who regard that as a bizarre and barbaric notion, and he says "everybody else is doing it!," we can probably guess he means every one of his friends, not everybody else in his entire junior high school. Friends can have a substantial influence on adolescents, but the effects of the entire peer group are weak (Berndt, 1996).

What do you think of first when you think of how adolescents are influenced by their friends? Often, the assumption is that the influences adolescent friends have on each other are negative. The influence of friends is often blamed for adolescents' involvement in a wide range of risk behaviors, including alcohol and other drug use, cigarette smoking, and delinquent behavior (see Berndt, 1996).

Actually, however, evidence suggests that the influence of friends is important not only in encouraging adolescents to participate in risk behavior but also in *discouraging* risk behavior, as well as in supporting them emotionally and helping them cope with stressful life events (Berndt & Savin-Williams, 1993; Hartup, 1993). Both types of friends' influence—the type that pertains to risk behavior and the type that pertains to support—appear to follow a similar developmental pattern, rising in strength in early adolescence and peaking in the midteens, then declining in late adolescence (Berndt, 1996). Let's take a look at the research on each of these aspects of friends' influence.

THINKING CRITICALLY

What has been your experience with friends' influence? Has it ever led you to do something you wish you had not done? To what extent has it been positive or negative?

Friends' Influence: Risk Behavior

A correlation does exist between the rates of risk behaviors that adolescents report for themselves and the rates they report for their friends. This is true for alcohol use, cigarette use, use of illegal drugs, sexual behavior, risky driving practices, and criminal activity (Barrett, Simpson, & Lehman, 1988; Ferguson & Horwood, 1995; Fisher & Bauman, 1988; Millstein, Petersen, & Nightingale, 1993; Stone et al., 2000).

But what does this mean, exactly? Because a correlation exists between the behavior adolescents report and the behavior they report for their friends, can we conclude that adolescents' participation in these behaviors is *influenced* by their friends? Not on the basis of a correlation alone. One of the simplest and most important principles of statistics is that correlation is not the same as causation. Just because two events are correlated does not mean that one causes the other. Unfortunately, this principle is often overlooked in the conclusions drawn from studies of similarities among adolescent friends.

There are two good reasons to question whether the correlations in these studies reflect causation. One is that, in most studies, reports of both the adolescents' behavior and the behavior of their friends come from the adolescents themselves (Berndt, 1996). However, several studies that have obtained separate reports of behavior from adolescents and from their friends indicate that adolescents generally perceive their friends as more similar to themselves than they actually are (according to their friends' reports), in their alcohol use, cigarette use, use of illegal drugs, and sexual attitudes (Bauman & Fisher, 1986; Graham, Marks, & Hansen, 1991; Iannotti & Bush, 1992). Perhaps because of egocentrism, adolescents perceive more similarity between themselves and their friends than is actually the case, which inflates the correlations in the risk behavior they report for themselves and their friends.

The second and perhaps even more important reason for doubting that correlation can be interpreted as causation in studies of risk behavior among adolescents and their friends is **selective association**, the principle that most people (including adolescents) tend to choose friends who are similar to themselves (Berndt, 1996). As we discussed earlier, friends tend to be similar to one another in a variety of ways, and this is in part because people *seek out* friends who are similar to themselves. Thus, the correlation between adolescents' risk behavior and the risk behavior of their friends might be partly or even entirely because they have selected each other as friends on the basis of the similarities they have in common, not because they have influenced each other in their risk behavior. If one adolescent likes to drink beer, smoke cigarettes, and look for potential sexual partners in his leisure time, and another prefers to play computer games, play basketball, and do volunteer work, the two are unlikely to become friends. In friendships, the old cliché is true—birds of a feather flock together.

Adolescent friends tend to have similar levels of substance use. Is this similarity due to peer pressure or selective association?

Fortunately, several longitudinal studies have been conducted on risk behavior that help to unravel this issue. These studies indicate that both selection and influence contribute to similarities in risk behavior among adolescent friends. That is, adolescents are similar in risk behavior before they become friends, but if they stay friends they tend to become even more similar, increasing or decreasing their rates of participation in risk behavior so that they more closely match one another. This pattern has been found to be true for cigarette use (Engles et al., 1999; Ennett & Bauman, 1994), alcohol use (Curran, Stice, & Chassin, 1997), other drug use (Farrell & Danish, 1993; Kandel, 1978; Stein, Newcomb, & Bentler, 1987), delinquency (Dobkin et al., 1995), and aggressive behavior (Botvin & Vitaro, 1995).

As noted, evidence also suggests that friends can influence each other not only participation in risk behavior, but also *against* it. It depends on who your friends are, and some adolescents are adamantly against risk behavior. In one study, adolescents who did not smoke indicated that they believed their friends would disapprove if they started smoking (Urberg, Shyu, & Liang, 1990), and in another, adolescents were more likely to report that their friends pressured them *not* to use alcohol than to use it (Keefe, 1994). In a study that compared various types of friend influence, adolescents rated pressure to participate in risk behavior as the *weakest* of five areas of possible influence, well below pressure to participate in school activities and to conform to styles of dress and grooming (Clasen & Brown, 1985). This study also found that pressure against participation in risk behavior was more common than pressure in favor of it.

This is not meant to dismiss entirely the role of friends' influence in encouraging risk behavior in adolescence. No doubt friends' influence does occur, for some adolescents for some types of risk behavior on some occasions. But we must not overmagnify this influence, and we should interpret the research on this topic carefully. Friends' influence is one part of the story of some adolescents' participation in risk behavior, but it is only one part, and the closer you look at it the smaller it seems.

Friends' Influence: Support and Nurturance

"Julie was on the swimming team with me, and she was scared to compete because she thought she wouldn't beat the other person. I was trying to tell her, 'Come on, you can do it.' But she always thought she wasn't good enough. And that was the way she felt about everything, not just swimming. Since I was her best friend, I really talked to her. 'You can do it. You're great. Do it for our team.' I kept boosting her confidence, and you know, after awhile she did do it. We all cheered for her and she was terrific."

—*Marlianne, age 18 (Bell, 1998, p. 81)*

Harry Stack Sullivan (1953) tended to emphasize the positive over the negative aspects of adolescents' friendships. In Sullivan's view, intimate friendships in adolescence are important for building their self-esteem. These friendships also help them develop their social understanding, according to Sullivan, as they compare their own perspective with their friends' and thus begin to learn how to take another person's perspective (also see Youniss & Smollar, 1985). More recently, theorists on adolescents'

friendships have specified four types of support that friends may provide to each other in adolescence (Berndt, 1996):

- **Informational support** is advice and guidance in solving personal problems, such as those involving friends, romantic relationships, parents, or school. Because of their similar ages and the age-grading of American society, adolescents are often going through similar experiences. This is particularly true of friends, because they tend to choose one another partly because of their similarities. Intimate friendships give adolescents a source of support, because they can talk about their most personal thoughts and feelings with someone they believe will accept and understand them.

- **Instrumental support** is help with tasks of various kinds. Adolescent friends support each other by helping each other do homework, assisting each other with household chores, lending each other money, and so on.

- **Companionship support** is being able to rely on each other as companions in social activities. Did you ever experience the anxiety, in your teens, of having no friend to go with to the school dance, or the big basketball game, or a much-discussed party? Adolescent friends support each other by being reliable companions for these kinds of events, as well as for more routine daily events—having someone to eat with at lunch, or someone to sit with on the bus, and so on.

- **Esteem support** is the support adolescent friends provide by congratulating their friends when they succeed and encouraging them or consoling them when they fail. Adolescents support their friends by being "on their side" whether things go well or go badly for them.

THINKING CRITICALLY

Give an example of each of the four types of friendship support described in this section.

What sort of effects do these kinds of support have on adolescents' development? Thus far, most research on the effects of friends in adolescence has been focused on the potentially negative effects discussed above. Only in recent years have researchers begun to turn their attention to the effects of friends' support in adolescence (Berndt, 1996), and the studies on this topic have had inconsistent results. Some longitudinal studies have found supportive friendships to be related to improvements in attitudes toward classmates (Berndt, 1989) and toward schoolwork (Berndt & Keefe, 1995), and friends' support has been found to predict an easing of depressive symptoms among girls but not boys (Slavin & Rainer, 1990). However, other longitudinal studies have found that supportive friendships did not predict changes over time in self-esteem, depression, drug use, or academic achievement (DuBois et al., 1992; Vernberg, 1990; Windle, 1992). Research in this area is just beginning and can be expected to provide more detailed information over the years to come.

Friends spend a high amount of their leisure time together in emerging adulthood.

Friends and Leisure Activities in Emerging Adulthood

In general, far more research has been done on relationships with friends and peers in adolescence than in emerging adulthood. Nevertheless, friendships may be especially important in emerging adulthood for a number of reasons. Emerging adults typically leave home, and we might expect that attachments and activities with friends would rise in importance once young people have left home and no longer experience family relations as part of their daily environment. Similarly, because most emerging adults are unmarried, this status might be expected to give them a greater incentive than married persons to seek contacts with friends.

The best data on activities with friends in emerging adulthood comes from a study by Osgood and Lee (1993), who presented data on leisure activities from a telephone survey of a representative sample of 827 Nebraska residents aged 18 and older. Their data provide insights into activities with friends in emerging adulthood, and also allow us to make comparisons between emerging adulthood and older ages.

Osgood and Lee (1993) inquired about participation in a variety of types of leisure activities (such as going to parties or going to music concerts), most of which we can assume would take place with friends. The average emerging adult in the study spent a con-

siderable amount of time in leisure activities with friends. Most emerging adults (aged 18 to 28 in their study) said they get together with friends at least once a week, for no specific purpose. The typical emerging adult went to a party at least once a month and went to bars nearly that often. Emerging adults also went to movies once or twice a month, on average, and to music concerts at least a few times a year.

In all of these respects, average rates of participation in leisure activities with friends were considerably higher among emerging adults than among older adults. However, even within emerging adulthood these activities steadily declined. Eighteen-year-olds had a more active leisure life with friends than 23-year-olds, and 23-year-olds were more active than 28-year-olds.

Osgood and Lee (1993) found that little of this decline during emerging adulthood could be explained by entering marriage, but that having a child reduced participation in every aspect of leisure with friends. Even for those who did not become parents from age 18 to 28, however, leisure with friends declined substantially over this period. It may be that some kinds of leisure that emerging adult friends often engage in—parties, bars, and so on—simply lose their charm by the late twenties.

■ ───────── **THINKING CRITICALLY**

How would you explain the decline in leisure activities with friends that Osgood and Lee (1993) found between age 18 and age 28? Keep in mind that they found that marriage does not explain the decline; also keep in mind that for most people their first child is not born until their late twenties, and most of the decline takes place before then.

Cliques and Crowds

So far we have focused on close friendships. Now we turn to larger groups of friends and peers. Scholars generally make a distinction between two types of adolescent groups, cliques and crowds. **Cliques** are small groups of friends who know each other well, do things together, and form a regular social group (Brown, 1990; Dunphy, 1969). Cliques have no precise size—3 to 12 is a rough range—but they are small enough so that all the members of the clique feel they know each other well and they think of themselves as a cohesive group (Brown, 1990). Sometimes cliques are defined by distinctive shared activities—for example, working on cars, playing music, playing basketball, surfing the Internet—and sometimes simply by shared friendship (a group of friends who eat lunch together every day, for example).

Crowds, in contrast, are larger, reputation-based groups of adolescents who are not necessarily friends and do not necessarily spend much time together (Brown, 1990; Brown, Mory, & Kinney, 1994; Kinney, 1993; Stone & Brown, 1998). Some of the crowd labels typical in American high schools in recent years are:

- **Jocks** (athletically oriented, usually members of at least one school sports team);
- **Brains**, **dweebs**, **nerds**, or **geeks** (academically oriented, known for striving for good grades and for being socially inept);
- **Populars** or **trendies** (the socially elite crowd, recognized as having the highest social status in the school);
- **Druggies** (alienated from the school social environment, suspected by other students of using illicit drugs);
- **Headbangers** (fans of heavy-metal music, who often wear black t-shirts);

- **Nobodies** (low in social skills, mostly ignored by other adolescents); and
- **Normals** (students who do not stand out in any particular way, either positively nor negatively).

Within each of these crowds, of course, there are likely to be cliques and close friends. However, the main function of crowds is not to provide a setting for adolescents' social interactions and friendships. Crowds mainly serve the function of helping adolescents to locate themselves and others within the high school social structure. In other words, crowds help adolescents to define their own identities and the identities of others. Knowing that others think of you as a brain has implications for your identity—it means you are the kind of person who likes school, does well in school, and perhaps has more success in school than in social situations. Thinking of someone else as a druggie tells you something about that person (whether it's accurate or not)—he or she uses drugs, of course, probably dresses unconventionally, and does not seem to care much about school.

Cliques are groups of friends, so it is not surprising that many of the characteristics that apply to adolescent friendships also apply to adolescent cliques. In particular, members of cliques tend to be similar to each other in the same way that friends are—age, gender, and ethnicity, as well as educational attitudes, media/leisure preferences, and participation in risky activities (Brown, 1990; Kinney, 1993, 1999). Also, clique members, being friends, rely on each other for shared activities and mutual support. Crowds, however, are not so much groups of friends as social categories, so their characteristics differ in important ways from friendships, as we will explore below.

Sarcasm and Ridicule in Cliques

Recall from the chapter on cognitive development that the cognitive changes of adolescence, particularly the increased capacity for complex thinking, makes adolescents capable of appreciating and using sarcasm more than they did prior to adolescence. Sarcasm— and a sharper form of sarcasm, ridicule—plays a part in adolescent friendships and clique interactions. In one study, Gavin and Furman (1989) studied young people in 5th through 12th grades and found that critical evaluations of one another were a typical part of the social interactions in adolescent cliques. Sarcasm and ridicule were included in what they called "antagonistic interactions." Such interactions were common in the adolescents they studied. Antagonistic interactions were directed both at members within the group and at those outside the group and were more common in early and middle adolescence than in late adolescence.

The authors of the study suggested a number of possible reasons for these kinds of interactions. One function of antagonistic interactions is that they promote the establishment of a dominance hierarchy—higher status members dish out more sarcasm and ridicule than they take. Also, antagonistic interactions serve to bring nonconformist group members into line and reinforce clique conformity, which helps to buttress the cohesiveness of the group. If an adolescent boy comes to school wearing a shirt with monkeys on it (as a friend of mine once did), and all his friends laugh at him all day (as we did), he will know better than to wear that shirt again if he wants to remain part of their clique.

Sarcasm and ridicule of people outside the clique also serve to strengthen clique identity by clarifying the boundaries between "us" and "them." Erik Erikson remarked on this tendency among adolescents:

> They become remarkably clannish, intolerant, and cruel in their exclusion of others who are "different," in skin color or cultural background, in tastes and gifts, and often in entirely petty aspects of dress and gesture arbitrarily selected as *the* signs of an in-grouper or an out-grouper. (Erikson, 1959, p. 97)

To Erikson, the motive was mainly psychological—sarcasm and ridicule are used by adolescents at a time when they are unsure of their identities, as part of the process of sorting through what they are and what they are not. Antagonistic interactions are a way of easing their anxiety about these issues by drawing attention to others who are implied to be both inferior and very different from themselves.

Schlegel and Barry (1991) describe an interesting variation on the use of sarcasm and ridicule in traditional cultures. They provide several examples of cultures where groups of adolescent boys use sarcasm and ridicule to enforce conformity to cultural standards of behavior and punish those who violate them. Their uses of sarcasm and ridicule are directed not just toward other adolescents, but toward adults.

The Mbuti Pygmies of Africa, for example, consider it improper to be argumentative. Persons who violate this prohibition are likely to find themselves awakened very early the next morning by a group of adolescent boys making loud noises, climbing on their hut and

pounding on the roof, tearing off leaves and sticks. Among the Hopi in the American Southwest, when a man is known to be visiting a woman at night while her husband is away, the adolescent boys of the village publicize and punish his adultery by leaving a trail of ashes during the night between his house and hers for everyone to see the next morning. In a historical example, Gillis (1974) describes how in various parts of Europe in the 16th and 17th centuries, groups of unmarried males in their teens and early twenties had an unwritten responsibility for enforcing social norms. Using profane songs and mocking pantomimes, they would publicly mock violators of social norms—the adulterer, the old man who had married a young bride, the widow or widower who had remarried a bit hastily following the death of a spouse. In Gillis' description, "a recently remarried widower might find himself awakened by the clamor of the crowd, an effigy of his dead wife thrust up to his window and a likeness of himself, placed backward on an ass, drawn through the streets for his neighbors to see" (Gillis, 1974, p. 30).

Thus in some cultural and historical contexts, young people are given permission to do what under other circumstances would be seen by adults as intolerable, even criminal behavior (Schlegel & Barry, 1991). Allowing young people to use sarcasm and ridicule in a socially constructive way serves the purpose of enforcing community standards and saves the adults the trouble of doing so.

Crowds

> ❝*Like it's really easy to go, 'He's a jock, or he's a punk, or she's alternative' or whatever. There's lots of different groups, but once you start hanging out with one group, you pretty much get labeled, which kind of sucks, since I think, if anything, you find your group because of who you are, not because they influenced you to be like them. It's like you seek out people who you like, and you go hang out with them.*❞

> —*Maria, high school student (Bell, 1998, p. 71)*

If you attended an American high school, you can probably think of the different crowds that existed in high school—jocks, nerds, populars, druggies, and so on. Now think of your elementary school, say, fifth or sixth grade. Most likely you find it harder to name any crowds from elementary school. Crowd definition and membership seems to be something that becomes important in adolescence, and not before. This may be partly because of the cognitive changes of adolescence (Brown, 1990; O'Brien & Bierman, 1988). Crowd labels are abstract categories, each with some abstract defining characteristics—degree of popularity, attitudes toward school, and so on—and the capacity for abstract thinking is one of the cognitive advances of adolescence. As noted, crowds may also become more important in adolescence because identity issues become important in adolescence (Stone & Brown, 1998). Adolescents are more concerned than younger children with asking questions about who they are—and who others are. Crowds help adolescents ascribe definite characteristics to themselves and to others as they grow through the process of identity formation in adolescence.

Although the focus on crowds in adolescence reflects certain developmental characteristics such as cognitive changes and identity formation, the cultural basis of crowds is also important. In industrialized societies, the fact that most adolescents remain in school at least until their late teens and the fact that these schools are almost always strictly age-graded makes crowd definition especially important. Spending so much time around peers on a daily basis elevates the importance of peers as social reference groups, that is, as groups that influence how adolescents think about themselves and their place in their social world (Brown & Lohr, 1987). For adolescents in the many cultures around the world where adolescents spend most of their time with family members or with groups of mixed ages, crowds have no relevance to their lives.

For adolescents in American society, however, crowds are an important part of their social lives, especially in early to midadolescence. Adolescent scholars Bradford Brown and David Kinney and their colleagues (Brown, 1990; Brown, Mory, & Kinney, 1994; Kinney, 1993, 1999) have described how crowd structure changes during adolescence, becoming more differentiated and more influential from early to midadolescence, then less hierarchical and less influential from mid- to late adolescence (see Figure 8.3). In Kinney's (1993, 1999) research on adolescent crowds in a small Midwestern city, he found that early adolescents (grades 6 to 8) perceived only two distinct crowds— a small group of popular, high-status adolescents (the trendies), and a larger group composed of everybody else (the dweebs). By midadolescence (grades 9 to 10), however, the

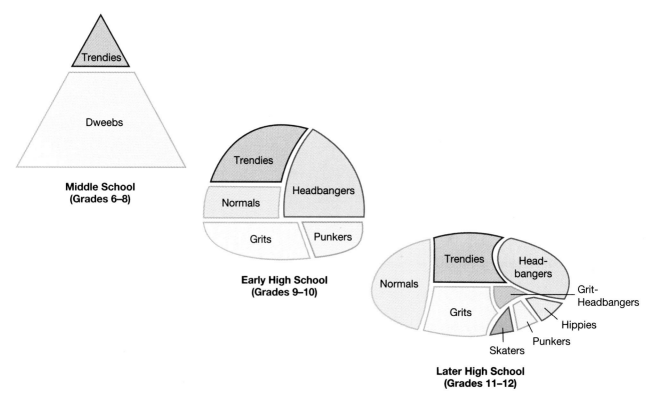

FIGURE 8.3 *Changes in crowd structure during adolescence.*
Source: Brown, Mory, & Kinney (1994).

RESEARCH FOCUS
Participant Observation of Adolescent Crowds

One fruitful way that adolescent crowds have been studied is through **participant observation**. This research method involves taking part in various activities with the people you are interested in studying. As the scholar, you participate in the activities but you also use that participation as an opportunity to observe and record the behavior of others. Participant observation is related to the ethnographic method we discussed in Chapter 1, which is typically used by anthropologists.

However, anthropologists using ethnographic methods actually live among the people they are studying. Participant observation does not go quite that far—the scholar takes part in many activities with the group of interest, but without actually living among them on a daily basis. Nevertheless, participant observation shares many of the strengths of the ethnographic method. Both methods allow the scholar to observe the behavior of people in action, as it actually occurs, rather than relying on later memories of behavior as questionnaires and interviews do.

One of the scholars who has done participant observation of adolescent crowds is sociologist David Kinney of Central Michigan University. For several years, Kinney's research has involved blending in with adolescent crowds in high schools and observing their behavior. He also conducts interviews with adolescents to supplement his observations.

Kinney's participant observation research has provided some of the best information we have on the composition of adolescent crowds and how they change from middle school through high school (e.g., Brown, Mory, & Kinney, 1994; Kinney, 1993; 1999). For example, he has observed how crowds in middle school tend to be divided simply into the popular crowd (trendies) and the unpopular crowd (dweebs), whereas in high school the crowds tend to be more diverse and defined by common interests and styles (e.g., skaters, hippies, headbangers). Kinney's interviews, too, provide valuable data on adolescent peer groups, for example, on the sometimes brutal process of establishing social hierarchies among peers through sarcasm and ridicule, as exemplified in these two quotes:

[In middle school] you were afraid of getting laughed at about anything you did because if you did one thing that was out of the ordinary, and you weren't expected to do anything out of the ordinary, then you were laughed at and made fun of, and you wouldn't fit the group at all, and then, of course, you were excluded and then you didn't even exist. (Kinney, 1993, p. 27)

If you have confidence, you can overlook people who put you down 'cause there are always people who are going to put you down. And [when you have confidence] you don't have to worry about what I think are the more trivial things in life, like appearance or being trendy. (Kinney, 1993, p. 33)

Kinney obtains permission from school officials first, of course. For the most part, the adolescents know he is not "one of them," and he does not attempt to hide that fact. However, effective participation does require blending into the social setting as thoroughly as possible, and Kinney takes steps to achieve that goal:

I attempted to carve out a neutral identity for myself at the school by making and maintaining connections with students in a wide variety of peer groups and by being open to their different viewpoints. . . . I also distanced myself from adult authority figures by dressing in jeans and casual shirts and by emphasizing my status as a college student writing a paper about teenagers' high school experiences. (Kinney, 1993, p. 25)

Of course, participant observation of adolescents is easier for someone who looks young, as Kinney did when he began his research as a graduate student. An older scholar, gray-haired and clearly a long way from adolescence, would be more conspicuous and would likely have a more difficult time being accepted by adolescents as a participant in their activities (Wulff, 1995a). In part because of his youth, Kinney has been able to "hang out" with various adolescent crowds, not just in school but at sports events, dances, and parties, and have them accept and even enjoy his presence.

adolescents identified five crowds in their high school. Trendies were still on top as the high-status crowd, followed in status by normals and headbangers, with grits (known for their rural attire, e.g., overalls) and punkers (known for liking punk music) on the bottom of the status hierarchy. Among late adolescents (grades 11 to 12), the same crowds were identified, but two others, skaters and hippies, had been added to the mix, as well as a hybrid crowd of grits-headbangers.

Kinney (1993, 1999) and Brown (Brown et al., 1999) have also noted changes in the role and importance of crowds in the adolescents' social lives. As crowds become more differentiated in midadolescence, they also become more central to adolescents' thinking about their social world. Among the ninth graders, nearly all agreed about their school's crowd structure, and their perceptions of the influence of these crowds was very high. By late adolescence, however, the significance of crowds had begun to diminish, and the adolescents saw them as less important in defining social status and social perceptions. This change parallels studies of friends' influence, which find friends' influence to be highest in intensity during midadolescence, diminishing in the later high school years (Berndt, 1996).

Scholars on adolescence generally see this pattern as reflecting the course of identity development (Brown, 1990; Varenne, 1982). During early to mid-adolescence, identity issues are especially prominent, and crowd structures help adolescents define themselves. The distinctive features of the crowd they belong to—the clothes they wear, the music they like best, the way they spend their leisure time, and so on—are ways for adolescents to define and declare their identities. By late adolescence, when their identities are better established, they no longer feel as great a need to rely on crowds for self-definition, and the importance of crowds diminishes. By that time, they may even see crowds as an impediment to their development as individuals. As they grow to adopt the individualism of the American majority culture, membership in any group—even a high-status one—may be seen as an infringement on their independence and uniqueness.

One reflection of this resistance to crowd identification is that adolescents do not always accept the crowd label attributed to them by their peers. According to one study (Brown, 1989), only 25% of the students classified by other students as jocks or druggies classified themselves this way, and only 15% of those classified as nobodies and loners by their peers also picked this classification for themselves. Thus, adolescents may readily sort their fellow students into distinct crowds, but they may be more likely to see themselves as the kind of person who is too distinctively individual to fit neatly into a crowd classification.

THINKING CRITICALLY

Why do you think adolescents resist identifying themselves as part of a particular crowd, even though they routinely apply crowd labels to others?

Crowds in American Minority Cultures Research on crowds in American minority cultures has revealed some interesting similarities and differences compared with the patterns in the American majority culture as described above (Brown & Mounts, 1989; Fordham & Ogbu, 1986; Peshkin, 1991). With respect to similarities, scholars have found that in high schools with mostly non-White students, the same kinds of crowds exist as among White adolescents—an athletic crowd, an academically oriented crowd, a deviant crowd, a popular crowd, and so on. This makes sense, because students in these schools would experience the same age-grading, the same cognitive changes, and the same identity issues that contribute to the formation of crowds among White adolescents. For minority adolescents, too, crowds serve as reference groups and as a way to establish a status hierarchy.

An interesting difference, however, applies to high schools that have multiethnic populations (Brown & Mounts, 1989). In these high schools, adolescents tend to see fewer crowd distinctions in other ethnic groups than they do in their own. To non-Asians, for example, all Asian American students are part of the Asian crowd, whereas the Asian students themselves distinguish among jocks, nerds, populars, and so on. Also of interest is that in multiethnic high schools there tends to be little crossing of ethnic boundaries in crowd membership, just as with clique membership and friendships. However, one exception to this rule is that adolescent boys with a common interest in sports—the jocks—are more likely than other adolescents in high school to form a multiethnic crowd (Damico & Sparks, 1986).

Crowds Across Cultures Although crowds as we know them in American schools do not really exist in

In multiethnic high schools, adolescents who belong to the same ethnic group are often seen by others as being part of one crowd.

mon in cultures in Africa, southern Asia, and the Pacific islands.

Another arrangement found in some traditional cultures is a **men's house**, a dormitory where adolescent boys sleep along with adult men who are widowed or divorced. Married men may also spend time there, during the day. The men's house serves a function similar to the adolescent dormitory, as a place to sleep and enjoy leisure, but it is not limited to adolescents. Rather than being a setting for an adolescent peer crowd, it is a setting mainly for male pursuits and for adult men to socialize adolescent boys into the male gender role, teaching them the kinds of things that men do with their spare time.

traditional cultures, many traditional cultures do have a distinct social group of young people. Traditional cultures often have one adolescent peer crowd in the community, rather than diverse crowds with different attributes and statuses as in American schools. The adolescent peer crowd in traditional cultures is also less strictly age-graded—adolescents of a variety of ages may be part of the adolescent peer crowd. Still, it could be called a peer crowd in the sense that it is a group of adolescents who spend time together on a daily basis and have a sense of themselves as being a distinct group with a distinct group identity.

In many traditional cultures the center of adolescent social life is a separate dwelling, a **dormitory** where the community's adolescents sleep and spend their leisure time (Schlegel & Barry, 1991). They do not spend all their time there, in most cases—adolescents typically work alongside their parents and have their meals with their families. The dormitory is a place for relaxing and having fun with other adolescents.

Often, this fun includes sexual experimentation. The adolescents sleep in the dormitory, and this setting provides the opportunity for their first sexual experiences. Even if there are separate dormitories for boys and girls, they may visit one another for sexual adventures. As Schlegel and Barry (1991) put it, the dorm is like an "extended slumber party as American teenagers know it, but often with the addition of sexual play" (p. 70). Adolescent dormitories are com-

THINKING CRITICALLY

Compare and contrast the peer relations of young people in the "dormitory" of traditional cultures with the peer relations of emerging adults in American college dormitories.

Changes in Clique and Crowd Composition During Adolescence and Emerging Adulthood

In industrialized societies, the end of formal education marks a key transition in friendships and peer relationships, usually at some point in the late teens or early twenties. The school is the main arena for adolescents' relationships, and the end of educational training removes young people from a setting where most of their daily social interactions are with people their own age doing the same kinds of things as they are. In the workplaces most young people enter following the end of their education, age-grading either does not exist or is much less intense. Also, in workplaces a hierarchy of social authority already exists, so that the anxiety adolescents experience about finding a place in a highly ambiguous and unstructured social hierarchy is no longer as much of an issue.

In a classic study now nearly 40 years old, Australian sociologist Dexter Dunphy (1963) described developmental changes in the structure of adolescent cliques and crowds. In the first stage, during early adolescence, according to Dunphy, most of adolescents' social lives take place within same-sex cliques. Boys hang around other boys and girls hang around other girls, each of them enjoying their separate activities apart from the other sex. In the second stage, a year or two later, boys and girls become more interested in one another, and boys' and girls' cliques begin to spend some of their leisure time near each other, if not actually doing much interacting across the gender gap. Picture the setting of a party, or a school dance, or the food court of a local mall, with small groups of adolescent boys and adolescent girls watching each other, checking each other out, but rarely actually speaking to members of the other sex clique.

In the third stage, the gender divisions of cliques begin to break down as the clique leaders begin to form romantic relationships. The other clique members soon follow, in the fourth stage (around the midteens), and soon all cliques and crowds are mixed-gender groups. In the fifth and final stage, during the late teens, males and females begin to pair off in more serious relationships, and the structure of cliques and crowds begins to break down and finally disintegrates.

Does Dunphy's model still make sense 40 years later? Probably more at the early stages than the later stages. Current research does confirm that early adolescents spend most of their time with same-sex friends, and that gradually these cliques of same-sex friends begin to spend time together in larger mixed-sex cliques and crowds (Berndt, 1996). However, whether the model holds beyond these early stages is questionable. As we have noted, the median age of marriage has risen dramatically since 1960. At that time the median marriage age in the United States was only about 20 for women and 22 for men (Arnett & Taber, 1994), meaning that most females were married or engaged just two years beyond high school. Now the median marriage age is 25 for women and 27 for men (U.S. Bureau of the Census, 2000) and is still rising, meaning that for most people marriage is far off during the high school years.

Thus, Dunphy's model of ending up in committed intimate pairings by the end of high school probably applies more to his time, when marriage took place relatively early, than to our time, when marriage takes place for most people much later. Most young people in the West are still experiment-ing with relationships, not just in high school but for many years after. This makes it less likely that they have paired up by the end of high school, and more likely that they maintain membership in a variety of same-sex and mixed-sex groups not just through high school but well into emerging adulthood.

Recent research shows how same-sex and other-sex friendships are balanced for current American adolescents and emerging adults. Several recent studies of adolescents' perceptions of emotional support concur that early adolescents derive more support from same-sex friendships than from other-sex relationships. However, during the teens other-sex relationships grow in importance, and late adolescents and emerging adults derive similar levels of support from their other-sex relationships as from their same-sex friendships (Berndt, 1996; Brown, Feiring & Furman, 1999; Furman & Buhrmester, 1992; Lempers & Clark-Lempers, 1993).

Also, ESM studies show the shifts that occur during adolescence in time spent with same-sex and other-sex friends (Csikszentmihalyi & Larson, 1984). As Figure 8.4 illustrates, the amount of time adolescents spend in other-sex groups or pairs increases from grade 9 through grade 12. However, even in grade 12 more time is spent with same-sex friends than with other-sex friends.

THINKING CRITICALLY

Little research has taken place on clique and crowd composition after high school. Based on your observations and experience, what hypothesis would you propose about peer group relations in emerging adulthood?

Popularity and Unpopularity

"When I got to school the first day, everyone looked at me like I was from outer space or something. It was like, Who's that? Look at her hair. Look at what she's wearing. That's all anybody cares about around here: what you look like and what you wear. I felt like a

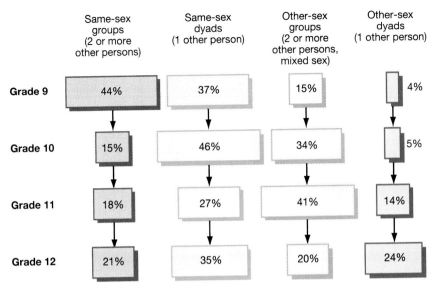

	Same-sex groups (2 or more other persons)	Same-sex dyads (1 other person)	Other-sex groups (2 or more other persons, mixed sex)	Other-sex dyads (1 other person)
Grade 9	44%	37%	15%	4%
Grade 10	15%	46%	34%	5%
Grade 11	18%	27%	41%	14%
Grade 12	21%	35%	20%	24%

FIGURE 8.4 *Amount of time adolescents spend in other-sex groups or pairs.*
Source: Csikszentmihalyi & Larson (1984).

total outcast. As soon as I got home, I locked myself in my room and cried for about an hour. I was so lonely."

—Tina, age 14 (Bell, 1998, p. 78)

A consistent finding in studies on peer crowds is that adolescents agree that certain of their peers are popular and certain others are unpopular. The popular, high-status crowds go by various names, including jocks, trendies, and (naturally) populars. The unpopular, low-status crowds have their characteristic names, too: nerds, dweebs, geeks, and druggies (Brown, 1990; Brown & Lohr, 1987; Kinney, 1993; Stone & Brown, 1998).

In addition to this research on crowd popularity, a great deal of research has been done at the individual level, investigating what makes some adolescents popular and others unpopular. Typically, this research has used a method known as **sociometry**, which involves having students rate the social status of other students. Students in a classroom or a school are shown the names and/or photographs of all the other students and asked about their attitudes toward them. They may be asked directly who is popular and who is unpopular, or whom they like best and whom they like least. Another approach is more indirect, asking students who they would most like and least like to be paired with on a class project or most and least like to have as a companion for social activities. In addition to the popularity ratings, students also

rate the other students on characteristics hypothesized to be related to popularity and unpopularity, such as physical attractiveness, intelligence, friendliness, and aggressiveness.

Sociometric research has revealed some aspects of adolescent popularity that are consistent with the basis of popularity at other ages and some aspects that are especially prominent in adolescence. Physical attractiveness, intelligence, and social skills are factors related to popularity at all ages (Hartup, 1996). Physically attractive persons tend to be popular and physically unattractive persons unpopular (Kennedy, 1990). For adolescents this is especially true at the extremes—adolescents considered highly good-looking have an advantage in the popularity poll, whereas adolescents whom others consider especially unattractive tend to be unpopular with their peers (Brown, 1990).

Intelligence is another characteristic related to popularity. Interestingly enough, high intelligence tends to be related to popularity, not to unpopularity (Hartup, 1996), in spite of the negative crowd labels applied to nerds, dweebs, and geeks. What stigmatizes the nerds and dweebs and makes them unpopular is not high intelligence but the perception that they focus on academics to the exclusion of a social life and that they lack social skills (Kinney, 1993). Overall, however, social intelligence and general intelligence are correlated—being intelligent usually goes along with being better at figuring out what people want and how to make them like you.

The Importance of Social Skills

At all ages, including adolescence, the qualities most often associated with popularity and unpopularity can be grouped under the general term **social skills**. People who are well-liked by others tend to be friendly, cheerful, good-natured, and humorous (Coie, Dodge, & Kupersmidt, 1990; Hartup, 1996). They treat other with kindness and are sensitive to others' needs. They listen well to others (that is, they are not simply wrapped up in their own concerns) and communicate their own point of view clearly

(Jarvinen & Nicholls, 1996; Kennedy, 1990). They participate eagerly in the activities of their group and often take the lead in suggesting group activities and drawing others in to participate (Bryant, 1992; Coie et al., 1990). They manage to be confident without appearing conceited or arrogant (Hartup, 1996). In all of these ways, they demonstrate the skills that contribute to social success.

Unpopular adolescents, on the other hand, tend to lack social skills. Scholars who have studied popularity and unpopularity in childhood and adolescence tend to distinguish between two types of unpopularity, reflecting different types of deficiencies in social skills (Coie et al., 1995; Inderbitzen et al., 1997; Parker & Asher, 1987). **Rejected adolescents** are actively disliked by their peers, usually because others find them to be excessively aggressive, disruptive, and quarrelsome. They tend to ignore what others want and respond to disagreements with selfishness and belligerence (Berndt & Das, 1987; Parker & Asher, 1987). These are the adolescents mentioned in sociometric ratings as peers who are disliked and whom other adolescents do *not* want as team members or companions. **Neglected adolescents** do not make enemies the way rejected adolescents do, but they do not have many friends, either. They are the nobodies, the ones who are barely noticed by their peers. They have difficulty making friendships or even normal peer contacts, usually because they are shy and withdrawn, and they avoid group activities. In sociometric ratings, they tend not to be mentioned as either liked or disliked—other adolescents have trouble remembering who they are. Both types of unpopular adolescents lack the social skills necessary to be accepted by others and establish durable relationships.

Social Skills and Social Cognition

One interesting line of research indicates that rejected adolescents' deficits in social skills are based on a deficit of social cognition, at least for males (Asher & Coie, 1990; Dodge & Feldman, 1990). According to the findings of this research, aggressive boys have a tendency to interpret other boys' actions as hostile even when the intention is ambiguous. Kenneth Dodge and his colleagues (Crick & Dodge, 1996; Dodge, 1983, 1993; Dodge & Feldman, 1990) came to this conclusion after showing videotapes to children and adolescents depicting ambiguous situations, such as where one boy would walk by and bump into another boy who was holding a drink, causing the boy to drop the drink. Boys who had been named as aggressive by their teachers and peers were more likely to see the bump as a hostile act intended to spill the drink, whereas other boys were more likely to see it as an accident. Part of lacking social skills, for rejected boys, is seeing the world as filled with potential enemies and being too quick to retaliate aggressively when events take place that could be interpreted as hostile. To put it another way, having social skills means, in part, giving others the benefit of the doubt and avoiding the tendency to interpret their actions as hostile when they may not be hostile after all.

Aggressiveness is not always a source of unpopularity in adolescence, however. Researchers have noted that some adolescents are high in aggressiveness but also in social skills (Inderbitzen et al., 1997; Newcomb, Bukowski, & Pattee, 1993). They are classified as **controversial adolescents**, because they tend to generate mixed responses among their peers. Rather than being consistently popular or unpopular, they may be strongly liked as well as strongly disliked, by different people and by the same people on different occasions.

Neglected adolescents lack the social skills necessary for making friends.

The Continuity of Popularity and Unpopularity

Popularity and unpopularity tend to be consistent from childhood through adolescence. Exceptions do exist, of course, but in general popular children become popular adolescents, and unpopular children remain unpopular as adolescents. This may be partly because of stability in the qualities that contribute to popularity and unpopularity, such as intelligence and aggressiveness. We have seen, in Chapter 3, that intelligence (or at least IQ) in childhood is highly correlated with intelligence in adolescence. Aggressiveness, which is such a distinguishing quality of rejected children, also tends to be consistent from childhood to adolescence (Moffitt, 1993).

THINKING CRITICALLY

Would you expect popularity and unpopularity to be more important or less important among adolescents in traditional cultures compared with adolescents in American society? Why?

In addition, scholars in this area emphasize that there is a certain self-perpetuating quality to both popularity and unpopularity in adolescence (Brendgen et al., 1998; Dodge & Feldman, 1990; Hymel, Wagner, & Butler, 1990). Children who are popular are reinforced every day in their popularity—other kids like them, are glad to see them, and want to include them in what they are doing. This kind of reinforcement strengthens their confidence in their popularity and also gives them daily opportunities to continue to develop the kinds of social skills that made them popular in the first place. Given this pattern, it makes sense that popular children tend to become popular adolescents.

Unfortunately, unpopularity is also self-perpetuating (Brendgen et al., 1998; Dodge & Feldman, 1990; Hymel et al., 1990). Children and adolescents who are unpopular develop a reputation with their peers as un-

> "To whom can I speak today? I am heavy-laden with trouble through lack of an intimate friend."
> —Anonymous, ca. 1990 B.C.

pleasant and hard to get along with (in the case of rejected children) or as submissive and weak (in the case of neglected children). These reputations, once developed, can be hard to break. Children and adolescents who have learned to see certain peers as unpopular may continue to view them negatively even if their behavior changes, because they are used to thinking of them that way (Coie & Dodge, 1997).

Also, as we have seen, rejected children may come to see the world as hostile, thus making it more likely that they will have the kinds of conflicts that reinforce their reputations as nasty kids and reinforce their belief that the world is out to get them (Asher & Coie, 1990; Dodge & Feldman, 1990). And for both rejected and neglected children, being unpopular makes it less likely that they will be included in the kinds of positive social exchanges that would help them develop social skills. Thus, the experience of being rejected or neglected may reinforce and deepen the kinds of characteristics that caused them to be rejected in the first place—aggressiveness, shyness, poor social skills, and so on (Buhrmester & Yin, 1997; Hecht et al., 1998; Inderbitzen et al., 1997; Parker & Seal, 1996). For these reasons, unpopular children find it difficult to shake off their unpopularity by adolescence.

THINKING CRITICALLY

Would you expect popularity and unpopularity to be more important or less important in emerging adulthood compared with adolescence? Why?

Interventions for Unpopularity

Although unpopularity is often self-perpetuating, this is not always the case. Many of us can remember a period in childhood or adolescence when we felt unpopular—rejected or neglected or both. If we are lucky, we grow out of it. We learn how to develop social skills, or we develop new interests and abilities that lead us to new social contacts with others who have similar interests, or we move to a new classroom or a new school where we can start fresh. Whatever the reasons, many of the young people who are considered dweebs and so on during late childhood and early adolescence go on to have more satisfying friendships in adolescence and beyond (Kinney, 1993).

Adolescents who remain unpopular, however, suffer a number of negative consequences. Overall, a correlation exists between unpopularity and such consequences as depression, behavior problems, and academic problems (Brendgen et al., 1998; Hecht et al., 1998; Kupersmidt & Coie, 1990; Morrison & Masten, 1991; Parker & Asher, 1987; Patterson & Stoolmiller, 1991). Rejected children and adolescents are at greater risk for problems than neglected children and adolescents (Dishion & Spracklen, 1996; Wentzel & Asher, 1998). For rejected children, the aggressiveness that is often the basis of their rejection is also the basis of their other problems. They tend to end up becoming friends with other aggressive adolescents, and they have higher rates of aggression-related problems such as conflicts with peers, teachers, and parents (Feldman et al., 1995; French, Conrad, & Turner, 1995; Underwood, Kupersmidt, & Coie, 1996). They are also more likely than their peers to drop out of school (Kupersmidt & Coie, 1990).

Neglected children tend to have a different set of problems in adolescence, such as low self-esteem, loneliness, depression, and alcohol abuse (Hecht et al., 1998; Hops et al., 1997; Kupersmidt & Coie, 1990). Some children and adolescents are both rejected and neglected, and they are at risk for the problems associated with both types of unpopularity (Morrison & Masten, 1991; Parker & Asher, 1987; Rubin, LeMare, & Lollis, 1990).

Responding to the problems associated with unpopularity, educators and psychologists have devised a variety of programs intended to ameliorate unpopularity and its effects. Programs like this, which are designed to apply social science knowledge to change people's cognitions or behavior, are called **interventions**. Because social skills are the primary basis of both popularity and unpopularity, interventions for unpopularity tend to focus on learning social skills. For rejected children and adolescents, this means learning how to control and manage anger and aggressiveness. In one program (Weissberg, Caplan, & Harwood, 1991), adolescents were taught by teachers to follow a sequence of six steps when they felt themselves losing control:

1. Stop, calm down, think before you act.

2. Go over the problem and say or write down your feelings.

3. Set a positive goal for the outcome of the situation.

4. Think of possible solutions that will lead toward that goal.

5. Try to anticipate the consequences of the possible solutions.

6. Choose the best solution and try it out.

In this intervention, the adolescents who took part improved their abilities to generate constructive solutions to problem situations, and their teachers reported improvement in their social relations in the classroom following the intervention.

For neglected adolescents, interventions are designed to teach the social skills involved in making friends. Typically, adolescents are taught, through instruction, modeling, and role playing, how to enter a group, how to listen in an attentive and friendly way, and how to attract positive attention from their peers (Murphy & Schneider, 1994; Repinski & Leffert, 1994). These programs generally report some degree of success in improving adolescents' relations with their peers.

Interventions of this kind have also been developed for college students, with "neglected" status based on self-reports of loneliness rather than on sociometric ratings. In one effort, Gerald Adams and his colleagues (Adams et al., 1988) developed an intervention designed to improve the social skills of lonely college students. Their research had indicated that lonely college students are less perceptive than other students about nonverbal communication, less effective in their efforts to influence people, less likely to take risks in interpersonal relations, and less likely to have good listening skills. The intervention, designed to address these deficits in social skills, was found to have positive effects on social skills and feelings of being included in social situations, both immediately following the program and 3 months later.

However, most of these interventions with rejected and neglected adolescents and college students have had few follow-up studies to see the long-term effects. A variety of programs have demonstrated success in improving social skills during and immediately following the program, but whether such interventions result in long-term changes in unpopularity is currently unknown.

Youth Culture

So far in this chapter we have looked at various aspects of friendship and at peer groups such as cliques and crowds, including issues of popularity and unpopularity. In addition to research in these areas, scholars have written extensively on **youth culture**. This is the idea that, along with their smaller social groups—friendships, cliques, and crowds—young people also constitute a group as a whole, separate from children and separate from adult society, with their own distinct culture (Brake, 1985). The analysis of youth culture has a long history in the field of sociology. Sociologists generally agree that a distinctive youth culture first arose in the West during the 1920s (Frith, 1983). (More detail on the rise of youth culture is provided in the Historical Focus box.)

What are the distinctive features of youth culture? What qualifies it as a culture? Recall from Chapter 1 that a culture is a group's distinctive way of life, including its beliefs and values, its customs, and its art and technologies. According to Talcott Parsons (1964), the

HISTORICAL FOCUS
The "Roaring Twenties" and the Rise of Youth Culture

Youth culture is viewed by sociologists as originating in the United States and other Western countries during the 1920s (Brake, 1985; Parsons, 1964; Wulff, 1995a). Previous historical periods may have had some small-scale youth cultures, but the 1920s was the first time that youth culture became a widespread social phenomenon. Then as now, the participants in youth culture were mainly emerging adults in their late teens and twenties.

The youth culture values of hedonism, leisure, and the pursuit of adventure and excitement were vividly displayed in the youth culture of the 1920s. This was especially evident in sexual behavior (Allen, 1964). The sexual code for young people of previous eras was highly restrictive, especially for girls. Adolescent girls were taught to keep themselves pure and virginal until the right man came along to lead them to the altar. This meant not only no sexual intercourse but no petting, no kissing even, until the right man appeared. There was no such thing as dating (Bailey, 1989); instead, there was courtship, in which a young man would visit a young woman in her home—only if he had serious intentions, of course.

This standard changed dramatically in the 1920s. "Petting parties" became popular, at which boys and girls would meet and pair up for kissing, petting, and possibly more. In the Middletown study of high school boys and girls in a typical Midwestern town, half of them marked as true the statement, "Nine out of every ten boys and girls of high school age have petting parties" (Lynd & Lynd, 1929/1957). In *This Side of Paradise* (1920), one of F. Scott Fitzgerald's novels depicting the lives of emerging adults during the 1920s, the narrator observed that "None of the Victorian mothers—and most of the mothers were Victorian—had any idea how casually their daughters were accustomed to being kissed." One of the heroines brazenly confessed, "I've kissed dozens of men. I suppose I'll kiss dozens more."

Sexual behavior was not the only form of pleasure seeking that marked the new youth culture. Use of alcohol and cigarettes was also pervasive

According to scholars, a distinct youth culture first developed during the 1920s.

(Johnson, 1992). Sale of alcohol was illegal at the time all over the United States, due to Prohibition. But this had an ironic and unintended effect—instead of alcohol use taking place mostly among men in the social setting of bars and restaurants, as had previously been the case, Prohibition drove alcohol use out of the public arena and into the "speakeasy," illegal bars catering to both men and women, as well as private parties (Allen, 1964). Because speakeasies and parties were attended by men and women rather than by men alone, they became settings for sexual contacts as well. Cigarettes, also previously used by men only, now became used by women as well.

Jazz and dancing to jazz was also part of the hedonism and leisure of 1920s youth culture—in fact, the 1920s are sometimes referred to as the "Jazz Age" because jazz was so popular then and because that was when jazz was first created. Jazz music was regarded by many as stimulating sexual desire—something the participants in youth culture found attractive but many adults considered dangerous. Jazz dancing, too, was regarded as sexually provocative. One Cincinnati newspaper of the time observed, "The music is sensuous, the embracing of partners—the female only half dressed—is absolutely indecent; and the motions—they are such as may not be described, with any respect for propriety, in a family newspaper" (Allen, 1964, p. 5).

Numerous aspects of the style of youth culture in the 1920s reflected the changes in sexual norms. The hems of women's dresses, previously considered improper if they rose any higher than 7 inches off the ground, now rose relentlessly until they reached the knee, a height many adults considered scandalous. The typical dress worn by a **flapper**—the term for a young woman of the youth culture—was thin, long-waisted, and short-sleeved or even sleeveless. Flesh-colored stockings became popular to enhance the now-exposed knee and calf. Short, bobbed hair became the most popular hairstyle for young women. Cosmetics became widely used for the first time—rouge and lipstick, wrinkle creams, and methods for plucking, trimming, and coloring the eyebrows.

The argot of 1920s youth culture was also distinctive. There was "23-skiddoo" and "the bee's knees" to describe something young people today would call "cool"; "rumble seat" for the back seat of an automobile, where sexual encounters frequently took place; and "spooning" for having a sexual encounter.

What historical influences led to the rise of youth culture in the 1920s? One important influence was the end of World War I, which had just preceded the 1920s (Allen, 1964; Johnson, 1992). Over 2 million American young people in their late teens and twenties had gone to Europe as part of the war effort. The savagery of the war promoted an emphasis on seeking enjoyment *now*, rather than waiting for a later that might never arrive. Furthermore, participation in the war removed many young people from the narrow strictures of socialization in the families and communities from which they had come, and when they returned home they resisted returning to the old restraints and taboos.

Another influence was the ideas of Sigmund Freud, which became popularized after the war (Allen, 1964). In the popularized version of Freud's theories, an uninhibited sex life was viewed as promoting psychological health. To be well and happy, in this view, it was necessary to follow your sexual impulses. To many, this made self-control seem not just obsolete but harmful. Terms that had formerly been regarded as compliments became terms of reproach and even ridicule: Victorian, Puritan, wholesome, ladylike. The values reflected in these terms became regarded by many young people as old-fashioned and as incompatible with a healthy sex life.

A third factor in the rise of youth culture was the changing status of women (Johnson, 1992). The 19th amendment giving women the right to vote was made law in 1920, and this law both reflected and promoted a new status for women as more equal—if by no means entirely equal—to men. During the 1920s women also became substantially more likely to enter the workplace as emerging adults, although most of them quit working after marriage or after their first child was born. Having their own income gave young women independence and social opportunities that had been unavailable to them before.

Finally, one other factor that contributed to the rise of youth culture was the increased availability of automobiles, particularly automobiles with tops—in 1919 only 10% of American cars had tops, but by 1927 this figure had climbed to 83% (Allen, 1964). Automobiles gave middle-class young people a means of escaping from the watchful eyes of parents and neighbors to attend parties, dances, or clubs miles away. Cars also provided, then as now, a roomy enough setting for sexual escapades in the "rumble seat" (Lynd & Lynd, 1927/1957).

Not all young people take part in youth culture, and this was no less true in the 1920s than today. Many, perhaps even most, adolescents and emerging adults continued to abide by the traditional rules of morality and behavior with regard to sexuality as well as other aspects of life (Allen, 1964; Johnson, 1992). Youth culture then and now appeals most to young people who have sensation-seeking personalities (Arnett, 1994b, 1996) and who live in conditions affluent enough to allow them to pursue the allurements of hedonism and leisure that youth culture offers.

sociologist who first used the term *youth culture,* the values that distinguish youth culture are *hedonism* (which means the seeking of pleasure) and *irresponsibility* (that is, a postponement of adult responsibilities). He argued that the values of youth culture are the inverse of the values of adult society. Adult society emphasizes a regular routine, delay of gratification, and acceptance of responsibilities; youth culture turns these values upside down and prizes hedonism and irresponsibility instead. Similarly, Matza and Sykes (1961) wrote that youth culture is based in **subterranean values**, such as hedonism, excitement, and adventure. These are values held by adults as well, but adults are allowed to express them only in restricted forms of leisure, whereas the youth culture of adolescents and emerging adults expresses them more openly. Recent sociologists have also emphasized the central values of hedonism and the pursuit of adventure in youth culture (Brake, 1985; Osgood & Lee, 1993).

This inversion of values is, of course, temporary. According to Parsons (1964), participation in youth culture is a "rite of passage" in Western societies. Young people enjoy a brief period in which they live by hedonism and leisure, before entering the adult world and accepting its responsibilities. This period lasts only from the time young people become relatively independent of their parents—especially after they leave home—until they marry. Marriage represented, for Parsons, the formal entry into adulthood and thus the departure from youth culture. At the time Parsons was writing, the typical age of marriage was much lower than it is now (Arnett, 1998a). This means that the years available for participation in youth culture have expanded dramatically and are mainly experienced in emerging adulthood rather than adolescence.

It is not only values that distinguish youth culture. British sociologist Michael Brake (1985) has proposed that there are three essential components to the **style** of youth culture:

1. **Image** refers to dress, hairstyle, jewelry, and other aspects of appearance. An example would be rings worn in the nose, navel, or eyebrow, which are worn by some young people but rarely by adults.

2. **Demeanor** refers to distinctive forms of gesture, gait, and posture. For example, certain ways of shaking hands (e.g., a "high five") have sometimes distinguished youth cultures.

3. **Argot** (pronounced *ar-go´*) is a certain vocabulary and a certain way of speaking. Examples of this include "cool" to refer to something desirable, and "chill out" to mean relax or calm down.

One useful way to look at these aspects of style is that each of them constitutes a custom complex (Shweder et al., 1998), as we discussed in Chapter 4. That is, each distinctive form of image, demeanor, and argot in youth culture symbolizes certain values and beliefs that distinguish youth culture from adult society. For example, dressing in tattered jeans and t-shirts could be interpreted as signifying the emphasis on leisure and hedonism in youth culture and a resistance to the more formal dress requirements of adult society. Using a youthful argot considered obscene and objectionable by adults could be interpreted as signifying a resistance of the manners and expectations of adults in favor of something more down-to-earth and authentic (Arnett, 1996; Brake, 1985). More generally, all aspects of style in youth culture serve to mark the boundaries between young people and adults.

Why do youth cultures develop? Sociologists have offered a variety of explanations. One condition necessary for the development of a youth culture is a pluralistic society (Brake, 1985), in other words, a society that is broad enough in its socialization that it condones a high degree of variability among individuals and groups, including many forms of behavior and belief that depart from the norms of society as a whole. A related view has been proposed by sociologists who see youth culture as arising in modern societies as a result of increasing individualism and the weakening of personal ties that results. In this view, youth culture is a way of constructing a coherent and meaningful worldview in a society that fails to provide one (Brake, 1985).

There is also Parson's (1964) view, as we have noted, that youth cultures arise in societies that allow young people an extended period between the time they gain substantial independence from parents and the time they take on adult responsibilities. From this perspective, youth culture is an arena for focusing on the pursuit of pleasure and fun for a few years before the responsibilities of adulthood descend permanently (Wulff, 1995b). In a related view, Michael Brake (1985) proposes that youth culture provides opportunities for young people to experiment with different possible identities. According to Brake,

> Young people need a space in which to explore an identity which is separate from the roles and expectations imposed by family, work and school. Youth culture offers a collective identity, a reference group from which youth can develop an individual identity. It provides cognitive material from which to develop an **alternative script**. . . . It represents a free area to relax with one's peers outside the scrutiny and demands of the adult world. (p. 195, emphasis added)

Youth culture does not necessarily exist in opposition or rebellion to adult society. As mentioned in Chapter 7, adolescents and their parents generally share many common values, such as the value of education, honesty, and hard work (Gecas & Seff, 1990). This is not inconsistent with also believing that the teens and early twenties represent a unique opportunity to pursue pleasure and leisure. Both young people and their parents know that this period is temporary

and that the responsibilities of adult life will eventually be assumed (Brake, 1985).

Of course, one could argue that there is not just one youth culture but many youth subcultures (Stone & Brown, 1998). The crowds we discussed earlier in this chapter represent different youth subcultures—jocks, dweebs, and headbangers all have their distinctive styles. And not all of these crowds could even be said to

1920s

1950s

1960s

1990s

The changing styles of youth cultures.

be part of the youth culture just described. Crowds such as dweebs and normals are conventional in style and do not participate in the pursuit of pleasure and leisure that defines youth culture. In contrast, crowds such as punkers and headbangers clearly have a style that represents resistance to the routine and conventions of adult life (Arnett, 1996). An illustration of the involvement of various crowds in youth culture and in adult institutions is shown in Figure 8.5.

Thus, adolescents participate in youth culture to different degrees—some not at all, some moderately, some intensely. Adolescence and emerging adulthood are years when some young people take part in youth culture, but most young people do so only to a limited degree and some do not at all (Stone & Brown, 1998).

Some scholars have observed that youth culture is increasing worldwide (Barber, 1995). Driven by worldwide media, new youth styles make their way quickly around the world. Of course, in all countries, young people vary in how much they take part in youth culture. Nevertheless, the image, argot, and media popular among adolescents in Western youth cultures have been influential among many adolescents in non-Western countries (Arnett, 2000d; Schlegel, 2000). Western countries also influence one another, and although the youth culture of the United States is typically viewed as dominant in the West (Barber, 1995; Dasen, 1999), youth cultures in other Western countries also influence some American

adolescents. The next section describes a new form of youth culture that has recently migrated from England to the United States.

A New Youth Subculture: Raves

One of the interesting features of youth subcultures is that they are constantly mutating into new forms (Brake, 1985; Wulff, 1995b). A constant interplay exists between youth culture's pursuit of spontaneous pleasure and adult society's efforts to make the activity of young people in youth subcultures more controllable and predictable. This is partly because the behavior of young people in youth subcultures can be disruptive to adult society—it can be loud, offensive, and obnoxious. Another reason for adults' efforts at control is that youth subcultures represent money to be made—every new manifestation of youth culture represents a potential gold mine to those who can be the first to sell the accoutrements of the latest youth culture style—the clothes, cosmetics, jewelry, music, and so on. But youth subcultures change in rapid and unexpected ways that make the "next big thing" hard to predict.

One new manifestation of youth culture that has appeared in recent years is the **rave**, an impromptu all-night dance party (Montgomery, 1999; Reynolds, 1998). The idea is to choose a place—an old warehouse, perhaps, or an empty field—as the site for the rave, then spread the word as widely as possible, via homemade posters, word of mouth, and the Internet. Sometimes dozens of people show up, sometimes hundreds, sometimes thousands. They are mostly emerging adults (it is difficult for adolescents, even those with permissive parents, to make it to an all-night party), although there is also a group called Ravers Geriatric—for ravers over age 25!

Raves first appeared in England in the late 1980s and spread throughout the United States during the 1990s (Montgomery, 1999). The music of the rave scene is a kind of electronic dance music called **techno**

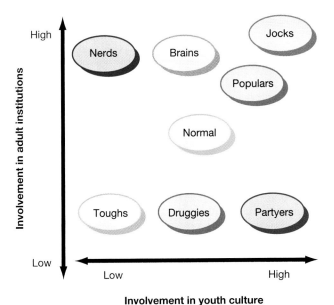

FIGURE 8.5 *Crowds in relation to youth culture.*
Source: Brown (1990).

or "house music" that is characterized by a pounding beat and the use of electronically produced sounds and rhythms (Reynolds, 1998). Youth subcultures often center on a particular kind of music, as we will see in more detail in Chapter 12. Disc jockeys at raves create original music by blending rhythms and patterns from a variety of different recordings. Raves also involve widespread use of drugs such as Ecstasy, an amphetamine that produces feelings of euphoria (Reynolds, 1998)—but ravers are quick to assert that many of them do not use drugs (Montgomery, 1999).

The rave subculture has an explicit set of values: peace, love, unity, and respect, which ravers refer to by the acronym PLUR. In this sense the rave subculture is a revival of the 1960s youth culture, which emphasized similar values. The rave culture emphasizes creating an environment that is open and accepting of everyone who comes. A rave is "a place you can go up and give somebody a hug and introduce yourself and have no problem," said "Elmo," age 19. "People who are not accepted come to raves and their self-esteem is raised so high. The acceptance you feel is life-altering" (Montgomery, 1999, p. C8). Some ravers see the rave scene as a refuge from the brutalities of the larger society. "It's about caring about each other," said a 25-year-old female raver. "You see too much stuff on the news and in regular life and you just shake your head and go, 'Gosh, why can't it be better?'" Similarly, a 19-year-old male raver observed, "I see this as my religion. My club is my church, my music is my religion, dancing is my prayer. . . . I have not found any other group of people more loving about each other and more caring about each other" (Montgomery, 1999, p. C8).

The rave style is diverse in its unconventionality, but typical aspects of style include baggy pants, moussed or spiked hair, and piercings in various body parts (Montgomery, 1999). Some ravers adopt nicknames for use in the rave setting, such as "Elmo" above.

The rave subculture has lasted long enough by now to inspire efforts to tame it and make it less disruptive. Raves have been often regarded as deplorable and obnoxious by adults, not just because drug use is common at raves but because raves have typically taken place in deserted buildings or outdoor settings without the benefit of official permits, insurance, and amenities such as restroom facilities (Montgomery, 1999). Thus, in recent years night clubs have begun to sponsor "rave" parties, featuring all-night techno music but in a regular setting, complete with permits and restrooms, same time every week. It will be interesting to see whether the rave subculture will survive its transi-

tion into respectability, or if the taming of the rave will inspire another mutation of youth culture. Given the history of youth culture, further mutations seem not just likely but inevitable.

Technological Change and the Power of Youth Culture

Youth culture is largely created and spread by young people themselves (Brake, 1985). To learn the latest styles of dress, hair, and argot, and the hot new forms of music and other media, young people look mainly to each other for cues. Adults may try to control or monitor this process—to make youth culture less disruptive or to profit from selling the items popular in youth culture—but young people learn the ways of youth culture from one another, not from adults (Frith, 1983). According to anthropologist Margaret Mead (1928/1978), in times of rapid technological change young people tend to look to one another for instruction in a variety of aspects of life.

Writing during the time youth culture was first forming, Mead (1928) described how the rate of technological change in a culture influences the degree to which adolescents receive teachings from adults or from each other. In cultures where the rate of technological change is very slow, which Mead called **postfigurative cultures**, what children and adolescents need to learn to function as adults changes little from one generation to the next. As a result, children and adolescents can learn all they need to know from their elders. For example, if a culture's economy has been based on farming for many generations and has always used the same methods, the elders will be the authorities young people will want to look to for instruction in how to plant, cultivate, and harvest their crops. In the example of the Zapotecs of Mexico discussed earlier in this chaper, adolescent girls learn the arts of sewing and embroidery from adult females who pass on this traditional knowledge.

Most cultures through most of human history have been postfigurative cultures. However, since the industrial revolution began about 500 years ago, the pace of technological change has increased with each century. Particularly in the past 100 years in industrialized countries, technological change has occurred with such speed that the skills most important in the economy change with each generation. The result is what Mead called **cofigurative cultures**, where young people learn what they need to know not only from adults but also from other young people. Learning about the styles and media of youth culture would be one example of this kind of learning. Another example would be

In a cofigurative culture, adolescents learn a great deal from one another, not just from adults.

the use of computers. An adolescent who wanted to learn how to make charts and graphs on her computer might be more likely to ask a computer-savvy friend for advice than to ask her grandparents, who may have reached retirement age before personal computers became popular.

Traditional cultures are likely to move from postfigurative to cofigurative status as globalization proceeds. We have seen an example of this in Chapter 4, where we discussed changing views among adolescent Aborigines in Australia. In the present generation of adolescents, the traditional Law describing relations between adults and children and between men and women has become viewed by many adolescents as obsolete (Burbank, 1988). The world they are growing up in differs too much from the world of their elders for the traditions of their elders to be relevant to their lives. Consequently, they are rejecting these traditions in favor of the global media of youth culture that they share with their friends and peers. These media seem to them to show where their futures lie, and with their peers they share a desire to look forward to the world shaped by globalization rather than backward to their cultural traditions.

Postfigurative and cofigurative describe levels of technological change and orientations to peers and adults in two kinds of cultures. Mead believed that in

the future, as the pace of technological change continues to accelerate, a third type, **prefigurative cultures**, may emerge. In prefigurative cultures, the direction of learning would come full circle—young people would teach adults how to use the latest technology. Mead proposed this theory in 1928, long before the computer age, and in many ways her prediction has come to pass in our time. Children and adolescents in industrialized societies now grow up with computers and the Internet, and many of them soon achieve a level of skill far beyond that of their elders. A recent *New York Times* article contained profiles of several adolescents in their teens who had thriving and lucrative businesses creating Web sites and developing computer software—with all of their business coming from adults much older than themselves (Morris, 1999).

THINKING CRITICALLY

Margaret Mead wrote her prediction of the arrival of prefigurative cultures in 1928. Would you say the culture you live in has reached a prefigurative state by now, at least in some respects? What examples could you give of the prefigurative pattern?

The history of the personal computer provides many other examples of revolutionary developments being led by adolescents and emerging adults. William Gates, now chairman of Microsoft, developed the DOS operating system that is now the basis of most personal computer operations when he was still in his twenties. Stephen Jobs started the Apple Computer Corporation by making a personal computer in his garage when he was still in his teens. Many of the older, more experienced executives and inventors at more established companies such as IBM have borrowed many of their ideas from Gates, Jobs, and other young people—one sign that the prefigurative culture predicted by Mead may have begun to arrive.

Still, it is difficult to believe that the day will ever come when *most* knowledge will be conveyed from adolescents to adults. Inevitably, adults have more experience than adolescents and have had more years to accumulate knowledge. Even now, the computer examples described above are the exception, not the rule. Most knowledge remains communicated from adults to young people rather than the other way around; the schools that adolescents and emerging adults attend are created for this purpose. And although young people learn a great deal about youth culture from their peers during adolescence and emerging adulthood, for nearly all young people youth culture is largely left behind after emerging adulthood ends and the role responsibilities of adult life begin.

Thus, highly technological, information-based societies can most accurately be described as having some of the characteristics of each of the cultures that Mead described. Adolescents learn from adults (postfigurative), adolescents learn from one another (cofigurative), and—in rare cases—adolescents teach adults (prefigurative).

Summing Up

The following are the key points of this chapter:

- Friends become increasingly important during adolescence. The amount of time spent with friends increases (and time spent with family decreases), and friends become increasingly significant as confidants and as sources of personal advice and emotional support.

- A key change in friendships from preadolescence to adolescence is the increased importance of intimacy, with a focus on issues such as trust and loyalty and with an increased amount of time together spent in conversation about significant issues rather than on shared activities.

- The most important basis for friendships in adolescence is similarity, particularly in ethnicity, educational orientation, media and leisure preferences, and participation in risk behavior.

- Although peer pressure is often used as a negative term to describe how adolescent friends encourage each other to participate in risk behavior, studies indicate that the extent of this influence may be exaggerated because of selective association and that adolescent friends may influence each other against risk behavior as well as toward it. Friends also have a variety of influences on one another involving support and nurturance.

- Emerging adults take part in frequent leisure activities with friends, such as attending parties, going to movies, and getting together for no particular purpose. However, participation in leisure activities with friends declines during emerging adulthood.

- The age-graded school setting of Western societies lends itself to the development of reputation-based crowds as a way of defining and organizing a social structure. Crowds become especially important in midadolescence, when issues of identity formation are paramount. Traditional cultures sometimes have a version of a peer crowd, with a separate dormitory where adolescents hang out, relax, and (in some cases) engage in sexual play.

- The most important determinant of popularity and unpopularity in adolescence is social skills.

- A distinctive youth culture first appeared in the West during the 1920s. According to sociologists, youth cultures are characterized by subterranean values of hedonism and irresponsibility and by a distinctive style consisting of image, demeanor, and argot. Late adolescents and emerging adults are the main participants in youth culture, but the degree of their participation varies from highly intense to not at all.

A common thread running through all the topics we have considered in this chapter is that the influence of peers on development during adolescence and emerging adulthood is substantial, and it has grown in the past century. Because of economic and social changes during the 20th century, adolescents now spend considerably more time with their peers on a typical day, in school and in play, and considerably less time with parents. Although peers are also important to young people in traditional cultures, the influence of peers is enhanced in industrialized societies because school brings peers together for many hours each day, away from their parents, and because by adolescence many young people become part of a media-driven youth culture in which what is viewed as most valued, most desirable, most "cool" is based on the preferences of peers and friends, not adults.

Just how much power do peers have on young people's development? This is a question still being debated by scholars. In a controversial recent book, Judith Harris (1999) argued that peers are far more important than parents in children's development, especially by adolescence. In her view, by adolescence children have entered a peer culture of which their parents have little knowledge and less control. Although most scholars on adolescence would view her conclusions as exaggerated, the diversity of opinions scholars have expressed about her book suggests that the extent of peer influence on young people's development is far from a settled issue (Begley, 1998). As you follow this debate, keep in mind that the influences of friends and peers are diverse and are often positive, a fact often overlooked even by scholars.

Although we have examined a wide range of issues on peers and friends in this chapter, one crucial area we have not discussed is romantic partnerships in adolescence and emerging adulthood. Rather than discussing it as part of this chapter, we will examine it in detail in the following chapter, on dating, love, and sex.

Key Terms

peers	brains	dormitory	style
friends	dweebs	men's house	image
intimacy	nerds	sociometry	demeanor
selective association	geeks	social skills	argot
informational support	populars	rejected adolescents	alternative script
instrumental support	trendies	neglected adolescents	rave
companionship support	druggies	controversial adolescents	techno
esteem support	headbangers	interventions	postfigurative cultures
cliques	nobodies	youth culture	cofigurative cultures
crowds	normals	flapper	prefigurative cultures
jocks	participant observation	subterranean values	

For Further Reading

Berndt, T. J. (1996). Transitions in friendship and friends' influence. In J. A. Graber, J. Brooks-Gunn, & A. C. Petersen (Eds.), *Transitions through adolescence: Interpersonal domains and context* (pp. 57–84). Mahwah, NJ: Erlbaum. An excellent summary of research on friendship in adolescence by one of the top scholars in the area.

Brake, M. (1985). *Comparative youth culture: The sociology of youth cultures and youth subcultures in America, Britain, and Canada.* London: Routledge and Kegan Paul. A perceptive, insightful analysis of youth culture by British sociologist Michael Brake.

Contains a history of the scholarship on youth culture.

Mead, M. (1928/1978). *Culture and commitment.* Garden City, NY: Anchor. Mead's analysis of changes in the relative importance of peers and adults based on a culture's rate of technological change.

Youniss, J., & Smollar, J. (1985). *Adolescents' relations with mothers, fathers, and friends.* Chicago: University of Chicago Press. A classic study of how changes in relationships to family and friends are intertwined during adolescence.

Applying Research

Josselson, R., & Apter, T. (1999). *Best friends: The pleasures and perils of girls' and women's friendships.* New York: Crown. Provides a guide to understanding and navigating girls' and women's friendships

from early adolescence through adulthood. Includes discussion of the difficulties of friendship, such as betrayal and shifting affections, as well as friendship's rewards.

Dating, Love, and Sexuality

Do you remember your first kiss? I know I'll never forget mine. It took place at a junior high school dance, when I was in ninth grade (I was a late-maturing adolescent). I had taken my sort-of girlfriend there, and I think that may well have been my first real "date." So far, we had progressed only as far as me going over to visit her at her home now and then. She never slammed the door in my face—always seemed kind of glad to see me, in fact, so I asked her to go to the dance with me.

I spent most of the evening trying to gather up sufficient courage to kiss her. We didn't dance much—we were both too chicken—so I had a lot of opportunities, with both of us sitting alongside the gymnasium watching as our bolder peers danced together. It took me a long time to get up the guts to try it, but as the evening waned I knew it was soon getting to be now or never. At last she smiled at me sweetly—probably thinking, "Will this fool ever get around to it?"— and I leaned over to place my lips against hers, and . . .

The vice principal grabbed me by the hair, snapped my neck back, and yelled "What do you think you're doing?! That's not allowed in here!" He dragged us down to his

259

office, and it was only after repeated assurances that we were not sex maniacs that he was persuaded not to call our parents and add to our already substantial humiliation.

I hope your first kiss was more fun than that! As we will see in this chapter, the beginnings of dating, love, and sexuality can be a source of many emotions for adolescents—pleasure, delight, and wonder, but also fear, anxiety, and confusion.

The chapter is divided into three sections on dating, love, and sexuality. In all cultures, part of developing into sexual maturity in adolescence and emerging adulthood is forming close relationships with persons outside the family. In current American society, forming these close relationships takes place in the particular cultural context of dating. We discuss dating in its cultural context, as well as the developmental progression that dating tends to follow in American society, the purposes of dating, and the different dating scripts that adolescent boys and girls learn.

Through dating, most young people in American society eventually form a relationship in which they experience love. We begin the section on love by discussing Sternberg's theory of love and how it applies to adolescents and emerging adults. Like dating, love is also discussed in its cultural context, with an examination of how various cultures allow or discourage adolescent passion. This is followed by a discussion about the reasons young people select a particular partner and the problems that rise when love goes bad.

Love in adolescence and emerging adulthood often includes sexuality, but sexual activity among young people may also take the form of sexual play or experimentation, not necessarily including love.

We look at rates in various kinds of sexual activity among American adolescents and emerging adults. Then we examine the wide variety in cultures' restrictiveness or permissiveness with regard to sex before marriage, as well as the different sexual scripts for adolescent boys and girls in American society. The development of homo-sexuality and the difficulties faced by homosexual adolescents in a society that severely disapproves of their sexual orientation are considered. In American society, sexuality in adolescence and emerging adulthood is considered problematic in a number of ways, and toward the close of the chapter we address those problems, including contraceptive use and non-use; pregnancy, abortion, and parenthood in adolescence; and sexually-transmitted diseases. The chapter ends with an examination of sex education programs.

Dating

It is not so easy to define exactly what counts as a date in the United States of the new millennium (Brown, Feiring, & Furman, 1999). Prior to the 1970s, dating usually followed more or less formal rules (Gordon & Miller, 1984). Boy asked girl to accompany him to some well-defined event—for example, a movie, a football game, or a school dance. Boy picked up girl at her house, where he would meet her parents and tell them what time he would bring her home. Boy and girl would go to the event and he would bring her home by

Dating today tends to be less formal than in the past.

the appointed time, perhaps after a quick stop somewhere for a bite to eat or some necking.

Today, dating tends to be much less formal. Even the terms "date" and "dating" have fallen out of fashion, replaced by "going with" or "hanging out with" or "seeing" someone (Miller & Benson, 1999). Adolescent boys and girls still go together to movies, football games, and school dances, of course, but they are much more likely than before to spend time together informally. As we saw in Chapter 5, prior to the women's movement of the 1960s gender roles were much more sharply drawn in the West, and adolescent boys and girls were less likely simply to hang out together as friends. Now they often know each other as friends before they become involved romantically (Kuttler, La Greca, & Prinstein, 1999).

This makes it harder now than before to tell what really counts as a date. One way to approach the question is to ask adolescents themselves. In one study, when 15-year-old adolescents were asked to name their typical dating activities, they most often named going to a movie, going to dinner, hanging out at a mall or at school, going to parties, and visiting each other's homes (Feiring, 1996). This indicates that the traditional concept of a date still endures—going to a movie, going to dinner, and going to a party all fit the traditional definition of a date as an outing in which a boy and a girl go to a specific event together at a specific time. However, hanging out at a mall or at school and visiting each other at home seem to fit the more recent, less formal concept of dating.

Dating tends to be even less formal in European societies than in American societies. In fact, European scholars on adolescence indicate that the concept of a formal date hardly exists any more in European countries (Alsaker & Flammer, 1999). Adolescents and emerging adults do pair up and become boyfriend and girlfriend. However, they rarely date in a formal way, by

HISTORICAL FOCUS
The Birth of Dating

Dating is not a universal practice but a relatively recent cultural invention, originating in Western societies in the early 20th century. The birth of dating in the United States is described in a book by historian Beth Bailey (1989) called *From Front Porch to Back Seat: Courtship in Twentieth-Century America.* Bailey describes how, at the beginning of the 20th century, the primary system of courtship in the American middle class was not dating but "calling." A young man would "call" on a young woman, at her invitation, by visiting her at her home. There he would meet her family and then the two young people would be allowed some time together, probably in the family parlor. They would talk, perhaps have some refreshments she had prepared, and she might play piano for him.

Dating became increasingly popular in the first two decades of the 20th century, and by the early 1920s dating had essentially replaced calling as the accepted mode of courtship for young people in the American middle class. This amounted to a revolution in American

By the 1920s, dating had become common among American young people.

courtship. Dating meant *going out* on a date to take part in some kind of shared activity. This moved the location of courtship out of the home and into the public world—restaurants, theaters, and dance halls. It also removed the young couple from the watchful eye of the girl's family to the anonymity of the public world.

Why did calling decline and dating arise? A number of changes in American society contributed to this. One was that Americans were becoming increasingly concentrated into large urban areas. Families living in urban areas tended to have less space in their homes, so that the parlor and the piano that had been the focus of calling were not as likely to be available. The cities also offered more excitement, more things for young people to go out and do than small towns did. The invention and mass production of the automobile also contributed, because it gave young people greater mobility, a greater range of places they could go.

The birth of dating greatly diminished the amount of control that could be exercised by parents and gave young people new opportunities for sexual exploration. When calling was the norm, not much was likely to go on between young lovers in the parlor that the rest of the family would not know about. It is certainly no coincidence that a sexual revolution took place at the same time as the change from calling to dating, with sexual experimentation before marriage—up to intercourse—becoming more accepted. Dating made the sexual revolution of the 1920s possible by providing more sexual opportunities. Although the change from calling to dating marked a decline in parental control and an increase in young people's independence, parents maintained a degree of control in part by setting curfews (as many still do) for when the date should end.

A second important consequence of the birth of dating was that it changed the balance of power in courtship from the female to the male. In the calling system, it was the girl who took the initiative. She could ask a young man to call on her, or not ask him. He could *not* ask her if it would be okay for him to call—not without being regarded as rude and unmannerly. But in the dating system, the male became the initiator. He could ask her on a date, but she could not ask him. And of course going on a date almost always meant spending money, *his* money, which further increased his power in the relationship. This promoted a view that she "owes" him sexual favors of some kind, in return for what he spends on the date. As one boy of the 1920s wrote, "When a boy takes a girl out and spends $1.20 on her (like I did the other night) he expects a little petting in return (which I didn't get)" (Bailey, 1989, p. 81).

One other point that should be mentioned is that both calling and the early decades of dating took place mostly among emerging adults rather than adolescents. Calling was considered a serious step, a prelude to a possible marriage proposal rather than simply a form of youthful recreation. Because early in the 20th century marriage did not take place for most young people until they were in their mid-twenties, they rarely took part in calling until they were in their early twenties. When dating replaced calling, at first dating, too, was an activity mainly of young people in their twenties. Young people in their teens were rarely allowed to go out as unchaperoned couples. It was only toward the middle of the century, as the marriage age declined and as enrollments in high school grew, that dating began to be acceptable for young people in their teens.

designating a specific event at a specific time and going out with the connotation of trying out what they would be like as a couple. More typically, they go out in mixed-gender groups, without any specific pairing-up. Or, a boy and a girl may go out simply as friends, without thinking of themselves as potential boyfriend and girlfriend, without the boy having the responsibility to pay the expenses, and without any implication of possible sexual activity as the evening progresses. In non-Western cultures, dating is also rare (Schlegel & Barry, 1991), for a variety of reasons we will discuss later in the chapter. Thus dating, even in its less formal style, appears to exist mainly as an American cultural phenomenon (Alsaker & Flammer, 1999).

Developmental Patterns in Adolescent Dating

American adolescents today begin dating—in one form or another—earlier than in previous generations. Most adolescent girls begin dating around age 12 or 13, and most boys begin dating around age 13 or 14 (Padgham & Blyth, 1991). About 20% of adoles-

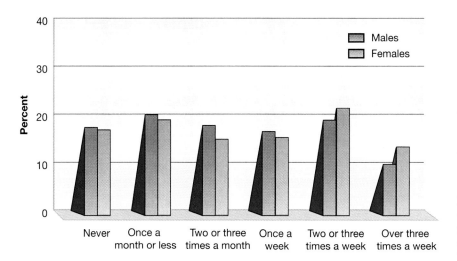

FIGURE 9.1 *Frequency of dating among U.S. high school seniors.*
Source: Bachman et al. (1995).

cents say they have "gone with" someone (i.e., had a romantic relationship that lasted at least a few weeks) by age 15 (Thornton, 1990). By their senior year in high school, the majority of adolescents date at least two or three times a month (see Figure 9.1).

Dating behavior among American adolescents tends to follow a sequence of four steps (Padgham & Blyth, 1991). In the first step, adolescents in same-gender groups go to places where they hope to find other-gender groups (the mall or fast-food restaurants are popular spots for today's American adolescents). In the second step, adolescents take part in social gatherings arranged by adults, such as parties and school dances, that include interactions between boys and girls. In the third step, mixed-gender groups arrange to go to some particular event together, such as a movie. In the final step, adolescent couples begin to date as pairs in activities such as movies, dinners, concerts, and so on. This pattern of couple dating continues through emerging adulthood.

Although most studies agree that dating rarely takes place before adolescence, actual biological maturity has little to do with the timing of beginning to date among adolescents. One especially interesting analysis exploring this question was carried out by Dornbusch and his colleagues (Dornbusch et al., 1981). They used data from a large national study of adolescents (aged 12 to 17) that included physicians' ratings of the adolescents' physical maturity, using the Tanner stages described in Chapter 2.

In two ways they demonstrated that physical maturation did not predict whether adolescents had begun

dating. First, they looked at adolescents who were of different ages (12 to 15) but who were all at Tanner's Stage 3 of physical maturity and found that the older adolescents were more likely to have begun dating even though all the adolescents were at the same level of physical maturity (see Figure 9.2). Second, they showed that adolescents of a particular age were more or less equally likely to have begun dating regardless of their level of physical maturity. For example, nearly all 12-year-olds had not yet begun dating, even though they varied widely in their level of physical maturation.

Adolescents' reports of the reasons they date include the following (Paul & White, 1990):

- *Recreation* (fun and enjoyment);
- *Learning* (becoming more skilled at dating interactions);
- *Status* (impressing others according to how often one dates and whom one dates);
- *Companionship* (sharing pleasurable activities with another person);
- *Intimacy* (establishing a close emotional relationship with another person); and
- *Courtship* (seeking someone to have as a steady partner or a potential marriage partner).

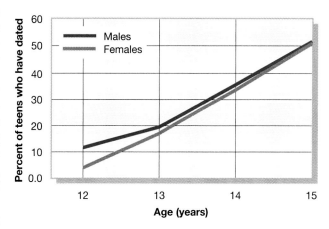

FIGURE 9.2 *Proportion of adolescents at Tanner's Stage 3 of maturity who have ever had a date.*
Source: Dornbusch et al. (1981).

■

THINKING CRITICALLY

Given that sexual contact in some form is often part of dating, why do you suppose sex was not mentioned among adolescents' and emerging adults' reasons for dating in the studies described here?

However, adolescents' reasons for dating tend to change as they enter emerging adulthood. One study investigated views of the functions of dating among early adolescents (6th grade), late adolescents (11th grade), and college students (Roscoe, Dian, & Brooks, 1987). The early and late adolescents were similar in their views. Both considered recreation to be the most important function of dating, followed by intimacy and then status. In contrast, for the college students intimacy ranked highest, followed by companionship, with recreation a bit lower, and status much lower.

What adolescents look for in a romantic partner also changes with age, at least for boys. During middle adolescence boys mention physical attractiveness prominently as a quality they look for, whereas girls emphasize interpersonal qualities such as support and intimacy. By late adolescence, however, both males and females emphasize interpersonal qualities, and what they seek is highly similar: support, intimacy, communication, com-

mitment, and passion (Feiring, 1996; Levesque, 1993; Shulman & Scharf, 2000).

Although adolescent girls have become a lot more assertive over the past 25 years in their relationships with boys, this does not mean that the old standards have expired entirely. Evidence indicates that **dating scripts**, the cognitive models that guide dating interactions, are still highly influenced by gender (Rose & Frieze, 1993). In general, males still follow a **proactive script**, females a **reactive script**. The male script includes initiating the date, deciding where they will go, controlling the public domain (driving the car and opening the doors), and initiating sexual contact. The female script focuses on the private domain (spending considerable time on dress and grooming prior to the date), responding to the male's gestures in the public domain (being picked up, waiting for him to open the doors), and responding to his sexual initiatives.

Thus, surveys indicate that adolescent boys are usually the ones who initiate a date, and most adolescent girls are reluctant to ask a boy out, although they are more likely to do so than in past generations. Bell (1988) interviewed adolescents about a variety of aspects of dating, and some of the things they had to say about initiating a date are revealing.

From the boy's perspective:

"I think boys have it really hard. Once you get to be a teenager, suddenly everybody expects you to start calling up girls and going out with them. But, hey, I think it takes a lot of courage to call a girl up and ask her out. You know, you always worry that she'll say no. . . . It's not so easy for me to just pick up the phone and act cool. I get nervous." (Bell, 1988, p. 68)

From the girl's perspective:

"Sitting around waiting for the phone to ring is a big part of my life—you know, wondering if some boy's going to call and ask you out for the weekend. Like on Monday night I'll sit there and say to myself, 'Well, the phone's going to ring by the time I count to twenty-five.' Then if it doesn't ring

Intimacy becomes more important in dating by late adolescence and emerging adulthood.

I count to a new number. It makes me so nervous I can't concentrate on anything else and I'm always yelling at everybody else in my family to get off the phone if they're using it." (Bell, 1988, p. 68)

Even in college, males are more likely than females to initiate a date, but by that time it is also common for females to initiate. In one study, 72% of college women had asked a man out within the past 6 months (McNamara & Grossman, 1991).

Dating is generally associated with positive development in adolescence. Adolescents who date regularly tend to be more popular and have a more positive self-image (Franzoni, Davis, & Vasquez-Suson, 1994; Long, 1989). However, this association to positive functioning depends partly on the age of the adolescents. In particular, for early adolescent girls, participating in mixed-gender group activities such as parties and dances may be positive, but dating in a serious relationship tends to be related to negative outcomes such as depressed mood (Graber et al., 1997; Hayward et al., 1997). Research has not yet identified why this would be the case, but some scholars have suggested that it may be because early adolescent girls in a serious relationship may find themselves under their boyfriends' pressure to participate in sexual activity before they feel ready (Simmons & Blyth, 1987).

Love

Sternberg's Theory of Love

After two adolescents have dated for a while, the dating relationship sometimes develops into love. The best-known theory of love has been developed by Robert Sternberg (1986, 1987, 1988). Sternberg proposes that different types of love involve combining three fundamental qualities of love in different ways. These three qualities are passion, intimacy, and commitment. *Passion* involves physical attraction and sexual desire. It is emotional as well as physical and may involve intense emotions such as desire, anxiety, delight, anger, and jealousy. *Intimacy* is feelings of closeness and emotional attachment. It includes mutual understanding, mutual support, and open communication about issues not discussed with anyone else. *Commitment* is the pledge to love someone over the long run, through the ups and downs that are often part of love. Commitment is what sustains a long-term relationship through fluctuations in passion and intimacy.

These three qualities of love can be combined into seven different forms of love, as follows:

- **Liking** is intimacy alone, without passion or commitment. This is the type of love that characterizes most friendships. Friendships often involve some level of intimacy, but without (sexual) passion, and without an enduring commitment. Most people have many friendships that come and go in the course of their lives.

- **Infatuation** is passion alone, without intimacy or commitment. Infatuation involves a great deal of physiological and emotional arousal, and a heightened level of sexual desire, but without emotional closeness to the person or an enduring commitment.

- **Empty love** is commitment alone, without passion or intimacy. This might apply to a couple who have been married for many years and who have lost the passion and intimacy in their relationship but nevertheless remain together. It also applies to the early stage of marriage in cultures where marriages are arranged by the parents rather than chosen by the young people themselves (Hatfield & Rapson, 1996; Schlegel & Barry, 1991). However, arranged marriages that begin as empty love may also develop passion and intimacy.

- **Romantic love** combines passion and intimacy, but without commitment. This is the kind of love people mean when they talk about being "in love." It is often experienced as intense and joyful.

- **Companionate love** combines intimacy and commitment, but without passion. It may be applied to married or long-term couples who have gradually decreased in their passion for each other but have maintained the other qualities of their love. It could also be applied to unusually close friendships, as well as to close family relationships.

- **Fatuous** (which means "silly" or "foolish") **love** involves passion and commitment without intimacy. This kind of love would apply to a "whirlwind" courtship where two people meet, fall passionately in love, and get married, all within a few weeks, before they even have time to know each other well.

- **Consummate love** integrates all three aspects of love into the ultimate love relationship. Of course, even if consummate love is reached in a relationship, over time passion may fade, or intimacy may falter, or commitment may be betrayed. But this is the kind of love that represents the ideal for many people.

■

THINKING CRITICALLY

Do you think most people are capable of consummate love by the time they reach emerging adulthood? Why or why not?

How does Sternberg's theory of love apply to adolescence? Perhaps most obvious would be that in most adolescent love relationships, commitment is either missing or highly tentative (Feldman & Cauffman, 1999). Most adolescent relationships last only a few weeks or months; few of their relationships last a year or longer (Feiring, 1996; Furman & Simon, 1999). This does not mean that adolescents are incapable of commitment, only that in industrialized countries today most people are not likely to get married until they are in their mid- to late twenties. Most adolescents, in fact, when asked to imagine their future, do not expect to be married until at least their late twenties (Greene, Wheatley, & Aldava, 1992). Under these circumstances, it is understandable that adolescents' love relationships would involve commitment much less than passion or intimacy. Commitment tends to develop in emerging adulthood, when young people begin looking more seriously for someone with whom they may have a lifelong love relationship.

One study indicated the relative strength of passion, intimacy, and commitment in adolescent love (Feiring, 1996). In this study, although the majority of the 15-year-old adolescents had had a relationship that lasted for a few months, only 10% had had a relationship that lasted for a year or longer (indicating weak commitment). However, during the relationship, contact was frequent (perhaps reflecting passion). Adolescents reported seeing their loved ones and talking to them on the phone on an almost daily basis during the relationship. Furthermore, the adolescents rated companionship, intimacy, and support as the most valued dimensions of their relationships (showing the importance of intimacy), whereas security—an aspect of commitment—ranked low.

The absence of long-term commitment in adolescence means that there are two principal types of adolescent love, infatuation and romantic love. (I do not include liking because it applies mainly to friends, not lovers.) Infatuation is common among adolescents, partly because they are new to love and the first few times they "fall in love" they may take passion alone as enough evidence of love, due to passion's intensity of feeling and of sexual desire. For example, imagine two adolescents who sit next to one another in math class, exchange occasional smiles, maybe flirt a little before and after class. She finds herself daydreaming of him as she lies in her bedroom and listens to loves songs; he starts writing her name surreptitiously in the margins of his notebook when his mind drifts during class. It feels like love, to both of them, and it *is* a certain kind of love, but it lacks the element of intimacy that people come to desire and expect from love once they become more experienced with it.

Adolescents can experience intimacy in their relationships, too, and combine passion and intimacy to create romantic love (Collins & Sroufe, 1999). The passion is there, with its heightened emotions and sexual desire, but now it is combined with intimacy, as two adolescents spend time together and come to know each other, and begin to share thoughts and feelings that they share with no one else. The prominence of intimacy in romantic relationships tends to grow through adolescence and into emerging adulthood (Brown, 1999; Furman & Wehner, 1997; Levesque, 1993).

Adolescents could even experience consummate love, combining passion, intimacy, and commitment.

Infatuation and romantic love are the most common types of love in adolescence.

Some "high school sweethearts" continue their relationship long after high school, and even marry and stay together their whole lives. However, this is rare among adolescents, especially in the current generation. With the typical marriage age so high, it is not until emerging adulthood that most young people begin thinking about finding someone to commit themselves to for years to come (Brown, 1999; Greene et al., 1992). For this reason, adolescent love relationships rarely progress past infatuation and romantic love to consummate love.

Adolescent Passion in Non-Western Cultures

It is not only in the West, and not only in industrialized countries, that adolescents experience infatuation and romantic love. On the contrary, feelings of passion appear to be a virtually universal characteristic of young people. Jankowiak and Fischer (1992) investigated this issue systematically by analyzing information compiled in the *Standard Cross-Cultural Sample*, a collection of data provided by anthropologists on 186 traditional cultures chosen to represent six distinct geographical regions around the world. They concluded that there was evidence that young people fell passionately in love in *all but one* of the cultures studied. In all the other cultures, even though they differed widely in geographical region, economic characteristics, and many other ways, young lovers experienced the delight and despair of passionate love, told stories about famous lovers, and sang love songs.

However, this does not mean that young people in all cultures are allowed to act on their feelings of love. On the contrary, romantic love as the basis for marriage is a fairly new cultural idea (Hatfield & Rapson, 1996). As we will see in more detail later in this chapter, in most cultures throughout most of history marriages have been arranged by parents, with little regard for the passionate desires of their adolescent children. Consequently, many cultures also have some version of the Romeo and Juliet story, about a tragic young couple whose love was thwarted by adults who would not let them marry, and who defied this prohibition by committing suicide together (Hatfield & Rapson, 1996). These stories are commemorated and passed down through poems, songs, plays, and legends. Although these tales of dual suicide for love have a powerful appeal to adolescents all over the world, in real life eloping is a more popular strategy for evading the obstacles to love erected by adults and by cultural customs (Jankowiak & Fischer, 1992).

Falling in Love

How do adolescents and emerging adults choose romantic partners? Do "opposites attract," or do "birds of a feather flock together"? The bird metaphor prevails for adolescents and emerging adults and throughout adulthood (Laursen & Jensen-Campbell, 1999). Just as we have seen with friendships, people of all ages tend to be most likely to have romantic relationships with people who are similar to them in characteristics such as intelligence, social class, ethnic background, religious beliefs, and physical attractiveness (Lykken & Tellegen, 1993; Michael et al., 1995). Of course, sometimes opposites *do* attract, and partners fall in love even though (and perhaps because) they may differ widely in their characteristics. For the most part, however, people are attracted to others who are like themselves. Social scientists attribute this to **consensual validation**, meaning that people like to find in others an agreement, or *consensus*, with their own characteristics. Finding this consensus supports, or *validates*, their own way of looking at the world.

> "FALL IN LOVE, FALL INTO DISGRACE."
> —CHINESE PROVERB

For example, if you have a partner who shares your religious beliefs, the two of you will validate each other in the beliefs that you possess and in the prescriptions for behavior that follow from those beliefs. However, if one of you is devout and the other is an atheist, you are likely to find that your different ways of looking at the world lead to conflicts of beliefs and behavior. One of you wants to go to religious services, the other scoffs that it is a waste of time. Most people find this kind of regular collision of preferences disagreeable, so they seek people who are like themselves to minimize the frequency of collisions (Rosenbaum, 1986; Laursen & Jensen-Campbell, 1999).

After the initial attraction, how does love develop? There has been surprisingly little research on romantic relationships in adolescence (Furman, Brown, & Feiring, 1999). However, one promising line of theory and research has explored similarities between attachments to romantic partners and attachments to parents (Furman & Simon, 1999; Furman & Wehner, 1994; Shaver & Hazan, 1993). Romantic partners try to maintain regular proximity to each other, the way children try to maintain proximity to parents. Romantic partners also seek each other out for comfort and protection in times of crisis, as children do their parents. Romantic partners also use one another as a "secure base," a source of

psychological security, as they go out to face the challenges in the world, the way children use their parents
as a secure base. Also, whether the attachment is to a
lover or a parent, extended separation is experienced as
a source of distress, and the loss of the person is deeply
painful. Of course, there are differences as well between
attachments to lovers and attachments to parents, most
notably that attachments between lovers include a sexual element that attachments to parents do not.

Attachment styles between lovers have been found to
resemble the parent–child attachment styles we have
discussed—secure, anxious-ambivalent, and anxious-
avoidant (Shaver & Hazan, 1993). Secure attachments
in romantic relationships are characterized by emotional support and concern for the partner's well-being.
Anxious-ambivalent attachments are characterized by
overdependence on the romantic partner along with in-
sensitivity to the partner's needs. Anxious-avoidant attachments involve keeping emotional distance from the
romantic partner and inhibiting self-disclosure. It has
been suggested that these attachment styles to romantic
partners may be based on earlier attachments to parents
(Collins & Sroufe, 1999; Gray & Steinberg, 1999).

Research on attachments in romantic relationships
has focused on college students and adults, and some
scholars have suggested that attachments are rare between romantic partners in adolescence (Furman et al.,
1999; Hazan & Zeifman, 1994). In this view, the brief
and transient quality of romantic relationships in adolescence means that those relationships lack the sense of
security that develops in a genuine attachment—they
lack the element of commitment, as we have noted in
terms of Sternberg's theory. Attachments may be more
likely to develop in emerging adulthood, when romantic relationships often become longer, more intimate,
and more serious (Furman & Wehner, 1997). However,
age is not all that matters—some adolescent lovers do
have genuine attachments, and many emerging adults
have a variety of brief romantic relationships that contain little in the way of commitments or attachments.

Another way that romantic relationships tend to be
different in adolescence than in emerging adulthood
or adulthood is that in adolescence the peer context of
romantic relationships tends to be especially important (Brown, 1999). We have noted, especially in the
previous chapter, that adolescence is a time when responsiveness to the opinions of friends and peers
reaches its peak. Adolescents tend to be highly aware
of and concerned about the social worlds of friendships, cliques, and crowds, and consequently friends
and peers exercise considerable power over their love

lives. A considerable amount of the conversation
among friends, especially in early adolescence, involves questions of who likes whom and who is "going
with" or "hooking up with" whom, questions often explored with much joking and teasing (Brown, 1999;
Eder, 1993). Adolescent friends often monitor each
other's romantic interests and are quick to offer inspiration, guidance, support, or scorn (Thompson, 1994).

Bradford Brown (1999) has proposed a developmental model of adolescent love that recognizes the important role played by peers and friends. Brown's model
contains four phases: the **initiation phase**, the **status
phase**, the **affection phase**, and the **bonding phase**. The
initiation phase usually takes place in early adolescence,
when the first tentative explorations of romantic interests begin. These explorations are usually superficial
and brief, and are often fraught with anxiety and fear, in
addition to excitement. The anxiety and fear result in
part from the novelty of romantic feelings and behaviors, but also from adolescents' awareness that these
new feelings and behaviors are subject to scrutiny and
potential ridicule from their friends and peers.

In the status phase, adolescents begin to gain confidence in their skills at interacting with potential romantic partners, and they begin to form their first romantic
relationships. In forming these relationships, they remain acutely aware of the evaluations of their friends
and peers. In considering a potential romantic partner,
they assess not just how much they like and are attracted
to the person, but also how their status with friends and
peers would be influenced. Peer crowds represent a
clear status hierarchy, and adolescents usually date others who have similar crowd status, but lower status adolescents often fantasize about and may attempt a
romantic relationship with someone of higher status—
this is a popular premise for many a movie and television show involving adolescents. Friends may also act as
messengers in the status phase, inquiring for a friend to
a potential love partner to see if he or she might be interested. This is a way of gaining information without
risking the direct humiliation—and loss of status—that
may result from inquiring one's self.

In the affection phase, adolescents come to know
each other better and express deeper feelings for each
other, as well as engaging in more extensive sexual activity. Relationships in this phase tend to last for several
months, rather than for weeks or days as in the previous
two phases. Because intimacy is greater in this phase,
romantic relationships become more emotionally
charged, and adolescents face greater challenges in
managing these strong emotions. The role of peers and

friends changes, too. Peers become less important as the relationship grows and the importance of status diminishes, but friends become even more important as *private eyes* who keep an eye on the friend's romantic partner to monitor faithfulness, as *arbitrators* between romantic partners when conflicts occur, and as *support systems* who provide a sympathetic ear when romantic difficulties or compexities arise. Issues of jealousy may also arise, if friends begin to resent the amount of time and closeness the adolescent devotes to the romantic partner at the expense of the friendship.

In the bonding phase, the romantic relationship becomes more enduring and serious, and partners begin to discuss the possibility of a lifelong commitment to each other. This phase usually occurs in emerging adulthood rather than adolescence. The role of friends and peers recedes in this phase, as the question of others' opinions becomes less important than issues of compatibility and commitment between the romantic partners. Nevertheless, friends may continue to provide guidance and advice, as someone to talk with about whether the romantic partner is the right person with whom to form a lifelong commitment.

When Love Goes Bad: Breaking Up, Sexual Harassment, and Date Rape

Love in adolescence and emerging adulthood is not only about affection and bonding. On the contrary, love is often the source of anxiety and distress as well. Three aspects of the dark side of love are breaking up, sexual harassment, and date rape.

Breaking Up Because most young people have a series of love relationships, most of them experience "breaking up," the dissolution of a relationship, at least once (Battaglia et al., 1998). What is breaking up like for adolescents and emerging adults?

For adolescents, the egocentrism of adolescence may contribute to the intensity of the unhappiness following a breakup. Egocentrism's personal fable can contribute to adolescents feeling that their suffering in the aftermath of a breakup is something that no one has ever experienced as deeply as they experience it and that the pain of it will never end. "I just feel like my life's over, like there's never going to be anything to smile about again," one 17-year-old girl lamented after breaking up (Bell, 1998, p. 71). However, few systematic studies of breaking up in adolescence have been done (Brown et al., 1999).

> "WE ARE NEVER SO DEFENSELESS AGAINST SUFFERING AS WHEN WE LOVE, NEVER SO FORLORNLY UNHAPPY AS WHEN WE HAVE LOST OUR LOVE OBJECT OR ITS LOVE."
> —SIGMUND FREUD

In contrast, quite a few studies have been conducted on college students' experiences with breaking up. One of the best of these studies was conducted in the late 1970s (Hill, Rubin, & Peplau, 1979). The authors followed over 200 college couples for 2 years. By the end of the 2-year period, 45% of the couples had broken up. A variety of factors were related to likelihood of breaking up. Couples who had broken up reported lower levels of intimacy and love in their relationship at the beginning of the study and were also less likely to be similar on characteristics such as age, SAT scores, and physical attractiveness (note the role of consensual validation here). The broken-up couples were also less balanced at the beginning of the study, in the sense that one partner indicated substantially more commitment to the relationship than the other partner did.

Reasons the students stated for breaking up included boredom and differences in interests. However, couples rarely agreed on what had caused the breakup. Also, the two were rarely equal in how the breakup affected them. Contrary to stereotypes that portray females as more susceptible to love than males, the study found (as other studies have found) that the woman was more likely to end the relationship, and that men who had been broken up with tended to be lonelier, unhappier, and more depressed than women who had been broken up with. Rejected men also found it harder than rejected women to accept the end of the relationship and to stay friends with their former partner.

More recently, Sprecher (1994) interviewed 101 college couples who had broken up, and compiled a list of the 10 most common reasons the couples gave for breaking up (Table 9.1). In contrast to Hill and colleagues (1979), Sprecher (1994) found that couples generally agreed about why they had broken up. However, like Hill and colleagues, the couples studied by Sprecher gave boredom and lack of common interests as prominent reasons for breaking up, along with factors such as different backgrounds and different attitudes regarding sex and marriage. Broken-up couples appear to lack the consensual validation that most people find attractive in an intimate relationship.

The emotions involved in love are intense, and breaking up often provokes sadness and a sense of loss. In one study of college students, over half of those who had broken up were at least moderately depressed

TABLE 9.1: REASONS FOR BREAKING UP

Reasons Referring to the Self

I desired to be independent.
I became bored with the relationship.

Reasons Referring to the Partner

My partner desired to be independent.
My partner became bored with the relationship.
My partner became interested in someone else.

Reasons Referring to the Couple's Interaction

We had different interests.
We had communication problems.
We had conflicting sexual attitudes and/or problems.
We had conflicting marriage ideas.
We had different backgrounds.

Source: Sprecher (1994), p. 217.

2 months later (Means, 1991). Breaking up can also inspire romantic harassment that includes anger and even violence. In one study, Jason and colleagues (1984) defined romantic harassment as "the persistent use of psychological or physical abuse in an attempt to continue dating someone after they have clearly indicated a desire to terminate a relationship" (p. 261). Using this definition, Jason and colleagues (1984) found that *over half* of female college students had been romantically harassed at some time. Romantic harassment included behavior such as telephoning the person late at night, repeatedly telephoning the person at home or at work, systematically watching or following the person in public, sending repeated love letters, insulting the person, physically attacking the person, and threatening to kill the person.

The women in the study indicated that when they confronted their harassers, the men rarely conceded that what they were doing was harassment. According to the men, they were merely trying to break through the woman's resistance and establish or reestablish a love relationship.

The experience was highly stressful for the women. They reported feeling acute fear, anxiety, and depression during the harassment and experiencing nervous physical symptoms such as stomachaches and nervous tics. The women tried a variety of strategies to deter their harassers, from ignoring them to trying to reason with

them to being rude to threatening them. Some changed their phone number or moved; some had a parent or boyfriend talk to or threaten them. None of these strategies worked very well in the short term. The best defense was simply time—eventually the harasser gave up.

Sexual harassment   In addition to the harassment that sometimes takes place in the context of the end of a romantic relationship, **sexual harassment** is a pervasive part of the peer interactions of adolescents. Sexual harassment is usually defined as including a wide range of behaviors, from mild harassment such as name-calling, jokes, and leering looks to severe harassment involving unwanted touching or sexual contact (AAUW, 1993; Connolly & Goldberg, 1999). Rates of sexual harassment in adolescence are strikingly high. Among early adolescents, research by Connolly and colleagues indicates that the incidence of sexual harassment increases from grade 5 through 8, with over 40% of eighth graders reporting that they have been victims of sexual harassment from their peers (Connolly & Goldberg, 1999; Connolly, McMaster, Craig, & Pepler, 1998; McMaster, Connolly, Pepler, & Craig, 1997). Rates of sexual harassment for adolescents in high school are even higher, around 80% for girls and 60% to 75% for boys (AAUW, 1993; Lee et al., 1996).

As noted earlier, sexual and romantic joking and teasing is a common part of adolescents' peer interactions, and this can make it difficult to tell where the border is between harmless joking and harmful harassment. Indeed, the majority of adolescents who report being sexually harassed also report sexually harassing others (Lee et al., 1996). Teachers and other school personnel who witness adolescents' interactions may be reluctant to intervene, unsure of what should qualify as harassment (Lee et al., 1996; Stein, 1995). However, being the victim of persistent harassment can be extremely unpleasant for adolescents, and can result in anxiety and depression as well as declining school performance (AAUW, 1993; Connolly & Goldberg, 1999).

Sexual harassment in adolescence is often the continuation of patterns of aggressive behavior or **bullying** that were established before adolescence. Both bullying and sexual harassment involve the aggressive assertion of power by one person over another. Thus, adolescents who bully others are also more likely to sexually harass others (Connolly & Goldberg, 1999). Furthermore, aggressive adolescents tend to bring their aggressiveness into their romantic relationships. Young people who are physically aggressive with their peers are more likely than others to be physically violent with their romantic partners as well, from early adolescence through emerging adulthood (Connolly & Goldberg, 1999; Connolly et al., 1998; O'Leary, Malone, & Tyree, 1994; Riggs, O'Leary, & Breslin, 1990).

Sexual harassment continues into emerging adulthood and beyond. It has been estimated that over half of American women will experience sexual harassment at some time during their professional life (Siegel, 1992). From early adolescence through adulthood, females are more likely than males to be the victims of sexual harassment, and males are more likely than females to be the harassers (AAUW, 1993; Connolly et al., 1998; Carroll & Wolpe, 1996).

Date rape   **Date rape** takes place when a person, usually a woman, is forced by a romantic partner, date, or acquaintance to have sexual relations against her will. Studies indicate that 15% of adolescent girls and 25% of emerging adult women (aged 18 to 24) have experienced date rape (Michael et al., 1995; Vicary, Klingaman, & Harkness, 1995). Rates are highest of all for girls who have sex at an early age: nearly three-fourths of girls who have intercourse before age 14 report having had intercourse against their will (Alan Guttmacher Institute, 1994).

Alcohol plays a big part in date rape on college campuses (Carroll & Wolpe, 1996). Being intoxicated makes women less effective in communicating a reluctance to have sex and makes men more likely to ignore or overpower a woman's resistance. When intoxicated, men are more likely to interpret women's behavior, such as talking to them or dancing with them, as indicating sexual interest (Carroll & Wolpe, 1996). However, even when sober, young men and women often interpret date rape incidents differently (Miller & Benson, 1999). In their accounts of such incidents, young men often deny they forced sex on the woman and say they interpreted the way the young woman dressed or offered affection as cues that she wanted sex. In contrast, young women describing the same incident deny that their dress or behavior was intended to be sexually alluring and say that the men were coercive and ignored their verbal or nonverbal resistance to sex.

Choosing a Marriage Partner

Although love has its dark sides, for most people love is a source of joy and contentment, and the positive emotions experienced with love become steadily stronger from early adolescence through emerging adulthood (Fehr, 1993; Fitness & Fletcher, 1993; Larson, Clore, & Woods, 1999). Perhaps for this reason, it has been true

consistently for many decades that about 90% of people in most societies eventually marry (Carroll & Wolpe, 1996). How do people choose a marriage partner?

In the chapter on gender we discussed the kinds of characteristics that adolescents use to describe the ideal man and the ideal woman. The most important qualities considered ideal for both genders were personal qualities such as being kind and honest, whereas qualities such as having a lot of money and being popular ranked quite low (Gibbons & Stiles, 1997).

The same kinds of results have been found in studies that ask young people about the qualities they consider most important in the person they marry. Psychologist David Buss (1989) carried out a massive study of over 10,000 young people in 37 countries on this question. The countries were from all over the world, including Africa, Asia, Eastern and Western Europe, and North and South America. The questionnaire had to be translated into 37 languages, with great care taken to make the meanings of the words (e.g., love) equivalent in every country. In many of the countries, a high proportion of the young people were illiterate, so the questions had to be read aloud to them.

Despite all of these challenges, the results showed impressive consistencies across countries and across genders (see Table 9.2). "Mutual attraction—love" ranked first across countries, followed by "dependable character," "emotional stability and maturity," and "pleasing disposition." Similarity in religious and political background ranked very low, which is surprising given that (as noted earlier) people tend to marry others who are similar to them in these ways. "Good financial prospects" also rated fairly low, as "having a lot of money" did in the studies of adolescents' views of the ideal man and the ideal woman.

> "WHEN TWO PEOPLE ARE UNDER THE INFLUENCE OF THE MOST VIOLENT, MOST INSANE, MOST DELUSIVE, AND MOST TRANSIENT OF PASSIONS, THEY ARE REQUIRED TO SWEAR THAT THEY WILL REMAIN IN THAT EXCITED, ABNORMAL, AND EXHAUSTING CONDITION CONTINUOUSLY UNTIL DEATH DO THEM PART."
> —GEORGE BERNARD SHAW, *GETTING MARRIED* (1908)

Although the cross-cultural similarities were strong and striking, some cross-cultural differences in what young people preferred in a marriage partner were also notable. The sharpest cross-cultural division was on the

TABLE 9.2: THE IMPORTANCE OF VARIOUS TRAITS IN MATE SELECTION THROUGHOUT THE WORLD	
Men's Ranking of Various Traits[1]	**Women's Ranking of Various Traits[1]**
1. Mutual attraction—Love	1. Mutual attraction—Love
2. Dependable character	2. Dependable character
3. Emotional stability and maturity	3. Emotional stability and maturity
4. Pleasing disposition	4. Pleasing disposition
5. Good health	5. Education and intelligence
6. Education and intelligence	6. Sociability
7. Sociability	7. Good health
8. Desire for home and children	8. Desire for home and children
9. Refinement, neatness	9. Ambition and industrious
10. Good looks	10. Refinement, neatness
11. Ambition and industrious	11. Similar education
12. Good cook and housekeeper	12. Good financial prospect
13. Good financial prospect	13. Good looks
14. Similar education	14. Favorable social status or rating
15. Favorable social status or rating	15. Good cook and housekeeper
16. Chastity (no previous experience in sexual intercourse)	16. Similar religious background
17. Similar religious background	17. Similar political background
18. Similar political background	18. Chastity (no previous experience in sexual intercourse)

[1]The lower the number, the more important men and women throughout the world consider this trait to be (on the average).

Source: Based on Hatfield & Rapson (1996).

issue of chastity (marrying someone who had never had sex before). In Eastern cultures (e.g., China, India, Indonesia) and Middle Eastern cultures (Iran, Palestinian Arabs in Israel), chastity was rated as highly important. However, in the West (e.g., Finland, France, Norway, Germany), chastity was generally considered unimportant.

Arranged Marriages   As noted earlier, although romantic love is found in all cultures, it is not considered the proper basis of marriage in all cultures. In fact, the idea that romantic love should be the basis of marriage is only about 300 years old in the West and is even newer in most of the rest of the world (Hatfield & Rapson, 1996). Marriage has more often been seen by cultures as an alliance between two *families*, rather than as the uniting of two individuals (Dion & Dion, 1993; Stone, 1990). Parents and other adult kin have often held the power to arrange the marriages of their adolescents, sometimes with the adolescent's consent, sometimes without it. The most important considerations in an **arranged marriage** did not usually include the prospective bride and

groom's love for one another—often they did not even know each other—or even their personal compatibility. Instead, the desirability of marriage between them was decided by each family on the basis of the other family's status, religion, and wealth. Economic considerations have often been of primary importance.

Currently, even cultures with a tradition of arranged marriage are beginning to change through the influence of globalization. India, for example, has a history of arranged marriage that has existed for 6,000 years (Prakasa & Rao, 1979; Saraswathi, 1999). Today, however, nearly 40% of adolescent Indians intend to choose their own mates (Prakasa & Rao, 1979; Sprecher & Chandak, 1992). This still leaves the majority (60%) who expect an arranged marriage, but for 40% to choose their own spouse is a high percentage compared with any time in the past in India, when the percentage would have been close to zero. A similar pattern is taking place in many other cultures with a tradition of arranged marriage, such as China (Chu & Ju, 1993), Japan (Kamagai, 1984), Egypt (Ahmed, 1992), and

Arranged marriages are still common in countries such as India.

sip that provide an education in how to cope with freedom. For other people the demands of freedom seem too much and they prefer to have a marriage arranged for them, perhaps with a clear-cut opportunity to veto the selected spouse. Thus one of the fascinating findings of studies of the newly created free marriage systems is the part some young people play in subverting their own freedom. (Rosenblatt & Anderson, 1981, p. 238)

Cultures with a tradition of arranged marriage may have different expectations for the marriage relationship. Hsu (1985) has observed that Eastern and Western cultures have distinct differences in expectations of intimacy in marriage. In the West, young people expect marriage to provide intimacy as well as passion and commitment. They leave their homes and families well before marriage, and they expect their closest attachment in adulthood to be with their marriage partner. However, in the East, much less is demanded of marriage. Commitment comes first, and passion is welcomed if it exists initially or develops eventually, but expectations of intimacy in marriage are modest. On the contrary, people expect to find intimacy mainly with their family of origin—their parents, their siblings—and eventually with their own children.

Turkey (Duben & Behar, 1991). Increasingly, young people in these cultures believe that they should be free to choose their mate or at least to have a significant role in whom their parents choose for them. Globalization has increased the extent to which young people value individual choice and the individual's pursuit of happiness, and these values are incompatible with the tradition of arranged marriage (Hatfield & Rapson, 1996).

The pace of social change and globalization in traditional cultures has been rapid, and the switch from a norm of arranged marriage to a norm of marriage by choice has sometimes taken place in just a few decades (Xu & Whyte, 1990). Given a sudden freedom of choice in marriage without a cultural tradition to support and guide it, some young people prefer to devise a path midway between arranged marriage and marriage by choice. As two scholars who have written on this topic observe:

> Perhaps the greatest tension in moving to a system based on freedom of choice is simply the lack of social skills and of attitudes necessary to cope with such a system. [Many scholars] have written about the uncertainties, insecurities, and bungling of young people, like young Japanese and Chinese, who have lacked models of how to behave, have been raised by kin who were reared under the arranged system, and who lacked confidence in their own criteria of choice. For some people the freedom creates a hunger for films, fiction, and gos-

These cultural differences in patterns of intimacy exist prior to marriage as well. Stella Ting-Toomey (1991) asked young people in the United States, France, and Japan about their willingness to share their thoughts and feelings with a romantic partner. Her hypothesis was that young people in individualistic cultures (such as the United States) would be more open to intimacy with a romantic partner than young people in more collectivistic cultures (such as Japan). France was chosen as a culture with some features of individualism and some of collectivism. The scale on openness to intimacy included items such as "To what extent did you reveal or disclose very intimate things about yourself or personal feelings to this person?" As predicted, Americans were highest in openness to intimacy, with Japanese least open, and the French in between.

However, these East–West differences in expectations and openness to intimacy may be disappearing in the face of globalization, at least for the more highly educated members of Eastern and Western cultures. Several recent studies have found that young people in Eastern cultures such as China (Xu & Whyte, 1990) and India (Yelsma & Athappilly, 1988) are increasingly requiring the same qualities in their love relationships as American young people do. For example, Ge Gao (1991) interviewed American and Chinese college students about their current romantic relationships. The findings in the two countries were surprisingly similar. In both the United States and China, the college students believed that a close, intimate relationship was a prerequisite for marriage. Young people were willing to consider marriage with their partner only if they were deeply involved with one another ("we see each other every day," "we do everything together"), when they communicated openly ("we talk about everything," "we share our problems with each other"), and when they were sensitive to one another's feelings ("we can understand each other without using words").

Cohabitation

For most young people in industrialized societies, marriage does not take place until at least the midtwenties. However, increasingly in industrialized countries, marriage no longer marks the beginning of living with a romantic partner. In the United States as well as in northern European countries, **cohabitation** before marriage is now experienced by at least two-thirds of emerging adults (Hurrelmann & Settertobulte, 1994; Michael et al., 1995; Nurmi & Siurala, 1994; Wu, 1999). The percentage is highest in Sweden, where nearly all young people—97%—cohabit before marriage (Hoem, 1992). In the United States, average age of first cohabitation is 22 for men and 20 for women (Michael et al., 1995). Most young Americans expect to marry their cohabiting partner, and two-thirds do so within 4 years of initiating cohabitation (Mensch, Bruce, & Greene, 1998).

In Europe, there are distinct differences in cohabitation between north and south and between east and west. Emerging adults in southern Europe are considerably less likely than their counterparts in the north to cohabit; most emerging adults in southern Europe live at home until marriage (Chisholm & Hurrelmann, 1995), especially females. Perhaps due to the Catholic religious tradition in the south, cohabitation carries a moral stigma in the south that it does not have in the north (Martinez, Miguel, & Fernandez, 1994).

Young people choose to cohabit in part because they wish to enhance the likelihood that when they marry, it will last (Carroll & Wolpe, 1996). However, cohabita-

tion before marriage is related to higher rather than lower likelihood of later divorce (Thomson & Colella, 1992). This may be because cohabiting couples become used to living together while maintaining separate lives in many ways, especially financially (Bennett, Blanc, & Bloom, 1988), so that they are unprepared for the compromises required by marriage. Also, even before entering cohabitation, emerging adults who cohabit tend to be different than emerging adults who do not—less religious, more skeptical of the institution of marriage, and more accepting of divorce (Carroll & Wolpe, 1996; Wu, 1999). Thus, it may not be that cohabiting makes divorce more likely, but that cohabiting is more likely to be chosen by emerging adults who are already at greater risk of future divorce than their peers.

THINKING CRITICALLY

Why do you think cohabitation before marriage is related to higher likelihood of divorce?

Sexuality

As we have discussed throughout this book, puberty and the development of sexual maturation are central to adolescence. We have seen how reaching sexual maturity has multiple effects on young people's development, from relationships with parents to gender intensification. However, like other aspects of development in adolescence and emerging adulthood, sex cannot be understood apart from its cultural context. Because human beings are shaped so much by their cultural and social environment, when considering sexual issues we have to think not just of sex but of **sexuality**, that is, not just biological sexual development but also sexual values, beliefs, thoughts, feelings, relationships, and behavior. Thus, our focus in this section will be not just on sex but on sexuality.

Rates of Adolescent Sexual Activity

"Even if you know [masturbation] is normal and all that, you still lock the door! You don't go around advertising that you're doing it. There are all these jokes like, 'What are you doing after school today?' 'Oh, I'm going home to beat off.' You know, Ha-ha-ha. That kind of thing. But even if everybody does it and everybody knows everybody does it, you still pretend you don't."

—*Johnny, age 15 (in Bell, 1998, p. 97)*

"When I was really little, my best girlfriend and I would sleep over at each other's house and we'd masturbate together in the same room. We even had our own name for it. We certainly didn't think there was anything wrong with what we were doing: It was just something we did that felt good. But in about fourth grade I found out more about sex and I realized that masturbating was sexual. Then, as far as I was concerned, it was definitely not OK to do anymore—especially not with somebody else in the same room. After that I used to feel guilty when I was doing it, like it was kind of humiliating, and I tried to stop myself. Then last year when I heard from a lot of my girlfriends that they do it too, I felt better about it."

—Caddie, age 15 (in Bell, 1988, pp. 98–99)

Most of the research on adolescent sexuality focuses on sexual intercourse, perhaps because of concerns about problems such as adolescent pregnancy and sexually transmitted diseases. However, intercourse is only one part of adolescent sexuality, and it is not the most widespread or the most frequent part of adolescent sexual activity. Most American adolescents have a considerable amount of other kinds of sexual experience before they have intercourse for the first time (Brooks-Gunn & Paikoff, 1997), and for most, intercourse is reached through a progression of stages lasting many years (Brooks-Gunn & Paikoff, 1993). The progression often begins with masturbation (almost always for boys, less often for girls), followed by necking and petting, sexual intercourse, and oral sex.

Masturbation Sexuality involves some of the most complex and intricate social interactions of any area of human behavior, so it is ironic that for many American adolescents their first sexual experiences take place alone. This is especially true for boys. Consistently for over a half century, studies have found that the majority of boys begin masturbating by age 13 and about 90% of boys masturbate by age 19 (Leitenberg, Detzer, & Srebnik, 1993; Masters, Johnson, & Kolodny, 1994). Masturbation among adolescent boys tends to occur frequently, about five times a week on average (Lopresto, Sherman, & Sherman, 1985).

For girls, the picture is quite different. In studies a half century ago only about 15% of females reported masturbating by age 13 and only about 30% reported masturbating by age 20 (Kinsey et al., 1953). In recent studies these percentages have increased, but it remains true that girls report considerably lower rates of mastur-

bation than boys. About 33% of girls report masturbating by age 13, and 60% to 75% by age 20 (Chilman, 1983; Masters et al., 1994). Girls who masturbate do so less frequently than boys, although with considerable individual variability (Chilman, 1983; Leitenberg et al., 1993). For both boys and girls, masturbation is not just a sexual release for adolescents who are not having intercourse. On the contrary, adolescents who have had sexual intercourse are more likely to masturbate than adolescents who have not (Chilman, 1983).

The increase in recent decades in adolescent girls' reports of masturbation is related to changes in cultural attitudes toward more acceptance of female sexuality and more acceptance of masturbation. By the late 1970s, over 70% of adolescents in their midteens agreed that "It's okay for a boy/girl my age to masturbate" (Hass, 1979). However, this is one of those findings where it is useful to ask about the validity of people's self-reports of their behavior. It could be that part of the increase in reported rates of girls' masturbation is due to girls' greater willingness to report it. For reasons of social desirability, they may have been less willing to report it 50 years ago than they are today. And even today, masturbation may be a particularly problematic topic in terms of self-report. Sex researchers find that both adolescents and adults are more reluctant to discuss masturbation than any other topic (Luria, Friedman, & Rose, 1987). Although masturbation is both normal and harmless, many young people still feel guilty and frightened by it (Bell, 1998; Stein & Reiser, 1994).

THINKING CRITICALLY

Do you think you would answer honestly if you were involved in a study on sexual behavior? Why or why not?

Necking and Petting After masturbation, sexual experience for White American adolescents tends to follow a sequence from kissing through intercourse and oral sex. Kissing and necking (mutual touching and stroking above the waist) are the first sexual experiences most White adolescents have with a sexual partner. Very little research has been done on this early stage of adolescent sexual experience, but one study found that 73% of 13-year-old girls and 60% of 13-year-old boys had kissed at least once (Coles & Stokes, 1985). The same study found that 35% of the girls reported having their

RESEARCH FOCUS
A New Approach to Studying Adolescent Sex

For obvious reasons, studies of adolescent sexuality are based almost entirely on self-report. This raises the question of how truthful people are about what they report. Sex involves many sensitive and private issues, and people may be unwilling to disclose information on these issues accurately even if they are promised that their responses will be anonymous.

Is there any way around this problem? The results of a recent study suggest that there is. A new approach to the study of adolescent sex involves having people respond on a computer to prerecorded questions given through headphones. The authors of the study used this approach in a national study of sexual behavior among 1,600 adolescent males aged 15 to 19 (Harmon, 1998). The results of the study showed that adolescents who listened to questions on the headphones and answered them on a computer screen were far more likely to report high-risk sexual behavior than adolescents who answered the questions in the traditional questionnaire format. The computer group was four times as likely to report having had sex with another male (5.5% to 1.5%), 14 times as likely to report sex with an intravenous drug user (2.8% to 0.2%), and five times as

likely to report that they were "always" or "often" drunk or high when they had heterosexual sex (10.8% to 2.2%). These differences remained after the researchers controlled statistically for ethnic background and school performance. The gap between computer answers and questionnaire answers was greatest among adolescents who did well in school, indicating that these adolescents felt they had more of an image to maintain and so were more influenced by social desirability.

Other studies of sensitive topics such as illegal drug use have also found that the use of a computer results in higher reports of the behavior (Harmon, 1998; Supple, Aquilino, & Wright, 1999). Scholars suggest that people generally experience a decrease in their inhibitions when a computer mediates their communication. One scholar, Sherry Turkle of the Massachusetts Institute of Technology, observed that "We know our computers are networked, but we still experience them as a blank screen for our own self-reflection" (Harmon, 1998, p. A-14). This may make it easier for adolescents (and others) to disclose their participation in behavior they perceive to be disapproved by their society.

breasts touched by a boy, and 20% of the boys reported touching a girl's breast. By age 16, a majority of boys and girls have engaged in this breast-touching aspect of necking. The next step in the sequence is usually petting (mutual touching and stroking below the waist). By age 18, 60% of boys and girls report vaginal touching, and 77% of boys and girls report penile touching (Coles & Stokes, 1985).

Sexual Intercourse and Oral Sex Probably the most researched topic on adolescent sexuality is the timing of adolescents' first episode of sexual intercourse, and research on this topic goes back almost to the beginning of the 20th century. These studies indicate that between 1925 and 1965 the proportion of high school students who reported having had intercourse at least once changed little. The rate was consistently 10% for females, 25% for males (Chilman,

1983). However, these rates have changed dramatically since 1965. The proportion of high school students who reported having sexual intercourse at least once rose through the seventies and eighties and had reached 52% for girls and 54% for boys in the most recent national survey (CDC, 1999). As you can see from Figure 9.3, the proportion of high school adolescents who have ever had intercourse rises steadily from 9th through 12th grades (CDC, 1999).

A similar historical pattern has been found for college students. For several decades prior to the 1960s, about 40% of college students reported having had intercourse at least once. A steep increase took place in the late 1960s and early 1970s, and by the mid-1970s 75% of college students reported having had intercourse (Dreyer, 1982). This proportion has continued to rise slowly over the past 20 years, and the most recent figure is 80% (Hatfield & Rapson, 1996).

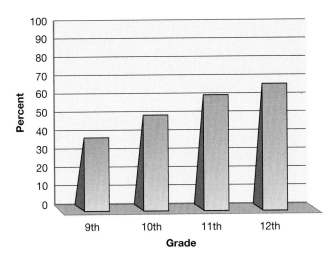

FIGURE 9.3 *Proportion of adolescents in grades 9 through 12 who have had sexual intercourse.*

Source: Centers for Disease Control and Prevention (1999).

Patterns of first sexual intercourse in American society have shown distinct ethnic differences, at least in recent years. According to national surveys by the Centers for Disease Control and Prevention (1999), the proportion of high school students in grades 9–12 who have had intercourse is lowest for White adolescents (49%), with Latino adolescents somewhat higher (58%), and Black adolescents (73%) highest. Black adolescents also reported earlier ages of first intercourse. Twenty-four percent of the African American adolescents report having intercourse by age 13, compared with just 9% of the Latino adolescents and 6% of the White adolescents.

Other studies have suggested that the earlier timing of intercourse among Black adolescents appears to be related in part to a different progression of stages in their sexual behavior. Rather than moving gradually from kissing through various stages of necking and petting and then to intercourse, African American adolescents are more likely to skip stages and move quickly to intercourse (Smith & Udry, 1985). This may help explain the high rates of adolescent pregnancy among African Americans, which we will discuss later in the chapter. The quick progression from kissing to intercourse may leave African American adolescents with less

time to consider the potential consequences of intercourse and to prepare themselves for it by obtaining contraception somewhere during the earlier steps of sexual contact.

Research has indicated that Asian Americans are considerably less likely to engage in sexual activity in adolescence, compared with any of the other major American ethnic groups (Feldman, Turner, & Araujo, 1999; McLaughlin et al., 1997). Asian American adolescents tend to have an especially strong sense of duty and respect toward their parents, and many of them view sexual relations in adolescence as something that would disappoint and shame their parents. Asian American adolescents' social interactions with the opposite sex tend to take place in groups through the late teens, and physical contact between adolescent boys and girls tends to be limited to holding hands and kissing. Boys as well as girls tend to view sexual intercourse as something that should wait until marriage or at least until they are "very seriously involved" (Feldman et al.,1999).

Having sexual intercourse once does not necessarily initiate a pattern of frequent intercourse from that point onward. On the contrary, the sexual activity of most adolescents is highly irregular for years after their first episode of intercourse. Although most studies of adolescent sexual behavior have focused on first episode of intercourse, a study by Sonenstein and colleagues (1991) explored patterns of adolescent intercourse in more detail. Their study involved an analysis of data from the National Survey of Adolescent Males, a nationally

For many adolescents, necking is their first sexual experience with a partner.

representative survey of American boys aged 15 to 19. Boys with a current sexual partner had had sex an average of 2.7 times in the past month. This is a considerably lower frequency than the typical rate of 4 to 8 times per month among married couples in young and middle adulthood (Michael et al., 1995). Furthermore, even the boys who had ever had intercourse spent about 6 months in the past year with no sexual partner. Only 20% had a sexual partner throughout the past year. Similarly, another national study found that 29% of the students who had ever had sexual intercourse had not had sex in the previous 3 months (CDC, 1999).

So, the term *sexually active* can be misleading. It is often used to refer to adolescents who have ever had sexual intercourse, without taking into account that such adolescents may have had sex only rarely or not at all since their first episode of intercourse. As Sonenstein and colleagues (1991) concluded, "A typical pattern of a [sexually active] adolescent male's year would be separate relationships with two partners, lasting a few months each, interspersed with several months without any sexual partner" (p. 166).

One other area for which rates of sexual behavior should be mentioned is oral sex. Most studies find that, for most young people, their first episode of oral sex comes at a later age than their first episode of sexual intercourse. According to one national study, 50% of high school males and 41% of high school females reported engaging in cunnilingus (male giving, female receiving), and 44% of males and 32% of females reported engaging in fellatio (female giving, male receiving) (Newcomer & Udry, 1985). Among college students, the reported rates are considerably higher. In one study, 86% of college males and 80% of college females reported at least one experience with oral sex in the past year (Gladue, 1990).

Cultural Beliefs and Adolescent Sexuality

Even though adolescents in all cultures go through similar biological processes in reaching sexual maturity, cultures vary enormously in how they view adolescent sexuality. The best description of this variation remains a book that is now almost 50 years old, *Patterns of Sexual Behavior* by Ford and Beach (1951). These two anthropologists compiled information about sexuality from over 200 cultures. On the basis of their analysis they described three types of cultural approaches to adolescent sexuality: restrictive, semirestrictive, and permissive.

CULTURAL FOCUS
Young People's Sexuality in the Netherlands

Young people's sexuality is viewed quite differently in northern Europe than in the United States. Northern Europeans tend to be considerably more liberal about sexuality than Americans and much more tolerant of sexual involvements by late adolescents and emerging adults (Jones et al., 1987). However, this does not mean that young people's sexuality in these countries is uncomplicated. Research by Manuela du Bois-Reymond and Janita Ravesloot (1996) provides interesting insights into young people's sexuality in northern Europe.

Bois-Reymond and Ravesloot (1996) interviewed young people (aged 15 to 22) and their parents in a city in the Netherlands, a country that has long been regarded as having liberal attitudes toward sexuality. Sixty young people and their parents (60 mothers and 60 fathers), from a variety of social classes, were in the study. The data collected in the study was mostly qualitative, based on interviews that were then coded in various ways. The focus of the interviews was on communication about sexual issues with peers and parents.

With regard to peers, most young people reported little pressure from peers to engage in sex. However, there was social pressure on girls—but not boys—to avoid changing sexual partners frequently. It was socially approved among peers for both boys and girls to be sexually active and to have intercourse with a steady partner, but girls experienced peer disapproval for having numerous partners. As one 18-year-old girl remarked, "My best friends do not allow me to date every boy . . . each week another one is not done . . . we think that's stupid" (p. 181). Thus, liberal attitudes toward sexuality among peers had limits, and a double standard was applied to the sexual behavior of boys and girls.

As for parents, for the most part they accepted sexual involvements by their adolescents and emerging adults. The authors noted that in the Netherlands as in most other northern European countries, "parents are prepared to either permit or tolerate premarital sexual behavior in their children, under one main condition: sexual relationships must be monogamous and serious, based on feelings of true love" (p. 182). However, this attitude did not mean that communication about sexuality was easy for young people and their parents. On the contrary, the authors observed "a certain embarrassment about communicating about sexuality among the parents. Their children feel this embarrassment and therefore refrain from confidential communication about their sexual lives" (p. 193). Fathers were particularly unlikely to be involved in communication about sexual issues with their children.

As a consequence of their mutual discomfort in discussing sexuality, Dutch young people and their parents often seemed to misunderstand each other. In particular, parents often perceived themselves as more permissive about sexual behavior and more open about sexual communication than their children perceived them to be. For example, one father described himself as lenient: "I do not interfere with anything . . . I am not able to do that . . . it's not my business" (p. 191); however, his 19-year-old daughter saw him much differently: "I am not allowed to go upstairs for a few hours [with my boyfriend]. . . . I'm using the pill in secret and that's annoying. . . . He badgers the life out of me to come home early . . . always restrictions" (p. 191).

The authors interpreted this conflict in perspectives as stemming from the fact that the parents had grown up in a much more sexually restrictive time. They viewed themselves as liberal and as tolerant of their children's sexual behavior—and by the standards of the previous generation they were, but not by the standards of their children, who had become still more liberal about sexuality. Parents worried about their children having sex too early, about STDs, and about premarital pregnancy. They liked to see themselves as allowing their children a great deal of freedom and autonomy, but given these concerns many of them attempted to manage their children's sex lives in ways the parents viewed as subtle and indirect but the children viewed as overbearing.

In sum, although Dutch society is certainly more permissive about young people's sexuality than American society, Bois-Reymond and Ravesloot's (1996) research indicates that in Dutch society, too, communication about sexuality is fraught with ambiguity. Young people must deal with the double standard that exists among their peers regarding males' and females' sexual behavior. And in their families, young people and their parents have difficulty discussing sexuality openly and often differ in how they perceive the parents' attitudes and behavior. The "divergent realities" that have been found to be common in relationships between young people and their parents in the United States (Larson & Richards, 1994) appear to exist in the Netherlands as well.

Restrictive cultures place strong prohibitions on adolescent sexual activity before marriage. One way of enforcing this prohibition is to have strict separation of boys and girls from early childhood through adolescence. Gilmore (1990) gives examples of cultures in several parts of the world, from East Africa to the rain-forest in Brazil, in which from about age 7 until marriage boys spend virtually all of their time in the company of men and other boys, with no females present. In other restrictive cultures, the prohibition on premarital sex is enforced through strong social norms. Young people in Asia and South America tend to disapprove strongly of premarital sex (Buss, 1989), reflecting the view they have been taught by their cultures.

In some countries, the sanctions against premarital sex even include the threat of physical punishment and public shaming. A number of Arab countries take this approach, including Algeria, Lebanon, Syria, and Saudi Arabia. Premarital female virginity is a matter of not only her honor but the honor of her family, and if she is known to lose her virginity before marriage, the males of her family may punish her, beat her, or even kill her (Shaaban, 1991). Although many cultures also value male premarital virginity, no culture has yet been found that punishes violations of male premarital chastity with such severity. Often, restrictive cultures are more restrictive for girls than for boys. A **double standard** in cultural views of adolescent sexuality is not uncommon worldwide (Hatfield & Rapson, 1996).

Female virginity before marriage is highly valued in Arab countries. Here, adolescent girls in Saudi Arabia.

THINKING CRITICALLY

What do you think explains the gender double standard regarding young people's sexuality that exists in so many cultures?

Semirestrictive cultures also have prohibitions on premarital adolescent sex. However, in these cultures the formal prohibitions are not strongly enforced and are easily evaded. Adults in these cultures tend to ignore evidence of premarital sexual behavior as long as young people are fairly discreet. However, if pregnancy results from premarital sex, the adolescents are often forced to marry. The Samoans studied by Margaret Mead (1928) are an example of this kind of culture. Adolescent love affairs were common among the

Samoans when Mead studied them, but pregnant girls were usually expected to marry.

Finally, **permissive cultures** encourage and expect adolescent sexuality. In fact, in some permissive cultures sexual behavior is encouraged even in childhood, and the sexuality of adolescence is simply a continuation of the sex play of childhood. One example of this type of culture is the people of the Trobriand Islands in the South Pacific. In Ford and Beach's (1951) description:

> Sexual life begins in earnest among the Trobrianders at six to eight years for girls, ten to twelve for boys. Both sexes receive explicit instruction from older companions whom they imitate in sex activities. . . . At any time an [adolescent] couple may retire to the bush, the bachelor's hut, an isolated yam house, or any other convenient place and there engage in prolonged sexual play with full approval of their parents. (pp. 188–191)

However, these are descriptions from the past, and the Trobriands as well as many other permissive cultures have become less permissive in response to globalization and the censure of Christian missionaries (Frayser, 1985).

Which of these categories best applies to the current norms in the American majority culture? When Ford and Beach published *Patterns of Sexual Behavior* in 1951, they classified American society as restrictive. However, a great deal has changed in adolescent sexuality in American society over the past 50 years. Adolescent sexual activity has become far more prevalent during this time, and the attitudes of both adults and adolescents toward adolescent sexuality have become much less restrictive. Semirestrictive is probably a better classification of the American majority culture by now. For the most part, American parents look the other way with respect to their adolescents' sexuality. Even though they may not approve of their adolescents having sexual intercourse, they allow dating and romantic relationships to flourish during adolescence, knowing that at least some expression of adolescent sexuality is likely under these circumstances.

However, the semirestrictive approach to adolescent sexuality in the American majority culture is tinged with ambivalence. In the best study conducted so far of American adults' sexual attitudes and behavior, 60% of a representative national sample of American adults aged 18 to 59 agreed with the statement that "Premarital sex among teenagers is always wrong" (Michael et al., 1995). Not only adults but young people are divided on this topic. A 1987 nationally representative telephone survey of young people aged 17 to 23 found that 87% believed that sex is wrong for adolescents aged 14 to 15 and 52% believed sex is wrong for adolescents aged 16 to 17 (Moore & Stief, 1991). These results indicate that although Americans may agree that sex in early adolescence is unwise and should be discouraged, there is little consensus in American society about the moral standing of adolescent sexuality in the late teens. Many Americans think that is wrong for adolescents in their late teens to have sexual intercourse, but many others do not.

Ford and Beach's (1951) framework was based on anthropologists' ethnographies. In recent years, other social scientists have conducted surveys in numerous countries that demonstrate the wide variability in cultural approaches to adolescent sexuality around the world. Table 9.3 shows some examples. In general, premarital sexual intercourse is engaged in by the majority of adolescents in their teens in most of the West. Premarital sex is most common in Western European countries. African countries such as Nigeria and Kenya report rates of premarital sex similar to the West. Premarital sex is somewhat less common in the countries of South America, although the large differences in reported premarital sex by male and female adolescents in countries such as Brazil and Chile suggest that males exaggerate their sexual behavior or females underreport theirs (or both). Finally, premarital sex is least common in Asian countries such as Japan and South Korea, where the emphasis on female virginity before marriage is still very strong. Missing from the table are figures from the Arab countries—no Arab country allows social scientists to ask adolescents about their sexual behavior—but ethnographic studies indicate that rates of premarital sex in those countries are even lower than in Asia because of the terrible penalties for girls who violate the prohibition.

Gender and the Meanings of Sex

“In our school, if you don't go around bragging about how far you got and what you did with the girl you were out with, well, then they start calling you fag or queer or something like that. . . . I think most guys lie about how far they go and what they do just to keep their image up.”

—*Henry, age 15 (in Bell, 1998, p. 105)*

“You know how it's okay for a guy to go around telling everybody about how horny he is and bragging about how he's going to get some this weekend?

Well if a girl ever said those things, everybody would call her a slut.”

—*Diana, age 16 (in Bell, 1998, p. 105)*

Although no one in the West advocates death for adolescent girls who engage in premarital sex, even in the West some degree of gender double standard exists in cultural attitudes toward adolescent sexuality. Just as in dating, adolescent girls and boys in the West learn different **sexual scripts** (Gagnon, 1973), that is, different cognitive frameworks for understanding how a sexual experience is supposed to proceed and how sexual experiences are to be interpreted. In general, both girls and boys expect the boy to "make the moves" (i.e., to be the sexual initiator), whereas the girl is seen as having the role of setting the limits on how far the sexual episode is allowed to progress (Fine, 1988). Studies have also found that girls are more likely than boys to have sexual scripts that include romance, friendship, and emotional intimacy, whereas for boys sexual attraction tends to outweigh emotional factors (Eyre & Millstein, 1999).

Evidence of differing sexual scripts for adolescent girls and boys can also be found in studies of adolescents' responses to their first sexual intercourse. Boys' responses to first intercourse are generally highly positive. They most commonly report feeling excitement, satisfaction, and happiness (Oswald, Bahne, & Feder, 1994), and they take pride in telling their friends about it (Miller & Simon, 1980). In contrast, girls are considerably more ambivalent about their first episode of sexual intercourse. Almost half of them indicate that the main reason for having first intercourse was affection/love for

Males and females tend to interpret their sexual experiences differently.

TABLE 9.3: PERCENTAGE OF MEN AND WOMEN WHO HAVE ENGAGED IN PREMARITAL SEXUAL RELATIONS

Culture	Age of Respondents (Average Age or Age Range)	Men (percent)	Women (percent)
United States	21	—	87
United States	20	84	61
Asian American	20	80	80
African American	20	95	90
African American	15–19	81	61
Chinese American	20	37	46
European American	20	80	80
European American	15–19	57	52
Hispanic	15–19	60	48
Hispanic	15–24	80	60
Mexican American	15–24	81	58
Puerto Rican American	15–24	77	68
Africa			
Liberia	18–21	93	82
Nigeria	19	86	63
Australia	By age 20	58	47
Brazil	15–19	73	28
	20–24	94	60
Chile	15–19	48	19
	20–24	86	57
Colombia	20	89	65
Federal Republic of Germany	By age 16	35	30
Hong Kong	13–18	6	4
	13–27	27	19
	By 27	38	24
India	20	75	60
Nigeria	14–19	68	43
Northern Ireland	20	50	44
Israel	14–19	42	11
Japan	21	27	10
Japan	16–21	15	7
Kenya	By age 19	80	—
Republic of Korea	12–21	17	4
Mexico	15–19	44	13
	20–24	86	39
Norway	20	78	86
United Kingdom	19–20	84	85
West Germany	20	78	83

Source: Hatfield & Rapson (1996), pp. 128–129.

their partner, compared with only one-fourth of males (Michael et al., 1995). However, they are less likely than boys to find the experience either physically or emotionally satisfying. Although many report feeling happy and excited about it, they are much more likely than boys to report also feeling afraid, worried, guilty, and concerned about becoming pregnant (Oswald et al., 1994), and they are much less likely than boys to tell their friends (Sprecher et al., 1995). This seems to indicate that the sexual script for girls is more fraught with ambivalence than the script for boys, as a result of cultural attitudes that view girls (but not boys) who engage in premarital sex as morally wrong.

Gender differences in sexual scripts are reflected in sexual fantasies as well as in interpretations of sexual experience. One study (Miller & Simon, 1980) found that although a majority of both male and female college students reported feeling sexual arousal when fantasizing about necking or intercourse with "someone you love or are fond of," fantasies of sexual episodes with strangers with whom they had no emotional attachment were much more common among males (79%) than among females (22%). Furthermore, females were more likely than males to be sexually aroused by thoughts of "doing nonsexual things with someone you are fond of or in love with." The authors of the study concluded that "For males, the explicitly sexual is endowed with erotic meaning regardless of the emotional context. For females, the emotional context is endowed with erotic meaning without regard for the presence or absence of explicitly sexual symbols" (1980, p. 403).

The fact that girls can get pregnant and boys cannot may partly explain why girls are more ambivalent about premarital sex, especially premarital sex in the absence of a committed relationship. If pregnancy results, the consequences are likely to be much more serious for her than for him, physically, socially, and emotionally. However, American cultural attitudes also reinforce the tendencies that arise from biological differences in consequences, and may in fact be more important than the biological differences. Many investigators of American sexual attitudes have observed that adolescent sex is more disapproved for girls than for boys (Brooks-Gunn & Paikoff, 1997; Durham, 1998; Michael et al., 1995; Rosenthal, 1994). Because of this double standard, adolescent girls who are engaging in sexual intercourse are more likely than boys to be seen as bad or unlovable, by themselves as well as others (Graber, Brooks-Gunn, & Galen, 1999). Under these circumstances, adolescent girls may find it difficult to experience their sexuality as a source of pleasure and joy (Fine, 1988).

Characteristics of Sexually Active Adolescents

As we have seen, even by grades 9 to 12 about half of American adolescents have never had sexual intercourse, and others may have had sex once or twice but are not currently in a sexual relationship. As noted earlier, different ethnic groups in American society have quite different rates of sexual intercourse in adolescence. What other characteristics distinguish adolescents who are having sex from adolescents who are not, and what factors are related to the timing of adolescents' first episodes of sexual intercourse?

At high school age, adolescents who remain virgins and adolescents who are nonvirgins are similar in some ways and different in others. The two groups have similar levels of self-esteem and of overall life satisfaction (Billy et al., 1988; Jessor et al., 1983). However, adolescents who remain virgins through high school are more likely than nonvirgins to be late maturing in the timing of their pubertal development (Caspi & Moffitt, 1991; Magnusson, Stattin, & Allen, 1986), and they are likely to have higher levels of academic performance and academic aspirations (Wyatt, 1990). They are also more likely to be politically conservative and to participate in religious activities (King et al., 1988).

Sharper differences exist between adolescents who have their first episode of sexual intercourse relatively early in adolescence (age 15 or younger) and other adolescents. Adolescents who have early sexual intercourse are more likely than other adolescents to be early users of drugs and alcohol as well (Jessor & Jessor, 1977; Miller & Moore, 1990). They are also more likely than other adolescents to be from single-parent families (Miller & Moore, 1990; Newcomer & Udry, 1987) and to have grown up in poverty (Brewster, Billy, & Grady, 1993; Brooks-Gunn et al., 1993). The early involvement of African American adolescents in sexual activity can be explained to a large extent by the higher rates of single-parent families and poverty among African Americans. Numerous scholars who have studied early sexual intercourse among African American adolescents in poor families have concluded that poverty gives these adolescents less to hope and plan for, so that they have less of an incentive to refrain from becoming sexually active to avoid pregnancy and preserve their future prospects (Crump et al., 1999; Lauritsen, 1994; Wilson, 1996).

Perhaps surprisingly, few differences exist in family relationships between early sexually active adolescents and other adolescents. Most studies find no differences between adolescents in these groups in *parental monitoring*—the extent to which parents know where their adolescents are and what they are doing (Casper, 1990; Moore, Peterson, & Furstenberg, 1986; Newcomer & Udry, 1985). Why parental monitoring does not discourage early intercourse is not clear at this point. As we will see in Chapter 13, parental monitoring does discourage a variety of other kinds of risky behavior in adolescence.

Communication between parents and adolescents about sexual issues also appears to make little difference in the timing of adolescents' first intercourse (Casper, 1990). In fact, according to one recent national study, girls whose mothers talk to them frequently about sex have their first sexual intercourse at a *younger* age than their peers do ("Mum's Not the Word," 1999). One problem with communication about sexuality appears to be that parents and adolescents often misunderstand each other. Parents often believe they have talked to their adolescents about sex when their adolescents report that they have not, and adolescents tend to underestimate how much their parents disapprove of their engaging in sexual activity (Jaccard, Dittus, & Gordon, 1998; Newcomer & Udry, 1985).

With respect to the influence of peers, girls who mature early tend to attract attention from older boys, which tends to result in the girls becoming sexually active earlier than other girls (Petersen, 1993). Also, when most of the adolescents in a clique are sexually active, they establish a norm within the clique that having sex is acceptable, and the remaining virgins in the clique may be influenced toward sexual involvements through their exposure to that norm (Furstenberg, Brooks-Gunn, & Morgan, 1987; Miller & Moore, 1990). Of course, selective association may be involved here. Adolescent virgins who are hanging around a group of nonvirgins are likely to have characteristics in common with the nonvirgins, such as lower academic goals and lower religiosity, that also contribute to decisions of whether to become sexually active. However, virgins would also be influenced by nonvirgins directly within cliques, because the nonvirgins are sexually experienced potential partners (Rodgers & Rowe, 1993).

Homosexuality

" *After people at school found out I was gay, a lot of them kind of kept a distance from me. I think they were scared that I was going to do something to them. . . .*

I guess that was one of the reasons I didn't come out sooner, because I was afraid that they would be scared of me. It's stupid and crazy, but a lot of people feel that way."

—Jamie, age 17 (in Bell, 1998, p. 141)

So far we have discussed adolescent dating, love, and sexuality in terms of the attractions and relationships between males and females. But what about young people who are sexually attracted to other persons of the same sex? What is it like for them to reach the age where issues of dating, love, and sex become more prominent?

Reaching sexual maturity can produce considerable confusion and anxiety (along with considerable excitement and joy, of course) in adolescents who are heterosexual. For adolescents who are homosexual, the degree of confusion and anxiety is often multiplied. Growing up, they are exposed almost entirely to heterosexual models of dating, love, and sex. The "presumption of heterosexuality" (Herdt, 1989) is part of their socialization from parents, friends, school, and media. Their parents may have laughed at how they were "flirting" if they were having fun with a member of the other sex. Their friends may have played doctor or spin the bottle under the assumption that everyone was attracted to the other sex. Their school dances and other social activities always assumed male–female couples. Television, movies, and magazines nearly always portray heterosexual dating, love, and sex.

But while all these socializers are assuming and promoting heterosexuality, there are some people who realize in early adolescence that they feel differently than their friends. They start to realize that, unlike most people, they are in fact attracted to others of the same sex. And at the same time, they realize that what they feel, and what they are, is regarded by their culture as sick, disgusting, even evil. How do they reconcile this terrible chasm between what other people expect them to be and what they know themselves to be?

Adolescence is especially important with respect to homosexuality because it is during adolescence that most homosexuals first become fully aware of their sexual orientation. In the past in Western cultures, and still today in many of the world's cultures, many people would keep this knowledge to themselves all their lives because of the certainty that they would be stigmatized and ostracized if they disclosed the truth. Today in the United States, however, homosexuals commonly engage in a process of **coming out**, beginning at an aver-

Adolescence is usually the time when homosexuals become fully aware of their orientation.

age age of about 14 for gay males and a year or two later for lesbians (Herdt, 1989). Coming out involves a person recognizing his or her own homosexuality, and then disclosing the truth to their friends, family, and others (Cass, 1979; Herdt, 1989). Usually, homosexuals come out first to a friend; fewer than 10% tell a parent first (Savin-Williams, 1998). Coming out is often a long process, as information is disclosed gradually to others. For many homosexuals the coming-out process is never complete, and they withhold information about their sexual orientation to some degree throughout their lives.

Given the presumption of heterosexuality and the pervasiveness of **homophobia** (fear and hatred of homosexuals) that exists in American society (Herek, 1986), coming to the realization of a homosexual identity can be traumatic for many adolescents. A 16-year-old girl wrote in her diary:

Help me please. My feelings are turning into gnawing monsters trying to clamber out. Oh please, I want to just jump out that window and try to kill myself. . . . I have to tell someone, ask someone. Who?!! Dammit all, would someone please help me? Someone, anyone. Help me. I'm going to kill myself if they don't. (Heron, 1995, p. 10)

This is not a unique example. Studies indicate that 20% to 35% of gay and lesbian adolescents have attempted suicide, a much higher rate than among straight adolescents (Herdt, 1989). Rates of substance abuse, school difficulties, and running away from home are also higher among homosexual adolescents (Savin-Williams, 1994). All these problems tend to increase after the adolescent discloses to parents, because parents' responses are often highly negative (Savin-Williams, 1998). However, many adolescents come out successfully and accept their homosexual identity. A 17-year-old gay male wrote:

I like who I am. I have come to accept myself on psychological as well as physical terms. I not only like myself, I like everyone around me. Today, for [homosexuals], that is really hard to say. (Heron, 1995, p. 15)

Distinguishing between having homosexual *experiences* and having a sexual *orientation* that is homosexual is important. A high percentage of adolescents and emerging adults (predominantly males) report some kind of homosexual sex play, but only about 2% of adolescents eventually become adults with a primarily homosexual orientation (Michael et al., 1995). One extensive study on this topic investigated the childhood and adolescent sexual feelings and sexual experiences of nearly 1,000 homosexuals and nearly 500 heterosexuals (Bell, Weinberg, & Hammersmith, 1981). The results of the study indicated that having predominantly homosexual feelings in childhood and adolescence was a better predictor of a homosexual orientation in adulthood than having homosexual experiences during the childhood and adolescent years. Among heterosexual adult males, about half (51%) had engaged in some kind of homosexual sex play in childhood and/or adolescence. However, only 1% of the heterosexual males reported having predominantly homosexual feelings in childhood and adolescence, compared with 59% of the gay males. Similarly, only 1% of heterosexual adult females reported having predominantly homosexual feelings while growing up, compared with 44% of lesbian adults.

Adolescents and emerging adults who are homosexual face a number of difficulties not faced by other adolescents because of the intense social stigma against homosexuality that still exists in the United States and most other countries, in the East as well as the West. In a 1991 national survey, 75% of Americans indicated that they thought that sexual relations between two persons of the same sex were always wrong or almost always wrong (Davis & Smith, 1991), and homosexual behavior remains illegal in some American states. Adolescents who are known to be homosexual typically face harassment, verbal abuse, and even physical abuse at the hands of their peers (Savin-Williams, 1994). For example in 1998 Matthew Shepherd, a young gay man, was tortured and killed by two other young men simply because he was gay. Parents are often deeply dismayed to learn that their adolescent is homosexual (Strommen, 1989). Given the unpleasant reception that often awaits them if they come out, it is not surprising that many adolescent homosexuals hide their homosexual feelings and behavior (Davis & Stewart, 1997; Gruskin, 1994; Malyon, 1981).

THINKING CRITICALLY

What do you think explains the pervasive homophobia of American society? Why does homosexuality make many people uncomfortable and even angry?

Girls in traditional cultures often marry by age 18, about 2 or 3 years after reaching menarche. Here, a young bride in Nepal.

Contraceptive Use and Nonuse

Just as cultures have a variety of ways of viewing adolescent sexuality, from strongly encouraging it to strictly prohibiting it, adolescent pregnancy is viewed by different cultures in a variety of ways. In most of the 186 traditional cultures described by Schlegel and Barry (1991), girls marry by the time they reach age 18. Thus, they tend to marry within 3 years of reaching menarche, because menarche tends to take place later in most traditional cultures—age 15 or 16—than in industrialized societies. Furthermore, the first 2 years after menarche are a period of **subfecundity** for most girls, meaning that they ovulate irregularly and are less likely to become pregnant during this time than later, after their cycle of ovulation has been established (Whiting, Burbank, & Ratner, 1986). This means that for most adolescent girls in traditional cultures, even if they begin having sexual intercourse before marriage, their first child is likely to be born in the context of marriage. And in many traditional cultures, even if a girl has a child before marriage it may be viewed positively, as an indication that she is fertile and will be able to have more children once she has married (Schlegel & Barry, 1991; Whiting, Burbank, & Ratner, 1986).

Clearly, the situation is quite different for adolescent girls in Western countries. They reach menarche much earlier, usually around age 12 or 13, and they tend to marry much later, usually in their mid- to late

twenties. Because the majority of adolescent girls in Western countries begin having sexual intercourse at some time in their mid- to late teens, this leaves a period of nearly a decade for many girls between the time they begin having intercourse and the time they enter marriage. Furthermore, for adolescent girls in the West, having a child while unmarried and in their teens has serious detrimental effects on their prospects for the future. Unlike in traditional cultures, the late teens and early twenties are crucial years in the West for educational and occupational preparation. For Western girls who have a child outside of marriage during those years, their educational and occupational prospects are often severely impeded, as we will see in the next section.

Of course, adolescents in industrialized societies also have the possibility of using various methods of contraception to prevent pregnancy, methods unavailable to girls in most traditional cultures. It is at least theoretically possible that adolescents who had begun having sexual intercourse and did not yet want to produce a child could use one of the highly effective methods of contraception available in industrialized societies.

However, this theoretical possibility is far removed from reality. The reality is that many American adolescents who are having sex do not use contraception responsibly and consistently. Over one million teenage American girls become pregnant each year (CDCP, 1998; Boyle, 2000). Over one-third of sexually active girls become pregnant at some time during their teen years. Although condom use among adolescents increased substantially during the 1980s and early 1990s, only half of the sexually active adolescents in a recent national survey reported that they or their partner had used a condom at their last episode of sexual intercourse and nearly one-fourth did not use any type of contraception (CDCP, 1999). Furthermore, even among sexually active adolescents who use contraception, their use of it is often inconsistent (Arnett & Balle-Jensen, 1993; Miller & Moore, 1990). Only about one-third of sexually active adolescents report that they always use birth control (Hayes, 1987).

Why do most sexually active adolescents fail to use contraception consistently? One the best analyses of this question is an integrative article by Diane Morrison (1985), in which she reviewed dozens of articles on this topic. She concluded that the core of the answer to this question is that most adolescent sexual activity is *unplanned* and *infrequent*. Adolescents typically do not anticipate that they will have sex on a given occasion. The opportunity is there—they start necking, they start taking their clothes off—and "it just happens." If contraception is available at that moment they may use it, but if it is not, they sometimes simply take their chances. Also, the fact that adolescent sex tends to be infrequent—only once or twice a month, much less often than adults—means that they may never get into the habit of preparing for sex as something that they take part in on a regular basis.

Some scholars have suggested that cognitive development in adolescence may play a role. Planning for and anticipating the future is enhanced by formal operations, and the ability for this kind of thinking is only just emerging when many adolescents become sexually active. One study of 300 sexually active adolescents aged 14 to 19 found that the adolescents who had higher scores on a measure of formal operations were more likely to report using contraception (Holmbeck et al., 1994). Also, the personal fable of adolescence makes it easy for adolescents to believe that getting pregnant "won't happen to me" (Arnett, 1990), especially when they are caught up in the heat of the moment.

Other scholars have identified a variety of other factors related to the likelihood that adolescents will use contraception. For both boys and girls, adolescents are more likely to use contraception if they are in their late rather than early teens, involved in an ongoing relationship with their partner, and doing well in school (Alan Guttmacher Institute [AGI], 1994; Civic, 1999; Cooper et al., 1999). Embarrassment over purchasing and using contraception is often stated as a reason for not using it (Helweg-Larsen & Collins, 1994; MacDonald et al., 1990). Also, some young people resist using contraception because they believe it interferes with the sexual mood and with romantic feelings (Helweg-Larsen & Collins, 1994; Sheer & Cline, 1994), and some males resist using condoms because they believe condoms reduce sexual pleasure (MacDonald et al., 1990).

Cultural factors are also involved in contraceptive use, because the United States has a higher rate of teenage pregnancy than any other industrialized country (AGI, 1994), as Figure 9.4 shows. This is not because adolescents in the United States have more sex than in other countries. The pregnancy rate among adolescents in Canada is less than half the rate in the United States, even though the percentages of adolescents in the two countries who are sexually active are nearly identical (Bibby & Posterski, 1992). Adolescents in European countries such as Sweden and Denmark are as likely as adolescents in the United States to be sexually active, but much less likely to become pregnant (Arnett & Balle-Jensen, 1993). What explains this? In part, higher American rates of adolescent pregnancy are due to higher rates of poverty, compared with European countries. Numerous studies have found that adolescents who are from low-income families are less likely than other adolescents to use contraception (e.g., AGI, 1994; Boyle, 2000; Chilman, 1986). However, even when analyses are restricted to White middle-class adolescents, Americans have higher rates of premarital pregnancy than adolescents in any other Western country (Jones et al., 1987; Manlove, 1998).

Most analyses of these cross-national differences have concluded that the core of the problem of inconsistent contraceptive use is the mixed messages that American adolescents receive about sexuality (AGI, 1994; Durham, 1998; Hayes, 1987; Jones et al., 1987). Earlier we discussed American society as having a semi-restrictive approach to adolescent sex. What this means, in practice, is that American adolescents are not strongly prohibited from having sex, but neither is adolescent sex widely accepted (Graber, Brooks-Gunn, & Galen, 1999). Adolescents receive different messages from different socialization sources, and few clear messages from any source, about the morality and desirability of premarital sex.

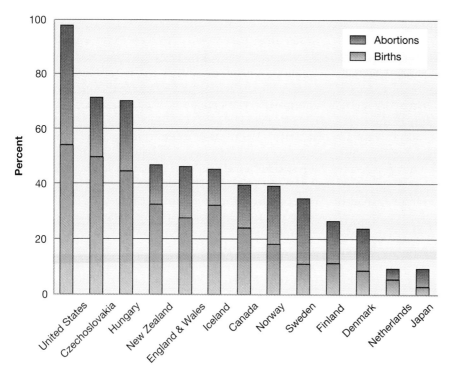

FIGURE 9.4 *Teen pregnancy rates in various Western countries.*
Source: Alan Guttmacher Institute (1994).

The media are often blamed for stoking adolescent sexual desires in a simplistic and irresponsible way (e.g., Jones et al., 1987). "Sex saturates American life" observes one scholar, "in television programs, movies, and advertisements—yet the media generally fail to communicate responsible attitudes toward sex, with birth control remaining a taboo subject" (Westoff, 1988, p. 254). In school, most adolescents receive sex education, but this "education" rarely includes an explicit discussion of contraceptive use. Communication between parents and adolescents about sexual issues tends to be low, in part because of the discomfort both feel about discussing such issues (Hutchinson & Cooney, 1998). Consequently, many American adolescents end up somewhere in the middle—having sex occasionally, but feeling guilty or at least ambivalent about it, and not really acknowledging that they are sexually active.

A number of studies find evidence of this ambivalence and of its relation to inconsistent contraceptive use (Tschann & Adler, 1997). For example, Gerrard (1987) found that adolescents who feel "very guilty" about having sex are less likely than other adolescents to report having sex, but when they do have sex they are less likely than other adolescents to use contracep-

tion. This suggests that their guilt leads them to deny to themselves that they are sexually active, with the result that they fail to be prepared for sexual intercourse when it takes place. Similarly, in a major study of adolescent males' sexual behavior, Miller and Moore (1990) concluded that a key reason that many adolescents fail to use contraception is that they are unwilling to admit to themselves that they are having sexual intercourse.

Two types of countries have low rates of teenage pregnancy: those that are permissive about adolescent sex and those that adamantly forbid it. Countries such as Denmark, Sweden, and Finland have low rates of adolescent pregnancy because they are permissive about adolescent sex (Jones et al., 1987). They have detailed and thorough sex education programs beginning in elementary school, with explicit information about contraception. Adolescents have easy access to all types of contraception. It is not uncommon for adolescents in these countries to have a boyfriend or girlfriend spend the night—in their bedroom, in their parents' home, a practice barely imaginable to most Americans (Arnett & Balle-Jensen, 1993). At the other end of the spectrum, restrictive countries such as Japan, South Korea, and Morocco strictly forbid adolescent sex (Davis & Davis, 1989; Hatfield & Rapson, 1996). Adolescents in these countries are even strongly discouraged from dating until they are well into emerging adulthood and are seriously looking for a marriage partner. It is rare for an adolescent boy and girl even to spend time alone together, much less have sex. Some adolescents follow the call of nature anyway and violate the taboo, but violations are rare because the taboo is so strong and the shame of being exposed for breaking it is so great.

American adolescents, then, have the worst of both worlds with respect to contraceptive use. Adolescent sex is not strictly forbidden, but neither is it widely accepted. As a consequence, most American adolescents have sexual intercourse at some time before they reach the end of their teens, but often those who are sexually active are not comfortable enough with their sexuality to acknowledge that they are having sex and to prepare for it responsibly by obtaining and using contraception.

Pregnancy, Abortion, and Parenthood in Adolescence

When adolescents fail to use contraceptives effectively and pregnancy takes place, what are the consequences for the adolescent parents and their child? About 40% of pregnancies to American adolescents in their teens end in abortion, and another 10% end in miscarriage (AGI, 1994; Hayes, 1987). Of the remaining 50%, only about 5% are put up for adoption. The others are raised by their adolescent mothers, sometimes with the help of the father, more often with the help of the adolescent mother's own mother.

About half a million children are born to teenage mothers in the United States every year. This may seem like a lot—and it is—but in fact the birth rate among teenage girls has declined steadily from the mid-1950s to the present (Furstenberg, 1991; www.childstats.gov; Lewin, 1998). Why, then, is there so much more concern about adolescent pregnancy in American society today than there was in the 1950s? The reason is that in the 1950s only about 15% of births to teenage mothers took place outside of marriage, whereas today about two-thirds of teenage births are to unmarried mothers (Furstenberg, 1991; www.childstats.gov). In the 1950s

and 1960s, the median age of marriage for females was just 20 years old (Arnett & Taber, 1994). This means that many girls at that time married in their teens and had their first child soon after. Today, however, with the median marriage age for females about age 25, it is very rare for young people to marry while still in their teens. If a teenage girl has a child, it is quite likely that she will be unmarried.

Birth rates among American teens rose sharply in the late 1980s but declined substantially (by about 12%) from 1991 to 1999 (Lewin, 1998; "Teen Birth Rate," 2000). The decline appears to be due to a variety of factors, including a slight decline in sexual activity, a slight increase in the use of injectable contraceptives, the effects of HIV/AIDS prevention programs, and—especially—a sharp increase in the use of condoms ("Teen Birth Rate," 2000). Birth rates for Black teenage girls especially declined in the first half of the 1990s, but even with that decline birth rates among Black teens remain over twice as high as for Whites (Boyle, 2000). In recent years, birth rates have become highest of all among Latina adolescents, as Figure 9.5 shows.

White adolescent girls are far more likely than Black or Latino adolescents to abort their pregnancy (Miller & Moore, 1990). Also, about two-thirds of White and Latino adolescents who become mothers are unmarried, but nearly all Black adolescent mothers are unmarried (Schellenbach, Whitman, & Borkowski, 1992).

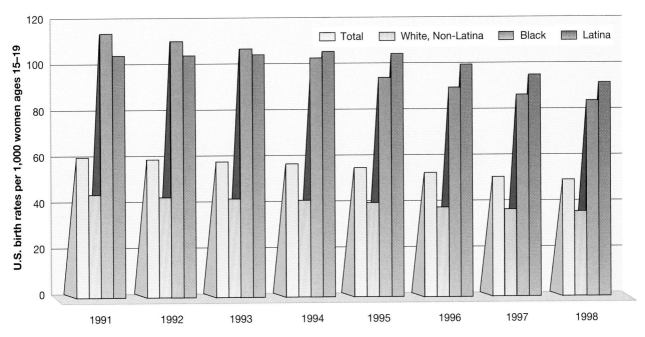

FIGURE 9.5 *Teen birth rates in different ethnic groups.*
Source: National Vital Statistics Report (1999).

Whether White, Black, or Latino, girls are more likely to become unmarried teenage mothers if they are from poor families and if they live in a single-parent household (Boyle, 2000; Manlove, 1998).

Before recent decades, adolescent pregnancy was often followed by a hasty "shotgun wedding" to avoid scandal and make certain the baby would be born to a married couple (Graber, Britto, & Brooks-Gunn, 1999). According to one estimate, about half of the teenage girls who married in the late 1950s were pregnant on their wedding day (Furstenberg et al., 1987). Today, the stigma of unmarried motherhood has receded (although certainly not disappeared), and adolescent girls who become pregnant are considerably more likely to have the child even while remaining unmarried. Figure 9.6 shows the pattern over the past half century.

The concern over adolescent pregnancy is not only moral, based on the view of many Americans that adolescents should not be having sex. The concern is also based on the practical consequences for the adolescent mother as well as for her child. For the unmarried adolescent mother, having a child means that she will be twice as likely as her peers to drop out of school and less likely to become employed or to go on to college after high school (Bachrach, Clogg, & Carver, 1993; Furstenberg, Brooks-Gunn, & Chase-Lansdale, 1989; Linares et al., 1991), even compared to peers who come from a similar economic background (Moore et al., 1993). Furthermore, adolescent mothers are less likely than their peers to get married and more likely to get divorced if they do marry (Furstenberg et al., 1989). In addition, many adolescent mothers are still a long way from maturity in their emotional and social development, and they feel overwhelmed by the responsibilities of motherhood (Osofsky, 1990). Adolescent mothers often had problems even before becoming pregnant, such as dropping out of school, conduct problems, and psychological problems, and becoming a parent only deepens their difficulties (Miller-Johnson et al., 1999; Stouthamer-Loeber & Wei, 1998; Woodward & Fergusson, 1998).

What about beyond adolescence? Do adolescent mothers eventually get back on track and catch up with their peers? The best evidence on this question is a study by Furstenberg, Brooks-Gunn, and Morgan (1987) that began with a sample of 300 urban, mostly Black, low-SES teenage mothers in 1966 when they first had their children, and followed both mothers and children every few years until 1984, when the children were 18 years old. Five years after giving birth, the disadvantages of teenage motherhood were evident in the ways that the mothers lagged behind their peers in their educational, occupational, and economic progress. However, by the last follow-up, 18 years after the study began, the life situations of the mothers were striking in their diversity. One-fourth of the mothers were still on welfare and had remained there for most of the 18-year period. In contrast, another one-fourth had succeeded in making it into the middle class, gaining enough education and occupational experience to make substantial progress economically. A majority of the mothers had eventually completed high school, and one-third had completed at least some college education.

Obtaining education was a key factor. Adolescent mothers who remained in high school became considerably more successful than those who had dropped out. Getting married eventually was related to more favorable outcomes than remaining single (although other studies have found that the effects of getting married depend crucially on the quality of the marriage and the degree of the couple's economic security)

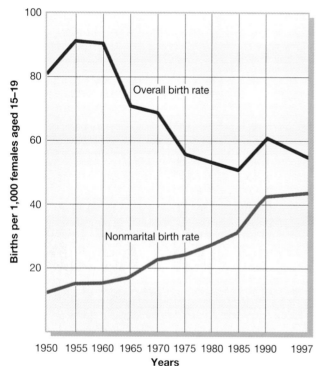

FIGURE 9.6 *Total teen birth rate and nonmarital rate, 1950–1997.*

Source: www.childstats.gov (1999).

Having a baby in adolescence puts both mother and baby at risk for a variety of difficulties.

(Teti & Lamb, 1989). Overall, the study showed both the perils of adolescent motherhood and the possibilities of eventual success for adolescent mothers.

Not nearly as many studies have been conducted on adolescent fatherhood as on adolescent motherhood, but the available studies indicate that becoming a father as a teen is also related to a variety of negative outcomes. Adolescent fathers are more likely than their male peers to become divorced, to have a lower level of education, and to have a lower-paying job (Nock, 1998; Resnick, Wattenberg, & Brewer, 1992). They are also more prone to a variety of problems, including use of drugs and alcohol, violations of the law, and feelings of anxiety and depression (Buchanan & Robbins, 1990; Elster et al., 1987). Like adolescent mothers, the problems of adolescent fathers often began prior to parenthood (Fagot et al., 1998; Nock, 1998; Thornberry et al., 1997). For the most part, adolescent fathers are unlikely to be involved very much in the life of their child. One study found that only one-fourth of adolescent fathers were viewed by the adolescent mother as having a "close" relationship

with the child by the time the child was 3 years old (Leadbetter et al., 1994).

What are the consequences for the children born to adolescent mothers? These children face a higher likelihood of a variety of difficulties in life, beginning even before they are born (Dryfoos, 1990). Only one in five adolescent mothers receives any prenatal care during the first 3 months of pregnancy. Partly for this reason, babies born to adolescent mothers are more likely to be born prematurely and to have a low birth weight; prematurity and low birth weight are in turn related to a variety of physical and intellectual problems in infancy and childhood. Children of adolescent mothers also face a greater likelihood than other children of behavioral problems throughout childhood, including school misbehavior, delinquency, and early sexual activity (Brooks-Gunn & Chase-Lansdale, 1995; Furstenberg et al., 1987).

However, scholars have stressed that the children's problems are due not just to the young age of their mothers but also to the fact that most adolescent mothers are not only young and unmarried but poor as well (Boyle, 2000; Schellenbach et al., 1992). Having a mother who is young, unmarried, or poor makes children at greater risk for a variety of developmental problems. Children whose mothers have all three characteristics—as the majority of adolescent mothers do—face an environment in which it will be difficult for them to thrive.

Abortion If having a child in adolescence often results in dire consequences for adolescent mothers and their babies, what about adolescent girls who have an abortion? Studies have consistently found little evidence of serious physical or psychological harm for adolescents who abort an unwanted pregnancy (Hayes, 1987). In fact, adolescent girls who abort are generally better off psychologically and economically 2 years later than adolescent girls who give birth (Zabin, Hirsch, & Emerson, 1989). Nevertheless, many experience guilt and emotional stress and feel highly ambivalent about their decision to abort (Franz & Reardon, 1992). Abortion remains tremendously controversial in American society, especially with respect to adolescents. By the mid-1990s, 16 states required minors (adolescents under age 18) to provide **parental notification** (that is, they were required to notify their parents before having the abortion), and another 21 states required minors to obtain **parental consent** (Carroll & Wolpe, 1996) (that is, they were required to obtain their parents' permission to have an abortion).

Sexually Transmitted Diseases

In addition to the problem of unwanted pregnancy, sex in adolescence and emerging adulthood carries a relatively high risk of sexually transmitted diseases (STDs). Few young people have sex with numerous partners, but most youthful love relationships do not endure for long. Young people typically get involved in a relationship, it lasts for a few months, sometimes sexual intercourse is part of it, and then they break up and move on. In this way young people gain experience in what love and sex involve and in what it is like to be involved with different people. Unfortunately, having sex with a variety of people, even if only one at a time, carries with it a substantial risk for STDs.

Consequently, many adolescents and emerging adults experience STDs. Approximately one-fourth of sexually active adolescents get an STD each year (or about 13% of all young people aged 13 to 19; AGI, 1994). Overall, two-thirds of all STDs occur in people who are under 25 years old (Carroll & Wolpe, 1996).

The symptoms and consequences of STDs vary widely, from the merely annoying ("crabs") to the deadly (HIV/AIDS). In between these extremes, many other STDs leave young women at higher risk for later infertility, because the female reproductive system is much more vulnerable than the male reproductive system to most STDs and to their consequences (Carroll & Wolpe, 1996). Another cause for concern about STDs is that rates of STDs are especially high among Black and Latino young people living in America's urban areas (Kassler & Cates, 1992), in part because rates of STD-promoting behaviors such as intravenous drug use and unsafe sex are higher in these populations.

Two other general characteristics of STDs bear mentioning before we discuss specific STDs. One is that many people who have STDs are **asymptomatic**, meaning that they show no symptoms of the disease, and they are especially likely to infect others because neither they nor others realize that they are infected. Second, some STDs (such as herpes and HIV) have a **latency period** that can last for years. This means that there may be years between the time people are infected and the time they begin to show symptoms, and during this time they may be infecting others without either themselves or their partners being aware of it.

Now we will consider briefly some of the major STDs, including chlamydia, gonorrhea, herpes, and HIV/AIDS.

> **THINKING CRITICALLY**
>
> Do you think adolescents and emerging adults would be more likely to use condoms if they knew that many people who have STDs are asymptomatic? Why or why not?

Chlamydia Chlamydia is a common STD, estimated to infect one in seven adolescent females and one in ten adolescent males (Hersch, 1991), with rates of up to 20% found on college campuses (Estrin & Do, 1988). It is the leading cause of female infertility, in part because if left untreated it can develop into pelvic inflammatory disease (PID), which in turn causes infertility. It is also highly infectious, with 70% of women and 25% of men contracting the disease during a single sexual episode with an infected partner. Seventy-five percent of women and 25% of men with the disease are asymptomatic (Kassler & Cates, 1992). When symptoms occur, they include pain during urination, pain during intercourse, and pain in the lower abdomen. Chlamydia can usually be treated effectively with antibiotics, but in recent years antibiotics have become less effective because widespread use of them has led to evolutionary changes in chlamydia that make it more resistant (Carroll & Wolpe, 1996).

Gonorrhea Gonorrhea (sometimes called the "clap" or the "drip") is caused by bacteria that thrive in the moist mucus membranes of the body, including the mouth, urethra, and vagina. Because sexual relations typically involve contact between the moist membranes of one person and the moist membranes of another, gonorrhea is very easily passed along during sex. Females are at least twice as likely as males to become infected through sexual relations with someone who has gonorrhea, because the vagina is an especially vulnerable place for contracting the disease. Although rates of gonorrhea have declined considerably since peaking in the mid-1970s, rates rose in the early 1990s, especially among young Black females (AGI, 1994).

Seventy-five percent of males and the majority of females who have gonorrhea are asymptomatic. When symptoms do occur, they develop within a week and include painful urination, increased frequency of urinating, and (for females) bleeding after sexual intercourse (Carroll & Wolpe, 1996). If left untreated, gonorrhea can cause pelvic inflammatory disease (PID) and subsequent infertility in females (Handsfield, 1992). If diagnosed and treated, antibiotics are highly effective against gonorrhea.

Herpes Simplex   Herpes simplex is an STD caused by a virus. It has two variations. Herpes simplex I (or *HSV-1*) is characterized by sores on the mouth and face. Herpes simplex II (*HSV-2*) is characterized by sores on the genitals. The two types are sometimes passed from mouth and face to genitals, and vice versa, through oral sex. The disease is highly infectious, and it is estimated that 75% of persons exposed to an infected partner contract the disease (Carroll & Wolpe, 1996).

Symptoms appear anywhere from one day to one month after infection. First there is a tingling or burning sensation in the infected area, followed by the appearance of sores. The sores last 3 to 6 weeks and can be painful. Blisters may appear along with the sores, and they eventually burst and emit a yellowish liquid. Other symptoms include fever, headaches, itching, and fatigue. These other symptoms peak within 4 days of the appearance of the blisters.

After the sores and blisters heal, the majority of people with herpes have at least one recurrent episode, with the symptoms for women being especially intense and enduring (Corey, Adams, & Brown, 1983). Treatment within 4 days of initial symptoms reduces the chance of recurrent episodes (Carroll & Wolpe, 1996). However, currently there is no cure for herpes. Once people are infected, the virus remains in their bodies for the rest of their lives, and the chance of a recurrent episode is ever present. For this reason, psychological distress including anxiety, guilt, anger, and depression frequently results when herpes is diagnosed (Aral, Vanderplate, & Madger, 1988). Nevertheless, because herpes is infectious only when an episode is occurring, the disease can be managed if the person has an understanding and supportive partner (Longo et al., 1988).

HIV/AIDS

> "*It's a really scary thing right now. If for some reason you're not careful or you forget to use protection, you're like paranoid for a long time, until you get tested. Nobody that I know has [HIV] right now, but everybody's scared about it. You never know for sure.*"
>
> —*Holly, age 18 (in Bell, 1998, p. 119)*

The STDs discussed so far have been around for a long time, but HIV/AIDS has appeared only recently, first diagnosed in 1981 (Carroll & Wolpe, 1996). In this STD, the human immunodeficiency virus (HIV) causes acquired immune deficiency syndrome (AIDS), which strips the body of its ability to fend off infections. Without this ability, the body is highly vulnerable to a wide variety of illnesses and diseases.

HIV is transmitted through bodily fluids, including semen, vaginal fluid, and blood. The virus typically enters the body through the rectum, vagina, or penis, during anal or vaginal intercourse. Another common form of transmission is through shared needles among intravenous drug users. Ninety percent of cases of HIV infection in the United States result from intercourse between homosexual or bisexual partners (CDCP, 1999), although in recent years the greatest percentage increase in cases of HIV/AIDS has been among heterosexuals (Carroll & Wolpe, 1996).

HIV/AIDS has an unusually long latency period. After the HIV virus is acquired, people who contract it tend to be asymptomatic for at least 5 years before the symptoms of AIDS appear, and in some cases as long as 10 years (Carroll & Wolpe, 1996). Thus, few adolescents have AIDS, but the incidence of AIDS rises sharply in the early twenties, and cases of AIDS that appear in the early twenties occur in people who contracted the HIV virus some time in their teens. The incidence of AIDS has risen dramatically since it was first diagnosed in 1981, and by the mid-1990s AIDS was the leading cause of death among persons aged 25 to 44 (CDCP, 1999). Rates of HIV/AIDS are especially high among homeless adolescents (Rotheram-Borus, Koopman, & Ehrhardt, 1991) and among minority adolescents living in America's urban areas (Smith et al., 1993). AIDS has been devastating in southern Africa, where 10 of every 11 new HIV infections take place, and where more than one-fourth of young adults are infected (Will, 2000).

No symptoms are evident when a person first contracts HIV, but evidence of HIV can be identified in a blood test about 6 weeks after infection (Friedman-Kien & Farthing, 1990). Later during the HIV latency period, a person may experience what may seem like the flu, with symptoms including fever, sore throat, fatigue, and swollen lymph nodes in the neck and armpits. After this initial outbreak of symptoms, no further evidence of the disease may appear until years later. Once AIDS does appear, it is usually in the form of symptoms of unusual diseases that people rarely get unless there is something seriously wrong with their immune system. AIDS-specific symptoms include **wasting syndrome**, in which the person loses a great deal of body weight and becomes extremely emaciated (Friedman-Kien & Farthing, 1990).

AIDS has proven to be extremely difficult to treat, because the virus has the ability to change itself and thus render medications ineffective. However, in recent years effective treatments for prolonging the lives of AIDS sufferers have begun to be developed. Nevertheless, the mortality rate for people who have AIDS remains extremely high.

Sex Education

One might think that with such high rates of pregnancy and STDs in adolescence and emerging adulthood there would be a broad consensus in the United States to do a better job at educating young people to avoid these problems. However, the issues are never so simple and clear when it comes to Americans and sexuality. Nowhere is the American ambivalence about adolescent sex so evident as on the topic of sex education.

Indeed, a broad consensus exists in American society that high rates of premarital pregnancy and STDs in adolescence are serious problems that must be reduced. However, there is vehement argument about what the solution to these problems might be. On one side are the proponents of **comprehensive sexuality education**, who advocate sex education programs beginning at an early age that include detailed information on sexual development and sexual behavior, with easy access to contraception for adolescents who choose to become sexually active. On the other side are the opponents of sexuality education, a minority of Americans but a vocal and well-organized political force, who advocate programs that promote abstinence until marriage and who believe that sex education programs encourage promiscuity and are a symptom of the moral breakdown of American society (Alexander, 1998). In between are America's adolescents, growing up in a socialization environment that includes both messages, and often choosing the "middle ground" of having premarital sex but not acknowledging their sexuality, thus failing to plan ahead for it and to use contraception responsibly.

School-based sex education programs must deal with this ambivalence and with the sharply divided opinions that may exist among the parents of the children they teach. Most schools do have some type of sex education program. As of the mid-1990s, 70% of American adolescents attending public schools received some type of sex education course (Carroll & Wolpe, 1996)—but note that this leaves 30% of adolescents who receive no sex education through the school, even now. By 1993, 17 states required schools to have a sex education program, and a total of 34 states required an education program focusing specifically on HIV/AIDS (www.siecus.org/pubs/facts).

Individual school systems usually choose the content of their sex education programs, resulting in a great deal of variability in the length and content of what children and adolescents are taught. Most often, such programs simply include information about the anatomy and physiology of sexual development (Stout & Rivera, 1989), often as part of a biology or physical education course, perhaps along with a little information about contraception and STDs (Carroll & Wolpe, 1996). Most of the programs avoid topics such as abortion and sexual orientation, and only one-third of sex education programs discuss sexual *behavior* at all (www.siecus.org/pubs/facts). Proponents of comprehensive sexuality education estimate that less than 10% of American adolescents receive this type of sex education by the time they leave high school (www.siecus.org/pubs/facts).

National analyses conducted in the 1980s on the effectiveness of sex education programs in the United States have generally found that the programs may increase adolescents' knowledge of their anatomy, their

Some studies have found school-based health clinics to be effective in lowering rates of adolescent pregnancy.

physiology, and to some extent even of contraception. Unfortunately, overall the programs have had little effect on (1) communication with partners or parents about sex or contraception; (2) frequency of sexual intercourse; or (3) use of contraception (Kirby, 1984, 2000; Stout & Rivera, 1989). However, because the programs vary so much across the United States, talking about the "overall" effects of sex education is misleading. Programs that focus on knowledge have little influence on adolescents' sexual behavior, but more extensive programs have often been found to be effective.

Perhaps the best known of these programs is one that was instituted in the early 1980s in the public schools in Baltimore (Zabin, 1986). The program established "family planning" clinics close to the schools, offering easy access to contraceptive services. The clinics provided nurses and social workers who made classroom presentations to students about contraceptive use, STDs, and the emotional and relationship aspects of sexuality. The nurses and social workers also offered after-school sessions of counseling, films, and educa-

tion. The effects of the program were substantial. Two years after the program began, students at the schools participating in the program were more likely than students at "control-group" schools (who did not participate) to delay the age of their first episode of intercourse. Also, the pregnancy rate among girls at the program schools fell 30% from where it had been before the program, whereas it rose 60% at the control-group schools.

In recent years a great deal of attention and money has been devoted to sex education programs that promote abstinence, encouraging adolescents to wait until marriage before having sexual intercourse. For the most part, programs that include only abstinence education have been found to be ineffective at decreasing rates of intercourse among adolescents (Lantier, 1998). However, some of the most effective sex education programs have been **abstinence-plus programs** that encourage adolescents to delay intercourse while also providing contraceptive information for adolescents who nevertheless choose to have intercourse (Dionne, 1999; Haffner, 1998).

Summing Up

In this chapter we have covered a variety of topics related to dating, love, and sexuality. Here are the main points we have discussed:

- Dating tends to begin with mixed-sex groups in early adolescence, developing into dating pairs by late adolescence. Most American adolescents begin dating in their early teens. Dating is a mostly American phenomenon; young people in other Western countries associate more informally, and young people in Eastern countries tend to be discouraged from dating until they are looking seriously for a marriage partner.

- Sternberg's theory of love describes a variety of types of love derived from various combinations of passion, commitment, and intimacy. Adolescent love usually lacks long-term commitment, so it is most often characterized by infatuation or romantic love. Adolescents in non-Western cultures also experience passion, but many cultures restrict adolescents' expressions of passionate love because they believe that marriage should be based on family interests rather than individual choice.

- With respect to their views on adolescent sexuality, cultures can be generally classified as restrictive,

semirestrictive, or permissive. The contemporary United States is probably best classified as semirestrictive, with a great deal of ambivalence and divided opinions about adolescent sexuality.

- Adolescent sexual activity tends to follow a progression that begins with masturbation, followed by kissing and necking, sexual intercourse, and oral sex. Having first intercourse at age 15 or younger tends to be associated with problems such as higher rates of drug and alcohol use. American adolescents tend to use contraceptives inconsistently or not at all, due to factors particular to American society such as a deep ambivalence about adolescent sexuality.

- Homosexual adolescents often have difficulty coping with their sexual orientation in a culture that stigmatizes homosexuality, and consequently they are more likely than other adolescents to have problems of suicide, substance abuse, school difficulties, and running away from home.

- Sexually transmitted diseases contracted by adolescents include chlamydia, gonorrhea, herpes simplex, and HIV/AIDS. Rates of all these STDs are especially high in the late teens and early twenties.

• Sex education is controversial in American society. Most sex education programs are ineffective, but some recent programs have shown promise in reducing adolescent pregnancy.

One striking characteristic of research on sexuality in adolescence and emerging adulthood is that it is so heavily weighted toward the problems that can arise from premarital sexual contact, such as unwanted pregnancies and STDs (Brooks-Gunn & Paikoff, 1997). This emphasis is understandable, given the profound effects that these problems can have on young people's lives. Still, such an emphasis can leave a distorted impression of how sexuality is experienced by young

people. If you knew nothing about sex except what you read in academic studies of adolescents, you would never guess that sex can be pleasurable (Fine, 1988). It is true that young people's sexuality can be a source of difficulties and problems, but what about sexuality as a source of enjoyment? What positive feelings and thoughts do adolescents and emerging adults have as they experience kissing, necking, petting, and intercourse? How are love and sex related in young people's relationships? In what ways does sexual contact enhance emotional intimacy between young people in love? We need to learn much more about these questions in order to have a complete picture of love and sexuality among young people.

Key Terms

dating scripts	consensual validation	cohabitation	subfecundity
proactive script	initiation phase	sexuality	parental notification
reactive script	status phase	restrictive cultures	parental consent
liking	affection phase	double standard	asymptomatic
infatuation	bonding phase	semirestrictive cultures	latency period
empty love	sexual harassment	permissive cultures	wasting syndrome
romantic love	bullying	sexual scripts	comprehensive sexuality
companionate love	date rape	coming out	education
fatuous love	arranged marriage	homophobia	abstinence-plus programs
consummate love			

For Further Reading

Bois-Reymond, M., & Ravesloot, J. (1996). The role of parents and peers in the sexual socialization of adolescents. In K. Hurrelmann & S. Hamilton (Eds.), *Social problems and social contexts in adolescence: Perspectives across boundaries* (pp. 175–197). Hawthorne, NY: Aldine de Gruyter. A study of adolescent sexuality in the Netherlands.

Hatfield, E., & Rapson, R. L. (1996). *Love & sex: Cross-cultural perspectives*. Boston: Allyn & Bacon. A lively, fascinating account of beliefs and behavior on love and sex around the world, including a wealth of material related to adolescents and emerging adults.

Herdt, G. (1989). *Gay and lesbian youth*. New York: Harrington Park Press. Anthropologist Gilbert Herdt is the editor of this book, which presents perspectives on gay and lesbian youth from a variety of disciplines.

Applying Research

Bass, E., & Kaufman, K. (1996). *Free your mind: The book for gay, lesbian and bisexual youth.* New York: Harper Perennial. Information for young people about coming to terms with being homosexual.

Gitchel, S., & Foster, L. (1985). *Let's talk about sex.* Fresno, CA: Planned Parenthood of Central California. Presents ways to promote communication between parents and adolescents about sexuality.

[14-year-old Mike] is slouching his way through another day of earth science. Around him, other students sit listening to the teacher and leafing through their textbooks, the thin white pages rustling softly through the room. He makes no pretense of following the lesson, however. He has not even bothered to take a book off the shelf. The teacher's trying to get him to join the rest of the class, but he's ignoring her. . . .

In a room at the end of B wing, an English teacher with short gray hair and a sly smile sits perched on a stool in front of one of her senior advanced placement classes. By tomorrow, she says, she wants the class to have read the final act of Henrik Ibsen's "A Doll's House."

A collective moan rises from the desks.

"Is that so much?" says [the teacher]. "One lousy act?"

Down the aisles, the kids mimic her in high-pitched, singsongy voices usually reserved for imitating parents.

"Is that so much? One lousy act?"

[The teacher] fights back a smirk, trying her best to look stern. This is a game that she and her seniors play. She assigns a reading, they pretend to pitch a fit, she pretends to be shocked.

But tomorrow, when the bell rings and they take their seats, she knows—and they know she knows—that most if not all of them will have read the one lousy act and will be prepared to dissect it with ruthless efficiency. These are advanced placement kids. This year they will read, among other things, Hamlet, Macbeth, Othello, Antigone, Medea, Lord of the Flies, Wuthering Heights, Lord Jim, *and Albert Camus's* The Stranger. *Furthermore, some of them will like it. (French, 1993, pp. 21, 151)*

These scenes from an American high school, taken from a book by journalist Thomas French (1993), provide an illustration of what occurs in today's **secondary school** (including middle school, junior high school, and high school). It is a place that contains all sorts of

An American high school.

students, with a vast range of interests and abilities. With nearly all of them, teachers wage a daily struggle to keep them engaged in learning, with only intermittent success. School competes for adolescents' attention with family problems, part-time work, and the many allurements of socializing and leisure with friends. Schools also struggle against the ambivalence of Americans' beliefs about adolescence—most Americans want adolescents to succeed in school and learn what they need to prepare themselves for work (or at least for further education), but most Americans also want adolescence to be a time when young people are free to enjoy life to the fullest before the responsibilities of adulthood permanently descend.

Given this formidable challenge, American secondary schools have generally achieved only mixed results. The great majority of American adolescents graduate from high school, and more than half of those who graduate from high school go on to obtain higher education. However, most evaluations of American secondary education have come to the conclusion that adolescents' academic achievements fall considerably short of what they could be and should be.

In this chapter, we examine young people's school experiences in the past and present, in the United States and in other countries, in secondary schools and in colleges and universities. The chapter begins with an extensive historical account of the rise of secondary schooling. This history is important because secondary schooling as a standard part of adolescence is relatively recent historically, and because it would be difficult to understand secondary schools today without knowing how they developed. Following this history, we look at the current state of educational achievement among American adolescents, including recent trends as well as international comparisons in which American adolescents compare unfavorably to adolescents in other industrialized countries.

American schools are extremely diverse, in part because the United States has no national educational policy as other industrialized countries do. Although the overall status of American secondary education is troubling in many ways, many schools do succeed, and we spend part of this chapter looking at the characteristics of effective schools. We also examine adolescents' school achievement in the context of the rest of their lives. Scholars have concluded that adolescents' academic performance is related in crucial ways to factors in their families, friendships, and work and leisure patterns. We examine these factors in relation to adolescents' academic achievement and also consider the role of cultural beliefs in what is required from adolescents academically.

Just as schools vary in their effectiveness, adolescents vary in their academic achievement. We focus especially on ethnic differences and gender differences in achievement, two areas that have been the focus of much research. We also consider the characteristics of adolescents who are at the extremes of achievement: gifted adolescents, disabled adolescents, adolescents who are in lower academic tracks, and adolescents who drop out of high school. At the end of the chapter we turn our attention to emerging adulthood and examine the characteristics of today's college students, the characteristics related to success and failure in college, and college students' accounts of their educational experiences.

The Rise of Schooling for Adolescents

Compulsory education through the midteens is relatively recent, historically. A hundred years ago, most American states did not have any laws requiring children to attend school beyond the elementary grades. It was during the "Age of Adolescence" (1890 to 1920) that this changed dramatically. During this time, many states passed laws requiring school attendance through the early teens, and the proportion of 14- to 17-year-olds in school rose from just 5% in 1890 to 30% by 1920 (Arnett & Taber, 1994). The trend did not stop there. By 1970, the proportion of 14- to 17-year-olds in school had risen to *90%*, and it has remained over 90% since that time (see Figure 10.1; Arnett & Taber, 1994).

In other Western countries a similar trend took place during these decades. Schooling became the normative experience for adolescents, and an increasing proportion of emerging adults also remained in school. For example, in Norway, as recently as 1950 only 20% of adolescents continued school past age 15; today, education is compulsory until age 16, and among emerging adults aged 17 to 24 over half are still in school (Stafseng, 1994).

In contrast, it is rare even now for adolescents to attend school in societies that are not industrialized (Schlegel & Barry, 1991). In those societies, education beyond childhood is only for the elite (just as it was in the West a century ago). Adolescents are usually engaged in productive work rather than attending

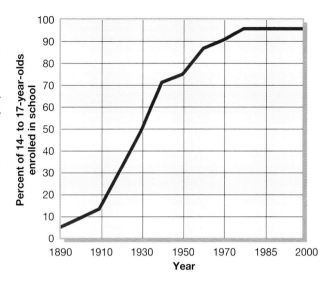

FIGURE 10.1 *Increasing enrollment in high school, 1890 to the present.*
Sources: Tanner (1972); Arnett and Taber (1994).

school. Their labor is needed by their families, and they can best learn the skills needed for adult work in their societies by working alongside adults rather than by attending school. However, these patterns are changing in many countries due to growing economic development. Virtually everywhere in the world, countries and cultures that were not industrialized 50 or more years ago are now becoming industrialized and entering the global economy. One consequence of economic development in these countries is that adolescents are increasingly likely to remain in school. Economic development introduces agricultural technologies that make children's and adolescents' labor less necessary to the family, while at the same time staying in school becomes a greater economic benefit because more jobs become available that require educational skills.

The effects of economic development on adolescents' education in developing countries is evident in the literacy of today's adolescents compared with their parents and grandparents (Bloom & Brender, 1993). Figure 10.2 shows the patterns in selected developing countries. For example, in Egypt, 74% of males aged 15 to 19 can read and write, compared with just 30% of males aged 65 and older; among females, 59% of girls aged 15 to 19 can read and write, compared with just 9% of women aged 65 and older. This suggests that as economic development continues in developing countries, the proportion of adolescents receiving education will continue to rise.

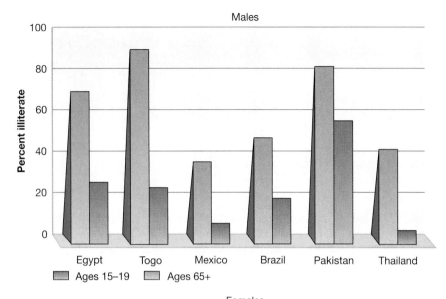

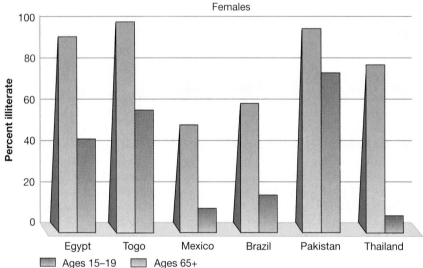

FIGURE 10.2 *Declining illiteracy in selected developing countries, males and females.*
Source: UNESCO (1991).

Changes in Schooling for Adolescents

Not only has the proportion of adolescents attending secondary school in the United States changed dramatically in the past century, but the kinds of things adolescents learn in school have changed as well. An examination of these changes is useful for understanding the kinds of requirements that exist for adolescents today. We begin in the 19th century and proceed up to the present.

The 19th and Early 20th Centuries In the 19th century, when few adolescents in the United States attended school, secondary education was mainly for the wealthy. The curriculum was constructed to provide young people (mainly males) with a broad liberal arts education—history, art, literature, science, philosophy, Latin, Greek, and so on (Church, 1976). Because the adolescents attending these schools were generally from families who were wealthy, the objective of their schooling was not practical training for employment but rather the cultivation of the mind and the attainment of knowledge of the broad range of subjects a member of the elite was expected to know about and to be able to discuss.

By 1920, following the steep rise in the proportion of young people attending secondary school, there was a widespread consensus that educational reform was needed. The composition of the student population in secondary schools had changed from the privileged few to a broad cross-section of the American population, and it was necessary to adapt the content of secondary education to respond to this change. Thus, the central goal of American secondary education shifted from education for its own sake to more practical goals focusing on training for work and citizenship. Secondary education for the privileged was merely a kind of leisure, with no particular application; but secondary education for the general public became oriented toward practical preparation for adult life in American society.

One of the motivations for this change in focus was the enormous wave of immigration from Europe to the United States during the first two decades of the 20th century by people seeking to escape economic and political instability and then the horrors of World War I. A backlash took place beginning about 1920 and immigration laws were tightened sharply, but by

HISTORICAL FOCUS
Higher Education and Cultural Beliefs

For the most part, today's colleges and universities in Western countries extol independent thinking and intellectual exploration. Although it may be tempting to think that these values are inherently part of the educational mission of higher education, a look at the colleges and universities of 100 years ago demonstrates that these are values based in cultural beliefs of individualism. A comparison of universities then and now also shows how much has changed in American higher education as well as in American cultural beliefs. This comparison was the subject of an essay by Dennis O'Brien (1997).

A century ago, the mission of most colleges and universities was grounded explicitly in religious beliefs. Courses in religious instruction were not only required but considered central to the curriculum. For example, the 1896–97 catalog of Lafayette College stated, "It is intended that the Bible shall be the central object of study throughout the [student's education]. It is dealt with reverently as the Word of God and as the inspired and infallible rule which God gives to His people."

Colleges and universities required not only religious study, but also religious practice—and not only at private colleges but at public universities as well. For example, at the University of North Dakota, every day began with a brief service in the chapel—with all students required to attend—featuring the singing of hymns, readings from the Bible, and recitation of the Lord's Prayer. The University of Maine required all students to attend daily morning prayer in the chapel. Missing 15% or more of these prayer sessions would lead to admonition by the president; if attendance did not improve, the student would be censured by the faculty.

Over the course of the 20th century, as the power of religious institutions waned and individualism became stronger as the basis of the cultural beliefs of the American majority culture, colleges and universities gradually ceased to promote religious beliefs. Instead, individualism became the basis of universities' educational mission. For example, in Gettysburg College's mission statement for 1997, the goal of the college is stated as helping students learn to "appreciate our common humanity in terms of such positive values as open-mindedness, personal responsibility, [and] mutual respect. . . . Students may develop greater freedom of choice among attitudes." The values stated are predominantly individualistic ones. Similarly, the University of North Dakota's 1997 catalog states that "Education concerning values is important in general education—not seeking one right to behave, but recognizing that choices cannot be avoided. Students should be aware of how many choices they make, how these choices are based on values, and how to make informed choices." Again, the individualistic nature of the university's mission is evident. The goal of most higher education today is not to communicate a specific way of looking at the world, but to teach students how to make "informed choices" as individuals, by themselves.

that time there was widespread concern about the social consequences of the arrival of millions of new immigrants. Secondary education was touted as a way to make the new immigrants "Americanized," by stamping a common American identity on immigrants arriving from a vast range of cultural backgrounds (Church, 1976; D. Tanner, 1972).

Thus it was in the 1920s that the framework for the American high school as we know it today was established, designed to educate a diverse population of adolescents for life in American society. Rather than being restricted to the liberal arts, education in the **comprehensive high school** (as it came to be known) includes classes in general education, college preparation, and vocational training.

The Mid-20th Century Between the 1920s and the middle of the 20th century, the proportion of young people attending secondary school continued to expand, and the diversity of the high school curriculum continued to expand as well. Now the curriculum was enlarged to include preparation for family life and leisure, with courses available on music, art, health, and physical education. In a sense, this was a combination of the two previous approaches. The practical focus on preparation for work and citizenship remained, but it was now combined with classes that had no particular purpose other than the enhancement of the appreciation of life. Now, however, the enjoyment of learning things in school about topics such as music and art was no longer restricted to adolescents from privileged families, but available to the majority of American adolescents through public high schools. The goal of secondary education, by midcentury, had become not just practical preparation for work and citizenship, and not just the appreciation of enjoyable but inessential knowledge, but a combination of the two with the goal of producing a "well-rounded" individual.

Midcentury to the Present   Since the 1950s, there have been periodic cries of alarm over the state of education in American schools, with much of the alarm focusing on the education of adolescents in secondary schools. In the late 1950s and early 1960s, concern focused on the perceived deficiencies in science education in the schools. The Soviet Union launched the first satellite (*Sputnik*) into space in 1957, stunning the United States with the prospect that this was the first step toward Soviet superiority in the military arms race. This event resulted in vigorous calls to teach children more science, in the belief that only through science education would the United States be able to raise children who would grow up to be able to design the military weapons that would allow the United States to stay ahead of the Soviets. This may sound extreme or even absurd to those of you who have grown up mostly after the breakup of the Soviet Union. But at the time the United States and the Soviet Union had been locked in a bitter Cold War struggle for world supremacy since World War II, and it was widely believed that the children of that time, and their children's children, would grow up to inherit that struggle. No one would have predicted then that 40 years later the Soviet Union would have ceased to exist.

In the early 1970s, the alarms were sounded again in response to several reports from committees of educational experts (Brown, 1973; Coleman, 1974; Martin, 1976). This time the inspiration for the alarms was the social upheaval of the 1960s and early 1970s. Although only a minority of adolescents and emerging adults held radical political views or participated in social or political protests over the Vietnam War, civil rights,

and other issues, those who did participate in the protests were highly visible and vocal, and concern over the state of America's youth was widespread. The various committees of educational experts reached similar conclusions, with all of them heaping blame on American high schools for the alienation and disillusionment of American young people.

The problem, according to these committees, was that the education provided by high schools was too far removed from real life. According to this view, high schools were teaching too much that was irrelevant to the kinds of roles adolescents would have to fulfill as adults (Church, 1976). *Relevance* became the new buzzword, and in the pursuit of relevance high schools were encouraged to develop programs that would involve less time in the traditional classroom and more time learning skills in the workplace, obtaining direct occupational training and experience. It was believed that this would not only improve education but also reduce adolescent alienation, as they would have more daily exposure to adults by working alongside them. Courses were also added that would provide greater opportunity for personal growth (National Commission on Excellence in Education, 1983), again in the hope of making the curriculum more relevant.

In the 1980s, a new alarm was sounded. Evidence began accumulating that students' educational achievement scores had declined steadily since the 1960s, and that the educational reforms of the 1970s had done little to halt or reverse the decline. Furthermore, cross-national comparisons of the United States in relation to other industrialized countries indicated that the United States ranked low, especially in relation to Asian countries (Stevenson & Stigler, 1992). Japan replaced the Soviet Union as the United States' most feared competitor, but the source of anxiety this time was economic rather than military. Japan was viewed as the rising economic power that would soon dominate the world, primarily as a consequence of their superior educational system.

New committees of educational experts were formed, and they arrived at a new diagnosis. The problem? All this relevance had reduced the rigor of American education, according to the experts (National Commission on Excellence in Education, 1983). Students were being given a great deal of freedom to choose their classes, and they tended to choose too many "fluffy" courses on personal development and not enough of the tougher academic courses, especially in math and science. Relevance became the problem rather than the solution, and "back to basics" became the popular new battle cry. The critics advocated more stringent requirements for high school students to take courses in math, science, and English, along with more homework, tighter discipline, and a longer school year. The back-to-basics movement continued through the 1990s with calls for more rigorous and demanding high school curriculums (National Education Commission on Time and Learning, 1994).

■ THINKING CRITICALLY

In your view, should high school courses be offered only on academic subjects such as math and English, or should courses in music and physical education also be available? Justify your view.

The Diversity of American Education   Something to keep in mind as you read about all of these educational reform movements over the past 50 years is that none of them has had much direct power to implement their proposed solutions in American schools. Unlike virtually every other industrialized country in the world, most decisions about education in the United States are controlled on the local and state levels, not on the national level. This has always been true in the United States, and local control of schools remains an issue of great importance to many people. For example, in recent years plans to develop national tests of academic performance in reading and math have met with fierce opposition, even though the plans specified that schools' participation would be voluntary. "Testing is just the next step in a liberal agenda for Washington to seize control of local schools" said one Congressman during the debate on the bill ("National Math, Reading Tests Fail in House," 1997), articulating a resistance to national school policies held by many Americans.

Because schools are funded and controlled by states and cities rather than nationally, a great deal of variability exists across the different U.S. school districts in the curriculums they use and in school rules and requirements. School quality varies depending on the financial resources available in the school district and on what the people in the state and the district decide is the best way for children to learn. Experts and critics can form all the committees they like and make recom-

mendations until they turn blue, but no state or school district is obliged to comply.

This does not mean that the experts and critics never have effects on how children and adolescents are educated. For example, the recommendations made in the early 1970s in favor of relevance had substantial effects in leading to more educational credits from applied work experience and more courses on personal growth (National Commission on Excellence in Education, 1983; Powell, Farrar, & Cohen, 1985). On the other hand, maybe these changes were not the result of expert recommendations and would have happened anyway—the recommendations of the back-to-basics movement appear to have had little effect (National Commission on Time and Learning, 1994).

Recently, however, definite steps toward a national educational policy have been taken. In 1994, the federal government took a major step by establishing a national program of educational standards. More important, the government backed the program by putting nearly a billion dollars in monetary incentives for states to adopt federal guidelines for educational excellence, and as a result virtually all the states have agreed to participate. The program is called "Goals 2000," because the aim was to reach various national educational goals by the year 2000, including high standards of student performance in subjects such as science, English, mathematics, geography, and history (Wilson, 1996). This is the most ambitious federal educational program yet attempted, but so far it has not succeeded in establishing an effective national educational policy (Cooper, 1999). Nevertheless, this goal has a great deal of public support—in a 1997 Gallup poll, 77% of American adults said that they support national standards for academic performance, and 66% supported a national curriculum.

Secondary Education Around the World

The United States is unusual in having only one institution—the comprehensive high school—as the source of secondary education. Canada and Japan also have comprehensive high schools as the norm, but most other industrialized countries have several different kinds of schools that adolescents may attend. For example, most European countries have three types of secondary schools (Arnett, 2000d). One type is a college-preparatory school that is similar in many ways to the American high school, in that it offers a variety of academic courses and the goal of it is general education rather than education for any specific profession. However, in Europe these schools do not include classes in recreational subjects such as music and physical education. In most European countries about one-fourth to one-half of adolescents attend this type of school. A second type of secondary school is the vocational school, where adolescents learn the skills involved in a specific blue-collar occupation such as plumbing or auto mechanics. Usually about one-third of adolescents in European countries attend this type of school. A third type of secondary school is a business-trade school, where adolescents prepare themselves for business-related professions such as accounting. About one-fourth of European adolescents usually attend this type of school. Some European countries, such as Germany, also have extensive apprenticeship systems, in which adolescents can attend a vocational or business-trade school part of the time and also spend part-time learning a profession in the workplace under the supervision of adults (Hamilton, 1990). We will discuss apprenticeships in more detail in the next chapter.

About one-third of adolescents in Europe attend a vocational school. Here, a French student learns to repair engines.

One consequence of the European system of different types of secondary schools is that adolescents must decide at a relatively early age what direction they want to pursue for their education and occupation. At age 15 or 16 adolescents must decide which type of secondary school they will enter, and this is a decision that is likely to have an enormous impact on the rest of their lives. Although adolescents sometimes change schools after a year or two, and adolescents who attend the vocational or business-trade schools sometimes attend college, these switches in direction are rare. Usually the decision is made by adolescents in conference with their parents and teachers, based on adolescents' interests as well as on their school performance (e.g., Motola, Sinisalo, & Guichard, 1998).

Do adolescents have the capacity to make this kind of decision by the age of 15 or 16? Clearly people in many countries have decided that the answer to this question is yes. As we have seen in Chapter 3, scholars differ in their views of whether adolescents have the capacity to make reasoned judgments as well as adults by the time they reach their midteens (Beyth-Marom et al., 1993; Steinberg & Cauffman, 1996). Adolescents' decision-making competence may depend on the specific area involved. However, few studies have specifically addressed adolescents' competence in making educational and occupational decisions.

Compared with the European system, the system of the comprehensive high school allows for greater flexibility. With the exception of adolescents who are directed into a lower track (whom we will discuss later in the chapter), all adolescents in a comprehensive high school have a broad range of courses to choose from. Because all adolescents attend the same high school, for most of them little about their occupational direction is decided by the time they graduate. At that point they may decide to end their education and enter work full-time, pursue training at a vocational school, attend a two-year college, attend a four-year college, or pursue some combination of work and school.

However, the great drawback of the comprehensive high school is that adolescents are all in the same school and in many of the same classes even though by their midteens they may have widely divergent educational and occupational interests and capacities. This makes it difficult for teachers to find a level of teaching that will appeal to all adolescents. It can also be frustrating for adolescents who would prefer to be obtaining job-specific skills to be forced instead to take further years of general education (Steinberg, 1996).

The Current State of Educational Achievement Among American Adolescents: Good News and Not So Good

Although the American secondary educational system has come under a great deal of criticism in recent decades, not all of the news about the current state of educational achievement among American adolescents is bad. Some of it is, in fact, quite good. As we have seen, far more adolescents attend and graduate from high school than 100 years ago or even 50 years ago. Among African American adolescents, the improvement in high school graduation rates in the past 30 years has been especially strong. Although the dropout rate among African American adolescents in some urban areas is alarmingly high, overall the high school graduation rate among African Americans has been rising steadily and is now 88%, nearly as high as for Whites (Pollard & O'Hare, 1999).

In addition to unprecedented levels of high school attendance and graduation, the rate of emerging adults attending college and graduate school is also higher than ever before (see Figure 10.3). Currently over 60%

of high school graduates go directly on to college (Bianchi & Spain, 1996), and about one-third of those who obtain an undergraduate degree go on to attend graduate school the following year (Mogelonsky, 1996). These are higher rates of college and graduate school attendance than in most other industrialized countries. In most Asian and European countries, for example, the rate of college attendance generally ranges from about 10% to 40% (Arnett, 2000d).

However, the educational achievement of American adolescents is also a cause for concern. The creation in recent decades of all those commissions of experts described in the previous section reflects a widespread dissatisfaction in American society over the state of secondary education. Despite various attempts at educational reform, dissatisfaction has persisted, because negative reports of the educational performance of American adolescents have continued to accumulate. Two kinds of evidence indicate that the concern over American secondary education is well-founded: patterns of academic performance over recent decades and comparisons of academic performance between American adolescents and adolescents in other industrialized countries.

Academic Performance in Recent Decades

Perhaps the most widely discussed indication of declining academic performance in American society is the pattern of scores in recent decades on the Scholastic Aptitude Test (SAT), the test that is taken by high school juniors and seniors who are planning to apply for admission to college. SAT scores declined steadily from the mid-1960s through the 1980s, before rising slightly during the 1990s. Although a wider range of students has taken the test each decade because more and more young people enter college after high school, the decline in SAT scores has been just as steep if the analysis is restricted to the White middle class (Steinberg, 1996).

The SAT is not the only indicator of decline in recent decades. A different evaluation, focusing not just on adolescents planning to attend college but on all high school students, reached similar

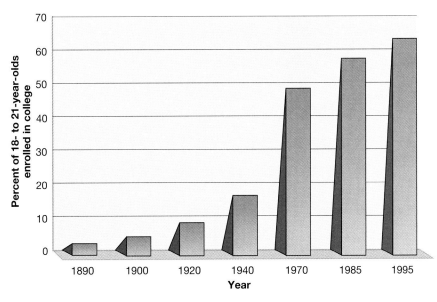

FIGURE 10.3 *College attendance over the past century.* Figures for college indicate percentage of 18- to 21-year-olds in the United States attending college during the year indicated.

Sources: Adapted from Arnett & Taber (1994); Bianchi & Spain (1996).

conclusions. This evaluation, the National Assessment of Educational Progress (NAEP), has examined students' performance since 1970 in four areas: math, science, reading, and writing. Throughout the 1970s and 1980s, the NAEP found declines in math, science, and reading, especially with respect to higher-order thinking (Newmann, 1992), that is, thinking that requires students to interpret, analyze, and evaluate information rather than just memorize it. Although some slight improvements were seen over this period in the proportion of younger adolescents who had a grasp of such basic skills as addition and subtraction, declines were seen in reading, math, and science among older adolescents. Specifically, the proportion of 17-year-olds who could synthesize and analyze advanced reading materials, solve math problems involving several steps, and synthesize detailed scientific information declined (Mullis, Owen, & Phillips, 1990). As with the SAT, the problems are not restricted to poor rural and urban schools but apply to affluent urban and suburban schools as well (Steinberg, 1996). Although students' performance on the NAEP rose slightly during the 1990s (Applebome, 1997), it remains well below the levels of the early 1970s.

Another confirmation of the serious academic problems of American adolescents comes from evaluations of entering freshmen at American colleges. Three-fourths of faculty at American colleges and universities indicate that their entering students lack basic academic skills (Steinberg, 1996). Over 30% of college freshmen must take "remedial" courses in reading, writing, and math before they are able to take higher-level college courses. This indicates that even though the proportion of American adolescents graduating from high school is quite high, a high school diploma no longer means that an adolescent has grasped even the most basic academic skills.

International Comparisons

The levels of educational achievement typical of American adolescents is alarming, not only in comparison to the past but also in comparison to adolescents in other industrialized countries. In the past 20 years numerous studies have compared the academic performance of adolescents in different industrialized countries. On virtually all of these comparisons, American students rank in the bottom half of the countries involved. A widely discussed report on American education released in the early 1980s, sharply titled *A Nation at Risk*, summarized 19 international comparisons of academic performance. The United States did not place first on any of these 19 comparisons, and placed *last* on 7 of them. Since that time, there is every indication that the place of American students in relation to other countries has grown worse, not better (Cooper, 1999; Steinberg, 1996).

Even the best students in American high schools, the ones enrolled in their schools' most challenging and advanced classes, compare unfavorably to the top students from other industrialized countries. In fact, with respect to math and science, the best students in the United States perform worse than the *average* students in other industrialized countries (Steinberg, 1996). Furthermore, the poor performance of American students in relation to students from other countries exists prior to the age at which adolescents in some of those countries are separated into different kinds of schools (Stevenson & Stigler, 1992). And in Japan, 95% of students graduate from high school, a higher percentage than in the United States (Armstrong & Savage, 1997), yet Japanese adolescents consistently perform better than American adolescents on international comparisons.

Not only are American adolescents not learning as much as their peers in other countries, they are not enjoying their classroom experience much, either. In the ESM studies, the most common mood adolescents report when beeped while in class is *boredom*. In a national study in which adolescents in grades 7 through 12 rated the quality of their teachers, over half said that teachers failed to make the subject matter interesting (Solarzano, 1984). But, as we will see later in the chapter, the blame for adolescents' low level of engagement in the classroom cannot be blamed entirely on poor teaching methods.

THINKING CRITICALLY

Based on what you have read so far about American and European secondary schools, what do you think explains the poor performance of American adolescents in international comparisons?

What Works? The Characteristics of Effective Schools

Although the academic performance of American adolescents indicates that American schools overall have a

CULTURAL FOCUS
Japanese High Schools and Colleges

Japan has been a frequent focus of international educational comparisons for Americans in recent decades, partly because Japan has emerged as a major economic competitor to the United States and partly because Japan is often at or near the top when children from a variety of countries are compared on academic achievement. Especially in math and science, Japanese children and adolescents consistently outperform Americans in cross-national comparisons (e.g., Educational Testing Service, 1992; McKnight et al., 1987), and the gap grows larger with age from childhood through adolescence (Chen, Lee, & Stevenson, 1996). Furthermore, 95% of Japanese adolescents graduate from high school, a percentage higher than in any Western country, and levels of college attendance and graduation are similar to the United States (Armstrong & Savage, 1997).

What are the characteristics of the Japanese educational system with regard to adolescents and emerging adults? One notable feature of the Japanese system is the length of the school year. Japanese adolescents attend their high schools for 243 days a year, more than American adolescents (typically about 180 days), Canadian adolescents, or adolescents in any Western European country. Japanese secondary education is also notable for how smoothly the parts of the curriculum fit together. Japanese adolescents have fewer courses to choose from than American students do (Armstrong & Savage, 1997), and a more structured ordering of courses from one level to the next. The curriculum and the textbooks for each course are chosen on a national basis by the Ministry of Education, so that all Japanese students in a particular grade are learning the same things at the same times (Rohlen, 1983; Stevenson, 1992). The curriculums are connected; for example, in math courses, students who have completed Math I have learned what they will need to know at the beginning of Math II. As a result, Japanese teachers spend much less time than American teachers simply reviewing material from previous courses before presenting fresh material for the current course (Armstrong & Savage, 1990).

However, Japanese high schools focus almost exclusively on rote learning and memorizing, with little time or encouragement given to critical thinking. Many Japanese have criticized their system as too rigid and as failing to teach students how to think (Rohlen, 1983). These critics hold up the American system in favorable contrast for encouraging independent and creative thinking, even though the American system is less successful than the Japanese system at teaching facts. Defenders of the Japanese system retort that school years should be the time for learning information, and that there is plenty of time in adulthood for the development of reflection and judgment.

Cultural beliefs are also important to the practices of Japanese schools. Teachers, adolescents, and parents believe that all children are capable of learning the material that teachers present (Armstrong & Savage, 1990; Stevenson, 1992; Stevenson & Stigler, 1992). The Japanese (as well as people in other Asian countries) generally believe that success or failure in school depends on effort, in contrast to the American belief that ability is what matters most (Stevenson & Stigler, 1992). When students do poorly in school, these beliefs result in intense socialization pressure to try harder, pressure that comes from teachers, parents, peers, and the struggling students themselves.

The major underlying source of pressure on adolescents is the national system of entrance exams to high school and college, which anthropologist Thomas Rohlen (1983), in his classic ethnography of Japanese high schools, called Japan's "national obsession." These two exams essentially determine young people's occupational fate for the rest of their lives, because in Japanese society obtaining a job is based primarily on the status of the schools a person has attended, and once young people obtain a job they tend to stay with the same company for their entire working lives.

To prepare for the entrance exams, the majority of Japanese students not only apply themselves seriously at school and in their homework, but from middle childhood through adolescence they attend "cram schools" after school or receive instruction from private tutors. This system goes a long way toward explaining the high level of performance of Japanese children and adolescents. They work intensely on their schoolwork because the stakes are so high, much higher than in the United States where the job market and the higher education system is much more open and fluid, and much less about people's occupational future is determined by the time they leave high school.

Is there a cost for the high performance of Japanese adolescents? Perhaps surprisingly, most evidence indicates that the intense academic pressure does not make Japanese children and adolescents unhappy and psychologically disturbed. Japanese adolescents do not show higher rates of stress, depression, or psychosomatic ailments than American adolescents do (Stevenson, 1992), and rates of suicide are *lower* for Japanese than for American adolescents. (Asian American adolescents also report *less* stress, *less* anxiety, and *fewer* psychosomatic problems such as headaches, compared with White students, despite their high rates of academic performance [Steinberg, 1996].)

However, Asian cultures, including Japanese culture, have a general taboo against disclosing personal information, so it may be that Japanese adolescents are underreporting their distress for reasons of social desirability. Many Japanese view the exam system as a problem for young people. There is a constant debate in Japanese society about the exam system, with many people objecting that it places too much pressure on young people and takes virtually all the fun out of childhood. Certainly it is true that with longer school days, a longer school year,

cram schools, and private tutors, Japanese adolescents have far less time for leisure and informal socializing with friends than American adolescents do (Rohlen, 1983).

For the Japanese, their time of leisure and fun comes during their college years. Getting into college is where all the pressure is; once they enter college, grades matter little and standards for performance are relaxed. Instead, they have "four years of university-sanctioned leisure to think and explore" (Rohlen, 1983, p. 168). Japanese college students spend a great deal of time in unstructured socializing, walking around the city and hanging out together. For most Japanese, this brief period in emerging adulthood is the only time in their lives, from childhood until retirement, that will be relatively free of pressure. Until they enter college the exam pressures are intense, and once they leave college they enter a work environment in which the hours are notoriously long. Only during their college years are they relatively free from responsibilities and free to enjoy extensive hours of leisure.

In Japan, pressure for academic achievement is much greater in high school than in college.

great deal of room for improvement, American schools vary enormously and some work better than others. Let's take a look at what educational research tells us about the characteristics of effective schools within the United States. Then we will examine the characteristics of schools in other countries where the educational system is particularly effective.

The Size Issue: Schools and Classes

What is the optimal size of schools and classes for adolescents? A considerable amount of educational research has been expended on this question. During this century, as the proportion of adolescents attending school has steadily grown, the tendency has been to build ever-larger schools to accommodate them. Within schools, school officials may attempt to fill classrooms to the maximum possible number of students to save money. But what size of school and class is best for the students?

Increased school size has both positives and negatives. Large schools have the advantage of being able to offer a more diverse range of classes than smaller schools. For example, students might benefit from having classes available on Medieval Literature, 19th Century English Literature, and 20th Century Poets rather than simply one course on English Literature. Larger schools also have the advantage of being able to offer a wider range of extracurricular activities. A school of 3,000 is likely to have a chess team, a debating team, and a school newspaper, whereas a school of 150 would probably be too small to have enough students or enough financial resources to make this range of activities available. With respect to academic achievement, no definite relationship to school size has been found (Rutter et al., 1979; Steinberg, 1996).

Although smaller schools offer less diversity in extracurricular activities, students in smaller schools are actually *more* likely to participate in them (Boyer, 1983; Goodlad, 1984). At larger schools most students end up being observers rather than participants. At smaller schools fewer students compete for the available positions, and students are more likely to be recruited because a team or club needs somebody to fill a spot. Consequently, students at smaller schools are more likely to be placed in positions of leadership and responsibility—vice-president of the drama club, treasurer of the girls' chorus, and so on. These students typically report that their participation makes them feel more confident in their abilities and more needed and important (Boyer, 1983; Goodlad, 1984).

All things considered, scholars have reached a consensus that the best school size for adolescents is be-

tween 500 and 1,000 students (Entwisle, 1990). Not too small, not too large, perhaps a size that combines the best of both.

With respect to class size, however, scholars disagree. Some claim that a direct and negative relationship exists between class size and students' academic performance (Boyesen & Bru, 1999). One team of scholars (Glass & Smith, 1978) analyzed a variety of studies and concluded that class size could have dramatic effects on students' academic performance. Students taught in classes of fewer than 15, they claimed, would typically perform up to 30 points better on national achievement tests than students taught in classes of 40. The difference was especially sharp for class sizes of less than 15, but even students taught in classes of 20 students were estimated to gain 10 points on national tests compared with students taught in classes of 40. Another team of scholars analyzed the same data through a different method and reached a similar conclusion (Hedges & Stock, 1983).

However, other scholars have reached a different conclusion about the effect of class size on academic performance. These scholars claim that variation within the typical range—20 to 40 students—has little effect on students' achievement (Bennett, 1987; Rutter, 1983). They agree that for students with academic difficulties, small classes are preferable because each student is likely to need more individual attention. However, in this view it would not benefit most students to have the size of their classes reduced from 40 to 20, and it would cost schools a great deal of money to do so.

Junior High, Middle School, or Neither?

Another issue of importance in the quality of adolescents' education is how their secondary school careers should be divided. Is it best for adolescents to attend junior high school from 7th through 9th grades, followed by high school from 10th through 12th grades? This is the so-called 6-3-3 plan: 6 years of elementary school, 3 years of junior high, and 3 years of high school. Or is it preferable for adolescents to attend middle school (rather than junior high) beginning in 6th grade, followed by a 4-year high school—the 5-3-4 plan? Or would it be best to dispense with junior high and middle school altogether, and have adolescents proceed directly from elementary school to high school—the 8-4 plan?

A number of studies have found that in both the 6-3-3 plan and the 5-3-4 plan, the first year of middle school or junior high school is a difficult time for many young adolescents (Eccles, Lord, & Midgely, 1991;

Hirsch & Rapkin, 1987; Simmons & Blyth, 1987). The main reason is that school transitions taking place in early adolescence are likely to coincide with a variety of other changes for most young people (Eccles et al., 1993; Fenzel, Blyth, & Simmons, 1991; Hawkins & Berndt, 1985). Any of the physical changes of puberty may coincide with the school transition, such as breast development (girls), growth spurt, changes in body shape, and increased acne. Peer relations change, too; early adolescence often marks the beginning of romantic and sexual experimentation.

The transition to middle school or junior high school also typically involves changes in school experience. It means moving from a small, personalized classroom setting to a larger setting where a student has not one teacher but five or six or more. It also usually means moving into a setting where the academic work is at a higher level, and grades are suddenly viewed as a more serious measure of academic attainment than they may have been in elementary school. These changes in school experience can add to early adolescents' anxieties and school-related stress (Eccles et al., 1993).

Because school transitions in early adolescence tend to be difficult, might it not be better to dispense with the junior high–middle school transition altogether, as in the 8-4 plan? This question was addressed in a classic study conducted by two sociologists, Roberta Simmons and Dale Blyth (1987). They studied adolescents in the Milwaukee, Wisconsin, school system over a period of 5 years, from 6th through 10th grades. About half of the students attended schools in districts with a 6-3-3 plan, and the other half attended schools in districts with an 8-4 plan. Simmons and Blyth focused on four aspects of adolescents' functioning: self-esteem, grade point average, extracurricular activities, and perceived anonymity (feelings of being unknown and insignificant). The results showed significant differences among students in the two types of school plans for every measure except grade point average, with the differences favoring students in the 8-4 plan.

Other studies have reported similar advantages of the 8-4 plan for outcomes such as self-esteem, school attendance, and student engagement in the classroom (Eccles et al., 1997). Studies focusing on African American and Latino adolescents have also found difficulties with school transitions in early adolescence. One study of mostly African American adolescents found that the transition to junior high school was followed by declines in their self-esteem, educational achievement, participation in extracurricular activities, and perceptions of the school environment (Seidman et

al., 1994). Another study found that African American and Latino adolescents experienced poor grades and more incidents of trouble with their teachers following the transition to junior high school—and that the difficulties they experienced were greater than for the White students who were attending the same schools (Munsch & Wampler, 1993).

Improving the School Experience of Adolescents

So, should we try to persuade all school districts to adopt the 8-4 plan on the basis of this research? Perhaps, but keep in mind that most studies comparing different school plans have focused on a limited range of variables such as self-esteem and extracurricular activities. Although most of the results favor the 8-4 plan, other characteristics not included in these studies may favor the 6-3-3 plan. One study found that 7th-grade adolescents made more positive than negative comments about the transition to junior high school, with positive comments about topics such as peer relationships (more people to "hang around" with), academics (greater diversity of classes available), and independence (Berndt & Mekos, 1995; also see Hirsch & DuBois, 1989).

Furthermore, considerable evidence suggests that the reason for difficulties with school transitions in early adolescence is not so much in the timing of the transition as in the nature of adolescents' school experiences in most junior high and middle schools. Jacquelynne Eccles, a scholar who has conducted several studies on early adolescents' school experiences, attributes the difficulties of these transitions to the fact that many adolescents find the environment of middle schools and junior high schools alienating and oppressive (Eccles et al., 1997). Compared with elementary schools, middle schools and junior high schools tend to have less individual contact between students and teachers and less opportunity for close relationships with teachers, in part because students have many teachers rather than just one. Also, there is a greater emphasis on teacher control. According to Eccles and her colleagues (1997), this increased emphasis on control is especially mismatched with early adolescents' increased abilities and desires for autonomy, and consequently undermines their motivation and self-esteem.

Early adolescents' difficulties with school transitions are also due in part to the kinds of beliefs that junior high teachers tend to hold about adolescents (Eccles et al., 1991; Eccles et al., 1993). Although why these teachers would differ from teachers in the 8-4 plan is not clear, Eccles and her colleagues have found that junior high teachers are considerably more negative in their views of adolescents. They are less likely to trust their students and more likely to see adolescents as inherently troublesome and unruly. When compared with elementary school teachers, junior high teachers report less confidence in their abilities, perhaps because the majority of them have not had any specialized training on adolescence (Eccles et al., 1993; Scales & McEwin, 1994). If the findings from Eccles's studies are widely true of middle school and junior high school teachers, it would go a long way toward explaining the difficulties adolescents have with school transitions in early adolescence.

Fortunately, other studies indicate that schools and parents can take steps to make school transitions more enjoyable and successful for early adolescents (Fenzel et al., 1991). One study compared two different junior high schools—one that grouped students into smaller teams of 100 students and 4 teachers, and one that was a more typical junior high school—and found that students in the team-organized school adjusted better to the transition, primarily because of the support they felt from their teachers (Hawkins & Berndt, 1985). In another study, some parents of adolescents in low-income families in Vermont participated in an 11-week program to provide parents with information about adolescence and promote their effectiveness as parents (Bronstein et al., 1994). The program took place just prior to the adolescents' transition to middle school. The results indicated that adolescents whose parents participated in the program did not show the typical decline in functioning after their transition to middle school and were better off following the transition than adolescents in a control group whose parents did not participate in the program. This finding is consistent with another study, which found that when parents are aware of and sensitive to adolescents' needs and developmental characteristics, their adolescents are more likely to make the transition to junior high school without experiencing a decline in their self-esteem (Lord, Eccles, & McCarthy, 1994).

School Climate

Although many studies indicate that school size and the timing of school transitions can be important influences on adolescents' school experience, most scholars on education would agree that these factors are important only insofar as they influence the kind of interactions that students and teachers have in the classroom. **School climate**, is the term for the quality of these interactions (Haynes, Emmons, & Ben-Avie, 1997; Rutter, 1983). It refers to how teachers interact with students, what sort of expectations and standards they have for students, and what kinds of methods are used in the classroom.

The term was coined by Michael Rutter (1983; Rutter et al., 1979), a British psychiatrist who has done extensive research on adolescents and schools. Rutter and his colleagues studied several thousand young adolescents in British secondary schools. Their study included observations in the classrooms as well as students' attendance records and achievement test scores, and students' self-reports of their participation in delinquent behavior.

The results indicated that the most important differences among the schools were related to school climate. Students were better off in schools where teachers tended to be supportive and involved with students but also applied firm discipline when necessary and held high expectations for students' conduct and academic performance. In particular, students in schools with this kind of school climate had higher attendance and achievement test scores and lower rates of delinquency compared with students in the schools where the school climate was not as favorable.

This was true even after taking into account statistically the differences in IQ and socioeconomic background of the students. So, it was not simply that the students in the better schools also came from more advantaged backgrounds—the schools themselves made a substantial difference in students' performance, based on differences in school climate.

Another large study compared public and private (mostly Catholic) schools in the United States, and reached conclusions similar to those of Rutter and his colleagues (Coleman & Hoffer, 1987; Coleman, Hoffer, & Kilgore, 1982). This study was led by James Coleman, a prominent scholar on adolescents and education, and focused on high school (in contrast to the Rutter study, which had focused on younger adolescents). Like Rutter and his colleagues (1979), Coleman and his colleagues found that students had higher levels of achievement and lower levels of delinquency in schools that maintained high expectations for students along with a spirit of involvement and dedication on the part of teachers. This was true regardless of whether the school was public or private, although private schools generally rated more favorably than public schools on various aspects of school climate. The findings remained true (as in the Rutter study) even after controlling statistically for differences in students' abilities and social class background.

Imagine that you have just become the principal of an American secondary school. What could you do to assess the school climate in your school? How would you go about improving it if it were less than satisfactory?

We can conclude from these studies that successful teaching looks a lot like successful parenting in that both combine demandingness and responsiveness. A combination of warmth, clear communication, high standards for behavior, and a moderate level of control seems to work as well in the classroom as it does in the home (Haynes et al., 1997). However, as with parenting, the practices that take place in schools are often rooted in a particular set of cultural beliefs. Coleman and his colleagues (1982) concluded that one of the key reasons for the success of the private schools was that a common set of Catholic religious beliefs was held by parents, teachers, and students. These beliefs included respect for authority (including teachers), consideration for and cooperation with others (including other students), and the importance of striving to make the most of one's abilities. Schools did not have to introduce these beliefs to students and persuade them to accept them. The beliefs were taught to the children from an early age, at home and in church, and school simply reinforced the values and attitudes shaped in these settings.

Violence in the School   Something that has put a chill on the climate of American secondary schools in recent years is the prospect of violence. The past decade has seen numerous highly publicized murders in schools. The worst of these took place in 1999 at Columbine High School in Littleton, Colorado, when 2 boys murdered 12 students and a teacher before killing themselves.

Ironically, these notorious murders have come during a period when violence in American schools is actually declining overall. According to the CDCP's National Youth Risk Behavior Survey, violence of a variety of types declined among high school students during the 1990s (Rook, 1999). For example, the proportion of high school students who reported carrying a gun to school in the past year declined by one-fourth, from 8% to 6%. Similarly, the proportion of students who reported being in a physical fight in the past year dropped from 43% to 36%. Adolescents remain far more likely to be the victims of violence outside of school than within school (Myers, 2000).

Nevertheless, there is a widespread perception that American secondary schools have become more dangerous in the past decade. In one 1999 survey, Americans named school security as their second greatest concern (Myers, 2000). The perception of increased danger of violence has affected school's security practices (Gibbs & Roche, 1999). An increasing number of schools use metal detectors to screen students at the school entrance and have hired additional security personnel to watch vigilantly for any sign of student misbehavior that might be interpreted as a precursor to violence. The fear of violence has also led to increased federal funding for school violence prevention programs (Myers, 2000).

Have students responded to this increased focus on the risk of violence in school with a greater sense of safety because of more extensive security measures and antiviolence programs? Or do they feel less safe than ever in school, because the focus on school violence has made them more fearful of it than they were in the past? These are urgent, and as yet unanswered, research questions.

Achievement in High School: Beyond the Classroom

The studies by Rutter and Coleman show that a favorable school climate succeeds in promoting adolescents' engagement while they are in school. **Engagement** is the quality of being psychologically committed to learning (Newmann, 1992). It means being alert and attentive in the classroom, and it means approaching educational assignments with the aim of truly learning the material, not just scraping by with minimal effort.

Unfortunately, engagement is the exception rather than the norm in the school experience of American adolescents. Research indicates that a remarkably high proportion of adolescents not only fall short of an ideal of engagement, but are strikingly disengaged during their time in school, "physically present but psychologically absent" (Steinberg, 1996, p. 67). In a comprehensive study of American high schools by Steinberg (1996) (described

"TODAY'S STUDENTS KNOW LESS, AND CAN DO LESS, THAN THEIR COUNTERPARTS COULD TWENTY-FIVE YEARS AGO. OUR HIGH SCHOOL GRADUATES ARE AMONG THE LEAST INTELLECTUALLY COMPETENT IN THE INDUSTRIALIZED WORLD. . . . THE ACHIEVEMENT PROBLEM WE FACE IN THIS COUNTRY IS DUE NOT TO A DROP IN THE INTELLIGENCE OF OUR CHILDREN, BUT TO A WIDESPREAD DECLINE IN CHILDREN'S INTEREST IN EDUCATION AND THEIR MOTIVATION TO ACHIEVE IN THE CLASSROOM; IT IS A PROBLEM OF ATTITUDE AND EFFORT, NOT ABILITY."

—STEINBERG (1996), PP. 183–184

Engagement is the exception rather than the rule in American secondary schools.

in the Research Focus box), more than one-third of the students in the study indicated that they rarely try hard, and a similar proportion indicated that they rarely pay attention in class. Over two-thirds admitted they had cheated on a test at least once in the past year, and *nine out of ten* said they had copied someone else's homework within the past year. These findings make a persuasive case that the majority of American adolescents are seriously disengaged from school. For many of them, their commitment seems to be not to learning but to getting by with the least effort possible.

Putting the Rutter and Coleman studies together with the Steinberg study, it seems reasonable to conclude that a favorable school climate enhances students' engagement, which in turn results in higher levels of achievement. Steinberg (1996) agrees that school climate makes a difference, and he makes various recommendations to improve the school climate in American high schools. However, he sees the principal problems with American secondary education as lying "beyond the classroom," in the family environments, peer relations, work and leisure patterns, and cultural beliefs experienced by American adolescents.

Family Environments and School

We saw in Chapter 7 that parenting styles are related to a variety of important aspects of adolescent development. Parenting affects not only the quality of the relationship between parents and adolescents but also a variety of other aspects of adolescents' lives, including their attitudes toward and performance in school.

One way parents influence adolescents' academic performance is through their expectations for achievement. Adolescents whose parents expect them to do well tend to live up to those expectations, as reflected in their grades in high school; adolescents whose parents have lower expectations for their school performance tend to perform less well (Patrikakou, 1996; Roeser, Lord, & Eccles, 1994; Schneider & Stevenson, 1999). Parents who have high expectations also tend to be more involved in their adolescents' education, assisting with course selection, attending school programs, and keeping track of their adolescents' performance, and this involvement contributes to adolescents' school success (Bogenschneider, 1997; Grolnick & Slowiaczek, 1994; Steinberg, Dornbusch, & Brown, 1992).

Parents' involvement in their adolescents' education tends to be a reflection of their overall parenting

RESEARCH FOCUS
The Mother of All Research Projects

You may notice that I draw a lot in this chapter from a study by Laurence Steinberg (1996). The reason I refer to this study so much is that it is perhaps the most comprehensive, in-depth study of American high school students ever conducted. Consider some of the features of this study:

- 20,000 students participated in the study.

- The students were from nine different schools in two states (Wisconsin and California). The schools were in urban, rural, and suburban communities.

- Forty percent of the sample was African American, Asian American, or Latino.

- Data was collected from the adolescents each year for four years, so that patterns of change over time could be investigated.

- Before any data was collected, planning and **pilot testing** of the measures took 2 years. (Pilot testing means trying out the measures on a small number

of potential participants before the larger study begins to make sure the measures have adequate reliability and validity.)

- Questionnaire measures were included on adolescents' academic attitudes and beliefs, academic performance, psychological functioning, and problem behavior, among other topics. Questionnaires were also included on adolescents' views of their parents' parenting practices, on their views of their peers' attitudes and behavior with regard to education and other areas, and on adolescents' work and leisure attitudes and behavior.

- Group interviews were conducted with 600 of the adolescents and 500 of the adolescents' parents.

The study has yielded an enormous amount of useful and interesting information, summarized in the book by Steinberg (1996) but also published in numerous papers in academic journals.

style (Paulson, 1994; Steinberg, 1996). For school as for other areas, authoritative parenting has the most favorable effects on adolescents' development. Adolescents whose parents combine high demandingness with high responsiveness have the highest levels of engagement in school and the highest levels of school success (Bronstein et al., 1996; Dornbusch et al., 1987; Steinberg, 1996). Authoritative parents contribute to adolescents' school success directly by being more involved than other parents in their adolescents' education (Paulson, 1994). Such parents also have a variety of favorable indirect effects on their adolescents' school performance. Adolescents with authoritative parents are more likely than other adolescents to develop personal qualities such as self-reliance, persistence, and responsibility, which in turn lead to favorable school performance (Steinberg, 1996).

Adolescents with authoritarian, indulgent, or indifferent parents all tend to perform worse in school than adolescents with authoritative parents (DeBaryshe,

Patterson, & Capaldi, 1993; Dornbusch et al., 1987; Melby & Conger, 1996). Adolescents' academic achievement tends to be worst when they have indifferent parents (low levels of both demandingness and responsiveness) (Dornbusch et al., 1987; Steinberg, 1996). These are adolescents whose parents know little about how they are doing in school and who also know little or nothing about how the adolescent's time is spent outside of school. Adolescents with such parents have the lowest estimation of their abilities, the weakest engagement to school, and the poorest grades (Steinberg, 1996).

Indifferent parents are not rare in American society. As noted in Chapter 7, studies indicate that at least one-third of American parents could be classified as indifferent. In the Steinberg (1996) study, one-third of adolescents indicated that their parents did not know how they were doing in school. Over half reported that their parents would not mind if they got Cs on their report card. Forty percent of the parents indicated that they never attend school programs. However, other studies have shown that schools can design effective programs to increase parents' involvement in their adolescents' education (Comer, 1993; Epstein & Dunbar, 1995). When parents become engaged, their adolescents' engagement and academic achievement also tends to improve. Such programs are especially important in the light of studies showing that, in general, parents tend to be less involved in their adolescents' education than they were when their children were younger (Eccles & Harold, 1993).

Family Social Class and School   One aspect of adolescents' families that has been recognized for decades as being strongly related to adolescents' academic achievement is the family's social class or socioeconomic status (SES). Numerous studies have found a positive association between family SES and adolescents' grades and achievement test scores, as well as between family SES and the highest level of education that adolescents or emerging adults ultimately attain (Featherman, 1980; Gutman & Eccles, 1999; Hanson, 1994; Lucas, 1996; Sewell & Hauser, 1972). These social class differences appear long before adolescence. Even before entering school, middle-class children score higher than working-class and lower-class children on tests of basic academic skills. By middle childhood these class differences are clearly established, and class differences in academic achievement remain strong through high school (Mullis & Jenkins, 1988). Middle-class emerging adults are also more likely than emerging adults from lower social classes to attend college following high school (Hanson, 1994; Lucas, 1996).

What makes social class so important in predicting academic achievement? Social class represents many other family characteristics that contribute to achievement. Middle-class parents tend to have higher IQs than lower-class parents, and they pass this advantage on to their children; in turn, IQ is related to academic achievement (Snow & Yalow, 1988). Middle-class children also tend to receive better nutrition and health care than lower-class children, beginning prenatally and continuing through adolescence; for lower-class children, health problems may interfere with their ability to perform academically (Children's Defense Fund, 1994; Teachman, 1996). Lower-class families tend to be subject to more stresses than middle-class families, in terms of major stresses (such as losing a job) as well as day-to-day minor stresses (such as the car breaking down), and these stresses are negatively related to adolescents' school performance (Dubois,

Eitel, & Felner, 1994; Felner et al., 1995; Gutman & Eccles, 1999).

Parents' behavior also varies by social class in ways that are related to adolescents' academic achievement. Middle-class parents are more likely than lower-class parents to have an authoritative parenting style that contributes to their children's school success (Dornbusch et al., 1987; Steinberg, 1996). Middle-class parents are also more likely than lower-class parents to be actively involved in their adolescents' education, through behavior such as guiding adolescents' selection of classes and attending parent–teacher conferences (Gutman & Eccles, 1999; Lee & Croninger, 1994). However, social classes are large categories, and substantial variability exists within each social class. In the lower class as well as the middle class, adolescents benefit in their academic performance from authoritative parents and from parents who are involved in their education and have high expectations for their academic achievement (Steinberg, 1996).

Peers, Friends, and School

*❝**W***ith my crowd, if you cut school and got away with it, that meant you were all right. You had a scam on those teachers. If you could still pass, you had an in. Everyone thought that was great. You'd be stoned in class and sit back and make a fool of yourself and everybody would laugh and you'd be considered fun. Like you'd be entertaining everyone. And if you didn't get caught, you were cool.❞*

—Annie, age 17 (in Bell, 1998, p. 76)

Although the influence of friends tends to be strongest in relatively less important areas such as dress, hair style, and music, school is one important area in which the influence of friends is in some respects greater than the influence of parents. Several studies have found that in high school, friends' influence is greater than the influence of parenting practices in a variety of school-related ways—how consistently adolescents attend class, how much time they spend on homework, how hard they try in school, and the grades they achieve (Midgely & Urdan, 1995; Steinberg, 1996).

Of course, as we have seen in Chapter 8, the influence of peers is not necessarily negative and may in fact be quite positive. Adolescent friends with high educational achievements and aspirations tend to give each other support and encouragement for doing well in school (Steinberg, 1996). This is true even taking into account selective association (the fact that adolescents tend to choose friends who are similar to themselves). When low-achieving adolescents have high-achieving friends, over time the high achievers tend to have a positive influence, such that the low achievers' grades improve (Davies & Kandel, 1981; Epstein, 1983). Low-achieving adolescents with high-achieving friends are also more likely to plan to attend college, compared with low achievers whose friends are not high achievers (Epstein, 1983).

Nevertheless, some studies do suggest reason for concern about the influence of friends and peers on adolescents' school performance. By the time they reach middle school, many adolescents become concerned with concealing a high-achievement orientation from their peers. For example, in one study eighth-grade students indicated that they wanted their teachers to know that they worked hard in school—but not their peers, because they feared that their peers would disapprove (Juvonen & Murdock, 1995). Also, adolescents who are more concerned than other adolescents about what their friends think of them tend to perform poorly in school (Fuligni & Eccles, 1992).

In school as in other areas, the influences of parents and peers are often intertwined. On the one hand,

parents influence adolescents' choices of friends, which can in turn influence school performance (Brown et al., 1993; Gonzales et al., 1996). On the other hand, having friends who denigrate school tends to be related to lower school success, even for adolescents with authoritative parents (Brown et al., 1993; Steinberg, 1996).

Work, Leisure, and School

Part-time work in high school tends to be damaging to school performance in a variety of ways, especially for adolescents who work more than 20 hours per week (Steinberg, 1996). The more adolescents work, the lower their grades, the less time they spend on homework, the more they cut class, the more they cheat on their schoolwork, the less committed they are to school, and the lower their educational aspirations. Figure 10.4 illustrates some of these patterns. In Steinberg's 1996 study, one-third of adolescents said they took easier courses because of their jobs, and the same proportion said they were frequently too tired from their jobs to do their homework. These relationships were causal, not merely correlational—in the course of the 3-year study, students who increased the number of hours they worked also reported declines in school

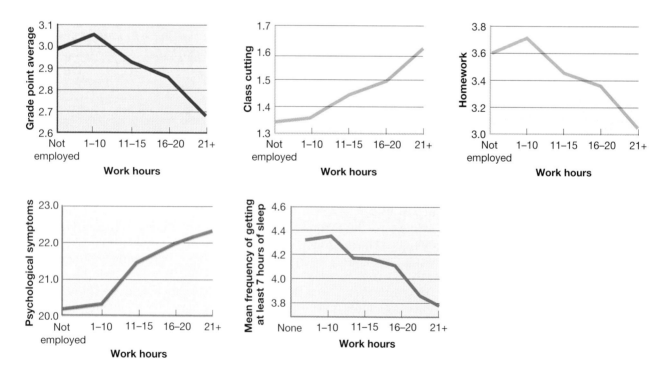

FIGURE 10.4 *Relation between work hours and school performance.* Beyond about 10 hours per week, the more adolescents work, the poorer their school performance.

Sources: Steinberg & Dornbusch (1991); Bachman & Schulenberg (1993).

commitment, whereas those who decreased the number of hours they worked reported increased school commitment.

However, it is not only work that interferes with adolescents' attention to school and schoolwork, but also leisure. Steinberg (1996) found that *socializing* was adolescents' most common daily activity. Adolescents reported socializing—activities such as "hanging out with friends" and "partying"—an average of 20 to 25 hours per week, more than the average time they worked and more than the amount of time they spent in school. In turn, amount of time spent socializing was strongly associated with lower grades in school.

For both work and leisure, the ethnic comparisons are striking, especially with respect to Asian Americans. According to Steinberg (1996), Asian American adolescents are less likely than other adolescents to have a part-time job and less likely to work 20 or more hours per week if they are employed. On average, Asian Americans spend only half as much time socializing, compared with adolescents in other ethnic groups. Because they spend less time on part-time employment, less time on socializing, and more nonschool time on academics, Asian Americans have the highest levels of academic achievement of any ethnic group, including Whites (Chen & Stevenson, 1995; Fuligni & Tseng, 1999).

Cultural Beliefs and School

The practices of schools and the attitudes of parents, peers, and adolescents themselves toward school are ultimately rooted in cultural beliefs about what is valuable and important (Arnett, 1995a). Although Americans do a lot of public hand-wringing about the state of their educational system, the truth is that education—at least at the high school level—is not as highly valued by Americans as it is by people of many other industrialized countries (Stevenson & Stigler, 1992). Sure, Americans would like to see their adolescents do better on the SAT and perform better in international comparisons with adolescents from other countries. But would most Americans support a law restricting employment for persons under 18 to no more than 10 hours a week? Would Americans support restricting participation in high school athletics to a similar time commitment, no more than 10 hours a week? Would parents of American adolescents be pleased if high school teachers began assigning homework that routinely required 3 or 4 hours per day after school and began handing out failing grades to adolescents who did not measure up to a high and inflexible standard of performance?

All the evidence indicates that the answer to these questions is a resounding *NO* (Stevenson & Stigler, 1992; Steinberg, 1996). For example, in a Gallup poll released in August 1997, the majority of American adults were opposed to lengthening the school day or the school year. The majority also indicated satisfaction with the state of the public schools, with most giving the schools a "grade" of A or B.

THINKING CRITICALLY

Steinberg (1996) asserts that to change American adolescents' school performance, Americans would have to change their beliefs about what should be required of adolescents. Do you think more should be required of American adolescents in high school? Why or why not?

Academic Achievement in High School: Individual Differences

Adolescents' academic achievement is related not only to characteristics of their environments but also to characteristics of the adolescents themselves. In this area, ethnic differences and gender differences in achievement are two issues that have been of particular interest to scholars. We will examine these two issues first, then examine the characteristics of students at the extremes of achievement: gifted adolescents, disabled adolescents, adolescents tracked into lower academic curriculums, and adolescents who drop out of high school.

Ethnic Differences

"You don't have to go to school to necessarily become successful. You can go about it another way. . . . If you do drop out, you can still make it in life, because I know people who dropped out at an early age like 14 and they're still making it."

—*Tony, urban African American adolescent (in Figueira-McDonough, 1998)*

Although looking at the overall academic performance of American adolescents provides interesting insights and information, the overall patterns obscure the sharp differences that exist between different ethnic groups. It is well established that Asian American adolescents have the best academic performance of any ethnic group in American society, followed by Whites, with the performance of African American and Latino adolescents below Whites (Chen & Stevenson, 1995; Steinberg, 1996; Warren, 1996). These differences exist even in early elementary school, but they become more pronounced in adolescence (Fuligni, 1994).

What explains these differences? To some extent, the explanation lies in ethnic group differences in the factors we have already discussed as important in school success, such as social class, parenting practices, and friends' influences. With regard to social class, African Americans and Latinos are more likely than Asian Americans or Whites to live in poverty, and living in poverty is negatively associated with academic performance regardless of ethnicity (Gillock & Reyes, 1999; Gutman & Eccles, 1999; National Center for Education Statistics, 1998).

We have seen the importance of parental expectations in adolescents' educational achievement, and ethnic differences exist here as well. Although the majority of parents in all ethnic groups value education highly, the emphasis on education is especially strong in Asian cultures (Asakawa & Csikszentmihalyi, 1999; Lee & Larson, 2000), and Asian American parents tend to have higher educational expectations than parents in other ethnic groups (Chen & Stevenson, 1995; Fuligni & Tseng, 1999; Steinberg, 1996; Stevenson & Stigler, 1992). Furthermore, Asian American parents and adolescents tend to believe that academic success is due mainly to *effort*; in contrast, parents and adolescents in other ethnic groups are more likely to believe that academic success is due mainly to *ability* (Holloway, 1988; Stevenson & Stigler, 1992). Consequently, Asian American parents are less likely than parents in the other ethnic groups to accept mediocre or poor academic performance as due to fixed limitations in their adolescents' academic abilities, and more likely to insist that their adolescents address academic difficulties by trying harder and spending more time on their schoolwork.

However, one ethnic difference that does not correspond to other findings on adolescents' academic performance concerns parenting styles. Asian American parents are less likely than White parents to be classified by researchers as authoritative, and more likely to be classified as authoritarian (Steinberg, 1996); Asian American adolescents excel even though, more gener-

ally, authoritative parenting is more likely than authoritarian parenting to be associated with academic success in adolescence. However, as we discussed in the chapter on families, it makes sense to view most Asian American parents as traditional rather than authoritarian, because they tend to combine a high level of demandingness with strong attachments to their adolescents and intense involvements in their lives (Chao, 1994; Fuligni, Tseng, & Lam, 1999).

Ethnic differences can also be seen in friends' attitudes toward education. The differences correspond to ethnic differences in academic achievement—Asian Americans are most likely to have academically oriented friends, African Americans and Latinos least likely, with Whites somewhere in between (Steinberg, 1996). Specifically, Asian American adolescents are most likely to study with friends, most likely to say their friends think it is important to do well in school, and most likely to say they work harder on schoolwork to keep up with their friends. Although the influence of friends on school performance is usually positive for Asian Americans, for adolescents in other ethnic groups the influence is more likely to be negative (Steinberg, 1996).

Although ethnic groups differ in social class, parenting, and friends' influence in ways that explain ethnic differences in adolescents' academic achievement, many scholars have argued that other forces are at work as well, forces related specifically to prejudice and discrimination against ethnic groups in American society. In particular, they have argued that the relatively low achievement of African American and Latino adolescents is due substantially to these adolescents' perception that even if they excel educationally, their prospects for occupational success would be limited due to prejudices against them (Ogbu, 1989, 1990a; Taylor et al., 1994). Studies have found that minority adolescents who believe that their opportunities are unfairly limited by ethnic discrimination have lower achievement than their minority peers who do not believe this (Taylor et al., 1994; Wood & Clay, 1996). And evidence suggests that perceptions of prejudice are not unfounded. In adulthood, African Americans who have obtained a college degree earn substantially less than Whites who have the same level of education (Entwistle, 1990). The perception of a "job ceiling" that exists to inhibit their career progress may be an influence in discouraging African American and Latino adolescents from striving for academic achievement (Ogbu, 1990a).

However, in a contradictory finding, Steinberg (1996) reported that African American and Latino students were equal to White and Asian students in their perceptions of the potential value of academic achievement for promoting future career success. Where the adolescents in the Steinberg study differed was in their perceptions of the consequences of *not* succeeding academically. African American and Latino students tended to believe that they could succeed in a career even if they did not obtain a high level of academic achievement, whereas White and Asian American students—especially Asian American students—tended to believe that failing to succeed academically would have more serious negative consequences. Thus, contrary to the view that African American and Latino adolescents are inhibited from academic achievement by a pessimistic view of the value of academic success, this study indicates that these adolescents may have less motivation to strive academically because they are optimistic about their chances of succeeding in the future even without excelling academically. Similar findings were reported by Figueira-McDonough (1998) in a qualitative study of urban African American and Latino adolescents.

For adolescents whose families have immigrated to the United States in recent generations, one consistent finding is that their school performance is related to how long their families have been in the United States. One would reasonably expect that the longer an adolescent's family has been in the United States, the better the adolescent would do in school, because English would more likely be the language spoken at home, the adolescent would be more familiar with the expectations of American schools, the parents would more likely be comfortable communicating with teachers and other school personnel, and so on.

However, research shows *just the opposite.* The more generations an Asian American or Latino adolescent's family has been in the United States, the *worse* the adolescent tends to do in school (Fuligni, 1997; Kao & Tienda, 1995; Steinberg, 1996). The main reason seems to be that the longer the family has been in the United States, the more "Americanized" the adolescent is likely to become—that is, the more likely the adolescent is to value socializing, dating, and part-time work over striving for academic excellence. Becoming American means becoming more likely to have adopted the American cultural value of placing good times before academic achievement in adolescence and getting by in high school with as little work as possible (Steinberg, 1996).

Nevertheless, every ethnic group has a substantial amount of individual differences. Not all Asian American adolescents do well in school; many African American and Latino adolescents excel. The kinds of parenting practices that we have discussed as important to academic achievement—high expectations, high involvement, and so on—make a difference within every ethnic group (Steinberg, 1996).

Black Adolescents and "Acting White" Despite the overall lower academic achievement of African American adolescents in comparison to Asian Americans and Whites, a number of positive trends can be seen in the educational achievement of African American adolescents. As noted earlier, the percentages of African American adolescents completing high school rose substantially during the 1980s and is now almost as high as for Whites (Pollard & O'Hare, 1999). Rates of college enrollment among African Americans *tripled* from 1960 to 1980 and has remained stable since then (U.S. Bureau of the Census, 1998). Between 1976 and 1992, the average SAT scores for African American adolescents rose 20 points on the verbal score and 31 points on the math score, whereas the average for White students declined slightly in both areas.

However, problems remain in Black adolescents' educational achievement. Black students' high school grades and SAT scores remain well below Whites'

Educational performance among Black adolescents has improved in recent years but remains well below that of Whites.

despite recent improvements (Steinberg, 1996), and although the proportion of Blacks obtaining a college degree has increased in recent decades, it remains only half as high as for Whites (Pollard & O'Hare, 1999).

Part of the explanation for lower academic achievement of Black adolescents is obvious and widely acknowledged. Adolescents' academic achievement tends to be related to the academic achievement of their parents, and Black adolescents are more likely than White adolescents to have parents who have low levels of academic achievement. Adolescents from single-parent and low-income families tend to be less successful in school than other adolescents, and Black adolescents are more likely to come from families with a single parent and/or a low income.

However, another explanation has been presented that is more controversial. Some scholars have argued that racism and long-term exclusion from equal educational and occupational opportunities have led African Americans to view educational attainment as something distinctively "White" and therefore to reject it. According to this view, "What appears to have emerged in some segments of the black community is a kind of cultural orientation which defines academic learning in school as 'acting white'" (Fordham & Ogbu, 1986).

According to this theory, articulated most notably by John Ogbu (1990a, 1990b; Fordham & Ogbu, 1986), Blacks believe that even if they obtain higher education they will be discriminated against occupationally, and this perception of racial discrimination in employment discourages their pursuit of educational success. According to Ogbu (1990a, 1990b), a crucial difference exists between the experience of African Americans and the experience of minorities such as Latinos and Asian Americans. Latinos and Asian Americans are for the most part immigrants (or the descendants of immigrants) who came to the United States voluntarily. In contrast, African Americans are what Ogbu calls a **subordinate/castelike minority**, whose ancestors came to the United States through slavery. For African Americans (according to this theory), one result has been an enduring resistance to adopting the cultural values of the majority culture, including the value placed on education. The inferior schooling received by most urban Black children further promotes their alienation from the educational process. As a result of these experiences, striving for educational achievement is discouraged among African Americans, especially within adolescent peer groups (Hemmings, 1998; Price, 1999; Steinberg et al., 1992).

■ **THINKING CRITICALLY**

How does Ogbu's theory fit or fail to fit the educational performance of Latino adolescents? What would you predict about the performance of Native American adolescents, based on Ogbu's theory?

Does Ogbu's model apply to a high proportion of African American adolescents? Ogbu's ethnographic research offers a number of striking examples of African American adolescents who view educational achievement and even educational effort as "acting White." However, his research has taken place only on African Americans. As we have seen, most White adolescents do not exactly revere high academic achievement in high school, either. The widespread use among White adolescents of epithets such as nerd, geek, dweeb, and so on reflect a certain contempt for adolescents who pursue academic goals at the expense of social ones.

One study has compared the educational aspirations of Black and White adolescents nationwide, and the results do not support the "acting White" theory. Solarzano (1992) analyzed responses from a national survey on the educational aspirations of eighth-grade students. The results indicated that over 80% of the Black students aspired to attend college. This figure was similar to the figure for Whites, but when family socioeconomic status (SES) was taken into account, Blacks had *higher* aspirations than Whites of similar SES levels. Similarly, nearly 90% of both Blacks and Whites perceived their mothers as wanting them to go to college, but within each SES grouping, Black adolescents viewed their mothers as having *higher* educational goals for them, compared with Whites. Occupationally, similar proportions of Blacks and Whites aspired to attain a professional job (e.g., lawyer, accountant, nurse, teacher) by age 30, but in the two lowest SES groupings, Blacks expressed higher occupational aspirations than Whites did.

These results seem to contradict the cultural deficit model espoused by Ogbu and others, which suggests that the experience of racism dampens the educational and occupational aspirations of Black children. On the contrary, the aspirations of Black children appear to be as high or higher than those of Whites. However, important questions remain unanswered. Solarzano's data is from eighth-graders, whereas Ogbu studied adolescents in 10th through 12th grades. Do African American adolescents' educational aspirations suddenly plummet toward the end of high school as they face the reality of limited opportunities once they leave high school? One recent study indicated that educational expectations do indeed decline from eighth grade through high school for many Black adolescents, especially for those from lower SES families (Trusty, Harris, & Morag, 1999). The basis for this decline should be investigated further by future research.

Gender Differences

As we discussed in Chapter 5, few differences in intellectual abilities exist between males and females. However, gender differences do exist in academic achievement. For the most part, these differences favor females. From the first grade of elementary school to the last grade of high school, girls tend to achieve higher grades than boys and have higher educational aspirations (Sommers, 2000). Girls are also less likely to have learning disabilities, less likely to be held back a grade, and less likely to drop out of high school (National Center for Education Statistics, 1998). Girls are more likely to attend college and more likely to graduate from college (Bianchi & Spain, 1996). The female advantage in academic achievement exists not only in the United States but across all Western countries (Arnett, 2000d; Chisholm & Hurrelmann, 1995).

What explains girls' superior performance in school and the relatively poor performance of boys? One reason is that girls tend to enjoy the school environment more. Adolescent girls report more positive experiences and interactions in the classroom than adolescent boys and have more favorable relationships with their teachers (Sommers, 2000). For example, in one nationwide survey, nearly one-third of boys in grades 7 through 12 stated that they feel that teachers do not listen to what they have to say, compared with one-fifth of girls (Public Education Network, 1997). In another survey, adolescent girls had more contact with teachers and were more likely to feel that teachers and administrators cared about them (Horatio Alger Association, 1998). A second reason lies "beyond the classroom." Adolescent girls are more likely than adolescent boys to feel supported by their parents, academically as well as in other areas, and are more likely to have supportive relationships with adults outside the family as well (Sommers, 2000).

The one exception to the pattern of girls' higher academic performance is in the area of math and science achievement, where males have greater levels of achievement in adolescence and beyond. This is an important area of difference because math and science education is necessary for many high-paying, high-status professions such as engineering, medicine, computer science, and other high-technology fields. In college, females form only a small proportion of the students majoring in math and in math-based subjects such as engineering and the physical sciences (Dey & Hurtado, 1999; Smith, 1992). This pattern is not true only in the United States. In one study comparing adolescents in the United States, Taiwan, Japan, & Hungary, males indicated greater liking than females for math and science in all four countries, and in all four countries females indicated greater liking than males for the language arts (Evans, 1992).

However, the most recent evidence indicates that gender differences in math and science orientation may be fading. By the late-1990s, girls were as likely as boys to take math courses in high school (National Center for Education Statistics, 1998), and they performed as well as boys in those courses (Voyer, 1996). Although women continue to be less likely than males to choose college majors such as engineering and the physical sciences, female representation has grown in all traditionally male-dominated majors in the past two decades (Bianchi & Spain, 1996; Dey & Hurtado, 1999; Smith, 1992), as we will see in more detail later in the chapter. These trends indicate that progress is being made in eroding the gender biases that have kept females out of traditionally male fields, although those biases certainly still exist.

Gender differences in academic performance are important, and have been the subject of heated debates among scholars and in the public arena (Sommers, 2000). However, for this topic as for others, it is important to keep in mind that gender comparisons involve comparing one half of the population to the other half, and there is a great deal of variability within each group. Girls generally do better academically than boys, but many boys excel and many girls struggle. More boys than girls pursue professions based in

■ THINKING CRITICALLY

Much more research has been conducted on why adolescent girls do less well than adolescent boys in math and science than on why boys generally do worse than girls on virtually every other measure of academic achievement. What hypotheses would you propose to explain why boys generally do worse than girls academically, from grade school through adolescence?

math and science, but an increasing number of girls pursue these professions as well. Although the group differences are genuine, we should avoid stereotypes that might lead us to prejudge the abilities and performance of any individual boys or girls.

Extremes of Achievement

Because American secondary schools place all students in the same school regardless of their abilities and interests, schools often have policies for addressing variations in students' learning abilities and particular talents or problems that students may have. Here we examine the characteristics of adolescents at the high end of achievement—gifted students—as well as students who have disabilities that interfere with their academic achievement. We also look at the controversial issue of tracking, specifically at students who are tracked into a less rigorous secondary school curriculum. Then we examine the characteristics of adolescents who drop out of school, including a look at programs for preventing dropping out.

Gifted and Disabled Students   In recent decades, programs for **gifted students** have become more common. Usually the criterion for considering students gifted is an IQ of at least 130 (Horowitz & O'Brien, 1985), but some schools have gifted programs that also recognize special talents that students may have, for example, in art or music. Sometimes gifted students are not in special classes but are simply given extra assignments or assignments at a higher level. Also, many high schools have **Advanced Placement (AP) classes** for gifted students, in specific subjects such as math or English. These classes have higher-level material than normal classes to provide a challenging curriculum for gifted students (Zeidner & Schleyer, 1999). By performing well on national AP exams at the end of their AP classes, gifted high school students can earn college credits.

At the other extreme of achievement are adolescents who have disabilities of various kinds that make it difficult for them to succeed in school. The most common disabilities related to school difficulties are speech handicaps, mental retardation, emotional disorders, and learning disabilities (Hallahan & Kauffman, 1998). Children and adolescents with disabilities have inspired debates over how they should be educated and the extent to which they should be included in regular classrooms. In the 1980s the U.S. Congress passed a landmark bill, **Public Law 94-142**, requiring school authorities to provide all children and adoles-

cents who have disabilities with an individualized educational program suited to their particular needs. The educational program for each student must be developed by school officials in consultation with parents and with the children and adolescents themselves.

Public Law 94-142 also required that children and adolescents with disabilities be kept in the classroom with their peers whenever possible (Gearhart, Gearhart, & Mullen, 1993; Hallahan & Kauffman, 1998). This approach is known as **mainstreaming** or **inclusion**. The goal of inclusion is to make the education of disabled adolescents similar to the experience of other adolescents and avoid shunting them off into separate classrooms where they have little contact with students who are not disabled (Lovitt, 1989). When this approach is taken, usually disabled students also have a "resource room" where they can go for extra help, staffed by teachers who have special training and skills for working with disabled students (Gearhart et al., 1997; Hallahan & Kauffman, 1998). Some schools also have a special education consultant who meets with teachers who have disabled students in their classrooms and talks to them about ways to address the needs of these students.

Mainstreaming keeps disabled students in regular classrooms.

Tracking   Another way that American secondary schools address the diversity in interests and abilities that exists among their students is through placing students into different groups, or "tracks." Not all secondary schools use tracking, and schools that do use tracking vary in the number and types of tracks. However, typically a tracking system includes an upper-level, college preparatory track, a general education track for average students, and a remedial or special education track for students who are academically behind their peers. Some schools also have a vocational education track, in which students learn skills such as welding or auto mechanics. Students in different tracks attend some classes together—physical education, music, some general education classes—but take other classes only with students in the same track.

Tracking has been a target of fierce debate among educators for many years. Advocates of tracking argue that tracking is the best way to ensure that all students are engaged in the schoolwork that is best suited to their varying levels of ability and achievement (Hallinan, 1992). According to this perspective, placing all high school students in the same classes makes no sense. The brightest and most advanced ones will be bored to death, and the slowest will be not only bored but humiliated that all the other students are more advanced than they are. Also, not all students plan to attend college. As we have noted, even today nearly 40% of American adolescents begin working full-time after high school instead of going to college. Advocates of tracking argue that it would be better to give these students some useful vocational preparation as part of their high school education, instead of alienating them by forcing them to sit through courses on topics that do not interest them.

However, critics of tracking argue that it dooms students in the lower tracks to a second-rate education. The critics point to research indicating that students in the highest tracks often have the most skilled and most experienced teachers (Gamoran, 1993), and that the teaching in high-track classes is more likely to require complex thinking rather than simple memorization. Meanwhile, students in the lower tracks are often labeled as slow or stupid by their peers, and often come to see themselves that way as well (Rutter, 1983).

Furthermore, students in the lower tracks tend to fall further and further behind their classmates with each year of school. Once students are placed in a low track, they receive a lower level of academic materials and a lower level of requirements compared with students in the higher tracks, making it difficult for stu-

dents ever to get out of a low track once they are placed in one (Alexander & Cook, 1982; Dornbusch, 1994; Hallinan, 1992). Over time, tracking increases the gap in learning between high-track and low-track students; ultimately, tracking influences students' achievement in high school and how much education they go on to obtain after high school (Gamoran, 1992; Natriello, Pallas, & Alexander, 1989). Finally, some scholars have argued that Black and Latino students are more likely to be placed in a low track than White students of similar abilities (Rosenbaum, 1976; Vanfossen, Jones, & Spade, 1987).

High School Dropouts

"I didn't like school. I just didn't like it. There was nothing I liked about it. Having to do all this reading and writing, and all that stuff. I had better things to do. I didn't want to be tied down with some schoolwork that I wasn't even going to remember in six weeks, or six days. I just found it all pointless. I'd rather go out in real life and learn real-life things than sit in a classroom and read a book, and answer questions from a teacher."

—*Rich, age 17, high school dropout*
(in Arnett, 1996, p. 120)

Fifty years ago in American society, leaving high school before graduation was not unusual and did not severely affect a young person's occupational prospects. Many well-paying manufacturing jobs were available in automobile factories, steel mills, and the like, which made it possible for a young person to earn an adequate income without obtaining a high school degree. Today, however, with the economy having changed from a manufacturing base to a services and information base, the consequences of having low education are much more severe. Young people who fail to obtain a high school degree are at high risk for unemployment (Rumberger, 1995). Dropouts who do obtain employment often find themselves in low-paying service jobs that leave them in poverty despite their employment.

As the importance of obtaining education has increased over the past half century, the proportion of young people who fail to obtain a high school degree has steadily declined. By the late 1990s, only 14% of young people had not obtained a high school degree by age 24 (Education Trust, 1996). A higher percentage, about 25%, actually leave high school before graduating, but many of them obtain a General Education

Development (GED) afterward—which is considered to be equivalent to a high school degree—to lower the overall "dropout rate" to 14% by age 24.

Distinct ethnic differences exist in dropout rates. Latinos have a relatively high dropout rate, about 30% among those born in the United States (Youth Indicators, 1996). African Americans have experienced the steepest decline in dropout rates over the past 25 years, and currently their dropout rate is just 12% (Pollard & O'Hare, 1999). Dropout rates are lowest among Whites (7%) and Asian Americans (10%) (Pollard & O'Hare, 1999). In all ethnic groups except Asian Americans, males are more likely than females to drop out.

What leads adolescents to drop out of school? For most, dropping out is not a sudden event but the culmination of many years of school problems (McDougall, Schonert-Reichl, & Hymel, 1996). Adolescents who drop out are more likely than other adolescents to have repeated a grade (Connell et al., 1995; Rumberger, 1995). They are also more likely to have had a history of other school difficulties, including low grades, behavior problems, and low scores on achievement and intelligence tests (Cairns et al., 1989; Connell et al., 1995; Goertz, Ekstrom, & Rock, 1991; Jordan, Lara, & McPartland, 1996). Given the difficulties they have in school, it is not surprising that dropouts often report that they disliked school and found it boring and alienating (Jordan et al., 1996; Reyes & Jason, 1993).

Personal characteristics and problems are also related to adolescents' risk of dropping out. Dropouts sometimes have aggressive, active, high-sensation-seeking personalities that make it difficult for them to endure the typical classroom environment, which often involves working alone quietly or listening to someone else talk (Cairns et al., 1989). Adolescents who have learning disabilities of various kinds are more likely than other adolescents to drop out (Lovitt, 1989), in part because their difficulties in learning may have left them hopelessly behind their peers by the time they reach high school. For girls, having a child puts them at high risk for dropping out (Goertz et al., 1991), although such girls often report lower school engagement even before becoming pregnant (Manlove, 1998).

A variety of family factors also predict adolescents' risk for dropping out of school. Parents' education and income is a strong predictor; adolescents with parents who have dropped out of school are at high risk of dropping out themselves, as are adolescents whose families are in poverty (National Center for Education

Statistics, 1995; Rumberger, 1995). The two often go together, of course—parents who have dropped out often have low incomes. Parents who have dropped out provide a model of dropping out to their adolescents, and often have lower educational expectations for their children (Rumberger, 1995). Also, families with low incomes often live in low-income neighborhoods where the quality of the schools is lower (Wilson, 1996). In addition, the stresses of living in a low-income family make it more difficult for parents to support their children's education, for example, by helping them with their homework or attending school conferences. Rates of dropping out are higher for adolescents in single-parent families, largely due to the lower incomes and higher stresses experienced in such families (Amato, 1993; Buchanan, 2000). Among Latinos, difficulty using English is an important contributor to dropping out (National Center for Education Statistics, 1995; Singh & Hernandez-Gantes, 1996).

School characteristics also predict adolescents' risk of dropping out. Here as in other areas we have discussed, school climate is of primary importance. Dropout rates are lower in schools where teachers are supportive of students and dedicated to teaching and the classroom environment is orderly (Connell et al., 1995). Dropout rates are higher in larger schools (Bryk & Thum, 1989), at least partly because a healthy school climate is more difficult to sustain in large schools (Pittman & Haughwout, 1987).

Because dropping out predicts a variety of future problems, intervention programs have been designed to assist adolescents who drop out or who are at risk for dropping out because of poor school performance or because of attending a school where the dropout rate is high. In general, these programs have concluded that because the problems that lead to dropping out are diverse, programs to prevent dropping out need to be adapted to adolescents' individual needs and problems (Bloch, 1989). The most promising approach so far is the establishment of alternative middle schools for students who are at risk for dropping out (Boyle & Lutton, 1999). Evaluations of these programs have shown that students in the alternative schools are half as likely to drop out as students in control groups who did not participate in the program.

The key to the success of the programs appears to lie in three factors: attention from caring adult staff members who serve as counselors and social workers; low student–teacher ratios, so each student receives a substantial amount of attention from teachers; and starting the program in middle school, because by high school students may have fallen too far behind for the interventions to succeed as well. As one administrator of these programs observed: "If you get kids into a controlled environment where the expectations are high and there is a lot of adult contact and a lot of adult supervision, guess what: They do pretty well" (Boyle & Lutton, 1999, p. 19).

Privately sponsored dropout prevention programs have also achieved success by identifying at a young age children who are at risk for dropping out and offering them extra assistance and incentives long before they reach high school. Perhaps the best known of these programs is the I Have a Dream (IHAD) program founded in 1986 by philanthropist Eugene Lang (Kahne, 1999). The program began when Lang, speaking to a class of sixth graders in inner-city New York about their educational prospects, spontaneously offered them this incentive: for any of them who graduated from high school with at least a B average, he would pay all of their expenses through college. The dropout rate in that area of New York was 75%, but among Lang's "adopted" class only 10% dropped out and 60% attended college!

Since that time, IHAD has established over 160 projects in 28 states involving over 12,000 children (Kahne, 1999). Local project administrators "adopt" a third- or fourth-grade class in an area where the high school dropout rate is high. The children in these classes are provided with special academic, cultural, and recreational activities through high school, and those who graduate from high school and enter college or vocational school are supported during the time they receive higher education. A key part of the program is the personal involvement of the project staff in the lives of the children, just as Lang became deeply involved with the lives of the children in the New York city class he first adopted. The success of the program has attracted national attention, and it has been suggested that some form of this program should be instituted as a federal program. Some states (e.g., Georgia) now provide financial support throughout college to any student who attains a B average by the end of high school and then attends a state college.

Education in Emerging Adulthood: College and University

As we have noted, the proportion of Americans attending college has risen dramatically in recent decades. Furthermore, about one-third of people who obtain an undergraduate degree enter graduate studies within one year (Mogolensky, 1996). The extension of education has been an important influence in creating a distinct period of emerging adulthood (Arnett, 2000a). Emerging adulthood is characterized by experimentation and exploration in a variety of aspects of life, and attending college allows young people to experiment with various possible educational directions that offer different occupational futures. College also allows for the exploration of ideas that may be unrelated to any occupational future. You may be a business major and nevertheless enjoy courses on literature or art or philosophy that lead you to explore a variety of ideas about what it means to be human. You may be a psychology major and yet find it engaging to explore ideas in courses about astronomy or chemistry.

In this section we will first examine current characteristics of college undergraduates. This will be followed by a discussion of what leads to educational success in college—or the lack of it. We will also examine college students' perspectives on the quality of their educational experiences.

Alternative schools have been found to be effective with adolescents who would otherwise drop out of school. Here, a biology class in an alternative school in Hartford, Connecticut.

Characteristics of College Students

In the United States, although over 60% of recent high school graduates enter college, rates of college attendance are not equal in all groups in American society. Females are more likely than males to enter college; currently, the undergraduate population is about 56% female (Dey & Hurtado, 1999). Asian Americans are the ethnic group most likely to attend college. About two-thirds of Asian Americans enter college after high school, compared with 60% of Whites, half of Blacks, and one-third of Latinos (Pollard & O'Hare, 1999). In the past two decades, these percentages have increased for all ethnic groups except Latinos.

Most undergraduates are in their late teens or early twenties. However, it is increasingly common for people to enter college or return to college in their later twenties or beyond. In 1974, only 22% of entering students were nontraditional students (older than 18 to 23); by 1994, this proportion had risen to 32% (Dey & Hurtado, 1999). In this section we will focus on traditional students, because our interest is in the emerging adulthood age period of the late teens and early twenties.

The areas of study chosen by college students have changed over the decades. UCLA's Higher Education Research Institute has been surveying entering college students every few years since 1966 (Dey & Hurtado, 1999). Business has consistently been among the top preferred majors, but the proportion of entering students preferring business fluctuated from 14% in 1966 to 27% in 1987 to 16% in 1993. Education and engineering have also ranked consistently among the top preferred majors, at about 10% each. The major area that has increased most in preference over the past three decades is health professions, which rose from 5% in 1966 to 16%—tied for first with business—in 1993. Declining major areas over this period were mainly in the liberal arts—English, history, fine arts, and humanities.

There are distinct gender differences in the major preferences stated by college students, and the extent of some of these gender differences has changed substantially over recent decades (Dey & Hurtado, 1999). Females are about three times as likely as males to major in education and about two and a half times as likely to major in the social sciences. Males and females are about equally represented in biological sciences, business, premed, and prelaw; in all of these areas, female representation has increased since 1972. Females are only about half as likely as males to major

The proportion of women in fields such as medicine and law has increased dramatically since 1970.

in the physical sciences, but in 1972 they were only one-fourth as likely.

Gender differences have also narrowed in attainment of postgraduate degrees (Bianchi & Spain, 1996). Women earn 34% of dentistry degrees, up from just 1% in 1970. They also earn one-third of medical doctor degrees (8% in 1970), one-third of master of business administration (MBA) degrees (4% in 1970), and 42% of law degrees (5% in 1970). Across fields, women earn over 40% of postgraduate degrees, up dramatically from just 10% in 1960.

For most young people, it takes longer now to obtain a 4-year undergraduate degree than it did two or three decades ago. Currently, it takes an average of 6 years for students to obtain a "4-year" degree. A number of factors explain why it now takes students longer to graduate (Dey & Hurtado, 1999). Financial concerns are at the top of the list. During the 1980s and early 1990s, tuition costs at most institutions rose at a steep rate, in part because of declining support from federal and state governments. Financial aid also shifted markedly from grants to loans, which has led many students to work many hours while attending college in order to avoid accruing excessive debt before they graduate (Dey & Hurtado, 1999). Also, some students prefer to extend their college years to switch majors, add a minor field of study, or take advantage of internship programs or study abroad programs.

Educational Success in College

Although college students take an average of 6 years now to graduate with a 4-year degree, even at 6 years or more graduation is by no means inevitable. In fact, about one-half of college students drop out before obtaining a degree (National Center for Education Statistics, 1999). For years, researchers have been studying different factors that contribute to individual decisions to stay in or leave higher education—**retention** is the term used for maintaining students in college until they graduate. Some factors related to retention are students' previous academic performance, ethnic background, and family SES. A variety of studies have found that retention is higher among students of higher academic ability and better precollege academic performance (Arnold, Mares, & Calkins, 1986; Moline, 1987; Nora, 1987; Tinto, 1993). Retention is higher among White students than among African American or Latino students, in part because minority students often come from high schools where they received poor academic preparation for college (Arnold et al., 1986; Tinto, 1993). Additionally, retention is positively related to students' family SES (Tinto, 1993; National Center for Education Statistics, 1998)—the higher students' family SES, the more likely they are to stay in college until they graduate.

THINKING CRITICALLY

Do you think that by the end of the 21st century nearly all emerging adults will attend college, just as high school education became nearly universal for adolescents in the 20th century? Why or why not?

Financial aid is another important factor in students' persistence in higher education (Moline, 1987). Lack of adequate financial support often causes students' premature departure (Arnold et al., 1986; Dey & Hurtado, 1999). Students who receive financial aid are more likely to get a bachelor's degree than students who do not get any aid, regardless of the type of the aid (loan or grant) (National Center for Education Statistics, 1998). Finally, personal concerns may also contribute to students' decisions to leave a university or college before graduating. Some of these personal concerns include marriage, family responsibilities, health problems, and accepting a new job (Arnold et al., 1986; Tinto, 1993).

Students' College Learning Experiences

Most college students believe that the education they receive at college is of high quality. In surveys, about 90% of students have indicated that they are satisfied with the quality of the teaching they receive (Dey & Hurtado, 1999). Overall satisfaction with their college education increased from about 75% of students in the late 1960s to nearly 90% by the early 1990s.

What kind of educational experiences do students have in college, and how do they evaluate their experiences? In one of the most intensive studies on this topic, Marcia Baxter Magolda (1997) interviewed a randomly selected group of nearly 100 students during each of their first 4 years at a large university. Each year she asked them a variety of questions about their educational experiences, such as "What observations do you have about instructors who you think are effective?" and "Tell me about the interactions you have with other students that help you learn."

In general, students rated large lecture classes as the least effective way to learn. Students often found lectures impersonal and boring. They preferred smaller classes where they had the opportunity to engage in discussions with the professor and their peers, and came to know their professor and peers personally. In general, students had smaller classes in their junior and senior years than in their freshman and sophomore years.

Students reported a variety of both positive and negative experiences with their professors. They had encountered some professors who were arrogant and intimidating. Some professors were perceived as not involved in their teaching and not receptive to students' questions and concerns; for example, some students reported being hurried out of office-hour conferences with professors. However, for the most part professors were viewed positively. Students appreciated professors who treated students courteously as learners, who clearly wanted them to learn, and who seemed to enjoy teaching. Especially in their junior and senior years, students reported many helpful interactions in and out of the classroom. Professors helped students with their course work, with internship applications, and with job searches; some professors even invited classes into their homes. Students found these positive interactions with professors inspiring and spoke of how the interactions increased their interest in learning as well as their ability to learn.

Students had strong opinions on the methods professors used to evaluate them. A common complaint was that much evaluation was ineffective because it did not truly reflect what they had learned. Students generally believed that tests should be on material covered in class, and they emphasized the importance of fairness in the test items. Tests on which the majority of students did poorly were regarded as unfair. Students expressed a strong desire for tests that would accurately reflect their ability to understand, think about, and apply the knowledge they had learned in class.

Of course, this is only one study, which took place at one university, and colleges and universities certainly vary a lot in the experiences they provide for students. How does your college experience compare with the experiences described above?

Summing Up

In this chapter we have discussed a variety of topics related to adolescents' and emerging adults' school experiences and performance. Here is a summary of the main points:

- Over the past century, the secondary school curriculum in the United States has changed from a focus on liberal arts, to a curriculum intended to prepare students for work and citizenship, to a curriculum that includes a wide range of courses from math and English to music and physical education. These changes have taken place partly in response to the changing characteristics of the young people attending high school, and partly in response to changes in cultural beliefs about what adolescents need to learn.

- Over recent decades, an increasing proportion of American young people have graduated from high school and attended college. However, current performance on most measures of academic competence is disturbingly poor. In international comparisons, the academic performance of American high school students tends to be poorer than the performance of students in most other industrialized countries.

- School climate, which is the quality of the classroom interactions between teachers and students, affects students' academic performance and their participation in delinquency. The same qualities of warmth and moderate control that are effective in parenting are also effective in schools.

- Adolescents' school performance is influenced not only by factors within the school but also by many influences beyond the classroom, including family, friends, work and leisure, and cultural beliefs.

- Ethnic differences in adolescents' academic performance are explained in part by social class differences and in part by different influences from family and friends. Some scholars have asserted that African Americans perceive striving for academic achievement as "acting White," but thus far the evidence on this issue is mixed.

- Although girls perform better than boys on many measures of academic performance, they are less likely than boys to pursue the math and science training necessary for many high-paying, high-status occupations. However, in recent years girls have become increasingly likely to pursue math and science.

- Tracking is a controversial practice in the United States, with advocates arguing that it results in a better fit between students' abilities and interests and their curriculum, whereas critics argue that it relegates students in lower tracks to a second-rate education in which they fall steadily further behind other students.

- Dropping out of high school is predicted by a variety of factors, including previous problems in school, personality characteristics, and family difficulties. Successful programs to prevent dropping out have focused on providing alternative schools or on promising adolescents long-term financial help for their education if they perform well in school.

- College students who obtain a bachelor's degree now take an average of 6 years to do so, but many students drop out of college before obtaining a degree. Factors related to dropping out of college include previous academic performance, ethnic background, and socioeconomic status.

The practice of having adolescents spend many hours each day in school is fairly recent historically and has developed in response to economic changes that require young people to have academic skills to fulfill the requirements of jobs in an increasingly information-based economy. As the material in this chapter shows, to some extent industrialized societies are still struggling with how best to teach their young people. European societies allow young people to begin specialized education by the time they are just 14 or 15 years old. This may make young people more engaged in their education, because they will be studying topics in areas they have chosen themselves, but such a system makes it difficult for them to change directions in their later teens or their early twenties. In the United States, no such early decision is required, and young people often postpone a decision about occupational choice until after a year or two of college or even until deciding on graduate school. Such a system allows for a substantial amount of individual choice, but during adolescence it means that all students are together in the same schools despite their widely varying abilities and interests, and this system seems inadequate and unstimulating to many of them. Perhaps the European and American systems involve different but inevitable trade-offs, or perhaps both systems will eventually be seen as early experiments on the way to other educational forms that will prove to be more effective.

For adolescents in economically developing countries, secondary school and higher education are currently restricted mainly to the elite, just as they were in industrialized countries a century ago. The proportion of young people in secondary school and beyond in developing countries is growing and is likely to continue to grow as a consequence of globalization and the requirements of the global economy (Arnett, 2000a; Mensch et al., 1998). Currently, however, the focus of daily activity for adolescents in developing countries is not school but work. In the next chapter we will explore in depth the nature of their work experiences and discuss the work experiences of young people in industrialized countries as well.

Key Terms

secondary school	engagement	gifted students	mainstreaming/inclusion
comprehensive high school	pilot testing	Advanced Placement (AP) classes	retention
school climate	subordinate/castelike minority	Public Law 94-142	

For Further Reading

Steinberg, L. (in collaboration with B. Brown & S. M. Dornbusch) (1996). *Beyond the classroom: Why school reform has failed and what parents need to do.* New York: Simon & Schuster. A detailed description of the authors' excellent study of adolescents' school experiences.

Applying Research

Dryfoos, J. G. (1998). *Full-service schools: A revolution in health and social services for children, youth, and families.* San Francisco: Jossey-Bass. Joy Dryfoos, a leading expert on interventions for adolescents, proposes in this book that schools extend their mission far beyond education to include services in areas such as drug abuse prevention, contraceptive and pregnancy services, and violence prevention. According to Dryfoos, providing such services through the school would enhance adolescents' educational performance and would make dropping out less common. Two "full-service" schools are described in detail.

"Love and work" was Sigmund Freud's terse response when he was asked what a person should be able to do well in order to be considered psychologically healthy. Work is, in all cultures and in all historical times, one of the fundamental areas of human activity. Earlier, we discussed preparation for adult roles as one of the three principal goals of socialization, and adult roles in all cultures include work of one kind or another. All cultures expect their members to contribute some kind of work, whether it be paid employment; cooperative hunting, fishing, or farming; or taking care of children and running a household. Adolescence is often a key time in preparation for adult work roles. Whatever work young people may have contributed as children, adolescence is the time when work expectations grow more serious, as adolescents prepare to take their place as full members—which always means working members—of their culture.

In this chapter, we begin by discussing adolescent work in traditional cultures. This is a good place to begin, because work has a special prominence for adolescents in traditional cultures. Unlike adolescents in industrialized societies, most adolescents in traditional cultures are no longer in school, and most of their day is devoted to work. As noted in earlier chapters, in traditional cultures adolescents typically work alongside adults, doing the kind of work that adults do. Thus we begin this chapter by taking a look at the types of work that occupy adolescents and adults in most traditional cultures: hunting, fishing, and gathering; farming; and child care.

Adolescents in traditional cultures are now in a position, with regard to work, that is similar to what was experienced by adolescents in industrialized societies a century ago. Both cases involve an economy rapidly becoming industrialized. In both cases, prolonged schooling was rarely available or useful to adolescents, given the jobs available in their economy. In both cases, industrialization left adolescents vulnerable to exploitation in unhealthy and unsafe working conditions. In the second part of the chapter, we examine these issues in the history of adolescent work in industrialized societies.

Following this, we will take a look at various issues related to adolescent work as it currently takes place in industrialized societies. This will include a look at what adolescents typically do in their jobs, and how work influences various aspects of their development. We will also look at the transition from school to work, both for emerging adults who attend college and for those who do not. This will include an examination of the influences on the occupational choices that young people make. At the end of the chapter we will examine the characteristics and experiences of young people who perform volunteer work.

Adolescent Work in Traditional Cultures

For many millenia of human history prior to industrialization, most human work involved the same basic activities: hunting, fishing, and gathering edible fruits and vegetables; farming and caring for domestic animals; and caring for children while doing household work. These kinds of work are still common in many traditional cultures, and we will first look at adolescents' participation in such work. However, virtually all traditional cultures are in the process of industrializing, so it will be important to look also at adolescents' experiences in industrial settings in traditional cultures.

Hunting, Fishing, and Gathering

Hunting and fishing in traditional cultures are typically undertaken by men, and adolescent boys learn how it is done by accompanying their fathers and

Adolescent boys in traditional cultures learn the work of adult men. Here, a boy in the Abouri tribe of West Africa learns to carve a dugout canoe.

other men on hunting or fishing expeditions. Females are rarely the principal hunters, but they sometimes assist in the hunting enterprise by holding nets, setting traps, or beating the bushes to flush out game (Gilmore, 1990).

Hunting often provides not only food but also materials for tools, clothing, and other purposes (Gilmore, 1990). As such, it serves many important functions in cultures that rely on it, and success at hunting may be required of adolescent boys as a way of showing that they are ready for manhood. For example, among the nomadic Bushmen of the Kalahari desert in southwest Africa, an adolescent boy is not considered a man—and is not allowed to marry—until he has successfully killed his first antelope. Doing so is a way of demonstrating that he will be able to provide for a family as part of his adult work role.

Fishing is another form of work that is learned by adolescent boys through observing and assisting their fathers and other men. The skills required for success at fishing include not only fishing itself but boating and navigation. For example, adolescents in the South Sea islands in the Pacific Ocean learn complex systems of night-time navigation from their fathers, using a "star compass" through which they set their course according to the position of the constellations (Gladwin, 1970; Hutchins, 1983).

Often in cultures where males have the responsibility for hunting or fishing, women have a complementary responsibility for gathering. This means that they find edible wild fruits and vegetables growing in the surrounding area and collect them to contribute to their families' food supply. This can be a substantial contribution—anthropologists have observed that in cultures that rely on a combination of hunting and gathering, women contribute as much or more to the family food supply through gathering than men do through hunting (Dahlberg, 1981).

Hunting and gathering cultures have rapidly changed in the past half century in response to globalization, and only a few such cultures exist in the present (Schlegel & Barry, 1991). The nomadic way of life typical of hunting and gathering cultures—moving from place to place, following the food supply—is not well-suited to the global economy, with its stable communities and its property boundaries. Fishing, too, has largely disappeared as a central basis for a culture's economy. Even in cultures that have a long tradition of fishing, such as in Norway and Japan, modern fishing techniques are so advanced that a very small proportion of people engaged in fishing can provide more than enough fish to feed the entire population.

Farming and Care of Domestic Animals

Farming and care of domestic animals often go together in the same way that hunting and gathering tend to go together—one for providing meat, the other for providing grains, vegetables, and fruit. Adolescents in cultures with economies based on farming and care of domestic animals often provide useful work to their families. Perhaps because such work requires little in the way of skill or experience, care of domestic animals is a frequent responsibility of adolescents or even of preadolescents all over the world (Schlegel & Barry, 1991)—cattle in southern Africa, sheep and goats in northern Africa and southern Europe, small livestock in Asia and Eastern Europe. Farming often requires a higher level of training and skill, particularly if the amount of land to be farmed is large. This enterprise is typically carried out by fathers and sons (and any other adult men in the family) working together, with the sons not only contributing to their families in the present but also learning how to manage the land they will eventually inherit (Schlegel & Barry, 1991).

Even today, farming remains the main occupation of a substantial proportion of the world's population. In developing countries such as Brazil, India, and the Philippines, over half of the adult males are employed in agricultural work (Treiman & Yip, 1989). However, in all developing countries, the proportion of people in farming is declining in the course of industrialization.

Child Care and Household Work

When it comes to child care, women and girls have the main responsibility in most traditional cultures, with men and boys occasionally providing support. The work of child care usually begins quite early in life for girls. If they have younger siblings, girls often become at least partly responsible for taking care of them as early as age 6 or 7 (Whiting & Edwards, 1988). By the time she reaches adolescence, the oldest girl in a family may have several younger siblings to help care for, and perhaps cousins as well.

Along with child care, working alongside her mother often means household work as well for an adolescent girl living in a traditional culture. A great deal of household work needs to be done in a traditional culture that has no access to electricity and the many conveniences that go along with it. Chores such as collecting firewood, starting and tending the fire, and fetching water must be done on a daily basis. Preparing food is also heavily labor intensive in such

Adolescent girls in traditional cultures typically have responsibility for household work such as food preparation. Here, a girl of the Sahelia culture of northern Africa prepares a meal.

cultures. Want a chicken for dinner? You have to do more than defrost it and zap it in the microwave oven (or stop by the drive-through window at Chuck-Full-O-Chicks)—you have to kill it, trim it, and pluck it before you can think about cooking it.

With so much work to be done, women in these cultures often enlist the help of their daughters from an early age, and by adolescence, daughters are typically working alongside their mothers and other women of the family as partners (e.g., Chinas, 1991). By doing this kind of work, the adolescent daughter prepares herself for her adult work role and also demonstrates to others, including potential marriage partners, that she is capable of fulfilling the expectations for running a household that are typically required of women in traditional cultures (e.g., Davis & Davis, 1989).

Globalization and Adolescent Work in Traditional Cultures

Adolescents and adults in traditional cultures have been doing the kinds of work described above for many hundreds and even thousands of years. However, as we have seen, all traditional cultures today are being influenced by globalization. An important aspect of globalization is economic integration, including increasing trade between countries and increasingly large-scale agriculture and manufacturing in many cultures and countries that have known only small, local, family-based economic activity until very recently. Globalization has certainly conferred some benefits to economic life for the people in these cultures. Preindustrial economic life can be hard. Simply providing the everyday necessities of life is a lot of work without industrialization, as the chicken example above illustrates. Entry into the global economy is usually accompanied by increased access to electricity, which often makes food preparation, clothes washing, heating, and other tasks considerably easier. Entry into the global economy is also usually accompanied by increased access to education and medical care.

The globalization of economic life thus holds the promise of eventually making life better for the many cultures around the world that are just now being introduced to it. However, the transition from a preindustrial economy to the global economy is proving to be problematic in many places. Currently, what is resulting for many people is not increased comfort but brutal work in terrible conditions for miserable pay. And the burden of much of this work is falling on the shoulders of adolescents, mainly those between 10 and 15 years old, who are more capable than children of doing useful industrial work and less capable than adults of asserting their rights and resisting maltreatment.

The **International Labor Organization (ILO)** has estimated that as many as *200 million* children and (mostly) adolescents are employed worldwide, and that 95% of them are in developing/industrializing countries (U.S. Department of Labor, 1994). They are numerous in Latin America and Africa, but the greatest number of adolescent workers and the worst working conditions are found in Asia (including countries such as India, Bangladesh, Thailand, Indonesia, Philippines, and Vietnam). Agricultural work is the most common form of employment for adolescents, usually on commercial farms or plantations, often working alongside their parents but for only one-third to one-half the pay (U.S. Department of Labor, 1995).

In addition, many adolescents in these countries work in factories and workshops where they perform labor such as weaving carpets, sewing clothes, gluing shoes, curing leather, and polishing gems. The working conditions are often almost unbelievably horrible—crowded garment factories where the doors are locked and the adolescents (and adults) work 14-hour shifts, small poorly lit huts where they sit at a loom weaving carpets for hours on end, glass factories where the temperatures are unbearably hot and adolescents carry hot rods of molten glass from one station to another (U.S. Department of Labor, 1994). Other adolescents work in cities in a wide variety of jobs including domestic service, grocery shops, tea stalls, road construction, and prostitution.

In India, a common and particularly brutal system for exploiting adolescent labor is called **debt bondage**. Debt bondage begins when a person needs a loan and has no money to offer for security, so he instead pledges his labor or that of his children. Because literacy is rare among the poor of India, who are most often the ones who are desperate enough to accept this kind of loan, they are easily exploited by lenders who manipulate the interest and the payments in such a way that the loan becomes virtually impossible to pay back. In desperation, parents sometimes offer the labor of their children in an effort to pay off the debt.

Adolescents are especially valuable for this purpose because they are more productive than children. According to the ILO, the areas that adolescents (and others) most often end up in as bonded laborers are agriculture, domestic service, prostitution, and industries such as the manufacture of hand-knitted carpets. Once adolescents have been committed by their parents to debt bondage, it is extremely difficult for them to free themselves of it, and in fact debt bondage has been condemned as a modern form of slavery by the United Nations (U.S. Department of Labor, 1994).

Perhaps the worst form of exploitation of adolescents' work is prostitution. Estimates of the number of adolescent prostitutes in developing countries vary, but it is widely agreed that adolescent prostitution is a pervasive and growing problem, especially in Asia, and within Asia especially in Thailand (U.S. Department of Labor, 1995). Of course, adolescent prostitutes exist in industrialized countries as well, but the problem is much more pervasive in developing countries.

Adolescent girls in these countries become prostitutes in several ways. Some are kidnapped and taken to a separate country. Isolated in a country where they are not citizens and where they do not know the language, they are highly vulnerable and dependent on their kidnappers. Some are rural adolescent girls who are promised jobs in restaurants or domestic service, then forced to become prostitutes once the recruiter takes them to their urban destination. Sometimes parents sell the girls into prostitution, out of desperate poverty or simply out of the desire for more consumer goods (U.S. Department of Labor, 1995). A large proportion of the customers in Asian brothels are Western tourists; the proportion is large enough that the

United States and several European countries now have laws permitting prosecution of their citizens for sexually exploiting young adolescent girls in other countries. The demand is increasingly for younger adolescent girls, because of the perception that they are less likely than older girls to be carrying the HIV virus. And indeed, studies have found that from 30% to 70% of the girls in Thai brothels are HIV positive (U.S. Department of Labor, 1995).

As horrifying and brutal as the current situation is regarding exploitation of adolescents in developing countries, signs of positive changes can be seen. In recent years the issue of child and adolescent labor has received increased attention from the world media, governments, and international organizations such as the ILO and the United Nations Children's Fund (UNICEF). This attention has resulted in legislative action in several countries to raise the number of years children and adolescents are legally required to attend school and to enforce the often-ignored laws in many countries against employing children younger than their midteens (U.S. Department of Labor, 1995). For example, India now has a program, monitored by UNICEF, to mark carpets that have not involved child labor with a RUGMARK label—a logo of a smiling child superimposed on a drawing of a carpet. In another example, in 1995 in Bangladesh an agreement was reached among industry, the government, and international organizations (including UNICEF) to launch a comprehensive effort to phase children and adolescents out of the garment factories and into schools. International organizations will facilitate and monitor young people's entry into schools, and adult relatives will be given first preference to fill the jobs left by the children and adolescents, so that families will not be hurt economically from the young people attending school rather than working.

These are signs of progress, but it remains true that millions of adolescents work in miserable conditions all around the world. As a UNICEF representative stated

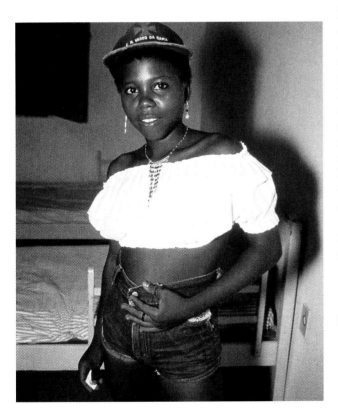

Many adolescent girls in developing countries have been forced into prostitution. Here, a young prostitute at a rehabilitation center in Brazil.

THINKING CRITICALLY

Do you think people living in the West have any responsibility for the conditions of adolescent work in developing countries? Why or why not? Do they have more responsibility if they buy the items that such adolescents produce through their labor?

recently, "we are now seeing growing commitment and increased action toward the goal of eliminating exploitative child labor—although there is no question that progress remains uneven and we obviously have a very long way to go" (U.S. Department of Labor, 1995, p. 7).

The History of Adolescent Work in the West

As noted at the outset of the chapter, adolescents' work in the West has followed a historical path similar to the one now being experienced by adolescents in traditional cultures: involvement in farming and family economic activities became exploitation in the factories and other early settings of industrialization. In response to this exploitation, adolescent work became restricted by governments in industrialized countries early in the 20th century. By midcentury most adolescents attended high school, and few high school students held part-time jobs. Since 1950, adolescents have increasingly combined school with part-time work, especially in the United States.

Adolescent Work Before 1900

Before industrialization began in the 17th and 18th centuries, adolescent work in the West was much like adolescent work is now in traditional cultures whose economies center on farming and care of domestic animals. Boys helped their fathers on the farm from middle childhood onward, and in adolescence they gradually learned to take over the responsibilities for running the farm they would eventually inherit. Girls helped with the care of the domestic animals and worked alongside their mothers in turning the harvests and the animals into meals on the table, with adolescent girls becoming near-equal partners to their mothers in running the household.

As noted in Chapter 1, in Europe from about 1500 to 1700, it was common for young people to leave their homes to take part in life-cycle service (Ben-Amos, 1994) during their late teens and twenties. This involved moving out of their parents' household and into the household of a "master" for a period lasting typically 7 years, during which they would engage in domestic service (maid or nanny), farm service, or apprenticeship in various trades and crafts. Young women were less likely than young men to leave home for a period of life-cycle service, but even among females many left home before marriage, most often to take part in domestic service (Ben-Amos, 1994). Life-cycle service was also common

among young people in the early European settlements in the United States (Kett, 1977), but in colonial New England the service was typically in the home of a relative or family friend rather than in the home of a previously unknown master.

As industrialization proceeded in the 18th and 19th centuries, it became increasingly common for adolescents to work in factories. Over the course of the 19th century, the proportion of the labor force working in farming in the United States declined from over 70% to under 40% (Hernandez, 1997). For many adolescents, this meant a transition from working alongside their parents on a family farm to working in a city, often in a factory setting. Industrialization created a huge demand for cheap labor, and adolescents were often recruited to fill this demand. By the 1870s, young men aged 16 to 20 comprised nearly half the male workforce in New England textile mills and about one-third of the workers in rubber factories and agricultural tool factories. In boot and shoe factories, over 40% of the female workers were aged 16 to 20 (Kett, 1977). Adolescents also worked in large numbers in coal mines, food canneries, and seafood processing plants (Freedman, 1994).

Working in factories, mines, and processing plants often meant working long hours under dangerous and unhealthy conditions. A typical work schedule was 10 to 14 hours a day, 6 days a week. Of course, adults were subject to the same conditions, but children and adolescents were more vulnerable to accident and injury. It is estimated that the accident rate for children and adolescents in factories was twice as high as for adults (Freedman, 1994). Their developing bodies also made them more vulnerable than adults to illness from unhealthy working conditions. For example, young millworkers often developed tuberculosis,

> "A TWELVE-YEAR-OLD BOY FELL INTO A SPINNING MACHINE AND THE UNPROTECTED GEARING TORE OUT TWO OF HIS FINGERS. 'WE DON'T HAVE ANY ACCIDENTS IN THIS MILL,' THE OVERSEER TOLD ME. 'ONCE IN A WHILE A FINGER IS MASHED OR A FOOT, BUT IT DON'T AMOUNT TO ANYTHING.'"
> —LEWIS HINE, PHOTOGRAPHER OF CHILD AND ADOLESCENT WORKERS, 1908 (IN FREEDMAN, 1994, P. 35)

bronchitis, and other respiratory diseases. Children and adolescents who worked in cotton mills were only half as likely to live past age 20 as those outside the mills.

HISTORICAL FOCUS
Work Among British Adolescents in the 19th Century

As we have seen in this chapter, the working conditions currently experienced by adolescents in developing countries are in many ways dangerous, unhealthy, underpaid, and exploitative. Adolescents in industrialized countries generally work in conditions that are much more favorable, but this is a relatively recent development. In fact, the working conditions of adolescents in the 19th century in industrialized countries were remarkably similar to the conditions experienced today by adolescents in developing countries.

Information on child and adolescent labor in the 19th century is especially abundant in Great Britain, where government statistics were kept much more

In the 19th century, adolescents often worked in dangerous and unhealthy conditions.

systematically and accurately than in the United States. The history of child and adolescent labor in Great Britain is described in a book by Pamela Horn (1994), *Children's Work and Welfare, 1780–1890*.

Because Britain was the first country in which industrialization took place, it was also the first country in which child and adolescent labor was widely used. Textiles was the first area, beginning in the 1770s when for the first time textiles were mass produced in factories rather than made one at a time in homes. Children and adolescents were especially attractive to employers, partly because there was a shortage of adult workers and partly because younger workers could be paid lower wages, and with their nimble fingers they could perform much of the work even better than adults.

Many of these children and adolescents had no parents and were sent to the mills by officials in city orphanages and institutions for the poor, who were glad to be relieved of the cost of caring for them. Young people had no choice but to go and were not free to leave until they reached age 21. For those who did have parents, their parents usually did not object to their children working in textile mills, but encouraged it in order to increase the family's income.

Working conditions varied in the mills, but 12- to 14-hour workdays were common, with an hour break for lunch. The work was monotonous, exhausting, and dangerous. A momentary lapse of attention could lead to serious injury, and crushed hands and fingers were common. Dust and residue from the spinning process damaged their lungs and caused stomach illnesses and eye infections.

The first attempts at government regulation of the mills were tentative, to say the least. Because the British economy depended so heavily on the young millworkers, even reformers were reluctant to advocate an end to their labor. There was also little public support for abolishing child and adolescent labor, and labor restrictions were fiercely resisted by parents who depended on their income. Thus the first law, the Health and Morals of Apprentices Act of 1802, simply limited young workers to 12 hours of labor a day! The act also mandated minimum standards of ventilation and sanitation in the mills, but these provisions were widely ignored by mill owners.

In addition, the act required employers to provide daily schooling to young workers. Employers generally complied with this, because they believed that educated children would be more compliant and more valuable as workers, so the result was a significant increase in literacy among young workers. This requirement spread to other industries over the following decades and became the basis of the *half-time system* in which young workers in factories received schooling for a half day and worked for a half day. This system survived in British society until the end of the 19th century.

In the 1830s, regulatory attention turned to mining. Just as changes in textile production had created a boom in jobs in the late 1700s, an increase in the need for coal in the early 1800s created a mining boom. Once again, children and adolescents were sought as workers because they were cheap, manageable, and could do some jobs better than adults. Once again, parents urged their children to become laborers as early as possible to contribute to

the family income, even though the work in the mines was especially hazardous.

A workday of 12 to 14 hours per day 6 days a week was common for young miners. Many of them descended into the mine before sunrise and came up again after sunset, so that they never saw daylight for weeks at a time except on Sunday. Accidents were common, and coal dust damaged young miners' lungs. The first reforms, in the 1842 Mines Act, prohibited boys under 10 from working in mines and required boys over age 10 to be provided with schooling by the mine owners, but did nothing about the working conditions in the mines. As this law and others restricted the employment of children, adolescents became even more in demand and employment among adolescents became even more widespread.

Over the second half of the 19th century, legal regulations on child and adolescent labor slowly and gradually reduced the exploitation of young workers in British industrial settings. Regulations increased concerning the work young workers could be required to do. The half-time system, once celebrated as a way of protecting young workers from exploitation, became viewed as an obstacle to their educational opportunities. Public schools were established, and attendance at school became legally required for all children in the 1880s.

Adolescent Work in the 20th Century

As we have seen in Chapter 1, this pattern of adolescents being typically engaged in full-time work changed during the Age of Adolescence, 1890 to 1920. Concern developed over the exploitation of children and adolescents by employers—a striking parallel to what is going on currently in developing countries—and laws were passed that restricted the times and places children and adolescents could work and that required children to attend school. Nevertheless, the changes in patterns of child and adolescent labor took place slowly. Even as recently as 1925 the majority of adolescents had left school by age 15 to become full-time workers (Horan & Hargis, 1991; Modell, Furstenberg, & Hershberg, 1976). Most families viewed the labor of their adolescents as an important contributor to the family income, and only relatively affluent families could afford the luxury of keeping their adolescents in school past their early teens.

However, the trend toward increasing time in school that had begun early in the century continued steadily,

and in the 1930s the proportion of adolescents staying in school through their midteens continued to grow. Furthermore, increasingly adolescents were either in school or working, but not both. By 1940, fewer than 5% of the 16- to 17-year-olds attending high school were also employed (U.S. Department of Commerce, 1940). American adolescents lived in two separate worlds, with 70% of 14- to 17-year-olds in high school and most of the other 30% in the labor force.

THINKING CRITICALLY

Compare the history of adolescent work in the West to the recent history of adolescent work in developing countries. What are the similarities and differences?

This pattern changed dramatically in the decades following World War II, toward combining school with part-time work. One reason for this was that the American

By 1980, part-time work had become typical for American high school students.

economy changed. From 1950 through the 1970s, the fastest growing sectors of the American economy were retail trade and service (Ginzberg, 1977). Jobs were numerous for young people who were willing to work part-time for relatively low wages in jobs such as salesperson in a clothing store, cook at a fast-food joint, waitress, or clerk in a department store.

And American adolescents proved to be willing. By 1980, one-half of high school sophomores and two-thirds of high school seniors were working in part-time jobs (Lewin-Epstein, 1981), and by the late 1990s over 80% of seniors had held at least one part-time job by the time they left high school (Barling & Kelloway, 1999). In just 40 years, from 1940 to 1980, part-time employment for American adolescents in high school changed from the rare exception to the typical pattern.

The current rate of adolescent employment in the United States is much higher than in any other industrialized country. In Japan, adolescent employment is almost nonexistent. In Western Europe, if adolescents work it is typically as part of an apprenticeship program connected to their schooling (Hamilton, 1990, 1994), and it is uncommon for adolescents to be engaged in other types of part-time work. In Canada, the proportion of adolescents who work (42%) is higher than in Japan or Western Europe, but still substantially lower than in the United States (Posterki & Bibby, 1988). In many of these countries, adolescents have a longer school day and have more homework on a typical evening, leaving less time for part-time jobs (Steinberg, 1996). American adolescents are not only willing to work but also able because of the relatively low demands on them made by their schools. In turn, pervasive employment among adolescents makes it diffi-

cult for high schools to require more, because many adolescents have little time or energy left over for homework after school and work (Steinberg, 1996).

The Adolescent Workplace: "Like Some Fries With That?"

We have seen what kind of work adolescents do in traditional cultures, and what kinds of work they did in Western countries prior to the 20th century. What kinds of jobs are held by contemporary American adolescents?

You won't find many American adolescents these days whose work involves hunting, fishing, farming, or factory work. Interestingly enough, however, American girls in early adolescence have something in common with girls in traditional cultures in that their first kind of work involves child care. Babysitting is the most common kind of work done by eighth-grade American girls (Schneider & Shouse, 1991). For boys, the most common kind of work in eighth grade is yard work—mowing lawns, trimming bushes, and so on. But the work done at this age in these kinds of jobs is more or less informal (Greenberger & Steinberg, 1986) and does not require a substantial commitment of time. As an eighth-grade girl maybe you babysit for Mr. and Mrs. Jones Saturday night every couple of weeks, and for Mr. and Mrs. Peabody on the occasional afternoon until they get home from work. As an eighth-grade boy maybe you mow a couple of neighbors' lawns once a week from early spring to late fall. Typically, these jobs are unlikely to interfere much with the rest of an adolescent's life.

For older adolescents, the work is different, and the amount of time involved tends to be greater. The majority of jobs held by American adolescents in high school involve restaurant work (waitress, cook, busboy/girl, hostess, etc.) or retail sales (Loughlin & Barling, 1999; Steinberg, Fegley, & Dornbusch, 1993). These jobs involve a more formal commitment. You are assigned a certain number of hours a week, and you are expected to be there at the times you are assigned. Typically this does not mean simply a few hours one week and a few the next. On average, employed high school sophomores work 15 hours per week, and employed high school seniors work 20 hours per week (Steinberg & Cauffman, 1995).

That is a substantial amount of time. What are adolescents typically doing during that time? One important source of information on this topic comes from a study by Ellen Greenberger and Laurence Steinberg (1986), who studied over 200 adolescent 10th and 11th graders in Orange County, California. Rather than relying only on adolescents' reports of what goes in the places they work, the research team observed adolescents directly in their work settings, recording the behavior of the adolescents, the things the adolescents said, and the people with whom the adolescents interacted. The researchers also interviewed the adolescents and had them fill out questionnaires about their work experiences.

The kinds of work performed by the adolescents fell into five general categories: restaurant work, retail, clerical (e.g., secretarial work), manual labor (e.g., working for a moving company), and skilled labor (e.g., carpenter's apprentice). With the exception of the jobs involving skilled labor, the work performed by the adolescents tended to be repetitive and monotonous, involving little that would challenge them or help them develop new skills. Twenty-five percent of their time on the job was spent cleaning or carrying things, not exactly work that entails much of a cognitive challenge. Furthermore, the work was almost never connected to anything the adolescents were learning or had previously learned in school. Again, if you think about the work—flipping burgers, taking food orders, answering the phone, helping people find their size in clothes—this is hardly surprising.

With respect to the people they interacted with at work, adolescents spent about an equal proportion of their time interacting with other adolescents and interacting with adults. However, their relationships with adult bosses and coworkers were rarely close. For the most part they did not see these adults except at work, they were reluctant to speak to them about personal issues, and they felt less close to them than they felt to the other people in their lives, such as parents and friends.

You can see how different the work experience of American adolescents is, compared with adolescents in traditional cultures (prior to industrialization) or adolescents in European countries who work in apprenticeships. Unlike these other adolescents, American adolescents rarely do work that involves close partnership with an adult who teaches them and provides a model. Unlike these other adolescents, the work done by American adolescents does little to prepare them for the kind of work they are likely to be doing as adults. You might expect that, given the dreary work they do and lack of connection between this work and their futures, for the most part the work done by American adolescents does little to promote their development in favorable ways.

There is some evidence that this is true, as we will see in the next section. We discussed in the previous chapter the relationship between part-time work and school performance. Now let's look at the relationships between work and two other aspects of development: psychological functioning and problem behavior.

Work and Adolescent Development

Three large-scale studies published in the past decade provide important insights into the relationship between work and adolescent development. One is the Monitoring the Future (MTF) study we have discussed in earlier chapters. A second study, by Jeylan Mortimer and her colleagues (Mortimer, Harley, & Aronson, 1999; Mortimer et al., 1992), focused on a sample of 1,000 ninth-grade adolescents in St. Paul, Minnesota, and followed them longitudinally for the next 13 years. The third study, by Steinberg and Dornbusch (1991) and their colleagues, included 4,000 adolescents in grades 10 and 12 in two states. All of these were questionnaire studies, which is usually the method used with large-scale studies. Together, they tell us a great deal about how work is related to a wide variety of aspects of adolescent development.

Work and Psychological Functioning

"I need to work because I need the money for car insurance and the prom. I like being involved in everything, but sometimes I feel really overloaded with my job and schoolwork and baseball and committees, and I need to take time to just chill out."

—Brian, a 17-year-old high school senior working 20 to 40 hours per week as a busboy for a catering company (in Salzman, 1993)

Both for psychological functioning and for problem behavior, the amount of time worked per week is an important variable. Most studies find that up to 10 hours a week, working at a part-time job has little effect on adolescents' development. However, beyond 10 hours a week problems arise, and beyond 20 hours a week the problems become considerably worse (Frone, 1999).

Steinberg and Dornbusch (1991) found that working up to 10 hours a week was not related to an index of psychological symptoms such as anxiety and depression.

However, reports of psychological symptoms jumped sharply for adolescents working more than 10 hours a week and continued to rise among adolescents working 20 hours a week or more (see Figure 10.4 on p. 318).

Up to 10 hours a week, working has little effect on the amount of sleep adolescents get. However, according to the Monitoring the Future (MTF) studies, beyond 10 hours a week, amount of sleep per night declines steadily as work hours increase (see Figure 10.4 on p. 318). The MTF studies also show that working more than 10 hours a week is disruptive to eating and exercise habits (Bachman & Schulenberg, 1993).

Mortimer's study (Mortimer et al., 1992), which examined closely the relationship between the kind of work adolescents do and their psychological functioning, found differences depending on gender. For boys, the amount of stress they reported experiencing at work was the best predictor of psychological functioning. More stress at work—from time pressure or from work conditions involving excessive noise, cold, or heat, for example—was related to symptoms of depression and feelings of inadequacy. For girls, the best predictor of their psychological functioning in relation to work was the extent to which they felt a conflict between the demands of work and the demands of school. The more they felt work interfered with school, the more likely they were to feel depressed and the less control they felt they had over their lives.

The Mortimer study also had some positive findings concerning psychological functioning. For both boys and girls, working at a job that involved learning new skills was positively related to psychological well-being and self-esteem (Mortimer et al., 1992). Also, in the MTF studies, learning and using new skills on the job was related to higher life satisfaction (Schulenberg & Bachman, 1993). We will consider the case in favor of adolescent work shortly.

Work and Problem Behavior

"Last week I cut off a pair of jeans to make shorts and my father got angry. He said I was wasting money. But I don't care, because I have a job now and can buy my own clothes. I feel more like an adult."

—*Chonita, age 16 (in Salzman, 1993, p. 72)*

One strong and consistent finding in research on adolescents and work, in the three major studies described above as well as in other studies, is that adolescents who work are more likely to use alcohol, cigarettes, and drugs, especially if they work more than 10 hours a week (Bachman & Schulenberg, 1993; Frone, 1999; Mortimer et al., 1999; Steinberg & Dornbusch, 1991; Steinberg et al., 1993). However, scholars disagree on whether this relationship means that working leads to greater substance use or whether this means that adolescents who work already have a tendency toward substance use. Scholars working with the MTF data have argued that the relationship is merely correlational—adolescents who work more than 10 hours a week also have a tendency toward substance use, but their tendency toward substance use was evident even before they began working long hours (Bachman & Schulenberg, 1993). However, Mortimer and colleagues (1993) and Steinberg and colleagues (1993) claim their longitudinal data indicates that increases in work hours *precede* increases in drug and alcohol use, suggesting that working long hours causes an increase in substance use. But these explanations are not incompatible, and both may be valid. Adolescents who work relatively long hours may already have a tendency toward substance use that is further amplified by working long hours. (For further information on this topic, see the Research Focus box.)

Not only is working related to problem behavior outside of work, but there is also a considerable amount of on-the-job deviance among adolescents who work. Greenberger and Steinberg investigated a variety of behaviors they called **occupational deviance** as part of their research on adolescents and work (Ruggiero, Greenberger, & Steinberg, 1982). They had first-time adolescent workers indicate on a confidential questionnaire how often they had engaged in each of nine behaviors that involved some kind of occupational deviance, such as falsely calling in "sick" and stealing things at work. A summary of the results is shown in Figure 11.1. Altogether, over 60% of the working adolescents had engaged in at least one type of occupational deviance after being employed for 9 months.

That may seem like a lot, and it is, but keep in mind that the study included only adolescents. Adults have also been known to call in sick when they were not, take things from work that did not belong to them, and so on. We have no way of knowing, from this study alone, whether adolescents tend to do these things more than adults do.

Nevertheless, the combination of these results and the results concerning substance use indicates a relationship between work and problem behavior in adolescence. Why would this be the case? The answer seems to be different for occupational deviance than it

RESEARCH FOCUS
A Longitudinal Study of Adolescents and Work

One of the most ambitious and impressive studies of adolescents and work has been conducted by Jeylan Mortimer of the University of Minnesota and her colleagues (Mortimer & Finch, 1996; Mortimer et al., 1996, 1999; Mortimer & Johnson, 1998). The focus of the study was on work in relation to mental health and in relation to role transitions to adulthood. The study began in 1987 with a sample of 1,000 adolescents who were randomly selected from a list of ninth graders attending public schools in St. Paul, Minnesota. The adolescents completed questionnaires in each year of high school and each year after high school—every year from age 14 through 27, so far (the study is still continuing). Their parents also completed questionnaires when the adolescents were in 9th grade and again when they were in 12th grade.

One of the impressive features of the study is the **retention rate**, which means the percentage of participants who continued to take part in the study after the first year. Retention rates are sometimes a problem in longitudinal studies, because people move, change phone numbers, or fail to return the questionnaire mailed to them. This would especially be likely to be a problem in a study like this one, in which young people are being followed beyond high school, a time that involves frequent changes of residence for many people. In Mortimer's study, the retention rate was 93% after 4 years of high school, and 78% over 8 years (Mortimer et al., 1999). Normally, 50% would be considered adequate after 8 years. They were able to keep the retention rate so high in this study by keeping in regular contact with the participants annually to see whether they had moved or were planning to move.

The longitudinal design of the study enabled Mortimer and her colleagues to provide insights into important aspects of the influences of work on adolescent development. One of the key questions

in this area is, does working influence adolescents' problem behavior, especially substance use? It is well-established that adolescents who work report higher rates of problem behavior (Greenberger & Steinberg, 1986), especially if they work more than 20 hours a week (Mortimer et al., 1996) but this leaves open the question: does working long hours cause adolescents to engage in problem behavior, or do adolescents who engage in problem behavior also choose to work more? Mortimer and her colleagues (1999), focusing on alcohol use, found that adolescents who work long hours in high school already have higher rates of alcohol use in ninth grade, *before* they start working long hours. However, they also found that working long hours contributed to greater alcohol use.

A second, related question is, does the higher rate of alcohol use among adolescents working long hours in high school establish a pattern that continues beyond high school? Again, this could only be determined through a longitudinal study that follows adolescents beginning in high school and extending several years beyond. Mortimer and Johnson (1997) found that 4 years after high school, the emerging adults who had worked long hours in high school had rates of alcohol use in their early twenties that were no higher than for emerging adults who had worked less in high school. It was not that the high-working adolescents had decreased their use of alcohol as emerging adults, but that the other adolescents had "caught up," reporting higher rates of alcohol use by the time they reached their early twenties.

Longitudinal studies like this one require a great deal of effort and patience (not to mention a considerable amount of money), but they often provide results that help considerably in unraveling complex questions of cause and effect with respect to development among adolescents and emerging adults.

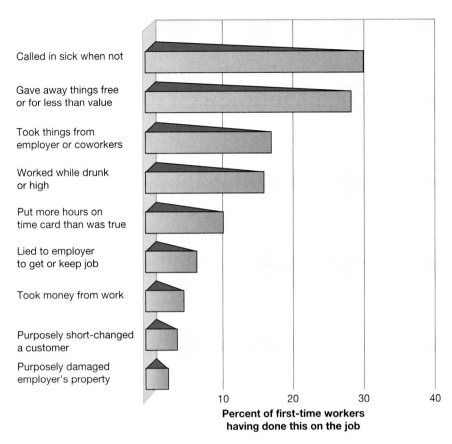

FIGURE 11.1 *Rates of occupational deviance.*

Source: Ruggiero et al. (1982).

For the higher substance use among adolescents who work, as we have noted some scholars believe that this tendency exists among adolescents who work even before they start working (Bachman & Schulenberg, 1993). However, other scholars have found that adolescents who work in jobs with a high level of stress are more likely to use drugs and alcohol than adolescents who work in lower-stress jobs (Greenberger, Steinberg, & Vaux, 1981). This suggests that the substance use may be serving as a stress reliever, and provides further evidence that the role of work in adolescent substance use is causal, not just correlational.

Also important is that having a part-time job gives adolescents more money to spend on leisure. Very little of the money they make goes to their family's living expenses or saving for their future education (Mortimer et al., 1992; Thomas, 1998). Instead, it goes toward purchases for themselves, here and now: snazzy clothes, CDs, car payments, gas and insurance for a car, concert tickets, movies, eating out—and drugs and alcohol (Bachman, 1983; Greenberger & Steinberg, 1986; Thomas, 1998). Adolescents tend to spend the money they make at their jobs in pursuit of good times, and for some of them the pursuit of good times includes use of drugs and alcohol (Greenberger & Steinberg, 1986).

The Case in Favor of Adolescent Work

Jeylan Mortimer and her colleagues (1999) at the University of Minnesota argue that the case against adolescent work has been overstated, and that in fact a strong case can be made in favor of adolescent work. Although, as we have seen above, some of Mortimer's own research has revealed certain problems associated with adolescent work, she argues that on the whole, the benefits outweigh the problems.

She points out that her research indicates that adolescents themselves see many benefits from their work. As you can see from Table 11.1, far more of them see benefits in their work than see problems. They believe

is for substance use. For occupational deviance, the characteristics of the typical adolescent workplace seem to offer likely explanations (Steinberg et al., 1993). The work is often boring and tedious, and adolescents do not see the jobs as leading to anything they plan to be doing in the future, so they rarely have much of a feeling of personal investment in the job. If you get caught doing these things, you might get fired, but who cares? There are plenty of other jobs of the same type (i.e., low skilled and low paying) easily available. Also, the adolescent workplace has little adult supervision, and adolescents do not feel close to the adults they work with, so they may feel they have little obligation or responsibility to these adults to behave ethically. Furthermore, adolescents who work are more likely than adolescents who do not to be cynical in their attitudes toward work (Steinberg et al., 1982)—more likely to agree, for example, that "Hard work really doesn't get you much of anything in this world"—and this cynicism may make it easier to justify occupational deviance.

they gain a sense of responsibility from working, improve their abilities to manage money, develop better social skills, and learn to manage their time better. Over 40% believe that their jobs have helped them develop new occupational skills, in contrast to the portrayal of adolescent work as involving nothing but dreary tasks (although we might add that 40%, while substantial, is still a minority).

Mortimer and her colleagues (1999) concede that nearly half of adolescents report that working gives them less time for homework, and over one-fourth believe that working has negatively affected their grades, as you can see in Table 11.1. However, Mortimer argues that the main activity that working adolescents spend less time on is watching television. According to her argument, American adolescents simply spend too little time on homework for working to make much difference in their school performance (also see Steinberg & Cauffman, 1995). She claims that no consistent relationship exists across studies between working and school performance in adolescence, even among adolescents who work 20 or more hours per week.

My own judgment is that the case against adolescent work at over 20 hours per week is quite strong. Even Mortimer's own data indicate that adolescents perceive negative effects of working on their school performance, and enough studies find a relationship between working long hours and poor grades to make this case convincingly (e.g., Committee on Child Labor, 1998; Greenberger & Steinberg, 1986; Marsh, 1991). Also, there is little dispute that working over 20 hours per week leads to higher substance use. However, Mortimer's research is a useful reminder that the effects of work on adolescent development are complex and that work does offer certain benefits to many adolescents.

THINKING CRITICALLY

American adolescents clearly prefer to work, even though the work is often boring and is frequently related to negative outcomes (though some positive outcomes as well). Given this situation, would you be for or against national legislation to limit adolescents' work (under age 18) to 10 hours a week? Justify your answer in terms of development in adolescence and in emerging adulthood.

TABLE 11.1: PERCENTAGES OF ADOLESCENTS INDICATING BENEFITS AND COSTS OF EMPLOYMENT

	Girls	Boys
Benefits		
Responsibility	90.2	80.3
Money management	65.7	57.4
Learned social skills	87.7	78.3
Work experience/ skill development	43.4	42.1
Work ethics	73.3	68.1
Independence	75.0	77.7
Time management	78.6	74.5
Learned about life/ shaped future	26.2	29.0
Problems		
Less leisure time	49.4	49.0
Lower grades	28.1	24.6
Less time for homework	47.9	48.8
Think about work during class	7.7	11.4
Fatigue	51.2	45.1

Source: Aronson et al. (1996), Table 2.10.

From School and Part-Time Work to a "Real Job"

As we have observed, few adolescents see their part-time jobs as the beginning of the kind of work they expect to be doing as adults. Waitressing, washing dishes, mowing lawns, sales clerking, and the like are fine for bringing in enough money to finance an active leisure life, but generally these are jobs that adolescents view as temporary and transient, not as forming the basis of a long-term career (Hamilton, 1990). Full-time work in a "real job" comes only after adolescents have completed their education—the end of high school, for some, the end of college or graduate school, for others. Let's take a look at the transition to work, first for those who take on full-time work immediately after high school, then for those who make the transition to full-time work following college or graduate school.

The Post-High-School Transition to Work

Although the proportion of American adolescents attending college after high school has risen steadily in the 20th century and now exceeds 60% (Bianchi & Spain, 1996; Schneider & Stevenson, 1999), that still leaves nearly 40% of adolescents who begin full-time work after high school instead of attending college. In European countries, the proportion of young people entering work immediately after secondary school is even higher, ranging from 60% to 90% in different countries (Arnett, 2000d). What are the work prospects like for these adolescents, and how successfully are they able to make the transition from school to the workplace?

In 1987, a distinguished panel of scholars and public policy officials was assembled by the William T. Grant Foundation and asked to address this question with respect to young Americans. They produced an influential and widely read report titled *The Forgotten Half: Non-College Youth in America* (William T. Grant Commission on Work, Family, and Citizenship, 1988), which contained an analysis of the circumstances of **the forgotten half** of young Americans who do not attend college and a set of policy suggestions for promoting a successful transition from high school to work.

The report begins by describing the changes in the American economy in recent decades, with a special focus on the loss of manufacturing jobs (for example, working in a steel mill or automobile factory) that used to provide well-paying jobs for unskilled workers. "A fast-changing economy has produced millions of new jobs in the service and retail sectors, but with wages at only half the level of a typical manufacturing job," the report states. "Stable, high wage employment in manufacturing, communications, transportation, utilities, and forestry that was once open to young people leaving high school is rapidly declining. For male high school graduates, employment in these high-wage sectors fell remarkably, from 57 percent in 1968 to 36 percent in 1986" (pp. 1, 19). Largely because of the decline in the number of these high-wage jobs available, the average income of male high school graduates aged 20 to 24 actually *declined* by 28% (adjusted for inflation) between 1973 and 1986. The decline for dropouts was even steeper—42%.

Given those statistics, clearly all is not well with the transition from school to work for high school graduates. What could be done to improve their prospects? The Commission's recommendations were of two kinds: *better occupational preparation in high schools* and *government job-training programs.*

Occupational Preparation in High School Better occupational preparation in high school does not mean simply more attention to "vocational education," which involves teaching applied skills (such as welding or auto mechanics) in high school classrooms. This approach, the Commission noted, has not worked well because "employers find that job-specific training is taught better on the job or in specialized post-secondary institutions than it is in high school classrooms that must often make do with outdated machinery and methods" (p. 50). A more promising approach is better coordination between schools and employers in programs that integrate what is learned in school with direct training in the workplace (also see Lewis et al., 1998; Stern, Rahn, & Chung, 1998).

An example of this kind of program is the Experience-Based Career Education (EBCE) program, a federally funded program that has been conducted in four sites around the country. Under this program, students spend up to 80% of their school time in the workplace over an entire school year. Program coordinators at the school supervise the placements, and over the course of the year all students experience several different placements so that they can explore a wide variety of career possibilities in both blue-collar and white-collar fields. Another link between school and the workplace is that the students attend regular seminars to discuss their experiences and to work on academic projects related to the work they are doing at their internships. This program bears strong similarities to the German apprenticeship program described in the Cultural Focus box.

Another example of a program linking school to work is the Executive High School Internships program in New York City, a semester-long program in which high school students are paired with executives

Teaching skills to adolescents directly in the workplace tends to be effective.

from various professions. During that semester students receive high school credits, but instead of attending classes they assist their executive role models in the workplace and learn from them. As in the EBCE program described above, school and workplace are linked through seminars in which students work on projects connecting their work experiences to academic subjects.

Government Job-Training Programs The Commission also described several government-sponsored job-training programs. Perhaps the most promising of these is the Jobs for America's Graduates (JAG) program. Unlike the school-to-work programs described above, which were open to all high school students, JAG focuses on students identified by their schools as at-risk for dropping out and being unemployed. About 70% of JAG participants are minorities, and over half (53%) are from low-income families.

The JAG program is multifaceted and includes not only training in specific job skills, but also job placement assistance from trained job specialists and follow-up monitoring and support from these specialists for 9 months following high school graduation. The program links school to work by providing classroom instruction in "employment abilities" such as career planning, job search and interviewing skills, leadership, and basic academics.

Unlike the school-to-work programs described in the previous section, the JAG program conducts regular evaluations to monitor its effectiveness. The results have been impressive. Evaluations have compared program participants with a control group of adolescents who were similar to the participants but did not take part in the program. Results show that 20 months after graduation, JAG participants averaged 8 more weeks of employment than nonparticipants and had earned 36% more; among African American and Latino participants, the income advantage was even higher, 55%. The job placement rate for JAG graduates was extremely high, nearly 90%, about double the rate for nonparticipants.

The "Forgotten Half," Ten Years Later

The Commission's report was published in 1988, at a time when the U.S. economy was sliding into a recession. How has the situation changed since that time? In 1998, a follow-up report was published, entitled *The Forgotten Half Revisited* (Halpern, 1998). This report concluded that in the decade since the Commissions original report, prospects for the "forgotten half" have become worse, not better. Young people who do not

attend college are "still in a free-fall of declining earnings and diminished expectations" (p. xii), despite a booming American economy.

Recently, Richard Murnane (an economist) and Frank Levy (a scholar on education) published a book looking at changes in the job skills needed by members of the "forgotten half" (Murnane & Levy, 1997). The book is entitled *Teaching the New Basic Skills: Principles for Educating Children to Thrive in a Changing Economy*.

Murnane and Levy conducted observations in a variety of factories and offices to gain information about the kinds of jobs now available to high school graduates and the kinds of skills required by those jobs. They focused not on routine jobs that require little skill and pay low wages, but on the most promising new jobs available to high school graduates in the changing economy, jobs that offer the promise of career development and middle-class wages. They concluded that six basic skills are necessary for success at these new jobs:

- Reading at a ninth-grade level or higher
- Doing math at a ninth-grade level or higher
- Solving semistructured problems
- Communicating orally and in writing
- Using a computer for word processing and other tasks
- Collaborating in diverse groups

The good news is that all of what Murnane and Levy (1997) call **the new basic skills** could be taught to adolescents by the time they leave high school. The bad news is that many American adolescents currently graduate from high school without learning them adequately. Murnane and Levy focused on reading and math skills because those are the skills on which the most data are available; they concluded that the data reveal "a sobering picture: close to half of all seventeen-year-olds cannot read or do math at the level needed" to succeed at the new jobs. The half who do have these skills are also the half who are most likely to go to college rather than seeking full-time work after high school. The result of this shortfall in skills is a vicious circle: employers are wary of hiring high school graduates for the new jobs because they are unimpressed with the skills typical of these graduates; for adolescents the awareness that a high school diploma will be of little help to them in securing a good job gives them little incentive to apply themselves in school; their lack of adequate skills reinforces employers' perceptions that it is not wise to hire high school graduates.

Of course, this does not mean that the current situation cannot be changed. There is certainly no reason why schools could not be expected to require that high school students can read and do math at a ninth-grade level or higher by the time they graduate. Ensuring that students are capable of "solving semistructured problems" and "communicating effectively orally and in writing" are also quite reasonably part of any high school's objectives and responsibility. Learning to use computer skills is a growing part of the school curriculum, not just at the high school level but from grade school on up. The ability to work in diverse groups is perhaps a less definitely teachable skill, but certainly practice in such situations in the school setting would help promote the development of this skill. Altogether, the results of Murnane and Levy's research suggest that it may be wise for administrators of job-training programs such as those described in the William T. Grant Commission's report to revise those programs to fit the requirements of the new information- and technology-based economy.

Apprenticeships in Western Europe

The William T. Grant Commission's main recommendation was to make programs such as JAG available to a wider proportion of the "forgotten half." All of the school-to-work and job-training programs tried thus far in the United States have been limited in scale, serving only one community or a small number of communities. Even the JAG program, although a federal program, was serving only 11,000 adolescents spread across 12 states at the time of the Commission's report.

> "AMERICA HAS THE WORST SCHOOL-TO-WORK TRANSITION PROCESS OF ANY INDUSTRIALIZED NATION. PUT SIMPLY, WE HAVE NO SYSTEMATIC PROCESSES TO ASSIST HIGH SCHOOL GRADUATES TO MOVE SMOOTHLY FROM SCHOOL INTO EMPLOYMENT."
> —RAY MARSHALL (1994), EDUCATOR

What would it be like to have a coherent national program available to all adolescents, coordinating the curriculum of the schools with the needs of employers and focused on training in the workplace that would lead directly to long-term employment? We don't need to use only our imaginations to find out. Western European countries have had such programs for a long time.

The focus of work preparation programs in Western Europe is on apprenticeships (Hamilton, 1994; Hamilton & Hurrelman, 1994). In an **apprenticeship**, an adolescent "novice" serves under contract to a "master" who has substantial experience in a profession, and through working under the master the novice learns the skills required to enter the profession successfully. Although apprenticeships originally began centuries ago in craft professions such as carpentry and blacksmithing, today they are undertaken to prepare for a wide range of professions, from auto mechanics and carpenters to police officers, personnel officers, and travel agents (Hamilton, 1990, 1994; Hamilton & Hurrelman, 1994). Although they are rare in the United States, apprenticeships are common in Western Europe, especially in German-speaking countries. For example, Germany's apprenticeship program includes over 60% of all 16- to 18-year-olds (Hamilton, 1990), and Switzerland's includes about one-third of the adolescents who do not attend college after secondary school (William T. Grant Commission on Work, Family, and Citizenship, 1988). The Cultural Focus box in this chapter provides more detail about Germany's apprenticeship program.

Common features of apprenticeship programs are (Hamilton, 1994; Hamilton & Hurrelman, 1994):

- Entry at age 16, with the apprenticeship lasting 2 to 3 years;
- Continued part-time schooling while in the apprenticeship, with the school curriculum closely connected to the training received in the apprenticeship;
- Training takes place in the workplace, under real working conditions;
- Preparation is for a career in a respected profession that provides an adequate income.

This kind of program requires close coordination between schools and employers, so that what adolescents learn at school during their apprenticeships will complement and reinforce what is being learned in the workplace. This means that schools consult employers with respect to the skills required in the workplace, and employers make opportunities available for adolescent apprentices and provide masters for them to work under. In Europe, the employers see this as worth their trouble because apprenticeships provide them with a reliable supply of well-qualified entry-level employees. In the United States, although employers have expressed great concern in recent years over the lack of sufficient skills in their young job applicants (Murnane & Levy, 1997), no system currently exists in

Apprenticeships are common in some European countries. Here, an apprentice in Poissy, France, learns to become a chef.

the United States that coordinates the requirements of the workplace—for example, as in the "new basic skills" described above—with the educational efforts of the schools.

In response to growing national concern over this problem, in 1994 the United States Congress passed the School-to-Work Opportunities Act (STWOA). The bill is intended to provide the beginning of a framework for a national school-to-work program, beginning with voluntary demonstration projects in states and local areas where businesses and educators work together to reform school systems and integrate school and work (Wilson, 1996). The initial funding for the program is rela-

CULTURAL FOCUS
Germany's Apprenticeship Program

Anna is only a few months away from the completion of her apprenticeship in a large [German] manufacturing firm. At age 17, Anna has worked in the firm's accounting, purchasing, inventory, production, personnel, marketing, sales, and finance departments, and studied those functions in school. She is very enthusiastic about the recent news that the company will give her an additional 18 months of training in electronic data processing before hiring her as a regular employee. She is already skilled and reliable enough to have substituted for two weeks in cost accounting during her supervisor's vacation.

This case example is taken from a book by developmental psychologist Stephen Hamilton (1990) of Cornell University about Germany's apprenticeship

system. Hamilton describes Germany's system and suggests how a similar system might be established in the United States.

Germany has an apprenticeship system that has existed in various forms for several hundred years. In the present, more than 60% of all 16- to 18-year-olds are apprentices, making apprenticeships the most common form of education for midadolescents and the primary passage from school to work. As Anna's example illustrates, the apprenticeships train young people not just for trades or skilled labor, but for professional and managerial positions as well. Usually young people are in the program for 3 years, and during that time they spend one day a week in a vocational school and the other four in their apprenticeship placement. More than half of apprentices remain with the company that trained them for at least 2 years after they complete the apprenticeship.

Employers pay all the costs of training their apprentices, including paying them a modest salary during the apprenticeship. About 10% of industrial and commercial (e.g., insurance or banking) businesses and 40% of craft businesses take part in the apprenticeship program. What is the incentive for employers? They participate partly out of German social tradition and partly because once an apprentice learns to do useful work the employer will have relatively cheap labor during the rest of the apprenticeship and a well-trained employee after the apprenticeship is completed.

Hamilton's ethnographic research demonstrates the effectiveness of the German apprenticeship system. Apprentices have numerous opportunities for learning on the job, and what they learn on the job is coordinated with and reinforced by what they learn in school. Motivation for learning in school is enhanced by the awareness that the knowledge they gain in school will have a direct and immediate application in the workplace. Adolescents work closely with adults who are in charge of instructing them and providing them with learning opportunities, and typically they have a variety of different positions during the apprenticeship so that they learn a variety of skills.

Furthermore, Hamilton notes, "Germany's apprenticeship system is more than a training program intended to teach the knowledge and skills related to a specific job. In addition to fulfilling that function, it is a form of general education and an institution for socializing youth to adulthood" (1990, p. 63). Although Hamilton's book was written before the reunification of Germany and was based mainly on the West German system, East Germany had a similar system (based in a common historical tradition) and the two systems have been combined into one since reunification (Hamilton, 1994).

Could a system like this work in the United States? In some places it already does, but it very rare—less than 5% of adolescents have participated by the time they leave high school (Hamilton, 1990, 1994). A vast government-sponsored system would be required to coordinate the schools with employers. It would also require earlier decisions about what road to take occupationally—this decision would have to be made by age 15 or 16, rather than putting it off until well after high school.

However, the benefits would be great. Young people would leave their teens much better prepared for the workplace than they are now. School would be less boring to them and more clearly related to their futures. Hamilton and others are currently conducting small-scale apprenticeship programs in the United States, and if the benefit of these programs can be demonstrated, increased enthusiasm may be seen for a national apprenticeship system.

tively small, but if the demonstration projects are successful, they may be expanded eventually into a national program.

THINKING CRITICALLY

Apprenticeships in Europe appear to work quite well, but they require that adolescents make career decisions by their midteens, much earlier than is typical in American society. Do you think the benefits of apprenticeships outweigh the fact that they require these early decisions, or do you prefer the American system of allowing for a longer period of experimentation and exploration—well into emerging adulthood—before such decisions are made? Is it a question of what is best developmentally, or just a question of different values?

From College to Work: Is College Worth It?

Although the United States does not have any widespread, unified program of internships or apprenticeships or other job-training programs for adolescents, we have noted that over 60% of American adolescents attend college after high school, a proportion higher than in any other country in the world. Perhaps young people in the United States are receiving in college the kind of occupational training that Western Europeans receive through their apprenticeships and other programs.

In some respects this may be true, but a recent book calls this assumption into serious question. James Coté and Anton Allahar, two Canadian sociologists, are the authors of *Generation on Hold: Coming of Age in the Late Twentieth Century* (1996). They argue that it is not the knowledge received at college that is most important in obtaining a decent job, but the *credential*—the fact of having a college degree—and they attack this **credentialism** for unnecessarily delaying young people's entry into well-paying full-time work:

> We are challenging the persistent belief that more and more education is required of *all* the population for the economy to be viable and for individuals to be fully competent in the modern workplace. . . . Many young people suffer because they believe that they must have postsecondary credentials to find jobs or because they have no choice but to get the credentials to compete for jobs which, in fact, do not require specific skills related to their degrees. (p. 37)

As a result, according to Coté and Allahar (1996), the majority of American and Canadian young people spend anywhere from one to four (or more) years in college, racking up debts from their educational costs and their living expenses, to obtain a credential that is required for most middle-class professions but is not necessary in terms of the skills they will apply in the workplace. Furthermore, because it has become so common for young people to obtain a college degree, many young people find that the job market is glutted with other young people who have similar credentials, with the result that it is difficult for them to obtain a job in the field they were supposed to be training for in college.

Coté and Allahar (1996) cite numerous American studies to support their thesis, but perhaps their most interesting and persuasive data come from studies of Canadian emerging adults in the years after college graduation. These studies show that a remarkably high proportion of college graduates are **underemployed**—that is, working in jobs that explicitly did not require a college degree. As Figure 11.2 illustrates, underemployment after college exists across a wide range of fields. In a nationwide Canadian study, 35% of the emerging adults who graduated from college in 1982 reported 5 years later that they were in a job that did not require a university degree (ranging from 24% in engineering to 40% in the social sciences and 45% in general arts and sciences). Underemploy-

ment was even higher (nearly 50%) for those who had obtained a 2-year (community college) degree. However, getting even more education did not help—57% of the people with Master's degrees were underemployed 5 years after graduation, and 40% of those with Doctorate degrees. Although data this detailed is not available for the United States, one analyst has estimated that for emerging adults who graduated from college in the 1980s, "almost 40 percent of the graduates awarded bachelor's degrees . . . reported that they thought a degree was not needed to obtain the job they held a year after graduation" (Hecker, 1992, p. 7).

However, it is important not to take this too far. Although it appears to be true that many people find themselves working during emerging adulthood in jobs that have no clear relation to their educational training, for the majority of adults the number of years of education completed is the *single best predictor of occupational success*—better than social class background, better than grades in school (Garbarino & Asp, 1981), better than *anything* else (Alexander & Eckland, 1975; Schneider & Stevenson, 1999). And the credential is not all that matters. Each year of education completed adds to occupa-

THINKING CRITICALLY

Based on your college experience, how would you evaluate Coté and Allahar's argument about the dubious usefulness of a college education? Are there benefits to a college education that they may have overlooked?

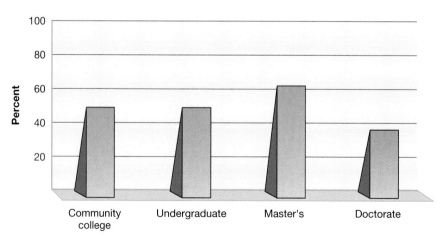

FIGURE 11.2 *Underemployment among Canadian young people, five years after graduation.*
Source: Nobert et al. (1992).

tional success, even if no credential is achieved, so that (for example) the person who completes 3 years of college is likely to be more successful than the person who completes only 1 year, even though neither received a college degree. So, although there may be some truth to the argument that there are many jobs for which a specific credential may be required even if it is not really necessary, in general education does pay off in workplace performance and success.

In addition, attending college has other benefits besides enhanced occupational success. A college education is related to a variety of other positive outcomes, including better critical-thinking skills, greater participation in political and community activities, more positive self-image, and greater interpersonal and intellectual competence (Pascarella & Terenzini, 1991; Rabow, Choi, & Purdy, 1998).

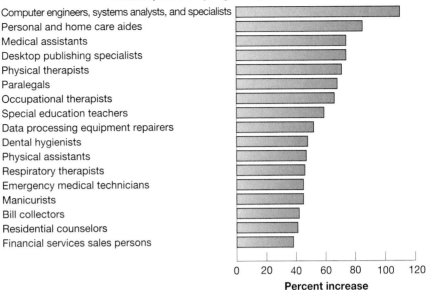

FIGURE 11.3 *Predicted job growth.*
Source: U.S. Department of Labor (2000).

Occupational Choice

As we saw at the outset of the chapter, adolescents in preindustrial traditional cultures (and in Western cultures historically) work alongside their parents—boys with their fathers and other men, girls with their mothers and other women—doing the kind of work adults do. Because the economies in such cultures are usually not diverse, there are few "occupations" to choose from. Boys learn to do what men do, whether it is hunting or farming or something else, and girls learn to do what women do, which is usually child care and running the household, and perhaps some gathering or gardening or other work. There is a certain security in this—you grow up knowing that you will have useful and important work to do as an adult, and you grow up gradually learning the skills required for it. On the other hand, there is a certain narrowness and limitation to it as well—if you are a boy, you must do the work that men do whether you care for it or not; and if you are a girl, your role is to learn child care and running a household regardless of what your individual preferences or talents might be.

Adolescents in cultures with industrialized economies face a different kind of trade-off. Industrialized economies are astonishingly complex and diverse. That means that, as an adolescent, you have a tremendous range of possible occupations to choose from. Figure 11.3 shows predicted job growth in a variety of fields through the early years of the 21st century, and it also gives you some idea of the range of occupations that now exists. However, every adolescent has to find a place for himself or herself among all of that fabulous diversity of choice. And even once you make your choice, you have to hope that the occupation you decide you want will be achievable for you. More young people would like to be medical doctors, veterinarians, musicians, and professional athletes than is possible (Sandberg et al., 1991; Schneider & Stevenson, 1999).

Let us take a look now at the developmental pattern in how American adolescents make occupational choices, and the various influences that play a part in their choices.

The Development of Occupational Goals

Although children and adolescents may have occupational dreams—fantasies of being a famous basketball player, singer, or movie star—adolescence and especially emerging adulthood are times when more serious reflection on occupational goals often begins. For emerging adults, decisions must be made about educational and occupational preparation that will have potential long-term effects on their occupational direction and success.

One influential theory of the development of occupational goals, by Donald Super (1967, 1976, 1980, 1992), begins with adolescence and continues through five stages into adulthood, as follows:

- *Crystallization*, ages 14 to 18. In this initial stage, adolescents begin to move beyond fantasizing and start to consider how their talents and interests match up with the occupational possibilities available to them. This requires a considerable capacity for self-reflection, which is one of the characteristics of cognitive development in adolescence. This new capacity allows them to think, "What am I good at? What would I most like to do?" During this time they may begin to seek out information about careers that are of interest to them, perhaps by talking over various possibilities with family and friends. Also, as adolescents begin to decide on their own beliefs and values (Arnett, 1997), this helps to guide their occupational explorations as they consider how various job possibilities may confirm or contradict those values.

- *Specification*, ages 18 to 21. During this stage, occupational choices become more focused and specific. For example, an adolescent who decided during the crystallization stage to seek an occupation that involves working with children may now decide whether that means being a child psychologist, a teacher, or a pediatrician. Making this specific choice usually involves seeking information about what is involved in these occupations, as in the crystallization stage, but with more of a focus on specific occupations rather than a general field. It also usually involves beginning to pursue the education or training required to obtain the desired occupation.

- *Implementation*, ages 21 to 24. This stage involves completing the education or training that was begun in the specification stage and entering the job itself. In part, this may mean that young people must reconcile any discrepancy between what they would like to do and what is available in the work world. You may have been educated to be a teacher, but find out after graduation that there are more teachers than available jobs, so that you end up working in a social service agency or a business.

- *Stabilization*, ages 25 to 35. This is the stage in which young adults establish themselves in their careers. The initial period of getting their feet wet in a job comes to an end, and they become more stable and experienced in their work.

- *Consolidation*, age 35 and up. From this point onward, occupational development means continuing to gain expertise and experience and seeking advancement into higher-status positions as expertise and experience grow.

Although this theory remains important in shaping the way scholars think about occupational development as well as in shaping the way that career counselors provide advice to young people, not everyone fits the pattern prescribed by the theory, and certainly not according to these precise ages. Because education is stretching out further and further into the twenties for more and more people, it is not unusual for the implementation stage to begin in the midtwenties rather than the early twenties. Perhaps more important, it is less and less common for occupational development to follow the kind of linear path through the life course that is described in Super's theory. Increasingly, people have not just one career or occupation, but two or more in the course of their working lives. Many of today's adolescents and emerging adults will change career directions at least once (Murnane & Levy, 1997).

Also, for women and increasingly for men, balancing work and family goals may mean taking time off or at least working fewer hours during the years when they have young children to care for. This point has been stressed by Celia Romm (1980–81), who has criticized the occupational development theories of Super and others for excluding the kinds of considerations often faced by women. She questions the assumptions that she believes are made by traditional theories of occupational development. One key assumption is that occupational development follows a single path.

According to Romm, this assumption ignores the fact that most women in Western societies both expect to lead and then actually do lead a dual-career life, with their role as homemaker and mother as a "second career" in addition to the out-of-home occupation they hold. Most women have a period of their lives, during the time they have one or more young children, when they spend as much or more time in the homemaker-mother role as they do in the role of their paid occupation. And throughout the time their children are growing up women face the challenge of integrating these two roles, more so than men because even now in Western cultures (as in Eastern and traditional cultures), women end up taking the great majority of the responsibility for child care. For this reason, theories of career development that neglect the challenge of this integration are not applicable to the career paths of most women.

Influences on Occupational Goals

Theories of occupational development provide a general outline of how adolescents and emerging adults may progress through their working lives. But how do adolescents and emerging adults make choices among the great variety of occupations available to them? What sorts of influences go into their decisions? A great deal of research has been conducted on these questions, especially focusing on the influence of personality characteristics, family social class, and gender.

Personality Characteristics One of the influences on occupational choice in cultures where people are allowed to choose from a wide range of possible occupations is the individual's judgment of how various occupations would be suited to his or her personality. People seek occupations that they judge to be consistent with their interests and talents. One influential theorist, John Holland (1985, 1987, 1996; Gottfredson, Jones, & Holland, 1993) has been investigating this topic for several decades by investigating the kinds of personality characteristics that are typical of people who hold various jobs and of adolescents who aspire to various jobs. Holland's theory describes six personality categories to consider when matching a person with a prospective occupation:

- *Realistic.* High physical strength, practical approach to problem solving, and low social understanding. Best occupations: those that involve physical activity and practical application of knowledge, such as farming, truck driving, and construction.
- *Intellectual.* High on conceptual and theoretical thinking. Prefer thinking problems through rather than applying knowledge. Low on social skills. Best occupations: scholarly fields such as math and science.
- *Social.* High in verbal skills and social skills. Best professions: those that involve working with people, such as teaching, social work, and counseling.
- *Conventional.* High on following directions carefully, dislike of unstructured activities. Best occupations: those that involve clear responsibilities but require little leadership, such as bank teller or secretary.

- *Enterprising.* High in verbal abilities, social skills, and leadership skills. Best occupations: sales, politics, management, running a business.
- *Artistic.* Introspective, imaginative, sensitive, unconventional. Best occupations: artistic occupations such as painting or writing fiction.

You can probably see the potential for overlap in some of these categories—obviously, they are not mutually exclusive. A person could have some Artistic qualities as well as some Social qualities, or some Intellectual qualities as well as some Enterprising qualities. Holland (1987) does not claim that all people fall neatly into clear types. However, he and others (Lowman, 1991; Vondracek, 1991) believe that most people will be happiest and most successful in their careers if they are able to find a match between their personality qualities and an occupation that allows them to express and develop those qualities. Holland's ideas have been used widely by career counselors to help adolescents gain insights into the types of fields that might be best for them to pursue (Vondracek, 1991). The Strong-Campbell Vocational Interest Inventory, a widely used scale, is based on Holland's ideas.

However, keep in mind the limitations of this approach to understanding occupational choice. Within any particular profession, you are likely to find persons with a considerable variety of personality traits. If you think of teachers you have known, for example, you will probably find that they varied widely in their personalities, even if they may have had some characteristics in common. Their different personalities may have allowed them each to bring a different combination of strengths and weaknesses to the job. So, there probably is not just one personality type that is potentially well-suited to a particular type of job.

In the same way, any one person's personality could probably fit well with a wide variety of the jobs available in a diverse economy. Because most people's personalities are too complex to fall neatly into one type or another, different occupations may bring out different combinations of strengths and weaknesses in a particular person. For this reason, assessing your personality traits may narrow somewhat the range of fields that you think of as being suitable for you, but for most people in industrialized countries that would still leave a considerable number of possible occupations to choose from.

Family Social Class Numerous studies find a relationship between adolescents' occupational goals and the socioeconomic status (SES) of their families (e.g., Hannah & Kohn, 1989; Holms & Esses, 1988; Wilson, Peterson, & Wilson, 1993). Adolescents from high-SES families tend to aspire to high-SES careers, and adolescents from low-SES families tend to have occupational goals consistent with their families' SES. To put it in more concrete terms, the adolescent sons and daughters of parents who are doctors, lawyers, and executives tend to aspire to similar professions, and the adolescent sons and daughters of laborers, factory workers, waitresses, and truck drivers tend to see themselves following similar paths.

There are several reasons why parents' SES would have an influence on adolescents' occupational choices. For one, parents provide occupational models that their children observe (Barber & Eccles, 1992; Grotevant & Cooper, 1988). If mom has become a physician, it is likely that her children will learn a lot during the time they are growing up about what it is like to be a physician, and these observations will lead them to imagine what their own lives would be like if they decided to go into medicine. If, in contrast, mom is a waitress, it is waitressing rather than medicine that the children are likely to learn about when mom comes home from work.

Second, parents of different social classes tend to differ in their access to various resources in ways that make it likely that their adolescents will follow the same occupational paths as they have. Middle-class parents usually make more money than lower- or working-class parents, which makes it more likely that they will be able to provide their children the kinds of educational experiences—such as private schools and attendance at college or university—that tend to lead to the attainment of middle-class occupations. Middle-class parents are also more likely than parents of lower SES to have connections within the middle-class work world—friends, neighbors, and other adults who are employers or who know about various opportunities—and this can be especially helpful to adolescents and emerging adults who are entering their careers.

A third reason for the connection between parents' SES and adolescents' occupational choices is that parents of different social classes raise their children in ways that lay a groundwork of personality and attitudes that propels children in the direction of some careers rather than others. Sociologist Melvin Kohn (1977) has described how parents of different social classes in the United States tend to have different methods of parenting, and how differences in these parenting methods prepare their children for different types of

occupations. Specifically, lower-SES parents tend to raise their children according to narrow socialization values of obedience and conformity, and learning these values prepares their children for blue-collar jobs that involve taking orders from others and following simple directions without innovating or deviating from the task (Ryu & Mortimer, 1996). In contrast, middle-class parents tend to possess the broad socialization values of the American majority culture and teach these values to their children—independence, self-direction, and self-reliance. These values prepare their children for middle-class jobs, which typically require people to think and work independently and to be self-directed rather than being constantly supervised. In a similar vein, scholars have described how parents influence their adolescents' educational aspirations, which in turn influence adolescents' educational achievement (Sewell & Hauser, 1975; Hogan & Astone, 1986). Educational achievement in turn influences occupational choice, because different kinds of jobs require different levels of education.

Although family SES has been shown to be consistently related to adolescents' occupational expectations and to emerging adults' occupational choices, this does not mean that adolescents inevitably end up in the same social class as their parents. The influence of SES on young people's job choices is weaker now than it has been in the past (Biblarz, Bengtson, & Bucur, 1996). For example, a substantial Black middle-class has developed in the United States over the past 40 years (Pollard & O'Hare, 1999), as a result of many young Black people achieving a higher SES level than their parents.

Also, when young people take occupations at the same SES level as their parents, this may be due not to SES itself but to other similarities between parents and children. As we have noted in previous chapters, any time we discuss patterns of similarity in biological families between the characteristics of parents and the characteristics of their children, we need to consider the possibility that at least part of the basis for this similarity is the fact that parents provide their children's genes, through passive genotype–environment interactions.

One aspect of passive–genotype environment interactions that plays a role in occupational choice is intelligence. If mom is a physician, and her adolescent daughter decides she'd like to become one as well, the model provided by mom and the connections available through mom will not be enough by themselves—the daughter will also need a high level of intelligence. Numerous studies indicate that heredity makes a substantial contribution to IQ (e.g., Neisser et al., 1996; Plomin & Rende, 1991). So, adolescents who make occupational choices that are similar to the occupational paths taken by their parents are likely to have similarities in intelligence as well as the other factors we have discussed.

Gender   Gender has a substantial influence on job choice. We observed in the last chapter the strong relation between gender and choice of major in college. This strong relation holds in the workplace as well. Although the proportion of young women who are employed has risen steeply in the 20th century, and although women aged 18 to 25 are now nearly as likely as young men to be employed (U.S. Bureau of the Census, 1999), it remains true that certain jobs are held mainly by men and certain jobs are held mainly by women (Reskin, 1993). Jobs held mainly by women are concentrated in the service sector—for example, teacher, nurse, secretary, and child-care worker. Jobs held mainly by men include engineer, chemist, surgeon, and computer software designer. In general, "women's jobs" tend to be low paying and low status, whereas "men's jobs" tend to be high paying and high in status. These patterns have changed somewhat in recent years—for example, women are now nearly as likely as men to become lawyers and medical doctors (Bianchi & Spain, 1996). However, for jobs such as the ones mentioned above, the gender differences have proven to be remarkably stable.

Why do these gender differences in job choice persist, despite the fact that women now exceed men in terms of overall educational attainment? Gender socialization is certainly part of it. Children learn early on that some jobs are "appropriate" for either males or females, in the same way that they learn other aspects of gender roles (Maccoby, 1990). By the time young people reach the age when it is time for them to choose an occupational direction, their gender identities are well-established and constitute a powerful influence on their job selection (Desmairis & Curtis, 1999).

Another important influence is that already in emerging adulthood, young women anticipate the difficulties they are likely to face in balancing their work and family roles, and this too influences their job selection. It has long been true that wives spend considerably more time on family tasks than husbands do, especially when the couple has young children (Rexroat & Shehan, 1987; Shelton & John, 1993). Although men now do more of the child care than in previous generations (Higgins, Duxbury, & Lee, 1994), wives still do about twice as much housework as their husbands, even when both of them work full-time (Blair & Johnson, 1992). Sociologists have called this the **second shift** (Hochschild, 1990, 1998), to refer to the domestic work shift that women must perform after they complete their first shift in the workplace.

THINKING CRITICALLY

How would you explain the fact that wives usually end up doing most of the household work and child care even when they work as many hours as their husbands? Do you think this is likely to change in the current generation of emerging adults?

Occupations such as nursing continue to be highly gender segregated.

While they are still emerging adults, young women often anticipate the crunch they are likely to face with their roles as worker, spouse, and mother. This realization affects their occupational choices, making them less likely to choose jobs that will be highly demanding and time consuming, even if the job is high paying and high status and in an area they enjoy and for which they have talent (Hochschild, 1990, 1998). They anticipate, too, that they will leave the workplace at some point to spend full-time caring for their young children. For example, one study asked college seniors majoring in business about their future work and family plans (Dey & Hurtado, 1999). The young women expected to work a total of 29 years full-time, nearly 8 years less than their male classmates. Even though these young women were majoring in business, an area that is traditionally "male," they too expected to take time away from the workplace to care for their young children.

In contrast, it is extremely rare for young men to take time away from the workplace to raise young children. Even in European countries where the government pays 100% of a person's salary for up to a year for those wish to leave the workplace temporarily while they have infant children, and even though the government guarantees by law that the employer must rehire the person at the same pay and the same status once they return, few young men take advantage of these policies (Hoem, 1992). However, this does not mean these patterns will never change. The period of women's entry into the workplace is still relatively brief in historical terms—less than 50 years. Many dramatic changes in gender roles have already taken place that could not have been anticipated a half century ago. The changes appear to be continuing—one recent survey found that young men gave time with family a higher priority than prestigious or high-paying work, more than older men and similar to young women (Grimsley, 2000). Furthermore, technologically driven changes in work that are likely to allow an increasing proportion of work to be done at home or in flexible shifts may make it easier for both men and women to balance successfully—and equally—the demands of work and family.

Unemployment

> *"I feel trapped. When you work hard and you're motivated, they should give you a chance. They don't."*
>
> —*Stephanie, age 25, unemployed emerging adult in Paris (in Swardson, 1999)*

Although most young people in the United States are able to find a job once they leave high school or college, this is not true for all of them. Unemployment is a problem particularly for African American and Latino young people in urban areas. Even in late 1999, after an 8-year economic boom, the unemployment rate among Black teenagers was 29%—a decline from 41% in 1993, but much higher than the overall U.S. unemployment rate of 4.2% (Smart, Stoughton, & Behr, 1999).

Most European countries have much higher unemployment rates than the United States does, especially for young people (Lowe & Krahn, 1999). In most European countries, the unemployment rate for emerging adults is at least twice as high as for adults beyond age 25 (Arnett, 2000d). For example, in Sweden the unemployment rate is 8.4% for adults aged 25 to 44, but 18% for 20- to 24-year-olds (Westin, 1998).

Unemployed does not just mean that the person does not have a job. A large proportion of young people in their late teens and early twenties are attending high school or college, but they are not classified as "unemployed" because school is considered to be the focus of their efforts, not work. A young woman whose time is mainly devoted to caring for her child or children also would not be classified as unemployed. Unemployment refers only to young people who are not in school, are not working, and are looking for a job.

This status applies to a substantial proportion of young people in the United States. Figure 11.4 shows the unemployment rates for young people in their late teens and early twenties. As you can see from the figure, unemployment is especially concentrated among Black and Latino adolescents, even though rates of unemployment in all groups of young people decreased in the 1990s. Also, unemployment is extremely high among young people who drop out of high school.

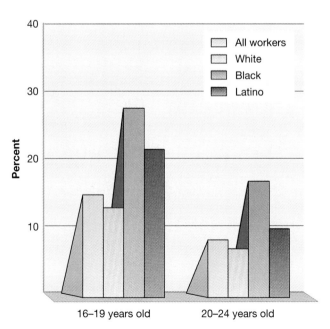

FIGURE 11.4 *Youth unemployment by ethnicity.*
Source: U.S. Bureau of the Census (2000).

Over half of high school dropouts aged 18 to 21 are unemployed (U.S. Bureau of the Census, 1999).

What explains the high rates of unemployment among minority groups? This was not always the case. Consider that in 1954, the teenage unemployment rate for Blacks was only slightly higher than for Whites— 16.5% for Blacks, lower than it is today, and 12% for Whites. To a large extent, the explanation for the change lies in shifting employment patterns in the American economy. Over the past several decades, as the economy has become more strongly focused toward information and technology rather than manufacturing, the number of jobs available to unskilled workers has diminished sharply (Lowe & Krahn, 1999; Murnane & Levy, 1997). The days are gone in the United States when stable, high-paying jobs were plentiful in settings such as automobile factories and steel mills. Today, young people with few or no skills are likely to have difficulty finding a job that pays well enough to support themselves and may have difficulty finding any job at all. As we have seen earlier in this chapter, most of the new jobs, and certainly the best jobs, require people to have at least a minimal level of information skills such as basic math knowledge and ability to use a computer.

For most people those skills come from education, and young African Americans or Latinos are less likely to obtain education past high school than young Whites or Asian Americans. This is especially true for Latinos. Educational attainment is lower among Latinos than among Whites, African Americans, or Asian Americans (O'Hare 1992). In 1990, only 44% of Latinos over the age of 25 had even completed high school, and only 5% had earned a college degree (Oritz, 1995). Among African American adolescents, the dropout rate from high school is only slightly higher than for Whites, but the proportion of Blacks obtaining a college degree is still only half as high as for Whites (O'Hare et al., 1991). Without educational credentials, gaining access to jobs in the new economy is difficult.

However, there is more to the problem of minority unemployment than a lack of college education. Changes that have taken place in urban areas in recent decades have resulted in a combination of dire conditions that is proving difficult to reverse. The changes began with the decline in high-paying, low-skilled manufacturing jobs (Wilson, 1996). These jobs became scarcer as technology was developed to require fewer workers and as the factories and plants moved overseas for cheaper labor or out to the suburbs for cheaper land. As economic activity in the inner cities declined, many people followed the movement of jobs out of the cities into the suburbs. The people who took the initiative to move were often the most able, the most educated, and the most ambitious, including community leaders who had been important in building and sustaining institutions such as churches, businesses, social clubs, and political organizations (Lemann, 1986; Wilson, 1996).

With the departure of these community leaders, the downward spiral of life in the cities accelerated. Neighborhoods eroded and crime increased, giving the businesses that had remained in the cities more incentive to join the exodus (Wilson, 1996). As the tax base of the cities declined with the departure of businesses and the more affluent citizens, the quality of schools also declined from lack of adequate funding. By the early 1980s, many young people living in the cities lacked the basic skills of reading and arithmetic necessary even for low-paying, entry-level jobs. With few jobs available, and with many of them lacking the skills to qualify for the available jobs, rates of crime, drug use, and gang violence among young people in urban areas climbed steadily higher (Wilson, 1996).

What can be done about this complex and so far intractable situation? Most scholars and policy makers agree by now that, given the number and seriousness of the problems in the cities, simply offering job-training programs will not be enough (Children's Defense Fund [CDF], 1995; Smith, 1993). William Julius Wilson (1996), one of the most prominent sociologists on this topic, has proposed an approach with the following elements:

- *Upgrade education.* The current system of local funding of schools perpetuates inequality because poor areas such as the inner cities have a smaller tax base to draw from than wealthy areas do. Financial support for schools should be more central and more equal. Also, the quality of teachers in the inner cities should be enhanced through scholarships to attract promising young people to teach in city schools and through reforms in teacher licensing and certification that require teachers to demonstrate competence in the subjects they teach.

- *Improve school-to-work programs.* Young people in the inner-city ghettos are especially harmed by the lack of effective school-to-work programs in the United States, as shown in their high rates of unemployment. The programs currently available (such as those described earlier in this chapter) are a good start, but should be expanded.

- *Improve access to employment.* Because most new jobs are opening up in suburban rather than urban locations, young people in the inner cities are at a disadvantage because few of them own automobiles and public transportation between cities and suburbs is inadequate in many American urban areas. Organized car pool and van pool networks to carry inner-city young people to jobs in suburban areas would improve their access to employment. Also, because newly available jobs are most often filled not through want ads but through personal contacts, young people in urban areas with high concentrations of unemployment have less information about available jobs. Creating job information and placement centers in urban areas would address this problem.

- *Provide government-funded public service jobs.* Urban areas have many needs that less skilled workers could help to address in public service jobs. Having young people serve in jobs such as nurse's aides, playground supervisors, bridge painters, pothole fillers, and library staffers would not only give them useful work experience—and provide a substitute for unemployment payments and welfare—but would also enhance the quality of life in the areas they live in, for themselves and for others.

Wilson notes that the current political mood of the American people is "away from, not toward, social programs" (1996, p. 236) of the kind he advocates in these proposals. However, if the effectiveness of such programs can be demonstrated on a small scale, political support for them may increase.

Volunteer Work— Community Service

In addition to the paid work that adolescents and emerging adults do, a substantial proportion of them also do volunteer work for little or no pay. Scholars refer to such work as **community service**, because it involves volunteering to serve members of the young person's community without monetary compensation (Yates & Youniss, 1996; Youniss & Yates, 1997).

A strikingly high proportion of American adolescents take part in volunteer work. According to the MTF surveys, consistently from the mid-1970s through the 1990s about 22% of high school seniors have reported taking part in volunteer work on a weekly or monthly basis, and an *additional* 45% have reported

yearly participation (Yates & Youniss, 1996). Taking these two figures together, then, two-thirds of American adolescents report community service at least once per year. This service encompasses a wide variety of activities, such as serving meals to the homeless, cleaning up parks and playgrounds, and collecting money, food, and clothing for the poor. Often, the service takes place under the guidance of a community organization, such as religious organizations, 4-H, Boy and Girl Scouts, and Boys and Girls clubs. Also local, state, and federal governments have made numerous efforts to promote community service among adolescents. Since 1992, the state of Maryland has required a minimum number of community service hours in order for adolescents to graduate from high school.

Community Service and Adolescent Development

Research on adolescents and community service has focused on two main questions. What are the distinctive characteristics of adolescents who do volunteer work? And what effects does volunteer work have on adolescents who take part in it?

Adolescents who volunteer tend to have a high sense of personal competence (Serow, Ciechalski, Daye, 1990), and they tend to have higher educational goals and performance than other adolescents (Johnson et al., 1998). They tend to have high ideals and to perceive a higher degree of similarity between their "actual selves" and their "ideal selves" than other adolescents do (Hart & Fegley, 1995). Not surprisingly, they also have a greater desire to help others and a greater sense of social responsibility compared with other adolescents (Yates & Youniss, 1996). Adolescents who participate in community service often indicate that one or both parents do so as well (Tierney & Branch, 1992). By their participation, parents provide both a model for community service and concrete opportunities for adolescents to participate (Yates & Youniss, 1996).

For most adolescents, their community service is motivated by both individualistic and collectivistic values. Often, of course, they are motivated by collectivistic values such as wanting to help others or a concern for those who have been less fortunate than themselves (Fitch, 1987). However, perhaps less obviously, studies have found that individualistic values are equal to collectivistic values as a motivation for adolescents' community service. In addition to wanting to help others, adolescents also volunteer because it makes them feel good, it gives them a sense of satisfaction, and they enjoy doing the work (Fitch, 1987; Hodgkinson & Weitzman, 1990). As

Yates and Youniss (1996) suggest, it may be that performing community service "requires a personal investment in which the action of helping others becomes part of one's identity and, thus, is understood and articulated in terms of what makes one feel good" (p. 91).

With regard to the effects of community service, scholars have observed that such service is often part of adolescents' political socialization in the sense that through their participation adolescents connect themselves to their society and develop an understanding of themselves as members of their society (Flanagan et al., 1998; Johnson et al., 1998). In one example of this effect, Youniss and Yates (1997) studied adolescents who were volunteering in a soup kitchen for the homeless. Through the course of the year of their service, the adolescents began to reassess themselves, not only reflecting on their fortunate lives in comparison to the people they were working with but also seeing themselves as potential actors in working for the reforms needed to address the problem of homelessness. Furthermore, the adolescents began to raise questions about characteristics of the American political system in relation to homelessness, such as policies regarding affordable housing and job training. Thus their participation made them more conscious of themselves as American citizens but also led them to be more critical of American political policies and also more aware of their own responsibility in addressing social problems in American society.

Studies have also examined the long-term effects of taking part in volunteer work in adolescence. In general, these studies indicate that people who take part in volunteer work in adolescence are also more likely to be active in political activities and volunteer organizations as adults (Ladewig & Thomas, 1987; Yates & Youniss, 1996). Of course, these studies do not show that community service in adolescence causes people to volunteer in adulthood as well. As we have seen, adolescent volunteers already differ from their peers in ways that explain their greater participation in community service. Nevertheless, the study by Youniss and Yates (1997) and other studies (e.g., Flanagan et al., 1998; Johnson et al., 1998) indicate that community service does have effects on the young people who take part in it.

Community Service in Emerging Adulthood: The Peace Corps and AmeriCorps

Like many adolescents, many emerging adults also do volunteer work, such as working with children and collecting and distributing food, clothing, and other resources to the poor. However, in emerging adulthood, volunteer work in American society has also taken the distinctive form of two major, government-sponsored institutions, the Peace Corps and AmeriCorps.

The **Peace Corps** is an organization that sends American volunteers all around the world to assist people in other nations by providing knowledge and skills in areas such as medical care, housing, sanitation, and food production. The organization began in 1961, when President John F. Kennedy exhorted young college graduates to give 2 years of their time in service to those in other nations who lacked the basic necessities of life. The Peace Corps is open to adults (age 18 and

Volunteers in the Peace Corps and AmeriCorps tend to be emerging adults.

older) of any age, but the main participants have been emerging adults. Over half of Peace Corps volunteers are aged 18 to 25 (Peace Corps, 2000a).

From its beginnings, the size of the Peace Corps grew rapidly, to a peak of 15,000 volunteers in 1966. Altogether, over 150,000 people have served as of 1999. Currently, about 7,000 volunteers are in the field in 134 countries. They are a highly educated group: 80% have undergraduate degrees, and another 15% have graduate training. Volunteers serve in a variety of areas, including education, environment, business, agriculture, and health. During their service they receive a monthly living allowance only high enough to enable them to live at the level of others in their community—not much, in other words. However, after the completion of their 2 years of service, they receive a bonus of about $6,000 to assist them in making the transition back to American society.

As benefits of serving in the Peace Corps, the organization points to the usefulness in future career development of overseas experience, cross-cultural knowledge, and learning the language of the host country (Peace Corps, 2000b). Although numerous personal accounts have been written by returning Peace Corps volunteers, few systematic studies have been conducted on the volunteers' experience and how it affects them. However, in 1996 the first comprehensive survey of returning volunteers was published (Peace Corps, 2000c). Among the findings were that 94% of them indicated they would make the same decision to join if they had it to do again. Also, 78% of returned volunteers had been involved in community service once they returned home.

In contrast to the Peace Corps, the **AmeriCorps** program is relatively recent, with the first group of volunteers serving in 1994. However, AmeriCorps has been larger than the Peace Corps from its inception. Over 20,000 volunteers served in 1994, and by 1999 over 40,000 AmeriCorp volunteers were serving each year (AmeriCorps, 2000a). About half the volunteers are White, 25% are African American, and 13% Latino (Aguirre International, 1999).

The AmeriCorps program does not originate volunteer programs but instead sponsors volunteers to work in local community organizations, doing such work as tutoring children and adults, rehabilitating housing for low-income families, immunizing children against diseases, and helping persons with disabilities and elderly persons to maintain independent living. Although AmeriCorps is open to any person age 18 or older, nearly all volunteers in the program are emerging adults aged 18 to 25. In return for their service they receive a small living allowance, health insurance, and an education award of $4,725 for each year served (1 or 2 years) to be applied toward college expenses, existing student loans, or an approved vocational training program (AmeriCorps, 2000b).

Evaluations of the AmeriCorps program have shown the benefits that it provides both to emerging adults and to their communities. An assessment of a random sample of volunteers before and after their participation in the program showed that 76% gained significantly in all five "life skills areas" examined: Communication, Interpersonal, Analytical Problem Solving, Understanding Organizations, and Using Information Technology (Aguirre International, 1999). One independent study showed that each tax dollar spent on the AmeriCorps program results in a direct and demonstrable benefit of $1.60 to $2.60 for the community in which the volunteer serves (AmeriCorps, 2000c).

Summing Up

In this chapter we have discussed work in traditional cultures, the history of young people's work in the West, and current patterns of work among adolescents and emerging adults in the West. The main points we have discussed are as follows:

- Adolescents in traditional cultures have typically worked alongside their parents, the boys in work such as hunting, fishing, and farming, the girls in work such as gathering, child care, and household work. However, because of globalization virtually all traditional cultures are moving toward indus-

trialization. The result of this in many countries is that people in traditional cultures, especially adolescents, are being subjected to hard work in terrible conditions for very low pay, such as on commercial farms and plantations, in factories, and in prostitution.

- Before industrialization, adolescents in the West typically worked alongside their parents, boys with their fathers mostly in farming, girls with their mothers mostly in child care and household work. During the 19th century, adolescents were a substantial proportion of the workforce in factories.

- Since World War II the proportion of American adolescents in part-time work has risen steeply, so that by now over three-fourths of high school seniors have a part-time job. Research results on the effects of working part-time during high school are complex, but evidence is quite strong that working more than 20 hours per week has a variety of negative effects.

- For the "forgotten half" of American adolescents who move to full-time work after high school rather than going to college, prospects have dimmed over the past 30 years as high-paying jobs for low-skilled workers have become more scarce in the American economy and high schools have failed to provide young people with the skills necessary for obtaining the best jobs available in the new technological economy.

- Super's widely used theory of occupational development focuses on adolescence and emerging adulthood as an important period containing stages of crystallization, specification, and implementation.

- Holland's theory describes six personality types and the jobs to which they are likely to be best suited. However, most people have personality characteristics that fit into more than one type, and most occupations can be performed with success and satisfaction by persons with a variety of personality characteristics.

- Unemployment is highly prevalent among African American and Latino emerging adults living in American cities due to the decline in low-skilled but high-paying manufacturing jobs in the cities over the past 30 years.

- Volunteer work (community service) is common among American adolescents and emerging adults. Two prominent volunteer programs for emerging adults are the Peace Corps and AmeriCorps.

Because school extends for so many years for most adolescents and emerging adults in industrialized countries, work plays less of a role in their lives than it does for young people in developing countries. The work that most adolescents do in their jobs is not work that many of them expect or want to be doing beyond adolescence. Still, it is striking how many American adolescents spend 20 hours or more per week in employment, especially since they recognize that their employment as adolescents does little to help them develop skills for adult work. They work in adolescence to finance an active leisure life, and their leisure is important enough to them that they are willing to spend a considerable number of hours a week in employment to be able to pay for it. It is a paradox—they give up leisure hours for employment, in order to be able to spend more money on their remaining leisure. But in doing so, they often sacrifice their school performance, which can have real effects on the success they are likely to have in their future occupations.

Emerging adults face different kinds of work challenges than adolescents. Work becomes more serious for emerging adults as a foundation for their occupations as adults. The central challenge for emerging adults in industrialized countries is to sort through the sometimes daunting range of possible occupations available to them and choose one occupational path they will find reasonably fulfilling and well-paying. They have to hope, too, that the path they choose will be open to them, and that they will succeed in the pursuit of the work they want.

For young people in developing countries, work is especially a problem. The economy of their parents' and grandparents' generations is disappearing under the influence of globalization, so they may feel that learning the skills that were central to work in their culture in the past is now pointless. However, the alternatives open to them right now in their industrializing economies are grim for the most part, and usually involve arduous work under dangerous, unhealthy, exploitative conditions.

The history of the work experience of adolescents in the West suggests that for young people in developing countries, changes in the 21st century will be in the direction of better work conditions, higher pay, and an increasing number of years in adolescence and emerging adulthood devoted to education and preparation for meaningful work that they choose for themselves. However, this will not happen automatically, if it happens at all, through some inevitable mechanism of history, but through the activism of committed people in their own countries as well as in industrialized countries.

Key Terms

International Labor Organization (ILO)	retention rate	credentialism	community service
debt bondage	the forgotten half	underemployed	Peace Corps
occupational deviance	the new basic skills	second shift	AmeriCorps
	apprenticeship	unemployed	

For Further Reading

Barling, J., & Kelloway, E. K. (1999). *Young workers: Varieties of experience.* Washington, DC: American Psychological Association. The authors of the chapters in this edited book emphasize that employment is not necessarily good or bad for adolescents, but can have different effects depending on the characteristics of the work and the characteristics of the adolescent.

Booth, A., Crouter, A. C., & Shanahan, M. (Eds.) (1999). *Transitions to adulthood in a changing economy: No work, no family, no future?* Westport, CT: Praeger. Contains a variety of interesting articles on work in emerging adulthood, mostly by sociologists.

Greenberger, E., & Steinberg, L. (1986). *When teenagers work: The psychological and social costs of adolescent employment.* New York: Basic Books. A classic study of the effects of work on adolescents by two prominent psychologists. The emphasis is on the negative effects of work, especially for adolescents who work over 15 hours per week.

Applying Research

Murnane, R. J. & Levy F. (1997). *Teaching the new basic skills: Principles for educating children to thrive in a changing economy.* New York: Free Press. The authors examine the employment prospects of emerging adults who do not attend college, 10 years after the publication of *The forgotten half: Non-college youth in America.* They conclude that many promising opportunities exist, but noncollege emerging adults often have not learned enough in high school to take advantage of those opportunities. The authors also supply specific suggestions for rectifying this problem.

CHAPTER 12

Media

In 1774, the great German writer Johann Wolfgang von Goethe (pronounced gur'-tuh*) published* The Sorrows of Young Werther, *about a young man who kills himself in despair over his unrequited love for a married woman. The novel immediately became immensely popular all over Europe, inspiring poems, plays, operas, songs, even jewelry and an "Eau de Werther" scent for ladies. At the same time, however, the novel inspired immense controversy. It was banned in some parts of Germany due to fear that impressionable adolescent readers might interpret it as recommending suicide, and in Denmark a proposed translation was prohibited for the same reason. Although claims that Werther caused an epidemic of suicide in Europe are now regarded as unfounded (Hulse, 1989), in one verified case a young woman who had been deserted by her lover drowned herself in the river behind Goethe's house in Weimar, Germany, a copy of* Werther *in her pocket. Goethe was sufficiently disturbed by the controversy over the book to add an epigraph to the 1775 edition of the novel urging his readers not to follow Werther's example.*

In Goethe's time as well as our own, the question of media effects has been a source of public debate and concern, often with a particular focus on the lives of adolescents. One example took place in the autumn of 1993, concerning a movie called *The Program* released by the Walt Disney Company. The movie, about the players and coach of a college football program, quickly became controversial because of a scene in which one of the players demonstrates his manly toughness by lying down in the middle of a busy highway at night as cars and trucks whoosh by him. Some adolescents who had seen the movie proceeded to try the stunt for themselves. An 18-year-old Pennsylvania boy was killed and two other boys were critically injured, one of them paralyzed. In response to the resulting outcry, Disney hastily recalled the film and deleted the scene in question, while strenuously denying responsibility for the boys' reckless acts.

This is about as definite an example of media effects as it is possible to find. There can be little doubt that the boys were imitating the behavior they had witnessed in the movie. They had seen the movie just days before, and the friends who accompanied them that night testified later that they were imitating the stunt they had seen in the film.

At the same time, this example illustrates why drawing a simple cause-and-effect relationship between the media adolescents consume and their subsequent behavior is problematic. Most obvious is that literally hundreds of thousands of people (mostly adolescents) saw the movie with the controversial scene—it was playing in 1,220 theaters at the time, and even estimating modestly at 100 persons per theater would put the total number of viewers over 100,000—yet the total number of reported incidents that resulted from adolescents imitating the scene was *three*. Even if it were generously estimated that 100 times as many adolescents imitated the scene as were injured in the process, the total number of adolescents who were affected by the scene to the point of imitating it would amount to one-fourth of 1% of the people who watched it. Evidently, then, the adolescents who imitated the scene had traits or circumstances that led them to imitate it even though the vast majority of the people who watched it did not.

This incident illustrates both the potentially profound effects of the media on adolescents and the complexity involved in tracing those effects. Debates over media effects are often polarized, with those at one extreme glibly blaming media for every social ill and those at the other extreme dismissing (just as glibly) all claims of media effects as unverifiable. I believe both extremes are mistaken, and in this chapter I will present you with a more complex (and hopefully more true-to-life) approach to understanding young people's uses of media.

THINKING CRITICALLY

If one or two people out of a million who watch a particular movie or listen to a particular song are negatively affected by it, is that reason enough to ban or withdraw the movie or song? Or should people—even adolescents—be responsible for how they respond to media?

Media and Young People's Development

No account of young people's development would be complete without a description of the media they use. Music, television, movies, and magazines are part of the environment of nearly every young person currently growing up in industrialized countries (and increasingly, as we will see, in developing countries as well). The typical American adolescent listens to music for about 4 to 6 hours a day (Christenson & Roberts, 1998; Fine, Mortimer, & Roberts, 1990), and watches television for another 2 to 4 hours (Lichty, 1989; Roberts, Foehr, Rideout & Brodie, 1999). Adolescents in Europe and Japan also watch TV for an average of about 2 hours a day (Flammer, Alsaker, & Noack, 1999; Rohlen, 1983). Seventy percent of all popular music recordings are bought by 12- to 20-year-olds (Brake, 1985). Adolescents watch more movies than any other segment of the population; over 50% of adolescents aged 12 to 17 go to at least one movie per month (Fine et al., 1990). Over a third of high school juniors and seniors claim daily magazine reading (Fine et al., 1990), and three-fourths of adolescent girls read at least one magazine regularly (Klein et al., 1993).

A new medium that is growing rapidly in popularity among young people is the Internet. In a 1998 survey by *Consumers' Research* magazine, 79% of high school students in the United States reported having regular Internet access, compared with just 13% of persons over age 50. Similar or even higher percentages are reported for other Western countries and for Eastern

American adolescents listen to music for an average of 4 to 6 hours a day.

countries such as Tiawan (Anderson, 2000). Internet access for young people in industrialized countries is expected to become nearly universal in the next decade, in part because schools are increasingly becoming linked to the Internet and encouraging students to use it for finding information (Cravatta, 1997).

Add videos, computer games, books, and newspapers, and the total amounts to a large proportion of the daily experience of adolescents. Altogether American adolescents typically spend about 8 hours per day using media, either as their primary activity or as background to other activities (Fine et al., 1990; Roberts et al., 1999). There are few statistics on media use among emerging adults, but there is no reason to expect media use to decline between adolescence and emerging adulthood.

Another reason for looking at media in relation to young people's development is that a great deal of concern exists, in our time, about the potential effects that media have on them. These effects are generally viewed as negative. Television is blamed for inspiring young people to drink alcohol, have sex, and hold stereotyped beliefs about gender roles. Music is blamed for motivating young people to commit violent acts toward others or toward themselves. Movies and computer games, too, are blamed for violence. Magazines are held re-

sponsible for promoting an ideal female form that is so emaciated that many girls become emaciated themselves attempting to emulate it. Given all this controversy over young people and media, it is important for us to consider what the research evidence tells us about the merit of the accusations. And it is important to consider the possibility of positive media effects, as well.

In this chapter, then, we will first look at some of the uses of media that are typical among young people and how those uses reflect certain developmental needs. This will include a discussion of how socialization through the media is related to socialization from other sources, such as parents, peers, and school. In the second half of the chapter we will examine the research concerning various controversial media, from violent television and computer games to sex in music to cigarette advertising. Then we will consider the role that media play in the globalization of adolescence.

The Uses and Gratifications Approach

For a long time, research on media was presented mainly in terms of media effects, with the media consumer depicted as passive and easily manipulated. However, in recent years a new approach has developed that recognizes that the role media play in the lives of adolescents and others is usually more complex than a simple cause-and-effect relationship. This new approach is known as the **uses and gratifications approach**, and the emphasis is on viewing people as active media consumers (Rubin, 1993).

The uses and gratifications approach is based on two key principles. The first is that people differ in numerous ways that lead them to make different choices about which media to consume. For example, not all adolescents like violent TV shows; the uses and gratifications approach assumes that adolescents who like such shows differ from adolescents who do not, even prior to any effect that watching violent shows may have. The second principle is that even people consuming the same media product will respond to it in a variety of ways, depending on their individual characteristics. For example, some adolescent girls may read teen magazines and respond by feeling extremely insecure about the way they look compared with the models in the magazine, whereas other girls may read the same magazines and be relatively unaffected.

Rather than viewing young people as the passive, easily manipulated targets of media influences, the uses and gratifications approach asks, "What sort of *uses* or purposes do young people have in mind when they watch a television show, or go to a movie, or listen to a CD, or read a magazine? And what sort of *gratifications* or satisfactions do they get from the media they choose?" We will keep these questions at the forefront as we discuss media in this chapter. Let's start out by taking a look at five of the principal uses that young people make of media.

Five Uses

Five uses of media by adolescents can be specified (Arnett, 1995b): entertainment, identity formation, high sensation, coping, and youth culture identification. This does not mean that these are the only uses of media that exist among young people, but these five represent their most common uses (for other typologies see Blumler, 1979; Lull, 1980; Rubin, 1979). All of the uses described except entertainment are *developmental* in the sense that they are more likely to be uses of media for adolescents and emerging adults than for children or adults (Arnett, 1995b).

Entertainment

Adolescents and emerging adults, like children and adults, often make use of media simply for entertainment, as an enjoyable part of their leisure lives (Brake, 1985; Roberts et al., 1999). Music is the most-used media form among adolescents and emerging adults, and listening to music often accompanies young people's leisure, from driving around in a car to hanging out with friends to secluding themselves in the privacy of their bedrooms for contemplation (Larson, 1995). This applies to music videos, too—adolescents state that one of their top motivations for watching music videos is simply entertainment (Sun & Lull, 1986). Television is used by many adolescents as a way of diverting themselves from personal concerns with entertainment that is passive, distracting, and undemanding (Larson, 1995; Roberts et al., 1999). Entertainment is clearly one of the uses young people seek in movies and magazines as well. Media are used by young people toward the entertainment purposes of fun, amusement, and recreation.

Identity Formation

" *[I'd like to be like] Cher, Madonna, and Tina Turner all rolled together, because they all have attitude and they know what they want.*"

—*Stephanie, age 13 (in Currie, 1999, p. 262)*

Adolescents often admire media stars.

" *I like it in* YM *and* Seventeen *magazines how they have like your horoscope and what you're like—your color and if you're an 'earth person' or a 'water person,' something like that. They tell you what you are.*"

—*Lauren, age 14 (in Currie, 1999, p. 154)*

One of the most important developmental challenges of adolescence and emerging adulthood is identity formation—the cultivation of a conception of one's values, abilities, and hopes for the future. In cultures where media are available, media can provide materials that young people use toward the construction of an identity (Swidler, 1986). Part of identity formation is thinking about the kind of person you would like to become, and in media adolescents find ideal selves and feared selves (Steele & Brown, 1995), to emulate and to avoid. The use of media for this purpose is reflected in the pictures and posters adolescents put up in their rooms, which are often of media stars from entertainment and sports (see the Research Focus box). After their parents, media celebrities of various kinds are mentioned most often by adolescents when they are asked whom they most admire (Arnett, 1996).

Media can also provide adolescents with information that would otherwise be unavailable to them, and some of this information may be used toward constructing an identity. For example, adolescents may learn about different possible occupations in part by watching television or reading magazines (Clifford,

RESEARCH FOCUS
Media Use in Adolescents' Bedrooms

Jane Brown and her colleagues have used a number of creative methods to study adolescents' uses of media. In one study (Brown, White, Nikopolou, 1993) they asked adolescent girls to keep a daily journal about whatever they saw in the media about sex and relationships. In another study (Steele & Brown, 1995), they had high school seniors interview each other about how they used media in their bedrooms at home, including television, magazines, and stereos as well as room decorations that reflected media use (posters of rock musicians, sport stars, etc.). Another method they have used in their research is what they call "room touring," where the researchers actually "tour" adolescents' bedrooms and have the adolescents describe everything that holds special meaning or significance for them, usually including numerous media artifacts (posters, pictures from magazines, CDs and cassette tapes, etc.).

All of these research methods are qualitative. This means (as described in Chapter 1) that the focus is not on quantifying experience into patterns that can be reflected in numbers and analyzed in statistical tests, but on the experience of individuals and how they interpret and articulate their experiences.

Qualitative methods can result in rich data about the lives of individual adolescents, as in these two descriptions:

> In [14 year-old] Rachel's room the bed is covered with clothes, cassette tapes and magazines, a red phone, and the cassette player. The walls are plastered with posters of the Beatles, the B52s, and a leering rock musician with his hand stuck down in his pants. The posters cover over an Impressionist art print of a little girl with flowers. One wall is full of advertisements torn from magazines featuring muscular men and thin women modeling the latest fashions. . . .
>
> Sixteen years old and a sophomore in high school, Jack safeguards an eclectic mix of childhood artifacts and teenage fantasies and aspi-

rations in his bedroom. On one wall a wooden box displays a fleet of multihued model cars, painstakingly crafted during grade school. A shelf is piled high with the audiotaped "mixes" that now occupy his time. Perched on top is a teddy bear dressed in a white sailor suit, and behind the portable TV are a hand-drawn "drugs kill" poster, GI Joe cutouts, and a pen-and-pencil rendering of *Lady and the Tramp*, the flotsam of earlier years. On the wall next to his bed are more current concerns: a Ferrari Testarossa poster, and pictures of girls clipped from magazines. "If they look good," Jack explains, "I just put them up on the wall." (Steele & Brown, 1995, pp. 551–552)

In addition to such individual examples, qualitative research such as the research conducted by Brown and her colleagues allows scholars to describe general patterns of development. However, for qualitative researchers these general patterns are usually ascertained through the researcher's insights and judgment rather than on the basis of statistical analyses. For example, in the study in which adolescent girls kept journals of their responses to sexual media content, the researchers concluded that the girls' responses fell into three general patterns (Brown et al., 1993). Those they termed "Disinterested" tended to ignore sexual content in media, and preferred not to talk or think about it even when prodded to do so. Their rooms tended to be filled with stuffed animals and dolls rather than media items. In contrast, a second group labeled "Intrigued" had rooms filled with magazines, musical recordings, and television, and their walls were filled with images of popular media stars, including media items with sexual content. A third group, "Resisters," also had rooms with evidence of high media use, but they tended to select images from less mainstream media—political leaders and female sports stars rather than popular music performers. They were termed "Resisters" because they were often critical of sexual media content, particularly the media depiction of women as sexual objects. In the journal of Audrey, age 14, was this critique of cosmetic ads:

> I think that they use these beautiful people to sell their products because they want fat old ladies sitting at home with curlers in their hair watching the soaps to think that if they buy Loreal's [sic] 10 day formula they'll end up looking that beautiful. I think that's really stupid because for one, I know perfectly well I don't look like Cybil Shepard and Loreal's

[sic] 10 day formula's not going to change that. (Steele & Brown, 1995, p. 564)

In this and many other examples, Brown and her colleagues show that adolescents are not just passive targets of media, but active consumers who *use* media for a variety of purposes. At the same time, their qualitative focus on the experience of individuals also allows for revealing examples suggesting media effects. Audrey, seemingly so adept at deflecting the lure of media images, reported in her journal a couple of days after the entry above that she had spent the afternoon buying "basically cosmetics!"

Gunter, & McAleer, 1995). I once interviewed a young man who was studying to become an environmental biologist. He had been introduced to the idea from watching television specials on animals and the environment during childhood and adolescence. Also, in my research on adolescent heavy metal fans (discussed in more detail later in the chapter), over one-third of them, inspired by their heavy metal heroes, stated their intention to go into music as a career, preferably as heavy metal heroes themselves (Arnett, 1996).

An important aspect of identity formation, and one for which adolescents may especially make use of media, is gender role identity (Brown & Hendee, 1989; Greenberg, Brown, & Buerkel-Rothfuss, 1992; Larson, 1995; Steele & Brown, 1995). Adolescents take ideals of what it means to be a man or a woman partly from the media, which present physical and behavioral gender ideals in images through music, movies (Greenberg et al., 1986), television (Brown, Childers, & Waszak, 1990), and magazines (Evans et al., 1991). Adolescents use the information provided in media to learn sexual and romantic scripts (Arnett, 2000f; Brown et al., 1990)—for example, how to approach a potential romantic partner for the first time, what to do on a date, and even how to kiss. For both girls and boys, gender, sexuality, and relationships are central to the kind of identity exploration and identity formation for which adolescents use media (Ward, 1995).

Magazines are a medium where gender role identity formation is an especially common implicit theme, particularly in magazines for adolescent girls. As noted in Chapter 5, nearly half of the space of the most popular magazines for teenage girls is devoted to advertisements, mostly for fashion and beauty products, and fashion/beauty is a prominent topic of the articles in

these magazines as well (Currie, 1999; Evans et al., 1991). Magazines for adolescent girls also provide abundant "information" about boys and the intricacies of heterosexual relationships. These relationships are the most common topic of feature articles in these magazines (Evans et al., 1991). In contrast, the magazines most popular among adolescent boys are devoted to sports, computer games, humor, and cars—with little or no mention of how to improve physical appearance or how to form relationships with girls (Kantrowitz & Wingert, 1999).

THINKING CRITICALLY

What do you think explains why physical appearance and relationships are virtually the only topic in magazines read by adolescent girls, but these topics scarcely exist in magazines read by adolescent boys?

High Sensation

Sensation seeking is a personality characteristic that is defined by the extent to which a person enjoys *novelty* and *intensity* of sensation. Adolescents and emerging adults tend to be higher in sensation seeking than adults (Arnett, 1994b), and certain media provide the intense and novel sensations that appeal to many young people. Many media products appeal to adults as well as young people, but some appeal almost exclusively to young people, at least partly because of the high-sensation quality of the stimulation. The audience for "action" films is composed mostly of males in adolescence and emerging adulthood, because this is the segment of the population that is highest in sensation seeking and consequently most likely to be drawn to films that portray high-sensation scenes involving explosions, car chases (and car crashes), gunfire, and the like (Arnett, 1994b). Adolescent boys also dominate the audiences for the high-sensation musical forms of rap and heavy metal (Arnett, 1996), and these are two types of music that are popular among teens (Chadwin & Heaton, 1996; Roberts et al., 1999). Heavy-metal fans use high-sensation words like *intense, fast,* and *powerful* to describe why they like the music (Arnett, 1996). Similar high-sensation terms could be applied to rap music, with the addition of vicarious high-sensation excitement from the depiction of urban violence (Samuels, 1991).

Heightened sensation seeking in adolescence and emerging adulthood may help explain why television viewing decreases during the adolescent years while music listening increases (Larson, Kubey, & Colletti, 1989). In general, television shows are created by adults with the intention of appealing to the widest possible audience, and for the most part the stimulation provided by television is not highly novel or intense. In the ESM studies, adolescents' emotional states during television viewing are usually low, slightly depressed, kind of *blah* (Larson, 1995). Most popular music, in contrast, is created by people who are adolescents and emerging adults or just beyond (with exceptions such as the Rolling Stones), and the sensory stimulation of most popular music is much higher than for television (think of the volume level of the last rock concert you attended). ESM studies find that adolescents' emotional arousal when listening to music tends to be high, at least partly because of the greater sensory and emotional intensity of music compared to television (Larson, 1995).

Coping

Young people use media to relieve and dispel negative emotions. Several studies indicate that "Listen to music" and "Watch TV" are the coping strategies most commonly used by adolescents when they are angry, anxious, or unhappy (Kurdek, 1987; Moore & Schultz, 1983). Music may be particularly important in this respect. Larson (1995) reports that adolescents often listen to music in the privacy of their bedrooms while pondering the themes of the songs in relation to their own lives, as part of the process of emotional self-regulation. In early adolescence, when the amount of problems, conflict, and stresses at home, at school, and with friends increases, time spent listening to music also increases, while time spent watching television decreases (Larson et al., 1989).

Certain types of music, such as rap or heavy metal, may appeal especially to young people who use music for coping. Little research exists on rap music, but adolescent fans of heavy metal report that they listen to heavy metal especially when they are angry, and that the music typically has the effect of purging their anger and calming them down (Arnett, 1991, 1996; we will discuss this in more detail below). Heavy metal is the most popular musical preference of male adolescents with serious emotional problems (Epstein, Pratto, & Skipper, 1990), which suggests that boys with emotional problems may use heavy metal as a way of coping with their problems.

Young people also sometimes use television for coping purposes. Larson (1995) reports that adolescents use television as a way of turning off the stressful emotions that have accumulated during the day. Similarly, Kurdek (1987) found that adolescents use watching TV as a deliberate coping strategy when experiencing negative emotions. Adolescents also may choose media materials for specific coping purposes. A study of Israeli adolescents, in the aftermath of the 1991 Persian Gulf war, indicated that the media were an important source of information during the war and that adolescents used the information obtained through the media to help them cope with the stress of the war (Zeidner, 1993).

THINKING CRITICALLY

Why do you think watching television and listening to music have calming effects on adolescents' emotions? Do you think the same effect would be true for emerging adults?

Youth Culture Identification

Media consumption can give adolescents a sense of being connected to a youth culture or subculture that is united by certain youth-specific values and interests. In cultures where people change residence frequently (such as the United States) the media provide common ground for all adolescents. No matter where they move within the United States, adolescents will find peers in their new area who have watched the same television programs and movies, have listened to the same music, and are familiar with the same advertising slogans and symbols. Music, especially, is a medium for the expression of adolescent-specific values (Roe, 1985).

Youth subcultures are often constructed around a specific type of music.

(Roe, 1987; Arnett, 1996). In recent decades, distinct youth subcultures have been defined by punk, heavy metal, rap, and techno music.

Media and Adolescent Socialization

We have seen that media use is a big part of the lives of most adolescents in the West. This prominent role for media is even more striking to think about in historical perspective. At the beginning of the 20th century, most adolescents' exposure to media would have been limited to print media such as books, magazines, and newspapers. Television, radio, record players, stereos, CD players, videos, and computer games did not even exist. In less than a century, all these media have become a central part of the cultural environment of industrialized societies.

Adolescents' identification may be not to youth culture as a whole but to a youth subculture. For example, recently in Europe a subculture of neo-fascist skinheads has developed, mostly adolescent boys and emerging adults. One of the unifying trademarks of this subculture is their music, known as "Oi" music. It is characterized by punk-style music, and lyrics that hurl insults and threats at foreigners and ethnic residents of their countries. Sales of the music reached hundreds of thousands annually by the early 1990s, across Europe ("Racism rock," 1992). Recently a similar type of music, dubbed "hatecore," has gained a following among several thousand young people in the United States, mainly young men in their twenties (Segal, 2000).

This is one example of the ways that young people may use media to establish a subculture, to carve out a subcultural identity that is distinct not only from the larger society but from other youth subcultures as well. Of course, as noted in Chapter 8, only a minority of adolescents ever become part of a distinct youth subculture. Roe's (1987, 1995) studies of Swedish adolescents suggest that one source of self-selection into youth subcultures is success or failure in school. In particular, adolescents who fail at school develop an oppositional view of the world and seek out similar peers as well as oppositional music that gives a voice to their alienation and their group identity (also see Lull, 1987). Media, particularly music, provide a way of defining and uniting the members of a youth subculture as well as expressing their shared view of the world

What does this transformation in the cultural environment imply for young people's development? Essentially it amounts to the creation of a new source of socialization (Arnett, 1995b). Of course, the media have become part of the social environment of people of all ages, but the potential role of media in the socialization of young people is perhaps especially strong. As noted, adolescence and emerging adulthood are times when important aspects of socialization are taking place, especially with regard to identity-related issues such as beginning occupational preparation, learning gender roles, and developing a set of values and beliefs. It is also a time when the presence and influence of the family has diminished relative to childhood (Larson & Richards, 1994; Youniss & Smollar, 1985). At the same time that parents' influence on socialization recedes during adolescence, the role of the media in socialization grows. In one national survey of 10- to 15-year-olds, 49% said they "learn a lot from" television and movies, a higher percentage than learned a lot from their mothers (38%) or their fathers (31%) (Kantrowitz & Wingert, 1999).

A common theme in the five uses of media described above is that, in all of these respects, adolescents draw materials from media that contribute to their socialization. When they seek entertainment or high sensation from media, when they use media materials toward identity formation or for coping, when they participate in a media-based youth subculture, adolescents are also, in a larger sense, participating in activities that are part of their socialization. That is, media are part of the process by which adolescents acquire—or resist acquiring—the behaviors and beliefs of the social world, the culture, in which they live (Arnett, 1995a). For this reason, we will address the properties of media with regard to the socialization process.

As a socialization influence, the media tend toward broad socialization in societies that have freedom of speech and where the media are relatively uncontrolled and uncensored by government agencies. In such societies, there is tremendous diversity in the media offerings available, providing adolescents a diverse array of potential models and influences to choose from. This is likely to promote a broad range of individual differences in values, beliefs, interests, and personality characteristics, because adolescents can choose from diverse media offerings the ones that resonate most strongly with their own particular inclinations.

Most Western societies value free speech highly, and so a diverse range of media content is allowed. However, the United States takes this principle further than European countries do. For example, Germany has a legal prohibition against music lyrics that express hatred and advocate violence toward immigrants and Jews. (The "Oi" music described above is among the prohibited music.) In Norway, one person in the government reviews all movies before they are allowed to be shown in theaters and prohibits the showing of movies judged to be too violent. Neither of these prohibitions would be likely to survive a legal challenge in the United States because of the protection of free speech in the First Amendment of the Constitution.

Nevertheless, the principle of free speech does not mean that all media must be accessible to all persons regardless of age. Age restrictions on access to media are allowable under the First Amendment, and the United States has rating systems for movies, music, television, and computer games that are designed to indicate to children, adolescents, and their parents which media may be unsuitable for persons under a certain age (Funk et al., 1999). However, the enforcement of these guidelines and restrictions requires substantial involvement on the part of parents (for the most part they are guidelines, not legal requirements). Because parents are often either unaware of the media their adolescents are using or hesitant to place restrictions, most American adolescents easily gain access to whatever media they like (Funk et al., 1999; Strasburger & Donnerstein, 1999).

Media and Other Sources of Socialization

An important difference exists between media and other socialization agents in the adolescent's environment, such as family members, teachers, community members, law enforcement agents, and religious authorities. Typically, these other socializers have an interest in encouraging the adolescent to accept the attitudes, beliefs, and values of adults in order to preserve social order and pass the culture on from one generation to the next (Wrong, 1994). In contrast, media are typically presented by people who have the economic success of the media enterprise as their primary concern. As a result, the content of media consumed by adolescents is driven not by a desire to promote successful socialization but by the uses adolescents themselves can make of media. Because the media are market-driven to a large extent, media providers are likely to provide adolescents with whatever it is they believe adolescents want—within the limits imposed on media providers by the other adult socializers such as parents and legal authorities.

This means that adolescents have greater control over their socialization from the media than they do over socialization from family or school. This has two important consequences. First, it results in a great deal of diversity in the media available to adolescents, from hip hop to heavy metal, from public television to MTV, from *Seventeen* to *Mad* magazine, as media providers try to cover every potential niche of the market for media products. Adolescents can choose from among this diversity whatever media materials best suit their personalities and preferences, and on any given occasion adolescents can choose the media materials that best suit the circumstances and their emotional state.

Second, to some extent this socialization goes *over the heads* of the other socializing adults in an adolescent's environment (Strasburger & Donnerstein, 1999). Parents may try to impose restrictions on the music, television shows, movies, and magazines their adolescents consume, but these restrictions are unlikely to be successful if an adolescent is determined to avoid them. The limited time parents and adolescents spend in each others' company make such restrictions difficult for parents to enforce (Larson & Richards, 1994).

As a source of adolescent socialization, media bear the most similarity to peers. With media as with peers, adolescents have substantial control over their own socialization, as they make choices about media and peers with only limited influence from their parents and other adult socializers. In both cases, adolescents sometimes make choices, from the range of options available to them, that adults find troublesome. Both media and peers are central to youth subcultures, and adolescents' participation in youth subcultures is often disturbing to adults because such subcultures are often oppositional and explicitly reject the authority of adults (Brake, 1985; Lull, 1987).

Examples of how adolescents may use media in ways that are disturbing to their parents and other adults in their immediate social environment can be seen in relation to each of the five uses of media described above. They may find *entertainment* in "action" movies and other media that many adults consider disturbingly violent. In assembling materials toward *identity formation* they may develop admiration for media stars, decorating their bedroom walls with the images of stars who seem to reject the values of the adult world, stars who may in fact reject the very idea of "growing up" to a responsible adulthood (Steele & Brown, 1995). Adolescents also may be attracted to *high-sensation* media that adults find disagreeable for precisely the reason it is so appealing to adolescents—the extraordinary high-sensation intensity of it (Arnett, 1996). Adolescents may seclude themselves in their rooms and use media in *coping* with their problems in a way that seems to shut out their parents (Larson, 1995). Finally, adolescents may become involved in a media-based *youth subculture* that actively and explicitly rejects the future that adult society holds out to them. In all of these ways, socialization from the media may be subversive to the socialization promoted by other adult socializers (Lull, 1987).

However, this portrayal of adolescents' media use as oppositional should be modified in several respects. First, it bears repeating that media are diverse, and not all of the media used by adolescents are contrary to the aims and principles of adult society. Much of it is, in fact, quite conservative; many media providers, especially in television, shrink from controversy (Brown et al., 1990; Larson, 1990) and tend to avoid topics that could subject them to public attack (and advertisers' boycotts). In most cases, television programs are perceived by adolescents as reinforcing conventional values such as "honesty is the best policy," "good wins over evil," and "hard work yields rewards." Second, adolescents do not come to media as blank slates, but as members of a family, community, and culture who have socialized them from birth and from whom they

have learned ideals and principles that are likely to influence their media choices and how they interpret the media they consume.

Third, the range of media available to adolescents, though vast, is not unlimited. Parents can place restrictions on how adolescents may use media at least when the parents are present; schools often restrict adolescents' media use during and between classes; and the United States has guidelines for the content of television programs (at least on the major networks) and for the magazines and movies that may be sold to adolescents under age 18. Fourth, profit is not the only motive of media providers. They have lives outside of their occupational roles, and they have interests as members of their families, communities, and culture that, at least for some of them, limit the extent to which they are willing to be perceived as undermining the socialization goals of the rest of society.

Also, the portrait of media socialization presented here applies to the contemporary West, and media socialization may be quite different in traditional cultures. Legal and parental controls over adolescents' access to media are likely to be tighter in traditional cultures with narrow socialization, so that adolescents are unlikely to be able to use media toward self-socialization to the same degree. However, today even in many traditional cultures, the introduction of Western media is opening up new possibilities to adolescents, loosening the extent of parental control and increasing the extent to which adolescents choose the materials of their socialization (Burbank, 1988; Condon, 1988, 1995; Davis & Davis, 1995). Later in this chapter, we will look at examples of Western media influencing adolescents in traditional cultures.

◼   **THINKING CRITICALLY**

Suppose you had an adolescent who liked to listen to a kind of music you believed was potentially harmful because of the level of violence in it. How would you handle it—would you forbid it, ignore it, discuss it—and why?

Controversial Media

Because adolescents spend a lot of time daily consuming media, and because media play an important role in adolescent socialization, parents and other adults express concern when they perceive the media as containing material that may have potentially damaging or disruptive influences on adolescents. In this section, we consider criticisms of controversial media and examine the available research evidence in relation to those criticisms. The areas of controversy discussed here are television and aggressiveness, computer games and aggressiveness, television and adolescent sex, rap and heavy metal music, and cigarette advertising.

Television and Aggressiveness

A great deal of research attention has focused on the extent to which media promote and provoke violence in young people. Virtually all of this research has concerned television, and the majority of it has concerned preadolescent children (Cantor, 1998, 2000; Comstock & Strasburger, 1990; Strasburger, 1995). However, this is an issue of particular importance with regard to adolescents and emerging adults, because the overwhelming majority of violent crimes are committed by young males, and because the rate of violent crimes rose sharply in the United States from 1960 to 1990 (Federal Bureau of Investigation, 1993), a period in which there was also an increase in the pervasiveness of television.

Unfortunately, most of the studies on adolescents and television violence are correlational studies, which ask adolescents about the television programs they watch and about their aggressive behavior. Correlational studies cannot prove causality and merely indicate the unremarkable finding that aggressive adolescents prefer aggressive television programs. These studies cannot answer the crucial question, "Does watching violence on TV cause adolescents to become more aggressive, or are adolescents who are more aggressive also more likely to enjoy watching violence on TV?"

In an effort to address this question, numerous **field studies** have been conducted on the effects of television on adolescent aggression, in which adolescents (usually boys) in a setting such as a residential school or summer camp were separated into two groups, and one group was shown TV or movies with violent themes whereas the other viewed TV or movies with nonviolent themes. However, the findings of these studies are weak and inconsistent, and overall they do not provide support for the claim that viewing violent media causes adolescents to be more aggressive (Freedman, 1984; Strasburger, 1995).

Nevertheless, two studies provide compelling support for the argument that watching violent television causes violent behavior. One study, by Huesmann and his colleagues (Huesmann et al., 1984), studied children's TV viewing in 3rd grade and their aggressive behavior in 3rd grade and again at age 19. A significant relationship was found for boys between viewing TV violence in 3rd grade and aggressive behavior at age 19. What makes the finding more compelling is that, in contrast, *no* relationship was found between boys' aggressive behavior in 3rd grade and their viewing of TV violence at age 19. This seems to indicate that the relationship between watching TV violence in 3rd grade and aggressiveness at age 19 was *causal*, rather than being based on a personality tendency for aggressiveness that was simply consistent from age 9 to age 19. However, this impressive pattern was not found for girls, and even among boys it was found for only one out of three measures of aggressiveness (Freedman, 1984).

Another intriguing study (Williams, 1986) involved a natural experiment in which a Canadian community (called "Notel" by the researchers) was studied before and after the introduction of television into the community. Aggressive behavior among children in Notel was compared with the behavior of children in two comparable communities, one with only one television channel ("Unitel") and one with multiple TV channels ("Multitel"). In each community several ratings of aggressiveness were obtained, including teachers' ratings, self-reports, and observers' ratings of children's verbal and physical aggressiveness. Aggressive behavior was lower among children in Notel than among children in Unitel or Multitel initially, but increased significantly among children in Notel after TV was introduced, so that Notel children were equal in aggressive behavior to their Unitel and Multitel peers 2 years after the introduction of TV. However, the study involved children in middle childhood rather than adolescents, and it is difficult to say how the adolescents of the community reacted.

> "SERIOUS AGGRESSION NEVER OCCURS UNLESS THERE IS A CONVERGENCE OF LARGE NUMBERS OF CAUSES, BUT ONE OF THE VERY IMPORTANT FACTS WE HAVE IDENTIFIED IS EXPOSURE TO MEDIA VIOLENCE. . . . IF WE DON'T DO SOMETHING, WE ARE CONTRIBUTING TO A SOCIETY THAT WILL BE MORE AND MORE VIOLENT."
> —PSYCHOLOGIST L. ROWELL HUESMANN (QUOTED IN STRASBURGER, 1995, P. 18)

Although the findings of these two studies are intriguing, overall the research in the area provides only mixed support for the claim that watching violent television causes adolescents to behave aggressively (Freedman, 1984). Hundreds of studies on television and aggressiveness have been conducted over the past 40 years, but in my judgment they have not conclusively shown that a causal relationship exists from violent television to aggression, in spite of the claims and hopes of some of the leading researchers in the area (e.g., Cantor, 2000; Comstock & Strasburger, 1990; Eron, 1993; Strasburger, 1995; Strasburger & Donnerstein, 1999). We can say with certainty that a *correlation* exists between adolescents' aggressiveness and their preferences for watching violent television, but it is not surprising that adolescents who behave aggressively also find it entertaining to watch other people behave aggressively. It is probably true that, for some adolescents, watching television violence acts as a model for their own aggressiveness (Strasburger, 1995). However, if watching violent television were a substantial contributor to aggressiveness among adolescents, the relationship would be stronger than it is in the many field studies and longitudinal studies that have been conducted (Freedman, 1984).

Does watching violent television programs cause adolescents to become aggressive?

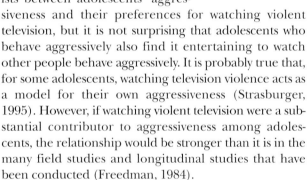

THINKING CRITICALLY

Do the two studies described here persuade you that television causes aggression in children and adolescents, or not? How would you design a study that would answer the question more clearly—or is that not possible?

Computer Games and Aggressiveness

A relatively new type of media that has become popular among adolescents is computer video games. It used to be that you had to go to a video arcade to play video games, but now these games are played mostly at home on personal computers (Funk, 1993). This form of media use is especially popular among young adolescents, and especially among boys. One survey of 7th and 8th graders found that boys reported spending over 4 hours a week playing computer games, and girls about 2 hours (Funk, 1993). Another survey, of 11-year-olds in Great Britain, found that 80% of boys and 67% of girls reported playing computer games either "every day" or "most days" (Griffiths, 1997).

Many of these computer games are in the category of harmless entertainment. A substantial proportion of the games simply involve having a computerized character jump from one platform to the next; or sports simulations of baseball, tennis, or hockey; or fantasies in which the player can escape to other worlds and take on new identities (Griffiths, 1997). However, many computer games involve depictions of extreme violence. In fact, the majority of adolescents' favorite computer games involve violence (Provenzo, 1991). Because violent

> "THE BLOOD AND GORE [IN QUAKE II] HAVE BEEN BEEFED UP A BIT. WE SHOWED AN EARLIER VERSION, AND THE FEEDBACK WE GOT WAS THAT THERE WASN'T ENOUGH BLOOD, SO WE ADDED SOME MORE."
> —JOHN CORMACK, DEVELOPER OF QUAKE II (IN TAKAHISHI & RAMSTAD, 1997)

games have proven to be so popular, manufacturers have steadily increased the levels of violence in computer games over the past decade (Funk et al., 1999). Here are a few examples of violent games (Ingalls, 1998; Strasburger, 1995; Takahashi & Ramstad, 1997):

- *Quake II.* A Marine lands on an alien planet to seek and destroy a huge weapon known as "the big gun." Players, controlling the Marine, blast away at aliens called Scroggs using an arsenal of weapons such as rocket launchers and "rail guns" that can pierce several aliens in a row.
- *Mortal Kombat.* Two opponents engage in a three-round martial arts contest. In the "gory" version, the winner finishes off the loser by either cutting his head off or tearing his heart out of his chest.
- *Night Trap.* Vampires attack attractive young women while the player tries to save them. If they are not defeated, the vampires end the game by drilling the young women through the neck with a power tool.
- *Terminator 2.* Players battle androids with a shotgun, a machine gun, and a rocket launcher.
- *Postal.* Players try to slaughter an entire high school marching band using various weapons such as flame throwers.

This all sounds potentially unhealthy, on the face of it, and there have been some notorious cases of the games appearing to promote violence. For example, one of the two boys who murdered 12 students and a

Many of the computer games most popular with adolescent boys have violent themes.

teacher in the massacre at Columbine High School in 1999 named the gun he used in the murders "Arlene," after a character in the gory Doom video game. And in a video the boys made before the murders, the same boy said of the murders they would commit, "It's going to be like fucking Doom. Tick, tick, tick, tick . . . Haaa! That fucking shotgun is straight out of Doom!" (Gibbs & Roche, 1999).

However, only a handful of studies thus far have examined the relation between video games and aggressiveness (Funk et al., 1999). One found that aggressiveness and hostility were heightened after playing arcade video games (Mehrabian & Wixen, 1986). Another found that the content of computer video games was related to adolescents' emotional responses, with adolescents' levels of hostility and anxiety increasing in correlation with the level of violence in the computer game they were playing (Anderson & Ford, 1987). One study in which college undergraduates played computer games with varying levels of violence found that the students reported decreased feelings of aggressiveness after playing a moderately violent game, but increased feelings of aggressiveness after playing a highly violent game (Scott, 1995).

It seems likely that with computer games, as with other violent media, there is a wide range of individual differences in responses, with young people who are already at risk for violent behavior—such as the Columbine murderers—being most likely to be affected by the games, as well as most likely to be attracted to them (Funk et al., 1999). However, with regard to computer games specifically, there is not much evidence to go on at this point. Because of the growing popularity and growing levels of violence in computer games, this will be an area to watch for future research.

Television and Movies and Sex

Sex is second only to violence as a topic of public concern with respect to the possible effects of television on adolescents (Strasburger & Donnerstein, 1999). A high proportion of prime-time television shows contain sexual themes. What sort of information about sexuality does television present to adolescents?

A study by Monique Ward (1995) provides a detailed examination of the sexual content of the television shows most often viewed by adolescents. Ward analyzed three episodes from each of the 10 television shows most often watched by adolescents aged 12 to 17 during the 1992–93 television season (based on the official

Neilsen ratings). This included shows such as "Fresh Prince of Bel Air," "Blossom," "Roseanne," "Martin," and "Beverly Hills 90210." Each episode of each show was segmented into a series of interactions, and the interactions were coded into one of 17 categories.

The analysis found that 29% of the interactions in the shows most popular among adolescents contained statements related to sexuality. The most common type of message in these sexual interactions involved references to the male sexual role. Males were portrayed in these interactions as preoccupied with sex, always ready and willing. For example, referring about his lust for a female coworker, one young man on a "Martin" episode moaned, "I don't know how long I can hold out." Interactions in this category also included males' views of women, in which women were portrayed as sexual objects valued mainly for their physical appearance. "These are going to be the most awesome girls we've ever seen," one adolescent boy said to another in an episode of "Beverly Hills 90210." "Girls with legs all the way up to their necks. Not an ounce out of place."

Women were sometimes portrayed as having similar views of men, valuing them mainly for their physical appeal, although not as often. Encouraging her mother to date a new man, a female adolescent on "Roseanne" urged "Come on, Ma, he's kinda cute. He's got a cute butt." However, in contrast to men, women were also portrayed as valuing the wealth and status of men. "Are you crazy?" said one sister to another on "Fresh Prince." "That man had a business, car, and money. Now what's love got to do with it?"

Both men and women were often portrayed as having what Ward termed a "recreational" orientation toward sex. Part of this recreational orientation was that sexual relations were frequently portrayed as a competition, a "battle of the sexes" in which men and women discuss "scoring," cheating on partners, stealing partners, and how to outmaneuver one another. Another part of the recreational orientation was the view of sexual relations as fun, a natural source of play and amusement that can be enjoyed without concern over commitment or responsibility. One adolescent girl said to her elderly mother on "Roseanne," "Is he going to be our new Dad, or is he just another one of your nooners?" However—in contrast to the early days of television when the word *pregnant* was considered too racy to be mentioned and even married characters slept in separate beds—there were also occasional discussions of contraception. "Don't be ashamed to carry a condom," said an adolescent in a safe sex video made by some adolescent characters on

"Blossom." "It doesn't mean you're going to have sex. It just means you're prepared if you do."

What sort of uses do adolescents make of the portrayals of sexuality on television? We can start out by noting that, because adolescents watch TV for at least 2 hours a day on average, the messages in these programs form a significant part of their socialization environment. In TV programs adolescents learn cultural ideas about how male and female roles differ in sexual interactions and what is considered physically attractive in males and females (Unger & Crawford, 1996; Ward & Rivadeneyra, 1999). Television also provides information to adolescents about appropriate sexual scripts (Gagnon, 1973; Roberts, 1980; Ward & Rivadeneyra, 1999), that is, the expected patterns of sexual interactions based on cultural norms of what is acceptable and desirable. For adolescents, who are just beginning to date, this information may be eagerly received, especially in a culture such as the American majority culture which provides little in the way of explicit instruction in male and female sexual roles.

Of course, the "information" they receive about sexual scripts from TV may not be the kind most adults would consider most desirable. Often, the sexual scripts in TV shows portray a "sniggering attitude" toward sexuality (Smith, 1991, p. 131). However, this may be mainly because most of the TV shows popular among adolescents are situation comedies, and they rely on standard comedic devices such as sexual innuendo, double entendre (words or phrases that have two meanings), irony, and exaggeration. Most adolescents are cognitively capable of separating what is intended to be humorous from what is intended to be a true portrayal of sexuality (Ward, 1995).

THINKING CRITICALLY

To what extent is the portrayal of sexuality in television shows watched by adolescents similar to and different from the way adolescents regard sexuality in real life?

Beyond this, however, we cannot say a great deal at this point about the uses that adolescents make of the sexual interactions they watch on TV. Scholars have done a great deal of theorizing about the uses and "effects" of these interactions, but they have produced very little in the way of useful data, so far. As Ward (1995) concluded in her analysis, "Much more research is needed to understand for certain why particular programs and particular characters hold appeal for young viewers, and, more importantly, how they interpret and use these messages in their sexual decision making" (p. 612).

One other issue that bears mention with respect to TV and adolescent sexuality is contraceptive advertising on TV. Although, as we have seen, sexual topics are common in television shows popular among adolescents, and sexual appeals are a common part of television commercials (Strasburger, 1995), the major television networks refuse to show advertisements or public service announcements about contraception. Network representatives claim that running such advertisements would offend a substantial proportion of their viewers, but they provide no evidence to support this claim (Strasburger, 1995). They continue this policy even though surveys indicate that a majority of Americans favor allowing contraceptive advertising on TV (Harris & Associates, 1987). Evidence from European countries suggests that contraceptive advertising on television in those countries contributes to their lower rates of adolescent pregnancy compared to the United States (Jones et al., 1988).

Movies (in theaters and on video) are another medium where adolescents witness portrayals of sexual behavior. Although adolescents spend less time watching movies than they do watching TV, the movies they watch tend to have more frequent and explicit portrayals of sexuality than TV shows do. As one prominent researcher in this area has observed, "What television suggests, movies and videos do" (Greenberg, 1994, p. 180). In one study by Greenberg and colleagues (1986) that compared content in prime time television programs to content in R-rated movies, the movies had seven times as many sexual acts or references as the TV programs did, and in the movies sexual intercourse between unmarried people was *32 times* more common than between married people. Of course, adolescents under age 18 are not supposed to be able to see R-rated movies (unless accompanied by an adult), but Greenberg and colleagues (1993) found that the majority of the 15- and 16-year-olds they surveyed had seen the most popular R-rated movies either in the theater or on video.

Sex and Violence on Music Television

Today's adolescents have grown up with a new medium that combines television and music: music television,

often referred to by the initials of the most popular music television network, MTV. MTV began in 1981 and was instantly popular among adolescents (Burnett, 1990). Studies indicate that most American adolescents watch MTV for about 30 to 60 minutes per day (Christenson & Roberts, 1998). Although MTV began in the United States, by 1990 MTV was being broadcast in 40 countries worldwide, making it a significant force toward globalization.

What uses are made of MTV by its adolescent listeners? Music videos can be divided into two general categories (Strasburger, 1995): **performance videos**, which show an individual performer or a group singing a song in a concert setting or a studio, and **concept videos**, which enact a story to go along with the lyrics of the song. For the most part, performance videos simply convey the song and have generated no more (or less) controversy than the songs themselves. More attention has been directed at the concept videos and the stories they depict. The targets of concern among critics are the same as for television more generally: violence and sex.

In one analysis of concept videos (Sherman & Dominick, 1986), more than half of the videos were found to contain violence such as wrestling and punching. Sexual themes appeared in more than three-fourths of the videos, but for the most part the sexuality was implied rather than shown—that is, the videos were more likely to contain provocatively dressed women than actually to show people kissing, fondling, and so forth. Sex and violence often appeared in the same video; over half the violent videos also contained sexual themes, often involving violence against women. Other analyses have found similar prevalence of violent and sexual themes (Baxter et al., 1985; Vincent, Davis, & Bronszkowski, 1987). Rap videos have been found to be especially high in sexual content, compared to other videos (Jones, 1997). Content analyses also show that the characters in music videos tend to be highly gender stereotyped, with the men aggressive and the women sexual and subservient (Gow, 1996; Sommers-Flanagan et al., 1993).

It is unclear what effects, if any, violent or sexual content in music videos might have on the adolescents who watch and listen to them. Few studies investigating adolescents' responses to music videos have yet been conducted (Strasburger, 1995). However, the handful of studies we have to go on so far show considerable diversity in how adolescents interpret the stories in concept videos (Brown & Schulze, 1990; Christenson

& Roberts, 1990). For example, in a study of adolescents' responses to the Madonna video "Papa Don't Preach," Black adolescents tended to interpret the story differently from White adolescents, and Black males interpreted it differently from Black females (Brown & Schultze, 1990). This is consistent with the theme of uses and gratifications we have emphasized in this chapter. Adolescents may watch the same music video, yet the messages they perceive in it and the uses they make of it may be quite variable.

Controversial Music: Rap and Heavy Metal

Television is not the only medium that has been criticized for promoting unhealthy and morally questionable tendencies in adolescents. Music has been criticized just as much, and the criticism goes back

even longer. Jazz was criticized in the 1920s for promoting promiscuity and alcohol use. Rock and roll was criticized throughout the fifties and sixties for promoting rebellion and sexual license (see the Historical Focus box in this chapter). In recent years, the criticism has focused on two particular genres of popular music: rap and heavy metal.

Rap   Rap music (also called hip hop) began in the late 1970s as street music in urban New York City (Berry, 1995; Decker, 1994). It started out with disc jockeys "rapping" (speaking or shouting rhythmically) spontaneous lyrics to a background of a lively beat and perhaps a repeated line of music, and only gradually developed into "songs" that were recorded. It was not until the late 1980s that rap attained widespread popularity. MTV had no program devoted to rap until 1988, but when MTV

HISTORICAL FOCUS
Elvis the Pelvis

In the spring of 1953 an 18-year-old delivery truck driver named Elvis Presley walked into a recording studio in Memphis, Tennessee, and paid four dollars for the opportunity to record two songs as a birthday present for his mother. Three years later, Elvis Presley was 21 years old, a multimillionaire entertainer, and the most famous person on the planet.

How did this happen? Part of the explanation, of course, lies in Elvis's extraordinary talents. He had a uniquely rich, expressive, and versatile singing voice, and he sang with a unique sensual intensity. He had grown up in the South listening to the early rock-and-roll songs being performed by Black musicians, and he incorporated the sensuality and power of their styles into his own. Many people recognized the Black influence in his singing, and Elvis himself acknowledged it.

Not only his singing but his performing was influenced by Black musicians he had seen, as he developed a performance style of bracing himself against the microphone stand and thrusting his pelvis back and forth in a distinctly sexual way (leading to the nickname "Elvis the Pelvis"), his legs pumping

rhythmically, his body shaking all over. He made Black rock-and-roll music and styles popular to White audiences at a time in American history when racist beliefs about Black people possessing an uncontrolled sexuality would have made it difficult for a Black person to be accepted by the American majority culture singing in that style.

However, in addition to Elvis's talents, four media forms interacted to fuel his fame: radio, newspapers, television, and movies. His career got its initial burst through radio, when a Memphis radio station played a recording of him singing "That's All Right (Mama)" and within days thousands of adolescents were storming Memphis record stores seeking copies of the record (which had not actually been printed yet). Soon radio stations all over the South were playing "That's All Right" and every other Elvis song as he recorded more of them.

Next, newspapers came into the mix. A Memphis newspaper printed a front-page story with the title "He's Sex!," and it was reprinted in newspapers all over the South. This, along with increasingly widespread exposure on radio stations, gave Elvis a hot reputation as he and his band began to tour and perform in cities throughout the South. Everywhere he performed, newspapers covered his concerts, mostly with rave reviews, further enhancing his popularity.

But it was television that made Elvis a world-famous star. Following his first television appearance on "The Ed Sullivan Show" early in 1956, when he was still relatively unknown outside the South, CBS was flooded with phone calls and letters from aroused adolescent fans. He appeared several more times on television in 1956, each time to an enormous national audience.

As he became increasingly popular, his critics grew louder and more numerous, calling his performances "lewd" and "obscene." Jackie Gleason, a popular TV performer of the day, sneered "The kid has no right behaving like a sex maniac on a national show" (Lichter, 1978, p. 22). A newspaper critic was one of many to express concern about the potential effects on young people: "When Presley executes his bumps and grinds, it must be remembered by [CBS] that even the twelve-year-old's curiosity may be overstimulated" (Lichter, 1978, p. 34). By the time Elvis appeared on "The Ed Sullivan Show" again in September of 1956, CBS executives decided he would be shown on TV only from the waist up, so as not to provoke any unruly sexual impulses among America's adolescents.

Elvis's first performance on "The Ed Sullivan Show" still ranks as the highest-rated television show ever broadcast in the United States, with an astonishing 83% of the television sets in the country tuned in. It is worth noting that the rise of Elvis coincided fortuitously with the rise of TV. In 1950, just 9% of American households owned a television; by the time of Elvis's first TV performance over half of American households had one, and by 1960 the figure would rise to nearly 90% (Lichty, 1989). Television propelled Elvis into unprecedented national fame. His fame became international as his performances and stories of his performances were distributed in newspapers, radio stations, and television networks all over the world.

Soon Elvis added movies to his media machine. His first film, *Love Me Tender*, was released near the end of 1956. Neither this film nor any of his 32 other films was highly regarded by movie critics, but Elvis's adolescent fans worldwide had a different opinion.

Elvis was wildly popular among adolescents.

They made this film and many of the others huge box office hits. Even in the mid-1960s, after Elvis's musical career had been eclipsed by the Beatles and other new performers, his movies continued to bring in millions of dollars (Lichter, 1978).

These four interacting media contributed substantially to Elvis's fame, but from the beginning their attention to him was driven by the responses of his adolescent fans—their calls to radio stations demanding to hear his songs again and again, the raucous screaming crowds at the concerts covered by newspaper reporters, the rapt and enormous television audiences, and a devoted movie-going audience even for Elvis movies that were (to put it mildly) less than memorable. Although corporate business people have tried hard ever since Elvis to control the highly lucrative business of popular music, the enthusiasms of adolescents have usually proven difficult to predict (Brake, 1985), and ultimately it is the enthusiasm of adolescents that drives the direction of popular music.

Rap has become one of the most popular types of music among adolescents. Here, the rap group NWA.

added "Yo! MTV Raps" it quickly became one of the station's most popular programs and helped to spread the influence of rap. By the 1990s, a wide range of rap groups were appearing on lists of the highest-selling albums. Rap now equals rock in popularity among American adolescents (Chadwin & Heaton, 1996; Roberts et al., 1999). Although rap is especially popular among Black and Latino adolescents, White adolescents also comprise a substantial proportion of rap fans (Roberts et al., 1999; Samuels, 1991).

Not all rap is controversial. Hammer, one of the most popular rap performers of the 1990s, focuses on themes of racial harmony, nonviolence, and tolerance for others. Queen Latifah, a popular female rap performer, stresses themes of self-esteem for young Black women. Other rap performers also enjoy a wide mainstream audience for their themes of love, romance, and celebration. The controversy over rap has focused on "gangsta rap" performers such as Ice Cube, Snoop Doggy Dogg, Tupac Shakur, Notorious B.I.G., and N.W.A. (Niggas with Attitude), and has concerned three themes (Berry, 1995): sexual exploitation of women, violence, and racism.

Controversial rap has been criticized for presenting images of women as objects of contempt, deserving sexual exploitation and even sexual assault. Women in controversial rap songs are often referred to as "hos" (whores) and "bitches," and sexuality is

frequently portrayed as a man's successful assertion of power over a woman (Berry, 1995; Decker, 1994; Peterson-Lewis, 1991). Although some rap performers defend their lyrics as "meant to be funny" (Berry, 1995, p. 172), an analysis by Peterson-Lewis disputes this defense:

> Their lyrics lack the wit and strategic use of subtle social commentary necessary for effective social satire; thus they do not so much debunk myths as create new ones, the major one being that in interacting with black women 'anything goes.' Their lyrics not only fail to satirize the myth of the hypersexual black, they also commit the moral blunder of sexualizing the victimization of women, black women in particular. (quoted in Berry, 1995, p. 172)

Violence is another common theme in the lyrics of controversial rap performers. Their songs depict scenes such as drive-by shootings, gang violence, and violent confrontations with the police. One song by N.W.A., called "Fuck the Police," caused so much outrage when it was released that their record company was ultimately forced by public pressure to withdraw the album. The violence spouted by gangsta rap performers is not just a pose but is part of the world many of them live in. In the late 1990s Tupac Shakur and Notorious B.I.G. were shot to death, and other gangsta rap performers have been arrested for offenses from illegal possession of firearms to sexual assault to attempted murder.

The performers of such songs, and their defenders, have argued that their lyrics simply reflect the grim realities of life for young Black people in America's inner cities. According to Chuck D, the leader of Public Enemy, "Rap is Black America's TV station. It gives a whole perspective of what exists and what Black life is about" (Decker, 1994, p. 103). However, critics have accused the performers of contributing to the stereotype of young Black men as dangerous criminals (e.g., Samuels, 1991).

With regard to racism, critics of rap have denounced the views that rap performers have expressed in songs and interviews toward Whites and Asians. Several popular rappers are members of the Black Muslim movement (Decker, 1994), whose leaders have written about White people as "devils" and "snakes," and these views have found expression in their lyrics. Asians have also been targets of attack in rap lyrics, for example, in Ice Cube's "Black Korea".

What effect—if any—does listening to rap lyrics with themes of sexism, violence, and racism have on the development of adolescents? Unfortunately, although many academics have speculated about the uses of rap by adolescents, thus far few credible studies have been done that provide research evidence on the topic. Looking at the question from the uses and gratifications perspective, we could point out that many of the controversial themes in rap songs reflect the realities faced daily by Black adolescents in urban America. As rock critic Jon Pareles has observed, "Rap's internal troubles reflect the poverty, violence, lack of education, frustration, and rage of the ghetto" (Pareles, 1992). Perhaps, then, rap is used by some adolescents as an expression of their frustration and rage in the face of the difficult conditions they live in. But does rap also reinforce and perhaps magnify tendencies toward sexism, violence, and racism? At this point, we lack an informed answer to this question.

Heavy Metal

"*There's a lot of anger in my generation. You can hear it in the music. Kids are angry for a lot of reasons, but mostly because parents aren't around.*"

—*Robertino, age 17 (in Begley, 2000)*

"*Sometimes I'm upset and I like to put on heavy metal. It kind of releases the aggression I feel. I can just drive along, put a tape in, and turn it up. It puts me in a better mood. It's a way to release some of your pressures, instead of going out and starting a fight with somebody, or taking it out on your parents or your cat or something like that.*"

—*Ben, age 21 (in Arnett, 1996, p. 82)*

The history of heavy metal goes back to the late 1960s and early 1970s and groups such as Led Zeppelin, Iron Maiden, and Black Sabbath. The peak of heavy metal's popularity—and controversy—came during the 1980s, with performers such as Metallica, Ozzy Ozbourne, Megadeth, Judas Priest, and Slayer selling millions of albums and performing in large arenas all over the world. Heavy metal's popularity waned some in the 1990s, but the most popular "metal" groups still sell millions of albums and play to packed concert halls of fervently devoted fans.

As with rap, not all heavy metal is controversial. Metal is quite diverse, from "lite metal" groups such as Motley Crue and Kiss that sing mostly about partying and sex, to groups such as Metallica and Megadeth that address serious social issues such as war and environmental destruction, to groups such as Slayer whose themes are relentlessly violent. Controversy and criticism has focused not on the "lite metal" groups but on the other heavy-metal groups, especially concerning issues of suicide and violence.

Two widely publicized incidents led to the public association between heavy metal and suicide. The first took place in 1985, when a U.S. Senate committee held hearings on the topic of whether there should be "Parental Advisory" warning stickers on some popular music recordings, with a focus on heavy metal. The committee's inquiry highlighted a song by Ozzy Ozbourne called "Suicide Solution," which some critics interpreted as an incitement to suicide. Ozzy and his defenders claimed that, far from advocating suicide, the song is actually an antialcohol song, warning about the dangers of alcohol abuse (and I agree that this claim holds up, if you look at the lyrics). However, the wide publicity the hearing received led to an association in the public mind between heavy metal and suicide.

The second incident took place in the early 1990s, when the parents of an adolescent boy who had attempted suicide sued members of the heavy metal band Judas Priest for allegedly inspiring the boy to attempt to take his own life. According to the lawsuit, the boy was influenced by a subliminal message on a song recorded by the band, a message that was allegedly spoken during the song so that it could not be heard consciously but would nevertheless penetrate the unconscious and affect the listener's behavior. The message that allegedly drove the boy to such an extreme of despair that he shot his own face off with a shotgun was just "Do it." There is, in fact, no scientific evidence that subliminal messages actually effect even behavior such as which soft drink to buy much less suicide, and the parents eventually lost their case. Once again, however, a public association was made between heavy metal and suicide.

The other accusation against heavy metal is that it promotes violence. It is true that violence is a common theme in heavy-metal songs; in fact, it is the most common theme (Arnett, 1996). However, this alone is not evidence that heavy metal causes violent behavior in those who listen to it. What the listeners hear in it, how they *use* it, is the crucial question.

Is there any credible evidence that heavy metal promotes suicide or violence? Some of my own research has concerned the heavy metal subculture, and this is one of the questions I investigated in a study of over 100 heavy metal fans (Arnett, 1991, 1996). I found that it is true that heavy metal fans (metalheads or headbangers as they call themselves) tend to have a dark view of the world. They are alienated from mainstream society; cynical about teachers, politicians, and religious leaders; and highly pessimistic about the future of the human race. They also tend to be more reckless than other adolescents, reporting higher rates of behavior such as high-speed driving, drug use, and vandalism.

However, I do not believe that their alienation or their recklessness can accurately be blamed on the music. I asked them if they *listen* to the music when they are in any particular mood, and if the music *puts* them in any particular mood. Consistently, they said they listen to the music especially when they are angry—not surprising, in view of the violent, angry quality of the music and lyrics. However, they also said consistently that the music has the effect of *calming them down.* Heavy metal songs have a **cathartic effect** on their anger; in other words, they *use* the music as a way of purging their anger harmlessly. The songs express their alienated view of the world and help them cope with the anger and frustration of living in a world they see as hopelessly corrupt. Because it has this

> "MUSIC HAS CHARMS TO SOOTHE A SAVAGE BREAST."
> —WILLIAM CONGREVE, 1697

cathartic effect on their anger and frustration, if anything the music makes them *less* likely to commit suicide or violence than they would be if they did not have the music available to use for this purpose. This cathartic effect of heavy metal music has also been demonstrated experimentally (Wooten, 1992).

We cannot and should not rule out the possibility that the despair and violence of the songs could act as an inspiration to suicide or violence in some extreme cases. As noted, adolescents can respond to the same media stimulus in widely different ways. However, for the great majority of the millions of adolescent metalheads around the world, heavy metal appears to act as a useful outlet for difficult youthful emotions.

THINKING CRITICALLY

Thus far the cathartic effect has been studied only for heavy metal music. Do you think this effect would be found for other types of music as well? What about for television? Computer games?

Controversial Advertising: Joe Camel and Friends

Most media used by adolescents contain advertising in some form. Television, of course, has commercials punctuating every program every few minutes. Radio is similar—ads every few minutes, interspersed among the talk and music. Almost all magazines and newspapers have numerous advertisements, and this is especially true of the magazines most popular among adolescent girls (Evans et al., 1991). Even movies have advertisements in a subtle form called "product placements," which means that companies pay to have their products used by actors in movies. The only exception to the pervasiveness of advertisements in the media used most by adolescents is recorded music.

In recent years, the most controversial form of advertising with respect to adolescents has been cigarette advertising. Advertising

Heavy metal fans often report that the music has a cathartic effect on their anger.

cigarettes on television or radio has been illegal in the United States since 1971, but since that time cigarette companies have simply poured more money into other forms of advertising and promotion, such as billboards, magazines, newspapers, movie product placements, and sponsorship of sporting events and concerts. In fact, cigarettes are the most heavily promoted consumer product in the United States, with cigarette advertising and promotion totaling over *six billion dollars* in 1993 (Pollay, 1997).

Critics of cigarette advertising claim that it is targeted especially toward adolescents (Gilpin & Pierce, 1997; Pierce, Lee, & Gilpin, 1994; Pollay, 1997). The tobacco companies claim that their advertising is intended only to persuade adult smokers to switch brands, but the critics note that only a small percentage of adults switch brands in a given year, a percentage far too small to justify the tobacco companies' massive advertising budgets. Where the real market lies is among adolescents. Ninety percent of smokers begin smoking by age 18 (U.S. Department of Health and Human Services, 1994), which means that adolescence is the time when virtually all smokers establish their first brand choice, making them a ripe target for cigarette companies seeking to expand their share of the market. Furthermore, because few people begin smoking after age 18, critics argue that tobacco companies try to persuade adolescents to smoke so that they will become addicted to nicotine before they are mature enough to realize fully the potential risks of smoking (Arnett, 2000e; Gerrard et al., 1996; Slovic, 1998). Thus, according to the critics, cigarette companies present images of independence (the Marlboro Man), youthful fun and vigor (Newport, Kool), and "coolness" (Joe Camel) in order to appeal to adolescents.

Several studies have established a relationship between cigarette advertising campaigns and adolescent smoking. Pollay et al. (1996) traced tobacco companies' advertising expenditures in relation to rates of smoking among adolescents (aged 12 to 18) and adults over the period 1979 to 1993. They concluded that the effect of advertising on brand choice was *three times as strong* for adolescents as for adults. The "Joe Camel" campaign provides an example of this effect.

Between 1988, when the "Joe" character was introduced, and 1993, Camel's market share among 12- to 17-year-olds rose from less than 1% to 13%. Under criticism, RJR Nabisco canceled the Joe Camel ad campaign in 1998.

Pierce and his colleagues (1994) examined trends in smoking initiation from 1944 to 1988. They found that for girls aged 14 to 17, a sharp rise in smoking initiation coincided with the introduction of three brands targeted at females—Virginia Slims, Silva Thins, and Eve—between 1967 and 1973. No such increase occurred during this period for girls aged 18 to 20 or 10 to 13, or for males. The ad campaigns were evidently particularly effective among—and targeted to?—adolescent girls in the age range when smoking initiation is most likely to take place, ages 14 to 17.

Also, in a study I and a colleague published (Arnett & Terhanian, 1998), adolescents were shown ads for five different brands of cigarettes (Camel, Marlboro, Lucky Strike, Benson & Hedges, and Kool) and asked various questions about their responses. The ads for Camel and Marlboro were the ads the adolescents had seen the most, the ads they liked the best, and the ads they were most likely to see as making smoking appealing (Figure 12.1). In a number of respects, smokers' responses to the ads were more favorable than the responses of nonsmokers. For all brands, smokers were significantly more likely to indicate that they liked the ad. For the Camel and Marlboro ads (but not for the other brands), smokers were more likely than nonsmokers to indicate that the ad made smoking more appealing.

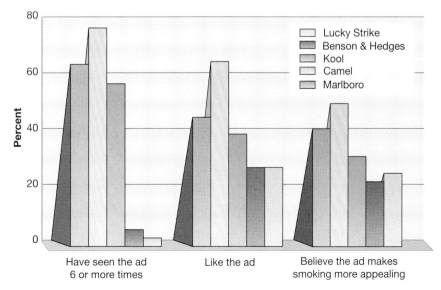

FIGURE 12.1 *Adolescents' responses to cigarette ads.*
Source: Arnett & Terhanian (1998).

Marlboro and Camel are two of the brands most popular among adolescents. Marlboro is by far the most popular, smoked by about half of 12- to 17-year-old smokers, with Newport second (25%) and Camel third at about 13% (King et al., 1998). These are also the three most heavily-promoted brands, indicating the influence of advertising and promotion in adolescent smoking (Arnett, 2000e). The fact that the ads for the most popular brands are so attractive to adolescents, especially to adolescent smokers, also suggests that cigarette advertising is one of the influences that leads them to smoke (Arnett & Terhanian, 1998).

Of course, findings of a relationship between the appeal of cigarette advertisements and rates of adolescent smoking or brand preferences do not prove that the cigarette companies *intended* to appeal to adolescents. However, in recent lawsuits against the tobacco companies, the companies have been forced to release literally tons of internal documents, many of which provide stark evidence that for decades these companies have discussed the psychological characteristics of adolescents and have been acutely aware of the importance of adolescents as the perpetually new market for cigarettes. For example, an R.J. Reynolds document from the mid-1970s stated, "Realistically, if our Company is to survive and prosper over the long term, we must get our share of the youth market" (Pollay, 1997). This evidence has strengthened the claim that tobacco companies have directly attempted to market their cigarettes to adolescents.

Marlboro is both the most heavily advertised cigarette brand and the brand by far the most popular among adolescents.

Cultural Differences in Media Uses

A number of cultural differences exist in American society with respect to adolescents' media use. Black adolescents watch more TV than Whites do (Fine et al., 1990; Roberts et al., 1999). Latino adolescents have also been found to watch more TV than Whites, at least in early adolescence (Blosser, 1988). Rap music has become highly popular among all adolescents, but 67% of Black adolescents name rap as their favorite type of music compared with just 17% of Whites (Chadwick & Heaton, 1996). In addition to these ethnic differences in the United States, there are interesting similarities and differences in the media uses of adolescents across cultures. Some of the similarities reflect the globalization of adolescence.

Media and Globalization

One of the most important aspects of media use among adolescents is that media are an important force behind the globalization of adolescence. All over the world, on every continent, adolescents are increasingly familiar with the same television shows, the same movies, and the same musical recordings and performers. (Magazines are the only exception; they still tend to be locally produced.) The Simpsons and other American TV

Media are a potent and pervasive force in globalization. Here, young Muslim women in Malaysia.

compete for their attention even if they also learn the songs and arts of their own culture. Second, adolescents are more capable than younger children of exploring for themselves the environment outside of the family, so that they are more capable than younger children of obtaining media products that their parents would not have provided for them. Third, adolescence is a time when young people are forming an identity, a sense of themselves and their place in the world. When social and economic change is rapid and they sense that the world of their future is going to be different from the world that has been familiar to their parents and grandparents, they look outside the family for information and instruction in what that world is going to be like and how they might find a place in it (Goode, 1999; Mead, 1970; see the Cultural Focus box for an example). For many adolescents today, the media provide information and instruction about what the global village of their future will be like.

Several of the ethnographies from the Harvard Adolescence Project provide examples of the impetus of the media toward globalization in the lives of adolescents. Among the Moroccan adolescents studied by Davis and Davis (1989, 1995), this influence is especially notable with respect to gender roles. In the past Moroccan culture had strictly defined gender roles, which is true in many traditional cultures. Marriages were arranged by parents and were made on the basis of practical family considerations rather than romantic love. Female virginity at marriage was considered essential (but not male virginity), and adolescent girls were forbidden to spend time in the company of adolescent boys.

These gender differences and the narrower socialization for girls continue to be part of Moroccan culture today, particularly in rural areas, and they are reflected in different standards for adolescent boys and girls with respect to their access to media. Adolescent boys attend movies frequently (in Davis and Davis's [1995] data, 80% attended movies occasionally or more), whereas for adolescent girls attendance at movies—*any* movie—is considered shameful (only

shows are popular not just in the United States, but in Norway, Malaysia, and Brazil. "Action" movies featuring actors such as Arnold Schwarzenegger and Steven Seagal are popular with adolescents not only in the United States, but in Italy, Mexico, and South Korea. Metallica, U2, and R.E.M. are listened to by adolescents not only in the United States, but in Japan, Chile, and Russia. This pattern is evident in the worldwide sales of these media products, but to give you an example of a study that actually quantified this, over 90% of young people in Poland (aged 16 to 25) preferred British and American rock as their favorite kind of music (Sasinska-Klas, 1988; cited in Robinson, Buck, & Cuthbert, 1991). Similar patterns of music preference among adolescents and emerging adults have been observed in other countries around the world (see Robinson et al., 1991).

Adolescents are not the only ones in these countries who enjoy Western—especially American—media. However, Western media tend to be especially appealing to adolescents, for several reasons. First, in developing countries around the world, social and economic change has been extremely rapid in the past 50 years. The current generation of adolescents in these countries often have parents and grandparents who grew up in a time when their country had less economic and technological contact with the West, so that these adults are more familiar with and more attached to their native traditions, such as their native musical forms and songs. The adolescents, in contrast, have grown up with Western media, which

CULTURAL FOCUS
"Teenagers" in Kathmandu, Nepal

Few places in the world have been more remote and more isolated from the West historically than Nepal, which is located between southwest China and northeast India. Not only is Nepal thousands of miles from the nearest Western country, but until 1951 the government made a concerted effort to isolate its citizens, banning all communications (travel, trade, books, movies, etc.) between Nepal and "the outside." Since then, Nepal, and especially its largest city, Kathmandu, has been undergoing a rapid transition into the world of global trade, Western tourism, and electronic mass media. Ethnographic research by anthropologist Mark Liechty (1995) provides a vivid look at how adolescents and emerging adults in Kathmandu are responding to Western media, and at how media are a potent force toward globalization.

According to the observations of Liechty and his colleagues, a variety of imported media are highly popular with young people in Kathmandu. Movies and videos from both India and the United States find a broad audience of young people. American and Indian television shows are also popular, and televisions and VCRs are a standard feature of middle-class homes. There is an avid audience among the young for Western music, including rock, heavy metal, and rap. Sometimes young people combine local culture with imported Western styles; Liechty gives the example of a local rock band that had recorded an original Nepali language album in the style of the Beatles. However, older traditions such as Nepali folk songs are rejected by many urban young people.

A locally produced magazine called *Teens* embodies the appeal of Western media to young people in Kathmandu. In addition to features such as comic strips, Nepali folktales, puzzles, and games, each issue contains pages of profiles devoted to Western pop music heroes, including biographical data and lyrics to popular songs. Each issue also includes a list of the top ten English-language albums of the month and a list of recent English video releases. A substantial proportion of the magazine is devoted to fashion, much like in American teen magazines, and the fashions shown are Western.

Nepalese people use the terms *teen* and *teenager* in English, even when speaking Nepali, to refer to young people who are oriented toward Western tastes, especially Western media. Not all Nepalese young people are "teenagers," even if they are in their teen years—the term is not an age category but a social category that refers to young people who are pursuing a Western identity and style based on what they have learned through media. To many young people in Kathmandu, being a "teenager" is something they covet and strive for. They associate it with leisure, affluence, and expanded opportunities. However, many adults use "teenager" with less favorable connotations to refer to young people who are disobedient, antisocial, and potentially violent. Their use of the term in this way reflects their view that Western media have had corrupting effects on many of their young people.

Even to "teenagers" themselves, the availability of Western media is a mixed blessing. They enjoy it and it provides them with information about the wider world beyond the borders of Nepal. Many of them use media to help them make sense of their own lives, growing up as they are in a rapidly changing society, and as material for imagining a broad range of possible selves. However, Western media also tend to disconnect them from their own culture and from their cultural traditions, leaving many of them confused and alienated. The media ideals of Western life raise their expectations for their own lives to unrealizable levels, and they eventually collide with the incompatibility between their expectations and their real lives. As 21-year-old Ramesh told Liechty:

> "You know, now I know sooooo much [from films, books, and magazines about the West]. Being a frog in a pond isn't a bad life, but being a frog in an ocean is like hell. Look at this. Out here in Kathmandu there is nothing. We have nothing." (p. 187)

20% had *ever* been to see a movie in a theater, in the Davis & Davis study). Adolescent boys are also allowed freer access to cassette tapes and players, and to video-cassettes. However, for both adolescent boys and adolescent girls, their exposure to television, music, and (for boys) movies is changing the way they think about gender relations and gender roles. The TV programs, songs, and movies they are exposed to are produced not only in Morocco and other Islamic countries but also include many from France (Morocco was once a French colony) and the United States.

From these various sources, Moroccan adolescents are seeing portrayals of gender roles quite different from what they see among their parents, grandparents, and other adults around them. In the media the adolescents use, romance and passion are central to male–female relationships. Love is the central basis for entering marriage, and the idea of accepting a marriage arranged by parents is either ignored or portrayed as something to be resisted. Young women are usually portrayed not in traditional roles but in professional occupations and as being in control of their lives and unashamed of their sexuality.

All of this is being used by young people to construct a conception of gender roles that is quite different from the traditional conception in their culture. Altogether it amounts to an influence toward globalization and toward the broad socialization of the West, as media are "used by adolescents in a period of rapid social change to reimagine many aspects of their lives, including a desire for more autonomy, for more variety in heterosexual interactions, and for more choice of a job and of a mate" (Davis & Davis, 1995, p. 578). Here we see an example of socialization from the media going "over the heads" of parents and other adult socializers, as we discussed earlier in the chapter.

Another example of media and globalization comes from Richard Condon's (1988, 1995) study of the Inuit (Eskimos) of the Canadian Arctic. Condon's ethnography is of particular interest with respect to media because he first observed Inuit adolescents in 1978, just prior to when television first became available (in 1980), and he subsequently returned there for further observations several times during the 1980s. Between his first visit and his subsequent visits he observed striking changes in adolescents' behavior with respect to competition in sports and with respect to romantic relationships, changes that Condon and many of the Inuit he interviewed attributed to the introduction of television.

With respect to sports, before TV arrived Inuit adolescents rarely played sports, and when they did they were reluctant to appear that they were trying hard to win and establish superior skills over other players because of Inuit cultural traditions that discourage competition and encourage cooperation. All of this changed after the introduction of television. Baseball, football, and hockey games quickly became among the most popular TV programs, especially among adolescents, and participation in these sports (especially hockey) became a central part of the recreational activities of adolescent boys, with adolescent girls often coming to watch. Furthermore, adolescent boys became intensively competitive in the games they played, no longer shy about trying hard to win, and talking loudly about their superior talent when they did win—clearly emulating the players they watched on TV. It is rare to see such an unambiguous example of the *effects* of media on adolescents.

The other area in which the influence of television was observed by Condon was male–female relationships. Prior to the introduction of television, adolescents' dating and sexual behavior was furtive and secretive. Couples rarely displayed affection for one another in public; in fact, couples rarely even acknowledged any special relationship between them when they were around others. Condon described one adolescent boy whom he had known closely for a year before the boy confided that he had a girlfriend he had been dating for the past 4 years—and even then, the boy refused to reveal her name!

However, all this changed after a couple of years of exposure to TV. Teenage couples were frequently seen together in public, holding hands or hugging. At community dances, young couples no longer ignored each other at opposite ends of the dance hall but sat together as couples and danced as couples. When Condon inquired about the reason for the change, many of the adolescents told him they thought it was due to the introduction of television. "Happy Days," a program about American teens in the 1950s, was a particular favorite.

Does all of this mean that, eventually, Western (especially American) media will obliterate all the other media of the world and establish a homogeneous global culture dominated by the United States? It is difficult to say. In some countries, locally produced media are having difficulty competing with the popularity of American media (Robinson et al., 1991). However, what seems to be happening in most places, at least so far, is that local media are coexisting with "imported" American media. Young people watch American television shows, but also shows in their own language produced in their own country, and perhaps shows from other countries as well (e.g., Davis & Davis, 1989,

1995). They go to American movies, but also to movies that are locally produced. They listen to American and British music, but also to the music of their own culture and their own artistic traditions (Robinson et al., 1991).

In some places, new blends of music are resulting from increasing globalization (Robinson et al., 1991). For example, in Britain, immigrant musicians from India have begun to develop a musical style dubbed "Indipop," a combination of traditional Indian musical forms and instruments with British and American popular music forms and technology. Whether creative and original new forms will continue to develop from globalization or whether globalization will lead to a relentless homogenization into one global media culture will be substantially determined by what appeals most to the adolescents and emerging adults of the world.

Summing Up

In this chapter we have discussed a wide range of media and how they are used by young people. The main points we have covered are as follows:

- Media use is an important part of young people's daily experience in industrialized countries and increasingly in traditional cultures as well. Altogether, adolescents in industrialized countries are estimated to spend about 8 hours per day in media use.
- The uses and gratifications approach depicts young people as active media users rather than as the passive recipients of media stimulation. This approach recognizes that young people vary in the media choices they make and that they vary in their responses to the same media experience. Uses of media among young people include entertainment, identity formation, high sensation, coping, and youth culture identification.
- Although hundreds of studies have been conducted on television and aggression, mostly on children, the evidence that television is a motivator of aggressive behavior in adolescents is mixed. Computer games have also been accused of promoting violence, but little is known at this point about the uses that adolescents may make of these games.
- The television shows most popular among adolescents contain a high proportion of interactions concerning sexuality. Generally these interactions emphasize the importance of physical appearance in male–female relationships and display a "recreational" attitude toward sex.
- Criticisms of "gangsta" rap target themes of sexual exploitation of women, violence, and racism in rap songs. Little is known about the responses of adolescents who like rap music.

- Heavy metal music has been accused of promoting suicidal and violent tendencies. However, adolescent heavy metal fans generally report that the music has a cathartic effect on their anger.
- Studies find that cigarette advertisements for Marlboro, Camel, and Newport are highly attractive to adolescents, especially adolescent smokers, and that these are also the brands adolescents are most likely to smoke. Internal tobacco company documents show evidence that tobacco companies have explicitly sought to appeal to adolescents.
- Media are a powerful force in the globalization of adolescence, but in most traditional cultures young people use local media as well as Western media.

Perhaps the most striking characteristic of young people's immersion in media today is that it marks such a dramatic change from the environment they experienced just a century ago. Eight hours a day is a lot of time to spend on *anything*, and it is remarkable that today's young people in industrialized countries spend this much time with media. Young people in developing countries are headed in this same direction; in fact, current trends in these countries represent a research opportunity to study them before and after their immersion in a media environment, as we have seen in Condon's (1988) study of the Inuit. Causes—rather than correlations—of media use are much easier to discern under these circumstances.

And what of the future? There is every indication that young people's time spent with media will continue to grow. Media are becoming increasingly mobile—music can now be listened to while walking, running, or riding a bus; some automobiles now come with televisions for the kids to watch in the back seat, and more will have this feature in the decades to come.

The Internet is new and use of it is likely to grow further among young people. School, previously a place where adolescents' media use was tightly curtailed, is now being opened up to new media uses. Forty percent of American secondary schools now begin their day with news *and advertisements* transmitted by Channel One, an in-school TV news program for teens (Manning, 1999).

Media are used by young people in many different ways, as we have emphasized in this chapter, and their media uses may have positive as well as negative impli-

cations for their development. Still, given the relentless and continuing increase in media use among young people, it is not unreasonable to wonder, is there a point at which the effect of media on their development is negative simply because of the amount of time devoted to it? It may be that ultimately the most important effect of young people's media use is a **displacement effect** (Strasburger & Donnerstein, 1999), in the sense that media use takes time away from activities such as exercising and spending time with others.

Key Terms

uses and gratifications approach	sensation seeking field studies	performance videos concept videos	cathartic effect displacement effect

For Further Reading

Christenson, P. G., & Roberts, D. F. (1998). *It's not only rock and roll: Popular music in the lives of adolescents.* Cresskill, NJ: Hampton Press. A good summary of research on adolescents and music.

Currie, D. (1999). *Girl talk: Adolescent magazines and their readers.* Toronto, Canada: University of Toronto Press. A fascinating and disturbing description of the characteristics of magazines aimed at adolescent girls and of girls' responses to them.

Funk, J. B., Flores, G., Buchman, D. D., & Germann, J. N. (1999). Rating electronic games: Violence is in the eye of the beholder. *Youth & Society, 30,* 283–312. The most recent research by the scholar

who has pioneered research on adolescents and computer games. Contains an excellent summary of the rating systems for various media, including not only computer games but movies, television, and music.

Strasburger, V. (1995). *Adolescents and the media: Medical and psychological impact.* Thousand Oaks, CA: Sage. An excellent summary of the research on adolescents and media, with a focus on television. Strasburger's position is clearly that violence and sex in media cause harm to adolescents' development, but he presents all the relevant research fairly and accurately so that you can make your own judgment.

Applying Research

Gore, T. (1987). *Raising PG kids in an X-rated society.* Nashville: Abingdon Press. Tipper Gore was widely ridiculed in the mid-1980s when she and several other wives of prominent politicians started the Parents Music Resource Center (PMRC) to alert parents to media (especially music) that they be-

lieved might have a harmful effect on children. However, the book is actually a quite thoughtful analysis of how to balance the vulnerability of children and adolescents with the cherished American value (and First Amendment right) of free expression and freedom of speech.

CHAPTER

13

Problems

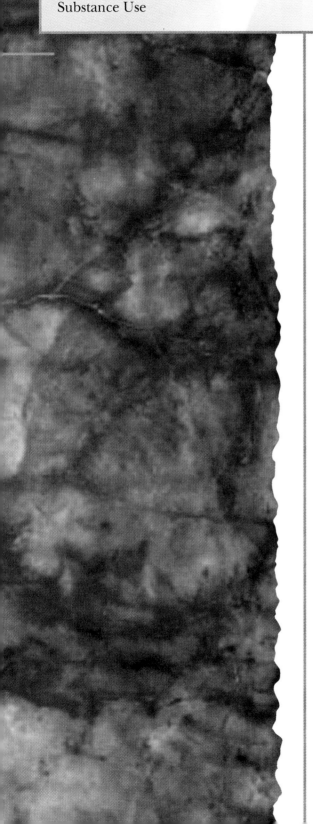

You do not have to look very far to find evidence of young people's problems in American society. Your local newspaper is likely to provide plenty of examples on a daily basis. A typical story appeared recently in my local newspaper, the Washington Post. *It described an incident in which three cars full of adolescent boys, high school students, pulled up alongside three men, got out of their cars, and allegedly demanded money. The men were middle-aged recent immigrants from El Salvador, who were walking home from their jobs washing dishes at a local restaurant. When the boys demanded money, the men panicked and tried to run. Two of them escaped, but the other one was caught by the boys, who allegedly beat him, kicked him, and slammed his head on the sidewalk. The next day the man died in the hospital as a result of his injuries. The boys have been charged with his murder.*

Terrible stories like this are probably familiar to you, and you may have noticed that these stories frequently involve young men in their teens and early twenties. Scholars sometimes complain that such stories promote stereotypes about young people, especially the stereotype that adolescence is inherently a time of "storm and stress" and that adolescents are disproportionately the cause of social problems such as crime (e.g., Steinberg & Levine, 1997). To the extent such a stereotype exists, applying it to all adolescents and emerging adults would be unfair. In examining many aspects of development in the various chapters of this book, we have seen that the teens and early twenties are years of many changes, some of them profound and dramatic. However, for most young people, these changes are manageable, and they develop through adolescence and emerging adulthood without suffering any serious or enduring problems.

Nevertheless, the teens and twenties are a period of life, at least in American society, when various problems are *more likely* to occur than at other times (Arnett,

395

A variety of problems are more common in adolescence and emerging adulthood than at other periods of life.

1999a). Most adolescents and emerging adults do not develop serious problems, but the *risk* of a wide range of problems is higher for them than it is for children or adults. These problems range from automobile accidents to criminal behavior to eating disorders to depressed mood. We will explore all of these problems in this chapter.

Before we examine specific types of problems, you should be introduced to some of the ideas that provide a context for understanding the problems. These ideas will be the topic of the next section.

Two Broad Types of Problems

Scholars studying young people's problems often make a distinction between **internalizing problems** and **externalizing problems** (Achenbach & Edelbrock, 1986). Internalizing problems take place when people turn their distress inward, toward themselves. This results in problems such as depression, anxiety, and eating disorders. Internalizing problems tend to go together (Compas, Connor, & Hinden, 1998; Petersen et al., 1993). For example, adolescents who have an eating disorder are also more likely than other adolescents to be depressed. Adolescents who are depressed are also more likely than other adolescents to have anxiety disorders. Young people who have internalizing problems are sometimes called **overcontrolled**. They tend to come from families in which parents have tight psychological control (Barber, Olsen, & Shagle, 1994). As a result,

their own personalities are often overly controlled, overly self-punishing. Internalizing problems are more common among females than among males (Compas et al., 1998).

Externalizing problems are problems that are directed outward rather than inward. Types of externalizing problems include delinquency, fighting, substance use, risky driving, and unprotected sex. Like internalizing problems, externalizing problems tend to go together (Elliott, Huizinga, & Menard, 1989; Jessor & Jessor, 1977; Jessor, 1998; Loeber et al., 1998). For example, adolescents who fight are also more likely than other adolescents to commit crimes; adolescents who have unprotected sex are also more likely than other adolescents to use substances such as alcohol and marijuana. Young people with externalizing problems are sometimes called **undercontrolled**. They tend to come from families where parental monitoring and control is lacking (Barber et al., 1994). As a result, they tend to lack self-control themselves, which then manifests itself in their externalizing problems. Externalizing problems are more common among males than among females (Elliott et al., 1989; Loeber et al., 1998).

Another key difference between internalizing and externalizing problems is that young people with internalizing problems usually experience distress, whereas

> "ONE BOY I WENT TO HIGH SCHOOL WITH DIED JUMPING A TRAIN. . . . [THE BROTHER OF MY BEST FRIEND] LOST A BROTHER. HE DIED IN A CAR CRASH, AS DID THE SISTER OF ANOTHER GIRL IN MY CLASS. . . . WHEN WE WERE TEENAGERS, I REALIZE NOW, WE LIVED VERY NEAR DEATH, MUCH NEARER THAN IN THE DECADES SINCE. ANY GIVEN SATURDAY NIGHT COULD BRING A GOOD PARTY, OR IT COULD BRING DEATH; SOMETIMES THE TWO WENT HAND IN HAND. IT DIDN'T SEEM LIKE WE WERE LIVING WITH DEATH. IT SEEMED LIKE WE WERE HAVING FUN, WHEN IN TRUTH WE WERE AS CLOSE TO DEATH AS BABIES ARE. LIKE BABIES, WE WERE CONSTANTLY DOING THINGS WE SHOULDN'T, TESTING THINGS WE SHOULDN'T; THE WORLD, TO US, WAS ONE BIG ELECTRICAL SOCKET INTO WHICH WE WERE ALWAYS PLUNGING OUR FINGERS."
>
> —LIZA MUNDY (1999)

young people with externalizing problems often do not (Maggs, 1999). The majority of young people take part in externalizing behaviors from time to time. Although externalizing behaviors may be a manifestation of problems with family, friends, or school, many young people who take part in externalizing behaviors have no such problems. Externalizing behaviors are often motivated not by underlying unhappiness or psychopathology but by the desire for excitement and intense experiences (Arnett, 1992a, 1994b), and can also be one way of having fun with friends (Maggs, 1999). Externalizing behaviors are almost always viewed as problems by adults but young people themselves may not see them that way.

The distinction between internalizing and externalizing problems is useful, but it should not be taken to be absolute. In general the problems within each category occur together, but some young people have both kinds of problems. For example, delinquent adolescents are sometimes depressed as well (Capaldi, 1991, 1992; Loeber et al., 1998), and depressed adolescents sometimes abuse drugs and alcohol (Henry et al., 1993). Some studies have found that adolescents with both externalizing and internalizing problems have had especially difficult family backgrounds (Capaldi & Stoolmiller, 1992).

We will examine externalizing problems first, then internalizing problems.

Externalizing Problems

Externalizing problems in adolescence have been intensively studied by social scientists, especially in the past 30 years. Various terms have been used by scholars in studying this topic, including not only externalizing problems but also **risk behavior** and **problem behavior**. Regardless of the terms used, these behaviors generally include risky sexual behavior, risky driving behavior, substance use, and crime. We will discuss each of these types of behavior except for risky sexual behavior, which was discussed in Chapter 9. Then we will discuss the various factors that have been found to be related to these behaviors. First, however, we will examine a widely used theory of how these behaviors are related.

Problem Behavior Theory
A great deal of research in recent years has established that young people who have one type of externalizing problem often have other types as well. Scholars con-

ducting this research have focused on a set of problems that are pervasive among young people—such as unprotected sex, substance use, and minor types of crime such as small theft—and the correlations between them. Richard Jessor, the scholar best known for this idea, calls the pattern of correlations **problem behavior syndrome** (Jessor, 1987, 1998; Jessor, Donovan, & Costa, 1991; Jessor & Jessor, 1977). In Jessor's view, the various kinds of externalizing problems have a common origin. To describe this origin, Jessor's **problem behavior theory** presents a complex model including background factors such as family income, personality factors such as self-esteem, and social factors such as parental controls and friends' involvement in problem behavior. If young people are at risk for one type of problem behavior on the basis of the factors in Jessor's model, they tend to be at risk for others as well.

Jessor has focused his research on externalizing problems such as drug use and theft. His studies (and others') support his view that different problems in adolescence and emerging adulthood tend to be correlated. Also, he has found that his model can be used to explain why some young people are more likely than others to engage in problem behavior (Donovan & Jessor, 1985; Jessor, 1987; Jessor et al., 1991; Jessor & Jessor, 1977).

Jessor's idea of the problem behavior syndrome has been highly influential in the study of young people's externalizing problems, and scholars generally accept that externalizing problems tend to be correlated. However, scholars have also criticized problem behavior theory in some respects (Arnett, 1992). A number of scholars have noted that, although problems of various kinds tend to be correlated, the correlations are not always high and should not be overstated (e.g., McCord, 1990; Osgood et al., 1988). For example, young people who commit crimes may be *more likely* than other young people to use hard drugs, but *most* young people who commit crimes do not use hard drugs (Elliott et al., 1989). As we will see in more detail later in this chapter, prevalence rates of the various kinds of externalizing problems vary widely, from over 80% for driving at high speeds to under 5% for using hard drugs. This means that many young people engage in behavior like driving at high speeds but never do things like using hard drugs.

Now we proceed to an examination of specific externalizing problems: risky automobile driving, substance use, and delinquency and crime.

Risky Automobile Driving

"I love to drive fast. But after awhile driving fast just wasn't doing it any more, so I started driving without the lights on [at night], going about ninety on country roads. I even got a friend to do it. We'd go cruising down country roads, turn off the lights, and just fly. It was incredible. We'd go as fast as we could, [and] at night, with no lights it feels like you're just flying."

—*Nick, age 23 (in Arnett, 1996, p. 79)*

The most serious threat to the lives and health of American adolescents and emerging adults comes from automobile driving. Young people aged 16 to 24 have the highest rates of automobile accidents, injuries, and fatalities of any age group in the American population (Figure 13.1; National Highway Traffic Safety Administration, 1999). Automobile accidents are also the leading cause of death in this age group (National Center for Health Statistics, 1999).

What is responsible for these grim statistics? Is it due to young drivers' inexperience or to their risky driving behavior? Inexperience probably does play a role. Rates of accidents and fatalities are highest in the late teens, during the years when adolescents have first begun to drive. Studies that have attempted to disentangle experience and age in young drivers have generally concluded that inexperience is partly responsible for young drivers' accidents and fatalities (e.g., Jonah, 1986).

However, these studies and others have also concluded that inexperience is not the only fac-

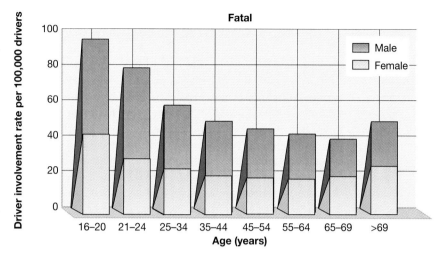

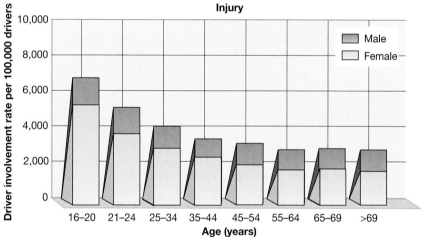

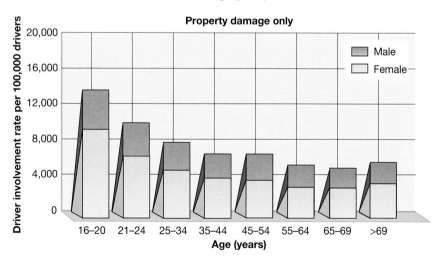

FIGURE 13.1 *Driver crash involvement rates per 100,000 drivers by age, 1997.*
Source: NHTSA (1999), p. 99.

Young drivers tend to take more risks than older drivers.

tor involved. More important is the way young people drive and the kinds of risks they take (U.S. Department of Transportation, 1995; Williams, 1998; Williams, Preusser, Ulmer, & Weinstein, 1995). Young people in their late teens and early twenties report driving faster than older drivers and closer to vehicles in front of them, and observational studies show that they take more risks in their lane-changing and passing behavior (Jonah, 1986; U.S. Department of Transportation, 1995). They are also more likely than older drivers to report driving under the influence of alcohol, and drivers aged 21 to 24 involved in fatal accidents are more likely to have been intoxicated at the time of the accident than persons in any other age group (National Highway Traffic Safety Administration, 1999). Nearly half of college students report driving while intoxicated in the past year (Finken, Jacobs, & Laguna, 1998). Young people are also less likely than older drivers to wear seatbelts, and in serious car crashes occupants not wearing seatbelts are twice as likely to be killed and three times as likely to be injured, compared with those wearing seatbelts (National Highway Traffic Safety Administration, 1999).

Preventing Automobile Accidents and Fatalities

What can be done to reduce the rates of automobile accidents and fatalities among young drivers? The two approaches that have been tried most often in the United States are **driver education**, which generally has not worked very well, and a program of restricted driving privileges called **graduated licensing**, which has been much more effective.

On the face of it, driver education would seem promising as a way to improve adolescents' driving

practices. It seems logical that if beginning drivers were taught how to drive by professional educators, they would become more proficient more quickly, and therefore be safer drivers. However, studies that have compared rates of crash involvement for adolescents who have taken driver education courses and for adolescents who have not have found that crash involvements tend to be as high or *higher* for the adolescents who have taken driver education (e.g., Potvin, Champagne, & Laberge-Nadeau, 1988). What seems to be happening is that when driver education is available, adolescents tend to obtain their licenses more quickly than when it is not. The increased risk of crash involvement as a result of obtaining an earlier license is stronger than any decreased risk that might result from taking driver education.

An alternative approach, one favored strongly by most scholars on adolescent driving, is graduated licensing. Graduated licensing is a program in which young people obtain driving privileges gradually, contingent on a safe driving record, rather than all at once. These programs typically include three stages (National Highway Traffic Safety Administration, 1996). **Learning license** is the stage in which the young person undergoes a period of obtaining driving experience under the supervision of an experienced driver. For example, a program implemented in 1998 in California requires young people to complete learning license training of 50 hours under the supervision of a parent, 10 of which must be at night.

The second stage is a period of **restricted license** driving. In this stage adolescents are allowed to drive unsupervised, but with tighter restrictions than those that apply to adults. One of the most effective restrictions has been found to be **driving curfews**, which prohibit young drivers from driving late at night (e.g., in New York, between 9 P.M. and 5 A.M.) except for a specific purpose such as going back and forth to work. This restriction has been found to reduce young people's crash involvement dramatically (Preusser et al., 1990; Preusser, Zador, Williams, 1993). Other restrictions include requirements for seat belt use and a **zero tolerance** rule for alcohol use, which means that young drivers are in violation if they drive with any alcohol at all in their blood. In the restricted stage, any violations of these restrictions may result in a suspended license. It is only after the restricted period has passed—usually no more than one year—that a young person obtains a **full license** and has the same driving privileges as adults.

Studies in the past decade have shown the effectiveness of graduated licensing programs (National Highway Traffic Safety Administration, 1996; Williams, 1998), and legislators in many states have responded to this evidence by passing more of these programs. As of 1998, 46 states had zero tolerance alcohol use laws for young drivers. Also by 1998, 12 states had some form of driving curfew for young drivers, up from 6 states just 2 years before. Several states with the lowest license ages have raised their minimum age of licensure from 15 to 16, so that only 6 states have a driving age less than 16. (Five of these 6 states have a driving age of 15. South Dakota has a driving age of 14. The minimum driving age is 16 in all other states except New Jersey, where it is 17.) Research indicates that these changes in state laws will lead to a significant reduction in automobile accidents and fatalities among young drivers. In other Western countries, a higher minimum driving age (usually 18) and more difficult driving tests have made their rates of accidents and fatalities among young people far lower than in the United States (Arnett & Balle-Jensen, 1993).

THINKING CRITICALLY

Are you in favor of a graduated licensing program for your state? If so, what provisions would you include? Are such programs unfair to young people who drive safely and nevertheless have their driving privileges restricted?

Substance Use

One of the problems that has drawn the most public attention in American society in the past 20 years is the use of alcohol and other drugs. Scholars often use the term **substance use** to refer to this topic, with "substances" including alcohol, cigarettes, and illegal drugs such as marijuana, LSD, and cocaine. Substance use, especially among adolescents, became the target of a great deal of political attention, scientific research, and public policy programs in the 1980s. It has remained a high-profile public issue through the 1990s and into the 21st century, especially in recent years as substance use has increased among adolescents (as we shall see in more detail shortly).

Current and Past Rates of Substance Use The Monitoring the Future (MTF) studies we have discussed at various points in this book were first developed with the primary goal of tracking rates of drug use among adolescents in the United States, and the MTF studies remain the best source of data on adolescent drug use. Throughout this section, the MTF studies will be the source unless otherwise specified (Monitoring the Future, 2000).

Is substance use a common part of going through adolescence and emerging adulthood in the United States? It depends very much on which substance you look at. If the substance is alcohol, the answer is yes. Fifty-one percent of high school seniors in 1999 reported using alcohol at least once in the past month, and 31% reported **binge drinking**—drinking five or more alcoholic drinks in a row—at least once in the past 2 weeks. Cigarettes are the next most common substance used in adolescence. In 1999, 35% of high school seniors reported smoking cigarettes at least once in the past 30 days. Cigarettes are followed in prevalence by marijuana, which 23% of high school seniors reported using in the past month in the 1999 MTF survey. In general, substance use in adolescence is highest among Native Americans, followed by White and Latino adolescents, with African American and Asian American adolescents lowest (Bachman et al., 1991; Gil, Vega, & Biafora, 1998).

Although the statistics in the preceding paragraph all concern high school seniors, for many adolescents substance use begins well before their senior year of high school. In 1999, half of American eighth graders had tried alcohol, one-fourth had been drunk, and 22% had tried marijuana (Monitoring the Future, 2000). Adolescents who smoke cigarettes typically begin between ages 13 and 15, and few people begin smoking after age 17 (U.S. Department of Health and Human Services, 1994).

Other than alcohol, cigarettes, and marijuana, substance use is uncommon among American adolescents. A small proportion of adolescents experiment with other substances. For example, in 1999, 17% of high school seniors had tried amphetamines; 15% had tried inhalants (e.g., glue, gasoline); 14% had tried hallucinogens (e.g., LSD); and 10% had tried cocaine. However, frequent use of these substances was very rare. None of them had been used by more than 5% of high school seniors in the past 30 days. Even so, use of illicit drugs (i.e., not including alcohol and cigarettes) is higher among adolescents in the United States than in any other industrialized country (Arnett, 2000d).

The peak of substance use actually comes not in adolescence but in emerging adulthood (Schulenberg & Maggs, 2000). The MTF studies have followed up several cohorts after high school through their twenties, and

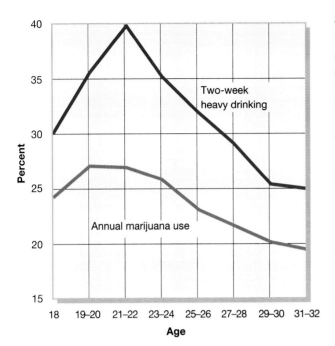

FIGURE 13.2 *Alcohol and marijuana use by age.*
Source: Bachman et al. (1997), p. 248.

now provide excellent data on substance use in emerging adulthood as well. These data show that substance use of all kinds continues to rise through the late teens and peaks in the early twenties before declining in the late twenties. Figure 13.2 shows the pattern for binge drinking and marijuana use (Bachman et al., 1997).

What explains the higher rates of substance use among emerging adults? Wayne Osgood has proposed a useful answer to this question. Osgood (Osgood et al., 1996) borrows from a sociological theory that explains all deviance on the basis of **propensity and opportunity** (see Gottfredson & Hirschi, 1990). People behave deviantly when they have a combination of sufficient propensity (that is, sufficient motivation for behaving deviantly) along with sufficient opportunity. In his explanation, Osgood especially focuses on the high degree of opportunity that emerging adults have for engaging in substance use and other deviant behavior, as a result of spending a high proportion of their time in unstructured socializing.

Osgood uses the term **unstructured socializing** to include behavior such as riding around in a car for fun, going to parties, going shopping, and going out with friends. Using MTF data, he shows that unstructured socializing is highest in the late teens and early twenties, and that within this age period, emerging adults

who are highest in unstructured socializing are also highest in the use of alcohol and marijuana (Osgood et al., 1996). Rates of most types of substance use are especially high among emerging adults who are college students (Kalb & McCormick, 1998; Schulenberg, 2000), perhaps because they have so many opportunities for unstructured socializing. Substance use (and other kinds of problem behavior) declines in the mid- to late twenties, as role transitions such as marriage, parenthood, and full-time work cause a sharp decline in unstructured socializing (Bachman, Johnston et al., 1996; Schulenberg et al., 1996).

How do the current rates of substance use in adolescence and emerging adulthood compare with previous decades? Because the MTF studies go back to 1975, there is excellent data on this question for adolescents over the past 23 years. As you can see from Figure 13.3, rates of most types of substance use (past month) declined from the late 1970s to the early 1990s. Alcohol use declined from about 70% to about 50%. Cigarette smoking declined from nearly 40% to under 30%. Marijuana use declined from a peak of 37% in 1978 to just 12% in 1992. Use of stimulants peaked at 15% in 1981 and had declined to under 5% by 1990. During this period, an increasing proportion of young people defined themselves as **straight-edge**, meaning that they abstain from all substance use (Kalb & McCormick, 1998).

However, this pattern of decline reversed during the 1990s. Thirty-day prevalence of marijuana use among high school seniors rose from 14% in 1990 to 23% in 1999. Prevalence of cigarette smoking rose from 29% in 1990 to 35% in 1999. Even the rates of most of the rarely used drugs rose during this time. For example, use of hallucinogens (such as LSD) rose from 2.3% in 1990 to 3.5% in 1999. A similar pattern of increase in the use of these substances took place among 8th and 10th graders (the MTF surveys have included adolescents at these ages since 1992), and the increases have been confirmed by other national surveys. However, alcohol use has been an exception to the upward trend. Alcohol use within the past 30 days declined among high school seniors from 57% in 1990 to 51% in 1999.

What is responsible for the recent upward trend in substance use among adolescents? The authors of the MTF surveys attribute the increase to a decline in the perceived risks of substance use (Johnston, O'Malley, & Bachman, 1996). They point out that throughout more than two decades of MTF surveys, substance use has been negatively correlated with the perceived risks of using various substances. In the 1990s perceived risks of using substances declined, and substance use

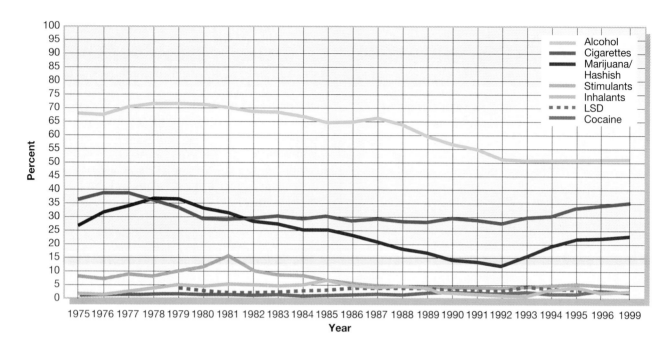

FIGURE 13.3 *Substance use, 1975–1999.*

Source: Johnston, Bachman, & O'Malley (1997), p. 408; Monitoring the Future, 2000.

rose. However, this begs the question of why the perceived risks of substance use declined in the 1990s. So far, scholars have not come up with a complete answer to the question of why substance use increased during the 1990s.

The Sequence of Substance Use Through Adolescence and Emerging Adulthood Substance use in adolescence and emerging adulthood has been found to follow a typical sequence of four stages: (1) drinking beer and wine; (2) smoking cigarettes and drinking hard liquor; (3) smoking marijuana; and (4) using "hard" drugs (e.g., cocaine, LSD). Almost all adolescents who begin to smoke cigarettes or use hard liquor have already tried beer and wine; almost all adolescents who try marijuana have already tried cigarettes and hard liquor; and almost all adolescents who use hard drugs have already tried marijuana (Kandel, 1975; Mills & Noyes, 1984; Van Kammen, Loeber, & Stouthamer-Loeber, 1991). Beer, wine, cigarettes, and marijuana have been referred to as **gateway drugs** because most adolescents who try hard drugs have already passed through the "gates" of these substances.

Of course, this does not mean that all or even most of the people who try one type of substance will go on to try the next substance in the sequence. It simply means that young people who try one type of substance are *more likely* than young people who have not tried it to move along the sequence to the next substance. So, for example, most young people who try marijuana will never try hard drugs; but among young people who try hard drugs, almost all of them have used marijuana first.

THINKING CRITICALLY

Some people have interpreted the "gateway drug" theory as indicating that if adolescents could be prevented from using alcohol and cigarettes, they would also be less likely to use marijuana and hard drugs. Do you think this is true, or would they be *more* likely to use other drugs if their access to alcohol and cigarettes was curtailed?

A good example of the sequence of substance use comes from the study by Kandel and Faust (1975) that originally inspired the "gateway drug" theory. The study assessed high school students' substance use on two occasions 6 months apart. At the 6-month follow-up, 27% of the students who had smoked or drank alcohol at the time of the original study had subsequently tried marijuana, compared with only 2% of the students who had not smoked or drank. Similarly, 26% of the students who had used marijuana at the time of the original study had subsequently tried hard drugs, compared with only 1% of the students who had never used marijuana. From this we can see both that young people who use one substance in the sequence are more likely to use the next one, and that most young people who use one substance do not proceed right away to use the next one in the sequence.

Substance Use and Abuse   Young people use substances for a variety of purposes, which can be classified as experimental, social, medicinal, and addictive (Weiner, 1992). Young people who take part in **experimental substance use** try a substance once or perhaps a few times out of curiosity, to "see what it was like," and then do not use it again. A substantial proportion of substance use in adolescence and emerging adulthood is experimental. "To see what it was like" has been found to be the most common motivation given by young people themselves when asked why they used an illicit drug (Arnett, 1992).

   Social substance use involves the use of substances during social activities with one or more friends. Parties and dances are common settings for social substance use in adolescence and emerging adulthood.

   Medicinal substance use is undertaken to relieve an unpleasant emotional state such as sadness, anxiety, stress, or loneliness. Using substances for these purposes has been described as a kind of **self-medication**. Young people who use

> "DRINK TODAY, AND DROWN
> ALL SORROW."
> —JOHN FLETCHER, 1639

substances for this purpose tend to use them more frequently than those whose purposes are mainly social or experimental (Novacek, Raskin, & Hogan, 1991).

   Finally, **addictive substance use** takes place when a person has come to depend on regular use of substances to feel good physically and/or psychologically. Addictive substance users experience **withdrawal symptoms** such as high anxiety and tremors when they stop taking the substance to which they are addicted. Addictive substance use involves the most regular and frequent substance use of the four categories described here.

   All substance use in adolescence and emerging adulthood is considered "problem behavior" in the

Some young people use substances for the purpose of self-medication.

sense that it is something that adults generally view as a problem if young people engage in it. However, the four categories described above indicate that young people may use substances in very different ways, with very different implications for their development. Research has found that young people who engage in experimental or social substance use are healthier psychologically in a variety of ways compared with adolescents who are frequent substance users (the "medicinal" and "addictive" users described above) (Barnes & Welte, 1986; Brook et al., 1989; Kandel, 1998; Shedler & Block, 1990). However, an important and provocative finding of recent research is that young people who engage in experimental or social substance use are at least as healthy as "abstainers" who never engage in substance use (Baumrind, 1991; Newcomb & Bentler, 1989; Shedler & Block, 1990).

   The best example of this phenomenon is from a longitudinal study described by Shedler and Block (1990). Shedler and Block used data from a well-known study by Block and Block (1980) that followed about 100 San Francisco children from ages 3 through 18. Shedler and Block (1990) reported distinct psychological differences among experimenters, frequent users, and abstainers at age 18. Experimenters had used marijuana "once or twice," "a few times," or "once a month," and had tried *no more* than one drug other than marijuana (not including alcohol or cigarettes). Frequent users reported using marijuana once a week or more and had tried *at least* one drug other than marijuana. Abstainers had never tried marijuana or any other drug.

   The personalities of the adolescents were rated at age 18 on the basis of interviews conducted by psychologists who knew nothing about their drug use. Frequent users were the least psychologically healthy. They tended to be rated by the psychologists as alienated, impulsive, self-indulgent, distrustful, and unhappy. The abstainers also had certain personality problems, although not as severe as the frequent users. Abstainers tended to be rated as overcontrolled, anxious, unexpressive, and socially isolated. The experimenters were rated as the most psychologically healthy. They tended to be rated as more likable, socially at ease, open, and personally charming, compared with adolescents in the other two groups.

Does this mean that experimental drug use should be recommended to adolescents as a way of enhancing their personalities? Not exactly. First, the study made only psychological judgments, and moral, religious, health, and legal arguments could be made against drug use at any level, however, it may be related to psychological functioning. Second, the study showed that the personality differences among the adolescents in the three groups existed long before they reached adolescence. Even in early childhood, the children who would become frequent users in adolescence were insecure and impulsive and had difficulty getting along with others. Similarly, the abstainers were overcontrolled, timid, and anxious even as young children, and experimenters as young children were warm, cheerful, and open to new experiences. Thus, the longitudinal data allow us to determine that their levels of drug use in adolescence did not cause their personality characteristics but simply reflected them.

More important than the differences between abstainers and experimenters is the finding, in Shedler and Block's (1990) study as well as others, that frequent substance use in adolescence—substance abuse rather than occasional substance use—reflects serious developmental problems. In addition to the personality difficulties found by Shedler and Block (1990), frequent users are more likely to have problems in school, to be withdrawn from peers, to have problems in their relationships with their parents, and to engage in delinquent behavior (Barnes & Welte, 1986; Brook et al., 1989). Frequent users are also three times more likely than other adolescents to be depressed, which suggests the role of self-medication as a motivation for frequent substance use (Belfer, 1993; Deykin, Buka, & Zeena, 1992).

Preventing Substance Use Efforts to prevent or reduce substance use among young people have gener-

ally been delivered through schools (Dryfoos, 1990, 1998). A variety of approaches have been tried. Some programs attempt to raise students' self-esteem, in the belief that the main cause of substance use is low self-esteem. Some programs present information about the health dangers of substance use, in the belief that becoming more knowledgeable about the effects of substance use will make students less likely to use them. Other programs, including the most widely used program, Project DARE, have focused on teaching students to resist "peer pressure," in the belief that peer pressure is the main reason young people use drugs. None of these approaches has worked very well (Ennett et al., 1994; Newcomb & Bentler, 1989; Wilson & Herrnstein, 1985).

More successful programs have been those that combine a variety of strategies and are implemented not only in school but through families and media as well (Dielman, 1994; Leventhal & Keeshan, 1993; Rohrbach et al., 1995). Successful programs also start young, in early middle school, and continue on a yearly basis through high school (Bruvold, 1993; Perry et al., 1996).

With regard to emerging adults, substance use prevention has focused especially on college students and especially on binge drinking. Approaches include providing freshman orientation workshops on alcohol use and abuse, handing out alcohol awareness pamphlets, sponsoring alcohol-free events, and pressuring local bars to limit offers for cheap drinks (Kalb & McCormick, 1998). Overall, these programs have had little effect on college students' drinking behavior. However, one approach that has shown promise is to increase students' awareness of how many of their peers *do not* binge drink. Students often believe the percentage is higher than it is, and this can create a norm that encourages binge drinking. For example, at Northern Illinois University, a study showed that students believed the percentage of binge drinkers among their peers was 70% when it was actually 45%. After an information campaign, students' estimates of the prevalence of binge drinking plunged to 33%—and the actual proportion of binge drinkers shrank to 25% (Kalb & McCormick, 1998).

Delinquency and Crime

Because criminal acts are so disruptive to societies, and because crime became increasingly pervasive with the development of modern cities, crime is one of the oldest and most intensively studied topics in the social sciences. In more than 150 years of research on crime, one finding stands out prominently with remarkable

"I WOULD THAT THERE WERE
NO AGE BETWEEN TEN AND
THREE-AND-TWENTY, OR THAT
YOUTH WOULD SLEEP OUT THE
REST; FOR THERE IS NOTHING
IN BETWEEN BUT GETTING
WENCHES WITH CHILD,
WRONGING THE ANCIENTRY,
STEALING, FIGHTING. . . ."
—WILLIAM SHAKESPEARE,
1610, "THE WINTER'S TALE,"
ACT III, SCENE 3

consistency: The great majority of crimes are committed by young people—mostly males—who are between the ages of 12 and 25. Because most crimes are committed by adolescents and emerging adults, this topic merits considerable attention for us in this chapter.

First, however, some definitions are necessary. Crimes, of course, are acts that violate the law. When violations of the law are committed by persons defined by the legal system as **juveniles**, these violations are considered acts of **delinquency**. About three-fourths of the states in the United States define juveniles as persons under 18 years of age.

There are three kinds of delinquent acts. **Status offenses** are offenses that are defined as violations of the law only because they are committed by juveniles. For example, adults can move away from home any time they wish, but juveniles who leave home without their parents' consent may be found guilty of *running away from home*. Other examples of status offenses include *truancy* (failure to attend school), consensual sex (legal ages for this vary widely among states), and purchasing alcohol.

Index crimes are serious crimes, and they are offenses that would be considered violations of the law if committed by a person of any age, juvenile or adult. Index offenses include two subcategories, **violent crimes**, such as rape, assault, and murder, and **property crimes**, such as robbery, motor vehicle theft, and arson. **Nonindex crimes** are less serious offenses such as illegal gambling and disorderly conduct. Like index crimes, nonindex crimes would be considered violations of the law no matter what the age of the person committing them.

By definition, status offenses are committed entirely by adolescents—they are acts that would not be criminal if performed by someone who is legally an adult. However, the dramatic relationship between age and crime—the finding that criminal acts are committed mostly by males aged 12 to 25—is true for index and nonindex offenses as well. In the West, this finding is remarkably consistent over a period of greater than 150 years. Figure 13.4 shows the age–crime relationship at two points, one in the 1840s and one quite recent. At any point in between these times, in most countries, the pattern would look very similar (Gottfredson & Hirschi, 1990; Wilson & Herrnstein, 1985).

Although young people aged 12 to 25 have committed most of the crimes in every historical period of the past two centuries, there have also been quite substantial historical fluctuations in the rates of crimes committed by young people. Of particular interest is that crime rates among young people rose sharply from the mid-1960s to the mid-1970s (Wilson & Herrnstein, 1985), and sharply again from the mid-1980s to the early 1990s (Federal Bureau of Investigation, 1999), before declining slightly in the mid- to late 1990s. During the late 1980s and early 1990s, the increase in crime was especially strong among young people aged 14 to 17 (Fox, 1996). Adolescents and emerging adults are not only more likely than children or adults to commit crimes, but also more likely to be the victims of crimes (Cohen & Potter, 1999).

What explains the strong and consistent relationship between age and crime? Some of the most influential theories have implicated school experiences, perhaps because of the well-established finding that delinquents tend to do poorly in school (Gottfredson & Hirschi, 1990; Wilson & Herrnstein, 1985). **Labeling theory** argues that delinquency results when young children do poorly in school and are labeled as failures. This causes them to develop an identity as a failure and as deviant, which in adolescence is expressed as delinquency. **Strain theory** argues that children from lower social classes frequently do poorly in school because they do not believe that hard work in school will be rewarded with economic success once they leave school. The result is frustration (strain) that becomes expressed in adolescence as delinquency. In this theory, delinquency is a way of explicitly rejecting middle-class values of cooperation, conformity, and delay of gratification, and this rejection takes place among lower-class adolescents who believe they are unfairly excluded from the opportunities that would allow them to reach the middle class.

Labeling and strain theories have a number of problems, perhaps the most important of which is that the

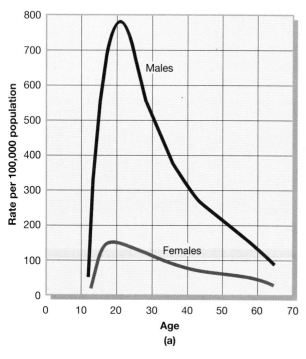

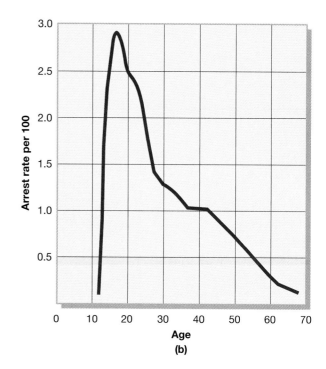

FIGURE 13.4 *Age and crime in (a) 1842 and (b) 1977.*
Source: Gottfredson & Hirschi (1990), p. 125.

behavior problems of most delinquents and criminals first appear in early childhood, before they ever enter the school system (Gottfredson & Hirschi, 1990; Kasen, Cohen, & Brook, 1998; Moffitt, 1993; Wilson & Herrnstein, 1985). Another, perhaps more plausible theory suggests that the key to explaining the age–crime relationship is that adolescents and emerging adults combine increased independence from parents and other adult authorities with increased time with peers and increased orientation toward peers (Wilson & Herrnstein, 1985). A consistent finding of research on crime is that crimes committed by young people in their teens and early twenties usually take place in a group, much more so than is the case among adult offenders (Gottfredson & Hirschi, 1990; Wilson & Herrnstein, 1985).

Of course, as we have noted, peers and friends can influence each other in a variety of ways, including toward conformity to adult standards, not just toward deviance and norm-breaking. However, adolescence and emerging adulthood appear to be the times of life when peer groups that value and reinforce norm-breaking are most likely to form (Wilson & Herrnstein, 1985). In seeking out excitement and sensation-seeking adventure, young people in these peer groups may en-

gage in activities that violate the law (Arnett, 1992, 1994b). Their motives are rarely economic—even when their activities involve theft, the thefts tend to be for small amounts. When they reach their mid-twenties, these antisocial peer groups break up as emerging adults enter the various roles of young adulthood, and participation in crime subsequently declines (Sampson & Laub, 1994).

Two Kinds of Delinquency Breaking laws of various kinds is quite common in the teens and early twenties, especially for males. Most surveys find that over three-fourths of adolescents commit at least one criminal offense some time before the age of 20 (Johnson & Fennell, 1992; Tolan & Loeber, 1993; Wilson & Herrnstein, 1985). However, there are obvious differences between committing one or two acts of minor crime—vandalism or small theft, for example—and committing crimes frequently over a long period, including more serious crimes such as rape and assault. Ten percent of young people commit over two-thirds of all offenses (Yoshikawa, 1994). What are the differences in delinquent behavior between adolescents in general and adolescents who are at risk for more serious, long-term criminal behavior?

CULTURAL FOCUS
The Young Males of Truk Island

Externalizing problems such as fighting, stealing, and substance use are far more common among males than among females, everywhere in the world and in every era of the historical record (Wilson & Herrnstein, 1985). The reasons for this may be partly biological, but they are also clearly connected to gender role socialization. In a wide range of cultures, what we have been calling "externalizing problems" are in fact part of the requirements for demonstrating an adolescent male's readiness for manhood (Gilmore, 1990).

One vivid example of this can be found among the people of Truk Island, an island that is part of a string of small islands in the South Pacific known as Micronesia. The culture of Truk Island has been vividly described by anthropologist Mac Marshall (1979) and summarized by David Gilmore (1990). Their accounts provide an excellent demonstration not only of the importance of gender role socialization in the externalizing behavior of young males, but also of the effect of globalization on young people even in cultures in the remotest parts of the world.

The globalization of the Trukese culture goes back more than a hundred years. Even long before that, the Trukese were known far and wide as fierce warriors who fought frequently among themselves and made short work of any Western sailors unlucky enough to drift nearby. However, in the late 1800s, German colonists arrived and took control of the islands and of the Trukese people. They stamped out local warfare, introduced Christianity, and introduced alcohol, which soon became widely and excessively used by young men. After World War II, the Americans replaced the Germans on Truk Island and introduced television, baseball, and other features of Western life. Today, Truk Island remains an American territory.

Much has changed on Truk Island during the century of Western influence, but there remains a strong emphasis on strictly defined gender roles. When they reach puberty, girls learn the traditional female role of cooking, sewing, and performing other household duties. Meanwhile, boys are expected to demonstrate their manhood principally in three ways: fighting, drinking large quantities of alcohol, and taking daredevil risks.

Fighting among young Trukese men is a group activity. It takes place in the context of rivalries between clans (extended family networks). Young men fight not just for their own prestige but for the honor and prestige of their clan. On weekend evenings, they roam the streets in clan groups looking for other groups to challenge, and taking part in brawls when they find them.

Drinking alcohol is also part of the weekend group activities of young males. By the time they are 13, getting drunk with their clan pals is a regular part of weekend evenings for adolescent boys. The drinking contributes to the fighting because it has the effect of diminishing any trepidation a boy might have over becoming injured. Also, on weekend days groups of young men sometimes take long risky trips in motor boats. They take long trips with limited fuel, a small motor, and nothing for sustenance except beer, risking the open sea in a small boat in order to demonstrate their bravery and thereby prove their readiness for manhood.

Although nearly all Trukese males in their teens and twenties engage in these activities, their externalizing escapades are limited to the weekends, and they rarely drink or fight during the week. In fact, Marshall's (1979) book on them is entitled *Weekend Warriors*. Also, when they reach about age 30, the expectations for manhood change. At that point, they are expected to marry and settle down. They rarely fight after reaching that age, and most stop drinking alcohol entirely. The externalizing behavior of males in adolescence and emerging adulthood is not viewed as a social problem, but rather as an expected part of a limited period of their lives, when their culture demands it as part of fulfilling the expectations for becoming a man.

Terrie Moffitt (1993) has proposed a provocative theory in which she distinguishes between adolescence-limited delinquency and life-course-persistent delinquency. In Moffitt's view, these are two distinct types of delinquency, each with different motivations and different sources. However, the two types may be hard to distinguish from one another in adolescence, when criminal offenses are more common than in childhood or adulthood. The way to tell them apart, according to Moffitt, is to look at behavior prior to adolescence.

Life-course-persistent delinquents (LCPDs) show a pattern of problems from birth onward. Moffitt believes their problems originate in neuropsychological deficits that are evident in a difficult temperament in infancy and a high likelihood of attention deficit disorder with hyperactivity (ADD-H) and learning disabilities in childhood. Children with these problems are also more likely than other children to grow up in a high-risk environment (e.g., low-income family, single parent, parents who have a variety of problems of their own). Consequently, their neurological deficits tend to be made worse rather than better by their environments. When they reach adolescence, children with the combination of neurological deficits and a high-risk environment are highly prone to engage in criminal activity. Furthermore, they tend to continue their criminal activity long after adolescence has ended, well into adulthood.

The **adolescence-limited delinquents (ALDs)** follow a much different pattern. They show no signs of problems in infancy or childhood, and few of them engage in any criminal activity after their mid-twenties. It is just during adolescence—actually, adolescence and emerging adulthood, about age 12 to about age 25—that they have a period of occasional criminal activity, breaking the law with behavior such as vandalism, theft, and use of illegal drugs.

The sources of LCPDs' delinquency are easy to see as an extension of their history of problems, but what explains delinquency among the ALDs? According to Moffitt, delinquency among ALDs is motivated by a desire to seize access to the power and privileges of adulthood. She emphasizes that in the past century biological maturity has become earlier while "social maturity" (including entry into adult roles such as full-time work) has been steadily more delayed. According to Moffitt, other adolescents see LCPDs as overcoming this maturity gap by obtaining possessions (through theft), becoming sexually experienced, and declaring an early independence from their families. ALDs mimic the behavior of LCPDs, including their delin-

quency, in order to obtain the adultlike advantages they believe LCPDs possess. AL delinquency subsides once adolescents are able to obtain adult privileges through more legitimate means—sex through marriage, material possessions through full-time work, independence as a result of moving out on their own.

Moffitt's theory is provocative and original, and it makes a valuable contribution in identifying two distinct types of delinquency in adolescence. However, the theory has certain limitations. In particular, the developmental explanation for AL delinquency is weak. There is no evidence that adolescents are eager to take on the roles of adulthood—marriage, parenthood, and full-time work. If anything, the steady rise in the median age of these transitions over the past 50 years suggests quite the opposite (Arnett, 1998a; Modell, 1989). More important, there is no evidence that adolescents view LCPDs as models of any kind. On the contrary, LCPDs tend to be unpopular in adolescence, as they had been in childhood, because of their aggressiveness and their lack of impulse control (Moffitt, 1993). Still, Moffitt's distinction between ALDs and LCPDs is useful for drawing our attention to the fact that adolescents who engage in delinquent behaviors may have very different pasts and futures, even if their current behavior is similar.

THINKING CRITICALLY

What do you think of Moffitt's claim that adolescence-limited delinquents are motivated by a desire to claim access to adult power and privileges? What other motivations do you think may be involved in AL delinquency?

Preventing Crime and Delinquency As noted above, the disruption to society that results from crime has made this area the focus of an enormous amount of social science research for many decades. Similarly, the seriousness of crime as a social problem has drawn a great deal of attention to preventing young people from committing crimes and, for young people who have already begun to commit crimes, toward trying to rehabilitate them so that they will no longer do so. For most young people, as we have discussed, criminal acts are limited to adolescence, and once they grow beyond their teens or early twenties they no longer have any inclination to commit such acts. The real focus of concern is the life-course-persistent offenders, the young people who have problems from early childhood onward, who become chronic delinquents in adolescence, and who are headed for a life of continued crime in adulthood.

Prevention programs to help children who show signs of being headed for trouble in adolescence or to help adolescents who have become involved in serious delinquency are enormously varied. They include individual therapy, group therapy, vocational training, "Outward Bound" kinds of programs that involve group activities in the outdoors, "Scared Straight" programs that take young offenders into a prison to show them the grim conditions of prison life, and many, many, many others. These programs, in all their diversity, have one thing in common. None of them has worked very well (McCord, 1990). The overall record of delinquency prevention and intervention programs is frustratingly poor, despite the best intentions of the many dedicated and highly skilled people who have undertaken them.

Two problems seem to be at the heart of the failure of these programs. One is that delinquents rarely welcome the opportunity to participate in the programs (Marohn, 1993; Stone, 1993). Typically they are required to participate in the programs against their will, often because the legal system commands them to participate or face incarceration. They do not see themselves as having a problem that needs to be "cured," and their resistance makes progress extremely difficult.

Most delinquency prevention programs have had little success. Here, young offenders watch a "Scared Straight" program.

A second problem is that prevention programs typically take place in adolescence, after a problem of delinquency is already clearly established, rather than earlier in childhood when signs of problems first appear (Yoshikawa, 1994). This is due partly to the limited resources expended on addressing these problems; the money tends to go to where the problems are most obvious and serious—current offenders, rather than possible future offenders. Furthermore, the problems of children frequently originate at least partly in the family, and in Western societies, especially in the United States, the state has limited authority to intervene in family life until a clear and serious problem is established.

Nevertheless, some programs do show definite, if limited, success. One sometimes successful approach has been to intervene at several levels, including the home, the school, and the neighborhood (Borduin et al., 1995; Borduin, 1999). These programs include parent training, job training and vocational counseling, and the development of neighborhood activities such as youth centers and athletic leagues (Henggeler, Melton, & Smith, 1992; Borduin, 1999). The goal is to direct the energy and exuberance of delinquents into more socially constructive directions.

Another approach that has shown some degree of success is to focus on teaching delinquents specific academic and job skills. Chronic delinquents tend to lack basic skills, and the idea is to help them to develop skills that would enable them to be successful and rewarded outside of the delinquent peer subculture. A number of studies have shown that this approach can achieve positive results (Cunliffe, 1992; Jensen & Howard, 1990).

Joy Dryfoos (1990), in a major review of delinquency intervention programs, concluded that the most successful programs have certain common features, including:

- A focus on multiple aspects of the delinquent's life—not just family or peer group involvement or academic and job skills, but multiple components.

- Tailoring the program to the problems of each delinquent. Although delinquents do have some common problems, each delinquent may have factors that make his or her situation unique, and it cannot be assumed that one strategy will work with all.

- Programs should provide long-term assistance. Even in successful programs, the effects tend to fade before long unless an effort is made to follow up and provide assistance for many years.

Factors Involved in Risk Behavior

At the beginning of the chapter I described how the various types of problem behavior or risk behavior tend to be correlated. Adolescents who take one kind of risk also tend to take others as well. For this reason it makes sense to look at the factors involved in risk behaviors as a group of behaviors, rather than separately. At the same time, it will be important to mention factors that are distinctive to one type of risk behavior but not others. We will focus on a variety of sources of socialization, including family, friends/peers, school, neighborhood/community, and religious beliefs. Then we will consider individual characteristics such as sensation seeking and aggressiveness that are related to participation in risk behavior. We will focus mostly on substance use and crime/delinquency, because a great deal of research has been conducted in these areas and surprisingly little on risky automobile driving.

As we discuss the factors involved in risk behavior, keep in mind that the *majority* of American adolescents and emerging adults take occasional risks of the kind that have been described in this chapter. Many of them have no evidence of problems in their socialization environment. Thus, although problems in the environment tend to be *related* to degree of participation in risk behavior, this does not mean that such problems *necessarily* exist among all or even most young people who engage in risk behavior. In general, the more serious a young person's involvement in risk behavior, the more likely these problems are to exist in the socialization environment.

Family A great deal of research has focused on the ways that family characteristics are related to risk behavior. This research is mainly on adolescents rather than emerging adults, because most emerging adults leave home by their late teens, so parents' control and influence over them diminishes. Consistently, this research supports a relationship between parenting styles and risk behavior. Specifically, adolescents who have authoritative parents—parents who combine warmth and control in their relationships with their adolescents—take part in risk behavior to a lesser extent than other adolescents (Baumrind, 1991). In contrast, adolescents whose parents are authoritarian (harshly controlling but not warm), indulgent (high warmth, low control), or indifferent (low in both warmth and control) tend to have higher rates of participation in risk behavior.

Thus, adolescents with substance abuse problems are more likely than other adolescents to have parents who are indulgent, detached, or hostile (Barnes & Farrell, 1992; Block, Block, & Keyes, 1988; Brook et al., 1990). In contrast, adolescents in families where closeness and warmth are high are less likely to have substance abuse problems (Bogenschneider et al., 1998; Needle, Su, & Doherty, 1990; Shedler & Block, 1990). Other family factors related to adolescent substance abuse are high levels of family conflict and family disorganization (Martin & Pritchard, 1991; Protinsky & Shilts, 1990). Also, adolescents are more likely to use substances when one or more other family members also use substances or have a lenient attitude toward substance use (Bogenschneider et al., 1998; Peterson et al., 1994). One of the reasons for the low rates of substance use among African American adolescents is that many African American parents are vehemently against substance use and make this clear to their adolescents (Peterson et al., 1994).

A similar pattern of family factors has been found in studies of delinquency. Several decades ago McCord and McCord (1959) found that delinquents were about twice as likely as nondelinquents to come from homes where discipline was inconsistent or lenient, and this finding has been confirmed numerous times since then. An especially important concept in research on delinquency has been **parental monitoring**— the extent to which parents know where their adolescents are and what they are doing at any given time. Parental monitoring is one reflection of the control dimension of parenting, and it has been found to be an especially important factor in adolescent delinquency (Jacobson & Crockett, 2000; Patterson & Stouthamer-Loeber, 1984). When parental monitoring is lacking, adolescents are considerably more likely to engage in delinquent acts (Dornbusch et al., 1985; Steinberg, Fletcher, & Darling, 1994; Patterson & Yoerger, 1997).

■ THINKING CRITICALLY

Is it possible that passive genotype–environment interactions are involved in crime and delinquency? Explain how you would test this possibility.

Parental monitoring is especially likely to be low once adolescents move out of their parents' household and enter emerging adulthood. This may help to explain why emerging adults consistently have higher rates of risk behavior than adolescents (Arnett, 1998b; Bachman et al., 1996). Emerging adults have neither parents nor spouses to provide social control (Gottfredson & Hirschi, 1990; Sampson & Laub, 1994), and this relative freedom makes risk behavior more likely.

Friends' Influence Because of the widespread belief that peers play a strong role in risk behavior, risk behavior has been the most common focus of research on the influence of peers and friends in adolescence (Berndt, 1996). However, this research has shown that the role of friends' influence in adolescents' risk behavior is considerably more complicated than originally supposed. In particular, studies have shown that similarity between friends in their risk behavior is due both to selective association and to friends' influence. That is, young people tend to seek out friends who are like themselves—in their tendencies for risk behavior as well as in other respects—but if they remain friends, they tend to influence each other, that is, they become more alike in their levels of risk behavior (Coombs, Paulson, & Richardson, 1991; Dishion et al., 1991; Steinberg et al., 1994).

Friends' influence has been found to promote risky driving. Young drivers are more likely than older drivers to believe their friends would approve of risky driving behavior such as speeding, closely following another vehicle, and passing another car in risky circumstances (U.S. Department of Transportation, 1995). Also, one reason young people are less likely than adults to wear seat belts is that some of them believe putting on a seat belt would subject them to ridicule by their friends (Rothe, 1992).

In studies of delinquency, friends' influence has been argued to play an especially strong role in socialized delinquency (Arbuthnot, Gordon, & Jurkovic, 1987; Dishion et al., 1991; Quay, 1987), which involves committing acts of delinquency as part of a group or gang. **Socialized delinquents** rarely commit crimes unless as part of a group, and other than their criminal activity they are very similar to other, nondelinquent adolescents in their psychological functioning and family relationships (Arbuthnot et al., 1987; Quay, 1987). In contrast, **unsocialized delinquents** usually have few friends and commit their crimes alone (Arbuthnot et al., 1987; Dishion et al., 1991; Quay, 1987).

The reason that socialized delinquents commit offenses despite being similar in many ways to adolescents who do not is that within their friendship group or gang, illegal behavior is supported and rewarded. Although they may be alienated from school and other adult institutions (Gottfredson & Hirschi, 1990), they tend to form close interpersonal relationships within their delinquent friendship group. They see their delinquent behavior not as immoral or deviant but as a way of finding excitement, proving their manly bravery, and demonstrating their support and loyalty to one another (Arbuthnot et al., 1987; Quay, 1987). The idea of unstructured socializing, discussed earlier in this chapter, also fits here. Unstructured socializing is often the setting for socialized delinquency (Osgood, 1991; Osgood et al., 1996).

A number of studies have explored the connections between family factors and peer factors in relation to risk behavior. Judith Brook and her colleagues (Brook et al., 1990; Kasen, Cohen, & Brook, 1998) have argued that the path to drug abuse in adolescence begins in early childhood with a lack of warmth from parents and a high level of conflict in the family. Children who experience this kind of family environment develop alienation and low self-control, which are expressed in adolescence through drug use and affiliation with drug-using peers. In contrast, experiencing close and supportive relationships with parents in childhood can serve as a protective factor against substance use even in a peer environment where drug use is common (Brook et al., 1990). Other studies have also found that close relationships to parents in adolescence tend to be related to lower orientation to peers, which is in turn related to lower substance use (Bogenschneider et al., 1998; Myers, Wagner, & Brown, 1997).

Gerald Patterson and his colleagues have developed a similar model to explain delinquency (Dishion et al., 1991; Patterson, 1986; Patterson, Reid, & Dishion, 1992). In their extensive longitudinal research, Patterson and colleagues have found that the first risk factors for delinquency begin in infancy, with an infant temperament that is aggressive and difficult. This kind of temperament is especially challenging for parents, and some parents respond not with the extra measure of love and patience that would be required to ameliorate it but with harsh, inconsistent, or indulgent discipline. This family environment leads by middle childhood to the development of personality characteristics such as aggressiveness and low self-control, which makes friendships with most other children problematic. Children with these characteristics are often left with no one to have as friends but each other, and associations in friendship groups of aggressive and rejected children lead in turn to delinquency in adolescence (also see Kim, Hetherington, & Reiss, 1999; Pettit et al., 1999).

Other Socialization Influences

Family and peer factors have been the areas studied most in relation to risk behavior in adolescence, but some research also exists on the ways that other aspects of socialization are related to risk behavior, including school, neighborhood/community, and religious beliefs. School has been of some interest because of the consistent finding that poor school performance is associated with a variety of types of risk behavior, especially substance use and delinquency (Wilson & Herrnstein, 1985). As noted above, problems in school have fared poorly as an explanation for risk behavior because tendencies toward the

Community norms regarding substance use influence adolescents' substance use.

most serious and enduring involvement in risk behavior begin before children enter school.

However, some studies have found that the overall school environment can have an influence on adolescents' risk behavior (Kasen et al., 1998). A classic study demonstrating this was conducted in the 1970s by the British scholar Michael Rutter and his colleagues (Rutter, 1983; Rutter et al., 1979). They studied young people in 12 schools in London, beginning at age 10 and following them for 4 years. The results indicated that school environment had a significant effect on rates of delinquency in early adolescence, even after controlling for such influences as social class and family environment. Two qualities of the school environments stood out as having the most positive effects. One was having an intellectual balance in the school that included a substantial proportion of bright and achievement-oriented students who identified with the aims and rules of school. These students tended to be leaders and discouraged misbehavior by setting norms for behavior that other students followed. The other important quality was what Rutter and his colleagues called the **ethos** of the school, meaning a kind of within-school belief system. A favorable ethos—one that emphasized the value of schoolwork, rewarded good performance, and established

fair but firm discipline—was related to lower rates of delinquency through early adolescence.

Neighborhood and community factors have also been studied in relation to risk behavior in adolescence, particularly in relation to delinquency. A number of classic studies in sociology focused on the ways that neighborhood factors promote or discourage delinquency (e.g., Whyte, 1943). These studies described how a sense of neighborhood identity and cohesion has the effect of discouraging delinquency. More recent studies on neighborhood and community factors have noted that high rates of residential mobility tend to be related to high rates of crime and delinquency, perhaps because when there are people moving in and out of a neighborhood frequently, residents tend to have weaker attachments to their neighbors and less regard for neighborhood opinion (e.g., Sampson, Castellano, & Laub, 1981; Wilson, 1996). Also, neighborhood and community norms regarding drug use and the availability of drugs in a community have been found to be related to substance use in adolescence (Petraitis, Flay, & Miller, 1995).

Finally, in recent years religious beliefs have become a topic of interest in relation to risk behavior. Numerous studies have found that religiosity is inversely related to participation in risk behavior in adolescence and emerging adulthood (Arnett, 1998b; Jessor et al., 1991; Wallace & Williams, 1999). It may be that religious beliefs and religious participation, like good schools, act as a **protective factor** that makes participation in risk behavior less likely. However, unlike with schools, with religious beliefs self-selection has to be considered as a possible explanation. That is, it may be that it is not so much that religious involvement causes adolescents and emerging adults to be less likely to take part in risk be-

havior, but rather that young people who strive for a high standard of moral behavior are both less likely to be interested in risk behavior and more likely to be interested in religious involvement (Arnett, 1998b).

Individual Factors in Risk Behavior We have examined various aspects of socialization that have been found to promote or discourage risk behavior. Within any particular socialization context, what makes some young people more likely than others to

RESEARCH FOCUS
The Gluecks' Longitudinal Study of Delinquency

Longitudinal studies of crime and delinquency go back far enough into the early part of the 20th century that the boys who originally took part in them have long since become men, and we have information on what became of their lives in adulthood. One of the most influential and informative of these studies was conducted by Sheldon and Eleanor Glueck, a husband-and-wife team of scholars who followed delinquent and nondelinquent boys in the Boston area from their teens until their early thirties. The study provides rich information on the factors involved in delinquency as well as the implications of delinquency for adult development.

The Gluecks' study began in the early 1940s with 1,000 Boston boys aged 10 to 17, including 500 delinquents and 500 nondelinquents (Glueck & Glueck, 1950). The delinquent boys were residents at correctional schools for delinquents. The nondelinquent boys were recruited from public schools. The nondelinquent boys were not randomly selected, but rather were matched case-by-case with the delinquent boys for age, ethnic group, IQ, and neighborhood socioeconomic status. The Gluecks chose this method because they wanted to be able to show that any differences between the two groups were not due to these kinds of preexisting characteristics. Boys in both groups grew up in family and neighborhood environments that were characterized by poverty and high exposure to delinquency and crime.

The Gluecks' study lasted 18 years, and their research team collected data on the boys at three times: adolescence (ages 10 to 17), emerging adult-

hood (ages 21 to 28), and young adulthood (ages 28 to 35). At each time, an abundance of information was collected. In adolescence, information was collected from the boys themselves as well as from parents, teachers, social workers, and local police. In the two follow-ups, information was collected from the young men and their families as well as from employers, neighbors, and officials in criminal justice and social welfare agencies. Ninety-two percent of the participants remained in the study through all three times of data collection, an exceptionally high rate across an 18-year period.

An enormous amount of information was collected in the study, and only the outlines of the results can be described here (see Glueck & Glueck, 1950, 1968; Sampson & Laub, 1994). Briefly, the Gluecks found that the key to delinquency lay in an interaction between *constitutional factors* and *family environments*. By constitutional factors they meant biological predispositions. The constitutional factors they found to be related to delinquency were *body type* and *temperament*. Delinquent adolescent boys were more likely than nondelinquents to have a *mesomorphic* body type, that is, a body that was stocky and muscular rather than rounded (*endomorphic*) or tall and slim (*ectomorphic*). Also, delinquents were more likely than nondelinquents to have had a *difficult temperament* as children. That is, they were more likely to be reported by their parents as having cried often as infants and children, as having been difficult to soothe when upset, and as having irregular patterns of eating and sleeping.

With regard to family environment, delinquent boys were more likely to be from families in which one or both parents were neglectful or hostile toward them. Parents' discipline in the families of delinquents tended to be either permissive or inconsistent, alternating periods of neglect with outbursts of punishment. This is now a familiar pattern to scholars, but the Gluecks were among the first to establish systematically the relationship between parenting and outcomes in adolescence.

And how did the boys "turn out" once they reached their twenties and early thirties? For the most part, their behavior in adolescence was highly predictive of their later development. By age 25, the 500 boys in the delinquent group had been arrested for 7 homicides, 100 robberies, 172 burglaries, 225 larcenies, and numerous other offenses (Wilson & Herrnstein, 1985). These rates were more than five times higher than for the nondelinquent group. However, it was not just crime that was predicted by delinquent status in adolescence. In young adulthood, those who had been adolescent delinquents were four times more likely than nondelinquents to abuse alcohol, seven times more likely to have a pattern of unstable employment, three times more likely to be divorced, and far less likely to have finished high school (Sampson & Laub, 1990).

In sum, delinquent status in adolescence was a strong predictor of a wide range of serious future problems. However, not all of the adolescent delinquents went on to have difficulties in adulthood. For those who did not, *job stability* and *attachment to spouse* were the best predictors of staying out of trouble in adulthood (Sampson & Laub, 1990). Income itself was a poor predictor, but job stability made a difference. Similarly, simply getting married was a poor predictor by itself, but a close emotional attachment to a spouse made a positive difference.

The Gluecks' study has been criticized on methodological grounds. The most serious criticism is that the persons collecting data on the boys and their environments were not *blind* to the boys' status as delinquent or nondelinquent. This means that researchers who interviewed the boys' parents or conducted psychological interviews with the boys knew in advance whether a boy was part of the delinquent or nondelinquent group. Because the conclusions for much of the study were based on interpretations from interviews rather than from questionnaires or objective tests, the interpretations may have been biased by what the researchers knew about the boys in advance. However, the Glueck's conclusions have stood the test of time quite well, and their study continues to be regarded as a classic of social science research.

participate in risk behavior? Given the same or similar types of family, peer, school, and community environments, some adolescents take part in risk behavior and others do not. Thus, in addition to the socialization influences, a variety of individual factors need to be considered in relation to various types of risk behavior in adolescence and emerging adulthood.

One individual factor related to a variety of risk behaviors is **aggressiveness**. Aggressiveness is obviously related to delinquency and crime, because many delinquent and criminal acts—destroying property, assault, rape—inherently involve aggressiveness (Wilson & Herrnstein, 1985). However, aggressiveness is also related to reckless driving behavior in the teens and twenties. In several studies, Dennis Donovan and his colleagues have found aggressiveness to be related to risky driving and accidents (Donovan, Marlatt, & Salzberg, 1983; Donovan et al., 1985; Donovan, Umlauf, & Salzberg, 1988). Based on their findings, they have argued that risky driving is often an expression of anger and hostility (Donovan et al., 1988). Similarly,

John Donovan (1993) has found aggressiveness to be part of the personality profile of emerging adults (aged 18 to 25) who report that they have driven while intoxicated. Aggressiveness has also been found to be related to substance use (Brook et al., 1986), for reasons that are not clear. Perhaps substances are used by some adolescents as a self-medication for aggressiveness, just as for anxiety and depression.

> "*I* was good at [theft]. The intensity of being in someone else's room when they're sleeping, taking their jewelry, their money, and their car keys, right there while they're sleeping in the bed, and you're looking right over them. . . . It was real intense, it was a rush. You know, 'What can you get away with? How far can you push your limit?' I found out."
>
> —*Jack, age 18 (in Arnett, 1996, p. 4)*

Another characteristic consistently related to risk behavior is sensation seeking. As discussed in Chapter 12, sensation seeking is a personality trait characterized by the degree to which a person seeks out **novelty and intensity** of experience (Arnett, 1994b; Zuckerman, 1995). Many types of risk behavior provide novelty and intensity of experience—for example, substance use leads to novel mental states, and breaking the law in delinquent and criminal acts is often described in terms of the intensity of the experience (Lyng, 1991). For this reason, young people who are high in sensation seeking also are more likely to engage in a variety of risk behaviors, including substance use, risky driving, delinquency, and risky sexual behavior (Arnett, 1994b; Beirness & Simpson, 1988; Zuckerman, 1995). Sensation seeking also tends to be higher in the teens and early twenties than in adulthood, which helps to explain why risk behavior is more common among the young (Arnett, 1994b; Zuckerman, 1995).

A third individual factor often related to risk behavior is *poor school achievement.* Although we have noted that future delinquents often exhibit problems even before they begin school, it has been a long-standing and consistent finding that poor school achievement is a predictor of delinquency (Moffitt, 1993; Wilson & Herrnstein, 1985). Poor school achievement has also been found in numerous studies to be related to substance use (Boyle et al., 1992; Brook et al., 1986; Kasen et al., 1998). To some extent, poor school achievement is a reflection of other characteristics. Sensation seeking (Zuckerman, 1995) and aggressiveness (Farrington & West, 1991; Moffitt, 1993) are related to poor school achievement, as well as to risk behavior. **Attention deficit disorder with hyperactivity (ADD-H)** is related to poor school achievement and to delinquency (Farrington, 1989; Moffitt, 1993; Stanger, Achenbach, & McConaughy, 1993). Low performance on intelligence tests is also related both to poor school achievement and to delinquency (Farrington, 1989; Moffitt & Silva, 1988). The fact that poor school achievement may represent such a wide range of other problems makes it an especially strong predictor of risk behavior in adolescence.

Low impulse control, which means difficulty in exercising self-control, is another characteristic related to risk behaviors in adolescence such as substance use and delinquency (Boyle et al., 1992; Brook et al., 1986; Gottfredson & Hirschi, 1990). Low impulse control is often a reflection of a family environment that is either too harsh or too permissive (Dishion et al., 1991; Moffitt, 1993). Finally, the *optimistic bias* also contributes to a variety of risk behaviors. As discussed in Chapter 3, adolescents have a tendency to assume that accidents, diseases, and other misfortunes are more likely to happen to other people than to themselves (Weinstein,

1998). Thus, young people who participate in risk behavior tend to be more likely than others to believe that nothing bad will happen to them as a result of such behavior (Arnett, 1992). For example, adolescents who take up smoking are less likely than adolescent nonsmokers to believe that smoking will result in addiction and early death (Arnett, 2000e; Gerrard et al., 1996). Adolescents and emerging adults tend to have a stronger optimistic bias than adults for behavior such as risky driving and substance use (Arnett, 2000e; U.S. Department of Transportation, 1995).

For every one of the individual factors described here, males are more at-risk than females. Males tend to be higher in aggressiveness (Maccoby, 1990), higher in sensation seeking (Arnett, 1994b), more likely to have poor school achievement (Moffitt, 1993), lower in impulse control (Gottfredson & Hirschi, 1990; Wilson & Herrnstein, 1985), and higher in optimistic bias (Weinstein, 1989). Together, these gender differences in individual risk factors largely explain why males are more likely than females to engage in risk behavior during adolescence and emerging adulthood.

Culture and Risk Behavior So far we have been focusing on the American majority culture, because that is the population that has been the focus of most research on risk behavior among young people. To what extent is young people's risk behavior a problem in cultures worldwide, and to what extent is it peculiar to American society? Schlegel and Barry (1991), in their analysis of traditional cultures, concluded that "For boys but not for girls, adolescence tends to be the stage during which antisocial behavior most often occurs, if it occurs at all" (p. 39). (By "antisocial behavior" they meant behavior such as fighting and stealing.) However, they found notable evidence of adolescent antisocial behavior in *less than half* of the traditional cultures they studied. Thus, traditional cultures have less of a problem with antisocial behavior than cultures in the West, and antisocial behavior is especially rare among adolescent girls in traditional cultures, in part because they are often monitored closely by adults.

American adolescents have higher rates of most types of risk behavior than adolescents in other Western countries. This is true for risky driving behavior, delinquency, and substance use. With regard to automobile driving, the main reason young people in other Western countries engage in less risky driving behavior is simply that they are much less likely to have access to automobiles. Other Western countries typically have a minimum legal driving age of 18, rather than 16 as in the United States. Even after age 18, in most Western countries automobiles are heavily taxed and therefore extremely expensive, whereas public transportation is inexpensive, safe, and widely available (Arnett & Balle-Jensen, 1993). For these reasons, rates of automobile accidents and fatalities among young people in their teens and early twenties are considerably lower in other Western countries than they are in the United States.

With regard to delinquency and crime, rates are substantially higher in the United States than in other Western countries for a wide variety of offenses, but especially for violent crimes (Wilson & Herrnstein, 1985). As shown in Figure 13.5, among young men aged 15 to 24 the firearm homicide rate in the United States is 5 times as high as in Canada, 12 times as high as in Denmark, and more than 50 times as high as in Great Britain (Rockett, 1998). High rates of violent crime in the Unites States appear to be due in part to higher rates of poverty. In poor urban areas of the United States, homicide rates among the young are appallingly high; homicide is the leading cause of death among young Blacks and Latinos (National Center for Health Statistics, 1999).

Another important reason for the high homicide rate among young people in the United States is the easy availability of firearms. Because of the widespread availability of firearms in American society—an estimated 200 million—what might be a fist fight between young men in London or Paris easily becomes murder in Chicago or Washington, DC.

Illicit drug use among the young, which is a topic of widespread public concern in the United States, is much less of a problem in Europe. For example, in a survey of Belgian adolescents (aged 14 to 19), only 4% had ever used illicit drugs, and of these, three of four had used only marijuana (Goossens, 1994). In Switzerland, only 25% of young people aged 15 to 25 report *ever* smoking marijuana and only 3% report ever using opiates, despite the Swiss policy of decriminalizing drug use (Buchmann, 1994). These figures are considerably lower than the rates for American adolescents (Monitoring the Future, 2000). Canadian adolescents also report higher rates of drug use than European adolescents. In a survey of 15- to 19-year-old Canadians, 27% had used stimulants (Galambos & Kolaric, 1994). It is unclear why drug use is so much higher among North American adolescents than among European adolescents.

In contrast to illegal drugs, use of alcohol and cigarettes tends to be at least as high in Europe as in North America. For example, 69% of 13- to 19-year-olds in Poland report regular alcohol use (Wlodarek, 1994). Cigarette smoking among young people is of particular concern, because it is the source of more illness and mortality in the long run than all illegal drugs combined and because the majority of persons who smoke begin in their mid-teens (U.S. Department of Health and Human Services, 1994). Substantial proportions of young people smoke in all Western countries, with rates generally in the 20% to 50% range (e.g., Galambos & Kolaric, 1994; Hurrelmann & Settertobulte, 1994). Rates of smoking are especially high among young people in eastern and southern Europe (Martinez, de Miguel, & Fernandez, 1994; Wlodarek, 1994). Smoking has decreased among young people in most Western countries since the 1960s (e.g., Buzzi & Cavalli, 1994; Galambos & Kolaric, 1994), due to growing public awareness of the health hazards of smoking and to increased government efforts to discourage smoking among young people and to restrict

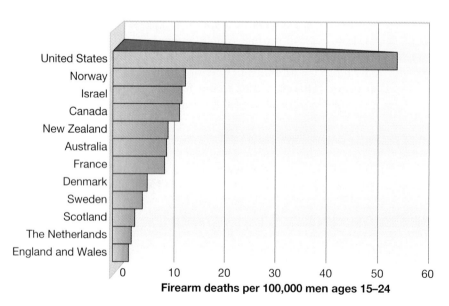

FIGURE 13.5 *Firearm homicide rates among young men in selected countries.*
Source: National Center for Health Statistics (1997).

cigarette advertising. Nevertheless, rates of smoking among young people have increased in recent years and remain strikingly high.

Within the United States, substantial cultural/ethnic differences exist in rates of risk behavior. As noted, Whites have higher rates of substance use in adolescence than African Americans, Latinos, or Asian Americans (Bachman et al., 1991; Bettes et al., 1990; Gil et al., 1998). African American and Latino adolescents are considerably more likely than White adolescents to be arrested for index crimes (Federal Bureau of Investigation, 1999). However, the higher crime rates among Blacks and Latinos are more a reflection of social class than of ethnicity or culture—growing up in a family that has a low socioeconomic status (SES) is associated with a greater likelihood of delinquency for adolescents of *all* ethnic backgrounds, but African American and Latino adolescents are more likely than White adolescents to come from a low-SES family. In addition, African American adolescents are more likely than White adolescents to be arrested for similar crimes, and tend to receive more severe penalties if found guilty (Fletcher, 2000; Krisberg et al., 1986).

Internalizing Problems

So far we have been discussing externalizing problems. Now we turn to the class of problems known as internalizing problems. We will focus on two of the most common types of internalizing problems in adolescence and emerging adulthood: depression and eating disorders.

Depression

Depression, as a general term, means an enduring period of sadness. However, psychologists make distinctions between different levels of depression (Compas et al., 1998). **Depressed mood** is a term for an enduring period of sadness by itself, without any related symptoms. **Depressive syndrome** means an enduring period of sadness along with other symptoms such as frequent crying, feelings of worthlessness, and feeling guilty, lonely, or worried. The most serious form of depression is **depressive disorder**. Depressive disorder is a clinical diagnosis that includes the following specific symptoms (American Psychiatric Association, 1994):

1. Depressed or irritable mood for most of the day, for more days than not, for at least one year.

2. The presence, when depressed, of at least two of the following:
   a. Poor appetite or overeating.
   b. Insomnia or oversleeping.
   c. Low energy or fatigue.
   d. Poor concentration or difficulty making decisions.
   e. Feelings of hopelessness.
3. The symptoms cause clinically significant distress or impairment in social, school, or other important areas of functioning.

Depressed mood is the most common kind of internalizing problem in adolescence. Several studies find that adolescents have higher rates of depressed mood than adults or children (Compas et al., 1998; Fleming & Offord, 1990; Petersen et al., 1993). Episodes of depressed mood prior to adolescence are relatively rare (Compas, Ey, & Grant, 1993), although they do sometimes occur. The beginning of adolescence marks a steep increase in the pervasiveness of depressed mood. Studies of rates of depressed mood at different ages have concluded that there is a **midadolescence peak** in depressed mood (Petersen et al., 1993). Rates of depressed mood rise steeply from age 10 to about ages 15 to 17, then decline in the late teens and twenties.

One analysis of 14 studies of adolescents concluded that the proportion of adolescents who reported

Depressed mood peaks in midadolescence.

experiencing depressed mood within the past 6 months was 35% (Petersen et al., 1993). In contrast, rates of depressive syndrome and depressive disorder among adolescents range in various studies from about 3% to about 7% (Achenbach et al., 1991; Compas et al., 1993; Lewinsohn, Hops et al., 1993), which is about the same rate found in studies of adults. Among adolescents as well as adults, rates of all types of depression are considerably higher among females than among males (Achenbach et al., 1991; Compas et al., 1998; Culbertson, 1997; Leadbeater, Blatt, & Quinlan, 1995; Petersen et al., 1993).

Causes of Depression   The causes of depression in adolescence and emerging adulthood differ somewhat depending on whether the diagnosis is depressed mood or the more serious forms of depression, depressive syndrome and depressive disorder. The most common causes of depressed mood tend to be common experiences among young people—conflict with or rejection from friends or family members, disappointment or rejection in love, and poor performance in school (Larson & Richards, 1994).

THINKING CRITICALLY

Few studies have been conducted on depressed mood among emerging adults. How would you expect the sources of depressed mood in emerging adulthood to be similar to or different from the sources of depressed mood in adolescence?

The causes of the more serious forms of depression are more complicated and less common. Studies have found that both genetic and environmental factors are involved (Petersen et al., 1993). Of course, both genetic and environmental influences are involved in most aspects of development, but the interaction of genes and environment is especially well-established with respect to depression. One useful model of this interaction that has been applied to depression as well as to other mental disorders is the **diathesis-stress model**. The theory behind this model is that mental disorders such as depression often begin with a *diathesis*, which means *a biologically-based vulnerability*. Often, this diathesis will have a genetic basis, but not necessarily. For example, being born prematurely is a diathesis for many physical and psychological problems in devel-

opment, but it is not genetic. However, a diathesis is only a vulnerability, a potential for problems. For that vulnerability to be expressed, it requires a *stress* as well, meaning *environmental conditions* that interact with the diathesis to produce the disorder.

The role of a genetic diathesis in depression has been established in twin studies and adoption studies. Identical twins have a much higher *concordance rate* for depression—meaning that if one gets the disorder, the other gets it as well—than fraternal twins do (Nurnberger & Gershon, 1992). This is true even for identical twins who are raised in different homes and who thus have different family environments (Farber, 1981). Also, adopted children whose biological mothers have experienced depression are more likely than other adopted children to develop depression themselves (Wender et al., 1986). There is also evidence that the genetic contribution to depression may be stronger when its onset is in childhood or adolescence rather than adulthood (Puig-Antich, 1987).

What sort of stresses bring out the diathesis to lead to depression in adolescence? A variety of family and peer factors have been found to be involved. In the family, factors contributing to depression in adolescence include emotional unavailability of parents, high family conflict, economic difficulties, and parental divorce (Asarnov & Horton, 1990; Forkel & Silbereisen, in press; Lee & Gotlib, 1990). With respect to peers, less contact with friends and more experiences of rejection contribute to depression over time (Vernberg, 1990). Unfortunately, poor peer relationships tend to be self-perpetuating for depressed adolescents, because other adolescents tend to avoid being around adolescents who are depressed (Petersen et al., 1993). Studies on depression in adolescence have also taken the approach of calculating an overall stress score, which usually includes stress in the family and in peer relationships as well as stresses such as changing schools. These studies find consistently that overall stress is related to depression in adolescence (Allgood-Merton et al., 1990; Compas & Grant, 1993; Rubin et al., 1992).

Gender Differences in Depression   One of the factors that constitutes the highest risk for depression in adolescence is simply being female. In childhood, when depression is relatively rare, rates are actually higher among boys. However, in adolescence the rates become substantially higher among females, and they remain higher among females throughout adulthood (Achenbach et al., 1991; Compas et al., 1998; Compas

& Grant, 1993; Petersen et al., 1993). What explains the gender difference in adolescent depression?

A variety of explanations have been proposed, but scholars believe the difference is not yet well-understood (Petersen et al., 1993; Peterson, 2000). There is little evidence that biological differences (such as the earlier entry of females into puberty) can explain it. Some scholars have suggested that the female gender role itself leads to depression in adolescence. As we have discussed in earlier chapters, some scholars argue that girls face a conflict in adolescence between the desire to achieve and the fear that achievement will be perceived as unfeminine and unattractive (Gilligan, 1982; Jack, 1991). Also, because of the gender intensification that takes place in adolescence (Hill & Lynch, 1983), concerns about physical attractiveness become a primary concern, especially for girls. There is evidence that adolescent girls who have a poor body image are more likely than other girls to be depressed (Allgood-Merton et al., 1990).

Other explanations have also been offered. Stress is related to depression in adolescence, and adolescent girls generally report experiencing more stress than adolescent boys (Allgood-Merton et al., 1990; Petersen, Kennedy, & Sullivan, 1991). Also, when faced with the beginning of a depressed mood, males are more likely to distract themselves (and forget about it), whereas females have a greater tendency to ruminate on their depressed feelings and thereby amplify them (Nolen-Hoeksma, 1987; Gjerde & Westenberg, 1998). Adolescent girls are also more likely than adolescent boys to devote their thoughts and feelings to their personal relationships, and these relationships can be a source of distress and sadness (Gore, Aseltine, & Colten, 1993; Larson & Richards, 1994).

Males and females generally differ in their responses to stress and conflict, which helps explain both the greater tendency toward externalizing problems in boys and the greater tendency toward internalizing problems in girls (Gjerde & Westenberg, 1998). In adolescence as well as in childhood and adulthood, males tend to respond to stress and conflict by directing their feelings *outward*—in the form of aggressive behavior (Gjerde, Block, & Block, 1988; Nolen-Hoeksma & Girgus, 1994). Females, in contrast, tend to respond to these problems by turning their distress *inward*, in the form of critical thoughts *toward themselves*. Thus, studies have found that *even when exposed to the same amount of stress* as adolescent boys, adolescent girls are more likely to respond by becoming depressed (Ge et al., 1996). Furthermore, depression in

adolescence is often accompanied for boys (but not for girls) by externalizing problems such as fighting and disobedience (Block, Gjerde, & Block, 1991; Gjerde et al., 1988; Loeber et al., 1998).

Treatments for Depression Just because depression in adolescence is common does not mean that it should be ignored or viewed as something that will go away eventually, especially when it persists over an extended period or reaches the level of depressive syndrome or depressive disorder. Depressed adolescents are at risk for a variety of other problems, including school failure, delinquency, and suicide (Compas et al., 1998; Fleming, Boyle, & Offord, 1993; Pfeffer, 1986). For many adolescents, symptoms of depression that begin in adolescence persist into emerging adulthood (Gjerde & Westenberg, 1998). Symptoms of depression in adolescence should be taken seriously, and treatment provided when necessary.

For adolescents as for adults, the two main types of treatment for depression are antidepressant medications and psychotherapy. However, the use of medication has been surprisingly ineffective in the treatment of adolescent depression. Controlled studies of the effects of antidepressants have found that for most adolescents the drugs do little to alleviate the symptoms of depression (Geller, Reising, Leonard, Riddle, & Walsh, 1999). Two studies (Boulos et al., 1991; Geller et al., 1990) used a **placebo design**, meaning that all of the depressed adolescents took pills but only the pills taken by adolescents in the treatment group contained the drug. Adolescents in the control group took a *placebo*, that is, a pill that did not contain any medication, although the adolescents did not know this. Both studies found no differences in subsequent symptoms of depression between the treatment group and the control group.

What makes this surprising is that antidepressants have been highly effective among adults, resulting in improvement in about 70% of cases (Paykel, 1996). The reason for the differences in response between adolescents and adults is not known (Petersen et al., 1993). However, recent studies indicate that newly developed antidepressants such as Prozac may be more effective in treating adolescent depression (Bostic, Wilens, Spencer, & Biederman, 1999; Emslie, Walkup, Pliszka, & Ernst, 1999).

Psychotherapy for adolescent depression takes a variety of forms, including individual therapy, group therapy, and skills training (Petersen et al., 1993). Studies that have randomly assigned depressed adolescents to either a treatment group (which received

Psychotherapy is often effective in treating young people's depression.

psychotherapy) or a control group (which did not) have found that therapy tends to be effective in reducing the symptoms of depression (Kahn et al., 1990; Lewinsohn et al., 1990; Reynolds & Coats, 1986). Few studies have compared the effectiveness of different types of psychotherapy, and to this point no clear differences have been found (Petersen et al., 1993).

Suicide

"*When Sandy told me she wanted to break up, I thought there was no point in going on. I loved her so much. I wanted to spend the rest of my life with her. So I started thinking about killing myself. I imagined how I could do it and what kind of note I'd leave my parents. Then I started thinking about my parents and my little sister, and I thought of them at the funeral crying and being so sad, and I knew I couldn't go through with it. I realized I didn't really want to die; I just wanted everything to be okay again.*"

— *Donnie, age 16 (in Bell, 1998, p. 176)*

One reason for taking young people's depression seriously is that it is a risk factor for suicide. Suicide attempts are usually preceded by symptoms of depression (Pfeffer, 1986; Shagle & Barber, 1994). However, often young people's suicide attempts take place as the symptoms of depression appear to be abating (Pfeffer,

1986). At the depths of depression, young people are often too dispirited to engage in the planning required to commit suicide. As they improve slightly, they remain depressed but now have enough energy and motivation to make a suicide attempt. Making a plan to commit suicide may also raise the mood of deeply depressed young people, because they may believe that the suicide will mean an end to all the problems they feel are plaguing them.

Rates of suicidal thoughts, suicide attempts, and completed suicides among American adolescents and emerging adults are alarming. One in three adolescents reports having had suicidal thoughts, and one in six reports a suicide attempt (Gans, 1990). Suicide is the third most common cause of death among young people aged 15 to 19, after automobile accidents and homicide (National Center for Health Statistics [NCHS], 1999). Furthermore, the suicide rate among American teens in the 1990s was *four times higher* than the suicide rate among teens in the 1950s (Garland & Zigler, 1993). The reason for this increase is not well understood. The rate among emerging adults aged 20 to 24 also increased during this time and is even higher than among 15- to 19-year-olds (NCHS, 1999). The suicide rate among White males rises again in late adulthood and is highest after age 60, but the rate among Black males is higher at ages 20 to 24 than at any other age (NCHS, 1999). Nevertheless, rates of suicide in adolescence and emerging adulthood are higher among Whites than among Blacks, and highest of all among Native Americans (NCHS, 1999; Grossman, Milligan, & Deyo, 1991).

Sharp gender differences also exist in rates of suicide and suicide attempts. Females are about four times as likely as males to attempt suicide in adolescence and emerging adulthood, but males are about four times as likely as females actually to kill themselves (Garland & Zigler, 1993; NCHS, 1999). These gender differences exist in adulthood as well. The reason for the higher rate of attempts among females is not well understood, but it is probably a consequence of their higher rates of depression. The reason for the higher rate of completed suicides among males seems to be due mainly to gender differences in the methods used. Males are more likely to use guns or hang themselves, and these methods are more deadly than the method of taking poison or pills that is more commonly used by females in their suicide attempts (McIntosh, 1992; NCHS, 1999).

Other than depression, what are the risk factors for suicide? One major factor for adolescents is *family dis-*

ruption. Attempted and completed suicide has frequently been found to be related to a family life that is chaotic, disorganized, high in conflict, and low in warmth (Bolger et al., 1989; Kosky, Silbum, & Zubrick, 1990; Wagner & Cohen, 1997). Furthermore, an adolescent's suicide is often preceded by a period of months in which family problems have worsened (Brent et al., 1993; de Wilde et al., 1992). One study found that among adolescents who had been hospitalized for attempted suicide, only 10% were from families the researchers characterized as harmonious at the time of the attempt (Withers & Kaplan, 1987).

In addition to family difficulties, suicidal adolescents often have substance abuse problems (Pfeffer et al., 1993), perhaps as an attempt at self-medication for their distress over their family problems and their depression. Also, suicidal adolescents have usually experienced problems in their relationships outside the family. Because they often come from families where they receive little in the way of emotional nurturance, suicidal adolescents may be more vulnerable to the effects of experiences such as school failure, loss of a boyfriend or girlfriend, or feelings of being rejected by their peers (Maris, Silverman, & Canetto, 1997).

However, in almost all cases, adolescent suicide takes place not in response to a single stressful or painful event but only after a series of difficulties extending over months or even years (Brown, Overholser et al., 1991; Garrison et al., 1991). It is very rare for sui-cidal adolescents to show no warning signs of emotional or behavioral problems prior to attempting suicide (see Table 13.1; Lewinsohn et al., 1993; Rao et al., 1993). Often, they have made efforts to address the problems in their lives, and the failure of these efforts has sent them on a downward spiral that deepened their hopelessness and led them to suicide (Dixon, Heppner, & Anderson, 1991; Rotheram-Borus et al., 1991).

Eating Disorders

"At 102 pounds I thought I would be happy. But when I lost another two pounds, I was even happier. By the time I was down to 98 pounds, I stopped getting my period. . . . Also, my hair, which was normally healthy and shiny, became very brittle and dull, and it started falling out. . . . [My skin] took on a yellowish tone that on me looked sick, but I didn't care. I thought I looked better than I ever had in my whole life."

—**Alicia (in Bell, 1998, p. 191)**

Puberty involves profound biological changes in the shape and functioning of the body, and these biological changes have numerous social and psychological effects. Adolescents find that people in their environment, such as peers and parents, respond differently to them as they show outward signs of reaching sexual maturity. These responses from others, along with

---

TABLE 13.1: EARLY WARNING SIGNS OF ADOLESCENT SUICIDE

1. Direct suicide threats or comments such as "I wish I were dead." "My family would be better off without me." "I have nothing to live for."
2. A previous suicide attempt, no matter how minor. Four out of five people who commit suicide have made at least one previous attempt.
3. Preoccupation with death in music, art, and personal writing.
4. Loss of a family member, pet, or boy/girl friend through death, abandonment, break-up.
5. Family disruptions such as unemployment, serious illness, relocation, divorce.
6. Disturbances in sleeping and eating habits and in personal hygiene.
7. Declining grades and lack of interest in school or hobbies that had previously been important.
8. Drastic changes in behavior patterns, such as a quiet, shy person becoming extremely gregarious.
9. Pervasive sense of gloom, helplessness, and hopelessness.
10. Withdrawal from family members and friends and feelings of alienation from significant others.
11. Giving away prized possessions and otherwise "getting their affairs in order."
12. Series of "accidents" or impulsive, risk-taking behaviors. Drug or alcohol abuse, disregard for personal safety, taking dangerous dares.

Source: From "Living with 10- to 15-Year-Olds, A Parent Education Curriculum," © 1984 Center for Early Adolescence, Suite 223, Carr Mill Mall, Carrboro, NC 27510.

their own self-reflection, lead to changes in the way adolescents think about their bodies.

For many adolescents in American society, changes in the way they think about their bodies are accompanied by changes in the way they think about food. Girls, in particular, pay more attention to the food they eat once they reach adolescence, and worry more about eating too much and getting "fat." Presented with a cultural ideal that portrays the ideal female body as slim, at a time when their bodies are biologically tending to become less slim and more rounded, many of them feel distressed at the biological changes taking place in their bodies, and they attempt to resist or at least modify those changes. Various studies have found that up to three-fourths of adolescent girls believe they weigh too much, even though less than 20% are actually overweight by medical standards (Davies & Furnham, 1986; French et al., 1995; Paxton et al., 1991).

This dissatisfaction exists far more often among girls than among boys (Vincent & McCabe, 2000). Boys are much less likely to believe they are overweight (Paxton et al., 1991), and much more likely to be satisfied with their bodies (Phelps et al., 1993). Even prior to adolescence, as early as fourth grade, girls are more likely to worry about becoming overweight and to desire to be thinner than they are (Thelen et al., 1992). Furthermore, body dissatisfaction among girls increases during the teens and continues through emerging adulthood and beyond (Rosenblum & Lewis, 1999). In fact, extreme weight-loss behaviors among adolescent girls, such as fasting, "crash dieting," and skipping meals, are related to their mothers' own extreme weight-loss behavior (Benedikt, Wertheim, & Love, 1998).

Exposed to this cultural emphasis on slimness as part of social and sexual attractiveness for women, some girls take the goal of controlling their food intake to an extreme and develop eating disorders. The path from the cultural emphasis on slimness to eating disorders is evident in studies that find that dieting and a negative body image are predictive of the development of eating problems (APA, 1994; Attie & Brooks-Gunn, 1989; Striegel-Moore, 1997). About 90% of eating disorders occur among females (Caspar, 1992).

The two most common eating disorders are **anorexia nervosa** (intentional self-starvation) and **bulimia** (binge eating combined with purging). About 1 of every 200 American adolescents have anorexia nervosa and about 3% have bulimia (APA, 1994; Whitaker et al., 1990). About half of anorexics are also bulimic, and avoid food except for episodes of binge-

ing and purging (Walsh, 1993). Most cases of eating disorders have their onset among females in their teens and early twenties (APA, 1994; Caspar, 1992).

For persons with anorexia nervosa, food intake is reduced so much that the person loses at least 15% of body weight. This reduction in food intake is accompanied by an intense fear of gaining weight, a fear that persists even when the person has lost so much weight as to be in danger of literally starving to death. One of the most striking symptoms of anorexia is this cognitive distortion. Young women with anorexia sincerely believe themselves to be too fat, even when they have become so thin that their lives are threatened. Standing in front of a mirror with them and pointing out how emaciated they look does no good—the anorexic looks in the mirror at herself and sees a fat person, no matter how thin she is. As anorexics become increasingly thin, they frequently develop physical problems that are symptoms of their starvation, such as constipation, high sensitivity to cold, and low blood pressure. About 10% of anorexics eventually die from starvation or from physical problems caused by their weight loss (Linscheid, Tarnowski, & Richmond, 1988; Thompson & Gans, 1985).

Even when they are so thin they risk starving to death, anorexic girls see themselves as "too fat."

HISTORICAL FOCUS
From Fasting Saints to Anorexic Girls

Anorexia nervosa is generally viewed by scholars to be a modern disorder, resulting primarily from current cultural pressures for young women to be thin. However, the phenomenon of young women voluntarily, willfully reducing their food intake, even to the point of self-starvation, has a surprisingly long history in the West, extending back many centuries. An examination of that history, with its illuminating similarities to and differences from present-day anorexia, is provided by Dutch scholars Walter Vandereycken and Ron Van Deth (1994) in their book *From Fasting Saints to Anorexic Girls: A History of Self-Starvation.*

Fasting, involving partial or total abstinence from food, has long been a part of both Eastern and Western religions. It has been undertaken for a variety of purposes—to purify the body while engaging in prayer, to demonstrate the person's elevation of spiritual concerns over bodily needs, or as a sign of penance or remorse for sins. Fasting has been a part of the religious ideal in the Eastern religions of Hinduism and Buddhism for millennia. In ancient Egypt, Pharaohs fasted for days before important decisions and religious celebrations. In the Bible, Moses and Jesus undertake periods of fasting. Fasting was required for all believers during the first millennium of the Christian church, at various times of the year including prior to Christmas. It remains a requirement of Islam, during the yearly holy period of Ramadan.

It was only from the 12th century onward that religious fasting in the West became associated mainly with young women. Why this happened when it did is not entirely clear, but it appears to be linked to females being allowed greater participation in church life. For both males and females during the Medieval period, piety was demonstrated in ways that seem extreme from the modern perspective. Men, during this time, would often demonstrate their piety by such practices as self-flagellation; piercing their tongues, cheeks, or other body parts with iron pins; or sleeping on beds of thorns or iron points. For women, in contrast, extreme fasting became the characteristic path to holiness.

Young women who engaged in extreme fasting often gained great fame and were regarded by their contemporaries with reverence and awe. For example, in the 13th century an English girl became known far and wide as "Joan the Meatless" for reputedly abstaining from all food and drink except on Sundays, when she fed only on the Eucharist. Many of these young women became anointed as saints by the Church, although official Church policy discouraged extreme fasting as detrimental to physical and mental well-being. In the 16th and 17th centuries, Catholic officials sharply tightened the rules for proving fasting "miracles," in response to exposed cases of fraud as well as in response to concern over the health of girls seeking sainthood, and extreme fasting lost its religious allure.

In place of extreme religious fasting, extreme fasting as a commercial spectacle arose. From the 16th through the 19th century, young women were exhibited at fairs who had supposedly fasted for months or even years. Their renown now came not from the piety their fasting demonstrated but from the way their fasting supposedly enabled them to transcend the requirements of nature. When these "miraculous maidens" were put to the test in conditions where they could be monitored closely, some starved to death trying to prove their legitimacy, whereas others were exposed as frauds, such as the young woman who had sown a substantial quantity of gingerbread into the hem of her dress.

During this same period, cases of self-starvation received increasing attention from physicians. The first medical description of anorexia nervosa was made by the British physician Richard Morton in 1689. All of the characteristics of Morton's clinical description of the disorder remain part of the clinical diagnosis of anorexia nervosa in the present, over three centuries later:

1. Occurs primarily in females in their teens and twenties;

2. Characterized by striking emaciation as a consequence of markedly decreased intake of food;

3. Often accompanied by constipation and amenorrhea (absence of menstruation);

4. Affected persons usually lack insight into the illness (that is, they do not believe anything is wrong with them); consequently, treatment is resisted;

5. No physical cause is responsible for the symptoms; they are psychological in origin.

Although these symptoms still characterize anorexia nervosa, it was only from the early 19th century onward that the disorder became motivated by a desire to conform to cultural standards of female attractiveness. In the early 19th century, the standard of beauty for young women in the West became the "hour-glass figure," characterized by a substantial bosom and hips and the slimmest waist possible. In pursuit of this figure young women had themselves laced tightly into corsets (often made of whale bone or some other similarly unforgiving material), ignoring the physicians who warned against the unhealthiness of the fashion. By the early 20th century, corsets had gone out of fashion, but in their place came an ideal of the female form as slim all over, not just the waist but the bosom and hips as well—not unlike the ideal that exists today.

That this thin ideal motivated self-starvation among girls is evident from clinical reports of the time, for example, by this late 19th-century physi-cian who, while examining an anorexic patient, "found that she wore on her skin, fashioned very tight around her waist, a rose-colored ribbon. He obtained the following confidence; the ribbon was a measure which the waist was not to exceed. 'I prefer dying of hunger to becoming as big as mamma'" (Vandereycken & Deth, 1994, p. 171).

Although the fasting saints may seem a long way from the anorexic girls, Vandereycken and Deth (1994) point out the striking similarities. In both cases the self-starvers were striving for an elusive perfection—the fasting girls for sainthood and the anorexic girls for the feminine ideal, a kind of secular sainthood—and typically their perfectionism extended into all aspects of their lives, not just their eating habits. In both cases, their unwillingness to eat was often evident in childhood before developing into a fixed pattern in adolescence. Perhaps most important, in both cases their self-starvation was often a way of asserting power in a social environment that offered them limited opportunities for self-fulfillment. By abstaining from food, they were able to establish an area over which they would have complete control, no matter what the threats or pleas from clergy, friends, or family.

Bulimia is an eating disorder characterized by **binge eating** and **purging**. Bulimics engage in binge eating, which means eating a large amount of food in a short time. Then they purge themselves, that is, they use laxatives or induce vomiting to get rid of the food they have just eaten during a binge episode. Unlike anorexics, bulimics typically maintain a normal weight, because they have more or less normal eating patterns in between their episodes of bingeing and purging (Herzog et al., 1991). Another difference from anorexics is that bulimics do not regard their eating patterns as normal. Bulimics view themselves as having a problem and often hate themselves in the aftermath of their binge episodes. However, both anorexics and bulimics have strong fears that their bodies will become big and fat (Cooper & Fairburn, 1992; Home, Van Vactor, & Emerson, 1991). Unlike anorexics, bulimics often suffer damage to their teeth from repeated vomiting.

Studies of anorexics and bulimics provide evidence that these eating disorders have cultural roots (Condit, 1990; Gowen et al., 1999). First, eating disorders are more common in cultures that emphasize slimness as part of the female physical ideal, especially Western countries (Gowen et al., 1999). Second, eating disorders are most common among females who are part of the middle to upper socioeconomic classes, which place more emphasis on female slimness than lower classes do. Third, most eating disorders occur among females in their teens and early twenties (Caspar, 1992; Kinder, 1991), which is arguably when gender intensification and cultural pressures to comply with a slim female physical ideal are at their strongest. Fourth, girls who read magazines such as *Seventeen*, which contain numerous ads and articles featuring thin models, are especially likely to strive to be thin themselves and to have eating problems that indicate a risk for eating disorders (Levine et al., 1994).

Although many girls in cultures that emphasize a thin female ideal strive for thinness themselves, only a small percentage reach the extreme of actually having an eating disorder. What factors lead some young females but not others to develop an eating disorder? In general, the same factors are involved for both anorexia and bulimia (Garner & Garfinkel, 1997).

One factor appears to be a general susceptibility to internalizing disorders. Females who have an eating disorder are also more likely than other females to have other internalizing disorders, especially depression (Munoz & Amado, 1986).

Family factors may also be involved. Some evidence suggests that girls with eating disorders tend to have parents who are warm but also highly controlling (Caspar, 1992; Kenny & Hart, 1992; Minuchin, Rosman, & Baker, 1978). The girls are outwardly well behaved and even perfectionist in trying to please their parents, but some clinicians believe that eating disorders are a way that some girls assert an area of control of their lives in the face of overly controlling parents (Caspar, 1992). However, critics of this theory argue that the "controlling" behavior of the parents is actually a worried response to their daughter's eating disorder rather than a cause of it.

Another clinical theory is that girls with eating disorders have fears of becoming physically mature and sexually attractive (Crisp, 1983). To some extent anorexia interferes with pubertal development, because it reduces breast development and results in an emaciated, asexual appearance. As weight loss continues it also results in **amenorrhea**, which means that the girls stop menstruating, seemingly returning them to a prepubescent state. Research also indicates that girls with eating disorders often fear becoming involved in intimate relationships (Pruitt, Kappius, & Gorman, 1992) and claim they are too busy with school and weight-reducing exercise to be interested in boys (Fagan & Anderson, 1990).

> ■ **THINKING CRITICALLY**
>
> What other causes of eating disorders would you hypothesize, besides the ones stated here?

Treatments for Eating Disorders Because anorexia is eventually life threatening, a hospital-based program is usually recommended as a first step to begin to restore the person's physical functioning (Linscheid et al., 1988; Powers, 1990). In addition to physical treatment, a variety of treatment approaches have been found to be effective for anorexia and bulimia, including family therapy (to address the family issues that may contribute to or be caused by the problem), individual therapy, and antidepressant medications (Agras et al., 1989; Condit, 1990).

However, the success of treating anorexia and bulimia is often limited. About two-thirds of anorexics treated in hospital programs improve, but one-third remain chronically ill despite treatment and remain at high risk for chronic health problems or even death from the disorder (Linscheid et al., 1988; Lucas, 1991; Steinhausen, 1995). Similarly, although treatments for bulimia are successful in about 50% of cases, there are repeated relapses in the other 50% of cases, and recovery is often slow (Garner & Garfinkel, 1997; Herzog et al., 1991).

Summing Up

In this chapter we have discussed a wide range of problems in adolescence and emerging adulthood, including both externalizing and internalizing problems. The main points we have discussed are as follows:

- Richard Jessor's problem behavior theory states that adolescents who have one kind of problem also tend to have other problems as well. Research by Jessor and others has supported this view. However, it is also true that some types of risk behavior are far more common than others.

- Automobile accidents are the leading cause of death among Americans in their late teens and early twenties, and young people at these ages have the highest rates of automobile accidents and fatalities of any age group. These high rates appear to be due to the risks they take while driving more than to inexperience. Graduated licensing programs have been shown to be highly effective at reducing accidents and fatalities among young people.

- With regard to substance use, emerging adults have higher rates than adolescents do, partly because they spend more time in unstructured socializing. Substance use among American young people declined in the late seventies through the 1980s but rose in the 1990s. Young people in the United States are more likely to use illegal drugs than young people in other Western countries, but young people in Europe use alcohol and cigarettes just as much or more than Americans.

- Alcohol and cigarettes have been called "gateway drugs" because they typically precede use of illegal drugs. However, most young people who drink alcohol do not use marijuana or harder drugs. Patterns of substance use can be classified as experimental, social, medicinal, and addictive.

- Studies over the past 150 years have found consistently that rates of a variety of types of crime peak in the late teens, and that crimes are committed mainly by males. Wilson and Herrnstein have argued that crime is highest in adolescence and emerging adulthood because these periods combine independence from parents with a high amount of time spent with peers, and peer groups sometimes seek out crime as a source of excitement. Programs to deter delinquents from committing further crimes have been generally unsuccessful. However, some promise has been shown in programs that intervene in a variety of contexts, including family, peer group, and neighborhood.

- Family factors that contribute to adolescent risk behavior include high conflict and parents who are neglectful, harsh, or inconsistent. Parental monitoring has been found to be an especially important predictor of adolescent delinquency. Other factors involved in risk behavior include friends' influence, schools' "ethos," neighborhood cohesion, and religious beliefs. Individual factors that predict involvement in risk behavior include aggressiveness, sensation seeking, poor school achievement, low impulse control, and optimistic bias.

- Depressed mood is more common in adolescence than in adulthood. Rates of depression in adolescence are considerably higher among girls than among boys. Explanations for this difference include gender differences in coping with problems, girls' greater concern with body image, higher overall stress among girls, and girls' greater tendency to internalize their difficulties.

- Rates of suicide among Americans in their teens and twenties increased sharply in the 1960s and 1970s and have remained high since that time. Females attempt suicide four times as often as males, but males are about four times more likely actually to kill themselves. Family disruptions and substance abuse are among the strongest predictors of suicide among adolescents.

- Anorexia nervosa and bulimia are most common among females in their teens and early twenties. Factors proposed to explain eating disorders include overcontrolling parents, fear of becoming sexually mature, and a cultural emphasis on slimness. Treatment for anorexia generally requires hospitalization. Relapse rates are high for both anorexia and bulimia.

We have focused on young people's tendencies for risk behavior as a source of problems in this chapter. In most societies, it is adolescents and emerging adults who are most likely to break the rules, to violate social norms for behavior. This tendency can indeed be disruptive and threatening to others, whether it be expressed in fighting, stealing, substance use, risky driving, or many other behaviors. Adolescence and (especially) emerging adulthood are times that are relatively free from the constraints of social roles (Arnett, 2000a). In childhood, behavior is restrained by parental control; in adulthood, obligations and expectations as spouse, parent, and employer/employee include restraints. It is in between, during adolescence and emerging adulthood, that social control is most lenient, and increased rates of risk behavior are one consequence (Gottfredson & Hirschi, 1990).

However, not all risky or norm-breaking behavior is negative. Young people have often been the ones willing to take risks for political and social changes by defying oppressive authorities. As we have seen, young people were at the forefront of the political changes in eastern Europe in 1989, and this is only one of many historical examples. Their relative freedom from role obligations provides the opportunity not just for socially disruptive behavior, but for socially constructive risks as well. They are often the explorers, the creative thinkers, the innovators, in part because they have fewer roles that structure and constrict their daily thoughts and behavior.

Key Terms

internalizing problems	binge drinking	violent crimes	attention deficit disorder
externalizing problems	propensity and	property crimes	with hyperactivity
overcontrolled	opportunity	nonindex crimes	(ADD-H)
undercontrolled	unstructured socializing	labeling theory	low impulse control
risk behavior	straight-edge	strain theory	depression
problem behavior	gateway drugs	life-course-persistent	depressed mood
problem behavior	experimental substance	delinquents (LCPDs)	depressive syndrome
syndrome	use	adolescence-limited	depressive disorder
problem behavior theory	social substance use	delinquents (ALDs)	midadolescence peak
driver education	medicinal substance use	parental monitoring	diathesis-stress model
graduated licensing	self-medication	socialized delinquents	placebo design
learning license	addictive substance use	unsocialized delinquents	anorexia nervosa
restricted license	withdrawal symptoms	ethos	bulimia
driving curfews	juveniles	protective factor	binge eating
zero tolerance	delinquency	aggressiveness	purging
full license	status offenses	novelty and intensity	amenorrhea
substance use	index crimes		

For Further Reading

Bachman, J. G., Wadsworth, K. N., O'Malley, P. M., Johnston, L. D., & Schulenberg, J. E. (1997). *Smoking, drinking, and drug use in young adulthood: The impacts of new freedoms and new responsibilities.* Mahwah, NJ: Erlbaum. This book describes patterns of substance use from adolescence through emerging adulthood, using data from the Monitoring the Future studies.

Jessor, R. (1998). *New perspectives on adolescent risk behavior.* New York: Cambridge University Press. A recent collection of writings on adolescent risk behavior, edited by a prominent scholar in the area, Richard Jessor.

Petersen, A. C., Compas, B. E., Brooks-Gunn, J., Stemmler, M., Ey, S., & Grant, K. E. (1993). Depression in adolescence. *American Psychologist, 48,* 155–168. An excellent brief summary of the research on adolescent depression.

Wilson, J. Q., & Herrnstein, R. J. (1985). *Crime and human nature.* New York: Simon and Schuster. Although it is over a decade old, in my view this remains the best book written on crime and delinquency. Covers every aspect of the topic, from constitutional factors to developmental factors to culture and history.

Applying Research

Dryfoos, J. (1990). *Adolescents at risk.* New York: Oxford University Press. A wide-ranging review of programs for helping adolescents with a variety of problems or potential problems.

Scales, P. C., & Leffert, N. (1998). *Developmental assets: A synthesis of scientific research on adolescent development.* Minneapolis, MN: Search Institute. Focuses on ways to address adolescent problems by helping them to build the "developmental assets" that promote healthy development. Integrates and applies a vast range of research articles on adolescent problems and on programs to treat and prevent those problems.

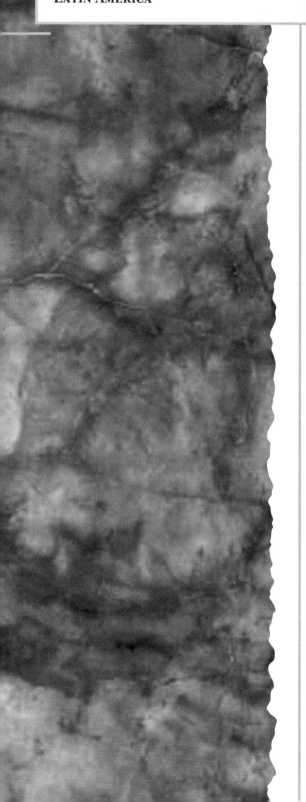

The 20th century was a time of astounding change for adolescents and emerging adults in the West. In 1900, typical 15-year-olds in Europe and North America had long ago completed any schooling they would receive and spent most of their days working alongside adults on farms and in factories (Kett, 1977). Their leisure, too, was often spent with family or at least under the watchful eyes of parents or other adults (Bailey, 1989). In 2000, typical 15-year-olds in these countries are in school among their peers for the better part of each day (Flammer & Alsaker, 1999). After school as well, a substantial amount of their time is spent among peers and friends—playing sports, hanging around, and in part-time service jobs (Flammer, Alsaker, & Noack, 1999; Steinberg & Cauffman, 1995). Much of their leisure includes electronic media, on an average day about two hours of television and two or more hours of music (Arnett, 1995b; Flammer et al., 1999). As for emerging adulthood, it barely existed in 1900, as a period of frequent change and independent exploration of possible identities and life options, whereas by 2000 it had become typical for young people in the West (Arnett, 2000a).

The degree of change in the 20th century was also dramatic for young people in non-Western countries. Most non-Western countries had not industrialized nearly as much as the West in 1900, but by 2000 countries such as Japan and South Korea had developed highly industrialized, information-based economies much like the West, and countries in many other parts of the world were headed in the same direction. Young people in non-Western countries were also deeply affected in the 20th century by historical events specific to their countries, such as the rise and dominance of communism in China and the independence movement in India.

What can we say about young people's prospects for the 21st century in countries around the world? Predicting the future is always a risky enterprise. Who would have predicted, in 1900, that the young people of 2000 would typically remain in school through their late teens and often into their early twenties; or that they would

429

typically postpone marriage into their late twenties; or that they would spend a considerable amount of their leisure time listening to recorded music, watching images flicker on a television, or surfing the Internet?

Nevertheless, speculating about the future can be a useful way of assessing the present. In this chapter, we will examine the prospects for adolescence and emerging adulthood in the 21st century in six regions of the world: sub-Saharan Africa, northern Africa and the Middle East, India, Asia, Latin America, and the West. Then we will discuss common issues likely to affect young people in the 21st century, including the future of globalization, disparities of wealth and opportunity, and the increasing cultural gap within countries between urban and rural areas.

Sub-Saharan Africa

In 1900, most African countries were not countries at all but colonies dominated by European countries such as Great Britain, France, and Germany. Gradually in the course of the 20th century, all of Africa gained political independence. However, for most African countries independence was not the end of their troubles but just the beginning. Sub-Saharan Africa has especially struggled during the 20th century, and as the 21st century begins it is plagued by numerous serious problems including chronic poverty, war, and an epidemic of HIV/AIDS.

Africa has been described as "a rich continent whose people are poor" (Nsemenang, 1998). The countries of Africa are extremely rich in natural resources such as oil, gold, and diamonds. Unfortunately, due to exploitation by the West followed by corruption, waste, and war in the post-colonial period, this natural wealth has not translated to economic prosperity for the people of Africa. On the contrary, living standards in Africa have actually declined in the past 50 years, and an increasing number of young Africans live in poverty (Nsemenang, 1998). Furthermore, sub-Saharan Africa has the worst performance of any region of the world on virtually any measure of living standards, including per capita income, access to clean water, life expectancy, infant mortality, and prevalence of disease (Nsemenang, 2000).

War was also a frequent part of life for Africans in the 20th century. The wars of independence were followed by many wars between African countries. There were many civil wars as well; the country boundaries drawn by European powers often ignored traditional tribal boundaries and antagonisms, and after independence tribal ri-

Adolescent boys are often recruited as soldiers in African wars. Here, a young soldier in Monrovia, Liberia.

valries often revived and resulted in civil wars. Young people have been and continue to be at the heart of these wars, as soldiers in the armies. Those who are not soldiers also find their lives disrupted when their parents are involved in the fighting, when the war comes to their own village, or when they are forced to become refugees.

As if poverty and war were not enough to daunt the prospects of young people in Africa, an even bigger threat to their future appeared on the threshold of the 21st century: an epidemic of HIV/AIDS. Of the deaths that took place from AIDS worldwide in 1999, 85% were in Africa (Bartholet, 2000). In some African countries, more than one-fourth of adults are currently infected with HIV. Already 10 million African children under age 15 have lost their mother or both parents to AIDS—90% of the world's total of AIDS orphans.

The AIDS epidemic will affect young Africans mainly in three ways (Bartholet, 2000; Nsemenang, 2000). First, many of them will be required to assume the leadership of their families due to their parents' deaths. Second, many of them will be forced into even deeper poverty by their parents' deaths and may end up joining the millions of AIDS orphans who have already become street children in African cities, where they are vulnerable to illness, malnutrition, and sexual exploitation. Third, many young Africans will become AIDS victims themselves in the 21st century if vast changes are not made soon in the prevalence of safe sex practices.

For young people growing up in sub-Saharan Africa in the 21st century, these conditions present a grim prospect. Growing up in poverty means that young people often will be struggling simply to survive, rather than being able to develop their abilities and enjoy their youth. War brings disruption to their lives and death to many of them. HIV/AIDS has the potential to devastate the continent and is already doing so. However, young people may be the ones who will reverse these grim trends and set Africa on a path toward a better future in the 21st century.

North Africa and the Middle East

North Africa and the Middle East are mostly Arab countries in which the Muslim religion is the predominant influence on all aspects of cultural life. For the young people of this region in the 21st century, three key issues are the continued strength of Islam, patriarchal family relationships, and the position of women.

Currently, the strength of Islam varies from countries in which all government policies are based on Islamic principles and texts (e.g., Kuwait and Saudi Arabia) to countries in which the influence of Islam is strong but a semblance of democracy and diversity of opinion also exists (e.g., Jordan and Morocco). During the 20th century the West generally moved toward secularism, as the influence of the Christian religion faded in the cultural life of most Western countries. Will North Africa and the Middle East follow a similar path in the 21st century? The young people of these countries may be the ones to determine the answer. Right now evidence suggests that many of them have been influenced by globalization and are highly attracted to the popular culture and information technologies of the West (e.g., Davis & Davis, 1989; Malik, 2000). Nevertheless, Islam currently remains strong, even among the young.

Patriarchal authority—meaning that the father's authority in the family is to be obeyed unquestioningly—has a long tradition in Arab societies and is supported by Islam (Malik, 2000). "Authoritative" discussion of family rules in Muslim families is uncommon; even to suggest such a thing would be considered an unacceptable affront to the authority of the parents, especially the father. Will this view of the father's authority survive the 21st century? Again, a look at the West would suggest that it would not, because the West also had a tradition of patriarchal authority in the family that no longer exists. Globalization, with its promotion of a worldwide youth culture, would also seem to undermine patriarchal authority. Nevertheless, it would be a mistake to assume that North African countries will follow the same path as the West. The strength of Islam may keep patriarchal authority strong in North Africa through the 21st century.

The third issue of importance with regard to young people in North Africa and the Middle East in the 21st century is the position of women. Islamic societies have a long tradition of keeping tight control over women's appearance and behavior. It is common in many Islamic societies to see girls and women wearing a **chador**, which is a garment that covers the hair and most of the face. Muslim women are often expected to

Will the position of women in Middle Eastern societies change in the 21st century?

wear a chador as a way of being modest. Typically, Muslim women are not allowed to go out of the house unaccompanied by a male (Malik, 2000). Virginity before marriage is highly prized, and violation of this taboo results in the most severe punishments, even death (Constable, 2000). Women are generally discouraged from working outside the home, although the percentage of working women varies from a high of 24% in Egypt to a low of 4% in Saudi Arabia (Makhlouf & Abdelkader, 1997). As discussed in Chapter 5, the terribly painful practice of female circumcision continues to be prevalent in most northern African and Middle Eastern countries.

Will these practices continue through the 21st century? Or will young women in this region gain a wider scope of autonomy and equal rights as the century progresses? It is impossible to say right now. So far, the practices described here have remained remarkably resistant to the influence of globalization and to criticisms within these countries as well.

India

India is a complex society with numerous religions, dozens of languages, and a population of over one billion people. In the 20th century, India gained its independence from Great Britain through peaceful means, following the strategy of nonviolent resistance devised by Mohandas K. Gandhi. India has maintained a democracy since obtaining independence in 1947, a remarkable feat given the diversity of its people and the high rate of illiteracy. In the 21st century, the main issues facing young people in India will be school versus work, the tradition of early arranged marriages, the caste system, and the rights of women.

Currently, India is one of the few countries in the world that does not have compulsory education for children (Verma & Saraswathi, 2000). Consequently, about one-third of 15- to 19-year-olds are illiterate. Illiteracy is especially high among adolescent girls, nearly 50% (PROBE, 1999). Many parents, especially in rural areas, do not believe that girls should be educated beyond a minimal ability to write letters and keep household accounts. Access to education is much higher in urban areas, for girls as well as boys; and despite high illiteracy, India also has a large number of highly educated young people, especially in fields such as medicine and information technologies. Nevertheless, many rural areas in India have few schools, and those that exist tend to be poorly funded and staffed by teachers who are poorly trained.

Many Indian adolescents work rather than attend school.

Also contributing to high illiteracy in India is widespread child and adolescent labor, with jobs ranging from carpet weaving to mines, cigarette manufacturing, and gem polishing, often in extremely unsafe and unhealthy conditions (Burra, 1997). Parents often prefer to have their children and adolescents working, and thus contributing to the family income, rather than attending school. Consequently, the government has taken few steps to restrict child and adolescent labor.

We can see, then, that the state of child and adolescent labor in India is very similar to the situation in Western countries 100 years ago. It is possible that during the 21st century primary and secondary education in India will become compulsory, and children and adolescents will focus on developing knowledge and skills for adult work rather than entering the workplace at an early age. However, this will happen only if an organized movement develops to abolish child and adolescent labor, as happened in the West.

With regard to marriage, India has a long tradition of young marriages. In the past, children were often married even before reaching puberty, and even now about half of India's young people marry in their teens (Verma & Saraswathi, 2000). Early marriages are especially common in rural areas. Furthermore, most marriages in India are arranged by the parents. Young people often contribute to the decision and may reject a person their parents recommend, but for the most part they rely on their parents to choose a marriage partner for them. Even most urban, highly educated Indians prefer to have an arranged marriage (Pathak, 1994).

The endurance of the tradition of arranged marriage is a reflection of the collectivist beliefs of Indian society and the trust and closeness that often exists between Indian young people and their parents (Larson et al., 2000). But will this practice survive the 21st century? The continued pervasiveness of arranged marriages even among highly educated, urban young people suggests that it may.

Another issue facing young Indians in the 21st century is the status of the **caste system**. According to this tradition, people are believed to be born into a particular caste based on their moral and spiritual conduct in their previous life (reincarnation is central to the Hindu beliefs held by most Indians). A person's caste then determines his or her status in Indian society. Only persons of elite castes are considered to be eligible for positions of wealth and power; persons of lower castes are considered worthy only of the lowest paying, dirtiest, lowest status jobs. Also, marrying outside one's caste is strongly discouraged.

Attempts were made in India throughout the 20th century to abolish the caste system, especially since independence, and the attempts have been partially successful. The Indian government has affirmative-action-type programs that give preference to persons from lower castes for certain government jobs and educational opportunities. However, the caste system is deeply embedded in Indian tradition, and it remains strong. Young people from lower castes continue to be less likely to attend school than young people from higher castes, which restricts the jobs available to them (Verma & Sarawathi, 2000). Although the lower castes are becoming increasingly well-organized and effective as a political force in India, it is difficult to believe the caste system will be entirely abolished by the end of the 21st century.

Finally, rights for women is likely to be an important issue affecting the lives of young people in India during the 21st century. Like many societies, India has a long tradition of holding women to be of inferior status from birth onward. As noted, girls are less likely than boys to receive even enough education to become literate. Even for girls who are fortunate to obtain a good education, often they have little opportunity to develop a career because of the belief that the role of women should be restricted to that of wife and mother. Prostitution of adolescent girls has also become a major prob-

lem in India. Increasingly, brothel owners seek out young adolescent girls as prostitutes; because of their youth, they are regarded as not as likely to have HIV/AIDS, and so men are willing to pay more to have sex with them (Thapar, 1998).

Will the opportunities for young women in India improve over the 21st century? One hopeful sign is that, for girls who do get the opportunity to attend school, they generally outperform boys academically (Verma & Saraswathi, 2000). Given the challenges that face their country in the 21st century, Indians may decide that they cannot afford to neglect the intellectual resources available in one-half of their population.

Asia

Asia comprises a vast and diverse area, ranging from countries that are highly industrialized (e.g., Japan) to countries that have recently industrialized (e.g., South Korea) to countries that are rapidly industrializing (e.g., China). Nevertheless, these countries share certain common characteristics and challenges in the 21st century. Some of the major issues affecting young people are likely to be the tradition of filial piety, arranged marriages and dating, intense pressure at the secondary school level, and the rights of women.

The cultures of Asia have been profoundly influenced by Confucianism, which is a set of beliefs and precepts attributed to the philosopher Confucious, who lived around 550 to 480 B.C. One of the tenets of Confucianism is **filial piety**, which means that children are expected to respect, obey, and revere their parents, especially the father. This principle applies not just in childhood, but in adolescence and adulthood as well, as long as their parents live. In fact, it even applies beyond death; ancestor worship is common in Asian cultures. Part of filial piety is the expectation that the children, in particular the oldest son, have the responsibility for caring for their parents when the parents become elderly. Often, this includes having the parents live in their children's household.

Asian cultures are becoming more individualistic under the influence of globalization (Stevenson & Zusho, 2000). Can filial piety survive this trend? Evidence suggests that adolescents' relationships with their parents are changing. Some studies indicate that parents are much less likely to demand obedience from their adolescents now than in the past (Park & Cho, 1995). However, in general, Asian adolescents still expect that they will take care of their parents as their parents grow older (e.g., Feldman et al., 1992).

Thus, the tradition of filial piety may endure in the 21st century, but in a modified, less rigid form.

One aspect of the authority of parents in Asian cultures is the tradition of arranged marriages, in which parents choose a mate for their children. This tradition remains strong in Asian cultures, even in cultures that have become highly industrialized (Cho & Shin, 1996). However, like filial piety, the tradition of arranged marriage has become modified in response to increased individualism. Today in Asian cultures, the "semi-arranged marriage" is the most common practice (Lee, 1998). This means that parents influence the mate selection of their children, but do not simply decide it without the children's consent. Parents may introduce a potential mate to their child. If the child has a favorable impression of the potential mate, they date a few times. If they agree that they are compatible, they marry. Another variation of semi-arranged marriage is that young people meet a potential mate, but seek their parents' approval before proceeding to date the person.

It is difficult to say if semi-arranged marriage will be an enduring form, or if it is a transitional stage on the way to the end of the tradition of arranged marriage. Although semi-arranged marriages are now common, it is also increasingly common for young people to choose their own marriage partner. Recreational dating remains rare in Asian cultures, but it is more common than in the past, and it seems likely to grow in the future.

The Confucian tradition places a strong emphasis on education, which is one of the reasons for the intense focus on education in the lives of young people in Asian cultures today. As we saw in the example of Japan in Chapter 10, high school tends to be highly pressured for young people in Asian societies, because performance on college entrance exams determines to a large extent their path through adult life. In South Korea, many high school students spend more than 70 hours a week in class or studying (Lee & Larson, 2000; Migliazzo, 1993)! This system is facing increasing criticism within Asian societies by those who argue that young people should not be subjected to such pressure at a young age and should be allowed more time for fun. Also, as Asian economies are becoming more flexible in response to global economic pressures, attending a certain college is no longer an absolute guarantee of a secure, well-paying job for life. However, the tradition of intense focus on secondary school education continues to be strong and seems likely to endure well into the 21st century.

In Asian societies as in so much of the world, females have fewer rights and opportunities than males.

The traditional emphasis on education in Asian societies is likely to endure through the 21st century.

With regard to education, boys receive more support from parents than girls for pursuing higher education. In Japan, for example, girls are discouraged from applying to the elite universities and are expected instead to enter junior colleges and pursue traditionally female occupations such as early childhood education (Stevenson & Zusho, 2000). Parents are reluctant to make the same sacrifices for higher education for girls as they do for boys, in part because it is sons and not daughters who are expected to take care of the parents in their old age. In the workplace, similar discrimination exists, with women being the first to be fired when cutbacks are made because of the view that they are less likely to need the money to support a family (Stevenson & Zusho, 2000). Given the pervasiveness of sexism in human societies throughout history, it is difficult to be optimistic that it will be totally eliminated in the 21st century, in Asia or anywhere else.

Latin America

Like Asia, Latin America comprises a vast land area of diverse cultures. And like Asia, Latin America has certain common characteristics that unite these cultures. Latin American countries share a common history of colonization by southern European powers, particularly Spain, and a common allegiance to the Catholic religion. For young people in Latin America, two of the key issues for the 21st century are political stability and economic growth.

The 20th century was one of great political instability in most of Latin America. Most Latin American countries became independent (mostly from Spain) in the 19th century or early in the 20th century. However, during the 20th century, most of them suffered continued instability. Sources of this instability included military coups followed by military dictatorships, communist revolutions, and civil wars between communist and anticommunist forces.

As the 20th century begins, prospects look much brighter for young people in Latin America. Although political instability continues in some countries, for the most part, Latin American countries have now established stable democracies. This means that young Latin Americans of the 21st century are much less likely than in the 20th century to have to fight in a war and much more likely to be able to express their ideas and beliefs freely.

The political instability of the 20th century led to considerable economic instability. Despite having great natural resources, the countries of Latin America have not prospered economically. Even now, with mostly stable democracies, Latin American countries continue to experience economic difficulties due to governmental corruption and mismanagement as well as to large international debt burdens accumulated from previous economic crises. The period from 1980 to 1990 is known in Latin America as the "lost decade" (Chanes, 2000), because the economies of the continent fared so poorly, and the 1990s were not much better.

For the young people of Latin America, this means that their economic prospects are grim as they enter the 21st century. Unemployment among adults is high throughout Latin America, and unemployment among young people is even higher, in most countries at least double the rate for adults, as high as 50% (Chanes, 2000). However, prospects for young people are likely to improve during the 21st century. With more enduring political stability, economic growth in Latin America is likely to improve. Young people in Latin America are obtaining increased education, which should help prepare them for the increasingly information-based global economy. Also, the birth rate has declined sharply in Latin America in the past two decades, and consequently the children who are now growing up should face less competition in the job market as they enter adolescence and emerging adulthood.

Unemployment is high among young people in most Latin American countries. Here, unemployed young men in Mexico.

The West

For young people in the West, in many ways the 21st century holds bright prospects. Western societies have well-established, stable democracies and economies that are generally healthier than in the rest of the world. Young people in the West generally have access to opportunities for secondary and higher education, and they have a wide range of occupations to choose from. Because Western societies are highly affluent, most young people have a wide range of leisure opportunities, such as sports and music. However, the West has its problems as well. For young people, the principle issues of the 21st century involve education, unemployment, immigrants, and health risk behavior.

As noted often in this book, young people in Western countries are obtaining increased education, with many of them remaining in school through their early twenties. However, educational opportunities are not evenly distributed in most Western countries. Young people in minority groups often attend college at rates considerably lower than among young people in the majority culture. Furthermore, some critics have argued that Western countries produce far more college graduates than the economy really needs, so that many of them end up underemployed, in jobs with skills that do not require a college education (Coté &

Allahar, 1996). Still, it seems likely that in the 21st century, with the economy headed rapidly toward an increased focus on information technologies, the jobs available requiring higher education will continue to expand, and the proportion of young people obtaining higher education will continue to expand accordingly.

Unemployment is another problem faced by young people in the West as we enter the 21st century. Despite the impressive efforts that European countries make to promote a smooth entry into the workplace for young people, unemployment among the young is a serious problem in most European countries. This is especially true for the countries of southern Europe, where youth unemployment (ages 15 to 24) has remained stubbornly over 20% for many years (Lagree, 1995; Lowe & Krahn, 1999). Unemployment among adults (age 25 and older) is also high in southern Europe relative to the north, but youth unemployment is especially high. Consistently across Europe, in the north as well as the south, and the east as well as the west, the youth unemployment rate is about twice as high as the unemployment rate for adults (Arnett, 2000d).

In the United States, unemployment is also higher among young people than among adults, and it is especially high among young Latinos and African Americans living in urban areas (Wilson, 1996). Similar disparities are reported in Europe between minority youth and the majority population (e.g., Bois-Reymond & van der Zande, 1994; Sansone, 1995). Throughout Western countries, young minorities are disadvantaged in the workplace in part because of lower levels of education and training and in part because of prejudice and discrimination from the majority (Kracke et al., 1998; Liebkind & Kosonen, 1998). Although opportunities for minorities have improved in most Western countries during the 20th century, it is an open question whether minorities in the West will reach true equality of opportunity with the majority populations in the course of the 21st century.

The issue of minorities is important in the West, not just with respect to employment but with regard to their treatment more generally. In the United States, young Blacks or Latinos are far more likely than Whites to grow up in poverty and are treated more harshly by the criminal justice system (Fletcher, 2000). European societies tend to be much more homogeneous than the United States, but most European countries have allowed substantial immigration in recent decades, from eastern Europe and from a variety of developing countries.

Most Europeans have been tolerant and accepting of immigration, and young people tend to be more favorable toward immigration than older people (Kracke et al., 1998; Westin, 1998). However, when anti-immigrant acts do occur, they tend to be committed by groups of young working-class men in their late teens and early twenties (Westin, 1998), especially young men who are members of the "skinhead" youth subculture. These acts include verbal harassment, attacks on refugee centers, and even random murders of immigrants. Immigration will be an important issue in Europe in the next century, as European countries make decisions about how much immigration to allow and how to address the problem of the small proportion of young people who are disposed to commit violent acts against immigrants.

Finally, young people in the West are more likely than young people in the rest of the world to engage in behavior that holds risks for their health. In many ways, Western young people at the dawn of the 21st century are the healthiest generation in history. Unlike the Western young people of 1900, and unlike young people in developing countries today, very few

Although most Europeans have accepted the immigrants to their countries, some groups of young men have rejected them. Here, a right-wing group rallies in Leipzig, Germany.

Western young people of the 21st century will die of infectious diseases before they reach maturity, nor are they subject to unsafe and unhealthy working conditions in mines and factories (Kett, 1977).

Nevertheless, young people in the West face health problems and challenges of their own in the 21st century. For Western adolescents and emerging adults today, the primary threats to their health arise from their behavior. As we have seen in previous chapters, the most serious threats are automobile fatalities and homicides, both of which are far more prevalent in the United States than in other Western countries (U.S. Department of Transportation, 1995; Rockett, 1998). Graduated licensing shows promise in reducing automobile fatalities among young people in the United States (Preusser et al., 1993), but rates of fatalities are likely to remain high as long as young people in American society rely heavily on automobiles for transportation and leisure—far into the 21st century, in other words.

The prevalence of unregulated firearms in American society—200 million, by recent estimates—makes it difficult to be hopeful that homicides among young people will be reduced any time soon. Regulation of gun ownership is a controversial issue in American society, and the United States has been reluctant to adopt the kind of gun control laws that have long been typical of other Western countries. Even if such laws were passed in the 21st century, one can only speculate how long it would take to achieve any kind of legal control over 200 million firearms.

Cigarette smoking among young people is another health risk behavior worth noting, because it is—in the long run—the source of more illness and mortality than automobile fatalities and homicides combined, and because the majority of persons who smoke begin as adolescents (U.S. Department of Health and Human Services, 1994). As noted in the previous chapter, smoking has decreased among young people in most Western countries since the 1960s (e.g., Buzzi & Cavalli, 1994; Galambos & Kolaric, 1994). However, rates of smoking among young people have changed little (or even increased) in recent years and remain strikingly high, so that is difficult to predict whether smoking will remain a common form of health risk behavior for young people through the 21st century.

Common Issues

Although young people in various parts of the world face challenges distinctive to their region and their so-ciety, some issues will be common to young people all over the world in the 20th century. Three of these issues are globalization, equality of wealth and opportunity, and the urban–rural split.

The Future of Globalization

We have discussed globalization often as a theme of this book. Globalization is affecting cultures around the world, as increased economic integration brings cultures and countries into more frequent contact with each other and as media spread common information and entertainment to every part of the globe. For the most part the direction of influence has been from the West outward, as Western political forms, economic practices, and media content are adopted by cultures in other parts of the world. Western influences have often been embraced first and most enthusiastically by young people in non-Western cultures (Schlegel, 2000).

Globalization is certain to continue into the 21st century, but two questions concerning globalization are: How far will it extend? And will its effects be positive or negative for young people? The first of these questions is difficult to answer. Globalization took place at a rapid pace in the second half of the 20th century, but this does not mean it will continue to occur at the same pace. As we have seen in earlier chapters, some evidence suggests that many cultures are devising new forms of dress, media, and economic practices that combine Western influences with indigenous forms. Will these hybrid forms continue to occur? Or is this a middle stage on the way to total Westernization and the creation of a more or less homogeneous global culture? The answer will probably become clear in the 21st century.

Is globalization good or bad for young people? There is probably not a clean either/or answer to this question. Globalization may be good if it provides young people with greater opportunities than they have had in the past. That is, as their economies develop and become more connected to the rest of the world, young people in developing countries may have a wider range of educational and occupational possibilities to choose from. Girls, in particular, may see their opportunities increase as globalization proceeds (Mensch et al., 1998). Also, as more countries develop stable democratic institutions, ethnic and religious hatreds may diminish, and young people may become less likely to die in ethnic and religious conflicts.

On the other hand, globalization holds a variety of perils for young people, as well. As we saw in the chapter on work, currently many young people in developing countries are being exploited, often by international companies that regard them as a source of plentiful, desperate, and easily exploitable labor. We have also seen examples of how young people may become alienated from the ways of their own culture as a consequence of globalization, and how conflict with parents often increases as young people in changing societies develop interests and beliefs that differ sharply from those of their parents. Also, young people in developing countries may develop aspirations and expectations for their lives, based on what they have seen or read about the West, that are unattainable in the cultures where they live. The result may be increased disenchantment and frustration among the young.

Equality of Wealth and Opportunity

Currently, resources of wealth and opportunity available to young people are distributed extremely unevenly around the world. Young people in the middle class and above in the majority cultures of industrialized countries have many advantages. They have access to high-quality health care from the womb onward. They are provided with a reasonably good education throughout childhood and adolescence, and most of them are able to obtain higher education if they wish. They have access to a variety of leisure opportunities, including a vast range of media and often the opportunity to travel to various parts of their own country and the world.

At the other extreme are young people around the world who are growing up in extremely desperate conditions. Even now, at the beginning of the 21st century, many children grow up without even the most basic health care such as childhood vaccinations, so that they reach adolescence in poor health if they reach it

at all. Hundreds of millions of young people—in fact, the majority of the world's young people—grow up with almost nothing in the way of material resources, and spend their youth as well as their adult lives working strenuously to survive from one day to the next. There are tens of millions of street children in the world, who live without families and who are subject daily to threats to their health and their lives (Raffaeli & Larson, 1999). Their prospects in adolescence and beyond are bleak. In the West, too, particularly in the United States, many young people grow up with few resources, with little to inspire hope for their futures.

Will these conditions change in the 21st century? Will the world move toward greater equality of opportunity for all young people, regardless of the conditions they have been born into through no choice of their own? It is difficult to say, but currently there is little question that the world is moving in the opposite direction—toward greater inequality of wealth and opportunity, as the rich get richer in industrialized countries, and the poor get poorer and more numerous around the world (Ratzan, Filerman, & Le Sar, 2000).

The Urban–Rural Split

Although I have been discussing young people in this chapter according to region and country, each region and country is diverse. In particular, in developing countries young people in urban areas face conditions much different than young people in rural areas (Gelbard, Haub, & Kent, 1999). In urban areas young people typically have greater access to education and health care. On the other hand, they are also more likely to be subject to exploitation by adults, in prosti-

Will the availability of resources for young people continue to be highly unequal in the 21st century?

tution or industrial labor. In rural areas, young people are less likely to attend school and often spend their days working in agriculture or other work with adults. On the other hand, they are more likely to have the support and care of a stable extended family.

Globalization is affecting urban areas in developing countries far more than rural areas, so far. Consequently, young people in urban areas are growing up in ways that are increasingly different than young people in rural areas. Will this disparity become more extreme in the 21st century? Or will young people in rural areas become increasingly swept up in globalization, like their urban counterparts? Currently in many developing countries, young people are leaving their rural villages when they reach adolescence or emerging adulthood and are heading for what they believe to be the promise of greater wealth and opportunity in the big cities. However, many of them are finding that when they reach the cities, opportunities are not what they expected, and there are threats of exploitation that they had not anticipated. It is difficult to predict what will happen with regard to the urban–rural split in the 21st century, but it is important to keep it in mind when considering the prospects for young people in developing countries.

A Final Summing Up

In this chapter we have looked ahead to what adolescence and emerging adulthood may be like during the century to come. We have seen that the young people of the world face futures of remarkable diversity, from the challenges of disease, exploitation, and illiteracy in developing countries to the challenges of unemployment, relations between minority and majority cultures, and health risk behavior in industrialized countries.

One of the reasons predicting the future for young people is difficult is that each generation of adolescents and emerging adults takes the material for life provided by their culture and reshapes it, recreates it in ways that are uniquely their own. Adolescence and emerging adulthood are times of rapid and often dramatic change. In adolescence, young people gain greater autonomy from their families and a deeper sense of what their capabilities are as individuals. In emerging adulthood, young people typically move out of their parents' household and into the world on their own. As they explore possibilities in love, work, and worldviews, they form a foundation for their adult lives. Often, they attempt to remake themselves during emerging adulthood, to form an identity that will be truly their own, drawn from the influences of their childhood and adolescence but not simply the sum of those influences. In remaking themselves, sometimes they also, collectively, remake their cultures and their societies.

In the course of many years of studying young people, conducting hundreds of interviews, and spending countless hours in informal conversations with them, I have been struck again and again by how adolescence and emerging adulthood are times of life when hopes for the future tend to be high. There are exceptions, of course, but for the most part even if their lives have so far been difficult and filled with problems, young people tend to see their futures as bright and filled with promise. Adolescents and emerging adults are setting the foundation for their adult lives and making decisions that will affect their futures. But for now, while they remain adolescents and emerging adults, the fate of their dreams has yet to be determined, the possible lives lying before them have yet to harden into accomplished facts. For the most part, they still believe their dreams will be fulfilled and they will achieve the kind of life they want (Arnett, 2000c).

Given the formidable problems that lie before today's young people, as we have seen in this chapter, should we conclude that any high hopes are misplaced, that such hopes would constitute a distortion of the realities they face? Perhaps it is rather that their hopes provide them with the fuel to proceed with confidence in a world that is fraught with peril. And who can say, ultimately, what will be the form of the future they will create?

Key Terms

chador

caste system

filial piety

Glossary

Absolute performance. In IQ tests, performance results compared to other persons, regardless of age.

Abstinence-plus programs. Sex education programs that encourage adolescents to delay intercourse while also providing contraceptive information for adolescents who nevertheless choose to have intercourse.

Abstract thinking. Thinking in terms of symbols, ideas, and concepts.

Active genotype–environment interactions. Occur when people seek out environments that correspond to their genotypic characteristics.

Actual self. A person's perception of the self as it is, contrasted with the possible self.

Addictive substance use. Pattern of substance use in which a person has come to depend on regular use of substances to feel good physically and/or psychologically.

Adolescence. A period of the life course between the time puberty begins and the time adult status is approached, when young people are in the process of preparing to take on the roles and responsibilities of adulthood in their culture.

Adolescence-limited delinquents (ALDS). In Moffitt's theory, young persons who commit delinquent acts in adolescence but show no evidence of problems prior to or following adolescence.

Adolescent egocentrism. Type of egocentrism in which adolescents have difficulty distinguishing their thinking about their own thoughts from their thinking about the thoughts of others.

Adolescent growth spurt. The rapid increase in height that takes place at the beginning of puberty.

Adrenocorticotropic hormone (ACTH). The hormone that causes the adrenal glands to increase androgen production.

Advanced Placement (AP) classes. Classes for gifted students in high schools that have higher-level material than normal classes in order to provide a challenging curriculum.

Affection phase. In Brown's developmental model of adolescent love, the third phase, in which adolescents come to know each other better and express deeper feelings for each other, as well as engaging in more extensive sexual activity.

Affective functions. Emotional, pertaining to love, nurturance, and attachment.

Age-graded. Practice in which children are grouped on the basis of age rather than developmental maturity.

Age norms. Technique for developing a psychological test, in which a typical score for each age is established by testing a large random sample of people from a variety of geographical areas and social class backgrounds.

Aggressiveness. A personality characteristic, related to a variety of kinds of risk behavior, that is characterized by angry and hostile feelings and/or actions toward others.

Alfred Binet. French psychologist who developed the first intelligence test in the early 20th century, which later became known as the Stanford-Binet.

Alternative script. According to Brake, the temporary identity offered by participation in youth culture that is different from the script or style of life followed by most adults.

Amenorrea. Cessation of menstruation, sometimes experienced by girls whose body weight falls extremely low.

AmeriCorps. The national service program in the United States in which young people serve in a community organization for up to 2 years for minimal pay.

Androgens. The sex hormones that have especially high levels in males from puberty onward and are mostly responsible for male primary and secondary sex characteristics.

Androgyny. The combination of "masculine" and "feminine" traits in one person.

Anorexia nervosa. Intentional self-starvation.

Apprenticeship. An arrangement, common in Europe, in which an adolescent "novice" serves under contract to a "master" who has substantial experience in a profession, and through working under the master, learns the skills required to enter the profession.

Areola. Area surrounding the nipple on the breast; enlarges at puberty.

Argot. (pronounced *ar-go'*). In youth culture, a certain vocabulary and a certain way of speaking.

Arranged marriage. A marriage in which the marriage partners are determined not by the partners themselves but by others, usually the parents or other family elders.

Assimilation. In the formation of ethnic identity, the option that involves leaving behind the ways of one's ethnic group and adopting the values and way of life of the majority culture.

Asymptomatic. A condition common with STDs in which an infected person shows no symptoms of the disease but may potentially infect others.

Asynchronicity. Uneven growth of different parts of the body during puberty.

Attachment theory. Theory originally developed by British psychiatrist John Bowlby, asserting that among humans as among other primates, attachments between parents and children have an evolutionary basis in the need for vulnerable young members of the species to stay in close proximity to adults who will care for and protect them.

Attention deficit disorder with hyperactivity (ADD-H). Disorder characterized by difficulty in maintaining attention on a task along with a high activity level that makes self-control problematic.

Authoritarian parents. Parenting style in which parents are high in demandingness but low in responsiveness, i.e., they require obedience from their children and punish disobedience without compromise, but show little warmth or affection toward them.

Authoritative parents. A parenting style in which parents are high in demandingness and high in responsiveness, i.e., they love their children but also set clear standards for behavior and explain to their children the reasons for those standards.

Automaticity. Degree of cognitive effort a person needs to devote to processing a given set of information.

Autonomous morality. Piaget's term for the period of moral development from about age 10 to age 12, involving a growing realization that moral rules are social conventions that can be changed if people decide they should be changed.

Autonomy. The quality of being independent and self-sufficient, capable of thinking for one's self.

Bar Mitzvah. Jewish religious ritual for boys at age 13 that signifies the adolescents' new responsibilities with respect to Jewish beliefs.

Barometric self-esteem. The fluctuating sense of worth and well-being people have as they respond to different thoughts, experiences, and interactions in the course of a day.

Baseline self-esteem. A person's stable, enduring sense of worth and well-being.

Bat Mitzvah. Jewish religious ritual for girls at age 13 that signifies the adolescents' new responsibilities with respect to Jewish beliefs.

Behavioral decision theory. Theory of decision making that describes the decision-making process as including (1) identifying the range of possible choices; (2) identifying the consequences that would result from each choice; (3) evaluating the desirability of each consequence; (4) assessing the likelihood of each consequence; and (5) integrating this information.

Biculturalism. In the formation of ethnic identity, the approach that involves developing a dual identity, one based in the ethnic group of origin and one based in the majority culture.

441

Bidirectional effects. In relations between parents and children, the concept that children not only are affected by their parents but affect their parents in return. Also called reciprocal effects.

Binge drinking. Drinking a large number of alcoholic drinks in one episode, usually defined as drinking five or more alcoholic drinks in a row.

Binge eating. Consumption of a large amount of food in a short period of time.

Bonding phase. In Brown's developmental model of adolescent love, the final phase, in which the romantic relationship becomes more enduring and serious and partners begin to discuss the possibility of a lifelong commitment to each other.

Brains. In adolescent crowds, the group known for doing well in school.

Breast bud. The first slight enlargement of the breast in girls at puberty.

Broad socialization. The process by which persons in an individualistic culture come to learn individualism, including values of individual uniqueness, independence, and self-expression.

Buddy relationship. Between siblings, a relationship in which they treat each other as friends.

Bulimia. An eating disorder characterized by episodes of binge eating followed by purging (self-induced vomiting).

Bullying. In peer relations, the aggressive assertion of power by one person over another.

Capacity. In information-processing theories, the concept that refers to how many aspects of a situation persons can keep in their mind at once.

Cardiac output. The quantity of blood flow from the heart; peaks around age 25.

Care orientation. Gilligan's term for the type of moral orientation that involves focusing on relationships with others as the basis for moral reasoning.

Caregiver relationship. Between siblings, a relationship in which one sibling serves parental functions for the other.

Caste system. Hindu belief that people are born into a particular caste based on their moral and spiritual conduct in their previous life. A person's caste then determines their status in Indian society.

Casual relationship. Between siblings, a relationship that is not emotionally intense, in which they have little to do with one another.

Cathartic effect. Effect sometimes attributed to media experiences, in which media experience has the effect of relieving unpleasant emotions.

Chador. A garment that covers the hair and most of the face, worn by many girls and women in Muslim societies.

Child study movement. Late 19th century group, led by G. Stanley Hall, that advocated research on child and adolescent development and the improvement of conditions for children and adolescents in the family, school, and workplace.

Cliques. Small groups of friends who know each other well, do things together, and form a regular social group.

Clitoris. Part of vulva in which females' sexual sensations are concentrated.

Closed question. Questionnaire format that entails choosing from specific responses provided for each question.

Cofigurative cultures. Cultures in which young people learn what they need to know not only from adults but also from other young people.

Cognitive development. Changes over time in how people think, how they solve problems, and how their capacities for memory and attention change.

Cognitive developmental approach. Approach to understanding cognition that emphasizes the changes that take place at different ages.

Cognitive developmental theory of gender. Kohlberg's theory, based on Piaget's ideas about cognitive development, asserting that gender is a fundamental way of organizing ideas about the world and that children develop through a predictable series of stages in their understanding of gender.

Cohabitation. Living with a romantic partner outside of marriage.

Collectivism. A set of beliefs asserting that it is important for persons to mute their individual desires in order to contribute to the well-being and success of the group.

Combinatorial reasoning. Cognitive skill of generating all possible combinations of a set of elements.

Coming out. For homosexuals, the process of acknowledging their homosexuality and then disclosing the truth to their friends, family, and others.

Commitment. Cognitive status in which persons commit themselves to certain points of view they believe to be the most valid while at the same time being open to reevaluating their views if new evidence is presented to them.

Communal manhood. Anthony Rotundo's term for the norm of manhood in 17th- and 18th-century colonial America, in which the focus of gender expectations for adolescent boys was on preparing to assume adult male role responsibilities in work and marriage.

Community service. Volunteer work provided as a contribution to the community, without monetary compensation.

Companionate love. In Sternberg's theory of love, the type of love that combines intimacy and commitment, but without passion.

Companionship support. Between friends, reliance on each other as companions in social activities.

Complex thinking. Thinking that takes into account multiple connections and interpretations, such as in the use of metaphor, satire, and sarcasm.

Componential approach. Description of the information-processing approach to cognition, indicating that it involves breaking down the thinking process into its various components.

Componential intelligence. Sternberg's term for the kind of intelligence that involves acquiring, storing, analyzing, and retrieving information.

Comprehensive high school. The form of the American high school that arose in the 1920s and is still the main form today, which encompasses a wide range of functions and includes classes in general education, college preparation, and vocational training.

Comprehensive sexuality education. Sex education programs that begin at an early age and include detailed information on sexual development and sexual behavior, with easy access to contraception for adolescents who choose to become sexually active.

Concept videos. Music videos that enact a story to go along with the lyrics of the song.

Concrete operations. Cognitive stage from age 7 to 11 in which children learn to use mental operations but are limited to applying them to concrete, observable situations rather than hypothetical situations.

Consensual validation. In social science studies of interpersonal attraction, the principle that people like to find in others an agreement, or consensus, with their own characteristics, in order to validate their own way of looking at the world.

Consent form. Written statement provided by a researcher to potential participants in a study, informing them of who is conducting the study, the purposes of the study, and what their participation would involve, including potential risks.

Consummate love. In Sternberg's theory of love, the type of love that combines passion, intimacy, and commitment.

Context. The environmental settings in which development takes place.

Contextual intelligence. Practical intelligence involving the ability to apply information to the kinds of problems faced in everyday life, including the capacity to evaluate social situations.

Controversial adolescents. Adolescents who are aggressive but who also possess social skills, so that they evoke strong emotions both positive and negative from their peers.

Conventional reasoning. In Kohlberg's theory of moral development, the level of moral reasoning in which the person advocates the value of conforming to the moral expectations of others. What is right is whatever agrees with the rules established by tradition and by authorities.

Credentialism. Coté and Allahar's term for requiring educational credentials such as a college degree even for jobs for which the knowledge learned in the course of obtaining the degree is irrelevant to the job.

Critical relationship. Between siblings, a relationship characterized by a high level of conflict and teasing.

Critical thinking. Thinking that involves not merely memorizing information but analyzing it, making judgments about what it means, relating it to other information, and considering ways in which it might be valid or invalid.

Cross-sectional study. Study that examines individuals at one point in time.

Crowds. Large, reputation-based groups of adolescents.

Crystallized intelligence. Accumulated knowledge and enhanced judgment based on experience.

Cultural beliefs. The predominant beliefs in a culture about right and wrong, what is most important in life, and how life should be lived. May also include beliefs about where and how life originated and what happens after death.

Cultural psychology. Approach to human psychology emphasizing that psychological functioning cannot be separated from the culture in which it takes place.

Culture. The total pattern of a group's customs, beliefs, art, and technology. A group's common way of life, passed on from one generation to the next.

Custodial parent. The parent who lives in the same household as the children following a divorce.

Custom complex. A customary practice and the beliefs, values, sanctions, rules, motives, and satisfactions associated with it; that is, a normative practice in a culture and the cultural beliefs that provide the basis for that practice.

Date rape. An act of sexual aggression in which a person, usually a woman, is forced by a romantic partner, date, or acquaintance to have sexual relations against her will.

Dating scripts. The cognitive models that guide dating interactions.

Debt bondage. Arrangement in which a person who is in debt pledges his labor or the labor of his children as payment.

Delinquency. Violations of the law committed by juveniles.

Demandingness. The degree to which parents set down rules and expectations for behavior and require their children to comply with them.

Demeanor. In Brake's description of youth cultures, refers to distinctive forms of gesture, gait, and posture.

Depressed mood. An enduring period of sadness, without any other related symptoms of depression.

Depression. An enduring period of sadness.

Depressive disorder. A clinical diagnosis that includes a range of specific symptoms such as depressed mood, appetite disturbances, sleeping disturbances, and fatigue.

Depressive syndrome. An enduring period of sadness along with other symptoms such as frequent crying, feelings of worthlessness, and feeling guilty, lonely, or worried.

Developing countries. Formerly traditional, preindustrial cultures that are in the process of becoming industrialized.

Dialectical thought. Type of thinking that develops in emerging adulthood, involving a growing awareness that most problems do not have a single solution and that problems must often be addressed with crucial pieces of information missing.

Diathesis-stress model. A theory that mental disorders result from the combination of a diathesis (biological vulnerability) and environmental stresses.

Differential gender socialization. The term for socializing males and females according to different expectations about what attitudes and behavior are appropriate to each gender.

Disequilibrium. In the family systems approach, this term is used in reference to a change that requires adjustments from family members.

Displacement effect. The extent to which media use takes time away from other activities.

Distancing hypothesis. Hypothesis that it may be adaptive for young people to move away from closeness to their parents when they reach sexual maturity so that they will mate and reproduce with persons outside the family, thus avoiding the genetic problems that often result from incest.

Divided attention. The ability to focus on more than one task at a time.

Dormitory. In some traditional cultures, a dwelling in which the community's adolescents sleep and spend their leisure time.

Double standard. Two different sets of rules for sexual behavior, one applying to males and the other females, with rules for females usually being more restrictive.

Driver education. Programs designed to teach young drivers safe driving skills before they receive their driver's licence.

Driving curfews. In graduated licensing programs, a feature of the restricted license stage in which young drivers are prohibited from driving late at night except for a specific purpose such as going back and forth to work.

Druggies. In adolescent crowds, the group known for drug use and alienation from school.

Dual-earner family. A family in which both parents are employed.

Dualistic thinking. Cognitive tendency to see situations and issues in polarized, absolute, black-and-white terms.

Dweebs. In adolescent crowds, the group known for lacking social skills.

Dyadic relationship. A relationship between two persons.

Early adolescence. Period of human development lasting from about age 10 to about age 14.

Effect size. The difference between two groups in a meta-analysis, represented by the letter *d*.

Emerging adulthood. Period from roughly ages 18 to 25 in industrialized countries during which young people become more independent from parents and explore various life possibilities before making enduring commitments.

Emotional loneliness. Condition that occurs when people feel that the relationships they have lack sufficient closeness and intimacy.

Empty love. In Sternberg's theory of love, the type of love that is based on commitment alone, without passion or intimacy.

Endocrine system. A network of glands in the body. Through hormones, the glands coordinate their functioning and affect the development and functioning of the body.

Engagement. The quality of being psychologically committed to learning, including being alert and attentive in the classroom and making a diligent effort to learn.

Esteem support. The support friends provide each other by providing congratulations for success and encouragement or consolation for failure.

Estradiol. The estrogen most important in pubertal development among girls.

Estrogens. The sex hormones that have especially high levels in females from puberty onward and are mostly responsible for female primary and secondary sex characteristics.

Ethnographic research. Research in which scholars spend a considerable amount of time among the people they wish to study, usually living among them.

Ethnography. A book that presents an anthropologist's observations of what life is like in a particular culture.

Ethos. The beliefs about education that characterize a school as a whole.

Evocative genotype–environment interactions. Occur when a person's inherited characteristics evoke responses from others in their environment.

Experience Sampling Method (ESM). Research method that involves having people wear beepers, usually for a period of one week. When they are beeped at random times during the day, they record a variety of characteristics of their experience at that moment.

Experiential intelligence. The ability to combine information in creative ways to produce new insights, ideas, and problem-solving strategies.

Experimental substance use. Trying a substance once or perhaps a few times out of curiosity.

Exploration. In research on identity formation, the term preferred by most current scholars for describing the process by which young people try out various possibilities in love, work, and ideology.

Expressive traits. Personality characteristics such as gentle and yielding, more often ascribed to females, emphasizing emotions and relationships.

Externalizing problems. Problems directed outward, such as delinquency and fighting.

Extremities. The feet, hands, and head.

False self. The self a person may present to others while realizing that it does not represent what he or she is actually thinking and feeling.

Familism. Concept of family life characteristic of Latino cultures that emphasizes the love, closeness, and mutual obligations of family life.

Family process. The quality of relationships among family members.

Family structure. The outward characteristics of a family, such as whether or not the parents are married.

Family systems approach. An approach to understanding family functioning that emphasizes how each relationship within the family influences the family as a whole.

Fatuous love. In Sternberg's theory of love, the type of love that involves passion and commitment without intimacy.

Feared self. The self a person imagines it is possible to become but dreads becoming.

Feedback loop. System of hormones involving the hypothalamus, the pituitary gland, and the gonads, which monitors and adjusts the levels of the sex hormones.

Field studies. Studies in which people's behavior is observed in a natural setting.

Filial piety. Confucian belief, common in many Asian societies, that children are obligated to respect, obey, and revere their parents, especially the father.

First-generation families. The status of persons who were born in one country and then immigrated to another.

Flapper. A young woman of the youth culture in the 1920s.

Fluid intelligence. Mental abilities that involve speed of analyzing, processing, and reacting to information.

Follicle-stimulating hormone (FSH). Along with LH, stimulates the development of gametes and sex hormones in the ovaries and testicles.

Follicles. Immature eggs in females' ovaries.

Formal operations. Cognitive stage from age 11 on up in which people learn to think systematically about possibilities and hypotheses.

Friends. Persons with whom an individual has a valued, mutual relationship.

Full license. In graduated licensing programs, the final stage, in which the young person has the same driving privileges as adults.

Gametes. Cells, distinctive to each sex, that are involved in reproduction (egg cells in the ovaries of the female and sperm in the testes of the male).

Gateway drugs. Term sometimes applied to alcohol, cigarettes, and marijuana because young people who use harder drugs usually use these drugs first.

Geeks. In adolescent crowds, the group known for doing well in school but lacking social skills. Also known as nerds.

Gender identity. Children's understanding of themselves as being either male or female, reached at about age 3.

Gender intensification hypothesis. Hypothesis that psychological and behavioral differences between males and females become more pronounced at adolescence because of intensified socialization pressures to conform to culturally prescribed gender roles.

Gender schema theory. Theory in which gender is viewed as one of the fundamental ways that people organize information about the world.

Gender. The social categories of male and female, established according to cultural beliefs and practices rather than being due to biology.

Generalizable. Characteristic of a sample that refers to the degree to which findings based on the sample can be used to make accurate statements about the population of interest.

Genital mutilation. Puberty ritual common in African cultures, in which parts of girls' genitals are cut off. Also known as female circumcision.

Gifted students. Students who have unusually high abilities in academics, art, or music.

Globalization. Increasing worldwide technological and economic integration, which is making different parts of the world increasingly connected and increasingly similar culturally.

Gonadotropin-releasing hormone (GnRH). Hormone released by the hypothalamus that causes gonadotropins to be released by the pituitary.

Gonadotropins. Hormones (FSH and LH) that stimulate the development of gametes.

Gonads. The ovaries and testicles. Also known as the sex glands.

Graduated licensing. Program in which young people receive driving privileges in steps, contingent on a safe driving record at each step.

Harvard Adolescence Project. Project initiated by Beatrice and John Whiting of Harvard University in the 1980s, in which they sent young scholars to do ethnographic research in seven different cultures in various parts of the world.

Headbangers. In adolescent crowds, the group known for liking heavy-metal music. Also known as metalheads.

Health promotion. Efforts to reduce health problems in young people through encouraging changes in the behaviors that put young people at risk.

Heteronomous morality. Piaget's term for the period of moral development from about age 4 to about age 7, in which moral rules are viewed as having a sacred, fixed quality, handed down from figures of authority and alterable only by them.

Holistic perspective. In theories of cognitive development, the quality of focusing on how human cognition works as a whole rather than as a set of isolated parts.

Homophobia. Fear and hatred of homosexuals.

Hormones. Chemicals, released by the glands of the endocrine system, that affect the development and functioning of the body, including development during puberty.

Howard Gardner. Psychologist who has proposed a theory of multiple intelligences.

Hypothalamus. The "master gland," located in the lower part of the brain beneath the cortex, that affects a wide range of physiological and psychological functioning and stimulates and regulates the production of hormones by other glands, including the initiation of puberty.

Hypothetical-deductive reasoning. Piaget's term for the process by which the formal operational thinker systematically tests possible solutions to a problem and arrives at an answer that can be defended and explained.

Ideal self. The self a person would like to be.

Identifications. Relationships formed with others, especially in childhood, in which love for another person leads one to want to be like that person.

Identity. Individuals' perceptions of their characteristics and abilities, their beliefs and values, their relations with others, and how their lives fit into the world around them.

Identity achievement. The identity status of young people who have made definite personal, occupational, and ideological choices following a period of exploring possible alternatives.

Identity crisis. Erikson's term for the intense period of struggle that adolescents may experience in the course of forming an identity.

Identity diffusion. An identity status that combines no exploration with no commitment. No commitments have been made among the available paths of identity formation, and the person is not seriously attempting to sort through potential choices and make enduring commitments.

Identity foreclosure. An identity status in which young people have not experimented with a range of possibilities but have nevertheless committed themselves to certain choices—commitment, but no exploration.

Identity moratorium. An identity status that involves exploration but no commitment, in which young people are trying out different personal, occupational, and ideological possibilities.

Identity versus identity confusion. Erikson's term for the crisis typical of the adolescent stage of life, in which individuals may follow the healthy path of establishing a clear and definite sense of who they are and how they fit into the world around them, or follow the unhealthy alternative of failing to form a stable and secure identity.

Image. In Brake's description of the characteristics of youth culture, refers to dress, hair style, jewelry, and other aspects of appearance.

Imaginary audience. Belief that others are acutely aware of and attentive to one's appearance and behavior.

Implicit personality theories. Judgments about what other persons are like and why they behave the way they do.

Inclusion. The policy of striving to make the education of disabled adolescents similar to the experience of other adolescents by having them learn in regular classrooms as much as possible. Also known as mainstreaming.

Independent self. A conception of the self typically found in individualistic cultures, in which the self is seen as existing independently of relations with others, with an emphasis on independence, individual freedoms, and individual achievements.

Index crimes. Serious crimes divided into two categories: violent crimes such as rape, assault, and murder, and property crimes such as robbery, motor vehicle theft, and arson.

Indifferent parents. Parenting style in which parents are low in both demandingness and responsiveness and relatively uninvolved in their children's development.

Individual differences. Approach to research that focuses on how individuals differ within a group, for example, in performance on IQ tests.

Individualism. Cultural belief system that emphasizes the desirability of independence, self-sufficiency, and self-expression.

Individuating-reflective faith. Fowler's term for the stage of faith most typical of late adolescence and emerging adulthood, in which people rely less on what their parents believed and develop a more individualized faith based on questioning their beliefs and incorporating their personal experience into their beliefs.

Indulgent parents. Parenting style in which parents are low in demandingness and high in responsiveness. They show love and affection toward their children but are permissive with regard to standards for behavior.

Industrialized countries. The countries of the West and Eastern countries such as Japan and South Korea. All of them have highly developed economies that are based mainly on services and information.

Infatuation. In Sternberg's theory of love, the type of love that is based on passion alone, without intimacy or commitment.

Information-processing approach. An approach to understanding cognition that seeks to delineate the steps involved in the thinking process and how each step is connected to the next.

Informational support. Between friends, advice and guidance in solving personal problems.

Informed consent. Standard procedure in social scientific studies that entails informing potential participants of what their participation would involve, including any possible risks.

Initiation phase. In Brown's developmental model of adolescent love, the first phase, usually in early adolescence, when the first tentative explorations of romantic interests begin, usually superficial and brief, often fraught with anxiety, fear, and excitement.

Insecure attachment. Type of attachment to caregiver in which infants are timid about exploring the environment and resist or avoid the caregiver when she attempts to offer comfort or consolation.

Instrumental support. Between friends, help with tasks of various kind.

Instrumental traits. Personality characteristics such as self-reliant and forceful, more often ascribed to males, emphasizing action and accomplishment.

Intelligence quotient. A measure of a person's intellectual abilities based on a standardized test.

Interdependence. The web of commitments, attachments, and obligations that exist in some human groups.

Interdependent self. A conception of the self typically found in collectivistic cultures, in which the self is seen as defined by relations with others, with an emphasis on cooperation, mutual support, maintaining harmonious social relations, and contributing to the group.

Internal consistency. A statistical calculation that indicates the extent to which the different items in a scale or subscale are answered in a similar way.

Internal working model. In attachment theory, the term for the cognitive framework, based on interactions in infancy with the primary caregiver, that shapes expectations and interactions in relationships to others throughout life.

Internalizing problems. Problems such as depression and anxiety that take place when people turn their distress inward, toward themselves.

International Labor Organization (ILO). An organization that seeks to prevent children and adolescents from being exploited in the workplace.

Interventions. Programs designed to apply social science knowledge to change people's cognitions or behavior.

Interview. Research method that involves asking people questions in a conversational format, such that people's answers are in their own words.

Intimacy versus isolation. Erikson's term for the central issue of young adulthood, in which persons face alternatives between committing themselves to another person in an intimate relationship or becoming isolated as a consequence of an inability to form an enduring intimate relationship.

Intimacy. The degree to which two people share personal knowledge, thoughts, and feelings.

Inventionist view. Theory that adolescence was invented during the early 20th century as a way of keeping young people excluded from adult work by putting them in educational institutions where they would be dependent on adults.

Isolation of variables. Cognitive skill of systematically changing one variable while the others are held constant.

Jean Piaget. Influential Swiss developmental psychologist, best known for his theories of cognitive and moral development.

Jocks. In adolescent crowds, the group known for excelling in athletics.

Justice orientation. A type of moral orientation that places a premium on abstract principles of justice, equality, and fairness.

Juveniles. Persons defined by the legal system as being younger than adult status.

Koran. The holy book of the religion of Islam, believed by Muslims to have been communicated to Muhammad from God through the angel Gabriel.

Labeling theory. Theory that delinquency results when young children do poorly in school and are labeled as failures, which causes them to develop an identity as a failure and as deviant, expressed in adolescence as delinquency.

Labia majora. Part of vulva; Latin for "large lips."

Labia minora. Part of vulva; Latin for "small lips."

Lamarckian. Reference to Lamarck's ideas, popular in the late 19th and early 20th centuries, that evolution takes place as a result of accumulated experience such that organisms pass on their characteristics from one generation to the next in the form of memories and acquired characteristics.

Late adolescence. Period of human development lasting from about age 15 to about age 18.

Latency periods. A period, common with STDs, between the time a person is infected with the a disease and the time symptoms appear.

Learning license. In graduated licensing programs, the stage in which the young person undergoes a period of obtaining driving experience under the supervision of an experienced driver.

Life-course persistent delinquents (LCPDs). In Moffitt's theory, adolescents who show a history of related problems both prior to and following adolescence.

Life-cycle service. A period in their late teens and twenties in which young people from the 16th to the 19th century engaged

in domestic service, farm service, or apprenticeship in various trades and crafts.

Liking. In Sternberg's theory of love, the type of love that is based on intimacy alone, without passion or commitment.

Long-term memory. Memory for information that is committed to longer-term storage, so that it can be drawn upon after a period when attention has not been focused on it.

Longitudinal study. Study in which the same individuals are followed across time and data on them is collected on more than one occasion.

Low impulse control. Difficulty in exercising self-control, often found to be related to risk behavior in adolescence.

Luteinizing hormone (LH). Along with FSH, stimulates the development of gametes and sex hormones in the ovaries and testicles.

Machismo. Ideology of manhood, common in Latino cultures, which emphasizes males' dominance over females.

Mainstreaming. The policy of striving to make the education of disabled adolescents similar to the experience of other adolescents by having them learn in regular classrooms as much as possible. Also known as inclusion.

Majority culture. The culture in a society that sets most of the norms and standards and holds most of the positions of political, economic, intellectual, and media power. The term *American majority culture* refers to the mostly White middle-class majority in American society.

Marginality. In the formation of ethnic identity, the option that involves rejecting one's culture of origin but also feeling rejected by the majority culture.

Maturation. Process by which abilities develop through genetically based development with limited influence from the environment.

Maximum oxygen uptake (VO$_2$ max). A measure of the ability of the body to take in oxygen and transport it to various organs; peaks in the early twenties.

Measures. Approaches and instruments used in scientific studies.

Median. In a distribution of scores, the point at which half of the population scores above and half below.

Medicinal substance use. Substance use undertaken for the purpose of relieving an unpleasant emotional state such as sadness, anxiety, stress, or loneliness.

Men's house. In some traditional cultures, a dormitory where adolescent boys sleep and hang out along with adult men who are widowed or divorced.

Menarche. A girl's first menstrual period.

Mental operations. Cognitive activity involving ability to manipulate objects mentally and reason about them in a way that accurately represents how the world works.

Mental structure. The organization of cognitive abilities into a single pattern, such that thinking in all aspects of life is a reflection of that structure.

Meta-analysis. A statistical technique that integrates the data from many studies into one comprehensive statistical analysis.

Metacognition. The capacity for "thinking about thinking" that allows adolescents and adults to monitor and reason about their thought processes.

Midadolescence peak. In research on depression, the peak risk for depressed mood that falls in the mid-teens.

Midlife crisis. The popular belief, largely unfounded according to research, that most people experience a crisis when they reach about age 40, involving intensive reexamination of their lives and perhaps sudden and dramatic changes if they are dissatisfied.

Mikveh. Among Orthodox Jews, the traditional ritual bath taken by a woman seven days after her menstrual period was finished, as a way of ridding herself of the uncleanness believed to be associated with menstruation.

Mnemonic devices. Memory strategies.

Multiple thinking. Cognitive approach entailing recognition that there is more than one legitimate view of things and that it can be difficult to justify one position as the true or accurate one.

Mutual perspective taking. Stage of perspective taking, often found in early adolescence, in which persons understand that their perspective-taking interactions with others are mutual, in the sense that each side realizes that the other can take their perspective.

Narrow socialization. The process by which persons in a collectivistic culture come to learn collectivism, including values of obedience and conformity.

National survey. Questionnaire study that involves asking a sample of persons in a country to respond to questions about their opinions, beliefs, or behavior.

Natural experiment. A situation that occurs naturally but that provides interesting scientific information to the perceptive observer.

Nature–nurture debate. Debate over the relative importance of biology and the environment in human development.

Negative identity. Erikson's term for an identity based on what a person has seen portrayed as most undesirable or dangerous.

Neglected adolescents. Adolescents who are ignored by their peers.

Nerds. In adolescent crowds, the group known for doing well in school but lacking social skills. Also known as geeks.

Nobodies. In adolescent crowds, the adolescents mostly ignored by their peers.

Nonindex crimes. Crimes such as illegal gambling, prostitution, and disorderly conduct, considered less serious offenses than index crimes.

Normals. In adolescent crowds, the adolescents not affiliated with any distinctive group.

Novelty and intensity. The two characteristics believed to underlie the personality trait of sensation seeking.

Occupational deviance. Deviant acts committed in relation to the workplace, such as stealing supplies.

Ontogenetic. Something that occurs naturally in the course of development as part of normal maturation; that is, it is driven by innate processes rather than by environmental stimulation or a specific cultural practice.

Open-ended question. Questionnaire format that involves writing in responses to each question.

Optimistic bias. The tendency to assume that accidents, diseases, and other misfortunes are more likely to happen to other people than to one's self.

Organizational core. Term applied especially to cognitive development, meaning that cognitive development affects all areas of thinking, no matter what the topic.

Overcontrolled. Personality characterized by inhibition, anxiety, and self-punishment, sometimes ascribed to adolescents who have internalizing problems.

Overevaluation. Evaluating persons favorably because they violate gender norms.

Ovum. Mature egg that develops from follicle in ovaries about every 28 days.

Parental consent. A legal requirement, in some states, that minors must obtain their parents' permission to have an abortion.

Parental monitoring. The degree to which parents keep track of where their adolescents are and what they are doing.

Parental notification. A legal requirement, in some states, that minors must notify their parents before having the abortion.

Parenting styles. The patterns of practices that parents exhibit in relation to their children.

Participant observation. A research method that involves taking part in various activities with the people being studied, and learning about them through participating in the activities with them.

Passionate manhood. Anthony Rotundo's term for the norm of manhood in the 20th-century United States, in which self-expression and self-enjoyment replaced self-control and self-denial as the paramount virtues young males should learn in the course of becoming a man.

Passive genotype–environment interactions. Situation in biological families that parents provide both genes and environment for their children, making genes and environment difficult to separate in their effects on children's development.

Patriarchal. Social rules or system in which males dominate and the rights and opportunities of women are limited.

Peace Corps. An international service program in which Americans provide service to a community in a foreign country for 2 years.

Peak height velocity. The point at which the adolescent growth spurt is at its maximum rate.

Peers. People who share some aspect of their status, such as being the same age.

Pendulum problem. Piaget's classic test of formal operations, in which persons are asked to figure out what determines the speed at which a pendulum sways from side to side.

Performance subtests. In the Wechsler IQ tests, subtests that examine abilities for attention, spatial perception, and speed of processing.

Performance videos. Music videos that show an individual performer or a group singing a song in a concert setting or a studio.

Permissive cultures. Cultures that encourage and expect sexual activity from their adolescents.

Personal fable. A belief in one's personal uniqueness, often including a sense of invulnerability to the consequences of taking risks.

Perspective taking. The ability to understand the thoughts and feelings of others.

Pilot testing. In research, trying out the measures on a small number of potential participants before the larger study begins to make sure the measures have adequate reliability and validity.

Pituitary gland. A gland about half an inch long located at the base of the brain that releases gonadotropins as part of the body's preparation for reproduction.

Placebo design. Research design in which some persons in a study receive medication and others receive placebos, which are pills that appear to be medication but actually contain no medication.

Poetic-conventional faith. Fowler's term for the stage of faith development most typical of early adolescence, in which people become more aware of the symbolism used in their faith and religious understanding becomes more complex in the sense that early adolescents increasingly believe that there is more than one way of knowing the truth.

Populars. In adolescent crowds, the group known for having the highest social status. Also known as trendies.

Population. The entire group of people of interest in a study.

Possible selves. A person's conceptions of the self as it potentially may be. May include both an ideal self and a feared self.

Postconventional reasoning. In Kohlberg's theory of moral development, the level in which moral reasoning is based on the individual's own independent judgments rather than on egocentric considerations or considerations of what others view as wrong or right.

Postfigurative cultures. Cultures in which what children and adolescents need to learn to function as adults changes little from one generation to the next, and therefore children and adolescents can learn all they need to know from their elders.

Postformal thinking. Type of thinking beyond formal operations, involving greater awareness of the complexity of real-life situations, such as in the use of pragmatism and reflective judgment.

Pragmatism. Type of thinking that involves adapting logical thinking to the practical constraints of real-life situations.

Preconventional reasoning. In Kohlberg's theory of moral development, the level in which moral reasoning is based on perceptions of the likelihood of external rewards and punishments.

Prefigurative cultures. Cultures in which young people teach knowledge to adults.

Premenstrual syndrome (PMS). The combination of behavioral, emotional, and physical symptoms that occur in some females the week before menstruation.

Preoperational stage. Cognitive stage from age 2 to 7 during which the child becomes capable of representing the world symbolically—for example, through the use of language—but is still very limited in ability to use mental operations.

Primary caregiver. The person mainly responsible for caring for an infant or young child.

Primary sex characteristics. The production of eggs and sperm and the development of the sex organs.

Proactive script. A dating script, more common for males than for females, that includes initiating the date, deciding where they will go, controlling the public domain (e.g., driving the car and opening the doors), and initiating sexual contact.

Problem behavior syndrome. The pattern of correlations between various types of problem behavior.

Problem behavior theory. Richard Jessor's theory of the basis for young people's problem behavior, including background factors such as family income, personality factors such as self-esteem, and social factors such as parental controls and friends' involvement in problem behavior.

Problem behavior. Behavior that young people engage in that is viewed by adults as a source of problems, such as unprotected premarital sex and substance use.

Problem finding. Type of postformal thinking that involves generating a variety of possible solutions to complex problems and seeing old problems in new ways.

Procedure. Standards for the way a study is conducted. Includes informed consent and certain rules for avoiding biases in the data collection.

Procreate. In the manhood requirements of traditional cultures, the requirement of being able to function sexually well enough to produce children.

Propensity and opportunity. The two factors believed by some sociologists to explain all deviance. Propensity means motivation for behaving deviantly.

Property crimes. Crimes that involve taking or damaging others' property, for example, robbery and arson.

Proportional reasoning. Cognitive skill of understanding how different variables in a given situation are related to each other.

Protect. In the manhood requirements of traditional cultures, the requirement of being able to assist in protecting one's family and community from human and animal attackers.

Protective factor. Characteristics of young people that are related to lower likelihood of participation in risk behavior.

Provide. In the manhood requirements of traditional cultures, the requirement of being able to provide economically for one's self as well as a wife and children.

Psychohistory. The psychological analysis of important historical figures.

Psychometric approach. Attempt to understand human cognition by evaluating cognitive abilities using intelligence tests.

Psychosocial moratorium. Erikson's term for a period during adolescence when adult responsibilities are postponed as young people try on various possible selves.

Puberty. The changes in physiology, anatomy, and physical functioning that develop a person into a mature adult biologically and prepare the body for sexual reproduction.

Public Law 94-142. A federal law requiring school authorities to provide all children and adolescents with disabilities with an individualized educational program suited to their particular needs.

Purging. Self-induced vomiting that follows binge eating for persons who have bulimia.

Qualitative. Data that is collected in verbal rather than numerical form, usually in interviews.

Quantitative. Data that is collected in numerical form, usually on questionnaires.

Ramadan. A month in the Muslim year that commemorates the revelation of the Koran from God to the prophet Muhammad, requiring fasting from sunrise to sunset each day and refraining from all sensual indulgences.

Random sample. Sampling technique in which the people selected for participation in a study are chosen randomly, meaning that no one in the population has a better or worse chance of being selected than anyone else.

Rave. An impromptu all-night dance party.

Reaction range. Term meaning that genes establish a range of possible development and environment determines where development takes place within that range.

Reactive script. A dating script, more common for females than males, that focuses on the private domain (e.g., spending considerable time on dress and grooming prior to the date), responding to the date's gestures in the public domain (e.g., being picked up, waiting for him to open the doors), and responding to his sexual initiatives.

Recapitulation. Now-discredited theory that held that the development of each individual recapitulates the evolutionary development of the human species as a whole.

Reciprocal effects. In relations between parents and children, the concept that children not only are affected by their parents but affect their parents in return. Also called bidirectional effects.

Reductionism. Breaking up a phenomenon into separate parts to such an extent that the meaning and coherence of the phenomenon as a whole becomes lost.

Reflective judgment. The capacity to evaluate the accuracy and logical coherence of evidence and arguments.

Rejected adolescents. Adolescents who are actively disliked by their peers.

Relatedness. The quality of being emotionally close to another person.

Relative performance. In IQ tests, performance results compared to other persons of the same age.

Relativism. Cognitive ability to recognize the legitimacy of competing points of view but also compare the relative merits of competing views.

Reliability. Characteristic of a measure that refers to the extent to which results of the measure on one occasion are similar to results of the measure on a separate occasion.

Representative. Characteristic of a sample that refers to the degree to which it accurately represents the population of interest.

Response bias. On a questionnaire, the tendency to choose the same response for all items.

Responsiveness. The degree to which parents are sensitive to their children's needs and express love, warmth, and concern for them.

Restricted license. In graduated licensing programs, the stage in which adolescents are allowed to drive unsupervised, but with tighter restrictions than those that apply to adults.

Restrictive cultures. Cultures that place strong prohibitions on adolescent sexual activity before marriage.

Retention rate. In a longitudinal study, the percentage of participants who continued to take part in the study after the first year.

Retention. The term used for the degree to which college students persist in their studies until they graduate.

Risk behavior. Problems that involve the risk of negative outcomes, such as risky driving and substance use.

Rival relationship. Between siblings, a relationship in which they compete against each other and measure their success against one another.

Robert Sternberg. Psychologist who has proposed a triarchic theory of intelligence and a triarchic theory of love.

Role preparation. An outcome of socialization that includes preparation for occupational roles, gender roles, and roles in institutions such as marriage and parenthood.

Roles. Defined social positions in a culture, containing specifications of behavior, status, and relations with others. Examples include gender, age, and social class.

Romantic love. In Sternberg's theory of love, the type of love that combines passion and intimacy, but without commitment.

Sample. The people included in a given study, who are intended to represent the population of interest.

Sampling. Collecting data on a subset of the members of a group.

Schema. Piaget's term for a structure for organizing and processing information.

School climate. The quality of interactions between teachers and students, including how teachers interact with students, what sort of expectations and standards they have for students, and what kinds of methods are used in the classroom.

Scientific method. A systematic way of finding the answers to questions or problems that includes standards of sampling, procedure, and measures.

Second shift. The domestic work shift performed in the household by women after they complete their first shift in the workplace.

Second-generation families. The status of persons who were born in the country they currently reside in but whose parents were born in a different country.

Secondary school. The schools attended by adolescents, including middle school and junior high school followed by high school.

Secondary sex characteristics. Bodily changes resulting from the hormonal changes of puberty, not including the ones related directly to reproduction.

Secular trend. A change in the characteristics of a population over time.

Secular. Based on nonreligious beliefs and values.

Secure attachment. Type of attachment to caregiver in which infants use the caregiver as a "secure base from which to explore" when all is well, but seek physical comfort and consolation from her if frightened or threatened.

Selective association. The principle that most people tend to choose friends who are similar to themselves.

Selective attention. The ability to focus on relevant information while screening out information that is irrelevant.

Self-concept. Persons' views of themselves, usually including concrete characteristics (such as height and age) as well as roles, relationships, and personality characteristics.

Self-esteem. A person's overall sense of worth and well-being.

Self-image. A person's evaluation of his or her qualities and relations with others. Closely related to self-esteem.

Self-made manhood. Anthony Rotundo's term for the norm of manhood in 19th-century America, in which males were increasingly expected to become independent from their families in adolescence and emerging adulthood as part of becoming a man.

Self-medication. The use of substances for relieving unpleasant states such as sadness or stress.

Self-perception. A person's view of his or her characteristics and abilities. Closely related to self-esteem.

Self-reflection. The capacity for thinking about one's self and one's characteristics, abilities, motivations, and desires.

Self-regulation. The capacity for exercising self-control in order to restrain one's impulses and comply with social norms.

Self-socialization. In gender socialization, refers to the way that children seek to maintain consistency between the norms they have learned about gender and their behavior.

Semenarche. A male's first ejaculation.

Semirestrictive cultures. Cultures that have prohibitions on premarital adolescent sex, but the prohibitions are not strongly enforced and are easily evaded.

Sensation seeking. A personality characteristic defined by the extent to which a person enjoys novelty and intensity of sensation.

Sensorimotor stage. Cognitive stage in first 2 years of life that involves learning how to coordinate the activities of the senses with motor activities.

Separation. In the formation of ethnic identity, the approach that involves associating only with members of one's own ethnic group and rejecting the ways of the majority culture.

Set point. Optimal level of sex hormones in the body. When this point is reached, responses in the glands of the feedback loop cause the production of sex hormones to be reduced.

Sex hormones. Androgens and estrogens that cause the development of primary and secondary sex characteristics.

Sex. The biological status of being male or female.

Sexist. Discriminating against other persons on the basis of their being male or female.

Sexual harassment. A wide range of threatening or aggressive behaviors related to sexuality, from mild harassment such as name-calling, jokes, and leering looks to severe harassment involving unwanted touching or sexual contact.

Sexual scripts. Cognitive frameworks, often different for males and females, for understanding how a sexual experience is supposed to proceed and how sexual experiences are to be interpreted.

Sexuality. Biological sexual development as well as sexual values, beliefs, thoughts, feelings, relationships, and behavior.

Short-term memory. Memory for information that is currently the focus of attention, with limited capacity and retention.

Social and conventional system perspective taking. Realizing that the social perspectives of self and others are influenced not just by their interaction with each other but by their roles in the larger society.

Social cognition. How people think about other people, social relationships, and social institutions.

Social desirability. The tendency for people participating in social science studies to report their behavior as they believe it would be approved by others rather than as it actually occurred.

Social loneliness. Condition that occurs when people feel that they lack a sufficient number of social contacts and relationships.

Social roles theory. Theory that social roles for males and females enhance or suppress different capabilities, so that males and females tend to develop different skills and attitudes, which leads to gender-specific behaviors.

Social skills. Skills for successfully handling social relations and getting along well with others.

Social substance use. The use of substances in the course of social activities with one or more friends.

Socialization. The process by which people acquire the behaviors and beliefs of the culture in which they live.

Socialized delinquents. Adolescents who commit acts of delinquency as part of a group or gang.

Society. A group of people who interact in the course of sharing a common geographical area. A single society may include a variety of different cultures.

Socioeconomic status (SES). A person or group's social class, which includes educational level, income level, and occupational status.

Sociometry. A method for assessing popularity and unpopularity that involves having students rate the social status of other students.

Sources of meaning. The ideas and beliefs that people learn as part of socialization, indicating what is important, what is to be valued, what is to be lived for, and how to explain and offer consolation for the individual's mortality.

Spermarche. Beginning of development of sperm in boys' testicles at puberty.

Stage. A period in which abilities are organized in a coherent, interrelated way.

Stanford-Binet. Widely used IQ test developed by Alfred Binet and revised by scholars at Stanford University.

Status offenses. Offenses such as running away from home that are defined as violations of the law only because they are committed by juveniles.

Status phase. In Brown's developmental model of adolescent love, the second phase, in which adolescents begin to gain confidence in their skills at interacting with potential romantic partners and begin to form their first romantic relationships, assessing not just how much they like and are attracted to the person, but also how their status with friends and peers would be influenced.

Stereotype. A belief that others possess certain characteristics simply as a result of being a member of a particular group.

Storm and stress. Theory promoted by G. Stanley Hall asserting that adolescence is inevitably a time of mood disruptions, conflict with parents, and antisocial behavior.

Straight-edge. Young people who abstain from all substance use.

Strain theory. Theory that children from lower social classes frequently do poorly in school because they do not believe that hard work in school will be rewarded with economic success once they leave school, resulting in frustration (strain) that becomes expressed in adolescence as delinquency.

Stratified sampling. Sampling technique in which researchers select participants so that various categories of people are represented in proportions equal to their presence in the population

Style. The distinguishing features of youth culture, including image, demeanor, and argot.

Subfecundity. The condition for girls in the first 2 years after menarche, in which they ovulate irregularly and are less likely to become pregnant during this time than later, after their cycle of ovulation has been established.

Subordinate/castelike minority. Ogbu's term for the condition of minority groups whose ancestors did not voluntarily become part of the United States, such as African Americans and Native Americans.

Substance use. Use of substances that have cognitive and mood-altering affects, including alcohol, cigarettes, and illegal drugs such as marijuana, LSD, and cocaine.

Subterranean values. Values such as hedonism, excitement, and adventure, asserted by sociologists to be the basis of youth culture.

Survey. A questionnaire study that involves asking a large number of people questions about their opinions, beliefs, or behavior.

Symbolic inheritance. The set of ideas and understandings, both implicit and explicit, about persons, society, nature, and divinity that serve as a guide to life in a particular culture. Expressed symbolically through stories, songs, rituals, sacred objects, and sacred places.

Techno. Music popular at raves, characterized by a pounding beat and the use of electronically produced sounds and rhythms. Also known as house music.

Test-retest reliability. Type of reliability that examines whether or not persons' scores on one occasion are similar to their scores on another occasion.

Testosterone. The androgen most important in pubertal development among boys.

The forgotten half. The nearly half of young Americans who enter the workplace following high school rather then attending college.

The new basic skills. Skills identified by Murnane and Levy that are required for high school graduates who wish to be able to obtain the best jobs available in the new information-based economy.

The West. Majority cultures of the United States, Canada, Western Europe, Australia, and New Zealand. Common features include industrialization, free-market economies, and representative democracies.

Theory of genotype–environment interactions. Theory that both genetics and environment make essential contributions to human development but are difficult to unravel because our genes actually influence the kind of environment we experience.

Theory of multiple intelligences. Howard Gardner's theory that there are eight separate types of intelligence.

Traditional cultures. Cultures that have maintained a way of life based on stable traditions passed from one generation to the next. Often—but not always—traditional cultures are preindustrial.

Traditional parenting style. The kind of parenting typical in traditional cultures, high in responsiveness and high in a kind of demandingness that does not encourage discussion and debate but rather expects compliance by virtue of cultural beliefs supporting the inherent authority of the parental role.

Trendies. In adolescent crowds, the group known for having the highest social status. Also known as populars.

Triarchic theory of intelligence. Sternberg's theory that intelligence can be understood as comprising three distinct but related forms: componential, experiential, and contextual.

Undercontrolled. Personality characterized by a lack of self-control, sometimes ascribed to adolescents who have externalizing problems.

Underemployed. Working at a job that requires a lower level of skills or credentials than the person possesses.

Unemployed. The status of persons who are not in school, not working, and who are looking for a job.

Unsocialized delinquents. Delinquent adolescents who have few friends and commit their crimes alone.

Unstructured socializing. The term for young people spending time together with no specific event as the center of their activity.

Uses and gratifications approach. Approach to understanding media that emphasizes that people differ in numerous ways that lead them to make different choices about which media to consume and that even people consuming the same media product will respond to it in a variety of ways, depending on their individual characteristics.

Validity. The truthfulness of a measure, that is, the extent to which it measures what it claims to measure.

Verbal subtests. In the Wechsler IQ tests, subtests that examine verbal abilities.

Violent crimes. Crimes that involve physical harm to others, for example, assault and murder.

Vital capacity. The amount of air that can be exhaled after a deep breath, which increases rapidly during puberty, especially for boys.

Vulva. External female sex organs, including the labia majora, the labia minora, and the clitoris.

Wasting syndrome. A symptom of AIDS, in which the person loses a great deal of body weight and becomes extremely emaciated.

Wechsler Adult Intelligence Scale (WAIS-III). Intelligence test for persons aged 16 and up, with six Verbal and five Performance subtests.

Wechsler Intelligence Scale for Children (WISC-III). Intelligence test for children aged 6 to 16, with six Verbal and five Performance subtests.

Withdrawal symptoms. States such as high anxiety and tremors experienced by persons who stop taking the substance to which they are addicted.

Women's movement. Organized effort in the 20th century to obtain greater rights and opportunities for women.

Young people. Combined term for adolescents and emerging adults.

Youth. Prior to the late 19th century, the term used to refer to persons in their teens and early twenties.

Youth culture. The culture of young people as a whole, separate from children and separate from adult society, characterized by values of hedonism and irresponsibility.

Zero tolerance. In graduated licensing programs, a feature of the restricted license stage in which young drivers are in violation if they drive with any alcohol at all in their blood.

References

AAUW. (1993). *Hostile hallways: The AAUW survey on sexual harassment in America's schools.* Washington, DC: American Association of University Women Educational Foundation.

Aboud, F. E., & Mendelson, M. J. (1998). Determinants of friendship selection and quality: Developmental perspectives. In W. M. Bukowski, W. H. Hartup, & A. F. Newcomb (Eds.), *The company they keep: Friendship in childhood and adolescence* (pp. 87–112). New York: Cambridge University Press.

Achenbach, T. M., & Edelbrock, C. (1986). *Manual for the teacher's report form and teacher version of the child behavior profile.* Burlington: University of Vermont, Department of Psychiatry.

Achenbach, T. M., Howell, C. T., Quay, H. C., & Conners, C. K. (1991). National survey of problems and competencies among four- to sixteen-year-olds. *Monographs of the Society for Research in Child Development, 56* (3, Serial No. 225).

Adams, G. R. (1999). *The objective measure of ego identity status: A manual on test theory and construction.* Guelph, Canada: Author.

Adams, G. R., Gullotta, T. P., & Montemayor, R. (Eds.). (1992). *Adolescent identity formation.* Newbury Park, CA: Sage.

Adams, G. R., Openshaw, D. K., Bennion, L., Mills, T., & Noble, S. (1988). Loneliness in late adolescence: A social skills training study. *Journal of Adolescent Research, 3,* 81–96.

Adegoke, A. (1993). The experience of spermarche (the age of onset of sperm emission) among selected adolescent boys in Nigeria. *Journal of Youth and Adolescence, 22,* 201–209.

Adelson, J. (1971). The political imagination of the young adolescent. *Daedalus, 100,* 1013–1050.

Adelson, J. (1991). Political development. In R. M. Lerner, A. C. Petersen, & J. Brooks-Gunn (Eds.), *Encyclopedia of adolescence* (Vol. 2, pp. 792–793). New York: Garland.

Adler, P., & Adler, P. (1998). *Peer power.* New Brunswick, NJ: Rutgers University Press.

Agras, W. S., Schneider, J., Arnow, B., Raeburn, S., & Teich, C. (1989). Cognitive-behavioral and response-prevention treatments for bulimia nervosa. *Journal of Consulting and Clinical Psychology, 57,* 215–221.

Aguirre International. (1999). *Making a difference: Impact of AmeriCorps state/national direct on members and communities, 1994–95 and 1995–96.* San Mateo, CA: Author.

Ahmed, L. (1992). *Women and gender in Islam.* New Haven, CT: Yale University Press.

Ainsworth, M. D. S. (1967). *Infancy in Uganda: Infant care and the growth of love.* Baltimore, MD: Johns Hopkins University Press.

Ainsworth, M. D. S. (1982). Attachment: Retrospect and prospect. In C. M. Parkes & J. Stevenson-Hinde (Eds.), *The place of attachment in human behavior.* New York: Basic Books.

Akhtar, S. (1984). The syndrome of identity diffusion. *American Journal of Psychiatry, 141,* 1381–1385.

Alan Guttmacher Institute (AGI). (1994). *Sex and America's teenagers.* New York: Author.

Alexander, B. (1998, June). Abstinence fund watchdog bites states. *Youth Today, 7,* 1, 18.

Alexander, K., & Cook, M. (1982). Curricula and coursework: A surprise ending to a familiar story. *American Sociological Review, 47,* 626–640.

Alexander, K., & Eckland, B. (1975). School experience and status attainment. In S. Dragastin & G. Elder, Jr. (Eds.), *Adolescence in the life cycle.* Washington, DC: Hemisphere.

Alexander, P. C., Moore, S., & Alexander, E. R., III (1991). What is transmitted in the intergenerational transmission of violence? *Journal of Marriage and the Family, 53,* 657–668.

Allen, F. L. (1964). *Only yesterday: An informal history of the 1920s.* New York: Harper & Row.

Allen, J. P., & Bell, K. L. (1995, March). *Attachment and communication with parents and peers in adolescence.* Paper presented at the meeting of the Society for Research in Child Development, Indianapolis.

Allen, J. P., & Kuperminc, G. P. (1995, March). *Adolescent attachment, social competence, and problematic behavior.* Paper presented at the meeting of the Society for Research in Child Development, Indianapolis.

Allen, J. P., Moore, C., Kuperminc, G., & Bell, K. (1998). Attachment and adolescent psychosocial functioning. *Child Development, 69,* 1406–1419.

Allen, J., & Land, P. (1999). Attachment in adolescence. In J. Cassidy & P. R. Shaver (Eds.), *Handbook of attachment: Theory, research, and clinical applications.* New York: Guilford.

Allen, J., Hauser, S., Bell, K., & O'Connor, T. (1994). Longitudinal assessment of autonomy and relatedness in adolescent–family interactions as predictors of adolescent ego development and self-esteem. *Child Development, 65,* 179–194.

Allen, L. S., & Gorski, R. A. (1992). Sexual orientation and the size of the anterior commissure in the human brain. *Proceed-ings of the National Academy of Sciences, USA, 89,* 7199–7202.

Allgood-Merten, B., Lewinson, R., & Hops, H. (1990). Sex differences and adolescent depression. *Journal of Abnormal Psychology, 99,* 55–63.

Allison, R., & Furstenberg, F., Jr. (1989). How marital dissolution affects children: Variations by age and sex. *Developmental Psychology, 25,* 540–549,

Almquist, E. M. (1989). The experiences of minority women in the United States: Intersections of race, gender, and class. In J. Freeman (Ed.), *Women: A feminist perspective* (4th ed., pp. 414–456). Mountain View, CA: Mayfield.

Alsaker, F. D., & Flammer, A. (1999). Cross-national research in adolescent psychology: The Euronet project. In F. D. Alsaker & A. Flammer (Eds.), *The adolescent experience: European and American adolescents in the 1990s* (pp. 1–14). Mahwah, NJ: Erlbaum.

Alsaker, F. D., & Flammer, A. (1999a). *The adolescent experience: European and American adolescents in the 1990s.* Mahwah, NJ: Erlbaum.

Alsaker, F. D., & Flammer, A. (1999b). Cross-national research in adolescent psychology: The Euronet project. In F. D. Alsaker & A. Flammer (Eds.), *The adolescent experience: European and American adolescents in the 1990s* (pp. 1–14). Mahwah, NJ: Erlbaum.

Alwin, D. F. (1988). From obedience to autonomy: Changes in traits desired in children, 1928–1978. *Public Opinion Quarterly, 52,* 33–52.

Alwin, D. F., Xu, X., & Carson, T. (1994, October). *Childrearing goals and child discipline.* Paper presented at the Public World of Childhood Project workshop on Children Harmed and Harmful, Chicago.

Amato, P. R. (1993). Children's adjustment to divorce: Theories, hypotheses, and empirical support. *Journal of Marriage and the Family, 55,* 23–38.

Amato, P. R., & Keith, B. (1991). Parental divorce and the well-being of children: A meta-analysis. *Psychological Bulletin, 100,* 26–46.

Amato, P. R., Loomis, L. S., & Booth, A. (1995). Parental divorce, marital conflict, and offspring well-being during early adulthood. *Social Forces, 73,* 895–915.

American Association of University Women (1991). *The AAUW Report: How schools shortchange girls.* Washington, DC: Author.

American Association of University Women. (1993). *Hostile hallways.* Washington, DC: Author.

American Psychiatric Association. (1994). *Diagnostic and statistical manual of mental disorders* (4th ed.). Washington, DC: Author.

AmeriCorps. (2000a). Research: The history of AmeriCorps. Available: www.cns.gov/americorps/research/history.html

AmeriCorps. (2000b). Joining AmeriCorps: Check out the benefits. Available: www.cns.gov/americorps/joining/step2.html

AmeriCorps. (2000c). Partners in service: About partnerships: How partnerships deliver. Available: www.cns.gov/partners/summary/deliver.html

Ammerman, R. T., & Hersen, M. (1992). Current issues in the assessment of family violence. In R. T. Ammerman & M. Hersen (Eds.), *Assessment of family violence* (pp. 3–11). New York: Wiley.

Anastasi, A. (1988). *Psychological testing*, 6th ed. New York: Macmillan.

Anderson, C., & Ford, C. M. (1987). Affect of the game player: Short-term effects of highly and mildly aggressive video games. *Personality and Social Psychology Bulletin, 12*, 390–402.

Anderson, E. R., Hetherington, E. M., & Clingempeel, W. G. (1989). Transformations in family relations at puberty: Effects of family context. *Journal of Early Adolescence, 9*, 310–334.

Anderson, E., & Starcher, L. (1992, March). *Transformations in sibling relationships during adolescence.* Paper presented at the biennial meeting of the Society for Research on Adolescence, Washington, DC.

Anderson, R. E. (2000). *Youth and information technology.* Unpublished manuscript, University of Minnesota.

Andersson, T., & Magnusson, D. (1990). Biological maturation in adolescence and the development of drinking habits and alcohol abuse among young males: A prospective longitudinal study. *Journal of Youth and Adolescence, 19*, 33–42.

Appell, L. W. R. (1988). Menstruation among the Rungus of Borneo: An unmarked category. In T. Buckley & A. Gottlieb (Eds.), *Blood magic: The anthropology of menstruation* (pp. 94–116). Berkeley: University of California Press.

Applebome, P. (1997, September 3). Students' test scores show slow but steady gains at nation's schools. *New York Times,* p. A-17.

Apter, D., & Vihko, R. (1977). Serum pregnenolone, progesterone, 17-hydroxy-progesterone, testosterone and 5-alpha-dihydrotestosterone during female puberty. *Journal of Clinical Endocrinology and Metabolism, 45*, 1039–1048.

Apter, T. (1990). *Altered loves: Mothers and daughters during adolescence.* New York: St. Martin's.

Aral, S., Vanderplate, C., & Madger, L. (1988). Recurrent genital herpes: What helps adjustment? *Sexually Transmitted Diseases, 15*, 164–166.

Arbuthnot, J., Gordon, D. A., & Jurkovic, G. J. (1987). Personality. In H. C. Quay (Ed.), *Handbook of juvenile delinquency* (pp. 139–183). New York: Wiley.

Archer, S. L. (1989). Gender differences in identity development: Issues of process, domain, and timing. *Journal of Adolescence, 12*, 117–138.

Archer, S. L., & Waterman, A. S. (1994). Adolescent identity development: Contextual perspectives. In C. B. Fisher & R. M. Lerner (Eds.), *Applied developmental psychology.* New York: McGraw-Hill.

Arehart, D. M., & Smith, P. H. (1990). Identity in adolescence: Influences on dysfunction and psychosocial task issues. *Journal of Youth and Adolescence, 19*, 63–72.

Arlin, P. K. (1989). Problem solving and problem finding in young artists and young scientists. In M. L. Commons, J. D. Sinnott, F. A. Richards, & C. Armon (Eds.), *Adult development, Vol. 1: Comparisons and applications of developmental models* (pp. 197–216). New York: Praeger.

Arlin, P. K. (1990). Wisdom: The art of problem finding. In R. J. Sternberg (Ed.), *Wisdom: Its nature, origins, and development* (pp. 230–243). New York: Cambridge University Press.

Armstrong, D. G., & Savage, T. V. (1997). *Secondary education: An introduction.* Upper Saddle River, NJ: Prentice-Hall.

Arnett, J. (1990). Contraceptive use, sensation seeking, and adolescent egocentrism. *Journal of Youth and Adolescence, 19*, 171–180. Reprinted in M. L. Patten (Ed.), *Educational and psychological research* (pp. 73–78). Los Angeles: Pyrczak Publishing.

Arnett, J. (1991). Adolescents and heavy metal music: From the mouths of metalheads. *Youth and Society, 23*, 76–98.

Arnett, J. (1992). Reckless behavior in adolescence: A developmental perspective. *Developmental Review, 12*, 339–373.

Arnett, J. (1994a). Are college students adults? Their conceptions of the transition to adulthood. *Journal of Adult Development, 1*, 154–168.

Arnett, J. (1994b). Sensation seeking: A new conceptualization and a new scale. *Personality and Individual Differences, 16*, 289–296.

Arnett, J. J. (1995a). Broad and narrow socialization: The family in the context of a cultural theory. *Journal of Marriage and the Family, 57*, 617–628.

Arnett, J. J. (1995b). Adolescents' uses of media for self-socialization. *Journal of Youth & Adolescence, 24*, 519–533.

Arnett, J. J. (1996). *Metalheads: Heavy metal music and adolescent alienation.* Boulder, CO: Westview Press.

Arnett, J. J. (1997). Young people's conceptions of the transition to adulthood. *Youth & Society, 29*, 1–23.

Arnett, J. J. (1998a). Learning to stand alone: The contemporary American transition to adulthood in cultural and historical context. *Human Development, 41*, 295–315.

Arnett, J. J. (1998b). Risk behavior and family role transitions during the twenties. *Journal of Youth & Adolescence, 27*, 301–320.

Arnett, J. J. (1999a). Adolescent storm and stress, reconsidered. *American Psychologist, 54*, 317–326.

Arnett, J. J. (2000a). Emerging adulthood: A theory of development from the late teens through the twenties. *American Psychologist, 55*, 469–480.

Arnett, J. J. (2000b). High hopes in a grim world: Emerging adults' views of their futures and of "Generation X." *Youth & Society, 31*, 267–286.

Arnett, J. J. (2000c). Conceptions of the transition to adulthood from adolescence through midlife. *Journal of Adolescent Development.*

Arnett, J. J. (2000d). *Adolescents in Western countries on the threshold of the 21st century.* Paper prepared for the meeting of the Study Group on Adolescence in the 21st Century. Washington, D.C.

Arnett, J. J. (2000e). Optimistic bias in adolescent and adult smokers and nonsmokers. *Addictive Behaviors.*

Arnett, J. J. (2000f). The sounds of sex: Sex in teens' music and music videos. In J. D. Brown, J. Steele, & K. Walsh-Childers (Eds.), *Sexual teens, sexual media.* Mahwah, NJ: Erlbaum.

Arnett, J. J., & Balle-Jensen, L. (1993). Cultural bases of risk behavior: Danish adolescents. *Child Development, 64*, 1842–1855.

Arnett, J. J., & Jensen, L. A. (2000). *A congregation of one: Individualized religious beliefs among emerging adults.* Manuscript submitted for publication.

Arnett, J. J., Ramos, K. D., & Jensen, L. A. (in press). Ideologies in emerging adulthood: Balancing the ethics of autonomy and community. *Journal of Adult Development.*

Arnett, J. J., & Taber, S. (1994). Adolescence terminable and interminable: When does adolescence end? *Journal of Youth & Adolescence, 23*, 517–537.

Arnett, J. J., & Terhanian, G. (1998). Adolescents' responses to cigarette advertising: Exposure, liking, and the appeal of smoking. *Tobacco Control, 7*, 129–133.

Arnold, L., Mares, K. R., & Calkins, E. V. (1986). Exit interviews reveal why students leave a BA-MD degree program prematurely. *College & University, 62* (1), 34–47.

Asakawa, K., & Csikszentmihalyi, M. (1999). The quality of experience of Asian American adolescents in activities related to future goals. *Journal of Youth & Adolescence, 27*, 141–163.

Asarmov, J. R., & Horton, A. A. (1990). Coping and stress in families of child psychiatric inpatients: Parents of children with depressive and schizophrenic spectrum disorders. *Child Psychiatry and Human Development, 21,* 145–157.

Asher, S. R., Parkhurst, J. E., Hymel, S., & Williams, G. A. (1990). Peer rejection and loneliness in childhood. In S. R. Asher & J. D. Coie (Eds.), *Peer rejection in childhood* (pp. 253–273). New York: Cambridge University Press.

Asher, S., & Coie, J. (Eds.). (1990). *Peer rejection in childhood.* New York: Cambridge University Press.

Astone, N. M., & McLanahan, S. S. (1995). Family structure, residential mobility, and school dropout: A research note. *Demography, 9,* 375–388.

Astrachan, A. (1989). Dividing lines. In M. S. Kimmel & M. A. Messner (Eds.), *Men's lives* (pp. 63–73). New York: Macmillan.

Attie, I., & Brooks-Gunn, J. (1989). Development of eating problems in adolescent girls: A longitudinal study. *Development Psychology, 25,* 70–79.

Bachman, J. (1983, Summer). Premature affluence: Do high school students earn too much? *Economic Outlook USA,* 64–67.

Bachman, J. G., Johnston, L. D., & O'Malley, P. M. (1995). *Monitoring the future: Questionnaire responses from the nation's high school seniors.* Ann Arbor: Institute for Social Research, University of Michigan.

Bachman, J. G., Johnston, L. D., O'Malley, P., & Schulenberg, J. (1996). Transitions in drug use during late adolescence and young adulthood. In J. A. Graber, J. Brooks-Gunn, & A. C. Petersen (Eds.), *Transitions through adolescence: Interpersonal domains and context* (pp. 111–140). Mahwah, NJ: Erlbaum.

Bachman, J. G., & O'Malley, P. M. (1986). Self-concepts, self-esteem, and educational experiences: The frog pond revisited (again). *Journal of Personality and Social Psychology, 50,* 35–46.

Bachman, J. G., & Schulenberg, J. (1993). How part-time work intensity relates to drug use, problem behavior, time use, and satisfaction among high school seniors: Are these consequences or just correlates? *Developmental Psychology, 29,* 220–235.

Bachman, J. G., Wadsworth, K. N., O'Malley, P. M., Johnston, L. D., & Schulenberg, J. E. (1997). *Smoking, drinking, and drug use in young adulthood: The impacts of new freedoms and new responsibilities.* Mahwah, NJ: Erlbaum.

Bachman, J. G., Wadsworth, K. N., O'Malley, P. M., Schulenberg, J., & Johnston, L. D. (1999). Marriage, divorce, and parenthood during the transition to adulthood: Impacts on drug use and abuse. In J. Schulenberg, J. L. Maggs, & K. Hurrelmann (Eds.), *Health risks and developmental transitions during adolescence* (pp. 246–282). New York: Cambridge University Press.

Bachman, J. G., Wallace, J. M., Jr., O'Malley, P. M., Johnston, L. D., Kurth, C. L., & Neighbors, H. W. (1991). Racial/ethnic differences in smoking, drinking, and illicit drug use among American high school seniors, 1976–89. *American Journal of Public Health, 81,* 372–377.

Bachrach, C. A., Clogg, C. C., & Carver, K. (1993). Outcomes of early childbearing: Summary of a conference. *Journal of Research on Adolescence, 3,* 337–348.

Bailey, B. L. (1989). *From front porch to back seat: Courtship in twentieth-century America.* Baltimore, MD: Johns Hopkins University Press.

Bailey, J. M., Pillard, R. C., Neale, M. C., & Agyei, Y. (1993). Heritable factors influence sexual orientation in women. *Archives of General Psychiatry, 50,* 217–223.

Baker, D. P., & Perkins-Jones, D. (1993). Creating gender equality: Cross-national gender stratification and mathematical performance. *Sociology of Education, 66,* 91–103.

Balikci, A. (1970). *The Netsilik Eskimo.* Prospect Heights, IL: Waveland Press.

Banks, R. (1995). *The rule of the bone.* New York: HarperCollins.

Barbarin, O., & Soler, R. (1993). Behavioral, emotional, and academic adjustment in a national probability sample of African-American children. *Journal of Black Psychology, 19,* 423–446.

Barber, B. R. (1995). *Jihad vs. McWorld: How globalism and tribalism are reshaping the world.* New York: Ballantine.

Barber, B., & Eccles, J. (1992). Long-term influence of divorce and single parenting on adolescent family- and work-related values, behaviors, and aspirations. *Psychological Bulletin, 111,* 108–126.

Barber, B., Olsen, J., & Shagle, S. (1994). Associations between parental psychological and behavioral control and youth internalized and externalized behaviors. *Child Development, 6S,* 1120–1136.

Barenboim, C. (1981). The development of person perception in childhood and adolescence: From behavioral comparisons to psychological construction to psychological comparisons. *Child Development, 52,* 129–144.

Barling, J., & Kelloway, E. K. (1999). *Young workers: Varieties of experience.* Washington, DC: American Psychological Association.

Barnes, G. M., & Farrell, M. (1992). Parental support and control as predictors of adolescent drinking, delinquency, and related problem behaviors. *Journal of Marriage and the Family, 54,* 763–776.

Barnes, G. M., & Welte, J. W. (1986). Adolescent alcohol abuse: Subgroup differences and relationships to other problem behaviors. *Journal of Adolescent Research, 1,* 79–94.

Barrett, M. E., Simpson, D. D., & Lehman, W. E. (1988). Behavioral changes of adolescents in drug abuse prevention programs. *Journal of Clinical Psychology, 44,* 461–473.

Barry, D. (1995). *Dave Barry's complete guide to guys.* New York: Fawcett Columbine.

Barsalou, L. W. (1992). *Cognitive psychology: An overview for cognitive scientists.* Hillsdale, NJ: Erlbaum.

Bartholet, J. (2000, January 17). The plague years. *Newsweek,* pp. 32–37.

Basow, S. A., & Rubin, L. R. (1999). Gender influences on adolescent development. In N. B. Johnson, M. C. Roberts, & J. Worell (Eds.), *Beyond appearance: A new look at adolescent girls* (pp. 25–52). Washington, DC: American Psychological Association.

Bass, E., & Kaufman, K. (1996). *Free your mind: The book for lesbian, gay, and bisexual youth and their allies.* New York: HarperTrade.

Basseches, M. (1984). *Dialectical thinking and adult development.* Norwood, NJ: Ablex.

Basseches, M. (1989). Dialectical thinking as an organized whole: Comments on Irwin and Kramer. In M. L. Commons, J. D. Sinnott, F. A. Richards, & C. Armon (Eds.), *Adult development, Vol. 1: Comparisons and applications of developmental models* (pp. 161–178). New York: Praeger.

Battaglia, D. M., Richard, F. D., Datteri, D. L., & Lord, C. G. (1998). Breaking up is (relatively) easy to do: A script for the dissolution of close relationships. *Journal of Social and Personal Relationships, 15,* 829–845.

Bauman, K. E., & Fisher, L. A. (1986). On the measurement of friend behavior in research on friend influence and selection: Findings from longitudinal studies of adolescent smoking and drinking. *Journal of Youth & Adolescence, 15,* 345–353.

Baumrind, D. (1968). Authoritative vs. authoritarian parental control. *Adolescence, 3,* 255–272.

Baumrind, D. (1971). Current patterns of parental authority. *Developmental Psychology Monographs, 4* (1, Pt. 2).

Baumrind, D. (1987). A developmental perspective on adolescent risk taking in contemporary America. In C. E. Irwin, Jr. (Ed.), *Adolescent social behavior and health. New Directions for Child Development, 37,* 93–125.

Baumrind, D. (1991). The influence of parenting style on adolescent competence and substance use. *Journal of Early Adolescence, 1,* 56–95.

Baumrind, D. (1991a). Effective parenting during the early adolescent transition. In P. A. Cowan & E. M. Hetherington (Ed.), *Advances in family research* (Vol. 2, pp. 111–163). Hillsdale, NJ: Erlbaum.

Baumrind, D. (1991b). The influence of parenting style on adolescent competence and substance use. *Journal of Early Adolescence, 11,* 56–95.

Baumrind, D. (1993). The average expectable environment is not enough: A response to Scarr. *Child Development, 64,* 1299–1317.

Baxter, B. L., De Riemer, C., Landini, A., Leslie, L., & Singletary, M. W. (1985). A content analysis of music videos. *Journal of Broadcasting and Electronic Media, 29,* 333–340.

Bayley, N. (1968). Behavioral correlates of mental growth: Birth to thirty-six years. *American Psychologist, 23,* 1–17.

Becker, E. (1973). *The denial of death.* New York: Free Press.

Bednar, R. L., Wells, M. G., & Peterson, S. R. (1995). *Self-esteem* (2nd ed.). Washington, DC: American Psychological Association.

Bee, H. (1998). *Lifespan development.* New York: Addison-Wesley.

Begley, S. (1998, September 7). Do parents matter? *Newsweek,* pp. 52–59.

Begley, S. (2000, May 8). A world of their own. *Newsweek,* pp. 52–56.

Beirness, D. J., & Simpson, H. M. (1988). Lifestyle correlates of risky driving and accident involvement among youth. *Alcohol, Drugs and Driving, 4,* 193–204.

Belfer, M. L. (1993). Substance abuse with psychiatric illness in children and adolescents: Definitions and terminology. *American Journal of Orthopsychiatry, 63,* 70–79.

Bell, A., Weinberg, M., & Hammersmith, S. (1981). *Sexual preference: Its development in men and women.* Bloomington: Indiana University Press.

Bell, R. (1998). *Changing bodies, changing lives* (3rd ed.). New York: Times Books.

Bellah, R. N., Madsen, R., Sullivan, W. M., Swidler, A., & Tipton, S. M. (1985). *Habits of the heart: Individualism and commitment in American life.* New York: Harper & Row.

Bem, S. L. (1974). The measurement of psychological androgyny. *Journal of Consulting and Clinical Psychology, 42,* 155–162.

Bem, S. L. (1975). Sex role adaptability: One consequence of psychological androgyny. *Journal of Personality and Social Psychology, 31,* 634–643.

Bem, S. L. (1977). On the utility of alternative procedures for assessing psychological androgyny. *Journal of Consulting and Clinical Psychology, 45,* 196–205.

Bem, S. L. (1981). Gender schema theory: A cognitive account of sex-typing. *Psychological Review, 88,* 354–364.

Bem, S. L. (1993). *The lenses of gender: Transforming the debate on sexual inequality.* New Haven: Connecticut University Press.

Ben-Amos, I. K. (1994). *Adolescence and youth in early modern England.* New Haven, CT: Yale University Press.

Benbow, C. P., & Stanley, J. C. (1980). Sex differences in mathematical ability: Fact or artifact? *Science, 210,* 1262–1264.

Benedict, R. (1934/1989). *Patterns of culture.* New York: Houghton Mifflin.

Benedikt, R., Wertheim, E. H., & Love, A. (1998). Eating attitudes and weight-loss attempts in female adolescents and their mothers. *Journal of Youth & Adolescence, 27,* 43–57.

Bennett, N., Blanc, A., & Bloom, D. E. (1988). Commitment and the modern union: Assessing the link between premarital cohabitation and subsequent marital stability. *American Sociological Review, 53,* 127–138.

Bennett, S. (1987). *New dimensions in research on class size and academic achievement.* Madison, WI: National Center on Effective Secondary Schools.

Bensley, L. S., Van Eeenwyk, J., Spieker, S. J., & Schoder, J. (1999). Self-reported abuse history and adolescent problem behaviors. I: Antisocial and suicidal behaviors. *Journal of Adolescent Health, 24,* 163–172.

Benson, M., Harris, P., & Rogers, C. (1992). Identity consequences of attachment to mothers and fathers among late adolescents. *Journal of Research on Adolescence, 2,* 187–204.

Benson, P., Donahue, M., & Erickson, J. (1989). Adolescence and religion: Review of the literature from 1970–1986. *Research in the Social Scientific Study of Religion, 1,* 153–181.

Bernard, J. (1987). *The female world from a global perspective.* Bloomington: Indiana University Press.

Berndt, T. J. (1989). Obtaining support from friends during childhood and adolescence. In D. Belle (Ed.), *Children's social networks and social supports* (pp. 308–331). New York: Wiley.

Berndt, T. J. (1992). Friendship and friends' influence in adolescence. *Current Directions in Psychological Science, 1,* 156–159.

Berndt, T. J. (1996). Transitions in friendship and friends' influence. In J. A. Graber, J. Brooks-Gunn, & A. C. Petersen (Eds.), *Transitions through adolescence: Interpersonal domains and context* (pp. 57–84). Mahwah, NJ: Erlbaum.

Berndt, T. J., & Das, R. (1987). Effects of popularity and friendship on perceptions of the personality and social behavior of peers. *Journal of Early Adolescence, 7,* 429–439.

Berndt, T. J., & Heller, K. A. (1986). Gender stereotypes and social influences: A developmental study. *Journal of Personality and Social Psychology, 50,* 889–898.

Berndt, T. J., & Keefe, K. (1995). Friends' influence on adolescents' adjustment to school. *Child Development, 66,* 1312–1329.

Berndt, T. J., & Mekos, D. (1995). Adolescents' perceptions of the stressful and desirable aspects of the transition to junior high school. *Journal of Research on Adolescence, 5,* 123–142.

Berndt, T. J., & Perry, T. B. (1990). Distinctive features and effects of early adolescent friendships. In R. Montemayor (Ed.), *Advances in adolescent research.* Greenwich, CT: JAI Press.

Berndt, T. J., & Savin-Williams, R. C. (1993). Variations in friendships and peer-group relationships in adolescence. In P. Tolan & B. Cohler (Eds.), *Handbook of clinical research and practice with adolescents* (pp. 203–219). New York: Wiley.

Berry, V. (1995). Redeeming the rap music experience. In J. S. Epstein (Ed.), *Adolescents and their music* (pp. 165–188). New York: Garland.

Berzonsky, M. D. (1992). A process perspective on identity and stress management. In G. R. Adams, T. P. Gullotta, & R. Montemayor (Eds.), *Adolescent identity formation* (pp. 193–215). Newbury Park, CA: Sage.

Bettes, B. A., Dusenbury, L., Kerner, J., James-Ortiz, S., & Botvin, G. J. (1990). Ethnicity and psychosocial factors in alcohol and tobacco use in adolescence. *Child Development, 61,* 557–565.

Beyth-Marom, R., Austin, L., Fischoff, B., Palmgren, C., & Jacobs-Quadrel, M. (1993). Perceived consequences of risky behaviors: Adults and adolescents. *Developmental Psychology, 29,* 549–563.

Beyth-Maron, R., & Fischoff, B. (1997). Adolescents' decisions about risks: A cognitive perspective. In J. Schulenberg & J. L. Maggs (Eds.), *Health risks and developmental transitions during adolescence* (pp. 110–135). New York: Cambridge University Press.

Bianchi, S. M., & Spain, D. (1996). Women, work, and family in America. *Population Bulletin, 51,* 1–48.

Bibby, R. W., & Posterski, D. C. (1992). *Teen trends: A nation in motion.* Toronto: Stoddart.

Biblarz, T. J., Bengtson, V. L., & Bucur, A. (1996). Social mobility across three generations. *Journal of Marriage and the Family, 58,* 188–200.

Billson, J. M. (1996). *Pathways to manhood: Young black males struggle for identity.* New Brunswick, NJ: Transaction.

Billy, J., Landale, N., Grady, W., & Zimmerle, D. (1988). Effects of sexual activity on adolescent social and psychological development. *Social Psychology Quarterly, 51,* 190–212.

Blain, M. D., Thompson, J. M., & Whiffen, V. E. (1993). Attachment and perceived social support in late adolescence. *Journal of Adolescent Research, 8,* 226–241.

Blair, S. L., & Johnson, M. P. (1992). Wives' perceptions of the fairness of the division of household labor: The intersection of housework and ideology. *Journal of Marriage and the Family, 54,* 570–581.

Blanchard-Fields, F. (1986). Reasoning on social dilemmas varying in emotional saliency: An adult development perspective. *Psychology and aging, 1,* 325–332.

Blasi, A., & Hoeffel, E. C. (1974). Adolescence and formal operations. *Human Development, 17,* 344–363.

Bloch, D. P. (1989). Using career information with dropouts and at-risk youth. *Career Development Quarterly, 38,* 160–171.

Block, J., & Block, J. H. (1980). *The California child Q-set.* Palo Alto, CA: Consulting Psychologists Press.

Block, J., Block, J., & Keyes, S. (1988). Longitudinally foretelling drug usage in adolescence: Early childhood personality and environmental precursors. *Child Development, 59,* 336–355.

Block, J., Gjerde, P. F., & Block, J. H. (1991). Personality antecedents of depressive tendencies in 18-year-olds: A prospective study. *Journal of Personality and Social Psychology, 60,* 726–738.

Block, J., & Robins, R. (1993). A longitudinal study of consistency and change in self-esteem from early adolescence to early adulthood. *Child Development, 64,* 909–923.

Bloom, D. E., & Brender, A. (1993). Labor and the emerging world economy. *Population Bulletin, 48,* 1–39. Washington, DC: Population Reference Bureau.

Blosser, B. J. (1988). Ethnic differences in children's media use. *Journal of Broadcasting & Electronic Media, 32,* 453–470.

Blum, H. M., Boyle, M. H., & Offord, D. R. (1988). Single-parent families: Child psychiatric disorder and school performance. *Journal of the American Academy of Child and Adolescent Psychiatry, 27,* 214–219.

Blume, J. (1970). *Are you there, God? It's me, Margaret.* New York: Yearling.

Blumler, J. G. (1979). The role of theory in uses and gratifications studies. *Communication Research, 6,* 9–36.

Blyth, D., Hill, J., & Thiel, K. (1982). Early adolescents' significant others: Grade and gender differences in perceived relationships with familial and non-familial adults and young people. *Journal of Youth and Adolescence, 11,* 425–450.

Blyth, D., Simmons, R., & Zakin, D. (1985). Satisfaction with body image for early adolescent females: The impact of pubertal timing within different school environments. *Journal of Youth and Adolescence, 14,* 227–236.

Bogenschneider, K. (1997). Parental involvement in adolescent schooling: A proximal process with transcontextual validity. *Journal of Marriage and the Family, 59, 1–16.*

Bogenschneider, K., & Steinberg, L. (1994). Maternal employment and adolescent academic achievement: A developmental analysis. *Sociology of Education, 67,* 60–77.

Bogenschneider, K., Wu, M., Raffaelli, M., & Tsay, J. C. (1998). Parent influences on adolescent peer orientation and substance use: The interface of parenting practices and values. *Child Development, 69,* 1672–1688.

Bois-Reymond, M., & Ravesloot, J. (1996). The roles of parents and peers in the sexual and relational socialization of adolescents. In K. Hurrelmann & S. Hamilton (Eds.), *Social problems and social contexts in adolescence: Perspectives across boundaries* (pp. 175–197). Hawthorne, NY: Aldine de Gruyter.

Bois-Reymond, M., & van der Zande, I. (1994). *The Netherlands.* In K. Hurrelmann (Ed.), *International handbook of adolescence* (pp. 270–286). Westport, CT: Greenwood Press.

Bolger, N., Downey, G., Walker, E., & Steininger, P. (1989). The onset of suicidal ideation in childhood and adolescence. *Journal of Youth and Adolescence, 18,* 175–190.

Bond, S., & Cash, T. F. (1992). Black beauty: Skin color and body images among African American college women. *Journal of Applied Social Psychology, 22,* 874–888.

Bonkowski, S. E. (1989). Lingering sadness: Young adults' responses to parental divorce. *The Journal of Contemporary Social Work, 70,* 219–223.

Booth, A., Crouter, A. C., & Shanahan, M. (Eds.). (1999). *Transitions to adulthood in a changing economy: No work, no family, no future?* Westport, CT: Praeger.

Borduin, C. M. (1999). Multisystemic treatment of criminality and violence in adolescents. *Journal of the American Academy of Child & Adolescent Psychiatry, 38,* 242–249.

Borduin, C. M., Mann, B. J., Cone, L. T., Henggler, S. W., Fucci, B. R., Blaske, D. M., & Williams, R. A. (1995). Multisystemic treatment of serious juvenile offenders: Long-term prevention of criminality and violence. *Journal of Consulting and Clinical Psychology, 63,* 569–578.

Bornholdt, L., Goodnow, J., & Cooney, G. (1994). Influences of gender stereotypes on adolescents' perceptions of their own achievement. *American Educational Research Journal, 31,* 675–692.

Bostic, J. Q., Wilens, T. E., Spencer, T., & Beiderman, J. Antidepressant treatment of juvenile depression. *International Journal of Psychiatry in Clinical Practice, 3,* 171–179.

Botvin, M., & Vitaro, F. (1995). The impact of peer relationships on aggression in childhood: Inhibition through coercion or promotion through peer support. In. J. McCord (Ed.), *Coercion and punishment in long-term perspective* (pp. 183–197). New York: Cambridge University Press.

Boulos, C., Kutcher, S., Marton, P., Simeon, J., Ferguson, G., & Roberts, D. (1991). Response to desipramine treatment in adolescent major depression. *Psychopharmacology Bulletin, 27,* 59–65.

Bowlby, J. (1969). *Attachment and loss, Vol. 1: Attachment.* New York: Basic Books.

Bowlby, J. (1973). *Attachment and loss, Vol. 2: Separation, anxiety, and anger.* New York: Basic Books.

Bowlby, J. (1980). *Attachment and loss, Vol. 3: Loss, sadness, and depression.* New York: Basic Books.

Boyer, E. (1983). *High school.* New York: Harper & Row.

Boyesen, M., & Bru, E. (1999). Small school classes, small problems? A study of peer harassment, emotional problems and student perception of social support at school in small and large classes. *School Psychology International, 20,* 338–351.

Boyle, M. H., Offord, D. R., Racine, Y. A., & Szatmari, P. (1992). Predicting substance use in late adolescence: Results from the Ontario Child Health Study follow-up. *American Journal of Psychiatry, 149,* 761–767.

Boyle, P. (2000, December/January). Latinas' perplexing lead in teen births. *Youth Today, 9,* 1, 47–49.

Boyle, P., & Lutton, L. (1999, November). Hard lessons in dropout prevention. *Youth Today, 8,* pp. 1, 17–20.

Brady, B., & Kendall, P. (1992). Comorbidity of anxiety and depression in children and adolescents. *Psychological Bulletin, 111,* 244–255.

Brake, M. (1985). *Comparative youth culture: The sociology of youth cultures and youth subcultures in America, Britain, and Canada.* London: Routledge and Kegan Paul.

Brandtstader, J., & Baltes-Gotz, B. (1990). Personal control over development and quality of perspectives in adulthood. In P. Baltes & M. M. Baltes (Eds.), *Successful aging* (pp. 197–224). Cambridge, England: Cambridge University Press.

Brandtstader, J., & Greve, W. (1994). The aging self: Stabilizing and protective processes. *Developmental Review, 14,* 52–80.

Brendgen, M., Vitaro, F., & Bukowski, W. M. (1998). Affiliation with delinquent friends: Contributions of parents, self-esteem, delinquent behavior, and rejection by peers. *Journal of Early Adolescence, 18,* 244–265.

Brent, D. A., Kolko, A., Wartella, M. E., Boylan, M. B., Moritz, G., Baugher, M., & Zelenak, J. P. (1993). Adolescent psychiatric inpatients' risk of suicide attempts at 6-month follow-up. *Journal of the American Academy of Child and Adolescent Psychiatry, 32,* 95–105.

Brewster, K., Billy, J., & Grady, W. (1993). Social context and adolescent behavior: The impact of community on the transition to sexual activity. *Social Forces, 71,* 713–740.

Briere, J. N. (1992). *Child abuse trauma.* Newbury Park, CA: Sage.

Briere, J., & Runtz, M. (1989). Symptomatology associated with childhood sexual victimization in a nonclinical adult sample. *Child Abuse and Neglect, 12,* 51–59.

Briere, J., & Runtz, M. (1991). The long-term effects of sexual abuse: A review and synthesis. In J. Briere (Ed.), *Treating victims of child sexual abuse* (pp. 3–13). *New Directions for Mental Health Services, 51.* San Francisco: Jossey-Bass.

Briggs, C. L. (1989). *Learning how to ask: A sociolinguistic appraisal of the role of the interview in social science research.* New York: Cambridge University Press.

Brody, N. (1992). *Intelligence* (2nd ed.). San Diego, CA: Academic Press.

Bronstein, P., Duncan, P., D'Ari, A., Pieniadz, J., Fitzgerald, M., Abrams, C., Frankowski, B., Franco, O., Hunt, C., & Cha, S. (1996). Family and parenting behaviors predicting middle school adjustment: A longitudinal study. *Family Relations, 45,* 110–121.

Bronstein, P., Duncan, R., Clauson, J., Abrams, C., Yannett, N., Ginsburg, G., & Milne, M. (1994). *Enhancing middle school adjustment for children from lower-income families: A parenting intervention.* Unpublished manuscript, University of Vermont.

Brook, J. S., Brook, D. W., Gordon, A. S., & Whiteman, M. (1990). The psychosocial etiology of adolescent drug use: A family interactional approach. *Genetic, Social, and General Psychology Monographs, 116,* 111–267.

Brook, J. S., Gordon, A. S., Brook, A., & Brook, D. W. (1989). The consequences of marijuana use on intrapersonal and interpersonal functioning in black and white adolescents. *Genetic, Social, and General Psychology Monographs, 111,* 317–330.

Brook, J., Whitman, M., Gordon, A., & Cohen, P. (1986). Dynamics of childhood and adolescent personality traits and adolescent drug use. *Developmental Psychology, 22,* 403–414.

Brooks-Gunn, J., & Chase-Lansdale, P. L. (1995). Adolescent parenthood. In M. H. Bornstein (Ed.), *Children and parenting* (Vol. 3). Hillsdale, NJ: Erlbaum.

Brooks-Gunn, J., Duncan, G., Klebanov, P., & Sealand, N. (1993). Do neighborhoods influence child and adolescent development? *American Journal of Sociology, 99,* 353–395.

Brooks-Gunn, J., & Paikoff, R. (1993). 'Sex is a gamble, kissing is a game': Adolescent sexuality and health promotion. In S. Millstein, A. Petersen, & E. Nightingale (Eds.), *Promoting the health of adolescents: New directions for the twenty-first century* (pp. 180–208). New York: Oxford University Press.

Brooks-Gunn, J., & Paikoff, R. (1997). Sexuality and developmental transitions during adolescence. In J. Schulenberg, J. L. Maggs, & K. Hurrelmann (Eds.), *Health risks and developmental transitions during adolescence* (pp. 190–219). New York: Cambridge University Press.

Brooks-Gunn, J., & Reiter, E. (1990). The role of pubertal processes. In S. Feldman & G. Elliott (Eds.), *At the threshold: The developing adolescent* (pp. 16–23). Cambridge, MA: Harvard University Press.

Brooks-Gunn, J., & Ruble, D. (1982). The development of menstrual-related beliefs and behaviors during early adolescence. *Child Development, 53,* 1567–1577.

Brown, A., & Finkelhor, D. (1986). The impact of child sexual abuse: A review of the research. *Psychological Bulletin, 99,* 66–77.

Brown, B. (1990). Peer groups. In S. Feldman & G. Elliott (Eds.), *At the threshold: The developing adolescent* (pp. 171–196). Cambridge, MA: Harvard University Press.

Brown, B., & Lohr, M. J. (1987). Peer group affiliation and adolescent self-esteem: An integration of ego-identity and symbolic interaction theories. *Journal of Personality and Social Psychology, 52,* 47–55.

Brown, B., & Mounts, N. (1989, April). *Peer group structures in single versus multiethnic high schools.* Paper presented at the biennial meeting of the Society for Research in Child Development, Kansas City.

Brown, B., Mounts, N., Lamborn, S., & Steinberg, L. (1993). Parenting practices and peer group affiliation in adolescence. *Child Development, 64,* 467–482.

Brown, B. B. (1989). The role of peer groups in adolescents' adjustment to secondary school. In T. J. Berndt & G. W. Ladd (Eds.), *Peer relationships in child development* (pp. 188–215). New York: Wiley.

Brown, B. B. (1999). "You're going out with who?" Peer group influences on adolescent romantic relationships. In W. Furman, B. B. Brown, & C. Feiring (Eds.), *The development of romantic relationships in adolescence* (pp. 291–329). New York: Cambridge University Press.

Brown, B. B., Feiring, C., & Furman, W. (1999). Missing the love boat: Why researchers have shied away from adolescent romance. In W. Furman, B. B. Brown, & C. Feiring (Eds.), *The development of romantic relationships in adolescence* (pp. 1–18). New York: Cambridge University Press.

Brown, B. B., & Lohr, M. J. (1987). Peer group affiliation and adolescent self-esteem: An integration of ego-identity and symbolic interaction theories. *Journal of Personality and Social Psychology, 52,* 47–55.

Brown, B. B., Mory, M., & Kinney, D. A. (1994). Casting adolescent crowds in relational perspective: Caricature, channel, and context. In R. Montemayor, G. R. Adams, & T. P. Gullotta (Eds.), *Advances in adolescent development: Vol. 6. Personal relationships during adolescence.* Newbury Park, CA: Sage.

Brown, E. F., & Hendee, W. R. (1989). Adolescents and their music. *Journal of the American Medical Association, 262,* 1659–1663.

Brown, F. (1973). *The reform of secondary education: Report of the national commission on the reform of secondary education.* New York: McGraw-Hill.

Brown, J. D., Childers, K. M., & Waszak, C. S. (1990). Television and adolescent sexuality. *Journal of Adolescent Health Care, 11,* 62–70.

Brown, J. D., & Schulze, L. (1990). The effects of race, gender, and fandom on audience interpretations of Madonna's music videos. *Journal of Communication, 40,* 88–102.

Brown, J. D., White, A. B., & Nikopolou, L. (1993). Disinterest, intrigue, and resistance: Early adolescent girls' use of sexual media content. In B. Greenberg, J. D. Brown, & N. Buerkel-Rothfuss (Eds.), *Media, sex, and the adolescent.* Cresskill, NJ: Hampton Press.

Brown, L. K. I., Overholser, J., Spirito, A., & Fritz, G. K. (1991). The correlates of planning in adolescent suicide attempts. *Journal of the American Academy of Child and Adolescent Psychiatry, 30,* 95–99.

Brown, L. M., & Gilligan, C. (1992). *Meeting at the crossroads: Women's psychology and girls' development.* Cambridge, MA: Harvard University Press.

Bruer, J. T. (1993). The mind's journey from novice to expert. *American Educator, 17,* 6–15, 38–46.

Brumberg, J. J. (1997). *The body project: An intimate history of American girls.* New York: Random House.

Bruvold, W. (1993). A meta-analysis of adolescent smoking prevention programs. *American Journal of Public Health, 83,* 872–880.

Bryant, B. K. (1992). Conflict resolution strategies in relation to children's peer relations. *Developmental Psychology, 13,* 35–50.

Bryk, A. S., & Thum, Y. M. (1989). The effects of high school organization on dropping out: An exploratory investigation. *American Educational Research Journal, 26,* 353–383.

Buchanan, C. M. (2000). The impact of divorce on adjustment during adolescence. In R. D. Taylor & M. Weng (Eds.), *Resilience across contexts: Family, work, culture, and community.* Mahwah, NJ: Erlbaum.

Buchanan, C. M., Eccles, J. S., Flanagan, C., Midgley, C., Feldlaufer, H., & Harold, R. D. (1990). Parents' and teachers' beliefs about adolescents: Effects of sex and experience. *Journal of Youth & Adolescence, 19,* 363–394.

Buchanan, C. M., Eccles, J., & Becker, J. (1992). Are adolescents the victims of raging hormones? Evidence for activational effects of hormones on moods and behavior at adolescence. *Psychological Bulletin, 111,* 62–107.

Buchanan, C. M., & Holmbeck, G. N. (1998). Measuring beliefs about adolescent personality and behavior. *Journal of Youth & Adolescence, 27,* 609–629.

Buchanan, C. M., Maccoby, E. E., & Dornbusch, S. M. (1996). *Adolescents after divorce.* Cambridge, MA: Harvard University Press.

Buchanan, C., Maccoby, E., & Dornbusch, S. (1991). Caught between parents: Adolescents' experience in divorced homes. *Child Development, 62,* 1008–1029.

Buchanan, M., & Robbins, C. (1990). Early adult psychological consequences for males of adolescent pregnancy and its resolution. *Journal of Youth and Adolescence, 19*, 413–424.

Buchmann, M. (1994). *Switzerland.* In K. Hurrelmann (Ed.), *International handbook of adolescence* (pp. 386–399). Westport, CT: Greenwood Press.

Buckley, T., & Gottlieb, A. (1988). *Blood magic: The anthropology of menstruation.* Berkeley, CA: University of California Press.

Buhrmester, D., & Carbery, J. (1992, March). *Daily patterns of self-disclosure and adolescent adjustment.* Paper presented at the biennial meeting of the Society for Research on Adolescence, Washington, DC.

Buhrmester, D., & Furman, W. (1987). The development of companionship and intimacy. *Child Development, 58*, 1101–1113.

Buhrmester, D., & Furman, W. (1990). Perceptions of sibling relationships during middle childhood and adolescence. *Child Development, 61*, 1387–1396.

Buhrmester, D., & Yin, J. (1997, April). *A longitudinal study of friends' influence on adolescents' adjustment.* Paper presented at the biennial meeting of the Society for Research in Child Development, Washington, DC.

Bukowski, W. M., Newcomb, A. F., & Hoza, B. (1987). Friendship conceptions among early adolescents: A longitudinal study of stability and change. *Journal of Early Adolescence, 7*, 143–152.

Bullough, V. L. (1981). Age at menarche: A misunderstanding. *Science, 213*, 365–366.

Burbank, V. K. (1988). *Aboriginal adolescence: Maidenhood in an Australian community.* New Brunswick, NJ: Rutgers University Press.

Burn, S. M. (1996). *The social psychology of gender.* New York: McGraw-Hill.

Burnett, R. (1990). From a whisper to a scream: Music video and cultural form. In K. Roe & U. Carlsson (Eds.), *Popular music research* (pp. 21–27). Goteborg, Sweden: Nordicom-Sweden.

Burns, A. (1992). Mother-headed families in Australia: An international perspective and the case of Australia. *Social Policy Report, Society for Research in Child Development, 6*, 1–22.

Burns, G. L., & Farina, A. (1992). The role of physical attractiveness in adjustment. *Genetic, Social, and General Psychology Monographs, 118*, 159–194

Burra, N. B. (1997). *Born to work: Child labor in India.* New Delhi: Oxford University Press.

Busch-Rossnagel, N. A., & Zayas, L. H. (1991). Hispanic adolescents. In R. M. Lerner, A. C. Petersen, & J. Brooks-Gunn (Eds.), *Encyclopedia of Adolescence* (pp. 492–498). New York: Garland.

Buss, D. M. (1989). Sex differences in human mate preferences: Evolutionary hypothesis tested in 37 cultures. *Behavioral and Brain Sciences, 12*, 1–49.

Buss, D. M. (1995). *The evolution of desire: Strategies of human mating.* New York: Basic Books.

Bussey, K., & Bandura, A. (1992). Self-regulatory mechanisms governing gender development. *Child Development, 63*, 1236–1250.

Buzzi, C., & Cavalli, A. (1994). Italy. In K. Hurrelman (Ed.), *International handbook of adolescence* (pp. 224–233). Westport, CT: Greenwood Press.

Byrnes, J. P., Miller, D. C., & Reynolds, M. (1999). Learning to make good decisions: A self-regulation perspective. *Child Development, 70*, 1121–1140.

Cairns, R. B., Cairns, B. D., Neckerman, H. J., Ferguson, L. L., & Gariepy, J. (1989). Growth and aggression: 1. Childhood to early adolescence. *Developmental Psychology, 25*, 320–330.

Cairns, R., Cairns, B., Neckerman, H., Gest, S., & Gariepy, J. L. (1988). Social networks and aggressive behavior: Peer support or peer rejection? *Developmental Psychology, 24*, 815–823.

Cantor, J. (1998). *Mommy, I'm scared: How TV and movies frighten children and what we can do to protect them.* New York: Harcourt.

Cantor, J. (2000). Violence in films and television. In R. Lee (Ed.), *Encyclopedia of international media and communications.* New York: Academic Press.

Capaldi, D. (1991). Co-occurrence of conduct problems and depressive symptoms in early adolescent boys, I: Familial factors and general adjustment at grade 6. *Development and Psychopathology, 3*, 277–300.

Capaldi, D. M., & Stoolmiller, M. (1999). Co-occurrence of conduct problems and depressive symptoms in early adolescent boys, III: Prediction to young adult adjustment. *Development and Psychopathology, 11*, 59–84.

Capaldi, D., & Patterson, G. (1991). Relation of parental transitions to boys' adjustment problems, I: A linear hypothesis; II: Mothers at risk for transitions and unskilled parenting. *Developmental Psychology, 27*, 489–504.

Caplow, T., Bahr, H. D. M., & Chadwick, B. E. A. (1982). *Middletown families: Fifty years of change and continuity.* Minneapolis: University of Minnesota Press.

Cappell, C., & Heiner, R. B. (1990). The intergenerational transmission of family aggression. *Journal of Family Violence, 5*, 135–152.

Carnegie Council on Adolescent Development. (1992). *A matter of time: Risk and opportunity in the after-school hours.* Washington, DC: Author.

Carroll, J. L., & Wolpe, P. R. (1996). *Sexuality and gender in society.* New York: Harper-Collins.

Carson, D. K., Chowdhury, A., Perry, C. K., & Pati, C. (1999). Family characteristics and adolescent competence in India: Investigation of youth in southern Orissa. *Journal of Youth & Adolescence, 28*, 211–233.

Case, R. (1985). *Intellectual development: Birth to adulthood.* New York: Academic Press.

Case, R. (1997). The development of conceptual structures. In D. Kuhn & R. S. Siegler (Eds.), *Handbook of child psychology* (5th ed., Vol. 2). New York: Wiley.

Cash, T. F. (1995). Developmental teasing about physical appearance: Retrospective descriptions and relationships with body image. *Social Behavior and Personality, 23*, 123–129.

Cash, T. F., & Henry, P. E. (1995). Women's body images: The results of a national survey in the USA. *Sex Roles, 33*, 19–28.

Cashmore, J., & Goodnow, J. (1987). Influences of Australian parents' values: Ethnicity versus socioeconomic status. *Journal of Cross-Cultural Psychology, 17*, 441–454.

Caspar, R. C. (1992). Risk factors for the development of eating disorders. In S. C. Feinstein (Ed.), *Adolescent psychiatry* (pp. 91–103). Chicago: University of Chicago Press.

Casper, L. (1990). Does family interaction prevent adolescent pregnancy? *Family Planning Perspectives, 22*, 109–114.

Caspi, A., & Moffitt, T. (1991). Individual differences and personal transitions: The sample case of girls at puberty. *Journal of Personality and Social Psychology, 61*, 157–168.

Caspi, A., Lynam, D., Moffitt, T., & Silva, P. (1993). Unraveling girls' delinquency: Biological, dispositional, and contextual contributions to adolescent misbehavior. *Developmental Psychology, 29*, 19–30.

Cass, V. C. (1979). Homosexual identity formation: A theoretical model. *Journal of Homosexuality, 4*, 219–235.

Casteel, M. (1993). Effects of inference necessity and reading goal on children's inferential generation. *Developmental Psychology, 29*, 346–357.

Catsambis, S. (1994). The path to math: Gender and racial-ethnic differences in mathematics participation from middle school to high school. *Sociology of Education, 67*, 199–215.

Cejka, M. A., & Eagly, A. H. (1999). Gender-stereotypic images of occupations correspond to the sex segregation of employment. *Personality and Social Psychology Bulletin, 25*, 413–423.

Centers for Disease Control and Prevention (CDCP). (1999). *1996 Youth Risk Behavior Surveillance System (YRBSS).* Available: www.cdc.gov/nccdphp/dash/yrbs/suse.htm

Chadwick, B. A., & Heaton, T. B. (1996). *Statistical handbook on adolescents in America.* New York: Oryx Press.

Chalmers, D., & Lawrence, J. (1993). Investigating the effects of planning aids on adults' and adolescents, Organization of a complex task. *International Journal of Behavioural Development, 16*, 191–214.

Chanes, C. W. (2000, February). *Adolescents in Latin America toward the 21st century.* Paper prepared for the meeting of the Study Group on Adolescence in the 21st Century, Washington, DC.

Chao, R. (1994). Beyond parental control and authoritarian parenting style: Understanding Chinese parenting through the cultural notion of training. *Child Development, 65*, 1111–1119.

Chase, W. G., & Simon, H. A. (1973). Perception in chess. *Cognitive Psychology, 4*, 55–81.

Chase-Lansdale, P. L., Cherlin, A. J., & Kiernan, K. E. (1995). The long-term effects of parental divorce on the mental health of young adults: A developmental perspective. *Child Development, 66*, 1614–1634.

Chen, C., & Stevenson, H. W. (1995). Motivation and mathematics achievement: A comparative study of Asian American, Caucasian American, and East Asian high school students. *Child Development, 66*, 1215–1234.

Chen, S., Lee, S., & Stevenson, H. (1996). Long-term prediction of academic achievement of American, Chinese, and Japanese adolescents. *Journal of Educational Psychology, 18*, 750–759.

Cherlin, A. J. (1992). *Marriage, divorce, and remarriage.* Cambridge, MA: Harvard University Press.

Cherlin, A. J. (1999). Going to extremes: Family structure, children's well-being, and social science. *Demography, 36*, 421–428.

Cherlin, A. J., Chase-Lansdale, P. L., & McCrae, C. (1998). Effects of parental divorce on mental health throughout the life course. *American Sociological Review, 63*, 239–249.

Cherlin, A. J., Furstenberg, F. F., Jr., Chase-Lansdale, P. L., Kiernan, K. E., Robins, P. K., Morrison, D. R., & Teitler, J. O. (1991). Longitudinal studies of effects of divorce on children in Great Britain and the United States. *Science, 252*, 1386–1388.

Chi, M. T. H., Glaser, R., & Rees, E. (1982). Expertise in problem solving. In R. J. Sternberg (Ed.), *Advances in the psychology of human intelligence.* Hillsdale, NJ: Erlbaum.

Children's Defense Fund (CDF). (1994). *The state of America's children, 1994.* Washington, DC: Author.

Children's Defense Fund (CDF). (1995). *The state of America's children, 1995.* Washington, DC: Author.

Chilman, C. (1986). Some psychosocial aspects of adolescent sexual and contraceptive behaviors in a changing American society. In J. Lancaster & B. Hamburg (Eds.), *School-age pregnancy and parenthood: Biosocial dimensions.* New York: Aldine de Gruyter.

Chilman, C. S. (1983). *Adolescent sexuality in a changing American society* (2nd ed.). New York: Wiley.

Chinas, L. (1992). *The Isthmus Zapotecs: A matrifocal culture of Mexico.* New York: Harcourt Brace Jovanovich College Publishers.

Chisholm, L., & Hurrelmann, K. (1995). Adolescence in modern Europe: Pluralized transition patterns and their implications for personal and social risks. *Journal of Adolescence, 18*, 129–158.

Cho, B. E., & Shin, H. Y. (1996). State of family research and theory in Korea. In M. B. Sussman & R. S. Hanks (Eds.), *Intercultural variation in family research and theory: Implications for cross-national studies* (pp. 101–135). New York: Haworth Press.

Christenson, P. G., & Roberts, D. F. (1990). *Popular music in early adolescence.* Washington, DC: Carnegie Council on Adolescent Development.

Christenson, P. G., & Roberts, D. F. (1998). *It's not only rock & roll: Popular music in the lives of adolescents.* Cresskill, NJ: Hampton Press.

Christopherson, B. B., Jones, R. M., & Sales, A. P. (1988). Diversity in reported motivations for substance use as a function of ego-identity development. *Journal of Adolescent Research, 3*, 141–152.

Chu, G. C., & Ju, Y. (1993). *The Great Wall in ruins.* New York: State University of New York Press.

Church, R. (1976). *Education in the United States.* New York: Free Press.

Cicchetti, D., & Carlson, V. (Eds.). (1989). *Child maltreatment: Theory and research on the causes and consequences of child abuse and neglect.* New York: Cambridge University Press.

Civic, D. (1999). The association between characteristics of dating relationships and condom use among heterosexual young adults. *AIDS Education and Prevention, 11*, 343–352.

Claes, M. (1998). Adolescents' closeness with parents, siblings, and friends in three countries: Canada, Belgium, and Italy. *Journal of Youth & Adolescence, 27*, 165–184.

Clark, C. A., & Worthington, E. V., Jr. (1987). Family variables affecting the transition of religious values from parents to adolescents: A review. *Family Perspectives, 21*, 1–21.

Clasen, D., & Brown, B. (1985). The multidimensionality of peer pressure in adolescence. *Journal of Youth and Adolescence, 14*, 451–468.

Clausen, C. (1996, Summer). Welcome to post-culturalism. *American Scholar, 65* (3), 379–388.

Clausen, J. A. (1966). *Socialization and society.* Boston: Little, Brown.

Clifford, B. R., Gunter, B., & McAleer, J. L. (1995). *Television and children.* Hillsdale, NJ: Erlbaum.

Clingempeel, W., Colyar, J., Brand, E., & Hetherington, E. (1992). Children's relationships with maternal grandparents: A longitudinal study of family structure and pubertal status effects. *Child Development, 63*, 1404–1422.

Cohen, J. (1969). *Statistical power analysis for the behavioral sciences.* New York: Academic Press.

Cohen, L. R., & Potter, L. B. (1999). Injuries and violence: Risk factors and opportunities. *Adolescent Medicine: State of the Art Reviews, 10*, 125–135.

Cohn, D. (1999, November 24). Parents prize less a child's obedience. *The Washington Post,* p. A8.

Coie, J. D., & Dodge, K. A. (1997). Aggression and antisocial behavior. In N. Eisenberg (Ed.), *Handbook of child psychology* (5th ed., Vol. 3). York: Wiley.

Coie, J. D., Dodge, K. A., & Kupersmidt, J. B. (1990). Peer group behavior and social status. In S. R. Asher & J. D. Coie (Eds.), *Peer rejection in childhood* (pp. 17–59). New York: Cambridge University Press.

Coie, J., Terry, R., Lenox, K., Lochman, J., & Hyman, C. (1995). Childhood peer rejection and aggression as predictors of stable patterns of adolescent disorder. *Development and Psychopathology, 7*, 697–713.

Colby, A., & Kohlberg, L. (1987). *The measurement of moral judgment.* New York: Cambridge University Press.

Colby, A., Kohlberg, L., Gibbs, J., & Lieberman, M. (1983). A longitudinal study of moral judgment. *Monographs of the Society for Research in Child Development, 48.*

Cole, M. (1996). *Cultural psychology: A once and future discipline.* Cambridge, MA: Harvard University Press.

Coleman, J. (1961). *The adolescent society.* Glencoe, IL: Free Press.

Coleman, J., & Hoffer, T. (1987). *Public and private high schools: The impact of communities.* New York: Basic Books.

Coleman, J., Hoffer, T., & Kilgore, S. (1982). *High school achievement: Public, Catholic and other private schools compared.* New York: Basic Books.

Coleman, M., & Ganong, L. H. (1990). Remarriage and stepfamily research in the 1980s: Increased interest in an old form. *Journal of Marriage and the Family, 52*, 925–939.

Coleman, J. S. (1974). *Youth: Transition to adulthood.* Report of the Panel on Youth of the President's Science Advisory Committee. Chicago: University of Chicago Press.

Coles, R., & Stokes, G. (1985). *Sex and the American teenager.* New York: Harper & Row.

Collins, W. A. (1990). Parent–child relationships in the transition to adolescence: Continuity and change in interaction, affect, and cognition. In R. Montemayor, G. Adams, & T. Gullotta (Eds.), *Advances in adolescent development, Vol. 2: The transition from childhood to adolescence* (pp. 85–106). Beverly Hills, CA: Sage.

Collins, W. A., Laursen, B., Mortenson, N., & Ferreira, M. (1997). Conflict processes and transitions in parent and peer relationships: Implications for autonomy and regulation. *Journal of Adolescent Research, 12,* 178–198.

Collins, W. A., Maccoby, E. E., Steinberg, L., Hetherington, E. M., & Bornstein, M. H. (2000). Contemporary research on parenting: The case for nature and nurture. *American Psychologist, 55,* 218–232.

Collins, W. A., & Sroufe, L. A. (1999). Capacity for intimate relationships: A developmental construction. In W. Furman, B. B. Brown, & C. Feiring (Eds.), *The development of romantic relationships in adolescence* (pp. 125–147). New York: Cambridge University Press.

Comer, J. P. (1993). *African American parents and child development: An agenda for school success.* Paper presented at the biennial meeting of the Society for Research in Child Development, New Orleans.

Committee on Child Labor. (1998). *Protecting youth at work.* Washington, DC: National Academy of Sciences.

Compas, B. E., Connor, J. K., & Hinden, B. R. (1998). New perspectives on depression during adolescence. In R. Jessor (Ed.), *New perspectives on adolescent risk behavior* (pp. 319–364). New York: Cambridge University Press.

Compas, B., Ey, S., & Grant, K. (1993). Taxonomy, assessment, and diagnosis of depression during adolescence. *Psychological Bulletin, 114,* 323–344.

Comstock, G., & Strasburger, V. C. (1990). Deceptive appearances: Television violence and aggressive behavior. *Journal of Adolescent Health Care, 11,* 31–44.

Condit, V. (1990). Anorexia nervosa: Levels of causation. *Human Nature, 1,* 391–413.

Condon, R. G. (1987). *Inuit youth: Growth and change in the Canadian Arctic.* New Brunswick, NJ: Rutgers University Press.

Condon, R. G. (1995). The rise of the leisure class: Adolescence and recreational acculturation in the Canadian Arctic. *Ethos, 23,* 47–68.

Connell, J., Halpern-Flesher, B., Clifford, E., Crichlow, W., & Usinger, P. (1995). Hanging in there: Behavioral, psychological, and contextual factors affecting whether African American adolescents stay in high school. *Journal of Adolescent Research, 10,* 41–63.

Connolly, J., & Goldberg, A. (1999). Romantic relationships in adolescence: The role of friends and peers in their emergence and development. In W. Furman, B. B. Brown, & C. Feiring (Eds.), *The development of romantic relationships in adolescence* (pp. 266–290). New York: Cambridge University Press.

Connolly, J., & Konarski, R. (1994). Peer self-concept in adolescence: Analysis of factor structure and of associations with peer experience. *Journal of Research on Adolescence, 4,* 385–403.

Connolly, J., McMaster, L., Craig, W., & Pepler, P. (1998, February). *Romantic relationships of bullies in early adolescence.* Paper presented at the biennial meeting of the Society for Research on Adolescence, San Diego, CA.

Constable, P. (2000, May 8). In Pakistan, women pay the price of "honor." *Washington Post,* pp. A1–A14.

Coombs, R., Paulson, M., & Richardson, M. (1991). Peer vs. parental influence in substance use among Hispanic and Anglo children and adolescents. *Journal of Youth and Adolescence, 20,* 73–88.

Cooney, T. M. (1994). Young adults' relations with parents: The influence of recent parental divorce. *Journal of Marriage and the Family, 56,* 45–56.

Cooney, T. M., Smyer, M. A., Hagestad, G. O., & Klock, R. (1986). Parental divorce in young adulthood: Some preliminary findings. *American Journal of Orthopsychiatry, 56,* 470–477.

Cooper, C., & Grotevant, H. (1987). Gender issues in the interface of family experience and adolescents' friendship and dating identity. *Journal of Youth and Adolescence, 16,* 247–264.

Cooper, C. R., & Ayers-Lopez, S. (1985). Family and peer systems in early adolescence: New models of the role of relationships in development. *Journal of Early Adolescence, 5,* 9–22.

Cooper, K. J. (1999, October 1). Clinton, governors assess efforts to improve education. *Washington Post,* p. A13.

Cooper, M. J., & Fairburn, C. G. (1992). Thoughts about eating, weight and shape in anorexia nervosa and bulimia nervosa. *Behaviour Research and Therapy, 30,* 501–511.

Cooper, M. L., Bede, A. V., & Powers, A. M. (1999). Motivations for condom use: Do pregnancy prevention goals undermine disease prevention among heterosexual young adults? *Health Psychology, 18,* 464–474.

Corby, B. (1993). *Child abuse: Toward a knowledge base.* Buckingham, PA: Open University Press.

Corey, L., Adams, H. G., & Brown, Z. A. (1983). Genital herpes simplex virus infections. *Annals of Internal Medicine, 98,* 958–972.

Cota-Robles, S., Neiss, M., & Hunt, C. B. (2000, April). *Future selves, future scholars: A longitudinal study of adolescent "possible selves" and adult outcomes.* Poster presented at the biennial meeting of the Society for Research on Adolescence, Chicago.

Coté, J. (1994). *Adolescent storm and stress: An evaluation of the Mead–Freeman controversy.* Hillsdale, NJ: Erlbaum.

Coté, J. (2000). *Arrested adulthood: The changing nature of maturity and identity in the late modern world.* New York: New York University Press.

Coté, J. E., & Allahar, A. L. (1996). *Generation on hold: Coming of age in the late twentieth century.* New York: New York University Press.

Cozby, P. C., Worden, P. E., & Kee, D. W. (1989). *Research methods in human development.* Mountain View, CA: Mayfield.

Cravatta, M. (1997). Online adolescents. *American Demographics, 19,* 29.

Crick, N., & Dodge, K. (1996). Social information-processing mechanisms in reactive and proactive aggression. *Child Development, 67,* 993–1002.

Crisp, A. (1983). Some aspects of the psychopathology of anorexia nervosa. In P. Darby, P. Garfinkel, D. Garner, & D. Cosina (Eds.), *Anorexia nervosa: Recent developments in research* (pp. 15–28). New York: Alan R. Liss.

Crouter, A. C., Manke, B. A., & McHale, S. M. (1995). The family context of gender intensification in early adolescence. *Child Development, 66,* 317–329.

Crump, A. D., Haynie, D. L., Aarons, S. J., Adair, E., Woodward, K., & Simons-Morton, B. G. (1999). Pregnancy among urban African-American teens: Ambivalence about prevention. *American Journal of Health Behavior, 23,* 32–42.

Csikszentmihalyi, M., & Larson, R. W. (1984). *Being adolescent: Conflict and growth in the teenage years.* New York: Basic Books.

Culbertson, F. M. (1997). Depression and gender. *American Psychologist,* 25–31.

Cunliffe, T. (1992). Arresting youth crime: A review of social skills training with young offenders. *Adolescence, 27,* 891–900.

Curran, P., Stice, E., & Chassin, L. (1997). The relation between adolescent alcohol and peer alcohol use: A longitudinal random coefficients model. *Journal of Consulting and Clinical Psychology, 65,* 130–140.

Currie, D. (1999). *Girl talk: Adolescent magazines and their readers.* Toronto: University of Toronto Press.

Cutrona, C. E. (1982). Transition to college: Loneliness and the process of social adjustment. In L. A. Peplau & D. Perlman (Eds.), *Loneliness: A sourcebook of theory, research, and therapy* (pp. 291–309). New York: Wiley.

Dahlberg, F. (1981). *Woman the gatherer.* New Haven, CT: Yale University Press.

Damico, S., & Sparks, C. (1986). Cross-group contact opportunities: Impact on interpersonal relationships in desegregated middle schools. *Sociology of Education, 59,* 113–123.

Daniels, D., Dunn, J., Furstenberg, F., Jr., & Plomin, R. (1985). Environmental differences within the family and adjustment differences within pairs of adolescent siblings. *Child Development, 56,* 764–774.

Dasen, P. (1998). Rapid social change and the turmoil of adolescence: A cross-cultural perspective. *World Psychology.*

Davies, E., & Furnham, A. (1986). The dieting and body shape concerns of adolescent females. *Journal of Child Psychology & Psychiatry, 27,* 417–428.

Davies, M., & Kandel, D. B. (1981). Parental and peer influences on adolescents' educational plans: Some further evidence. *American Journal of Sociology, 87,* 363–387.

Davis, J. A., & Smith, T. W. (1991, July). *General social surveys, 1972–1991.* Chicago: National Opinion Research Center, University of Chicago.

Davis, K., & Kirkpatrick, L. (1998). Attachment style, gender, and relationship stability: A longitudinal analysis. *Journal of personality and Social Psychology, 66,* 505–512.

Davis, L., & Stewart, R. (1997, July). *Building capacity for working with lesbian, gay, bisexual, and transgender youth.* Paper presented at the conference on Working with America's Youth, Pittsburgh, PA.

Davis, S. S., & Davis, D. A. (1989). *Adolescence in a Moroccan town.* New Brunswick, NJ: Rutgers.

Davis, S. S., & Davis, D. A. (1995). "The mosque and the satellite": Media and adolescence in a Moroccan town. *Journal of Youth & Adolescence, 24,* 577–594.

De Mey, L., Baartman, H. M., & Schultze, H. J. (1999). Ethnic variation and the development of moral judgment of youth in Dutch society. *Youth & Society, 31,* 54–75.

de Wilde, E. J., Kienhorts, I., Diekstra, R., & Wolters, W. (1992). The relationship between adolescent suicidal behavior and life events in childhood and adolescence. *American Journal of Psychiatry, 149,* 45–51.

Deaux, K., & Lewis, L. L. (1984). Structure of gender stereotypes: Interrelationships among components and gender label. *Journal of Personality and Social Psychology, 46,* 991–1004.

DeBaryshe, K., Patterson, G., & Capaldi, D. (1993). A performance model for academic achievement in early adolescent boys. *Developmental Psychology, 29,* 795–804.

Decker, J. L. (1994). The state of rap: Time and place in hip hop nationalism. In A. Ross & T. Rose (Eds.), *Microphone fiends: Youth music & youth culture* (pp. 99–121). New York: Routledge.

Deihl, L. M., Vicary, J. R., & Deike, R. C. (1997). Longitudinal trajectories of self-esteem from early to middle adolescence and related psychosocial variables among rural adolescents. *Journal of Research on Adolescence, 7,* 393–411.

Delaney, C. (1988). Mortal flow: Menstruation in Turkish village society. In T. Buckley & A. Gottlieb (Eds.), *Blood magic: The anthropology of menstruation* (pp. 75–93). Berkeley: University of California Press.

DeLisi, R., & Soundranayagam, L. (1990). The conceptual structure of sex role stereotypes in college students. *Sex Roles, 23,* 593–611.

Demorest, A., Meyer, C., Phelps, E., Gardner, H., & Winner, E. (1984). Words speak louder than actions: Understanding deliberately false remarks. *Child Development, 55,* 1527–1534.

Dempster, N. W. (1984). Model of cognitive development across the lifespan. *Developmental Review, 4,* 171–191.

Desmairis, S., & Curtis, J. (1999). Gender differences in employment and income experiences among young people. In J. Barling & E. K. Kelloway (Eds.), *Youth workers: Varieties of experience* (pp. 59–88). Washington, DC: American Psychological Association.

Dey, E. L., & Hurtado, S. (1999). Students, colleges, and society: Considering the interconnections. In P. G. Altbach, R. O. Berndahl, & P. J. Gumport (Eds.), *American higher education in the twenty-first century: Social, political, and economic challenges* (pp. 298–322). Baltimore: Johns Hopkins University Press.

Deyhle, D. (1995). Navajo youth and Anglo racism: Cultural integrity and resistance. *Harvard Educational Review, 65,* 403–444.

Deyhle, D. (1998). From break dancing to heavy metal: Navajo youth, resistance, and identity. *Youth & Society, 30,* 3–31.

Deykin, E. Y., Buka, S. L., & Zeena, T. H. (1992). Depressive illness among chemically dependent adolescents. *American Journal of Psychiatry, 149,* 1341–1347.

Diaz, R., & Berndt, T. (1982). Children's knowledge of a best friend: Fact or fancy? *Developmental Psychology, 18,* 787–794.

Dielman, T. (1994). School-based research on the prevention of adolescent alcohol use and misuse: Methodological issues and advances. *Journal of Research on Adolescence, 4,* 271–293.

Dinges, N. G., Trimble, J. E., & Hollenbeck, A. R. (1979). American Indian adolescent socialization: A review of the literature. *Journal of Adolescence, 2,* 259–296.

Dion, K. K., & Dion, K. L. (1993). Individualistic and collectivistic perspectives on gender and the cultural context of love and intimacy. *Journal of Social Issues, 49,* 53–69.

Dionne, E. J., Jr. (1999, July 16). Abstinence-plus. *The Washington Post,* p. A-23.

Dishion, T. J., & Spracklen, K. M. (1996, March). *Childhood peer rejection in the development of adolescent substance abuse.* Paper presented at the meeting of the Society for Research on Adolescence, Boston.

Dishion, T., Patterson, G., Stoolmiller, M., & Skinner, M. (1991). Family, school, and behavioral antecedents to early adolescent involvement with antisocial peers. *Developmental Psychology, 27,* 172–180.

DiTommaso, E., & Spinner, B. (1997). Social and emotional loneliness: A reexamination of Weiss' typology of loneliness. *Personality and Individual Differences, 22,* 417–427.

Dixon, W. A., Heppner, P. P., & Anderson, W. (1991). Problem-solving appraisals, stress, hopelessness, and suicidal ideation in a college population. *Journal of Counseling Psychology, 38,* 51–56.

Dobkin, P., Tremblay, R., Masse, L., & Vitaro, F. (1995). Individual and peer characteristics in predicting boys' early onset of substance abuse: A seven-year longitudinal study. *Child Development, 66,* 1198–1214.

Dodd, J. M., Nelson, J. R., & Hofland, B. H. (1994). Minority identity and self-concept: The American Indian experience. In T. M. Brinthaupt & R. P. Lipka (Eds.), *Changing the self: Philosophies, techniques, and experiences* (pp. 307–336). Albany, NY: State University of New York Press.

Dodge, K. A. (1983). Behavioral antecedents of peer social status. *Child Development, 54,* 1386–1399,

Dodge, K. A. (1993, March). *Social information processing and peer rejection factors in the development of behavior problems in children.* Paper presented at the biennial meeting of the Society for Research in Child Development, New Orleans.

Dodge, K. A., & Feldman, E. (1990). Issues in social cognition and sociometric status. In S. R. Asher & J. D. Coie (Eds.), *Peer rejection in childhood* (pp. 119–155). Cambridge, England: Cambridge University Press.

Donahue, M. (1994, February). *Positive youth development in religiously-based youth programs.* Paper presented at the biennial meeting of the Society for Research on Adolescence, San Diego.

Donnelly, D., & Finkelhor, D. (1992). Does equality in custody arrangement improve the parent–child relationship? *Journal of Marriage and the Family, 54,* 837–845.

Donovan, D. M., Marlatt, G. A., & Salzberg, P. M. (1983). Drinking behavior, personality factors, and high-risk driving: A review and theoretical formulation. *Journal of Studies on Alcohol, 44,* 395–428.

Donovan, D. M., Queisser, H. R., Salzberg, P. M., & Umlauf, R. L. (1985). Intoxicated and bad drivers: Subgroups within the same population of high-risk men drivers. *Journal of Studies on Alcohol, 46,* 375–382.

Donovan, D. M., Umlauf, R. L., & Salzberg, P. M. (1988). Derivation of personality subtypes among high-risk drivers. *Alcohol, Drugs and Driving, 4,* 233–244.

Donovan, J. E. (1993). Young adult drinking-driving: Behavioral and psychosocial correlates. *Journal of Studies on Alcohol, 54,* 600–613.

Donovan, J., & Jessor, R. (1985). Structure of problem behavior in adolescence and young adulthood. *Journal of Consulting and Clinical Psychology, 53,* 890–904.

Dornbusch, S. (1994, February). *Off the track.* Presidential address to the Society for Research on Adolescence, San Diego.

Dornbusch, S., Carlsmith, J., Bushwall, S., Ritter, P., Leiderman, P., Hastorf, A., & Gross, R. (1985). Single parents, extended households, and the control of adolescents. *Child Development, S6,* 326–341.

Dornbusch, S. M., Carlsmith, J. M., Gross, R. T., Martin, J. A., Jennings, D., Rosenberg, A., & Duke, P. (1981). Sexual development, age, and dating: A comparison of biological and social influences upon one set of behaviors. *Child Development, 52,* 179–185.

Dornbusch, S., M. Ritter, R., Liederman, P., Roberts, D., & Fraleigh, M. (1987). The relation of parenting style to adolescent school performance. *Child Development, 58,* 1244–1257.

Dornbusch, S. M., Ritter, P. L., Mont-Reynaud, R., & Chien, Z. (1990). Family decision making and academic performance in a diverse high school population. *Journal of Adolescent Research, 5,* 143–160.

Douvan, E., & Adelson, J. (1966). *The adolescent experience.* New York: Wiley.

Dreyer, P. (1982). Sexuality during adolescence. In B. Wolman (Ed.), *Handbook of developmental psychology.* Englewood Cliffs, NJ: Prentice-Hall.

Dryfoos, J. (1990). *Adolescents at risk: Prevalence and prevention.* New York: Oxford University Press.

Dryfoos, J. G. (1998). *Full-service schools: A revolution in health and social services for children, youth, and families.* San Francisco: Jossey-Bass.

Dubas, J. S., & Petersen, A. C. (1996). Geographical distance from parents and adjustment during adolescence and young adulthood. In J. A. Graber & J.S. Dubas (Eds.), *New Directions for Child Development, 71,* 3–19.

Dubas, J., Graber, J., & Petersen, A. (1991). A longitudinal investigation of adolescents' changing perceptions of pubertal timing. *Developmental Psychology, 27,* 580–586.

Duben, A., & Behar, C. (1991). *Istanbul households.* Cambridge, England: Cambridge University Press.

DuBois, D. L., & Hirsch, B. J. (1990). School and neighborhood friendship patterns of blacks and whites in early adolescence. *Child Development, 61,* 524–536.

DuBois, D. L., & Hirsch, B. J. (1993). School/nonschool friendship patterns in early adolescence. *Journal of Early Adolescence, 13,* 102–122.

DuBois, D. L., & Tevendale, H. D. (1999). Self-esteem in childhood and adolescence: Vaccine or epiphenomenon? *Applied & Preventive Psychology, 8,* 103–117.

DuBois, D. L., Bull, C. A., Sherman, M. D., & Roberts, M. (1998). Self-esteem and adjustment in early adolescence: A social-contextual perspective. *Journal of Youth & Adolescence, 27,* 557–584.

DuBois, D., Eitel, S., & Felner, R. (1994). Effects of family environment and parent–child relationships on school adjustment during the transition to early adolescence. *Journal of Marriage and the Family, 56,* 405–414.

DuBois, D., Felner, R., Brand, S., Adan, A., & Evans, E. (1992). A prospective study of life stress, social support, and adaptation in early adolescence. *Child Development, 63,* 542–557.

DuBois, D., Felner, R., Brand, S., Phillip, R., & Lease, A. (1996). Early adolescent self-esteem: A developmental-ecological framework and assessment strategy. *Journal of Research on Adolescence, 6,* 543–579.

Dudley, J. R. (1991). Increasing our understanding of divorced fathers who have infrequent contact with their children. *Family Relations, 40,* 279–285.

Duffy, M., & Gotcher, J. M. (1996). Crucial advice on how to get the guy: The rhetorical vision of power and seduction in the teen magazine *YM. Journal of Communication Inquiry, 20,* 32–48.

Duncan, P., Ritter, P., Dornbusch, S., Gross, R., & Carlsmith, J. (1985). The effects of pubertal timing on body image, school behavior, and deviance. *Journal of Youth and Adolescence, 14,* 227–236.

Dunphy, D. (1969). *Cliques, crowds, and gangs.* Melbourne: Ghesire.

Dunphy, D. (1963). The social structure of urban adolescent peer groups. *Sociometry, 26,* 230–246.

Durbin, D. L., Darling, N., Steinberg, L., & Brown, B. B. (1993). Parenting style and peer group membership among European-American adolescents. *Journal of Research on Early Adolescence, 3,* 87–100.

Durham, M. G. (1998). Dilemmas of desire: Representations of sexuality in two teen magazines. *Youth & Society, 29,* 369–389.

Dyk, P., & Adams, G. (1990). Identity and intimacy: An initial investigation of three theoretical models using crosslag panel correlations. *Journal of Youth and Adolescence, 19,* 91–110.

Eagly, A. H. (1987). *Sex differences in social behavior: A social-role interpretation.* Hillsdale, NJ: Erlbaum.

Eccles, J. S. (1993, March). *Psychological and social barriers to women's participation in mathematics and science.* Paper presented at the biennial meeting of the American Educational Research Association, Atlanta.

Eccles, J. S., & Harold, R. D. (1993). Parent-school involvement during the adolescent years. In R. Takanishi (Ed.), *Adolescence in the 1990s.* New York: Columbia University Press.

Eccles, J. S., Lord, S. E., Roeser, R. W., Barber, B. L., & Hernandez Jozefowicz, D. M. (1997). The association of school transitions in early adolescence with developmental trajectories through high school. In J. Schulenberg, J. L. Maggs, & K. Hurrelmann (Eds.), *Health risks and developmental transitions during adolescence* (pp. 283–320). New York: Cambridge University Press.

Eccles, J., Lord, S., & Midgley, C. (1991). What are we doing to early adolescents? The impact of educational contexts on early adolescents. *American Journal of Education, 99,* 521–542.

Eccles, J., Midgley, C., Wigfield, A., Buchanan, C., Reuman, D., Flanagan, C., & Mac Iver, D. (1993). Development during adolescence: The impact of stage-environment fit on young adolescents' experiences in schools and families. *American Psychologist, 48,* 90–101.

Eckenrode, J., Laird, M., & Doris, J. (1993). School performance and disciplinary problems among abused and neglected children. *Developmental Psychology, 29,* 53–62.

Eder, D. (1993). "Go get ya a French!" Romantic and sexual teasing among adolescent girls. In D. Tannen (Ed.), *Gender and conversational interaction* (pp. 17–31). New York: Oxford University Press.

Eder, D. (1995). *School talk: Gender and adolescent culture.* New Brunswick, NJ: Rutgers University Press.

Education Trust. (1996). *Education watch: The 1996 Education Trust state and national data book.* Washington, DC: Author.

Educational Testing Service. (1992). *Crossnational comparisons of 9–13 year olds' science and math achievement.* Princeton, NJ: Author.

Eichorn, D. H. (1970). Physiological development. In P. H. Mussen (Ed.), *Carmichael's manual of child psychology* (Vol. 2, 3rd ed., pp. 152–183). New York: Wiley.

Eichorn, D. H. (1975). Asynchronizations in adolescent development. In S. Dragastin & G. H. Elder, Jr. (Eds.), *Adolescence in the life cycle: Psychological change and the social context* (pp. 81–96). New York: Halsted.

El-Bakri, Z. B., & Kameir, E. M. (1983). Aspects of women's political participation in Sudan. *International Social Science Journal, 35,* 605–623.

Elder, G. H., Jr. (1974/1999). *Children of the Great Depression: Social change in life experience.* Boulder, CO: Westview Press.

Elder, G. H., Jr., Caspi, A., & van Nguyen, T. (1986). Resourceful and vulnerable children: Family influences in stressful times. In R. Silbereisen, K. Eyferth, & G. Rudinger (Eds.), *Development as action in context.* Heidelberg: Springer.

Elder, G. H., Jr., van Nguyen, T., & Caspi, A. (1985). Linking family hardship to children's lives. *Child Development, 56,* 361–375.

Elkind, D. (1967). Egocentrism in adolescence. *Child Development, 38,* 1025–1034.

Elkind, D. (1978). Understanding the young adolescent. *Adolescence, 13,* 127–134.

Elkind, D. (1985). Egocentrism redux. *Developmental Review, 5*, 218–226.

Elliott, D. S., Huizinga, D., & Menard, S. (1989). *Multiple problem youth: Delinquency, substance abuse, and mental health problems.* New York: Springer.

Ellis, N. (1991). An extension of the Steinberg accelerating hypothesis. *Journal of Early Adolescence, 11*, 221–235.

Elster, A., Lamb, M., Peters, L., Kahn, J., & Tavare, J. (1987). Judicial involvement and conduct problems of fathers of infants born to adolescent mothers. *Pediatrics, 79*, 230–234.

Emery, R. E. (1999). *Marriage, divorce, and children's adjustment* (2nd ed.). Newbury Park, CA: Sage.

Emery, R. E., & Tuer, M. (1993). Parenting and the marital relationship. In T. Luster & L. Okagaki (Eds.), *Parenting: An ecological perspective.* Hillsdale, NJ: Erlbaum.

Emslie, G. J., Graham, J., Walkup, J. T., Pliszka, S. R., & Ernst, M. (1999). Nontricyclic antidepressants: Current trends in children and adolescents. *Journal of the American Academy of Child & Adolescent Psychiatry, 38*, 513–528.

Engles, R. C. M. E., Knibbe, R. A., de Vries, H., Drop, M. J., & van Breukelen, G. J. P. (1999). Influences of parental and best friends' smoking and drinking on adolescent use: A longitudinal study. *Journal of Applied Social Psychology, 29*, 337–361.

Ennett, S., & Bauman, K. (1994). The contribution of influence and selection to adolescent peer group homogeneity: The case of adolescent cigarette smoking. *Journal of Personality and Social Psychology, 67*, 653–663.

Ennett, S., Tobler, N., Ringwalt, C., & Flewelling, R. (1994). How effective is drug abuse resistance education? A meta-analysis of Project DARE outcome evaluations. *American Journal of Public Health, 84*, 1394–1401.

Entwisle, D. (1990). Schools and the adolescent. In S. Feldman & G. Elliott (Eds.), *At the threshold: The developing adolescent* (pp. 197–224). Cambridge, MA: Harvard University Press.

Ephron, N. (2000). *Crazy salad: Some things about women.* New York: Random House.

Epstein, J. (1983). Selecting friends in contrasting secondary school environments. In J. Epstein & N. Karweit (Eds.), *Friends in school.* New York: Academic Press.

Epstein, J. L., & Dunbar, S. L. (1995). Effects on students of an interdisciplinary program linking social studies, art, and family volunteers in the middle grades. *Journal of Early Adolescence, 15*, 114–144.

Epstein, J. S., Pratto, D. J., & Skipper, J. K. (1990). Teenagers, behavioral problems, and preferences for heavy metal and rap music: A case study of a Southern middle school. *Deviant Behavior, 11*, 381–394.

Ericsson, K. A. (1990). Peak performance and age: An examination of peak performance in sports. In P. Baltes & M. M. Baltes (Eds.), *Successful aging* (pp. 164–196). Cambridge, MA: Cambridge University Press.

Erikson, E. H. (1950). *Childhood and society.* New York: Norton.

Erikson, E. H. (1958). *Young man Luther.* New York: Norton.

Erikson, E. H. (1959). Identity and the life cycle. *Psychological Issues, 1*, 1–171.

Erikson, E. H. (1968). *Identity: Youth and crisis.* New York: Norton.

Eron, L. R. (1993). *The problem of media violence and children's behavior.* New York: Henry Frank Guggenheim Foundation.

Espin, O. M. (1997). *Latina realities: Essays on healing, migration, and sexuality.* Boulder, CO: Westview Press.

Estrin, H. M., & Do, S. H. (1988). Chlamydia trachomatis, monoclonal antibody testing, wet mount screening, and the university health service. *Journal of American College Health, 37*, 61–64.

Evans, E. D., Rutberg, J., Sather, C., & Turner, C. (1991). Content analysis of contemporary teen magazines for adolescent females. *Youth & Society, 23*, 99–120.

Evans, M. E. (1992, March). *Achievement and achievement-related beliefs in Asian and Western contexts: Cultural and gender differences.* Paper presented at the biennial meeting of the Society for Research on Adolescence, Washington, DC.

Eveleth, P. B., & Tanner, J. M. (1990). *Worldwide variation in human growth.* Cambridge, MA: Cambridge University Press.

Eyre, S. L., & Millstein, S. G. (1999). What leads to sex? Adolescent preferred partners and reasons for sex. *Journal of Research on Adolescence, 9*, 277–307.

Fagan, P. J., & Anderson, A. E. (1990). Sexuality and eating disorders in adolescence. In M. Sugar (Ed.), *Atypical adolescence and sexuality* (pp. 108–126). New York: Norton.

Fagot, B. I., Pears, K. C., Capaldi, D. M., Crosby, L., & Leve, C. S. (1998). Becoming an adolescent father: Precursors and parenting. *Developmental Psychology, 34*, 1209–1219.

Faludi, S. (1991). *Backlash: The undeclared war against American women.* New York: Crown.

Farber, S. L. (1981). *Identical twins reared apart.* New York: Basic Books.

Farrell, A. D., & Danish, S. J. (1993). Peer drug association and emotional restraint: Causes or consequences of adolescent drug use? *Journal of Consulting and Clinical Psychology, 61*, 327–334.

Farrington, D. (1989). Early predictors of adolescent aggression and adult violence. *Violence and Victims, 4*, 79–100.

Farrington, D., & West, D. (1991). The Cambridge Study in Delinquent Development: A long-term follow-up of 411 London males. In H. Kerner & G. Kaiser (Eds.), *Criminality: Personality, behavior, and life history* (pp. 115–138). New York: Springer-Verlag.

Featherman, D. (1980). Schooling and occupational careers: Constancy and change in worldly success. In O. Brim, Jr., & J. Kagan (Eds.), *Constancy and change in human development.* Cambridge, MA: Harvard University Press.

Federal Bureau of Investigation. (1993). *Uniform crime reports for the United States.* Washington, DC: U.S. Government Printing Office.

Federal Bureau of Investigation. (1999). *Uniform crime reports for the United States.* Washington, DC: U.S. Government Printing Office.

Federal Interagency Forum on Child and Family Statistics. (1999). *America's children: Key national indicators of well-being, 1999.* Washington, DC: U.S. Government Printing Office.

Fehr, B. (1993). How do I love thee? Let me consult my prototype. In S. Duck (Ed.), *Individuals in relationships: Understanding relationship process series* (Vol. 1, pp. 87–120). Newbury Park, CA: Sage.

Feiring, C. (1996). Concepts of romance in 15-year-old adolescents. *Journal of Research on Adolescence, 6*, 181–200.

Feiring, C., & Lewis, M. (1991). The transition from middle childhood to early adolescence: Sex differences in the social network and perceived self-competence. *Sex Roles, 24*, 489–310.

Feldman, S. S., & Cauffman, E. (1999). Sexual betrayal among late adolescents: Perspectives of the perpetrator and the aggrieved. *Journal of Youth & Adolescence, 28*, 235–258.

Feldman, S. S., & Elliott, G. R. (1990). *At the threshold: The developing adolescent.* Cambridge, MA: Harvard University Press.

Feldman, S. S., Feldman, D., Brown, N., & Canning, R. (1995). Predicting sexual experience in adolescent boys from peer acceptance and rejection during childhood. *Journal of Research on Adolescence, 5*, 387–411.

Feldman, S. S., Mont-Reynaud, R., & Rosenthal, D. A. (1992). When East meets West: The acculturation of values of Chinese adolescents in the U.S. and Australia. *Journal of Research on Adolescence, 2*, 147–173.

Feldman, S. S., Rosenthal, D. A., Mont-Reynaud, R., Leung, K., & Lau, S. (1991). Ain't misbehavin': Adolescent values and family environments as correlates of misconduct in Australia, Hong Kong, and the United States. *Journal of Research on Adolescence, 1*, 109–134.

Feldman, S. S., Turner, R. A., & Araujo, K. (1999). Interpersonal context as an influence on the sexual timetables of youths: Gender and ethnic effects. *Journal of Research on Adolescence, 9*, 25–52.

Felner, R., Brand, S., DuBois, D., Adan, A., Mulhall, P., & Evans, E. (1995). Socioeconomic disadvantage, proximal environmental experiences, and socio-emotional and academic adjustment in adolescence: Investigation of a mediated effects model. *Child Development, 66,* 774–792.

Female genital mutilation: Is it crime or culture? (1999, February 13). *The Economist,* p. 45.

Fenzel, L. M., Blyth, D. A., & Simmons, R. G. (1991). School transitions, secondary. In R. M. Lerner, A. C. Petersen, & J. Brooks-Gunn (Eds.), *Encyclopedia of adolescence* (Vol. 2). New York: Garland.

Ferguson, D., & Horwood, L. (1995). The role of adolescent peer affiliations in the continuity between childhood behavioral adjustment and juvenile offending. *Journal of Abnormal Child Psychology, 24,* 533–553.

Ferrier, M. B. (1996, July/August). Alphas apply "each one, teach one" rule to help turn boys to men. *Youth Today,* pp. 46, 48.

Figueira-McDonough, J. (1998). Environment and interpretation: Voices of young people in poor inner-city neighborhoods. *Youth & Society, 30,* 123–163.

Fine, G. A., Mortimer, J. T., & Roberts, D. F. (1990). Leisure, work, and the mass media. In S. S. Feldman & G. R. Elliott (Eds.), *At the threshold: The developing adolescent.* (pp. 225–254). Cambridge, MA: Harvard University Press.

Fine, M. (1988). Sexuality, schooling, and adolescent females: The missing discourse of desire. *Harvard Educational Review, 58,* 29–53.

Finkelhor, D. (1990). Early and long-term effects of child sexual abuse: An update. *Professional Psychology, 21,* 325–330.

Finken, L. L., Jacobs, J. E., & Laguna, K. D. (1998). Risky driving and driving/riding decisions: The role of previous experience. *Journal of Youth & Adolescence, 27,* 493–511.

Fischer, J. L. (1981). Transitions in relationship styles from adolescence to young adulthood. *Journal of Youth and Adolescence, 10,* 11–24.

Fischoff, B. (1992). Risk taking: A developmental perspective. In J. Yates (Ed.), *Risk taking behavior* (pp. 133–162). New York: Wiley.

Fisher, L. A., & Bauman, K. E. (1988). Influence and selection in the friend-adolescent relationship: Findings from studies of adolescent smoking and drinking. *Journal of Applied Social Psychology, 18,* 289–314.

Fisher, M., Trieller, K., & Napolitano, B. (1989). Premenstrual symptoms in adolescence. *Journal of Adolescent Health Care, 10,* 369–375.

Fitch, R. T. (1987). Characteristics and motivations of college students volunteering for community service. *Journal of College Student Development, 32,* 534–540.

Fitness, J., & Fletcher, G. J. O. (1993). Love, hate, anger, and jealousy in close relationships: A prototype and cognitive appraisal analysis. *Journal of Personality and Social Psychology, 65,* 942–958.

Fitzgerald, F. S. (1920/1995). *This side of paradise.* New York: Barnes and Noble Books.

Flammer, A., & Alsaker, F. D. (1999). Time use by adolescents in international perspective: The case of necessary activities. In F. D. Alsaker & A. Flammer (Eds.), *The adolescent experience: European and American adolescents in the 1990s* (pp. 61–84). Mahwah, NJ: Erlbaum.

Flammer, A., Alsaker, F. D., & Noack, P. (1999). Time use by adolescents in international perspective: The case of leisure activities. In F. D. Alsaker & A. Flammer (Eds.), *The Adolescent experience: European and American adolescents in the 1990s* (pp. 33–60). Mahwah, NJ: Erlbaum.

Flanagan, C. A., Bowes, J. M., Jonsson, B., Csapo, B., & Sheblanova, E. (1998). Ties that bind: Correlates of adolescents' civic commitments in seven countries. *Journal of Social Issues, 54,* 457–475.

Flanagan, C., & Botcheva, L. (1999). Adolescents' preference for their homeland and other countries. In F. D. Alsaker & A. Flammer (Eds.), *The adolescent experience: European and American adolescents in the 1990s* (pp. 131–144). Mahwah, NJ: Erlbaum.

Flanagan, T. J., & Maguire, K. (Eds.). (1992). *Sourcebook of criminal justice statistics—1991.* Washington, DC: U. S. Department of Justice.

Flavell, J. H. (1985). *Cognitive development* (2nd ed.). Englewood Cliffs, NJ: Prentice-Hall.

Flavell, J. H. (1992). Cognitive development: Past, present, and future. *Developmental Psychology, 28,* 998–1005.

Flavell, J. H., Miller, P. A., & Miller, S. A. (1993). Cognitive development (3rd ed.). Englewood Cliffs, NJ: Prentice-Hall.

Fleming, J. E., & Offord, D. R. (1990). Epidemiology of childhood depressive disorders: A critical review. *Journal of the American Academy of child and Adolescent Psychiatry, 29,* 571–580.

Fleming, J. E., Boyle, M. H., & Offord, D. R. (1993). The outcome of adolescent depression in the Ontario Child Health Study follow-up. *Journal of the American Academy of Child and Adolescent Psychiatry, 32,* 28–83.

Fletcher, M. A. (2000, February 3). California minority youth treated more harshly, study says. *Washington Post,* p. A-16.

Ford, C., & Beach, F. (1951). *Patterns of sexual behavior.* New York: Harper & Row.

Fordham, S., & Ogbu, J. U. (1986). Black students' school success: The "burden of 'acting white'." *The Urban Review, 18,* 176–206.

Forkel, I., & Silbereisen, R. K. (in press). Family economic hardship and depressed mood among young adolescents in the former East and West Germany. *American Behavioral Scientist.*

Fors, S., & Rojek, D. G. (1991). A comparison of drug involvement between runaways and school youths. *Journal of Drug Education, 21,* 13–25.

Forum on Child and Family Statistics. (1999). America's children, 1999 [Online]. Available: www.childstats.gov

Fowler, J. W. (1981). *Stages of faith: The psychology of human development and the quest for meaning.* San Francisco: Harper & Row.

Fowler, J. W. (1991). Stages in faith consciousness. In F. K. Oser & W. O. Scarlett (Eds.), *New directions for child development: Special issue on religious development in childhood and adolescence* (Vol. 52, pp. 27–45). San Francisco: Jossey-Bass.

Fox, J. A. (1996). Trends in juvenile violence: A report to the United States Attorney General on the current and future rates of juvenile offending. Washington, DC: U.S. Department of Justice.

Frank, A. (1942/1997). *The diary of Anne Frank.* New York: Bantam.

Franklin, C. W., II (1984). *The changing definition of masculinity.* New York: Plenum.

Franz, W., & Reardon, D. (1992). Differential impact of abortion on adolescents and adults. *Adolescence, 27,* 161–172.

Franzoni, S. L., Davis, M. H., & Vasquez-Suson, K. A. (1994). Two social worlds: Social correlates and stability of adolescent status groups. *Journal of Personality and Social Psychology, 67,* 462–473.

Frayser, S. G. (1985). *Varieties of sexual experience: An anthropological perspective on human sexuality.* New Haven, CT: Human Relations Area Files Press.

Freedman, J. L. (1984). Effects of television violence on aggressiveness. *Psychological Bulletin, 96,* 227–246.

Freedman, R. (1994). *Kids at work: Lewis Hine and the crusade against child labor.* New York: Clarion.

Freeman, H. S. (1993, March). *Parental control of adolescents through family transitions.* Paper presented at the biennial meeting of the Society for Research in Child Development, New Orleans.

French, D., Conrad, J., & Turner, T. (1995). Adjustment of antisocial and nonantisocial rejected adolescents. *Development and Psychopathology, 7,* 857–874.

French, M. (1992). *The war against women.* New York: Summit Books.

French, S., Story, M., Downes, B., Resnick, M., & Blum, R. (1995). Frequent dieting among adolescents: Psychosocial and health behavior correlates. *American Journal of Public Health, 85,* 695–701.

French, T. (1993). *South of heaven: Welcome to the American high school at the end of the twentieth century.* New York: Pocket Books.

Freud, A. (1946). *The ego and the mechanisms of defense.* New York: International Universities Press.

Freud, A. (1958). Adolescence. *Psychoanalytic Study of the Child, 15,* 255–278. New York: International Universities Press, Inc.

Freud, A. (1968). Adolescence. In A. E. Winder & D. Angus (Eds.), *Adolescence: Contemporary studies* (pp. 13–24). New York: American Book.

Freud, A. (1969). Adolescence as a developmental disturbance. In G. Caplan & S. Lebovici (Eds.), *Adolescence: Psychosocial perspectives* (pp. 5–10). New York: Basic Books.

Freud, S. (1940/64). *An outline of psychoanalysis.* Standard edition of the works of Sigmund Freud. London: Hogarth Press.

Friedman, L. (1989). Mathematics and the gender gap: A meta-analysis of recent studies on sex differences in mathematical tasks. *Review of Educational Research, 59,* 185–213.

Friedman-Klein, A. E., & Farthing, C. (1990). Human immunodeficiency virus infection: A survey with special emphasis on mucocutaneous manifestations. *Seminars in Dermatology, 9,* 167–177.

Frith, S. (1983). *Sound effects.* London: Constable.

Frone, M. R. (1999). Developmental consequences of youth employment. In J. Barling & E. K. Kelloway (Eds.), *Youth workers: Varieties of experience* (pp. 89–128). Washington, DC: American Psychological Association.

Fry, A. F., & Hole, S. (1996). Processing speed, working memory, and fluid intelligence: Evidence for a developmental cascade. *Psychological Science, 7,* 237–241.

Fuentes, C. D. L., & Vasquez, M. J. T. (1999). Immigrant adolescent girls of color: Facing American challenges. In N. B. Johnson, M. C. Roberts, & J. Worell (Eds.), *Beyond appearance: A new look at adolescent girls* (pp. 131–150). Washington, DC: American Psychological Association.

Fukuyama, F. (1993). *The end of history and the last man.* New York: Free Press.

Fuligni, A. (1994, February). *Academic achievement and motivation among Asian-American and European-American early adolescents.* Paper presented at the biennial meetings of the Society for Research on Adolescence, San Diego.

Fuligni, A. (1997). The academic achievement of adolescents from immigrant families: The roles of family background, attitudes and behavior. *Child Development, 68,* 351–363.

Fuligni, A., & Eccles, J. (1992, March). *The effects of early adolescent peer orientation on academic achievement and deviant behavior in high school.* Paper presented at the biennial meeting of the Society for Research on Adolescence, Washington.

Fuligni, A., & Eccles, J. (1993). Perceived parent–child relationships and early adolescents' orientation toward peers. *Developmental Psychology, 29,* 622–632.

Fuligni, A. J., & Tseng, V. (1999). Family obligation and the academic motivation of adolescents from immigrant and American-born families. *Advances in Motivation and Achievement, 11,* 159–183.

Fuligni, A. J., Tseng, V., & Lam, M. (1999). Attitudes toward family obligations among American adolescents with Asian, Latin American, and European backgrounds. *Child Development, 70,* 1030–1044.

Funk, J. (1993). Reevaluating the impact of video games. *Clinical Pediatrics, 32,* 86–90.

Funk, J. B., Flores, B., Buchman, D. D., & Germann, J. N. (1999). Rating electronic video games: Violence is in the eye of the beholder. *Youth & Society, 30,* 283–312.

Furby, M., & Beyth-Marom, R. (1992). Risk-taking in adolescence: A decision-making perspective. *Developmental Review, 12,* 1–44.

Furman, W., Brown, B. B., & Feiring, C. (Eds.). (1999). *The development of romantic relationships in adolescence.* New York: Cambridge University Press.

Furman, W., & Buhrmester, D. (1985). Children's perceptions of the personal relationships in their social networks. *Developmental Psychology, 21,* 1016–1024.

Furman, W., & Buhrmester, D. (1992). Age and sex differences in perceptions of networks of personal relationships. *Child Development, 63,* 103–115.

Furman, W., & Simon, V. A. (1999). Cognitive representations of adolescent romantic relationships. In W. Furman, B. B. Brown, & C. Feiring (Eds.), *The development of romantic relationships in adolescence* (pp. 75–98). New York: Cambridge University Press.

Furman, W., & Wehner, E. A. (1994). Romantic views: Toward a theory of adolescent romantic relationships. In R. Montemayor, G. R. Adams, & G. P. Gullotta (Eds.), *Advances in adolescent development: Vol. 6, Relationships during adolescence: Developmental perspectives* (pp. 21–36). Thousand Oaks, CA: Sage.

Furman, W., & Wehner, E. A. (1997). Adolescent romantic relationships: A developmental perspective. In S. Shulman & W. A. Collins (Eds.), *Romantic relationships in adolescence: Developmental perspectives* (pp. 21–36). San Francisco: Jossey-Bass.

Furnham, A., & Singh, A. (1986). Memory for information about sex differences. *Sex Roles, 15,* 479–486.

Furstenberg, E. F., Jr., Brooks-Gunn, J., & Morgan, S. P. (1987). *Adolescent mothers in later life.* New York: Cambridge University Press.

Furstenberg, F. (1991). Is teenage sexual behavior rational? *Journal Applied Social Psychology, 21,* 957–986.

Furstenberg, F. F., Jr. (1990). Coming of age in a changing family system. In S. Feldman & G. Elliott (Eds.), *At the threshold: The developing adolescent* (pp. 147–170). Cambridge, MA: Harvard University Press.

Furstenberg, F. F., Jr., & Cherlin, A. J. (1991). *Divided families: What happens to children when parents part.* Cambridge, MA: Harvard University Press.

Furstenberg, F., Jr., Brooks-Gunn, J., & Chase-Lansdale, L. (1989). Teenaged pregnancy and childbearing. *American Psychologist, 44,* 313–320.

Gaddis, A., & Brooks-Gunn, J. (1985). The male experience of pubertal change. *Journal of Youth and Adolescence, 14,* 61–69.

Gagnon, J. H. (1973). Scripts and the coordination of sexual conduct. *Nebraska Symposium on Motivation, 21,* 27–59.

Galambos, N. L., & Ehrenberg, M. F. (1997). The family as health risk and opportunity: A focus on divorce and working families. In J. Schulenberg, J. L. Maggs, & K. Hurrelmann (Eds.), *Health risks and developmental transitions during adolescence* (pp. 139–160). New York: Cambridge University Press.

Galambos, N. L., & Tilton-Weaver, L. C. (1998). Multiple-risk behavior in adolescents and young adults. *Statistics Canada, Health Reports, 10,* 9–20.

Galambos, N., Almeida, D., & Petersen, A. (1990). Masculinity, femininity, and sex role attitudes in early adolescence: Exploring gender intensification. *Child Development, 61,* 1905–1914.

Galambos, N., & Kolaric, G. C. (1994). Canada. In K. Hurrelmann (Ed.), *International handbook of adolescence* (pp. 92–107). Westport, CT: Greenwood Press.

Galambos, N., & Maggs, J. (1991). Out-of-school care of young adolescents and self-reported behavior. *Developmental Psychology, 27,* 644–655.

Gallagher, W. (1993, May). Midlife myths. *The Atlantic Monthly,* pp. 51–68.

Gallup, G., Jr. (1990). *America's youth in the 1990s.* Princeton, NJ: Author.

Gallup, G., Jr., & Castelli, J. (1989). *The people's religion: American faith in the '90s.* New York: Macmillan.

Gallup, G., Jr., & Lindsay, D. M. (1999). *Surveying the religious landscape: Trends in U.S. beliefs.* Harrisburg, PA: Morehouse.

Gallup, G. W., & Bezilla, R. (1992). *The religious life of young Americans.* Princeton, NJ: Gallup Institute.

Galotti, K. (1989). Gender differences in self-reported moral reasoning: A review and new evidence. *Journal of Youth and Adolescence, 18,* 475–488.

Galotti, K., Kozberg, S., & Farmer, M. (1991). Gender and developmental differences in adolescents' conceptions of moral reasoning. *Journal of Youth and Adolescence, 20,* 13–30.

Gamoran, A. (1992). The variable effects of high school tracking. *American Sociological Review, 57*, 812–828.

Gamoran, A. (1993). Alternative uses of ability grouping in secondary schools: Can we bring high-quality instruction to low-ability classes? *American Journal of Education, 69*, 1–21.

Ganong, L. H., & Coleman, M. (1994). *Remarried family relationships.* Thousand Oaks, CA: Sage.

Ganong, L. H., & Coleman, M. (1999). *Changing families, changing responsibilities: Family obligations following divorce and remarriage.* Mahwah, NJ: Erlbaum.

Gans, J. (1990). *America's adolescents: How healthy are they?* Chicago: American Medical Association.

Gao, G. (1991). Stability of romantic relationships in China and the United States. In S. T. Toomey & F. Korzenny (Eds.), *Cross-cultural interpersonal communication* (Vol. 15, pp. 99–115). London: Sage Publications.

Garbarino, J. (1989). Troubled youth, troubled families: The dynamics of adolescent maltreatment. In D. Cicchetti & V. Carlson (Eds.), *Child maltreatment: Theory and research on causes and consequences of child abuse and neglect* (pp. 685–706). New York: Cambridge University Press.

Garbarino, J., & Asp, C. (1981). *Successful schools and competent students.* Lexington, MA: Lexington Books.

Garbarino, J., Schellenbach, C. J., & Sebes, J. M. (1986). *Troubled youth, troubled families: Understanding families at risk for adolescent maltreatment.* New York: Aldine de Gruyter.

Garcia, A. M. (1991). The development of Chicana feminist discourse. In J. Lorber & S. A. Farrell (Eds.), *The social construction of gender* (pp. 269–287). Newbury Park, CA: Sage.

Gardner, H. (1983). *Frames of mind.* New York: Basic Books.

Gardner, H. (1989). Beyond a modular view of mind. In W. Damon (Ed.), *Child development today and tomorrow.* San Francisco: Jossey-Bass.

Gardner, H. (1999, February). Who owns intelligence? *Atlantic Monthly,* 67–76.

Garland, A., & Zigler, E. (1993). Adolescent suicide prevention: Current research and social policy implications. *American Psychologist, 48*, 169–182.

Garner, D. M., & Garfinkel, P. E. (1997). *Handbook of treatment for eating disorders.* New York: Plenum.

Garrison, C. Z., Abby, C. L., Jackson, K. L., McKeown, R. E., & Walter, J. L. (1991). A longitudinal study of suicidal ideation in young adolescents. *Journal of the American Academy of Child and Adolescent Psychiatry, 30*, 597–603.

Gavin, L., & Furman, W. (1989). Age differences in adolescents' perceptions of their peer groups. *Developmental Psychology, 25*, 827–834.

Ge, X., Best, K., Conger, R., & Simons, R. (1996). Parenting behaviors and the occurrence and co-occurrence of adolescent depressive symptoms and conduct problems. *Developmental Psychology, 32*, 717–731.

Ge, X., Conger, R. D., & Elder, G. H., Jr. (1996). Coming of age too early: Pubertal influences on girls' vulnerability to psychological distress. *Child Development, 67*, 3386–3400.

Gearheart, B., Gearheart, C., & Mullen, R. (1993). *Exceptional individuals: An introduction.* New York: Brooks/Cole.

Gecas, V., & Seff, M. (1990). Families and adolescents: A review of the 1980s. *Journal of Marriage and the Family, 52*, 941–958.

Gelbard, A., Haub, C., & Kent, M. M. (1999). World population beyond six billion. *Population Bulletin, 54* (1), 1–40

Geller, B., Cooper, T. B., Graham, D. L., Marsteller, F. A., & Bryant, D. M. (1990). Double-blind placebo-controlled study of nortriptyline in depressed adolescents using a "fixed plasma level" design. *Psychopharmacology Bulletin, 26*, 85–90.

Geller, B., Reising, D., Leonard, H. L., Riddle, M. A., & Walsh, B. (1999). Critical review of tricyclic antidepressant use in children and adolescents. *Journal of the American Academy of Child & Adolescent Psychiatry, 38*, 513–528.

Gentile, D. A. (1993). Just what are sex and gender, anyway? A call for a new terminological standard. *Psychological Science, 4*, 120–122.

Gerrard, M. (1987). Sex, sex guilt, and contraceptive use revisited: The 1980s. *Journal of Personality and Social Psychology, 52*, 975–980.

Gerrard, M., Gibbons, F. X., Benthin, A. C., & Hessling, R. M. (1996). A longitudinal study of the reciprocal nature of risk behaviors and cognitions in adolescents: What you do shapes what you think, and vice versa. *Health Psychology, 15*, 344–354.

Gibbons, J. L., & Stiles, D. A. (1997, July). *International studies of adolescents' ideal persons.* Paper presented at the regional meeting of the International Council of Psychologists, Padova, Italy.

Gibbs, N., & Roche, T. (1999, December 20). The Columbine tapes. *Time,* pp. 40–51.

Gibbs, N., & Roche, T. (1999, December). The Columbine tapes. *Time,* pp. 40–51.

Gil, A. G., Vega, W. A., & Biafora, F. (1998). Temporal influences of family structure and family risk factors on drug use initiation in a multiethnic sample of adolescent boys. *Journal of Youth & Adolescence, 27*, 373–394.

Gilbert, L. A., Lee, R. N., & Chiddix, S. (1981). Influence of presenter's gender on students' evaluations of presenters discussing sex fairness in counseling: An analogue study. *Journal of Counseling Psychology, 28*, 258–264.

Gilligan, C. (1982). *In a different voice.* Cambridge, MA: Harvard University Press.

Gilligan, C., Lyons, N. P., & Hanmer, T. J. (1990). *Making connections.* Cambridge, MA: Harvard University Press.

Gilligan, C., Lyons, N., & Hanmer, T. (Eds.). (1990). *Making connections: The relational worlds of adolescent girls at Emma Willard School.* Cambridge, MA: Harvard University Press.

Gillis, J. R. (1974). *Youth and history.* New York: Academic Press.

Gillock, K. L., & Reyes, O. (1999). Stress, support, and academic performance of urban, low-income Mexican-American adolescents. *Journal of Youth & Adolescence, 28*, 259–282.

Gilmore, D. (1990). *Manhood in the making: Cultural concepts of masculinity.* New Haven: Yale University Press.

Gilpin, E. A., & Pierce, J. P. (1997). Trends in adolescent smoking initiation in the United States: Is tobacco marketing an influence? *Tobacco Control, 6.*

Ginsburg, H. P., & Opper, S. (1988). Piaget's theory of intellectual development (3rd ed.). Englewood Cliffs, NJ: Prentice-Hall.

Ginzberg, E. (1977). The job problem. *Scientific American, 237*, 43–51.

Gitchel, S., & Foster, L. (1985). *Let's talk about sex.* Fresno, CA: Planned Parenthood of Central California.

Gjerde, P. F., Block, J., & Block, J. H. (1988). Depressive symptoms and personality during late adolescence: Gender differences in the externalization-internalization of symptom expression. *Journal of Abnormal Psychology, 97*, 475–486.

Gjerde, P. F., & Westenberg, P. M. (1998). Dysphoric adolescents as young adults: A prospective study of the psychological sequelae of depressed mood in adolescence. *Journal of Research on Adolescence, 8*, 377–402.

Gladue, B. (1990, November). Adolescents' sexual practices: Have they changed? *Medical Aspects of Human Sexuality,* 53–54.

Gladwin, E. T. (1970). *East is a big bird.* Cambridge, MA: Harvard University Press.

Glass, G. V., & Smith, M. L. (1978, September). *Meta-analysis of research on the relationship of class size and achievement.* San Francisco: Far West Educational Laboratory.

Glick, P. (1989). Remarried families, stepfamilies, and stepchildren: A brief demographic review. *Family Relations, 38*, 24–27.

Glueck, S., & Glueck, E. (1950). *Unraveling juvenile delinquency.* New York: Commonwealth Fund.

Glueck, S., & Glueck, E. (1968). *Delinquents and nondelinquents in perspective.* Cambridge, MA: Harvard University Press.

Goertz, M. E., Ekstrom, R. B., & Rock, D. (1991). Dropouts, high school: issues of race and sex. In R. M. Lerner, A. C. Petersen, & J. Brooks-Gunn (Eds.), *Encyclopedia of adolescence* (Vol. I). New York: Garland.

Gold, D. P., Andres, D., Etezadi, J., Arbuckle, T., Schwartzman, A., & Chaikelson, J. (1995). Structural equation model of intellectual change and continuity and predictors of intelligence in older men. *Psychology and Aging, 10,* 294–303.

Gold, M., & Yanof, D. (1985). Mothers, daughters, and girlfriends. *Journal of Personality and Social Psychology, 49,* 654–659.

Goldberg, A. P., Dengel, D. R., & Hagberg, J. M. (1996). Exercise physiology and aging. In E. L. Schneider & J. W. Rowe (Eds.), *Handbook of the biology of aging* (4th ed., pp. 331–354). San Diego, CA: Academic Press.

Goldberg, P. H. (1968). Are women prejudiced against women? *Transaction, 5,* 28–30.

Goldscheider, F., & Goldscheider, C. (1994). Leaving and returning home in 20th century America. *Population Bulletin, 48* (4).

Goldscheider, F., & Goldscheider, C. (1999). *The changing transition to adulthood: Leaving and returning home.* Thousand Oaks, CA: Sage.

Goldstein, B. (1976). *Introduction to human sexuality.* Belmont, CA: Star.

Goleman, D. (1997). *Emotional intelligence.* New York: Bantam.

Gonzales, N., Cauce, A., Friedman, R., & Mason, C. (1996). Family, peer, and neighborhood influences on achievement among African American adolescents: One-year prospective effects. *American Journal of Community Psychology, 24,* 365–387.

Goode, E. (1999, May 20). Study finds TV trims Fiji girls' body image and eating habits. *New York Times,* p. A1.

Goodlad, J. A. (1984). *A place called school.* New York: McGraw-Hill.

Goodwin, C. J. (1995). *Research in psychology: Methods and design.* New York: Wiley.

Goodwin, M. P., & Roscoe, B. (1990). Sibling violence and agonistic interactions among middle adolescents. *Adolescence, 25,* 451–467.

Goosens, L. (1994). Belgium. In K. Hurrelmann (Ed.), *International handbook of adolescence* (pp. 51–64). Westport, CT: Greenwood Press.

Goossens, L. (1994). *Belgium.* In K. Hurrelmann (Ed.), *International handbook of adolescence* (pp. 51–64). Westport, CT: Greenwood Press.

Goossens, L., Seiffge-Krenke, L., & Marcoen, A. (1992). The many faces of adolescent egocentrism: Two European replications. *Journal of Adolescent Research, 7,* 43–48.

Gordon, M., & Miller, R. L. (1984). Going steady in the 1980s: Exclusive relationships in six Connecticut high schools. *Sociology and Social Research, 68,* 463–479.

Gore, S., Aseltine, R. H., & Colten, M. E. (1993). Gender, social-relational involvement, and depression. *Journal of Research on Adolescence, 3,* 101–125.

Gottfredson, G. D., Jones, E. M., & Holland, J. L. (1993). Personality and vocational interests: The relation of Holland's six interest dimensions to five robust dimensions of personality. *Journal of Counseling Psychology, 40,* 518–524.

Gottfredson, M., & Hirschi, T. (1990). *A general theory of crime.* Stanford, CA: Stanford University Press.

Gould, S. J. (1981). *The mismeasure of man.* New York: Norton.

Gow, J. (1996). Reconsidering gender roles on MTV: Depictions in the most popular music videos of the early 1990s. *Communication Reports, 9,* 151–161.

Gowen, L. K., Hayward, C., Killen, J. D., Robinson, T. N., & Taylor, C. B. (1999). Acculturation and eating disorder symptoms in adolescent girls. *Journal of Research on Adolescence, 9,* 67–83.

Graber, J., Brooks-Gunn, J., & Warren, M. (1995). The antecedents of menarcheal age: Heredity, family environment, and stressful life events. *Child Development, 66,* 346–359.

Graber, J. A., Britto, P. R., & Brooks-Gunn, J. (1999). What's love got to do with it? Adolescent and young adult's beliefs about sexual and romantic relationships. In W. Furman, B. B. Brown, & C. Feiring (Eds.), *The development of romantic relationships in adolescence* (pp. 364–395). New York: Cambridge University Press.

Graber, J. A., Brooks-Gunn, J., & Galen, B. R. (1999). Betwixt and between: Sexuality in the context of adolescent transitions. In R. Jessor (Ed.), *New perspectives on adolescent risk behavior* (pp. 270–318). New York: Cambridge University Press.

Graber, J. A., Brooks-Gunn, J., Paikoff, R. L., & Warren, M. P. (1994). Prediction of eating problems: An 8-year study of adolescent girls. *Developmental Psychology, 30,* 823–834.

Graber, J. A., Brooks-Gunn, J., & Warren, M. P. (1995). The antecedents of menarcheal age: Heredity, family environment, and stressful life events. *Child Development, 66,* 346–359.

Graber, J. A., & Dubas, J. S. (1996). Leaving home: Understanding the transition to adulthood. *New Directions for Child Development, 71.*

Graber, J. A., Lewinsohn, P. M., Seeley, J. R., & Brooks-Gunn, J. (1997). Is psychopathology associated with the timing of pubertal development? *Journal of the American Academy of Child and Adolescent Psychiatry, 36,* 1768–1776.

Graham, J. W., Marks, G., & Hansen, W. B. (1991). Social influence processes affecting adolescent substance abuse. *Journal of Applied Developmental Psychology, 76,* 291–298.

Gray, M. R., & Steinberg, L. (1999). Adolescent romance and the parent–child relationship. In W. Furman, B. B. Brown, & C. Feiring (Eds.), *The development of romantic relationships in adolescence* (pp. 235–265). New York: Cambridge University Press.

Gray, W. M. (1990). Formal operational thought. In W. F. Overton (Ed.), *Reasoning, necessity, and logic: Developmental perspectives* (pp. 227–253). Hillsdale, NJ: Erlbaum.

Graystone, A. D., de Luca, R. V., & Boyes, D. A. (1992). Self-esteem, anxiety, and loneliness in preadolescent girls who have experienced sexual abuse. *Child Psychiatry and Human Development, 22,* 277–286.

Green, A. H. (1991). Child sexual abuse and incest. In M. Lewis (Ed.), *Child and adolescent psychiatry* (pp. 1019–1029). Baltimore, MD: Williams & Wilkins.

Greenberg, B. S. (1994). Content trends in media sex. In D. Zillman, J. Bryant, & A. C. Huston (Eds.), *Media, children and the family: Social scientific, psychodynamic, and clinical perspectives* (pp. 165–182). Hillsdale, NJ: Erlbaum.

Greenberg, B. S., Brown, J. D., & Buerkel-Rothfuss, N. (1992). *Media, sex, and the adolescent.* Cresskill, NJ: Hampton Press.

Greenberg, B. S., Siemicki, M., & Dorfman, S. (1986). *Sex content in R-rated films viewed by adolescents.* Project CAST Report #3. East Lansing: Michigan State University.

Greenberger, E., & Steinberg, L. (1986). *When teenagers work: The psychological social costs of adolescent employment.* New York: Basic Books.

Greenberger, E., Steinberg, L., & Vaux, A. (1981). Adolescents who work: Health and behavioral consequences of job stress. *Developmental Psychology, 17,* 691–703.

Greenberger, E., Steinberg, L., Vaux, A., & McAuliffe, S. (1980). Adolescents who work: Effects of part-time employment on family and peer relations. *Journal of Youth and Adolescence, 9,* 189–202.

Greene, A. L., Wheatley, S. M., & Aldava IV, J. F. (1992). Stages on life's way: Adolescents' implicit theories of the life course. *Journal of Adolescent Research, 7,* 364–381.

Greene, C. G., & Maccoby, E. E. (1986). How different is the "different voice"? *Signs, 11,* 310–316.

Griffiths, M. (1997). Computer game playing in early adolescence. *Youth & Society, 29,* 223–237.

Grimsley, K. D. (2000, April 3). Family a priority for young workers: Survey finds change in men's thinking. *Washington Post,* pp. E1-2.

Grolnick, W., & Slowiaczek, M. (1994). Parents' involvement in children's schooling: A multidimensional conceptualization and motivational model. *Child Development, 65,* 230–252.

Grossman, D., Milligan, C., & Deyo, R. (1991). Risk factors for suicide attempts among Navajo adolescents. *American Journal of Public Health, 81,* 870–874.

Grotevant, H. D. (1987). Toward a process model of identity formation. *Journal of Adolescent Research, 2*, 202–222.

Grotevant, H. D., & Adams, G. R. (1984). Development of an objective measure to assess ego identity in adolescence: Validation and replication. *Journal of Youth and Adolescence, 13*, 419–438.

Grotevant, H., & Cooper, C. (1988). The role of family experience in career exploration during adolescence. In R. Baltes, D. Featherman, & R. Lerner (Eds.), *Life-span development and behavior* (Vol. 8). Hillsdale, NJ: Erlbaum.

Grumbach, M., Roth, J., Kaplan, S., & Kelch, R. (1974). Hypothalamic-pituitary regulation of puberty in man: Evidence and concepts derived from clinical research. In M. Grumbach, G. Grave, & F. Mayer (Eds.), *Control of the onset of puberty*. New York: Wiley.

Gruskin, E. (1994, February). *A review of research on self-identified gay, lesbian, and bisexual youth from 1970–1993*. Paper presented at the meeting of the Society for Research on Adolescence, San Diego.

Gupta, A. K. (1987). *Parental influences on adolescents*. New Delhi, India: Ariana.

Gutman, L. M., & Eccles, J. S. (1999). Financial strain, parenting behaviors, and adolescents' achievement: Testing model equivalence between African American and European American single- and two-parents families. *Child Development, 70*, 1464–1476.

Gutmann, D. (1987). *Reclaimed powers: Toward a new psychology of men and women in later life*. New York: Basic Books.

Haffner, D. (1998, March/April). Realism in sex ed. *Youth Today, 7*.

Haidt, J., Koller, S. H., & Dias, M. G. (1993). Affect, culture, and morality, or is it wrong to eat your dog? *Journal of Personality and Social Psychology, 65*, 613–628.

Hale, S. (1990). A global developmental trend in cognitive processing speed. *Child Development, 61*, 653–663.

Hall, G. S. (1904). *Adolescence: Its psychology and its relation to physiology, anthropology, sociology, sex, crime, religion, and education* (Vols. 1 & 2). Englewood Cliffs, NJ: Prentice-Hall.

Hallahan, D. P., & Kauffman, J. M. (1998). *Introduction to learning disabilities*. New York: Simon & Schuster Trade.

Hallinan, M. (1992). The organization of students for instruction in the middle school. *Sociology of Education, 65*.

Hallinan, M., & Sorensen, A. (1987). Ability grouping and sex differences in mathematics achievement. *Sociology of education, 60*, 63–72.

Halpern, S. (1998). *The forgotten half revisited: American youth and young families, 1988–2008*. Washington, DC: American Youth Policy Forum.

Hamer, D. H., Hu, S., Magnuson, V. L., Hu, N., & Pattatucci, A. M. L. (1993). A linkage between DNA markers on the X chromosome and male sexual orientation. *Science, 261*, 321–327.

Hamilton, S. F. (1990). *Apprenticeship for adulthood: Preparing youth for the future*. New York: Free Press.

Hamilton, S. F. (1994). Employment prospects as motivation for school achievement: Links and gaps between school and work in seven countries. In R. K. Silbereisen & E. Todt (Eds.), *Adolescence in context: The interplay of family, school, peers, and work in adjustment* (pp. 267–284). New York: Springer-Verlag.

Hamilton, S. F., & Hurrelmann, K. (1994). The school-to-career transition in Germany and the United States. *Teachers College Record, 96*, 329–344.

Handsfield, H. (1992). Recent developments in STDs: Viral and other syndromes. *Hospital Practice, 14*, 175–200.

Hannah, J. S., & Kohn, S. E. (1989). The relationship of socioeconomic status and gender to the occupational choices of grade 12 students. *Journal of Vocational Behavior, 34*, 161–178.

Hansen, D. J., & Warner, J. E. (1992). Child physical abuse and neglect. In R. T. Ammerman & M. Hersen (Eds.), *Assessment of family violence* (pp. 123–147). New York: Wiley.

Hansen, D. J., Conaway, L. P., & Christopher, J. S. (1990). Victims of child physical abuse. In R. T. Ammerman & M. Hersen (Eds.), *Treatment of family violence* (pp. 17–49). New York: Wiley.

Hanson, S. (1994). Lost talent: Unrealized educational aspirations and expectations among U.S. youths. *Sociology of Education, 67*, 159–183.

Hardaway, C. K., Marler, P. L., & Chaves, M. (1993). What the polls don't show: A closer look at U.S. church attendance. *American Sociological Review, 58*, 741–752.

Harevan, T. K. (1984). Themes in the historical development of the family. In R. D. Parke (Ed.), *Review of child development research* (Vol. 7) (pp. 137–178). Chicago: University of Chicago Press.

Harkness, S., & Super, C. M. (1995). *Parents' cultural belief systems: Their origins, expressions, and consequences*. New York: Guilford.

Harlan, W. R., Harlan, E. A., & Grillo, G. R. (1980). Secondary sex characteristics of girls 12–17 years of age: The U.S. Health Examination Survey. *Journal of Pediatrics, 96*, 1074–1087.

Harmon, A. (1998, May 8). Underreporting found on male teen-age sex. *New York Times*, p. A-14.

Harris & Associates (1987). *Attitudes about television, sex and contraceptive advertising*. New York: Planned Parenthood Federation of America.

Harris, J. R. (1999). *The nurture assumption: Why children turn out the way they do*. New York: Free Press.

Harris, R. L., Ellicott, A. M., & Holmes, D. S. (1986). The timing of psychosocial transitions and changes in women's lives: An examination of women aged 45 to 60. *Journal of Personality and Social Psychology, 51*, 409–416.

Hart, D., & Fegley, S. (1995). Prosocial behavior and caring in adolescence: Relations to self-understanding and social judgment. *Child Development, 66*, 1346–1359.

Harter, S. (1986). Processes underlying the enhancement of the self-concept of children. In J. Suis & A. Greenald (Eds.), *Psychological perspective on the self* (Vol. 3). Hillsdale, NJ: Erlbaum.

Harter, S. (1988). *Self-perception profile for adolescents*. Denver: University of Denver.

Harter, S. (1989). Causes, correlates, and the functional role of global self-worth: A life-span perspective. In J. Kolligian & R. Sternberg (Eds.), *Perceptions of competence and incompetence across the life-span*. New Haven, CT: Yale University Press.

Harter, S. (1990a). Processes underlying adolescent self-concept formation. In R. Montemayor, G. R. Adams, & T. P. Gullotta (Eds.), *From childhood to adolescence: A transitional period?* Newbury Park, CA: Sage.

Harter, S. (1990b). Self and identity development. In S. S. Feldman & G. R. Elliott (Eds.), *At the threshold: The developing adolescent* (pp. 352–387). Cambridge, MA: Harvard University Press.

Harter, S. (1993). Causes and consequences of low self-esteem in children and adolescents. In R. F. Baumeister (Ed.), *Self esteem: The puzzle of low self-regard* (pp. 87–116). New York: Plenum.

Harter, S. (1997). The development of self-representations. In N. Eisenberg (Ed.), *Handbook of child psychology* (5th ed., Vol. 3). New York: Wiley.

Harter, S. (1997). The personal self in social context: Barriers to authenticity. In R. D. Ashmore & L. J. Jussim (Eds.), *Self and identity: Fundamental issues* (pp. 81–105). New York: Oxford University Press.

Harter, S. (1999). *The construction of the self: A developmental perspective*. New York: Guilford.

Harter, S., Bresnick, S., Bouchey, H. A., & Whitesell, N. R. (1997). The development of multiple role-related selves during adolescence. *Development and Psychopathology, 9*, 835–853.

Harter, S., & Lee, L. (1989). *Manifestations of true and false selves in adolescence*. Paper presented at the meeting of the Society for Research in Child Development, Kansas City.

Harter, S., Marold, D. B., Whitesell, N. R., & Cobbs, G. (1996). A model of the effects of perceived parent and peer support on adolescent false self behavior. *Child Development, 67*, 360–374.

Harter, S., Marold, D. B., Whitesell, N. R., & Cobbs, G. (1996). A model of the effects of parent and peer support on adolescent false self behavior. *Child Development, 67*, 360–374.

Harter, S., Waters, P. L., & Whitesell, N. R. (1997). Lack of voice as a manifestation of false-self behavior among adolescents: The school setting as a stage upon which the drama of authenticity is enacted. *Educational Psychologist, 32*, 153–173.

Harter, S., Waters, P., & Whitesell, N. (1996, March). *False self behavior and lack of voice among adolescent males and females.* Paper presented at the meeting of the Society for Research on Adolescence, Boston.

Harter, S., Waters, P., Whitesell, N. R., & Kastelic, D. (1998). Predictors of level of voice among high school females and males: Relational context, support, and gender orientation. *Developmental Psychology, 34*, 1–10.

Hartup, W. W. (1993). Adolescents and their friends. In B. Laursen (Ed.), *New directions for child development: Close friendships in adolescence* (pp. 3–22). San Francisco: Jossey-Bass.

Hartup, W. W. (1996). The company they keep: Friendships and their developmental significance. *Child Development, 67*, 1–13.

Hartup, W. W., & Overhauser, S. (1991). Friendships. In R. M. Lerner, A. C. Petersen, & J. Brooks-Gunn (Eds.), *Encyclopedia of adolescence* (pp. 378–384). New York: Garland.

Hass, A. (1979). *Teenage sexuality: A survey of teenage sexual behavior.* New York: Macmillan.

Hatfield, E., & Rapson, R. L. (1996). *Love and sex: Cross-cultural perspectives.* Boston: Allyn & Bacon.

Haugaard, J. J. (1992). Epidemiology and family violence involving children. In R. I. Ammerman & M. Hersen (Eds.), *Assessment of family violence* (pp. 89–120). New York: Wiley

Haugaard, J. J., & Reppucci, N. D. (1988). *The sexual abuse of children.* San Francisco: Jossey-Bass.

Hauser, S. L., Borman, R., Jacobson, A. M., & Powers, S. L. (1991). Understanding family contexts of adolescent coping: A study of parental ego development and adolescent coping strategies. *Journal of Early Adolescence, 11*, 96–124.

Hawkins, J. A., & Berndt, T. J. (1985, April). *Adjustment following the transition to junior high school.* Paper presented at the biennial meeting of the Society for Research in Child Development, Toronto.

Hayes, C. (Ed.). (1987). *Risking the future: Adolescent sexuality, pregnancy, and childbearing* (Vol. 1). Washington, DC: National Academy Press.

Haynes, N. M., Emmons, C., & Ben-Avie, M. (1997). School climate as a factor in student adjustment and achievement. *Journal of Educational & Psychological Consultation, 8*, 321–329.

Hayward, C., Killen, J. D., Wilson, D. M., & Hammer, L. D. (1997). Psychiatric risk associated with early puberty in adolescent girls. *Journal of the American Academy of Child and Adolescent Psychiatry, 36*, 255–262.

Hazan, C., & Zeifman, D. (1994). Sex and the psychological tether. In K. Bartholomew & D. Perlman (Eds.), *Advances in personal relationships, Vol. 5: Attachment processes in adulthood* (pp. 151–180). London: Jessica Kingsley.

Hechinger, F. (1993). Schools for teenagers: An historic dilemma. *Teachers' College Record, 94*, 522–539.

Hecht, D. B., Inderbitzen, H. M., & Bukowski, A. L. (1998). The relationship between peers status and depressive symptoms in children and adolescents. *Journal of Abnormal Child Psychology, 26*, 153–160.

Hecker, D. E. (1992, July). Reconciling conflicting data on jobs for college graduates. *Monthly Labor Review*, 3–12.

Hedges, L. V., & Stock, W. (1983, Spring). The effects of class size: An examination of rival hypotheses. *American Educational Research Journal*, 63–85.

Heilman, E. E. (1998). The struggle for self: Power and identity in adolescent girls. *Youth & Society, 30*, 182–208.

Heilman, M. E., Martell, R. F., & Simon, M. C. (1988). The vagaries of sex bias: Conditions regulating the undervaluation, equivalation, and overvaluation of female job applicants. *Organizational Behavior and Human Decision Processes, 41*, 98–110.

Hein, K. (1988). *Issues in adolescent health: An overview.* Washington, DC: Carnegie Council on Adolescent Development.

Helweg-Larsen, M., & Collins, B. E. (1994). The UCLA multidimensional condom attitudes scale: Documenting the complex determinants of condom use in college students. *Health Psychology, 13*, 224–237.

Hemmer, J. D., & Kleiber, D. A. (1981). Tomboy and sissies: Androgynous children? *Sex Roles, 7*, 1205–1211.

Hemmings, A. (1998). The self-transformations of African American achievers. *Youth & Society, 29*, 330–368.

Henderson, V. L., & Dweck, C. S. (1990). Motivation and achievement. In S. S. Feldman & G. R. Elliott (Eds.), *At the threshold: The developing adolescent* (pp. 308–329). Cambridge, MA: Harvard University Press.

Henggeler, S. W., Melton, G. B., & Smith, L. A. (1992). Family preservation using multisystemic therapy: An effective alternative to incarcerating serious juvenile offenders. *Journal of Consulting and Clinical Psychology, 60*, 935–961.

Henry, B., Feehan, M., McGee, R., Stanton, W., Moffitt, T., & Silva, R. (1993). The importance of conduct problems and depressive symptoms in predicting adolescent substance use. *Journal of Abnormal Child Psychology, 21*, 469–480.

Herdt, G. (1987). *The Sambia: Ritual and gender in New Guinea.* New York: Holt, Rinehart & Winston.

Herdt, G. (1989). *Gay and lesbian youth.* New York: Harrington Park Press.

Herek, G. M. (1986). The social psychology of homophobia: Toward a practical theory. *New York University Review of Law and Social Changes, 14*, 923–935.

Herman-Giddens, M., Slora, E., Wasserman, R., Bourdony, C., Bhapkar, M., Koch, G., & Hasemeier, C. (1997). Secondary sexual characteristics and menses in young girls seen in office practice: A study from the Pediatric Research in Office Settings Network. *Pediatrics, 88*, 505–512.

Hernandez, D. J. (1994). Children's changing access to resources: A historical perspective. *SRCD Social Policy Report, VIII(1)*.

Hernandez, D. J. (1997). Child development and the social demography of childhood. *Child Development, 68*, 149–169.

Heron, A. (1995). *Two teenagers in twenty: Writings by gay and lesbian youth.* New York: Alyson Press.

Herrnstein, R. J., & Murry, C. (1995). *The bell curve: Intelligence and class structure in American life.* New York: Simon & Schuster.

Hersch, P. (1991). Sexually transmitted diseases are ravaging our children: Teen epidemic. *American Health, 10*, 42–45.

Hersch, P. (1998). *A tribe apart: A journey into the heart of American adolescence.* New York: Fawcett Columbine.

Hertzog, C., & Schaie, K. W. (1986). Stability and change in adult intelligence: 1. Analysis of longitudinal covariance structures. *Psychology and Aging, 1*, 159–171.

Herzog, D. B., Keller, M. B., Lavori, P. W., & Bradbum, L. S. (1991). Bulimia nervosa in adolescence. *Journal of Development and Behavioral Pediatrics, 12*, 191–195.

Hetherington, E. M. (1991). Presidential address: Families, lies, and videotapes. *Journal of Research on Adolescence, 1*, 323–348.

Hetherington, E. M. (1993). An overview of the Virginia longitudinal study of divorce and remarriage with a focus on early adolescence. *Journal of Family Psychology, 7*, 39–56.

Hetherington, E. M., Arnett, J., & Hollier, E. A. (1986). Adjustments of parents and children to remarriage. In S. Wolchik & P. Karoly (Eds.), *Children of divorce: Perspectives on adjustment* (pp. 132–151). New York: Gardner Press.

Hetherington, E. M., Bridges, M., & Insabella, G. M. (1998). What matters? What does not? Five perspectives on the association between marital transitions and children's adjustment. *American Psychologist, 53*, 167–184.

Hetherington, E. M., & Clingempeel, W. G. (1992). Coping with marital transition: A family systems perspective. *Monographs of the Society for Research in Child Development* (Vol. 57, No. 2-3, Serial No. 227).

Hetherington, E. M., Stanley-Hagan, M., & Anderson, E. (1989). Marital transitions: A child's perspective. *American Psychologist, 44*, 303–312.

Higgins, C., Duxbury, L., & Lee, C. (1994). Impact of life-cycle stage and gender on the ability to balance work and family responsibilities. *Family Relations, 43*, 144–150.

Hill, C., Rubin, Z., & Peplau, L. (1979). Breakups before marriage: The end of 103 affairs. In G. Levinger & O. Moles (Eds.), *Divorce and separation.* New York: Basic Books.

Hill, J. P. (1987). Research on adolescents and their families: Past and prospect. In C. E. Irwin (Ed.), *Adolescent social behavior and health* (pp. 13–31). San Francisco: Jossey-Bass.

Hill, J., & Holmbeck, G. (1986). Attachment and autonomy during adolescence. In G. Whitehurst (Ed.), *Annals of child development.* Greenwich, CT: JAI Press.

Hill, J., & Holmbeck, G. (1987). Disagreements about rules in families with seventh-grade girls and boys. *Journal of Youth & Adolescence, 16*, 221–246.

Hill, J., & Lynch, M. (1983). The intensification of gender-related role expectations during early adolescence. In J. Brooks-Gunn & A. Petersen (Eds.), *Female puberty.* New York: Plenum.

Hill, J., & Palmquist, W. (1978). Social cognition and social relations in early adolescence. *International Journal of Behavioral Development, 1*, 1–36.

Hingson, R., & Howland, J. (1993). Promoting safety in adolescents. In S. Millstein, A. Petersen, & E. Nightingale (Eds.), *Promoting the health of adolescents: New directions for the twenty-first century.* (pp. 305–327). New York: Oxford University Press.

Hirsch, B. J., & DuBois, D. L. (1989). The school–nonschool ecology of early adolescent friendships. In D. Belle (Ed.), *Children's social networks and social supports* (pp. 260–274). New York: Wiley.

Hirsch, B. J., & Rapkin, B. D. (1987). The transition to junior high school: A longitudinal study of self-esteem, psychological symptomatology, school life, and social support. *Child Development, 58*, 1235–1243.

Hirsch, B., & DuBois, D. (1991). Self-esteem in early adolescence: The identification and prediction of contrasting longitudinal trajectories. *Journal of Youth and Adolescence, 20*, 53–72.

Ho, D. Y. F., & Chiu, C-Y. (1994). Component ideas of individualism, collectivism and social organization: An application in the study of Chinese culture. In

U. Kim, H. C. Triandis, C. Kagitcibasi, S-C. Choi, & G. Yoon (Eds.), *Individualism and collectivism: Theory, method, and application.* Newbury Park, CA: Sage.

Hochschild, A. R. (1990). *The second shift.* New York: William Morrow.

Hochschild, A. R. (1998). *The time bind: When work becomes home and home becomes work.* New York: Henry Holt.

Hodgkinson, V. A., & Weitzman, M. S. (1990). *Volunteering and giving among American teenagers 14 to 17 years of age.* Washington, DC: Independent Sector.

Hoem, B. (1992). Early phases of family formation in contemporary Sweden. In M. K. Rosenheim & M. F. Testa (Eds.), *Early parenthood and coming of age in the 1990s* (pp. 183–199). New Brunswick, NJ: Rutgers University Press.

Hofferth, S. (1992). The demand for and supply of child care in the 1990s. In A. Booth (Ed.), *Child care in the 1990s: Means, ends and consequences* (pp. 3–25). Hillsdale, NJ: Erlbaum.

Hoffman, L. (1991). The influence of the family environment on personality: Accounting for sibling differences. *Psychological Bulletin, 110*, 187–203.

Hoffman, L. W. (1984). Work, family, and the socialization of the child. In R. D. Parke (Ed.), *Review of child development research* (Vol. 7, pp. 223–281). Chicago: University of Chicago Press.

Hoffman, M. L. (1988). Moral development. In M. H. Bornstein & M. E. Lamb (Eds.), *Developmental psychology: An advanced textbook* (2nd ed.). Hillsdale, NJ: Erlbaum.

Hofstede, G. (1980). *Culture's consequences.* Newbury Park, CA: Sage.

Hogan, D. P., & Astone, N. M. (1986). The transition to adulthood. *Annual Review of Sociology, 12*, 109–130.

Hoge, D. R., Johnson, B., & Luidens, D. A. (1993). Determinants of church involvement of young adults who grew up in Presbyterian churches. *Journal for the Scientific Study of Religion, 32*, 242–255.

Hoge, D., Smit, E., & Hanson, S. (1990). School experiences and predicting changes in self-esteem of sixth- and seventh-grade students. *Journal of Educational Psychology, 82*, 117–127.

Holland, J. (1985). *Making vocational choice: A theory of careers* (2nd ed.). Englewood Cliffs, NJ: Prentice-Hall.

Holland, J. L. (1987). Current status of Holland's theory of careers: Another perspective. *Career Development Quarterly, 36*, 24–30.

Holland, J. L. (1996). Exploring careers with a typology: What we have learned and some new directions. *American Psychologist, 51*, 397–406.

Hollinger, D. (Ed.). (1993). *Single-sex schooling: Perspectives from practice and research.* Washington, DC: U.S. Department of Education, Office of Educational Research and Improvement.

Hollinger, P. C., & Lester, D. (1991). Suicide, homicide, and demographic shifts: An epidemiologic study of regional and national trends. *Journal of Nervous and Mental Disease, 179*, 574–575.

Hollos, M., & Leis, P. E. (1989). *Becoming Nigerian in Ijo society.* New Brunswick, NJ: Rutgers University Press.

Hollos, M., & Richards, F. A. (1993). Gender-associated development of formal operations in Nigerian adolescents. *Ethos, 21*, 24–52.

Holloway, S. (1988). Concepts of ability and effort in Japan and the United States. *Review of Educational Research, 58*, 327–345.

Holmbeck, G. N., Crossmaii, R. E., Wandrei, M. L., & Gasiewski, E. (1994). Cognitive development, egocentrism, self-esteem, and adolescent contraceptive knowledge, attitudes, and behavior. *Journal of Youth and Adolescence, 23*, 169–193.

Holmbeck, G., & Hill, J. (1991). Conflictive engagement, positive affect, and menarche in families with seventh-grade girls. *Child Development, 62*, 1030–1048.

Holmes, J., & Silverman, E. L. (1992). *We're here, listen to us: A survey of young women in Canada.* Ottawa: Canadian Advisory Council on the Status of Women.

Holms, V. L., & Esses, L. M. (1988). Factors influencing Canadian high school girls' career motivation. *Psychology of Women Quarterly, 12*, 313–328.

Home, R. L., Van Vactor, J. C., & Emerson, S. (1991). Disturbed body image in patients with eating disorders. *American Journal of Psychiatry, 148*, 211–215.

Hooks, B. (1981). *Ain't I a woman?* Boston: South End Press.

Hops, H., Davis, B., Alpert, A., & Longoria, N. (1997, April). *Adolescent peer relations and depressive symptomatology.* Paper Presented at the meeting of the Society for Research in Child Development, Washington, DC.

Horan, P., & Hargis, P. (1991). Children's work and schooling in the late nineteenth-century family economy. *American Sociological Review, 56*, 583–596.

Horatio Alger Association. (1998). *Back-to-school survey, 1998.* New York: Author.

Horn, J. L. (1982). The aging of human abilities. In B. B. Wolman (Ed.), *Handbook of developmental psychology* (pp. 847–870). Englewood Cliffs, NJ: Prentice-Hall.

Horn, P. (1994). Children's work and welfare, 1780–1890. New York: Cambridge University Press.

Horowitz, F. D., & O'Brien, M. (1985). *The gifted and talented: Developmental perspectives.* Washington, DC: American Psychological Association.

Hsu, F. L. K. (1983). *Rugged individualism reconsidered.* Knoxville: University of Tennessee Press.

Hsu, F. L. K. (1985). The self in cross-cultural perspective. In A. J. Marsella, G. DeVos, & F. L. K. Hsu (Eds.), *Culture and self: Asian and Western perspectives* (pp. 24–55). London, England: Tavistock.

Huesmann, L. R., Eron, L. D., Lefkowitz, M. M., & Walder, L. O. (1984). Stability of aggression over time and generations. *Developmental Psychology, 20,* 1120–1134.

Hulse, M. (1989). *The sorrows of young Werther, by Johann Wolfgang von Goethe, translated with an Introduction and Notes.* London, England: Penguin.

Hunt, E. (1989). Cognitive science: Definition, status, and questions. *Annual Review of Psychology, 40,* 603–629.

Hurrelmann, K. (1996). The social world of adolescents: A sociological perspective. In K. Hurrelmann & S. Hamilton (Eds.), *Social problems and social contexts in adolescence: Perspectives across boundaries* (pp. 39–62). Hawthorne, NY: Aldine de Gruyter.

Hurrelmann, K., & Settertobulte, W. (1994). Germany. In K. Hurrelmann (Ed.), *International handbook of adolescence* (pp. 160–176). Westport, CT: Greenwood Press.

Huston, A., & Alvarez, M. (1990). The socialization context of gender role development in early adolescence. In R. Montemayor, G. Adams, & T. Gullotta (Eds.), *Advances in adolescent development, Vol. 2: The transition from childhood to adolescence* (pp. 156–179). Beverly Hills, CA: Sage.

Hutchins, E. (1983). Understanding Micronesian navigation. In D. Gentner & A. Stevens (Eds.), *Mental models.* Hillsdale, NJ: Erlbaum.

Hutchinson, M. K., & Cooney, T. M. (1998). Patterns of parent–teen sexual risk communication: Implications for intervention. *Family Relations, 47,* 185–194.

Hyde, J. S. (1985). *Half the human experience: The psychology of women* (3rd ed.). Lexington, KY: D.C. Heath.

Hyde, J. S. (1992). Gender and sex: So what has meta-analysis done for me? *The Psychology Teacher Network Newsletter, 2,* 2–6.

Hymel, S., Wagner, E., & Butler, L. J. (1990). Reputational bias: View from the peer group. In S. R. Asher & J. D. Coie (Eds.), *Peer rejection in childhood* (pp. 156–186). New York: Cambridge University Press.

Iannotti, R. J., & Bush, P. J. (1992). Perceived vs. actual friends' use of alcohol, cigarettes, marijuana, and cocaine: Which has the most influence? *Journal of Youth & Adolescence, 21,* 375–389.

Inclan, J. E., & Herron, D. G. (1990). Puerto Rican adolescents. In J. T. Gibbs & L. N. Huang (Eds.), *Children of color: Psychological interventions with minority youth* (pp. 251–277). San Francisco: Jossey-Bass.

Inderbitzen, H. M., Walters, K. S., & Bukowski, A. L. (1997). The role of social anxiety in adolescent peer relations: Differences among sociometric status groups and rejected subgroups. *Journal of Clinical Child Psychology, 26,* 338–348.

Ingalls, M. (1998, February). Killer games. *Computer Life,* pp. 59–60, 75.

Inhelder, B., & Piaget, J. (1958). *The growth of logical thinking from childhood to adolescence.* New York: Basic Books.

Irwin, C. E., Jr., Igra, V., Eyre, S., & Millstein, S. (1997). Risk-taking behavior in adolescents: The paradigm. In M. S. Jacobson, J. M. Rees, N. H. Golden, & C. E. Irwin (Eds.), *Adolescent nutritional disorders: Prevention and treatment* (pp. 1–35). New York: New York Academy of Sciences.

Irwin, C., Jr. (1993). Topical areas of interest for promoting health: From the perspective of the physician. In S. Millstein, A. Petersen, & E. Nightingale (Eds.), *Promoting the health of adolescents: New directions for the twenty-first century.* (pp. 328–332). New York: Oxford University Press.

Jaccard, J., Dittus, P. J., & Gordon, V. V. (1998). Parent–adolescent congruency in reports of adolescent sexual behavior and in communications about sexual behavior. *Child Development, 69,* 247–261.

Jack, D. J. (1991). *Silencing the self: Women and depression.* Cambridge, MA: Harvard University Press.

Jacobs, J. W. (1983). Treatment of divorcing fathers: Social and psychotherapeutic considerations. *American Journal of Psychiatry, 140,* 1294–1299.

Jacobson, K. C., & Crockett, L. J. (2000). Parental monitoring and adolescent adjustment: An ecological perspective. *Journal of Research on Adolescence, 10,* 65–98.

Jankowiak, W. R., & Fischer, E. F. (1992). A cross-cultural perspective on romantic love. *Ethology, 31,* 149–155.

Jarvinen, D., & Nicholls, J. (1996). Adolescents' social goals, beliefs about the causes of social success, and satisfaction in peer relations. *Developmental Psychology, 32,* 435–441.

Jason, L. A., Reichler, A., Easton, J., Neal, A., & Wilson, M. (1984). Female harassment after ending a relationship: A preliminary study. *Alternative Lifestyles, 6,* 259–269.

Jensen, J. M., & Howard, M. O. (1990). Skill deficits, skills training, and delinquency. *Children and Youth Services Review, 12,* 213–228.

Jensen, L. A. (1995). Habits of the heart revisited: Autonomy, community and divinity in adults' moral language. *Qualitative Sociology, 18,* 71–86.

Jensen, L. A. (1997a). Culture wars: American moral divisions across the adult life span. *Journal of Adult Development, 4,* 107–121.

Jensen, L. A. (1997b). Different worldviews, different morals: America's culture war divide. *Human Development, 40,* 325–344.

Jensen, L. A. (2000). *A cultural-developmental approach to moral psychology.* Manuscript submitted for publication.

Jessor, R. (1987). Risky driving and adolescent problem behavior: An extension of problem-behavior theory. *Alcohol, Drugs, and Driving, 3,* 1–11.

Jessor, R. (1999). New perspectives on adolescent risk behavior. In R. Jessor (Ed.), *New perspectives on adolescent risk behavior* (pp. 1–10). New York: Cambridge University Press.

Jessor, R., Colby, A., & Shweder, R. A. (1996). *Ethnography and human development: Context and meaning in social inquiry.* Chicago: University of Chicago Press.

Jessor, R., Costa, F., Jessor, L., & Donovan, J. (1983). Time of first intercourse: A prospective study. *Journal of Personality and Social Psychology, 44,* 608–626.

Jessor, R., Donovan, J. E., & Costa, F. M. (1991). *Beyond adolescence: Problem behavior and young adult development.* New York: Cambridge University Press.

Jessor, R., & Jessor, S. (1977). *Problem behavior and psychosocial development: A longitudinal study of youth.* New York: Academic Press.

Jeynes, W. H. (1999). Effects of remarriage following divorce on the academic achievement of children. *Journal of Youth & Adolescence, 28,* 385–393.

John, R. (1998). Native American families. In C. H. Mindel, R. W. Habenstein, & R. Wright, Jr. (Eds.), *Ethnic families in America: Patterns and variations* (pp. 382–421). Upper Saddle River, NJ: Prentice-Hall.

Johnson, B. M., Shulman, S., & Collins, W. A. (1991). Systemic patterns of parenting as reported by adolescents: Developmental differences and implications for psychosocial outcomes. *Journal of Adolescent Research, 6,* 235–252.

Johnson, J. H., & Fennell, E. B. (1992). Aggressive, antisocial, and delinquent behavior in childhood and adolescence. In C. E. Walker & M. C. Roberts (Eds.), *Handbook of clinical child psychology* (2nd ed., pp. 341–358). New York: Wiley.

Johnson, M. K., Beebe, T., Mortimer, J. T., & Snyder, M. (1998). Volunteerism in adolescence: A process perspective. *Journal of Research on Adolescence, 8,* 309–332.

Johnson, P. (1992). *Modern times: The world from the twenties to the nineties.* New York: HarperCollins.

Johnston, L., Bachman, J., & O'Malley, P. (1996). *Monitoring the future.* Ann Arbor, MI: Institute for Social Research.

Johnston, L. D., O'Malley, P. M., & Bachman, J. G. (1995). *National survey results on drug use from the Monitoring the Future Study, Vol. I: Secondary school students.* Ann Arbor, MI: Institute for Social Research.

Jonah, B. A. (1986). Accident risk and risk-taking behaviour among young drivers. *Accident Analysis and Prevention, 18,* 255–271.

Jones, E. F., Forrest, J. D., Goldman, N., Henshaw, S., Lincoln, R., Rosoff, J. I., Westoff, C. F., & Wulf, D. (1986). *Teenage pregnancy in industrialized countries.* New Haven: Yale University Press.

Jones, E. F., Forrest, J. D., Goldman, N., Henshaw, S., Lincoln, R., Rosoff, J. I., Westoff, C. F., & Wulf, D. (1987). *Teenage pregnancy in industrialized Countries.* New Haven: Yale University Press.

Jones, E. F., Forrest, J. D., Henshaw, S. K., Silverman, J., & Torres, A. (1988). Unintended pregnancy, contraceptive practice and family planning services in developed countries. *Family Planning Perspectives, 20,* 53–67.

Jones, K. (1997). Are rap videos more violent? Style differences and the prevalence of sex and violence in the age of MTV. *Howard Journal of Communications, 8,* 343–356.

Jordan, W., Lara, J., & McPartland, J. (1996). Exploring the causes of early dropout among race-ethnic and gender groups. *Youth & Society, 28,* 62–94.

Josselson, R. (1988). *Finding herself: Pathways to identity development in women.* San Francisco: Jossey-Bass.

Josselson, R. (1989). Identity formation in adolescence: Implications for young adulthood. In S. C. Feinstein (Ed.), *Adolescent psychiatry* (Vol. 16, pp. 142–154). Chicago: University of Chicago Press.

Juang, L. P., & Nguyen, H. H. (1997, April). *Autonomy and connectedness: Predictors of adjustment in Vietnamese adolescents.* Paper presented at the meeting of the Society for Research in Child Development, Washington, DC.

Juvonen, J., & Murdock, T. (1995). Grade-level differences in the social value of effort: Implications for self-presentation tactics of early adolescents. *Child Development, 66,* 1694–1705.

Kahn, J. S., Kehle, T. J., Jensen, W. R., & Clark, E. (1990). Comparison of cognitive-behavioral, relaxation, and self-modeling interventions for depression among middle-school students. *School Psychology Review, 19,* 196–211.

Kahne, J. (1999). Personalized philanthropy: Can it support youth and build civic commitments? *Youth & Society, 30,* 367–387.

Kail, R. (1991a). Processing time declines exponentially during childhood and adolescence. *Developmental Psychology, 27,* 259–266.

Kail, R. (1991b). Developmental change in speed of processing during childhood and adolescence. *Psychological Bulletin, 109,* 490–501.

Kail, R., & Pellegrino, J. W. (1985). *Human intelligence.* New York: Freeman.

Kakar, S. (1998). Asian Indian families. In R. L. Taylor (Ed.), *Minority families in the United States: A multicultural perspective* (pp. 208–223). Upper Saddle River, NJ: Prentice Hall.

Kalb, C., & McCormick, J. (1998, September 21). Bellying up to the bar. *Newsweek,* p. 89.

Kalin, R., & Tilby R. (1978). Development and validation of a sex-role ideology scale. *Psychological Reports, 42,* 731–738.

Kallman, D. A., Plato, C. C., & Tobin, J. D. (1990). The role of muscle loss in the age-related decline of grip strength: Cross-sectional and longitudinal perspectives. *Journals of Gerontology: Medical Sciences, 45,* M82–88.

Kamagai, F. (1984). The life cycle of the Japanese family. *Journal of Marriage and the Family, 46,* 191–204.

Kandel, D. B. (1975). Stages in adolescent involvement in drug use. *Science, 190,* 912–914.

Kandel, D. B. (1978). Homophily, selection, and socialization in adolescent friendships. *American Journal of Sociology, 84,* 426–437.

Kandel, D. B. (1998). Persistent themes and new perspectives on adolescent substance use: A lifespan perspective. In R. Jessor (Ed.), *New perspectives on adolescent risk behavior* (pp. 43–89). New York: Cambridge University Press.

Kandel, D. B., & Faust, R. (1975). Sequence and stages in patterns of adolescent drug use. *Archives of General Psychiatry, 32,* 923–932.

Kantrowitz, B., & Wingert, P. (1999, October 18). The truth about teens. *Newsweek,* pp. 62–72.

Kao, G., & Tienda, M. (1995). Optimism and achievement: The educational performance of immigrant youth. *Social Science Quarterly, 76,* 1–19.

Kaplan, S. J. (1991). Physical abuse and neglect. In M. Lewis (Ed.), *Child and adolescent psychiatry* (pp. 1010–1018). Baltimore, MD: Williams & Wilkins.

Kasen, S., Cohen, P., & Brook, J. S. (1998). Adolescent school experiences, and dropout, adolescent pregnancy, and young adult deviant behavior. *Journal of Adolescent Research, 13,* 49–72.

Kasen, S., Cohen, P., Brook, J. S., & Hartmark, C. (1996). A multiple-risk interaction model: Effects of temperament and divorce on psychiatric disorder in children. *Journal of Abnormal Child Psychology, 24,* 121–150.

Kashani, J. H., Daniel, A. E., Dandoy, A. C., & Holcomb, W. R. (1992). Family violence: Impact on children. *Journal of the American Academy of Child and Adolescent Psychiatry, 31,* 181–189.

Kassler, W. J., & Cates, W. (1992). The epidemiology and prevention of sexually transmitted diseases. *Urology Clinics of North America, 19,* 1–12.

Katchadourian, H., & Boli, J. (1985). *Careerism and intellectualism among college students.* San Francisco: Jossey-Bass.

Katz, J. (Ed.). (1995). *Messengers of the wind: Native American women tell their life stories.* New York: Ballantine.

Kaufman, D. R. (1991). *Rachel's daughters: Newly orthodox Jewish women.* New Brunswick, NJ: Rutgers University Press.

Keating, D. (1975). Precocious cognitive development at the level of formal operations. *Child Development, 46,* 476–480.

Keating, D. (1990). Adolescent thinking. In S. Feldman & G. Elliott (Eds.), *At the threshold: The developing adolescent* (pp. 54–89). Cambridge, MA: Harvard University Press.

Keating, D. (1991). Cognition, adolescent. In R. M. Lerner, A. C. Petersen, & J. Brooks-Gunn (Eds.) *Encyclopedia of adolescence* (Vol. 1, pp. 119–129). New York: Garland.

Keating, D. P., & Sasse, D. K. (1996). Cognitive socialization in adolescence: Critical period for a critical habit of mind. In G. R. Adams, R. Montemayer, & T. Gullotta (Eds.), *Psychosocial development during adolescence* (pp. 232–258). Thousand Oaks, CA: Sage.

Keefe, K. (1994). Perceptions of normative social pressure and attitudes toward alcohol use: Changes during adolescence. *Journal of Studies on Alcohol, 55,* 46–54.

Keel, P. K., Fulkerson, J. A., & Leon, G. R. (1997). Disordered eating precursors in pre- and early-adolescent girls and boys. *Journal of Youth & Adolescence, 26,* 203–216.

Kelly, J. A., O'Brien, G. G., & Hosford, R. (1981). Sex roles and social skills: Considerations for interpersonal judgment. *Psychology of Women Quarterly, 5,* 758–766.

Kendall-Tackett, K. A., Williams, L. M., & Finkelhor, D. (1993). Impact of sexual abuse on children: A review and synthesis of recent empirical studies. *Psychological Bulletin, 113,* 164–180.

Kennedy, J. H. (1990). Determinants of peer social status: Contributions of physical appearance, reputation, and behavior. *Journal of Youth and Adolescence, 19,* 233–244.

Kenny, M. E., & Hart, K. (1992). Relationship between parental attachment and eating disorders in an inpatient and a college sample. *Journal of Counseling Psychology, 39,* 521–526.

Kerber, L. K. (1997). *Toward an intellectual history of women.* Chapel Hill: University of North Carolina Press.

Kerns, K. (1994). Individual differences in friendship quality: Links to child–mother attachment. In W. Bukowski, A. Newcomb, & W. Hartup (Eds.), *The company they keep: Friendship in childhood and adolescence.* New York: Cambridge University Press.

Kett, J. (1977). *Rites of passage: Adolescence in America, 1790 to the present.* New York: Basic Books.

Killen, M., & Wainryb, C. (1998). Independence and interdependence in diverse cultural contexts. *New Directions for Child Development.*

Kim, J. E., Hetherington, E., & Reiss, D. (1999). Associations among family relationships, antisocial peers, and adolescents' externalizing behaviors: Gender and family type differences. *Child Development, 70,* 1209–1230.

Kinder, B. N. (1991). Eating disorders (anorexia nervosa and bulimia nervosa). In M. Hersen & S. M. Turner (Eds.), *Adult psychopathology and diagnosis* (2nd ed., pp. 392–409). New York: Wiley.

King, A. J. C., Beazley, R. P., Warren, W. K., Hankins, C. A., Robertson, A. S., & Radford, J. L. (1988). *Canadian youth & AIDS study.* Ottawa, Canada: Health and Welfare Canada.

King, C., Siegel, M., Celebucki, C., & Connolly, G. (1998). Adolescent exposure to cigarette advertising in magazines: An evaluation of brand-specific advertising in relation to youth readership. *Journal of the American Medical Association, 279,* 516–520.

King, H. E. (1992). The reactions of children to divorce. In C. E. Walker & M. C. Roberts (Eds.), *Handbook of clinical child psychology* (2nd ed., pp. 1009–1023). New York: Wiley.

Kinney, D. (1993). From nerds to normals: The recovery of identity among adolescents from middle school to high school. *Sociology of Education, 66,* 21–40.

Kinney, D. A. (1999). From "headbangers" to "hippies": Delineating adolescents' active attempts to form an alternative peer culture. *New Directions for Child Development, 84,* 21–35.

Kinsey, A. C., Pomeroy, W., Martin, C. E., & Gebhard, P. (1953). *Sexual behavior in the human female.* Philadelphia: Saunders.

Kirby, D. (1984). *Sexuality education: An evaluation of programs and their effects: An executive summary.* Bethesda, MD: Mathtech, Inc.

Kirby, D. (2000). School-based interventions to prevent unprotected sex and HIV among adolescents. In J. L. Peterson & R. J. DiClemente (Eds.), *Handbook of HIV prevention* (pp. 83–101). New York: Plenum.

Kiser, L. J., Heston, J., Millsap, P. A., & Pruitt, D. B. (1991). Physical and sexual abuse in childhood: Relationship with post-traumatic stress disorder. *Journal of the American Academy of Child and Adolescent Psychiatry, 30,* 776–783.

Kitahara, M. (1982). Menstrual taboos and the importance of hunting. *American Anthropologist, 84,* 901–903.

Kitchener, K. S., & King, P. M. (1990). The reflective judgment model: Ten years of research. In M. L. Commons, C. Armon, L. Kohlberg, F. A. Richards, T. A. Grotzer, & J. Sinnott (Eds.), *Adult development* (Vol. 2, pp. 63–78). New York: Praeger.

Kitchener, K. S., Lynch, C. L., Fischer, K. W., & Wood, P. K. (1993). Developmental range of reflective judgment: The effect of contextual support and practice on developmental stage. *Developmental Psychology, 29,* 893–906.

Klebanov, P., & Brooks-Gunn, J. (1992). Impact of maternal attitudes, girls' adjustment, and cognitive skills upon academic performance in middle and high school. *Journal of Research on Adolescence, 2,* 81–102.

Klein, J. D., Brown, J. D., Childers, K. W., Oliveri, J., Porter, C., & Dykers, C. (1993). Adolescents' risky behavior and mass media use. *Pediatrics, 92,* 24–31.

Klein, J. R., & Litt, I. F. (1983). Menarche and dysmenorrhea. In J. Brooks-Gunn & A. C. Petersen (Eds.), *Girls at puberty: Biological, psychological, and social perspectives.* New York: Plenum.

Kobak, R., & Cole, H. (1994). Attachment and metamonitoring: Implications for adolescent autonomy and psychopathology. In D. Cicchetti & S. Toth (Eds.), *Rochester symposium on developmental psychopathology, Vol. 5: Disorders and dysfunctions of the self.* Rochester, NY: University of Rochester Press.

Kobak, R., Cole, H., Ferenz-Gillies, R., Fleming, W., & Gamble, W. (1993). Attachment and emotion regulation during mother–teen problem-solving: A control theory analysis. *Child Development, 64,* 231–245.

Kobak, R., & Sceery, A. (1988). Attachment in late adolescence: Working models, affect regulation, and representations of self and others. *Child Development, 59,* 135–146.

Kohlberg, L. (1958). *The development of modes of moral thinking and choice in the years 10 to 16.* Unpublished doctoral dissertation, University of Chicago.

Kohlberg, L. (1966). A cognitive-developmental analysis of children's sex role concepts and attitudes. In E. E. Maccoby (Ed.), *The development of sex differences.* Palo Alto, CA: Stanford University Press.

Kohlberg, L. (1976). Moral stages and moralization: The cognitive-development approach. In T. Lickona (Ed.), *Moral development and behavior.* New York: Holt, Rinehart and Winston.

Kohlberg, L. (1981). *Essays on moral development. Vol. 1: The philosophy of moral development.* New York: Harper & Row.

Kohlberg, L. (1986). A current statement on some theoretical issues. In S. Modgit & C. Modgil (Eds.), *Lawrence Kohlberg.* Philadelphia: Falmer.

Kohn, M. (1977). *Class and conformity* (2nd ed.). Chicago: University of Chicago Press.

Konopka, G. (1985). *Young girls: A portrait Of adolescence.* New York: Harrington Park Press.

Kosky, R., Silbum, S., & Zubrick, S. R. (1990). Are children and adolescents who have suicidal thoughts different from those who attempt suicide? *Journal of Nervous and Mental Disease, 178,* 38–43.

Kracke, B., Oepke, M., Wild, E., & Noack, P. (1998). Adolescents, families, and German unification: The impact of social change on antiforeigner and antidemocratic attitudes. In J. Nurmi (Ed.), *Adolescents, cultures, and conflicts* (pp. 149–170). New York: Garland.

Kramer, L., & Lin, L. (1997, April). *Mothers' and fathers' responses to sibling conflict.* Paper presented at the meeting of the Society for Research in Child Development, Washington, DC.

Krisberg, B., Schwartz, I., Fishman, G., Eisikovits, Z., & Guttman, E. (1986). *The incarceration of minority youth.* Minneapolis, MN: Hubert H. Humphrey Institute of Public Affairs, National Council on Crime and Delinquency.

Kroger, J. (1999). *Identity development: Adolescence through adulthood.* London, England: Sage.

Kufeldt, K., & Nimmo, M. (1987). Youth on the street: Abuse and neglect in the eighties. *Child Abuse and Neglect, 11,* 531–543.

Kuhn D. (1992). Cognitive development. In M. H. Bornstein & M. Lamb (Eds.), *Developmental psychology: An advanced textbook* (3rd ed., pp. 211–272). Hillsdale, NJ: Erlbaum.

Kuhn, D. (1999). Metacognitive development. In L. Balte & C. S. Tamis-LeMonde (Eds.), *Child psychology: A handbook of contemporary issues* (pp. 259–286). Philadelphia, PA: Psychology Press.

Kupersmidt, J. B., & Coie, J. D. (1990). Preadolescent peer status, aggression, and school adjustment as predictors of externalizing problems in adolescence. *Child Development, 61,* 1350–1363.

Kurdek, L. (1987). Gender differences in the psychological symptomatology and coping strategies of young adolescents. *Journal of Early Adolescence, 7,* 395–410.

Kurdek, L. A., & Krile, D. (1982). A developmental analysis of the relation between peer acceptance, interpersonal understanding and perceived social self-competence. *Child Development, 53,* 1485–1491.

Kurtz, D. A., Cantu, C. L., & Phinney, J. S. (1996, March). *Group identities as predictors of self-esteem among African American, Latino, and White adolescents.* Paper presented at the meeting of the Society for Research on Adolescence, Boston.

Kuttler, A. F., La Greca, A. M., & Prinstein, M. J. (1999). Friendship qualities and social-emotional functioning of adolescents with close, cross-sex friendships. *Journal of Research on Adolescence, 9,* 339–366.

Labouvie-Vief, G. (1982). Dynamic development and mature autonomy: A theoretical prologue. *Human Development, 25,* 161–191.

Labouvie-Vief, G. (1990). Modes of knowledge and the organization of development. In M. L. Commons, J. D. Sinnott, F. A. Richards, & C. Armon (Eds.), *Models and methods in the study of adolescent and adult thought* (pp. 43–62). New York: Praeger.

Labouvie-Vief, G. (1998). Cognitive-emotional integration in adulthood. In K. W. Schaie & M. P. Lawton (Eds.), *Annual review of gerontology and geriatrics, Vol. 17: Focus on emotion and adult development* (pp. 206–237). New York: Springer.

Lacombe, A. C., & Gay, J. (1998). The role of gender in adolescent identity and intimacy decisions. *Journal of Youth & Adolescence, 27,* 795–802.

Ladd, G. W., & Le Sieur, K. D. (1995). Parents and children's peer relationships. In M. H. Bornstein (Ed.), *Children and parenting* (Vol. 4). Hillsdale, NJ: Erlbaum.

Ladewig, H., & Thomas, J. K. (1987). *Assessing the impact of 4-H on former members.* College Station: Texas A&M University Press.

Ladurie, E. L. (1979). *Montaillou: The promised land of error.* New York: Random House.

Laframboise, T. D., & Low, K. G. (1989). American Indian children and adolescents. In J. T. Gibbs, L. N. Huang (Eds.), *Children of color: Psychological interventions with minority youth* (pp. 114–147). San Francisco: Jossey-Bass.

Lagree, J. C. (1995). Young people and employment in the European Community: Convergence or divergence? In L. Chisholm, P. Buchner, H. H. Kruger, & M. du Bois-Reymond (Eds.), *Growing up in Europe: Contemporary horizons in childhood and youth studies* (pp. 61–72). New York: Walter de Gruyter.

Laible, D. J., Carlo, G., & Rafaelli, M. (2000). The differential relations of parent and peer attachment to adolescent adjustment. *Journal of Youth & Adolescence, 29,* 45–60.

Lakatta, E. G. (1990). Heart and circulation. In E. L. Schneider & J. W. Rowe (Eds.), *Handbook of the biology of aging* (3rd ed., pp. 181–217). San Diego, CA: Academic Press.

Lamborn, S. D., Mounts, N. S., Steinberg, L., & Dornbusch, S. M. (1991). Patterns of competence and adjustment among adolescents from authoritative, authoritarian, indulgent, and neglectful families. *Child Development, 62,* 1049–1065.

Lantier, G. (1998, June). Do abstinence lessons lessen sex? *Youth Today, 7,* 19.

Lapsley, D. K. (1990). Continuity and discontinuity in adolescent social cognitive development. In R. Montemayor, G. R. Adams, & T. P. Gullotta (Eds.), *From childhood to adolescence: A transitional period?* Newbury Park, CA: Sage.

Lapsley, D. K., Enright, R. D., & Serlin, R. C. (1985). Toward a theoretical perspective on the legislation of adolescence. *Journal of Early Adolescence, 5,* 441–466.

Laron, Z., Arad, J., Gurewitz, R., Grunebaum, M., & Dickerman, Z. (1980). Age at first conscious ejaculation: A milestone in male puberty. *Helevetica Paediatrica Acta, 5,* 13–20.

Larose, S., & Boivin, M. (1998). Attachment to parents, social support expectations, and socioemotional adjustment during the high school–college transition. *Journal of Research on Adolescence, 8,* 1–27.

Larson, E. (1990, July/August). Censoring sex information: The story of Sassy. *Utne Reader,* 96–97.

Larson, R. (1990). The solitary side of life: An examination of the time people spend alone from childhood to old age. *Developmental Review, 10,* 155–183.

Larson, R. (1995). Secrets in the bedroom: Adolescents' private use of media. *Journal of Youth & Adolescence, 24,* 535–550.

Larson, R., Clore, G. L., & Wood, G. A. (1999). The emotions of romantic relationships: Do they wreak havoc on adolescents? In W. Furman, B. B. Brown, & C. Feiring (Eds.), *The development of romantic relationships in adolescence* (pp. 19–49). New York: Cambridge University Press.

Larson, R., Csikszentmihalyi, M., & Graef, R. (1982). Time alone in daily experience: Loneliness or renewal? In L. A. Peplau & D. Perlman (Eds.), *Loneliness: A sourcebook of theory, research, and therapy* (pp. 40–53). New York: Wiley.

Larson, R., & Ham, M. (1993). Stress and "storm and stress" in early adolescence: The relationship of negative life events with dysphoric affect. *Developmental Psychology, 29,* 130–140.

Larson, R., Kubey, R., & Colletti, J. (1989). Changing channels: Early adolescent media choices and shifting investments in family and friends. *Journal of Youth & Adolescence, 18,* 583–599.

Larson, R., & Richards, M. H. (1994). *Divergent realities: The emotional lives of mothers, fathers, and adolescents.* New York: Basic Books.

Larson, R., & Richards, M. (1998). Waiting for the weekend: Friday and Saturday nights as the emotional climax of the week. *New Directions for Child and Adolescent Development, 82,* 37–52.

Larson, R., Verman, S., & Dworkin, J. (2000, March). *Adolescence without family disengagement: The daily family lives of Indian middle-class teenagers.* Paper presented at the biennial meeting of the Society for Research on Adolescence, Chicago.

Larson, R. W., Csikszentmihalyi, M., & Graef, R. (1980). Mood variability and the psycho-social adjustment of adolescents. *Journal of Youth & Adolescence, 9,* 469–490.

Larson, R. W., Richards, M. H., Moneta, G., Holmbeck, G., & Duckett, E. (1996). Changes in adolescents' daily interactions with their families from ages 10 to 18: Disengagement and transformation. *Developmental Psychology, 32,* 744–754.

Lasch, C. (1979). *Haven in a heartless world.* New York: Basic Books.

Lau, S. (1988). The value orientations of Chinese university students in Hong Kong. *International Journal of Psychology, 23,* 583–596.

Lauritsen, J. (1994). Explaining race and gender differences in adolescent sexual behavior. *Social Forces, 72,* 859–884.

Laursen, B., & Collins, W. (1994). Interpersonal conflict during adolescence. *Psychological Bulletin, 115,* 197–209.

Laursen, B., & Jensen-Campbell, L. A. (1999). The nature and functions of social exchange in adolescent romantic relationships. In W. Furman, B. B. Brown, & C. Feiring (Eds.), *The development of romantic relationships in adolescence* (pp. 50–74). New York: Cambridge University Press.

Laursen, B., Coy, K. C., & Collins, W. A. (1998). Reconsidering changes in parent–child conflict across adolescence: A meta-analysis. *Child Development, 69,* 817–832.

Lave, J. (1988). *Cognition in practice: Mind, mathematics, and culture in everyday life.* Cambridge: Cambridge University Press.

Leadbeater, B. J., Blatt, S. J., & Quinlan, D. M. (1995). Gender-linked vulnerabilities to depressive symptoms, stress, and problem behaviors in adolescence. *Journal of Research on Adolescence, 5,* 1–30.

Leadbetter, B. J. (1994, February). *Reconceptualizing social supports for adolescent mothers: Grandmothers, babies, fathers, and beyond.* Paper presented at the meeting of the Society for Research on Adolescence, San Diego.

Lee, B. (1998). *The changes of Korean adolescents' lives.* Unpublished manuscript, Department of Human Development and Family Studies, University of Missouri.

Lee, C. M., & Gotlib, I. H. (1990). Family disruption, parental availability, and child adjustment. In R. Prinz (Ed.), *Advances in behavioral assessment of children and families* (Vol. 5, pp. 173–202). New York: Kingsley.

Lee, M., & Larson, R. (2000). The Korean "examination hell": Long hours of studying, distress, and depression. *Journal of Youth & Adolescence, 29,* 249–271.

Lee, M. M. C., Chang, K. S. F., & Chan, M. M. C. (1963). Sexual maturation of Chinese girls in Hong Kong. *Pediatrics, 32,* 389–398.

Lee, P. A. (1980). Normal ages of pubertal events among American males and females. *Journal of Adolescent Health Care, 1,* 26–29.

Lee, V. E., Burkam, D. T., Zimiles, H., & Ladewski, B. (1994). Family structure and its effect on behavioral and emotional problems in young adolescents. *Journal of Research on Adolescence, 4,* 405–437.

Lee, V., & Bryk, A. (1986). Effects of single-sex secondary schools on achievement and attitudes. *Journal of Educational Psychology, 78,* 381–395.

Lee, V., & Croninger, R. (1994). The relative importance of home and school in the development of literacy skills for middle-grade students. *American Journal of Education, 102*, 286–329.

Lee, V., Croninger, R., Linn, E., & Chen, X. (1996). The culture of harassment in secondary schools. *American Educational Research Journal, 33*, 383–417.

Lee, V., Marks, H., & Byrd, T. (1994). Sexism in single-sex and co-educational independent secondary school classrooms. *Sociology of Education, 67*, 92–120.

Lefley, H. P. (1976). Acculturation, child-rearing, and self-esteem in two North American Indian tribes. *Ethos, 4*, 385–401.

Leitenberg, H., Detzer, M. J., & Srebnik, D. (1993). Gender differences in masturbation and the relation of masturbation experience in preadolescence and/or early adolescence to sexual behavior and sexual adjustment in young adulthood. *Archives of Sexual Behavior, 22*, 87–98.

Lemann, N. (1986, June). The origins of the underclass. *Atlantic Monthly*, pp. 31–55.

Lempers, J. D., & Clark-Lempers, D. S. (1993). A functional comparison of same-sex and opposite-sex friendships during adolescence. *Journal of Adolescent Research, 8*, 89–108.

Lepper, M. R., & Gurtner, J. (1989). Children and computers: Approaching the 21st century. *American Psychologist, 44*, 170–178.

LeVay, S. (1991). A difference in hypothalamic structure between heterosexual and homosexual men. *Science, 253*, 1034–I037.

Leventhal, H., & Keeshan, P. (1993). Promoting healthy alternatives to substance abuse. In S. Millstein, A. Petersen, & E. Nightingale (Eds.), *Promoting the health of adolescents: New directions for the 21st century* (pp. 260–284). New York: Oxford University Press.

Levesque, R. J. (1993). The romantic experience of adolescents in satisfying love relationships. *Journal of Youth & Adolescence, 22*, 219–251.

LeVine, D. N. (1966). The concept of masculinity in Ethiopian culture. *International Journal of Social Psychiatry, 12*, 17–23.

Levine, M., Smolak, L., & Hayden, H. (1994). The relation of sociocultural factors to eating attitudes and behaviors among middle school girls. *Journal of Early Adolescence, 14*, 471–490.

Levinson, D. J. (1978). *The seasons of a man's life*. New York: Knopf.

Levitt, M. J., Guacci-Franco, N., & Levitt, J. L. (1993). Convoys of social support in childhood and early adolescence: Structure and function. *Developmental Psychology, 29*, 811–818.

Lewin, T. (1998, May 1). Birth rates for teenagers declined sharply in the 90's. *New York Times*, p. A-17.

Lewin-Epstein, N. (1981). *Youth employment during high school*. Washington, DC: National Center for Education Statistics.

Lewinsohn, P. M., Clarke, G. N., Hops, H., & Andrews, J. (1990). Cognitive, behavioral treatment for depressed adolescents. *Behavior Therapy, 21*, 385–401.

Lewinsohn, P. M., Rohde, P., & Seeley, J. R. (1993). Psychosocial characteristics of adolescents with a history of suicide attempts. *Journal of the American Academy of Child and Adolescent Psychiatry, 32*, 60–68.

Lewinsohn, P., Hops, H., Roberts, R., Seeley, J., & Andrews, J. (1993). Adolescent psychopathology, I: Prevalence and incidence of depression and other DSM-III R disorders in high school students. *Journal of Abnormal Psychology, 102*, 133–144.

Lewis, C. G. (1981). How adolescents approach decisions: Changes over grades seven to twelve and policy implications. *Child Development, 52*, 538–554.

Lewis, D. O., Mallouh, C., & Webb, V. (1989). Child abuse, delinquency, and violent criminality. In D. Cicchetti & V. Carlson (Eds.), *Child maltreatment: Theory and research in the causes and consequences of child abuse and neglect* (pp. 707–721). New York: Cambridge University Press.

Lewis, T., Stone, J., Shipley, W., & Madzar, S. (1998). The transition from school to work: An examination of the literature. *Youth & Society, 29*, 259–292.

Lichter, P. (1978). *The boy who dared to rock: The definitive Elvis*. New York: Dolphin Books.

Lichty, L. W. (1989). Television in America: Success story. In P. S. Cook, D. Gomery, & L. W. Lichty (Eds.), *American media* (pp. 159–176). Los Angeles, CA: Wilson Center Press.

Liebkind, K., & Kosonen, L. (1998). Acculturation and adaptation: A case of Vietnamese children and youths in Finland. In J. Nurmi (Ed.), *Adolescents, cultures, and conflicts* (pp. 199–224). New York: Garland.

Liechty, M. (1995). Media, markets, and modernization: Youth identities and the experience of modernity in Kathmandu, Nepal. In V. Amit-Talai & H. Wulff (Eds.), *Youth cultures: A cross-cultural perspective* (pp. 166–201). New York: Routledge.

Lin, C. C., & Fu, V. R. (1990). A comparison of child-rearing practices among Chinese, immigrant Chinese, and Caucasian-American parents. *Child Development, 61*, 429–433.

Linares, L. O., Leadbeater, B. J., Kato, P. M., & Jaffe, L. (1991). Predicting school outcomes for minority group mothers: Can subgroups be identified? *Journal of Research on Adolescence, 1*, 379–400.

Linden-Ward, B., & Green, C. H. (1993). *American women in the 1960s: Changing the future*. New York: Twayne.

Linn, M. C., De Benedictus, T., & Delucchi, K. (1982). Adolescent reasoning about advertising: Preliminary investigations. *Child Development, 53*, 1599–1613.

Linn, M., & Songer, N. (1991). Cognitive and conceptual change in adolescence. *American Journal of Education, 99*, 379–417.

Linn, M., & Songer, N. (1993). How do students make sense of science? *Merrill-Palmer Quarterly, 39*, 47–73.

Linscheid, I. R., Tarnowski, K. J., & Richmond, D. A. (1988). Behavioral approaches to anorexia nervosa, bulimia, and obesity. In D. K. Routh (Ed.), *Handbook of pediatric psychology* (pp. 332–362). New York: Guilford.

Lips, H. M. (1993). *Sex and gender: An introduction*. Mountain View, CA: Mayfield.

Litt, I. F., & Vaughan, V. C., III (1987). Growth and development during adolescence. In R. E. Behrman, V. C. Vaughan, & W. E. Nelson (Eds.), *Textbook of pediatrics* (13th ed., pp. 20–24). Philadelphia: Saunders.

Liu, L. L., Slap, G. B., Kinsman, S. B., & Khalid, N. (1994). Pregnancy among American Indian adolescents: Reactions and prenatal care. *Journal of Adolescent Health, 15*, 336–341.

Liu, X., Kaplan, H. B., & Risser, W. (1992). Decomposing the reciprocal relationships between academic achievement and general self-esteem. *Youth & Society, 24*, 124–148.

Livesley, W. J., & Bromley, D. B. (1973). *Person perception in childhood and adolescence*. New York: Wiley.

Livson, N., & Peskin, H. (1980). Perspectives on adolescence from longitudinal research. In J. Adelson (Ed.), *Handbook of adolescent psychology* (pp. 47–98). New York: Wiley.

Loeber, R., Farrington, D. P., Stouthamer-Loeber, M., & Van Kammen, W. B. (1998). Multiple risk factors for multiproblem boys: Co-occurrence of delinquency, substance use, attention deficit, conduct problems, physical aggression, covert behavior, depressed mood, and shy/withdrawn behavior. In R. Jessor (Ed.), *New perspectives on adolescent risk behavior* (pp. 90–149). New York: Cambridge University Press.

Long, B. (1989). Heterosexual involvement of unmarried undergraduate females in relation to self-evaluations. *Journal of Youth and Adolescence, 18*, 489–500.

Long, N., Slater, E., Forehand, R., & Fauber, R. (1988). Continued high or reduced interparental conflict following divorce: Relation to young adolescent adjustment. *Journal of Consulting and Clinical Psychology, 56*, 467–469.

Longo, D. J., Clum, G. A., & Yaeger, N. J. (1988). Psychosocial treatment for recurrent genital herpes. *Journal of Consulting and Clinical Psychology, 56*, 61–66.

Lopresto, C. T., Sherman, M. F., & Sherman, N. C. (1985). The affects of a masturbation seminar on high school males' attitudes, false beliefs, and behavior. *Journal of Sex Research, 21,* 142–156.

Lord, S., Eccles, J. S., & McCarthy, K. (1994). Risk and protective factors in the transition to junior high school. *Journal of Early Adolescence, 14,* 162–199.

Loughlin, C., & Barling, J. (1999). The nature of youth employment. In J. Barling & E. K. Kelloway (Eds.), *Youth workers: Varieties of experience* (pp. 17–36). Washington, DC: American Psychological Association.

Lovitt, T. (1989). *Introduction to learning disabilities.* Boston: Allyn & Bacon.

Lowe, G. S., & Krahn, H. (1999). Reconceptualizing youth unemployment. In J. Barling & E. K. Kelloway (Eds.), *Youth workers: Varieties of experience* (pp. 201–223). Washington, DC: American Psychological Association.

Lowman, R. L. (1991). *The clinical practice of career assessment.* Washington, DC: American Psychological Association.

Lucas, A. R. (1991). Eating disorders. In M. Lewis (Ed.), *Child and adolescent psychiatry* (pp. 573–583). Baltimore, MD: Williams & Wilkins.

Lucas, S. (1996). Selective attrition in a newly hostile regime: The case of 1980 sophomores. *Social Forces, 75,* 511–533.

Lull, J. (1980). The social uses of television. *Human Communication Research, 6,* 197–209.

Lull, J. (1987). Listeners' communicative uses of popular music. In J. Lull (Ed.), *Popular music and communication* (pp. 140–174). Beverly Hills, CA: Sage.

Lundberg-Love, P. K. (1990). Adult survivors of incest. In R. T. Ammerman & M. Hersen (Eds.), *Treatment of Family violence* (pp. 211–240). New York: Wiley.

Luo, Q., Fang, X., & Aro, P. (1995, March). *Selection of best friends by Chinese adolescents.* Paper presented at the meeting of the Society for Research in Child Development, Indianapolis.

Luria, Z., Friedman, S., & Rose, M. D. (1987). *Human sexuality.* New York: Wiley.

Lykken, D. T., & Tellegen, A. (1993). Is human mating advantageous or the result of lawful choice? A twin study of mate selection. *Journal of Personality and Social Psychology, 65,* 56–68.

Lynch, M. E. (1991). Gender intensification. In R. M. Lerner, A. C. Petersen, & J. Brooks-Gunn (Eds.), *Encyclopedia of adolescence* (Vol. 1). New York: Garland.

Lynd, R. S., & Lynd, H. M. (1927/1957). *Middletown: A study of modern American culture.* New York: Harvest.

Lynd, R. S., & Lynd, H. M. (1929). *Middletown: A study in modern American culture.* New York: Harvest Books.

Lyng, S. (1991). Dysfunctional risk taking: Criminal behavior as edgework. In N. J. Bell & R. W. Bell (Eds.), *Adolescent risk taking* (pp. 107–130). Newbury Park, CA: Sage.

Lytle, L. J., Bakken, L., & Romig, C. (1997). Adolescent female identity development. *Sex Roles, 37,* 175–185.

Lytton, H., & Romney, D. M. (1991). Parents' differential socialization of boys and girls: A meta-analysis. *Psychological Bulletin, 109,* 267–296.

Maccoby, E. (1990). Gender and relationships: A developmental account. *American Psychologist, 45,* 755–775.

Maccoby, E. E., & Jacklin, C. N. (1974). *The psychology of sex differences.* Stanford, CA: Stanford University Press.

Maccoby, E. E., Depner, C. E., & Mnookin, R. H. (1988). Custody of children following divorce. In E. M. Hetherington & J. D. Aresteh (Eds.), *Impact of divorce, single parenting, and stepparenting* (pp. 91–114). Hillsdale, NJ: Erlbaum.

Maccoby, E., & Martin, J. (1983). Socialization in the context of the family: Parent-child interaction. In E. M. Hetherington (Ed.), *Handbook of child psychology: Socialization, personality, and social development* (Vol. 4). New York: Wiley.

MacDonald, N. E., Wells, G. A., Fisher, W. A., Warren, W. K., King, M. A., Doherty, J. A., & Bowie, W. R. (1990). High-risk STD/HIV behavior among college students. *Journal of the American Medical Association, 263,* 3155–3159.

Macek, P., & Rabusic, L. (1994). Czechoslovakia. In K. Hurrelman (Ed.), *International handbook of adolescence* (pp. 117–130). Westport, CT: Greenwood.

Maggs, J. L. (1999). Alcohol use and binge drinking as goal-directed action during the transition to post-secondary education. In J. Schulenberg, J. L. Maggs, & K. Hurrelmann (Eds.), *Health risks and developmental transitions during adolescence* (pp. 345–371). New York: Cambridge University Press.

Magnusson, D., Stattin, H., & Allen, V. (1986). Differential maturation among girls and its relation to social adjustment in a longitudinal perspective. In P. Baltes, D. Featherman, & R. Lerner (Eds.), *Life span development and behavior* (Vol. 7). Hillsdale, NJ: Erlbaum.

Magolda, M. B. B. (1997). Students' epistemologies and academic experiences: Implications for pedagogy. In K. Arnold & I. C. King (Eds.), *Contemporary higher education: International issues for the 21st century* (pp. 117–140). New York: Garland.

Majors, R. (1989). Cool pose: The proud signature of black survival. In M. S. Kimmel & M. A. Messner (Eds.), *Men's lives* (pp. 83–87). New York: Macmillan.

Majors, R., & Billson, J. M. (1992). *Cool pose.* New York: Lexington.

Makhlouf, H., & Abdelkader, M. (1997). *The current status of research and training in population and health in the Arab region and the future needs.* Cairo: Cairo Demographic Center.

Malik, S. (2000, February). *Arab adolescents facing the 3rd millennium.* Paper prepared for the meeting of the Study Group on Adolescence in the 21st Century, Washington, DC.

Malyon, A. K. (1981). The homosexual adolescent: Developmental issues and social bias. *Child Welfare, 60,* 321–330.

Manchester, W. (1973). *The glory and the dream: A narrative history of America, 1932–1972.* New York: Bantam.

Manis, F. R., Keating, D. P., & Morrison, F. J. (1980). Developmental differences in the allocation of processing capacity. *Journal of Experimental Child Psychology, 29,* 156–169.

Manlove, J. (1998). The influence of high school dropout and school disengagement on the risk of school-age pregnancy. *Journal of Research on Adolescence, 8,* 187–220.

Manning, S. (1999, September 27). Students for sale: How corporations are buying their way into America's classrooms. *The Nation,* pp. 11–18.

Marcia, J. (1966). Development and validation of ego identity status. *Journal of Personality and Social Psychology, 3,* 551–558.

Marcia, J. (1980). Identity in adolescence. In J. Adelson (Ed.), *Handbook of adolescent psychology.* New York: Wiley.

Marcia, J. (1989). Identity and intervention. *Journal of Adolescence, 12,* 401–410.

Marcia, J. E. (1993). The relational roots of identity. In J. Kroger (Ed.), *Discussions on ego identity* (pp. 101–120). Hillsdale, NJ: Erlbaum.

Marcia, J. E. (1994). The empirical study of ego identity. In H. A. Bosma & L. G. Tobi (Ed.), *Identity and development: An interdisciplinary approach* (pp. 67–80). Thousand Oaks, CA: Sage.

Marcia, J. E. (1999). Representational thought in ego identity, psychotherapy, and psychosocial developmental theory. In I. E. Siegel (Ed.), *Development of mental representation: Theories and applications* (pp. 391–414). Mahway, NJ: Erlbaum.

Margolin, G. (1988). Marital conflict is not marital conflict is not marital conflict. In R. D. Peters & R. J. McMahon (Eds.), *Social learning and systems approaches to marriage and the family* (pp. 193–216). New York: Brunner/Mazel.

Maris, R. W., Silverman, M., & Canetto, S. S. (1997). *Review of suicidology, 1997.* New York: Guilford.

Markstrom-Adams, C. (1989). Androgyny and its relation to adolescent psychological well-being: A review of the literature. *Sex Roles, 21,* 469–473.

Markstrom-Adams, C. (1992). A consideration of intervening factors in adolescent identity formation. In G. R. Adams, T. P. Gullotta, & R. Montemayor (Eds.), *Adolescent identity formation* (pp. 173–192). Newbury Park, CA: Sage.

Markus, H., & Kitayama, S. (1991). Culture and the self: Implications for cognition, emotion, and motivation. *Psychological Review, 98,* 224–253.

Markus, H., & Nurius, R. (1986). Possible selves. *American Psychologist, 41,* 954–969.

Marohn, R. C. (1993). Residential services. In P. H. Tolan & B. J. Cohler (Eds.), *Handbook of clinical research and practice with adolescents* (pp. 453–466). New York: Wiley.

Marsh, H. W. (1991). Employment during high school: Character building or subversion of academic goals? *Sociology of Education, 64,* 172–189.

Marshall, M. (1979). *Weekend warriors.* Palo Alto, CA: Mayfield.

Marshall, R. (1994). *School to work processes in the United States.* Paper presented at the Carnegie Council/Johann Jacobs Foundation, November 3–5, Marbach Castle, Germany.

Marshall, W. (1978). Puberty. In F. Falkner & J. Tanner (Eds.), *Human growth* (Vol. 2). New York: Plenum.

Marshall, W. A., & Tanner, J. M. (1969). Variations in pattern of pubertal changes in girls. *Archives of Disease in Childhood, 44,* 291–303.

Marshall, W. A., & Tanner, J. M. (1970). Variations in the pattern of pubertal changes in boys. *Archives of Disease in Childhood, 45,* 13–23.

Marston, P. J., Hecht, M. L., & Robers, T. (1987). "True love ways": The subjective experience and communication of romantic love. *Journal of Social and Personal Relationships, 4,* 387–407.

Martin, C. L. (1987). A ratio measure of sex stereotyping. *Journal of Personality and Social Psychology, 52,* 489–499.

Martin, J. (1976). *The education of adolescents.* Washington, DC: U.S. Office of Education.

Martin, M. J., & Pritchard, M. E. (1991). Factors associated with alcohol use in later adolescence. *Journal of studies on Alcohol, 52,* 5–9.

Martin, N. C. (1997, April). *Adolescents' possible selves and the transition to adulthood.* Paper presented at the meeting of the Society for Research in Child Development, Washington, DC.

Martinez, R., de Miguel, M., & Fernandez, S. (1994). Spain. In K. Hurrelmann (Ed.), *International handbook of adolescence* (pp. 360–373). Westport, CT: Greenwood Press.

Mason, M. G., & Gibbs, J. C. (1993). Social perspective taking and moral judgment among college students. *Journal of Adolescent Research, 8,* 109–123.

Massad, C. (1981). Sex role identity and adjustment during adolescence. *Child Development, 52,* 1290–1298.

Masters, W. H., Johnson, V. E., & Kolodny, R. C. (1994). *Heterosexuality.* New York: HarperCollins.

Matyas, M. L. (1987). Keeping undergraduate women in science and engineering: Contributing factors and recommendations for action. In J. Z. Daniels & J. B. Kahle (Eds.), *Contributions to the fourth GASAT conference* (Vol. 3, pp. 112–122). Washington, DC: National Science Foundation.

Matza, D., & Sykes, G. (1961). Juvenile delinquency and subterranean values. *American Sociological Review, 26,* 712–719.

May, P. A. (1996). Overview of alcohol abuse epidemiology for American Indian populations. In G. D. Sandefur, R. R. Rindfuss, & B. Cohen (Eds.), *Changing numbers, changing needs: American Indian demography and public health* (pp. 235–261). Washington, DC: National Academy Press.

McAdoo, H. P. (1996). *Black families* (3rd ed.). Newbury Park, CA: Sage.

McAdoo, H. P. (Ed.). (1993). *Family ethnicity.* Newbury Park, CA: Sage.

McAdoo, H. P. (1998). African American families. In C. H. Mindel, R. W. Haberstein, & R. Wright, Jr. (Eds.), *Ethnic families in America: Patterns and variations* (pp. 361–381). Upper Saddle River, NJ: Prentice-Hall.

McCarthy, B. (1994). Youth on the street: Violent offenders and victims. In H. Coward (Ed.), *Anger in our city: Youth seeking meaning* (pp. 69–107). Victoria, BC: Centre for Studies in Religion and Society.

McCarthy, B., & Hagan, J. (1992). Surviving on the street: The experiences of homeless youth. *Journal of Adolescent Research, 7,* 412–430.

McCord, J. (1990). Problem behaviors. In S. Feldman & G. Elliott (Eds.), *At the threshold: The developing adolescent* (pp. 414–430). Cambridge, MA: Harvard University Press.

McCord, W., & McCord, J. (1959). *Origins of crime: A new evaluation of the Cambridge-Somerville study.* New York: Columbia University Press.

McDougall, P., Schonert-Reichl, K., & Hymel, S. (1996, March). *Adolescents at risk for high school dropout: The role of social factors.* Paper presented at the meeting of the Society for Research on Adolescence, Boston.

McFalls, J. A., Jr. (1990). The risks of reproductive impairment in the later years of childbearing. *Annual Review of Sociology, 16,* 491–519.

McIntosh, J. L. (1992). Methods of suicide. In R. W. Maris, A. L. Berman, J. T. Maltsberger, & R. I. Yufit (Eds.), *Assessment and prediction of suicide* (pp. 381–397). New York: Guilford.

McKenry, P. C., & Price, S. J. (1995). Divorce: A comparative perspective. In B. B. Ingoldsby & S. Smith (Eds.), *Families in Multicultural Perspective* (pp. 187–212). New York: Guilford.

McKnight, C. C., Crosswhite, F. J., Dossey, J. A., Kifer, E., Swafford, J. O., Travers, K. J., & Cooney, T. J. (1987). *The underachieving curriculum: Assessing U.S. school mathematics from an international perspective.* Champaign, IL: Stipes.

McLanahan, S., & Bumpass, L. (1988). Intergenerational consequences of family disruption. *American Journal of Sociology, 94,* 130–152.

McLanahan, S., & Sandefur, G. (1994). *Growing up in a single-parent family: What hurts, what helps.* Cambridge, MA: Harvard University Press.

McLaughlin, C. S., Chen, C., Greenberger, E., & Biermeier, C. (1997). Family, peer, and individual correlates of sexual experience among Caucasian and Asian American late adolescents. *Journal of Research on Adolescence, 7,* 33–54.

McLeer, S. V., Deblinger, E., Henry, D., & Orvaschel, H. (1992). Sexually abused children at high risk for posttraumatic stress disorder. *Journal of the American Academy of Child and Adolescent Psychiatry, 31,* 875–879.

McMaster, L., Connolly, J., Pepler, D., & Craig, W. (1997, June). *Peer to peer sexual harassment in early adolescence: A developmental perspective.* Paper presented at the annual meeting of the Canadian Psychological Association, Toronto, Canada.

McNamara, J. R., & Grossman, K. (1991). Initiation of dates and anxiety among college men and women. *Psychological Reports, 69,* 252–254.

McNelles, L. R., & Connolly, J. A. (1999). Intimacy between adolescent friends: Age and gender differences in intimate affect and intimate behaviors. *Journal of Research on Adolescence, 9,* 143–159.

McRobbie, A. (1994). Shut up and dance: Youth culture and changing modes of femininity. In A. McRobbie (Ed.), *Postmodernism and popular culture* (pp. 177–197). London: Routledge.

Mead, M. (1928). *Coming of age in Samoa.* New York: Morrow.

Mead, M. (1928/1978). *Culture and commitment.* Garden City, NY: Anchor.

Mead, M. (1970). *Culture and commitment: A study of the generation gap.* Garden City, NY: Doubleday.

Means, J. (1991). Coping with a breakup: Negative mood regulation expectancies and depression following the end of a romantic relationship. *Journal of Personality and Social Psychology, 60,* 327–334.

Mechanic, D., & Hansell, S. (1989). Divorce, conflict, and adolescent well-being. *Journal of Health and Social Behavior, 30,* 105–116.

Meeus, W., Iedema, J., Helsen, M., & Vollebergh, W. (1999). Patterns of adolescent identity development: Review of literature and longitudinal analysis. *Developmental Review, 19*, 419–461.

Mehrabian, A., & Wixen, W. J. (1986). Preferences for individual video games as a function of their emotional effects on players. *Journal of Applied Social Psychology, 16*, 3–15.

Melby, J., & Conger, R. (1996). Parental behaviors and adolescent academic performance: A longitudinal analysis. *Journal of Research on Adolescence, 6*, 113–137.

Mensch, B. S., Bruce, J., & Greene, M. E. (1998). *The uncharted passage: Girls' adolescence in the developing world.* New York: Population Council.

Michael, R. T., Gagnon, J. H., Laumann, E. O., & Kolata, G. (1994). *Sex in America.* Boston: Little, Brown.

Michael, R. T., Gagnon, J. H., Laumann, E. O., & Kolata, G. (1995). *Sex in America: A definitive survey.* New York: Warner Books.

Midgely, C., & Urdan, T. (1995). Predictors of middle school students' use of self-handicapping strategies. *Journal of Early Adolescence, 15*, 389–411.

Migliazzo, A. C. (1993, Winter). Korean leadership in the 21st century: A profile of the coming generation. *Korea Journal*, pp. 60–67.

Miller, B. C., & Benson, B. (1999). Romantic and sexual relationship development during adolescence. In W. Furman, B. B. Brown, & C. Feiring (Eds.), *The development of romantic relationships in adolescence* (pp. 99–121). New York: Cambridge University Press.

Miller, B. D. (1995). Precepts and practices: Researching identity formation among India Hindu adolescents in the United States. *New Directions for Child Development, 67*, 71–85.

Miller, B., & Moore, K. (1990). Adolescent sexual behavior, pregnancy, and parenting: Research through the 1980s. *Journal of Marriage and the Family, 52*, 1025–1044.

Miller, J. B. (1991). The development of women's sense of self. In J. V. Jordan, A. G. Kaplan, J. B. Miller, I. P. Stiver, & J. L. Surrey (Eds.), *Women and growth in connection* (pp. 11–26). New York: Guilford.

Miller, P., & Simon, W. (1980). The development of sexuality in adolescence. In J. Adelson (Ed.), *Handbook of adolescent psychology* New York: Wiley.

Miller, P. H., & Weiss, M. G. (1981). Children's attention allocation, understanding of attention, and performance on the incidental learning task. *Child Development, 52*, 1183–1190.

Miller-Johnson, S., Winn, D. M., Coie, J., Maumary-Gremaud, A., Hyman, C., Terry, R., & Lochman, J. (1999). Motherhood during the teen years: A developmental perspective on risk factors for childbearing. *Development and Psychopathology, 11*, 85–100.

Miller-Jones, D. (1989). Culture and testing. *American Psychologist, 44*, 360–366.

Millett, K. (1970/2000). *Sexual politics.* Urbana-Champaign: University of Illinois Press.

Mills, C. J., & Noyes, H. L. (1984). Patterns and correlates of initial and subsequent drug use among adolescents. *Journal of Consulting and Clinical Psychology, 52*, 231–243.

Millstein, S. (1989). Adolescent health: Challenges for behavioral scientists. *American Psychologist, 44*, 837–842.

Millstein, S., Petersen, A., & Nightingale, E. (Eds.) (1993). *Promoting the health of adolescents: New directions for the twenty-first century.* New York: Oxford University Press.

Mines, M. (1988). Conceptualizing the person: Hierarchical society and individual autonomy in India. *American Anthropologist, 90*, 568–579.

Minuchin, S. (1974). *Families and family therapy.* Cambridge, MA: Harvard University Press.

Minuchin, S., Rosman, B., & Baker, L. (1978). *Psychosomatic families: Anorexia nervosa in context.* Cambridge, MA: Harvard University Press.

Mirchev, M. (1994). Bulgaria. In K. Hurrelman (Ed.), *International handbook of adolescence* (pp. 77–91). Westport, CT: Greenwood.

Modell, J. (1989). *Into one's own: From youth to adulthood in the United States, 1920–1975.* Berkeley: University of California Press.

Modell, J., Furstenberg, E., Jr., & Hershberg, T. (1976). Social change and transitions to adulthood in historical perspective. *Journal of Family History, 1*, 7–32.

Modell, J., & Goodman, M. (1990). Historical perspectives. In S. S. Feldman & G. Elliott (Eds.), *At the threshold: The developing adolescent.* Cambridge, MA: Harvard University Press.

Moffitt, T. (1993). Adolescence-limited and life-course persistent antisocial behavior: A developmental taxonomy. *Psychological Review, 100*, 674–701.

Moffitt, T. E., Caspi, A., Belsky, J., & Silva, P. A. (1992). Childhood experience and onset of menarche: A test of a sociobiological model. *Child Development, 63*, 47–58.

Moffitt, T., & Silva, P. (1988). IQ and delinquency: A direct test of the differential detection hypothesis. *Journal of Abnormal Psychology, 97*, 330–333.

Moffitt, T., Caspi, A., Harkness, A., & Silva P. (1993). The natural history of change in intellectual performance: Who changes? How much? Is it meaningful? *Journal of Child Psychology and Psychiatry, 34*, 455–506.

Mogelonsky, M. (1996, May). The rocky road to adulthood. *American Demographics, 26–36, 56.

Molina, B., & Chassin, L. (1996). The parent-adolescent relationship at puberty: Hispanic ethnicity and parent alcoholism as moderators. *Developmental Psychology, 32*, 675–686.

Moline, A. E. (1987). Financial aid and student persistence: An application of causal modeling. *Research in Higher Education, 26* (2), 130–147.

Money, J. (1980). *Love and love sickness: The science of sex, gender difference, and pairbonding.* Baltimore: Johns Hopkins University Press.

Money, J. (1988). *Gay, straight, and in-between: The sexology of erotic orientation.* New York: Oxford University Press.

Monitoring the Future (2000). Available: www.monitoringthefuture.org

Montemayor, R. (1982). The relationship between parent–adolescent conflict and the amount of time adolescents spend alone and with parents and peers. *Child Development, 53*, 1512–1519.

Montemayor, R. (1984). Maternal employment and adolescents' relations with parents, siblings, and peers. *Journal of Youth and Adolescence, 13*, 543–557.

Montemayor, R., & Flannery, D. J. (1989). A naturalistic study of the involvement of children and adolescents with their mothers and friends: Developmental differences in expressive behavior. *Journal of Adolescent Research, 4*, 3–14.

Montgomery, D. (1999, May 14). No rant. Just rave: Peaceful protesters defend party scene. *Washington Post*, pp. C-1, C-6.

Moore, D., & Schultz, N. R. (1983). Loneliness at adolescence: Correlates, attributes, & coping. *Journal of Youth & Adolescence, 12*, 95–100.

Moore, K. A., & Stief, T. M. (1991). Changes in marriage and fertility behavior: Behavior versus attitudes of young adults. *Youth & Society, 22*, 362–386.

Moore, K., Myers, D., Morrison, D., Nord, C., Brown, B., & Edmonston, B. (1993). Age at first childbirth and later poverty. *Journal of Research on Adolescence, 3*, 393–422.

Moore, K., Peterson, J., & Furstenberg, E., Jr. (1986). Parental attitudes and the occurrence of early sexual activity. *Journal of Marriage and the Family, 48*, 777–782.

Morris, B. R. (1999, February 25). You want fries with that website? For some young techies, after-school tinkering turns into work and wealth. *New York Times*, pp. E-1, E-7.

Morrison, D. M. (1985). Adolescent contraceptive behavior: A review. *Psychological Bulletin, 98*, 538–568.

Morrison, P., & Masten, A. S. (1991). Peer reputation in middle childhood as a predictor of adaptation in adolescence: A seven-year follow-up. *Child Development, 62*, 991–1007.

Mortimer, J., & Finch, M. (1996). *Adolescents, work, and family: An intergenerational developmental analysis.* Newbury Park, CA: Sage.

Mortimer, J., Finch, M., Ryu, S., Shanahan, M., & Call, K. (1993, March). *The effects of work intensity on adolescent mental health, achievement and behavioral adjustment: New evidence from a prospective study.* Paper presented at the biennial meeting of the Society for Research in Child Development, New Orleans.

Mortimer, J., Finch, M., Ryu, S., Shanahan, M. J., & Call, K. (1996). The effects of work intensity on adolescent mental health, achievement, and behavioral adjustment: New evidence from a prospective study. *Child Development, 67,* 1243–1261.

Mortimer, J. T., Finch, M., Shanahan, M., & Ryu, S. (1992). Work experience, mental health, and behavioral adjustment in adolescence. *Journal of Research on Adolescence, 21,* 24–57.

Mortimer, J. T., Harley, C., & Aronson, P. J. (1999). How do prior experiences in the workplace set the stage for transitions to adulthood? In A. Booth, A. C. Crouter, & M. J. Shanahan (Eds.), *Transitions to adulthood in a changing economy: No work, no family, no future?* (pp. 131–159). Westport, CT: Praeger.

Mortimer, J. T., & Johnson, M. K. (1998). New perspectives on adolescent work and the transition to adulthood. In R. Jessor (Ed.), *New perspectives on adolescent risk behavior* (pp. 425–496). New York: Cambridge University Press.

Motola, M., Sinisalo, P., & Guichard, J. (1998). Social habitus and future plans. In J. Nurmi (Ed.), *Adolescents, cultures, and conflicts* (pp. 43–73). New York: Garland.

Mounts, N. S. (1997, April). *Parental management of adolescent friendships.* Paper presented at the meeting of the Society for Research in Child Development, Washington, DC.

Mullatti, L. (1995). Families in India: Beliefs and realities. *Journal of Comparative Family Studies, 26,* 11–26.

Mullis, I., & Jenkins, L. B. (1988). *The science report card: Elements of risk and recovery: Trends and achievement based on the 1986 national assessment.* Princeton, NJ: Educational Testing Service.

Mullis, I., Owen, E., & Phillips, G. (1990). *America's challenge: Accelerating academic achievement. A summary of findings from 20 years of NAEP.* Washington, DC: U.S. Department of Education.

Mum's Not the Word. (1999, September). *Population Today,* p. 3.

Mundy, L. (1999, May 16). Teen angels. *Washington Post Magazine,* p. 6.

Munoz, R. A., & Amado, H. (1986). Anorexia nervosa: An affective disorder. *New Directions for Mental Health Services, 31,* 13–19.

Munro, G., & Adams, G. (1977). Ego-identity formation in college students and working youth. *Developmental Psychology, 13,* 523–524.

Munsch, J., & Wampler, R. (1993). Ethnic differences in early adolescents' coping with school stress. *American Journal of Orthopsychiatry, 63,* 633–646.

Murnane, R. J., & Levy, F. (1997). *Teaching the new basic skills: Principles for educating children to thrive in a changing economy.* New York: Free Press.

Murphy, K., & Schneider, B. (1994). Coaching socially rejected early adolescents regarding behaviors used by peers to infer liking: A dyad-specific intervention. *Journal of Early Adolescence, 14,* 83–95.

Mussen, P. H., Conger, J. J., Kagan, J., & Huston, A. (1990). *Child development and personality* (7th ed.). New York: Harper & Row.

Myers, D. G. (1990). *Social psychology* (3rd ed.). New York: McGraw Hill.

Myers, J. (2000, December/January). Columbine's shadow shades U.S. budget. *Youth Today,* p. 9.

Myers, M. G., Wagner, E. E., & Brown, S. A. (1997). Substance abuse. In V. B. Van Hasselt & M. Hersen (Eds.), *Handbook of psychological treatment protocols for children and adolescents.* Mahwah, NJ: Erlbaum.

Nash, S. C., & Feldman, S. S. (1981). Sex role and sex-related attributes: Continuity and change across the family life cycle. In M. E. Lamb & A. L. Brown (Eds.), *Advances in developmental psychology* (pp. 1–36). Hillsdale, NJ: Erlbaum.

National Center for Education Statistics (1995). *The condition of education, 1995.* Washington, DC: U.S. Department of Education.

National Center for Education Statistics (1998). *The condition of education, 1998.* Washington, DC: U.S. Department of Education.

National Center for Education Statistics (1999). *The condition of education, 1999.* Washington, DC: U.S. Department of Education.

National Center for Health Statistics. (1999). Worktable GM291. Available: www.cdc.gov/nchswww/datawh/statab/unpubd/mortabs/gmwk291.htm

National Commission on Excellence in Education. (1983). *A nation at risk: The imperative for educational reform.* Washington, DC: U.S. Department of Education.

National Education Commission on Time and Learning. (1994). *Prisoners of time.* Washington, DC: U.S. Government Printing Office.

National Highway Traffic Safety Administration (NHTSA). (1996). *Graduated driver licensing system for novice drivers.* Washington, DC: U.S. Department of Transportation.

National Highway Traffic Safety Administration (NHTSA). (1999). *Traffic safety facts, 1998.* Washington, DC: Author.

National Math, Reading Tests Fail in House (1997, September 17). *St. Louis Post-Dispatch,* p. A-1.

Natriello, G., Pallas, A., & Alexander, K. (1989). On the right track? Curriculum and academic achievement. *Sociology of Education, 62,* 109–118.

Needle, R., Su, S., & Doherty, W. (1990). Divorce, remarriage, and adolescent substance use: A prospective longitudinal study. *Journal of Marriage and the Family, 52,* 157–169.

Neinstein, L. S. (1984). *Adolescent health care: A practical guide.* Baltimore/Munich: Urban & Schwarzenberg.

Neisser, U., Boodoo, G., Bouchard, T. J., Boykin, A. W., Brody, N., Ceci, S. J., Halpern, D. F., Loehlin, J. C., Perloff, R., Sternberg, R. J., & Urbina, S. (1996). Intelligence: Knowns and unknowns. *American Psychologist, 51,* 77–101.

Newcomb, A. F., Bukowski, W. M., & Pattee, L. (1993). Children's peer relations: A meta-analytic review of popular, rejected, neglected, controversial, and average sociometric status. *Psychological Bulletin, 113,* 99–128.

Newcomb, M. D., & Bentler, P. M. (1989). Substance use and abuse among children and teenagers. *American Psychologist, 44,* 242–248.

Newcomer, S., & Udry, J. R. (1985). Oral sex in an adolescent population. *Archives of Sexual Behavior, 14,* 41–56.

Newcomer, S., & Udry, J. R. (1987). Parental marital status effects on adolescent sexual behavior. *Journal of Marriage and the Family, 49,* 235–240.

Newmann, F. (1992). Higher-order thinking and prospects for classroom thoughtfulness. In F. Newmann (Ed.), *Student engagement and achievement in American high schools.* New York: Teachers College Press.

Noble, J., Cover, J., & Yanagishita, M. (1996). *The world's youth.* Washington, DC: Population Reference Bureau.

Nock, S. L. (1998). The consequences of premarital fatherhood. *American Sociological Review, 63,* 250–263.

Nolen-Hoeksma, S. (1987). Sex differences in unipolar depression: Evidence and theory. *Psychological Bulletin, 101,* 259–282.

Nolen-Hoeksma, S., & Girgus, J. (1994). The emergence of gender differences in depression during adolescence. *Psychological Bulletin, 115,* 424–443.

Nora, A. (1987). Determinants of retention among Chicano college students: A structural model. *Research in Higher Education, 26* (1), 31–59.

Nottelmann, E. D., Susman, E. J., Blue, J. H., Inoff-Germain, G., Dorn, L. D., Loriaux, D. L., Cutler, G. B., & Chrousos, G. P. (1987). Gonadal and adrenal hormone correlates of adjustment in early adolescence. In R. M. Lerner & T. T. Foch (Eds.), *Biological-psychological interactions in early adolescence.* Hillsdale, NJ: Erlbaum.

Novacek, J., Raskin, R., & Hogan, R. (1991). Why do adolescents use drugs? Age, sex, and user differences. *Journal of Youth and Adolescence, 20,* 475–492.

Nsemenang, A. B. (1998). Work organization and economic management in sub-Saharan Africa: From a Eurocentric orientation toward an Afrocentric perspective. *Psychology and Developing Societies, 10,* 75–97.

Nsemenang, A. B. (2000, February). *Adolescence in sub-Saharan Africa.* Paper prepared for the meeting of the Study Group on Adolescence in the 21st Century, Washington, DC.

Nurcombe, J., & Parlett, D. (1994). *Child mental health and the law.* New York: Free Press.

Nurmi, J., & Siurala, L. (1994). *Finland.* In K. Hurrelmann (Ed.), *International handbook of adolescence* (pp. 131–145). Westport, CT: Greenwood Press.

Nurnberger, J. I., Jr., & Gershon, E. S. (1992). Genetics. In E. S. Paykell (Ed.), *Handbook of affective disorders* (2nd ed., pp. 131–148). New York: Guilford.

Nussbaum, M. (1992). Human functioning and social justice: In defense of Aristotelian essentialism. *Political Theory, 20,* 202–246.

O'Brien, D. (1997). The disappearing moral curriculum. *The Key Reporter, 62* (4), 1–4.

O'Brien, S., & Bierman, K. (1988). Conceptions and perceived influence of peer groups: Interviews with preadolescents and adolescents. *Child Development, 59,* 1360–1365.

O'Connor, T. G., Allen, J. P., Bell, K. L., & Hauser, S. T. (1996). Adolescent–parent relationships and leaving home in young adulthood. *New Directions in Child Development, 71,* 39–52.

O'Hare, W. P. (1992). America's minorities: The demographics of diversity. *Population Bulletin, 47* (4), 1–47. (Washington, DC: Population Reference Bureau.).

O'Hare, W. P., Pollard, K. M., Mann, T. L., & Kent, M. M. (1991). African Americans in the 1990s. *Population Bulletin, 46* (1), 1–40. (Washington, DC: Population Reference Bureau.)

O'Leary, K. D., Malone, J., & Tyree, A. (1994). Physical aggression in early marriage: Prerelationship and relationship effects. *Journal of Consulting and Clinical Psychology, 62,* 594–602.

O'Malley, P., & Bachman, J. (1983). Self-esteem: Change and stability between ages 13 and 23. *Developmental Psychology, 19,* 257–268.

O'Malley, P. M., Bachman, J. G., & Johnston, L. D. (1988). Period, age, and cohort effects on substance use among young Americans: A decade of change, 1976–1986. *American Journal of Public Health, 78,* 1315–1321.

Offer, D. (1969). *The psychological world of the teenager.* New York: Basic Books.

Offer, D., Ostrov, E., & Howard, K. L. (1981). *The adolescent: A psychological self-portrait.* New York: Basic Books.

Offer, D., & Schonert-Reichl, K. A. (1992). Debunking the myths of adolescence: Findings from recent research. *Journal of the American Academy of Child & Adolescent Psychiatry, 31,* 1003–1014.

Ogbu, J. (1989, April). *Academic socialization of black children: An inoculation against future failure?* Paper presented at the biennial meeting of the Society for Research in Child Development, Kansas City.

Ogbu, J. (1990a). Minority status and literacy in comparative perspective. *Daedalus, 119,* 141–168.

Ogbu, J. (1990b). Minority education in comparative perspective. *Journal of Negro Education, 59,* 45–57.

Oritz, V. (1995). The diversity of Latino families. In R. E. Zambrana (Ed.), *Understanding Latino families: Scholarship, policy and practice.* Thousand Oaks, CA: Sage.

Orr, E., & Ben-Eliahu, E. (1993). Gender differences in idiosyncratic sex-typed self-images and self-esteem. *Sex Roles, 29,* 271–296.

Osgood, D. W., & Lee, H. (1993). Leisure activities, age, and adult roles across the life span. *Society and Leisure, 16,* 181–208.

Osgood, D. W., Johnston, L., O'Malley, P., & Bachman, J. (1988). The generality of deviance in late adolescence and early adulthood. *American Sociological Review, 53,* 81–93.

Osgood, D. W., Wilson, J. K., Bachman, J. G., O'Malley, P. M., & Johnston, L. D. (1996). Routine activities and individual deviant behavior. *American Sociological Review, 61,* 635–655.

Osofsky, J. D. (1990, Winter). Risk and protective factors for teenage mothers and their infants. *SRCD Newsletter,* 1–2.

Oswald, H., Bahne, J., & Feder, M. (1994, February). *Love and sexuality in adolescence: Gender-specific differences in East and West Berlin.* Paper presented at the biennial meeting of the Society for Research on Adolescence, San Diego.

Overton, W. F., & Byrnes, J. P. (1991). Cognitive development. In R. M. Lerner, A. C. Petersen, & J. Brooks-Gunn (Eds.) *Encyclopedia of adolescence* (Vol. 1, pp. 151–156). New York: Garland.

Oyserman, D., & Markus, H. (1990). Possible selves and delinquency. *Journal of Personality and Social Psychology, 59,* 112–125.

Padgham, J. J., & Blyth, D. A. (1991). Dating during adolescence. In R. M. Lerner, A. C. Petersen, & J. Brooks-Gunn (Eds.), *Encyclopedia of adolescence* (pp. 196–198). New York: Garland.

Page, K. (1999, May 16). The graduate. *Washington Post Magazine,* pp. 18, 20.

Pahl, K., Greene, M., & Way, N. (2000, April). *Self-esteem trajectories among urban, low-income, ethnic minority high school students.* Poster presented at the biennial meeting of the Society for Research on Adolescence, Chicago.

Paikoff, R. L., & Brooks-Gunn, J. (1991). Do parent–child relationships change during puberty? *Psychological Bulletin, 110,* 47–66.

Paludi, M. A., & Strayer, L. A. (1985). What's in an author's name? Differential evaluations of performance as a function of author's name. *Sex Roles, 12,* 353–362.

Papini, D. R., Micka, J. C., & Barnett, J. K. (1989). Perceptions of intrapsychic and extrapsychic functioning as bases of adolescent ego identity status. *Journal of Adolescent Research, 4,* 462–482.

Papini, D., & Sebby, R. (1988) Variations in conflictual family issues by adolescent pubertal status, gender, and family member. *Journal of Early Adolescence, 8,* 1–15.

Pareles, J. (1992, February 2). Fear and loathing along pop's outlaw trail. *New York Times,* pp. 1, 23.

Park, I. H., & Cho, L. J. (1995). Confucianism and the Korean family. *Journal of Comparative Family Studies, 26,* 1134–1170.

Parker, H., & Parker, S. (1986). Father-daughter sexual abuse: An emerging perspective. *American Journal of Orthopsychiatry, 56,* 531–549.

Parker, J., & Asher, S. (1987). Peer acceptance and later personal adjustment. Are low accepted children at risk? *Psychological Bulletin, 102,* 357–389.

Parker, J., & Seal, J. (1996). Forming, losing, renewing, and replacing friendships: Applying temporal parameters to the assessment of children's friendship experiences. *Child Development, 67,* 2248–2268.

Parker, S., Nichter, M., Vuckovic, N., Sims, C., & Ritenbaugh, C. (1995). Body image and weight concerns among African American and White adolescent females: Differences which make a difference. *Human Organization, 54,* 103–114.

Parsons, J., Eccles, J., Adler, T., & Kaczala, C. (1982). Socialization of achievement attitudes and beliefs: Parental influences. *Child Development, 53,* 310–321.

Parsons, T. (1964). *Essays in sociological theory.* Chicago: Free Press.

Pascarella, E., & Terenzini, P. (1991). *How college affects students: Findings and insights from twenty years of research.* San Francisco: Jossey-Bass.

Pasley, K., & Gecas, V. (1984). Stresses and satisfactions of the parental role. *Personnel and Guidance Journal, 2,* 400–404.

Pathak, R. (1994, January 31). The new generation. *India Today,* 72–87.

Patrikakou, E. (1996). Investigating the academic achievement of adolescents with learning disabilities: A structural modeling approach. *Journal of Educational Psychology, 88,* 435–450.

Patterson, G. (1986). Performance models for antisocial boys. *American Psychologist, 41,* 432–444.

Patterson, G., Reid, J., & Dishion, T. (1992). *Antisocial boys.* Eugene, OR: Castalia.

Patterson, G., & Stoolmiller, M. (1991). Replications of a dual failure model for boys' depressed mood. *Journal of Consulting and Clinical Psychology, 59,* 491–498.

Patterson, G., & Stouthamer-Loeber, M. (1984). The correlation of family management practices and delinquency. *Child Development, 55,* 1299–1307.

Patterson, G. R., & Yoerger, K. (1997). A developmental model for late-onset delinquency. In D. W. Osgood (Ed.), *Motivation and delinquency* (pp. 119–177). Lincoln: University of Nebraska Press.

Patterson, S. J., Sochting, I., & Marcia, J. E. (1992). The inner space and beyond: Women and identity. In G. R. Adams, T. P. Gullotta, & R. Montemayor (Eds.), *Adolescent identity formation* (pp. 9–24). Newbury Park, CA: Sage.

Paul, E. L., & White, K. M. (1990). The development of intimate relationships in late adolescence. *Adolescence, 25,* 375–400.

Paulson, S. E. (1994, February). *Parenting style or parental involvement: Which is more important for adolescent achievement?* Paper presented at the meeting of the Society for Research on Adolescence, San Diego.

Paxton, S., Wertheim, E., Gibbons, K., Szmukler, G., Hillier, L., & Petrovoch, J. (1991). Body image satisfaction, dieting beliefs, and weight loss behaviors in adolescent girls and boys. *Journal of Youth and Adolescence, 20,* 361–380.

Paykel, E. (1996). Tertiary prevention: Longer-term drug treatment in depression. In T. Kendrick & A. Tylee (Eds.), *The prevention of mental illness in primary care* (pp. 281–293). Cambridge, England: Cambridge University Press.

Peace Corps. (2000a). Peace Corps facts. Available: www.peacecorps.gov/about/facts/index.html

Peace Corps. (2000b). Two years of service, a lifetime of benefits. Available: www.peacecorps.gov/volunteer/benefits.html

Peace Corps. (2000c). Peace Corps history. Available: www.peacecorps.gov/about/history/chronology.html

Perry, C., Williams, C., Veblen-Mortenson, S., Toomey, T., Komro, K., Anstine, P., McGivern, P., Finnegan, J., Forster, J., Wagenar, A., & Wolfson, M. (1996). Project Northland: Outcomes of a community-wide alcohol use prevention program during early adolescence. *American Journal of Public Health, 86,* 956–965.

Perry, W. G. (1970/1999). *Forms of ethical and intellectual development in the college years: A scheme.* San Francisco: Jossey-Bass.

Peshkin, A. (1991). *The color of strangers, the color of friends.* Chicago: University of Chicago Press.

Peskin, H. (1967). Pubertal onset and ego functioning: A psychoanalytic approach. *Journal of Abnormal Psychology, 72,* 1–15.

Petersen, A. (1985). Pubertal development as a cause of disturbance: Myths, realities, and unanswered questions. *Genetic, Social, and General Psychology Monographs, 111,* 205–232.

Petersen, A. (1988). Adolescent development. *Annual Review of psychology, 39,* 583–607.

Petersen, A. C. (1987, September). Those gangly years. *Psychology Today,* 28–34.

Petersen, A. C. (1993). Creating adolescents: The role of context and process in developmental trajectories. *Journal of Research on Adolescence, 3,* 1–18.

Petersen, A. C. (2000, March). *Biology, culture, and behavior: What makes young adolescent boys and girls behave differently?* Paper presented at the biennial meeting of the Society for Research on Adolescence, Chicago.

Petersen, A. C., Compas, B. E., Brooks-Gunn, J., Stemmler, M., Ey, S., & Grant, K. E. (1993). Depression in adolescence. *American Psychologist, 48,* 155–168.

Petersen, A. C., Kennedy, R. E., & Sullivan, P. (1991). Coping with adolescence. In M. E. Colten & S. Gore (Eds.), *Adolescent stress: Causes and consequences* (pp. 93–110). New York: Aldine de Gruyter.

Petersen, A., & Taylor, B. (1980). The biological approach to adolescence: Biological change and psychological adaptation. In J. Adelson (Ed.), *Handbook of adolescent psychology.* New York: Wiley.

Peterson, J. L., & Zill, N. (1986). Marital disruption, parent–child relationships, and behavior problems in children. *Journal of Marriage and the Family, 48,* 295–307.

Peterson, P., Hawkins, J., Abbott, R., & Catalano, R. (1994). Disentangling the effects of parental drinking, family management, and parental alcohol norms on current drinking by Black and White adolescents. *Journal of Research on Adolescence, 4,* 203–227.

Peterson-Lewis, S. (1991). A feminist analysis of the defenses of obscene rap lyrics. *Black sacred music: A journal of theomusicology, 5,* 68–80.

Petraitis, J., Flay, B., & Miller, T. (1995). Reviewing theories of adolescent substance use: Organizing pieces in the puzzle. *Psychological Bulletin, 117,* 67–86.

Pettit, G. S., Bates, J. E., Dodge, K. A., & Meece, D. W. (1999). The impact of after-school peer contact on early adolescent externalizing problems is mediated by parental monitoring, perceived neighborhood safety, and prior adjustment. *Child Development, 70,* 768–778.

Pfeffer, C. R. (1986). *The suicidal child.* New York: Guilford Press.

Pfeffer, C. R., Klerman, G. L., Hurt, S. W., Kakuma, T., Peskin, J. R., & Siefkeer, C. A. (1993). Suicidal children grown up: Rates and psychosocial risk factors for suicide attempts during follow-up. *Journal of the American Academy of Child and Adolescent Psychiatry, 32,* 106–113.

Phelps, L., Johnson, L. S., Jiminez, D. P., Wilczenski, F. L., Andrea, R. K., & Healy, R. W. (1993). Figure preference, body dissatisfaction, and body distortion in adolescence. *Journal of Adolescent Research, 8,* 297–310.

Phinney, J. S. (1990). Ethnic identity in adolescents and adults: A review of research. *Psychological Bulletin, 108,* 499–514.

Phinney, J. S. (2000, March). *Identity formation among U.S. ethnic adolescents from collectivist cultures.* Paper presented at the biennial meeting of the Society for Research on Adolescence, Chicago.

Phinney, J. S., & Alipuria, L. (1987). *Ethnic identity in older adolescents from four ethnic groups.* Paper presented at the biennial meeting of the Society for Research in Child Development, Baltimore.

Phinney, J. S., & Devich-Navarro, M. (1997). Variation in bicultural identification among African American and Mexican American adolescents. *Journal of Research on Adolescence, 7,* 3–32.

Phinney, J. S., Devich-Navarro, M., DuPont, S., Estrada, A., & Onwughala, M. (1994, February). *Bicultural identity orientations of African American and Mexican American Adolescents.* Paper presented at the biennial meetings of the Society for Research on Adolescence, San Diego.

Phinney, J. S., DuPont, S., Espinosa, A., Revill, J., & Sanders, K. (1994). Ethnic identity and American identification among ethnic minority adolescents. In E. van de Vijver (Ed.), *Proceedings of 1992 conference of the International Association for Cross-cultural Psychology.* Tilburg, The Netherlands: Tilburg University Press.

Phinney, J. S., Ong, A., & Madden, T. (2000). Cultural values and intergenerational value discrepancies in immigrant and nonimmigrant families. *Child Development, 71,* 528–539.

Phinney, J. S., & Rosenthal, D. A. (1992). Ethnic identity in adolescence: Process, context, and outcome. In G. R. Adams, T. P. Gullotta, & R. Montemayor (Eds.), *Adolescent identity formation* (pp. 145–172). Newbury Park, CA: Sage.

Piaget, J. (1932). *The moral judgment of the child.* New York: Harcourt Brace Jovanovich.

Piaget, J. (1967). *Six psychological studies.* New York: Random House.

Piaget, J. (1972). Intellectual evolution from adolescence to adulthood. *Human Development, 15,* 1–12.

Piaget, J., & Inhelder, B. (1969). *The psychology of the child.* New York: Basic Books.

Picard, C. L. (1999). The level of competition as a factor for the development of eating disorders in female collegiate athletes. *Journal of Youth & Adolescence, 28,* 583–594.

Pierce, J. P., Lee, L., & Gilpin, E. A. (1994). Smoking initiation by adolescent girls, 1944 through 1988: An association with targeted advertising. *Journal of the American Medical Association, 271,* 608–611.

Pierce, K. (1993). Socialization of teenage girls through teenage magazine fiction: The making of a new woman or an old lady. *Sex Roles, 29,* 59–68.

Piotrowski, C. C. (1997, April). *Mother and sibling triads in conflict: Linking conflict style and the quality of sibling relationships.* Paper presented at the meeting of the Society for Research in Child Development, Washington, DC.

Pipher, M. (1994). *Reviving Ophelia: Saving the selves of adolescent girls.* New York: Ballantine.

Pittman, R. B., & Haughwout, P. (1987). Influence of high school size on dropout rate. *Educational Evaluation and Policy Analysis, 9,* 337–343.

Pleck, J. H. (1983). The theory of male sex role identity: Its rise and fall, 1936–present. In M. Lewin (Ed.), *In the shadow of the past: Psychology portrays the sexes.* New York: Columbia University Press.

Pleck, J. H., Sonnenstein, F., & Ku, L. (1998). Problem behaviors and masculine ideology in adolescent males. In R. Ketterlinus & M. E. Lamb (Eds.), *Adolescent problem behaviors* (pp. 165–186). Hillsdale, NJ: Erlbaum.

Plomin, R., & Daniels, D. (1987). Why are children in the same family so different from one another? *Behavioral and Brain Sciences, 10,* 1–60.

Plomin, R., & Rende, R. (1991). Human behavioral genetics. *Annual Review of Psychology, 42,* 161–190.

Plowman, S. A., Drinkwater, B. L., & Horvath, S. M. (1979). Age and aerobic power in women: A longitudinal study. *Journal of Gerontology, 34,* 512–520.

Podolskij, A. I. (1994). Russia. In K. Hurrelman (Ed.), *International handbook of adolescence* (pp. 332–345). Westport, CT: Greenwood.

Pollack, W. (1998). *Real boys: Rescuing our sons from the myths of boyhood.* New York: Henry Holt.

Pollard, K. M., & O'Hare, W. P. (1999). America's racial and ethnic minorities. *Population Bulletin, 54,* 1–48.

Pollay, R. W. (1997). Hacks, flacks, and counterattacks: Cigarette advertising, sponsored research, and controversies. *Journal of Social Issues, 53,* 53–74.

Pollay, R. W., Siddarth, S., Siegel, M., Haddix, A., Merritt, R. K., Giovino, G. A., & Eriksen, M. P. (1996). The last straw? Cigarette advertising and realized market shares among youths and adults, 1979–1993. *Journal of Marketing, 60,* 1–16.

Posterski, D., & Bibby, R. (1988). *Canada's youth, ready for today: A comprehensive survey of 15- to 24-year-olds.* Ottawa: Canadian Youth Foundation.

Postman, N. (1985). *Amusing ourselves to death: Public discourse in the age of show business.* New York: Penguin.

Potvin, L., Champagne, F., & Laberge-Nadeau, C. (1988). Mandatory driver training and road safety: The Quebec experience. *American Journal of Public Health, 78,* 1206–1209.

Powell, A., Farrar, E., & Cohen, D. (1985). *The shopping mall high school.* Boston: Houghton Mifflin.

Powers, P. S. (1990). Anorexia nervosa: Evaluation and treatment. *Comprehensive Therapy, 16,* 24–34.

Prakasa, V. V., & Rao, V. N. (1979). Arranged marriages: An assessment of the attitudes of college students in India. In G. Kurian (Ed.), *Cross-cultural perspectives on mate selection and marriage* (pp. 11–31). Westport, CT: Greenwood Press.

Presser, S., & Stinson, L. (1998). Data collection mode and social desirability bias in self-reported religious attendance. *American Sociological Review, 63,* 137–146.

Pressley, M., & Schneider, W. (1997). *Introduction to memory development during childhood and adolescence.* Mahwah, NJ: Erlbaum.

Preusser, D. F., Williams, A. F., Lund, A. K., & Zador, P. L. (1990). City curfew ordinances and motor vehicle injury. *Accident Analysis and Prevention, 22,* 391–397

Preusser, D. F., Zador, P. L., & Williams, A. F. (1993). City curfew ordinances and teenage motor vehicle fatalities. *Accident Analysis and Prevention, 25,* 641–645.

Price, J. N. (1999). Racialized masculinities: The diploma, teachers, and peers in the lives of young, African American men. *Youth & Society, 31,* 224–263.

PROBE. (1999). *Peoples' report on basic education.* New Delhi: Oxford University Press.

Protinsky, H., & Shilts, L. (1990). Adolescent substance use and family cohesion. *Family Therapy, 17,* 173–175.

Provenzo, E. F., Jr. (1991). *Video kids: Making sense of Nintendo.* Cambridge, MA: Harvard University Press.

Pruitt, J. A., Kappius, R. E., & Gorman, P. W. (1992). Bulimia and fear of intimacy. *Journal of Clinical Psychology, 48,* 472–476.

Psychological Corporation. (2000). Technical/product information [On-line]. Available: www.psychcorp.com

Public Education Network (PEN). (1997). *The American teacher 1997: Examining gender issues in public schools.* New York: Author.

Puig-Antich, J. (1987). Sleep and neuroendocrine correlates of affective illness in childhood and adolescence. *Journal of Adolescent Health Care, 8,* 505–529.

Quadrel, M., Fischoff, B., & Davis, W. (1993). Adolescent(in)vulnerability. *American Psychologist, 48,* 102–116.

Quay, H. C. (1987). Patterns of delinquent behavior. In H. C. Quay (Ed.), *Handbook of Juvenile delinquency* (pp. 118–138). New York: Wiley.

Rabow, J., Choi, H., & Purdy, D. (1998). The GPA perspective: Influences, significance, and sacrifices of students. *Youth & Society, 29,* 451–470.

Racism rock (1992, April 27). *Chicago Tribune,* p. 2.

Raffaelli, M., & Duckett, E. (1989). "We were just talking": Conversations in early adolescence. *Journal of Youth and Adolescence, 18,* 567–582.

Raffaelli, M., & Larson, R. W. (1999). *Homeless and working youth around the world: Exploring developmental issues.* San Francisco: Jossey-Bass.

Raja, S. N., McGee, R., & Stanton, W. R. (1992). Perceived attachment to parents and peers and psychological well-being in adolescence. *Journal of Youth and Adolescence, 21,* 471–485.

Rao, U., Weissman, M. M., Martin, J. A., & Hammond, R. W. (1993). Childhood depression and risk of suicide: A preliminary report of a longitudinal study. *Journal of the American Academy of Child and Adolescent Psychiatry, 32,* 21–27.

Ratzan, S. C., Filerman, G. L., & LeSar, J. W. (2000). Attaining global health: Challenges and opportunities. *Population Bulletin, 55* (1), 1–48.

Rebok, G. W. (1987). *Life-span cognitive development.* New York: Holt, Reinhart and Winston.

Reddy, R., & Gibbons, J. L. (1999). School socioeconomic contexts and self-descriptions in India. *Journal of Youth & Adolescence, 28,* 619–631.

Repinski, D., & Leffert, N. (1994, February). *Adolescents' relations with friends: The effects of a psychoeducational intervention.* Paper presented at the biennial meeting of the Society for Research on Adolescence, San Diego.

Reskin, B. (1993). Sex segregation in the workplace. *Annual Review of Sociology, 19,* 241–270.

Resnick, M. D., Wattenberg, E., & Brewer, R. (1992, March). *Paternity avowal/disavowal among partners of low income mothers.* Paper presented at the meeting of the Society for Research on Adolescence, Washington, DC.

Rest, J. (1983). Morality. In J. Flavell & E. Markman (Eds.), *Handbook of child psychology, Vol. III: Cognitive development.* New York: Wiley.

Rest, J. R. (1986). *Moral development: Advances in theory and research.* New York: Praeger.

Retschitzki, J. (1989). Evidence of formal thinking in Baoule airele players. In D. M. Keats, D. Munro, & L. Mann (Eds.), *Heterogeneity in cross-cultural psychology.* Amsterdam: Swets & Zeitlinger.

Rexroat, C., & Shehan, C. (1987). The family life cycle and spouses' time in housework. *Journal of Marriage and the Family, 49,* 737–750.

Reyes, O., & Jason, L. A. (1993). Pilot study examining factors associated with academic success for Hispanic high school students. *Journal of Youth and Adolescence, 22,* 57–72.

Reynolds, S. (1998). *Generation ecstasy: Into the world of techno and rave culture*. New York: Little, Brown.

Reynolds, W. W., & Coats, K. I. (1986). A comparison of cognitive-behavioral therapy and relaxation training for the treatment of depression in adolescents. *Journal of Consulting and Clinical Psychology, 54*, 653–660.

Richards, M., & Duckett, E. (1994). The relationship of maternal employment to early adolescent daily experience with and without parents. *Child Development, 65*, 225–236.

Richardson, J., Dwyer, K., McGuigan, K., Hansen, W., Dent, C., Johnson, C., Sussman, S., Brannon, B., & Flay, B. (1989). Substance use among eighth-grade students who take care of themselves after school. *Pediatrics, 84*, 556–566.

Riggs, D. S., O'Leary, K. D., & Breslin, F. C. (1990). Multiple correlates of physical aggression in courting couples. *Journal of Interpersonal Violence, 5*, 61–73.

Roberts, D. F., Foehr, U. G., Rideout, V. J., & Brodie, M. (1999). *Kids & media @ the new millennium: A comprehensive national analysis of children's media use*. New York: Henry J. Kaiser Family Foundation.

Roberts, E. (1980). *Childhood sexual learning: The unwritten curriculum*. Cambridge, MA: Ballinger.

Robinson, D. C., Buck, E. B., & Cuthbert, M. (1991). *Music at the margins: Popular music and global cultural diversity*. Newbury Park, CA: Sage.

Robinson, N. S. (1995). Evaluating the nature of perceived support and its relation to perceived self-worth in adolescents. *Journal of Research on Adolescence, 5*, 253–280.

Rockett, I. R. H. (1998). Injury and violence: A public health perspective. *Population Bulletin, 53* (4), 1–40.

Rodgers, J., & Rowe, D. (1993). Social contagion and adolescent sexual behavior: A developmental EMOSA model. *Psychological Review, 100*, 479–510.

Roe, K. (1985). Swedish youth and music: Listening patterns and motivations. *Communication Research, 12*, 353–362.

Roe, K. (1987). The school and music in adolescent socialization. In J. Lull (Ed.), *Popular music and communication* (pp. 212–230). Beverly Hills, CA: Sage.

Roe, K. (1992). Different destinies, different melodies: School achievement, anticipated status and adolescents' tastes in music. *European Journal of Communication, 7*, 335–337.

Roe, K. (1995). Adolescents' use of socially disvalued media: Toward a theory of media delinquency. *Journal of Youth & Adolescence, 24*, 595–616.

Roeser, R., Lord, S., & Eccles, J. (1994, February). *A portrait of academic alienation in adolescence: Motivation, mental health, and family experience*. Paper presented at the biennial meeting of the Society for Research on Adolescence, San Diego.

Rogoff, B. (1990). *Apprenticeship in thinking: Cognitive development in social context*. New York: Oxford University Press.

Rogoff, B. (1993). Children's guided participation and participatory appropriation in sociocultural activity. In R. Wozniak & K. Fischer (Eds.), *Development in context: Acting and thinking in specific environments*. Hillsdale, NJ: Erlbaum.

Rogoff, B. (1997). Cognition as a collaborative process. In D. Kuhn & R. S. Siegler (Eds.), *Handbook of child psychology* (5th ed., Vol. 2). New York: Wiley.

Rohlen, T. P. (1983). *Japan's high schools*. Berkeley, CA: University of California Press.

Rohrbach, L. A., Hodgson, C. S., Broder, B. I., Montgomery, S. B., Flay, B. F., Hansen, W. B., & Pentz, M. A. (1995). Parental participation in drug abuse prevention: Results from the Midwestern Prevention Project. In G. M. Boyd, J. Howard & R. A. Zucker (Eds.), *Alcohol problems among adolescents*. Hillsdale, NJ: Erlbaum.

Romm, T. (1980–81). Interaction of vocational and family factors in the career planning of teenage girls. *Interchange, 11*, 13–24.

Roof, W. C. (1993). *A generation of seekers*. New York: HarperCollins.

Rook, A. (1999, September). High school violence down, but does anybody notice? *Youth Today*, p. 58.

Roscoe, B., Dian, M. S., & Brooks, R. H. (1987). Early, middle, and late adolescents' views on dating and factors influencing partner selection. *Adolescence, 22*, 59–68.

Rose, S., & Frieze, L. R. (1993). Young singles' contemporary dating scripts. *Sex Roles, 28*, 499–509.

Rosen, R. (2000). *The world split open: How the modern women's movement changed America*. New York: Viking.

Rosenbaum, J. (1976). *Making inequality: The hidden curriculum of high school tracking*. New York: Wiley.

Rosenbaum, M. E. (1986). The repulsion hypothesis: On the nondevelopment of relationships. *Journal of Personality and Social Psychology, 51*, 1156–1166.

Rosenberg, M. (1986). Self concept from middle childhood through adolescence. In J. Suls & A. Greenwald (Eds.), *Psychological perspectives on the self* (Vol. 3). Hillsdale, NJ: Erlbaum.

Rosenberg, M., Schooler, C., & Schoenbach, C. (1989). Self-esteem and adolescent problems: Modeling reciprocal effects. *American Sociological Review, 54*, 1004–1018.

Rosenblatt, P. C., & Anderson, R. M. (1981). Human sexuality in cross-cultural perspective. In M. Cook (Ed.), *The bases of human sexual attraction* (pp. 215–250). London, England: Academic Press.

Rosenblum, G. D., & Lewis, M. (1999). The relations between body image, physical attractiveness, and body mass in adolescence. *Child Development, 70*, 50–64.

Rosenthal, D. (1984). Intergenerational conflict and culture: A study of immigrant and non-immigrant adolescents and their parents. *Genetic Psychology Monographs, 109*, 53–79.

Rosenthal, D. (1987). *Child-rearing and cultural values: A study of Greek and Australian mothers*. Paper presented at the biennial meeting of the International Society for the Study of Behavioral Development, Tours, France.

Rosenthal, D. (1994, February). *Gendered constructions of adolescent sexuality*. Paper presented at the biennial meeting of the Society for Research on Adolescence, San Diego.

Rosenthal, M. (1986). *The character factory: Baden-Powell and the origins of the Boy Scout movement*. New York: Pantheon.

Rothe, P. (1992). Traffic sociology: Social patterns of risk. *International Journal of Adolescent Medicine and Health, 5*, 187–197.

Rotheram-Borus, M. J. (1990). Adolescents' reference group choices, self-esteem, and adjustment. *Journal of Personality and Social Psychology, 59*, 1075–1081.

Rotheram-Borus, M. J. (1993). Suicidal behavior and risk factors among runaway youth. *American Journal of Psychiatry, 150*, 103–107.

Rotheram-Borus, M. J., Koopman, C., & Ehrhardt, A. (1991). Homeless youths and HIV infection. *American Psychologist, 46*, 1188–1197.

Rotundo, E. A. (1993). *American manhood: Transformations in masculinity from the Revolution to the Modern Era*. New York: Basic Books.

Rowe, D. C. (1995). *The limits of family influence*. New York: Guilford.

Rubin, A. M. (1979). Television use by children and adolescents. *Human Communication Research, 5*, 109–120.

Rubin, A. M. (1993). Uses, gratifications, and media effects research. In J. Bryant & D. Zillman (Eds.), *Perspectives on media effects*. Hillsdale, NJ: Erlbaum.

Rubin, C., Rubenstein, J. L., Stechler, G., & Heeren, T. (1992). Depressive affect in "normal" adolescents: A relationship to life stress, family, and friends. *American Journal of Orthopsychiatry, 62*, 430–441.

Rubin, K., LeMare, L., & Lollis, S. (1990). Social withdrawal in childhood: Developmental pathways to peer rejection. In S. Asher & J. Coie (Eds.), *Peer rejection in childhood* (pp. 217–249). New York: Cambridge University Press.

Ruggiero, M., Greenberger, E., & Steinberg, L. (1982). Occupational deviance among first-time workers. *Youth and Society, 13*, 423–448.

Rumberger, R. (1995). Dropping out of middle school: A multilevel analysis of students and schools. *American Educational Research Journal, 32,* 583–625.

Russell, D., Cutrona, C. E., Rose, J., & Yurko, K. (1984). Social and emotional loneliness: An examination of Weiss's typology of loneliness. *Journal of Personality and Social Psychology, 46,* 1313–1321.

Rust, J. O., & Troupe, P. A. (1991). Relationships of treatment of child sexual abuse with school achievement and self-concept. *Journal of Early Adolescence, 11,* 420–429.

Rutter, M. (1983). School effects on pupil progress: Research findings and policy implications. *Child Development, 54,* 1–29.

Rutter, M., Maughan, B., Mortimore, P., & Ouston, J. (1979). *Fifteen thousand hours: Secondary schools and their effects on children.* Cambridge, MA: Harvard University Press.

Ryan, R. M., & Lynch, J. H. (1989). Emotional autonomy versus attachment: Revisiting the vicissitudes of adolescence and young adulthood. *Child Development, 60,* 340–356.

Ryu, S., & Mortimer, J. T. (1996). The 'occupational linkage hypothesis' applied to occupational value formation in adolescence. In J. T. Mortimer & M. D. Finch (Eds.), *Adolescents, work, and family: An intergenerational developmental analysis* (pp. 167–190). Thousand Oaks, CA: Sage.

Saadawi, N. (1980). *The hidden face of Eve: Women in the Arab world.* London: Zed Press.

Sadker, M., & Sadker, D. (1982). *Sex equity handbook for schools.* New York: Longman.

Sadker, M., & Sadker, D. (1994). *Failing at fairness: How America's schools cheat girls.* New York: Scribner.

Sagestrano, L. M., McCormick, S. H., Paikoff, R. L., & Holmbeck, G. N. (1999). Pubertal development and parent–child conflict in low-income, urban, African American adolescents. *Journal of Research on Adolescence, 9,* 85–107.

Sahay, S., & Piran, N. (1997). Skin-color preferences and body satisfaction among South Asian-Canadian and European-Canadian female university students. *Journal of Social Psychology, 137,* 161–172.

Salinger, J. D. ([1951] 1964). *The catcher in the rye.* New York: Bantam.

Salzinger, S., Feldman, R. S., Manner, M., & Rosario, M. (1993). The effects of physical abuse on children's social relationships. *Child Development, 64,* 169–187.

Salzman, A. (1993, May 17). Mom, Dad, I want a job. *U.S. News & World Report,* pp. 68–72.

Sampson, R. J., Castellano, T. C., & Laub, J. H. (1981). *Juvenile criminal behavior and its relation to neighborhood characteristics.* Washington, DC: Office of Juvenile Justice and Delinquency Prevention.

Sampson, R. J., & Laub, J. H. (1990). Crime and deviance over the life course: The salience of adult social bonds. *American Sociological Review, 55,* 609–627.

Sampson, R. J., & Laub, J. H. (1994).Urban poverty and the family context of delinquency: A new look at structure and process in a classic study. *Child Development, 65,* 523–540.

Samuels, D. (1991, November 11). The rap on rap. *The New Republic,* 24–29.

Sandberg, D. E., Ehrhardt, A. A., Ince, S. E., & MeyerBahlburg, H. (1991). Gender differences in children's and adolescents' career aspirations: A follow-up study. *Journal of Adolescent Research, 6,* 371–386.

Sansone, L. (1995). The making of a black youth culture: Lower-class young men of Surinamese origin in Amsterdam. In V. Amit-Talai & H. Wulff (Eds.), *Youth cultures: A cross-cultural perspective* (pp. 114–143). New York: Rutledge.

Saraswathi, T. S. (1999). Adult–child continuity in India: Is adolescence a myth or an emerging reality? In T. S. Saraswathi (Ed.), *Culture, socialization, and human development: Theory, research, and applications in India* (pp. 213–232). Thousand Oaks, CA: Sage.

Sasinska-Klas, T. (1988). *Turbulence of the masses: The sociological phenomenon of rock music in Poland.* Paper presented at the ICYC conference, Geltow, German Democratic Republic.

Savin-Williams, R. (1994). Verbal and physical abuse as stressors in the lives of lesbian, gay male, and bisexual youths: Associations with school problems, running away, substance abuse, prostitution, and suicide. *Journal of Consulting and Clinical Psychology, 62,* 261–269.

Savin-Williams, R. C. (1998). The disclosure to families of same-sex attractions by lesbian, gay, and bisexual youth. *Journal of Research on Adolescence, 8,* 49–68.

Savin-Williams, R., & Berndt, T. (1990). Friendship and peer relations. In S. Feldman & G. Elliott (Eds.), *At the threshold: The developing adolescent* (pp. 277–307). Cambridge, MA: Harvard University Press.

Savin-Williams, R., & Demo, D. (1984). Developmental change and stability in adolescent self-concept. *Developmental Psychology, 20,* 1100–1110.

Scales, E., & McEwin, C. (1994). *Growing pains: The making of America's middle schoolteachers.* Columbus, OH: National Middle School Association.

Scales, P. C., & Leffert, N. (1998). *Development assets: A synthesis of scientific research on adolescent development.* Minneapolis, MN: Search Institute.

Scarr, D., Phillips, D., & McCartney, K. (1989). Working mothers and their families. *American Psychologist, 44,* 1402–1409.

Scarr, S. (1992). Developmental theories for the 1990s: Development and individual differences. *Child Development, 63,* 1–19.

Scarr, S. (1993). Biological and cultural diversity: The legacy of Darwin for development. *Child Development, 64,* 1333–1353.

Scarr, S., & McCartney, K. (1983). How people make their own environments: A theory of genotype environment effects. *Child Development, 54,* 424–435.

Scheer, S. D., Unger, D. G., & Brown, M. (1994, February). Adolescents becoming adults: Attributes for adulthood. Poster presented at the biennial meeting of the Society for Research on Adolescence, San Diego, CA.

Scheidel, D. G., & Marcia, J. E. (1985). Ego identity, intimacy, sex role orientation, and gender. *Developmental Psychology, 21,* 149–160.

Schellenbach, C., Whitman, T., & Borkowski, J. (1992). Toward an integrative model of adolescent parenting. *Human Development, 35,* 81–99.

Schiff, A., & Knopf, I. (1985). The effects of task demands on attention allocation in children of different ages. *Child Development, 56,* 621–630.

Schlegel, A. (1973). The adolescent socialization of the Hopi girl. *Ethnology, 4,* 449–462.

Schlegel, A. (2000). The global spread of adolescent culture. In L. Crockett & R. K. Silbereisen (Eds.), *Negotiating adolescence in a time of social change.* Cambridge: Cambridge University Press.

Schlegel, A., & Barry, H. (1991). *Adolescence: An anthropological inquiry.* New York: Free Press.

Schneider, B., & Shouse, R. (1991, April). *The work lives of eighth graders: Preliminary findings from the National Educational Longitudinal Study of 1988.* Paper presented at the biennial meeting of the Society for Research in Child Development, Seattle.

Schneider, B., & Stevenson, D. (1999). *The ambitious generation: America's teenagers, motivated but directionless.* New Haven, CT: Yale University Press.

Schulenberg, J. (2000, April). *College students get drunk, so what? National panel data on binge drinking trajectories before, during and after college.* Paper presented at the biennial meeting of the Society for Research on Adolescence, Chicago.

Schulenberg, J., & Bachman, J. (1993, March). *Long hours on the job? Not so bad for some adolescents in some types of jobs: The quality of work and substance use, affect, and stress.* Paper presented at the biennial meeting of the Society for Research in Child Development, New Orleans.

Schulenberg, J., Bachman, J. G., Johnston, L. D., & O'Malley, P. M. (1995). American adolescents' views on family and work: Historical trends from 1976–1992. In P. Noack, M. Hofer, & J. Youniss (Eds.), *Psychological responses to social change: Human development in changing environments* (pp. 37–64). New York: Walter De Gruyter.

Schulenberg, J., & Maggs, J. L. (2000). *A developmental perspective on alcohol use and heavy drinking during adolescence and the transition to adulthood.* Washington, DC: National Institute on Alcohol Abuse and Alcoholism.

Schulenberg, J., O'Malley, P. M., Bachman, J. G., Wadsworth, K. N., & Johnston, L. D. (1996). Getting drunk and growing up: Trajectories of frequent binge drinking during the transition to adulthood. *Journal of Studies on Alcohol, 57,* 1–15.

Schultz, R., & Curnow, C. (1988). Peak performance and age among superathletes: Track and field, swimming, baseball, tennis, and golf. *Journal of Gerontology: Psychological Sciences, 43,* P113–P120.

Scott, D. (1995). The effect of video games on feelings of aggression. *Journal of Psychology, 129,* 121–132.

Segal, D. (2000, January 12). The pied piper of racism: William Pierce wants young people to march to his hate records. *Washington Post,* pp. C-1, C-8.

Segal, U. A. (1998). The Asian Indian-American family. In C. H. Mindel, R. W. Habenstein, & R. Wright, Jr. (Eds.), *Ethnic families in America* (4th ed.; pp. 331–360). Upper Saddle River, NJ: Prentice Hall.

Seginer, R. (1998). Adolescents' perceptions of relationships with older siblings in the context of other close relationships. *Journal of Research on Adolescence, 8,* 287–308.

Seidman, E., Allen, L., Aber, J., Mitchell, C., & Feinman, J. (1994). The impact of school transitions in early adolescence on the self-system and perceived social context of poor urban youth. *Child Development, 6S,* 507–522.

Seligman, M. E. P. (1993). *What you can change and what you can't: The complete guide to successful self-improvement.* New York: Fawcett.

Sells, C. W., & Blum, R. W. (1996). Morbidity and mortality among U.S. adolescents: An overview of data and trends. *American Journal of Public Health, 86,* 513–519.

Selman, R. (1976). Social-cognitive understanding. In T. Lickona (Ed.), *Moral development and behavior.* New York: Holt, Rinehart & Winston.

Selman, R. (1980). *The growth of interpersonal understanding: Developmental and clinical analyses.* New York: Academic Press.

Selman, R., & Byrne, D. (1974). A structural developmental analysis of levels of role-taking in middle childhood. *Child Development, 45,* 803–806.

Serbin, L. A., Powlishta, K. K., & Gulko, J. (1993). The development of sex typing in middle childhood. *Monographs of the Society for Research in Child Development, 58,* 1–74.

Serow, R. C., Ciechalski, J., & Daye, C. (1990). Students as volunteers: Personal competence, social diversity, and participation in community service. *Urban Education, 25,* 157–168.

Sewell, W. H., & Hauser, R. M. (1975). *Education, occupation, and earnings: Achievement in the early career.* New York: Academic Press.

Sewell, W., & Hauser, R. (1972). Causes and consequences of higher education: Models of the status attainment process. *American Journal of Agricultural Economics, 54,* 851–861.

Sexton, M. A., & Geffen, G. (1979). Development of three strategies of attention in dichotic monitoring. *Developmental Psychology, 15,* 299–310.

Shaaban, B. (1991). *Both right and left handed: Arab women talk about their lives.* Bloomington: Indiana University Press.

Shagle, S. C., & Barber, B. K. (1994, February). *Effects of parenting variables, self-derogation, and depression on adolescent suicide ideation.* Paper presented at the meeting of the Society for Research on Adolescence, San Diego.

Shakin, M., Shakin, D., & Sternglanz, S. H. (1985). Infant clothing: Sex labeling for strangers. *Sex Roles, 12,* 955–964.

Shantz, C. U. (1983). Social cognition. In P. H. Mussen (Ed.), *Handbook of child psychology* (Vol. 3, pp. 495–555). New York: Wiley.

Shaughnessy, J. J., & Zechmeister, E. B. (1985). *Research methods in psychology.* New York: Knopf.

Shaver, P. R., & Hazan, C. (1993). Adult romantic attachment: Theory and evidence. In D. Perlman & W. Jones (Eds.), *Advances in personal relationships* (Vol. 4, pp. 29–70). London: Jessica Kingsley.

Shaver, P., Furman, W., & Buhrmester, D. (1985). Transition to college: Network changes, social skills, and loneliness. In S. Duck & D. Perlman (Eds.), *Understanding personal relationships: An interdisciplinary approach.* Newbury Park, CA: Sage.

Shedler, J., & Block, J. (1990). Adolescent drug use and psychological health. *American Psychologist, 45,* 612–630.

Sheer, V. C., & Cline, R. J. (1994). The development and validation of a model explaining sexual behavior among college students: Implications for AIDS communication campaigns. *Health Communication Research, 21,* 280–304.

Shelton, B. A., & John, D. (1993). Ethnicity, race, and difference: A comparison of White, Black, and Hispanic men's household labor time. In J. C. Hood (Ed.), *Men, work, and family* (pp. 131–150). Newbury Park, CA: Sage.

Sherman, B. L., & Dominick, J. R. (1986). Violence and sex in music videos: TV and rock 'n' roll. *Journal of Communication, 36,* 79–93.

Shrum, W., Cheek, N., Jr., & Hunter, S. D. (1988). Friendship in school: Gender and racial homophily. *Sociology of Education, 61,* 227–239.

Shukla, M. (1994). India. In K. Hurrelmann (Ed.), *International handbook of adolescence* (pp. 191–206). Westport, CT: Greenwood.

Shulman, S., & Scharf, M. (2000). Adolescent romantic behaviors and perceptions: Age- and gender-related differences, and links with family and peer relationships. *Journal of Research on Adolescence, 10,* 99–118.

Shulman, S., Laursen, B., Kalman, Z., & Karpovsky, S. (1997). Adolescent intimacy revisited. *Journal of Youth & Adolescence, 26,* 597–617.

Shweder, R. A. (Ed.). (1998). *Welcome to middle age! (And other cultural fictions).* Chicago: University of Chicago Press.

Shweder, R. A., Goodnow, J., Hatano, G., Levine, R. A., Markus, H., & Miller, P. (1998). The cultural psychology of development: One mind, many mentalities. In W. Damon (Ed.), *Handbook of child development* (5th ed., Vol. 1, pp. 865–937) New York: Wiley.

Shweder, R. A., Mahapatra, M., & Miller, J. G. (1990). Culture and moral development. In J. W. Stigler, R. A. Shweder, & G. Herdt (Eds.), *Cultural psychology* (pp. 130–204). New York: Cambridge University Press.

Shweder, R. A., Much, N. C., Mahapatra, M., & Park, L. (1997). The "big three" of morality (autonomy, community, divinity), and the "big three" explanations of suffering. In A. Brandt & D. Rozin (Eds.), *Morality and heath.* New York: Routledge.

Sidorowicz, L. S., & Lunney, G. S. (1980). Baby X revisited. *Sex Roles, 6,* 67–73.

Siegel, B. (1997, April). *Developmental and social policy issues and the practice of educational mainstreaming and full inclusion.* Paper presented at the biennial meeting of the Society for Research on Child Development, Washington, DC.

Siegel, D. L. (1992). *Sexual harassment: Research and resources.* Washington, DC: National Council for Research on Women.

Siegler, R. (1988). Individual differences in strategy choices: Good students, not-so-good students, and perfectionists. *Child Development, 59,* 833–851.

Sigelman, C., & Toebben, J. (1992). Tolerant reactions to advocates of disagreeable ideas in childhood and adolescence. *Merrill-Palmer Quarterly, 38,* 542–557.

Silbereisen, R. K., Meschke, L. L., & Schwarz, B. (1996). Leaving the parental home: Predictors for young adults raised in the former East and West Germany. *New Directions in Child Development, 71,* 71–86.

Silbereisen, R., Petersen, A., Albrecht, H., & Kracke, B. (1989). Maturational timing and the development of problem behavior: Longitudinal studies in adolescence. *Journal of Early Adolescence, 9,* 247–268.

Silverberg, S., & Steinberg, L. (1990). Psychological well-being of parents at midlife: The impact of early adolescent children. *Developmental Psychology, 26,* 658–666.

Simmons, R. G., & Blyth, D. A. (1987). *Moving into adolescence.* New York: Aldine de Gruyter.

Simmons, R., Blyth, D., & McKinney, K. (1983). The social and psychological effects of puberty on white females. In J. Brooks-Gunn & A. Petersen (Eds.), *Girls at puberty.* New York: Plenum.

Simons, R., Whitbeck, L., Conger, R., & Chyi-In, W. (1991). Intergenerational transmission of harsh parenting. *Developmental Psychology, 27,* 159–171.

Singh, G., & Hernandez-Gantes, V. (1996). The relation of English language proficiency to educational aspirations of Mexican-American eighth graders. *Journal of Early Adolescence, 16,* 154–167.

Singh, G., & Yu, S. (1996). U.S. childhood mortality, 1950 through 1993: Trends and socioeconomic differentials. *American Journal of Public Health, 86,* 505–512.

Sinnott, J. D. (1998). *The development of logic in adulthood: Postformal thoughts and its applications.* New York: Plenum.

Skoe, E. E., & Gooden, A. (1993). Ethic of care and real-life moral dilemma content in male and female early adolescents. *Journal of Early Adolescence, 13,* 154–167.

Skultans, V. (1988). Menstrual symbolism in South Wales. In T. Buckley & A. Gottlieb (Eds.), *Blood magic: The anthropology of menstruation* (pp. 137–160). Berkeley: University of California Press.

Slavin, L. A., & Rainer, K. L. (1990). Gender differences in emotional support and depressive symptoms among adolescents: A prospective analysis. *American Journal of Community Psychology, 18,* 407–421.

Slovic, P. (1998). Do adolescent smokers know the risks? *Duke Law Journal, 47,* 1133–1141.

Smart, T., Stoughton, S., & Behr, P. (1999, September 12). Working their way up: Economy's expansion has lifted those on the bottom rung, but will gains last? *Washington Post,* p. H-1.

Smetana, J. (1988). Concepts of self and social convention: Adolescents' and parents' reasoning about hypothetical and actual family conflicts. In M. Gunnar & W. A. Collins (Eds.), *Minnesota Symposium on Child Psychology* (Vol. 21, pp. 79–122). Hillsdale, NJ: Erlbaum.

Smetana, J. (1989). Adolescents' and parents' reasoning about actual family conflict. *Child Development, 59,* 1052–1067.

Smetana, J., & Asquith, R. (1994). Adolescents' and parents' conceptions of parental authority and personal autonomy. *Child Development, 65,* 1147–1162.

Smetana, J. G. (1993). Morality in context: Abstractions, ambiguities, and applications. *Annals of Child Development, 10,* 83–130.

Smetana, J., Yau, J., Restrepo, A., & Braeges, J. (1991). Adolescent–parent conflict in married and divorced families. *Developmental Psychology, 27,* 1000–1010.

Smith, C. (1991). Sex and gender on prime time. *Journal of Homosexuality, 12,* 119–138.

Smith, D. (2000, May 6). Jocks and couch potatoes. *Washington Post,* p. A13.

Smith, E., & Udry, J. (1985). Coital and noncoital sexual behaviors of white and black adolescents. *American Journal of Public Health, 75,* 1200–1203.

Smith, K., McGraw, S., Crawford, S., Costa, L., & McKinlay, J. (1993). HIV risk among Latino adolescents in two New England cities. *American Journal of Public Health, 83,* 1395–1399.

Smith, R. C., & Crockett, L. J. (1997, April). *Positive adolescent peer relations: A potential buffer against family adversity.* Paper presented at the meeting of the Society for Research in Child Development, Washington, DC.

Smith, T. (1992). Gender differences in the scientific achievement of adolescents: Effects of age and parental separation. *Social Forces, 71,* 469–484.

Smith, T. (1993, March). *Federal employment training programs for youth: Failings and opportunities.* Paper presented at the biennial meeting of the Society for Research in Child Development, New Orleans.

Smock, P. J. (1993). The economic costs of marital disruption for young women over the past two decades. *Demography, 30,* 353–371.

Smoll, F., & Schutz, R. (1990). Quantifying gender differences in physical performance: A developmental perspective. *Developmental Psychology, 26,* 360–369.

Snarey, J. R. (1985). Cross-cultural universality of social moral development: A review of Kohlbergian research. *Psychological Bulletin, 97,* 202–232.

Snow, R. E., & Yalow, E. (1988). Education and intelligence. In R. J. Sternberg (Ed.), *Handbook of human intelligence* (pp. 493–585). New York: Cambridge University Press.

Solarzano, D. G. (1992). An exploratory analysis of the effects of race, class, and gender on student and parent mobility aspirations. *Journal of Negro Education, 61,* 30–44.

Solarzano, L. (1984, August 27). Students think schools are making the grade. *U.S. News & World Report,* pp. 49–51.

Sommers, C. H. (2000, May). The war against boys. *Atlantic Monthly,* pp. 59–74.

Sommers-Flanagan, R., Sommers-Flanagan, J., & Davis, B. (1993). What's happening on music television? A gender role content analysis. *Sex Roles, 28,* 745–753.

Sommerville, J. (1982). *The rise and fall of childhood.* Beverly Hills, CA: Sage.

Sonenstein, E. L., Pleck, J. H., & Ku, L. C. (1991). Levels of sexual activity among adolescent males in the United States. *Family Planning Perspectives, 23,* 162–167.

Sparrow, P. R., & Davies, D. R. (1988). Effects of age, tenure, training, and job complexity on technical performance. *Psychology and Aging, 3,* 307–314.

Spence, J., & Helmreich, R. (1978). *Masculinity and femininity: Their psychological dimensions, correlates, and antecedents.* Austin: University of Texas Press.

Spencer, M., & Dornbusch, S. (1990). Challenges in studying minority youth. In S. Feldman & G. Elliott (Eds.), *At the threshold: The developing adolescent* (pp. 123–146). Cambridge, MA: Harvard University Press.

Spencer, M., & Markstrom-Adams, C. (1990). Identity processes among racial and ethnic minority children in America. *Child Development, 61,* 290–310.

Spencer, P. (1965). *The Samburu: A study of gerontocracy in a nomadic tribe.* Berkeley: University of California Press.

Spiro, M. (1993). Is the Western conception of the self "peculiar" within the context of the world's cultures? *Ethos, 21,* 107–153.

Sprecher, S. (1994). Two sides to the breakup of dating relationships. *Personal Relationships, 1,* 199–222.

Sprecher, S., & Chandak, R. (1992). Attitudes about arranged marriages and dating among men and women from India. *Journal of Sex Research, 32,* 3–15.

Sprecher, S., Barbee, A., & Schwartz, P. (1995). "Was it good for you, too?" Gender differences in first sexual intercourse experiences. *Journal of Sex Research, 32,* 3–15.

Sroufe, L. A., Carlson, E., & Schulman, S. (1993). Individuals in relationships: Development from infancy through adolescence. In D. C. Funder, R. D. Parke, C. Tomlinson-Keasey, & K. Widaman (Eds.), *Studying lives through time: Personality and development* (pp. 51–60). Norwood, NJ: Ablex.

Stafseng, O. (1994). *Norway.* In K. Hurrelmann (Ed.), *International handbook of adolescence* (pp. 287–298). Westport, CT: Greenwood Press.

Stanger, C., Achenbach, T., & McConaughy, S. (1993). Three-year course of behavioral/emotional problems in a national sample of 4- to 16-year-olds, 3: Predictors of signs of disturbance. *Journal of Consulting and Clinical Psychology, 61,* 839–848.

Stangor, C., & Ruble, D. N. (1987). Development of gender role knowledge and gender constancy. In L. Liben & M. Signorella (Eds.), *Children's gender schemata* (pp. 5–22). San Francisco: Jossey Bass.

Stangor, C., & Ruble, D. N. (1989). Differential influences of gender schemata and gender constancy on children's information processing and behavior. *Social Cognition, 7*, 353–372.

Stedman, L., & Smith, M. (1983). Recent reform proposals for American education. *Contemporary Education Review, 2*, 85–104.

Steele, J. R., & Brown, J. D. (1995). Adolescent room culture: Studying media in the context of everyday life. *Journal of Youth & Adolescence, 24*, 551–576.

Stein, J. A., Newcomb, M. D., & Bentler, P. M. (1994). Psychosocial correlates and predictors of AIDS risk behaviors, abortion, and drug use among a community sample of young adult women. *Health Psychology, 13*, 308–318.

Stein, J. H., & Reiser, L. W. (1993). A study of White middle-class adolescent boys' responses to "semenarche" (the first ejaculation). *Journal of Youth & Adolescence, 23*, 373–383.

Stein, J., & Reiser, L. (1994). A study of white middle-class adolescent boys' responses to "semenarche" (the first ejaculation). *Journal of Youth & Adolescence, 23*, 373–384.

Stein, J., Newcomb, M., & Bentler, P. (1987). An 8-year study of the multiple influences on drug use and drug use consequences. *Journal of Personality and Social Psychology, 53*, 1094–1105.

Stein, N. (1995). Sexual harassment in school: The public performance of gendered violence. *Harvard Educational Review, 65*, 145–162.

Steinberg, L. (1986). Latchkey children and susceptibility to peer pressure: An ecological analysis. *Developmental Psychology, 22*, 433–439.

Steinberg, L. (1987a). The impact of puberty on family relations: Effects of pubertal status and pubertal timing. *Developmental Psychology, 23*, 451–460.

Steinberg, L. (1987b, September). Bound to bicker: Pubescent primates leave home for good reasons. Our teens stay with us and squabble. *Psychology Today*, 36–39.

Steinberg, L. (1987c). Single parents, stepparents, and the susceptibility of adolescents to antisocial peer pressure. *Child Development, 58*, 269–275.

Steinberg, L. (1988). Reciprocal relation between parent–child distance and pubertal maturation. *Developmental Psychology, 24*, 122–128.

Steinberg, L. (1989). Pubertal maturation and parent–adolescent distance: An evolutionary perspective. In G. Adams, R. Montemayor, & T. Gullotta (Eds.), *Advances in adolescent development* (Vol. 1, pp. 71–97). Beverly Hills, CA: Sage.

Steinberg, L. (1990). Autonomy, conflict, and harmony in the family relationship. In S. Feldman & G. Elliott (Eds.), *At the threshold: The developing adolescent* (pp. 255–276). Cambridge, MA: Harvard University Press.

Steinberg, L. (in collaboration with B. Brown & S. Dornbusch) (1996). *Beyond the classroom: Why school reform has failed and what parents need to do*. New York: Simon & Schuster.

Steinberg, L. (2000, April). *We know some things: Parent–adolescent relations in retrospect and prospect*. Presidential Address, presented at the biennial meeting of the Society for Research on Adolescence, Chicago, IL.

Steinberg, L., & Cauffman, E. (1995). The impact of employment on adolescent development. In R. Vasta (Ed.), *Annals of Child Development* (Vol. 11, pp. 131–166). London: Jessica Kingsley Publishers.

Steinberg, L., & Cauffman, E. (1996). Maturity of judgment in adolescence: Psychosocial factors in adolescent decision making. *Law and Human Behavior, 20*, 249–272.

Steinberg, L., & Dornbusch, S. M. (1991). Negative correlates of part-time employment during adolescence: Replication and elaboration. *Developmental Psychology, 27*, 304–313.

Steinberg, L., Dornbusch, S. M., & Brown, B. B. (1992). Ethnic differences in adolescent achievement: An ecological perspective. *American Psychologist, 47*, 723–729.

Steinberg, L., Fegley, S., & Dornbusch, S. M. (1993). Negative impact of part-time work on adolescent adjustment: Evidence from a longitudinal study. *Developmental Psychology, 29*, 171–180.

Steinberg, L., Fletcher, A., & Darling, N. (1994). Parental monitoring and peer influences on adolescent substance use. *Pediatrics, 93*, 1060–1064.

Steinberg, L., Greenberger, E., Garduque, L., Ruggiero, M., & Vaux, A. (1982). Effects of working on adolescent development. *Developmental Psychology, 18*, 385–395.

Steinberg, L., Lamborn, S., Darling, N., Mounts, N., & Dornbusch, S. (1994). Over-time changes in adjustment and competence among adolescents from authoritative, authoritarian, indulgent, and neglectful families. *Child Development, 65*, 754–770.

Steinberg, L., & Levine, A. (1997). *You and your adolescent: A parents' guide for ages 10 to 20* (rev. ed.). New York: HarperCollins.

Steinberg, L., Mounts, N., Lamborn, S., & Dornbusch, S. (1991). Authoritative parenting and adolescent adjustment across various ecological niches. *Journal of Research on Adolescence, 1*, 19–36.

Steinberg, L., & Steinberg, W. (1994). *Crossing paths: How your child's adolescence triggers your own crisis*. New York: Simon & Schuster.

Steinhauer, J. (1995, January 4). Teen-age girls talk back on exercise. *New York Times*, pp. B1, B4.

Steinhausen, H. (1995). The course and outcome of anorexia nervosa. In K. D.

Brownwell & C. G. Fairburn (Eds.), *Eating disorders and obesity: A comprehensive handbook* (pp. 234–237). New York: Guilford.

Stern, D., Rahn, M. L., & Chung, Y. (1998). Design of work-based learning for students in the United States. *Youth & Society, 29*, 471–502.

Sternberg, R. (1977). *Intelligence, information processing, and analogical reasoning: The componential analysis of human abilities*. Hillsdale, NJ: Erlbaum.

Sternberg, R. (1983). Components of human intelligence. *Cognition, 15*, 1–48.

Sternberg, R. (1988). *The triarchic mind: A new theory of human intelligence*. New York: Viking Penguin.

Sternberg, R. J. (1986). *Intelligence applied*. San Diego: Harcourt Brace Jovanovich.

Sternberg, R. J. (1986). A triangular theory of love. *Psychological Review, 93*, 119–135.

Sternberg, R. J. (1987). Liking versus loving: A comparative evaluation of theories. *Psychological Bulletin, 102*, 331–345.

Sternberg, R. J. (1988). Triangulating love. In R. J. Sternberg & M. L. Barnes (Eds.), *The psychology of love* (pp. 119–138). New Haven, CT: Yale University Press.

Sternberg, R. J. (1990). *Metaphors of mind: Conceptions of the nature of intelligence*. New York: Cambridge University Press.

Sternberg, R. J. (1997, April). *Practical intelligence differs from academic intelligence*. Paper presented at the meeting of the Society for Research in Child Development, Washington, DC.

Sternberg, R. J., Conway, B. E., Ketron, J. L., & Berstein, M. (1981). People's conceptions of intelligence. *Journal of Personality and Social Psychology, 41*, 37–55.

Sternberg, R. J., & Nigro, C. (1980). Developmental patterns in the solution of verbal analogies. *Child Development, 51*, 27–38.

Sternberg, R., & Rifkin, B. (1979). The development of analogical reasoning processes. *Journal of Experimental Child Psychology, 27*, 195–232.

Stevens, J. H. (1984). Black grandmothers' and black adolescent mothers' knowledge about parenting. *Developmental Psychology, 20*, 1017–1025.

Stevenson, H. W. (1992, December). Learning from Asian schools. *Scientific American* pp. 6, 70–76.

Stevenson, H. W., & Zusho, A. (2000, February). *Adolescence in China and Japan*. Paper prepared for the meeting of the Study Group on Adolescence in the 21st Century, Washington, DC.

Stevenson, H., & Stigler, J. (1992). *The learning gap: Why our schools are failing and what we can learn from Japanese and Chinese education*. New York: Simon & Schuster.

Stewart, R. B., Beilfuss, M. L., & Verbrugge, K. M. (1995, March). *That was then, this is now: An empirical typology of adult sibling relationships*. Paper presented at the biennial meeting of the Society for Research on Child Development, Indianapolis.

Stigler, J. W., Shweder, R. A., & Herdt, G. (Eds.) (1990). *Cultural psychology.* New York: Cambridge University Press.

Stiles, D. A., Gibbons, J. L., & Schnellman, J. (1990). The smiling sunbather and the chivalrous football player: Young adolescents' images of the ideal women and man. *Journal of Early Adolescence, 7,* 411–427.

Stone, L. (1990). *Road to divorce: England 1530–1987.* New York: Oxford University Press.

Stone, M. H. (1993). Long-term outcome in personality disorders. *British Journal of Psychiatry, 162,* 299–313.

Stone, M. R., & Brown, B. B. (1998). In the eye of the beholder: Adolescents' perceptions of peer crowd stereotypes. In R. Muuss (Ed.), *Adolescent behavior and society: A book of readings* (5th ed., pp. 158–169). San Francisco: Jossey-Bass.

Stone, M. R., Barber, B. L., & Eccles, J. S. (2000, April). *Adolescent "crowd" clusters: An adolescent perspective on persons and patterns.* Paper presented at the biennial meeting of the Society for Research on Adolescence, Chicago.

Stone, M. R., & Brown, B. B. (1999). Identity claims and projections: Descriptions of self and crowds in secondary schools. *New Directions for Child and Adolescent Development, 84,* 7–20.

Stones, M. J., & Kozma, A. (1996). Activity, exercise, and behavior. In J. E. Birren & K. W. Schaie (Eds.), *Handbook of psychology of aging* (4th ed., pp. 338–352). San Diego, CA: Academic Press.

Stout, J., & Rivera, E (1989). Schools and sex education: Does it work? *Pediatrics, 83,* 375–379.

Stouthamer-Loeber, M., & Wei, E. H. (1998). The precursors of young fatherhood and its effects on delinquency of teenage males. *Journal of Adolescent Health, 22,* 56–65.

Strachen, A., & Jones, D. (1982). Changes in identification during adolescence: A personal construct theory approach. *Journal of Personality Assessment, 46,* 139–148.

Strahan, D. B. (1983). The emergence of formal operations in adolescence. *Transcendence, 11,* 7–14.

Strasburger, V. C. (1995). *Adolescents and the media: Medical and psychological impact.* Thousand Oaks, CA: Sage.

Strasburger, V. C., & Donnerstein, E. (1999). Children, adolescents, and the media: Issues and solutions. *Pediatrics, 103,* 129–139.

Strickland, B. R. (1995). Research on sexual orientation and human development: A commentary. *Developmental Psychology, 31,* 137–140.

Striegel-Moore, R. H. (1997). Risk factors for eating disorders. In M. S. Jacobson & J. M. Rees (Eds.), *Adolescent nutritional disorders: Prevention and treatment* (pp. 98–109). New York: New York Academy of Sciences.

Striegel-Moore, R. H., & Cachelin, F. M. (1999). Body image concerns and disordered eating in adolescent girls: Risk and protective factors. In N. B. Johnson, M. C. Roberts, & J. Worell (Eds.), *Beyond appearance: A new look at adolescent girls* (pp. 85–108). Washington, DC: American Psychological Association.

Strommen, E. F. (1989). "You're a what?" Family member reactions to the disclosure of homosexuality. *Journal of Homosexuality, 19,* 37–58.

Studer, J. (1993). A comparison of the self-concepts of adolescents from intact, maternal custodial, and paternal custodial families. *Journal of Divorce and Remarriage, 19,* 219–227.

Suarez-Orozco, C., & Suarez-Orozco, M. (1996). *Transformations: Migration, family life and achievement motivation among Latino adolescents.* Palo Alto, CA: Stanford University Press.

Substance Abuse and Mental Health Services Administration. (1999). *1998 National Survey on drug abuse.* Rockville, MD: Author.

Sudman, S., & Bradburn, N. M. (1989). *Asking questions: A practical guide to questionnaire design.* San Francisco: Jossey-Bass.

Sullivan, H. S. (1953). *The interpersonal theory of psychiatry.* New York: Norton.

Sullivan, L. C., & Sullivan, A. (1980). Adolescent–parent separation. *Developmental Psychology, 16,* 93–99.

Sun, S., & Lull, J. (1986). The adolescent audience for music videos and why they watch. *Journal of Communication, 36,* 115–125.

Sung, B. L. (1979). *Transplanted Chinese children.* Washington, DC: Department of Health, Education, and Welfare. (ERIC Document Reproduction Service No. ED 182-040)

Sung, B. L. (1985). Bicultural conflicts in Chinese immigrant children. *Journal of Comparative Studies, 16,* 255–270.

Super, D. (1992). Toward a comprehensive study of career development. In D. H. Montross & C. J. Shinkman (Eds.), *Career development: Theory and practice* (pp. 35–64). Springfield, IL: Charles C. Thomas.

Super, D. E. (1967). *The psychology of careers.* New York: Harper & Row.

Super, D. E. (1976). *Career education and the meanings of work.* Washington, DC: U.S. Office of Education.

Super, D. E. (1980). A life-span life-space approach to career development. *Journal of Vocational Behavior, 16,* 282–298.

Supple, A. J., Aquilino, W. S., & Wright, D. L. (1999). Collecting sensitive self-report data with laptop computers: Impact on the response tendencies of adolescents in a home interview. *Journal of Research on Adolescence, 9,* 467–488.

Surbey, M. (1990). Family composition, stress, and human menarche. In F.

Bercovitch & T. Zeigler (Eds.), *The socioendocrinology of primate reproduction.* New York: Alan R. Liss.

Surrey, J. L.(1991). The self-in-relation: A theory of women's development. In J. V. Jordan, A. G. Kaplan, J. B. Miller, L. R. Stiver, & J. L. Surrey (Eds.), *Women and growth in connection* (pp. 51–66). New York: Guilford.

Susman, E. J. (1997). Modeling developmental complexity in adolescence: Hormones and behavior in context. *Journal of Research on Adolescence, 7,* 283–306.

Susman, E., Koch, R., Maney, D., & Finkelstein, J. (1993). Health promotion in adolescence: Developmental and theoretical considerations. In R. Lerner (Ed.), *Early adolescence: Perspectives on research, policy, and intervention.* (pp. 247–260). Hillsdale, NJ: Erlbaum.

Swanson, D. P., Spencer, M. B., & Petersen, A. (1998). Identity formation in adolescence. In K. Borman & B. Schneider (Eds.), *The adolescent years: Social influences and educational challenges: Ninety-seventh yearbook of the National Society for the Study of Education, Part 1* (pp. 18–41). Chicago, IL: National Society for the Study of Education.

Swardson, A. (1999, September 28). In Europe's economic boom, finding work is a bust. *Washington Post,* pp. 1, 20.

Swensen, C. H., Eskew, R. W., & Kohlhepp, K. A. (1981). Stage of family life cycle, ego development, and the marriage relationship. *Journal of Marriage and the Family, 43,* 841–853.

Swidler, A. (1986). Culture in action: Symbols and strategies. *American Sociological Review, 51,* 273–286.

Szeszulski, R., Martinez, A., & Reyes, B. (1994, February). *Patterns and predictors of self-satisfaction among culturally diverse high school students.* Paper presented at the biennial meeting of the Society for Research on Adolescence, San Diego.

Takahashi, D., & Ramstad, E. (1997, December 9). Quake sequel beefs up blood and guts. *Wall Street Journal,* pp. B-1, B-16.

Tamir, L. M. (1982). *Men in their forties: The transition to middle age.* New York: Springer.

Tanner, D. (1972). *Secondary education.* New York: Macmillan.

Tanner, J. M. (1962). *Growth at adolescence.* Oxford: Blackwell Scientific Publications.

Tanner, J. M. (1970). *Physical growth.* In P. H. Mussen (Ed.), *Carmichael's manual of child psychology* (Vol. 2, 3rd ed., pp. 77–156). New York: Wiley.

Tanner, J. M. (1971). Sequence, tempo, and individual variation in the growth and development of boys and girls aged twelve to sixteen. *Daedalus, 100,* 907–930.

Tanner, J. M. (1991). Growth spurt, adolescent. In R. M. Lerner, A. C. Petersen, & J. Brooks-Gunn (Eds.), *Encyclopedia of adolescence* (Vol. 2, pp. 419–424). New York: Garland.

Tavris, C. (1992). *The mismeasure of woman: Why women are not the better sex, the inferior sex, or the opposite sex.* New York: Touchstone.

Taylor, R. D. (1994, February). *Kinship support and family management in African-American families.* Paper presented at the biennial meeting of the Society for Research in Adolescence, San Diego.

Taylor, R. D. (1996). Adolescents' and perceptions of kinship support family management practices: Association with adolescent adjustment in African American families. *Developmental Psychology, 32,* 687–695.

Taylor, R. D. (1997). The effects of economic and social stressors on parenting and adolescent adjustment in African-American families. In R. D. Taylor & M. C. Wang (Eds.), *Social and emotional adjustment and family relations in ethnic minority families.* Mahwah, NJ: Erlbaum.

Taylor, R., Casten, R., & Flickinger, S. (1993). The influence of kinship social support on the parenting experiences and psychosocial adjustment of African American adolescents. *Developmental Psychology, 29,* 382–388.

Taylor, R., Casten, R., Flickinger, S., Roberts, D., & Fulmore, C. (1994). Explaining the school performance of African-American adolescents. *Journal of Research on Adolescence, 4,* 21–44.

Taylor, R. L. (1998). Minority families in America: An introduction. In R. L. Taylor (Ed.), *Minority families in the United States: A multicultural perspective* (pp. 1–16). Upper Saddle River, NJ: Prentice-Hall.

Teachman, J. (1996). Intellectual skill and academic performance: Do families bias the relationship? *Sociology of Education, 69,* 35–48.

Teen Birth Rate Continues to Drop. (January, 2000). *Population Today, 3.*

Terrelonge, P. (1989). Feminist consciousness and Black women. In J. Freeman (Ed.), *Women: A feminist perspective* (4th ed., pp. 556–566). Mountain View, CA: Mayfield.

Teti, D., & Lamb, M. (1989). Socioeconomic and marital outcomes of adolescent marriage, adolescent childbirth, and their co-occurrence. *Journal of Marriage and the Family, 51,* 203–212.

Thapar, V. (1998, November). *Family life education in India: Emerging challenges.* Background paper for the National Convention on Family Life Education, New Delhi, India.

Tharinger, D. (1990). Impact of child sexual abuse on developing sexuality. *Professional Psychology, 21,* 331–337.

Thelen, M. H., Powell, A. L., Lawrence, C., & Kuhnert, M. E. (1992). Eating and body image concerns among children. *Journal of Clinical Child Psychology, 21,* 41–46.

Thio, A. (1997). *Sociology: A brief introduction.* New York: Addison Wesley Longman.

Thomas, J. (1998, May 13). Experts take a second look at virtue of student jobs. *New York Times,* p. A-16.

Thompson, M. G., & Gans, M. T. (1985). Do Anorexics and bulimics get well? In S. W. Emmett (Ed.), *Theory and treatment of anorexia nervosa and bulimia* (pp. 291–303). New York: Brunner/Mazel.

Thompson, S. (1994). Changing lives, changing genres: Teenage girls' narratives about sex and romance, 1978–1986. In A. S. Rossi (Ed.), *Sexuality across the life course* (pp. 209–232). Chicago: University of Chicago Press.

Thomson, E., & Colella, U. (1992). Cohabitation and marital stability: Quality or commitment? *Journal of Marriage and the Family, 54,* 259–267.

Thornberry, T. P., Smith, C. A., & Howard, G. J. (1997). Risk factors for teenage fatherhood. *Journal of Marriage and the Family, 59,* 505–522.

Thornton, A. (1990). The courtship process and adolescent sexuality. *Journal of Family Issues, 11,* 239–273.

Tierney, J. P., & Branch, A. Y. (1992). *College students as mentors for at-risk youth.* Philadelphia: Public/Private Ventures.

Ting-Toomey, S. (1991). Intimacy *expressions* in three cultures: France, Japan, and the United States. *International Journal of Intercultural Relations, 15,* 29–46.

Tinto, V. (1993). *Leaving college: Rethinking the causes and cures of student attrition research.* Chicago: University of Chicago.

Tolan, P. H., & Loeber, R. (1993). Antisocial behavior. In P. H. Tolan & B. J. Cohler (Eds.), *Handbook of clinical research and practice with adolescents* (pp. 307–331). New York: Wiley.

Tomb, D. A. (1991). The runaway adolescent. In M. Lewis (Ed.), *Child and adolescent psychiatry* (pp. 1066–1071). Baltimore, MD: Williams & Wilkins.

Tomlinson-Keasey, C., & Eisert, D. C. (1981). From a structured "ensemble" to separate organizations for cognitive and affective development. In J. A. Meacham & R. Santilli (Eds.), *Social development in youth. Structure and content* (pp. 1–19). Basel: S. Karger.

Top, T. J. (1991). Sex bias in the evaluation of performance in the scientific, artistic, and literary professions: A review. *Sex Roles, 24,* 73–106.

Torney-Purta, J. (1990). From attitudes and knowledge to schemata: Expanding the outcomes of political socialization research. In O. Ichilov (Ed.), *Political socialization, citizenship, education, and democracy* (pp. 98–115). New York: Columbia University Press.

Torney-Purta, J. (1992). Cognitive representations of the political system in adolescents: The continuum from pre-novice to expert. In H. Haste & J. Torney-Purta (Eds.), *New directions for child development: The development of political understanding* (Vol. 56, pp. 11–25). San Francisco: Jossey-Bass.

Treiman, D. J., & Yip, K. (1989). Educational and occupational attainment in 21 countries. In M. L. Kohn (Ed.), *Cross-national research in sociology* (pp. 373–394). Newbury Park, CA: Sage.

Triandis, H. C. (1995). *Individualism and collectivism.* Boulder, CO: Westview Press.

Trommsdorff, G. (1994). Parent–adolescent relations in changing societies: A cross-cultural study. In P. Noack, M. Hofer, & J. Youniss (Eds.), *Psychological responses to social change* (pp. 189–218). New York: Walter de Gruyter.

Trusty, J., Harris, C., & Morag, B. (1999). Lost talent: Predictors of the stability of educational expectation across adolescence. *Journal of Adolescent Research, 14,* 359–382.

Tschann, J. M., & Adler, N. E. (1997). Sexual self-acceptance, communication with partner, and contraceptive use among adolescent females: A longitudinal study. *Journal of Research on Adolescence, 7,* 413–430.

Turnbull, C. M. (1983). *The human cycle.* New York: Simon & Schuster.

Turner, R. A., Irwin, C. E., & Millstein, S. G. (1991). Family structure, family processes, and experimenting with substances during adolescence. *Journal of Research on Adolescence, 1,* 93–106.

Tyack, D. B. (1990). *The one best system: A history of American urban education.* Cambridge, MA: Harvard University Press.

U.S. Bureau of the Census. (1991). *Current population reports, population characteristics series P-20, #433.* Washington, DC: U.S. Government Printing Office.

U.S. Bureau of the Census. (1996). *Statistical abstracts of the United States.* Washington, DC: Author.

U.S. Bureau of the Census. (1998). *Statistical abstracts of the United States.* Washington, DC: U.S. Government Printing Office.

U.S. Bureau of the Census. (1999). *Statistical abstracts of the United States.* Washington, DC: U.S. Government Printing Office.

U.S. Bureau of the Census. (2000). *Statistical abstracts of the United States: 2000.* Washington, DC: U.S. Bureau of the Census.

U.S. Bureau of the Census. (2000). Geographic mobility: March 1997 to March 1998. *Current Population Reports* (Series P-20, No. 520). Washington, DC: U.S. Government Printing Office.

U.S. Department of Commerce, Bureau of the Census. (1940). *Characteristics of the population.* Washington, DC: U.S. Government Printing Office.

U.S. Department of Health & Human Services. (1990). *Vital statistics of the United States, Volume III, Natality.* Washington, DC: U.S. Government Printing Office.

U.S. Department of Health and Human Services. (1994). *Preventing tobacco use among young people: A report of the surgeon general.* Atlanta, GA: Author.

U.S. Department of Labor. (1994). *By the sweat and toil of children, Vol. I: The use of child labor in American imports.* Washington, DC: U.S. Department of Labor.

U.S. Department of Labor. (1995). *By the sweat and toil of children, Vol. II: The use of child labor in U.S. agricultural imports and forced and bonded child labor.* Washington, DC: U.S. Department of Labor.

U.S. Department of Transportation. (1995). *Understanding youthful risk taking and driving.* (DOT Publication No. HS 808-318). Springfield, VA: National Technical Information Service.

U.S. public schools with access to the Internet, 1994, 1997, and 1998. (1999, April). *Population Today*, p. 6.

Underwood, L. E., & Van Wyk, J. J. (1981). Hormones in normal and aberrant growth. In R. H. Williams (Ed.), *Textbook of endocrinology* (6th ed., pp. 11–49). Philadelphia: Saunders.

Underwood, M. K., Kupersmidt, J. B., & Coie, J. D. (1996). Childhood peer sociometric status and aggression as predictors of adolescent childbearing. *Journal of Research on Adolescence, 6,* 201–223.

Unger, R., & Crawford, M. (1996). *Women and gender: A feminist psychology* (2nd ed.). New York: McGraw-Hill.

Unger, S. (1977). *The destruction of American Indian families.* New York: Association on American Indian Affairs.

Urberg, K. A., Degirmencioglu, S. M., & Tolson, J. M. (1998). Adolescent friendship selection and termination: The role of similarity. *Journal of Social and Personal Relationships, 15,* 703–710.

Urberg, K. A., Shyu, S., & Liang, J. (1990). Peer influence in adolescent cigarette smoking. *Addictive Behaviors, 15,* 247–255.

Van Kammen, W. B., Loeber, R., Stouthamer-Loeber, M. (1991). Substance use and its relationship to conduct problems and delinquency in young boys. *Journal of Youth and Adolescence, 20,* 399–414.

Vandereycken, W., & Van Deth, R. (1994). *From fasting saints to anorexic girls: The history of self-starvation.* New York: New York University Press.

Vanfossen, B., Jones, J., & Spade, J. (1987). Curriculum tracking and status maintenance. *Sociology of Education, 60,* 104–122.

Varenne, H. (1982). Jocks and freaks: The symbolic structure of the expression of social interaction among American senior high school students. In G. Spindler (Ed.), *Doing the ethnography of schooling* (pp. 213–235). New York: Holt, Rinehart and Winston.

Vasquez, M. J. T., & Fuentes, C. D. L. (1999). American-born Asian, African, Latina, and American Indian adolescent girls: Challenges and strengths. In N. B. Johnson, M. C. Roberts, & J. Worell (Eds.), *Beyond appearance: A new look at adolescent girls* (pp. 151–173). Washington, DC: American Psychological Association.

Verma, S., & Saraswathi, T. S. (2000, February). *The current state of adolescence in India: An agenda for the next millennium.* Paper prepared for the meeting of the Study Group on Adolescence in the 21st Century, Washington, DC.

Vernberg, E. M. (1990). Psychological adjustment and experience with peers during early adolescence: Reciprocal, incidental, or unidirectional relationships? *Journal of Abnormal Child Psychology, 18,* 187–198.

Vernberg, E., Ewell, K., Beery, S., & Abwender, D. (1994). Sophistication of adolescents' interpersonal negotiation strategies and friendship formation after relocation: A naturally occurring experiment. *Journal of Research on Adolescence, 4,* 5–19.

Vicary, J. R., Klingaman, L. R., & Harkness, W. L. (1995). Risk factors associated with date rape and sexual assault of adolescent girls. *Journal of Adolescence, 18,* 289–306.

Villee, D. B. (1975). *Human endocrinology: A developmental approach. Philadelphia:* Saunders.

Vincent, M. A., & McCabe, M. P. (2000). Gender differences among adolescents in family and peer influences on body dissatisfaction, weight loss, and binge eating disorders. *Journal of Youth & Adolescence, 29,* 205–221.

Vincent, R. C., Davis, D. K., & Bronszkowski, L. A. (1987). Sexism in MTV: The portrayal of women in rock videos. *Journalism Quarterly, 64,* 750–755.

Visher, E., & Visher, J. (1988). *Old loyalties, new ties: Therapeutic strategies with stepfamilies.* New York: Brunner/Mazel.

Vondracek, F. W. (1991). Vocational development and choice in adolescence. In R. M. Lerner, A. C. Petersen, & J. Brooks-Gunn (Eds.), *Encyclopedia of adolescence* (Vol. 2). New York: Garland.

Voyer, D. (1996). The relation between mathematical achievement and gender differences in spatial abilities: A suppression effect. *Journal of Educational Psychology, 88,* 563–571.

Vuchinich, S., Hetherington, E., Vuchinich, R., & Clingempeel, W. (1991). Parent–child interaction and gender differences in early adolescents' adaptation to stepfamilies. *Developmental Psychology, 27,* 618–626.

Wagner, B., & Cohen, P. (1997). Adolescent sibling differences in suicidal symptoms: The role of parent-child relationships. *Journal of Abnormal Child Psychology, 22,* 321–337.

Walker, A. (1992). *Possessing the secret of joy.* New York: Harcourt, Brace, Jovanovich.

Walker, L. J. (1984). Sex differences in the development of moral reasoning. A critical review. *Child Development, 51,* 131–139.

Walker, L. J. (1989). A longitudinal study of moral reasoning. *Child Development, 60,* 157–166.

Walker, L., de Vries, B., & Trevethan, S. (1987). Moral stages and moral orientations in real-life and hypothetical dilemmas. *Child Development, 58,* 842–858.

Wallace, J. M., & Williams, D. R. (1997). Religion and adolescent health-compromising behavior. In J. Schulenberg, J. L. Maggs, & K. Hurrelmann (Eds.), *Health risks and developmental transitions during adolescence* (pp. 444–468). New York: Cambridge University Press.

Wallerstein, J. S., & Blakeslee, S. (1996). *Second chances: Men, women and children a decade after divorce.* New York: Houghton Mifflin.

Wallerstein, J. S., & Corbin, S. B. (1991). The child and the vicissitudes of divorce. In M. Lewis (Ed.), *Child and adolescent psychiatry* (pp. 1108–1118). Baltimore, MD: Williams & Wilkins.

Walsh, T. B. (1993). Binge eating in bulimia nervosa. In C. G. Fairburn & G. T. Wilson (Eds.), *Binge eating* (pp. 37–49). New York: Guilford

Ward, J. V. (1990). Racial identity formation and transformation. In C. Gilligan, N. P. Lyons, & T. J. Haruner (Eds.), *Making connections* (pp. 215–232). Cambridge, MA: Harvard University Press.

Ward, L. M. (1995). Talking about sex: Common themes about sexuality in the prime-time television programs children and adolescents view most. *Journal of Youth & Adolescence, 24,* 595–616.

Ward, L. M., & Rivadeneyra, R. (1999). Contributions of entertainment television to adolescents' sexual attitudes and expectations: The role of viewing amount versus viewer involvement. *Journal of Sex Research, 36,* 237–249.

Warren, J. (1996). Educational inequality among White and Mexican-origin adolescents in the American Southwest: 1990. *Sociology of Education, 69,* 142–158.

Waterman, A. S. (1992). Identity as an aspect of optimal functioning. In G. R. Adams, T. P. Gullotta, & R. Montemayor (Eds.), *Adolescent identity formation.* Newbury Park, CA: Sage.

Waterman, A. S. (1999). Issues of identity formation revisited: United States and the Netherlands. *Developmental Review, 19,* 462–479.

Watkins, W. G., & Bentovim, A. (1992). The sexual abuse of male children and adolescents: A review of current research. *Journal of Child Psychology & Psychiatry, 33,* 197–248.

Weatherford, D. (1997). *Milestones: A chronology of American women's history.* New York: Facts on File.

Web envelopes young adults. (1999, August 9). *The Washington Post*, p. 5.

Weber, R., & Crocker, J. (1983). Cognitive processes in the revision of stereotypical beliefs. *Journal of Personality and Social Psychology, 45*, 961–977.

Weinberg, R. A. (1989). Intelligence and IQ: Landmark issues and great debates. *American Psychologist, 44*, 98–104.

Weinberg, R. A., Scarr, S., & Waldman, I. D. (1992). The Minnesota transracial adoption study: A follow-up of IQ test performance. *Intelligence, 44*, 98–104.

Weiner, I. B. (1992). *Psychological disturbance in adolescence* (2nd ed.). New York: Wiley.

Weinraub, M., & Wolf, B. M. (1983). Effects of stress and social supports on mother–child interactions in single and two-parent families. *Child Development, 54*, 1297–1311.

Weinreich, H. E. (1974). The structure of moral reasoning. *Journal of Youth and Adolescence, 3*, 135–143.

Weinstein, N. D. (1998). Accuracy of smokers' risk perceptions. *Annals of Behavioral Medicine, 20*, 135–140.

Weiss, B., Dodge, K. A., Bates, J. E., & Pettit, G. S. (1992). Some consequences of early harsh discipline: Child aggression and a maladaptive social information processing style. *Child Development, 63*, 1321–1335.

Weiss, R. S. (1973). *Loneliness: The experience of emotional and social isolation*. Cambridge, MA: MIT Press.

Weissberg, R., Caplan, M., & Harwood, R. (1991). Promoting competent young people in competence-enhancing environments: A systems-based perspective on primary prevention. *Journal of Consulting and Clinical Psychology, 59*, 830–841.

Wender, P. H., Kety, S. S., Rosenthal, D., Schulsinger, E., Ortmann, J., & Lunde, L. (1986). Psychiatric disorders in the biological and adoptive families of adopted individuals with affective disorders. *Archives of General Psychiatry, 43*, 923–929.

Wentzel, K. R., & Asher, S. R. (1995). The academic lives of neglected, rejected, popular, and controversial children. *Child Development, 66*, 754–763.

Wentzel, K. R., & Feldman, S. S. (1993). Parental predictors of boys' self-restraint and motivation to achieve at school: A longitudinal study. *Journal of Early Adolescence, 13*, 183–203.

Westin, C. (1998). Immigration, xenophobia, and youthful opinion. In J. Nurmi (Ed.), *Adolescents, cultures, and conflicts* (pp. 225–241). New York: Garland.

Westoff, C. (1988). Unintended pregnancy in America and abroad. *Family Planning Perspectives, 20*, 254–261.

Whipple, E. E., & Webster-Stratton, C. (1991). The role of parental stress in physically abusive families. *Child Abuse and Neglect, 15*, 279–291.

Whitaker, A., Johnson, J., Shaffer, D., Rapoport, J. L., Kalikow, K., Walsh, B. T., Davies, M., Braiman, S., & Dolinsky, A. (1990). Uncommon troubles in young people. *Archives of General Psychiatry, 47*, 487–496.

Whitbeck, L. B., & Hoyt, D. R. (1999). *Nowhere to grow: Homeless and runaway adolescents and their families*. New York: Aldine de Gruyter.

White, L., & Edwards, J. N. (1990). Emptying the nest and parental well-being: An analysis of national panel data. *American Sociological Review, 55*, 235–242.

White, L. K., Brinkerhoff, D. B., & Booth, A. (1985). The effect of marital disruption on child's attachment to parents. *Journal of Family Issues, 6*, 5–22.

Whiting, B. B., & Edwards, C. P. (1988). *Children of different worlds: The formation of social behavior*. Cambridge, MA: Harvard University Press.

Whiting, J. W. M., & Child, I. (1953). *Child training and personality*. New Haven, CT: Yale University Press.

Whiting, J. W. M., Burbank, V. K., & Ratner, M. S. (1986). The duration of maidenhood across cultures. In J. B. Lancaster & B. A. Hamburg (Eds.), *School-age pregnancy and parenthood: Biosocial dimensions* (pp. 273–302). New York: Aldine de Gruyter.

Whyte, W. F. (1943). *Street corner society*. Chicago: University of Chicago Press.

Wichstrom, L. (1999). The emergence of gender difference in depressed mood during adolescence: The role of intensified gender socialization. *Developmental Psychology, 35*, 232–245.

Wildavsky, R. (1997, June). What teens really want. *Reader's Digest*, 50–57.

Will, G. (2000, January 10). Aids crushes a continent. *Newsweek*, 64.

William T. Grant Foundation Commission on Work, Family, and Citizenship. (1988). *The forgotten half: Noncollege-bound youth in America*. New York: William T. Grant Foundation.

Williams, A. F. (1998). Risky driving behavior among adolescents. In R. Jessor (Ed.), *New perspectives on adolescent risk behavior* (pp. 221–240). New York: Cambridge University Press.

Williams, A. F., Preusser, D. F., Ulmer, R. G., & Weinstein, H. B. (1995). Characteristics of fatal crashes of 16-year-old drivers: Implications for licensure policies. *Journal of Public Health Policy, 16*, 347–390.

Williams, J. E., & Best, D. L. (1990). *Measuring sex stereotypes: A multination study*. Newbury Park, CA: Sage.

Williams, T. B. (Ed.). (1986). *The impact of television: A natural experiment in three communities*. New York: Academic Press.

Williamson, J., Borduin, C., & Howe, B. (1991). The ecology of adolescent maltreatment: A multilevel examination of adolescent physical abuse, sexual abuse,

and neglect. *Journal of Consulting and Clinical Psychology, 59*, 449–457.

Willits, F. K., & Crider, D. M. (1989). Church attendance and traditional religious beliefs in adolescence and young adulthood: A panel study. *Review of Religious Research, 31*, 68–81.

Wilson, B. J., & Gottman, J. M. (1995). Marital interaction and parenting. In M. H. Bornstein (Ed.), *Children and parenting* (Vol. 4). Hillsdale, NJ: Erlbaum.

Wilson, C. A., & Keye, W. R. (1989). A survey of dysmenorrhea and premenstrual symptom frequency: A model for prevention, detection, and treatment. *Journal of Adolescent Health Care, 10*, 317–322.

Wilson, J. Q., & Herrnstein, R. J. (1985). *Crime and human nature*. New York: Simon and Schuster.

Wilson, M. N. (1989). Child development in the context of the black extended family. *American Psychologist, 44*, 380–383.

Wilson, S. M., Peterson, G. W., & Wilson, P. (1993). The process of educational and occupational attainment of adolescent females from low-income, rural families. *Journal of Marriage and the Family, 55*, 158–175.

Wilson, W. J. (1987). *The truly disadvantaged: The inner city, the underclass, and public policy*. Chicago: University of Chicago Press.

Wilson, W. J. (1996). *When work disappears: The world of the new urban poor*. New York: Knopf.

Windle, M. (1989). Substance use and abuse among adolescent runaways: A four-year follow-up study. *Journal of Youth and Adolescence, 18*, 331–344.

Windle, M. (1992). A longitudinal study of stress buffering for adolescent problem behaviors. *Developmental Psychology, 28*, 522–530.

Wiseman, H. (1995). The quest for connectedness: Loneliness as process in the narratives of lonely university students. In R. Josselson & A. Lieblich (Eds.), *Interpreting experience: The narrative study of lives* (pp. 116–152). Thousand Oaks, CA: Sage.

Withers, L. E., & Kaplan, D. W. (1987). Adolescents who attempt suicide: A retrospective clinical chart review of hospitalized patterns. *Professional Psychology, 18*, 391–393.

Wlodarek, J. (1994). Poland. In K. Hurrelman (Ed.), *International handbook of adolescence* (pp. 309–321). Westport, CT: Greenwood Press.

Wolfe, D. A. (1985). Child-abusive parents: An empirical review and analysis. *Psychological Bulletin, 97*, 462–483.

Wolff, T. (1989). *This boys' life*. New York: HarperTrade.

Wong, C. A. (1997, April). *What does it mean to be African-American or European-American growing up in a multi-ethnic community?* Paper presented at the biennial meeting of the Society for Research in Child Development, Washington, DC.

Wood, P., & Clay, W. (1996). Perceived structural barriers and academic performance among American Indian high school students. *Youth & Society, 28,* 40–61.

Woods, P. D., Haskell, W. L., Stern, S. L., & Perry, C. (1977). Plasma lipoprotein distributions in male and female runners. *Annals of the New York Academy of Sciences, 301,* 748–763.

Woodward, K. L. (1993, November 29). The rites of Americans. *Newsweek,* 80–82.

Woodward, L., & Fergusson, D. (1999). Early conduct problems and later risk of teenage pregnancy in girls. *Development and Psychopathology, 11,* 127–142.

Wooten, M. A. (1992). The effects of heavy metal music on affect shifts of adolescents in an inpatient psychiatric setting. *Music Therapy Perspectives, 10,* 93–98.

Wright, L., Frost, C., & Wisecarver, S. (1993). Church attendance, meaningfulness of religion, and depressive symptomatology among adolescents. *Journal of Youth and Adolescence, 22,* 559–568.

Wright, M. R. (1989). Body image satisfaction in adolescent girls and boys: A longitudinal study. *Journal of Youth and Adolescence, 18,* 71–84.

Wrong, D. H. (1994). *The problem of order: What unites and divides society.* New York: Free Press.

Wu, Z. (1999). Premarital cohabitation and the timing of first marriage. *Canadian Review of Sociology and Anthropology, 36,* 109–127.

Wulff, H. (1995a). Inter-racial friendship: Consuming youth styles, ethnicity and teenage femininity in South London. In V. Amit-Talai & H. Wulff (Eds.), *Youth cultures: A cross-cultural perspective* (pp. 63–80). New York: Routledge.

Wulff, H. (1995b). Introducing youth culture in its own right: The state of the art and new possibilities. In V. Amit-Talai & H. Wulff (Eds.), *Youth cultures: A cross-cultural perspective* (pp. 1–18). New York: Routledge.

www.bsa.scouting.org

www.norc.uchicago.edu/gss

www.psychorp.com/sub/featured/fpwwfaq.htm

Wyatt, G. E. (1990). Changing influences on adolescent sexuality over the past 40 years. In J. Bancroft & J. M. Reinisch (Eds.), *Adolescence and puberty* (pp. 182–206). New York: Oxford University Press.

Xu, X., & Whyte, M. K. (1990). Love matches and arranged marriages: A Chinese replication. *Journal of Marriage and the Family, 52,* 709–722.

Yang, K. S. (1986). Chinese personality and its change. In M. H. Bond (Ed.), *The psychology of the Chinese people* (pp. 106–170). Hong Kong: Oxford University Press.

Yates, M., & Youniss, J. (1996). A developmental perspective on community service in adolescence. *Social Development, 5,* 85–101.

Yelsma, P., & Athappilly, K. (1988). Marital satisfaction and communication practices: Comparisons among Indian and American couples. *Journal of Comparative Family Studies, 19,* 37–54.

Yoder, K. A., Hoyt, D. R., & Whitbeck, L. B. (1998). Suicidal behavior in homeless and runaway adolescents. *Journal of Youth & Adolescence, 27,* 753–772.

Yoshikawa, H. (1994). Prevention as cumulative protection: Effects of early family support and education on chronic delinquency and its risks. *Psychological Bulletin, 115,* 28–54.

Youniss, J., McLellan, J. A., & Yates, M. (1999). Religion, community service, and identity in American youth. *Journal of Adolescence, 22,* 243–253.

Youniss, J., & Smollar, J. (1985). *Adolescent relations with mothers, fathers, and friends.* Chicago: University of Chicago Press.

Youniss, J., & Yates, M. (1997). *Community service and social responsibility in youth: Theory and policy.* Chicago: University of Chicago Press.

Youth Indicators. (1996). *Trends in the well-being of American youth.* Washington, DC: U.S. Government Printing Office.

Yussen, S. R. (1977). Characteristics of moral dilemmas written by adolescents. *Developmental Psychology, 13,* 162–163.

Zabin, L. S. (1986, May/June). Evaluation of a pregnancy prevention program for urban teenagers. *Family Planning Perspectives,* 119.

Zabin, L., Hirsch, M., & Emerson, M. (1989). When urban adolescents choose abortion: Effects on education, psychological status and subsequent pregnancy. *Family Planning Perspectives, 21,* 248–255.

Zeidner, M. (1993). Coping with disaster: The case of Israeli adolescents under threat of missile attack. *Journal of Youth & Adolescence, 22,* 89–108.

Zeidner, M., & Schleyer, E. J. (1999). The effects of educational context on individual difference variables, self-perceptions of giftedness, and school attitudes in gifted adolescents. *Journal of Youth & Adolescence, 28,* 687–703.

Zhou, M. (1997). Growing up American: The challenge confronting immigrant children and children of immigrants. *Annual Review of Sociology, 23,* 63–95.

Zigler, E., & Hall, N. W. (1989). Physical child abuse in America: Past, present, and future. In D. Cicchetti & V. Carlson (Eds.), *Child maltreatment: Theory and research on the causes and consequences of child abuse and neglect* (pp. 38–75). New York: Cambridge University Press.

Zill, N., & Nord, C. W. (1994). *Running in place: How American families are faring in a changing economy and an individualistic society.* Washington, DC: Child Trends.

Zill, N., Morrison, D. R., & Coiro, M. J. (1993). Long-term effects of parental divorce on parent–child relationships, adjustment, and achievement in young adulthood. *Journal of Family Psychology, 7,* 91–103.

Zimiles, H., & Lee, V. (1991). Adolescent family structure and educational progress. *Developmental Psychology, 27,* 314–320.

Zimmerman, M. A., Copeland, L. A., Shope, J. T., & Dielman, T. E. (1997). A longitudinal study of self-esteem: Implications for adolescent development. *Journal of Youth & Adolescence, 26,* 117–142.

Zuckerman, M. (1995). *Behavioral expressions and psychobiological bases of sensation seeking.* New York: Cambridge University Press.

Credits

Photos

Chapter 1 Opener Corbis Digital Stock; p. 4 Jeff Greenberg, PhotoEdit; p. 8 Corbis; p. 10 Culver Pictures, Inc.; p. 11 (top) Corbis; p. 11 (bottom) Corbis; p. 17 (left, middle, right) David Young Wolff, PhotoEdit; p. 18 Dean Chapman, Panos Pictures; p. 19 Luis Veiga, The Image Bank; p. 23 Courtesy of the Library of Congress; p. 26 M. L. Corvetto, The Image Works.

Chapter 2 Opener Larry Kolvoord, The Image Works; p. 36 Mary Steinbacher, PhotoEdit; p. 38 Gerard Vandystadt, Photo Researchers, Inc.; p. 44 Blackwell Science, Ltd.; p. 47 Sylvain Grandadam, Photo Researchers, Inc.; p. 48 The Image Works; p. 49 Bob Krist, Corbis; p. 52 Scott Swanson, Archive Photos; p. 54 David Young Wolff, PhotoEdit.

Chapter 3 Opener Corbis Digital Stock; p. 65 Corbis; p. 67 Mimi Forsyth, Monkmeyer Press; p. 71 David R. Austen, Stock Boston; p. 72 Eastcott/Momatiuk, Woodfin Camp & Associates; p. 74 J. Nordell, The Image Works; p. 75 Keystone View Co.; p. 77 (left) J. Pickerell, The Image Works; p. 77 (right) David Young Wolff, PhotoEdit; p. 81 John Neubauer, PhotoEdit; p. 86 Bob Daemmrich, Stock Boston; p. 91 The Chronicle, Gary J. Cichowski, AP/Wide World Photos; p. 92 John Terence Turner, FPG International LLC.

Chapter 4 Opener Paula Bronstein, Stone; p. 99 Jonathan Nourok, PhotoEdit; p. 101 (A) Nancy Richmond, The Image Works; p. 101 (B) Steve Rubin, The Image Works; p. 101 (C) J. Holmes, Panos Pictures; p. 102 D. Young Wolff, PhotoEdit; p. 105 Penny Tweedie, Panos Pictures; p. 108 Joseph Sohm, Corbis; p. 109 John Eastcott-Yva Momatiuk, The Image Works; p. 110 Lawrence Migdale, Photo Researchers, Inc.; p. 115 Nathan Benn, Corbis; p. 116 Archive Photos; p. 120 Richard Lord, The Image Works; p. 125 Andy Hernandez, Liaison Agency, Inc.

Chapter 5 Opener Corbis Digital Stock; p. 131 L. Dematteis, The Image Works; p. 134 Giacomo Pirozzi, Panos Pictures; p. 137 Copyright © Bettmann, Corbis; p. 139 YMCA archives/Courtesy of The Kautz Family YMCA and YMCA of the USA; p. 141 Bob Daemmrich, Stock Boston; p. 144 Telegraph Colour Library, FPG International LLC; p. 148 Mary Ellen Mark; p. 150 Lucas, The Image Works; p. 155 Morris Carpenter, Panos Pictures.

Chapter 6 Opener Corbis Digital Stock; p. 163 David Young Wolff, PhotoEdit; p. 168 Nancy Richmond, The Image Works; p. 169 Ellen B. Senisi, The Image Works; p. 172 Ted Streshinsky, Corbis; p. 178 Billy Barnes, Stock Boston; p. 179 Eastcott, The Image Works; p. 181 (top left) Ellen B. Senisi, The Image Works; p. 181 (bottom right) Mark Richards, PhotoEdit.

Chapter 7 Opener David Young Wolff, PhotoEdit; p. 189 M. Ferguson, PhotoEdit; p. 190 Zigy Kaluzny, Stone; p. 191 Giacomo Pirozzi, Panos Pictures; p. 192 Dick Luria, FPG International LLC; p. 197 John Lawlor, FPG International LLC; p. 201 Charles Gupton, Stock Boston; p. 203 Mark C. Burnett, Stock Boston; p. 204 Jim Whitmer, Stock Boston; p. 208 Culver Pictures, Inc.; p. 210 Hulton Getty, Liaison Agency, Inc.; p. 213 Richard Hutchings, Photo Researchers, Inc.; p. 216 Bruce Ayres, Stone.

Chapter 8 Opener Corbis Digital Stock; p. 224 Andy Sacks, Stone; p. 228 M&E Bernheim, Woodfin Camp & Associates; p. 229 (left) Bob Daemmrich, Stock Boston; p. 229 (right) Jeff Greenberg, Stock Boston; p. 232 Charles Gupton, Stock Boston; p. 235 Telegraph Colour Library, FPG International LLC; p. 237 Jeff Baker, FPG International LLC; p. 243 Don Smetzer, Stone; p. 246 Penny Tweedie, Stone; p. 249 Yeadon, Archive Photos; p. 252 (top left) Corbis; p. 252 (top right) Archive Photos; p. 252 (bottom left) FPG International LLC; p. 252 (bottom right) Catherine Karnow, Woodfin Camp & Associates; p. 255 Hunter Freeman, Stone.

Chapter 9 Opener Corbis Digital Stock; p. 260 Willinger, FPG International LLC; p. 261 Culver Pictures, Inc.; p. 264 Bob Daemmrich, Stock Boston; p. 266 Peter Correz, Stone; p. 273 Hari Mahidhar, The Image Works; p. 277 Telegraph Colour Library, FPG International LLC; p. 280 Robert Azzi, Woodfin Camp & Associates; p. 281 Jeffry W. Myers, Stock Boston; p. 285 Bob Daemmrich, Stock Boston; p. 286 David Hanson, Stone; p. 291 Bob Daemmrich, The Image Works; p. 294 Blair Seitz, Photo Researchers, Inc.

Chapter 10 Opener Corbis Digital Stock; p. 300 Bob Daemmrich Photography, Inc.; p. 306 Michael A. Dwyer, Stock Boston; p. 310 Charles Gupton, Stock Boston; p. 315 Will and Deni McIntyre, Photo Researchers, Inc.; p. 321 Bob Daemmrich, Stock Boston; p. 324 Bob Daemmrich, Stock Boston; p. 327 Bob Child, AP/Wide World Photos; p. 328 Ron Sherman, Stock Boston.

Chapter 11 Corbis Digital Stock; p. 334 M&E Bernheim, Woodfin Camp & Associates; p. 335 Jeremy Hartley, Panos Pictures; p. 336 Sean Spregue, Panos Pictures; p. 339 FPG International LLC; p. 341 Lawrence Migdale, Stock Boston; p. 347 Stock Boston; p. 350 Nubar Alexanian, Stock Boston; p. 357 Telegraph Colour Library, FPG International LLC; p. 361 Steve Maines, Stock Boston.

Chapter 12 Opener Dorothy Littell Greco, Stock Boston; p. 369 Dorothy Littell Greco, Stock Boston; p. 370 Karen Thomas, Stock Boston; p. 374 Spooner, Liaison Agency, Inc.; p. 378 Bob Daemmrich Photography, Inc.; p. 379 Michael Newman, PhotoEdit; p. 383 Corbis; p. 384 Corbis; p. 386 M. Benjamin, The Image Works; p. 388 J. Griffin, The Image Works; p. 389 Chris Brown, Stock Boston.

Chapter 13 Opener Corbis Digital Stock; p. 396 Bob Daemmrich, Stock Boston; p. 399 Chris Brown, Stock Boston; p. 403 Bob Daemmrich Photography, Inc.; p. 409 Mike Derer, AP/Wide World Photos; p. 412 Charles Gatewood, Pearson Education/PH College; p. 417 Steve Weber, Stock Boston; p. 420 Bob Daemmrich, Stock Boston; p. 422 Tony Latham, Stone.

Chapter 14 Opener Corbis Digital Stock; p. 430 Copyright © by P. Robert, Corbis Sygma; p. 431 Liba Taylor, Panos Pictures; p. 432 Copyright © by S. Elbaz, Corbis Sygma; p. 434 Copyright © by J.P. Laffont, Corbis Sygma; p. 435 Betty Press, Woodfin Camp & Associates; p. 436 Patrick Piel, Liaison Agency, Inc.; p. 438 (left) Penny Tweedie, Panos Pictures; p. 438 (right) Copyright © by N. Hashimoto, Corbis Sygma.

Cartoons, Figures, and Tables

Chapter 1 Figure 1.1 U.S. Bureau of the Census (2000). Geographic Mobility: March 1997 to March 1998. *Current Population Reports* (Series P–20, No. 520). Washington, D.C.: U.S. Government Printing Office; **Figure 1.2** Arnett, J.J. (2000). Emerging adulthood: A theory of development from the late teens through the twenties. *American Psychologist, 55,* 469–480; **Table 1.1** Courtesy of The Gallup Poll; **Table 1.2** U.S. Bureau of the Census (1991) (marriage) and U.S. Department of Health and Human Services (1990) (first birth); **Table 1.3** Noble, J., Cover, J., & Yanagishita, M. (1996). *The World's Youth.* Washington D.C.: Population Reference Bureau.

Chapter 2 Figure 2.6 Marshall, W. A., & Tanner, J. M. (1969). Variations in the pattern of pubertal changes in girls. *Archives of Disease in Childhood, 45,* 291–303; **Figure 2.7** Adapted from p. 22, Figure 8, of Marshall, W. A., & Tanner, J. M. (1970). Variations in the pattern of pubertal changes in boys. *Archives of Disease in Childhood, 45,* 13–23; **Figure 2.8** Eveleth, P. B., & Tanner, J. M. (1990) *Worldwide variation in human growth.* Cambridge, MA: Cambridge University Press. Reprinted with permission of Cambridge University Press; **Figure 2.9**

Eveleth, P. B., & Tanner, J. M. (1990) *Worldwide variation in human growth.* Cambridge, MA: Cambridge University Press. Reprinted with permission of Cambridge University Press; **Figure 2.10** Montemayor, R., & Flannery, D. J. (1989). A naturalistic study of children and adolescents with their mothers and friends: Developmental differences in expressive behavior. *Journal of Adolescent Research, 4,* 3–14.

Chapter 3 Figure 3.2 Bayley, N. (1968). Behavioral correlates of mental growth: Birth to thirty-six years. *American Psychologist, 23,* 1–7. Copyright © 1968 by the American Psychological Association. Reprinted by permission of the publisher and author; **Table 3.2** Tavris, C. & Wade, C. (1997). *Psychology,* 5th ed. Upper Saddle River, NJ: Prentice Hall. Copyright © 1997. Reprinted by permission of Prentice Hall, Inc.; **Cartoon** (top, p. 69) King Features Syndicate. Reprinted with special permission of King Features Syndicate; **Cartoon** (bottom, p. 69) Toles © 1993 The Buffalo News. Reprinted with permission of UNIVERSAL PRESS SYNDICATE. All rights reserved.

Chapter 4 Figure 4.1 Adapted from p. 158 of Feldman, S. S., Mont-Reynaud, R., & Rosenthal, D. A. (1992). When East meets West: The acculturation of Chinese adolescents in the U.S. and Australia. *Journal of Research on Adolescence, 2,* 147–173; **Table 4.2** Alwin, D. F. (1988). From obedience to autonomy: Changes in traits desired in children, 1928-1978. *Public Opinion Quarterly, 52,* 33–52. Reprinted with permission of Cambridge University Press; **Table 4.3** Shweder, R. A., Mahapatra, M., & Miller, J. G. (1990). Culture and moral development. In J. W. Stigler, R. A. Shweder, & G. Herdt (Eds.), *Cultural psychology: Essays on Comparative Human Development* (pp. 130–204). Cambridge, MA: Cambridge University Press. Reprinted with permission of Cambridge University Press.

Chapter 5 Figure 5.1 From Female Genital Mutilation: Is It Crime or Culture? *The Economist,* February 13, 1999, p. 45; **Figure 5.2** From p. 105 of Evans, E. D., Ruthberg, J., Sather, C., & Turner, C. (1991). Content analysis of contemporary teen magazines for adolescent females. *Youth & Society, 23,* 99–120; **Figure 5.3** Benbow, C. P., & Stanley, J. C. (1980). Sex differences in mathematical ability: Fact or artifact? *Science, 210,* 1262–1264. By permission of the authors; **Table 5.1** National Opinion Research Center (NORC); 1972-1982, 1994 (www.norc.uchicago.edu/gss); **Table 5.2** Bem, S. L. (1974). Measurement of psychological adrogeny. *Journal of Consulting and Clinical Psychology, 42,* 155–162; **Table 5.3** From Table 2-1 on p. 36 of Baker, D. P., & Perkins-Jones, D. (1993). Creating gender equality: Cross-national gender stratification and mathematical performance. *Sociology of Education, 66,* 91-103. Reprinted by permission of the American Sociological Association and the authors.

Chapter 6 Figure 6.1 Adapted from Hirsch, B., & DuBois, D. (1991). Self-esteem in early adolescence: The identification and prediction of contrasting longitudinal trajectories. *Journal of Youth and Adolescence, 20,* 53–72; **Table 6.3** Adapted from Phinney, J. S., & Devich-Navarro, M. (1997). Variation in bicultural identification among African American and Mexican American adolescents. *Journal of Research on Adolescence, 7,* 3–32.

Chapter 7 Figure 7.2 Hernandez, D. J. (1997): Child development and the social demography of childhood. *Child Development, 68,* 149–169; **Figure 7.3** Federal Interagency Forum on Child and Family Statistics (1999); **Table 7.1** Adapted from Maccoby, E., & Martin, J. (1983). Socialization in the context of the family: Parent and child interaction. In E. M. Hetherington (Ed.), *Handbook of child psychology: Socialization, personality, and social development,* Vol. 4. New York; **Cartoon** (p. 209) FOR BETTER OR WORSE reprinted by permission of United Features Syndicate, Inc. Copyright © 1992 FOR BETTER OR WORSE by Lynn.

Chapter 8 Figure 8.1 Larson, R. W., Richards, M. H., Moneta, G., Holmbeck, G., & Duckett, E. (1996). Changes in adolescents' daily interactions with their families from ages 10 to 18: Disengagement

and transformation. *Developmental Psychology, 32,* 744–754; **Figure 8.2** Youniss, J., & Smollar, J., (1985). *Adolescent relations with mothers, fathers, and friends,* p. 284, Figure 8.2. Chicago: University of Chicago Press. Reprinted with permission; **Figure 8.3** Brown, B. B., Mory, M., & Kinney, D. A. (1994). Casting adolescent crowds in relational perspective: Caricature, channel, and context. In R. Montemayor, G. R. Adams, & T. P. Gullotta (Eds.), *Advances in Adolescent Development: Vol. 6. Personal relationships during adolescence,* Newbury Park, CA: Sage; **Figure 8.4** Csikszentmihalyi, M., & Larson, R. (1984). *Being Adolescent:* Conflict and growth in the teenage years, p. 183, Figure 7-3. Perseus Books Group; **Figure 8.5** Brown, B. B. (1990). Peer groups. In S. Feldman & G. Elliot (Eds.), *At the threshold: The developing adolescent,* pp. 171–196. Cambridge, MA: Harvard University Press.

Chapter 9 Figure 9.1 Data from Bachman, J. G., Johnston, L. D., & O'Malley, P. M. (1995). *Monitoring the future: Questionnaire responses from the nation's high school seniors.* Ann Arbor: Institute for Social Research, University of Michigan; **Figure 9.2** Dornbusch, S. M., Carlsmith, J. M., Gross, R. T., Martin, J. A., Jennings, D., Rosenberg, A., & Duke, P. (1981). Sexual development, age, and dating: A comparison of biological and social influences upon one set of behaviors. *Child Development, 52,* 179–185. Copyright © 1981 by the Society for Research in Child Development, Inc. Reprinted with permission; **Figure 9.3** Centers for Disease Control and Prevention (CDCP) (1999). 1995 *Youth Risk Behavior Surveillance System (YRBSS).* Available: www.cdc.gov/nccdphp/dash/yrbs/suse.htm; **Figure 9.4** From The Alan Guttmacher Institute (1994). *Sex and America's teenager.* New York: The Alan Guttmacher Institute, p. 76, Fig. 55. Reproduced with the permission of the Alan Guttmacher Institute (AGI); **Figure 9.5** National Vital Statistics Reports, Oct. 25, 1999. Washington D.C.: US Centers for Disease Control and Prevention; **Figure 9.6** Federal Interagency Forum on Child and Family Statistics. (1999). *America's children: Key national indicators of well-being, 1999.* Washington D.C.: U.S. Government Printing Office; **Table 9.1** Sprecher, S. (1994). Two sides to the breakup of dating relationships. *Personal Relationships, 1,* 199–222. Reprinted with permission of the Cambridge Ur.iversity Press; **Table 9.2** Hatfield, E., & Rapson, R. L. (1996): *Love and Sex: Crosscultural Perspectives.* Needham: Allyn & Bacon; **Table 9.3** Hatfield, E., & Rapson, R. L. (1996): *Love and Sex: Crosscultural Perspectives.* Needham: Allyn & Bacon.

Chapter 10 Figure 10.1 Tanner, D. (1972): *Secondary Education.* New York: MacMillan and Arnett, J. & Taber, S. (1994) Adolescence terminable and interminable: When does adolescence end? *Journal of Youth and Adolescence, 23,* 517-537; **Figure 10.2** 1991 UNESCO Statistical Yearbook. Paris, UNESCO, 1991; **Figure 10.4** (top figures and bottom left) Steinberg, L. & Dornbusch, S. M. (1991). Negative correlates of part-time employment during adolescence: Replication and elaboration. *Developmental Psychology, 27,* 304–313, Figure 1. Copyright © 1991 The American Psychological Association. Reprinted with permission; **Figure 10.4** (bottom right) Bachman, J. G. & Schulenberg, J. (1993). How part-time work intensity relates to drug use, problem behavior, time use, and satisfaction among high school seniors. *Developmental Psychology, 29,* 220–235. Copyright © 1993 The American Psychological Association. Reprinted with permission.

Chapter 11 Figure 11.1 Ruggiero, M., Greenberger, E., & Steinberg, L. (1982). Occupational deviance among first-time workers. *Youth and Society, 13,* 423–448; **Figure 11.2** From Norbert, McDowell, & Goulet (1992). Profile of higher education in Canada, 1991 Edition. Ottowa, Canada: Department of the Secretary of State; **Figure 11.3** U.S. Department of Labor (2000); **Figure 11.4** U.S. Bureau of the Census (2000); **Table 11.1** Aronson, P. J., et al. (1996): Generational differences in early work experience and evaluations. In J. T. Mortimer & M.D. Finch (Eds.), *Adolescents, work, and family: An intergenerational developmental analysis* (pp. 25–62). Newbury Park: CA, Sage.

Chapter 12 Figure 12.1 Arnet, J. J., & Terhanian, G. (1998). Adolescents' responses to cigarette advertsing: Exposure, liking, and the appeal of smoking. *Tobacco Control, 7,* 129–133.

Chapter 13 Figure 13.1 FARS and GES: 1998 Motor Vehicle Crash Data. U.S. Department of Transportation; **Figure 13.2** Bachman, J. G., Johnston, L. D., O'Malley, P., & Schulenberg, J. (1997). Transitions in drug use during late adolescence and young adulthood. In J. A. Graber, J. Brooks-Gunn, & A. C. Petersen (Eds.), *Transitions through adolescence: Interpersonal domains and context* (pp. 111–140). Mahwah, NJ: Erlbaum; **Figure 13.3** Johnson, L., Bachman, J., & O'Malley, P. (1996). *Monitoring the Future.* Ann Arbor, MI: Institute for Social Research; **Figure 13.4** Gottfredson, M., & Hirschi, T. (1990). A *general theory of crime,* Stanford, CA: Stanford University Press; **Figure 13.5** National Center for Health Statistics: Health United States 1996-1997 and Injury Chartbook (1997): 32; **Table 13.1** From "Living with 10- to 15-year-olds," A parent education curriculum. Copyright © 1984 Center for Early Adolescence, Suite 223, Carr Mill Mall, Carrboro, NC 27510.

Name Index

Subject Index